July 15–18, 2014
Paris, France

Association for Computing Machinery

Advancing Computing as a Science & Profession

PODC'14

Proceedings of the 2014 ACM Symposium on Principles of Distributed Computing

Sponsored by:

ACM SIGACT & ACM SIGOPS

Supported by:

Ben-Gurion University of the Negev, CNRS, Facebook, Inria, LIP6, LRI, Lincs, Mairie de Paris, Microsoft Research, Oracle Labs, Qualcomm, Telecom ParisTech and University Pierre & Marie Curie

Association for
Computing Machinery

Advancing Computing as a Science & Profession

The Association for Computing Machinery
2 Penn Plaza, Suite 701
New York, New York 10121-0701

ISBN: 978-1-4503-2944-6

Additional copies may be ordered prepaid from:

ACM Order Department
PO Box 30777
New York, NY 10087-0777, USA

Phone: 1-800-342-6626 (USA and Canada)
+1-212-626-0500 (Global)
Fax: +1-212-944-1318
E-mail: acmhelp@acm.org
Hours of Operation: 8:30 am – 4:30 pm ET

ACM Order Number: 536140

Printed in the USA

Foreword, PODC'14 Chair's Welcome

It is our great pleasure to welcome you to the *2014 ACM Symposium on Principles of Distributed Computing – PODC'14.* This year's symposium continues its tradition of being the premier forum for presentation of research on all aspects of distributed computing, including the theory, design, implementation and applications of distributed algorithms, systems and networks. During the years, PODC has been the stage where many landmark results have been presented that have increased our understanding of this exciting and fundamental research endeavor. In the best tradition of theoretical discovery, the insights that have been provided have not only elucidated fundamental conceptual issues but also found their way into the real world of systems and applications.

The call for papers attracted 141 regular submissions and 23 brief announcements. The Program Committee accepted 39 papers and 11 brief announcements that cover a wide variety of topics. Every submitted paper was read and evaluated by at least three reviewers. The final decisions regarding acceptance or rejection of each paper were made through teleconference and electronic Program Committee discussions held during April 2014. Revised and expanded versions of a few selected papers will be considered for publication in a special issue of the journal *Distributed Computing* and in the *Journal of the ACM.*

The program committee has selected the paper "Signature-Free Asynchronous Byzantine Consensus" by Achour Mostéfaoui, Hamouma Moumen, and Michel Raynal for this year's Best Paper Award. In addition, the program committee selected the paper "Distributed Connectivity Decomposition" by Keren Censor-Hillel, Mohsen Ghaffari, and Fabian Kuhn for the Best Student Paper Award.

Leslie Lamport, the 2013 ACM A.M. Turing Award recipient, will give his Turing Lecture.

Three keynote talks will be given by Silvio Micali, Michael Luby, and Joseph Sifakis.

The 2013 Dijkstra Prize was given to the paper, "Locality in distributed graph algorithms", by Nati Linial published in *SIAM Journal on Computing, 21 (1992).* It was presented at the 27th International Symposium on Distributed Computing (DISC).

The 2014 Dijkstra Prize is given to the paper, "Distributed Snapshots: Determining Global States of Distributed Systems", by Kanianthra Mani Chandy and Leslie Lamport, published in *ACM Transactions on Computer Systems (1985).* It will be presented here.

Finally, this year we will celebrate the 60th birthday of Maurice Herlihy.

Putting together *PODC'14* was a team effort. We first thank the authors for providing the content of the program. We are grateful to the Program Committee and the sub-reviewers, who worked very hard in reviewing papers and providing feedback for authors. The help of the Steering Committee and of the Conference Committee was timely and invaluable. Finally, we thank our sponsors, ACM SIGOPS, and ACM SIGACT, and our generous corporate supporters, Ben-Gurion University of the Negev, CNRS, Facebook, Inria, LIP6, LRI, Lincs, Mairie de Paris (Paris City Hall), Microsoft Research, Oracle Labs, Qualcomm, Telecom ParisTech, and University Pierre and Marie Curie.

We hope that you will find this program interesting and thought-provoking and that the symposium will provide you with a valuable opportunity to share ideas with other researchers from institutions around the world.

I would like to extend my personal thanks to the organization committee and all sponsors.

Shlomi Dolev
PODC'14 Program Chair

Table of Contents

Session 4

Session Chair: Nitin H. Vaidya *(University of Illinois at Urbana-Champaign)*

Session 5

Session Chair: Moti Yung *(Google & Columbia University)*

Keynote Lecture

Session 6

Session Chair: Alexander Shvartsman *(University of Connecticut)*

Session 7

Session Chair: Panagiota Fatourou *(University of Crete & FORTH)*

Session 8

Session Chair: Vassos Hadzilacos *(University of Toronto)*

Session 9

Session Chair: Seth Gilbert *(National University of Singapore)*

2013 ACM A.M. Turing Award Lecture

Keynote Lecture

Session 10

Session Chair: Paul G. Spirakis *(CTI & University of Liverpool)*

PODC 2014 Symposium Organization

General Chair: Magnús Halldórsson (Reykjavik Univ., Iceland)

Program Chair: Shlomi Dolev (Ben-Gurion Univ., Israel)

Organizing Chairs: Sylvie Delaët (LRI, Univ. Paris Sud, France)
Maria Potop-Butucaru (LIP6, UMPC, France)
Sébastien Tixeuil (LIP6, UMPC, France)

Publicity Chair: Mark Tuttle (Intel, USA)

Treasurer Chair: Chryssis Georgiou (Univ. of Cyprus, Cyprus)

Steering Committee Chair: Alexander Shvartsman (Univ. of Connecticut, USA)

Steering Committee: Shlomi Dolev (Ben-Gurion Univ., Israel)
Chryssis Georgiou (Univ. of Cyprus, Cyprus)
Magnús Halldórsson (Reykjavik Univ., Iceland)
Alessandro Panconesi (Sapienza Univ., Italy)
Gadi Taubenfeld (IDC, Israel)
Nitin H.Vaidya (Univ. of Illinois, USA)

Program Committee: Joffroy Beauquier (LRI Univ. Paris Sud et CNRS, France)
Harry Buhrman (CWI & Univ. of Amsterdam, Netherlands)
Christian Cachin (IBM, Switzerland)
Reuven Cohen (Bar-Ilan Univ., Israel)
Shlomi Dolev, Chair (Ben-Gurion Univ., Israel)
Panagiota Fatourou (Univ. of Crete & FORTH, Greece)
Michael Fischer (Yale Univ., USA)
Paola Flocchini (Univ. of Ottawa, Canada)
Ian Foster (Argonne NL & Univ. of Chicago, USA)
Cyril Gavoille (LaBRI, Univ. of Bordeaux, France)
Seth Gilbert (National Univ. of Singapore, Singapore)
Niv Gilboa (Ben-Gurion Univ., Israel)
Vassos Hadzilacos (Univ. of Toronto, Canada)
Prasad Jayanti (Dartmouth College, USA)
Petr Kuznetsov (Telecom ParisTech, France)
Michael Luby (Qualcomm, USA)
Oded Maler (CNRS-VERIMAG, France)
Muriel Medard (MIT, USA)
Mike Paterson (Univ. of Warwick, UK)
Michel Raynal (IUF and IRISA (Univ. Rennes), France)
Luís Rodrigues (INESC-ID, Univ. Lisboa, Portugal)
Elad M. Schiller (Chalmers Univ. Tech., Sweden)

Program Committee (continued):

Stefan Schmid (TU Berlin & DT, Germany)
Alexander Shvartsman (Univ. of Connecticut, USA)
Joseph Sifakis (EPFL, Switzerland)
Paul G. Spirakis (CTI, Greece & Univ. of Liverpool, UK)
Nitin Vaidya (Univ. of Illinois Urbana-Champaign, USA)
Jennifer Welch (Texas A&M Univ., USA)
Jeannette Wing (Microsoft, USA)
Rebecca Wright (Rutgers Univ., USA)
Moti Yung (Google and Columbia Univ., USA)
Gil Zussman (Columbia Univ., USA)

Additional reviewers:

Marcos Aguilera
Dan Alistarh
Steve Alpern
Karine Altisen
James Aspnes
Hagit Attiya
Chen Avin
Hillel Avni
Yossi Azar
Leonid Barenboim
Ezio Bartocci
Reuven Bar-Yehuda
Michael Bender
Petra Berenbrink
Vartika Bhandari
Berk Birand
Peva Blanchard
Andrew Blumberg
François Bonnet
Silvia Bonomi
Zohir Bouzid
Trevor Brown
Dan Brownstein
Olga Brukman
Janna Burman
Shoaib Burq
Victor Bushkov
A. M. Chandrashekhar
Nikolaos Chatzipanagiotis
Hyun Chul Chung
Graham Cormode
Tyler Crain
Artur Czumaj
Sebastian Daum
Seda Davtyan
Oksana Denysyuk
Stéphane Devismes
Giuseppe Di Luna
Dave Dice
Nuno Diegues
Michael Dinitz
Danny Dolev
Eleni Drinea
Alon Efrat
Michael Elkin
Faith Ellen
Yuval Emek
Matthias Englert
Amir Epstein
Thomas Erlebach
Guy Even
Joel Falcou
Hugues Fauconnier
Uriel Feige
Thomas Ferrere
Sergey Frenkel
Luisa Gargano
Leszek Gasieniec
Georgios Georgiadis
Chryssis Georgiou
Mohsen Ghaffari
Phillip B. Gibbons

Additional reviewers (continued):

Emmanuel Godard
Wojciech Golab
Olga Goussevskaia
Maria Potop-Butucaru
Vincent Gramoli
Guy Grebla
Ehud Gudes
Rachid Guerraoui
Varun Gupta
Magnús Halldórsson
Moumen Hamouma
Carmit Hazay
Chinmay Hedge
Danny Hendler
Thomas Hérault
Maurice Herlihy
Ted Herman
Martin Hirt
Stephan Holzer
David Ilcinkas
Damien Imbs
Taisuke Izumi
Tomoko Izumi
Russel Jancewicz
Stanislaw Jarecki
Stephen Jarvis
Colette Johnen
Tomasz Jurdzinski
Nikolaos Kallimanis
Eleni Kanellou
Erez Kantor
Ronen Kat
Idit Keidar
Thomas Kesselheim
Maleq Khan
Gabriel Kliot
Alex Kogan
Sven Köhler
Kishori Konwar
Marina Kopeetsky
Eric Koskinen
Eleftherios Kosmas
Adrian Kosowski
Andreas Koutsopoulos
Eugene Kovalev
Darius Kowalski
Fabian Kuhn
Saptaparni Kumar
Ravi Kumar
Shay Kutten
Jan Lanik
João Leitão
Pierre Leone
Guy Leshem
Olivier Leveque
Xi Ming Li
Yun Li
Guanfeng Liang
Nati Linial
Thomas Locher
Zvi Lotker
Desmond Lun
Carlos Maltzahn
D. Manjunath
Jelena Marasevic
Robert Margolies
Toshimitsu Masuzawa
Alexandre Maurer
Stephen Maybank
Andrew McGregor
Hammurabi Mendes
Maged Michael
Othon Michail
Michael Mitzenmacher
Mark Moir
Oscar Morales Ponce
Adam Morrison
Thomas Moscibroda
Achour Mostéfaoui
Kiran-Kumar Muniswamy-Reddy
Lars Nagel
Danupon Nanongkai
Levon Nazaryan
Mikhail Nesterenko
Calvin Newport
Dejan Nickovic

Additional reviewers (continued):

Sotiris Nikoletseas
Nicolas Nisse
Ilan Orlov
Piya Pal
Panagiota Panagopoulou
Marina Papatriantafilou
Ali Parandehgheibi
Andrzej Pelc
Thomas Petig
Seth Pettie
Aditya Ramamoorthy
Christoforos Raptopoulos
Srivatsan Ravi
Pavel Raykov
Mike Reiter
Andrea Richa
Noam Rinetzky
Peter Robinson
Paolo Romano
Chris Rossbach
Christian Esteve Rothenberg
Matthieu Roy
Eric Ruppert
Jared Saia
Iosif Salem
Nicola Santoro
Srikanth Sastry
Gabriel Scalosub
Christian Scheideler
Ivan Seskar
Mayank Sharma
Shantanu Sharma
Scott Shenker
Maiko Shigeno
Tatiana Shpeisman
Chandramani Singh
Radu Sion
Michael Sirivianos
Michiel Smid
Saleh Soltan
Ulrich Speidel
Abhinav Srivastav
Damjan Strnad
Hsin-Hao Su
Adi Suissa
Malgosia Sulkowska
Chriti Symeonidou
Ewa Syta
Edward Talmage
Dan Tamir
Gadi Taubenfeld
Pranav Tendulkar
Justin Thaler
Dan-Cristian Tomozei
Lewis Tseng
Volker Turau
Shimrit Tzur-David
Przemysław Uznański
Jan Van Den Bussche
Victor Vianu
Giovanni Viglietta
Sheng Wang
Roger Wattenhofer
Wojciech Wawrzyniak
Joerg Widmer
Yukiko Yamauchi
Aylin Yener
Haifeng Yu
Shmuel Zaks
Hong-Sheng Zhou
Polina Zilberman

PODC 2014 Sponsors & Supporters

Sponsors:

Supporters:

The 2013 Edsger W. Dijkstra Prize in Distributed Computing

The Dijkstra Prize Committee has selected **Nati Linial** as the recipient of this year's Edsger W. Dijkstra Prize in Distributed Computing. The prize is given to him for his outstanding paper, "Locality in distributed graph algorithms", published in *SIAM Journal on Computing, 21* (1992), 193-201.

The Edsger W. Dijkstra Prize in Distributed Computing is awarded for an outstanding paper on the principles of distributed computing, whose significance and impact on the theory and/or practice of distributed computing has been evident for at least a decade.

This paper has had a major impact on distributed message-passing algorithms. It explored the notion of *locality* in distributed computation and raised interesting questions concerning the locality level in various problems, in terms of their time complexity in different classes of networks. Linial developed a clean model for studying locality that ignores message sizes, asynchrony and failures. The model allowed researchers to isolate the effects of locality and study the roles of distances and neighborhoods, as graph theoretic notions, and their interrelations with algorithmic and complexity-theoretic problems.

Linial's paper also presents an $O(\Delta^2)$-coloring algorithm for graphs with degree at most Δ that runs in $O(\log^* n)$ time. It is based on a new connection between extremal set theory and distributed computing. This result serves as a cornerstone for other coloring algorithms, including the current best algorithm. Whether one can get an $O(\Delta^{2-E})$-coloring within the same time bound remains a major open problem.

His paper also proves that, for any function f, any $f(\Delta)$-coloring algorithm requires $\Omega(\log^* n)$ time. Moreover, the same bound is shown for 3-coloring an oriented path or cycle. To obtain these lower bounds, Linial introduced the concept of the *neighborhood graph* of a distributed network and analyzed it. An enhanced form of his technique was recently used for establishing the best known lower bounds for Maximal Independent Set and Maximal Matching.

In summary, Linial's paper opened new approaches to distributed symmetry breaking and remains one of the most important papers in this area.

The Prize is sponsored jointly by the ACM Symposium on Principles of Distributed Computing (PODC) and the EATCS Symposium on Distributed Computing (DISC). This prize is presented annually, with the presentation taking place alternately at PODC and DISC. The 2013 Prize was presented at DISC.

Dijkstra Prize Committee 2013

Yehuda Afek, *Tel-Aviv University*
Faith Ellen, *University of Toronto*
Boaz Patt-Shamir, *Tel-Aviv University*
Sergio Rajsbaum, *UNAM*
Alexander Shvartsman, *University of Connecticut*
Gadi Taubenfeld, *IDC, Chair*

The 2014 Edsger W. Dijkstra Prize in Distributed Computing

The Dijkstra Prize Committee has selected **Kanianthra Mani Chandy** and **Leslie Lamport** as the recipients of this year's Edsger W. Dijkstra Prize in Distributed Computing. The prize is given to them for their outstanding paper "Distributed Snapshots: Determining Global States of Distributed Systems", published in ACM Transactions on Computer Systems, Vol. 3, No. 1, 1985, pages 63–75.

The ACM-EATCS Edsger W. Dijkstra Prize in Distributed Computing is awarded for an outstanding paper on the principles of distributed computing, whose significance and impact on the theory and/or practice of distributed computing has been evident for at least a decade. The prize is sponsored jointly by the ACM Symposium on Principles of Distributed Computing (PODC) and the EATCS Symposium on Distributed Computing (DISC).

In their paper, Chandy and Lamport describe a distributed algorithm to record a consistent global state of an asynchronous distributed computation. Determining such a distributed snapshot is essential for several fundamental tasks and it is for example at the basis of solutions for termination or deadlock detection or to verify whether some other stable global property holds. Note that the inherent lack of a common clock or a global observer means that global states that are asynchronously recorded can be potentially inconsistent. The solution provided by Chandy and Lamport is extremely elegant and also remarkably simple, a fact that certainly also contributed to its success. The correctness proof is based on swapping of prerecording and postrecording events without affecting the correctness of the observed state. It is very significant that the recorded global state may not have been any of the global states that the system passed through in a real-time view of its execution.

The paper provides the first clear understanding of the definition of consistent global states in distributed systems. Consistent global states form the cornerstone of asynchronous distributed execution observation, and subsequent concepts such as those of the hugely popular vector clocks and concurrent common knowledge are based on consistent global states. Further, the paper demonstrates that the recorded state in the global snapshot is a valid equivalent state in the sense that an equivalent execution may very well pass through that state, even though the actual execution may not have. In fact, the possibility of the occurrence of the recorded state is indistinguishable from the possibility of the occurrence of the actual states that occurred in the distributed execution. This property led to the definition of global predicates on entire executions, as opposed to the definition of global predicates on individual observations of executions. Similarly, this spawned the important concept of isomorphism of executions.

In conclusion, the paper by Chandy and Lamport has had a profound and lasting impact on the theory and implementation of distributed algorithms and systems. It has led to concepts such as vector time, isomorphism of executions, global predicate detection, and concurrent common knowledge. Applications of the results of observing the system in consistent states include the development of vector clocks, checkpointing and message logging protocols, correct protocols for detecting stable properties such as distributed deadlocks and termination, mutual exclusion algorithms, garbage collection protocols, cache coherency and file coherency protocols in distributed replicated file systems, distributed debugging protocols, protocols for total message order and causal message order in group communication systems, global virtual time algorithms used particularly in parallel and distributed simulations of discrete event systems, and collaborative sessions and editing protocols in wide area systems and on the grid.

Dijkstra Prize Committee 2014

Lorenzo Alvisi, *University of Texas at Austin*
Shlomi Dolev, *Ben-Gurion University of the Negev*
Rachid Guerraoui, *EPFL*
Idit Keidar, *Technion*
Fabian Kuhn, *University of Freiburg, Chair*
Shay Kutten, *Technion*

Rational and Resilient Protocols

Silvio Micali
MIT
silvio@csail.mit.edu

Abstract

Cryptography and distributed computation have been very successful in advancing the study of interaction of distinct computing agents. Moreover, both fields have been very successful in conversing with each other, sharing models and techniques. Notably, they both model agents as being either "good" (i.e., following their prescribed programs) or "bad" (i.e., deviating from their prescribed program, by stopping, by acting maliciously, or even by coordinating their malicious strategies). I believe however, that we have been neglecting a fundamental ingredient, *utility*, which has long been recognized and studied by another scientific field, *game theory*, and in particular by a beautiful subfield of it, *mechanism design*.

Mechanism design aims at obtaining a desired outcome by engineering a game that, rationally played, yields a desired outcome. In such games, multiple players interact very much as in a cryptographic/distributed protocol. But here players are not good or malicious. Rather, every player is RATIONAL, that is, always acts so as to maximize HIS OWN utility.

I believe that properly incorporating utility/rationality in our models will dramatically increase our range of action. Viceversa, mechanism design stands to gain a lot by properly incorporating cryptographic/distributed notions and techniques. In particular, rational players may, by colluding (and making side-payments to one another), increase their utilities. And they too value privacy, which may indeed represent their strategic interests in unforeseen and not yet modeled interactions. Thus, privacy and collusion can disrupt the intended course of an engineered game, and ultimately prevent a desired outcome from being achieved. Mechanism design has been only moderately successful in protecting against collusion, has largely ignored privacy, and might gain precious resiliency by taking into consideration our notions and techniques.

In sum, there is an opportunity for cryptography, distributed computation, and mechanism design to join forces to study more general and accurate models of interaction, and to design more realistic and resilient protocols that simultaneously take into account utility, collusion, and privacy. No sufficiently complex and sufficiently large system, no *organism* can successfully work or merely sustain its existence without recognizing and harmonizing these basic forces. To be successful, this designing effort will require a good deal of modeling and the development of new conceptual frameworks. It will require open minds and open hearts, so as to leverage past and successful scientific experiences, without being trapped or confined by them. There is the promise of a great deal of fun, challenge, and excitement, and we must recruit as much talent as possible to this effort.

As a concrete, simple, and hopefully provocative example, I will describe a (quite) resilient mechanism, designed by me and Jing Chen, for achieving a (quite) alternative revenue benchmark in unrestricted combinatorial auctions. In such auctions there are multiple distinct goods for sale, each player privately attributes an arbitrary value to any possible subset of the goods, and the seller has no information about the players' valuations.

Categories and Subject Descriptors:
F.0 General

Keywords
interaction; collusion; privacy; rationality; resiliency; cryptography; distributed computation; mechanism design

PODC'14, July 15–18, 2014, Paris, France.
ACM 978-1-4503-2944-6/14/07.
http://dx.doi.org/10.1145/2611462.2611516

Signature-Free Asynchronous Byzantine Consensus with $t < n/3$ and $O(n^2)$ Messages

Achour Mostéfaoui
LINA, Université de Nantes
44322 Nantes, France
Achour.Mostefaoui@univ-nantes.fr

Hamouma Moumen
University of Bejaia
Bejaia, Algeria
moumenh@gmail.com

Michel Raynal
Institut Universitaire de France
& IRISA, Université de Rennes
raynal@irisa.fr

ABSTRACT

This paper presents a new round-based asynchronous consensus algorithm that copes with up to $t < n/3$ Byzantine processes, where n is the total number of processes. In addition of not using signature, not assuming a computationally-limited adversary, while being optimal with respect to the value of t, this algorithm has several noteworthy properties: the expected number of rounds to decide is four, each round is composed of two or three communication steps and involves $O(n^2)$ messages, and a message is composed of a round number plus a single bit. To attain this goal, the consensus algorithm relies on a common coin as defined by Rabin, and a new extremely simple and powerful broadcast abstraction suited to binary values. The main target when designing this algorithm was to obtain a cheap and simple algorithm. This was motivated by the fact that, among the first-class properties, simplicity –albeit sometimes under-estimated or even ignored– is a major one.

Categories and Subject Descriptors

C.2.4 [**Computer-Communication Network**]: Distributed Systems *-distributed applications, network operating systems*; D.4.1 [**Operating Systems**] *-concurrency, synchronization*; D.4.5 [**Operating Systems**] Reliability *-fault-tolerance*; F.1.1 [**Computation by Abstract Devices**]: Models of Computation *-Computability theory*

General Terms: Algorithms, Reliability, Theory

Keywords: Abstraction, Asynchronous message-passing system, Broadcast abstraction, Byzantine process, Common coin, Consensus, Distributed algorithm, Optimal resilience, Randomized algorithm, Signature-free algorithm, Simplicity.

1. INTRODUCTION

Distributed computing.

Distributed computing occurs when one has to solve a problem in terms of physically distinct entities (usually called nodes, processors, processes, agents, sensors, etc.) such that each entity has only a partial knowledge of the many parameters involved in the problem. In the following, we use the term *process* to denote any computing entity. From an operational point of view this means that the processes of a distributed system need to exchange information, and agree in some way or another, in order to cooperate to a common goal. If processes do not cooperate, the system is no longer a distributed system. Hence, a distributed system has to provide the processes with communication and agreement abstractions.

Understanding and designing distributed applications is not an easy task [3, 11, 29, 38, 39, 40]. This is because, due to the very nature of distributed computing, no process can capture instantaneously the global state of the application it is part of. This comes from the fact that, as processes are geographically localized at distinct places, distributed applications have to cope with the uncertainty created by asynchrony and failures. As a simple example, it is impossible to distinguish a crashed process from a very slow process in an asynchronous system prone to process crashes.

As in sequential computing, a simple approach to facilitate the design of distributed applications consists in designing appropriate abstractions. More generally, computer science is a science of abstraction and distributed computing is the science of distributed abstractions [19]. With such abstractions, the application designer can think about solutions to solve problems at a higher conceptual level than the basic send/receive communication level.

Communication and agreement abstractions.

Broadcast abstractions are among the most important abstractions encountered in fault-tolerant distributed computing [3, 11, 13, 29, 38]. Roughly speaking, these abstractions allow processes to disseminate information in such a way that specific provable properties concerning this dissemination are satisfied. One of the most popular of these abstractions is reliable broadcast [8, 13].

As far as agreement abstractions are concerned, *non-blocking atomic commit* [24, 30] and *consensus* [18, 36] are certainly the most important abstractions of fault-tolerant distributed computing. Assuming that each process proposes a value, the consensus abstraction allows the non-faulty processes to agree on the same value, which has to satisfy some validity condition depending on both the proposed values and the failure model [3, 29, 38, 39].

Consensus in asynchronous Byzantine systems.

This paper is on consensus in asynchronous distributed systems where processes can commit Byzantine failures [27]. This failure type has first been introduced in the context of synchronous distributed systems [27, 36, 39], and then investigated in the context of asynchronous distributed systems [3, 29, 38]. A process has a *Byzantine* behavior when it arbitrarily deviates from its intended behavior: it then commits a Byzantine failure (otherwise we say it is *correct*). This bad behavior can be intentional (malicious) or sim-

PODC'14, July 15–18, 2014, Paris, France.

http://dx.doi.org/10.1145/2611462.2611468.

Protocol	$n >$	signatures	msgs/round	bits/msg	steps/round
Rabin 1983 [37]	$10t$	yes	$O(n^2)$	$O(1)$	2
Berman Garay 1993 [5]	$5t$	no	$O(n^2)$	$O(1)$	2
Friedman Mostefaoui Raynal 2005 [22]	$5t$	no	$O(n^2)$	$O(1)$	1
Bracha 1987 [7]	$3t$	no	$O(n^3)$	$O(\log(n))$	9
Srikanth Toueg 1987 [42]	$3t$	no	$O(n^3)$	$O(\log(n))$	5
Toueg 1984 [43]	$3t$	yes	$O(n^3)$	$O(n)$	3
Canetti Rabin 1993 [12]	$3t$	yes	$O(n^2)$	poly(n)	9
Cachin Kursawe Shoup 2000 [9]	$3t$	yes	$O(n^2)$	$O(\ell)$	2
This paper	$3t$	no	$O(n^2)$	$O(1)$	2 or 3

Table 1: Cost and constraint of different Byzantine binary consensus algorithms

ply the result of a transient fault that altered the local state of a process, thereby modifying its behavior in an unpredictable way. Let us notice that process crashes (unexpected halting) define a strict subset of Byzantine failures.

Related work.

Let t denote the model upper bound on the number of processes that can have a Byzantine behavior. It is shown in several papers (e.g., [16, 27, 36, 43]) that Byzantine consensus cannot be solved when $t \geq n/3$, be the system synchronous or asynchronous, be the algorithm allowed to use cryptography or not, or be the algorithm allowed to use random numbers or not. As far as synchronous systems are concerned, it has been been shown in [17] that $(t+1)$ rounds is a lower bound on the number of communication steps needed to solve Byzantine consensus. It has also been shown in [23] that, using randomization, this bound can be improved to an expected $O(\log n)$ value in systems that are full-information, synchronous, and where where $t \leq \frac{n}{3+\epsilon}$ and $\epsilon > 0$.

As far as asynchronous systems are concerned, it is well-known that there is no deterministic consensus algorithm as soon as one process may crash [18], which means that Byzantine consensus cannot be solved either as soon as one process can be faulty. Said another way, the basic asynchronous Byzantine system model has to be enriched with additional computational power. Such an additional power can be obtained by randomization (e.g., [4, 14, 22, 37]), assumption on message delivery schedules [8, 43], failure detectors suited to Byzantine systems (e.g., [21, 25]), additional – deterministic or probabilistic– synchrony assumptions (e.g., [8, 16, 31]), or restrictions on the vectors of input values proposed by the processes [20, 33].

This paper is on binary consensus algorithms in asynchronous Byzantine systems where the additional computational power is supplied by a *common coin*. Such an object, introduced by Rabin [37], is a distributed object that delivers the same sequence of random bits $b_1, b_2, \ldots, b_r, \ldots$ to each process. Some of the first randomized algorithms (such as the ones of Ben-Or [4] or Bracha [6]) use local coins. As a consequence they have an expected number of rounds which is exponential (unless $t = O(\sqrt{n})$), which makes them of theoretical interest, but of limited practical use. As randomized algorithms based on a common coin can have an expected number of rounds which is constant, this paper focuses only on such algorithms.

Round-based asynchronous Byzantine algorithms based on a common coin are listed in Table 1[1]. All these algorithms, which address binary consensus, are round-based, and, in each of them, each message carries a round number. Hence, when comparing their message size, we do not consider round numbers. We have the following.

- The first algorithm is such that $n < 10t$, has an $O(n^2)$ message complexity, and requires signatures.
- The algorithms of the two next lines are such that $t < n/5$, and their message complexity is $O(n^2)$. These algorithms are simple, signature-free, and use one or two communication steps per round, but none of them is optimal with respect to t-resilience.
- The algorithms of the next three lines are optimal with respect to t, but have an $O(n^3)$ message complexity. Moreover, [43] uses signed messages, while [7] does not use a common coin, and may consequently execute an exponential number of rounds. Due to their message complexity, and their number of communication steps per round, these algorithms are costly.
- The algorithm proposed in [12], although polynomial, has a huge bit complexity. The algorithm presented in [9] is optimal with respect to t, uses only $O(n^2)$ messages per round, has two communication steps per round, and uses signed messages (the value ℓ in the bit complexity corresponds to the size of RSA signatures). However, as noticed by its authors, "because of public key operations, the computational complexity of this protocol is typically higher than those using authentication codes".

Content of the paper.

The paper first introduces a simple broadcast abstraction suited to binary values, that we call BV-broadcast. This broadcast focuses on values and not on processes, which means that it does not consider the fact that "this" value has been broadcast by "this" process. BV-broadcast, whose implementation is particularly simple, reduces the power of Byzantine processes, in such a way that a value broadcast only by Byzantine processes is never delivered to the correct processes. This value-oriented broadcast abstraction is then used to solve Byzantine binary consensus is asynchronous systems enriched with a common coin. The resulting consensus algorithm is a round-based asynchronous algorithm that has the following noteworthy features.

- The algorithm requires $t < n/3$ and is consequently optimal with respect to t.
- The algorithm uses 2 or 3 communication steps per round (2 steps when the correct processes start a round with the same estimate of the decision value).
- The expected number of rounds to decide is 4.
- The message complexity is $O(n^2)$ messages per round.

[1]As far as synchronous systems are concerned, an efficient coin-based algorithm that solves consensus despite Byzantine processes is described in [26]. This algorithm assumes an adaptive adversary.

- Each message carries its type, a round number plus a single data bit.
- Finally, the algorithm does not require signed messages, and does not assume a computationally-limited adversary.

Hence, contrarily to what one could believe from existing asynchronous Byzantine binary consensus algorithms, the formula

$$[\text{quadratic message complexity}] \Rightarrow [(\text{use of signatures}) \vee (t < n/5)]$$

is false. The proposed algorithm shows that $t < n/3$ (as in [9]), quadratic message complexity (as in [5, 9]), and absence of signatures (as in [5, 22]) are not incompatible.

Simplicity is a first class property.

When designing this algorithm, an important issue was to obtain a *simple* Byzantine consensus algorithm. Our guiding mantra while designing the proposed algorithm was the famous sentence of Einstein "make it as simple as possible, but not simpler". This was not an easy task as simplicity is rarely obtained for free. Let us also remember the following sentence written by Pascal at the end of a letter to a friend "I apologize for having written such a long letter, I had not enough time to write a shorter one". The implication "simple ⇒ easy" is rarely true for non-trivial problems [1]. Simplicity requires effort, but is very rewarding. It is a first class scientific property which participates in the beauty of science[2] and makes pedagogy easier.

Roadmap.

The paper is composed of 5 sections. Section 2 presents the computation model. Section 3 presents and proves correct the binary-value broadcast abstraction, while Section 4 presents and proves correct the consensus algorithm. Finally, Section 5 concludes the paper.

2. COMPUTATION MODEL

Asynchronous processes.

The system is made up of a finite set Π of $n > 1$ asynchronous sequential processes, namely $\Pi = \{p_1, \ldots, p_n\}$. "Asynchronous" means that each process proceeds at its own pace, which may vary arbitrarily with time, and remains always unknown to the other processes.

Communication network.

The processes communicate by exchanging messages through an asynchronous reliable point-to-point network. "Asynchronous" means that a message that has been sent is eventually received by its destination process, i.e., there is no bound on message transfer delays. "Reliable" means that the network does not loss, duplicate, modify, or create messages. "Point-to-point" means that there is a bi-directional communication channel between each pair of processes. Hence, when a process receives a message, it can identify its sender.

A process p_i sends a message to a process p_j by invoking the primitive "send TAG(m) to p_j", where TAG is the type of the message and m its content. To simplify the presentation, it is assumed that a process can send messages to itself. A process receives a message by executing the primitive "receive()".

[2]To quote Dijkstra: "When we recognize the battle against chaos, mess, and unmastered complexity as one of computing science's major callings, we must admit that "Beauty is our Business"." [15].

The operation broadcast TAG(m) is a macro-operation which stands for "**for each** $j \in \{1, \ldots, n\}$ send TAG(m) to p_j **end for**".This operation is usually called *unreliable* broadcast (if the sender crashes in the middle of the **for** loop, it is possible that only an arbitrary subset correct processes receives the message).

Failure model.

Up to t processes may exhibit a *Byzantine* behavior. A Byzantine process is a process that behaves arbitrarily: it may crash, fail to send or receive messages, send arbitrary messages, start in an arbitrary state, perform arbitrary state transitions, etc. Hence, a Byzantine process, which is assumed to send a message m to all the processes, can send a message m_1 to some processes, a different message m_2 to another subset of processes, and no message at all to the other processes. Moreover, Byzantine processes can collude to "pollute" the computation. A process that exhibits a Byzantine behavior is called *faulty*. Otherwise, it is *correct*.

Let us notice that, as each pair of processes is connected by a channel, no Byzantine process can impersonate another process. Byzantine processes can modify the message delivery schedule, but cannot affect network reliability. More generally, the model does not assume a computationally-limited adversary.

Notation.

This computation model is denoted $\mathcal{BZ\_AS}_{n,t}[\emptyset]$. In the following, this model is both restricted with a constraint on t and enriched with an object providing processes with additional computational power. More precisely, $\mathcal{BZ\_AS}_{n,t}[n > 3t]$ denotes the model $\mathcal{BZ\_AS}_{n,t}[\emptyset]$ where the number of faulty processes is smaller than $n/3$, and $\mathcal{BZ\_AS}_{n,t}[n > 3t, \text{CC}]$ denotes the model $\mathcal{BZ\_AS}_{n,t}[n > 3t]$ enriched with the common coin (CC) abstraction as defined in [37].

3. THE BINARY-VALUE BROADCAST ABSTRACTION

3.1 Binary-value Broadcast

Definition.

This communication abstraction (in short, BV-broadcast) in an all-to-all abstraction that provides the processes with a single operation denoted BV_broadcast().

When a process invokes BV_broadcast TAG(m), we say that it "BV-broadcasts the message TAG(m)". The content of a message m is 0 or 1 (hence the term "binary-value" in the name of this communication abstraction).

In a BV-broadcast instance, each correct process p_i BV-broadcasts a binary value and obtains binary values. To store the values obtained by each process, BV-broadcast provides each correct process p_i with a read-only local variable denoted bin_values_i. This variable is a set, initialized to $\emptyset$, which increases when new values are received. VB-broadcast is defined by the four following properties.

- BV-Obligation. If at least $(t+1)$ correct processes BV-broadcast the same value v, v is eventually added to the set bin_values_i of each correct process p_i.
- BV-Justification. If p_i is correct and $v \in bin\_values_i$, v has been BV-broadcast by a correct process.
- BV-Uniformity. If a value v is added to the set bin_values_i of a correct process p_i, eventually $v \in bin\_values_j$ at every correct process p_j.
- BV-Termination. Eventually the set bin_values_i of each correct process p_i is not empty.

operation BV_broadcast $\text{MSG}(v_i)$ **is**
(1) broadcast $\text{B\_VAL}(v_i)$.

when $\text{B\_VAL}(v)$ **is received**
(2) **if** $\big(\text{B\_VAL}(v)$ received from $(t+1)$ different processes and $\text{B\_VAL}(v)$ not yet broadcast$\big)$
(3) **then** broadcast $\text{B\_VAL}(v)$ % a process echoes a value only once %
(4) **end if**;
(5) **if** $\big(\text{B\_VAL}(v)$ received from $(2t+1)$ different processes$\big)$
(6) **then** $bin\_values_i \leftarrow bin\_values_i \cup \{v\}$ % local delivery of a value %
(7) **end if**.

Figure 1: An algorithm implementing BV-broadcast in $\mathcal{BZ\_AS}_{n,t}[n > 3t]$

The following property is an immediate consequence of the previous properties.

PROPERTY 1. *Eventually the sets bin_values_i of the correct processes p_i become non-empty and equal, contain all the values broadcast by correct processes and no value broadcast only by Byzantine processes.*

3.2 A BV-broadcast Algorithm

A simple algorithm implementing the BV-broadcast abstraction is described in Figure 1. This algorithm is based on a particularly simple "echo" mechanism. Differently from previous echo-based algorithms (e.g., [7, 42]), echo is used here with respect to each value that has been received (whatever the number of processes that broadcast it), and not with respect to each pair composed of a value plus the identity of the process that broadcast this value. In the algorithm of Figure 1, a value entails a single echo, whatever the number of processes that have broadcast this value.

When a process invokes BV_broadcast $\text{MSG}(v)$, $v \in \{0, 1\}$, it broadcasts $\text{B\_VAL}(v)$ to all the processes (line 1). Then, when a process p_i receives (from any process) a message $\text{B\_VAL}(v)$, (if not yet done) it forwards this message to all the processes (line 3) if it has received the same message from at least $(t+1)$ different processes (line 2). Moreover, if p_i has received v from at least $(2t+1)$ different processes, the value v is added to bin_values_i.

Remark.

It is important to notice that no correct process p_i can know when its set bin_values_i has obtained its final value. (Otherwise, consensus will be directly obtained by directing each process p_i to deterministically extract the same value from bin_values_i). This impossibility is due to the net effect of asynchrony and process failures [18].

3.3 Proof and Cost of the Algorithm

THEOREM 1. *The algorithm described in Figure 1 implements the BV-broadcast abstraction in the system model $\mathcal{BZ\_AS}_{n,t}[t < n/3]$.*

Proof Proof of the BV-Obligation property. Let v be a value such that $(t+1)$ correct processes invoke BV_broadcast $\text{MSG}(v)$. It follows from the predicate of line 2 that each correct process eventually receives these $(t+1)$ messages, and consequently each correct process broadcasts exactly once the message $\text{B\_VAL}(v)$ to all the processes. As the channels are reliable, and $n - t \geq 2t + 1$, it follows that the predicate of line 5 is eventually satisfied at each correct process, and consequently, the property follows.

Proof of the BV-Justification property. To show this property, we prove that a value BV-broadcast only by faulty processes cannot be added to the set bin_values_i of a correct process p_i. Hence, let us assume that only faulty processes BV-broadcast v. It follows that a correct process can receive the message $\text{B\_VAL}(v)$ from at most t different processes. Consequently the predicate of line 2 cannot be satisfied at a correct process. Hence, the predicate of line 5 cannot be satisfied either at a correct process, and the property follows.

Proof of the BV-Uniformity property. If a value v is added to the set bin_values_i of a correct process p_i (local delivery), this process has received $\text{B\_VAL}(v)$ from at least $(2t+1)$ different processes (line 5), i.e., from at least $(t+1)$ different correct processes. As each of these correct processes has sent this message to all the processes, it follows that the predicate of line 2 is eventually satisfied at each correct process, which consequently broadcasts $\text{B\_VAL}(v)$ to all. As $n - t \geq 2t + 1$, the predicate of line 5 is then eventually satisfied at each correct process, and the BV-Uniformity property follows.

Proof of the BV-Termination property. As (a) there are at least $(n - t)$ correct processes, (b) each of them invokes BV_broadcast $\text{MSG}()$, (c) $n - t \geq 2t + 1 = (t+1) + t$, and (d) only 0 and 1 can be BV-broadcast, it follows that there is a value $v \in \{0, 1\}$ that is BV-broadcast by at least $(t+1)$ correct processes. The proof of the BV-Termination property is then an immediate consequence of the BV-Obligation property. $\Box_{Theorem\ 1}$

Cost of the algorithm.

As far as the cost of the algorithm is concerned, we have the following for each BV-broadcast instance.

- If all correct processes BV-broadcast the same value, the algorithm requires a single communication step. Otherwise, it can require two communication steps.
- Let $c \geq n - t$ be the number of correct processes.

  The correct processes send $c\,n$ messages if they BV-broadcast the same value, and send $2\,c\,n$ messages otherwise.
- In addition to the control tag B_VAL, a message carries a single bit. Hence, message size is constant.

4. A BYZANTINE CONSENSUS ALGORITHM

4.1 Byzantine Consensus and Enriched Model

Binary Byzantine consensus.

The Byzantine consensus problem has been informally stated in the Introduction. Assuming that each correct process p_i proposes a value $v_i \in \{0, 1\}$, each of them has to decide a value such that the following property are satisfied.

- BC-Validity. A decided value was proposed by a correct process.

- BC-Agreement. No two correct processes decide different values.
- BC-One-shot. A correct process decides at most once.
- BC-Termination. Each correct process decides.

The BC-Validity property states that no value proposed only by faulty processes can be decided. As we consider binary consensus, it is equivalent to the following property: if all correct processes propose the same value v, the value $\overline{v}$ cannot be decided (where $\overline{v}$ is the other binary value).

From binary to multivalued Byzantine consensus.
Interestingly, asynchronous multivalued Byzantine consensus (i.e., when more than two values can be proposed) can be solved on top of binary Byzantine consensus. Such constructions are described in [10, 14, 28, 32, 34, 35, 41] (see [44] for synchronous systems).

Enriching the basic asynchronous model: Rabin's common coin.
As indicated in the Introduction, the model $\mathcal{BZ\_AS}_{n,t}[t < n/3]$ has to be enriched so that Byzantine consensus can be solved. The additional computational power we consider here is a *common coin* (CC) as defined by Rabin [37]. As indicated, the corresponding enriched system model is denoted $\mathcal{BZ\_AS}_{n,t}[t < n/3, \text{CC}]$. A common coin can be seen as a global entity that delivers the very same sequence of random bits $b_1, b_2, \ldots, b_r, \ldots$ to processes, each bit b_r has the value 0 or 1 with probability $1/2$.

More precisely, this oracle provides the processes with a primitive denoted random() that returns a bit each time it is called by a process. In addition to being random, this bit has the following global property: the rth invocation of random() by a correct process p_i returns it the bit b_r. This means that the r^{th}invocations of random() by any pair of correct processes p_i and p_j return them b_r. A common coin is built in such a way that the processes need to cooperate to compute the value of each bit b_r. More precisely, no Byzantine process can obtain the value b_r before at least one correct process has started accessing b_r (see [11]). This is required to prevent Byzantine processes from computing bit values in advance and exploit these values to produce message delivery schedule that would prevent termination[3]. The reader interested in the implementation of such a common coin can consult [2, 9].

On randomized consensus.
When using additional computing power provided by common coins, the consensus termination property can no longer be deterministic. *Randomized consensus* is defined by BC-Validity (Obligation), BC-Agreement, plus the following BC-Termination property [4, 37]: Every non-faulty process decides with probability 1. For round-based algorithms, this termination property is re-stated as follows. For any correct process p_i, we have:

$$\lim_{r \to +\infty} \big(\text{Probability } [p_i \text{ decides by round } r]\big) = 1.$$

[3]As just indicated, this assumption on the common coin computation is due to the fact that Byzantine processes are not prevented from controlling message delivery schedule, thereby rendering random numbers helpless. It would be possible to let Byzantine processes know in advance the sequence of random bits, as long as they cannot control message delivery schedules (this assumption corresponds to the *oblivious scheduler* model [2]).

4.2 Randomized Byzantine Consensus Algorithm

Principles and description of the algorithm.
The consensus algorithm is described in Figure 2. It requires $t < n/3$ and is consequently optimal with respect to the maximal number t of Byzantine processes that can be tolerated. A process p_i invokes propose(v_i) where $v_i \in \{0, 1\}$ is the value it proposes. It decides when it executes the statement decide(v) at line 8.

The local variable est_i of a process p_i keeps its current estimate of the decision (initially $est_i = v_i$). The processes proceed by consecutive asynchronous rounds and a BV-broadcast instance is associated with each round. The local variable r_i denotes the current round of process p_i, while the local variable $bin\_values_i[r_i]$ denotes the local read-only variable bin_values_i associated with the BV-broadcast instance used at round r_i.

The behavior of a correct process p_i during a round r_i can be decomposed in three phases.

- Phase 1: lines 1-3. This first phase is an exchange phase. During a round r_i, a process p_i first invokes BV_broadcast $\text{EST}[r_i](est_i)$ (line 2) to inform the other processes of the value of its current estimate est_i. This message is tagged EST and associated with the round number r_i (hence the notation $\text{EST}[r_i]()$). Then, p_i waits until its underlying read-only BV-broadcast variable $bin\_values_i[r_i]$ is no longer empty (line 3). Due to the BV-Termination property, this eventually happens. When the predicate becomes satisfied, the set $bin\_values_i[r_i]$ has not yet necessarily its final value, but it contains at least one value $\in \{0, 1\}$. Moreover, due to the BV-Justification property, the values in $bin\_values_i[r_i]$ were BV-broadcast by correct processes.
- Phase 2: lines 4-5. The second phase is also an exchange phase during which each correct process p_i invokes the operation broadcast $\text{AUX}[r_i](w)$ where w is a value belonging to $bin\_values_i[r_i]$ (line 4). Let us notice that all the correct processes p_j broadcast a value of their set $bin\_values_j[r_j]$ (i.e., an estimate value of a correct process), while a Byzantine process can broadcast an arbitrary binary value. To summarize, the broadcasts of the second phase inform the other processes of estimate values that have been BV-broadcast by correct processes.

  A process p_i then waits until the predicate of line 5 becomes satisfied. This predicate is used to discard (if any) a value that would have been sent only by Byzantine processes. From an operational point of view, it states that there is a set $values_i$ containing only the values broadcast at line 4 by $(n - t)$ distinct processes, and these values originated from correct processes (which BV-broadcast them at line 2). Said in another way, the set $values_i$ of a correct process p_i cannot contain an estimate value broadcast only by Byzantine processes. Hence, after line 5, we have $values_i \in \{0, 1\}$, and for any $v \in values_i$, v is an estimate VB-broadcast by a correct process.
- Phase 3: lines 6-11. This last phase is a local computation phase. A correct process p_i first obtains the common coin value s associated with the current round (line 6).
  - If $|values_i| = 2$, both the value 0 and the value 1 are estimate values of correct processes. In this cases, p_i adopts the value s of the common coin (line 10).
  - If $|values_i| = 1$, p_i decides v (the single value present in $values_i$) if additionally $s = v$ (line 8). Otherwise it adopts v as its new estimate (line 9).

```
operation propose(v_i) is
est_i ← v_i; r_i ← 0;
repeat forever
(1)     r_i ← r_i + 1;
(2)     BV_broadcast EST[r_i](est_i);
(3)     wait until (bin_values_i[r_i] ≠ ∅);
        % bin_values_i[r_i] has not necessarily obtained its final value when the wait statement terminates %
(4)     broadcast AUX[r_i](w) where w ∈ bin_values_i[r_i];
(5)     wait until (∃ a set of (n − t) AUX[r_i](x) messages delivered from distinct processes such that
                values_i ⊆ bin_values_i[r_i] where values_i is the set of values x carried by these (n − t) messages);
(6)     s ← random();
(7)     if (values_i = {v})  % i.e.,|values_i| = 1 %
(8)       then if (v = s) then decide(v) if not yet done end if;
(9)             est_i ← v
(10)      else est_i ← s
(11)    end if
end repeat.
```

Figure 2: A BV-broadcast-based algorithm implementing binary consensus in $\mathcal{BZ\_AS}_{n,t}[n > 3t, \mathrm{CC}]$

The statement decide() used at line8 allows the invoking process p_i to decide but does not stop its execution. A process executes round forever. This facilitates the description and the understanding of the algorithm.

4.3 Proof and Cost of the Algorithm

Notation.

Let p_i be a correct process. $values_i^r$ denotes the value of the local variable $values_i$ which makes satisfied the predicate of line 5 at round r.

LEMMA 1. *Let $n > 3t$. Consider the situation where, at the beginning of a round r, all the non-faulty processes have the same estimate value v. These processes will never change their estimates, thereafter.*

Proof If all the correct processes (which are at least $n - t > t + 1$) have the same estimate value v at beginning of a round r, they all BV-broadcast $\mathrm{EST}[r](v)$ at line 2. It follows that the set $bin\_values_i[r]$ of each correct process p_i contains v (BV-Obligation property) and only v (BV-Justification property). Hence, due to the lines 4, 7, and 9, the estimate est_i of any correct process p_i is set to v, which concludes the proof of the lemma. $\Box_{Lemma\ 1}$

LEMMA 2. *Let $n > 3t$, and p_i and p_j be two correct processes.* $(values_i^r = \{v\}) \wedge (values_j^r = \{w\}) \Rightarrow (v = w)$.

Proof Let us consider a correct process p_i and assume $value_i^r = \{v\}$. It follows from the predicate of line 5 that p_i has received the same message $\mathrm{AUX}[r](v)$ from at least $(n - t)$ different processes. As at most t processes can be Byzantine, it follows that p_i has received $\mathrm{AUX}[r](v)$ from at least $(n - 2t)$ different correct processes, i.e., as $n - 2t \geq t + 1$, from at least $(t + 1)$ correct processes.

Let us consider another correct process p_j such that $value_j^r = \{w\}$. This process received the message $\mathrm{AUX}[r](w)$ from at least $(n - t)$ different processes. As $(n - t) + (t + 1) > n$, it follows that one correct process p_x sent $\mathrm{AUX}[r](v)$ to p_i and $\mathrm{AUX}[r](w)$ to p_j. As p_x is correct, it sent the same message to all the processes. Hence $v = w$, which concludes the proof of the lemma. $\Box_{Lemma\ 2}$

LEMMA 3. *Let $n > 3t$. A decided value is a value proposed by a correct process.*

Proof Let us consider the round $r = 1$. It follows from (a) the BV-Justification property of the BV-broadcast (line 2), (b) the wait statement at line 3, and (c) the broadcast by each correct process p_j of a value taken from its set $bin\_values_j[1]$, that, the set $values_i$ computed at line 5 by any correct process p_i contains only estimate values of correct processes. Then, if $values_i = \{v\}$ and v is equal to the value s of the common coin, v is decided. Be the value v decided or not, p_i adopts it as new estimate (line 9). If $values_i = \{0, 1\}$, both values have been proposed by correct processes and p_i adopts the one defined by the common coin as its new estimate (line 10). In all cases, the estimate value of a correct process is equal to a proposed value. Then the same reasoning applies to all other rounds, from which it follows that a decided value is an estimate value that was proposed by a correct process. $\Box_{Lemma\ 3}$

LEMMA 4. *No two non-faulty processes decide different values.*

Proof Let r be the first round at which processes decide. If two correct processes p_i and p_j decide at round r, they decide the same value, namely, the value of the common coin associated with round r, and update their estimates to the value of the common coin.

Moreover, due to Lemma 2, if p_i decides v during round r, there is no correct process p_j such that $value_i^r = \{w\}$, with $w \neq v$. Hence, if a process p_j does not decide during r, we necessarily have $values_j^r = \{v, w\} = \{0, 1\}$. It follows that such a process p_j executes line 10, and assigns the value of the common coin to its estimate est_j.

Hence, at the beginning of round $(r + 1)$, the estimates of all the correct processes are equal to the common coin, which is itself equal to the decided value v. It then follows from Lemma 1 that they keep this value forever. As a decided value is a an estimate value, only v can be decided. $\Box_{Lemma\ 4}$

LEMMA 5. *Each non-faulty process decides with probability* 1.

Proof Let us first prove that no correct process remains blocked forever during a round r. There are two **wait** statements. Due to the BV-Termination property, no correct process can block forever at line 3. To show that no correct process can block forever at line 5, we have to show that the predicate of line 5 becomes eventually true at every correct process p_i. This follows from the following observations: during round r, (a) the set $bin\_values_i[r]$ of each correct process contains only values BV-broadcast by correct processes (BV-Justification), and eventually the sets of all the correct processes are equal (BV-Uniformity); (b) each of the at least $(n-t)$ correct processes p_i broadcasts a message $\text{AUX}[r](w)$ such that $w \in bin\_values_i[r]$; (c) each of these messages is eventually received by each correct process.

Claim. With probability 1, there is a round r at the end of which all the correct processes have the same estimate value. (End of the claim.)

Assuming the claim holds, it follows from Lemma 1 that all the correct processes p_i keep their estimate value $est_i = v$ and consequently the predicate $values_i = \{v\}$ at line 7 is true at every round. Due to the common coin CC, it follows that, with probability 1, there is eventually a round in which random() outputs v. Then, the predicates of the lines 7 and 8 evaluate to true, and all the correct processes decide.

Proof of the claim. We need to prove that, with probability 1, there is a round at the end of which all the correct processes have the same estimate value. Let us consider a round r.

- If all the correct processes execute line 10, they all adopt the value of the common coin at the end of round r, and the claim directly follows.
- Similarly, if all the correct processes execute line 9, they adopt the same value v as their new estimate, and the claim follows.
- The third case is when some correct processes execute line 9 and adopt the same value v, while others execute line 10 and adopt the same value s.

  Due to the properties of the common coin, the value it computes at a given round is independent from the values it computes at the other rounds (and also from the Byzantine processes and the network scheduler). Thus, s is equal to v with probability $p = 1/2$. Let $P(r)$ be the following probability (where x^r is the value of x at round r): $P(r) = \text{Probability}[\exists r' : r' \le r : v^{r'} = s^{r'}]$. We have $P(r) = p + (1-p)p + \cdots + (1-p)^{r-1}p$. So, $P(r) = 1-(1-p)^r$. As $\lim_{r \to +\infty} P(r) = 1$, the claim follows. (End of the proof of the claim.)

$\Box_{Lemma\ 5}$

THEOREM 2. *The algorithm described in Figure 2 solves the randomized binary consensus problem in* $\mathcal{BZ\_AS}_{n,t}[t < n/3, \text{CC}]$.

Proof BC-Validity follows from Lemma 3. BC-Agreement follows from Lemma 4. BC-One-shot follows from line 8. BC-Termination follows from Lemma 5. $\Box_{Theorem\ 2}$

THEOREM 3. *Let $n > 3t$. The expected decision time is constant (four rounds).*

Proof As indicated in the proof of Lemma 5, termination is obtained in two phases. First, all the correct processes must adopt the same value v. Second, the outcome of the common coin has to be the same as the commonly adopted value v.

It follows from the proof of Lemma 5 that there is only one situation in which the correct processes do not adopt the same value. This is when the predicate of line 7 is satisfied for a subset of correct processes and not for the other correct processes. Thus, the expected number of rounds for this to happen is 2. As for the second phase, here again, the probability that the value output by the common coin is the same as the value held by all the correct processes is $1/2$. Thus, the expected time for this to occur is also 2. Combining the two phases, the expected termination time is 4 rounds (i.e., a small constant). $\Box_{Theorem\ 3}$

Cost of the algorithm.

As far as the cost of the algorithm is concerned, we have the following, where $c \ge n - t$ denotes the number of correct processes.

- If the correct processes propose the same value, each round requires two communication steps (one in the BV-broadcast and one broadcast), and the expected number of rounds to decide is two. Hence, the total number of messages sent by correct processes is $2\,c\,n$.
- If the correct processes propose different values, each round requires three communication steps (two in the BV-broadcast and one broadcast), and the expected number of rounds to decide is four. Moreover, the total number of messages sent by the correct processes is then $4\,c\,n$ per round.
- In addition to a round number, both a message $\text{EST}[r]()$ and a message $\text{AUX}[r]()$ sent by a correct process carry a single bit. An underlying message B_VAL() has to carry a round number and a bit.
- The total number of bits exchanged by the correct processes is $O(n^2 r \log r)$ where r is the number of rounds executed by the correct processes. Hence, the expected bit complexity is $O(n^2)$.

5. CONCLUSION

This paper has presented a new consensus algorithm suited to asynchronous systems composed of n processes, and where up to $t < n/3$ processes may have a Byzantine behavior. This algorithm relies on Rabin's common coin and an underlying binary-value broadcast algorithm which guarantees that a value broadcast only by Byzantine processes is never delivered to the correct processes. In addition to being t-resilient optimal, the algorithm, which is round-based and signature-free, uses two or three communication steps per round (this depends on the estimate values of the correct processes at the beginning of a round), and $O(n^2)$ messages per rounds. Moreover, each message carries a round number and a single bit, and the expected number of rounds to decide is four. Finally, as claimed in the Introduction, and in addition to its efficiency-related properties, a very important first class property of the proposed algorithm lies in its *design simplicity*.

6. ACKNOWLEDGMENTS

The authors want to thank the referees for their constructive comments. This work has been partially supported by the French ANR project DISPLEXITY devoted to computability and complexity in distributed computing.

7. REFERENCES

[1] Aigner M. and Ziegler G., *Proofs from THE BOOK* (4th edition). Springer, 274 pages, 2010 (ISBN 978-3-642-00856-6).

[2] Aspnes J., Lower bounds for distributed coin flipping and randomized consensus. *J. of the ACM*, 45(3):415-450, 1998.

[3] Attiya H. and Welch J., *Distributed computing: fundamentals, simulations and advanced topics*, (2d Edition), Wiley-Interscience, 414 pages, 2004.

[4] Ben-Or M., Another advantage of free choice: completely asynchronous agreement protocols. *Proc. 2nd Annual ACM Symposium on Principles of Distributed Computing(PODC'83)*, ACM Press, pp. 27-30, 1983.
[5] Berman P. and Garay J.A., Randomized distributed agreement revisited. *Proc. 33rd Annual Int'l Symposium on Fault-Tolerant Computing (FTCS'93)*, IEEE Computer Press, pp. 412-419, 1993.
[6] Bracha G., An asynchronous $(n-1)/3$-resilient consensus protocol. *Proc. 3rd Annual ACM Symposium on Principles of Distributed Computing (PODC'84)*, ACM Press, pp. 154-162, 1984.
[7] Bracha G., Asynchronous Byzantine agreement protocols. *Information & Computation*, 75(2):130-143, 1987.
[8] Bracha G. and Toueg S., Asynchronous consensus and broadcast protocols. *Journal of the ACM*, 32(4):824-840, 1985.
[9] Cachin Ch., Kursawe K., and Shoup V., Random oracles in Constantinople: practical asynchronous Byzantine agreement using cryptography. *Proc. 19th Annual ACM Symposium on Principles of Distributed Computing (PODC'00)*, ACM Press, pp. 123-132, 2000.
[10] Cachin Ch., Kursawe K., Petzold F., and Shoup V., Secure and efficient asynchronous broadcast protocols. *Proc. 21st Annual International Cryptology Conference CRYPTO'01*, Springer LNCS 2139, pp. 524âĂŞ541, 2001.
[11] Cachin Ch., Guerraoui R., and Rodrigues L., *Reliable and secure distributed programming*, Springer, 367 pages, 2011 (ISBN 978-3-642-15259-7).
[12] Canetti R., and Rabin T., Fast asynchronous Byzantine agreement with optimal resilience, *Proc. 25th Annual ACM Symposium on Theory of Computing (STOC'93)*, ACM Press, pp. 42-51, 1993.
[13] Chandra T. and Toueg S., Unreliable failure detectors for reliable distributed systems. *Journal of the ACM*, 43(2):225-267, 1996.
[14] Correia M., Ferreira Neves N., and Verissimo P., From consensus to atomic broadcast: time-free Byzantine-resistant protocols without signatures. *The Computer Journal*, 49(1):82-96, 2006.
[15] Dijkstra E.W., Some beautiful arguments using mathematical induction. *Algorithmica*, 13(1):1-8, 1980.
[16] Dwork C., Lynch N., and Stockmeyer L., Consensus in the presence of partial synchrony. *Journal of the ACM*, 35(2), 288-323, 1988.
[17] Fischer M. and Lynch N., A lower bound for the time to ensure interactive consistency. *Information Processing Letters*, 14:183-186, 1982.
[18] Fischer M.J., Lynch N.A., and Paterson M.S., Impossibility of distributed consensus with one faulty process. *Journal of the ACM*, 32(2):374-382, 1985.
[19] Fischer M.J. and Merritt M., Appraising two decades of distributed computing theory research. *Distributed Computing*, 16(2-3): 239-247, 2003.
[20] Friedman R., Mostéfaoui A., Rajsbaum S., and Raynal M., Distributed agreement problems and their connection with error-correcting codes. *IEEE Transactions on Computers*, 56(7):865-875, 2007.
[21] Friedman R., Mostéfaoui A. and Raynal M., $\diamond\mathcal{P}_{mute}$-based consensus for asynchronous Byzantine systems. *Parallel Processing Letters*, 15(1-2):162-182, 2005.
[22] Friedman R., Mostéfaoui A., and Raynal M., Simple and efficient oracle-based consensus protocols for asynchronous Byzantine systems. *IEEE Transactions on Dependable and Secure Computing*, 2(1):46-56, 2005.
[23] Goldwasser S., Pavlov E., and Vaikuntanathan V., Fault-tolerant distributed computing in full-information networks. *Proc. 47th Annual IEEE Symposium on Foundations of Computer Science (FOCS'06)*,IEEE Computer Society, pp. 15-26, 2006.
[24] Gray J. and Reuter A., *Transaction processing: concepts and techniques*, Morgan Kaufmann Pub., San Francisco (CA), 1045 pages, 1993, (ISBN 1-55860-190-2).
[25] Kihlstrom K.P., Moser L.E. and Melliar-Smith P.M., Byzantine fault detectors for solving consensus. *The Computer Journal*, 46(1):16-35, 2003.
[26] King V. and Saia J., Breaking the $O(n^2)$ bit barrier: scalable Byzantine agreement with an adaptive adversary. *Proc. 30th ACM Symposium on Principles of Distributed Computing (PODC'11)*, ACM Press, pp. 420-429, 2011.
[27] Lamport L., Shostack R., and Pease M., The Byzantine generals problem. *ACM Transactions on Programming Languages and Systems*, 4(3)-382-401, 1982.
[28] Liang G. and Vaidya N., Error-free multi-valued consensus with Byzantine failures. *Proc. 30th ACM Symposium on Principles of Distributed Computing (PODC'11)*, ACM Press, pp. 11-20, 2011.
[29] Lynch N.A., *Distributed algorithms*. Morgan Kaufmann Pub., San Francisco (CA), 872 pages, 1996 (ISBN 1-55860-384-4).
[30] Lynch N.A., Merritt M., Weihl W.E., and Fekete A., *Atomic Transactions*. Morgan Kaufmann Pub., San Francisco (CA), 500 pages, 1994 (ISBN 1-55860-104-X).
[31] Martin J.-Ph. and Alvizi L., Fast Byzantine consensus. *IEEE Transactions on Dependable and Secure Computing*, 3(3):202-215, 2006.
[32] Milosevic Z., Hutle M., and Schiper A., On the reduction of atomic broadcast to consensus with Byzantine faults. *Proc. 30th IEEE Int'l Symposium on Reliable Distributed Systems (SRDS'11)*, IEEE Computer Press, pp. 235-244, 2011.
[33] Mostéfaoui A., Rajsbaum S., and Raynal M., Conditions on input vectors for consensus solvability in asynchronous distrbuted systems. *Journal of the ACM*, 50(6):922-954, 2003.
[34] Mostéfaoui A. and Raynal M., Signature-free broadcast-based intrusion tolerance: never decide a Byzantine value. *Proc. 14th Int'l Conference On Principles Of Distributed Systems (OPODIS'10)*, Springer LNCS 6490, pp. 144-159, 2010.
[35] Patra A., Error-free multi-valued broadcast and Byzantine agreement with optimal communication complexity. *Proc. 15th Int'l Conference On Principles Of Distributed Systems (OPODIS'10)*, Springer LNCS 7109 pp. 34-49, 2011.
[36] Pease M., R. Shostak R., and Lamport L., Reaching agreement in the presence of faults. *Journal of the ACM*, 27:228-234, 1980.
[37] Rabin M., Randomized Byzantine generals. *Proc. 24th IEEE Symposium on Foundations of Computer Science (FOCS'83)*, IEEE Computer Society Press, pp. 116-124, 1983.
[38] Raynal M., *Communication and agreement abstractions for fault-tolerant asynchronous distributed systems*. Morgan & Claypool, 251 pages, 2010 (ISBN 978-1-60845-293-4).
[39] Raynal M., *Fault-tolerant agreement in synchronous message-passing systems*. Morgan & Claypool, 165 pages, 2010 (ISBN 978-1-60845-525-6).
[40] Raynal M., *Concurrent programming: algorithms, principles and foundations*. Springer, 515 pages, 2013 (ISBN 978-3-642-32026-2).
[41] Song Y.J. and van Renesse R., Bosco: one-step Byzantine asynchronous consensus. *Proc. 22th Symposium on Distributed Computing (DISC'08)*, Springer LNCS 5218, 438-450, 2008.
[42] Srikanth T.K. and Toueg S., Simulating authenticated broadcasts to derive simple fault-tolerant algorithms. *Distributed Computing*, 2:80-94, 1987.
[43] Toueg S., Randomized Byzantine agreement. *Proc. 3rd Annual ACM Symposium on Principles of Distributed Computing (PODC'84)*, ACM Press, pp. 163-178, 1984.
[44] Turpin R. and Coan B.A., Extending binary Byzantine agreement to multivalued Byzantine agreement. *Information Processing Letters*, 18:73-76, 1984.

Asynchronous MPC with a Strict Honest Majority Using Non-equivocation

Michael Backes[†] Fabian Bendun[†] Ashish Choudhury[‡] Aniket Kate[*]

[†]CISPA, Saarland University, Germany — {backes,bendun}@cs.uni-saarland.de
[‡]International Institute of Information Technology, Bangalore, India — partho31@gmail.com
[*]MMCI, Saarland University, Germany — aniket@mmci.uni-saarland.de

ABSTRACT

Multiparty computation (MPC) among n parties can tolerate up to $t < n/2$ active corruptions in a *synchronous* communication setting; however, in an *asynchronous* communication setting, the resiliency bound decreases to only $t < n/3$ active corruptions. We improve the resiliency bound for asynchronous MPC (AMPC) to match synchronous MPC using *non-equivocation*.

Non-equivocation is a message authentication mechanism to restrict a corrupted sender from making conflicting statements to different (honest) parties. It can be implemented using an increment-only counter and a digital signature oracle, realizable with trusted hardware modules readily available in commodity computers and smartphone devices. A non-equivocation mechanism can also be transferable and allows a receiver to verifiably transfer the authenticated statement to other parties. In this work, using transferable non-equivocation, we present an AMPC protocol tolerating $t < n/2$ faults. From a practical point of view, our AMPC protocol requires fewer setup assumptions than the previous AMPC protocol with $t < n/2$ by Beerliová-Trubíniová, Hirt and Nielsen [PODC 2010]: unlike their AMPC protocol, it does not require *any* synchronous broadcast round at the beginning of the protocol and avoids the threshold homomorphic encryption setup assumption. Moreover, our AMPC protocol is also efficient and provides a gain of $\Theta(n)$ in the communication complexity per multiplication gate, over the AMPC protocol of Beerliová-Trubíniová et al. In the process, using non-equivocation, we also define the first asynchronous verifiable secret sharing (AVSS) scheme with $t < n/2$, which is of independent interest to threshold cryptography.

Categories and Subject Descriptors

C.2.0 [**Computer-Communication Networks**]: General—*security and protection*; E.3 [**Data**]: Data Encryption—*Public key cryptosystems*

Keywords

Multiparty Computation (MPC); Asynchrony; Non-equivocation; Resiliency; Verifiable Secret Sharing (VSS); Reduced Assumptions

PODC'14, July 15–18, 2014, Paris, France.

ACM 978-1-4503-2944-6/14/07 ...$15.00.
http://dx.doi.org/10.1145/2611462.2611490 .

1. INTRODUCTION

Secure multi-party computation (MPC) is an important primitive in distributed systems. Informally, in a system of n mutually distrusting parties, an MPC protocol allows the parties to "securely" evaluate any agreed-on function f of their private inputs, in the presence of a centralized active adversary $\mathcal{A}$, controlling at most any t out of the n parties. In the synchronous communication model, where the message transfer delays are bounded by a known constant, the MPC problem has been studied extensively (e.g., [10, 18, 27, 36, 40]). In practice, there is growing interest in generalizing MPC to an asynchronous communication model [9, 14, 17] that does not place any bound on the communication delays. The weaker restrictions on the adversary in the asynchronous model not only worsen the required resiliency conditions and communication complexities, but also make designing protocols a more challenging task; intuitively this is because in a completely asynchronous setting, it is not possible to distinguish between a slow (but honest) sender and a crashed sender. Due to this, at any "stage" of an asynchronous protocol, no party can afford to wait to hear from all the parties and so the communication from t (potentially honest) parties may be ignored [17]. Due to their complexity, only a few asynchronous MPC (AMPC) protocols are available [5, 9, 11, 20, 31].

In this work, we focus on an asynchronous model with a *computationally bounded* adversary $\mathcal{A}$, where the parties are connected by pairwise authenticated links. In this setting, AMPC protocols are possible if and only if $t < n/3$ [30, 31]. This is in contrast to the synchronous world, where we can tolerate up to $t < n/2$ corruptions [29]. Interested in bridging this gap in the resilience, Beerliová-Trubíniová, Hirt and Nielsen [7] observed that it is possible to design an AMPC protocol tolerating $t < n/2$ corruptions in a "partial" synchronous network. More specifically, assuming one *synchronous broadcast* round at the beginning of the protocol, where each party can synchronously broadcast to every other party, they designed an AMPC protocol tolerating $t < n/2$ corruptions. Due to the availability of the synchronous broadcast round, their protocol could also ensure "input provision", i.e. the inputs of all the (honest) parties are considered for the computation, which otherwise is impossible to achieve in an asynchronous protocol [17]. Nevertheless, their requirement of one synchronous broadcast round per MPC instance may not always be realizable: deterministic broadcast protocols [24] require $\Theta(t)$ rounds of communication over the pairwise channels or randomized broadcast protocols [25, 39] require $\mathcal{O}(1)$ (with a large constant) expected rounds of communication. It was left as an open problem in [7] to see whether one can design an AMPC protocol with $t < n/2$ under other simplified assumptions.

In distributed computing research, a similar problem with asynchronous protocols has recently been addressed by introducing a small trusted hardware assumption [21–23, 32–34]. In particular, it was shown that, the resilience of asynchronous distributed computing tasks such as reliable broadcast, Byzantine agreement, and state machine replication (SMR) can be improved using a small *trusted hardware module* at each party. The hardware module utilized is just a trusted, increment-only local counter and a signature oracle, which can be realized with pervasively available trusted hardware-enabled devices. Using such trusted hardware with each party, one can design asynchronous reliable broadcast tolerating up to $t < n$ active faults [22,23], and asynchronous Byzantine agreement (ABA) and SMR protocols tolerating up to $t < n/2$ [21,33,34] active faults, all of which otherwise require $t < n/3$ [39].

At a conceptual level, such a trusted module makes it impossible for a corrupted party to perform *equivocation*, which essentially means making conflicting statements to different (honest) parties. The use of signatures (or transferable authentication) complements *non-equivocation* (i.e., making equivocation impossible) by making it transferable as required in the asynchronous communication environment. Clement et al. [22] generalized the results [21,23,34] and proved that non-equivocation with signatures (or *transferable* non-equivocation) allows treating Byzantine faults as crash faults for many distributed computing tasks. In particular, they present a generic transformation that enables any crash-fault tolerant distributed protocol to tolerate the same number of Byzantine faults using transferable non-equivocation. However, their generic transformation considers only the basic distributed computing requirements of safety and liveness. It does not apply to cryptographic tasks such as AMPC where *confidentiality (or privacy)* of inputs is also required. This presents an interesting challenge to assess the utility of transferable non-equivocation for the task of AMPC.

1.1 Contribution and Comparison

We study the power of transferable non-equivocation in the context of AMPC and demonstrate how to improve the resilience of AMPC from $t < n/3$ to $t < n/2$, without any synchrony assumption. In particular, we present a general MPC protocol in a completely asynchronous communication model with $n \geq 2t + 1$. Our protocol, called NeqAMPC , improves upon the previous AMPC protocol [7] with $n \geq 2t + 1$ in the following ways:

(a) Simplified assumptions. Our AMPC protocol needs a transferable non-equivocation mechanism, but unlike [7] neither makes a synchronous broadcast round assumption nor requires a threshold homomorphic encryption setup. Given the feasibility of realizing transferable non-equivocation over prevalent computing devices, we argue that transferable non-equivocation is a more practical assumption than the synchronous broadcast round assumption.

(b) Efficiency. For a security parameter κ, our AMPC protocol requires an amortized communication complexity of $\mathcal{O}(n^3\kappa)$ bits per multiplication gate, which improves upon the AMPC protocol of [7] by a factor of $\Theta(n)$.

To reduce the setup assumptions for the NeqAMPC protocol, we avoid the traditional threshold additive homomorphic encryption based circuit evaluation approach as used in [7,31]. Instead, we employ a secret-sharing based circuit evaluation approach [10,18,36], where privacy of the computation is maintained via secret sharing. Nevertheless, as detailed in our protocol overview (Section 2), secret-sharing based AMPC with $n = 2t + 1$ and $\mathcal{O}(n^3\kappa)$ communication complexity (per multiplication) presents several interesting challenges. As a result the NeqAMPC protocol is significantly different than those in the literature [5,7,31].

In the process, we also present the first computationally secure asynchronous verifiable secret sharing (AVSS) [2,3,14,17] scheme for $n \geq 2t + 1$ with $\mathcal{O}(n^2\kappa)$ communication complexity (using transferable non-equivocation), which otherwise requires $t < n/3$ [17]. Our AVSS scheme has an additional useful feature—it is the first publicly verifiable [38] AVSS scheme, as it allows any third party to publicly verify the "consistency" of the shares. With its efficiency and public verifiability, our AVSS scheme may be of independent interest to other cryptographic protocols.

Comparison with Existing Work. The best known computationally secure AMPC protocols are reported in [7, 31]. The protocol in [31] considers a *fully* asynchronous setting with $t < n/3$, whereas [7] assumes one synchronous broadcast round and can tolerate up to $t < n/2$ corruptions. Both the protocols require a threshold additive homomorphic encryption instantiation, and incur an (amortized) communication complexity of $\mathcal{O}(n^2\kappa)$ and $\mathcal{O}(n^4\kappa)$ bits per multiplication gate respectively.[1]

We do not employ a threshold encryption setup, but rather prefer a more standard public key encryption setup with the addition of transferable non-equivocation. Our NeqAMPC protocol with $t < n/2$ performs circuit evaluation by secret-sharing the inputs and incurs a communication complexity of $\mathcal{O}(n^3\kappa)$ bits per multiplication gate. Nevertheless, by modifying our protocol and employing a threshold encryption setup (coupled with transferable non-equivocation), we can tolerate $t < n/2$ faults with communication complexity $\mathcal{O}(n^2\kappa)$ bits per multiplication gate. However, we prefer the secret-sharing based AMPC, as we aim to reduce the assumptions relied upon.

We note that unlike [7], our AMPC protocol could not enforce *input provision*: the input from t potentially honest parties may be ignored for computation. As discussed earlier, this is inherent to asynchronous systems and presents a trade-off between our protocol and that of [7] based on what is more important: input provision or avoiding the synchrony assumption. Finally, we note that using a transferable non-equivocation mechanism, one can realize asynchronous reliable broadcast (see Section 3.3) with $t < n$ and consequently get rid of the synchronous broadcast round required in [7]. However, the resultant protocol will still require the threshold homomorphic encryption setup and $\mathcal{O}(n^4\kappa)$ communication per multiplication, and it will no longer support input provision.

2. OVERVIEW OF OUR PROTOCOL

Without loss of generality, we assume $n = 2t+1$; thus, $t = \Theta(n)$. We assume that the function f to be computed is expressed as an arithmetic circuit over the finite field $\mathbb{Z}_p$, where $p > n$ is a κ bit prime and κ is the security parameter. The circuit consists of two-input addition (linear) and multiplication (non-linear) gates, apart from random gates. The AMPC protocol consists of two phases: an input phase and a computation phase. During the input phase, the parties share their inputs, while during the computation phase, the parties jointly evaluate f on the shared inputs and publicly reconstruct the output. Linear gates can be evaluated locally if the underlying secret-sharing scheme is linear; so we use the Shamir secret-sharing scheme with threshold t [37]. We denote a sharing of a value s by $[s]$. It follows that locally adding the shares of $[x]$ and $[y]$ provides the shares for $[x + y]$.

Multiplication gates cannot be evaluated locally since multiplying the individual shares results in the underlying sharing polynomial having degree $2t$ instead of t. Therefore we evaluate multiplication gates using the standard Beaver's circuit-randomization

[1]Beerliová-Trubíniová et al. [7] focused on designing a protocol with $t < n/2$, and the communication complexity of $\mathcal{O}(n^4\kappa)$ of their protocol (measured by us in the extended version of the paper [1]) can possibly be improved.

technique [4]. This technique requires three "pre-processed" secret-shared values, say $([u],[v],[w])$, unknown to the adversary $\mathcal{A}$, such that $w = u \cdot v$. Given such a shared *multiplication triple*, and shared inputs of a multiplication gate, say $[x]$ and $[y]$, the multiplication gate is securely evaluated using the equation $[x \cdot y] = (x-u)\cdot(y-v) + [v]\cdot(x-u) + [u]\cdot(y-v) + [u \cdot v]$. In particular, the parties compute the sharings of $(x-u)$ and $(y-v)$, and publicly reconstruct the same. Once $(x-u)$ and $(y-v)$ are public, the parties can compute their shares of $x \cdot y$, using the above equation and employing linearity of the secret sharing. As u and v are random and unknown to $\mathcal{A}$, the public knowledge of $(x-u)$ and $(y-v)$ does not violate the privacy of x and y.

2.1 Pre-processing Phase

Although the idea of our AMPC protocol is the same as the existing information-theoretically secure MPC and AMPC protocols [5,6,20], our major challenge lies in generating the required shared multiplication triples with $n = 2t+1$ parties; the existing protocols [5,6,20] employ at least $n > 3t$ parties for this purpose[2]. These triplets are independent of the circuit and the inputs of the parties, and generated in an additional *pre-processing* phase. Generating these triplets efficiently is the important problem we solve in our protocol. In the rest of the section, we give an overview of how $(c_M + c_R)$ shared random triples are generated, where c_M and c_R are the number of multiplication gates and random gates in the circuit. As a first step, we describe how a single triple is generated (see Fig. 1 for a pictorial representation of the protocols involved) and then extend this to $c_M + c_R$ triples.

Supervised Triple Generation (Section 6). The idea for generating a random shared multiplication triple $[u],[v],[w]$ is to compute a random sharing $[v]$ and then combining "several" $[u^{(i)}]$s and $[u^{(i)} \cdot v]$s to get $[u]$ and $[w]$. The triple generation protocol uses two sub-protocols: Sup-Sh and Sup-PreMul-Sh. Protocol Sup-Sh allows a *dealer* D to "verifiably" generate the sharing $[u]$ of his value u, while Sup-PreMul-Sh allows a dealer D to "verifiably" generate a sharing $[u]$ and $[u \cdot v]$, given u and $[v]$. To generate $([u],[v],[w])$, we use Sup-Sh and Sup-PreMul-Sh in the following way: first, we ask each party P_i to act as a dealer D and invoke an instance of Sup-Sh to share a uniformly random value, say $v^{(i)}$. The parties then agree on a common subset (say $\mathcal{T}_v$) of $t+1$ dealers whose Sup-Sh instances will be eventually terminated by all the parties. We set $v = \sum_{P_i \in \mathcal{T}_v} v^{(i)}$. The shared value v will be random and unknown to $\mathcal{A}$, as $\mathcal{T}_v$ has at least one honest party. Next, each party P_i is asked to act as a D and invoke a Sup-PreMul-Sh instance to share a uniformly random value $u^{(i)}$ as well as $u^{(i)} \cdot v$. The parties then agree on a common subset of $t+1$ dealers, say $\mathcal{T}_u$, whose Sup-PreMul-Sh instances will be eventually terminated by all the parties. For $u = \sum_{P_i \in \mathcal{T}_u} u^{(i)}$ and $w = \sum_{P_i \in \mathcal{T}_u} u^{(i)} \cdot v$, the triple (u, v, w) is a random multiplication triple.

There is, however, an important subtlety: As a *precondition*, the Sup-PreMul-Sh protocol expects its dealer D to also have *encryptions* of all n shares of $[v]$, encrypted under the individual keys of the respective share-holders; here, the encryption scheme is additively homomorphic (and not threshold additively homomorphic). For any sharing, we call a party having such n encrypted shares to be *privileged*. Due to asynchronicity, the Sup-Sh protocol cannot guarantee that *all* the $n-t$ honest parties are privileged with respect to every $[v^{(i)}]$ sharing of $P_i \in \mathcal{T}_v$. We solve the problem by ensuring in Sup-Sh that there exists a designated (possibly

[2]Shared multiplication triples with $n = 2t+1$ have been generated in the synchronous setting [12]; however, their adaptability to the asynchronous setting is unclear.

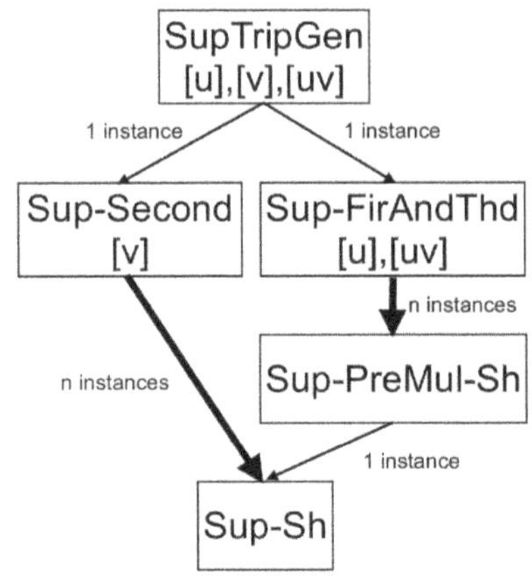

Figure 1: Supervised Multiplication Triple Generation

corrupted) *supervisor* P_{king} (called *king*), who is a privileged party with respect to *each* $[v^{(i)}]$. An honest P_{king} then computes all the n encrypted shares of $[v]$ using the homomorphic properties of encryption, and reliably broadcasts them. Using non-equivocation, the required asynchronous reliable broadcast is possible for $n > t$ (Section 3.3). Once P_{king} (correctly) broadcasts the n encrypted shares of v, each P_i can invoke its Sup-PreMul-Sh instance.

The resultant wrapper protocols are called Sup-Second, which generates $[v]$ under the supervision of P_{king} and Sup-FirAndThd, which generates $[u]$ and $[w = u \cdot v]$ under the supervision of P_{king}. A combination of Sup-Second and Sup-FirAndThd leads to the protocol SupTripGen under the supervision of P_{king}, which outputs a uniformly random and private multiplication triple $([u],[v],[w])$.

Preprocessing Phase Protocol. Protocol SupTripGen may not terminate for a *corrupted* P_{king}. Therefore, we ask each party P_i to act as a king and generate shared random multiplication triples under its supervision by invoking an instance of SupTripGen. As the instances of honest kings will eventually terminate, we distribute the load of generating $c_M + c_R$ shared random multiplication triples among n parties. Each party P_i is asked to act as a king and generate $\frac{c_M + c_R}{t+1}$ shared multiplication triples in its SupTripGen instance. The parties then agree on a common subset $\mathcal{T}_{\mathsf{king}}$ of $t+1$ kings whose SupTripGen instances will be eventually completed by everyone and the $|\mathcal{T}_{\mathsf{king}}| \cdot \frac{c_M + c_R}{t+1} = c_M + c_R$ shared triples obtained in these instances are considered as the final output.

2.2 Sub-protocols for the Preprocessing Phase

We now discuss the realization of the main sub-protocols Sup-Sh and Sup-PreMul-Sh for the preprocessing phase.

Protocol Sup-Sh (Section 5.1). Our Sup-Sh protocol is almost equivalent to the AVSS primitive [3,14,17]: it allows a *dealer* D to "verifiably" share a secret s, thus generating $[s]$, and ensures that at least *one* honest party is privileged to obtain all the n shares encrypted for the respective share holders. The existing computational AVSS protocols (e.g., [3,14]) are designed with $n = 3t+1$ and are based on sharing a secret using a bivariate polynomial of degree t in each variable and (homomorphic) commitments. In this paradigm, it is ensured that D has distributed "consistent" shares to $n - t = 2t+1$ parties such that (at least) $t+1$ *honest* parties among them can "enable" the remaining parties to get their shares. Unfortunately, this approach cannot be used with $n = 2t+1$, as here we can only ensure that D has distributed consistent shares to $n - t = t+1$ parties. In the worst case, there will be *only one* honest party in this set, who may not have sufficient information to help the other honest parties to complete a sharing.

We solve this problem by introducing encryptions of the shares[3], and by employing univariate polynomials instead of bivariate polynomials. Here, D provides a vector of n encrypted shares as well as homomorphic commitments of those shares to each party. The non-equivocation mechanism is used to ensure that a *corrupted* D does not distribute different sets of encrypted and committed shares to the different parties. Once $n - t = t + 1$ parties confirm that they have received "consistent" n encrypted and committed shares, there must exist at least one honest privileged party with all n encrypted shares, who can transfer the individual encrypted shares to the individual parties. Transferability of non-equivocation ensures that corrupted privileged parties do not transfer incorrect encryptions.

Protocol Sup-PreMul-Sh **(Section 5.2).** The protocol takes as input an existing sharing $[v]$ of a value v unknown to everybody including $\mathcal{A}$, such that *all* the parties are privileged, i.e., all the parties hold encryptions of all shares. The protocol then allows a dealer D to verifiably share its value u as well as $u \cdot v$ (i.e. $[u]$ and $[u \cdot v]$). The protocol ensures that $u \cdot v$ remains secure in general and u is secure for an *honest* D. The idea behind the protocol is that knowing the encrypted and committed shares of v and employing the homomorphic properties of encryptions and commitments, D can compute the encrypted and committed shares corresponding to $u \cdot v$ for his choice of u, even without knowing v. The dealer can then (non-equivocally) distribute the encrypted and committed shares to the parties. Once it is confirmed that $t + 1$ parties have received all the n encrypted and committed shares of $u \cdot v$, it is ensured that there exists a honest privileged party, who can relay the individual encrypted shares of $u \cdot v$ to the respective parties.

We take a more bottom-up approach in the rest of the paper. We describe our model, and define non-equivocation and other primitives in Section 3. We present our AVSS protocol in Section 4. We start our AMPC construction with subprotocols Sup-Sh and Sup-PreMul-Sh in Section 5. We then present our supervised multiplication triple generation in Section 6 and finally describe the complete AMPC protocol in Section 7. Due to space constraints, all proofs are shifted to the extended version [1].

3. PRELIMINARIES

3.1 Model

We consider a set $\mathcal{P} = \{P_1, \ldots, P_n\}$ of n parties connected by pairwise authenticated channels, where $n = 2t+1$. These communication channels are asynchronous with arbitrary but finite delay (i.e. the messages sent by the honest parties reach to their destinations eventually). A centralized static adversary $\mathcal{A}$ can actively corrupt any t out of the n parties and force them to deviate in any arbitrary manner during a protocol execution. A party not under the control of $\mathcal{A}$ is called *honest*. The adversary $\mathcal{A}$ is modeled as a probabilistic polynomial time (PPT) algorithm, with respect to a security parameter κ. During a protocol execution, the message delivery order is decided by a *scheduler* controlled by $\mathcal{A}$. Nevertheless, the scheduler cannot modify the messages exchanged between honest parties.

A protocol execution is considered as a sequence of *atomic* steps, where a single party is active in each such step. A party is activated upon receiving a message, after which it performs some computation and possibly outputs messages on its outgoing links. The scheduler controls the order of these atomic steps. At the beginning of the execution, each party will be in a special *start* state. A party is said to *terminate/complete* the execution if it reaches a *halt* state. A protocol execution is said to *be complete* when all honest parties complete it. We assume that every message sent by a party during an execution has a publicly known unique *identifier (key)* associated with it. We denote the set $\{y, y+1, \ldots, z\} \subset \mathbb{N}$ as $[y, z]$.

3.2 Definitions

Computationally Secure AVSS. Informally an AVSS scheme consists of two phases, a sharing phase, where a special party called *dealer* shares a secret and a reconstruction phase, where the parties reveal their shares to reconstruct the secret.

More formally, let (Sh, Rec) be a pair of protocols for parties in $\mathcal{P}$, where a dealer D $\in \mathcal{P}$ has a private input $s \in \mathbb{Z}_p$ for Sh. Then (Sh, Rec) is an computationally secure AVSS scheme, if the following requirements hold for every possible adversary $\mathcal{A}$, except with a negligible probability in κ:

- TERMINATION: **(a)** If D is *honest* and all the honest parties participate in the protocol Sh, then each *honest* party eventually terminates the protocol Sh; **(b)** If some *honest* party terminates Sh, then every *honest* party eventually terminates Sh; **(c)** If all the honest parties invoked Rec, then each *honest* party eventually terminates Rec.

- CORRECTNESS: If some honest party terminates Sh, then there exists a fixed value $\overline{s} \in \mathbb{Z}_p$ such that the following requirements hold except with a negligible probability in κ: **(a)** If D is *honest*, then $\overline{s} = s$, and all the honest parties output $\overline{s}$ upon terminating Rec; **(b)** Even if D is *corrupted*, all the honest parties output $\overline{s}$ upon terminating Rec.

- PRIVACY: If D is *honest* during the protocol Sh and no honest party has started to execute the protocol Rec, then the adversary $\mathcal{A}$ has no information about the secret s.

Computationally Secure AMPC. We briefly review computationally secure AMPC here, and refer the readers to [30,31] for a formal definition. Informally, in an AMPC protocol Π_{MPC}, every party first provides its input in $\mathbb{Z}_p$ to the computation (in a secure fashion). Due to the asynchronous nature of communication, the parties cannot wait to consider the inputs of all n parties, and instead they agree on inputs from a set $\mathcal{CORE}$ of $n-t$ parties. The parties then compute an "approximation" of f on the inputs from the $\mathcal{CORE}$ set and assuming a default value (say 0) as the remaining t inputs. For every possible $\mathcal{A}$ and for all possible inputs and random coins of the (honest) parties, we expect the following properties for a Π_{MPC} instance, except with a negligible probability in κ:

- TERMINATION: Every honest party eventually terminates the instance Π_{MPC}.

- CORRECTNESS: Every honest party obtains the correct output of the function f.

- PRIVACY: The adversary $\mathcal{A}$ obtains no additional information about the inputs of the honest parties other than what may be inferred from the inputs and outputs of the corrupted parties.

These properties are formalized to the standard simulation-based definition following the real-world/ideal-world paradigm [17,31].

(Transferable) Non-equivocation. Non-equivocation restricts a corrupted party from making conflicting statements to different parties. It has been used in several asynchronous distributed systems [21–23,33,34] to improve their resiliency. In particular, these systems employ transferable non-equivocation which (like digital signatures) allows a party to verifiably transfer a non-equivocation tag

[3]We argue that the problem is inherently not solvable for $n = 2t+1$ with only commitments usually employed in computationally secure VSS protocols [3,14], and that we have to employ encryptions which allow a *single honest* party to procure encrypted shares of all the parties. Interestingly, the problem persists even when we assume the adversary $\mathcal{A}$ is only passive (but crashable).

The Neq mechanism

Neq is parameterized by a polynomial $p(\cdot)$, and an implicit security parameter κ.

Setup: Upon receiving a (Setup) message from party $P_i \in \mathcal{P}$:

1. If a list L_i exists, return $\bot$.
2. Otherwise, create an empty list L_i of key-message-signature triplets of type $\{0,1\}^* \times \{0,1\}^* \times \{0,1\}^{p(\kappa)}$. Send a message (Registered, P_i) to all parties in $\mathcal{P}$.

Signing: Upon receiving an (Neq-Sign, P_i, ℓ, m) message from party $P_i \in \mathcal{P}$:

1. If the list L_i does not exist *or* $\langle \ell, \_, \_ \rangle \in L_i$, return $\bot$.
2. Otherwise, choose an arbitrary tag $\sigma_i^{\ell,m} \in \{0,1\}^{p(\kappa)}$, update $L_i \leftarrow L_i \cup \langle \ell, m, \sigma_i^{\ell,m} \rangle$ and return $\sigma_i^{\ell,m}$.

Verification: Upon receiving an (Neq-Verify, P_i, ℓ, m, σ) message from party $P_j \in \mathcal{P}$:

1. If the list L_i does not exist *or* $\langle \ell, m, \sigma \rangle \notin L_i$, then return 0, else return 1.

Figure 2: Simplified transferable non-equivocation mechanism

(or signature) provided by a sender to other parties. Clement et al. [22] justify the necessity of transferability of non-equivocation by proving that non-equivocation or signature alone are powerless in *asynchronous* distributed systems. Nevertheless, (transferable) non-equivocation has not been formalized so far, and we present a simplified, idealized definition for transferable non-equivocation.

In Figure 2, we define a simplified mechanism Neq, intended to model the event for a transferable non-equivocation instantiation: (1) during the setup phase, every party P_i gets associated with a unique non-equivocation list L_i characterized by its index i, and all parties are informed about this association. (2) The list owner party can create a non-equivocation signature for any key-message pair except that she cannot equivocate and obtain a signature for the *same* key twice. (3) Given a key-message-signature triplet associated with a sender, any party successfully verifies only correctly generated signatures except with a negligible probability.

We survey existing transferable non-equivocation instantiations and analyze their relations to Neq in the full version of the paper [1]. In most instantiations, the transferable non-equivocation is implemented using an increment-only counter for keys and signatures with public key infrastructure (PKI) [21–23, 34] or message authentication codes (MACs) generated with a replicated secret key [33]. In Neq, we generalize these using the list L_i of key-message-signature triplets associated with party P_i indexed by *party-defined ordered keys* ℓ. Similar to signatures, only P_i can use Neq-Sign to add triplets (one per each key) to L_i. Similar to PKI, anybody can Neq-Verify if a triplet $\langle \ell, m, \sigma \rangle$ belongs to L_i of P_i, and verifiably transfer authentication to others. Note that the increment-only counter provides a space-efficient way to implement a list L_i as only the counter value has to be maintained and not the whole list.

For ease of exposition, we use a phrase P_i *sends* m_{σ_i} *to* P_j and P_j *receives* m_{σ_i} *from* P_i to suggest that P_i sends a triplet $\langle \ell, m, \sigma_i^{\ell,m} \rangle$ for a key ℓ to P_j and P_j delivers it only after applying Neq-Verify to check if $\sigma_i^{\ell,m}$ is obtained by P_i using Neq-Sign on ℓ and m. Similarly, we use a phrase P_j *forwards* m_{σ_i} *to* P_k to suggest that P_j received (in the above sense) message m_{σ_i} (of P_i) from some party, and then forwards it to P_k who should also (non-equivocally) receive it. Note that we avoid the keys ℓ in the above phrases as they can be pre-assigned to protocol instance-step combinations in an unambiguous manner.

3.3 Employed Primitives

Homomorphic Encryptions and Commitments: We assume an IND-CPA secure encryption scheme (Enc, Dec), which is *linearly homomorphic*. Every party P_i has its own key-pair $(\mathsf{pk}_i, \mathsf{sk}_i)$, for which the public key pk_i is known to all parties. Given two ciphertexts $\mathbf{c}_{m_1} = \mathsf{Enc}_{\mathsf{pk}_i}(m_1, \cdot)$ and $\mathbf{c}_{m_2} = \mathsf{Enc}_{\mathsf{pk}_i}(m_2, \cdot)$, we require that there exist operations $\boxplus$ and $\boxdot$ on ciphertexts such that $\mathbf{c}_{m_1} \boxplus \mathbf{c}_{m_2} = \mathsf{Enc}_{\mathsf{pk}_i}(m_1 + m_2, \cdot)$ and $a \boxdot \mathbf{c}_{m_i} = \mathsf{Enc}_{\mathsf{pk}_i}(a \cdot m_i, \cdot)$ holds. We also assume an unconditional hiding and computational commitment scheme (Commit, Open), which is linearly homomorphic with analogous homomorphic operations; these are denoted by $\oplus$ and $\odot$. For the sake of readability, we sometimes leave the randomness of encryptions and commitments implicit.

For instantiating encryptions and commitments over messages in $\mathbb{Z}_p$, we use the encoding-free additive El-Gamal encryption scheme [19] and Pedersen commitment scheme [35] respectively. In particular, we only require that the scheme is CPA secure (Theorem 3 in [19]) and it is not necessary that applying homomorphism twice to the same encrypted values leads to different ciphertexts.

Zero-knowledge (ZK) Proofs: We assume the presence of the following two-party ZK protocols.

In the zero-knowledge proof of equality of encrypted and committed values (protocol PoE), there exists a prover $\mathsf{P} \in \mathcal{P}$ who computes and publishes a commitment $\mathsf{Com}_m = \mathsf{Commit}(m, r)$, and ciphertexts $\mathbf{c}_m = \mathsf{Enc}_{\mathsf{pk}_i}(m, \cdot)$ and $\mathbf{c}_r = \mathsf{Enc}_{\mathsf{pk}_i}(r, \cdot)$. Then using PoE, the prover P can prove to *any* verifier $\mathsf{V} \in \mathcal{P}$ (knowing $\mathsf{Com}_m, \mathbf{c}_m, \mathbf{c}_r$ and pk_i) that the message encrypted in $\mathbf{c}_m$ is also committed in Com_m, under the randomness encrypted in $\mathbf{c}_r$; i.e., $\exists m, r, r_1, r_2$, such that

$$\mathsf{Com}_m = \mathsf{Commit}(m, r) \quad \wedge \quad \mathbf{c}_m = \mathsf{Enc}_{\mathsf{pk}_i}(m, r_1) \\ \wedge \quad \mathbf{c}_r = \mathsf{Enc}_{\mathsf{pk}_i}(r, r_2).$$

In the zero-knowledge proof of correct pre-multiplication (protocol PoCM), publicly known commitments $\mathsf{Com}_{v_j} = \mathsf{Commit}(v_j, r_j)$ and corresponding ciphertexts $\mathbf{c}_{v_j} = \mathsf{Enc}_{\mathsf{pk}_j}(v_j, \cdot)$ and $\mathbf{c}_{r_j} = \mathsf{Enc}_{\mathsf{pk}_j}(r_j, \cdot)$ for $j \in [1, n]$ will be available. There exists a prover $\mathsf{P} \in \mathcal{P}$ who selects a random $u \in \mathbb{Z}_p$ and t-degree random polynomials $m(\cdot)$ and $\hat{m}(\cdot)$ in $\mathbb{Z}_p[x]$ with $m(0) = \hat{m}(0) = 0$. Let $m_j = m(j)$ and $\hat{m}_j = \hat{m}(j)$ for $j \in [0, n]$. In addition, P publishes $\mathsf{Com}_u = \mathsf{Commit}(u, \cdot)$ and $\mathsf{Com}_{m_j} = \mathsf{Commit}(m_j, \hat{m}_j)$. Using the homomorphic property of commitments and encryptions, P computes and publishes the commitment $\mathsf{Com}_{u \cdot v_j + m_j} = \mathsf{Commit}(u \cdot v_j + m_j, u \cdot r_j + \hat{m}_j)$ and encryptions $\mathbf{c}_{u \cdot v_j + m_j}$ and $\mathbf{c}_{u \cdot r_j + \hat{m}_j}$ of $u \cdot v_j + m_j$ and $u \cdot r_j + \hat{m}_j$ respectively. Then using PoCM, P can prove to *any* verifier $\mathsf{V} \in \mathcal{P}$ that all values $\mathsf{Com}_{u \cdot v_j + m_j}$ were generated by multiplying Com_{v_j} with the same u followed by re-randomization using the same $m(\cdot)$ and $\hat{m}(\cdot)$ polynomials, and that all $\mathbf{c}_{u \cdot v_j + m_j}$ and $\mathbf{c}_{u \cdot r_j + \hat{m}_j}$ values were generated by multiplying $\mathbf{c}_{v_j}$ and $\mathbf{c}_{r_j}$ respectively with the same u, followed by re-randomization using the same $m(\cdot)$ and $\hat{m}(\cdot)$ respectively. i.e.,

$$\exists u, \rho, m(\cdot), \hat{m}(\cdot), \{k_j, \hat{k}_j\}_{j \in [1,n]} : \mathsf{Com}_u = \mathsf{Commit}(u, \rho) \wedge \\ \deg(m(\cdot)) \leq t \wedge \deg(\hat{m}(\cdot)) \leq t \wedge m(0) = 0 = \hat{m}(0) \wedge \\ \mathsf{Com}_{u \cdot v_j + m_j} = u \odot \mathsf{Com}_{v_j} \oplus \mathsf{Commit}(m_j, \hat{m}_j) \wedge \\ \mathbf{c}_{u \cdot v_j + m_j} = u \boxdot \mathbf{c}_{v_j} \boxplus \mathsf{Enc}_{\mathsf{pk}_j}(m_j, k_j) \wedge \\ \mathbf{c}_{u \cdot r_j + \hat{m}_j} = u \boxdot \mathbf{c}_{r_j} \boxplus \mathsf{Enc}_{\mathsf{pk}_j}(\hat{m}_j, \hat{k}_j).$$

Both the ZK protocols are based on standard Σ-protocols [8] and have communication complexity $\mathcal{O}(\kappa)$ bits and $\mathcal{O}(n\kappa)$ bits respectively; see the extended version of the paper [1] for their instantiations based on the ZK protocols in [16].

Certificates of Claims: Hirt, Nielsen, and Przydatek [31] introduced this concept to allow a prover $\mathsf{P} \in \mathcal{P}$ to *publicly* prove correctness of a certain claim (like real-life certificates), without revealing any additional information. Here, to certify validity of a statement m, the prover P proves m to every *verifier* $P_i \in \mathcal{P}$ using an appropriate zero-knowledge (ZK) protocol. A verifier P_i, upon successful verification, sends a signature to P on an "appropriate" message (known publicly), corresponding to m. P cannot wait for all n signatures in the asynchronous environment; thus, upon receiving $(n-t) = t+1$ signatures, the prover P concatenates them to construct a certificate α for the claim m. These $t+1$ signatures ensure that at least one honest party has verified the claim, and that m is true with an overwhelming probability. Assuming each signature to be of size $\mathcal{O}(\kappa)$ bits, the size of α will be $\mathcal{O}(n\kappa)$ bits; this can be reduced to $\mathcal{O}(\kappa)$ bits using a *threshold signature scheme* with threshold t [7]. Here, the verifiers send signature *shares* and the prover P "combines" $(n-t)$ shares to a single signature[4].

Let zkp be the ZK protocol corresponding to the claim m. We denote by $\alpha = \mathsf{certify}_{\mathsf{zkp}}(m)$, the task of constructing a certificate α for m. Similarly we say that "P_i verifies the certificate α for the claim m" to mean that that P_i verifies that α is a valid (threshold) signature on the "appropriate message" corresponding to m. The communication cost of constructing α is the same as that of executing n instances of the corresponding ZK protocol zkp.

Reliable Broadcast (r-broadcast): This asynchronous primitive [13,28,39] allows a sender S to send a message m identically to *all* the parties: For a given instance τ_b of r-broadcast, when S is *honest*, all honest parties eventually terminate with output (τ_b, m); if S is *corrupted* and some honest party terminates with (τ_b, m'), then every honest party also eventually terminates with (τ_b, m'); for any instance, at most one message can be delivered by an honest party.

The resiliency bound for r-broadcast is $n \geq 3t+1$ [13,28,39]; however, assuming transferable non-equivocation, an r-broadcast protocol with $n \geq t+1$ and $\mathcal{O}(n^2(\ell+\kappa))$ bits of communication for broadcasting an ℓ-bit message is available [22, 23]. The high-level idea of the protocol is as follows: S first (non-equivocally) sends $m_{\sigma_{\mathsf{S}}}$ to all the parties; this prevents a corrupted S from sending different messages to different honest parties. However, a corrupted S can avoid sending $m_{\sigma_{\mathsf{S}}}$ to some honest parties. Thus, to ensure that all the honest parties eventually receive $m_{\sigma_{\mathsf{S}}}$, whenever an honest party (non-equivocally) receives some message $m_{\sigma_{\mathsf{S}}}$, before delivering the message, it non-equivocally forwards it to every other party. This ensures that whenever an honest party receives $m_{\sigma_{\mathsf{S}}}$ then it will be eventually received by every other honest party.

In the rest of the paper, the term "P_i *broadcasts* m" means that P_i as a sender invokes an r-broadcast instance for m. Similarly, "P_j *receives* m *from the broadcast of* P_i" means that P_j terminates the r-broadcast instance τ_b invoked by P_i with the output (τ_b, m).

Agreement on a Common Subset (ACS): This primitive allows the parties to agree on a common subset of $(n-t)$ parties, who correctly invoked some protocol, say Π, satisfying the following requirements: (a) If an honest party invokes an instance of Π then all the (honest) parties eventually terminate the instance; (b) If some honest party terminates an instance of Π invoked by a corrupted party, then every honest party eventually does the same. ACS can be realized by executing n instances (one for each party) of an asynchronous Byzantine agreement (ABA) protocol to decide if it should be included in the common subset. Assuming transferable non-equivocation, ABA, and hence ACS, can be implemented with $n \geq 2t+1$ [22,23,33]. An efficient ACS protocol with expected communication complexity of $\mathcal{O}(n^3\kappa)$ bits can be obtained by using the Neq mechanism in the multi-valued ABA of [15].

[4]Note that the AMPC protocols of [7, 31] also assume a threshold signature setup.

3.4 Secret Sharing Notations

Given a secret $s \in \mathbb{Z}_p$, let $\phi(\cdot), \psi(\cdot) \in \mathbb{Z}_p[x]$ be, respectively, a degree t *sharing polynomial* with $\phi(0) = s$ and a t-degree *randomness polynomial* required for commitments; here, p is a κ-bit prime. For party P_j, $s_j = \phi(j)$ and $r_j = \psi(j)$ are respectively her shares of s and the randomness polynomial. Let $\mathbf{c}_{s_j} = \mathsf{Enc}_{\mathsf{pk}_j}(s_j, \cdot)$, $\mathbf{c}_{r_j} = \mathsf{Enc}_{\mathsf{pk}_j}(r_j, \cdot)$ and $\mathsf{Com}_{s_j} = \mathsf{Commit}(s_j, r_j)$ and let $\mathsf{Com}_s = \mathsf{Commit}(s, \psi(0))$. We call $\{\mathbf{c}_{s_j}, \mathbf{c}_{r_j}\}_{j\in[1,n]}$ the encrypted shares and $\{\mathsf{Com}_{s_j}\}_{j\in[1,n]}$ the committed shares of s.

- **$[\cdot]$-sharing:** A secret s is said to be $[\cdot]$-shared, if every (honest) party $P_i \in \mathcal{P}$ holds s_i, r_i, $\{\mathsf{Com}_{s_j}\}_{j\in[1,n]}$ and Com_s. The information held by the (honest) parties corresponding to $[\cdot]$-sharing of s is denoted as $[s]$.
- **Privileged party:** P_i is called a privileged party of $[\cdot]$-sharing of s if it holds the encrypted shares $\{\mathbf{c}_{s_j}, \mathbf{c}_{r_j}\}_{j\in[1,n]}$.

Due to linearity of sharing and commitments, $[\cdot]$-sharing is also *linear*: given $[a]$, $[b]$ and a public constant c, every party can locally compute its information corresponding to $[a+b]$ and $[c \cdot a]$, as $[a+b] = [a] + [b]$ and $[c \cdot a] = c \cdot [a]$.

4. OUR AVSS PROTOCOL

Protocols Sh and Rec presented in Figure 3 constitutes an AVSS scheme with $n = 2t+1$. Protocol Sh allows a *dealer* D to "verifiably" generate $[s]$ for a secret $s \in \mathbb{Z}_p$. It ensures that if the protocol terminates then there exists a value (say $\overline{s}$) which will be $[\cdot]$-shared among the parties; if D is *honest* then $\overline{s} = s$, and $\mathcal{A}$ learns no new information on s. The protocol always terminates for an *honest* D and has communication complexity $\mathcal{O}(n^2\kappa)$. Protocol Rec allows the parties to reconstruct s, given that s is $[\cdot]$-shared.

In the Sh protocol, D polynomial-shares the secret s with threshold t to generate shares $\{s_j\}_{j\in[1,n]}$ and computes the commitments $\mathsf{Com}_{s_j} = \mathsf{Commit}(s_j, r_j)$, where r_j is a share of a random t-degree randomness polynomial $\psi(\cdot)$. It also computes the encryptions $\mathbf{c}_{s_j} = \mathsf{Enc}_{\mathsf{pk}_j}(s_j)$ and $\mathbf{c}_{r_j} = \mathsf{Enc}_{\mathsf{pk}_j}(r_j)$ of each share-pair s_j, r_j, and the commitment $\mathsf{Com}_s = \mathsf{Commit}(s, \psi(0))$. D then (non-equivocally) *sends* $\{\mathbf{c}_{s_j}\}_{\sigma_{\mathsf{D}}}$, $\{\mathbf{c}_{r_j}\}_{\sigma_{\mathsf{D}}}$ and $\{\mathsf{Com}_{s_j}\}_{\sigma_{\mathsf{D}}}$ for all $j \in [1,n]$, and $\{\mathsf{Com}_s\}_{\sigma_{\mathsf{D}}}$ to *every* party and claims that it has correctly $[\cdot]$-shared a secret: the claim involves proving that the plaintexts in $\mathbf{c}_{s_j}$ and $\mathbf{c}_{r_j}$ are committed in Com_{s_j} and that the values committed in $\{\mathsf{Com}_{s_j}\}_{j\in[1,n]}$ constitute shares of the secret committed in Com_s with threshold t. Note that although sending the full vector $\{\mathbf{c}_{s_j}\}_{\sigma_{\mathsf{D}}}$, $\{\mathbf{c}_{r_j}\}_{\sigma_{\mathsf{D}}}$ and $\{\mathsf{Com}_{s_j}\}_{\sigma_{\mathsf{D}}}$ to each party looks a bit non-intuitive, it is the *crux* of our Sh protocol to ensure that every party eventually receives its shares for $[s]$.

To verify D's claim, upon (non-equivocally) receiving information from D, every P_i verifies if the committed shares $\{\mathsf{Com}_{s_j}\}_{j\in[1,n]}$ constitute Shamir sharing of the secret committed in Com_s with threshold t. For this, the parties use the fact that given the commitments to at least $t+1$ distinct points on a t degree polynomial, it is possible to (homomorphically) compute the commitments of the coefficients of the polynomial [14, 26]. In particular, party P_i takes Com_s along with $\{\mathsf{Com}_{s_j}\}_{j\in[1,t]}$ and homomorphically computes the commitments of the sharing and randomness polynomial. Using these commitments, party P_i then computes the commitments of the remaining $n-t$ points and matches them with $\{\mathsf{Com}_{s_j}\}_{j\in[t+1,n]}$. Additionally P_i engages in n instances of PoE (one per triplet $\{\mathbf{c}_{s_j}, \mathbf{c}_{r_j}, \mathsf{Com}_{s_j}\}$) with D. By non-equivocally sending messages to the parties, it is ensured that the parties who receive the messages from D, receive the *same* messages. D then

Protocol $\mathsf{Sh}(\mathsf{D}, \tau, s)$: τ is the session id

I. **D-Dependent Phase**:

Share Computation and Certificate Generation—Given the secret $s \in \mathbb{Z}_p$, D executes the following code:

1. Select t-degree polynomials $\phi(\cdot)$, $\psi(\cdot)$ with $\phi(0) = s$. For $j \in [1, n]$, compute *share-pairs* $s_j = \phi(j), r_j = \psi(j)$, ciphertexts $\mathbf{c}_{s_j} = \mathsf{Enc}_{\mathsf{pk}_j}(s_j), \mathbf{c}_{r_j} = \mathsf{Enc}_{\mathsf{pk}_j}(r_j)$ and *committed share* $\mathsf{Com}_{s_j} = \mathsf{Commit}(s_j, r_j)$. Compute $\mathsf{Com}_s = \mathsf{Commit}(s, \psi(0))$.
2. Send messages $\{\mathbf{c}_{s_j}\}_{\sigma_\mathsf{D}}$, $\{\mathbf{c}_{r_j}\}_{\sigma_\mathsf{D}}$ and $\{\mathsf{Com}_{s_j}\}_{\sigma_\mathsf{D}}$ for all $j \in [1, n]$, and $\{\mathsf{Com}_s\}_{\sigma_\mathsf{D}}$ to each P_i. Start constructing a certificate $\alpha^{\mathsf{D},\tau} = \mathsf{certify}_{\mathsf{PoE}}(\mathsf{claim}_{\mathsf{D},\tau})$ claiming that "D has correctly shared a secret in session τ": This indirectly requires a proof that "$\exists \phi(\cdot), \psi(\cdot) : \mathsf{deg}(\phi(\cdot)) \leq t \wedge \mathsf{deg}(\psi(\cdot)) \leq t \wedge \mathbf{c}_{s_j} = \mathsf{Enc}_{\mathsf{pk}_j}(\phi(j), \cdot) \wedge \mathbf{c}_{r_j} = \mathsf{Enc}_{\mathsf{pk}_j}(\psi(j), \cdot) \wedge \mathsf{Com}_{s_j} = \mathsf{Commit}(\phi(j), \psi(j)) \wedge \mathsf{Com}_s = \mathsf{Commit}(\phi(0), \psi(0))$". For this, run an instance of PoE for each $(\mathbf{c}_{s_j}, \mathbf{c}_{r_j}, \mathsf{Com}_{s_j})$ triplet with every party P_i. Broadcast $\alpha^{\mathsf{D},\tau}$ once it is constructed.

Share Verification and Certification—Every party $P_i \in \mathcal{P}$ including D executes the following code:

1. On receiving $\{\mathbf{c}_{s_j}\}_{\sigma_\mathsf{D}}$, $\{\mathbf{c}_{r_j}\}_{\sigma_\mathsf{D}}$ and $\{\mathsf{Com}_{s_j}\}_{\sigma_\mathsf{D}}$ for all $j \in [1, n]$, and $\{\mathsf{Com}_s\}_{\sigma_\mathsf{D}}$ from D, perform the following verifications:
   (a) Verify if $\{\mathsf{Com}_{s_j}\}_{j \in [1,n]}$ and Com_s define unique t-degree polynomials.
   (b) If the above verification is successful, then participate in the PoE instances of D to verify $\mathsf{claim}_{\mathsf{D},\tau}$ and enable D to construct a certificate $\alpha^{\mathsf{D},\tau}$ for $\mathsf{claim}_{\mathsf{D},\tau}$.

II. **D-Independent Phase and Termination**—Every party $P_i \in \mathcal{P}$ including D executes the following code:

1. Upon receiving the broadcasted certificate $\alpha^{\mathsf{D},\tau}$ from D, verify $\alpha^{\mathsf{D},\tau}$ for $\mathsf{claim}_{\mathsf{D},\tau}$. Upon successful verification, if $\{\mathbf{c}_{s_j}\}_{\sigma_\mathsf{D}}$, $\{\mathbf{c}_{r_j}\}_{\sigma_\mathsf{D}}$ and $\{\mathsf{Com}_{s_j}\}_{\sigma_\mathsf{D}}$ for all $j \in [1, n]$ have been received from D,
   (a) then compute $s_i = \mathsf{Dec}_{\mathsf{sk}_i}(\mathbf{c}_{s_i}), r_i = \mathsf{Dec}_{\mathsf{sk}_i}(\mathbf{c}_{r_i})$, and $\forall j \in [1, n]$ forward *only* $\{\mathbf{c}_{s_j}\}_{\sigma_\mathsf{D}}, \{\mathbf{c}_{r_j}\}_{\sigma_\mathsf{D}}, \{\mathsf{Com}_{s_j}\}_{\sigma_\mathsf{D}}$ to P_j,
   (b) else wait for $\{\mathbf{c}_{s_i}\}_{\sigma_\mathsf{D}}$, $\{\mathbf{c}_{r_i}\}_{\sigma_\mathsf{D}}$, and $\{\mathsf{Com}_{s_i}\}_{\sigma_\mathsf{D}}$ to be forwarded by some party. Once received, compute the share-pair $s_i = \mathsf{Dec}_{\mathsf{sk}_i}(\mathbf{c}_{s_i})$ and $r_i = \mathsf{Dec}_{\mathsf{sk}_i}(\mathbf{c}_{r_i})$.
2. Forward $\{\mathsf{Com}_{s_i}\}_{\sigma_\mathsf{D}}$ to each P_j. On receiving $t+1$ $\{\mathsf{Com}_{s_j}\}_{\sigma_\mathsf{D}}$, homomorphically compute $\{\mathsf{Com}_{s_j}\}_{j \in [1,n]}$, Com_s and terminate.

Protocol $\mathsf{Rec}(\mathsf{D}, \tau, [s])$: τ is the session id

Every party $P_i \in \mathcal{P}$ executes the following code:

1. Send the share-pair (s_i, r_i) to every party $P_j \in \mathcal{P}$.
2. On receiving the share-pair (s_j, r_j) from party P_j, verify whether $\mathsf{Com}_{s_j} \stackrel{?}{=} \mathsf{Commit}(s_j, r_j)$. If the verification is successful, then include s_j in a set $\mathcal{T}_j$, initialized to $\emptyset$.
3. Once $|\mathcal{T}_j| = t+1$, construct a t-degree polynomial $\phi(\cdot)$ by interpolating the points $\{(j, s_j)\}_{s_j \in \mathcal{T}_j}$. Output $s = \phi(0)$ and terminate.

Figure 3: AVSS with $n = 2t + 1$ using Transferable Non-equivocation

constructs a certificate $\alpha^{\mathsf{D},\tau}$ (for session id τ) to support its claim of correct sharing and broadcasts it. A party proceeds further only upon receiving a valid certificate. A valid $\alpha^{\mathsf{D},\tau}$ ensures that at least one honest party, say P_h, has verified D's claim; P_h will be an *honest privileged party*.

A valid certificate from D does not ensure that every (honest) P_i will eventually hold its information corresponding to $[s]$: due to asynchrony or possible corrupted behavior of D, t honest parties may not receive their shares corresponding to $[s]$. We solve this problem by using *two* additional "rounds" of communication, which we call the D-*independent phase*. Each *privileged* party non-equivocally *forwards only* $\{\mathbf{c}_{s_j}\}_{\sigma_\mathsf{D}}$, $\{\mathbf{c}_{r_j}\}_{\sigma_\mathsf{D}}$, and $\{\mathsf{Com}_{s_j}\}_{\sigma_\mathsf{D}}$ to every party P_j, who can decrypt $\mathbf{c}_{s_j}$ and $\mathbf{c}_{r_j}$ to obtain s_j, r_j. Existence of at least one honest privileged party ensures that every P_j eventually receives s_j, r_j and Com_{s_j}. Next, every P_i forwards $\{\mathsf{Com}_{s_i}\}_{\sigma_\mathsf{D}}$ to all parties. As all $t+1$ honest parties would eventually receive their respective $\{\mathbf{c}_{s_i}\}_{\sigma_\mathsf{D}}$, $\{\mathbf{c}_{r_i}\}_{\sigma_\mathsf{D}}$, and $\{\mathsf{Com}_{s_i}\}_{\sigma_\mathsf{D}}$ messages at the end of first "round" of the D-independent phase, eventually every honest party will receive $t+1$ forwarded committed shares. Now using the homomorphic property of commitments every party can compute the remaining committed shares and Com_s, thus possessing all the necessary information of $[s]$.

Given $[s]$ generated using Sh, protocol Rec is based on the standard reconstruction protocol used in the existing computationally secure AVSS [3, 14], which allows the parties to *robustly* reconstruct s. In the protocol, each party sends its share-pair to all the parties, which are verified with the corresponding commitment, available with the parties (as part of $[s]$). Once $t+1$ "correct" share pairs are received, the sharing polynomial, and hence s, is reconstructed. As there exist at least $t+1$ honest parties whose shares will eventually be communicated among themselves, the Rec protocol eventually terminates. As stated in Lemma 4.1. the pair of protocols (Sh, Rec) constitutes an AVSS scheme with $n = 2t+1$ and communication complexity $\mathcal{O}(n^2\kappa)$ bits. Due to space constraints, the proof is shifted to the extended version [1].

LEMMA 4.1. *Protocols* (Sh, Rec) *constitute a computational secure AVSS scheme tolerating* $t < n/2$ *corruptions, where both* Sh *and* Rec *incur communication cost of* $\mathcal{O}(n^2\kappa)$ *bits.*

Notice that the above AVSS scheme is also publicly verifiable [38] as any third party can verify the consistency of the shares using the valid certificate broadcasted by D.

Commitment to Shares instead of Polynomial Coefficients during Sh: In most existing computational secure VSS schemes [3, 35], D commits to the polynomial coefficients of sharing and randomness polynomials during the sharing phase, and the parties homomorphically generates the committed shares from those. This approach makes VSS simpler as the parties are not required to verify whether the committed shares lie on degree t polynomial.

If we follow this approach in our Sh protocol, then D has to non-equivocally distribute the commitment to polynomial coefficients of the sharing and randomness polynomials. In that case, however, the homomorphically generated committed shares will not have the necessary non-equivocation tag as the non-equivocation mechanism is not required to be homomorphic in nature. As a result, a corrupted privileged party can forward some incorrect committed shares to the respective parties during the D-independent phase, and the correctness of the protocol. Although the privileged parties can be asked to non-equivocally forward the polynomial coefficients during the D-independent phase, and it will result in an additional $\Theta(n)$ communication overhead.

Protocol $\mathsf{Sup\text{-}PreMul\text{-}Sh}(\mathsf{D}, \tau, P_{\mathsf{king}}, \mathcal{P}, [v])$**:** τ **is the session id**

Let $\{\mathbf{c}_{v_j}, \mathbf{c}_{r_j}, \mathsf{Com}_{v_j} = \mathsf{Commit}(v_j, r_j)\}_{j\in[1,n]}$ and $\mathsf{Com}_v = \mathsf{Commit}(v, \cdot)$ be information corresponding to $[v]$ available to *all* parties;

I. **Generating** $[u]$: On having a value u, D invokes an instance $\mathsf{Sup\text{-}Sh}(\mathsf{D}, \tau, P_{\mathsf{king}}, u)$ of Sup-Sh to generate $[u]$ under the supervision of P_{king} and every party in $\mathcal{P}$ participates in this instance and wait for its termination. Let $\mathsf{Com}_u = \mathsf{Commit}(u, \cdot)$ be the commitment of u which is computed and communicated during this instance of Sup-Sh (along with the other information corresponding to $[u]$).

II. **Generating** $[u \cdot v]$—The following code is executed by the respective parties only upon terminating the Sup-Sh instance of D:

a. D**-Dependent Phase**

1. **Share Computation and Certificate Generation**—The following code is executed only by D:
   (a) Select random *masking polynomials* $m(\cdot)$ and $\hat{m}(\cdot)$ of degree at most t with $m(0) = \hat{m}(0) = 0$. For $j \in [1, n]$, compute $m_j = m(j), \hat{m}_j = \hat{m}(j), \mathsf{Com}_{m_j} = \mathsf{Commit}(m_j, \hat{m}_j)$ and $\mathsf{Com}_m = \mathsf{Commit}(m(0), \hat{m}(0))$.
   (b) For $j \in [1, n]$, using the homomorphic property of the encryption and commitment scheme, compute the *new encrypted share pair* $\mathbf{c}_{u\cdot v_j+m_j} = u \boxdot \mathbf{c}_{v_j} \boxplus \mathsf{Enc}_{\mathsf{pk}_j}(m_j, \cdot), \mathbf{c}_{u\cdot r_j+\hat{m}_j} = u \boxdot \mathbf{c}_{r_j} \boxplus \mathsf{Enc}_{\mathsf{pk}_j}(\hat{m}_j, \cdot)$ and the *new committed share* $\mathsf{Com}_{u\cdot v_j+m_j} = u \odot \mathsf{Com}_{v_j} \oplus \mathsf{Com}_{m_j}$. In addition, compute the *new commitment* $\mathsf{Com}_{u\cdot v} = u \odot \mathsf{Com}_v \oplus \mathsf{Com}_m$.
   (c) Send messages $\{\mathbf{c}_{u\cdot v_j+m_j}\}_{\sigma_{\mathsf{D}}}, \{\mathbf{c}_{u\cdot r_j+\hat{m}_j}\}_{\sigma_{\mathsf{D}}}, \{\mathsf{Com}_{u\cdot v_j+m_j}\}_{\sigma_{\mathsf{D}}}$ and $\{\mathsf{Com}_{m_j}\}_{\sigma_{\mathsf{D}}}$ for all $j \in [1, n]$ and $\{\mathsf{Com}_u\}_{\sigma_{\mathsf{D}}}, \{\mathsf{Com}_{u\cdot v}\}_{\sigma_{\mathsf{D}}}$ and $\{\mathsf{Com}_m\}_{\sigma_{\mathsf{D}}}$ to each P_i. Start constructing a certificate $\beta^{\mathsf{D},\tau} = \mathsf{certify}_{\mathsf{PoCM}}(\mathsf{claim}_{\mathsf{D},\tau})$ claiming that "D has correctly done the pre-multiplication in session τ." This claim indirectly requires the following proof:

$$\exists u, \rho, m(\cdot), \hat{m}(\cdot), \{k_j, \hat{k}_j\}_{j\in[1,n]} : \mathsf{Com}_u = \mathsf{Commit}(u, \rho) \wedge \mathsf{deg}(m(\cdot)) \leq t \wedge \mathsf{deg}(\hat{m}(\cdot)) \leq t \wedge m(0) = 0 = \hat{m}(0) \wedge$$

$$\mathsf{Com}_{u\cdot v_j+m_j} = u \odot \mathsf{Com}_{v_j} \oplus \mathsf{Com}_{m_j} \wedge \mathbf{c}_{u\cdot v_j+m_j} = u \boxdot \mathbf{c}_{v_j} \boxplus \mathsf{Enc}_{\mathsf{pk}_j}(m_j, k_j) \wedge \mathbf{c}_{u\cdot r_j+\hat{m}_j} = u \boxdot \mathbf{c}_{r_j} \boxplus \mathsf{Enc}_{\mathsf{pk}_j}(\hat{m}_j, \hat{k}_j)$$

   For this, run an instance of PoCM for $(\{\mathbf{c}_{v_j}, \mathbf{c}_{r_j}, \mathsf{Com}_{v_j}, \mathbf{c}_{u\cdot v_j+m_j}, \mathbf{c}_{u\cdot r_j+\hat{m}_j}, \mathsf{Com}_{u\cdot v_j+m_j}, \mathsf{Com}_{m_j}\}_{j\in[1,n]}, \mathsf{Com}_u, \mathsf{Com}_m)$ with every party P_i. Broadcast the certificate $\beta^{\mathsf{D},\tau}$ once it is constructed.
2. **Share Verification and Certification**—Every $P_i \in \mathcal{P}$ upon receiving $\{\mathbf{c}_{u\cdot v_j+m_j}\}_{\sigma_{\mathsf{D}}}, \{\mathbf{c}_{u\cdot r_j+\hat{m}_j}\}_{\sigma_{\mathsf{D}}}, \{\mathsf{Com}_{u\cdot v_j+m_j}\}_{\sigma_{\mathsf{D}}}$ and $\{\mathsf{Com}_{m_j}\}_{\sigma_{\mathsf{D}}}$ for all $j \in [1, n]$ and $\{\mathsf{Com}_u\}_{\sigma_{\mathsf{D}}}, \{\mathsf{Com}_{u\cdot v}\}_{\sigma_{\mathsf{D}}}$ and $\{\mathsf{Com}_m\}_{\sigma_{\mathsf{D}}}$ from D, participate (as a V) in the instance of PoCM with D to verify the claim $\mathsf{claim}_{\mathsf{D},\tau}$ and enable D to construct the certificate $\beta^{\mathsf{D},\tau}$ for $\mathsf{claim}_{\mathsf{D},\tau}$. Upon successful verification, broadcast the message (`approve`, D) if $P_i = P_{\mathsf{king}}$.

b. D**-Independent Phase and Termination**—Every party $P_i \in \mathcal{P}$ executes the following code:

1. Upon receiving the broadcasted certificate $\beta^{\mathsf{D},\tau}$ from D and the broadcasted message (`approve`, D) from P_{king}, verify $\beta^{\mathsf{D},\tau}$ for $\mathsf{claim}_{\mathsf{D},\tau}$. Upon successful verification:
   (a) If $\forall j \in [1, n], \{\mathbf{c}_{u\cdot v_j+m_j}\}_{\sigma_{\mathsf{D}}}, \{\mathbf{c}_{u\cdot r_j+\hat{m}_j}\}_{\sigma_{\mathsf{D}}}, \{\mathsf{Com}_{u\cdot v_j+m_j}\}_{\sigma_{\mathsf{D}}}$ have been received from D, then compute $w_i = \mathsf{Dec}_{\mathsf{sk}_i}(\mathbf{c}_{u\cdot v_i+m_i}), \hat{r}_i = \mathsf{Dec}_{\mathsf{sk}_i}(\mathbf{c}_{u\cdot r_i+\hat{m}_i})$, and forward *only* $\{\mathbf{c}_{u\cdot v_j+m_j}\}_{\sigma_{\mathsf{D}}}, \{\mathbf{c}_{u\cdot r_j+\hat{m}_j}\}_{\sigma_{\mathsf{D}}}, \{\mathsf{Com}_{u\cdot v_j+m_j}\}_{\sigma_{\mathsf{D}}}$ to each P_j,
   (b) else wait for $\{\mathbf{c}_{u\cdot v_i+m_i}\}_{\sigma_{\mathsf{D}}}, \{\mathbf{c}_{u\cdot r_i+\hat{m}_i}\}_{\sigma_{\mathsf{D}}}$, and $\{\mathsf{Com}_{u\cdot v_i+m_i}\}_{\sigma_{\mathsf{D}}}$ to be forwarded by some party. Once received, compute the share-pair $w_i = \mathsf{Dec}_{\mathsf{sk}_i}(\mathbf{c}_{u\cdot v_i+m_i})$ and $\hat{r}_i = \mathsf{Dec}_{\mathsf{sk}_i}(\mathbf{c}_{u\cdot r_i+\hat{m}_i})$.
2. Forward $\{\mathsf{Com}_{u\cdot v_i+m_i}\}_{\sigma_{\mathsf{D}}}$ to every P_j. On receiving $t + 1$ $\{\mathsf{Com}_{u\cdot v_i+m_i}\}_{\sigma_{\mathsf{D}}}$ messages, homomorphically compute $\{\mathsf{Com}_{u\cdot v_j+m_j}\}_{j\in[1,n]}, \mathsf{Com}_{u\cdot v}$ and terminate.

Figure 4: Supervised Pre-multiplication Protocol for generating $[u]$ **and** $[u \cdot v]$ **under** P_{king}

5. SUPERVISED SHARING PROTOCOLS

In this section, we present two protocols for generating $[\cdot]$-sharings with different properties under the supervision of a king P_{king}. Here, if the protocols terminate, then an *honest* P_{king} will be a *privileged* party with respect to the generated sharings.

5.1 Protocol Sup-Sh: Supervised $[\cdot]$-sharing

In our first supervised sharing protocol Sup-Sh, a *dealer* D verifiably generates $[s]$ for a secret s under the supervision of $P_{\mathsf{king}} \in \mathcal{P}$. If the protocol terminates then there exists a value (say $\overline{s}$) which will be $[\cdot]$-shared among the parties; if D is *honest* then $\overline{s} = s$, and $\mathcal{A}$ learns no new information on s from the protocol execution. Moreover, if P_{king} is *honest* then it will be a privileged party. The protocol always terminates for an *honest* D and P_{king} and has communication complexity $\mathcal{O}(n^2\kappa)$.

We obtain protocol Sup-Sh by adding two small verification steps during the D-dependent phase in the protocol Sh in Figure 3. Specifically, in the term of properties Sup-Sh is the same as Sh, with the additional requirement that P_{king} is a privileged party. To ensure the same, in protocol Sh, during the D-dependent phase, we ask P_{king} to broadcast an "acknowledgement" (a special message) after verifying the claim of D during the D-dependent phase. Additionally, we enforce that every party should this receive acknowledgement from P_{king}, before proceeding further. As an honest P_{king} will broadcast the acknowledgement only after verifying the claim of D, these additional steps ensure that indeed P_{king} will be a privileged party. To avoid repetition, we avoid giving the complete formal details of Sup-Sh and instead state the following lemma. The proof follows from the proof of Lemma 4.1 and the above discussion (for details, see [1]).

LEMMA 5.1. *Let s be the* D*'s secret. Then for every possible $\mathcal{A}$ and scheduler, protocol* Sup-Sh *achieves the following properties up to a negligible probability in κ:* (1) TERMINATION*: if* D *and* P_{king} *are honest then all the honest parties eventually terminate the protocol. Moreover, if some honest party terminates the protocol, then every other honest party eventually does the same.* (2) CORRECTNESS*: if some honest party terminates the protocol, then there exists a value $\overline{s}$ which will eventually be $[\cdot]$-shared among the parties. Moreover, if* D *is honest then $\overline{s} = s$. Furthermore if* P_{king} *is honest then* P_{king} *will be a privileged party.* (3) PRIVACY*: if* D *is honest then s remains private.* (4) COMMUNICATION COMPLEXITY*: the protocol has communication complexity of $\mathcal{O}(n^2\kappa)$ bits.*

5.2 Supervised Pre-multiplication Protocol

The Sup-PreMul-Sh protocol (Figure 4) takes input a $[\cdot]$-shared uniformally random and private value v and allows a dealer $\mathsf{D} \in \mathcal{P}$ to verifiably generate $[u]$ as well as $[u \cdot v]$ for a value u of his choice, under the supervision of a designated $P_{\mathsf{king}} \in \mathcal{P}$. As a *pre-condition*, the protocol assumes that every (honest) party is a privileged party with respect to the input $[v]$. The protocol ensures that v and $u \cdot v$ remains private, and when D is *honest* then $\mathcal{A}$ learns no new information on u. Finally if P_{king} is *honest* then it will be a privileged party with respect to $[u]$ as well as $[u \cdot v]$. The protocol always terminates for an *honest* D and P_{king} and has communication complexity $\mathcal{O}(n^2\kappa)$ bits.

Let $\{\mathbf{c}_{v_j}, \mathbf{c}_{r_j}, \mathsf{Com}_{v_j}\}_{j\in[1,n]}$ and Com_v be the encrypted shares and the committed shares corresponding to $[v]$ that is available to all the parties. Let $\phi(\cdot)$ and $\psi(\cdot)$ be the sharing and randomness polynomial corresponding to $[v]$. Thus $v_i = \phi(i)$, $r_i = \psi(i)$ is the share-pair available with P_i and $\mathbf{c}_{v_j} = \mathsf{Enc}_{\mathsf{pk}_j}(v_j), \mathbf{c}_{r_j} = \mathsf{Enc}_{\mathsf{pk}_j}(r_j), \mathsf{Com}_{v_j} = \mathsf{Commit}(v_j, r_j)$ and $\mathsf{Com}_v = \mathsf{Commit}(\phi(0), \psi(0))$. To generate $[u]$, D first invokes an instance of Sup-Sh. The next task for D would be to generate $[u \cdot v]$ and that too without knowing v. To do this, we observe that $u \cdot \phi(\cdot) + m(\cdot)$ and $u \cdot \psi(\cdot) + \hat{m}(\cdot)$ constitue correct sharing and randomness polynomial respectively for $[u \cdot v]$, where $m(\cdot)$ and $\hat{m}(\cdot)$ are random *masking polynomials* of degree at most t selected by D with the constraint $m(0) = \hat{m}(0) = 0$. This is because $u \cdot \phi(\cdot) + m(\cdot)$ and $u \cdot \psi(\cdot) + \hat{m}(\cdot)$ will have degree at most t, with the constant term of $u \cdot \phi(\cdot) + m(\cdot)$ being $u \cdot v$. Thus $w_j = u \cdot v_j + m(j)$ and $\hat{r}_j = u \cdot r_j + \hat{m}(j)$ constitute valid share-pair for $[u \cdot v]$ and so by using the homomorphic property of encryption and commitment, D can compute the encrypted shares and committed shares of $[u{\cdot}v]$ and distribute the same to the parties; the presence of masking polynomials preserves the privacy of u and $u \cdot v$.

The rest of the protocol is now similar to Sup-Sh, except that PoCM is used instead of PoE by D to construct the certificate that it has done "correct pre-multiplication". As nothing about the masking polynomials is revealed, u remains private. The properties of the protocol are stated in Lemma 5.2, with the proofs being shifted to [1] due to space constraints.

LEMMA 5.2. *Let v be a completely random and unknown value which is $[\cdot]$-shared among $\mathcal{P}$ and let u be a value selected by* D. *Then for every possible $\mathcal{A}$ and scheduler, protocol* Sup-PreMul-Sh *achieves the following properties up to a negligible probability in κ:* (1) TERMINATION*: if* D *and P_{king} are honest then all the honest parties eventually terminate the protocol. Moreover, if some honest party terminates the protocol, then every other honest party eventually does the same.* (2) CORRECTNESS*: if some honest party terminates the protocol, then there exists a value $\overline{u}$, such that $\overline{u}$ and $\overline{u} \cdot v$ will eventually be $[\cdot]$-shared among the parties. If* D *is honest then $\overline{u} = u$. Moreover if P_{king} is honest then P_{king} will be a privileged party with respect to $[\overline{u}]$ as well as $[\overline{u}{\cdot}v]$.* (3) PRIVACY*: v and $u \cdot v$ remains private at the end of the protocol. Additionally, if* D *is honest then u also remains private.* (4) COMMUNICATION COMPLEXITY*: the protocol has communication complexity of $\mathcal{O}(n^2\kappa)$ bits.*

6. SUPERVISED TRIPLE GENERATION

Protocol SupTripGen generates $[u], [v], [w]$ for a uniformly random and private multiplication triple (u, v, w) under the supervision of a king P_{king} with $\mathcal{O}(n^3\kappa)$ communication complexity. It employs sub-protocols, Sup-Second and Sup-FirAndThd. The pseudocodes and the proofs for all three protocols are shifted to the extended version [1].

6.1 Generating the Second Component

Sup-Second generates $[v]$ for a uniformly random and private value v, under the supervision of P_{king}. For a requirement clarified in the sequel, Sup-Second also ensures that each party becomes a privileged party with respect to $[v]$. In the protocol, each P_i invokes an instance Sup-Sh$_i$ of Sup-Sh (as a D) to generate $[v^{(i)}]$ for a uniformly random $v^{(i)}$. Let $\mathcal{T}_{\mathsf{king}}$ be the set of first $t+1$ parties whose instance of Sup-Sh is terminated by P_{king}, and let $v = \sum_{P_k \in \mathcal{T}_{\mathsf{king}}} v^{(k)}$. As at least one party in $\mathcal{T}_{\mathsf{king}}$ is honest, v is uniformly random and private. Next, P_{king} broadcasts $\mathcal{T}_{\mathsf{king}}$ and every party waits until it terminates all Sup-Sh$_k$ instances of $P_k \in \mathcal{T}_{\mathsf{king}}$; this ensures that every party obtains its share-pair and committed shares of v.

As P_{king} is privileged for *every* $[v^{(k)}]$, it computes all encrypted shares of $[v]$, using the homomorphic property of encryptions. However, unlike P_{king}, other honest parties may be non-privileged for one or more $[v^{(k)}]$s, and thus may not compute the encrypted shares of $[v]$. The way out is that P_{king} "helps" other parties by broadcasting the encrypted shares of v, which costs $\mathcal{O}(n^3\kappa)$ bits. To confirm whether P_{king} indeed broadcasted the correct encrypted shares of v, P_{king} is also asked to non-equivocally forward the encrypted shares corresponding to each $[v^{(k)}]$ to every other party. We stress that this information is *not* broadcasted, and rather communicated over the *point-to-point* channels, which costs $\mathcal{O}(n^3\kappa)$ bits. Once this information is *non-equivocally received* by a party, it *re-computes* the encrypted shares of v, verifies them with the P_{king}'s broadcast, and broadcasts the verification result. If $t+1$ parties broadcasts "positively" for P_{king}, then at least one honest party must have successfully verified those encrypted shares; so every party terminates the protocol with $[v]$ and the broadcasted encrypted shares of $[v]$. The properties of the Sup-Second protocol are stated in Lemma 6.1.

LEMMA 6.1. *For every possible $\mathcal{A}$ and every possible scheduler, protocol* Sup-Second *achieves the following properties up to a negligible probability in κ:* (1) TERMINATION: *if P_{king} is honest, all honest parties eventually terminate the protocol. Even if P_{king} is corrupted and some honest party terminates, then every other honest party eventually does the same.* (2) CORRECTNESS: *if the honest parties terminate the protocol, then the parties output $[\cdot]$-sharing $[v]$ of a value v. Moreover, each party will be a privileged party having all the encrypted share-pairs of v.* (3) PRIVACY: *the output shared value will be random from the viewpoint of $\mathcal{A}$.* (4) COMMUNICATION COMPLEXITY: *the protocol has communication complexity of $\mathcal{O}(n^3\kappa)$ bits.*

6.2 Generating First and Third Components

Protocol Sup-FirAndThd takes as input a $[\cdot]$-shared uniformly random, say v, unknown to $\mathcal{A}$ such that *every party is a privileged party for* $[v]$. It then generates $[u]$ for a uniformly random u, unknown to $\mathcal{A}$, along with the $[\cdot]$-sharing $[u \cdot v]$, under the supervision of P_{king}. The protocol follows the same principle as Sup-Second, except that each party P_i now invokes an instance Sup-PreMul-Sh$_i$ of Sup-PreMul-Sh with $[v]$ and a uniformly random value $u^{(i)}$ to generate $[u^{(i)}]$ and $[u^{(i)} \cdot v]$; this is possible as every P_i is a privileged party with respect to $[v]$. Now the parties set $u = \sum_{P_k \in \mathcal{T}_{\mathsf{king}}} u^{(k)}$ and $w = \sum_{P_k \in \mathcal{T}_{\mathsf{king}}} u^{(k)} \cdot v$, where $\mathcal{T}_{\mathsf{king}}$ is the set of $t+1$ parties P_k such that the instance Sup-PreMul-Sh$_k$ has been terminated by P_{king}. The properties of the protocol Sup-FirAndThd are presented in Lemma 6.2.

LEMMA 6.2. *For every possible A and every possible scheduler, the protocol* Sup-FirAndThd *achieves the following properties up to a negligible probability in κ:* (1) TERMINATION: *if P_{king} is honest, then all honest parties eventually terminate. Moreover, if one honest party terminates, then all honest parties eventually terminate.* (2) CORRECTNESS: *after termination, all parties hold a sharing $[u], [w]$ such that $[w] = [u \cdot v]$.* (3) PRIVACY: *the view of the adversary is indistinguishable for different values of u and v.*

(4) COMMUNICATION COMPLEXITY: *the protocol has communication complexity of $\mathcal{O}(n^3\kappa)$ bits.*

6.3 Sup-Second+Sup-FirAndThd⟹SupTripGen

Finally SupTripGen consists of two steps: **(1).** The parties execute Sup-Second and output $[v]$; **(2).** On terminating Sup-Second, the parties execute Sup-FirAndThd, output $[u]$ and $[w] = [u \cdot v]$ and terminate. Lemma 6.3 describes the SupTripGen properties, and follows easily from lemmas 6.1 and 6.2, and the protocol steps:

LEMMA 6.3. *For every possible $\mathcal{A}$ and every possible scheduler, the protocol SupTripGen achieves the following properties up to a negligible probability in κ:* (1) TERMINATION: *if P_{king} is honest then all honest parties eventually terminate the protocol. Moreover, even if P_{king} is corrupted and some honest party terminates the protocol, then every other honest party eventually does the same.* (2) CORRECTNESS: *if the honest parties terminate the protocol, then the parties output $[\cdot]$-sharing $([u], [v], [w])$ of a multiplication triple (u, v, w).* (3) PRIVACY: *the shared multiplication triple (u, v, w) will be random from the viewpoint of $\mathcal{A}$.* (4) COMMUNICATION COMPLEXITY: *the protocol has communication complexity of $\mathcal{O}(n^3\kappa)$ bits.*

7. THE NeqAMPC PROTOCOL

The key idea of the NeqAMPC protocol has already been discussed in Section 2. It is a sequence of three phases, where a party proceeds to the next phase only after completing the current phase:

1. **Pre-processing phase:** it generates $[\cdot]$-sharing of $c_M + c_R$ random multiplication triples;
2. **Input phase:** here each party $[\cdot]$-shares its private input, using an instance of Sh; due to the asynchronicity, the parties agree on a set of $(n-t)$ input providers and substitute 0 as the default input of the remaining t parties;
3. **Computation phase:** here the parties evaluate the circuit in a shared fashion, using the idea discussed in Section 2.

As this protocol is standard [30, 31], we shift it to the extended version [1] and state only the main theorem here.

THEOREM 7.1 *(The NeqAMPC Theorem). Let $f : \mathbb{Z}_p^n \rightarrow \mathbb{Z}_p$ be a function expressed as an arithmetic circuit over $\mathbb{Z}_p$, consisting of c_M multiplication gates and c_R random gates. Assume a non-equivocation oracle associated with every party. Then for every possible $\mathcal{A}$ and for every possible scheduler, there exists a computationally secure AMPC protocol to securely compute f with communication complexity of $\mathcal{O}(((c_M + c_R) \cdot n^3 + n^3)\kappa)$ bits.*

8. ACKNOWLEDGMENTS

We would like to thank the anonymous reviewers for their feedback, and Martin Hirt for his suggestions on an earlier draft of the paper. This work was supported by the German Ministry for Education and Research (BMBF) through funding for the Center for IT-Security, Privacy and Accountability (CISPA) and the German Universities Excellence Initiative.

9. REFERENCES

[1] M. Backes, F. Bendun, A. Choudhury, and A. Kate. Asynchronous MPC with $t < n/2$ Using Non-equivocation. Cryptology ePrint Archive, Report 2013/745.

[2] M. Backes, A. Datta, and A. Kate. Asynchronous Computational VSS with Reduced Communication Complexity. In *CT-RSA*, pages 259–276, 2013.

[3] M. Backes, A. Kate, and A. Patra. Computational Verifiable Secret Sharing Revisited. In *ASIACRYPT*, pages 590–609, 2011.

[4] D. Beaver. Efficient Multiparty Protocols Using Circuit Randomization. In *CRYPTO*, pages 420–432, 1991.

[5] Z. Beerliová-Trubíniová and M. Hirt. Simple and Efficient Perfectly-Secure Asynchronous MPC. In *ASIACRYPT*, pages 376–392, 2007.

[6] Z. Beerliová-Trubíniová and M. Hirt. Perfectly-Secure MPC with Linear Communication Complexity. In *TCC*, pages 213–230, 2008.

[7] Z. Beerliová-Trubíniová, M. Hirt, and J. B. Nielsen. On the Theoretical Gap between Synchronous and Asynchronous MPC Protocols. In *PODC*, pages 211–218, 2010.

[8] M. Bellare and O. Goldreich. On Defining Proofs of Knowledge. In *CRYPTO*, pages 390–420, 1992.

[9] M. Ben-Or, R. Canetti, and O. Goldreich. Asynchronous Secure Computation. In *STOC*, pages 52–61, 1993.

[10] M. Ben-Or, S. Goldwasser, and A. Wigderson. Completeness Theorems for Non-Cryptographic Fault-Tolerant Distributed Computation. In *STOC*, pages 1–10, 1988.

[11] M. Ben-Or, B. Kelmer, and T. Rabin. Asynchronous Secure Computation with Optimal Resilience . In *PODC*, pages 183–192, 1994.

[12] E. Ben-Sasson, S. Fehr, and R. Ostrovsky. Near-Linear Unconditionally-Secure Multiparty Computation with a Dishonest Minority. In *CRYPTO*, pages 663–680, 2012.

[13] G. Bracha. An Asynchronous [(n-1)/3]-Resilient Consensus Protocol. In *PODC*, pages 154–162, 1984.

[14] C. Cachin, K. Kursawe, A.Lysyanskaya, and R. Strobl. Asynchronous Verifiable Secret Sharing and Proactive Cryptosystems. In *CCS*, pages 88–97, 2002.

[15] C. Cachin, K. Kursawe, F. Petzold, and V. Shoup. Secure and Efficient Asynchronous Broadcast Protocols. In *CRYPTO*, pages 524–541, 2001.

[16] J. Camenisch and M. Stadler. Proof Systems for General Statements about Discrete Logarithms. Technical report, 1997. 260, Dept. of Computer Science, ETH Zurich.

[17] R. Canetti. *Studies in Secure Multiparty Computation and Applications*. PhD thesis, The Weizmann Institute of Science, 1996.

[18] D. Chaum, C. Crépeau, and I. Damgård. Multiparty Unconditionally Secure Protocols. In *STOC*, pages 11–19, 1988.

[19] B. Chevallier-Mames, P. Paillier, and D. Pointcheval. Encoding-Free Elgamal Encryption Without Random Oracles. In *PKC*, pages 91–104, 2006.

[20] A. Choudhury, M. Hirt, and A. Patra. Asynchronous Multiparty Computation with Linear Communication Complexity. In *DISC*, pages 388–402, 2013.

[21] B.-G. Chun, P. Maniatis, S. Shenker, and J. Kubiatowicz. Attested Append-only Memory: Making Adversaries Stick to their Word. In *SOSP*, pages 189–204, 2007.

[22] A. Clement, F. Junqueira, A. Kate, and R. Rodrigues. On the (limited) Power of Non-Equivocation. In *PODC*, pages 301–308, 2012.

[23] M. Correia, G. S. Veronese, and L. C. Lung. Asynchronous Byzantine Consensus with 2f+1 Processes. In *SAC*, pages 475–480, 2010.

[24] D. Dolev and H. R. Strong. Authenticated Algorithms for Byzantine Agreement. *SIAM J. Comput.*, 12(4):656–666, 1983.

[25] P. Feldman and S. Micali. Byzantine Agreement in Constant Expected Time (and Trusting No One). In *FOCS*, pages 267–276, 1985.

[26] R. Gennaro, M. Rabin, and T. Rabin. Simplified VSS and Fast-Track Multiparty Computations with Applications to Threshold Cryptography. In *PODC*, pages 101–111, 1998.

[27] O. Goldreich, S. Micali, and A. Wigderson. How to Play any Mental Game. In *STOC*, pages 218–229, 1987.

[28] V. Hadzilacos and S. Toueg. A Modular Approach to Fault-Tolerant Broadcasts and Related Problems. Technical report, Ithaca, NY, USA, 1994.

[29] M. Hirt and J. B. Nielsen. Robust Multiparty Computation with Linear Communication Complexity. In *CRYPTO*, pages 463–482, 2006.

[30] M. Hirt, J. B. Nielsen, and B. Przydatek. Cryptographic Asynchronous Multi-party Computation with Optimal Resilience (Extended Abstract). In *EUROCRYPT*, pages 322–340, 2005.

[31] M. Hirt, J. B. Nielsen, and B. Przydatek. Asynchronous Multi-Party Computation with Quadratic Communication. In *Proc. of ICALP'08*, pages 473–485, 2008.

[32] A. Jaffe, T. Moscibroda, and S. Sen. On the Price of Equivocation in Byzantine Agreement. In *PODC*, pages 309–318, 2012.

[33] R. Kapitza, J. Behl, C. Cachin, T. Distler, S. Kuhnle, S. V. Mohammadi, W. Schröder-Preikschat, and K. Stengel. CheapBFT: Resource-efficient Byzantine Fault Tolerance. In *EuroSys*, pages 295–308, 2012.

[34] D. Levin, J. R. Douceur, J. R. Lorch, and T. Moscibroda. TrInc: Small Trusted Hardware for Large Distributed Systems. In *NSDI*, pages 1–14, 2009.

[35] T. P. Pedersen. Non-Interactive and Information-Theoretic Secure Verifiable Secret Sharing. In *CRYPTO*, pages 129–140, 1991.

[36] T. Rabin and M. Ben-Or. Verifiable Secret Sharing and Multiparty Protocols with Honest Majority. In *STOC*, pages 73–85, 1989.

[37] A. Shamir. How to Share a Secret. *Commun. ACM*, 22(11):612–613, 1979.

[38] M. Stadler. Publicly Verifiable Secret Sharing. In *EUROCRYPT*, pages 190–199, 1996.

[39] S. Toueg. Randomized Byzantine Agreements. In *PODC*, pages 163–178, 1984.

[40] A. Yao. Protocols for secure computations. In *FOCS*, pages 160–164, 1982.

Distributing the Setup in Universally Composable Multi-Party Computation

Jonathan Katz[*]
Dept. of Computer Science,
University of Maryland
jkatz@cs.umd.edu

Aggelos Kiayias[†]
Dept. of Informatics and Telecommunications,
University of Athens
aggelos@di.uoa.gr

Hong-Sheng Zhou[‡]
Dept. of Computer Science,
Virginia Commonwealth University
hszhou@vcu.edu

Vassilis Zikas[§]
Dept. of Computer Science,
UCLA
vzikas@cs.ucla.edu

ABSTRACT

Universally composable (UC) protocols retain their security properties even when run concurrently alongside arbitrary other protocols. Unfortunately, it is known that UC multi-party computation (for general functionalities, and without assuming honest majority) is impossible without some form of setup. To circumvent this impossibility, various *complete* setup assumptions have been proposed.

With only a few exceptions, past work has viewed these setup assumptions as being implemented by some ideal, incorruptible entity. Any such entity is thus a *single point of failure*, and security fails catastrophically in case the setup entity is subverted by an adversary.

We propose here a clean, general, and generic approach for distributing trust among m arbitrary setups, by modeling potential corruption of setups within the UC framework, where such corruption might be fail-stop, passive, or arbitrary and is in addition to possible corruption of the parties themselves. We show several feasibility and impossibility results in this model, for different specifications of the corruptible sets. For example, we show that given m complete setups, up to t of which might be actively corrupted in an adaptive manner, general multiparty computation with no honest majority is possible if and only if $t < m/2$.

[*]Work supported in part by NSF awards #1111599 and #1223623.

[†]Work supported by ERC grant CODAMODA.

[‡]Work supported in part by an NSF CI postdoctoral fellowship, and mainly done while at the University of Maryland.

[§]Work supported in part by the Swiss National Science Foundation (SNF), project no. 200020-132794, and mainly done while at the University of Maryland.

PODC'14, July 15–18, 2014, Paris, France.

ACM 978-1-4503-2944-6/14/07 ...$15.00.
http://dx.doi.org/10.1145/2611462.2611480.

1. INTRODUCTION

Secure multi-party computation (MPC) is a quintessential cryptographic problem. The strongest and most desirable level of security that can be attained by such a protocol is universal composability (UC) [2]. Unfortunately, results by Canetti and Fischlin [5] and Canetti, Kushilevitz, and Lindell [6] show that unless a majority of the parties are honest, most "interesting" functionalities cannot be realized in the UC framework. These impossibility results can be circumvented if one is willing to assume a *trusted setup*: Canetti and Fischlin [5] showed that the existence of a (trusted) common reference string (CRS) allows for circumventing their impossibility result. Subsequently, Canetti et al. [7] showed that a CRS is *complete* in that it can be used for UC computation of arbitrary functionalities, for any number of corrupted parties. Similarly, oblivious transfer (OT) [24], a two-party primitive for sending one out of two inputs without learning which one was actually delivered, was proven to be complete for computing arbitrary functionalities with information-theoretic (aka unconditional or statistical) security [21]. Since then, researchers have suggested a variety of setups, e.g., [1, 18, 8, 20], and showed them to be complete; we refer to [3] for a (now slightly outdated) survey.

With only a few exceptions [15, 14, 12] (discussed below), prior work in this line of research has viewed setup assumptions as being implemented by some ideal, incorruptible entity. In reality, however, most setups would have to be implemented by some mechanism that could be subverted, or by some party that could be compromised. (As an example, NIST runs a "random beacon" that could function as a CRS—see `https://beacon.nist.gov/home` and `http://www.nist.gov/itl/csd/ct/nist_beacon.cfm`; their implementation could be hacked, or contain unexpected design flaws.) To cope with such situations, recent works [15, 14, 12] have suggested distributing trust among more than one such setup mechanisms, so that security is not compromised even if some of them fail.

1.1 Our Contribution

We propose here a new approach for modeling potential failure/corruption of setups within the UC framework that is more general and, arguably, more natural than prior attempts. Informally, for an arbitrary setup functionality $\mathcal{F}$ we consider three ways $\mathcal{F}$ might be compromised. In the *fail-stop* case, an adversary can cause $\mathcal{F}$ to halt at any point. *Passive* corruption allows the adversary to read the entire internal state of $\mathcal{F}$, but not change its behavior. Finally, in the *active* case the adversary gains complete control over $\mathcal{F}$ and can cause it to behave arbitrarily. This is in addition to any possible corruption of the parties running the protocol. Clearly, access to a single setup that can be actively corrupted is no different than having no setup at all. But our framework allows us to analyze the scenario where the parties have access to *multiple* setups, some subset of which might be corrupted, possibly in different ways.

In most of our results, we allow the adversary to *adaptively* choose the parties and setups to corrupt. Note that, similarly to party-corruption, adaptive corruption of setups is an important consideration: Consider, for example, the following mechanism used by two parties having access to several setups (some of which might be corrupted): in order to increase their probability of using uncorrupted setups, the parties start any protocol by agreeing on a random subset of setups to be used (e.g., by executing a coin-tossing protocol to determine this subset). Clearly adaptively choosing the corrupted setups (after the coins have been flipped and the decision of which setups to be used is taken) gives the adversary advantage in such a protocol over the adversary with static setup corruption.

As our main technical contribution, we study feasibility of general secure computation with no honest majority within the framework discussed above. We show, for example, that given m *arbitrary* complete setups, any t of which might be *actively* corrupted, secure computation of arbitrary (well-formed) functionalities is possible *if and only if* $t < m/2$. We also prove that this bound is tight even for *passive* corruption of setups. We further extend our characterization to the setting of mixed (i.e., active and passive) corruption: given m arbitrary complete setups, where any t_a might be *actively* corrupted and, simultaneously, any t_p might be passively corrupted, secure computation of arbitrary (well-formed) functionalities is possible *if and only if* $t_a + t_p < m/2$. We further generalize the above threshold results to the case of arbitrary "corruption structures" that enumerate the allowable sets of corruptible setups; there, we show that secure computation of arbitrary functionalities is possible if and only if no two corruptible sets cover the entire set of available setups.

Additionally, we show that for many setups considered in the literature, one can do better than the above generic bounds. (The negative results stated hold for arbitrary complete setups; for specific setups it may be possible to do better.) In particular, we introduce the class of *passively immune* setups (which includes a natural variant of the CRS functionality) we show that given m complete setups in this class, any t_a of which might be actively corrupted, secure computation of arbitrary functionalities is possible *if and only if* $t_a < m/2$ *even if all* m *setups can simultaneously be* passively *corrupted.*

All the above mentioned results hold for an adversary who, in addition to corrupting functionalities, *is allowed to actively corrupt arbitrary many parties.* In a slightly different direction, we give a "best-of-both worlds" result for the setting where there is either a corrupted majority of setups, or a corrupted majority of parties. Due to space limitation, some of the details of our results are deferred to the full version of the current extended abstract.

1.2 Prior Work on Corruptible Setups

Corruptible UC setups were first considered by Groth and Ostrovsky [15] for the special case of a Common Reference String (CRS). In particular, they studied the "multi-CRS" model where there are m common reference strings and the adversary is allowed to replace any t of them with strings of his own choice. Building on their work, Goyal and Katz [14] looked at the case where there is a *single* CRS, and either the CRS is compromised (as in [15]) but a majority of the parties are honest, or the CRS is not compromised but a majority of the parties is no longer honest. Finally, in TCC 2011 Garg et al. [12] initiated the study of feasibility of UC computation with *potentially different* setups that can "fail" in certain ways. Our work unifies, abstracts, and extends the above results, as we now explain.

Comparison to [15]. In contrast to the work of Groth and Ostrovsky [15], our corruption model is both more general and more broadly applicable. We consider active, passive, and fail-stop[1] corruption of setup functionalities, and in the active case we allow the adversary to *arbitrarily control* the setup (e.g., an actively corrupted CRS can send different strings of the adversary's choice to different parties, something not considered in [15]). Moreover, we consider corruption of general setup functionalities, not just a CRS, and give results for general corruption structures.

On a technical level, Groth and Ostrovsky [15, Theorem 4] prove impossibility of implementing non-interactive zero-knowledge for languages that are not in $\mathcal{P}/\mathsf{poly}$ when more than half the CRSs are faulty. In contrast, we show unconditionally that *any* set of arbitrary (even different) setup functionalities becomes *trivial* (i.e., implementable from secure channels without further assumptions) as soon as half of them are faulty.

Comparison to [12]. In the work of Garg et al. [12], corruption of setups is not modeled "directly"; rather, three types of "faulty" UC puzzles are introduced, and corruption of a setup $\mathcal{F}$ is *defined* by what type of "faulty" UC puzzle can be realized using $\mathcal{F}$. (UC puzzles were introduced by Lin et al. [22] and shown there to be complete for secure computation. We sketch the definition of UC puzzles in Appendix A.) A bit more specifically, given a setup $\mathcal{F}$ that can be used to construct a UC puzzle, and the assumption that an adversary can corrupt $\mathcal{F}$ to obtain the faulty setup $\mathcal{F}'$, the "type" of this corruption model is defined to be exactly the "type" of faulty UC puzzle that results from using $\mathcal{F}'$.

From a conceptual point of view we find our modeling more appealing, as it speaks *directly* of the different ways (fail-stop, passive, active) in which arbitrary setups can be

[1]The non-triviality of dealing with fail-stop corruption stems from the fact that we aim for secure computation with *unanimous* abort [13]. Thus, it is not sufficient for a single party to disqualify a setup when it observes a failure; rather, there needs to be consensus that a failure occurred. And running a consensus protocol is not an option as we allow arbitrary many corrupted parties.

compromised, rather than indirectly in terms of what sort of puzzle can be constructed from a compromised setup (something that, a priori, is unclear). Moreover, the framework of Garg et al. allows the faulty version $\mathcal{F}'$ of a setup $\mathcal{F}$ to be *arbitrary*, even having no relation to $\mathcal{F}$. (E.g., $\mathcal{F}$ could be a CRS, while $\mathcal{F}'$ implements oblivious transfer.) Our modeling, instead, uses well-defined "wrappers" that ensure a particular relationship between $\mathcal{F}$ and $\mathcal{F}'$. Although we only deal with fail-stop, passive, and active faults in this paper, our framework could easily be extended to deal with other faults, e.g., dropped messages.

Our choice of modeling has technical consequences as well, which are reflected both in our results and the corresponding proofs. The framework of Garg et al. *only* applies only to setups $\mathcal{F}$ that can be used to construct UC puzzles in the first place. In contrast, our framework applies to arbitrary, even incomplete, setups. Even restricting attention to complete setups (which is the more interesting case), it is not known whether all complete setups can be used to construct UC puzzles: Indeed, even for a UC-complete setup $\mathcal{R}$, the standard approach of replacing (in an $\mathcal{F}$-hybrid UC puzzle) calls to $\mathcal{F}$ by an $\mathcal{R}$-hybrid protocol computationally implementing $\mathcal{F}$ does not yield a $\mathcal{R}$-hybrid UC puzzle as it does not satisfy the *statistical* simulatability property [22]. Second, observe that applying the results of Garg et al. to some specific $\mathcal{F}$ (that is known to yield a UC puzzle) and its faulty version $\mathcal{F}'$, would require the protocol designer to know (or somehow figure out) what type of faulty UC puzzle can be constructed from $\mathcal{F}'$. It is not clear, in general, how (or even if) this can be done. Finally, we note that although Type 1 setups (as defined in [12]) can be shown to correspond to the active corruptions we consider here (at least for setups that can be handled by [12]), such a correspondence does not seem to hold for the other corruption types considered in our work.

With regard to differences in the results (as opposed to differences in the models), we first note that the positive results from [12] all rely on UC puzzles as an intermediate step. As a consequence, (1) their protocols can *only* be *computationally* secure, even when the assumed setups are complete for information-theoretic secure computation; (2) their work only handles static adversaries.[2] In contrast, our possibility results rely on constructions of MPC from oblivious transfer (OT), yielding *information-theoretic* constructions secure against *adaptive adversaries*.

Finally, we mention that proving tightness of the positive results was left as the main open question in [12]. Although our results do not directly answer this question in their model (since we use a different model), we are able to prove tightness of all the positive results shown in this work.

Comparison to using combiners. In other work similar in spirit to our own, researchers have studied the notion of *combiners* [16, 23, 26]. The goal of that work is to construct a single primitive securely realizing some task (e.g., oblivious transfer) from a collection of m such primitives, some t of which may fail. Our work is more general in several ways, in particular because we work in the UC framework, and do not require that each of our m setup functionalities realizes the same primitive. Rather, our impossibility results apply to arbitrary, even different setups. Additionally, we specify different ways in which setups might fail and provide characterizations for each of them individually as well as their combinations. In fact, a corollary of our impossibility result for passive corruption of setups (Lemma 6) gives a simpler proof of impossibility for third-party black-box OT combiners when half (or more) of the OT candidates are faulty [16, 23]. On the other hand, at the technical level, our main positive results are obtained by reduction to OT-combiners.

[2]Dachman-Soled et al. [11] show how to construct adaptively secure MPC from UC puzzles. Plugging this protocol into the feasibility result of [12] strengthens their result to hold for adaptive corruption of parties (but still static failure of setups). But the construction from [11] relies on even stronger (non-standard) complexity assumptions than those used in [12].

2. THE MODEL

We lay down the specifics of our model and fix some notation and conventions. We assume the reader has some familiarity with the Universal Composition (UC) framework [2]. We use the following notation: for $m \in \mathbb{Z}$ we denote by $[m]$ the set $[m] = \{1, \ldots, m\}$. We consider both the two-party and the multi-party case, where the parties can communicate over a complete network of bilateral authenticated channels. We denote by $\mathcal{P} = \{p_1, \ldots, p_n\}$ the player set ($\mathcal{P} = \{p_1, p_2\}$ for the two-party case). The adversary, denoted by $\mathcal{A}$, corrupts parties adaptively, i.e., might corrupt parties during the execution of the protocol. We consider standard (i.e., active) party corruption as defined in [2].

As usually in the UC literature we model setups as UC functionalities. The *setup-functionalities* $\mathcal{F}$ considered in this work have the following properties: **(1)** Whenever some input is received from some honest party, the functionality $\mathcal{F}$ notifies the adversary *(input notification)*, and **(2)** all outputs of the functionality are issued in a delayed manner as specified in [2], i.e., whenever $\mathcal{F}$ has an output to be sent to some party p_i, it notifies the adversary about this fact (the notification includes the PID of p_i) and delivers the input only when the adversary permits it *(delayed output)*. Furthermore, we only deal with setup-functionalities that are *efficiently computable*, where we assume that the inputs and outputs of the setup-functionalities are strings of a fixed length. Whenever the term "setup-functionality" is used in this work it refers to a functionality that satisfies the above properties.[3]

Consistently with the UC framework, assuming a (setup) functionality $\mathcal{F}$ implies assuming that every $\mathcal{F}$-hybrid protocol can instantiate its own (independent) instance(s) of $\mathcal{F}$.[4] Hence, assuming that the setup $\mathcal{F}$ fails (in our terminology, becomes corrupted) implies that its instances fail across all protocols using $\mathcal{F}$ as a hybrid. As pointed out in [2, 9], a side effect of this modeling choice is that in order to prove security of multiple protocols using the same (stateful) setup, e.g., the same public key infrastructure (PKI), one needs to use the *joint state composition theorem* (JUC) [9]. An alternative approach would be to model setups directly in the *UC with global setups* (GUC) model of Canetti et al [4]. Our modeling of corrupted functionalities can be easily extended to capture corrupted (global) setups in GUC. However, our proofs do not go through in that model; it is an interesting

[3]At times we might refer to setup-functionalities as *setups*.

[4]For example, when one speaks of UC completeness of Oblivious Transfer (OT) functionality, it is implicitly assumed that multiple independent instances of the OT functionality can be invoked with different sender and receivers.

open question to prove bounds for corrupted setups in the GUC model.

2.1 Modeling Corruption of Functionalities

To capture the fact that a setup might be, at least partially, controlled by the adversary we introduce the notion of corruptible functionalities. *Corruptible functionalities* are modeled as being enclosed into a *corruption wrapper* which behaves as follows: any message sent to/from the functionality is forwarded by the wrapper to its recipient (the wrapper also records all these messages and can access the random tape of the wrapped functionality). In addition to the standard communication with the functionality, the wrapper might accept from the adversary $\mathcal{A}$ messages of the form ($\texttt{fcorrupt}, type$)—where *type* specifies the way in which $\mathcal{A}$ wishes to corrupt the underlying functionality—and modify its behavior accordingly. Consistently with the multi-party computation (MPC) literature, in this work we focus on the following three corruption types

ACTIVE: Upon receiving a message ($\texttt{fcorrupt}, \texttt{active}$) from $\mathcal{A}$, the corruption wrapper sends $\mathcal{A}$ all the messages it has seen so far as well as the internal randomness of the wrapped functionality; from then on, the wrapper behaves as the "dummy" functionality which forwards every message it receives from any party to the adversary $\mathcal{A}$, and when instructed by the adversary to send (as output) some message y to some party, it does so.

PASSIVE: Upon receiving a message ($\texttt{fcorrupt}, \texttt{passive}$) from $\mathcal{A}$, the wrapper sends $\mathcal{A}$ all the messages it has seen so far as well as the internal randomness of the wrapped functionality.[5]

FAIL: Upon receiving a message ($\texttt{fcorrupt}, \texttt{fail}$) from $\mathcal{A}$, the wrapper enters a *crashed* stated, i.e., answers all messages sent to it from that point on with a special ($\texttt{crashed}$) message; we say then that the adversary has *forced $\mathcal{F}$ to to crash.*

A wrapped functionality which accepts active or passive corruption requests will be called *actively corruptible* or *passively corruptible*, respectively. A setup-functionality which does not accept any corruption requests (i.e., behaves as unwrapped) is called *incorruptible.* In order to model mixed-type corruption of functionalities, we also consider wrapped functionalities that accept corruption messages of more than one type. Unless explicitly stated otherwise, we assume that *the adversary might corrupt the setup-functionalities in an adaptive manner*, i.e, might corrupt (additional) setups during the execution of a protocol.

Consistent with the terminology used in the literature for party corruption we refer to a setup-functionality $\mathcal{F}$ which has been actively corrupted, i.e., the adversary has sent $\mathcal{F}$ ($\texttt{fcorrupt}, \texttt{active}$), as *malicious.* Similarly, a passively corrupted functionality is called *semi-honest.* $\mathcal{F}$ is called *honest* or *uncorrupted* if the adversary has not sent $\mathcal{F}$ any ($\texttt{fcorrupt}, type$) message.

Functionality Sets and Corruption Patterns.

Let $\mathcal{M} = \{\mathcal{F}_1, \ldots, \mathcal{F}_m\}$ be a set of (possibly different) setup functionalities. In slight abuse of terminology we often refer to $\mathcal{M}$ as a setup-functionality, where calls to $\mathcal{M}$ are addressed to the appropriate functionality. An *$\mathcal{M}$-hybrid* protocol π is a protocol that can make hybrid calls to all the functionalities in $\mathcal{M}$. We say that the adversary is *t-restricted* if he might corrupt up to a certain threshold t of the functionalities. We also consider the more general setting, where the adversary might corrupt any set of functionalities from a specific *corruption structure* $\mathcal{K}$; we refer to the latter as a *$\mathcal{K}$-restricted* adversary.[6] More precisely, $\mathcal{K}$ is a *monotone* set of subsets of the functionality-set $\mathcal{M}$, i.e., $\mathcal{K} = \{A_1, \ldots, A_n\}$, where each $A_i \subseteq \mathcal{M}$. A $\mathcal{K}$-restricted adversary might corrupt all the functionalities in some class $A^\star \in \mathcal{K}$.

Corruption Ignoring Strengthening.

Throughout this extended abstract we assume functionalities that allow for active and passive corruption. However, at times we need to refer to the corresponding honest functionality. Therefore we introduce the following notation: For a given setup-functionality $\mathcal{F}$, we define the *corruption-ignoring strengthening* of $\mathcal{F}$, denoted as $\mathcal{F}^{\not{C}}$, to be the "unwrapped" functionality that ignores all ($\texttt{fcorrupt}, \cdot$) requests. At times, we need to refer to the strengthening of a functionality that ignores only a specific type of corruption-requests; we refer to the strengthening of $\mathcal{F}$ that ignores only ($\texttt{fcorrupt}, \texttt{passive}$) (resp. ($\texttt{fcorrupt}, \texttt{active}$)) commands as the *passively ignoring* (resp. *actively ignoring*) strengthening of $\mathcal{F}$, and denote it as $\mathcal{F}^{\not{P}}$ (resp. $\mathcal{F}^{\not{A}}$). Note that (depending on $\mathcal{F}$), the corruption ignoring strengthening $\mathcal{F}^{\not{C}}$ might not necessarily be a useful setup, e.g., one could consider a functionality $\mathcal{F}$ which, upon receiving from the adversary the message ($\texttt{becomeDummy}$), acts as $\mathcal{F}^{\text{dum}}$.

Assumptions, Completeness, and Sufficiency.

For a pair of functionalities $\mathcal{F}$ and $\mathcal{F}'$ and a computational assumptions α, we say that a functionality $\mathcal{F}$ is *(UC) α-sufficient for $\mathcal{F}'$* if, assuming α, there exists an $\mathcal{F}$-hybrid protocol which UC-realizes $\mathcal{F}'$ (using authenticated communication). Furthermore, we say that a functionality $\mathcal{F}$ is *(UC) α-complete* if, assuming α, for every well-formed[7] functionality $\mathcal{F}'$ there exists an $\mathcal{F}$-hybrid protocol which UC-realizes $\mathcal{F}'$. Note that for the definition of UC completeness we make no restriction on the adversary's party-corruption capabilities, i.e., *the adversary might corrupt arbitrary many parties.* Some specific examples of assumptions α_ℓ used in this work are the existence of one-way permutation (OWP), denoted as $\alpha_{\texttt{OWP}}$, and the existence of an oblivious-transfer (OT) protocol secure for semi-honest adversaries, denoted as $\alpha_{\texttt{shOT}}$.

The definition of completeness naturally extends to functionality sets and/or assumption sets. In particular, for assumptions $\alpha_1, \ldots, \alpha_q$ we denote by $\{\alpha_1, \ldots, \alpha_q\}$ the assumption which holds if for every $\ell \in [q] : \alpha_\ell$ holds. We say that *a functionality-set $\mathcal{M} = \{\mathcal{F}_1, \ldots, \mathcal{F}_m\}$ is $\{\alpha_1, \ldots, \alpha_q\}$-complete* if, assuming $\{\alpha_1, \ldots, \alpha_q\}$ holds, for every well-formed functionality $\mathcal{F}'$ there exists an $\mathcal{M}$-hybrid protocol which UC-realizes $\mathcal{F}'$.

[5] Note that the adversary might send the ($\texttt{fcorrupt}, \texttt{passive}$) message several times in a protocol execution.

[6] This corruption pattern corresponds to the so called *general adversary* [17] from the MPC literature.

[7] Roughly speaking, a functionality is well-formed if its code does not depend on the ID's of the corrupted parties; for a detailed description we refer to [7].

3. IMPOSSIBILITY FOR MALICIOUS MAJORITY

We start our analysis with our main impossibility result for the case of actively corruptible functionalities. Informally, we prove the following:

> Any collection of setups becomes trivial (i.e., implementable via secure channels— denoted by $\mathcal{F}_{\text{SEC}}$) if the adversary is allowed to actively corrupt more than half of them.

We state the result in Theorem 1 in its most general form, i.e., for an adversary characterized by a functionality-corruption structure $\mathcal{K}$. We use the following notation borrowed from [17]: we say that a structure $\mathcal{K}$ is a Q^2 structure if condition $Q^2(\mathcal{M},\mathcal{K})$ holds, where

$$Q^2(\mathcal{M},\mathcal{K}) \iff \forall A_i, A_j \in \mathcal{K} \; : \; A_i \cup A_j \neq \mathcal{M}$$

THEOREM 1 (STATIC PARTY-CORRUPTION). *For a 2-party setup-functionality set $\mathcal{M} = \{\mathcal{F}_1, \ldots, \mathcal{F}_m\}$, and a functionality-corruption structure $\mathcal{K}$, if $Q^2(\mathcal{M},\mathcal{K})$ does not hold then there exists an $\mathcal{F}_{\text{SEC}}$-hybrid 2-party protocol which securely realizes (all the functionalities in) $\mathcal{M}$, in the presence of a $\mathcal{K}$-restricted adversary who might statically corrupt any (or even both) parties.*

PROOF. Let $A_1, A_2 \in \mathcal{K}$ be functionality sets such that $A_1 \cup A_2 = \mathcal{M}$ (such sets are guaranteed to exist by the assumption that $\mathcal{K}$ is not Q^2). Without loss of generality assume that $A_1 \cap A_2 = \emptyset$ (if this is not the case take $A_2 \setminus A_1$ instead of A_2).[8] The protocol Π for securely realizing $\mathcal{M}$ in the $\mathcal{F}_{\text{SEC}}$-hybrid world is as follows: The idea of the protocol is to have each p_i (for $i = 1, 2$) answer all queries that are for the functionalities in A_i. More precisely, each p_i internally simulates the code of every $\mathcal{F}_\ell \in A_i$ and stores the internal states of all (simulated) $\mathcal{F}_\ell$'s; whenever in the protocol some party sends a message to the other party, this is done by use of the secure channel $\mathcal{F}_{\text{SEC}}$. The detailed code of p_i is given in the following.

We show that protocol Π UC securely realizes the functionality $\mathcal{M}$. The simulator for an adversary $\mathcal{A}$ works as follows: We consider the following four cases: (I) Both p_1 and p_2 are corrupted, (II) only p_1 is corrupted, (III) only p_2 is corrupted, and (IV) both p_1 and p_2 are honest.

In Case I: The simulator acts as a forwarder between the adversary and $\mathcal{Z}$ (and never invokes the functionality $\mathcal{M}$).

In Case II: The simulator corrupts all $\mathcal{F}_\ell \in A_1$. Any message which is received from the environment is forwarded to the adversary; any message which the adversary generates for the environment is outputted to $\mathcal{Z}$.

- Whenever $\mathcal{S}$ receives from $\mathcal{A}$ a message z to be sent to p_2, $\mathcal{S}$ simulates the view of $\mathcal{Z}$ in the secure channel, i.e., sends $|z|$ to $\mathcal{Z}$, and if z is of the form $(\texttt{input}, \ell, x)$ for some $\mathcal{F}_\ell \in A_2$, $\mathcal{S}$ inputs z to $\mathcal{F}_\ell$.
- Whenever p_2 sends input $(\texttt{input}, \ell, x)$ to some $\mathcal{F}_\ell \in A_1$, $\mathcal{S}$ (who, recall, has actively corrupted $\mathcal{F}_\ell$) receives this input, he simulates the view of $\mathcal{Z}$ corresponding to $(\texttt{input}, \ell, x)$ being sent through the secure channel, i.e., sends $|(\texttt{input}, \ell, x)|$ to $\mathcal{Z}$ and hands $(\texttt{input}, \ell, x)$ to the adversary $\mathcal{A}$.

Protocol $\Pi(\{p_1, p_2\}, \mathcal{M}, A_1, A_2)$

Code for p_i:

- Upon receiving an input x for functionality $\mathcal{F}_\ell$, i.e., the command $(\texttt{input}, \ell, x)$, from the environment $\mathcal{Z}$:
  - if $\mathcal{F}_\ell \in A_i$ then p_i simulates the behavior of $\mathcal{F}_\ell$; if the simulated $\mathcal{F}_\ell$ would generate a message y for p_i then output $(\texttt{output}, \ell, y)$ to the environment, otherwise, if it would generate a message y for p_{3-i} then send $(\texttt{output}, \ell, y)$ to p_{3-i}.
  - else, i.e., if $\mathcal{F}_\ell \in A_{3-i}$, then p_i sends the message $(\texttt{input}, \ell, x)$ to p_{3-i}.
- Upon receiving a message $(\texttt{input}, \ell, x)$ from p_{3-i}, if $\mathcal{F}_\ell \notin A_i$ then ignore the message. Else, simulate the behavior of $\mathcal{F}_\ell$ on input x from p_{3-i}; if the simulated $\mathcal{F}_\ell$ would generate a message y for p_i then output $(\texttt{output}, \ell, y)$ to the environment $\mathcal{Z}$, otherwise, if it would generate a message y for p_{3-i} then send $(\texttt{output}, \ell, y)$ to p_{3-i}.
- Upon receiving a message $(\texttt{output}, \ell, y)$ from p_{3-i}, if $\mathcal{F}_\ell \in A_i$ then ignore the message, else output $(\texttt{output}, \ell, y)$ to the environment $\mathcal{Z}$.

- For every pending output $(\texttt{output}, \ell, y)$ (recall that the setup-functionalities $\mathcal{F}_\ell$ issue their output in a public delayed manner) for $\mathcal{F}_\ell \in A_2$, as long as $\mathcal{S}$ has finished simulating the protocol messages and the output should be delivered in the (simulated) protocol, $\mathcal{S}$ instructs $\mathcal{F}_\ell$ to deliver the message to the corresponding party.

In Case III: This case can be handled as in Case II, symmetrically.

In Case IV: If the adversary $\mathcal{A}$ (in the $\mathcal{F}_{\text{SEC}}$-hybrid world) corrupts no party, then the simulator simply needs to simulate the view of $\mathcal{A}$ from the secure channel $\mathcal{F}_{\text{SEC}}$. Note that the simulator can trivially do this as (1) all messages exchanged between the parties are of fixed length which allows the simulator to know the output of $\mathcal{F}_{\text{SEC}}$ whenever a message would be exchanged in the protocol, and (2) the functionality notifies the simulator for every input it receives and always asks for permission before delivering the outputs, which allows $\mathcal{S}$ to order the messages sent to the environment according to the order they would appear in the protocol.

It is straight-forward to verify that the above is a good simulator for Protocol Π. □

We stress that Theorem 1 only claims *static* corruption of parties. In fact, counter to the standard intuition, we cannot obtain the same statement for adaptive party corruption as a corollary; we refer to Section 3.1 for a justification and for a complete handling of adaptive party-corruption. As a corollary of Theorem 1 we obtain the following impossibility result for t-restricted adversaries.

COROLLARY 2. *For a 2-party setup-functionality set $\mathcal{M} = \{\mathcal{F}_1, \ldots, \mathcal{F}_m\}$, there exists an $\mathcal{F}_{\text{SEC}}$-hybrid 2-party protocol which securely realizes (all the functionalities in) $\mathcal{M}$, in the presence of a $m/2$-restricted adversary who can (simultaneously) statically corrupt any (or even both) parties.*

[8]Recall that by definition $\mathcal{K}$ is monotone, thus $A_2 \setminus A_1 \in \mathcal{K}$.

PROOF. Let $\mathcal{K}_t$ denote the structure including all subsets of $\mathcal{M}$ of cardinality at most t. When $t \geq m/2$, the the condition $Q^2(\mathcal{M}, \mathcal{K}_t)$ is violated. Thus the statement follows trivially from Theorem 1. □

Observe that the only impossibility result in the multi-setup UC model is due to Groth and Ostrovsky [15], who showed that if a language L has a non-interactive zero-knowledge (NIZK) proof system in the multi-string model, then either $L \in \mathsf{P/poly}$ or at most half of the common reference strings might be adversarially chosen. Their proof uses a completely different approach than the one used here. Furthermore, our impossibility result is more general than the result from [15] in several aspects: In particular, for the case of a static adversary it extends to arbitrary setups. Moreover, as we show in Section 3.1, for the special case of the CRS (in fact for any adaptively well-formed setup [7]) our impossibility extends adaptive corruption of parties, thereby *strictly* generalizing [15]. Finally, our result proves that when a majority of setups is corrupted, then the multi-setup functionality in not just insufficient for NIZKs, but it is trivial, in the sense that it can be realized from secure channels.

REMARK (A WEAKER CORRUPTION TYPE [15] ALSO COVERED BY THEOREM 1). In [15] the adversary is assumed to have less power on the CRS than our active corruption, i.e., $\mathcal{A}$ is merely allowed to change the value of the common string, but he cannot make the functionality distribute inconsistent (i.e., different) strings (see the discussion in Section 1.2). It is straight-forward to verify that our proof works, almost verbatim, even if we restrict the power of the simulator along these lines. The only difference is that in the protocol used in the proof, as soon as a value is output by some party the party does not output any different value in the future.

3.1 Adaptive Party Corruption

Although one is tempted to assume that Theorem 1 implies impossibility also for *adaptive* corruption of parties, this is not the case, as allowing the adversary to adaptively corrupt the parties makes simulation in the $\mathcal{M}$-hybrid world harder. In particular, the proof of Theorem 1 breaks down for an adversary who first corrupts one of the parties, say p_1, and later corrupts the other one p_2. Intuitively, the reason is that while emulating this adversary, the simulator needs, at the point when p_2 gets corrupted, to come up with internal states for the setups emulated by p_2 that are consistent with the outputs they generated so far. However, by that time the simulator has exhausted all his corruption resources in order to emulate the corruption of p_1 and is therefore stuck.

In this section we show that this limitation can be overcome if we assume that the setups are adaptively well-formed [7]. Roughly speaking, an adaptively well-formed setup hands the adversary its internal randomness as soon as every party gets corrupted (for a formal description we refer to [7]). We remark, that adaptive well-formedness is a natural assumption for setups and all natural (in particular all known) setups satisfy it or they can be trivially modified to satisfy it by adding an extra instruction to send their adversary their full internal randomness as soon as every party becomes corrupted). In particular, for the class of adaptively well-formed setups, the result of Theorem 1 holds even for an adversary who can corrupt parties in an adaptive manner.

Note that, because the CRS is adaptively well-formed, Theorem 1 holds for the CRS even assuming adaptive corruption of parties. The following theorem extends Theorem 1 to an adversary who corrupts parties adaptively.

THEOREM 3. *For a set $\mathcal{M} = \{\mathcal{F}_1, \dots, \mathcal{F}_m\}$ of adaptively well-formed 2-party setup-functionalities,*[9] *and a corruption structure $\mathcal{K}$, if $Q^2(\mathcal{M}, \mathcal{K})$ does not hold then there exists an $\mathcal{F}_{\text{SEC}}$-hybrid 2-party protocol which securely realizes (all the functionalities in) $\mathcal{M}$, in the presence of a $\mathcal{K}$-restricted adversary who might adaptively corrupt any (or even both) parties.*

PROOF (*Idea*). We can use the same protocol as in Theorem 1. Intuitively, the reason why this is simulatable is the following: as long as at most one party is corrupted, the simulator does not have a problem as he can choose which functionalities to corrupt depending on the adversary's choice of party corruption (recall that we assume that the corruption of functionalities is by default adaptive and the corruption wrapper keeps a record of past inputs and outputs). Hence a problem might occur only when the adversary corrupts both parties during the protocol execution. In that case, the adaptive well-formedness of the setups ensures that the simulator learns the randomness used by all (even the uncorrupted) setups and, as by corrupting both parties he learns all inputs/outputs, he can go on with the simulation. We refer to the full version for a formal proof. □

Similarly to Corollary 2, a threshold impossibility result (for $t \geq m/2$ corrupted setups) can be obtained also for the adaptive case as a corollary of Theorem 3.

4. ACTIVE CORRUPTION OF SETUPS

Having established our main impossibility result, we proceed to proving its tightness. Informally, the statement we prove is the following:

> For a set $\mathcal{M}$ of (possibly different) actively corruptible UC-complete setups, there exists a protocol which securely realizes any well-formed functionality while tolerating an adversary corrupting arbitrary many parties *if and only if* the adversary might (simultaneously) corrupt less than half of the setups.

The above statement is formalized in Theorem 4. Note that, throughout this section, the assumed functionalities only accept active corruption requests, i.e., they ignore any message of the form ($\texttt{fcorrupt}$, *type*) for *type* $\neq$ $\texttt{active}$.

For proving the following theorem we use a well-known result on robust combiners for Oblivious Transfer (OT). In [23] is was shown that from m copies of the OT functionality at most half of which might be faulty (in our terminology faulty corresponds to actively corrupted) we can implement the *incorruptible* OT functionality $\mathcal{F}_{\text{OT}}{}^{\not\mathcal{C}}$. We use this fact to prove our result; the idea of our proof is the following: We use each of the setups to implement an independent copy of $\mathcal{F}_{\text{OT}}$ and then we use the OT-combiner to construct a single copy of $\mathcal{F}_{\text{OT}}$ that behaves honestly (i.e., as being incorruptible). Note that because the combiner from [23] works even

[9]Note that if $\mathcal{F}$ is adaptively well-formed, then so is its corruption-ignoring strengthening $\mathcal{F}_{\ell}{}^{\not\mathcal{C}}$.

when the adversary corrupts the parties adaptively, our positive results also works for adaptive party-corruption. (The same holds also for tightness as long as the $\mathcal{F}_\ell$'s are adaptively well-formed.)

We remark that although the combiner from [23] does not explicitly claim adaptive corruption of the assumed OTs, or universal composability, we can use the combiner proposed by Wullschleger [26] which is explicitly claimed to be universally composable and to tolerate adaptive corruption of the assumed functionality.[10] Importantly, the combiner from [W09] uses only the input/output of the OLFE protocol (and *not* the OLFE-protocol instructions). We remark that, although the relevant theorem statement [26, Theorem 2] does not explicitly mention UC, it provides a simulation-based proof of the combiner, where the simulator is black-box, straight-line, and does not depend on the actual OLFE implementation but only on the inputs/outputs. Hence, we can use the same simulator-structure with the only difference that when both parties are honest (but some of the OT's are corrupted) one needs to additionally observe that the simulator can simulate the inputs of the (honest) parties to the t corrupted OLFEs; this follows trivially from the fact that (by construction of the combiner) these inputs are shares lying on random polynomials of degree more than t. In the full version we provide the details of how the proof of [26, Theorem 2] can be adapted to work in our setting.

THEOREM 4. *Let $\mathcal{M} = \{\mathcal{F}_1, \ldots, \mathcal{F}_m\}$ be a set of setup-functionalities and $\alpha_1, \ldots, \alpha_m$ be assumptions such that for each $\mathcal{F}_\ell \in \mathcal{M}$ the corruption-ignoring strengthening $\mathcal{F}_\ell^{\not{C}}$ is (UC) α_ℓ-sufficient for OT. Assuming that the adversary is t-restricted, $\mathcal{M}$ is (UC) $\{\alpha_1, \ldots, \alpha_m\}$-complete if and only if $t < m/2$.*

PROOF (*sketch*). The necessity of the $t < m/2$ bound follows immediately from Corollary 2 (the case of adaptive party-corruption and adaptively well-formed setups follows from Theorem 3). We next argue its sufficiency: Because each $\mathcal{F}_\ell \in \mathcal{M}$ is α_ℓ-complete, we can use each of them to UC implement an independent copy of the OT functionality $\mathcal{F}_{\text{OT}}$. If $\mathcal{F}_\ell$ is corrupted, then there is no guarantee on the corresponding emulated copy of $\mathcal{F}_{\text{OT}}$. However, if $\mathcal{F}_\ell$ is uncorrupted, then the resulting construction is a good UC-emulation of the OT functionality. Moreover, as more than half of the $\mathcal{F}_\ell$'s are uncorrupted, there are more than $m/2$ emulations of (honest) OT functionalities. But the results of [23, 26] state that from m copies of the OT functionality a majority of which is good (honest) we can implement an incorruptible copy of the OT functionality (in our terminology this corresponds to implementing the corruption-ignoring strengthening $\mathcal{F}_{\text{OT}}^{\not{C}}$ of $\mathcal{F}_{\text{OT}}$). The UC composition theorem ensures that plugging the $\mathcal{F}_\ell$-to-OT reductions into the OT-combiner (along with an appropriate addressing mechanism) yields a secure protocol for $\mathcal{F}_{\text{OT}}^{\not{C}}$, i.e., an $\mathcal{M}$-hybrid protocol π_{OT} for securely emulating an incorruptible copy of the OT functionality assuming $t < m/2$. The UC completeness of $\mathcal{M}$ follows then from the (unconditional) UC completeness of OT [21, 10, 19] by applying the UC composition theorem: For any given functionality $\mathcal{F}'$, let $\Pi^{\mathcal{F}_{\text{OT}}}$ denote the OT-hybrid protocol for $\mathcal{F}'$ which is guaranteed to exist from [21, 10, 19]. The UC composition theorem ensures that replacing in $\Pi^{\mathcal{F}_{\text{OT}}}$ every instance of $\mathcal{F}_{\text{OT}}$ by a call to π_{OT} yields a secure protocol for $\mathcal{F}'$.[11] □

As an immediate corollary of Theorem 4 and the UC $\alpha_{\texttt{shOT}}$-completeness of the CRS functionality [7], we get sufficiency of the $t < m/2$ bound for the m-multi-$\mathcal{F}_{\text{CRS}}$ functionality, which consists of m independent CRSs.

COROLLARY 5. *Let $\mathcal{M} = \{\mathcal{F}_1, \ldots, \mathcal{F}_m\}$, where for each $\ell \in [m]$: $\mathcal{F}_\ell$ is the CRS functionality. Assuming that the adversary is t-restricted, $\mathcal{M}$ is (UC) $\alpha_{\texttt{shOT}}$-complete if and only if $t < m/2$.*

A similar possibility result as in the above corollary—i.e., sufficiency of having a majority of "good" CRS's—was proved in [15] for a slightly restricted adversary, who cannot make the CRS send inconsistent values to different parties (i.e., the adversary can only choose the value of the reference string). In fact, this restriction is crucial in the security proof of [15] , as one can verify that otherwise their suggested protocol is insecure. Intuitively, the reason is that the CRS's are parsed as keys for the constructed commitment scheme, hence dropping this assumption means that the parties use inconsistent keys which leads to violation of correctness (an honest party might not be able to open its commitment towards another honest party). Note that the naïve approach for resolving inconsistencies in the distributed reference strings, i.e., have the parties exchange the values they received from the CRS, would not work for the *multi-party* setting, as it would require that all parties can achieve *consensus* on a common string, which is not possible when a majority of the parties is corrupted.

5. PASSIVE (AND MIXED) CORRUPTION OF SETUPS

In this section we investigate the setting where the adversary can passively corrupt setups. We show that the $m/2$ bound which was established in the previous section for active corruption of setups is in fact tight even in this setting. More precisely, we show that there are UC complete setups for which passive corruption is as severe as active corruption. Finally, combining the results from the current and the previous section we obtain a tight feasibility bound for *mixed* corruption of setups, i.e., for an adversary who might both actively and passively corrupt setups.

In the following we show that a collection of m (independent) copies of the OT functionality half of which might be *only passively corrupted* is no stronger than just secure communication. Because $\mathcal{F}_{\text{OT}}$ is deterministic, therefore adaptively well-formed in a trivial sense, the lemma holds even for adaptive party-corruption. The proof of the lemma follows the structure of the proof of Theorems 1 and 3.

[10] We point out that the combiner from [26] constructs a Rabin-OT from m copies of the so called *oblivious linear function evaluation (OLFE) functionality* less than half of which might be corrupted. However, one can unconditionally implement OLFE from OT (e.g., by using [19]).

[11] We implicitly assume that each instance of $\mathcal{F}_{\text{OT}}$ within $\Pi^{\mathcal{F}_{\text{OT}}}$ is replaced by an $\mathcal{M}$-hybrid protocol π_{OT} using an independent instance of (each functionality in) $\mathcal{M}$ (see Section 2). If the adversary corrupts some $\mathcal{F}_\ell \in \mathcal{M}$, then he is allowed to corrupt it across all protocols using it as a hybrid "for free" (i.e., this does not count as additional corruptions towards his threshold t). Alternatively, we could have all invocations of π_{OT} use the same hybrid $\mathcal{M}$ and apply the joint state composition theorem (JUC) [9].

LEMMA 6. *Let $\mathcal{M} = \{\mathcal{F}_1, \ldots, \mathcal{F}_m\}$, where for each $\ell \in [m]$: $\mathcal{F}_\ell$ is the OT functionality $\mathcal{F}_{\text{OT}}$. For a functionality-corruption structure $\mathcal{K}$, if $Q^2(\mathcal{M}, \mathcal{K})$ does not hold then there exists an $\mathcal{F}_{\text{SEC}}$-hybrid 2-party protocol which securely realizes $\mathcal{M}$, in the presence of an adversary who might corrupt any (or even both) parties.*

As a corollary of the above result (along the lines of Corollary 2) we obtain a simple proof of impossibility of OT-combiners when at least half of the candidates are passively corrupted which holds even for adaptive corruption of the assumed OT functionalities.

Mixed (active and passive) setup-corruption..

We next obtain a feasibility statement for the case of an adversary who might corrupt setups both actively and passively. Consistently with the terminology introduced in Section 2, we say that an adversary is (t_a, t_p)-*restricted* if he corrupts up to t_a functionalities actively and (at the same time) up to t_p functionalities passively. The proof of the theorem follows from Theorem 4 and the fact that passive corruption is weaker than active. The simplicity of the proof demonstrates the power of having corruption types that can be ordered with respect to their strength which is one of the advantages of our model with respect to [12].

THEOREM 7. *Let $\mathcal{M} = \{\mathcal{F}_1, \ldots, \mathcal{F}_m\}$ be a set of setup-functionalities and $\alpha_1, \ldots, \alpha_m$ be assumptions so that the corruption-ignoring strengthening ${\mathcal{F}_\ell}^{\mathbb{C}}$ of each $\mathcal{F}_\ell \in \mathcal{M}$ is (UC) α_ℓ-complete. Assuming the adversary is (t_a, t_p)-restricted, $\mathcal{M}$ is (UC) $\{\alpha_1, \ldots, \alpha_m\}$-complete if $t_a + t_p < m/2$.*

PROOF. Because passively corrupting a setup gives the adversary strictly less power than actively corrupting it, a protocol which tolerates $t_a + t_p$ actively corrupted setups is also secure for t_a actively and t_p passively corrupted setups. Because $t_a + t_p < m/2$, the existence of such a protocol is guaranteed by Theorem 4. □

5.1 Passive Immunity

The above feasibility result is tight for certain complete setups, e.g., for the OT. Indeed, tightness of the bound in Theorem 7 when $\mathcal{F}_\ell = \mathcal{F}_{\text{OT}}$ for all $\ell \in [m]$ follows easily from Lemma 6: Assume, towards contradiction that a generic MPC protocol exists tolerating t_a actively and t_p passively corrupted (arbitrary) setups, where $t_a + t_p > m/2$. Then this protocol can be use to implement a non-trivial functionality (e.g., OT) from m copies of the OT out of which $t_a + t_p$ could be passively corrupted, contradicting Lemma 6.

Interestingly, as it turns out for many of the setups used in the literature giving the power of passive corruption to the adversary "does *not* buy her much". These include, for example, the CRS or the version and the Key Registration functionality, denoted as $\mathcal{F}_{\text{KR}}(\mathcal{P}, f)$, where the keys are sampled according to a given distribution generated by a function f (still, corrupted parties get to choose their coins). To model this fact, we introduce the notion of *passively immune* setups which, informally, satisfy the property that their incorruptible version reduces to the version that might be at most passively (but not actively) corrupted.

Definition 1. For some assumption α, a (wrapped) functionality $\mathcal{F}$ is said to be α-*passively immune* if for the actively ignoring strengthening $\mathcal{F}^{\mathbb{A}}$ of $\mathcal{F}$ (which, recall, accepts only passive-corruption requests) there exists an $\mathcal{F}^{\mathbb{A}}$-hybrid protocol which securely realizes (assuming α) the corruption-ignoring strengthening $\mathcal{F}^{\mathbb{C}}$ of $\mathcal{F}$.

Note that the uniformly random reference string functionality $\mathcal{F}_{\text{URS}}$ is trivially passively immune as the adversary does not learn anything by passively corrupting it. Furthermore, for the case of the (imperfect) CRS functionality, $\mathcal{F}_{\text{CRS}}(\mathcal{P}, f)$ which samples the reference string using a sampling algorithm f, the results by Canetti, Pass, and shelat [8, 22, 25] imply that $\mathcal{F}_{\text{CRS}}(\mathcal{P}, f)$ is passively immune under the following assumption: f is polynomially computable and $\mu(\lambda) - d(\lambda) > \lambda^\varepsilon$ for some $\varepsilon > 0$, where $d(\lambda)$ is the size of the description of f and $\mu(\lambda)$ is the min-entropy of the corresponding distribution (λ denotes the length of the reference string).

In what follows, we show that under standard complexity assumptions, i.e., semi-honest OT ($\alpha_{\texttt{shOT}}$) and one-way permutations ($\alpha_{\texttt{OWP}}$), two additional important setups used in the UC literature are passively immune. To prove passively immunity of these setups $\mathcal{F}$ we use *UC puzzles* [22]. On a high level, a UC puzzle is a two party protocol with the following property: no adversary can successfully complete the puzzle while simultaneously obtaining a trapdoor associated with the puzzle; however, there does exist a simulator $\mathcal{S}$ who can generate statistically close puzzle transcripts and the associated trapdoors. We refer to the appendix for a more formal description and a "tweak" of the definition from [22] which is used in our proofs.

As proved in [22], UC puzzles are $\alpha_{\texttt{shOT}}$-complete. Thus, to prove our result, we show that there exists an $\mathcal{F}^{\mathbb{A}}$-hybrid UC puzzle, where $\mathcal{F}^{\mathbb{A}}$ denotes the actively ignoring strengthening of $\mathcal{F}$. For readers familiar with the use of UC puzzles, the high-level idea is to have the UC puzzle simulator "hide" the corresponding trapdoor in the pre-image of a one-way permutation. We point out that the lemma is stated and proved for the case of static party-corruption; however using ideas from [11] (and the stronger assumptions used there) one can extend the proof to the adaptive setting. A proof can be found in the full version.

LEMMA 8. *Let f be a second-preimage collision resistant function.*[12] *The functionalities for the Common Reference String $\mathcal{F}_{\text{CRS}}(\mathcal{P}, f)$ and the Key Registration $\mathcal{F}_{\text{KR}}(\mathcal{P}, f)$ are $\{\alpha_{\texttt{OWP}}, \alpha_{\texttt{shOT}}\}$-passively immune assuming the adversary statically chooses the set of corrupted parties.*

The following theorem establishes a tight feasibility bound for passively immune setups with a mixed (active/passive) adversary.

THEOREM 9. *For a setup set $\mathcal{M} = \{\mathcal{F}_1, \ldots, \mathcal{F}_m\}$ let $\alpha_1, \ldots, \alpha_m$ be assumptions such that for each $\mathcal{F}_\ell \in \mathcal{M}$ the following properties hold: $\mathcal{F}_\ell$ is α_ℓ-passively immune and the corruption-ignoring strengthening ${\mathcal{F}_\ell}^{\mathbb{C}}$ is α_ℓ-complete. Assuming that the adversary is (t_a, t_p)-restricted and corrupts parties non-adaptively, $\mathcal{M}$ is (UC) $\{\alpha_1, \ldots, \alpha_m\}$-complete if and only if $t_a < m/2$ (and thus for* arbitrary $t_p \leq m$).

PROOF *(sketch).* The necessity of the bound follows trivially from Corollary 2. We next argue the sufficiency: Because for each $\mathcal{F}_\ell \in \mathcal{M}$: $\mathcal{F}_\ell$ is α_ℓ-passively immune and ${\mathcal{F}_\ell}^{\mathbb{C}}$

[12] Note that existence of such f is implied by $\alpha_{\texttt{OWP}}$, and in particular f can be any injective function.

is α_ℓ-complete we can use each of them to generate an independent copy of the OT functionalities. The statement follows then from Theorem 4. □

6. EXTENSIONS

In the full version of this paper we demonstrate the flexibility of our model by using it to prove the following results. We provide a "best-of-both worlds" result for the setting where there is either a corrupt majority of setups, or a corrupt majority of parties.

THEOREM 10. *(informal) For a set of m UC-complete setup-functionalities and any given thresholds $s < n/2$ and t such that $s + t < n$, there exists a protocol which securely realizes any well-formed n-party functionality tolerating* static *party-corruption if some of the following holds: (1) at most s parties are corrupted and arbitrary many of the setup-functionalities are corrupted, or (2) up to $t > s$ parties are corrupted but at most $t' < m/2$ functionalities are actively-corrupted.*

Additionally, we extend our positive result for actively-corruptible functionalities by additionally considering fail-corruption.

THEOREM 11. *(informal) For a set of m UC complete setup-functionalities, if the adversary adaptively corrupts up to t_a of them actively and fail corrupts up to t_f of them (and corrupts arbitrarily many parties actively), then there exists a protocol which securely realizes any well-formed functionality if and only if $2t_a + t_f < m$.*

Finally, we we generalize our positive result to the setting of an arbitrary functionality-corruption structure $\mathcal{K}$ (instead of a threshold structure). Recall that $\mathcal{K}$ is an enumeration of all possible corruptible sets of functionalities.

THEOREM 12. *(informal) For a set $\mathcal{M}$ of (possibly different) actively corruptible UC-complete setups and a functionality corruption structure $\mathcal{K}$, there exists a protocol which securely realizes any well-formed functionality while tolerating a $\mathcal{K}$-restricted adversary corrupting arbitrary many parties* if and only if *$Q^2(\mathcal{M}, \mathcal{K})$ holds.*

7. ACKNOWLEDGMENTS

We thank Yuval Ishai for his comments during the early stages of our work.

8. REFERENCES

[1] B. Barak, R. Canetti, J. B. Nielsen, and R. Pass. Universally composable protocols with relaxed set-up assumptions. In E. Upfal, editor, *FOCS 2004*, pages 186–195. IEEE Computer Society Press, Oct. 2004.

[2] R. Canetti. Universally composable security: A new paradigm for cryptographic protocols. Cryptology ePrint Archive, Report 2000/067, 2005. An extended abstract appeared in FOCS 2001.

[3] R. Canetti. Obtaining universally compoable security: Towards the bare bones of trust (invited talk). In K. Kurosawa, editor, *ASIACRYPT 2007*, volume 4833 of *LNCS*, pages 88–112. Springer, Dec. 2007.

[4] R. Canetti, Y. Dodis, R. Pass, and S. Walfish. Universally composable security with global setup. In S. P. Vadhan, editor, *TCC 2007*, volume 4392 of *LNCS*, pages 61–85. Springer, Feb. 2007.

[5] R. Canetti and M. Fischlin. Universally composable commitments. In J. Kilian, editor, *CRYPTO 2001*, volume 2139 of *LNCS*, pages 19–40. Springer, Aug. 2001.

[6] R. Canetti, E. Kushilevitz, and Y. Lindell. On the limitations of universally composable two-party computation without set-up assumptions. *Journal of Cryptology*, 19(2):135–167, Apr. 2006.

[7] R. Canetti, Y. Lindell, R. Ostrovsky, and A. Sahai. Universally composable two-party and multi-party secure computation. In J. H. Reif, editor, *STOC 2002*, pages 494–503. ACM Press, May 2002.

[8] R. Canetti, R. Pass, and A. Shelat. Cryptography from sunspots: How to use an imperfect reference string. In A. Sinclair, editor, *FOCS 2007*, pages 249–259. IEEE Computer Society Press, Oct. 2007.

[9] R. Canetti and T. Rabin. Universal composition with joint state. In D. Boneh, editor, *CRYPTO 2003*, volume 2729 of *LNCS*, pages 265–281. Springer, Aug. 2003.

[10] C. Crépeau, J. van de Graaf, and A. Tapp. Committed oblivious transfer and private multi-party computation. In D. Coppersmith, editor, *CRYPTO'95*, volume 963 of *LNCS*, pages 110–123. Springer, Aug. 1995.

[11] D. Dachman-Soled, T. Malkin, M. Raykova, and M. Venkitasubramaniam. Adaptive and concurrent secure computation from new adaptive, non-malleable commitments. In *ASIACRYPT 2013*, pages 316–336. Springer, Dec. 2013.

[12] S. Garg, V. Goyal, A. Jain, and A. Sahai. Bringing people of different beliefs together to do UC. In Y. Ishai, editor, *TCC 2011*, volume 6597 of *LNCS*, pages 311–328. Springer, Mar. 2011.

[13] S. Goldwasser and Y. Lindell. Secure multi-party computation without agreement. *Journal of Cryptology*, 18(3):247–287, July 2005. Preliminary version appeared at DISC 2002.

[14] V. Goyal and J. Katz. Universally composable multi-party computation with an unreliable common reference string. In R. Canetti, editor, *TCC 2008*, volume 4948 of *LNCS*, pages 142–154. Springer, Mar. 2008.

[15] J. Groth and R. Ostrovsky. Cryptography in the multi-string model. In A. Menezes, editor, *CRYPTO 2007*, volume 4622 of *LNCS*, pages 323–341. Springer, Aug. 2007.

[16] D. Harnik, J. Kilian, M. Naor, O. Reingold, and A. Rosen. On robust combiners for oblivious transfer and other primitives. In R. Cramer, editor, *EUROCRYPT 2005*, volume 3494 of *LNCS*, pages 96–113. Springer, May 2005.

[17] M. Hirt and U. M. Maurer. Complete characterization of adversaries tolerable in secure multi-party computation (extended abstract). In *16th ACM PODC*, pages 25–34. ACM Press, Aug. 1997.

[18] D. Hofheinz and J. Müller-Quade. Universally composable commitments using random oracles. In

M. Naor, editor, *TCC 2004*, volume 2951 of *LNCS*, pages 58–76. Springer, Feb. 2004.

[19] Y. Ishai, M. Prabhakaran, and A. Sahai. Founding cryptography on oblivious transfer - efficiently. In D. Wagner, editor, *CRYPTO 2008*, volume 5157 of *LNCS*, pages 572–591. Springer, Aug. 2008.

[20] J. Katz. Universally composable multi-party computation using tamper-proof hardware. In M. Naor, editor, *EUROCRYPT 2007*, volume 4515 of *LNCS*, pages 115–128. Springer, May 2007.

[21] J. Kilian. Founding crytpography on oblivious transfer. In *STOC '88*, pages 20–31, New York, NY, USA, 1988. ACM.

[22] H. Lin, R. Pass, and M. Venkitasubramaniam. A unified framework for concurrent security: universal composability from stand-alone non-malleability. In M. Mitzenmacher, editor, *STOC 2009*, pages 179–188. ACM Press, May / June 2009.

[23] R. Meier, B. Przydatek, and J. Wullschleger. Robuster combiners for oblivious transfer. In S. P. Vadhan, editor, *TCC 2007*, volume 4392 of *LNCS*, pages 404–418. Springer, Feb. 2007.

[24] M. Rabin. How to exchange secrets by oblivious transfer. Technical Report TR-81,Harvard Aiken Computation Laboratory, 1981.

[25] M. Venkitasubramaniam. A universal framework for concurrent security. PhD thesis, Cornell University, 2010.

[26] J. Wullschleger. Efficiently from semi-honest to malicious ot via OLFE. Cryptology ePrint Archive, Report 2009/428, 2009.

APPENDIX

A. UC PUZZLES

We sketch the (general) definition of UC puzzles from [22] to the standard setting, i.e., with a non-uniform PPT environment $\mathcal{Z}$, a uniform PPT adversary $\mathcal{A}$ and a uniform PPT simulator $\mathcal{S}$. We let $\langle S, R\rangle$ represent a protocol between two parties, the sender S and the receiver R. We consider a concurrent puzzle execution in which $\mathcal{A}$ participates as a sender concurrently in $m = poly(k)$ puzzles (where k is a security parameter) with honest receivers $R_1, \dots, R_m$. We now describe the real and the ideal executions.

Real execution. In the real execution, the adversary $\mathcal{A}$ on input 1^k, interacts with a puzzle-environment $\mathcal{Z}$ and participates as a sender in m interactions using $\langle S, R\rangle$. After every puzzle-interaction, $\mathcal{A}$ sends trans to $\mathcal{Z}$, where trans is the puzzle-transcript. We denote the probability ensemble corresponding to the output of $\mathcal{Z}$ at the end of the execution by $\{\text{REAL}_{\mathcal{A},\mathcal{Z}}(k)\}_{k\in\mathbb{N}}$.

Ideal execution. In the ideal execution, there is a simulator $\mathcal{S}$ that on input 1^k interacts with puzzle-environment $\mathcal{Z}$. Note that $\mathcal{S}$ has a special output tape which is not accessible to $\mathcal{Z}$. We denote the probability ensemble corresponding to the output of $\mathcal{Z}$ at the end of the execution by $\{\text{IDEAL}_{\mathcal{S},\mathcal{Z}}(k)\}_{k\in\mathbb{N}}$.

Definition (UC PUZZLE [22]). A pair $(\langle S, R\rangle, \mathcal{R})$, where $\mathcal{R}$ is a polynomial time computable binary relation, is a UC-puzzle if the following conditions hold:

SOUNDNESS: For every malicious PPT receiver R^*, there exists a negligible function $negl(\cdot)$ such that the probability that R^*, after an execution with S on common input 1^k, outputs τ such that $\mathcal{R}(\mathsf{trans}, \tau) = 1$ (where trans is the transcript of the messages exchanged in the interaction) is at most $negl(k)$.

STATISTICAL SIMULATABILITY: For every adversary $\mathcal{A}$ participating in a concurrent puzzle execution there is a simulator $\mathcal{S}$ such that for all puzzle environments $\mathcal{Z}$, the ensembles $\{\text{REAL}_{\mathcal{A},\mathcal{Z}}(k)\}_{k\in\mathbb{N}}$ and $\{\text{IDEAL}_{\mathcal{S},\mathcal{Z}}(k)\}_{k\in\mathbb{N}}$ are statistically close over $k \in \mathbb{N}$; moreover, whenever $\mathcal{S}$ outputs a message of the form trans to $\mathcal{Z}$, it also outputs τ in a special output tape (which cannot be accessed by $\mathcal{Z}$) such that $\mathcal{R}(\mathsf{trans}, \tau) = 1$.

Lin et al. [22, 25] proved the following theorem stating that UC puzzles are $\alpha_{\mathtt{shOT}}$-complete.

THEOREM 13 ([22, 25]). *Assume the existence of a $t_1(\cdot)$-round UC-secure puzzle Σ using some set-up $\mathcal{F}$, the existence of a $t_2(\cdot)$-round standalone secure semi-honest oblivious transfer protocol. Then for every m-ary functionality $\mathcal{G}$, there exists an $O(t_1(\cdot) + t_2(\cdot))$-round protocol Π—using the same set-up $\mathcal{F}$—that UC-realizes $\mathcal{G}$.*

UC puzzles with Strong Statistical Simulatability. In order to be able to tolerate adaptive corruption of the assumed setups, our protocols need puzzles that satisfy a somewhat strengthened version of the statistical simulatability property, namely we want to ensure that the simulator (playing as the receiver) is able to simulate *even if the adversarial sender corrupts the hybrid (i.e., the setup) used by the puzzle protocol during its execution* (however, if such a corruption request occurs we no longer require the simulator to output a trapdoor for the puzzle). We refer to this property as *strong statistical simulatability*.

Note that for an adversary who (non-adaptively) corrupts the hybrid functionality before the beginning of any puzzle, the strong statistical simulatability property is implied by the definition of the UC puzzle: Indeed, if $\mathcal{Z}$ requests to corrupt the hybrid $\mathcal{F}$ at the beginning then the simulator simply sends $\mathcal{Z}$ the code and randomness and forwards all calls of the (simulated) puzzle protocol to $\mathcal{Z}$ from that point on; otherwise, strong simulatability follows trivially from the statistical simulatability property of the UC puzzle. However, for an adversary who might (adaptively) corrupt the hybrid functionality at any point in the protocol execution, the strong statistical simulatability property is not necessarily implied from the definition of UC puzzles. Nevertheless, one can verify that for most, if not all, setups for which a UC puzzle is described in the literature [25, 12] this property is indeed satisfied, as the simulator considered in these puzzles explicitly emulates the execution of the hybrid. Furthermore, most of these puzzles exist under the semi-honest OT assumption $\alpha_{\mathtt{shOT}}$ which, as shown in [25, 12] is also sufficient for the completeness of standard UC puzzles.

The Future(s) of Shared Data Structures

Alex Kogan
Oracle Labs
Burlington, MA, USA
alex.kogan@oracle.com

Maurice Herlihy*
Brown University and Oracle Labs
Providence, RI, USA
mph@cs.brown.edu

ABSTRACT

This paper considers how to use futures, a well-known mechanism to manage parallel computations, to improve the performance of long-lived, mutable shared data structures in large-scale multicore systems. We show that futures can enable type-specific optimizations such as combining and elimination, improve cache locality and reduce contention. To exploit these benefits in an effective way, however, it is important to define clear notions of correctness. We propose new extensions to linearizability appropriate for method calls that return futures as results. To illustrate the utility and trade-offs of these extensions, we describe implementations of three common data structures: stacks, queues, and linked lists, designed to exploit futures. Our experimental results show that optimizations enabled by futures lead to substantial performance improvements, in some cases up to two orders of magnitude, compared to well-known lock-free alternatives.

Categories and Subject Descriptors

E.1 [**Data**]: Data Structures—*lists, stacks, and queues*; D.1.3 [**Software**]: Programming Techniques—*concurrent programming*

General Terms

Algorithms, Design, Theory

Keywords

Concurrent data structures; futures; elimination; combining; linearizability

1. INTRODUCTION

Futures [5] are widely considered an attractive way to manage parallel computations: they are simple to use, and they lend themselves well to efficient scheduling mechanisms such as work-stealing. In this paper, we consider the use of futures for different purposes: improving the performance of long-lived concurrent data structures in large-scale multicore systems.

We are interested in the design and implementation of long-lived objects shared by many threads. Calling an operation of such an object might take a long time, perhaps because there is contention, or because the object resides on a remote node in a non-uniform memory access (NUMA) architecture. One way to alleviate these problems is to have the object's operations return futures as return values. By using futures, threads can accumulate multiple pending operations, that is, operations that were invoked, but not yet applied to the object. These pending operations can be evaluated in a flexible way, perhaps exploiting type-specific optimizations such as combining and elimination intended to reduce contention, improve cache locality and reduce communication costs.

Our use of futures in this paper departs in important ways from the original proposal, where futures were benign annotations that did not affect a program's meaning, and future computations had no side-effects [5]. By contrast, our use of futures centers on operations that exist for their side-effects on shared, long-lived state, operations that can interact and interfere with one another.

As a result, it is essential to define clear and useful notions of correctness for objects whose operations return futures. A major observation of this paper is that no single notion of correctness is likely to cover all reasonable cases. Instead, we propose three new extensions to linearizability [11], called *strong*, *medium*, and *weak futures linearizability*. Each notion makes a different trade-off between determinism, which reduces the number of possible interleavings, and the flexibility to apply various optimizations, which yields more efficient programs. Like standard linearizability, however, these notions require that any concurrent execution be equivalent, in some sense, to a sequential computation.

To demonstrate the utility of these notions, we describe strong, medium, and weak futures linearizable implementations of three common data structures: stacks, queues, and linked lists, and compare their performance on a multicore system to well-known lock-free algorithms. These experiments illustrate in a quantitative way the trade-offs between performance and determinism. In particular, we show that implementations satisfying the weak and medium correctness conditions typically significantly outperform lock-free alternatives, in some cases by up to two orders of magnitude.

*Supported by NSF 1301924.

PODC'14, July 15–18, 2014, Paris, France.
Copyright 2014 ACM 978-1-4503-2944-6/14/07 ...$15.00.
http://dx.doi.org/10.1145/2611462.2611496.

```
Future<T> f = submit(task); // start task
...                         // do something else
T x = f.eval ();            // pick up task's result
```

Figure 1: Use of futures

Even though the versions satisfying the strong correctness condition typically perform worse than other future-based versions, we show cases where they achieve better performance than the lock-free alternatives.

The rest of the paper is organized as follows. We discuss the benefits of using futures with long-lived concurrent data structures in Section 2. In Section 3 we informally define three extensions to linearizability that support operations returning futures. We exploit these extensions by constructing three common data structures in Section 4. These constructions are evaluated and compared to lock-free alternatives in Section 5. The formal model and proofs appear in Section 6. The related work is surveyed in Section 7. Finally, we conclude the paper with discussion in Section 8.

2. FUTURES AND LONG-LIVED OBJECTS

A *future* [5] is a data object that represents a *promise* to deliver the result of an asynchronous computation when it is ready. Figure 1 shows a simple code fragment that uses a future. In Line 1, a thread creates a future to hold the result of an asynchronous computation. In Line 2, the thread does something unrelated, and in Line 3, it calls the future's eval() method to retrieve the task's result, blocking if necessary until that result is ready. (Calling a future's eval() method is called *evaluating* or *touching* that future.)

While futures were originally proposed as a way of managing short-lived functional computations, here we focus on long-lived mutable objects, like maps, lists, queues, or stacks, shared by multiple threads in a multicore architecture. These objects return future values in response to method calls. These method calls typically have side-effects (such as binding a key to a value), and the results may return information about the object state (such as the result of a map look-up) or confirmation that a side-effect has taken place (such as confirming that map has finished binding a key to a value).

The principal contribution of this paper is the observation that futures, properly redefined, can provide substantial benefits to long-lived concurrent data structures. These benefits include:

- *Combining*: multiple operations may be combined into a single operation on the shared object, reducing computation and communication latency.
- *Elimination*: some operations may "cancel" each other out, eliminating the need to access the shared object at all.
- *Delegation*: one thread might be able to apply pending operations on behalf of others. This thread may be selected dynamically (as is done here) or it may be designated statically.
- *Contention reduction and cache efficiency*: combining and elimination may cause the shared data structure to be accessed less frequently, alleviating synchronization bottlenecks and incurring less cache coherence traffic.

```
Future<Nil> fx = queue.enq(x);
Future<Nil> fy = queue.enq(y);
Future<T> fz = queue.deq();
fx.eval ();          // force enq(x) to happen?
fy.eval ();          // force enq(x) to happen?
T z = fz.eval ();    // value at the head of queue?
```

Figure 2: A FIFO queue example

- *Scheduling*: the implementation is free to choose whether to apply pending method calls eagerly or lazily.

However, to apply these optimizations correctly, we need a careful definition what it means when a method call to a mutable object returns a future, and how a result retrieved from the evaluated future is related to the state of that mutable object.

3. FUTURES AND LINEARIZABILITY

A future's value is calculated sometime between when that future is created and when it is evaluated. As originally conceived, future computations were short-lived tasks without side-effects, so it was impossible to observe when these computations actually happened. Here, by contrast, we are interested in futures returned by methods that do have side-effects, such as adding or removing an item into or from a container. It is important to define when a future-returning method can "take effect", and, indirectly, how such effects might be interleaved.

In the absence of futures, it is common to define the behavior of concurrent method calls through properties such as linearizability [11]. Each object is assumed to provide a sequential specification, which describes its behavior in sequential executions where method calls do not overlap. To describe an object's concurrent behavior, each method call is split into two instantaneous events: the *invocation*, when control leaves the caller, and the *response*, when control (and perhaps a result) returns to the caller. Informally, an execution is *linearizable* if each method call appears to take effect instantaneously between its invocation and its response events.

To make effective use of futures, and to determine which optimizations are permitted, we will need to define extensions to linearizability. For ease of presentation, we define these extensions informally here. The formal definitions are postponed to Section 6.

There are several natural ways to extend linearizability to futures, and each has its own advantages and disadvantages. We will illustrate these choices using the code fragment in Figure 2, where a FIFO queue, initially empty, provides enq() and deq() methods that return futures. The thread first calls enq(x), returning future fx, then enq(y), returning future fy, and finally deq(), returning future fz. It then evaluates first fx, then fy, and finally fz. What can we assume about the value returned from fz? There are several reasonable choices.

Strong Futures Linearizability (Strong-FL).

One natural correctness condition is to require that each method call takes effect at some instant between its call (creating the future), and its response (returning the future), just as if it were a regular method call. In Figure 2, enq(x) precedes enq(y), which precedes deq(), so (assuming no other thread is accessing the queue) evaluating fz must yield x.

This property is easy to reason about, since it is essentially the same as linearizability, treating futures as benign hints for optimizations. Implementations are free to delay the actual computation until the future is evaluated, as long as no thread can tell the difference. As we show in Section 5, this separation of how operations are ordered from when they are evaluated can be very beneficial in some cases. For many applications, however, strong futures linearizability rules out certain attractive optimizations.

Weak Futures Linearizability (Weak-FL).

Another natural correctness condition is to require that each method call takes effect at some instant between its call (creating the future), and the return from that future's evaluation. In Figure 2, the calls to enq(x), enq(y), and deq() are free to take effect in any order, so evaluating fz could yield either Nil (if deq() takes effect first), x (enq(x) first), or y (enq(y) first). This choice gives the run-time system considerable freedom for optimization.

For some applications, however, this condition may be too permissive. A thread that wants to enqueue x before y would have to evaluate fx *before* calling enq(y), making optimizations such as combining impossible. Furthermore, if fx is not evaluated before calling enq(y), this condition may seem counter-intuitive, as (probably, a different) thread may see the effect of the second enqueue before the effect of the first one.

Medium Futures Linearizability (Medium-FL).

Here is an intermediate proposal that balances the programmer's guarantees with the flexibility for optimization. We separate two issues: (1) when a future's computation takes effect, and (2) how a future's computation is ordered with respect to other futures' computations. For question (1), we require each method call to take effect at some instant between that method's future's creation and its evaluation, just as in weak futures linearizability. For question (2), we require two future method calls issued by the *same thread* to the *same object* to take effect in the same order as their future creation operations. In Figure 2, enq(x) precedes enq(y), which precedes deq(), so evaluating fz must yield x. Notice that medium future linearizability does *not* constrain the perceived order of operations issued to distinct objects.

Informally, a correctness property is *non-blocking* if by itself it never forces a thread T with a pending operation to wait for another pending operation to complete before T can evaluate its own operation's future. In Section 6, we show that strong, medium, and weak futures linearizability are all non-blocking. Examples of correctness notions that are *not* non-blocking include *serializability* [1].

A correctness property is *compositional* if any combination of two or more objects, each individually satisfying that property, collectively also satisfies that same property. In Section 6, we show that strong, medium, and weak futures linearizability are all compositional.

Compositionality should not be taken for granted. For example, consider the following natural generalization of medium futures linearizability, which we call *futures sequential consistency*: (1) as before, each method call takes effect

```
1   Future<Nil> f1 = p.enq(x);
2                                       Future<Nil> f2 = q.enq(y);
3   Future<Nil> f3 = q.enq(x);
4                                       Future<Nil> f4 = p.enq(y);
5   f1.eval();                          f2.eval();
6   f3.eval();                          f4.eval();
7
8   Future<T> fp = p.deq();
9   fp.eval(); // returns y
10                                      Future<T> fq = q.deq();
11                                      fq.eval(); // returns x
```

Figure 3: Why futures sequential consistency is not compositional

at some instant between that method's future's creation and its evaluation, but (2) two future method calls issued by the same thread *to any object* (not just an individual object) take effect in the same order as their future creation operations.

Futures sequential consistency, like the classical notion of sequential consistency [12], is not compositional. Figure 3 shows a simple counterexample. Each column represents a thread, A and B, and the lines represent the interleaving. There are two FIFO queues, p and q. In Lines 1–4, A enqueues x on p, B enqueues y on q, A enqueues x on q, and B enqueues y on p. All four resulting futures are then evaluated (Lines 5–6). Futures sequential consistency requires that each thread's method calls take effect in the order their futures were created: Line 1 takes effect before Line 3, and Line 2 before Line 4. Since y is the first item dequeued from p, Line 4 takes effect before Line 1, and similarly, Line 3 takes effect before Line 2, resulting in a cyclic order. It is easy to check, however, that this interleaving is medium futures linearizable, because a thread's enqueue calls to different objects are unordered.

4. EXPLOITING FUTURES

This section describes how to use futures to encapsulate type-specific optimizations for three basic data types: queues, stacks, and linked lists (or more precisely, linked list-based sets). For brevity and simplicity, we treat all return values as futures. (Non-future return values can be treated as futures that are evaluated immediately.) We first describe high-level designs common to all three data types. In the following subsections, we provide additional details specific to each considered data type.

Threads share an instance of the data structure (queue, stack, or list, respectively). In weak and medium-FL implementations, this shared instance is similar to a lock-free version of the data structure[1], except that it supports single-operation insertion or removal of multiple nodes. For instance, pushing multiple nodes (organized in a list) into a stack is a straightforward extension of the single-node code, where the last node of the list is connected to the first node in the stack and the head of stack is updated with a single compare-and-swap (CAS) instruction to point the first node in the list. The strong-FL implementation employs a

[1]We use standard lock-free data structures from the literature: Michael and Scott's lock-free queue [14], Harris's linked list [6], and Treiber's stack [18].

sequential instance of the data structure, for reasons discussed below.

In our prototype implementations, futures are realized as objects with `opCode`, `value`, `result` and `resultReady` fields. The first two fields store the type of the corresponding operation (e.g., enq() or deq()) and an optional parameter. The evaluation of a future is completed by writing the corresponding result into the `result` field and setting the `resultReady` flag. An operation is *pending* if its invocation has occurred, but the operation itself has not yet been applied to its object. A thread may check quickly if an operation is still pending by reading the `resultReady` flag of that operation's corresponding future.

For the weak and medium-FL implementations, each thread uses thread-local list(s) to store and evaluate its own pending operations. Each such list presents an opportunity to apply type-specific optimizations (such as combining or canceling compatible operations). The exact details on how these local lists are maintained and used are given in the following subsections.

For the strong-FL implementations, each operation appears to take effect before its future is returned. To achieve that, all threads share a single queue of pending operations, which allows adding new operations (more precisely, future objects) in a lock-free manner. This queue is based on the lock-free queue by Michael and Scott [14]. When a thread invokes an operation, it allocates and enqueues a future object describing that operation, and returns the future to the caller. The evaluation of pending operations is protected by a lock. When a thread T evaluates a future F, it tries to acquire the lock. If it succeeds, and if F is still pending, T records the current last pending operation that is in the queue. (If T fails to acquire the lock, it waits until the lock becomes available again, checking periodically that F is still pending.) Then T evaluates all operations in the queue, including F, starting from the head (or, more precisely, from the operation next to the head, as the first operation is a dummy [14]) and up to the last recorded operation. Note that while T is holding the lock, other threads can keep adding new operations to the queue, but those operations might not be evaluated by T. However, the number of pending operations evaluated by T (and thus the time T possesses the lock) is limited. While evaluating pending operations, T is free to apply type-specific optimizations such as combining and eliminating multiple operations. Moreover, once T has exclusive access to the shared data structure, the (possibly combined) operations can be applied directly to the shared data structure instance, without any synchronization. When T is done, it updates the head of the queue to point the recorded last operation, effectively removing evaluated operations from the queue, and releases the lock.

The particular implementations described in this paper were chosen for simplicity. There are many other ways one could implement these objects while satisfying the correctness conditions presented in Section 3. For example, we note that our strong-FL implementations may have limited scalability, because the shared queue of pending operations or the lock protecting evaluations might become bottlenecks under high contention. Such limitations may matter more for objects whose operations are lightweight, such as queues and stacks. In particular, one might achieve better performance by applying the elimination optimization in the strong-FL stack before resorting to the shared queue of pending operations. In this paper, we opted to exploit futures by presenting an approach, which is not necessarily optimal, yet general enough to be applied for different data structures with minimal efforts. As we will see in Section 5, by enabling a clean separation between how operations are *ordered* from how they are *evaluated*, this approach is most beneficial for objects with heavyweight operations, such as long linked lists.

4.1 Stack Algorithm

Since the weak-FL condition permits each operation to take effect at any instant between its invocation and its future's evaluation, we can reorder pending push() and pop() operations, increasing the potential for the elimination optimization. As a result, we will never have both pending push() and pop() operations for the same thread at any given time. Thus, each thread maintains only one local list to store pending operations, each having the same type (that is, all operations in the local list are either push() or pop()).

When a thread invokes a push(), it checks whether its local list contains pending pop() operations. If so, the push() provides a result to one of the pending pop() operations. (That is, the `value` of the future for the push() operation is copied into the `result` field of the future for the pop() operation, and `resultReady` flag is set for both futures). Otherwise, the new push() is added to the list of pending push() operations. The code for pop() operations is symmetric.

When a thread evaluates a future, it actually evaluates all the futures stored in that thread's local list, in order to combine multiple operations and reduce traffic to the shared stack instance. Specifically, for pop() operations, as many items as there are pending pop() invocations are popped from the shared stack using a single CAS instruction. If the stack does not have enough items, all items are removed and excess pop() operations are paired with a special "empty stack" value. Symmetrically, the items associated with all pending push() operations are pushed onto the stack with a single CAS instruction.

The medium-FL stack cannot cancel complementary operations quite as aggressively since it has to respect the ordering of thread's operations. As a result, the local list may contain pending operations of distinct types. The medium-FL property implies that a push() operation cannot be combined with a prior pending pop() operation, but a pop() operation can be combined with the most recent prior push(). Multiple pending operations of the same thread and of the same type are combined before modifying the shared stack, allowing the thread to add or remove multiple items with a single CAS.

The strong-FL implementation is straightforward. When a thread attempts to evaluate a future, it tries to acquire the lock associated with the shared queue of pending operations. If it succeeds, it traverses that queue starting from its head. When possible, it eliminates pending pop() operations with preceding pending push() operations. At the end, it applies the remaining pop() and push() operations to the shared stack and releases the lock.

4.2 Queue Algorithm

Queue semantics does not allow operations to be eliminated as easily as stacks, yet it does allow for efficient combining. For the weak-FL queue, each thread keeps two thread-local lists of pending operations: one for pending enq() operations, and another for pending deq() operations. When a future returned by a method call is evaluated, so are all futures of the same operation type. This is again to combine a number of operations and reduce the number of accesses to the shared queue instance. The latter is achieved by inserting (removing) multiple nodes into (from) the shared queue, using just two (one, respectively) CAS operations.

For the medium-FL queue, each thread maintains one local list that contains all its pending operations in the order they were invoked. A thread evaluates a future F by traversing its local list, starting from the head (the oldest pending operation). It removes a sequence of pending operations of the same type (either enq() or deq()), combines operations in the sequence and applies those combined operations to the shared queue. This process is repeated until F is evaluated. Here, again, multiple nodes are inserted or removed to/from the shared queue with one or two CAS operations.

Similarly to stacks, the strong-FL implementation of queues is straightforward. A thread that acquires the lock, runs on the queue of pending operations and applies them to the shared queue.

4.3 Linked List Algorithm

The weak-FL linked list implementation keeps each thread's local list of pending operations sorted by key. A thread evaluates a future by traversing the shared list (which also maintains nodes in sorted order) and applying the pending operations from its local list. Multiple pending operations with the same key are combined, so that at most one modification per key is done to the global list. This implementation traverses the shared list just once to apply all pending operations.

Due to ordering restrictions on thread's operations, the medium-FL linked list implementation keeps each thread's local list of pending operations sorted in temporal order, not by key. A thread evaluates a future F by traversing the local list, starting from the oldest operation, and applying pending operations subject to the following optimization. In the shared lock-free list [6], all operations on the list employ an auxiliary search() function that accepts a key and traverses the list, looking for the last node holding a value less than or equal to the given key. When done applying a pending operation op(), if the next pending operation has a key larger than or equal to the key of op(), the thread resumes searching from the position in the list where op() was applied. Otherwise, and if F is not yet evaluated, it resumes searching from the head of the list.

Finally, in the strong-FL linked list implementation, a thread that evaluates a future acquires the shared lock. Next, it runs through the shared queue of pending operations, and sorts the operations by key. The sort is stable, meaning that the temporal (linearization) order of operations with the same key is preserved. Then it traverses the shared list just once, to apply the pending operations. Finally, it releases the lock.

5. EVALUATION

We evaluated the implementations described in Section 4 and compared them to well-known lock-free alternatives, namely Michael and Scott's lock-free queue [14], Harris's linked list [6], and Treiber's stack [18]. The implementations were done in C++. To avoid effects of memory management on our results, the memory required by any implementation was pre-allocated. We used a simple benchmark in which each thread performs a preset number (100K) of operations on a data structure, initialized as described below. No external work was performed by threads between operations on a shared data structure. The operations were chosen randomly from distributions described below.

A future-based implementation must choose how many pending operations to permit, a quantity we refer to as *slack*. We experimented with different choices of slack: after every X (=slack) operations returning futures (where X is 1, 10, 20 or 100), the thread evaluates all those futures before proceeding with the next X operations. For $X = 1$, each future is evaluated immediately, allowing a direct comparison between the overheads of the future-based versus lock-free implementations.

Our experiments were run on a 1-socket, 8-core SPARC T4 system featuring 64 hardware thread contexts and powered by Solaris 11 operating system. The sources were compiled by g++ 4.7.1 compiler with -O4 optimization level. We varied the number of threads between 1 and 64, and measured the time for all threads to complete their operations. The results shown are the mean of 10 runs performed with exactly the same parameters. The variance of the majority of the results is negligible.

5.1 Stacks

Figure 4 shows the stack benchmark performance with different values for the slack (in log scale for y-axis). The stack is initially empty, and each thread executes 100K operations, choosing between push() and pop() with equal probability. As Figure 4(a) shows, with slack=1 and a single thread, futures-based stacks perform worse than the lock-free stack due to the additional overhead required for managing local lists of pending operations (for the weak-FL and medium-FL versions) or managing the shared queue and lock (for the strong-FL version). When the number of threads increases, this overhead is mitigated by the contention created by threads accessing the stack. Thus, in multi-threaded experiments with slack=1, futures-based stacks perform competitively with the lock-free implementation.

As the slack increases, the weak-FL and medium-FL stacks significantly outperform the lock-free stack, by up to two orders of magnitude. It is interesting to note that the gap between those two future-based stacks shrinks with the increase in slack. This is because the medium-FL stack manages to eliminate more operations, thus accessing the shared stack less frequently. Interestingly, the strong-FL stack performs competitively with the lock-free counterpart, and even slightly outperforms it on high thread counts. We believe that this is because the contention on the head of the stack in the lock-free stack is more severe than on the access to the shared queue of pending operations and on the lock protecting this queue in the strong-FL stack. We have seen the effect of one bottleneck relieving the contention on another bottleneck (and thus improving the overall performance) in other contexts as well [2].

5.2 Queues

Figure 5 shows the queue benchmark performance for different levels of the slack. The queue is initially empty, and each thread executes 100K operations, choosing between enq() and deq() with equal probability. As with stacks, both

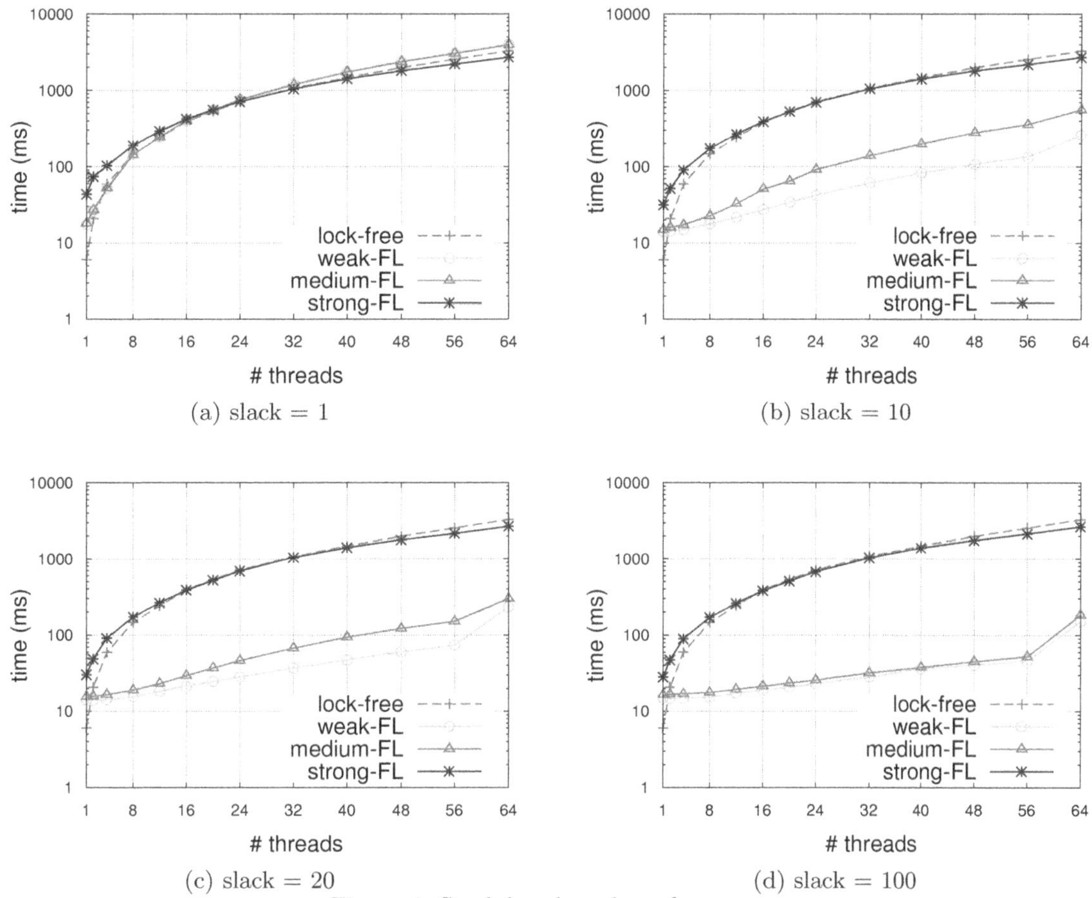

Figure 4: Stack benchmark performance

weak-FL and medium-FL queues perform similarly to the lock-free queue when the slack is just 1. In contrast, the strong-FL queue performs worse than the lock-free queue. The gap remains the same even when increasing the slack. The reasons are twofold. First, while in the strong-FL queue, all threads insert new pending operations at the tail of the queue of pending operations, the shared queue in the lock-free version is accessed from both ends, resulting in less contention. Second, queue semantics dictates that queue operations cannot be eliminated as aggressively as stack operations. Thus, the synchronization overhead of evaluating pending operations is not compensated by elimination.

The remaining queue performance phenomena shown in Figure 5 are also quite different from the stack results. First, the performance of the medium-FL queue relative to the lock-free queue stays the same for levels of slack larger than 1. This is because, in the medium-FL queue, future evaluation combines sequences of operations of the same type (cf. Section 4.2). Increasing the bound on the number of pending operations does not significantly increase the chance for larger sequences.

The weak-FL queue, however, does benefit from increasing the slack, as it can combine operations more aggressively. As the number of threads increases, however, this version's running time spikes sharply. It is interesting to note that the spike occurs at increasing thread counts as the slack increases. This happens because, even with aggressive combining, this version encounters contention on the shared queue with the increased number of threads. We validated this claim by measuring the average number of CAS operations issued by the weak-FL version per one high-level operation on the shared queue. We found out that there was strong correlation between the running time of the weak-FL version and the average number of CAS operations.

5.3 Linked Lists

We evaluated the list benchmark performance in the following setting. The list is initialized with a number of randomly chosen keys. The number of keys is equal to half of the key range, which is set to 10K. Each thread executes 100K operations: 20% `insert()`, 20% `remove()`, and 60% `contains()`, chosen randomly. Each operation returns a Boolean flag indicating whether the list was changed or the required key was found. The results for different slack levels are shown in Figure 6.

Similarly to stacks and queues, the performance of the weak-FL list improves relatively to that of the lock-free list as the slack increases. This is because we combine more operations and apply them all by traversing the shared list just once. The medium-FL list achieves better performance than the lock-free list for slack larger than 1, but the relative gap stays constant. This is because, just as for queues, increasing the slack does not significantly increase the chance to apply more operations in one list traversal.

The strong-FL list shows some interesting behavior. As in the previous case, its performance is significantly worse rela-

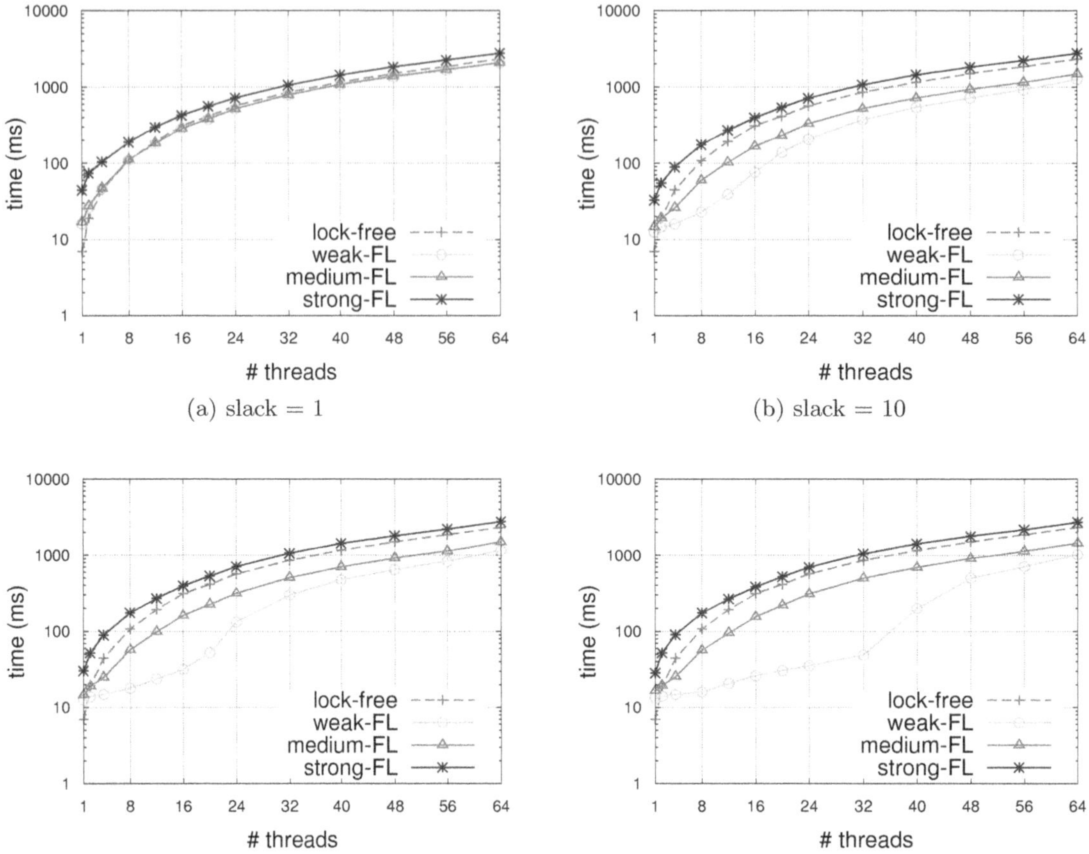

(a) slack = 1
(b) slack = 10
(c) slack = 20
(d) slack = 100

Figure 5: Queue benchmark performance

tive to all other versions when the slack is 1. However, once the slack increases, it beats the lock-free alternative (and the medium-FL list). This is because it enables one thread to effectively combine multiple pending operations produced by other threads, while those threads can continue to work in parallel on producing new operations. Given that the strong-FL property implies the medium-FL property, this example shows that, at least in our prototype implementations, the stronger correctness condition does not necessarily imply worse performance.

6. FORMAL MODEL

The formal definitions of the three kinds of futures linearizability are straightforward generalizations of the standard linearizability definition [10]. For simplicity and brevity, we assume that each future is evaluated at most once, and only by the thread that created it.

6.1 Model

We first describe the standard linearizability model, and then discuss extensions to encompass the different degrees of futures linearizability.

Threads are *sequential*: they perform one method call at a time. (Later, we will relax this condition for method calls that return futures, allowing method calls issued by a single thread to overlap in constrained ways.) A method call is split into two events: an *invocation* event and a later *response* event. An execution of a concurrent system is modeled by a *history*, a finite sequence of method invocation and response events. A *subhistory* of a history H is a subsequence of the events of H. We write a method invocation as $\langle x\ m\ A\rangle$, where x is an object, m is a method (and arguments) and A is a thread. We write a method response as $\langle x\ t\ A\rangle$ where t is a value (possibly *void*) or an exception. Sometimes we refer to an event labeled with thread A as a *step* of A.

A response *matches* an invocation if they have the same object and thread. A *method call* in a history H is a pair consisting of an invocation and the next matching response. For a method call m, its delimiting events are denoted $inv(m)$ and $res(m)$. An invocation is *pending* in H if no matching response follows the invocation. An *extension* of H is a history constructed by appending responses to some (possibly zero) pending invocations of H. The history $complete(H)$ is the subsequence of H consisting of all matching invocations and responses.

For a thread A, the *thread subhistory*, $H|A$ is the subsequence of events in H whose thread names are A. For an object x, the *object subhistory* $H|x$ is similarly defined. Histories H and H' are *equivalent* if for every thread A, $H|A = H'|A$. A thread or object history is *well-formed* if every response has an earlier matching invocation.

A method call m_0 *precedes* a method call m_1 in history H if m_0 finished before m_1 started: that is, m_0's response event occurs before m_1's invocation event in H. Precedence defines a *partial order* on the method calls of H: $m_0 \prec_H m_1$.

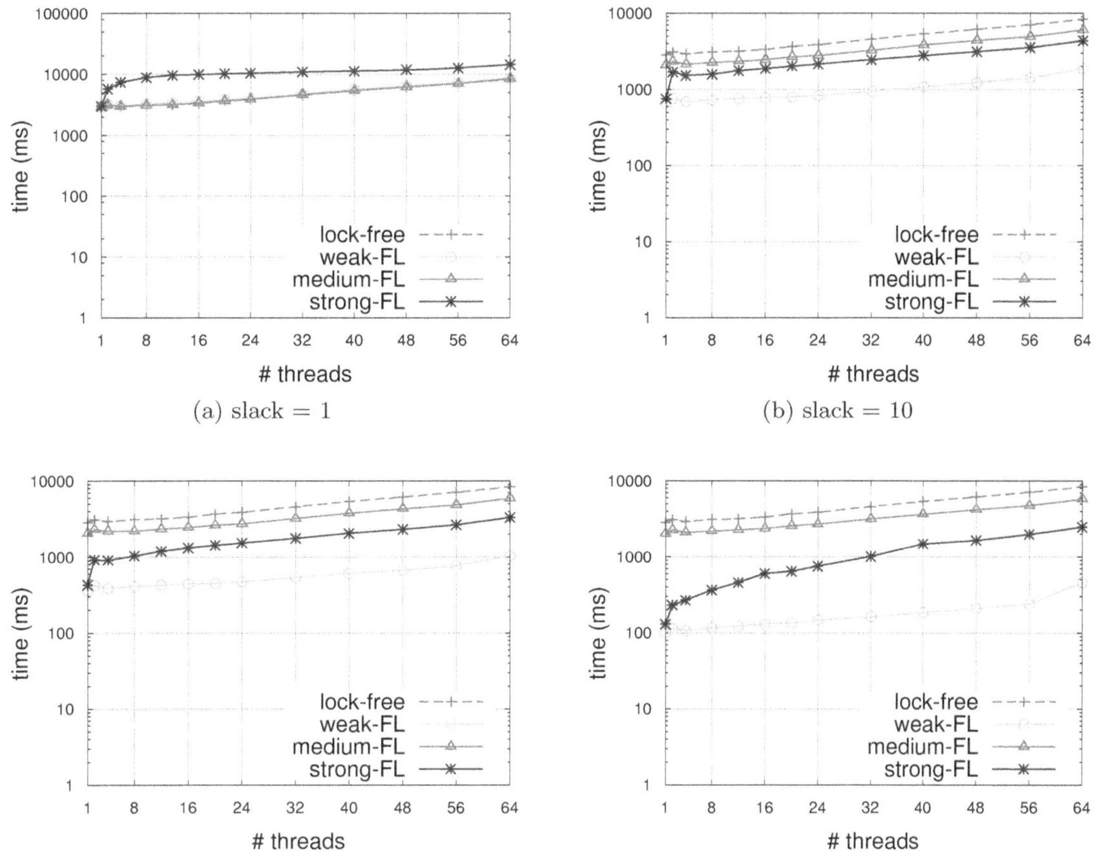

(a) slack = 1 (b) slack = 10

(c) slack = 20 (d) slack = 100

Figure 6: Linked list benchmark performance

A history H is *sequential* if the first event of H is an invocation, and each invocation, except possibly the last, is immediately followed by a matching response. If S is a sequential history, then $\prec_S$ is a total order. A *sequential specification* for an object x is a prefix-closed set of sequential histories called the *legal* histories for x. A sequential history H is *legal* if each object subhistory $H|x$ is legal for x.

For a history H, a partial order $\prec$ *extends* $\prec_H$ if for method calls m_0, m_1 of H, $m_0 \prec_H m_1$ implies $m_0 \prec m_1$, but not necessarily vice-versa. (Informally, different choices for $\prec$ will correspond to strong, medium, and weak futures linearizability.)

DEFINITION 6.1. *For history H, and partial order $\prec$ extending $\prec_H$, H is* $\prec$-linearizable *if it has an extension H' and there is a legal sequential history S, with no pending invocations, such that*

L1 *complete(H') is equivalent to S, and*

L2 *if method call $m_0 \prec_{H'} m_1$, then $m_0 \prec_S m_1$ in S.*

We refer to S as a *$\prec$-linearization* of H.

Definition 6.1 generalizes the usual notion of linearizability in two ways: first, we do not require thread histories to be sequential, and second, we require that $\prec_S$ extends $\prec$ as well as $\prec_H$, a stronger requirement than the linearizability condition that $\prec_S$ extends $\prec_H$. We will use the partial order $\prec$ to capture the additional constraints on method ordering imposed by the various futures linearizability conditions.

6.2 Properties

A method is *total* if it is defined for every object state: for example, a deq() method that throws an exception on an empty queue. We now show that $\prec$-linearizability by itself never forces a thread with a pending invocation of a total method to block.

THEOREM 6.2. *Let inv(m) be an invocation of a total method. If $\langle x\ inv\ P\rangle$ is a pending invocation in a $\prec$-linearizable history H, then there exists a response $\langle x\ res\ P\rangle$ such that $H \cdot \langle x\ res\ P\rangle$ is also $\prec$-linearizable.*

PROOF. Let S be any $\prec$-linearization of H. If S includes a response $\langle x\ res\ P\rangle$ to $\langle x\ inv\ P\rangle$, we are done, since S is also a $\prec$-linearization of $H \cdot \langle x\ res\ P\rangle$. Otherwise, $\langle x\ inv\ P\rangle$ does not appear in S either, since $\prec$-linearizations, by definition, include no pending invocations. Because the method is total, there exists a response $\langle x\ res\ P\rangle$ such that

$$S' = S \cdot \langle x\ inv\ P\rangle \cdot \langle x\ res\ P\rangle$$

is legal. S', however, is a $\prec$-linearization of $H \cdot \langle x\ res\ P\rangle$, and hence is also a $\prec$-linearization of H. □

We have just shown that like linearizability, $\prec$-linearizability is *non-blocking*: a pending invocation of a total method is never required to wait for another pending invocation to complete.

Also like linearizability, $\prec$-linearizability is *compositional*:

THEOREM 6.3. *H is $\prec$-linearizable if, and only if, for each object x, $H|x$ is $\prec$-linearizable.*

PROOF. The "only if" part is immediate from the definitions.

For each object x, pick a $\prec$-linearization H_x of $H|x$. Let R_x be the set of responses appended to $H|x$ to construct that $\prec$-linearization, and let $\prec_x$ be the resulting total order on method calls of x. Let H' be the history constructed by appending to H each response in R_x, for all objects x, in any order.

To show that H is $\prec$-linearizable, we argue by induction on the number of method calls in H'. For the base case, if H' contains only one method call, then it is sequential, thus trivially $\prec$-linearizable. Otherwise, assume the claim for every H' containing fewer than $k > 1$ method calls. For some object x, the last method call m in $H'|x$ must be maximal with respect to $\prec$: that is, there is no m' such that $m \prec m'$. Let G' be the history defined by removing m from H'. Because m is maximal with respect to $\prec$, H' is equivalent to $G' \cdot m$. By the induction hypothesis, G' is $\prec$-linearizable to a sequential history S', and both H' and H are $\prec$-linearizable to $S' \cdot m$. □

A compositional property is sometimes called *local* [11].

6.3 Extension to Futures

For simplicity, we assume each future is evaluated at most once by the thread that created it. For each method m that returns a Future<T> object, we assume there is a corresponding method $\tilde{m}$ that returns a T object, and that the meaning of m is given by the object's sequential specification.

We model futures through simple re-writing rules. Let H be a history. Each Future<T> object in H is associated with two method calls: a first call m that creates the future, and a second call that evaluates it, both executed by a thread A. We will rewrite each such pair as a single call $\tilde{m}$ that returns a value of type T, yielding a new history $\tilde{H}$. While the method call precedence order $\prec_H$ is assumed to be total on $H|A$, the rewritten precedence order $\prec_{\tilde{H}}$ is not necessarily total on $\tilde{H}|A$. We then specify a partial order $\prec_F$ extending $\prec_{\tilde{H}}$, and require that $\tilde{H}$ be $\prec_F$-linearizable.

The exact rewriting rule depends on whether we are considering strong, medium, or weak futures linearizability.

Strong Futures Linearizability.

Construct $\tilde{H}$ by replacing m with $\tilde{m}$, treating the future object as a regular variable, and the future evaluation step as a simple assignment.

DEFINITION 6.4. *H is* strong futures linearizable *if $\tilde{H}$ is $\prec_{\tilde{H}}$-linearizable.*

Weak Futures Linearizability.

Construct $\hat{H}$ by replacing the invocation step of m with the invocation step of $\tilde{m}$, deleting the response step of m, deleting the future evaluation's invocation step, and replacing the future evaluation's response step with the response step of $\tilde{m}$.

DEFINITION 6.5. *H is* weak futures linearizable *if $\hat{H}$ is $\prec_{\hat{H}}$-linearizable.*

Medium Futures Linearizability.

Construct $\hat{H}$ just as for weak futures linearizability. If m_0 and m_1 are future creation calls in H, by the same thread on the same object, such that $\tilde{m}_0$ and $\tilde{m}_1$ are overlapping in $\hat{H}$, then they are unordered by weak futures linearizability, but should be ordered by medium futures linearizability. We define $\prec_m$ by strengthening $\prec_{\hat{H}}$ to order such calls.

$$\tilde{m}_0 \prec_m \tilde{m}_1 \text{ if } \begin{cases} \tilde{m}_0 \prec_{\hat{H}} \tilde{m}_1, \text{ or} \\ \tilde{m}_0, \tilde{m}_1 \in \hat{H}|A \cap \hat{H}|x \text{ and } m_0 \prec_H m_1. \end{cases}$$

DEFINITION 6.6. *H is* medium futures linearizable *if $\hat{H}$ is $\prec_m$-linearizable.*

COROLLARY 6.7. *Strong, medium, and weak futures linearizability are all non-blocking.*

COROLLARY 6.8. *Strong, medium, and weak futures linearizability are all compositional.*

7. RELATED WORK

Halstead [5] originally proposed futures as benign annotations for side-effect-free computations. These futures were untyped and implicit: any object reference could be a future, and a run-time check was needed on each dereference. Modern futures are usually typed, and future creation and evaluation are explicit.

Liskov and Shrira [13] propose the notions of *call-streams* and *promises*. A call-stream allows one thread to make a sequence of remote procedure calls to another. Each such call returns immediately with a *promise* object, a kind of typed future that can be evaluated later to get the call's results. In our terminology, call-streams and promises satisfy medium futures linearizability, except with respect to streams instead of objects. Call-streams are intended for remote procedure calls, and make use of batching to reduce communication costs. Our treatment here is intended for shared objects in multicore systems, and utilizes type-specific optimizations, e.g., combining and elimination.

As noted, futures were originally proposed for side-effect-free computations. Welc et al. [19] consider the question of how futures should behave in languages like Java, where side-effects are common. They propose that futures should satisfy strong futures linearizability, and describe how to extend a JVM to support a speculative implementation of futures satisfying this property. Their futures implementation is general-purpose, and does not consider type-specific optimizations such as combining and elimination.

Scherer and Scott [16] propose *dual data structures*, objects whose methods are split into a request method, that registers the invocation and returns a ticket, and a follow-up method that takes the ticket as an argument, and returns either the request's response or a "not ready" indicator (for example, if trying to dequeue from an empty queue). If we interpret the ticket returned by a request as a kind of future, and the matching successful follow-up as that future's evaluation, then dual data structures satisfy weak futures linearizability. Note that the motivation for dual data structures is to provide a new way to implement linearizable partial methods, which is distinct from our motivation of using futures as a means of deploying highly-concurrent, type-specific techniques for scalable shared-memory data structures.

Futures provide a systematic and clean way to encapsulate a variety of optimization techniques, including *elimination* [8, 15, 17], where operations cancel one another without synchronizing at the object, *combining* [3, 4, 9] and *flat combining* [7], where a single thread executes method calls on behalf of multiple concurrent threads.

8. DISCUSSION

We have considered the use of futures in a novel context of long-lived shared data structures. We have shown that, in this context, futures enable multiple efficient optimizations, such as combining, elimination, flexible evaluation scheduling, contention reduction, etc. To make effective use of futures and to define which optimizations are permitted, we have proposed several correctness conditions, each extending linearizability. We have constructed three standard data structures – queues, stacks and linked lists – satisfying different correctness conditions and compared their performance with well-known lock-free alternatives. Our experience shows that in most cases the versions of the data structures satisfying the weakest correctness condition provide significantly better performance, up to two orders of magnitude. Furthermore, even the versions satisfying the strongest correctness condition substantially outperform the lock-free alternatives in certain cases.

Finally, a word about future work. We have not exhausted the optimizations permitted by futures. For example, our implementation of the linked list under medium futures linearizability does not allow a thread that issues operations such as inserting 3 and then inserting 2 to reorder those operations, because if it did, another thread might observe 2 but not 3 in the list. This danger could be averted, and the operations reordered, if the thread were to lock the shared list and apply multiple operations in a kind of atomic transaction. A promising area of future work is to determine whether such transaction-based approaches are scalable.

9. ACKNOWLEDGMENTS

We are grateful to Tim Harris, Yossi Lev, Mark Moir and anonymous reviewers for valuable feedback.

10. REFERENCES

[1] Bernstein, P., Hadzilacos, V., and Goodman, N. *Concurrency Control and Recovery in Database Systems.* Addison Wesley Publishing Company, 1987.

[2] Calciu, I., Dice, D., Harris, T., Herlihy, M., Kogan, A., Marathe, V. J., and Moir, M. Message passing or shared memory: Evaluating the delegation abstraction for multicores. In *Proceedings of OPODIS* (2013), pp. 83–97.

[3] Goodman, J. R., Vernon, M. K., and Woest, P. J. Efficient synchronization primitives for large-scale cache-coherent multiprocessors. In *Proceedings of the International Conference on Architectural Support for Programming Languages and Operating Systems (ASPLOS)* (1989), pp. 64–75.

[4] Gottlieb, A., Lubachevsky, B. D., and Rudolph, L. Basic techniques for the efficient coordination of very large numbers of cooperating sequential processors. *ACM Trans. Program. Lang. Syst. 5*, 2 (Apr. 1983), 164–189.

[5] Halstead, R. H. Multilisp: A Language for Concurrent Symbolic Computation. *ACM Trans. Program. Lang. Syst. 7*, 4 (Oct. 1985), 501–538.

[6] Harris, T. L. A pragmatic implementation of non-blocking linked-lists. In *Proceedings of the International Conference on Distributed Computing (DISC)* (2001), pp. 300–314.

[7] Hendler, D., Incze, I., Shavit, N., and Tzafrir, M. Flat combining and the synchronization-parallelism tradeoff. In *Proceedings of ACM SPAA* (2010), pp. 355–364.

[8] Hendler, D., Shavit, N., and Yerushalmi, L. A scalable lock-free stack algorithm. *J. Parallel Distrib. Comput. 70*, 1 (2010), 1–12.

[9] Herlihy, M., Lim, B.-H., and Shavit, N. Scalable concurrent counting. *ACM Trans. Comput. Syst. 13*, 4 (Nov. 1995), 343–364.

[10] Herlihy, M., and Shavit, N. *The Art of Multiprocessor Programming.* Morgan Kaufmann Publishers Inc., San Francisco, CA, USA, 2008.

[11] Herlihy, M. P., and Wing, J. M. Linearizability: a correctness condition for concurrent objects. *ACM Trans. Program. Lang. Syst. 12*, 3 (July 1990), 463–492.

[12] Lamport, L. How to Make a Multiprocessor Computer That Correctly Executes Multiprocess Programs. *IEEE Transactions on Computers C-28*, 9 (Aug. 1979), 690–691.

[13] Liskov, B., and Shrira, L. Promises: Linguistic support for efficient asynchronous procedure calls in distributed systems. In *Proceedings of the ACM Conference on Programming Language Design and Implementation (PLDI)* (1988), pp. 260–267.

[14] Michael, M. M., and Scott, M. L. Simple, fast, and practical non-blocking and blocking concurrent queue algorithms. In *Proceedings of the ACM Symposium on Principles of Distributed Computing (PODC)* (1996), pp. 267–275.

[15] Moir, M., Nussbaum, D., Shalev, O., and Shavit, N. Using elimination to implement scalable and lock-free fifo queues. In *Proceedings of ACM SPAA* (2005), pp. 253–262.

[16] Scherer, W. N., and Scott, M. L. Nonblocking concurrent data structures with condition synchronization. In *Proceedings of DISC* (2004), pp. 174–187.

[17] Shavit, N., and Touitou, D. Elimination trees and the construction of pools and stacks: Preliminary version. In *Proceedings of the ACM Symposium on Parallel Algorithms and Architectures (SPAA)* (1995), pp. 54–63.

[18] Treiber, R. *Systems Programming: Coping with Parallelism.* Technical Report RJ 5118. IBM Almaden Research Center, 1986.

[19] Welc, A., Jagannathan, S., and Hosking, A. Safe futures for java. In *Proceedings of the ACM Conference on Object-oriented Programming, Systems, Languages, and Applications (OOPSLA)* (2005), pp. 439–453.

A Paradox of Eventual Linearizability in Shared Memory

Rachid Guerraoui
EPFL, Switzerland

Eric Ruppert
York University, Canada

ABSTRACT

This paper compares, for the first time, the computational power of linearizable objects with that of eventually linearizable ones. We present the following paradox. We show that, unsurprisingly, no set of eventually linearizable objects can (1) implement any non-trivial linearizable object, nor (2) boost the consensus power of simple objects like linearizable registers. We also show, perhaps surprisingly, that any implementation of an eventually linearizable complex object like a fetch&increment counter (from linearizable base objects), can itself be viewed as a fully linearizable implementation of the same fetch&increment counter (using the exact same set of base objects).

Categories and Subject Descriptors

D.1.3 [**Programming Techniques**]: Concurrent Programming

Keywords

Concurrent; asynchronous; linearizable; consistency; wait-free; obstruction-free; fetch-and-increment; consensus

1. INTRODUCTION

A central activity in shared-memory computing is that of raising the abstraction level of synchronization primitives by building, in software, higher-level inter-process communication objects than those provided in hardware. The goal is usually to ensure that, even if the constructed objects have richer semantics, they appear as if they were provided in hardware. In particular, every process should be able to access the shared object independently of contention, i.e., even when other processes may be accessing the same object. This property, called *wait-freedom* [9], says that if we build, for instance, a fetch&increment counter in software, then every process should be able to increment the counter and get its new value, independently of whether other processes that are accessing the counter concurrently have been swapped or paged out. This requirement rules out the usage of locks. However, in order to provide the illusion of a single shared object, processes must synchronize using underlying hardware primitives, such as compare&swap. This illusion, in turn, is typically captured by the property of being *linearizable* [11]. This property says that even if they are actually performed concurrently, the operations issued on that object appear as if they are executed sequentially.

Ensuring either linearizability or wait-freedom alone is simple. What is challenging, and sometimes considered too expensive, is to ensure both at the same time. Two major research directions have been considered to reduce the difficulty. The first is to weaken wait-freedom and devise algorithms that "simply" ensure lock-freedom, obstruction-freedom, or even use locks in specific portions of the code [10]. The rationale here is that the conditions under which the operating system swaps out a process for a long period of time do not happen very often. A lot of theoretical work has been devoted in the last decades to this avenue of research. The second approach is to weaken linearizability: for some applications, weaker consistency conditions suffice [19]. Consider a shared fetch&increment abstraction used to count references of objects in a concurrent setting. As pointed out, this would typically be implemented in software using the system's compare&swap objects. If several compare&swap tentatives fail due to unusually high contention, it may be acceptable to return a temporary value of the counter, as long as, eventually, all increments of concurrent processes are taken into account in some future value of the counter. In other words, in the implementation, if a process is taking too long to synchronize perfectly, because of contention, it could give up trying to get the most up-to-date value and (a) do its increment locally, making sure later that its increments are eventually counted, and (b) get a value of the counter to return that is lower than the true value, assuming that the process will get information about concurrent increments later.

The notion of *eventual consistency* [19] aims to capture precisely this notion of "intermittent inconsistency". The approach is analogous to the way *self-stabilization* was defined, namely stating that the system should eventually work correctly forever beyond some stabilization time, with the goal of modelling intermittent failures and the return of the system to normal after the failure. Obviously, if instead of consistency, implementations only need to implement an eventual form of it, they would offer weaker guarantees. In our example above, the value returned by the counter might be temporarily inconsis-

PODC'14, July 15–18, 2014, Paris, France.

http://dx.doi.org/10.1145/2611462.2611484 .

tent with the eventual value. But would these implementations be easier to implement? Maybe surprisingly, we show that the answer is no in some situations. More specifically, we highlight the following paradox.

- On the one hand, unsurprisingly, eventual linearizability is strictly weaker than linearizability in the following two senses. (1) No set of eventually linearizable objects can implement any non-trivial linearizable object. (A trivial object is one that can be implemented without inter-process communication.) This is true even if we only require the resulting linearizable object to be obstruction-free, whereas the eventually linearizable base objects are wait-free. (2) No set of eventually linearizable objects can boost the consensus power of simple linearizable objects like registers, i.e., help solve consensus among two processes in conjunction with linearizable registers. In short, eventually linearizable objects can neither implement linearizable ones (1) nor augment the power of shared linearizable registers (2).
- On the other hand, eventual linearizability can be as hard to implement as linearizability: any implementation of an eventually linearizable fetch&increment counter (from a set of linearizable base objects), yields an implementation of a fully linearizable fetch-&increment counter (from the same set of base objects). Roughly speaking, this is because a fetch&increment object continues to require synchronization forever. In contrast, such a result does not hold for objects that require synchronization only in the beginning of an execution: for example, consensus and test&set objects are trivial to implement in an eventually linearizable manner. Thus, an eventually linearizable implementation of consensus (respectively, test&set) will clearly *not* yield a linearizable implementation of consensus (respectively, test&set).

In fact, we show that any algorithm A that implements an eventually linearizable fetch&increment object, starting from a given initial state of the object, can itself be viewed as an algorithm A' that implements a fully linearizable fetch&increment object, simply starting from a different initial state of the counter than A. Basically, the variables of A' are those of A, initialized after a global "stabilization time" of eventual linearizability. Interestingly, this is in spite of the fact that the stabilization time is not *a priori* fixed: it could be different in different executions (and this is allowed by our definition of eventual linearizability). The main difficulty of the proof is to show that there must exist a stable configuration C of algorithm A where *every* possible run that passes through C has already stabilized *at* C. (Then, we initialize the variables of A as they are in C to get A'.)

2. RELATED WORK

Eventual consistency originated in the context of replicated systems where updates to the replicas are propagated using gossipping to improve latency and tolerate asynchrony and partitions [4, 6, 18]. Because gossipping is used, replicas are not always consistent, but eventually become so if the updates stop. More recently, researchers argued eventual consistency is a reasonable alternative to consistency in the cloud context. The argument is that consistency does not scale and is not necessary for many applications, e.g., [1, 17, 19]. So far, research on eventual consistency has focused on describing systems that implement some form of eventual consistency.

Some attempts have been made to formalize the semantics of eventual consistency. In [14, 15], for instance, the focus was on abstract properties, while in [2] the goal was to show how to verify replication schemes that ensure only eventual consistency. However, little effort has been devoted to theoretical studies that would precisely measure the power and limitations of eventual consistency (beyond artifacts related to specific implementations). Two notable exceptions are [16] and [5].

In [16], Serafini et al. introduced the concept of eventual linearizability and addressed the problem of the weakest failure detector to implement objects for which some operations are linearizable and some operations are not. In a sense, their work is orthogonal to ours. The main common feature is the definition of eventual linearizability. There are however two differences between our definition of an eventually linearizable implementation and the definition used by Serafini et al. The first is a minor difference. Serafini et al. used a timed model of computation, and talked about stabilizing after time t rather than after t events. This is due to their underlying message-passing model equipped with failure detectors where timing assumptions are used, while we consider a totally asynchronous shared-memory model, where time plays no role. The second, more important difference, has to do with quantifiers. Serafini et al. defined eventual linearizability of an implementation by saying that there is a *single* time t such that *all* executions stabilize by time t. We do not require a single t for all executions: the number of events before executions stabilize may vary, and even be unbounded. Serafini et al. motivate their choice of focusing only on *finite* executions by arguing that any finite history is trivially linearizable after some t (because t can be chosen large enough to satisfy the definition vacuously), and thus the notion of eventual linearizability makes sense only if there is a single t for all executions. We take a different approach. We consider *infinite* executions, which do not trivially satisfy the property of being t-linearizable for some t. We made this choice following an analogy with the literature on self-stabilization, which also deals with a property describing eventual good behaviour.

Dubois et al. [5] consider a message-passing environment and compare the weakest failure detector to implement total order broadcast with the weakest failure detector to implement eventual total order broadcast. Their results do not provide a comparison between linearizable and eventually linearizable implementations of specific objects. We show in this paper that some eventually linearizable objects are trivial to implement in an asynchronous system (and would thus not require any failure detector), whereas others are as hard to implement as their linearizable counterparts. Note that the fact that two abstractions have the same weakest failure detectors does not mean that any implementation of the first is also an implementation of the second (which is what we show for fetch&increment objects in this paper). For instance, [3] shows that two object types T_1 and T_2 can have the same weakest failure detectors even if the consensus number of T_1 is greater than that of T_2, meaning that T_2 cannot implement T_1.

To our knowledge, this paper is the first to compare the computational power of linearizable and eventually linearizable objects in a shared-memory context.

3. MODEL, DEFINITIONS AND PROPERTIES

A shared-memory system consists of a collection of processes that communicate by accessing shared objects of various types. Each type of object has a *sequential specification*, which consists of

- a set Q of possible states,
- a set of possible initial states $Q_0 \subseteq Q$,
- a set INV of possible operation invocations,
- a set RES of possible operation response values, and
- a transition relation $\delta \subseteq Q \times OP \times RES \times Q$.

Intuitively, if $(q, op, r, q') \in \delta$, it means that when the object is in state q and operation op is applied to it, the object can return the response r and move into state q'. We consider the name of an operation in OP to include all of the operation's arguments. A type T is *deterministic* if, for each state q and each operation op, there is a unique result r and state q' such that $(q, op, r, q') \in \delta$. A type T has *finite non-determinism* if, for each state q and each operation op, there are finitely many pairs (r, q') such that $(q, op, r, q') \in \delta$.

An *event* is a tuple $\langle p, o, x\rangle$ where p is a process name, o is the name of an object of some type T and x is either an invocation or response for type T. A computation of the distributed system is described by a sequence of such events, called a *history*. We use $H|o$ to denote the subsequence of history H consisting of events at object o and $H|p$ to denote the subsequence H consisting of events performed by process p. A history is *sequential* if it consists of operation invocation and response events, starting with an invocation, where each invocation $\langle p, o, inv\rangle$ (except possibly the last, if the history is finite) is immediately followed by a matching response $\langle p, o, res\rangle$. Any history H mentioned in this paper is assumed to be *well-formed*, i.e., the subsequence $H|p$ is sequential for each process p. An *operation* consists of an invocation event and its matching response event (if it exists).

A sequential history H is *legal* if, for each object o, the subsequence $H|o = \langle p_1, o, i_1\rangle, \langle p_1, o, r_1\rangle, \langle p_2, o, i_2\rangle, \langle p_2, o, r_2\rangle, \ldots$ satisfies the following with respect to o's sequential specification $(Q, Q_0, INV, RES, \delta)$: there is a sequence of states $q_0, q_1, \ldots$ in Q such that $q_0 \in Q_0$ and, for each $j \geq 0$, $(q_j, i_j, r_j, q_{j+1}) \in \delta$.

An *implementation* of an object of type $T = (Q, Q_0, INV, RES, \delta)$ provides, for each $q_0 \in Q_0$, a programme that each process can follow to perform each operation op in INV. When the programme terminates, it outputs a result in RES. Since we focus on a shared-memory model, the programme can make use of shared base objects: it can invoke an operation on a base object and await a response from it. In a concurrent *execution* of the implementation, each process repeatedly executes the programme to perform an operation until the programme generates a response to the operation, and the steps of different processes may be interleaved in an arbitrary way. Each execution defines a history, the sequence of invocations and responses on the object of type T. In Section 3.1, we define eventual linearizability, which is a correctness condition for an implementation, that constrains the set of possible histories that can arise from executions of the implementation.

An implementation is *wait-free* if each operation completes within a finite number of steps of the process performing it. An implementation is *non-blocking* if, whenever some operation is pending and processes continue to take steps, some operation is eventually completed. (Some authors call the non-blocking progress property lock-freedom.) An implementation is *obstruction-free* if, there is no execution where only one process takes steps in an infinite suffix without completing its operation.

Generally, the focus of distributed computing research is on the interprocess communication, and the computational power of the processes is not specified. For this work, we assume that the programmes are written in a programming language that has equivalent power to the Turing machine model (but includes a mechanism for accessing the shared base objects). Correspondingly, we assume that the transition relations of object type specifications are Turing-computable.

3.1 Eventual Linearizability

We now give several definitions that are used in defining eventual linearizability. These are based on the definitions in [16], but differ in the ways described in Section 2. The first property, weak consistency, ensures that operations cannot return responses that are "out of left field," even during the initial period when absolute consistency is not enforced. In particular, the response to each operation should take into account earlier operations done by the same process and should be a possible response if the process knows only about a subset of the operations performed by other processes.

DEFINITION 1. *A history H is* weakly consistent *if, for each operation op that has a response in H, there is a legal sequential history S that*

- *contains only operations that are invoked in H before op terminates,*
- *contains all operations that are performed by the same process that does op and precede op in H, and*
- *ends with the same response to op as in H.*

Now we define the notion of being linearizable "after the first t events have occurred."

DEFINITION 2. *Let H be a history and t be a natural number. Let H' be the suffix of H obtained by removing the first t events. Then, a legal sequential history S is called a* t-linearization *of H if*

- *each operation invoked in S is invoked in H,*
- *each operation completed in H is completed in S,*
- *if op_1's response is before op_2's invocation and both of these events are in H' and op_2 is in S, then op_1 precedes op_2 in S, and*
- *each operation that has a response in H' has the same response in S.*

A history is t-linearizable *if it has a t-linearization.*

DEFINITION 3. *A history is* eventually linearizable *if it is weakly consistent and t-linearizable for some t.*

DEFINITION 4. *An implementation of an object is* eventually linearizable *if every history is eventually linearizable. (Note that different histories can be t-linearizable for different values of t.)*

3.2 Basic Properties

We start with some easy properties of t-linearizability.

LEMMA 5. *If a history H is t-linearizable, then it is also t'-linearizable for any $t' > t$.*

PROOF. If S is a t-linearization of H, then S is also a t'-linearization of H. □

LEMMA 6. *If a history H is t-linearizable, then every prefix of H is also t-linearizable.*

SKETCH OF PROOF. Let S be a t-linearization of H. A prefix of H of length at most t is trivially t-linearizable. So, consider a prefix H_1H_2 of H where $|H_1| = t$. Let S_1 be the shortest prefix of S containing all operations that terminate in H_2. Let S_2 be an arbitrary permutation of the operations that terminate in H_1 but do not appear in S_1 (with the responses they would have if executed in that order after S_1). Then, it is easy to check that S_1S_2 is a t-linearization of H_1H_2. □

Serafini et al. [16] prove the following proposition using their slightly different definition of t-linearizability. Note, however, that the proof holds only for histories involving a finite number of objects (an assumption that should have been included in [16]).

LEMMA 7. *(Proved in [16]) A history H involving a finite number of objects is t-linearizable for some t if and only if, for each object o, there is a t_o such that $H|o$ is t_o-linearizable.*

The proof of Lemma 7 is based on the proof in [11] that linearizability is a local property, and it carries over to our definition. For the "only if" direction, we can take $t_o = t$. For the "if" direction, we choose t large enough so that the first t events of H include the first t_o events of $H|o$ for each o. This is possible because the set of objects o is finite.

The proof of the following lemma in [16] has a small error, so for completeness, we provide a detailed proof.

LEMMA 8. *A history H is weakly consistent if and only if, for each object o, $H|o$ is weakly consistent.*

PROOF. Suppose H is weakly consistent. Let o be any object and *op* be any operation with a response in $H|o$. Since H is weakly consistent, there is a sequential history S that satisfies Definition 1 for *op* in H. Then, $S|o$ satisfies Definition 1 for *op* in $H|o$. So, $H|o$ is weakly consistent.

Now, suppose $H|o$ is weakly consistent for each object o. Let *op* be any operation that has a response in H. Let p be the process that performs *op* and o be the object *op* is performed on. Let S be the legal sequential history that satisfies Definition 1 for *op* in $H|o$. Let S' be obtained from S by inserting at the beginning of S any operations performed by p before *op* in H on objects other than o, with responses as dictated by the objects' sequential specifications. Then, S' satisfies Definition 1 for *op* in H. Thus, H is weakly consistent. □

The next proposition is immediate from Lemma 7 and 8.

PROPOSITION 9. *A history H that involves a finite number of objects is eventually linearizable if and only if, for each object o, $H|o$ is eventually linearizable.*

Proposition 9 does not hold for some histories that use infinitely many objects. For example, consider the following sequential history H that uses read/write registers $R_1, R_2, \ldots$, all initialized to the value 0.
$\langle p, R_1, write(1)\rangle, \langle p, R_1, ack\rangle, \langle q, R_1, read\rangle, \langle q, R_1, 0\rangle,$
$\langle p, R_2, write(1)\rangle, \langle p, R_2, ack\rangle, \langle q, R_2, read\rangle, \langle q, R_2, 0\rangle,$
$\langle p, R_3, write(1)\rangle, \langle p, R_3, ack\rangle, \langle q, R_3, read\rangle, \langle q, R_3, 0\rangle, \ldots$
If t_i is chosen so that the response to the read of R_i occurs before the t_ith event of H, then $H|R_i$ is t_i-linearizable and it is easy to see that $H|R_i$ is weakly consistent, so $H|R_i$ is eventually linearizable for every i. However, H is not eventually linearizable: for any t, there is an i such that the write to R_i is invoked after the tth event of H, and $H|R_i$ is not t-linearizable, so H is not t-linearizable.

A *safety property* is a set of histories that is non-empty, prefix-closed and limit-closed. A *liveness property* is a set of histories such that every finite history is the prefix of some history in the set. The following lemma follows easily from the definition of weak consistency.

LEMMA 10. *Weak consistency is a safety property.*

PROOF. The empty execution (consisting of no events) vacuously satisfies Definition 1, so the set of weakly consistent histories is non-empty.

Next, we prove that the set of weakly consistent histories is prefix-closed. Suppose H is weakly consistent. Let H' be a prefix of H. Let *op* be an operation that terminates in H'. Let S be the sequential history that satisfies definition 1 for *op* in H. Then S also satisfies Definition 1 for *op* in H'. Thus, H' is weakly consistent.

To show the set of weakly consistent histories is limit-closed, let $H_1, H_2, \ldots$ be an infinite sequence of histories such that, for each i, H_i is weakly consistent and H_i is a prefix of H_{i+1}. We show that $H = \lim_{i\to\infty} H_i$ is weakly consistent. Let *op* be an operation that terminates in H. Then there exists an i such that *op* terminates in H_i. Let S be a sequential history that satisfies Definition 1 for *op* in H_i. Then, S also satisfies Definition 1 for *op* in H. □

0-linearizability is equivalent to linearizability [11]. For deterministic objects, Lynch [13] proved that linearizability is a safety property. The proof extends easily to objects with finite non-determinism [8]. However, linearizability is *not* a safety property for objects with infinite non-determinism [8].

For $t > 0$, t-linearizability is *not* a safety property, even for deterministic types. Consider a fetch&increment object, which stores a natural number and provides a single operation, *fetch&inc*, which adds one to the value stored and returns the old value. Consider the infinite sequential history which uses a single fetch&increment object X initialized to the value 0.
$\langle p, X, fetch\&inc\rangle, \langle p, X, 0\rangle, \langle q, X, fetch\&inc\rangle, \langle q, X, 0\rangle,$
$\langle q, X, fetch\&inc\rangle, \langle q, X, 1\rangle, \langle q, X, fetch\&inc\rangle, \langle q, X, 2\rangle, \ldots$
Every finite prefix is t-linearizable if event t is the response to the first operation: the t-linearization moves the first operation to the end. However, the whole infinite history is not t-linearizable.

Thus, t-linearizability is neither a safety nor a liveness property. However, the property of being t-linearizable for *some* t is trivially a liveness property: for any finite history H, just take t to be equal to the number of events in H, and then any permutation of the operations in H yields a legal, sequential history that is a t-linearization of H. Thus, eventual linearizability is the intersection of a safety property (weak consistency) and a liveness property (being t-linearizable for some t).

3.3 Using Registers to Obtain Weak Consistency

Our definition of eventual linearizability combines a safety property (weak consistency) and a liveness property (being t-linearizable for some t). If our underlying system includes linearizable read/write registers, then we can easily modify any non-blocking implementation that satisfies the liveness property to also satisfy the safety property.

PROPOSITION 11. *Consider a system that includes linearizable registers as base objects. Let T be an object type with finite nondeterminism. There is an eventually linearizable non-blocking implementation of T if and only if there is a non-blocking implementation of T such that for every history there is a t such that the history is t-linearizable.*

This proposition is proved in detail in the appendix. The basic idea is to announce all operations by writing them to shared memory. Then, when a response to an operation has been computed, a process reads all announced operations and returns the response only if it can verify that the response does not violate weak consistency. If a violation of weak consistency is detected, the process is free to return any response that is consistent with just its own prior operations.

4. EVENTUAL LINEARIZABILITY IS WEAK

It is fairly easy to prove that eventually linearizable objects by themselves are useless for implementing linearizable objects. The intuition is that a linearizable implementation must eventually produce the correct output for some operations, but if the eventually linearizable base objects used by the implementation are still behaving badly when that output is produced, that output can be incorrect. The following theorem says that there is no linearizable implementation of any non-trivial object that is useful for inter-process communication from any collection of eventually linearizable objects.

THEOREM 12. *For $n \geq 2$, the following are equivalent for any type T with finite non-determinism.*

1. *There is an n-process linearizable wait-free implementation of T using no shared objects.*
2. *There is an n-process linearizable obstruction-free implementation of T using no shared objects.*
3. *There is an n-process linearizable wait-free implementation of T from some collection of eventually linearizable objects.*
4. *There is an n-process linearizable obstruction-free implementation of T from some collection of eventually linearizable objects.*

PROOF. It is trivial to see that $1 \Rightarrow 3 \Rightarrow 4$ and $1 \Rightarrow 2 \Rightarrow 4$. So, it remains to prove that $4 \Rightarrow 1$.

Suppose there is an obstruction-free linearizable implementation I of an object of type T from some collection of eventually linearizable objects for n processes $p_1, \ldots p_n$. We construct an n-process wait-free linearizable implementation I' of an object of type T simply by replacing each shared object o by n local copies $o_1, \ldots, o_n$. (Since we assume that transition functions are Turing-computable, a process can simulate the object in its local memory.) Whenever process p_i must perform an operation op on shared object o according to I, p_i instead performs op on its local copy o_i.

Then, any finite history H of I' is also a possible finite history of I since the eventually linearizable objects used by I can return arbitrary answers (that satisfy weak consistency) in any finite prefix of an execution. (Note that using a local copy of each object ensures the responses satisfy weak consistency.) Thus, every finite history H of I' must be linearizable, since I guarantees linearizability. Since linearizability is a safety property for T (which is assumed to have finite non-determinism), this means that every history of I' is linearizable.

It remains to show that I' is wait-free. Consider any execution α of I' and any process p_i that takes infinitely many steps in α. Since there is no communication between processes in α, p_i cannot distinguish α from $\alpha|p_i$, where p_i runs solo. But $\alpha|p_i$ is also a solo execution of I and I is obstruction-free, so every operation that p_i invokes in this execution must terminate. □

Theorem 12 allows us to characterize the trivial deterministic types that have linearizable implementations from eventually linearizable objects as follows.

DEFINITION 13. *A deterministic type T is called* trivial *if and only if there is a computable function r that maps each initial state q_0 and operation op to a response $r(q_0, op)$ that is the correct response to op for every state reachable from q_0.*

PROPOSITION 14. *A deterministic type T has a linearizable obstruction-free implementation for 2 processes from some collection of eventually linearizable objects if and only if T is trivial.*

PROOF. ($\Leftarrow$): Suppose T is trivial. For any initial state q_0, an object of type T initialized to state q_0 can be implemented by having op simply return $r(q_0, op)$.

($\Rightarrow$): Suppose there is an obstruction-free linearizable implementation from eventually linearizable objects. By Theorem 12, there is also an obstruction-free linearizable implementation using no shared objects at all for two processes p_1 and p_2. To compute $r(q_0, op)$, we simply run the programme for p_1 that implements op for an object initialized to state q_0 until it produces a response. Let α be this solo execution of the implementation. Let q be any state that can be reached from q_0 via some sequence of operations. We must show that $r(q_0, op)$ is the correct response for op when an object of type T is in state q. Consider an execution β of the implementation in which process p_2 runs solo, performing a sequence of operations that takes the implemented object from the initial state q_0 to state q. (This uses the assumption that T is deterministic, so that we can force the implemented object into any reachable state.) Since the implementation uses no shared objects, $\beta\alpha$ is a also possible execution of the implementation. Since this execution is linearizable, and p_1 returns $r(q_0, op)$ as the response for op in α, there must be a transition $(q, op, r(q_0, op), q')$ in the transition relation that specifies type T. □

In particular, Proposition 14 says that even weak objects like read/write registers do not have linearizable implementations from any collection of eventually linearizable objects.

Eventual Linearizability is Still Weak Even With Linearizable Registers

Theorem 12 tells us that if T is a non-trivial type (i.e., cannot be implemented linearizably without any communication) then a linearizable implementation of T cannot be built from eventually linearizable objects. But what if we also have linearizable registers available? Then, could we build a linearizable object of type T? We use a valency argument [7] to show the answer is still no if T is strong enough to solve two-process consensus.

PROPOSITION 15. *Let T be any object type that can solve wait-free two-process consensus. There is no wait-free linearizable implementation of T from linearizable registers and any collection of eventually linearizable objects (of any types).*

PROOF. Suppose there were such an implementation to derive a contradiction. Then we could build a wait-free consensus algorithm for two processes p_0 and p_1 from that same collection of eventually linearizable objects and linearizable registers. Consider the tree of all possible histories of this consensus algorithm in which process p_i has input i for $i = 0, 1$. (In this tree, nodes represent configurations of the algorithm and the edge connecting a parent to a child are labelled by an invocation or response on one of the base objects.) A node C is 0-valent (or 1-valent) if all decisions made in the subtree rooted at C are 0 (or 1, respectively). A node is multivalent if it is neither 0- nor 1-valent. The root of this tree is multivalent, since a solo run by p_i must produce output i. So there must be a critical configuration C (i.e., C is multivalent, but each child of C in the tree is 0- or 1-valent).

Thus, there must be one event s_0 at p_0 and one event s_1 at p_1 that take the system from C to configurations C_0 and C_1 with opposite valencies. If s_0 and s_1 do not involve the same shared object o, then the events commute: the configurations reached from C by doing s_0s_1 or s_1s_0 are indistinguishable to all processes. So, a solo execution by p_0 from either one leads to the same outcome, contradicting the fact that C_0 and C_1 have opposite valencies. We consider three cases.

CASE 1 (s_0 is an invocation event on o): Let α be any solo run by p_1 continuing from C_1 until p_1 decides. Then $s_1\alpha$ is also a legal continuation from the configuration C_0, contradicting the fact that C_0 and C_1 have opposite valencies.

CASE 2 (s_1 is an invocation event on o): symmetric to Case 1.

CASE 3 (s_0 and s_1 are both response events from o): We show s_0s_1 and s_1s_0 could both occur after C.

First, suppose o is a linearizable register. Then, whatever response p_0 gets in event s_0 from configuration C is still a valid response to p_0's pending operation after s_1 occurs. In particular, if s_0 returns a null response to a write by p_0, the write would receive exactly the same response after s_1. Likewise, if s_0 returns a value v as the response to a read by p_0, that value is still a valid response to the read if p_1 gets the response to its operation first. So, s_1s_0 is a valid sequence of events following C. Similarly, s_0s_1 is a valid sequence of events following C.

Now suppose o is an eventually linearizable object, then there is no constraint that the responses from o in any finite prefix of the execution must satisfy (beyond weak consistency). So s_0s_1 and s_1s_0 are both possible sequences of events following C.

Let $s_0s_1\alpha$ be an execution onward from C where α is a solo execution by p_0 until it decides. Then, $s_1s_0\alpha$ is a possible execution from C, contradicting the fact that C_0 and C_1 have opposite valencies. □

Implementing Eventually Linearizable Objects Using Registers

We next consider whether eventually linearizable objects are easier to implement than their linearizable counterparts. Here, we focus on implementations from registers: we show that it is possible to obtain eventually linearizable implementations of some objects that have no linearizable implementations.

Any one-shot type has a trivial eventually linearizable implementation using no shared objects since the implementation may behave badly during the finite prefix when all operations are performed. Similarly, some long-lived types whose behaviour is "interesting" only in a finite prefix of each execution have eventually linearizable implementations using no shared memory. For example, a *test&set object* has an eventually linearizable implementation where each process simply returns 0 for its first invocation of test&set and 1 for all subsequent invocations.

A *consensus object* provides one operation *propose*(v), where v is a value drawn from some domain D. Each *propose* operation returns the value used as the argument of the first *propose* operation to be linearized. This object is essentially the hardest object to implement in a linearizable way (since it can be used to build linearizable implementations of every other type [9]), but it is trivial to implement it in an eventually linearizable way using only linearizable registers. In fact, the following proposition states that such an implementation can be built even from eventually linearizable registers.

PROPOSITION 16. *A consensus object has a wait-free, eventually linearizable implementation from eventually linearizable registers.*

PROOF. The implementation for n processes uses an array *Proposals*[1..n] of single-writer multi-reader registers, each initially holding the value $\bot \notin D$. When process p_i invokes Propose(v), it runs the following programme.

```
1 PROPOSE(v)
2    if Proposal[i] = ⊥ then Proposal[i] := v
3    read Proposal[1..n] and return leftmost non-⊥ value
4 end PROPOSE
```

The weak consistency property of the base registers ensures that p_i's first read of *Proposal*[i] returns $\bot$ and all of p_i's subsequent reads of *Proposal*[i] returns the argument of p_i's first PROPOSE operation. Thus, p_i always sees a non-$\bot$ value on line 3, so the leftmost non-$\bot$ value is well-defined. Moreover, if p_i performs a write, then it only performs one write (during its first execution of PROPOSE); all subsequent executions of line 2 must see a non-$\bot$ value in *Proposal*[i].

The implementation is clearly wait-free. Consider any concurrent execution of the implementation. Let H be the history of invocations and responses on the consensus object during this execution and let H' be the history of invocations and responses on the base objects.

We first show that H is weakly consistent. Let *op* be a PROPOSE operation by p_i that terminates in H and returns the value v it read from *Proposal*[j]. Then, the

$\text{PROPOSE}(v)$ operation op' by process p_j that wrote v must have been invoked before op terminated. Thus, a sequential history that starts with op' can be used to show that the result returned by op satisfies Definition 1 in H.

Our next goal is to define a value of t such that H is t-linearizable. By Lemma 7, there is a t' such that H' is t'-linearizable (since each of the finitely many base registers are eventually linearizable). Let P be the set of PROPOSE operations, all of whose reads terminate after event t' in H' and appear after all writes in the t'-linearization of H'. (Note that there are only finitely many PROPOSE operations that are *not* in P because there are at most n writes during the execution.) Then, all PROPOSE operations in P read exactly the same set of values on line 3 and therefore return the same result v_0.

Choose t such that a $\text{PROPOSE}(v_0)$ operation op_0 begins before event t of H and the finitely many terminating PROPOSE operations that are not in P all terminate before event t of H. To create a t-linearization of H, we put op_0 first, followed by all other complete operations, in the order that they terminate. In this sequential history, all operations return v_0, as do all operations in the concurrent history that terminate after step t. □

5. EVENTUAL LINEARIZABILITY CAN BE HARD TO IMPLEMENT

We prove in Proposition 18, below, that if we have an eventually linearizable *implementation* of a fetch&increment object from linearizable base objects, we can "fix" the implementation so that it is linearizable. We use the following technical lemma.

LEMMA 17. *Suppose we have an eventually linearizable implementation of a fetch&increment object. Let $t > 0$ and let α be an infinite history of this implementation. If every finite prefix of α is t-linearizable, then α is t-linearizable.*

PROOF. Since the implementation is eventually linearizable, there is some t' such that α has a t'-linearization S'. If $t' \leq t$, then the claim follows from Lemma 5. So, for the remainder of the proof, we assume $t' > t$.

We partition the operations of α into four sets according to their response events as follows.

- Let A_1 contain the operations whose response is among the first t events of α.
- Let A_2 contain the operations whose response is among events $t+1, \ldots, t'$.
- Let A_3 contain the operations whose response occurs after event t'.
- Let A_4 contain the operations that do not terminate.

Our goal is to construct a t-linearization S of α. We describe how to do this by assigning operations to positions in S. We assume the positions are numbered starting from 0. If an operation in A_2 or A_3 returns a value v, we assign it to position v in S. (Note that this cannot assign two operations to the same position, since if two operations op_1 and op_2 return the same result v, the prefix of α that includes the responses of both op_1 and op_2 would not be t-linearizable.) Let $E = \{v :$ no operation in A_2 or A_3 returns $v\}$. This is the set of slots that have not yet been assigned an operation.

We first show that $|A_1| \leq |E| \leq |A_1| + |A_4|$. Let $E' = \{v :$ no operation in A_3 returns $v\}$. Then, S' fills all positions of E' with operations in A_1 and A_2 and some subset $A_4' \subseteq A_4$. Thus, $|A_1|+|A_2| \leq |E'| \leq |A_1|+|A_2|+|A_4|$ (and all of these quantities are finite). Each operation of A_3 is assigned the same slot by S and S' (since both are t'-linearizations of α). So, $|E| = |E'| - |A_2|$. Thus, $|A_1| \leq |E| \leq |A_1| + |A_4|$.

For our linearization S, we fill in the first $|A_1|$ slots of E with operations in A_1, in the order they are invoked in α. Then, we fill in the remaining slots with the first $|E| - |A_1| \leq |A_4|$ operations of A_4 in the order of their invocations in α. It remains to prove that S is a t-linearization of α.

- Each operation invoked in S is invoked in α: This follows from the definition of S.
- Each operation that terminates in α appears in S: By definition of S, all operations in $A_1 \cup A_2 \cup A_3$ are assigned slots in S.
- If op_1 terminates after event t and op_2 begins after op_1 terminates and op_2 appears in S, then op_1 precedes op_2 in S: Then, $op_1 \in A_2 \cup A_3$ and $op_2 \in A_2 \cup A_3 \cup A_4$. We consider several cases.

  First, suppose op_2 is in $A_2 \cup A_3$. Then, op_1 must return a smaller value than op_2, since the prefix containing the responses of both op_1 and op_2 is t-linearizable. Thus, op_1 is assigned an earlier slot than op_2 in S.

  Now, suppose op_2 is in A_4. Let v be the response returned by op_1. Consider a prefix of α that contains all response events of α that return values less than or equal to v. By the hypothesis of the lemma, there is a t-linearization of this prefix. In that t-linearization, all the slots of E prior to slot v are filled using operations of A_1 and operations of A_4 that begin before op_1's response (and hence before op_2 is invoked). This means that the number of operations in A_1 and the number of operations in A_4 that begin before op_2 begins is at least $|E \cap \{0, 1, \ldots, v\}|$. In S, all of these operations are linearized before op_2, so op_2 is assigned a slot greater than v. Thus, op_1 precedes op_2 in S.
- Each operation that has a response after event t of α has the same response in S: Each operation of $A_2 \cup A_3$ is assigned to the slot that would cause it to return the same response in S as it does in α.

□

For Lemma 17, the hypothesis that the implementation is eventually linearizable is necessary since t-linearizability is not a safety property of fetch&increment implementations (see Section 3.2).

PROPOSITION 18. *If there is an n-process eventually linearizable, non-blocking implementation of a fetch&increment object from a set $\mathcal{O}$ of linearizable objects, then there is an n-process linearizable, non-blocking implementation of a fetch&increment object from $\mathcal{O}$.*

PROOF. Let A be an n-process eventually linearizable implementation of a fetch&increment object from $\mathcal{O}$. Consider the execution tree of all possible executions of this implementation in which n processes $p_1, \ldots, p_n$ each repeatedly perform fetch&inc operations forever. Each edge in the tree represents either a local event or an atomic action on an object in $\mathcal{O}$.

Consider a node C in this tree. Let α_C be the finite execution represented by the path from the root to C. We say that C is *stable* if *every* execution with prefix α_C is $|\alpha_C|$-linearizable. (In other words, the behaviour of the implemented fetch&increment object has "stabilized" by C.)

It follows from the definition of stable and Lemma 5 that if C is stable, then so are C's descendants.

CLAIM 1: There is a stable node in the tree.

PROOF OF CLAIM 1: To derive a contradiction, suppose no node in the tree is stable. We inductively construct a sequence of finite paths $p_0, p_1, \ldots$ that have the following properties, where $\ell_i = |p_0 p_1 \ldots p_i|$:

1. For $i \geq 0$, $p_0 p_1 \cdots p_i$ is a path starting at the root of the tree.
2. For $i \geq 1$, p_i is non-empty.
3. For $i \geq 1$, $p_0 p_1 \ldots p_i$ is not ℓ_{i-1}-linearizable.

Let p_0 be the empty execution. For the inductive step of the construction, let $i \geq 1$. Given $p_0, \ldots, p_{i-1}$ with the properties listed above, we construct p_i as follows.

Let C be the endpoint of the path $p_0 p_1 \ldots p_{i-1}$. By the assumption, C is not stable. So, there is some execution α with prefix $p_0 p_1 \ldots p_{i-1}$ that is not ℓ_{i-1}-linearizable. By Lemma 17, some finite prefix α' of α is not ℓ_{i-1}-linearizable. That prefix has length greater than ℓ_{i-1}, so let p_i be the non-empty path such that $\alpha' = p_0 p_1 \ldots p_{i-1} p_i$.

Now, consider the infinite execution $\pi = p_0 p_1 \ldots$. Since the implementation is eventually linearizable, there is a t such that this execution is t-linearizable. Choose i such that $\ell_{i-1} > t$. (Such a choice is possible because all of the p_j's are non-empty, so we have $\ell_0 < \ell_1 < \cdots$.) Since π is t-linearizable, it is also ℓ_{i-1} linearizable, by Lemma 5. By Lemma 6, the prefix $p_0 p_1 \ldots p_i$ of π is also ℓ_{i-1} linearizable, which contradicts the third property of the construction. This completes the proof of Claim 1.

Let C be a stable node. Let t be the number of events in the execution α_C. Consider the configuration C_{idle} reached from C by allowing each process to run solo until it completes its current fetch&inc operation. Then, we let one process p run fetch&inc operations repeatedly. We argue that, eventually, some operation op_0 that p performs must return a value that is equal to the number of fetch&inc operations that were invoked before op_0. (If not, there would be no way to t-linearize the infinite execution where p continues forever.) Let C_0 be the configuration at the end of op_0. Let v_0 be the number of fetch&inc operations invoked in the path from the root to C_0.

Now, we construct a linearizable implementation A' of a fetch&increment object using $\mathcal{O}$. Initialize each object in $\mathcal{O}$ to the state it has in C_0. Similarly, each process uses the same local variables as in A, and they are initialized in A' to the values they have in C_0. In A', to perform a fetch&inc operation, a process executes the algorithm A for fetch&inc until it obtains a result v, and then it returns $v - v_0$.

If β is an execution of A', there is a corresponding execution $\alpha\beta'$ of A, where α is the execution described above that takes the system to configuration C_0, and β' is the same as β except that v_0 is not subtracted from the output values. Since C is stable, $\alpha\beta'$ is t-linearizable, and the t-linearization must linearize before op_0 all v_0 operations invoked before op_0. Moreover, the t-linearization respects the real-time order of operations in β' since they are invoked after event t of $\alpha\beta'$. The suffix of the t-linearization obtained by removing the first v_0 operations is a linearization of all operations in β. $\square$

Remark: The preceding proposition can also be proved for other progress conditions: if the eventually linearizable implementation is obstruction-free or wait-free, then it can be used to create an obstruction-free or wait-free linearizable implementation.

COROLLARY 19. *There is no non-blocking eventually linearizable implementation of a fetch&increment object for two processes from linearizable registers.*

PROOF. If there were such an implementation, we could build a linearizable implementation of a fetch&increment object for two processes from linearizable registers, by Proposition 18. This is impossible since a fetch&increment object and registers can solve two-process consensus and registers alone cannot [9, 12]. $\square$

6. OPEN QUESTIONS

We have shown that eventually linearizable implementations can be much easier to build (and weaker) than linearizable ones for some types (e.g., consensus objects). For other types (such as fetch&increment), an eventually linearizable implementation appears to be just as hard to build as a linearizable one. It would be interesting to characterize the exact situations where an eventually linearizable implementation is easier to attain than a linearizable one.

One of the fundamental results about linearizable objects is Herlihy's wait-free universal construction [9]. It is natural to ask whether there is a lock-free universal construction of eventually linearizable objects from some natural eventually linearizable primitive objects (possibly in conjunction with linearizable registers). The results of [5] may provide some ideas for doing this.

APPENDIX: PROOF OF PROPOSITION 11

PROOF. The "only if" direction is trivial by the definition of eventually linearizable. It remains to prove the "if" direction. Consider a system of n processes $p_1, \ldots, p_n$. Let A be an implementation of T with the property that for every history there is a t such that the history is t-linearizable. We define a new implementation A' that is eventually linearizable.

In addition to whatever shared objects are used by implementation A, A' uses a sequence of single-writer registers $R_i[0, 1, 2, \ldots]$ for each process p_i. All of these additional registers are initialized to the value $\perp$. Each process p_i also stores a local counter c_i, initially 0, that counts how many operations p_i has performed, and a local variable q_i (initialized to the initial state of the implemented object) that stores the state of the implemented object that would result if only p_i's own operations were performed on it. In the implementation A', p_i performs an operation op by executing the algorithm in Figure 1.

First, we prove A' is non-blocking. The call to algorithm A on line 5 is non-blocking, by the hypothesis. The

```
1  EXECUTE(op)
2     write op in R_i[c_i]    ▷ announce op
3     c_i := c_i + 1
4     ⟨q_i, r_private⟩ := a possible new state and result if
          op is applied to object in state q_i
          (according to sequential specification)
5     r_shared := result of running op in implementation A
6     for j = 1..n          ▷ read all announced operations
7        k = 0
8        do until R_j[k] = ⊥
9           read R_j[k]
10          k := k + 1
11       end do
12    end for
13    if a permutation of a subset of the operations read
          in the loop (including all read in R_i) yields a
          legal sequential execution where op returns
          r_shared then return r_shared
14    else return r_private
15 end EXECUTE
```

Figure 1: Algorithm to guarantee weak consistency.

only way the loop (line 8–11) can run forever without terminating is if process p_j increments its counter c_j infinitely many times, meaning that p_j completes infinitely many operations. Also, there are only finitely many permutations to try in line 13, since T has finite nondeterminism.

We now show that any history H generated by this implementation is eventually linearizable.

Consider an operation *op* that terminates in H and is performed by some process p. If *op* returns on line 14, let $S_{private}$ be the sequential execution defined by the sequence of operations performed by p up to and including *op*, with the responses chosen on line 4. Then $S_{private}$ satisfies Definition 1 for *op* in H. If *op* returns on line 13, then the permutation described on line 13 defines a sequential execution S_{shared} that satisfies Definition 1 for *op* in H. (Note that all operations included in the permutation begin before *op* terminates.) Thus, H is weakly consistent.

Next, we prove that H is t-linearizable for some t. Consider the execution that consists of all steps inside the calls to implementation A on line 5. These define a history H_A. By the hypothesis about implementation A, H_A is t_A-linearizable for some t_A. Let S be a t_A-linearization of H_A.

Let O be the set of operations *op* such that *op* terminates in H and *op*'s call to A on line 5 terminates within the first t_A events in H_A. Note that O is finite, because only finitely many operations terminate before event t_A in H_A. Choose t large enough that that all operations in O terminate before event t of H. (This is possible because O is a finite set of operations, all of which terminate in H.) We prove that the legal sequential execution S is a t-linearization of H by showing it satisfies the four properties in Definition 2.

Since S is a t_A-linearization of H_A, each operation invoked in S is also invoked in H_A, and is therefore invoked in H.

Each operation that terminates in H also must terminate in H_A, and therefore terminates in S (since S is a t_A-linearization of H_A).

Consider any two operations op_1 and op_2 such that op_1 terminates before op_2 is invoked in H and both of these events occur after event t of H, and op_2 is in S. Let op_1' and op_2' be the operations in H_A called at line 5 of op_1 and op_2, respectively. Note that op_1' exists because op_1 terminates, and op_2' exists because the operation appears in S, which is a t_A-linearization of H_A. Since op_1 terminates after event t of H, op_1 does not belong to O, so op_1' terminates after the first t_A events of H_A. Moreover, op_2's call to A on line 5 is after op_2 begins, which is after op_1 terminates, which is after op_1's call to A terminates. Thus, op_1' terminates before op_2' begins in H_A. Since S is a t_A-linearization of H_A, op_1 precedes op_2 in S.

Suppose *op* is an operation that terminates in H after the first t events. We first argue that the test performed by *op* at line 13 evaluates to true, so that *op* returns r_{shared} at line 13. Let op_p be any operation that precedes *op* in S. Let op' and op_p' be the operations in H_A called at line 5 of *op* and op_p, respectively. Note that op' exists because *op* terminates, and op_p' exists because it appears in S, which is a t_A-linearization of H_A. Since *op* terminates after event t of H, *op* does not belong to O, so op' terminates after the first t_A events of H_A. So, op_p' must begin before op' terminates in H_A (otherwise, *op* would have to precede op_p in S). This means that op_p begins executing line 5 before *op* finishes executing line 5. So, op_p executes line 2 before *op* reaches line 6. Since this is true for every operation op_p that precedes *op* in S, *op* will see the announcement of every operation that precedes *op* in S when it reads the registers. Thus, one possible permutation that *op* considers in the test on line 13 will be the prefix of S up to *op*, which yields the response r_{shared} for *op*, so the test will evaluate to true, and *op* will return r_{shared}, which is the same value that *op* returns in S. □

7. REFERENCES

[1] P. Bailis and A. Ghodsi. Eventual consistency today: Limitations, extensions and beyond. *Commun. ACM*, 56(5):55–63, May 2013.

[2] A. Bouajjani, C. Enea, and J. Hamza. Verifying eventual consistency of optimistic replication systems. In *Proc. 41st ACM Symposium on Principles of Programming Languages*, pages 285–296, 2014.

[3] C. Delporte-Gallet, H. Fauconnier, and R. Guerraoui. Tight failure detection bounds on atomic object implementations. *J. ACM*, 57(4), Apr. 2010.

[4] A. Demers, D. Greene, C. Hauser, W. Irish, J. Larson, S. Shenker, H. Sturgis, D. Swinehart, and D. Terry. Epidemic algorithms for replicated database maintenance. In *Proc. 6th ACM Symposium on Principles of Distributed Computing*, pages 1–12, 1987.

[5] S. Dubois, R. Guerraoui, P. Kouznetsov, F. Petit, and P. Sens. The weakest failure detector for eventual consistency. Unpublished manuscript, 2014.

[6] A. Fekete, D. Gupta, V. Luchangco, N. Lynch, and A. Shvartsman. Eventually-serializable data services. *Theoretical Comput. Sci.*, 220(1):113–156, June 1999.

[7] M. J. Fischer, N. A. Lynch, and M. S. Paterson. Impossibility of distributed consensus with one faulty process. *J. ACM*, 32(2):374–382, Apr. 1985.

[8] R. Guerraoui and E. Ruppert. Linearizability is not always a safety property. In *Proc. 2nd International Conference on Networked Systems*, 2014. To appear.

[9] M. Herlihy. Wait-free synchronization. *ACM Trans. Prog. Lang. Syst.*, 13(1):124–149, Jan. 1991.

[10] M. Herlihy and N. Shavit. On the nature of progress. In *Proc. 15th International Conference on Principles of Distributed Systems*, pages 313–328, 2011.

[11] M. P. Herlihy and J. M. Wing. Linearizability: a correctness condition for concurrent objects. *ACM Trans. Prog. Lang. Syst.*, 12(3):463–492, July 1990.

[12] M. C. Loui and H. H. Abu-Amara. Memory requirements for agreement among unreliable asynchronous processes. In F. P. Preparata, editor, *Advances in Computing Research*, volume 4, pages 163–183. JAI Press, Greenwich, Connecticut, 1987.

[13] N. Lynch. *Distributed Algorithms*, chapter 13. Morgan Kaufmann, 1996.

[14] Y. Saito and M. Shapiro. Optimistic replication. *ACM Computing Surveys*, 37(1):42–81, Mar. 2005.

[15] A. G. Sebastien Burckhard and H. Yang. Understanding eventual consistency. Technical report, Microsoft, 2013.

[16] M. Serafini, D. Dobre, M. Majuntke, P. Bokor, and N. Suri. Eventually linearizable shared objects. In *Proc. 29th ACM Symposium on Principles of Distributed Computing*, pages 95–104, 2010. Full version available from http://labs.yahoo.com/files/aurora.pdf.

[17] A. Singh, P. Fonseca, P. Kuznetsov, R. Rodrigues, and P. Maniatis. Zeno: Eventually consistent byzantine-fault tolerance. In *Proc. 6th USENIX Symposium on Networked Systems Design and Implementation*, pages 169–184, 2009.

[18] D. B. Terry, M. M. Theimer, K. Petersen, A. J. Demers, M. J. Spreitzer, and C. H. Hauser. Managing update conflicts in Bayou, a weakly connected replicated storage system. In *Proc. 15th ACM Symposium on Operating Systems Principles*, pages 172–182, 1995.

[19] W. Vogels. Eventually consistent. *Commun. ACM*, 52(1):40–44, Jan. 2009.

Brief Announcement: Are Lock-Free Concurrent Algorithms Practically Wait-Free?

Dan Alistarh*
Microsoft Research
daalista@microsoft.com

Keren Censor-Hillel†
Technion
ckeren@cs.technion.ac.il

Nir Shavit‡
MIT & Tel-Aviv University
shanir@csail.mit.edu

ABSTRACT

Lock-free concurrent algorithms guarantee that *some* concurrent operation will always make progress in a finite number of steps. Yet programmers would prefer to treat concurrent code as if it were *wait-free*, guaranteeing that *all* operations always make progress. Unfortunately, designing wait-free algorithms is in general a complex undertaking, and the resulting algorithms are not always efficient, so most non-blocking commercial code is only lock-free, and the design of efficient wait-free algorithms has been left to the academic community.

In [2], we suggest a solution to this problem. We show that, for a large class of lock-free algorithms, under scheduling conditions which approximate those found in commercial hardware architectures, lock-free algorithms behave as if they are wait-free. In other words, programmers can keep on designing simple lock-free algorithms instead of complex wait-free ones, and in practice, they will get wait-free progress.

Our main contribution is a new way of analyzing a general class of lock-free algorithms under a *stochastic scheduler*. Our analysis relates the individual performance of processes with the global performance of the system using *Markov chain lifting* between a complex per-process chain and a simpler system progress chain. We show that lock-free algorithms are not only wait-free with probability 1, but that in fact a broad subset of lock-free algorithms can be closely bounded in terms of the average number of steps required until an operation completes.

To the best of our knowledge, this is the first attempt to analyze progress conditions, typically stated in relation to a worst case adversary, in a stochastic model capturing their expected asymptotic behavior.

Categories and Subject Descriptors

E.1 [**Data Structures**]: Distributed Data Structures; F.2.2 [**Analysis of Algorithms and Problem Complexity**]: Nonnumerical Algorithms and Problems

Keywords

Distributed computing; shared memory; wait-free algorithms; lock-free algorithms; progress properties; schedulers

1. OVERVIEW

The introduction of multicore architectures as today's main computing platform has brought about a renewed interest in concurrent data structures and algorithms, and a considerable amount of research has focused on their modeling, design and analysis.

The behavior of concurrent algorithms is captured by *safety properties*, which guarantee their correctness, and *progress properties*, which guarantee their termination. Progress properties can be quantified using two main criteria. The first is whether the algorithm is *blocking* or *non-blocking*, that is, whether the delay of a single process will cause others to be blocked, preventing them from terminating. Algorithms that use locks are blocking, while algorithms that do not use locks are non-blocking. Most of the code in the world today is lock-based, though the fraction of code without locks is steadily growing [11].

The second progress criterion, and the one we will focus on, is whether a concurrent algorithm guarantees *minimal* or *maximal progress* [12]. Intuitively, minimal progress means that *some* process is always guaranteed to make progress by completing its operations, while maximal progress means that *all* processes always complete all their operations.

Most non-blocking commercial code is *lock-free*, that is, provides minimal progress without using locks [12, 7]. Most blocking commercial code is *deadlock-free*, that is, provides minimal progress when using locks. Over the years, the research community has devised ingenious, technically sophisticated algorithms that provide *maximal progress*: such algorithms are either *wait-free*, i.e. provide maximal progress without using locks [10], or *starvation-free* [13, 14], i.e. provide maximal progress when using locks. Unexpectedly, maximal progress algorithms, and wait-free algorithms in

*Part of this work was performed while the author was a Postdoctoral Associate at MIT CSAIL, where he was supported by SNF Postdoctoral Fellows Program, NSF grant CCF-1217921, DoE ASCR grant ER26116/DE-SC0008923, and by grants from the Oracle and Intel corporations.
†Shalon Fellow.
‡This work was supported in part by NSF grants CCF-1217921 and CCF-1301926, DoE ASCR grant ER26116/DE-SC0008923, and by grants from the Oracle and Intel corporations.

PODC'14, July 15–18, 2014, Paris, France.
ACM 978-1-4503-2944-6/14/07.
http://dx.doi.org/10.1145/2611462.2611502 .

particular, are not being adopted by practitioners, despite the fact that the completion of all method calls in a program is a natural assumption that programmers implicitly make.

Recently, Herlihy and Shavit [12] suggested that perhaps the answer lies in a surprising property of lock-free algorithms: in practice, they often behave as if they were wait-free (and similarly, deadlock-free algorithms behave as if they were starvation-free). Specifically, most operations complete in a timely manner, and the impact of long worst-case executions on performance is negligible. In other words, in real systems, the scheduler that governs the threads' behavior in long executions does not single out any particular thread in order to cause the theoretically possible bad behaviors. This raises the following question: could the choice of *wait-free* versus *lock-free* be based simply on what assumption a programmer is willing to make about the underlying scheduler, and, with the right kind of scheduler, one will not need wait-free algorithms except in very rare cases?

This question is important because the difference between a wait-free and a lock-free algorithm for any given problem typically involves the introduction of specialized "helping" mechanisms [10], which significantly increase the complexity (both the design complexity and time complexity) of the solution. If one could simply rely on the scheduler, adding a helping mechanism to guarantee wait-freedom (or starvation-freedom) would be unnecessary.

Unfortunately, there is currently no analytical framework which would allow answering the above question, since it requires predicting the behavior of a concurrent algorithm over long executions, under a scheduler that is not adversarial.

Contribution. In this paper, we take a first step towards such a framework. Following empirical observations, we introduce a *stochastic scheduler* model, and use this model to predict the long-term behavior of a general class of concurrent algorithms. The stochastic scheduler is similar to an adversary: at each time step, it picks some process to schedule. The main distinction is that, in our model, the scheduler's choices *contain some randomness.* In particular, a stochastic scheduler has a probability threshold $\theta > 0$ such that every (non-faulty) process is scheduled with probability at least θ in each step. In the following, we present an informal overview of our results. We direct the reader to [3] for a full version of our results.
We begin from the following observation.

THEOREM 1. *Let $\mathcal{S}$ be a stochastic scheduler with probability threshold $1 \geq \theta > 0$. Let A be bounded lock-free algorithm with progress bound T. Then A is wait-free with probability 1. Moreover, the expected time for an operation of A to complete is at most $(1/\theta)^T$.*

(Recall that a *bounded* lock-free algorithm guarantees that *some* process always makes progress within a finite progress bound.) In other words, for any such algorithm, the schedules which prevent a process from ever making progress must have probability mass 0. The intuition is that, with probability 1, each specific process eventually takes enough consecutive steps, implying that it completes its operation. This observation generalizes to any bounded minimal/maximal progress condition [12]: we show that under a stochastic scheduler, with probability 1, bounded minimal progress becomes maximal progress. However, this intuition is insufficient for explaining why lock-free data structures are *efficient* in practice; because it works for arbitrary algorithms,

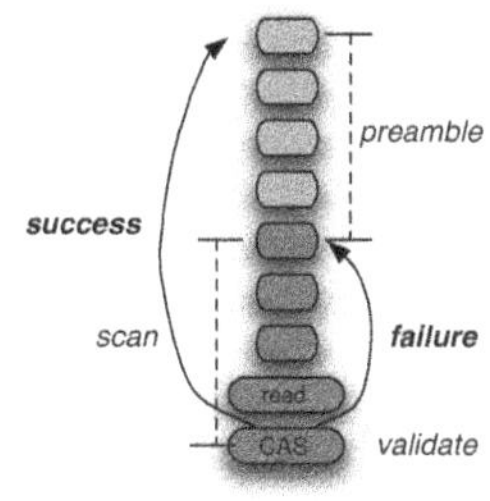

Figure 1: Structure of an algorithm in $SCU(q, s)$.

the upper bound it yields on the number of steps until an operation completes is unacceptably high.

Our main contribution is analyzing a general class of lock-free algorithms under a specific stochastic scheduler, and showing that not only are they wait-free with probability 1, but that in fact they provide a pragmatic bound on the number of steps until each operation completes.

We address a refined *uniform* stochastic scheduler, which schedules each non-faulty process with *uniform probability* in every step. Our experiments suggest that, in the long run, and for certain setups, the uniform stochastic scheduler is a reasonable approximation for a real-world scheduler.We emphasize that we do not claim real schedulers are uniform stochastic, but only that such a scheduler gives a good approximation of what happens in practice, for our complexity measures, over long executions.

We call the algorithmic class we analyze *single compare-and-swap universal* (SCU). An algorithm in this class is divided into a *preamble*, and a *scan-and-validate* phase. The preamble executes auxiliary code, such as local updates and memory allocation. In the second phase, the process first determines the data structure state by scanning the memory. It then locally computes the updated state, the state after its method is performed, and attempts to commit this state to memory by performing an atomic *compare-and-swap* (CAS) operation on one of the locations that was just read. If the CAS operation succeeds, then the state is updated, and the method call completes. Otherwise, if some other process changes the state inbetween the scan and the attempted update, then the CAS operation fails, and the process must restart its operation.

This algorithmic pattern is widely used to design lock-free data structures. It is known that every sequential object has a lock-free implementation in this class using a lock-free version of Herlihy's universal construction [10]. Instances of this class are used to obtain efficient data structures such as stacks [16], queues [15], or hash tables [7]. The read-copy-update (RCU) [8] synchronization mechanism employed by the Linux kernel is also an instance of this pattern.

We examine the class *SCU* under a uniform stochastic scheduler, and first observe that, in this setting, every such algorithm behaves as a Markov chain. The computational cost of interest is *system steps*, i.e. shared memory accesses by the processes. The complexity metrics we analyze are *individual latency*, which is the expected number of steps of the system until a specific process completes a method call, and *system latency*, which is the expected number of steps of the system to complete *some* method call. We bound these parameters by studying the stationary distribution of the Markov chain induced by the algorithm.

We prove two main results. The first is that, in the given setting, all algorithms in *SCU* have the property that the individual latency of any process is n times the system latency. In other words, the expected number of steps for any two processes to complete an operation is *the same*. Moreover, the expected number of steps for the system to complete any operation is the same as the expected number of steps for a specific process to complete an operation, divided by n. The second result is an upper bound of $O(q + s\sqrt{n})$ on the system latency, where q is the number of steps in the preamble, s is the number of steps in the scan-and-validate phase, and n is the number of processes. Specifically, the compare-and-swap operation at the end of a scan-and-validate loop is performed on a register R, and the register R is read immediately before the compare-and-swap operation. Please see Figure 1 for an illustration.

THEOREM 2. *Let A be an algorithm in $SCU(q, s)$. Then, under the uniform stochastic scheduler, the system latency of A is $O(q+s\sqrt{n})$, and the individual latency is $O(n(q+s\sqrt{n}))$.*

The key mathematical tool we use is *Markov chain lifting* [5, 9]. More precisely, for such algorithms, we prove that there exists a function which *lifts* the complex Markov chain induced by the algorithm to a simplified *system* chain. The asymptotics of the system latency can be determined directly from the minimal progress chain. In particular, we bound system latency by characterizing the behavior of a new type of *iterated* balls-into-bins game, consisting of iterations which end when a certain condition on the bins first occurs, after which some of the bins change their state and a new iteration begins. Using the lifting, we prove that the individual latency is always n times the system latency.

In summary, our analysis shows that, under an approximation of the real-world scheduler, a large class of lock-free algorithms provide virtually the same progress guarantees as wait-free ones, and that, roughly, the system completes requests at a rate that is n times that of individual processes. More generally, it provides for the first time an analytical framework for predicting the behavior of a class of concurrent algorithms, over long executions, under a scheduler that is not adversarial.

2. RELATED WORK

To the best of our knowledge, the only prior work which addresses a probabilistic scheduler for a shared memory environment is that of Aspnes [4], who gave a fast consensus algorithm under a probabilistic scheduler model different from the one considered in this paper. The observation that many lock-free algorithms behave as wait-free in practice was made by Herlihy and Shavit in the context of formalizing minimal and maximal progress conditions [12], and is well-known among practitioners. For example, reference [1, Figure 6] gives empirical results for the latency distribution of individual operations of a lock-free stack. A parallel line of work considered designing contention managers which convert lock-free or obstruction-free algorithms into wait-free ones, e.g. [6].

3. REFERENCES

[1] Samy Al-Bahra. Nonblocking algorithms and scalable multicore programming. *Commun. ACM*, 56(7):50–61, 2013.

[2] Dan Alistarh, Keren Censor-Hillel, and Nir Shavit. Are lock-free concurrent algorithms practically wait-free? To appear in Proceedings of the 46th Annual Symposium on the Theory of Computing (STOC), 2014.

[3] Dan Alistarh, Keren Censor-Hillel, and Nir Shavit. Are lock-free concurrent algorithms practically wait-free? *CoRR*, abs/1311.3200, 2013.

[4] James Aspnes. Fast deterministic consensus in a noisy environment. *J. Algorithms*, 45(1):16–39, 2002.

[5] Fang Chen, László Lovász, and Igor Pak. Lifting markov chains to speed up mixing. In *Proceedings of the thirty-first annual ACM symposium on Theory of computing*, STOC '99, pages 275–281, New York, NY, USA, 1999. ACM.

[6] Faith Ellen Fich, Victor Luchangco, Mark Moir, and Nir Shavit. Obstruction-free algorithms can be practically wait-free. In *Proceedings of the International Symposium on Distributed Computing*, pages 493–494, 2005.

[7] Keir Fraser. Practical lock-freedom. Technical Report UCAM-CL-TR-579, University of Cambridge, Computer Laboratory, February 2004.

[8] D. Guniguntala, P.E. McKenney, J. Triplett, and J. Walpole. The read-copy-update mechanism for supporting real-time applications on shared-memory multiprocessor systems with linux. *IBM Systems Journal*, 47(2):221–236, 2008.

[9] Thomas P. Hayes and Alistair Sinclair. Liftings of tree-structured markov chains. In *Proceedings of the 14th International conference on Randomization and Combinatorial Optimization*, APPROX/RANDOM'10, pages 602–616, Berlin, Heidelberg, 2010. Springer-Verlag.

[10] Maurice Herlihy. Wait-free synchronization. *ACM Transactions on Programming Languages and Systems*, 13(1):123–149, January 1991.

[11] Maurice Herlihy and Nir Shavit. *The art of multiprocessor programming.* Morgan Kaufmann, 2008.

[12] Maurice Herlihy and Nir Shavit. On the nature of progress. In *15th International Conference on Principles of Distributed Systems (OPODIS), Toulouse, France, December 13-16, 2011. Proceedings*, pages 313–328, 2011.

[13] Donald E. Knuth. Additional comments on a problem in concurrent programming control. *Commun. ACM*, 9(5):321–322, May 1966.

[14] Leslie Lamport. A new solution of Dijkstra's concurrent programming problem. *Commun. ACM*, 17(8):453–455, 1974.

[15] Maged M. Michael and Michael L. Scott. Simple, fast, and practical non-blocking and blocking concurrent queue algorithms. In *PODC*, pages 267–275, 1996.

[16] R. K. Treiber. Systems programming: Coping with parallelism. Technical Report RJ 5118, IBM Almaden Research Center, 1986.

Brief Announcement: A Generic Construction for Nonblocking Dual Containers*

Joseph Izraelevitz and Michael L. Scott
Computer Science Department, University of Rochester
Rochester, NY 14627-0226, USA
{jhi1, scott}@cs.rochester.edu

ABSTRACT

A dual container has the property that when it is empty, the remove method will insert an explicit reservation ("antidata") into the container, rather than returning an error flag. This convention gives the container explicit control over the order in which pending requests will be satisfied once data becomes available. The dual pattern also allows the method's caller to spin on a thread-local flag, avoiding memory contention. In this paper we introduce a new nonblocking construction that allows any nonblocking container for data to be paired with almost any nonblocking container for antidata. This construction provides a composite ordering discipline—e.g., it can satisfy pending pops from a stack in FIFO order, or satisfy pending dequeues in order of thread priority.

1. INTRODUCTION

Dual data structures [10] extend the definition of nonblocking progress to *partial* methods—those that must wait for a precondition to hold. Informally, a partial method is replaced with a total *request* method that either performs the original operation (if the precondition holds) or else modifies the data structure in a way that makes the caller's interest in the precondition (its *reservation*) visible to subsequent operations. The data structure can then assume full control over the order in which reservations should be satisfied when data becomes available, and each waiting thread can spin on a separate local flag, avoiding memory contention.

Scherer et al. [9] report that dual versions of the java.util.concurrent.SynchronousQueue improved the performance of task dispatch by as much as an order of magnitude. The Java library also includes a dual Exchanger class, in which operations of a single type "match up." Other synchronous queues include the flat combining version of Hendler et al. [3] and the elimination-diffraction trees of Afek et al. [1]. Recently [4], we have developed two fast dual queues based on the LCRQ algorithm of Morrison and Afek [8].

To the best of our knowledge, all published nonblocking dual containers have shared a common design pattern: at any given time, the structure holds either data or reservations ("antidata"), depending on whether there have been more inserts or remove_requests in the set of operations completed to date (in some cases the structure may also contain already-*satisfied* reservations, whose space has yet to be reclaimed). As the balance of completed operations changes over time, the structure "flips" back and forth between the two kinds of contents.

This design strategy has two significant drawbacks. First, adapting an existing container to make it a dual structure is generally nontrivial: not only must an operation that flips the structure linearize with respect to all other operations; if it satisfies a reservation it must both remove the reservation and unblock the waiting thread, all atomically. Second, since the same structure is used to hold either data or reservations, straightforward adaptations will apply the same ordering discipline to each.

We introduce a new construction that eliminates these drawbacks by joining a pair of subcontainers—one for data and one for antidata. Any existing concurrent container can be used for the data side; on the antidata side, we require that the remove method be partitioned into a peek method and a separate remove_conditional. Full details can be found in a companion technical report [5].

2. THE GENERIC DUAL CONSTRUCTION

When a thread calls the public insert method of our outer, "joined" container, we refer to its operation (and sometimes the thread itself) as having *positive polarity*. When a thread calls the public remove method, we refer to its operation (and sometimes the thread itself) as having *negative polarity*. Positive and negative operations are said to *correspond* when the former provides the datum for the latter.

We maintain the invariant that at any given linearization point, at most one of the underlying subcontainers is nonempty. Thus, in a positive operation, we may *satisfy* and remove an element from the antidata subcontainer, allowing the thread that is waiting on that element to return. Alternatively, we may verify that the antidata subcontainer is empty and instead insert into the data subcontainer. In a negative operation, we either remove and return an element from the data subcontainer or verify that the data subcontainer is empty and insert into the antidata subcontainer.

The outer container is said to have positive polarity when its data subcontainer is nonempty; it has negative polarity when its antidata subcontainer is nonempty. The only asymmetry—and it is a crucial one—is that the public insert method is total, while remove is partial: negative threads must wait, spinning on a local variable, until a datum is available.

We assume a conventional API for the data subcontainer. The insert method takes a datum (typically a pointer) as argument, and returns no useful value. The remove method takes no argument; it returns either a previously inserted datum or an EMPTY flag. We assume that the data subcontainer maintains a total order $<^+$ on its elements, and remove returns the smallest.

*This work was supported in part by NSF grants CCF-0963759, CCF-1116055, CNS-1116109, CNS-1319417, and CCF-1337224, and by support from the IBM Canada Centres for Advanced Study.

PODC'14, July 15–18, 2014, Paris, France.
ACM 978-1-4503-2944-6/14/07
http://dx.doi.org/10.1145/2611462.2611510 .

For the antidata subcontainer, we assume a similar insert method, which takes an antidatum as argument, and a similar total order $<^-$ on elements. We require, however, that removal be partitioned into a pair of methods. The peek method takes no argument; it returns an antidatum and a special *key*. The key can then be passed to a subsequent call to remove_conditional. The remove_conditional call removes the key's associated antidatum, so long as it its still the smallest antidatum under $<^-$. Between a peek that returns (v, k) and the first remove_conditional that takes k as argument, we require that any intervening peek also return (v, k). At the time of the original peek, v must be the smallest antidatum present under $<^-$. As it turns out, many nonblocking container objects can be converted easily to support peek and remove_conditional.

To verify that one subcontainer is empty and insert into the other, atomically, we introduce the concept of *placeholders*. Instead of actually storing data or antidata in a subcontainer, we instead store a pointer to a placeholder object. Each placeholder contains a datum or an antidatum, together with a small amount of metadata. Specifically, a placeholder can be in one of four states: unvalidated, aborted, validated, and satisfied. An unvalidated placeholder indicates an ongoing operation—the associated thread has begun to check for emptiness of the opposite subcontainer, but has not yet finished the check. An aborted placeholder indicates that the associated thread took too long in its emptiness check, and any information it has regarding the status of the opposite subcontainer may be out of date. A validated placeholder indicates that the associated thread has completed its emptiness check successfully and has inserted into the subcontainer of like polarity. Finally, a satisfied placeholder indicates that the associated data or antidata has been "mixed" with antidata or data from its corresponding operation.

On beginning a positive or negative operation on the outer container, we first store an unvalidated placeholder in the subcontainer of like polarity. We then check for emptiness of the opposite subcontainer by repeatedly removing elements. If we find a validated placeholder, we mix it with our own data or antidata, transition it from validated to satisfied, and return, leaving our own unvalidated placeholder behind. If we find an unvalidated placeholder, we abort it, indicating that it has been removed from its subcontainer and that any information the owning thread may have had regarding the polarity of the outer container is now out of date. Finally, if we discover that the opposite subcontainer is empty, we can go back to our stored placeholder and attempt to validate it, completing our operation. If we find, however, that our placeholder has been aborted, then some thread of opposite polarity has removed us from our subcontainer. If that left our subcontainer empty, the other thread may have validated its own placeholder and returned successfully. We must therefore retry our operation from the beginning. The possibility that two threads, running more or less in tandem, may abort each other's placeholders—and both then need to retry—implies that our construction is merely obstruction free.

One detail remains to be addressed. While a partial method of a dual data structure may block when a precondition is not met, the definitions of Scherer and Scott place strict limits on this blocking [10]. In particular, if a thread inserts a datum into a container, and another thread is waiting for that datum, the waiting thread must wake up "right away." The description of our construction so far admits the possibility that a positive thread will remove a placeholder from the negative subcontainer and then wait an unbounded length of time (e.g., due to preemption by the operating system) before actually satisfying the placeholder and allowing its owner to return. In the meantime, an unbounded number of other operations (of either polarity) may complete.

We term this issue the *preemption window*. We close it with the peek and remove_conditional methods. A positive thread T, instead of simply removing a placeholder from the negative subcontainer, first peeks at the head placeholder and satisfies or aborts it. Only then does it remove that placeholder from the subcontainer. Any other thread that discovers a satisfied or aborted placeholder can help T's operation by removing the placeholder for it. By updating placeholders while they are still in the negative subcontainer, we order all waiting threads, guaranteeing that they are able to return without any further delay.

3. CORRECTNESS

Detailed proofs of safety and liveness can be found in a companion technical report [5]. We assume an API, suggested by Scherer & Scott [10], that divides remove into separate remove_request and remove_followup methods. The first of these returns a special *ticket* value; the latter takes this ticket as argument and *succeeds* or *fails* depending on whether a matching insert has yet occurred in the object's history. We term the sequential object that exports this API a *two-order container* (TOC). The key difference between a conventional (total) concurrent container and a dual container is that spins on remove_followup can be entirely thread-local, with no impact on the contention observed by other threads.

Using the divided API, we establish the following:

THEOREM 1 (SAFETY). *Any realizable history of the generic dual container that comprises only completed operations is equivalent to a legal history of the TOC.*

THEOREM 2 (LIVENESS). *If both subcontainers of the generic dual container are correct and nonblocking, then the generic dual container itself is obstruction free.*

THEOREM 3 (IMMEDIATE WAKEUP). *If a thread A performs an unsuccessful remove_followup operation, u^A, and some other thread B performs a successful remove_followup operation, s^B, between A's remove_request, r^A, and u^A, then $r^B <^- r^A$ or i^B linearizes before r^A, where i^B is the insert operation that matches r^B.* In other words, if r^A and r^B are in the antidata subcontainer at the same time, and if $r^A <^- r^B$, then it is not possible for A to experience an unsuccessful remove_followup after B has experienced a successful remove_followup. Even more informally, a waiting thread is guaranteed to wake up immediately after the corresponding insert.

THEOREM 4 (CONTENTION FREEDOM). *An unsuccessful remove_followup() operation performs no remote memory accesses.*

4. EXPERIMENTAL RESULTS

We implemented the generic dual, all subcontainers, and comparison structures in C++ 11. All code was compiled using gcc 4.8.2 at the -O3 optimization level, and run on Fedora Core 19 Linux. Our hardware was a machine with two six-core, two-way hyperthreaded Intel Xeon E5-2430 processors at 2.20 GHz, supporting up to 24 hardware threads. The L3 cache (15 MB) is shared by all cores of a given processor; L1 and L2 caches are per-core private. To maximize cache locality, we pinned each thread to its core, filling a processor first using each core and then each hyperthread before moving to the second processor.

We measure throughput using a *hot potato* microbenchmark [4]. This test, based on the children's game, allows each thread to access a dual structure randomly, choosing on each iteration whether to insert or remove an element. However, at the beginning of the test, one thread inserts the *hot potato*, a special data value, into

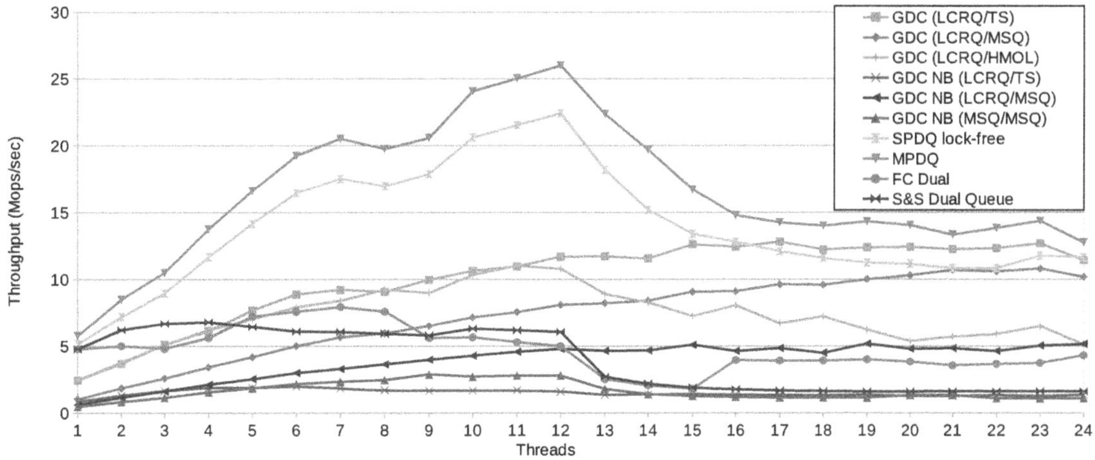

Figure 1: Performance on hot potato benchmark (second processor engaged at 13 cores)

the container. If any thread removes the hot potato, it waits a set amount of time ($1\mu s$) before reinserting the value then continues to randomly operate on the container. The reinsertion convention eliminates the possibility of deadlock. We ran each test for two seconds, and report the maximum throughput of five runs.

We test several combinations of subcontainers for our generic dual container (GDC), with and without the peek operation to close the preemption window: **LCRQ(+), Treiber stack(−), blocking**: the fastest combination; uses Morrison and Afek's LCRQ [8] for data and the Treiber stack [11] for antidata. **LCRQ(+), Treiber stack(−), nonblocking:** A comparison to demonstrate the impact of closing the preemption window. **LCRQ(+), M&S Queue** [7]**(−), blocking:** A FIFO dual queue, suitable for direct comparison to the MPDQ, SPDQ, or S&S dual queue. **LCRQ(+), M&S Queue(−), nonblocking:** Another comparison to demonstrate the impact of closing the preemption window, but with a more efficient peek than in the Treiber stack. **M&S Queue(+), M&S Queue(−), nonblocking:** demonstrates the baseline cost of our construction when compared directly to the S&S dual queue. **LCRQ(+), H&M Ordered List(−), blocking:** orders waiting threads based on priority, using the lock-free ordered list of Harris and Michael [2, 6].

For comparison purposes, we also test existing nonblocking dual containers: **MPDQ:** a fast but blocking dual queue derived from the LCRQ [4]. **SPDQ lock-free:** an alternative, lock-free derivative of the LCRQ [4]. **S&S Dual Queue:** the dual queue of Scherer & Scott [10]. **FC Dual Queue:** a flat-combining dual queue inspired by the work of Hendler et al. [3, 4].

With the LCRQ as the data subcontainer, and ignoring the preemption window, our generic dual outperforms traditional dual structures, including the S&S dual queue and the flat combining queue. Clearly, a fast base algorithm matters enormously. The antidata subcontainer also matters: using the Treiber stack over the M&S queue provides a consistent 25% speedup in the blocking case.

Closing the preemption window incurs a significant performance cost, especially when crossing the boundary between chips. With all threads competing to satisfy the same peeked-at placeholder, the cache line tends to bounce between processors. Additional contention arises when the peek modification requires internal caching of values (as in the Treiber stack). If all one wants in practice is a fast shared buffer, the "not quite nonblocking" version of our construction (with the preemption window intact) will deliver superior performance. Similarly, if mixed ordering disciplines are not required, the (non-generic) MPDQ and SPDQ will provide very fast FIFO handling of both data and antidata.

5. REFERENCES

[1] Y. Afek, G. Korland, M. Natanzon, and N. Shavit. Scalable producer-consumer pools based on elimination-diffraction trees. In *16th Intl. Euro-Par Conf. on Parallel Processing*, Ischia, Italy, Aug.–Sep. 2010.

[2] T. L. Harris. A pragmatic implementation of non-blocking linked-lists. In *15th Intl. Symp. on Distributed Computing (DISC)*, Lisbon, Portugal, Oct. 2001.

[3] D. Hendler, I. Incze, N. Shavit, and M. Tzafrir. Scalable flat-combining based synchronous queues. In *24th Intl. Conf. on Distributed Computing (DISC)*, Sept. 2010.

[4] J. Izraelevitz and M. L. Scott. Fast dual ring queues (brief announcement). In *26th ACM Symp. on Parallel Algorithms and Architectures (SPAA)*, Prague, Czech Republic, June 2014. Expanded version available as TR 990, Dept. of Computer Science, Univ. of Rochester, Jan. 2014.

[5] J. Izraelevitz and M. L. Scott. A generic construction for nonblocking dual containers. Technical Report TR 992, Dept. of Computer Science, Univ. of Rochester, May 2014.

[6] M. M. Michael. High performance dynamic lock-free hash tables and list-based sets. In *14th ACM Symp. on Parallel Algorithms and Architectures (SPAA)*, Winnipeg, MB, Canada, Aug. 2002.

[7] M. M. Michael and M. L. Scott. Simple, fast, and practical non-blocking and blocking concurrent queue algorithms. In *15th ACM Symp. on Principles of Distributed Computing (PODC)*, Philadelphia, PA, May 1996.

[8] A. Morrison and Y. Afek. Fast concurrent queues for x86 processors. In *18th ACM Symp. on Principles and Practice of Parallel Programming (PPoPP)*, Shenzhen, China, Feb. 2013.

[9] W. N. Scherer III, D. Lea, and M. L. Scott. Scalable synchronous queues. *Communications of the ACM*, 52(5):100–108, May 2009.

[10] W. N. Scherer III and M. L. Scott. Nonblocking concurrent data structures with condition synchronization. In *18th Intl. Symp. on Distributed Computing (DISC)*, Amsterdam, The Netherlands, Oct. 2004.

[11] R. K. Treiber. Systems programming: Coping with parallelism. Technical Report RJ 5118, IBM Almaden Research Center, Apr. 1986.

Multi-Message Broadcast with Abstract MAC Layers and Unreliable Links*

Mohsen Ghaffari
MIT CSAIL
Cambridge, MA
ghaffari@csail.mit.edu

Erez Kantor
MIT CSAIL
Cambridge, MA
erezk@csail.mit.edu

Nancy Lynch
MIT CSAIL
Cambridge, MA
lynch@csail.mit.edu

Calvin Newport
Georgetown University
Washington, DC
cnewport@cs.georgetown.edu

ABSTRACT

We study the multi-message broadcast problem using abstract MAC layer models of wireless networks. These models capture the key guarantees of existing MAC layers while abstracting away low-level details such as signal propagation and contention. We begin by studying upper and lower bounds for this problem in a *standard abstract MAC layer model*—identifying an interesting dependence between the structure of unreliable links and achievable time complexity. In more detail, given a restriction that devices connected directly by an unreliable link are not too far from each other in the reliable link topology, we can (almost) match the efficiency of the reliable case. For the related restriction, however, that two devices connected by an unreliable link are not too far from each other in geographic distance, we prove a new lower bound that shows that this efficiency is impossible. We then investigate how much extra power must be added to the model to enable a new order of magnitude of efficiency. In more detail, we consider an *enhanced abstract MAC layer model* and present a new multi-message broadcast algorithm that (under certain natural assumptions) solves the problem in this model faster than any known solutions in an abstract MAC layer setting.

Categories and Subject Descriptors

F.2.2 [**Analysis of Algorithms and Problem Complexity**]: Non-numerical Algorithms and Problems—*Computations on Discrete Structures*; G.2.2 [**Discrete Mathematics**]: Graph Theory—*Network Problems*

PODC'14, July 15–18, 2014, Paris, France.

ACM 978-1-4503-2944-6/14/07 ...$15.00. http://dx.doi.org/10.1145/2611462.2611492.

*Supported in a part by AFOSR FA9550-13-1-0042, the Ford University Research Grant Program, and NSF grants Nos. CCF-1320279, CCF-0939370, CCF-1217506, CCF-AF-0937274, and the MIT Center for Wireless Networks and Mobile Computing.

Keywords

wireless networks; abstract MAC layer; broadcast

1. INTRODUCTION

Most existing work on distributed algorithms for wireless networks assumes low-level synchronous models that require algorithms to deal directly with link-layer issues such as signal fading (e.g., [13, 21, 22]) and contention (e.g., [2, 12, 16, 28]). These low-level models are appropriate for answering basic science questions about the capabilities and limits of wireless communication. We argue, however, that they are often *not* appropriate for designing and analyzing algorithms meant for real world deployment, because: (1) they fail to capture the unpredictable reality of real radio signal propagation (which tends not to follow simple collision or fading rules [33]); (2) they do not address issues like network coexistence (it is rarely true that your algorithm is alone in using the wireless channel); and (3) they ignore the presence of general purpose MAC layers which are standard and hard to bypass in existing devices.

In [29,30], we introduced the *abstract MAC layer* approach as an alternative to low-level models for studying wireless algorithms. This approach moves the algorithm designer up the network stack by modeling the basic guarantees of most existing wireless MAC layers. In doing so, it abstracts away low level issues such as signal fading and contention, instead capturing the impact of this behavior on higher layers with model uncertainty. Because abstract MAC layers are defined to maintain the basic guarantees of most standard wireless MAC layers, algorithms developed in such models can be deployed on existing devices while maintaining their formally proved properties.

In this paper, we study the basic communication primitive of *multi-message broadcast* (a subset of devices start with one or more messages they need to disseminate to the whole network) in abstract MAC layer models that include unreliable links. We produce new upper and lower bounds, and explore new model variants. Our results, summarized below and in Figure 1, provide new theoretical insight into the relationship between unreliability and efficiency, and identify practical algorithmic strategies.

Abstract MAC Layer Models. Abstract MAC layer models provide devices with an acknowledged local broadcast primitive that guarantees to deliver a message to a device's reliable neighbors (captured by a graph G) and possibly some arbitrary subset of additional unreliable neighbors (captured by a graph G'). At some point after the message is delivered, the sender receives an acknowledgment.[1] The performance of the model in a given execution is defined by two constants: F_{ack}, the maximum time for a given local broadcast to complete and be acknowledged, and F_{prog}, the maximum time for a device to receive *some* message when at least one nearby device is broadcasting. We note that in both theory and practice, $F_{prog} \ll F_{ack}$.[2]

Results. In this paper, we consider the multi-message broadcast (MMB) problem. This problem distributes $k \geq 1$ messages to devices at the beginning of an execution, where k is not known in advance. It is considered solved once all messages are delivered to all nodes. We begin by studying a natural MMB strategy called Basic Multi-Message Broadcast (BMMB) in what we call the *standard abstract MAC layer* model: a basic model that captures the key guarantees of existing MAC layers. The BMMB algorithm implements an expected strategy for broadcast: on first receiving a message m, from the environment or from another device, add it to your FIFO queue of messages to broadcast; going forward, discard any additional copies of m that you receive. In previous work [30], we proved that BMMB solves the problem in $O(DF_{prog} + kF_{ack})$ time in the standard abstract MAC layer model under the strong assumption that $G' = G$, i.e., there are no unreliable links, and D is the diameter of G. In the first part of this paper, we investigate the performance of strategy in the presence of unreliability.

We begin by considering the case where G' is arbitrary; i.e., there are no constraints on the structure of unreliable links. Under this pessimistic regime, we reanalyze BMMB, proving a new guarantee of $O((D + k)F_{ack})$ time, which is (potentially) much slower than what is possible when $G' = G$. The presence of unreliable edges, it turns out, breaks the careful induction at the core of the $G' = G$ result, as they allow old messages to arrive unexpectedly from farther away in the network at inopportune points in an execution.

Not satisfied with this slow-down, we then consider the case of an *r-restricted* G'—a natural constraint that only allows G' edges between nodes within r hops in G. Under these constraints, we can now show that BMMB solves the problem in $O(DF_{prog} + r \cdot k \cdot F_{ack})$ time, which is close to the $G' = G$ case for small r. This proof discards the core strategy of the $G' = G$ case, which depends heavily on the lack of unreliable links, and instead uses a new type of pipelining argument that carefully accounts for the possible message behavior over r-restricted G' links.

We conclude our investigation of BMMB by studying the *grey zone* constraint [4, 20]: a natural geographic restriction on G' that generalizes the unit disk graph model. Here we prove the perhaps surprising lower bound result that *every MMB algorithm* requires $\Omega((D + k)F_{ack})$ time, in the worst case, to solve the problem under this constraint. This result establishes the optimality of our analysis of BMMB under the grey zone constraint, as well as for arbitrary G', and opens an intriguing gap between the grey zone and r-restricted assumptions. At the core of this lower bound is a careful scheduling strategy that synchronizes broadcasters in two parallel lines to a sufficient degree to allow their messages to cause mutual delay.

Having established the limits of MMB in the standard abstract MAC layer model, we then explore the possibility of adding more power to the model to enable more efficient solutions. In particular, we use the enhanced abstract MAC layer model of [30] which also allows nodes to abort transmissions in progress and use knowledge of F_{prog} and F_{ack}. Combining this model with the grey zone constraint on G', we describe and analyze a new algorithm, which we call Fast Multi-Message Broadcast (FMMB), that solves the MMB problem in $O((D \log n + k \log n + \log^3 n)F_{prog})$ time (with high probability in the network size, n^3)—avoiding an F_{ack} term altogether. This algorithm begins by building a maximal independent set (a subroutine of independent interest), then efficiently gathers and spreads messages over the overlay network defined by these nodes. We note that the assumptions that separate the enhanced from standard model were chosen in part because they are feasible to implement using existing technology.

Discussion. From a theoretical perspective, the new upper and lower bounds proved in this paper emphasize the perhaps surprising insight that the efficiency of message dissemination depends on the *structure* of unreliability, not the *quantity*. We are able, for example, to solve MMB fast with an r-restricted G'. This constraint allows for a large number of unreliable edges in every neighborhood, and only forbids these edges from covering long distances in G. Our lower bound, on the other hand, demonstrates that even a small number of unreliable edges is sufficient to slow down any MMB solution, so long as these edges are allowed to cover large distances in G.

From a practical perspective, our efficient time bounds for BMMB under the (reasonable) r-restricted assumption helps explain why straightforward flooding strategies tend to work well in real networks. In addition, our enhanced MAC layer results provide feedback to MAC layer designers, indicating that the ability to abort messages might prove crucial for enabling more efficient distributed protocols running on these layers.

Related Work. The study of broadcast in wireless networks has a long line of history, dating back to 1985 work

[1]The acknowledgment in this model describes the behavior of a standard MAC layer asking for the next message to broadcast from the send queue; i.e., after a CSMA back-off protocol finishes with a given packet. It does not represent an acknowledgment explicitly sent from the receivers.

[2]From a theory perspective, we note that standard probabilistic strategies like *decay* (cycle through an exponentially decreasing series of broadcast probabilities), when analyzed in graph-based, low-level wireless models, offer F_{prog} values that are polylogarthmic in the maximum possible contention, while F_{ack} values can be linear (or worse) in this same parameter (see [19] for more discussion). From a practical perspective, this gap is easily demonstrated. Consider, for example, a star network topology centered on device u where all points in the star have a message to broadcast. If these nodes are using standard back-off style strategies, u will receive *some* message quickly. But regardless of how contention is managed, there are some points in the star that will have to wait a long time (i.e., linear in the star size) for their turn.

[3]We define high probability to be at least $1 - 1/n$. We note that BMMB's guarantees are deterministic but that our lower bound works even for randomized solutions.

Model/G' Const.	$G' = G$	r-Restricted	Grey Zone
Standard	$O(DF_{prog} + kF_{ack})$ [30]	$O(DF_{prog} + rkF_{ack})$	$\Theta((D+k)F_{ack})$
Enhanced	*same as grey zone*	*open*	$O((D + k\log n + \log^3 n)F_{prog})$

Figure 1: A summary of results categorized by model type and constraints assumed regarding G'. With the exception of the $G' = G$ result for the standard model, the results in this table are proved for the first time in this paper. We note that the grey zone result for the standard model summarizes two separate results: an upper bound and matching lower bound. These two results also hold for arbitrary G'.

of Chalamatac and Kutten [5], and has since received a vast amount of attention (see e.g., [1,3,11,14,15,17,23,26,27,31, 34]). Most of this existing work deals directly with low-level issues such as managing contention on the shared medium.

The *abstract MAC layer* model was proposed in [29,30] as an alternative approach, which moves up the network stack and abstracts away low level issues with model uncertainty. This model has since been used to study a variety of problems; e.g., [6,7,9,10,24,25,32]. Most relevant to this paper is the work of [29] and subsequently [24], which study broadcast in various abstract MAC layer models, but under the assumption of no unreliable edges.

A core property of the abstract MAC layer models studied in this paper, by contrast, is the presence of unreliable links in addition to reliable links. A lower level model also assuming these dual link types was introduced by Clementi et al. [8], where it was called the *dynamic fault* model. We independently reintroduced the model in [29] with the name *dual graph* model. By now it is well-known that most problems that are simple in the absence of unreliability (when $G' = G$), become significantly harder in its presence (when $G' \neq G$); e.g., [4,19,20,29]. For instance, in the dual graph model with an offline adaptive adversary, single-message broadcast require $\Omega(n)$ rounds, even in constant diameter graphs [29]. We emphasize, however, that this existing work on dual graphs focuses on low level models, whereas this paper carries this behavior to a higher level of abstraction.

2. MODEL AND PROBLEM

There is no single abstract MAC layer model, but instead many different such models that all share the same strategy of abstracting standard wireless link layer behavior and therefore preventing the algorithm from having to deal directly with low level wireless behavior. Below we define the basics shared by these models, then specify the two variants studied in this paper. We conclude by formalizing the multi-message broadcast problem.

Abstract MAC Layer Basics. Abstract MAC layer models typically define the connectivity of a radio network with a pair of graphs, G and G', where $G = (V, E)$, $G' = (V, E')$, and $E \subseteq E'$. The n vertices in V correspond to the wireless devices (which we call *nodes* in this paper), while the edges in G and G' describe the communication topology. At a high-level, edges in E indicate reliable links over which the model can always deliver messages, while edges in $E' \setminus E$ indicate unreliable links over which the model sometimes delivers messages and sometimes does not.

The model provides an acknowledged local broadcast primitive. To simplify the definition of this primitive, assume without loss of generality that all local broadcast messages are unique. When a node $u \in V$ *broadcasts* a message m, the model delivers the message to all neighbors in E and (perhaps) *some* neighbors in $E' \setminus E$. It then returns an *acknowledgment* of m to u indicating the broadcast is complete. These are the only message deliveries performed by the model. We assume nodes are well-formed in the sense that they always wait for the acknowledgment of their current message before initiating a new broadcast.

This model provides two timing bounds, defined with respect to two positive constants, F_{ack} and F_{prog} which are fixed for each execution. The first is the *acknowledgment* bound, which guarantees that each broadcast will complete and be acknowledged within F_{ack} time. The second is the *progress* bound, which guarantees the following slightly more complex condition: fix some $(u, v) \in E$ and interval of length F_{prog} throughout which u is broadcasting a message m; during this interval v must receive some message (though not necessarily m). The progress bound, in other words, bounds the time for a node to receive some message when at least one of its neighbors is broadcasting. As mentioned in the introduction, in both theory and practice it is reasonable to assume that F_{prog} is much smaller than F_{ack}. We emphasize that in abstract MAC layer models, the choice of which neighbors in $E' \setminus E$ receive a given message, as well as the order of receive events, are determined non-deterministically by an arbitrary *message scheduler*. The timing of these events is also determined non-deterministically by the scheduler, constrained only by the above time bounds.

We assume that nodes have unique ids. We also assume that each node can differentiate between their neighbors in E and $E' \setminus E$, an assumption justified by the standard practice in real networks of assessing link quality. For a given network definition (G, G'), we use D to describe the diameter of G, and $d_G(u, v)$, for $u, v \in V$, to describe the shortest path distance between u and v in G. We define D' and $d_{G'}$ similarly, but for G'. Finally, when proving lower bounds, we explicitly model randomness by passing each node at the beginning of the execution sufficiently many random bits to resolve probabilistic choices.

The Standard Abstract MAC Layer. The standard abstract MAC layer models nodes as event-driven automata. It assumes that an environment abstraction fires a *wake-up* event at each node at the beginning of each execution. The environment is also responsible for any events specific to the problem being solved. In multi-message broadcast, for example, the environment provides the broadcast messages to nodes at the beginning of the execution.

The Enhanced Abstract MAC Layer. The enhanced abstract MAC layer model differs from the standard model in two ways. First, it allows nodes access to time (formally, they can set timers that trigger events when they expire), and assumes nodes know F_{ack} and F_{prog}. Second, the model also provides nodes an *abort* interface that allows them to abort a broadcast in progress.

Restrictions on G'. When studying a problem in an abstract MAC layer model, it is often useful to consider constraints on the graph G'. In the original paper on these models [29], for example, we considered the very strong constraint that $G' = G$. In this paper, we consider three more general constraints on G'.

First, we say G' is *arbitrary* to indicate that we place no restrictions on its definitions (other than the default constraint of $E \subset E'$). Second, we say G' is *r-restricted*, for some $r \geq 1$, if for every $(u, v) \in E'$, $d_G(u, v) \leq r$. In studying this constraint, we sometimes use the notation G^r to describe the graph with edges between every $u, v \in V$, $u \neq v$, where u and v are within r hops in G. An r-restricted G' is a subgraph of G^r. Third, we say G' is *grey zone restricted* if (in addition to the general constraint of $E \subseteq E'$), the following is also true: we can embed the nodes in the Euclidean plane, giving each $v \in V$ a position $p(v) \in \mathbb{R}^2$ such that (1) For each pair of nodes $v, u \in V$, $(v, u) \in E$ if and only if $\|p(v) - p(u)\|_2 \leq 1$, and (2) for each pair of nodes $v, u \in V$, if $(v, u) \in E'$, then $\|p(v) - p(u)\|_2 \leq c$, where c is a universal constant such that $c \geq 1$. The range between 1 and c, in other words, describes a *grey zone* in which communication is uncertain. We emphasize that the second property described above only states that edges in E' cannot be longer than c, it does not require that every pair of nodes that have distance less than or equal to c must be G'-neighbors.

The Multi-Message Broadcast Problem. The multi-message broadcast (MMB) problem assumes the environment injects $k \geq 1$ messages into the network at the beginning of an execution,[4] perhaps providing multiple messages to the same node. We assume k is not known in advance. The problem is solved once every message m, starting at some node u, reaches every node in u's connected component in G. To achieve strong upper bound we do not, in other words, assume that G is connected. We treat messages as black boxes that cannot be combined; for example, we do not consider network coding solutions. We also assume that only a constant number of these messages can fit into a single local broadcast message. In this paper, we consider both deterministic and randomized algorithms. We require randomized solutions to solve the problem with high probability (w.h.p.), which we define to be at least $1 - 1/n$.

3. MULTI-MESSAGE BROADCAST WITH A STANDARD ABSTRACT MAC LAYER

In this section we study multi-message broadcast in what we call the *standard abstract MAC layer model*. As mentioned in the introduction, in previous work [29, 30] we described the *Basic Multi-Message Broadcast* (BMMB) algorithm, which implements the standard strategy of broadcasting each message only the first time you receive it. In more detail, the BMMB protocol works as follows. Every process i maintains a FIFO queue and list of received messages. When a process i receives a message m from the MAC layer it checks whether it already received it. If it has already received it, it discards the message. Otherwise, process i adds m to the back of its queue. Process i broadcasts the message at the head of its queue (if its queue is not empty) and waits for acknowledgment from the MAC layer. When the MAC layer acknowledges the message, i removes it from the queue and moves on to the next message (if any).

[4] A general version of the MMB problem, in which the messages arrive in an online manner, is studied in [30] and elsewhere.

In [30], we proved that BMMB solves the MMB problem in $O(DF_{prog} + kF_{ack})$ time under the strong assumption that $G' = G$. In the two subsections that follow, we study its behavior under more general definitions of G'. We then prove a lower bound for all MMB solutions.

3.1 The BMMB Algorithm for Arbitrary G'

The natural next step in analyzing BMMB is considering its performance in our model when we assume an arbitrary G'. It is easy to show, of course, that the algorithm always terminates in $O(DkF_{ack})$ time, as a message m, on arriving at a new hop, must wait for at most $O(k)$ messages to be broadcast before it too is broadcast. Here we apply a more detailed pipeline argument to show that BMMB performs better than this basic bound in this difficult setting.

Theorem 3.1. *The BMMB algorithm solves the MMB problem in $O((D + k)F_{ack})$ time in the standard abstract MAC layer model for arbitrary G'.*

Proof. For the sake of analysis, assume each node u keeps a *sent* set to which it adds every message that it has successfully broadcast (i.e., broadcast and received an ack for). Next, fix some execution and an arbitrary message m from among the k messages provided to BMMB to broadcast in this execution. Let $u_m \in V$ be the node that is provided m by the environment at the start of the execution. For each node $v \in V$, let $d_v = d_G(v, u_m)$. For each $\ell \in [1, k]$, let $t_\ell(v) = d_v + \ell$.

Our strategy is to prove the following key claim: *for each $\ell \in [1, k]$ and node v, after $t_\ell(v)F_{ack}$ time, node v's sent set either: (1) contains m; or (2) contains at least ℓ other messages.* Once we prove this claim, it will then follow that after $t_k(v)F_{ack} \leq (D+k)F_{ack}$ time, v has sent (and thus also received) m. Applying this to all nodes and all k messages then yields the theorem statement. We prove our key claim using induction on $h = d_v + \ell$. For the base case of $h = 0$, notice that $h = 0$ implies $d_v = 0$. This, in turn, reduces the key claim to a statement about the local queue of v that follows directly from the definition of the algorithm.

For the inductive step, consider some v such that $d_v + \ell = h$. To show the key claim holds for $t_\ell(v) = h$, we leverage the inductive hypothesis for nearby nodes and combinations of relevant values that sum to $h - 1$. First, we note that if $d_v = 0$, then the base case argument once again applies. Assume, therefore, that $d_v \geq 1$. Next, fix some G-neighbor u of v such that $d_u = d_v - 1$. By the induction hypothesis, we know that after $s = t_{\ell-1}(v)F_{ack} = t_\ell(u)F_{ack}$ time: v has either sent m or sent $\ell - 1$ other messages, and u has either sent m or sent ℓ other messages. If v has sent m or at least ℓ messages by s then we are done. If it has not, then by time s, u will have either sent it m or a new message (i.e., distinct from the $\ell - 1$ messages v has already sent by time s). In either case, in the F_{ack} time that passes between s and $t_\ell(v)F_{ack}$, v will either send m or an ℓth message, establishing the key claim for $t_\ell(v) = h$. □

3.2 The BMMB Algorithm for r-Restricted G'

We have shown that moving from $G' = G$ to an unrestricted definition of G' slows down the performance of BMMB; i.e., replacing a DF_{prog} factor with DF_{ack}, which might be substantially slower. In this section we seek a middle ground—attempting to identify just enough constraints on G' to enable faster MMB performance. In more detail, we study BMMB with an r-restricted G' and prove that its performance scales well with r:

Theorem 3.2. *For any $r \geq 1$, the BMMB algorithm solves the MMB problem in $O(DF_{prog} + rkF_{ack})$ time in the standard abstract MAC layer model with an r-restricted G'.*

Notice that for small r, this bound is better than the $O((D+k)F_{ack})$ bound we established in Theorem 3.1 for arbitrary G', and comes close to matching the bound proved in [30] for the case where $G' = G$. This result implies the DF_{ack} factor of the arbitrary G' bound is somehow dependent on the possibility of G' edges between nodes distant in G. We emphasize that the above bound does not follow naturally from the $O(DF_{prog} + kF_{ack})$ bound for $G' = G$. The presence of unreliability fundamentally disrupts the core induction of this existing bound and requires a new approach.

The complete proof for Theorem 3.2 can be found in the full version of this paper [18]. To provide intuition for this argument, however, we present below a summary of the full proof and establish its key lemma.

In more detail, fix some execution and an arbitrary message m, among the k messages provided to BMMB to broadcast in this execution, that arrive at some node $i_0 \in V$ at time $t = 0$. For use in our complexity analysis, we define certain time bounds. For integers $\ell \geq 1$ and $d \geq 0$, we define:

$$t_{d,\ell} := (d + (r+1)\ell - 2) \cdot F_{prog} + r \cdot (\ell - 1) \cdot F_{ack} \ .$$

We also use the notation *completes*, with respect to a node u and message m, to describe the event of node u receiving an acknowledgment for m. The key lemma in our proof of Theorem 3.2 is:

Lemma 3.3. *Let j be a node at distance $d = d_G(i_0, j)$ from i_0 in G. Let ℓ be any positive integer. Then: (1) Either j receives m or it receives at least ℓ messages by time $t_{d,\ell}$. (2) Either j completes m or it completes at least ℓ messages by time $t_{d,\ell} + F_{ack}$.*

Given that $t_{D,k} = O(DF_{prog} + r \cdot k \cdot F_{ack})$, Theorem 3.2 follows directly from this lemma. We note that in the setting where $G' = G$, when a node j has completed sending a message, it follows that all of its neighbors must have received it. In our setting, however, where $G' \neq G$, we must also consider G' neighbors for which this is not true. In fact, although, one might expect that G' neighbors will receive all message within $r \cdot F_{ack}$ time, that too turns out to be not true, due to possible interference with other messages. To cope with such problems, we carry out a finer analysis of conditions that guarantee progress of messages through the network. Specifically, we define two *positive progress* scenarios, *fast positive progress* and *slow positive progress*, in which node i is guaranteed to receive some "new" message in F_{prog} time and in $z \cdot F_{ack}$ time, respectively (where z is some positive integer). (Recall that the basic progress definition does not require that the received message is "new": this is a condition we must established with respect to our given algorithm.)

- ***Fast positive progress:*** Suppose that at time t, (1) every message that i has received is already completed at all of i's neighbors in G'; and (2) some neighbor j of i in G has received some message that i has not yet received. Then i will receive a new message within F_{prog} time.
- ***Slow positive progress:*** Suppose that at time t, (1) j has completed at least $\ell - 1$ messages; (2) every message that j has completed is also completed at all of j's neighbors in G^z; and (3) there exists at least one neighbor of j in G^z that has received at least ℓ messages. Then j will receive at least ℓ messages by time $t + z \cdot F_{ack}$.

With these preliminaries established, we can now sketch our proof for our key lemma.

Proof Sketch (for Lemma 3.3). We use a double induction for ℓ as an "outer" induction and for distance d as an "inner" induction. Such a double induction was also used in [29, 30] for the case where $G' = G$. However, the current used different bounds and different inductive hypotheses, based on the two positive progress scenarios above. For the base where $\ell = 1$, we prove Part 1 by induction on d. We assume that Part 1 holds for $d - 1$. Thus, there exists a neighbor j' of j in G at distance $d - 1$ from i_0 (in G) such that j' receives at least one message by time $t_{d-1,1}$. Thus, j receives at least one message by time $t_{d-1,1} + F_{prog}$. Part 1 follows, since $t_{d,1} = t_{d-1,1} + F_{prog}$. Hence, also, j will complete its first message by time $t_{d,1} + F_{ack}$ as needed for Part 2.

Now, we are ready to show the inductive step for ℓ. Let $\ell \geq 2$. We assume the lemma statement for $\ell - 1$ (and for all d) and prove it for ℓ. To prove the lemma statement for ℓ, we use a second, "inner" induction, on the distance d (in G) from i_0 and the destination j. For the base, $d = 0$, Part 1 follows immediately. Part 2 follows, since (1) $\ell F_{ack} \leq t_{\ell,0}$; (2) if the position of m in $bcastq_{i_0}$ is $\leq \ell$, then i_0 completes m by time ℓF_{ack}; and (3) if the position of m in $bcastq_{i_0}$ is greater than ℓ, then i_0 completes at least ℓ messages by time ℓF_{ack}.

For the inductive step of the inner induction, we assume $d \geq 1$. Assume both parts of the lemma for (1) $\ell - 1$ (as "outer" induction hypothesis) for all distances; and (2) for ℓ for distance $d - 1$ (as "inner" induction hypothesis). We prove both parts of the lemma for ℓ and distance d.

We now sketch Part 1. (Part 2 follows from Part 1.) Let $t^* = t_{d+r,\ell-1}$. Note that $t^* + r \cdot F_{ack} \leq t_{d,\ell}$ (by a simple algebraic calculation). If either (1) j completes m by time t^* or (2) j completes at least ℓ messages by time t^*, then Part 1 follows, since $t^* < t_{d,\ell}$. So, suppose the contrary, that j does not completes m and it completes exactly $\ell - 1$ messages by time t^*. (By the outer inductive hypothesis for $\ell - 1$, if j does not complete m by time t^*, then it must complete at least $\ell - 1$ messages by that time.) We then show (by using the outer inductive hypothesis for $\ell - 1$ for all neighbors j' of j in G^r), that, if there exists some neighbor j' of j in G^r that completes, by time t^*, a different message set than the message set that j completes by that time, then the *slow positive progress scenario* occurs at time t^* with respect to some $z \leq d_G(j, j') \leq r$. This implies that j receives at least ℓ messages by time $t^* + r \cdot F_{ack} \leq t_{d,\ell}$, as needed for Part 1.

Finally, we consider the case where j and all of its neighbors in G^r complete exactly the same message set by time t^*. In that case, hypothesis (1) of the fast positive progress scenario holds at time t^*, but hypothesis (2) of that scenario does not necessarily holds for that time. We then use the outer inductive hypothesis for ℓ with the inner inductive hypothesis for $d - 1$ to show that there exists a neighbor j' of j in G at distance $d - 1$ from i_0 (in G) that receives at least ℓ messages by time $t_{d-1,\ell}$. This implies that, if j

receives exactly $\ell - 1$ messages by time $t_{d-1,\ell}$ (that is, j does not receive additional messages during the time interval $[t^*, t_{d-1,\ell}]$), then the *fast positive progress scenario* occurs at time $t_{d-1,\ell}$. Therefore, in both cases, j receives at least ℓ messages by time $t_{d-1,\ell} + F_{prog}$. Part 1 follows since $t_{d,\ell} = t_{d-1,\ell} + F_{prog}$ (by a simple algebraic calculation). □

3.3 Lower Bound for Grey Zone G'

We are left with two questions concerning MMB. First, does BMMB perform as well as the r-restricted case when we we consider other natural restrictions on G', such as the grey zone constraint? And second, if not BMMB, are there *any* MMB algorithms for the standard abstract MAC layer model model that can perform well given the grey zone restriction, or perhaps even perform well for arbitrary G'? Below, we answer both questions in the negative by proving that all MMB algorithms require $\Omega((D+k)F_{ack})$ time to solve MMB with a grey zone restricted G'. This result establishes that our analysis of BMMB from Section 3.1 is tight, and it opens an intriguing gap between the superficially similar r-restricted and grey zone constraints.

Theorem 3.4. *For any Multi-Message Broadcast algorithm $\mathcal{A}$, every $k > 1$, and random bit assignment, there exists a network, message assignment, and message scheduler such that $\mathcal{A}$ requires $\Omega((D+k)F_{ack})$ time to solve the MMB problem.*

To prove our main theorem, we handle the kF_{ack} and DF_{ack} terms separately. The kF_{ack} part is simple: consider a node u that represents the only bridge in G between a receiver v and the source(s) of k messages. Our message size limit restricts u to send only a constant number of messages to v at a time, inducing the $\Omega(kF_{ack})$ bound.

Lemma 3.5. *For every $k \in [1, n-2]$, algorithm $\mathcal{A}$, and random bit assignment, there exists a network with $G' = G$, a message assignment that has no node begins with more than one message—what we call a* singleton assignment*—and a message scheduler such that $\mathcal{A}$ requires $\Omega(kF_{ack})$ time to solve the MMB problem.*

Proof. We first fix our definition of $G' = G$. To define G, connect each node in $U = \{u_1, u_2, ..., u_{k-1}\}$ to u_k, forming a star. Then connect u_k to some other node v. Start each node in $U \cup \{u_k\}$ with a unique broadcast message. Consider a message schedule that requires the full F_{ack} time between each broadcast and its corresponding acknowledgment. We now bound the time for v to receive all k messages. The key observation is that u_k is a choke-point through which all messages must pass to arrive at v. To bound the time for messages to make it through this constriction, divide time into *rounds* of length F_{ack}. By our assumption on the scheduler, u_k can begin the transmission of at most a constant number of message per round. Therefore, v can receive at most a constant number of new messages per round. The $\Omega(kF_{ack})$ bound follows directly. □

The more interesting step is proving the $\Omega(DF_{ack})$ term. To accomplish this goal, we begin by defining the network used in our proof argument. Fix some diameter D that is divisible by 2 (the below proof can be easily modified to handle odd D). Fix two node sets $U_A = \{a_1, a_2, ..., a_D\}$ and $U_B = \{b_1, b_2, ..., b_D\}$. Let A and B be the two line graphs that connect, in order of their indices, the nodes in U_A and U_B, respectively. Let C be the dual graph network over nodes $U_A \cup U_B$ where: G consists of the edges in A, B, and G' is defined to include all the edges in G, as well as the following extra edges: for $i < D$, a_i (resp. b_i) is connected to b_{i+1} (resp. a_{i+1}). Notice that our definition of G' in C satisfies the definition of grey zone restricted for a sufficiently large value for the constant c (see Section 2). An example of this network is shown in Figure 2.

In the following, we define a *endpoint-oriented* execution to be an execution of an MMB broadcast algorithm for $k = 2$, in C, for message set $M = \{m_0, m_1\}$, where m_0 starts at a_1 and m_1 starts at b_1. Given a finite endpoint-oriented execution α, let $\ell_0(\alpha)$ be the largest node in A (by increasing index order) that has received m_0 in α, and $\ell_1(\alpha)$ be the largest node in B that has received m_1. Let q_0 and q_1 be defined in the same way, except now capturing the largest node in the relevant line to have received *and initiated a broadcast* of the relevant message. Finally, we call an execution (or execution prefix/extension) *valid*, if the message events and their timing satisfy the model guarantees.

The main insight in our proof argument is that given the right scheduling strategy, m_0's progress down A can slow m_1's progress down B, as well as the other way around. This strategy, however, requires that nodes that receive these messages proceed to then broadcast them as well. The below lemma argues that when m_0 and m_1 make progress, either the next hops start broadcasting, or we can show that at least one of the messages is delayed long enough to establish our desired result.

Lemma 3.6. *Let α be a finite endpoint-oriented execution of a MMB algorithm $\mathcal{A}$ with random bit assignment κ in network C, such that $q_0(\alpha) < \ell_0(\alpha) = a_i$ and $q_1(\alpha) < \ell_1(\alpha) = b_i$ for some $i \in \{1, ..., D-1\}$. There exists a message schedule that produces one of the following outcomes: (1) an extension α' of α in which no time passes and $q_0(\alpha') = \ell_0(\alpha') = a_i$ and $q_1(\alpha') = \ell_1(\alpha') = b_i$; or (2) an extension α'' of α of duration $\Omega(DF_{ack})$ in which the MMB problem is not yet solved.*

Proof. Let α be the finite execution specified by the lemma statement. By assumption a_i has m_0 and b_i has m_1 at the end of α, but neither node has yet initiated a broadcast of this message. We begin by extending α using the following message schedule behavior:

For every broadcast initiated by a node in $U_A \cup U_B \setminus \{a_i, b_i\}$, or broadcast by a_i (resp. b_i) but not containing m_0 (resp. m_1): deliver the message to the broadcaster's neighbors in G (but to *no* G'-only neighbors) and then return an acknowledgment to the broadcaster, instantaneously (i.e., with no time passing). In scheduling these events, construct the schedule to proceed in a round robin fashion through all nodes; that is, for each node in this order, if there is a receive or acknowledgment event to schedule (as specified in the above rule), schedule that event and allow the node to initiate its next broadcast (if its algorithm dictates), then move on to the next node in the round robin order.

Call this extension β. Notice, β is not necessarily a valid execution of our algorithm because if a_i or b_i initiate a broadcast of m_0 and m_1, respectively, in β, they are starved by the schedule. We now use β, however, to force our algorithm to satisfy one of the two lemma outcomes. In more detail, let s_a be the step in β where a_i initiates a broadcast containing m_0 (define $s_a = \perp$ if no such step exists). Define

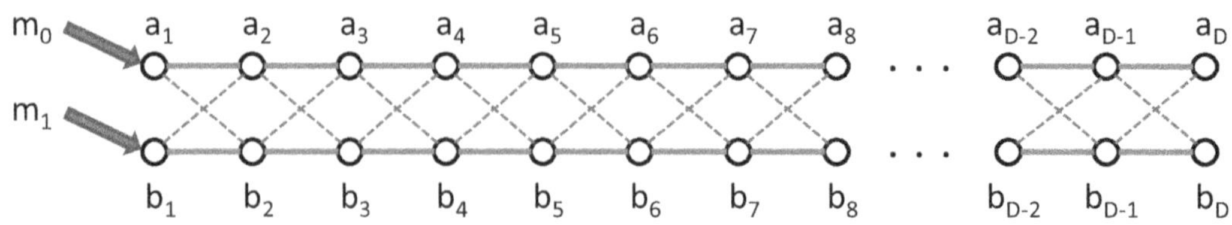

Figure 2: The lower bound network. The green solid lines represent the reliable edges, i.e., those in G, and the red dashed lines represent the unreliable edges, i.e., those in $G' \setminus G$.

s_b the same with respect to b_i and m_1. Because our schedule in β never allows these broadcasts to complete, there can only be at most one such step for a_i and b_i in β. We consider three cases depending on the values of s_a and s_b.

Case 1: Assume that $s_a \neq \bot$ and $s_b \neq \bot$. Let α' be the prefix of β that stops at whichever of these two steps happens later in β. Notice, α' provides a valid extension of α: even though either a_i or b_i might have been delayed from delivering a message in this extension, no time passed between α and the end of α', so no timing guarantees were violated. Accordingly, we see that α' satisfies outcome (1) of the lemma statement.

Case 2: $s_a = s_b = \bot$. In this case, β does not starve any node: every initiated broadcast is delivered to G neighbors and acknowledged. Let α' be a transformation of β where we: (1) allow F_{prog} time to pass between each broadcast and its corresponding acknowledgment; and (2) we stop after DF_{ack} time has passed since the end of α. Because our algorithms are event-driven (and therefore have no concept of time), it is straightforward to see that α' is indistinguishable from β for all nodes. We also node that the schedule in α' satisfies the necessary time constraints, as we never delay a pending delivery by more than F_{prog} time. It follows that α satisfies outcome (2) of the lemma statement.

Case 3: either $s_a = \bot$ or $s_b = \bot$, but not both. Assume, w.l.o.g., that $s_a = \bot$ (the other case is symmetric). Let β' be an extension of α defined with the same rules as β with two exceptions: (1) schedule b_i's broadcasts of m_1 the same as all other broadcasts; and (2) allow F_{prog} time to pass between each broadcast and its corresponding acknowledgment. Let α' be the prefix of β' that ends after DF_{ack} time has passed since the end of α. As in the previous case, we note that α' is indistinguishable from β with respect to nodes in A (the scheduling rules defined above for β do not allow messages from B to be delivered to nodes in A, therefore nodes in A cannot learn that, in β', b_i can succeed in its broadcasts of m_1) and that it still satisfies the model's time bounds. As a result, a_i behaves the same in α' as in β and does not broadcast m_0. Because a_i, by assumption, is the furthest node down the line in A to receive m_0 so far, it follows that by the end of α' there are nodes in A that have not yet received m_0. It follows that α' satisfies outcome (2). □

With the above lemma established, we can use it to prove the main lemma regarding the necessity of DF_{ack} rounds. Here is the main idea: As the messages arrive at each new hop in their respective lines, we apply the above lemma to force these new hops to initiate broadcasts (or, directly prove our time bound by delaying too long). Once we have established that the message frontiers on each line are broadcasting, we can allow these broadcasts to mutually interfere over $G' \setminus G$ edges in such a way that satisfies the progress bound while preventing useful dissemination.

Lemma 3.7. *For every algorithm $\mathcal{A}$ and random bit assignment κ, there exists a message assignment and schedule such that $\mathcal{A}$ requires $\Omega(DF_{ack})$ time to solve MMB in network C for $k = 2$.*

Proof. We construct an endpoint oriented execution of $\mathcal{A}$ in C with random bits κ, by defining the message schedule behavior. We start with α_0: the finite execution that captures the behavior of the above system only through a_1 receiving m_0 and b_1 receiving m_1. These events happen at the beginning of the execution, so no time passes in α_0.

Notice, α_0 satisfies the preconditions required to apply Lemma 3.6. Apply this lemma to α_0. By the definition of this lemma, there are two possible outcomes. If it is the second outcome, we have proved our theorem. Assume, therefore, that the lemma produces an extension α_0' of α_0 that satisfies the first outcome. At the end of α_0', we know that a_1 has initiated a broadcast of m_0 and b_1 has initiated a broadcast of m_1, and no time has passed since these broadcasts are initiated. We further note that at this point, m_0 has made it no further down the A line and b_1 has made it no further down the B line.

We now extend α_0' with a message schedule that delays m_0's arrival at a_2 and m_1's arrival at b_2 by the maximum F_{ack} time. To do so, partition an interval of F_{ack} time following α_0' into sub-intervals of length F_{prog}. At the end of each sub-interval, deliver m_0 from a_1 to b_2 (over a G' edge) and m_1 from b_1 to a_2 (also over a G' edge). At the end of this F_{ack} interval, allow m_0 to make it to a_2 and m_1 to make it to b_2, and acknowledge these broadcasts. Notice, this schedule satisfies both the progress and acknowledgment bounds for a_1 and b_1's broadcasts during this interval. During this F_{ack} interval, however, we must also schedule *other nodes'* broadcasts. To do so, we use a simple rule: for every other broadcast, allow the message to be delivered to all (and only) G neighbors and be acknowledged at the end of the next F_{prog} interval.

Notice, our above delay strategy leads to a finite execution α_1, of duration F_{ack} longer than α_0, where $q_0(\alpha_1) \neq \ell_0(\alpha_1) = a_2$ and $q_1(\alpha_1) \neq \ell_1(\alpha_1) = b_2$. We can, therefore, apply our above argument again, now replacing α_0 with α_1. Indeed, we can keep applying this argument until either we arrive at outcome (2) from Lemma 3.6, or we build up to α_{D-2}, an execution of length $\Omega(DF_{ack})$ in which m_0 and m_1 have not yet made it to the end of the A and B lines, respectively. Either way, we have proved the theorem statement. □

4. MULTI-MESSAGE BROADCAST WITH AN ENHANCED ABSTRACT MAC LAYER

In Section 3, we proved that in the standard abstract MAC layer model, $\Omega(kF_{ack})$ time is necessary to solve MMB, and for some definitions of G', an additional $\Omega(DF_{ack})$ time is also necessary. Our analysis of BMMB then established that this algorithm is essentially the best you can do in this model. In this section, we tackle the question of how much *additional power* we must add to our model definition to enable faster solutions under the assumption that $F_{prog} \ll F_{ack}$, pointing to the extra assumptions of the enhanced abstract MAC layer model as one possible answer. In particular, we describe a new algorithm, which we call *Fast Multi-Message Broadcast* (FMMB), that guarantees the following time complexity when run in the enhanced abstract MAC layer model with a grey zone restricted G':

Theorem 4.1. *The FMMB algorithm solves the MMB problem in $O((D\log n + k\log n + \log^3 n)F_{prog})$ time, w.h.p., in the enhanced abstract MAC layer model and grey zone restricted G'.*

This result has no F_{ack} term. As the size of F_{prog} decreases, this result's advantage over BMMB increases.

Preliminaries. In the following, for $v \in V$, we use $ID(v)$ to refer to v's unique id, $N_G(v)$ to describe *the ids* of v's neighbors in G, and $N_{G'}(v)$ to describe the ids of v's neighbors in G'. We use $\mathcal{M}$ to refer to the set of messages to be disseminated in a given execution of MMB. We call a set $S \subseteq V$ of nodes *G-independent* if for each pair of nodes $u, v \in S$, we have $(v, u) \notin E$.

4.1 Algorithm Outline

The FMMB algorithm divides time into lock-step *rounds* each of length F_{prog}. This can be achieved by leveraging the ability of a node to use time and *abort* a broadcast in progress in the enhanced abstract MAC layer. In more detail, when we say a node *broadcasts in round t*, we mean that it initiates the broadcast at the beginning of the time slot dedicated to round t, and aborts it (if not completed yet) at the end of the time slot.

The FMMB algorithm uses three key subroutines which we summarize here, but detail and analyze in the subsections that follow. All three subroutines are randomized and will be shown to hold with sufficiently high probability that their correctness guarantees can be combined with a union bound. The FMMB algorithms begins by having nodes construct a maximal independent set (MIS) in G using $O(\log^3 n)$ rounds. We note that this MIS subroutine might be of independent interest.[5] The FMMB algorithm then uses a gather subroutine to gather the broadcast messages at nearby MIS nodes in an additional $O(k + \log n)$ rounds. Finally, it uses an overlay dissemination subroutine that broadcasts the messages to all MIS nodes, and then to their neighbors (i.e., all nodes), in $O((D+k)\log n)$ rounds. The total combined running time of FMMB is therefore $O(D\log n + k\log n + \log^3 n)$ rounds, which requires $O((D\log n + k\log n + \log^3 n)F_{prog})$ total time.

We continue by describing each of the three subroutines. Theorem 4.1 follows directly from the analysis of these subroutines. Due to space constraints, we defer this analysis to the full version of this paper [18].

[5]The previously best known MIS solution for an abstract MAC layer model uses time that is linear in n [32].

4.2 The MIS Subroutine

We now describe an MIS subroutine that succeeds in building an MIS in G in $O(c^4 \log^3 n)$ rounds, w.h.p., where c is the universal constant from the grey zone definition (see Section 2). In more detail, the algorithm runs for a fixed length of time, $t_{MIS} \in O(c^4 \log^3 n)$. At the end of this period, some set $S \subseteq V$ of nodes *join* the MIS. The algorithm guarantees, w.h.p.,[6] that S is a *maximal G-independent set*: (1) all pairs of nodes in S are G-independent; and (2) every $u \in V$ is either in S or neighbors a node in S in G.

The subroutine (called "algorithm" from here forward) works as follows: initially, all nodes are active. In the course of the algorithm, some nodes join the MIS and some nodes become inactive. The algorithm runs in $O(c^2 \log^2 n)$ phases, each of which consists of $O(c^2 \log n)$ rounds, which are divided into two parts: *election* and *announcement*.

The election part has $4\log n$ rounds. At the start, each active node v picks a random bit-string $b(v) \in \{0,1\}^{4\log n}$. In each round $\tau \in [1, 4\log n]$ of this part, each active node v broadcasts its bit-string $b(v)$ iff the τth bit of $b(v)$ is 1. If node v did not broadcast but it received a message $b(u)$, be it from a G or a G' neighbor, then node v becomes temporarily inactive for the rest of this phase. At the end of $4\log n$ rounds of the election part, if a node v is still active, then v joins the MIS set S.

The announcement part has $O(c^2 \log n)$ rounds. In each round, each node v that joined the MIS in this phase broadcasts a message containing $ID(v)$ with probability $\Theta(1/c^2)$, and does not broadcast any message with probability $1 - \Theta(1/c^2)$. If a node u that has not joined the MIS receives a message $ID(v)$ from a G-neighbor, then u knows that one of its G-neighbors is in the MIS and thus node u becomes permanently inactive. At the end of the announcement part, each node that joined the MIS in this phase becomes permanently inactive, while each temporarily inactive node becomes active again.

4.3 The Message Gathering Subroutine

We now describe a message gathering subroutine (called "algorithm" in the rest of this subsection) that delivers each MMB message to a nearby MIS node in $O(c^2(k + \log n))$ rounds, w.h.p. In more detail, each node v maintains message-set $M_v \subseteq \mathcal{M}$ of messages that the node currently owns. When this algorithm is first called, these sets describe the initial assignment of MMB message to nodes. Throughout the algorithm, the message-set of MIS nodes grow while the message set of non-MIS nodes shrink. The goal is to arrive at a configuration where $\cup_{v\in S} M_v = \mathcal{M}$: at which point, all messages in $\mathcal{M}$ are owned by MIS nodes. The algorithm is divided into $O(c^2(k + \log n))$ *periods*, where each period consists of three rounds. At the start of each period, each MIS node decides to be active with probability $1/\Theta(c^2)$, and inactive otherwise. Then, in the first round of the period, each active MIS node broadcasts its ID, announcing that it is active. In the second round, each non-MIS node v that received a message from one of its G-neighbors in the first

[6]For this guarantee, as with the other subroutines we consider, we assume that the high probability is of the form $1 - n^{-c}$ for a sufficiently large constant c to enable a union bound on the fail probability for all three subroutines.

round and has at least one message left in its message-set M_v broadcasts one of the messages in M_v, along with its own ID. In the same round, if an MIS node u receives a message m from a G-neighbor, then node u updates its message-set as $M_u = M_u \cup \{m\}$. In the third round of the period, each MIS node u that received a message m in the second round sends an *acknowledgment* message, which contains message m and its own ID. In this round, if a non-MIS node v receives a message m from a G-neighbor, then v updates its message-set as $M_v = M_v \setminus \{m\}$.

4.4 The Message Spreading Subroutine

We conclude by describing the subroutine ("algorithm" in the following subsection) used by FMMB to efficiently spread the messages gathered at MIS nodes to the full network. This algorithm spreads the messages to all nodes in the network in $O((D+k)\log n)$ rounds, w.h.p. In more detail, in the following, let S be the set of MIS nodes when this algorithm is executed. Assume S is a valid MIS. Let E_S be the set of unordered pairs $(v,u) \in E$ such that the hop distance of u and v in graph G is at most 3. Consider the overlay graph $\mathcal{H} = (S, E_S)$. The algorithm works by spreading messages over $\mathcal{H}$. For this purpose, we explain a simple procedure, that uses $O(\log n)$ rounds, and that achieves the following: Suppose that each node $v \in S$ starts this procedure with at most one message m_v. Then, at the end of this procedure, w.h.p., we have that m_v is delivered to all $\mathcal{H}$-neighbors of v. We will then establish the final upper bound of $O((D+k)\log n)$ rounds by combining this procedure with a standard pipelining argument applied to messages in $\mathcal{H}$.

The Local Broadcast Procedure on the Overlay. The algorithm consists of $O(c^2 \log n)$ periods, each consisting of three rounds. In each period, each node v decides to be active with probability $1/\Theta(c^2)$ and remains inactive otherwise. If a node $v \in S$ is active, it broadcasts its message m_v in the first round, if it has a message m_v. For all the three rounds of the period, if a node $u \in V$ receives a message from a G-neighbor in one round, it broadcasts this message in the next round. At the end of the three rounds of the period, each node $u \in S$ adds the messages that it has received to its message-set.

This local broadcast on the overlay provides essentially the same guarantee as given by F_{ack} on the full network topology, but with respect to the overlay graph $\mathcal{H}$. Having this *simulated broadcast*, the problem can be solved by combining BMMB with this simulated broadcast, and then analyzing its performance with respect to $\mathcal{H}$. That is, we divide the time into phases, each of length $O(\log n)$ rounds, where the constants are such that one run of the above procedure fits in one phase. Then, in each phase, each MIS node sends a message that it has not sent so far, to all of its $\mathcal{H}$-neighbors. It follows from Theorem 3.1 that after $O(D_{\mathcal{H}} + k)$ phases, all messages are broadcast over $\mathcal{H}$, i.e., to all MIS nodes. Here $D_{\mathcal{H}}$ is the hop diameter of the overlay graph $\mathcal{H}$, and we clearly have $D_{\mathcal{H}} \leq D_G = D$. Below is a more detailed description of this part.

Broadcast on the Overlay Graph $\mathcal{H}$. Here, we explain a more detailed version of the algorithm that broadcasts messages on the overlay graph $\mathcal{H}$, in $O((D+k)\log n)$ rounds. We divide the $O((D+k)\log n)$ rounds into $O(D+k)$ phases, each of length $O(\log n)$ rounds, where the constants are such that one run of the above procedure fits in one phase. In the algorithm, each node $v \in S$ has a message-set M_v of messages that it has or it has received, and it also has a *sent-set* M'_v of messages that contains all the messages that v has sent throughout this algorithm. Initially, for each node v, $M'_v = \emptyset$. In each phase, each node v sets m_v to be equal to one of the messages in $M_v \setminus M'_v$ and runs the procedure explained above. At the end of the phase, node v adds m_v to M'_v and it also adds each message received during this phase to M_v. The following theorem shows that this algorithm broadcasts all messages to all MIS nodes.

5. CONCLUSION

In this paper, we applied the abstract MAC layer approach to a natural problem: disseminating an unknown amount of information starting at unknown devices through an unknown network (what we call multi-message broadcast). We proved that the presence of unreliable links has a significant but perhaps unexpected impact on the worst-case performance of multi-message broadcast. In particular, with no unreliability or unreliable links limited to nodes close in the reliable link graph, basic flooding (what we called the BMMB algorithm) is efficient. Once we shift to the similar constraint of unreliability limited to nodes close in geographic distance, however, all solutions are inherently slow. This indicates an interesting property of unreliability: the ability to unreliably connect nodes distant in the reliable link graph seems to be what degrades worst-case performance of broadcast algorithms. Finally, we demonstrated that if nodes have estimates of the model time bounds and can abort messages in progress, even more efficient solutions to this problem are possible. Most existing MAC layers do not offer an interface to abort messages. This result motivates the implementation of this interface (which seems technically straightforward).

In terms of future work, there exist many other important problems for which a similar analysis can be performed, such as leader election, consensus, and network structuring. It would be interesting to investigate whether there are properties of link unreliability that are universal to distributed computation in this setting, or if the properties of this type that matter differ from problem to problem. Another direction to study within this same general area is whether the strength of the scheduler strongly impacts worst-case performance. In our lower bound, for example, the scheduler knows the algorithm's random bits. This is a strong assumption and motivates the question of whether this bound can be circumvented with a weaker adversary and a more clever algorithm.

6. REFERENCES

[1] N. Alon, A. Bar-Noy, N. Linial, and D. Peleg. A Lower Bound for Radio Broadcast. *Journal of Computer and System Sciences*, 43(2):290–298, 1991.

[2] R. Bar-Yehuda, O. Goldreich, and A. Itai. On the Time Complexity of Broadcast in Radio Networks: an Exponential Gap Between Determinism and Randomization. In *Proceedings of the International Symposium on Principles of Distributed Computing*, 1987.

[3] R. Bar-Yehuda, O. Goldreich, and A. Itai. On the time-complexity of broadcast in multi-hop radio networks: An exponential gap between determinism and randomization. *J. Comput. Syst. Sci.*, 45(1):104–126, 1992.

[4] K. Censor-Hillel, S. Gilbert, N. Lynch, and C. Newport. Structuring Unreliable Radio Networks. In *Proceedings of the International Symposium on Principles of Distributed Computing*, 2011.

[5] I. Chlamtac and S. Kutten. On broadcasting in radio networks: Problem analysis and protocol design. *IEEE Transactions on Communications*, 33(12):1240–1246, 1985.

[6] H. C. Chung, P. Robinson, and J. L. Welch. Regional consecutive leader election in mobile ad-hoc networks. In *Proceedings of the 6th International Workshop on Foundations of Mobile Computing*, pages 81–90, 2010.

[7] H. C. Chung, P. Robinson, and J. L. Welch. Optimal regional consecutive leader election in mobile ad-hoc networks. In *Proceedings of the 7th ACM ACM SIGACT/SIGMOBILE International Workshop on Foundations of Mobile Computing*, FOMC '11, pages 52–61, 2011.

[8] A. E. F. Clementi, A. Monti, and R. Silvestri. Round Robin is Optimal for Fault-Tolerant Broadcasting on Wireless Networks. *Journal of Parallel and Distributed Computing*, 64(1):89–96, 2004.

[9] A. Cornejo, N. Lynch, S. Viqar, and J. L. Welch. Neighbor Discovery in Mobile Ad Hoc Networks Using an Abstract MAC Layer. In *Annual Allerton Conference on Communication, Control, and Computing*, 2009.

[10] A. Cornejo, S. Viqar, and J. L. Welch. Reliable Neighbor Discovery for Mobile Ad Hoc Networks. In *Proceedings of the Workshop on the Foundations of Mobile Computing*, 2010.

[11] A. Czumaj and W. Rytter. Broadcasting algorithms in radio networks with unknown topology. In *Proceedings of the Symposium on Foundations of Computer Science*, pages 492–501, 2003.

[12] A. Czumaj and W. Rytter. Broadcasting Algorithms in Radio Networks with Unknown Topology. *Journal of Algorithms*, 60:115–143, 2006.

[13] S. Daum, S. Gilbert, F. Kuhn, and C. Newport. Broadcast in the Ad Hoc SINR Model. In *Proceedings of the International Symposium on Distributed Computing*, 2013.

[14] S. Dolev, S. Gilbert, M. Khabbazian, and C. Newport. More channels is better: Efficient and robust wireless broadcast, 2010. Submitted for publication.

[15] L. Gasieniec, D. Peleg, and Q. Xin. Faster communication in known topology radio networks. *Distributed Computing*, 19(4):289–300, 2007.

[16] L. Gasieniec, A. Pelc, and D. Peleg. The Wakeup Problem in Synchronous Broadcast Systems. *SIAM Journal on Discrete Mathematics*, 14(2):207–222, 2001.

[17] M. Ghaffari, B. Haeupler, and M. Khabbazian. Randomized broadcast in radio networks with collision detection. In *Proceedings of the International Symposium on Principles of Distributed Computing*, 2013.

[18] M. Ghaffari, E. Kantor, N. Lynch, and C. Newport. Multi-message broadcast with abstract mac layers and unreliable links. *CoRR*, abs/1405.1671, 2014.

[19] M. Ghaffari, B. Haeupler, N. Lynch, and C. Newport. Bounds on Contention Management in Radio Networks. In *Proceedings of the International Symposium on Distributed Computing*, 2012.

[20] M. Ghaffari, N. Lynch, and C. Newport. The Cost of Radio Network Broadcast for Different Models of Unreliable Links. In *Proceedings of the International Symposium on Principles of Distributed Computing*, 2013.

[21] T. Jurdzinski, D. R. Kowalski, M. Rozanski, and G. Stachowiak. Distributed Randomized Broadcasting in Wireless Networks under the SINR Model. In *Proceedings of the International Symposium on Distributed Computing*, 2013.

[22] T. Kesselheim and B. Vöcking. Distributed Contention Resolution in Wireless Networks. In *Proceedings of the International Symposium on Distributed Computing*, 2010.

[23] M. Khabbazian and D. R. Kowalski. Time-efficient randomized multiple-message broadcast in radio networks. In *Proceedings of the International Symposium on Principles of Distributed Computing*, pages 373–380, 2011.

[24] M. Khabbazian, F. Kuhn, D. R. Kowalski, and N. Lynch. Decomposing Broadcast Algorithms Using Abstract MAC Layers. In *Proceedings of the Workshop on the Foundations of Mobile Computing*, 2010.

[25] M. Khabbazian, F. Kuhn, N. Lynch, M. Médard, and A. ParandehGheibi. MAC Design for Analog Network Coding. In *Proceedings of the Workshop on the Foundations of Mobile Computing*, 2011.

[26] D. R. Kowalski and A. Pelc. Broadcasting in undirected ad hoc radio networks. In *Proceedings of the International Symposium on Principles of Distributed Computing*, pages 73–82, 2003.

[27] D. R. Kowalski and A. Pelc. Optimal deterministic broadcasting in known topology radio networks. *Distributed Computing*, 19(3):185–195, 2007.

[28] D.R. Kowalski and A. Pelc. Broadcasting in Undirected Ad Hoc Radio Networks. *Distributed Computing*, 18(1):43–57, 2005.

[29] F. Kuhn, N. Lynch, and C. Newport. The Abstract MAC Layer. In *Proceedings of the International Symposium on Distributed Computing*, 2009.

[30] F. Kuhn, N. Lynch, and C. Newport. The Abstract MAC Layer. *Distributed Computing*, 24(3-4):187–206, 2011.

[31] E. Kushilevitz and Y. Mansour. An $O(Dlog(N/D))$ lower bound for broadcast in radio networks. In *Proceedings of the International Symposium on Principles of Distributed Computing*, pages 65–74, 1993.

[32] Nancy Lynch, Tsvetomira Radeva, and Srikanth Sastry. Asynchronous leader election and mis using abstract mac layer. In *Proceedings of the 8th International Workshop on Foundations of Mobile Computing*, pages 3:1–3:10, 2012.

[33] C. Newport, D. Kotz, Y. Yuan, R. S. Gray, J. Liu, and C. Elliott. Experimental Evaluation of Wireless Simulation Assumptions. *Simulation*, 83(9):643–661, 2007.

[34] A. Pelc. Algorithmic aspects of radio communication. pages 1–2, 2008.

Consensus with an Abstract MAC Layer

Calvin Newport
Georgetown University
Washington, D.C.
cnewport@georgetown.edu

ABSTRACT

In this paper, we study distributed consensus in the radio network setting. We produce new upper and lower bounds for this problem in an abstract MAC layer model that captures the key guarantees provided by most wireless MAC layers. In more detail, we first generalize the well-known impossibility of deterministic consensus with a single crash failure [15] from the asynchronous message passing model to our wireless setting. Proceeding under the assumption of no faults, we then investigate the amount of network knowledge required to solve consensus in our model—an important question given that these networks are often deployed in an ad hoc manner. We prove consensus is impossible without unique ids or without knowledge of network size (in multihop topologies). We also prove a lower bound on optimal time complexity. We then match these lower bounds with a pair of new deterministic consensus algorithms—one for single hop topologies and one for multihop topologies—providing a comprehensive characterization of the consensus problem in the wireless setting. From a theoretical perspective, our results shed new insight into the role of network information and the power of MAC layer abstractions in solving distributed consensus. From a practical perspective, given the level of abstraction used by our model, our upper bounds can be easily implemented in real wireless devices on existing MAC layers while preserving their correctness guarantees—facilitating the development of wireless distributed systems.

Categories and Subject Descriptors

F.2.2 [**Analysis of Algorithms and Problem Complexity**]: Non-numerical Algorithms and Problems—*Computations on Discrete Structures*; G.2.2 [**Discrete Mathematics**]: Graph Theory—*Network Problems*

Keywords

wireless networks; abstract MAC layer; consensus

PODC '14, July 15–18 2014, Paris, France.
Copyright 2014 ACM 978-1-4503-2944-6/14/07 $15.00.
http://dx.doi.org/10.1145/2611462.2611479.

1. INTRODUCTION

Consensus provides a fundamental building block for developing reliable distributed systems [20, 19, 21]. Motivated by the increasing interest in *wireless* distributed systems, in this paper we prove new upper and lower bounds for the consensus problem in wireless networks.

The Abstract MAC Layer. Consensus bounds are dependent on the model in which they are established. Accordingly, we must take care in selecting our model for studying the wireless version of this problem. Most existing work on distributed algorithms for wireless networks assumes low-level synchronous models that require algorithms to deal directly with link-layer issues such as signal fading and channel contention. Some of these models use topology graphs to determine message behavior (c.f., [6, 24, 27, 34, 13, 16]) while others use signal strength calculations (c.f., [35, 33, 17, 22, 23, 14]). These models are well-suited for asking basic science questions about the capabilities of wireless communication. They are not necessarily appropriate, however, for developing algorithms meant for deployment, as real wireless systems typically require an algorithm to operate on top of a general-purpose MAC layer which is hard to bypass and enables many key network functions such as managing co-existence.

Motivated by this reality, in this paper we adopt the *abstract MAC layer* approach [29], in which we model the basic guarantees provided by most existing wireless MAC layers—if you broadcast a message it will eventually be delivered with acknowledgment to nearby nodes in the network—but leverages a non-deterministic message scheduler to allow for unpredictability—there is no bound on when messages are delivered or in what order. The goal with this approach is to describe and analyze algorithms at a level of abstraction that makes it easy to subsequently implement theory results in real systems while still preserving their formally analyzed properties. (See Section 2 for a detailed model definition and motivation.)

Results. We begin with lower bounds. In Section 3.1, we generalize the oft-cited result on the impossibility of deterministic consensus with a single process failure [15] from the asynchronous message passing model to our abstract MAC layer model. (See Section 2 for details on how these two models differ.) The main difficulty in this generalization is the new assumption in our model that senders receive acknowledgments at some point after a given broadcast completes. To overcome this difficulty, we restrict our valency definitions to focus on a restricted class of schedulers.

Having established this impossibility, we proceed in this paper assuming no crash failures. Noting that wireless network deployments are often ad hoc, we next focus on determining how much *a priori* information about the network is required to solve deterministic consensus in our model. We start, in Section 3.2, by proving that consensus is impossible without unique ids, even if nodes know the size and diameter of the network. We then prove, in Section 3.3, that even with unique ids (and knowledge of the diameter), consensus is impossible in multihop networks if nodes do not know the network size. Finally, we prove that any solution to consensus in our model requires $\Omega(D \cdot F_{ack})$ time, where D is the diameter of the underlying network topology and F_{ack} is the maximum message delivery delay (a value unknown to the nodes in the network). All three bounds leverage partitioning arguments that rely on carefully-constructed worst-case network topologies and message scheduler behavior for which the relevant network knowledge assumptions do not break symmetry.

We then turn our attention to matching these lower bounds with a pair of new deterministic consensus algorithms. We begin, in Section 4.1, with a new algorithm that guarantees to solve consensus in single hop networks in an optimal $O(F_{ack})$ time, even without advance knowledge of the network size or participants (this opens up a gap with the asynchronous message passing model, where consensus is impossible under such assumptions [1]). This algorithm uses a two-phase structure. The key insight is that nodes wait to decide after their second phase broadcast until they have also heard this broadcast from a set of important *witnesses*.

In Section 4.2, the *wireless PAXOS* (wPAXOS) algorithm, which guarantees to solve consensus in multihop topologies of diameter D in an optimal $O(D \cdot F_{ack})$ time. This algorithm assumes unique ids and knowledge of n (as required by our lower bounds[1]), but no other advance knowledge of the network or participants. The wPAXOS algorithm combines the high-level logic of the PAXOS consensus algorithm [30] with a collection of support services that efficiently disseminate proposals and aggregate responses. We note that if the PAXOS (or similar consensus algorithm) logic is combined with a basic flooding algorithm, the result would be a $O(n \cdot F_{ack})$ time complexity, as bottlenecks are possible where $\Omega(n)$ value and id pairs must be sent by a single node only able to fit $O(1)$ such pairs in each message. To reduce this time complexity to an optimal $O(D \cdot F_{ack})$, we implement eventually stable shortest-path routing trees and show they allow fast aggregation once stabilized, and preserve safety at all times. These stabilizing support services and their analysis represent the main contribution of this algorithm. One could, for example, replace the PAXOS logic working with these services with something simpler (since we have unique ids and knowledge of n, and no crash failures, we could, for example, simply gather all values at all nodes). We choose PAXOS mainly for performance reasons, as it only depends on a majority nodes to make progress, and is therefore not slowed if a small portion of the network is delayed.

Related Work. Consensus provides a fundamental building block for reliable distributed computing [20, 19, 21]. It is particularly well-studied in asynchronous models [30, 40, 36, 2], where deterministic solutions are impossible with even a single crash failure [15]. Most existing distributed algorithm results for the wireless setting assume low-level models. Though consensus has been studied in such models (e.g., [10]), most efforts in the low-level setting focus on reliable communication problems such as broadcast (see [38] for a good survey). The abstract MAC layer approach to modeling wireless networks is introduced in [28] (later expanded to a journal version [29]), and has been subsequently used to study several different problems [11, 25, 26, 12]. This paper, however, is the first to consider consensus in the abstract MAC layer context.

Other researchers have also studied consensus in wireless networks at higher levels of abstraction. Vollset and Ezhilchelvan [41], and Alekeish and Ezhilchelvan [4], study consensus in a variant of the asynchronous message passing model where pairwise channels come and go dynamically—capturing some behavior of mobile wireless networks. Their correctness results depend on detailed liveness guarantees that bound the allowable channel changes. Wu et al. [42] use the standard asynchronous message passing model (with unreliable failure detectors [9]) as a stand-in for a wireless network, focusing on how to reduce message complexity (an important metric in a resource-bounded wireless setting) in solving consensus.

Finally, we note that a key focus in this paper is understanding the importance of network information in solving consensus, a topic previously studied in the classical models. Ruppert [39], and Bonnet and Raynal [7], for example, study the amount of extra power needed (in terms of shared objects and failure detection, respectively) to solve wait-free consensus in *anonymous* versions of the standard models. Attiya et al. [5] describe consensus solutions for shared memory systems without failures or unique ids. In this paper, by contrast, we prove consensus impossible without failures or unique ids. These results do not contradict, however, as we assume multihop message passing-style networks. A series of papers [8, 18, 3], starting with the work of Cavin et al. [8], study the related problem of *consensus with unknown participants* (CUPs), where nodes are only allowed to communicate with other nodes whose identities have been provided by a *participant detector* formalism. Results on the CUPs problem focus on the structure of the knowledge from such detectors required for consensus (e.g., if we create a graph with a directed edge indicating participant knowledge, then the resulting graph must satisfy certain connectivity properties). Closer to our own model is the work of Abboud et al. [1], which studies single hop networks in which participants are *a priori* unknown, but nodes do have a reliable broadcast primitive. They prove consensus is impossible in single hop networks under these assumptions without knowledge of network size. In Section 4.1, we describe an algorithm in our model that *does* solve consensus under these assumptions: opening an interesting gap.

2. MODEL AND PROBLEM

For simplicity, in the following we sometimes call our model *the* abstract MAC layer model. We emphasize, however, that there is no single abstract MAC layer model, but instead many variants that share the same basic assumptions of acknowledged local broadcast and an arbitrary scheduler. The major differences between our model and the standard

[1]Our algorithm still works even if provided only *good enough* knowledge of n to recognize a majority. This does not contradict our lower bound as the lower bound assumes *no* knowledge of n.

asynchronous message passing model are that: (1) we assume local broadcast instead of point-to-point communication; (2) senders receive an acknowledgment at some point after their broadcast completes (this acknowledgment captures the time at which the underlying link layer is done broadcasting its current message; e.g., after its slot in a TDMA schedule arrives or its CSMA algorithm finally detected a clear channel); and (3) we care about assumptions regarding network information knowledge as wireless networks are often deployed in an ad hoc manner where such information may be unknown to nodes.

Model Details. To formalize our abstract MAC layer model, fix a graph $G = (V, E)$, with the set V describing the $|V| = n$ wireless devices in the network (called *nodes* in the following), and the edges in E describing nodes within reliable communication range. In this model, nodes communicate with a local reliable (but not necessarily atomic[2]) broadcast primitive that guarantees to eventually deliver messages to a node's neighbors in G. At some point after a broadcast completes (see below), a node receives an ack. If a node attempts to broadcast additional messages before receiving an ack for the current message, those extra messages are discarded. To formalize the message delivery guarantees, fix some execution α of a deterministic algorithm in our model. To simplify definitions, assume w.l.o.g. that messages are unique. Let π be the event in α where u calls *broadcast*(m), and π' be the subsequent ack returned to u. Our abstract MAC layer model guarantees that in the interval from π to π' in α, every non-faulty neighbor of u in G receives m, and these are the only receive events for m in α (this is where we leverage message uniqueness in our definition).

We associate each message scheduler with an unknown (to the nodes) but finite value F_{ack} that bounds the maximum delay it is allowed between a broadcast and a corresponding acknowledgment. This property induces some notion of fairness: the scheduler must eventually allow each broadcast to finish. To simplify timing, we assume local non-communication steps take no time. That is, all non-determinism is captured in the message receive and ack scheduling. We note that in some definitions of abstract MAC layer models (see [29]), a second timing parameter, F_{prog}, is introduced to bound the time for a node to receive *some* message when one or more neighbors are broadcasting. We omit this parameter in this study as it is used mainly for refining time complexity analysis, while we are concerned here more with safety properties. Refining our upper bound results in a model that includes this second parameter remains useful future work. We also note that some definitions of the abstract MAC layer assume a second topology graph consisting of *unreliable* links that sometimes deliver messages and sometimes do not. We omit this second graph in this analysis, which strengthens our lower bounds. Optimizing our multihop upper bound to work in the presence of such links, however, is left an open question.

In some results that follow, we consider *crash* failures (a node halts for the remainder of the execution). The decision to crash a node and the timing of the crash is determined by the scheduler and can happen in the middle of a broadcast (i.e., after some neighbors have received the message but not all). We call a node *non-faulty* (equiv. *correct*) with respect to a given execution if it does not crash. For our upper bounds, we restrict the message size to contain at most a constant number of unique ids. For a given topology graph G, we use D to describe its diameter. Finally, for integer $i > 0$, let $[i] = \{1, 2, ..., i\}$.

The Consensus Problem. To better understand the power of our abstract MAC layer model we explore upper and lower bounds for the standard binary consensus problem. In more detail, each node begins an execution with an initial value from $\{0, 1\}$. Every node has the ability to perform a single irrevocable *decide* action for a value in $\{0, 1\}$. To solve consensus, an algorithm must guarantee the following three properties: (1) *agreement*: no two nodes decide different values; (2) *validity*: if a node decides value v, then some node had v as its initial value; and (3) *termination*: every non-faulty process eventually decides. By focusing on binary consensus, as oppose to the more general definition that assumes an arbitrary value set, we strengthen the lower bounds that form the core of this paper. Generalizing our upper bounds to the general case in an efficient manner (e.g., a solution more efficient than agreeing on the bits of a general value, one by one, using binary consensus) is non-trivial and remains an open problem.

3. LOWER BOUNDS

We begin by exploring the fundamental limits of our abstract MAC layer model with respect to the consensus problem. In Section 4, we provide matching upper bounds. In the following, we defer some proofs to the appendix for the sake of clarity and concision.

3.1 Consensus with Crash Failures

In this section we prove consensus is impossible in our model in the presence of even a single crash failure. To achieve the strongest possible bound we assume a clique topology. Our proof generalizes the FLP [15] result to hold in our stronger setting where nodes now have acknowledgments.[3]

Preliminaries. For this proof, assume w.l.o.g. that nodes always send messages; i.e., on receiving an ack for their current message they immediately begin sending a new message. We define a *step* of a node u to be either: (a) a node $v \neq u$ receiving u's current message; or (b) u receiving an ack for its current message (at which point its algorithm advances to sending a new message). We call a step of type (a) from above *valid* with respect to the execution so far if the node v receiving u's message has not previously received that message *and* all non-crashed nodes smaller than v (by some fixed but arbitrary ordering) have already received u's message. We call a step of type (b) *valid* with respect to the execution so far if every non-crashed neighbor of u has received its current message in a previous step. When we consider executions that consist only of valid steps we are, in effect, restricting our attention to a particular type of well-behaved message scheduler.

We call an execution fragment (equiv. prefix) α of a consensus algorithm *bivalent* if there is some extension of valid

[2]Local broadcast in wireless networks is not necessarily an atomic operation, as effects such as the hidden terminal problem might lead some neighbors of a sender to receive a message before other neighbors.

[3]The version of the FLP proof that we directly generalize here is the cleaned up and condensed version that appeared in the subsequent textbook of Lynch [32].

steps that leads to nodes deciding 0, and some extension of valid steps that leads to nodes deciding 1. By contrast, we call an execution α *univalent* if every extension of valid steps from α that leads to a decision leads to the same decision.[4] If this decision is 0 (resp. 1), we also say that α is 0-*valent* (resp. 1-*valent*). In the following, we use the notation $\alpha \cdot s$, for execution fragment α and step s, to describe the extension of α by s.

Result. Fix some algorithm $\mathcal{A}$. Assume for the sake of contradiction that $\mathcal{A}$ guarantees to solve consensus in this setting with up to 1 crash failure. The key to generalizing the FLP impossibility to our model is the following lemma, which reproves the main argument of this classical result in a new way that leverages our model-specific constraints.

LEMMA 3.1. *Fix some bivalent execution fragment α of $\mathcal{A}$ and some process u. There exists a finite extension α' of α such that $\alpha' \cdot s_u$ is bivalent, where s_u is a valid step of u with respect to α'.*

PROOF. Assume for contradiction that this property does not hold for some α and u. It follows that for every finite extension α' of α of valid steps, if we extend α' by a single additional valid step of u, the execution is univalent. Let s_u be the next valid step for u after α (by our definition of valid, s_u is well-defined). We start by considering $\alpha \cdot s_u$. By assumption, this fragment is univalent. Assume, w.l.o.g. that $\alpha \cdot s_u$ is 0-valent (the argument below is symmetric for the case where $\alpha \cdot s_u$ is instead 1-valent). Because α is bivalent, however, there is some other extension α'' consisting of valid steps that is 1-valent.

We now move step by step in α'', starting from α, until our growing fragment becomes 1-valent. Assume there are $k \geq 1$ steps in this extension. Label the k intermediate execution fragments from α to the α'': $\alpha_1, \alpha_2, ..., \alpha_k$, where α_k is the where the fragment becomes 1-valent. To simplify notation, let $\alpha_0 = \alpha$. For $0 < i < k$, we know α_i is bivalent, so, by our contradiction assumption, that step between α_{i-1} and α_i cannot be s_u. Let s^* be the step between α_{k-1} and α_k. (Notice that it *is* possible that $s^* = s_u$, as the execution is no longer bivalent after this final step.)

By our contradiction assumption, we know that for each $i \in \{0, ..., k-1\}$, $\alpha_i \cdot s_u$ is univalent. We also know that $\alpha_0 \cdot s_u$ is 0-valent. It follows that there must exist some $\hat{i} \in \{0, ..., k-1\}$, such that $\alpha_{\hat{i}} \cdot s_u$ is 0-valent and $\alpha_{\hat{i}} \cdot s_v \cdot s_u$ is 1-valent, where s_v is the next valid step of some node $v \neq u$. Notice this holds whether or not $s^* = s_u$ (if $s^* = s_u$ then α_k is a fragment ending with s_u that we know to be 1-valent, otherwise, $\alpha_k \cdot s_u$ is this fragment). We have found a fragment α^*, therefore, where $\alpha^* \cdot s_u$ is 0-valent but $\alpha^* \cdot s_v \cdot s_u$ is 1-valent. We now perform a case analysis on s_v and s_u to show that all possible cases lead to a contradiction. In the following, to simplify notation, let $\beta_0 = \alpha^* \cdot s_u$ and $\beta_1 = \alpha^* \cdot s_v \cdot s_u$.

Case 1*:* Both steps affect the same node w. It is possible that w is u or v (e.g., if s_u is an acknowledgment and s_v is u receiving v's message), it is also possible that w is not u or v (e.g., if s_u and s_v are both receives at some third node w). We note that w (and only w) can distinguish between β_0 and β_1. Imagine, however, that we extend β_1 such that every node *except for* w keeps taking valid steps. All non-w nodes must eventually decide, as this is equivalent to a fair execution where w crashes after β_1, and w is the only node to crash—a setting where termination demands decision. By our valency assumption, these nodes must decide 1. Now imagine that we extend β_0 with the exact same steps. For all non-w nodes these two executions are indistinguishable, so they will once again decide 1. We assumed, however, that β_0 was 0-valent: a contradiction.

Case 2*:* The steps affect two different nodes. In this case, it is clear that no node can distinguish between $\beta_0 \cdot s_v$ and β_1. We can, therefore, apply the same style of indistinguishability argument as in case 1, except in this case we can allow all nodes to continue to take steps. □

[4]Notice, not every extension need lead to a decision. If, for example, the extension does not give steps to two or more nodes, than this is equivalent to two or more nodes crashing—a circumstance for which we do not expect a 1-fault tolerant algorithm to necessarily terminate.

We now leverage Lemma 3.1 to prove our main theorem.

THEOREM 3.2. *There does not exist a deterministic algorithm that guarantees to solve consensus in a single hop network in our abstract MAC layer model with a single crash failure.*

PROOF. Assume for contradiction such an algorithm exists. Call it $\mathcal{A}$. Using the standard argument we first establish the existence of a bivalent initial configuration of $\mathcal{A}$ (e.g., Lemma 2 from [15]). Starting from this configuration, we keep applying Lemma 3.1, rotating through all n nodes in round robin order, to extend the execution in a way that keeps it bivalent. Because we rotate through all nodes when applying Lemma 3.1, the resulting execution is fair in the sense that all nodes keep taking steps. The termination property of consensus requires that nodes eventually decide. By agreement when any node decides the execution becomes univalent. By Lemma 3.1, however, our execution remains bivalent, so no node must ever decide. This violates termination and therefore contradicts the assumption that $\mathcal{A}$ solves consensus. □

3.2 Consensus without Unique Ids

Having proved that consensus is impossible with crash failures, we consider the conditions under which it remains impossible *without* crash failures. Recall, in wireless networks, unlike wired networks, the network configuration might be ad hoc, preventing nodes from having full *a priori* information on the participants. Accordingly, in this section and the next we explore the network information required to solve consensus. We start here by investigating the importance of unique ids. We call an algorithm that *does not* use unique ids an *anonymous* algorithm. We prove below that consensus is impossible with anonymous algorithms, even if nodes know the network size and diameter. We then provide a corollary that extends this result to the standard asynchronous network model. To the best of our knowledge, this is the first result on the necessity of unique ids for consensus in multihop message passing networks.

Result. To prove our main theorem we leverage an indistinguishability result based on the network topologies shown in Figure 1. Due to the careful construction of these networks, we cannot prove our impossibility holds for all n and D (network B, for example, requires that n be divisible by 3). We can, however, prove that for every sufficiently large (even) D and n, the problem is impossible for D and some $n' = \Theta(n)$.

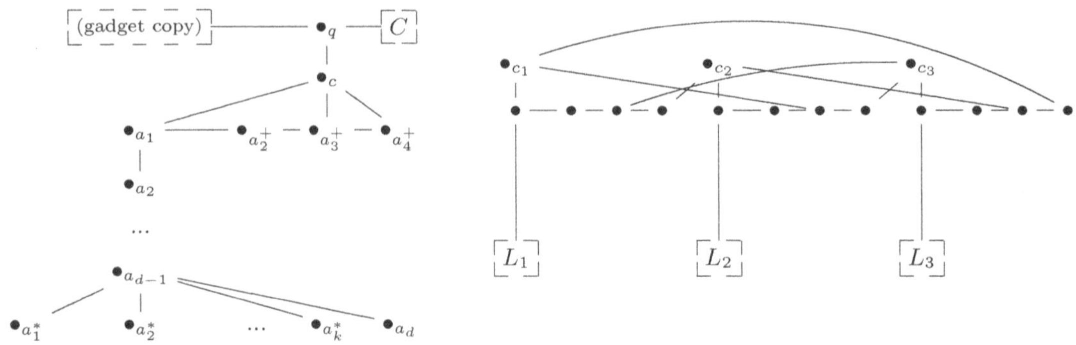

Figure 1: In Network A (left) the a nodes plus c combine to comprise a *gadget*. The bridge node q is connected to two copies of this gadget at their c nodes. It is also connected to all nodes in a clique C used to adjust the total network size. In Network B (right) the sub-graphs L_1, L_2, and L_3, are each a copy of the sub-graph of the gadget of Network A consisting of nodes at a_2 and below in the diagram (i.e., nodes labelled a_i for $i > 1$, as well as the a_j^* nodes.) L_1, L_2, and L_3, in other words, connect to the a_1 node of the Network A gadget.

THEOREM 3.3. *There exists a constant integer $c \geq 1$, such that for every even diameter $D \geq 4$ and network size $n \geq D$, there exists an $n' \in \{n, ..., c \cdot n\}$, such that no anonymous algorithm $\mathcal{A}$ guarantees to solve consensus in our abstract MAC layer model in all networks of diameter D and size n'.*

Given some D and n that satisfy the theorem constraints, let k be the smallest integer $k \geq 0$ such that $3(\frac{D-2}{2}+k)+12 \geq n$. Set $n' = 3(\frac{D-2}{2}+k)+12$. Consider networks A and B from Figure 1, instantiated with $d = \frac{D-2}{2}$ and k set to the value fixed above in defining n'. In the case of network A, set the clique C to contain enough nodes to bring the total count in that network to equal the number of nodes in B. The following claim follows from the structure of these networks and our definitions of k and d.

CLAIM 3.4. *Networks A and B, instantiated with the values described above, have size n' and diameter D.*

We define the *synchronous scheduler* in our model to be a message scheduler that delivers messages in lock step rounds. That is, it delivers all nodes' current message to all recipients, then provides all nodes with an ack, and then moves on to the next batch of messages. Furthermore, we assume no global time (or, equivalently, some small amount of time that we can define as needed in the below proof) passes between these *synchronous steps.* Fix some consensus algorithm $\mathcal{A}$ that does not use unique ids. For $b \in \{0,1\}$, let α_B^b be the execution of $\mathcal{A}$ in network B (see the right network in Figure 1) with all nodes starting with initial value b and message behaviors scheduled by the synchronous scheduler. The following lemma follows directly from the definition of consensus and the fairness of the synchronous scheduler.

LEMMA 3.5. *There exists some $t \geq 0$ such that for $b \in \{0,1\}$, α_B^b terminates by synchronous step t with all nodes deciding b.*

Next, let α_A be an execution of $\mathcal{A}$ in network A (see the left network in Figure 1) defined as follows: (1) all nodes in one gadget start with initial value 0 (call these nodes A_0), all nodes in the other copy of the gadget start with initial value 1 (call these nodes A_1); (2) the bridge node q and the nodes in component C start with arbitrary initial values; and (3) we fix the scheduler to schedule the steps of A_0 and A_1 like the synchronous scheduler for for t steps (for the t fixed in Lemma 3.5), while delaying any message from node q being delivered until after these t steps are complete. After this point, the scheduler can behave as the synchronous scheduler for the full network.

The key argument in our proof is that a node in A_b cannot distinguish itself during the first t steps of α_A from the same node in α_B^b. Intuitively, this follows because the network in B is carefully constructed to be symmetric, so nodes cannot tell if they are communicating with one copy of the network A gadget or multiple copies. To formalize this argument, we introduce some notion that relates network A to B. Notice that network B consists of three copies of the gadget from network A (with some of the edges from the connector node copies swapped to interconnect the copies). For each node u in a network A gadget, therefore, we can define S_u to be the set containing the three nodes in network B that correspond to u: that is, the nodes in u's position in the three gadget copies of B). For example, consider node c in the network A gadget shown in Figure 1. By our above definition, $S_c = \{c_1, c_2, c_3\}$. We can now formalize our indistinguishability.

LEMMA 3.6. *Fix some $b \in \{0,1\}$ and some node u in A_b. The first t steps of u in α_A are indistinguishable from the first t steps of the three nodes in S_u in α_B^b.*

PROOF. We begin by noting the following property of our networks that follows directly from its structure (in the following, we use the notation N_{A_b} to indicate the neighbor function of the subgraph of network A consisting only of the nodes in A_b): (*) *Fix any $u \in A_b$ and $u' \in S_u$. For every $v \in N_{A_b}(u)$, u' is connected to exactly one node in S_v. There are no other edges adjacent to u' in B.* We now leverage property (*) in proving the following induction argument, which directly implies our lemma statement. The below induction is on the number of synchronous steps in the α executions.

Hypothesis: $\forall u \in A_b$, $0 \leq r \leq t$: after r steps, u in α_A has the same state as the nodes in S_u in α_B^b.

Basis ($r = 0$): Because we assume no unique ids and the same initial values for all relevant nodes, the hypothesis is trivially true after 0 steps.

Step: Assume the hypothesis holds through some step $r, 0 \leq r < t$. We will now show it holds for step $r+1$. By our hypothesis, for each $w \in A_b$, the nodes in S_w will send the same message as w during step $r+1$ (as this message is generated deterministically by the nodes' state after step r). Now consider a particular $u \in A_b$ and a particular copy $u' \in S_u$ in network B. By property (*), for each node $v \in N_{A_b}(u)$ that sends a message to u in $r+1$, u' is connected to a single node in S_v. By our above argument, this node in S_v will send the same message to u' as v sends to u. Furthermore, (*) establishes that there are no other edges to u' that will deliver messages at this point. It follows that u' will receive the same message set in $r+1$ in α_B^b as u receives in $r+1$ in α_A. They will end $r+1$, therefore, in the same state. □

We now leverage Lemma 3.6 to prove our main theorem.

Proof Proof of Theorem 3.3.. Assume for contradiction that there exists an anonymous algorithm $\mathcal{A}$ that guarantees to solve consensus for a diameter D and network size n' specified to be impossible by the theorem statement. Fix some nodes $u \in A_0$ and $v \in A_1$ such that u and v are in the same position in their respective gadgets in network A. Fix some $w \in S_u = S_v$. By Lemma 3.5, w decides 0 within t steps of α_B^0. Combining this observation with Lemma 3.6, applied to u and $b = 0$, it follows that u will decide 0 in α_A. By agreement, it follows that all nodes must decide 0 in α_A—including v. We can, however, apply this same argument to α_B^1, v and $b = 1$, to determine that v decides 1 in α_A. A contradiction. □

We conclude with a corollary for the standard asynchronous model that follows from the fact that our model is strictly stronger and this result concerns a lower bound.

Corollary 3.7. *There exists a constant integer $c \geq 1$, such that for every even diameter $D \geq 4$ and network size $n \geq D$, there exists an $n' \in \{n, ..., c \cdot n\}$, such that no anonymous algorithm $\mathcal{A}$ guarantees to solve consensus in the asynchronous network model with broadcast communication and no advance knowledge of the network topology, in all networks of diameter D and size n'.*

3.3 Consensus without Network Size

In Section 3.2, we proved that consensus in our model requires unique ids. Here we prove that even with unique ids and knowledge of D, nodes still need knowledge of n to solve the problem (in multihop networks). Our strategy for proving this theorem is an indistinguishability argument of a similar style to that used in Section 3.2. In more detail, consider network K_D with diameter D shown in Figure 2. Imagine that we start the $D+1$ nodes in sub-graph L_D^1 (resp. L_D^2) with initial value 0 (resp. 1). If we delay message delivery long enough between L_{D-1} and its neighbors in K_D, the nodes in L_D^i cannot distinguish between being partitioned in K_D or executing by themselves in a network. Diameter knowledge does not distinguish these cases.

To formalize this argument, we first assume w.l.o.g. that nodes continually send messages. In the following, fix some consensus algorithm $\mathcal{A}$. Let L_d, for integer $d \geq 1$, be the network graph consisting of $d+1$ nodes in a line. Let α_d^b, for $b \in \{0, 1\}$ and some integer $d \geq 1$, be the execution of $\mathcal{A}$ in L_d, where all nodes begin with initial value 0 and message behavior is scheduled by the synchronous scheduler (defined in Section 3.2). The following lemma follows from the validity and termination properties of consensus.

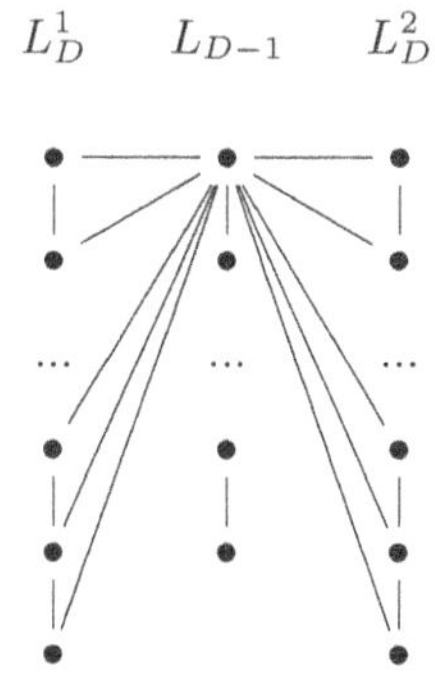

Figure 2: The K_D network. Note: L_{D-1} contains D nodes.

Lemma 3.8. *There exists some integer $t \geq 0$, such that for every $b \in \{0, 1\}$ and $d \geq 1$, α_d^b terminates after t synchronous steps with all nodes deciding b.*

For a given diameter $D > 1$, we define the network graph K_D to consist of two copies of L_D (call these L_D^1 and L_D^2) and the line L_{D-1}, with an edge added from every node in L_D^1 and L_D^2 to some fixed endpoint of the L_{D-1} line. Notice that by construction, K_D has diameter D. (See Figure 2.) Next, we define the *semi-synchronous scheduler*, in the context of network graph K_D, to be a message scheduler that delivers messages amongst nodes in L_D^1 and amongst nodes in L_D^2, in the same manner as the synchronous scheduler for t synchronous steps (for the t provided by Lemma 3.8). During this period, the semi-synchronous scheduler does *not* deliver any messages from the endpoint of the L_{D-1} line to nodes in L_D^1 or L_D^2. After this period, it behaves the same as the synchronous scheduler. Let β_D be the execution of $\mathcal{A}$ in K_D with: (1) all nodes in L_D^1 starting with initial value 0; (2) all nodes in L_D^2 starting with initial value 1; (3) all nodes in L_{D-1} starting with arbitrary initial values; and (4) the semi-synchronous scheduler controlling message actions. With these definitions established, we can prove our main theorem.

Theorem 3.9. *For every $D > 1$, no algorithm $\mathcal{A}$ guarantees to solve consensus in our abstract MAC layer model in all networks of diameter D.*

Proof. Assume for contradiction that $\mathcal{A}$ guarantees to solve consensus in all networks of diameter D, for some fixed $D > 1$. By the definition of the semi-synchronous scheduler, it is straightforward to see that β_D is indistinguishable from α_D^0 for nodes in L_D^1, and indistinguishable from α_D^1 for nodes in L_D^2, for the first t synchronous steps. Combining Lemma 3.8 with our indistinguishability, we note that nodes in L_D^1 will decide 0 in β_D while nodes in L_D^2 will decide 1. Therefore, $\mathcal{A}$ does not satisfy agreement in β_D. We constructed K_D, however, so that it has a diameter of D. Therefore, $\mathcal{A}$ guarantees to solve consensus (and thus satisfy agreement) in this network. A contradiction. □

3.4 Time Bound for Consensus

The preceding lower bounds all concerned computability. For the sake of completeness, we conclude by considering complexity. The $\Omega(D \cdot F_{ack})$ time bound claimed below is established by a partitioning argument.

THEOREM 3.10. *No algorithm can guarantee to solve consensus in our abstract MAC layer model in less than* $\lfloor \frac{D}{2} \rfloor F_{ack}$ *time.*

PROOF. Fix some D. Consider a line of diameter D consisting of nodes $u_1, u_2, ..., u_{D+1}$, arranged in that order. Consider an execution of a consensus algorithm in this network with a variant of the synchronous scheduler from Section 3.2 that delays the maximum F_{ack} time between each synchronous step. In $\lfloor \frac{D}{2} \rfloor F_{ack}$ time, the endpoints cannot hear from beyond their nearest half of the line. If we assume they must decide by this deadline we can apply a standard partitioning argument to create an agreement violation. In particular, if one half starts with initial value 0 and the other initial value 1, the endpoint of the first half must decide 0 and the endpoint of the second must decide 1 (by indistinguishability and validity), creating an agreement violation. □

4. UPPER BOUNDS

In Section 3, we proved fundamental limits on solving consensus in our model. In this section, we prove these bounds optimal with matching upper bounds. We consider both *single hop* (i.e., the network graph is a clique) and *multihop* (i.e., the network graph is an arbitrary connected graph) networks. Due to the impossibility result from Section 3.1, we assume no crash failures in the following.

4.1 Consensus in Single Hop Networks

Here we describe an algorithm—*two-phase consensus*—that guarantees to solve consensus in single hop network topologies in an optimal $O(F_{ack})$ time. It assumes unique ids but does not require knowledge of n. This opens a separation with the standard broadcast asynchronous model (which does not include acknowledgments) where consensus is known to be impossible under these conditions [1].

The pseudocode for our algorithm is presented in Algorithm 1. Here we summarize its operation: Each node u executes two *phases*. At the beginning of the first phase, u broadcasts its unique id and its initial value $v_u \in \{0, 1\}$. Node u considers its first phase complete once it receives an acknowledgment for its first broadcast. At this point, u will choose its *status*. If u has seen evidence of a different initial value in the system by this point (i.e., it sees a phase 1 message for a different value or a *bivalent* phase 2 message), it sets its status to *bivalent*. Otherwise, it sets it to *decided* v_u. Node u now begins phase 2 by broadcasting its status and id. Once u finishes this phase 2 broadcast, it has two possibilities. If its status is *decided*, then it can decide its initial value and terminate. Otherwise, it constructs a *witness set* W_u, consisting of every node it has heard from so far in the execution. It waits until it has received a phase 2 message from *every* node in W_u. At this point, if the set contains any message of the form *decided* v_w, then it decides v_w. Otherwise, it decides default value 1. We now establish the correctness of this strategy.

Algorithm 1 Two-Phase Consensus (for node u)

```
v ← initial value from {0, 1}
R1 ← {⟨phase 1, id_u, v⟩}
                                                        ▷ Phase 1
broadcast(⟨phase 1, id_u, v⟩)
while waiting for ack do
    add received messages to R1
end while
if ⟨phase 1,*,1 − v⟩ ∈ R1 or ⟨phase 2,*, bivalent⟩ ∈ R1 then
    status ← bivalent
else
    status ← decided(v)
end if
                                                        ▷ Phase 2
broadcast(⟨phase 2, id_u, status⟩)
R2 ← {⟨phase 2, id_u, status⟩}
while waiting for ack do
    add received messages to R2
end while
W ← every unique id in R1 and R2            ▷ Witness list created
while ∃id ∈ W s.t. ⟨phase 2, id,*⟩ ∉ R1 ∪ R2 do
    add received phase 2 messages to R2
end while
if ⟨phase 2, *, decided(0)⟩ ∈ R2 then
    decide 0
else
    decide 1
end if
```

THEOREM 4.1. *The two-phase consensus algorithm solves consensus in* $O(F_{ack})$ *time in our abstract MAC layer model in single hop networks with unique ids.*

PROOF. Validity and termination are straightforward to establish. We turn our attention, therefore, to agreement. If no node ends up with $status$ = *decided*(0), then 1 is the only possible decision value. The interesting case, therefore, is when some node u does set $status \leftarrow$ *decided*(0) after its phase 1 broadcast completes. Let S be the subset of nodes that began with initial value 1 (if any). By assumption, u's phase 1 broadcast completed before any node in S, as, otherwise, u would have seen evidence of a 1 before setting $status$, preventing it from choosing *decided*(0). It follows that every node in S must set $status$ to *bivalent*. We know, therefore, that it is impossible to have both *decided*(1) and *decided*(0) in the system. We are left to show that if there is *decided*(0) in the system, then all nodes end up deciding 0. As before, let u be a node with status *decided*(0). Now let v be a node with status *bivalent*. We consider two cases concerning u and v's interaction.

In the first case, assume v receives a message from u before v finishes its phase 2 broadcast. It follows that u will be placed in v's witness list, W. The algorithm now requires v to wait for u's phase 2 broadcast before deciding. It will therefore see that u has a status of *decided*(0), requiring v to decide 0. In the second case, v does not receive a message from u before v finishes its phase 2 broadcast. Accordingly, u is not in v's witness set W. This might be problematic as it could allow v to decide before it sees a *decided*(0) message. Fortunately, we can show this second case cannot happen. If v had not heard *any* message from u by the time it finished its phase 2 broadcast, it follows that u receives this broadcast before it finishes its phase 1 broadcast. But v's phase 2 broadcast has a *bivalent* status. By the algorithm, this would prevent u from setting its status to *decided*(0)—contradicting our assumption that u has a *decided* status. □

4.2 Consensus in Multihop Networks

We now describe a consensus algorithm for the multihop setting that guarantees to solve consensus in $O(D \cdot F_{ack})$ time. It assumes unique ids and knowledge of n (as required by the lower bounds of Section 3), but makes no additional assumptions about the participants or network topology. Notice, this solution does not *replace* the single hop algorithm of Section 4.1, as this previous algorithm: (1) is simpler; (2) has a small constant in its time complexity (i.e., 2); and (3) does not require knowledge of n.[5]

Due to the complexity of this algorithm and its analysis, we provide below only a high-level summary of the algorithm and its analysis. A detailed description (including pseudocode) and full proof arguments can be found in the full version of this paper [37].

Algorithm Strategy. Our strategy for solving consensus in this setting is to leverage the logic of the PAXOS consensus algorithm [30, 31]. This algorithm was designed and analyzed for the asynchronous network model with bounded crash failures. Here we apply the logic to our wireless model with no crash failures. The main difficulty we face in this effort is that nodes do not know the topology of the network or the identity of the other participants in advance. To overcome these issue we connect the PAXOS logic with a collection of sub-routines we call *services*, which are responsible for efficiently delivering messages, electing the leaders needed by PAXOS for liveness, and telling the proposers when to generate new proposal numbers. We call this combination of PAXOS logic with our model-specific services *wireless PAXOS* (wPAXOS).

If we were satisfied with a non-optimal $O(n \cdot F_{ack})$ time complexity, the communication services could be implemented with a simple flooding logic (the first time you see a message, re-broadcast), and the leader election service could simply return the largest id seen so far. To obtain an optimal $O(D \cdot F_{ack})$ time complexity, however, requires a more intricate solution. In particular, when a proposer is waiting to hear from a majority of acceptors, we cannot afford for it to receive each response individually (as each message can only hold a constant number of unique ids, and this would therefore require a proposer to receive $\Theta(n)$ messages). Our solution is to instead have nodes execute a distributed Bellman-Ford style iterative refinement strategy to establish shortest-path routing trees rooted at potential leaders. We design this service such that once the leader election service stabilizes, a tree rooted at this leader will complete soon after (if it is not already completed). These trees are then used to safely *aggregate* responses from acceptors: a strategy that leverages the fact that PAXOS only requires the total *count* of a given response type, not the individual responses.[6] This aggregation strategy reduces the time to gather responses (after stabilization) from $O(n \cdot F_{ack})$ to $O(D \cdot F_{ack})$.

The final optimization needed to adapt PAXOS to our model is the change service. We need the eventual leader to generate proposals *after* the leader election and tree services stabilize, so it can reap the benefits of efficient acceptor response aggregation. At the same time, however, the leader cannot generate *too many* new proposals after this point, or each new proposal may delay the previous. The key property of our change service is that it guarantees that the leader will generate $\Theta(1)$ new proposal after stabilization (assuming there is no decision yet in the network).

Analysis. We now summarize the correctness argument for wPAXOS. We begin with the main theorem.

THEOREM 4.2. *The wPAXOS algorithm solves consensus in $O(D \cdot F_{ack})$ time in our abstract MAC layer model in any connected network topology, where D is the network diameter and nodes have unique ids and knowledge of network size.*

The correctness of this theorem follows from the lemmata stated below. In the following, we provide a short note on the main proof idea for each. The full proofs can be found in the appendix.

Before continuing to the lemma statements, we first define a *proposition* to be either a prepare or propose (sometimes called accept) message generated by a proposer. Fix some execution of wPAXOS and some proposition p in that execution. We define $a(p)$ and $c(p)$ to describe the number of acceptors that accept proposition p and the count of acceptances calculated at the originator of p, respectively. Our first lemma establishes that this count is never too large, even though it might depend on aggregating responses in a tree structure that is still changing during this aggregation. The main strategy in proving the below is an induction on the message receive steps in the execution. The inductive hypothesis states that the sum of acceptances counted at the originator of p and the acceptance contained in messages in the system, is no larger than $a(p)$.

LEMMA 4.3. *Fix some execution of wPAXOS. Let p be a proposition generated by u in this execution. It follows that $c(p) \leq a(p)$.*

We then leverage this lemma to prove the following claim, which comes from [31]. As argued by Lamport in [31], proving this claim is the key to proving the safety of PAXOS. To establish this lemma we leverage a causality graph construction to show that receiving a given response count requires that you heard from (in a causal sense) that many acceptors.

LEMMA 4.4. *Fix an execution of wPAXOS. Assume proposer u generates a proposal with value val and proposal number x. It follows that there exists a set S consisting of a majority of acceptors such that either: (a) no acceptor in S has accepted a proposal with number smaller than x, or (b) val is the value of the highest-numbered proposal among all proposals with numbers less than x accepted by the acceptors in S.*

The final safety argument guarantees that the proposal numbers never get too large too fit in our bounded message size (i.e., larger than $\Theta(\log n)$ bits). The proof for the below lemma works by bounding the number of events in the network that can possibly generate new proposals.

[5]This lack of knowledge of n does not violate the lower bound of Section 3.3, as this lower bound requires the use of a multihop network topology.

[6]A technicality here is that these responses sometimes include prior proposals; we handle this issue by simply maintaining in aggregated responses the prior proposal—if any—with the largest proposal number of those being aggregated.

LEMMA 4.5. *There exists a constant k such that the tags used in proposal numbers of wPAXOS are bounded by $O(n^k)$.*

The final lemma needed to prove our main theorem concerns liveness; it establishes that wPAXOS terminates in $O(D \cdot F_{ack})$ time. The proof argument for this lemma first shows that the leader and tree services stabilize in $O(D \cdot F_{ack})$ time, and then shows that after this *global stabilization*, the stable leader will generate $\Theta(1)$ additional proposals—one of which must lead to a decision.

LEMMA 4.6. *Fix some execution of wPAXOS. Every node decides in $O(D \cdot F_{ack})$ time.*

5. CONCLUSION

Consensus is a key primitive in designing reliable distributed systems. Motivated by this reality and the increasing interest in wireless distributed systems, in this paper we studied the consensus problem in a wireless setting. In particular, we proved new upper and lower bounds for consensus in an abstract MAC layer model—decreasing the gap between our results and real deployment. We first proved that (deterministic) consensus is impossible with crash failures. We then proved that without crash failures, consensus requires unique ids and knowledge of the network size. We also establish a lower bound on the time complexity of any solution. We conclude by presenting two new consensus algorithms—one optimized for single hop networks and one that works in general multihop (connected) networks.

In terms of future work, there are three clear next steps that would help advance this research direction. The first step is to consider consensus in an abstract MAC layer model that includes unreliable links in addition to reliable links. Our multihop algorithm, for example, does not necessarily work once we allow unreliability. Identifying strategies that tolerate this uncertainty remains an open question.

The second step is to consider what additional formalisms might allow deterministic consensus solutions to circumvent the impossibility concerning crash failures. In the classical distributed systems setting, failure detectors were used for this purpose. In the wireless world, where, among other things, we do not always assume *a priori* knowledge of the participants, this might not be the most natural formalism to deploy.

The third direction is to consider randomized algorithms, which might provide better performance and the possibility of circumventing crash failures, unique id, and/or network size knowledge lower bounds.

6. ACKNOWLEDGMENTS

The research described in this paper was supported in a part by the Ford University Research Grant Program and NSF grant number CCF-1320279.

7. REFERENCES

[1] M. Abboud, C. Delporte-Gallet, and H. Fauconnier. Agreement without knowing everybody: a first step to dynamicity. In *Proceedings of the International Conference on New Technologies in Distributed Systems*, 2008.

[2] M. K. Aguilera, W. Chen, and S. Toueg. Failure detection and consensus in the crash-recovery model. *Distributed computing*, 13(2):99–125, 2000.

[3] E. A. Alchieri, A. N. Bessani, J. da Silva Fraga, and F. Greve. Byzantine consensus with unknown participants. In *Proceedings of the International Conference on the Principles of Distributed Systems*. 2008.

[4] K. Alekeish and P. Ezhilchelvan. Consensus in sparse, mobile ad hoc networks. *IEEE Transactions on Parallel and Distributed Systems*, 23(3):467–474, 2012.

[5] H. Attiya, A. Gorbach, and S. Moran. Computing in totally anonymous asynchronous shared memory systems. *Information and Computation*, 173(2):162–183, 2002.

[6] R. Bar-Yehuda, O. Goldreich, and A. Itai. On the Time Complexity of Broadcast in Radio Networks: an Exponential Gap Between Determinism and Randomization. In *Proceedings of the International Symposium on Principles of Distributed Computing*, 1987.

[7] F. Bonnet and M. Raynal. Anonymous Asynchronous Systems: the Case of Failure Detectors. In *Proceedings of the International Symposium on Distributed Computing*, 2010.

[8] D. Cavin, Y. Sasson, and A. Schiper. Consensus with unknown participants or fundamental self-organization. In *ADHOC-NOW*, 2004.

[9] T. D. Chandra and S. Toueg. Unreliable failure detectors for reliable distributed systems. *Journal of the ACM*, 43(2):225–267, 1996.

[10] G. Chockler, M. Demirbas, S. Gilbert, C. Newport, and T. Nolte. Consensus and collision detectors in wireless ad hoc networks. In *Proceedings of the International Symposium on Principles of Distributed Computing*, 2005.

[11] A. Cornejo, N. Lynch, S. Viqar, and J. L. Welch. Neighbor Discovery in Mobile Ad Hoc Networks Using an Abstract MAC Layer. In *Proceedings of the Annual Allerton Conference on Communication, Control, and Computing*, 2009.

[12] A. Cornejo, S. Viqar, and J. L. Welch. Reliable Neighbor Discovery for Mobile Ad Hoc Networks. *Ad Hoc Networks*, 12:259–277, 2014.

[13] A. Czumaj and W. Rytter. Broadcasting Algorithms in Radio Networks with Unknown Topology. *Journal of Algorithms*, 60:115–143, 2006.

[14] S. Daum, S. Gilbert, F. Kuhn, and C. Newport. Broadcast in the Ad Hoc SINR Model. In *Proceedings of the International Symposium on Distributed Computing*, 2013.

[15] M. J. Fischer, N. A. Lynch, and M. S. Paterson. Impossibility of distributed consensus with one faulty process. *Journal of the ACM*, 32(2), 1985.

[16] L. Gasieniec, D. Peleg, and Q. Xin. Faster Communication in Known Topology Radio Networks. *Distributed Computing*, 19(4):289–300, 2007.

[17] O. Goussevskaia, R. Wattenhofer, M. Halldorsson, and E. Welzl. Capacity of Arbitrary Wireless Networks. In *Proceedings of the IEEE International Conference on Computer Communications*, 2009.

[18] F. Greve and S. Tixeuil. Knowledge connectivity vs. synchrony requirements for fault-tolerant agreement in unknown networks. In *Proceedings of the IEEE/IFIP International Conference on Dependable Systems and Networks*, 2007.

[19] R. Guerraoui, M. Hurfinn, A. Mostéfaoui, R. Oliveira, M. Raynal, and A. Schiper. Consensus in asynchronous distributed systems: A concise guided tour. *Advances in Distributed Systems, Lecture Notes in Computer Science*, 1752:33–47, 2000.

[20] R. Guerraoui and A. Schiper. Consensus: the big misunderstanding [distributed fault tolerant systems]. In *Proceedings of the IEEE Computer Society Workshop on Future Trends of Distributed Computing Systems*, 1997.

[21] R. Guerraoui and A. Schiper. The generic consensus service. *IEEE Transactions on Software Engineering*, 27(1):29–41, 2001.

[22] M. M. Halldorsson and P. Mitra. Wireless Connectivity and Capacity. In *Proceedings of the ACM-SIAM Symposium on Discrete Algorithms*, 2012.

[23] T. Jurdzinski, D. R. Kowalski, M. Rozanski, and G. Stachowiak. Distributed Randomized Broadcasting in Wireless Networks under the SINR Model. In *Proceedings of the International Symposium on Distributed Computing*, 2013.

[24] T. Jurdziński and G. Stachowiak. Probabilistic Algorithms for the Wakeup Problem in Single-Hop Radio Networks. In *Algorithms and Computation*, pages 535–549. Springer, 2002.

[25] M. Khabbazian, F. Kuhn, D. Kowalski, and N. Lynch. Decomposing Broadcast Algorithms Using Abstract MAC Layers. In *Proceedings of the Workshop on the Foundations of Mobile Computing*, 2010.

[26] M. Khabbazian, F. Kuhn, N. Lynch, M. Medard, and A. ParandehGheibi. MAC Design for Analog Network Coding. In *Proceedings of the Workshop on the Foundations of Mobile Computing*, 2011.

[27] D. Kowalski and A. Pelc. Broadcasting in Undirected Ad Hoc Radio Networks. *Distributed Computing*, 18(1):43–57, 2005.

[28] F. Kuhn, N. Lynch, and C. Newport. The Abstract MAC Layer. In *Proceedings of the International Symposium on Distributed Computing*, 2009.

[29] F. Kuhn, N. Lynch, and C. Newport. The Abstract MAC Layer. *Distributed Computing*, 24(3-4):187–206, 2011.

[30] L. Lamport. The part-time parliament. *ACM Transactions on Computer Systems*, 16(2):133–169, 1998.

[31] L. Lamport. Paxos made simple. *ACM Sigact News*, 32(4):18–25, 2001.

[32] N. A. Lynch. *Distributed algorithms.* Morgan Kaufmann, 1996.

[33] T. Moscibroda. The Worst-Case Capacity of Wireless Sensor Networks. In *Proceedings of the ACM/IEEE International Conference on Information Processing in Sensor Networks*, 2007.

[34] T. Moscibroda and R. Wattenhofer. Maximal Independent Sets in Radio Networks. In *Proceedings of the International Symposium on Principles of Distributed Computing*, 2005.

[35] T. Moscibroda and R. Wattenhofer. The Complexity of Connectivity in Wireless Networks. In *Proceedings of the IEEE International Conference on Computer Communications*, 2006.

[36] A. Mostefaoui and M. Raynal. Solving consensus using chandra-touegÕs unreliable failure detectors: A general quorum-based approach. *Lecture Notes in Computer Science*, 1693:49–63, 1999.

[37] C. Newport. Consensus with an Abstract MAC Layer. (Available on arXiv; also online at `http://cs.georgetown.edu/~cnewport/pubs/consensus-abstract-full.pdf`).

[38] D. Peleg. Time-Efficient Broadcasting in Radio Networks: a Review. In *Proceedings of the Conference on Distributed Computing and Internet Technology*, 2007.

[39] E. Ruppert. The Anonymous Consensus Hierarchy and Naming Problems. In *Proceedings of the International Conference on Principles of Distributed Systems*, 2007.

[40] A. Schiper. Early consensus in an asynchronous system with a weak failure detector. *Distributed Computing*, 10(3):149–157, 1997.

[41] E. W. Vollset and P. D. Ezhilchelvan. Design and performance-study of crash-tolerant protocols for broadcasting and reaching consensus in MANETs. In *IEEE Symposium on Reliable Distributed Systems*, 2005.

[42] W. Wu, J. Cao, and M. Raynal. Eventual clusterer: A modular approach to designing hierarchical consensus protocols in manets. *IEEE Transactions onParallel and Distributed Systems*, 20(6):753–765, 2009.

Simple and Efficient Local Codes for Distributed Stable Network Construction*

Othon Michail
Computer Technology Institute & Press
"Diophantus" (CTI)
Patras, Greece
michailo@cti.gr

Paul G. Spirakis
Department of Computer Science, University of Liverpool, Liverpool, UK
& CTI, Patras, Greece
P.Spirakis@liverpool.ac.uk

ABSTRACT

In this work, we study protocols so that populations of distributed processes can *construct networks*. In order to highlight the basic principles of distributed network construction we keep the model minimal in all respects. In particular, we assume *finite-state processes* that all begin from the same initial state and all execute the same protocol. Moreover, we assume *pairwise interactions* between the processes that are scheduled by a fair adversary. In order to allow processes to construct networks, we let them *activate* and *deactivate* their pairwise connections. When two processes interact, the protocol takes as input the states of the processes and the state of their connection and updates all of them. Initially all connections are inactive and the goal is for the processes, after interacting and activating/deactivating connections for a while, to end up with a desired *stable network*. We give protocols (optimal in some cases) and lower bounds for several basic network construction problems such as *spanning line*, *spanning ring*, *spanning star*, and *regular network*. The *expected time to convergence* of our protocols is analyzed under a *uniform random scheduler*. Finally, we prove several *universality* results by presenting generic protocols that are capable of simulating a Turing Machine (TM) and exploiting it in order to construct a large class of networks. We additionally show how to partition the population into k *supernodes*, each being a line of $\log k$ nodes, for the largest such k. This amount of local memory is sufficient for the supernodes to obtain unique names and exploit their names and their memory to realize nontrivial constructions.

Categories and Subject Descriptors:
C.2.4 [Computer-communication Networks]: Distributed Systems; C.2.1 [Computer-communication Networks]: Network Architecture and Design—*distributed networks, network communications, network topology*; F.1.1 [Computation By Abstract Devices]: Models of Computation—*automata, computability theory, unbounded-action devices*; F.1.2 [Computation By Abstract Devices]: Modes of Computation—*parallelism and concurrency, probabilistic computation*; J.2 [Computer Applications]: Physical Sciences and Engineering—*Chemistry, Physics*

Keywords: network construction; distributed protocol; interacting automata; stabilization; population; fairness; random schedule; structure formation; self-organization

1. INTRODUCTION

1.1 Motivation

Suppose a set of tiny computational devices (possibly at the nanoscale) is injected into a human circulatory system for the purpose of monitoring or even treating a disease. The devices are incapable of controlling their mobility. The mobility of the devices, and consequently the interactions between them, stems solely from the dynamicity of the environment, the blood flow inside the circulatory system in this case. Additionally, each device alone is incapable of performing any useful computation, as the small scale of the device highly constrains its computational capabilities. The goal is for the devices to accomplish their task via cooperation. To this end, the devices are equipped with a mechanism that allows them to create bonds with other devices (mimicking nature's ability to do so). So, whenever two devices come sufficiently close to each other and interact, apart from updating their local states, they may also become connected by establishing a physical connection between them. Moreover, two connected devices may at some point choose to drop their connection. In this manner, the devices can organize themselves into a desired global structure. This network-constructing self-assembly capability allows the artificial population of devices to evolve greater complexity, better storage capacity, and to adapt and optimize its performance to the needs of the specific task to be accomplished.

1.2 Our Approach

In this work, we study the fundamental problem of *network construction* by a distributed computing system. The system consists of a set of processes that are capable of performing local computation (via pairwise interactions) and of forming and deleting connections between them. Connections between processes can be either *physical* or *virtual* depending on the application. In the most general case, a con-

*Supported in part by the project FOCUS, implemented under the "ARISTEIA" Action of the OP EdLL co-funded by the EU (ESF) and Greek National Resources. Full version: http://ru1.cti.gr/aigaion/?page=publication&kind=single&ID=989

PODC'14, July 15–18, 2014, Paris, France.

ACM 978-1-4503-2944-6/14/07 ...$15.00.
http://dx.doi.org/10.1145/2611462.2611466.

nection between two processes can be in one of a finite number of possible states. For example, state 0 could mean that the connection does not exist while state $i \in \{1, 2, \ldots, k\}$, for some finite k, that the connection exists and has strength i. We consider here the simplest case, which we call the *on/off* case, in which, at any time, a connection can either exist or not exist, that is there are just two states for the connections. If a connection exists we also say that it is *active* and if it does not exist we say that it is *inactive*. Initially all connections are inactive and the goal is for the processes, after interacting and activating/deactivating connections for a while, to end up with a desired *stable network*. In the simplest case, the output-network is the one induced by the active connections and it is stable when no connection changes state any more.

Our aim in this work is to initiate this study by proposing and studying a very *simple*, yet sufficiently generic, model for distributed network construction. To this end, we assume the computationally weakest type of processes. In particular, the processes are finite automata that all begin from the same initial state and all execute the same finite program which is stored in their memory (i.e. the system is *homogeneous*). The communication model that we consider is also very minimal. In particular, we consider processes that are inhabitants of an *adversarial environment* that has total control over the inter-process interactions. We model such an environment by an adversary scheduler that operates in discrete steps selecting in every step a pair of processes which then interact according to the common program. This represents very well systems of (not necessarily computational) entities that interact in pairs whenever two of them come sufficiently close to each other. When two processes interact, the program takes as input the states of the interacting processes and the state of their connection and outputs a new state for each process and a new state for the connection. The only restriction that we impose on the scheduler in order to study the constructive power of the model is that it is *fair*, by which we mean the weak requirement that, at every step, it assigns to every reachable configuration of the system a non-zero probability to occur. In other words, a fair scheduler cannot forever conceal an always reachable configuration of the system. Note that such a generic scheduler gives no information about the running time of our constructors. Thus, to estimate the efficiency of our solutions we assume a *uniform random scheduler*, one of the simplest fair probabilistic schedulers. The uniform random scheduler selects in every step independently and uniformly at random a pair of processes to interact from all such pairs. What renders this model interesting is its ability to achieve complex global behavior via a set of notably simple, uniform (i.e. with codes that are independent of the size of the system), anonymous, homogeneous, and cooperative entities.

We now give a simple illustration of the above. Assume a set of n very weak processes that can only be in one of two states, "black" or "red". Initially, all processes are black. We can think of the processes as small particles that move randomly in a fair solution. The particles are capable of forming and deleting physical connections between them, by which we mean that, whenever two particles interact, they can read and write the state of their connection. Moreover, for simplicity of the model, we assume that fairness of the solution is independent of the states of the connections. This is in contrast to schedulers that would take into account the geometry of the active connections and would, for example, forbid two non-neighboring particles of the same component to interact with each other. In particular, we assume that throughout the execution every pair of processes may be selected for interaction. Consider now the following simple problem. We want to identically program the initially disorganized particles so that they become self-organized into a *spanning star*. In particular, we want to end up with a unique black particle connected (via active connections) to $n-1$ red particles and all other connections (between red particles) being inactive. Equivalently, given a (possibly physical) system that tends to form a spanning star we would like to unveil the code behind this behavior. Consider the following program. When two black particles that are not connected interact, they become connected and one of them becomes red. When two connected red particles interact they become disconnected (i.e. reds repel). Finally, when a black and a red that are not connected interact they become connected (i.e. blacks and reds attract). The protocol forms a spanning star as follows. As whenever two blacks interact only one survives and the other becomes red, eventually a unique black will remain and all other particles will be red (we say "eventually", meaning "in finite time", because we do not know how much time it will take for all blacks to meet each other but from fairness we know that this has to occur in a finite number of steps). As blacks and reds attract while reds repel, it is clear that eventually the unique black will be connected to all reds while every pair of reds will be disconnected. Moreover, no rule of the program can modify such a configuration thus the constructed spanning star is stable. It is worth noting that this very simple protocol is optimal both w.r.t. to the number of states that it uses and w.r.t. to the time it takes to construct a stable spanning star under the uniform random scheduler.

Our model for network construction is strongly inspired by the Population Protocol model [3] and the Mediated Population Protocol model [18]. States on the connections were first introduced in the latter. The main difference to our model is that *in those models the focus was on the computation of functions of some input values and not on network construction*. Another important difference is that we allow the edges to choose between *only two possible states* which was not the case in [18]. Interestingly, when operating under a uniform random scheduler, population protocols are formally equivalent to *chemical reaction networks* (CRNs), which model chemistry in a *well-mixed solution* and are widely used to describe information processing occurring in natural cellular regulatory networks [13]. However, CRNs and population protocols can only capture the dynamics of molecular counts and not of structure formation. Our model then may also be viewed as an extension of population protocols and CRNs aiming to capture the stable structures that may occur in a well-mixed solution. From this perspective, our goal is to determine what stable structures can result in such systems (natural or artificial), how fast, and under what conditions (e.g. by what underlying codes/reaction-rules). Most computability issues in the area of population protocols have now been resolved. Finite-state processes on a complete interaction network, i.e. one in which every pair of processes may interact, (and several variations) compute the *semilinear predicates* [4]. Semilinearity persists up to $o(\log \log n)$ local space but not more than this [9]. If additionally the connections between processes can hold a state from a finite domain (note that this is a stronger requirement than the on/off that the present work assumes) then the computational power dramatically increases to the commutative subclass of $\mathbf{NSPACE}(n^2)$ [18]. Other important works include [16] and [7]. For a very recent introductory text see [19].

The paper essentially consists of two parts. In the first part, we give simple (i.e. small) and efficient (i.e. polynomial-time) protocols for the construction of several fundamental networks. In particular, we give protocols for spanning lines, spanning rings, cycle-covers, partitioning into cliques, and regular networks. We remark that the spanning line problem is of outstanding importance because it constitutes a basic ingredient of universal constructors. We give three different protocols for this problem each improving on the running time but using more states to this end. Additionally, we establish a $\Omega(n \log n)$ generic lower bound on the expected running time of all constructors that construct a spanning network and a $\Omega(n^2)$ lower bound for the spanning line, where n throughout this work denotes the number of processes. Our fastest protocol for the problem runs in $O(n^3)$ expected time and uses 9 states while our simplest uses only 5 states but pays in an expected time which is between $\Omega(n^4)$ and $O(n^5)$. In the second part, we investigate the more generic question of *what is in principle constructible by our model.* We arrive there at several satisfactory characterizations establishing some sort of universality of the model. The main idea is as follows. To construct a decidable graph-language L we (i) construct on k of the processes (called the *waste*) a network G_1 capable of simulating a Turing Machine (abbreviated "TM" throughout the paper) and of constructing a random network on the remaining $n-k$ processes (called the *useful space*), (ii) use G_1 to construct a random network $G_2 \in G_{n-k,1/2}$ on the remaining $n-k$ processes, (iii) execute on G_1 the TM that decides L with G_2 as input. If the TM accepts, then we output G_2 (note that this is not a terminating step - the reason why will become clear in Section 6; the protocol just freezes and its output forever remains G_2), otherwise we go back to (ii) and repeat. Using this core idea we prove several universality results for our model. Additionally, we show how to organize the population into a distributed system with names and logarithmic local memories.

In Section 2, we discuss further related literature. In Section 3, we formally define the model of network constructors and the network construction problems that are considered in this work. In Section 4, we study the spanning line problem. In Section 5, we provide direct constructors for all the other basic network construction problems. Section 6 presents our *universality* results. Finally, in Section 7 we conclude and give further research directions that are opened by our work.

2. FURTHER RELATED WORK

Algorithmic Self-Assembly. There are already several models trying to capture the self-assembly capability of natural processes with the purpose of engineering systems and developing algorithms inspired by such processes. For example, [12] proposes to learn how to program molecules to manipulate themselves, grow into machines and at the same time control their own growth. The model guiding the study in algorithmic self-assembly is the Abstract Tile Assembly Model (aTAM) [24, 21] and variations. In contrast to those models that try to incorporate the exact molecular mechanisms, we propose a very abstract combinatorial rule-based model, free of specific application-driven assumptions, with the aim of revealing the fundamental laws governing the distributed (algorithmic) generation of networks. Our model may serve as a common substructure to more applied models that may be obtained from our model by imposing restrictions on the scheduler, the degree, and the number of local states.

Distributed Network Construction. To the best of our knowledge, classical distributed computing has not considered the problem of constructing an actual communication network from scratch. From the seminal work of Angluin [1], that initiated the theoretical study of distributed computing systems, up to now, the focus has been more on assuming a given communication topology and constructing a virtual network over it, e.g. a spanning tree for the purpose of fast dissemination of information, most of the time under the assumption of unique identities and unbounded memories. An exception is the area of geometric pattern formation by mobile robots (cf. [23, 10]). A great difference, though, to our model is that in mobile robotics the computational entities have complete control over their mobility and thus over their future interactions. Additionally, as observed in [11], in the area of self-organizing particle systems, only very little theoretical work has been done. This further supports the importance of introducing a simple yet sufficiently generic model for distributed network construction.

Cellular Automata. A cellular automaton (cf. e.g. [22]) consists of a grid of cells each cell being a finite automaton. A cell updates its own state by reading the states of its neighboring cells. Cellular automata have been used as models for self-replication, for modeling several physical systems, and for understanding emergence, complexity, and self-organization issues. Though there are some similarities there are also significant differences between our model and cellular automata. Cellular automata are more suitable for studying the formation of patterns on e.g. a discrete surface of static cells while our model is more suitable for studying how a totally dynamic (e.g. mobile) and initially disordered collection of entities can self-organize into a network.

Social Networks. There is a great amount of work dealing with networks formed by a group of interacting individuals, called players, which usually have incentives and connections between them indicate some social relationship. The network is formed by allowing the individuals to form or delete connections usually selfishly by trying to maximize their own utility (see e.g. [17, 8]). This is a game-theoretic setting which is very different from the setting considered here as the latter does not include incentives and utilities. Another important line of research considers random social networks in which new links are formed according to some probability distribution (see e.g. [6]). Though, in principle, we allow processes to perform a coin tossing during an interaction, our focus is not on the formation of a random network but on cooperative (algorithmic) construction according to a common set of rules.

Network Formation in Nature. Nature has an intrinsic ability to form complex structures and networks via a process known as *self-assembly*. By self-assembly, small components (like e.g. molecules) automatically assemble into large, and usually complex structures (like e.g. a crystal)

[12]. There is an abundance of such examples in the physical world. Through billions of years of prebiotic molecular selection and evolution, nature has produced a basic set of molecules. By combining these simple elements, natural processes are capable of fashioning an enormously diverse range of fabrication units, which can further self-organize into refined structures, materials and molecular machines that not only have high precision, flexibility and error-correction capacity, but are also self-sustaining and evolving. In fact, nature shows a strong preference for bottom-up design which inspires the fabrication of biomaterials by attempting to mimic these phenomena with the aim of creating new and varied structures with novel utilities well beyond the gifts of nature [25]. Moreover, there is already a remarkable amount of work envisioning our future ability to engineer computing and robotic systems by manipulating molecules with nanoscale precision. Ambitious long-term applications include molecular computers [5] and miniature (nano)robots for surgical instrumentation, diagnosis and drug delivery in medical applications (e.g. it has very recently been reported that DNA nanorobots could even kill cancer cells [14]) and monitoring in extreme conditions (e.g. in toxic environments). However, the road towards this vision passes first through our ability to discover *the laws governing the capability of distributed systems to construct networks*. The gain of developing such a theory will be twofold: It will give some insight to the role (and the mechanisms) of network formation in the complexity of natural processes and it will allow us engineer artificial systems that achieve this complexity.

3. A MODEL OF NETWORK CONSTRUCTORS

DEFINITION 1. *A* Network Constructor *(NET) is a distributed protocol defined by a 4-tuple* $(Q, q_0, Q_{out}, \delta)$, *where* Q *is a finite set of* node-states, $q_0 \in Q$ *is the* initial node-state, $Q_{out} \subseteq Q$ *is the set of* output node-states, *and* $\delta : Q \times Q \times \{0,1\} \to Q \times Q \times \{0,1\}$ *is the* transition function.

If $\delta(a,b,c) = (a',b',c')$, we call $(a,b,c) \to (a',b',c')$ a *transition* (or *rule*) and we define $\delta_1(a,b,c) = a'$, $\delta_2(a,b,c) = b'$, and $\delta_3(a,b,c) = c'$. A transition $(a,b,c) \to (a',b',c')$ is called *effective* if $x \neq x'$ for at least one $x \in \{a,b,c\}$ and *ineffective* otherwise. When we present the transition function of a protocol we only present the effective transitions. Additionally, we agree that the *size* of a protocol is the number of its states, i.e. $|Q|$.

The system consists of a population V_I of n distributed *processes* (also called *nodes* when clear from context). In the generic case, there is an underlying *interaction graph* $G_I = (V_I, E_I)$ specifying the permissible interactions between the nodes. Interactions in this model are always pairwise. In this work, G_I is a *complete undirected interaction graph*, i.e. $E_I = \{uv : u, v \in V_I \text{ and } u \neq v\}$, where $uv = \{u, v\}$. Initially, all nodes in V_I are in the initial node-state q_0.

A central assumption of the model is that edges have binary states. An edge in state 0 is said to be *inactive* while an edge in state 1 is said to be *active*. All edges are initially inactive.

Execution of the protocol proceeds in discrete steps. In every step, a pair of nodes uv from E_I is selected by an *adversary scheduler* and these nodes interact and update their states and the state of the edge joining them according to the transition function δ. In particular, we assume that, for all distinct node-states $a, b \in Q$ and for all edge-states $c \in \{0,1\}$, δ specifies either (a,b,c) or (b,a,c). So, if a, b, and c are the states of nodes u, v, and edge uv, respectively, then the unique rule corresponding to these states, let it be $(a,b,c) \to (a',b',c')$, is applied, the edge that was in state c updates its state to c' and if $a \neq b$, then u updates its state to a' and v updates its state to b', if $a = b$ and $a' = b'$, then both nodes update their states to a', and if $a = b$ and $a' \neq b'$, then the node that gets a' is drawn equiprobably from the two interacting nodes and the other node gets b'.

A *configuration* is a mapping $C : V_I \cup E_I \to Q \cup \{0,1\}$ specifying the state of each node and each edge of the interaction graph. Let C and C' be configurations, and let u, v be distinct nodes. We say that C *goes to* C' *via encounter* $e = uv$, denoted $C \xrightarrow{e} C'$, if $(C'(u), C'(v), C'(e)) = \delta(C(u), C(v), C(e))$ or $(C'(v), C'(u), C'(e)) = \delta(C(v), C(u), C(e))$ and $C'(z) = C(z)$, for all $z \in (V_I \backslash \{u,v\}) \cup (E_I \backslash \{e\})$. We say that C' *is reachable in one step from* C, denoted $C \to C'$, if $C \xrightarrow{e} C'$ for some encounter $e \in E_I$. We say that C' is *reachable* from C and write $C \rightsquigarrow C'$, if there is a sequence of configurations $C = C_0, C_1, \ldots, C_t = C'$, such that $C_i \to C_{i+1}$ for all i, $0 \leq i < t$.

An *execution* is a finite or infinite sequence of configurations $C_0, C_1, C_2, \ldots$, where C_0 is an initial configuration and $C_i \to C_{i+1}$, for all $i \geq 0$. A *fairness condition* is imposed on the adversary to ensure the protocol makes progress. An infinite execution is *fair* if for every pair of configurations C and C' such that $C \to C'$, if C occurs infinitely often in the execution then so does C'. In what follows, every execution of a NET will by definition considered to be fair.

Note that NETs are *uniform* and *anonymous*, that is the size of the protocol does not depend on the number of nodes n and there is not enough room in the states of the nodes to store unique identifiers.

We define the *output of a configuration* C as the graph $G(C) = (V, E)$ where $V = \{u \in V_I : C(u) \in Q_{out}\}$ and $E = \{uv : u, v \in V,\ u \neq v, \text{ and } C(uv) = 1\}$. In words, the output-graph of a configuration consists of those nodes that are in output states and those edges between them that are active, i.e. the active subgraph induced by the nodes that are in output states. The output of an execution $C_0, C_1, \ldots$ is said to *stabilize* (or *converge*) to a graph G if there exists some step $t \geq 0$ s.t. $G(C_i) = G$ for all $i \geq t$, i.e. from step t and onwards the output-graph remains unchanged. Every such configuration C_i, for $i \geq t$, is called *output-stable*. The *running time* (or *time to convergence*) of an execution is defined as the minimum such t (or ∞ if no such t exists). Throughout the paper, whenever we study the running time of a NET, we assume that interactions are chosen by a *uniform random scheduler* which, in every step, selects independently and uniformly at random one of the $|E_I| = n(n-1)/2$ possible interactions. In this case, the running time becomes a random variable (abbreviated "r.v.") X and our goal is to obtain bounds on the expectation $E[X]$ of X. Note that the uniform random scheduler is fair with probability 1.

DEFINITION 2. *We say that an execution of a NET on* n *processes* constructs a graph *(or* network*)* G, *if its output stabilizes to a graph isomorphic to* G.

DEFINITION 3. *We say that a NET* $\mathcal{A}$ constructs a graph language L with useful space $g(n) \leq n$, *if* $g(n)$ *is the greatest function for which: (i) for all* n, *every execution of* $\mathcal{A}$

on n processes constructs a $G \in L$ of order at least $g(n)$ (provided that such a G exists) and, additionally, (ii) for all $G \in L$ there is an execution of $\mathcal{A}$ on n processes, for some n satisfying $|V(G)| \geq g(n)$, that constructs G. Equivalently, we say that $\mathcal{A}$ constructs L with waste $n - g(n)$.

DEFINITION 4. *Define* $\mathbf{REL}(g(n))$ *to be the class of all graph languages that are constructible with useful space $g(n)$ by a NET. We call* $\mathbf{REL}(\cdot)$ *the* relation *or* on/off *class.*

Also define $\mathbf{PREL}(g(n))$ in precisely the same way as $\mathbf{REL}(g(n))$ but in the extension of the above model in which every pair of processes is capable of tossing an unbiased coin during an interaction between them. In particular, in the weakest probabilistic version of the model, we allow transitions that with probability 1/2 give one outcome and with probability 1/2 another. Additionally, we require that all graphs have the same probability to be constructed by the protocol.

We denote by $\mathbf{DGS}(f(l))$ (for "Deterministic Graph Space") the class of all graph languages that are decidable by a TM of (*binary*) space $f(l)$, where l is the length of the adjacency matrix encoding of the input graph.

3.1 Problem Definitions

We here provide formal definitions of all the network construction problems that are considered in this work.

Global line. The goal is for the n distributed processes to construct a spanning line, i.e. a connected graph in which 2 nodes have degree 1 and $n-2$ nodes have degree 2.

Cycle cover. Every process in V_I must eventually have degree 2. The result is a collection of node-disjoint cycles spanning V_I.

Global star. The processes must construct a spanning star, i.e. a connected graph in which 1 node, called the *center*, has degree $n-1$ and $n-1$ nodes, called the *peripheral nodes*, have degree 1. (Already discussed in Section 1)

Global ring. The processes must construct a spanning ring, i.e. a connected graph in which every node has degree 2.

k-regular connected. The generalization of global ring in which every node has degree $k \geq 2$ (note that k is a constant and a protocol for the problem must run correctly on any number n of processes).

c-cliques. The processes must partition themselves into $\lfloor n/c \rfloor$ cliques of order c each (again c is a constant).

Replication. The protocol is given an input graph $G = (V, E)$ on a subset V_1 of the processes ($|V_1| = |V|$). The processes in V_1 are initially in state q_0 and the edges of E are the active edges between them. All other edges in E_I are initially inactive. The processes in $V_2 = V_I \backslash V_1$ are initially in state r_0. The goal is to create a *replica* of G on V_2, provided that $|V_2| \geq |V_1|$. Formally, we want, in every execution, the output induced by the active edges between the nodes of V_2 to stabilize to a graph isomorphic to G.

4. CONSTRUCTING A GLOBAL LINE

In this section, we study probably the most fundamental network-construction problem, which is the problem of constructing a spanning line. Its importance lies in the fact that a spanning line provides an ordering on the processes which can then be exploited (as shown in Section 6) to simulate a TM and thus to establish universality of our model.

We begin with a generic lower bound holding for all protocols that construct a spanning network.

THEOREM 1 (GENERIC LOWER BOUND). *The expected time to convergence (always under the uniform random scheduler) of any protocol that constructs a spanning network is* $\Omega(n \log n)$.

PROOF. Consider the time at which the last edge is activated. By that time, all nodes have some active edge incident to them, thus every node has interacted at least once. The latter can be shown to require an expected number of $\Theta(n \log n)$ steps. □

We now give an improved lower bound for the particular case of constructing a spanning line.

THEOREM 2 (LINE LOWER BOUND). *The expected time to convergence of any protocol that constructs a spanning line is* $\Omega(n^2)$.

We proceed by presenting our simplest protocol for the spanning line problem.

Protocol Simple-Global-Line: $(q_0, q_0, 0) \rightarrow (q_1, l, 1)$, $(l, q_0, 0) \rightarrow (q_2, l, 1)$, $(l, l, 0) \rightarrow (q_2, w, 1)$, $(w, q_2, 1) \rightarrow (q_2, w, 1)$, $(w, q_1, 1) \rightarrow (q_2, l, 1)$

THEOREM 3. *Protocol* Simple-Global-Line *constructs a spanning line. It uses 5 states and its expected running time is* $\Omega(n^4)$ *and* $O(n^5)$.

PROOF. *Correctness.* In the initial configuration C_0, all nodes are in state q_0 and all edges are inactive, i.e in state 0. Every configuration C that is reachable from C_0 consists of a collection of active lines and isolated nodes. Additionally, every active line has a unique leader which either occupies an endpoint and is in state l or occupies an internal node, is in state w, and moves along the line. Whenever the leader lies on an endpoint of its line, its state is l and whenever it lies on an internal node, its state is w. Lines can expand towards isolated nodes and two lines can connect their endpoints to get merged into a single line (with total length equal to the sum of the lengths of the merged lines plus one). Both of these operations only take place when the corresponding endpoint of every line that takes part in the operation is in state l.

We have to prove two things: (i) there is a set $\mathcal{S}$ of output-stable configurations whose active network is a spanning line, (ii) for every reachable configuration C (i.e. $C_0 \rightsquigarrow C$) it holds that $C \rightsquigarrow C_s$ for some $C_s \in \mathcal{S}$. For (i), consider a spanning line, in which the non-leader endpoints are in state q_1, the non-leader internal nodes in q_2, and there is a unique leader either in state l if it occupies an endpoint or in state w if it occupies an internal node. For (ii), note that any reachable configuration C is a collection of active lines with unique leaders and isolated nodes. We present a (finite) sequence of transitions that converts C to a $C_s \in \mathcal{S}$. If there are isolated nodes, take any line and if its leader is internal make it reach one of the endpoints by selecting the appropriate interactions. Then successively apply the rule $(l, q_0, 0) \rightarrow (q_2, l, 1)$ to expand the line towards all isolated nodes. Thus we may now w.l.o.g. consider a collection of lines without isolated nodes. By successively applying the rule $(l, l, 0) \rightarrow (q_2, w, 1)$ to pairs of lines while always moving the internal leaders that appear towards an endpoint it is not hard to see that the process results in an output-stable configuration from $\mathcal{S}$, i.e. one whose active network is a spanning line.

Running Time Upper Bound. For the running time upper bound, we have an expected number of $O(n^2)$ steps until further progress is made (i.e. for another merging to occur given that at least two l-leaders exist) and $O(n^4)$ steps for the resulting random walk (until state w reaches one endpoint of the line) to finish and to have again the system ready for progress. $O(n^4)$ follows because we have a random walk on a line with two absorbing barriers (see e.g. [15] pages 348-349) delayed on average by a factor of $O(n^2)$. As progress is made $n-2$ times, we conclude that the expected running time of the protocol is upper bounded from above by $(n-2)[O(n^2)+O(n^4)] = O(n^5)$.

Running Time Lower Bound. We next prove that we cannot hope to improve the above upper bound by a better analysis by more than a factor of n. For this we first prove that the protocol w.h.p. constructs $\Theta(n)$ different lines of length 1 during its course. A set of k disjoint lines implies that k distinct merging processes have to be executed in order to merge them all in a common line and each single merging results in the execution of another random walk. We exploit all these to prove the desired $\Omega(n^4)$ lower bound.

Recall that initially all nodes are in q_0. Every interaction between two q_0-nodes constructs another line of length 1. Call the random interaction of step i a *success* if both participants are in q_0. Let R be the r.v. of the number of nodes in state q_0; i.e. initially $R = n$. Note that, at every step, R decreases by at most 2, which happens only in a success (it may also remain unchanged, or decrease by 1 if a leader expands towards a q_0). Let the r.v. X_i be the number of successes up to step i and X be the total number of successes throughout the course of the protocol (e.g. until no further successes are possible or until stabilization). Our goal is to calculate the expectation of X as this is equal to the number of distinct lines of length 1 that the protocol is expected to form throughout its execution (note that these lines do not necessarily have to coexist). Given R, the probability of success at the current step is $p_R = [R(R-1)]/[n(n-1)] \geq (R-1)^2/n^2$. As long as $R \geq (n/2)+1 = z$ it holds that $p_R \geq (n^2/4)/n^2 = 1/4$. Moreover, as R decreases by at most 2 in every step, there are at least $(n-z)/2 = [(n/2)-1]/2 = (n/4)-1/2$ steps until R becomes less or equal to z. Thus, our process *dominates* a Bernoulli process Y with $(n/4)-1/2$ trials and probability of success $p' = 1/4$ in each trial. For this process we have $\mathrm{E}[Y] = [(n/4)-1/2](1/4) = (n/16)-1/8 = \Theta(n)$.

We now exploit the following Chernoff bound (cf. [20], page 70) establishing that w.h.p. Y does not deviate much below its mean $\mu = \mathrm{E}[Y]$:

Chernoff Bound. Let $Y_1, Y_2, \ldots, Y_t$ be independent Poisson trials such that, for $1 \leq i \leq t$, $\mathrm{P}[Y_i = 1] = p_i$, where $0 < p_i < 1$. Then, for $Y = \sum_{i=1}^t Y_i$, $\mu = \mathrm{E}[Y] = \sum_{i=1}^t p_i$, and $0 < \delta < 1$, $\mathrm{P}[Y < (1-\delta)\mu] < \exp(-\mu\delta^2/2)$.

Additionally, we have $\exp(-\mu\delta^2/2) = \epsilon \Leftrightarrow \delta = \sqrt{\frac{2\ln 1/\epsilon}{\mu}}$. Thus $\exp(-\mu\delta^2/2) = n^{-c}$ implies $\delta^2 = \frac{2c\ln n}{\mu} = \frac{2c\ln n}{(1/8)(n/2-1)} = \frac{16c\ln n}{n/2-1} \Rightarrow \delta = \sqrt{\frac{16c\ln n}{n/2-1}} \Rightarrow (1-\delta)\mu = \frac{1}{8}\left(1-\sqrt{\frac{16c\ln n}{n/2-1}}\right)\left(\frac{n}{2}-1\right) > \frac{1}{16}\left(n-2\sqrt{cn\ln n}-2\right) = \Theta(n)$.

So, for all $c = O(1)$, $\mathrm{P}[Y < \frac{1}{16}\left(n-2\sqrt{cn\ln n}-2\right)] < n^{-c} \Rightarrow \mathrm{P}[Y \geq \frac{1}{16}\left(n-2\sqrt{cn\ln n}-2\right)] > 1-n^{-c} \Rightarrow \mathrm{P}[Y = \Theta(n)] > 1-n^{-c}$ and as X dominates Y, we have $\mathrm{P}[X = \Theta(n)] > 1-n^{-c}$. In words, w.h.p. we expect $\Theta(n)$ lines of length 1 to be constructed by the protocol.

Now, given that $X = \Theta(n)$, we distinguish two cases: (i) At some point during the course of the protocol two lines both of length $\Theta(n)$ get merged. In this case, the corresponding random walk takes on average $\Theta(n^2)$ transitions involving the leader and on average the leader is selected every $\Theta(n^2)$ steps to interact with one of the 2 active edges incident to it. That is, the expected number of steps for the completion of such a random walk is $\Theta(n^4)$ and the expected running time of the protocol is $\Omega(n^4)$. (ii) In every merging process, at least one of the two participating lines has length at most $d_{max} = o(n)$. We have already shown that the protocol w.h.p. forms $k = \Theta(n)$ distinct lines of length 1. Consider now the interval $I = \{k/2 - d_{max}+1, \ldots, k/2\}$. As $h = \Theta(n) > d_{max}$ for all $h \in I$, only a single line can ever have length $h \in I$ and one, call it l_1, will necessarily fall in this interval due to the fact that the length of l_1 will increase by at most d_{max} in every merging until it becomes n. Consider now the time at which l_1 has length $h \in I$. As the total length due to lines of length 1 (ever to appear) is k and the length of l_1 is h there is still a remaining length of at least $k-h \geq k-k/2 = k/2 = \Theta(n)$ to be merged to l_1. As the maximum length of any line different than l_1 is d_{max}, l_1 will get merged to the $k-h$ remaining length via at least $j = \Theta(n)/d_{max}$ distinct mergings with lines of length at most d_{max}. These mergings, and thus also the resulting random walks, cannot occur in parallel as all of them share l_1 as a common participant (and a line can only participate in one merging at a time). Let d_i denote the length of the i-th line merged to l_1, for $1 \leq i \leq j$. If l_1 has length $d(l_1)$ just before the i-th merging, then the expected duration of the resulting random walk is $n^2 \cdot d(l_1) \cdot d_i$ and the new l_1 resulting from merging will have length $d(l_1)+d_i$. Let Y denote the duration of all random walks, and Y_i, $1 \leq i \leq j$, the duration of the i-th random walk. In total, the expected duration of all random walks resulting from the j mergings of l_1 is $\mathrm{E}[Y] = \mathrm{E}[\sum_{i=1}^j Y_i] = \sum_{i=1}^j \mathrm{E}[Y_i] = \sum_{i=1}^j n^2(h+d_1+\ldots+d_{i-1})d_i \geq n^2\sum_{i=1}^j hd_i = n^2 h\sum_{i=1}^j d_i = n^2\Theta(n)\Theta(n) = \Theta(n^4)$. The fifth equality follows from the fact that $\sum_{i=1}^j d_i = k-h = \Theta(n)$. We conclude that the expected running time of the protocol is also in this case $\Omega(n^4)$.

Now if we define the r.v. W to be the total running time of the protocol (until convergence), by the law of total probability and for every constant $c \geq 1$, we have that: $\mathrm{E}[W] = \mathrm{E}[W \mid X = \Theta(n)] \cdot \mathrm{P}[X = \Theta(n)] + \mathrm{E}[W \mid X = o(n)] \cdot \mathrm{P}[X = o(n)] \geq \mathrm{E}[W \mid X = \Theta(n)] \cdot \mathrm{P}[X = \Theta(n)] > \Theta(n^4)(1-n^{-c}) = \Theta(n^4 - n^{4-c}) = \Theta(n^4)$. Thus, the expected running time of the protocol is $\Omega(n^4)$. □

We now give our fastest protocol for the global line construction. [1] The main difference to the previous protocol is that we now totally avoid mergings as they seem to consume much time. The intuition is that when two disjoint lines in-

[1]In the full paper, we also give an intermediate protocol that performs a more "deterministic" merging. That protocol uses 3 more states than *Simple-Global-Line* but improves the expected running time to between $\Omega(n^3)$ and $O(n^4)$.

teract, instead of merging, the corresponding leaders play a pairwise game. The winner grows by one towards the other line and the loser sleeps. A sleeping line cannot increase any more and only loses nodes by lines that are still awake. A single leader is guaranteed to always win and eventually remain unique and this occurs quite fast. Then the leader makes progress (by one) in most interactions and every such progress is in turn quite fast.

Protocol Fast-Global-Line: $(q_0, q_0, 0) \to (q_1, l, 1)$, $(l, q_0, 0) \to (q_2, l, 1)$, $(l, l, 0) \to (q_2', l', 1)$, $(l', q_2, 1) \to (l'', f_1, 0)$, $(l', q_1, 1) \to (l'', f_0, 0)$, $(l'', q_2', 1) \to (l, q_2, 1)$, $(l, f_0, 0) \to (q_2, l, 1)$, $(l, f_1, 0) \to (q_2', l', 1)$

THEOREM 4. *Protocol* Fast-Global-Line *constructs a spanning line. It uses 9 states and its expected running time under the uniform random scheduler is* $O(n^3)$.

5. OTHER BASIC CONSTRUCTORS

Protocol Cycle-Cover: $(q_0, q_0, 0) \to (q_1, q_1, 1)$, $(q_1, q_0, 0) \to (q_2, q_1, 1)$, $(q_1, q_1, 0) \to (q_2, q_2, 1)$

THEOREM 5 (CYCLE COVER). *Protocol* Cycle-Cover *constructs a cycle cover with waste 2. It uses 3 states, its expected running time is* $\Theta(n^2)$*, and it is optimal w.r.t. time.*

THEOREM 6 (RING LOWER BOUND). *The expected time to convergence of any protocol that constructs a spanning ring is* $\Omega(n^2)$.

Protocol Global-Ring: The rules of Protocol *Simple-Global-Line* and additionally $(l, q_1, 0) \to (l', q_1', 1)$, $(x', y, 0) \to (x'', y, 0)$, for $x \in \{l, q_1\}$ and $y \in \{l, w, q_1, q_0\}$, $(x', y', 0) \to (x'', y'', 0)$, for $x \in \{l, q_1\}$ and $y \in \{l, q_1\}$, $(l'', q_1', 1) \to (l, q_1, 0)$, $(l', q_1'', 1) \to (l, q_1, 0)$, $(l'', q_1'', 1) \to (l, q_1, 0)$

THEOREM 7 (GLOBAL RING). *Protocol* Global-Ring *constructs a spanning ring using 9 states.*

The following protocols can be found in the full paper.

THEOREM 8 (k-REGULAR CONNECTED). *We provide a parameterized protocol (called* kRC*) which, for every fixed integer* $k \geq 2$ *and every population of size* $n \geq k+1$*, constructs a connected spanning network in which at least* $n - k + 1$ *nodes have degree* k *and each of the remaining* $l \leq k-1$ *nodes has degree at least* $l - 1$ *and at most* $k - 1$.

THEOREM 9 (MANY SMALL COMPONENTS). *We provide a parameterized protocol (*c-Cliques*) which, for every fixed positive integer* c*, constructs* $\lfloor n/c \rfloor$ *cliques of order* c *each.*

THEOREM 10 (REPLICATION). *We provide a protocol (*Leader-Replication*) that constructs a copy of any connected input graph* $G_1 = (V_1, E_1)$ *with no waste. It uses 12 states and its expected running time is* $\Theta(n^4 \log n)$.

Table 1 summarizes all upper and lower bounds that we established in Sections 1 (global star), 4 and 5.

6. GENERIC CONSTRUCTORS

In this section, we ask whether there is a generic constructor capable of constructing a large class of networks. We answer this in the affirmative by presenting (i) constructors that simulate a Turing Machine (TM) and (ii) a constructor that simulates a distributed system with names and logarithmic local memories. Denote by l the binary length of the input of a TM and by n the size of a population. Note that Theorems 11 to 14 construct a random graph in the useful space and that graph constitutes the input to a TM. Thus, if the useful space consists of h nodes, the input to the TM has size $l = \Theta(h^2)$ and, as all of our constructors have $h = \Theta(n)$, in what follows it holds that $l = \Theta(n^2)$. Moreover, the TM can use space at most $O((n-h)^2) = O(n^2)$, where $n - h$ is the waste.

THEOREM 11 (LINEAR WASTE-HALF). $\mathbf{DGS}(O(\sqrt{l})) \subseteq \mathbf{PREL}(\lfloor n/2 \rfloor)$. *In words, for every graph language* L *that is decidable by a* $O(\sqrt{l})$*-space TM, there is a protocol that constructs* L *equiprobably with useful space* $\lfloor n/2 \rfloor$.

PROOF. We present here the main idea. Given a population of size n, the protocol, call it $\mathcal{A}$, partitions the population (apart from one node when n is odd) into two equal sets U and D such that all nodes in U are in state q_u, all nodes in D are in state q_d and each $u \in U$ is matched via an active edge to a $v \in D$, i.e. there is an active perfect matching between U and D. By using the *Simple-Global-Line* protocol of Section 4 on the nodes of set U, $\mathcal{A}$ constructs a spanning line in U which has the endpoints in state q_1, the internal nodes in state q_2, and has additionally a unique leader on some node. We should mention that, though we use protocol *Simple-Global-Line* here as our reference, any protocol that constructs a spanning line would work. Given such a construction, $\mathcal{A}$ organizes the line into a TM. The goal is for the TM to compute a graph from L and construct it on the nodes of set D. To achieve this, the TM implements a binary counter ($\log n$ bits long) in its memory and uses it in order to uniquely identify the nodes of set D according to their distance from one endpoint, say e.g. the left one. Whenever it wants to modify the state of edge (i, j) of the network to be constructed, it marks by a special activating or deactivating state the D-nodes at distances i and j from the left endpoint, respectively. Then an interaction between two such marked D-nodes activates or deactivates, respectively, the edge between them. To compute a graph from L equiprobably, the TM performs the following random experiment. It activates or deactivates each edge of D equiprobably (i.e. each edge becomes active/inactive with probability 1/2) and independently of the other edges. In this manner, it constructs a random graph G in D and all possible graphs have the same probability to occur. Then it simulates on input G the TM that decides L in $\sqrt{l}$ space to determine whether $G \in L$. Notice that the $n/2$ space of the simulator is sufficient to decide on an input graph encoded by an adjacency matrix of $(n/2)^2$ binary cells (which are the edges of U). If the TM rejects, then $G \notin L$ and the protocol repeats the random experiment to produce a new random graph G' and starts another simulation on input G' this time. When the TM accepts for the first time, the constructed random network belongs to L and the protocol releases the constructed network by deactivating one after the other the active (q_u, q_d) edges and at the same time updates the state of each D-node to a special q_{out} state. Finally, we should point out that, whenever the *Simple-Global-Line* protocol makes progress, all edges in D are deactivated and the TM-configuration is *reinitialized* to ensure that, when the final progress is made (resulting in the final line spanning U) the TM will be executed from the beginning on a

Protocol	# states	Expected Time	Lower Bound
Simple-Global-Line	5	$\Omega(n^4)$ and $O(n^5)$	$\Omega(n^2)$
Fast-Global-Line	9	$O(n^3)$	$\Omega(n^2)$
Cycle-Cover	3	$\Theta(n^2)$ (optimal)	$\Omega(n^2)$
Global-Star	2 (optimal)	$\Theta(n^2 \log n)$ (optimal)	$\Omega(n^2 \log n)$
Global-Ring	9		$\Omega(n^2)$
kRC	$2(k+1)$		$\Omega(n \log n)$
c-Cliques	$5c-3$		$\Omega(n \log n)$
Leader-Replication	12	$\Theta(n^4 \log n)$	

Table 1: All upper and lower bounds established in this work. *Leader-Replication* is a randomized protocol thus it concerns class PREL, while all other protocols do not use randomization and concern REL.

correct configuration (free of residues from previous partial simulations). □

We now show an interesting trade-off between the space of the simulated TM and the order of the constructed network. In particular, we prove that if the constructed network is required to occupy 1/3 instead of half of the nodes, then the available space of the TM-constructor dramatically increases to $O(n^2)$ from $O(n)$.

THEOREM 12 (LINEAR WASTE-TWO THIRDS). **DGS**$(l+O(\sqrt{l})) \subseteq$ **PREL**$(\lfloor n/3 \rfloor)$.

PROOF. The idea is to partition the population into three equal sets U, D, and M instead of the two sets of Theorem 11. The purpose of sets U and D is more or less as in Theorem 11. The purpose of the additional set M is to constitute a $\Theta(n^2)$ memory for the TM to be simulated. The goal is to exploit the $(n/3)(n/3-1)/2$ edges of set M as the binary cells of the simulated TM (see Figure 1). The set U now, instead of executing the simulation on its own nodes, uses for that purpose the edges of set M. Reading and writing on the edges of set M is performed in precisely the same way as reading/writing the edges of set D (described in Theorem 11).

As everything works in precisely the same way as in Theorem 11, we only present the subroutine that constructs the (U, D, M) partitioning.

Constructing the (U, D, M) partitioning. The rules that guarantee the desired partitioning into the three sets are: $(q_0, q_0, 0) \to (q'_u, q_d, 1)$, $(q'_u, q_0, 0) \to (q_u, q_m, 1)$, $(q'_u, q'_u, 0) \to (q_u, q'_m, 1)$, and $(q'_m, q_d, 1) \to (q_m, q_0, 0)$. The idea is to consider a U-node as unsatisfied as long as it has not managed to obtain a q_m neighbor. The unsatisfied state of a U-node is q'_u. If a q'_u meets a q_0 then it makes that q_0 its q_m neighbor and becomes satisfied. Note that it is possible that at some point the population may only consist of q'_u nodes matched to D-nodes which is not a desired outcome. For this reason, we have allowed q'_u nodes to be capable of making other q'_u nodes their q_m neighbors. That is, when two q'_u nodes interact, one of them becomes satisfied, the other becomes q'_m, and the edge joining them becomes active. A q'_m just waits to meet its active connection to a D-node, deactivates it, isolates the D-node by making it q_0 again, and becomes q_m. Then, for the construction of the line spanning U, we only allow satisfied U-nodes to participate to the construction. As a satisfied U-node never becomes unsatisfied again, this choice is safe. □

We now relax our requirement for simulation space in order to reduce the waste.

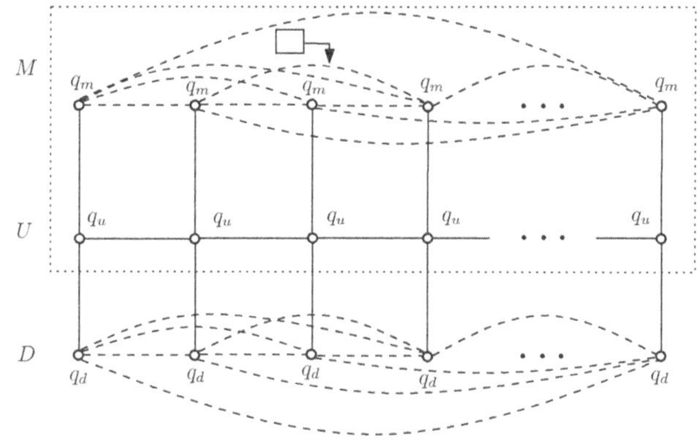

Figure 1: A partitioning into three equal sets U, D, and M. The line of set U plays the role of an ordering that will be exploited both by the random graph drawing process and by the TM-simulation. The line of set U instead of using its $\Theta(n)$ memory as the memory of the TM it now uses the $\Theta(n^2)$ memory of set M for this purpose. Set D is again the useful space on which the output-network will be constructed. Sets U and M constitute the waste.

THEOREM 13 (LOGARITHMIC WASTE). **DGS**$(O(\log l)) \subseteq$ **PREL**$(n - \log n)$.

PROOF. We give the main idea. The protocol first constructs a spanning line. Let us for now assume that the spanning line has been somehow constructed by the protocol. Then the protocol exploits the line to count the number of nodes in the network. We may assume that counting is performed in the rightmost cells of the line. The head visits one after the other the nodes from left to right and for each next move it increments the binary counter by one. When the head reaches the right endpoint, counting stops and the binary counter will have occupied approximately $\log n$ nodes (in fact, the rightmost $\log n$ nodes). Now the protocol releases the counter without altering its line structure and additionally makes all remaining $n - \log n$ nodes isolated by resetting their states and deactivating the edges between them. From now on, we may assume w.l.o.g. that there is a line of $\log n$ nodes with a unique leader and with a distributed variable containing a very good estimate of the number of isolated nodes (for this, we just compute in the logarithmic memory $n - \log n$, where n was already stored in binary and $\log n$ is the number of cells of the memory; another way to achieve this is to stop counting when the head -

moving from left to right - reaches the first, i.e. leftmost, cell occupied by the counter). All nodes of the memory are in a special m state while all remaining nodes are in some other state, e.g. f, so the two sets are distinguishable. Next the leader starts a random experiment in order to construct a random graph on the free nodes as follows. It picks the first free node that it sees, call it u_1, activates the edge between them and informs it to start tossing coins on each one of the edges joining it to other free nodes. Whenever u_1 tosses a coin on a new edge, it marks the corresponding node to avoid it in the future and informs the leader to decrement its $(n - \log n)$-counter by 1. When the counter becomes 0, u_1 has tossed coins on all its edges, by a similar counting process it removes all marks from the other free nodes, and remains marked so that the leader avoids picking it again in the future. Then the leader moves to some other free node u_2, repeating more or less the same process. At the same time the leader decrements another $(n - \log n)$-counter by one to know when all free u_is have been picked. In this manner, a random graph is drawn equiprobably on the set of free nodes. Next, the leader simulates a logarithmic TM in its memory trying to decide whether the random graph belongs or not to a given language L. If yes, then we are done. If not, then the TM just repeats the random experiment and restarts the simulation.

Reinitialization. The protocol cannot know when the line that it was initially trying to construct has become spanning. Due to this, after every expansion of the line it assumes that the line has become spanning and starts counting. It is clear that every counting process leads to the formation of a small line with a leader (of length logarithmic in the length of the original line) and several free nodes. The small line and its leader are kept forever by the simulation process. This implies that if there are more than one such lines, they will eventually interact and detect that their original line was not spanning. At that point, the interacting lines may merge to form a new line. It is clear that the only stable case is the one in which the original line was spanning and this will eventually occur. □

We next prove that a large class of graph-families can be constructed with no waste.

THEOREM 14 (NO WASTE). *Let L be a graph language such that: (i) there exists a natural number d s.t. for all $G \in L$ there is a subgraph G' of G of logarithmic order s.t. either G' or its complement is connected and has degree upper bounded by d and (ii) L is decidable in logarithmic space. Then $L \in$ **PREL**(n), i.e. there is a protocol that constructs L equiprobably with useful space n.*

PROOF. We give again the main idea. As in Theorem 13, the protocol first constructs a spanning line used to separate a subpopulation S of V_I of size approximately $\log n$. Before deactivating the line of $T = V_I \backslash S$ of length $n - \log n$ the protocol first exploits it to construct a random graph in S of active or inactive degree (choosing randomly between these) upper bounded by d (note that d is finite and thus it is known in advance by the protocol). Then the line of T organizes the bounded-degree graph of S into a TM M (which is feasible due to the fact that the degree is bounded; see Theorem 7 of [2]) of logarithmic space with a unique leader on some node. Next M draws (more or less as in Theorem 13) a random graph on the edges of $E_I \backslash E[S]$, i.e. on all edges apart from those between the nodes of S (to prevent destroying the structure of the TM). Note that, in order for the TM to be able to distinguish the nodes of S, the protocol has all these nodes in a special state that is not present in T. Observe now that, in this manner, the protocol has constructed on V_I a random graph from those having a connected subgraph of logarithmic order and degree upper bounded by d. It remains to verify whether the one constructed indeed belongs to L. To do this, M simulates the TM N that decides L in logarithmic space. If N rejects then M builds another line in T that repeats the whole process, i.e. draws a new random graph in S and so on. When N first accepts, the protocol sleeps (in the sense that it does not terminate but does not alter edges anymore either). □

REMARK 1. *If the graph-property L (in any of the above results) happens to occur with probability at least $1/f(n)$, where $f(n)$ is polynomial on n, in the $G_{n,1/2}$ random graph model, then its corresponding generic constructor runs in polynomial expected time (e.g. connectivity, hamiltonicity).*

Finally, we establish that a population consisting of n nodes can be partitioned into k *supernodes* each consisting of $\log k$ nodes, for the largest such k. The internal structure of each supernode is a line, thus it can be operated as a TM of memory logarithmic in the total number of supernodes. This amount of storage is sufficient for the supernodes to obtain unique names and exploit their names and their internal storage to realize nontrivial constructions. We are interested in the networks that can be constructed at the supernode abstraction layer.

THEOREM 15 (PARTITIONING INTO SUPERNODES). *For every network G that can be constructed by k nodes having local memories $\lceil \log k \rceil$ and unique names there is a NET that constructs G on $n = k\lceil \log k \rceil$ nodes.*

7. CONCLUSION AND OPEN PROBLEMS

There are many open problems related to the findings of the present work. Though our universal constructors show that a large class of networks is in principle constructible, they do not imply neither the simplest nor the most efficient protocols. To this end, we have provided direct constructors for some of the most basic networks, but there are still many other constructions to be investigated like grids or planar graphs. Moreover, a look at Table 1 makes it evident that there is even more work to be done towards the probabilistic analysis of protocols and in particular towards the establishment of tight bounds. Of special interest is the spanning line problem as it is a key component of universal construction. All of our attempts to give a protocol asymptotically faster than $O(n^3)$ have failed (our best lower bound for the problem is $\Omega(n^2)$). Is there a $\Theta(n^2 \log n)$ constructor?

Another very intriguing issue has to do with the size of network constructors. In particular, we would like to give problem-specific lower bounds and to formalize the apparent relationship between the size and the running time of a protocol. Is there some sort of hierarchy showing that with more states we can produce faster protocols (until optimality is obtained)? Moreover, it is worth considering non-uniform protocols that when executed on the correct number of nodes are required to construct a unique network. For example, given a population of 10 processes is there a protocol that stabilizes to the Petersen graph?

Another interesting open problem is to characterize the class **REL** in which protocols do not have access to (internal) randomness. Note that in **REL** we can again construct a sufficiently long line (as our protocols for global line are in **REL**) and exploit it as a space-bounded TM. It is also worth noting that our results on universal construction indicate that the constructive power increases as a function of the available waste. A complete characterization of this dependence would be of special value.

There is also a practically unlimited set of variations of the proposed model that is worth considering. An immediate extension of our model is to allow the connections to have more than just the two states that we considered in this work. Another route is to assume other natural probabilistic scheduling models, than the uniform considered here, which would probably require different algorithmic developments and techniques to achieve efficiency.

Finally, a very valuable and challenging interdisciplinary goal is to further investigate and formalize the apparent applicability of the model proposed here (and potential variations of it) in physical and chemical (possibly biological) processes. As already stated, we envision that a potential usefulness of such models is to unveil the algorithmic properties underlying the structure/network formation capabilities of natural processes.

Acknowledgments: We would like to thank Leslie Ann Goldberg for bringing to our attention the importance of constructing regular networks and also the reviewers of this work and some previous versions of it whose comments have helped us to improve our work substantially.

8. REFERENCES

[1] D. Angluin. Local and global properties in networks of processors. In *Proceedings of the 12th annual ACM symposium on Theory of computing (STOC)*, pages 82–93. ACM, 1980.

[2] D. Angluin, J. Aspnes, M. Chan, M. J. Fischer, H. Jiang, and R. Peralta. Stably computable properties of network graphs. In *1st IEEE International Conference on Distributed Computing in Sensor Systems (DCOSS)*, volume 3560 of *LNCS*, pages 63–74. Springer-Verlag, June 2005.

[3] D. Angluin, J. Aspnes, Z. Diamadi, M. J. Fischer, and R. Peralta. Computation in networks of passively mobile finite-state sensors. *Distributed Computing*, pages 235–253, March 2006.

[4] D. Angluin, J. Aspnes, D. Eisenstat, and E. Ruppert. The computational power of population protocols. *Distributed Computing*, 20(4):279–304, November 2007.

[5] A. Bandyopadhyay, R. Pati, S. Sahu, F. Peper, and D. Fujita. Massively parallel computing on an organic molecular layer. *Nature Physics*, 6(5):369–375, 2010.

[6] A.-L. Barabási and R. Albert. Emergence of scaling in random networks. *Science*, 286(5439):509–512, 1999.

[7] J. Beauquier, J. Burman, J. Clement, and S. Kutten. On utilizing speed in networks of mobile agents. In *Proceedings of the 29th ACM SIGACT-SIGOPS symposium on Principles of distributed computing (PODC)*, pages 305–314. ACM, 2010.

[8] L. Blume, D. Easley, J. Kleinberg, R. Kleinberg, and É. Tardos. Network formation in the presence of contagious risk. *ACM Transactions on Economics and Computation*, 1(2):6, 2013.

[9] I. Chatzigiannakis, O. Michail, S. Nikolaou, A. Pavlogiannis, and P. G. Spirakis. Passively mobile communicating machines that use restricted space. *Theoretical Computer Science*, 412(46):6469–6483, October 2011.

[10] S. Das, P. Flocchini, N. Santoro, and M. Yamashita. On the computational power of oblivious robots: forming a series of geometric patterns. In *Proceedings of the 29th ACM SIGACT-SIGOPS symposium on Principles of distributed computing (PODC)*, pages 267–276, 2010.

[11] S. Dolev, R. Gmyr, A. W. Richa, and C. Scheideler. Ameba-inspired self-organizing particle systems. *arXiv preprint arXiv:1307.4259*, 2013.

[12] D. Doty. Theory of algorithmic self-assembly. *Communications of the ACM*, 55:78–88, 2012.

[13] D. Doty. Timing in chemical reaction networks. In *Proc. of the 25th Annual ACM-SIAM Symp. on Discrete Algorithms (SODA)*, pages 772–784, 2014.

[14] S. M. Douglas, I. Bachelet, and G. M. Church. A logic-gated nanorobot for targeted transport of molecular payloads. *Science*, 335(6070):831–834, 2012.

[15] W. Feller. *An Introduction to Probability Theory and Its Applications, Vol. 1, 3rd Edition, Revised Printing.* Wiley, 1968.

[16] R. Guerraoui and E. Ruppert. Names trump malice: Tiny mobile agents can tolerate byzantine failures. In *36th International Colloquium on Automata, Languages and Programming (ICALP)*, volume 5556 of *LNCS*, pages 484–495. Springer-Verlag, 2009.

[17] M. O. Jackson. A survey of network formation models: Stability and efficiency. *Group Formation in Economics: Networks, Clubs and Coalitions, ed. G. Demange and M. Wooders*, pages 11–57, 2005.

[18] O. Michail, I. Chatzigiannakis, and P. G. Spirakis. Mediated population protocols. *Theoretical Computer Science*, 412(22):2434–2450, May 2011.

[19] O. Michail, I. Chatzigiannakis, and P. G. Spirakis. *New Models for Population Protocols.* N. A. Lynch (Ed), Synthesis Lectures on Distributed Computing Theory. Morgan & Claypool, 2011.

[20] R. Motwani and P. Raghavan. *Randomized algorithms.* Cambridge university press, 1995.

[21] P. W. K. Rothemund and E. Winfree. The program-size complexity of self-assembled squares. In *Proceedings of the 32nd annual ACM symposium on Theory of computing (STOC)*, pages 459–468, 2000.

[22] J. L. Schiff. *Cellular automata: a discrete view of the world*, volume 45. Wiley-Interscience, 2011.

[23] I. Suzuki and M. Yamashita. Distributed anonymous mobile robots: Formation of geometric patterns. *SIAM J. Comput.*, 28(4):1347–1363, Mar. 1999.

[24] E. Winfree. *Algorithmic Self-Assembly of DNA.* PhD thesis, California Institute of Technology, June 1998.

[25] S. Zhang. Fabrication of novel biomaterials through molecular self-assembly. *Nature biotechnology*, 21(10):1171–1178, 2003.

Linear-in-Δ Lower Bounds in the LOCAL Model

Mika Göös
mika.goos@mail.utoronto.ca
Department of Computer Science
University of Toronto, Canada

Juho Hirvonen
juho.hirvonen@aalto.fi

Jukka Suomela
jukka.suomela@aalto.fi

Helsinki Institute for Information Technology HIIT
Department of Information and Computer Science
Aalto University, Finland

ABSTRACT

By prior work, there is a distributed graph algorithm that finds a maximal fractional matching (maximal edge packing) in $O(\Delta)$ rounds, independently of n; here Δ is the maximum degree of the graph and n is the number of nodes in the graph. We show that this is optimal: there is no distributed algorithm that finds a maximal fractional matching in $o(\Delta)$ rounds, independently of n. Our work gives the first linear-in-Δ lower bound for a natural graph problem in the standard LOCAL model of distributed computing—prior lower bounds for a wide range of graph problems have been at best logarithmic in Δ.

Categories and Subject Descriptors

C.2.4 [**Computer-Communication Networks**]: Distributed Systems; F.2.2 [**Analysis of Algorithms and Problem Complexity**]: Nonnumerical Algorithms and Problems

Keywords

Local distributed algorithms; lower bounds; maximal edge packing; maximal fractional matching

1. INTRODUCTION

This work settles the distributed time complexity of the *maximal fractional matching* problem (see Section 1.2 for definitions) as a function of Δ, the maximum degree of the input graph.

By prior work [4], there is a distributed algorithm that finds a maximal fractional matching (also known as a maximal edge packing) in $O(\Delta)$ communication rounds, independently of the number of nodes. In this work, we show that this is optimal: there is no distributed algorithm that finds a maximal fractional matching in $o(\Delta)$ rounds.

This is the first linear-in-Δ lower bound for a natural graph problem in the standard LOCAL model of distributed computing. It is also a step towards understanding the complexity of the non-fractional analogue, the maximal matching problem, which is a basic symmetry breaking primitive in the field of distributed graph algorithms. For many related primitives, the prior lower bounds in the LOCAL model have been at best logarithmic in Δ.

PODC'14, July 15–18, 2014, Paris, France.

ACM 978-1-4503-2944-6/14/07 ...$15.00.
http://dx.doi.org/10.1145/2611462.2611467.

1.1 Matchings: State-of-the-art

Simple randomised distributed algorithms that find a maximal matching in time $O(\log n)$ have been known since the 1980s [1, 15, 22]. Currently, the fastest algorithms that compute a maximal matching stand as follows:

- **Dense graphs.** There is a recent $O(\log \Delta + \log^4 \log n)$-time randomised algorithm due to Barenboim et al. [6]. The fastest known deterministic algorithm runs in time $O(\log^4 n)$ and is due to Hańćkowiak et al. [12].
- **Sparse graphs.** There is a $O(\Delta + \log^* n)$-time deterministic algorithm due to Panconesi and Rizzi [26]. Here $\log^* n$ is the iterated logarithm of n, a very slowly growing function.

Our focus is on the sparse case. It is a long-standing open problem to either improve on the algorithm of Panconesi and Rizzi, or prove it optimal. As we are dealing with two independent parameters n and Δ, we must be careful what we mean by "proving it optimal". The meaning is: (1) there is no algorithm with run-time $O(\Delta) + o(\log^* n)$; (2) nor an algorithm with run-time $o(\Delta) + O(\log^* n)$.

The first type of lower bound follows from Linial's [21] seminal work. Linial shows that 3-colouring a cycle is not possible in time $o(\log^* n)$, so by a simple reduction:

(1) Linial's result: *Maximal matchings cannot be computed in time $f(\Delta) + o(\log^* n)$ for any function f.*

Hence we have an arbitrarily large lower bound in terms of Δ, since $\Delta = 2$ on cycles. However, viewing Linial's result from the perspective of Δ is not very meaningful: the source of hardness exhibited in Linial's proof is *not* the degree of the graph but its growing size.

The second type of lower bound has remained elusive (see Barenboim and Elkin [5, Open Problem 10.6]):

(2) Open problem: *Can maximal matchings be computed in time $o(\Delta) + O(\log^* n)$?*

We conjecture that there are no such algorithms. Our linear-in-Δ lower bound for the *fractional* version of this problem builds towards proving such conjectures: the source of hardness for maximal fractional matchings is *not* the size of the graph but the growing degree. The graphs in our lower bound construction end up satisfying $\Delta = \Theta(\log^* n)$; if this could be improved to a family where $\Delta = \omega(\log^* n)$, we would obtain a negative answer to (2).

1.2 Fractional matchings

While a matching associates a weight 0 or 1 with each edge of a graph, with 1 indicating that the edge is in a matching, a fractional matching (FM) associates a weight between 0 and 1 with each edge. In both cases, the total weight of the edges incident to any given node has to be at most 1.

Formally, let $G = (V, E)$ be a simple undirected graph and let $y\colon E \to [0,1]$ associate weights to the edges of G. Define, for each $v \in V$,

$$y[v] := \sum_{e \in E : v \in e} y(e).$$

The function y is called a *fractional matching*, or an FM for short, if $y[v] \leq 1$ for each node v. A node v is *saturated* if $y[v] = 1$.

There are two interesting varieties of fractional matchings.

- **Maximum weight.** An FM y is of *maximum weight*, if its total weight $\sum_{e \in E} y(e)$ is the maximum over all fractional matchings on G.
- **Maximality.** An FM y is *maximal*, if each edge e has at least one saturated endpoint $v \in e$.

See below for examples of (a) a maximum-weight FM, and (b) a maximal FM; the saturated nodes are highlighted.

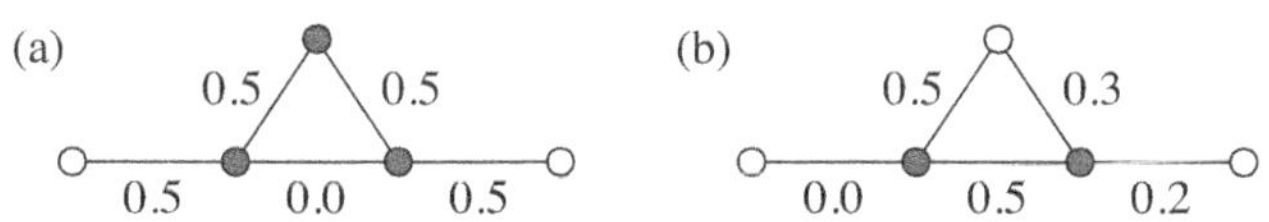

Distributed complexity.

The distributed complexity of computing maximum-weight FMs is completely understood. It is easy to see that computing an exact solution requires time $\Omega(n)$ already on odd-length path graphs (a node needs to learn the parity of its distance from an endpoint). If one settles for an approximate solution, then FMs whose total weight is at least a $(1 - \epsilon)$-fraction of the maximum can be computed in time $O(\epsilon^{-1} \log \Delta)$ by the well-known results of Kuhn et al. [16–18]. This is optimal: Kuhn et al. also show that any constant-factor approximation of maximum-weight FMs requires time $\Omega(\log \Delta)$.

By contrast, the complexity of computing maximal FMs has not been understood. A maximal FM is a 1/2-approximation of a maximum-weight FM, so the results of Kuhn et al. imply that finding a maximal FM requires time $\Omega(\log \Delta)$, but this lower bound is exponentially small in comparison to the $O(\Delta)$ upper bound [4].

1.3 Contributions

We prove that the $O(\Delta)$-time algorithm [4] for maximal fractional matchings is optimal:

THEOREM 1. *There is no (randomised)* LOCAL *algorithm that finds a maximal fractional matching in $o(\Delta)$ rounds.*

To our knowledge, this is the first linear-in-Δ lower bound in the LOCAL model for a classical graph problem. Indeed, prior lower bounds have typically fallen in one of the following categories:

- they are logarithmic in Δ [16–18],
- they analyse the complexity as a function of n for a fixed Δ [7, 8, 10, 11, 20, 21, 24],
- they only hold in a model that is strictly weaker than LOCAL [14, 19].

1.4 The LOCAL model

Our result holds in the standard LOCAL model of distributed computing [21, 27]. For now, we only recall the basic setting; see Section 3 for precise definitions.

In the LOCAL model an input graph $G = (V, E)$ defines both the problem instance and the structure of the communication network. Each node $v \in V$ is a computer and each edge $\{u, v\} \in E$ is a communication link through which nodes u and v can exchange messages. Initially, each node is equipped with a *unique identifier* and, if we study randomised algorithms, a source of randomness. In each *communication round*, each node in parallel (1) sends a message to each neighbour, (2) receives a message from each neighbour, and (3) updates its local state. Eventually, all nodes have to stop and announce their local outputs—in our case the local output of a node $v \in V$ is an encoding of the weight $y(e)$ for each edge e incident to v. The *running time* t of the algorithm is the number of communication rounds until all nodes have stopped. We call an algorithm *strictly local*, or simply *local*, if $t = t(\Delta)$ is only a function of Δ, i.e., independent of n.

The LOCAL model is the strongest model commonly in use—in particular, the size of each message and the amount of local computation in each communication round is unbounded—and this makes *lower bounds* in this model very widely applicable.

2. OVERVIEW

The maximal FM problem is an example of a *locally checkable* problem: there is a local algorithm that can check whether a proposed function y is a feasible solution.

It is known that randomness does not help a local algorithm in solving a locally checkable problem [24]: if there is a $t(\Delta)$-time worst-case randomised algorithm, then there is a $t(\Delta)$-time deterministic algorithm (see Appendix A). Thus, we need only prove our lower bound for deterministic algorithms.

2.1 Deterministic models

Our lower bound builds on a long line of prior research. During the course of the proof, we will visit each of the following deterministic models (see Figure 1), whose formal definitions are given in Section 3.

ID: *Deterministic* LOCAL. Each node has a unique identifier [21, 27]. This is the standard model in the field of deterministic distributed algorithms.

OI: *Order-invariance.* The output of an algorithm is not allowed to change if we relabel the nodes while preserving the relative order of the labels [24]. Equivalently, the algorithm can only compare the identifiers, not access their numerical value.

PO: *Port numbering and orientation.* For each node, there is an ordering on the incident edges, and all edges carry an orientation [23].

EC: *Edge colouring.* A proper edge colouring with $O(\Delta)$ colours is given [14].

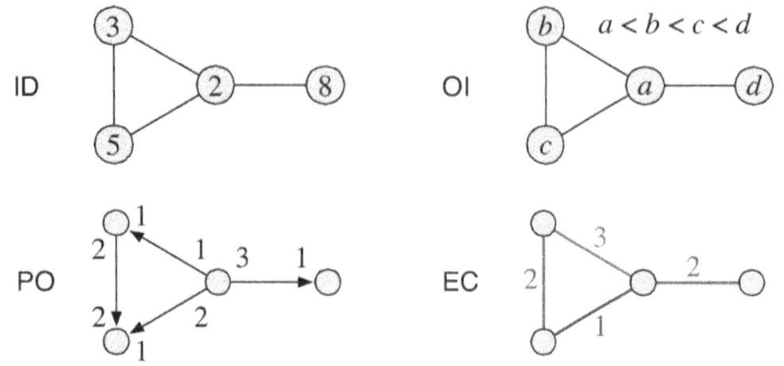

Figure 1: Deterministic models that are discussed in this work.

The models are listed here roughly in the order of decreasing strength. For example, the ID model is strictly stronger than OI, which is strictly stronger than PO. However, the EC model is not directly comparable: there are problems that are trivial to solve in ID, OI, and PO but impossible to solve in EC with any deterministic algorithm (example: graph colouring in 1-regular graphs); there are also problems that can be solved with a local algorithm in EC but they do not admit a local algorithm in ID, OI, or PO (example: maximal matching).

2.2 Proof outline

In short, our proof is an application of techniques that were introduced in two of our earlier works [10, 14]. Accordingly, our proof is in two steps.

A weak lower bound.

In our prior work [14] we showed that *maximal matchings* cannot be computed in time $o(\Delta)$ in the weak EC model. The lower-bound construction there is a regular graph, and as such, tells us very little about the fractional matching problem, since maximal fractional matchings are trivial to compute in regular graphs.

Nevertheless, we use a similar *unfold-and-mix* argument on what will be called *loopy* EC*-graphs* to prove the following intermediate result in Section 4:

STEP 1. *The maximal FM problem cannot be solved in time $o(\Delta)$ on loopy* EC*-graphs.*

The proof heavily exploits the limited symmetry breaking capabilities of the EC model. To continue, we need to argue that similar limitations exist in the ID model.

Strengthening the lower bound.

To extend the lower bound to the ID model, we give a series of local simulation results

$$\mathsf{EC} \rightsquigarrow \mathsf{PO} \rightsquigarrow \mathsf{OI} \rightsquigarrow \mathsf{ID},$$

which state that a local algorithm for the maximal fractional matching problem in one model can be simulated fast in the model preceding it. That is, even though the models EC, PO, OI, and ID are generally very different, we show that the models are roughly equally powerful for computing a maximal fractional matching.

This part of the argument applies ideas from another prior work [10]. There, we showed that, for a large class of optimisation problems, a run-time preserving simulation PO $\rightsquigarrow$ ID exists. Unfortunately, the maximal fractional matching problem is not included in the scope of this result (fractional matchings are not *simple* in the sense of [10]), so we may not apply this result directly in a black-box fashion. In addition, this general result does not hold for the EC model.

Nevertheless, we spend Section 5 extending the methods of [10] and show that they can be tailored to the case of fractional matchings:

STEP 2. *If the maximal FM problem can be solved in time $t(\Delta)$ on* ID*-graphs, then it can be solved in time $t(\Theta(\Delta))$ on loopy* EC*-graphs.*

In combination with Step 1, this proves Theorem 1.

3. TOOLS OF THE TRADE

Before we dive into the lower-bound proof, we recall the definitions of the four models mentioned in Section 2.1, and describe the standard tools that are used in their analysis.

3.1 Locality

Distributed algorithms are typically described in terms of networked state machines: the nodes of a network exchange messages for t synchronous communication rounds after which they produce their local outputs (cf. Section 1.4).

Instead, for the purposes of our lower-bound analysis, we view an algorithm $\mathcal{A}$ simply as a function that associates to each pair (G, v) an output $\mathcal{A}(G, v)$ in a way that respects *locality*. That is, an algorithm $\mathcal{A}$ is said to have run-time t, if the output $\mathcal{A}(G, v)$ depends only on the information that is available in the radius-t neighbourhood around v. More formally, define

$$\tau_t(G, v)$$

as the restriction of the structure (G, v) to the t-neighbourhood of v. That is, $\tau_t(G, v)$ consists of the nodes and edges of G that are within distance t from v; here the distance of an edge $\{u, w\}$ from v is defined as $\min\{\text{dist}(v, u), \text{dist}(v, w)\} + 1$. A t-time algorithm $\mathcal{A}$ is then a mapping that satisfies

$$\mathcal{A}(G, v) = \mathcal{A}(\tau_t(G, v)). \tag{1}$$

(Note that, according to our definition, a node needs to use an algorithm with run-time at least 1 to learn its own degree. While this might seem restrictive, we adopt this convention merely for technical convenience: our algorithms are at most 1 round slower than algorithms in the more natural model where the degree is known at the start.)

The information contained in $\tau_t(G, v)$ depends on which of the models EC, PO, OI, and ID we are studying. For each model we define an associated graph class.

3.2 Identifier-based networks

An ID*-graph* is simply a graph G whose nodes are assigned unique identifiers; namely, $V(G) \subseteq \mathbb{N}$. Any mapping $\mathcal{A}$ satisfying (1) is a t-time ID-algorithm.

An OI*-graph* is an ordered graph $(G, \preceq)$ where $\preceq$ is a linear order on $V(G)$. An OI-algorithm $\mathcal{A}$ operates on OI-graphs in such a way that if $(G, \preceq, v)$ and $(G', \preceq', v')$ are isomorphic (as ordered structures), then $\mathcal{A}(G, \preceq, v) = \mathcal{A}(G', \preceq', v')$.

Every ID-graph G is naturally an OI-graph $(G, \leq)$ under the usual order $\leq$ on $\mathbb{N}$. In the converse direction, we often convert an OI-graph $(G, \preceq)$ into an ID-graph by specifying an ID-assignment $\varphi\colon V(G) \to \mathbb{N}$ that *respects* $\preceq$ in the sense that $v \preceq u$ implies $\varphi(v) \leq \varphi(u)$. The resulting ID-graph is denoted $\varphi(G)$.

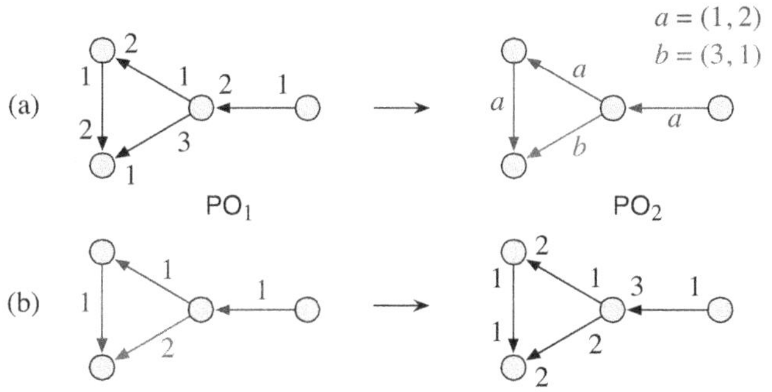

Figure 2: Two equivalent definitions of PO-graphs: (PO_1) a node of degree d can refer to incident edges with labels $1, 2, \ldots, d$; (PO_2) edges are coloured so that incoming edges have distinct colours and outgoing edges have distinct colours.

3.3 Anonymous networks

On anonymous networks the nodes do not have identifiers. The only symmetry breaking information is now provided in an *edge colouring* of a suitable type. This means that whenever there is an isomorphism between (G, v) and (G', v') that preserves edge colours, we will have $\mathcal{A}(G, v) = \mathcal{A}(G', v')$.

An EC-*graph* carries a proper edge colouring $E(G) \to \{1, \ldots, k\}$, where $k = O(\Delta)$. That is, if two edges are adjacent, they have distinct colours.

A PO-*graph* is a directed graph whose edges are coloured in the following way: if (u, v) and (u, w) are outgoing edges incident to u, then they have distinct colours; and if (v, u) and (w, u) are incoming edges incident to u, then they have distinct colours. Thus, we may have (v, u) and (u, w) coloured the same.

We find it convenient to treat PO-graphs as edge-coloured digraphs, even if this view is slightly nonstandard. Usually, PO-graphs are defined as digraphs with a *port numbering*, i.e., each node is given an ordering of its neighbours. This is equivalent to our definition as it is easy to give local simulations in both directions: A port numbering gives rise to an edge colouring where an edge (u, v) is coloured with (i, j) if v is the i-th neighbour of u and u is the j-th neighbour of v (see Figure 2a). Conversely, we can derive a port numbering from an edge colouring—using some agreed-upon ordering of the edge colours, first take all outgoing edges ordered by their colours, and then take all incoming edges ordered by their colours (see Figure 2b). (Note that this does not give a one-to-one correspondence between port-numbered graphs and edge-coloured graphs, but what matters is that we can simulate any algorithm designed for one model in the other model with the same run-time).

We are not done with defining EC and PO algorithms. We still need to restrict their power by requiring that their outputs are *invariant under graph lifts*, as defined next.

3.4 Lifts

A graph H is said to be a *lift* of another graph G if there exists an onto graph homomorphism $\alpha\colon V(H) \to V(G)$ that is a *covering map*, i.e., α preserves node degrees, $\deg_H(v) = \deg_G(\alpha(v))$; see Figure 3. Our discussion of lifts always takes place in either EC or PO; in this context we require that a covering map preserves edge colours.

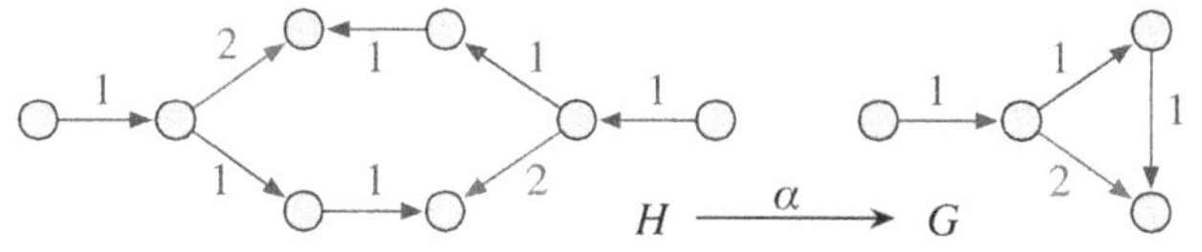

Figure 3: H is a lift of G.

The defining characteristic of anonymous models is that the output of an algorithm is invariant under taking lifts. That is, if $\alpha\colon V(H) \to V(G)$ is a covering map, then

$$\mathcal{A}(H, v) = \mathcal{A}(G, \alpha(v)), \qquad \text{for each } v \in V(H). \tag{2}$$

Since an isomorphism between H and G is a special case of a covering map, the condition (2) generalises the discussion in Section 3.3. We will be exploiting this limitation extensively in analysing the models EC and PO.

Graphs are partially ordered by the *lift* relation. For any connected graph G, there are two graphs U_G and F_G of special interest that are related to G via lifts.

Universal cover U_G.

The *universal cover* U_G of G is an unfolded tree-like version of G; see Figure 4. More precisely, U_G is the unique tree that is a lift of G. Thus, if G is a tree, $U_G = G$; if G has cycles, U_G is infinite. In passing from G to U_G we lose all the cycle structure that is present in G. The universal cover is often used to model the information that a distributed algorithm—even with unlimited running time—is able to collect on an anonymous network [2].

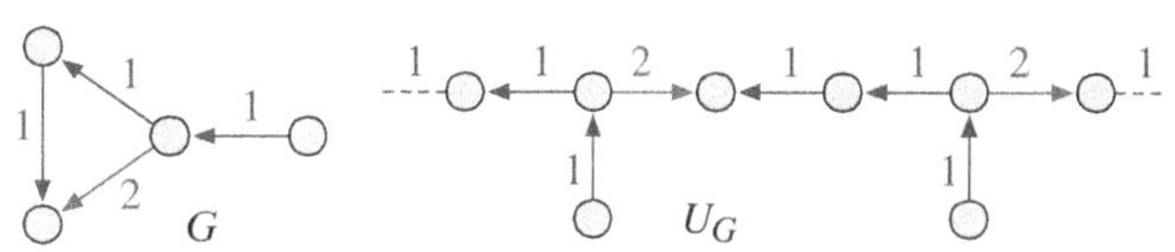

Figure 4: Universal cover U_G of G.

Factor graph F_G.

The *factor graph* F_G of G is the smallest graph F such that G is a lift of F; see Figure 5. In general, F_G is a multigraph with loops and parallel edges. It is the most concise representation of all the global symmetry breaking information available in G. For example, in the extreme case when G is vertex-transitive, F_G consists of just one node and some loops.

An input graph to an algorithm is always required to be simple (no loops or parallel edges). However, we find it convenient to *virtually* run EC and PO-algorithms $\mathcal{A}$ on multigraphs F with the understanding that the output $\mathcal{A}(F, v)$ is interpreted as if we had run $\mathcal{A}$ on a simple lift of F and then mapped the solution back to F according to (2). That is, to determine $\mathcal{A}(F, v)$ where F is a multigraph, do the following:

1. Lift F to a simple graph G (e.g., take $G = U_F$) via some $\alpha\colon V(G) \to V(F)$.
2. Execute $\mathcal{A}$ on (G, u) for some $u \in \alpha^{-1}(v)$.
3. Interpret the output of u as an output of v.

In what follows we refer to multigraphs simply as graphs.

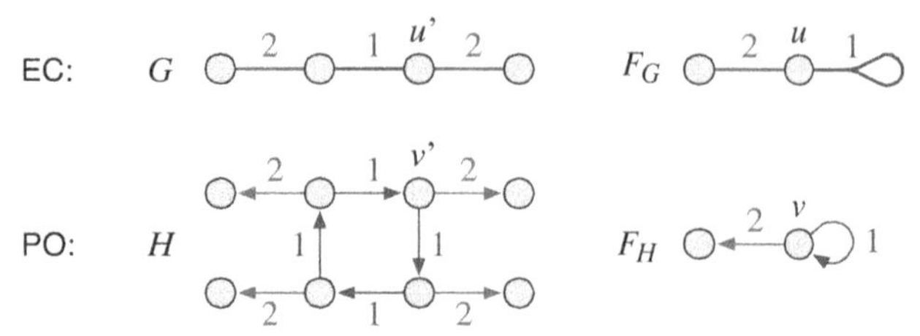

Figure 5: Factor graphs and loops. We follow the convention that undirected loops in EC-graphs count as a single incident edge, while directed loops in PO-graphs count as two incident edges: an incoming edge and an outgoing edge. In this example, both u and its preimage u' are nodes of degree 2; they are incident to one edge of colour 1 and one edge of colour 2. Both v and its preimage v' are nodes of degree 3; they are incident to two outgoing edges of colours 1 and 2, and one incoming edge of colour 1.

3.5 Loops

In EC-graphs, a single loop on a node contributes +1 to its degree, whereas in PO-graphs, a single (directed) loop contributes +2 to the degree, once for the tail and once for the head. This is reflected in the way we draw loops—see Figure 5.

The loop count on a node $v \in V(G)$ measures the inability of v to break local symmetries. Indeed, if v has ℓ loops, then in any simple lift H of G each node $u \in V(H)$ that is mapped to v by the covering map will have ℓ distinct neighbours $w_1, \ldots, w_\ell$ that, too, get mapped to v. Thus, an anonymous algorithm is forced to output the same on u as on each of $w_1, \ldots, w_\ell$.

We consider loops as an important resource.

Definition 1. An edge-coloured graph G is called *k-loopy* if each node in F_G has at least k loops. A graph is simply *loopy* if it is 1-loopy.

When computing maximal fractional matchings on a loopy graph G, an anonymous algorithm must saturate all the nodes. For suppose not. If $v \in V(G)$ is a node that does not get saturated, the loopiness of G implies that v has a neighbour u (can be $u = v$ via a loop) that produces the same output as v. But now neither endpoint of $\{u, v\}$ is saturated, which contradicts maximality; see Figure 6. We record this observation.

LEMMA 1. *Any EC-algorithm for the maximal FM problem computes a fully saturated FM on a loopy EC-graph.* □

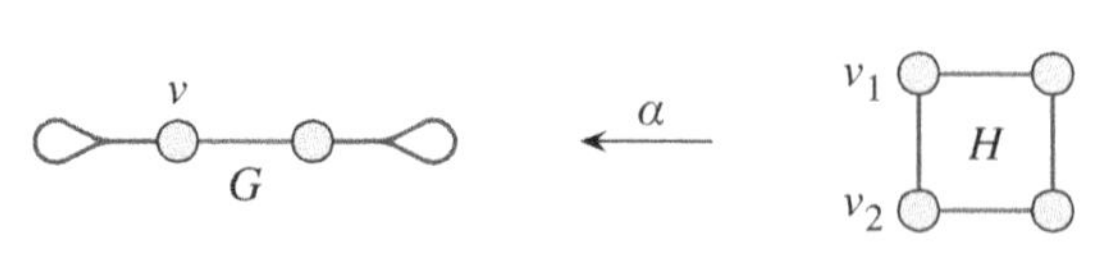

Figure 6: EC-graph G is loopy. Assume that an EC-algorithm $\mathcal{A}$ produces an output in which node v is unsaturated. Then we can construct a simple EC-graph H that is a lift of G via $\alpha\colon V(H) \to V(G)$ such that $\alpha(v_1) = \alpha(v_2) = v$ and $\{v_1, v_2\} \in E(H)$. If we apply $\mathcal{A}$ to H, both v_1 and v_2 are unsaturated; hence $\mathcal{A}$ fails to produce a maximal FM.

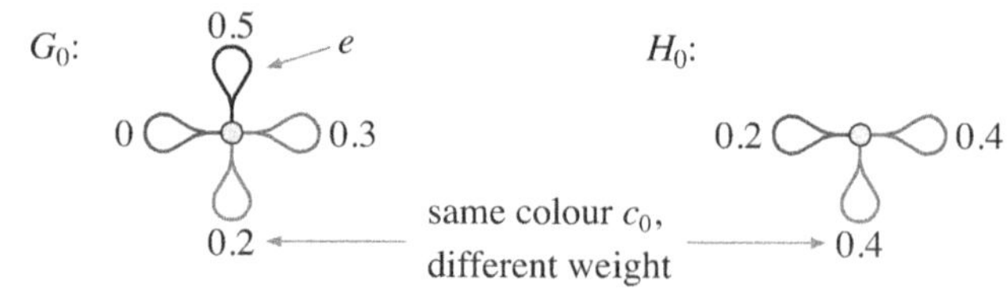

Figure 7: Base case. By removing a loop e with a non-zero weight, we force the algorithm to change the weight of at least one edge that is present in both G_0 and H_0.

4. LOWER BOUND IN EC

In this section we carry out Step 1 of our lower-bound plan. To do this we extend the previous lower bound result [14] to the case of maximal fractional matchings.

4.1 Strategy

Let $\mathcal{A}$ be any EC-algorithm computing a maximal fractional matching. We construct inductively a sequence of EC-graph pairs

$$(G_i, H_i), \quad i = 0, 1, \ldots, \Delta - 2,$$

that witness $\mathcal{A}$ having run-time greater than i. Each of the graphs G_i and H_i will have maximum degree at most Δ, so for $i = \Delta - 2$, we will have the desired lower bound. More precisely, we show that there are nodes $g_i \in V(G_i)$ and $h_i \in V(H_i)$ satisfying the following property:

(P1) The i-neighbourhoods $\tau_i(G_i, g_i)$ and $\tau_i(H_i, h_i)$ are isomorphic, yet

$$\mathcal{A}(G_i, g_i) \neq \mathcal{A}(H_i, h_i).$$

Moreover, there is a loop of some colour c_i adjacent to both g_i and h_i such that the outputs disagree on its weight.

We will also make use of the following additional properties in the construction:

(P2) The graphs G_i and H_i are $(\Delta - 1 - i)$-loopy. Consequently, $\mathcal{A}$ will saturate all their nodes by Lemma 1.

(P3) When the loops are ignored, both G_i and H_i are trees.

4.2 Base case (i = 0)

Let G_0 consist of a single node v that has Δ differently coloured loops. When $\mathcal{A}$ is run on G_0, it saturates v by assigning at least one loop e a non-zero weight; see Figure 7. Letting $H_0 := G_0 - e$ it is now easy to check that the pair (G_0, H_0) satisfies (P1–P3) for $g_0 = h_0 = v$. For example, we have $\tau_0(G_0, v) \cong \tau_0(H_0, v)$ because both 0-neighbourhoods consist of a single isolated node of degree 0. Recall our convention that the loops are at distance 1 from v.

4.3 Inductive step

Suppose (G_i, H_i) is a pair satisfying (P1–P3). For convenience, we write G, H, g, h, and c in place of G_i, H_i, g_i, h_i, and c_i. Also, we let $e \in E(G)$ and $f \in E(H)$ be the colour-c loops adjacent to g and h to which $\mathcal{A}$ assigns different weights.

To construct the pair (G_{i+1}, H_{i+1}) we unfold and mix; see Figure 8.

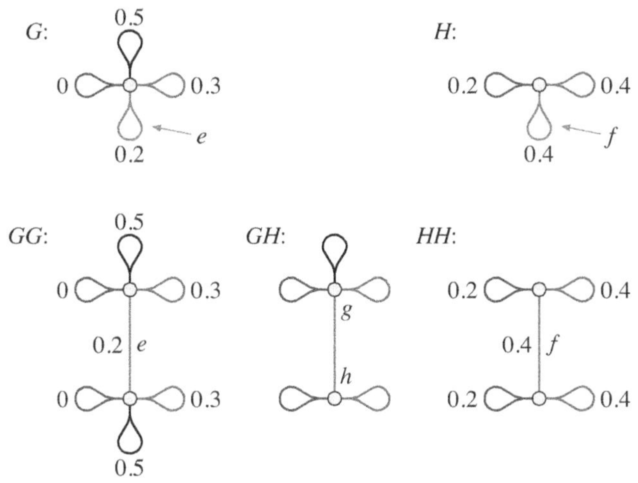

Figure 8: Unfold and mix. The weights of e and f differ; hence the weight of $\{g, h\}$ is different from the weight of e or f.

Unfolding.
First, we unfold the loop e in G to obtain a 2-lift GG of G. That is, GG consists of two disjoint copies of $G - e$ and a new edge of colour c (which we still call e) that connects the two copies of g in GG. For notational purposes, we fix some identification $V(G) \subseteq V(GG)$ so that we can easily talk about one of the copies. Similarly, we construct a 2-lift HH of H by unfolding the loop f.

Recall that $\mathcal{A}$ cannot tell apart G from GG, or H from HH. In particular $\mathcal{A}$ continues to assign unequal weights to e and f in these lifts.

Mixing.
Next, we mix together the graphs GG and HH to obtain a graph GH defined as follows: GH contains a copy of $G - e$, a copy of $H - f$, and a new colour-c edge that connects the nodes g and h. For notational purposes, we let $V(GH) := V(G) \cup V(H)$, where we tacitly assume that $V(G) \cap V(H) = \varnothing$.

Analysis.
Consider the weight that $\mathcal{A}$ assigns to the colour-c edge $\{g, h\}$ in GH. Since $\mathcal{A}$ gives the edges e and f different weights in GG and HH, we must have that the weight of $\{g, h\}$ differs from the weight of e or the weight of f (or both). We assume the former (the latter case is analogous), and argue that the pair

$$(G_{i+1}, H_{i+1}) := (GG, GH)$$

satisfies the properties (P1–P3). It is easy to check that (P2) and (P3) are satisfied by the construction; it remains is to find the nodes $g_{i+1} \in V(GG)$ and $h_{i+1} \in V(GH)$ that satisfy (P1).

To this end, we exploit the following property of fractional matchings:

FACT 1 (PROPAGATION PRINCIPLE). *Assume that y and y' are fractional matchings that saturate a node v. If y and y' disagree on some edge incident to v, there must be another edge incident to v where y and y' disagree.*

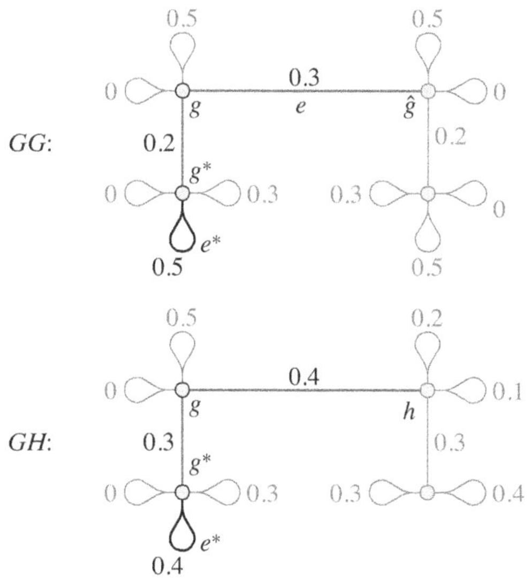

Figure 9: Propagation. The weights of e and $\{g, h\}$ differ. We apply the propagation principle towards the common part G that is shared by GG and GH. The graphs are loopy and hence all nodes are saturated by $\mathcal{A}$; we will eventually find a loop e^* that is present in both GG and GH, with different weights.

Our idea is to apply this principle in a fully saturated graph, where the disagreements propagate until they are resolved at a loop; this is where we locate g_{i+1} and h_{i+1}. See Figure 9 for an example.

We consider the following fully saturated fractional matchings on G:

$$\begin{aligned} y &= \text{the FM determined by } \mathcal{A}\text{'s output} \\ &\quad\ \text{on the nodes } V(G) \text{ in } GG, \\ y' &= \text{the FM determined by } \mathcal{A}\text{'s output} \\ &\quad\ \text{on the nodes } V(G) \text{ in } GH. \end{aligned}$$

Starting at the node $g \in V(G)$ we already know by assumption that y and y' disagree on the colour-c edge incident to g. Thus, by the propagation principle, y and y' disagree on some other edge incident to g. If this edge is not a loop, it connects to a neighbour $g' \in V(G)$ of g and the argument can be continued: because y and y' disagree on $\{g, g'\}$, there must be another edge incident to g' where y and y' disagree, and so on. Since G does not have any cycles (apart from the loops), this process has to terminate at some node $g^* \in V(G)$ such that y and y' disagree on a loop $e^* \neq e$ incident to g^*. Note that e^* is a loop in both GG and GH, too. Thus, we have found our candidate $g_{i+1} = h_{i+1} = g^*$.

To finish the proof, we need to show that

$$\tau_{i+1}(GG, g^*) \cong \tau_{i+1}(GH, g^*). \qquad (3)$$

The critical case is when $g^* = g$ as this node is the closest among $V(G)$ to seeing the topological differences between the graphs GG and GH. Starting from g and stepping along the colour-c edge towards the differences, we arrive, in GG, at a node $\hat{g}$ that is a copy of $g \in V(G)$, and in GH, at the node h. But these nodes satisfy

$$\tau_i(GG, \hat{g}) \cong \tau_i(GH, h)$$

by our induction assumption. Using this, (3) follows.

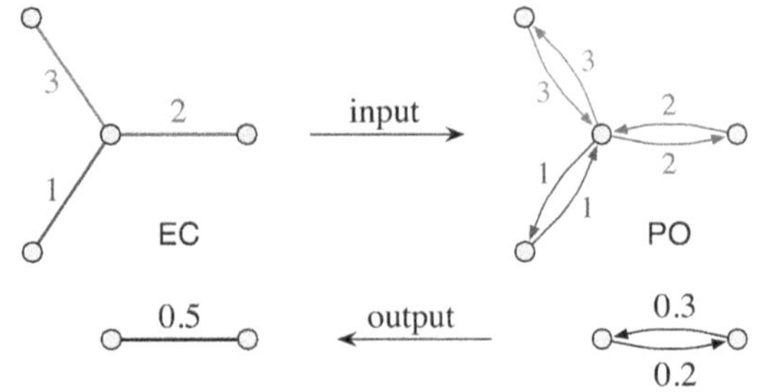

Figure 10: EC $\rightsquigarrow$ PO. Mapping an EC-graph G into a PO-graph $G_{\leftrightarrows}$, and mapping the output of a PO-algorithm back to the original graph.

5. LOCAL SIMULATIONS

Now that we have an $\Omega(\Delta)$ time lower bound in the EC model, our next goal is to extend this result to the ID model. In this section we implement Step 2 of our plan and give a series of local simulations

$$\mathsf{EC} \rightsquigarrow \mathsf{PO} \rightsquigarrow \mathsf{OI} \rightsquigarrow \mathsf{ID}.$$

Here, each simulation preserves the running time of an algorithm up to a constant factor. In particular, together with Step 1, this will imply the $\Omega(\Delta)$ time lower bound in the ID model.

5.1 Simulation EC $\rightsquigarrow$ PO

We start with the easiest simulation. Suppose there is a t-time PO-algorithm for the maximal fractional matching problem on graphs of maximum degree Δ; we describe a t-time EC-algorithm for graphs of maximum degree $\Delta/2$.

The local simulation is simple; see Figure 10. On input an EC-graph G we interpret each edge $\{u, v\}$ of colour c as two directed edges (u, v) and (v, u), both of colour c; this interpretation makes G into a PO-graph $G_{\leftrightarrows}$. We can now locally simulate the PO-algorithm on $G_{\leftrightarrows}$ to obtain an FM y as output. Finally, we transform y back to an FM of G: the edge $\{u, v\}$ is assigned weight $y(u, v) + y(v, u)$.

5.2 Tricky identifiers

When we are computing a maximal fractional matching $y\colon E(G) \to [0, 1]$, we have, a priori, infinitely many choices for the weight $y(e)$ of an edge. For example, in a path on nodes v_1, v_2, and v_3, we can freely choose $y(\{v_1, v_2\}) \in [0, 1]$ provided we set $y(\{v_2, v_3\}) = 1 - y(\{v_1, v_2\})$. In particular, an ID-algorithm can output edge weights that depend on the node identifiers whose magnitude is not bounded.

Unbounded outputs are tricky from the perspective of proving lower bounds. The main result of the recent work [10] is a run-time preserving local simulation PO $\rightsquigarrow$ ID, but the result only holds under the assumption that the solution can be encoded using finitely many values per node on graphs of maximum degree Δ. This restriction has its source in an earlier local simulation OI $\rightsquigarrow$ ID due to Naor and Stockmeyer [24] that is crucially using Ramsey's theorem. In fact, these two local simulation results fail if unbounded outputs are allowed; counterexamples include even natural graph problems [13].

In conclusion, we need an ad hoc argument to establish that an ID-algorithm cannot benefit from unique identifiers in case of the maximal fractional matching problem.

5.3 Simulation PO $\rightsquigarrow$ OI

Before we address the question of simulating ID-algorithms, we first salvage one part of the result in [10]: there is local simulation PO $\rightsquigarrow$ OI that applies to many locally checkable problems, regardless of the size of the output encoding. Even though this simulation works off-the-shelf in our present setting, we cannot use this result in a black-box fashion, as we need to access its inner workings later in the analysis. Thus, we proceed with a self-contained proof.

The following presentation is considerably simpler than that in [10], since we are only interested in a simulation that produces a *locally maximal* fractional matching, not in a simulation that also provides approximation guarantees on the *total weight*, as does the original result.

PO-*checkability*.

Maximal fractional matchings are not only locally checkable, but also PO-*checkable*: there is a local PO-algorithm that can check whether a given y is a maximal FM. An important consequence of PO-checkability is that if H is a lift of G then any PO-algorithm produces a feasible solution on H if and only if it produces a feasible solution on G.

Order homogeneity.

The key to the simulation PO $\rightsquigarrow$ OI is a *canonical linear order* that can be computed for any tree-like PO-neighbourhood. To define this ordering, let d denote the maximum number of edge colours appearing in the input PO-graphs that have maximum degree Δ, and let T denote the infinite $2d$-regular d-edge-coloured PO-tree. We fix a homogeneous linear order for T:

LEMMA 2. *There is a linear order $\preceq$ on $V(T)$ such that all the ordered neighbourhoods $(T, \preceq, v)$, $v \in V(T)$, are pairwise isomorphic (i.e., up to any radius).*

PROOF. The tree T can be thought of as a Cayley graph of the free group on d generators, and the free group admits a linear order that is invariant under the group acting on itself by multiplication; for details, see Neumann [25] and the discussion in [10, §5]. □

For an alternative, combinatorial proof of Lemma 2, see the extended version of this paper [9].

Simulation.

Let $\mathcal{A}_{\mathsf{OI}}$ be any t-time OI-algorithm solving a PO-checkable problem; we describe a t-time PO-algorithm $\mathcal{A}_{\mathsf{PO}}$ solving the same problem.

The algorithm $\mathcal{A}_{\mathsf{PO}}$ operates on a PO-graph G as follows; see Figure 11. Given a PO-neighbourhood $\tau := \tau_t(U_G, v)$, we first embed τ in T: we choose an arbitrary node $u \in V(T)$, identify v with u, and let the rest of the embedding $\tau \subseteq (T, u)$ be dictated uniquely by the edge colours. We then use the ordering $\preceq$ inherited from T to order the nodes of τ. By Lemma 2, the resulting structure $(\tau, \preceq)$ is independent of the choice of u, i.e., the isomorphism type of $(\tau, \preceq)$ is only a function of τ. Finally, we simulate

$$\mathcal{A}_{\mathsf{PO}}(\tau) := \mathcal{A}_{\mathsf{OI}}(\tau, \preceq). \tag{4}$$

To see that the output of $\mathcal{A}_{\mathsf{PO}}$ is feasible, we argue as follows. Embed the universal cover U_G as a subgraph of $(T, \preceq)$ in a way that respects edge colours. Again, all possible embeddings are isomorphic; we call the inherited ordering

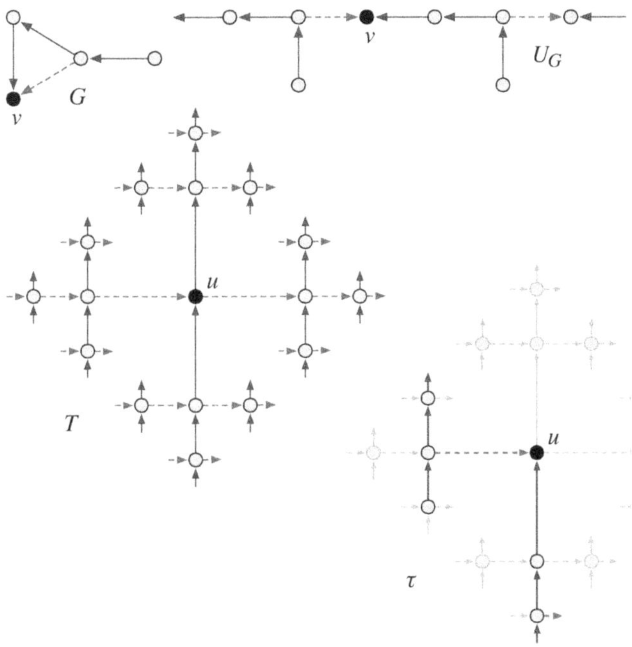

Figure 11: Given a PO-graph G, algorithm $\mathcal{A}_{\mathsf{PO}}$ simulates the execution of $\mathcal{A}_{\mathsf{OI}}$ on OI-graph τ. The linear order on $V(\tau)$ is inherited from the regular tree T. As T is homogeneous, the linear order does not depend on the choice of node u in T.

$(U_G, \preceq)$ the *canonical ordering* of U_G. Our definition of $\mathcal{A}_{\mathsf{PO}}$ and the order homogeneity of $(T, \preceq)$ now imply that

$$\mathcal{A}_{\mathsf{PO}}(U_G, v) = \mathcal{A}_{\mathsf{OI}}(U_G, \preceq, v) \qquad \text{for all } v \in V(U_G).$$

Therefore, the output of $\mathcal{A}_{\mathsf{PO}}$ is feasible on U_G. Finally, by PO-checkability, the output of $\mathcal{A}_{\mathsf{PO}}$ is feasible also on G, as desired.

5.4 Simulation OI ⇝ ID

The reason why an ID-algorithm $\mathcal{A}$ cannot benefit from unbounded identifiers is due to the propagation principle. We formalise this in two steps.

(i) We use the Naor–Stockmeyer OI ⇝ ID result to see that $\mathcal{A}$ can be forced to output fully saturated FMs on so-called *loopy* OI-neighbourhoods.

(ii) We then observe that, on these neighbourhoods, $\mathcal{A}$ behaves like an OI-algorithm: $\mathcal{A}$'s output cannot change if we relabel a node in an order-preserving fashion, because the changes in the output would have to propagate outside of $\mathcal{A}$'s run-time.

That is, our simulation OI ⇝ ID will work only on certain types of neighbourhoods (in contrast to our previous simulations), but this will be sufficient for the purposes of the lower bound proof.

Step (i).

Let $\mathcal{A}$ be a t-time ID-algorithm that computes a maximal fractional matching on graphs of maximum degree Δ.

From $\mathcal{A}$ we can derive, by a straightforward simulation, a t-time *binary-valued* ID-algorithm $\mathcal{A}^*$ that indicates whether $\mathcal{A}$ saturates a node. That is, $\mathcal{A}^*(G, v) := 1$ if $\mathcal{A}$ saturates v in G, otherwise $\mathcal{A}^*(G, v) := 0$. Such saturation indicators $\mathcal{A}^*$ were considered previously in [3, §4].

Because (and *only* because) $\mathcal{A}^*$ outputs finitely many values, we can now apply the Ramsey technique of Naor and Stockmeyer [24, Lemma 3.2]. To avoid notational clutter, we use a version of their result that follows from the application of the infinite Ramsey's theorem (rather than the finite):

Lemma 3 (Naor and Stockmeyer). *There is an infinite set $I \subseteq \mathbb{N}$ such that $\mathcal{A}^*$ is an OI-algorithm when restricted to graphs whose identifiers are in I.* □

We say that $\tau_t(U_G, \preceq, v)$ is a *loopy* OI-neighbourhood if G is a loopy PO-graph and $(U_G, \preceq)$ is the canonically ordered universal cover of G. We also denote by $B_t(v) \subseteq V(U_G)$ the node set of $\tau_t(U_G, v)$.

Our saturation indicator $\mathcal{A}^*$ is useful in proving the following lemma, which encapsulates step (i) of our argument.

Lemma 4. *Let $\tau := \tau_t(U_G, \preceq, v)$ be loopy. If $\varphi\colon B_t(v) \to I$ is an ID-assignment to the nodes of τ that respects $\preceq$, then $\mathcal{A}$ saturates v under φ.*

Proof. By loopiness of G, the node v has a neighbour $u \in V(U_G)$ such that $\tau_t(U_G, v) \cong \tau_t(U_G, u)$ as PO-neighbourhoods. By order homogeneity, $\tau_t(U_G, \preceq, v) \cong \tau_t(U_G, \preceq, v)$ as OI-neighbourhoods. By Lemma 3, this forces $\mathcal{A}^*$ to output the same on v and u under any ID-assignment $\varphi'\colon B_t(v) \cup B_t(u) \to I$ that respects $\preceq$. But $\mathcal{A}^*$ cannot output two adjacent 0's if $\mathcal{A}$ is to produce a maximal fractional matching. Hence, $\mathcal{A}^*$ outputs 1 on $\varphi'(\tau)$. Finally, by order-invariance, $\mathcal{A}^*$ outputs 1 on $\varphi(\tau)$, which proves the claim. □

Step (ii).

Define J as an infinite subset of I that is obtained by picking every $(m+1)$-th identifier from I, where m is the maximum number of nodes in a $(2t+1)$-neighbourhood of maximum degree Δ. That is, for any two $j, j' \in J$, $j < j'$, there are m distinct identifiers $i \in I$ with $j < i < j'$.

The next lemma states that $\mathcal{A}$ behaves like an OI-algorithm on loopy neighbourhoods that have identifiers from J.

Lemma 5. *Assume that $\tau := \tau_t(U_G, \preceq, v)$ is loopy. If $\varphi_1, \varphi_2\colon B_t(v) \to J$ are any two ID-assignments that respect $\preceq$, then $\mathcal{A}(\varphi_1(\tau)) = \mathcal{A}(\varphi_2(\tau))$.*

Proof. We first consider the case where φ_1 and φ_2 disagree only on a single node $v^* \in B_t(v)$. Towards a contradiction suppose that

$$\mathcal{A}(\varphi_1(\tau)) \neq \mathcal{A}(\varphi_2(\tau)). \tag{5}$$

We start with partial ID-assignments for U_G that are defined on the nodes $B_{2t+1}(v)$; this will suffice for running $\mathcal{A}$ on the nodes $B_{t+1}(v)$. Indeed, because $J \subseteq I$ is sufficiently sparse, we can extend φ_1 and φ_2 into assignments $\bar\varphi_1, \bar\varphi_2\colon B_{2t+1}(v) \to I$ such that

- $\bar\varphi_1$ and $\bar\varphi_2$ respect $\preceq$, and
- $\bar\varphi_1$ and $\bar\varphi_2$ still disagree only on the node v^*.

Let y_i, $i = 1, 2$, be the fractional matching defined on the edges incident to $B_{t+1}(v)$ that is determined by the output of $\mathcal{A}$ on the nodes $B_{t+1}(v)$ under the assignment $\bar\varphi_i$. By

Lemma 4, all the nodes $B_{t+1}(v)$ are saturated in both y_1 and y_2.

Let $D \subseteq U_G$ be the subgraph consisting of the edges e with $y_1(e) \neq y_2(e)$ and of the nodes that are incident to such edges; by (5), we have $v \in V(D)$. Now we can reinterpret the propagation principle from Section 4:

FACT 2 (PROPAGATION PRINCIPLE). *For each node $u \in B_{t+1}(v) \cap V(D)$ we have $\deg_D(u) \geq 2$.*

Using the fact that $D \subseteq U_G$ is a tree, we can start a simple walk at $v \in V(D)$, take the first step away from v^*, and finally arrive at a node $u \in B_{t+1}(v) \cap V(D)$ that has $\mathrm{dist}(u, v^*) \geq t + 1$, i.e, the node u does not see the difference between the assignments $\bar{\varphi}_1$ and $\bar{\varphi}_2$. But this is a contradiction: as the t-neighbourhoods $\bar{\varphi}_i(\tau_t(U_G, u))$, $i = 1, 2$, are the same, so should the weights output by $\mathcal{A}$.

General case. If $\varphi_1, \varphi_2 \colon B_t(v) \to J$ are any two assignments respecting $\preceq$, they can be related to one another by a series of assignments

$$\varphi_1 = \pi_1, \pi_2, \ldots, \pi_k = \varphi_2,$$

where any two consecutive assignments π_i and π_{i+1} both respect $\preceq$ and disagree on exactly one node. Thus, the claim follows from the analysis above. □

Let $\mathcal{A}_{\mathsf{OI}}$ be any t-time OI-algorithm that agrees with the order-invariant output of $\mathcal{A}$ on loopy OI-neighbourhoods that have identifiers from J. We now obtain the final form of our OI $\rightsquigarrow$ ID simulation:

COROLLARY 1. *If G is a loopy PO-graph, $\mathcal{A}_{\mathsf{OI}}$ produces a maximal fractional matching on the canonically ordered universal cover $(U_G, \preceq)$.*

PROOF. The claim follows by a standard argument [24, Lemma 3.2] from two facts: J is large enough; and maximal fractional matchings are locally checkable. □

5.5 Concluding Theorem 1

To get the final lower bound of Theorem 1 we reason backwards. Assume that $\mathcal{A}$ is a t-time ID-algorithm that computes a maximal fractional matching on any graph of maximum degree Δ.

- OI $\rightsquigarrow$ ID: Corollary 1 above gives us a t-time OI-algorithm $\mathcal{A}_{\mathsf{OI}}$ that computes a maximal fractional matching on the canonically ordered universal cover $(U_G, \preceq)$ for any loopy PO-graph G of maximum degree Δ.

- PO $\rightsquigarrow$ OI: Simulation (4) in Section 5.3 queries the output of $\mathcal{A}_{\mathsf{OI}}$ only on $(U_G, \preceq)$. This gives us a t-time PO-algorithm $\mathcal{A}_{\mathsf{PO}}$ that computes a maximal fractional matching on any loopy PO-graph G of maximum degree Δ.

- EC $\rightsquigarrow$ PO: The simple simulation in Section 5.1 gives us a t-time EC-algorithm $\mathcal{A}_{\mathsf{EC}}$ that computes a maximal fractional matching on any loopy EC-graph G of maximum degree $\Delta/2$.

But now we can use the construction of Section 4: there is a loopy EC-graph of maximum degree $\Delta/2$ where $\mathcal{A}_{\mathsf{EC}}$ runs for $\Omega(\Delta)$ rounds. Hence the running time of $\mathcal{A}$ is also $\Omega(\Delta)$.

6. ACKNOWLEDGEMENTS

This work is supported in part by the Academy of Finland, Grants 132380 and 252018, and by the Research Funds of the University of Helsinki. Much of this research was done while the authors were affiliated with the Department of Computer Science, University of Helsinki. We would like to thank Christoph Lenzen and Roger Wattenhofer for discussions and the anonymous reviewers for their helpful feedback.

7. REFERENCES

[1] Noga Alon, László Babai, and Alon Itai. A fast and simple randomized parallel algorithm for the maximal independent set problem. *Journal of Algorithms*, 7(4):567–583, 1986. doi:10.1016/0196-6774(86)90019-2.

[2] Dana Angluin. Local and global properties in networks of processors. In *Proc. 12th Annual ACM Symposium on Theory of Computing (STOC 1980)*, pages 82–93. ACM Press, 1980. doi:10.1145/800141.804655.

[3] Matti Åstrand, Patrik Floréen, Valentin Polishchuk, Joel Rybicki, Jukka Suomela, and Jara Uitto. A local 2-approximation algorithm for the vertex cover problem. In *Proc. 23rd International Symposium on Distributed Computing (DISC 2009)*, volume 5805 of *Lecture Notes in Computer Science*, pages 191–205. Springer, 2009. doi:10.1007/978-3-642-04355-0_21.

[4] Matti Åstrand and Jukka Suomela. Fast distributed approximation algorithms for vertex cover and set cover in anonymous networks. In *Proc. 22nd Annual ACM Symposium on Parallelism in Algorithms and Architectures (SPAA 2010)*, pages 294–302. ACM Press, 2010. doi:10.1145/1810479.1810533.

[5] Leonid Barenboim and Michael Elkin. *Distributed Graph Coloring: Fundamentals and Recent Developments.* Morgan & Claypool, 2013. doi:10.2200/S00520ED1V01Y201307DCT011.

[6] Leonid Barenboim, Michael Elkin, Seth Pettie, and Johannes Schneider. The locality of distributed symmetry breaking. In *Proc. 53rd Annual IEEE Symposium on Foundations of Computer Science (FOCS 2012)*, pages 321–330. IEEE Computer Society Press, 2012. doi:10.1109/FOCS.2012.60.

[7] Andrzej Czygrinow, Michał Hańćkowiak, and Wojciech Wawrzyniak. Fast distributed approximations in planar graphs. In *Proc. 22nd International Symposium on Distributed Computing (DISC 2008)*, volume 5218 of *Lecture Notes in Computer Science*, pages 78–92. Springer, 2008. doi:10.1007/978-3-540-87779-0_6.

[8] Patrik Floréen, Marja Hassinen, Joel Kaasinen, Petteri Kaski, Topi Musto, and Jukka Suomela. Local approximability of max-min and min-max linear programs. *Theory of Computing Systems*, 49(4):672–697, 2011. doi:10.1007/s00224-010-9303-6.

[9] Mika Göös, Juho Hirvonen, and Jukka Suomela. Linear-in-Δ lower bounds in the local model, 2013. arXiv:1304.1007.

[10] Mika Göös, Juho Hirvonen, and Jukka Suomela. Lower bounds for local approximation. *Journal of the ACM*, 60(5):39:1–23, 2013. doi:10.1145/2528405. arXiv:1201.6675.

[11] Mika Göös and Jukka Suomela. No sublogarithmic-time approximation scheme for bipartite vertex cover. In *Proc. 26th International Symposium on Distributed*

Computing (DISC 2012), volume 7611 of *Lecture Notes in Computer Science*, pages 181–194. Springer, 2012. doi:10.1007/978-3-642-33651-5_13. arXiv:1205.4605.

[12] Michał Hańćkowiak, Michał Karoński, and Alessandro Panconesi. On the distributed complexity of computing maximal matchings. *SIAM Journal on Discrete Mathematics*, 15(1):41–57, 2001. doi:10.1137/S0895480100373121.

[13] Henning Hasemann, Juho Hirvonen, Joel Rybicki, and Jukka Suomela. Deterministic local algorithms, unique identifiers, and fractional graph colouring. In *Proc. 19th International Colloquium on Structural Information and Communication Complexity (SIROCCO 2012)*, volume 7355 of *Lecture Notes in Computer Science*, pages 48–60. Springer, 2012. doi:10.1007/978-3-642-31104-8_5.

[14] Juho Hirvonen and Jukka Suomela. Distributed maximal matching: greedy is optimal. In *Proc. 31st Annual ACM Symposium on Principles of Distributed Computing (PODC 2012)*, pages 165–174. ACM Press, 2012. doi:10.1145/2332432.2332464. arXiv:1110.0367.

[15] Amos Israeli and Alon Itai. A fast and simple randomized parallel algorithm for maximal matching. *Information Processing Letters*, 22(2):77–80, 1986. doi:10.1016/0020-0190(86)90144-4.

[16] Fabian Kuhn, Thomas Moscibroda, and Roger Wattenhofer. What cannot be computed locally! In *Proc. 23rd Annual ACM Symposium on Principles of Distributed Computing (PODC 2004)*, pages 300–309. ACM Press, 2004. doi:10.1145/1011767.1011811.

[17] Fabian Kuhn, Thomas Moscibroda, and Roger Wattenhofer. The price of being near-sighted. In *Proc. 17th Annual ACM-SIAM Symposium on Discrete Algorithms (SODA 2006)*, pages 980–989. ACM Press, 2006. doi:10.1145/1109557.1109666.

[18] Fabian Kuhn, Thomas Moscibroda, and Roger Wattenhofer. Local computation: lower and upper bounds, 2010. arXiv:1011.5470.

[19] Fabian Kuhn and Roger Wattenhofer. On the complexity of distributed graph coloring. In *Proc. 25th Annual ACM Symposium on Principles of Distributed Computing (PODC 2006)*, pages 7–15. ACM Press, 2006. doi:10.1145/1146381.1146387.

[20] Christoph Lenzen and Roger Wattenhofer. Leveraging Linial's locality limit. In *Proc. 22nd International Symposium on Distributed Computing (DISC 2008)*, volume 5218 of *Lecture Notes in Computer Science*, pages 394–407. Springer, 2008. doi:10.1007/978-3-540-87779-0_27.

[21] Nathan Linial. Locality in distributed graph algorithms. *SIAM Journal on Computing*, 21(1):193–201, 1992. doi:10.1137/0221015.

[22] Michael Luby. A simple parallel algorithm for the maximal independent set problem. *SIAM Journal on Computing*, 15(4):1036–1053, 1986. doi:10.1137/0215074.

[23] Alain Mayer, Moni Naor, and Larry Stockmeyer. Local computations on static and dynamic graphs. In *Proc. 3rd Israel Symposium on the Theory of Computing and Systems (ISTCS 1995)*, pages 268–278. IEEE, 1995. doi:10.1109/ISTCS.1995.377023.

[24] Moni Naor and Larry Stockmeyer. What can be computed locally? *SIAM Journal on Computing*, 24(6):1259–1277, 1995. doi:10.1137/S0097539793254571.

[25] B. H. Neumann. On ordered groups. *American Journal of Mathematics*, 71(1):1–18, 1949. doi:10.2307/2372087.

[26] Alessandro Panconesi and Romeo Rizzi. Some simple distributed algorithms for sparse networks. *Distributed Computing*, 14(2):97–100, 2001. doi:10.1007/PL00008932.

[27] David Peleg. *Distributed Computing: A Locality-Sensitive Approach*. SIAM Monographs on Discrete Mathematics and Applications. Society for Industrial and Applied Mathematics, Philadelphia, 2000.

APPENDIX

A. DERANDOMISATION

As discussed in Section 5.2, unbounded outputs require special care. In this appendix we note that even though Naor and Stockmeyer [24] assume bounded outputs, their result on derandomising local algorithms applies in our setting, too.

Let $\mathcal{A}$ be a randomised $t(\Delta)$-time algorithm that computes a maximal FM on graphs of maximum degree Δ or possibly fails with some small probability. Given an assignment of random bit strings $\rho\colon V(G) \to \{0,1\}^*$ to the nodes of a graph G, denote by $\mathcal{A}^\rho$ the *deterministic* algorithm that computes as $\mathcal{A}$, but uses ρ for randomness.

The proof of Theorem 5.1 in [24] is using the following fact whose proof we reproduce here for convenience.

LEMMA 6. *For every n, there is an n-set $S_n \subseteq \mathbb{N}$ of identifiers and an assignment $\rho_n\colon S_n \to \{0,1\}^*$ such that $\mathcal{A}^{\rho_n}$ is correct on all graphs that have identifiers from S_n.*

PROOF. Denote by $k = k(n)$ the number of graphs G with $V(G) \subseteq \{1,\ldots,n\}$. Let $X_1,\ldots,X_q \subseteq \mathbb{N}$ be any q disjoint sets of size n. Suppose for the sake of contradiction that the claim is false for each X_i. That is, for any assignment $\rho\colon X_i \to \{0,1\}^*$ of random bits, $\mathcal{A}^\rho$ fails on at least one of the k many graphs G with $V(G) \subseteq X_i$. By averaging, this implies that for each i there is a particular graph G_i, $V(G_i) \subseteq X_i$, on which $\mathcal{A}$ fails with probability at least $1/k$. Consider the graph G that is the disjoint union of the graphs $G_1,\ldots,G_q$. Since $\mathcal{A}$ fails independently on each of the components G_i, the failure probability on G is at least $1-(1-1/k)^q$. But this probability can be made arbitrarily close to 1 by choosing a large enough q, which contradicts the correctness of $\mathcal{A}$. □

The deterministic algorithms $\mathcal{A}^{\rho_n}$ allow us to again obtain a $t(\Delta)$-time OI-algorithm, which establishes the $\Omega(\Delta)$ lower bound for $\mathcal{A}$. Only small modifications to Section 5.4 are needed:

- **Step (i).** Instead of the infinite set $I \subseteq \mathbb{N}$ as previously provided by Lemma 3, we can use the finite Ramsey's theorem to find arbitrarily large sets $I_n \subseteq S_n$ (i.e., $|I_n| \to \infty$ as $n \to \infty$) with the property that $\mathcal{A}^{\rho_n}$ fully saturates the nodes of a loopy OI-neighbourhood that has identifiers from I_n (Lemma 4).
- **Step (ii).** Then, passing again to sufficiently sparse subsets $J_n \subseteq I_n$, we can reprove Lemma 5 and Corollary 1, which only require that J is large enough.

This concludes the lower bound proof for randomised LOCAL algorithms.

Anonymous Networks: Randomization = 2-Hop Coloring

Yuval Emek
Faculty of Industrial Engineering and Management
Technion, Haifa
Israel
yemek@ie.technion.ac.il

Christoph Pfister
Distributed Computing
ETH Zurich
Switzerland
pfistchr@ethz.ch

Jochen Seidel
Distributed Computing
ETH Zurich
Switzerland
seidelj@ethz.ch

Roger Wattenhofer
Distributed Computing
ETH Zurich
Switzerland
wattenhofer@ethz.ch

ABSTRACT

This paper considers the computational power of *anonymous* message passing algorithms (henceforth, anonymous algorithms), i.e., distributed algorithms operating in a network of unidentified nodes. We prove that every problem that can be solved (and verified) by a *randomized* anonymous algorithm can also be solved by a *deterministic* anonymous algorithm provided that the latter is equipped with a *2-hop coloring* of the input graph. Since the problem of 2-hop coloring a given graph (i.e., ensuring that two nodes with distance at most 2 have different colors) can by itself be solved by a randomized anonymous algorithm, it follows that with the exception of a few mock cases, the execution of every randomized anonymous algorithm can be decoupled into a generic preprocessing randomized stage that computes a 2-hop coloring, followed by a problem-specific deterministic stage. The main ingredient of our proof is a novel simulation method that relies on some surprising connections between 2-hop colorings and an extensively used graph lifting technique.

Categories and Subject Descriptors

F.1.2 [**Theory of Computation**]: Modes of Computation—*Relations among modes*

General Terms

Theory

Keywords

Anonymous Networks; Derandomization; 2-Hop Coloring

PODC'14, July 15–18, 2014, Paris, France.
Copyright 2014 ACM 978-1-4503-2944-6/14/07 ...$15.00.
http://dx.doi.org/10.1145/2611462.2611478 .

1. INTRODUCTION

Computability in networks (a.k.a. distributed computability), where the processors are represented as nodes in a graph and the task is to produce an output at every node, is Turing machine-equivalent if the nodes are equipped with unique IDs. This fact remains intact even when the attention is restricted to *deterministic* distributed algorithms. In contrast, the distributed problems that can be solved deterministically in *anonymous* networks (where the nodes are not uniquely identified) are of a rather limited nature [38]. The question of distributed computability becomes interesting however once the nodes in an anonymous network gain access to random bits. For example, the extensively studied *maximal independent set (MIS)* problem [34, 3] is solvable in an anonymous network only if random bits are available.

Our goal in this paper is to investigate the role that (Las-Vegas type) randomness plays in the computational power of anonymous message passing algorithms (referred to hereafter as *anonymous algorithms*), regardless of round and message complexity considerations. However, before we can do so, care must be taken to rule out distributed problems in which unique IDs are (perhaps implicitly) encoded in the input instances as those mock cases obviously do not faithfully represent the properties of distributed computability in anonymous networks. To that end, we restrict our focus to the class GRAN (standing for Genuinely solvable by Randomized algorithms in Anonymous Networks) of distributed problems Π that satisfy (1) there exists a randomized anonymous algorithm that solves Π; and (2) there exists a randomized anonymous algorithm that decides whether a given graph is a legal input instance of Π; we refer to Section 1.1 for a formal definition. Notice that with the exception of some artificial cases generated for the purpose of investigating the leader election problem, essentially all interesting distributed problems studied in the existing literature in the context of anonymous networks belong, in fact, to GRAN.

What exactly characterizes the computational power of a randomized anonymous algorithm as opposed to a deterministic one? Surprisingly, randomization is only required to establish a *2-hop coloring* of the network: Once a 2-hop coloring is known, every problem in GRAN can be solved by a deterministic anonymous algorithm.

1.1 Model

Labeled Graphs.

We denote the node- and edge-set of a graph G by V and E, respectively. For a node $v \in V$, we denote the set containing all neighbors of v by $\Gamma(v)$. To make it explicit, we only consider finite connected simple[1] graphs G. A *labeling function* for V is a function $\ell : V \to L$ that assigns a *label* to every node in V. For the sake of simplicity, unless stated otherwise, we assume hereafter that all labels are finite bitstrings. Tuples $G = (V, E, \ell)$, where (V, E) is a graph and ℓ is a labeling function for V, are called *labeled graphs*. We often label vertices by more than one labeling function $\ell_1, \ldots, \ell_k$; in that case, we treat $G = (V, E, \ell_1, \ldots, \ell_k)$ as being labeled by a single labeling function ℓ that assigns $\ell(v) = \langle \ell_1(v), \ldots, \ell_k(v) \rangle$ to each node $v \in V$.

Distributed Problems.

A distributed problem Π is specified by a set of *input instances* and for every input instance I of Π, a set $\Pi(I)$ of *valid outputs* for I. The input instances of Π are labeled graphs $I = (V, E, i)$ and the labeling function i, called the *input labeling* of I, assigns an *input label* to every node in V. For the input instance $I = (V, E, i)$, the set of valid outputs $\Pi(I)$ for I consists of labeling functions o for V called *valid output labelings* for I. At the risk of abusing the notation, we use Π to denote the set of input instances as well as the problem itself. For the sake of simplicity we assume that in every input instance $I = (V, E, i)$, the input label $i(v)$ of every node v includes v's degree. A typical example for a distributed problem is *graph coloring*, where the input is an arbitrary graph and the output must obey the rule $o(u) \neq o(v)$ if (u, v) is an edge in the input instance.

2-Hop Colorings.

For a graph $G = (V, E)$, the labeling ℓ is said to be a *k-hop coloring* if $\ell(u) \neq \ell(v)$ for every $u, v \in V$, $u \neq v$, that are at most k hops away, i.e., G admits a path between u and v that consists of at most k edges. A labeling function that plays a central role in the present paper is the 2-hop coloring, i.e., a coloring that assigns a different label to each node in $\{u\} \cup \Gamma(u)$ for every $u \in V$. We say that a labeled graph $G = (V, E, \ell)$ is *2-hop colored* if ℓ is a 2-hop coloring. Note that in the context of the present paper, we do not pay attention to the number of distinct colors used by the nodes under ℓ.

Consider some distributed problem Π. The *2-hop colored variant* Π^c of Π is the problem defined as follows: the input instance set Π^c is

$$\Pi^c = \{(V, E, i, c) : (V, E, i) \in \Pi, \text{ and } c \text{ is a 2-hop coloring of } (V, E)\}$$

and given an input instance $I = (V, E, i) \in \Pi$, the valid output labeling set for every corresponding input instance $I^c = (V, E, i, c) \in \Pi^c$ is $\Pi^c(I^c) = \Pi(I)$.

Randomized Anonymous Algorithms.

Our model for randomized anonymous algorithms corresponds to the anonymous variant of the message passing model as defined in [40] (c.f. the port numbering model of [5]) with irrevocable outputs. In a labeled graph $I = (V, E, i)$, all nodes v execute the same message passing algorithm $\mathcal{A}$ with input $i(v)$. The input to a node v is fully specified by $i(v)$ — in particular, nodes are not equipped with a *(unique) identifier* nor do they possess an apriori knowledge of any global network parameter (unless specified as part of $i(\cdot)$). The execution of $\mathcal{A}$ on I is performed in synchronous rounds. In every round, each node v sends/receives messages of finite size to/from each of its neighbors, where v distinguishes between the ports corresponding to its incident edges. We consider randomized algorithms, where in every round, node v has access to one random bit. (Note that this is equivalent to accessing finitely many random bits per round as multiple rounds can be grouped together.)

Algorithm $\mathcal{A}$ is said to *solve* the distributed problem Π if the following two requirements hold for every $I \in \Pi$: (1) if $\mathcal{A}$ is executed on I, then $\mathcal{A}$ produces an irrevocable local output $\mathcal{A}(v)$ for every node v within finite time with probability 1; and (2) each output labeling o obtained with positive probability by setting $o(v) = \mathcal{A}(v)$ for every $v \in V$ satisfies $o \in \Pi(I)$ (i.e., we only consider Las-Vegas algorithms). Algorithm $\mathcal{A}$ is *deterministic* if it does not access any random bits. Note that the round and message complexities of $\mathcal{A}$ are not taken into consideration (as long as they are finite).

Genuine Solvability.

Let Y be a set of labeled graphs called *yes-instances*. The *distributed decision problem* Δ_Y obtained from Y (see, e.g., [21]) is the problem whose input instances I are all labeled graphs, and whose valid output labelings $o \in \Delta_Y(I)$ are such that all nodes output "YES" if $I \in Y$ and at least one node outputs "NO" if $I \notin Y$. We say that problem Π is *genuinely* solvable by randomized algorithms in anonymous networks if (1) there exists a randomized anonymous algorithm that solves Π; and (2) there exists a randomized anonymous algorithm that solves the distributed decision problem Δ_Π, namely, the problem of deciding whether a given labeled graph is an input instance of Π. Denote the class of such problems Π by GRAN (standing for Genuinely solvable by Randomized algorithms in Anonymous Networks).

Local Views.

Given a node v in the labeled graph $G = (V, E, \ell)$, we denote by $L_d(v, G)$ a rooted tree called the *depth-d local view* of v in G. (When G is clear from the context we may write $L_d(v)$ instead.) To avoid confusion, we distinguish between nodes and labels in G and *vertices* and *marks* in $L_d(v)$. The local view of node v is defined inductively as follows: $L_1(v)$ consists of a single vertex x marked with $\ell(v)$; $L_{d+1}(v)$ is the tree obtained by connecting the root of $L_d(u)$ as a child of $L_1(v)$'s root for every $u \in \Gamma(v)$. Refer to Figure 1 for an illustration. Notice that the the local view $L_d(v)$ in G essentially captures all information that a deterministic algorithm $\mathcal{A}$ executed by node v in G could possibly gather in d rounds of execution. The *depth-infinity local view* of a node v is the infinite tree $L_\infty(v)$ obtained from the inductive construction of $L_d(v)$ by taking d to infinity.

1.2 Our Contribution

Classic distributed symmetry breaking problems such as maximal independent set and graph (1-hop) coloring are known to be in GRAN. Common to these two problems

[1] A graph is simple if it is undirected and does not contain any loops or parallel edges.

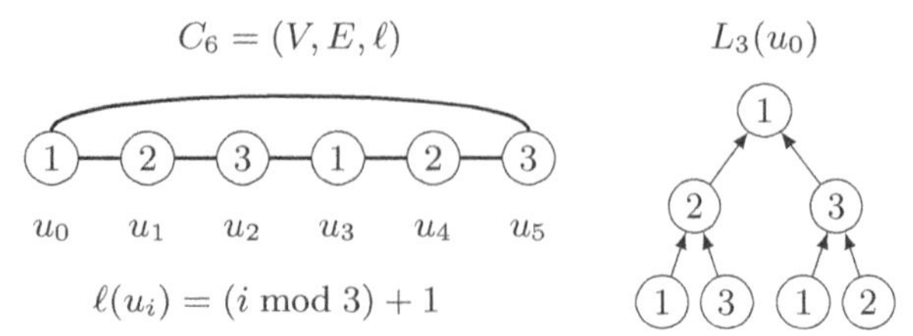

Figure 1: Depth-3 local view of node u_0 in the labeled graph C_6.

is the local nature of their symmetry breaking challenges.[2] While the 2-hop variant of graph coloring is still solvable by randomized anonymous algorithms and thus, belongs to GRAN, it is not difficult to show that this no longer holds for its k-hop variant for any $k > 2$. (In fact, the same can be said for maximal independent set under a natural extension to k-hop variants that are not discussed in the present paper, cf. [37].) Is this a coincidence? Does GRAN contain problems that require (systematic) symmetry breaking between nodes which are more than two hops apart? Our main result provides a negative answer to these questions.

THEOREM 1. *If $\Pi \in$ GRAN, then Π^c is solvable by a deterministic anonymous algorithm.*

1.3 Related Work

The seminal work by Angluin [5] established the connection between computation in networks and *factors/products* of graphs (see Section 2 for a definition) and marks the beginning of history for distributed computability theory. Her work employs a lifting technique from a graph to its products to establish impossibility of leader election (and equivalent problems, e.g., assigning IDs), even under the assumption of Las-Vegas algorithms. As stated in [23] graph products also characterize recognizable cases for graph rewriting systems, a localized model for distributed computation. Fibrations, i.e, a related generalization for directed graphs (see [13] for an extensive overview), were found to characterize problems solvable by self stabilization (a possibly incorrect output stabilizes to a correct one) in [14]. The lifting technique also plays a key role in our proof of Theorem 1.

Product graphs are also studied in their own right (see, e.g., [8, 31]), also products obtained from a random process [4]. For a graph G the *universal cover* $U(G)$ (cf. [5]) is a (possibly infinite) product of G closely related to the depth-infinity local view. (The un-rooted tree $U(G)$ can be obtained from $L_\infty(v)$ of any node v in G by (1) for every vertex x in $L_\infty(v)$ pruning x's child corresponding to x's parent; and (2) making every edge in the resulting tree undirected.) In Section 3 we apply the result of Norris [39] that isomorphism in $U(G)$ up to depth $|V| - 1$ implies isomorphism to all depths to obtain a finite representation of a specific factor of G.

Another line of research investigates (mock-anonymous) problems where the input instances permit leader election. For example, electing a leader in a ring network is possible if the size n of the ring is known [26, 27]. Later it was found that a $(2 - \varepsilon)$-approximation of n is enough [1], even in general networks [42]. The impact of prior knowledge (e.g., the network size) on the solvability of various problems was studied in [43, 11]. We restrict ourselves to problems in GRAN, which rules out cases that permit leader election.

Electing a leader with a Monte-Carlo algorithm (a randomized algorithm that is allowed to fail) was studied in rings [26, 27] and in general graphs [2, 41]. Recently, the problem was found to be solvable with high probability (i.e., with probability $1 - n^{-c}$ for any $c \geq 1$, w.h.p. for short) in [36]. Since electing a leader and assigning IDs are equivalent, any distributed problem solvable with IDs is w.h.p. solvable in an anonymous network. On the other hand it is known that some symmetry-breaking problems, e.g., MIS [34, 3] or coloring [33], are in GRAN. It is thus a natural question to ask what exactly distinguishes Las-Vegas algorithms from deterministic ones. We find that a 2-hop coloring suffices to completely characterize the capabilities of a Las-Vegas algorithm solving a GRAN problem.

Anonymous networks and electing a leader therein also plays a major role in self-stabilization research, e.g. [17]. Self-stabilizing leader election is possible with population protocols (nodes are controlled by asynchronous finite state machines, cf. [7]) if the network is a ring [10]. In the presence of an oracle the problem becomes solvable also in general networks, however, the required oracle is impossible to implement as a population protocol [9]. We hope that our contribution may also play a role towards a better understanding of randomization in self-stabilization (cf. [32, 18]).

Naor and Stockmeyer [38] introduced the notion of locally checkable labelings (LCL), a labeling that can be checked by a deterministic constant-time algorithm in a network with IDs. With IDs a randomized constant-time algorithm cannot solve more LCLs than a deterministic one. This is in contrast to the anonymous model, where the run-time is unbounded but finite and a deterministic algorithm requires a 2-hop coloring to replace randomization. The impact of having/not having identifiers on verifying a proof (solution) to a decision problem was studied in [28], and the authors observe that the existence of a uniquely determined leader cannot be verified without identifiers. A hierarchy of decision problems in terms of bit complexity required for a proof is established in [25]. In [21, 20] Monte-Carlo algorithms for decision problems are studied in networks with unidentified but distinguishable nodes and a strict hierarchy depending on the success probability is found. We utilize the notion of decision problems to characterize the problem class GRAN.

The notion of a 2-hop coloring (also referred to as distance-2 coloring) has been used to assign frequencies in radio networks [29], to solve optimization problems in parallel on shared memory computers [22], and to emulate Turing machines in population protocols [6]. The related k-local election problem, where a local leader needs to be unique only up to distance k, was studied in an asynchronous model in [37]. A solution to the 2-hop coloring problem can already be found in the weak model of [19], where nodes are controlled by finite state machines. Minimizing the number of colors in a k-hop coloring is, however, $\mathcal{NP}$-complete for any $k \geq 1$ due to a result in [35]. We would like to note that port numbers are not necessary under the assumption of randomized algorithms. Since each node v knows its degree a 2-hop coloring can be found even without port numbers and by including the sender's color in every message missing port

[2] Despite the inherent locality of the notions of maximal independent set and coloring, the results of [33, 30] show that the corresponding distributed computational tasks cannot be solved in constant time.

numbers can be emulated. We show that a 2-hop coloring uniquely determines a graph's prime factor.

2. THE CASE FOR INFINITY

Before presenting the proof of Theorem 1, we state and prove a slightly easier variant of it that captures some of its main ideas. To that end, for the moment, assume the following rather strong *infinity model* for anonymous computation. Fix some problem Π, let Π^c be its 2-hop colored variant, and let $I^c = (V, E, i, c) \in \Pi^c$ be some input instance. An algorithm under the infinity model is fully specified by a function $\mathcal{A}_\infty$ from the set of depth-infinity local views to the possible output labels. The algorithm sets the output of node $v \in V$ to be $o(v) = \mathcal{A}_\infty(L_\infty(v))$, namely, it applies the function $\mathcal{A}_\infty$ to $L_\infty(v)$ and uses the returned image as the output of v. We shall use $\mathcal{A}_\infty$ to denote the algorithm under the infinity model as well as the function that lies at its heart. Disregarding computability issues of $\mathcal{A}_\infty$ for the moment, we say that $\mathcal{A}_\infty$ *solves* Π^c if the labeling o satisfies $o \in \Pi^c(I^c)$. Note that the infinity model involves neither communication nor randomization. In other words, node v's output is completely determined by $L_\infty(v)$ in which the vertices are only marked with input labels and a 2-hop coloring. The remainder of this section is devoted to proving the following theorem.

THEOREM 2. *If $\Pi \in GRAN$, then Π^c is solvable in the infinity model.*

A key ingredient of our proof for Theorem 2 is the notion of an *infinite view graph* G_∞ of a 2-hop colored graph G.

Definition 1. Let $G = (V, E, \ell)$ be a 2-hop colored graph. We define the *infinite view graph* $G_\infty = (V_\infty, E_\infty, \ell_\infty)$ of G by identifying $L_\infty(v)$ with $\tilde{\tilde{v}}$ and setting

$$V_\infty := \{\tilde{\tilde{v}} : v \in V\} \qquad \text{(the different local views in } G),$$
$$E_\infty := \{(\tilde{\tilde{u}}, \tilde{\tilde{v}}) : (u, v) \in E\},$$
$$\ell_\infty(\tilde{\tilde{v}}) := \ell(v)$$

Note that $|V_\infty| \leq |V|$, where the inequality is strict when different nodes in G have the same depth-infinity local view For example in the graph C_6 from Figure 1 the local views of nodes with the same color are equal.

For the remainder of this section, fix some problem $\Pi \in$ GRAN, let $\mathcal{A}_R$ be a randomized anonymous algorithm solving Π, and let $I^c = (V, E, i, c)$ be some input instance of Π^c. We would like to construct an algorithm $\mathcal{A}_\infty$ that solves Π^c under the infinity model. The idea behind $\mathcal{A}_\infty$ is to perform the following three steps for each node $v \in V$:

i. construct the infinite view graph $I^c_\infty = (V_\infty, E_\infty, i_\infty, c_\infty)$ from $L_\infty(v)$;
ii. simulate a specific terminating execution of $\mathcal{A}_R$ on $J = (V_\infty, E_\infty, i_\infty)$; and
iii. use the output of node $\tilde{\tilde{v}}$ in that simulation as output for node v.

We now turn to explaining these three steps in detail.

2.1 Constructing I^c_∞

Consider $L_\infty(v, I^c)$ for some node $v \in V$. For every node $u \in V$, the local view $L_\infty(u)$ appears as a sub-tree in $L_\infty(v)$. Conversely, every depth-infinity sub-tree of $L_\infty(v)$ is the depth-infinity local view of some node (or nodes) in V. Therefore, the set of all depth-infinity sub-trees of $L_\infty(v)$ is exactly the node set of I^c's infinite view graph I^c_∞. Moreover, (u, u') is an edge in I^c if and only if $L_\infty(u')$ appears as a sub-tree of $L_\infty(u)$ rooted at a child of $L_\infty(u)$'s root. In other words, I^c_∞ can be uniquely constructed from $L_\infty(v)$.

Algorithm $\mathcal{A}_\infty$ and its analysis relies on a canonical representation of the depth-infinity trees $L_\infty(u)$, namely, fixing the order of the vertices in each depth-level. For that purpose, it suffices to fix a total order among the children of each vertex. Such a total order follows immediately by noticing that since I^c is 2-hop colored, every two siblings must have distinct marks. Using these canonical representations, two depth-infinity local views can now be compared level by level, thus implying a total order on V_∞; let $\tilde{\tilde{u}}_1, \ldots, \tilde{\tilde{u}}_k$ be the nodes in V_∞ indexed according to this total order.

2.2 Simulating $\mathcal{A}_R$

The second step in $\mathcal{A}_\infty$ is to simulate an execution of algorithm $\mathcal{A}_R$, the randomized anonymous algorithm solving Π. More precisely, multiple executions of $\mathcal{A}_R$ will be simulated on the input $J = (V_\infty, E_\infty, i_\infty)$. A t-round simulation σ of $\mathcal{A}_R$ on J (corresponding to executing $\mathcal{A}_R$ on J for t rounds) is fully determined by an assignment $b : V_\infty \to \{0,1\}^t$ of t random bits to every node in V_∞. We refer to this simulation σ as the simulation *induced by* b. The simulation σ is said to be *successful* if every node $\tilde{\tilde{v}} \in V_\infty$ produces an output under σ.

It will be essential for $\mathcal{A}_\infty$'s correctness that all nodes in I^c choose the same simulation of $\mathcal{A}_R$ on J — i.e., the same assignment b — to determine their output. This will be accomplished by using the total order on V_∞ to fix a total order among the possible assignments $b : V_\infty \to \{0,1\}^t$. To that end, given two assignments $b_1, b_2 : V_\infty \to \{0,1\}^t$, $b_1 \neq b_2$, the relation $b_1 < b_2$ holds if and only if $(b_1(\tilde{\tilde{u}}_1), \ldots, b_1(\tilde{\tilde{u}}_k)) < (b_2(\tilde{\tilde{u}}_1), \ldots, b_2(\tilde{\tilde{u}}_k))$, where the latter comparison is done lexicographically. For convenience, we extend the total order on the assignments b so that it also covers assignments $b_1 : V_\infty \to \{0,1\}^{t_1}$ and $b_2 : V_\infty \to \{0,1\}^{t_2}$, $t_1 \neq t_2$, by defining that $b_1 < b_2$ holds if and only if $t_1 < t_2$.

Assuming that there exists a successful simulation of $\mathcal{A}_R$ on J, algorithm $\mathcal{A}_\infty$ selects the successful simulation induced by the smallest assignment $b : V_\infty \to \{0,1\}^t$. We denote this simulation by σ_∞ and summarize in the following lemma.

LEMMA 1. *If algorithm $\mathcal{A}_R$ returns an output when executed on J, then in $\mathcal{A}_\infty$, all nodes select the same successful simulation σ_∞.*

2.3 The Output of $\mathcal{A}_\infty$

The output value $o(v) = \mathcal{A}_\infty(L_\infty(v))$ of node $v \in V$ is set to the output produced by node $\tilde{\tilde{v}}$ in simulation σ_∞ of $\mathcal{A}_R$ on J. For that to be well defined, there must exist an execution of $\mathcal{A}_R$ on J in which every node $\tilde{\tilde{v}}$ produces an output (leading to a successful simulation). We establish the existence of such an execution by using the well-known lifting lemma [5, 12] to assert that $J \in \Pi$ and thus, guarantee that a terminating execution of $\mathcal{A}_R$ on J exists. This requires developing a better understanding of the infinite view graph's fundamental properties based on the notion of factor graphs.

2.3.1 *Factor Graphs and 2-Hop Colorings*

The central concept of our analysis is that of *factor* and *product graphs.*[3] For two labeled graphs $G = (V, E, \ell)$ and

[3] Our notion of product graphs should not be confused with

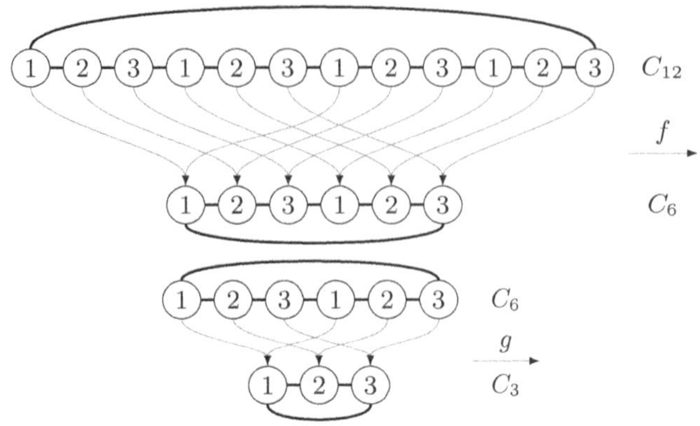

Figure 2: The labeled graph C_6 is a factor of C_{12} induced by the factorizing map f (and C_{12} is a product of C_6). Similarly, the labeled graph C_3 is a factor of C_6 induced by the factorizing map g.

$G' = (V', E', \ell')$, we say that G' is a *factor* of G and that G is a *product* of G' if there exists a function $f : V \to V'$, referred to as a *factorizing map*, that satisfies:

1. the mapping f is surjective (onto);
2. f respects the labeling functions, that is, $\ell(v) = \ell'(f(v))$ for every node $v \in V$; and
3. f is a *local isomorphism*, that is, for every node $v \in V$, the restriction $f|_{\Gamma(v)}$ is a bijection onto $\Gamma(f(v))$.

We shall use the notations $G' \preceq_f G$ (and $G \succeq_f G'$) to denote that G' is a factor of G (and G is a product of G'). The role of the factorizing map f is sometimes emphasized by saying that the factor/product is *induced* by f. Refer to Figure 2 for an illustration.

It is known that $|V| = m \cdot |V'|$ for some positive integer m (see, e.g., [24]). If $m = 1$, then the factorizing map is bijective and both $G' \preceq_f G$ and $G \preceq_{f^{-1}} G'$ hold. In that case, we refer to the two labeled graphs G and G' as being *isomorphic* (since f is a graph isomorphism that respects the node labels) and write $G \cong_f G'$ or $G \cong G'$ if the specific bijection is not relevant. Moreover, it is well-established that if $G \succeq_f G'$, then the graphs G and G' are indistinguishable from the perspective of a node v in G or G' (see, e.g., [39]) as cast in the following fact.

FACT 1. *Let G, G' be two labeled graphs. If $G \succeq_f G'$, then $L_\infty(v) = L_\infty(f(v))$ for every node v in G.*

It follows from Fact 1 that the factor of a 2-hop colored graph is also 2-hop colored. Let $G = (V, E, \ell)$ be a 2-hop colored graph and let $G_\infty = (V_\infty, E_\infty, \ell_\infty)$ be its infinite view graph. Lemmas 2 to 4 establish some important properties of G and G_∞. These three lemmas can be derived from the results on graph fibrations presented in [13] using an intricate construction. (we briefly sketch this connection in Section 4); for completeness, we also present stand-alone proofs. Our first Lemma 2 establishes that G_∞ is a factor of G induced by the factorizing map $f_\infty : V \to V_\infty$ that maps v to $\overset{\infty}{v}$; we subsequently refer to f_∞ as the *infinite view (factorizing) map* of G.

binary operations on two graphs referred to as *graph products*. The unlabeled counterpart of the concept of product graphs is often called graph lifts, or covering graphs in the existing literature. We extend the definition presented in [24] to incorporate node labels. Note that changes are required when considering non-simple or undirected graphs.

LEMMA 2. *Let $G = (V, E, \ell)$ be a 2-hop colored graph, $G_\infty = (V_\infty, E_\infty, \ell_\infty)$ its infinite view graph, and $f_\infty : V \to V_\infty$ the infinite view map. Then, G_∞ is a factor of G induced by f_∞, i.e., $G_\infty \preceq_{f_\infty} G$.*

PROOF. We show that f_∞ is a factorizing map inducing the factor G_∞ by verifying the properties required in the definition of factor graphs. (1) The function $f_\infty : V \to V_\infty$ is surjective by the definition of V_∞. (2) For every $v \in V$, the labeling functions satisfy $\ell(v) = \ell_\infty(f_\infty(v))$ by the definition of ℓ_∞. (3) Bijectivity of $f_\infty|_{\Gamma(v)}$ for every $v \in V$ is established by showing that $f_\infty|_{\Gamma(v)}$ is injective and surjective separately.

To see that $f_\infty|_{\Gamma(v)}$ is injective, observe that two nodes $u_1, u_2 \in \Gamma(v)$, $u_1 \neq u_2$, have different labels $\ell(u_1) \neq \ell(u_2)$ since ℓ is a 2-hop coloring. Property (2) thus ensures that $f_\infty(u_1) \neq f_\infty(u_2)$, i.e., $f_\infty|_{\Gamma(v)}$ is injective. Denote by $\overset{\infty}{v}$ the node $f_\infty(v)$ and let $\overset{\infty}{u}$ be some neighbor of $\overset{\infty}{v}$ in G_∞. It follows from the definitions of E_∞ and local views that the tree $\overset{\infty}{u}$ is a sub-tree rooted at a child of $\overset{\infty}{v}$'s root vertex. Thus, G admits some node $u \in \Gamma(v)$ with $L_\infty(u) = \overset{\infty}{u}$ and the function f_∞ satisfies $f_\infty|_{\Gamma(v)}(u) = \overset{\infty}{u}$. Hence, $f_\infty|_{\Gamma(v)}$ is also surjective. □

A labeled graph G is called *prime* (cf. [13]) if all factors of G are isomorphic to it. For example, the labeled 3-cycle C_3 in Figure 2 is prime, whereas C_{12} and C_6 are not. Both C_{12} and C_6 have C_3 as a prime factor. Lemma 3 states that the only prime factor of a 2-hop colored graph G is its infinite view graph (indeed, C_3 is isomorphic to the infinite view graph of C_{12} and C_6).

LEMMA 3. *If G is a 2-hop colored graph, then the infinite view graph G_∞ is the unique prime factor of G (up to isomorphism).*

PROOF. Let G and G' be 2-hop colored graphs with $G' \preceq_f G$. To establish the statement we show that G' is either isomorphic to G_∞ or not prime. The key to our proof is to show that G and G' have the same infinite view graph; this establishes the assertion due to Lemma 2.

To that end, let $G_\infty = (V_\infty, E_\infty, \ell_\infty)$ and $G'_\infty = (V'_\infty, E'_\infty, \ell'_\infty)$ be the infinite view graphs of G and G', respectively, i.e., $G_\infty \preceq_{f_\infty} G$ and $G'_\infty \preceq_{f'_\infty} G'$. Fact 1 implies that $V'_\infty = V_\infty$. The construction of E_∞ guarantees that an edge $(\overset{\infty}{u}, \overset{\infty}{v})$ is in E_∞ if and only if $\overset{\infty}{v}$ is a sub-tree rooted at one of the children of $\overset{\infty}{u}$'s root. Since $V'_\infty = V_\infty$, the same edge is also in E'_∞, and vice versa, every edge in E'_∞ is also in E_∞. Therefore, it also holds that $E'_\infty = E_\infty$. Finally, observe that $\ell_\infty(\overset{\infty}{w})$ and $\ell'_\infty(\overset{\infty}{w}')$ for any nodes $\overset{\infty}{w} \in V_\infty$ and $\overset{\infty}{w}' \in V'_\infty$, respectively, are completely determined by the marks attributed to the corresponding root vertices of $\overset{\infty}{w}$ and $\overset{\infty}{w}'$. We conclude that $(V_\infty, E_\infty, \ell_\infty) = (V'_\infty, E'_\infty, \ell'_\infty)$, i.e., $G_\infty = G'_\infty$. □

Note that the previous Lemma 3 does not hold for arbitrary graphs G, since, e.g., the uncolored 12-cycle has two distinct prime factors, namely, the 3-cycle and the 4-cycle. In prime 2-hop colored graphs however, based on the following key lemma, we can use $L_\infty(v)$ of node v in a prime 2-hop colored graph G as the *alias* of v in G.

LEMMA 4. *Let $G = (V, E, \ell)$ be a prime 2-hop colored graph and consider some $u, v \in V$. Then, $u = v$ if and only if $L_\infty(u) = L_\infty(v)$.*

PROOF. Let $G = (V, E, \ell)$ be a prime 2-hop colored graph and let $u, v \in V$ be two nodes in G. Since the "only-if" direction is true by the assumption $u = v$, we only need to show that $L_\infty(u) = L_\infty(v)$ implies $u = v$. To that end, consider the infinite view graph $G_\infty = (V_\infty, E_\infty, \ell_\infty)$ of G and assume for the sake of contradiction that $L_\infty(u) = L_\infty(v)$ in G but $u \neq v$. By the definition of G_∞, this implies that $|V_\infty| < |V|$ and thus, Lemma 2 guarantees that G admits a non-trivial factor, in contradiction to the assumption that G is prime. □

2.3.2 Establishing the Output's Validity

Getting back to $\mathcal{A}_\infty$, we have shown that the graph I^c_∞ constructed by $\mathcal{A}_\infty$ (independently, at every node v) satisfies $I^c_\infty \preceq_{f_\infty} I^c$. (Recall that $I^c = (V, E, i, c)$ is an input instance of Π's 2-hop colored variant Π^c and that $I = (V, E, i)$ is the corresponding input instance of Π.) Algorithm $\mathcal{A}_\infty$ simulates algorithm $\mathcal{A}_\mathrm{R}$ on the input $J = (V_\infty, E_\infty, i_\infty)$. Since $I^c_\infty \preceq_{f_\infty} I^c$, the input instance I satisfies $J \preceq_{f_\infty} I$ with the same factorizing map f_∞.

We argue that J is an input instance of Π. Indeed, as Π is genuinely solvable, there exists a randomized anonymous algorithm $\mathcal{B}$ that decides whether a given labeled graph is an input instance of Π. By the lifting lemma, $\mathcal{B}$ cannot distinguish J from I (cf. [5, 12]), hence the fact that $I \in \Pi$ implies that $J \in \Pi$, as required.

It follows that $\mathcal{A}_\mathrm{R}$ returns a correct output when executed on J, thus Lemma 1 ensures that the same successful simulation σ_∞ is selected by every node. Employing the lifting lemma once more, we conclude that the simulation obtained by lifting σ_∞ from nodes in V_∞ to nodes in V corresponds to a possible execution η of $\mathcal{A}_\mathrm{R}$ on I (cf. [5, 12]). The output labeling that $\mathcal{A}_\infty$ produces for the input instance I^c is exactly the output labeling produced by η in I and since the latter is valid, the former must also be valid by the definition of problem Π^c, thus establishing Theorem 2.

Since the description of $\mathcal{A}_\infty$ involves trees of infinite depth, one may wonder whether it can be replaced by a "real" algorithm. This issue is addressed in the next section, where we also establish Theorem 1.

3. DEALING WITH (IN)FINITY

Recall that under the infinity model introduced in Section 2, each node v in the graph essentially receives $L_\infty(v)$. This luxury, of course, cannot be realized in a standard anonymous algorithm, where node v can only obtain $L_d(v)$ for finite values of d. Nevertheless, in this section we show how the algorithm presented in Section 2 can be adapted to finite depth local views. A key ingredient in this adaptation is the following theorem established by Norris [39].[4]

THEOREM 3 ([39]). *Let G be a labeled graph with n nodes. The local view $L_n(v)$ fully determines $L_\infty(v)$ for every node $v \in V$.*

Employing Lemma 4, we obtain the following corollary that facilitates the usage of depth n local views as aliases for the nodes in an n-node prime 2-hop colored graph (instead of the depth-infinity local views that were used in Section 2).

[4] The result in [39] is described in terms of the depth $n-1$ sub-trees of a graph's universal cover. To prove the corresponding statement for depth-n local views the same refinement argument can be made.

COROLLARY 1. *Let $G = (V, E, \ell)$ be an n-node prime 2-hop colored graph and consider some $u, v \in V$. Then, $u = v$ if and only if $L_n(u) = L_n(v)$.*

Consider a 2-hop colored graph $G = (V, E, \ell)$ and denote by $n = |V_\infty|$ the number of different depth-infinity local views in G. For a node $v \in V$, denote by $\overset{*}{v} = L_n(v)$ the depth-n local view in G. The graph $G_* = (V_*, E_*, \ell_*)$, where $V_* = \{\overset{*}{v} : v \in V\}$, $E_* = \{(\overset{*}{u}, \overset{*}{v}) : (u, v) \in E\}$, and $\ell_*(\overset{*}{v}) = \ell(v)$ is called the *finite view graph* of G. The following corollary is established due to Theorem 3, where f_n is the *depth-n truncating function* that truncates every depth-k local view, $k \geq n$, to depth n, i.e., $f_n(\overset{\infty}{u}) = \overset{*}{v}$.

COROLLARY 2. *For a 2-hop colored graph G, it holds that $G_* \cong_{f_n} G_\infty$.*

The graph G_* can thus serve as a canonical representative for its equivalence class under the equivalence relation $\cong$. This is crucial because in contrast to G_∞, the graph G_* has a finite bitstring representation. Furthermore, each node v in a 2-hop colored graph G can identify its corresponding node in G_*, within $n = |V_*|$ rounds of the execution.

3.1 Algorithm $\mathcal{A}_*$

Fix some problem $\Pi \in$ GRAN and randomized anonymous algorithm $\mathcal{A}_\mathrm{R}$ that solves Π. Let Π^c be the 2-hop colored variant of Π and let $I^c = (V, E, i, c) \in \Pi^c$ be an arbitrary input instance of Π^c. To establish Theorem 1, we present a deterministic algorithm $\mathcal{A}_*$ that solves Π^c. Algorithm $\mathcal{A}_*$ resembles algorithm $\mathcal{A}_\infty$ presented in Section 2, however, the graph I^c_∞ is replaced by its finite representation I^c_* utilizing Corollary 2.

Algorithm $\mathcal{A}_*$, described from the perspective of an arbitrary node $v \in V$, proceeds in phases indexed by the positive integers. Throughout the execution of $\mathcal{A}_*$, node v keeps track of an initially empty bitstring $b(v)$, where the value of $b(v)$ for phase $p+1$ is determined during phase p. It will be convenient to denote by b^p the labeling function derived from the values $b(v)$ in phase p by setting $b^p(v) = b(v)$ for phase p. Correspondingly, we denote by $I^p = (V, E, i, c, b^p)$ the graph obtained by augmenting I^c with the labeling b^p. In each phase p, every node v invokes the three sub-procedures `Update-Graph`, `Update-Output`, and `Update-Bits` in this order. We now describe each sub-procedure individually. For convenience, we also include a pseudo-code style description of $\mathcal{A}_*$ in Figure 3.

`Update-Graph`.

We say that a labeled graph $\hat{G} = (\hat{V}, \hat{E}, \hat{\imath}, \hat{c}, \hat{b})$ is a *candidate* for phase p if it satisfies the following three conditions:

C1. $|\hat{V}| \leq p$;

C2. there exists a node $\hat{v} \in \hat{V}$ such that $L_p(\hat{v}, \hat{G}) = L_p(v, I^p)$; and

C3. $(\hat{V}, \hat{E}, \hat{\imath}, \hat{c})$ is an input instance of Π^c.

Denote by $\mathcal{F}$ the set containing the finite view graphs of all candidates for phase p. In phase p, node v computes $L_p(v, I^p)$ (requires p rounds) and based on that, constructs the set $\mathcal{F}$.

Note that the set $\mathcal{F}$ can be totally ordered in a predetermined way. To see this, observe that for any finite view graph $G_* = (V_*, E_*, \ell_*)$, the set V_* can be totally ordered in a predetermined way similarly to the order used in Sec-

Algorithm: $\mathcal{A}_*$, a deterministic algorithm solving Π^c at node v

▷ *Initialization of variables for node v:*
$(\hat{V}_*, \hat{E}_*, \hat{\imath}_*, \hat{c}_*, \hat{b}_*) \leftarrow$ the empty labeled graph.
$\overset{*}{v} \leftarrow$ NULL
$b(v) \leftarrow$ the empty bitstring
for *phase* $p \leftarrow 1, \ldots$ **do**
    `Update-Graph`(p)
    `Update-Output`(p)
    `Update-Bits`(p)

Procedure `Update-Graph`(p):
$L \leftarrow L_p(v, I^p)$ ▷ *$b(v)$ is treated as a labeling function*
construct the set $\mathcal{F}$ of candidates for phase p
if $\mathcal{F} = \emptyset$ **then**
    skip phase p
else
    $\hat{G}_* = (\hat{V}_*, \hat{E}_*, \hat{\imath}_*, \hat{c}_*, \hat{b}_*) \leftarrow$ the smallest graph in $\mathcal{F}$
    $\hat{G} = (\hat{V}, \hat{E}, \hat{\imath}, \hat{c}, \hat{b}) \leftarrow$ a candidate that corresponds to $\hat{G}_*$
    $\hat{v} \leftarrow$ the node $\hat{v} \in \hat{V}$ such that $L_p(\hat{v}, \hat{G}) = L_p(v, I^p)$ as assured by C2
    $q \leftarrow |\hat{V}_*|$
    $\overset{*}{v} \leftarrow$ the node $\overset{*}{v} = L_q(\hat{v}, \hat{G}) \in \hat{V}_*$ with $L_p(\hat{v}, \hat{G}) = L$

Procedure `Update-Output` (p):
$\sigma \leftarrow$ the simulation of $\mathcal{A}_{\mathrm{R}}$ on $(\hat{V}_*, \hat{E}_*, \hat{\imath}_*)$ induced by $\hat{b}_*$
if *σ is successful* **then set** $o(v)$ to be the output of $\overset{*}{v}$ in σ

Procedure `Update-Bits` (p):
$\mathcal{B} \leftarrow \{b : b$ is a p-extension of $\hat{b}_*$, and the simulation of $\mathcal{A}_{\mathrm{R}}$ on $(\hat{V}_*, \hat{E}_*, \hat{\imath}_*)$ induced by b is successful$\}$
if $\mathcal{B} \neq \emptyset$ **then**
    $b_{\min} \leftarrow$ the smallest $b \in \mathcal{B}$
    $b(v) \leftarrow b_{\min}(\overset{*}{v})$

Figure 3: The deterministic algorithm $\mathcal{A}_*$ that solves Π^c.

tion 2.1. This total order on V_* fully determines a representation of G_* as a finite bitstring $s = s(G_*)$ (encoding the ordinal number and label of every node as well as every edge in G_*). Given two finite view graphs $G_* = (V_*, E_*, \ell_*)$ and $G'_* = (V'_*, E'_*, \ell'_*)$, we write $G_* < G'_*$ if either $|V_*| < |V'_*|$ or $|V_*| = |V'_*|$ and $s(G_*) < s(G'_*)$ lexicographically.

If the set $\mathcal{F}$ is empty in phase p, then node v skips the remainder of this phase. Otherwise, `Update-Graph` selects the smallest finite view graph $\hat{G}_* = (\hat{V}_*, \hat{E}_*, \hat{\imath}_*, \hat{c}_*, \hat{b}_*) \in \mathcal{F}$. Let $\hat{G}$ be a candidate that corresponds to $\hat{G}_*$ and recall that condition C2 guarantees the existence of a node $\hat{v} \in \hat{V}$ such that $L_p(\hat{v}, \hat{G}) = L_p(v, I^p)$. Let $\overset{*}{v} = L_q(\hat{v}, \hat{G})$, where $q = |\hat{V}_*|$, be the node in $\hat{V}_*$ that corresponds to v.

`Update-Output.`

Node v simulates $\mathcal{A}_{\mathrm{R}}$ on the instance $J = (\hat{V}_*, \hat{E}_*, \hat{\imath}_*)$ using the bitstrings provided by $\hat{b}_*$ as a replacement for $\mathcal{A}_{\mathrm{R}}$'s random bits. Recall that $\hat{b}_*$ corresponds to the bitstring assignment $\hat{b}$ in some candidate $\hat{G}$ and as such, reflects the bitstring assignment b^p of I^p. Since b^p may assign bitstrings of varying lengths to the nodes in V, $\hat{b}_*$ may also assign bitstrings of varying lengths to the nodes in $\hat{V}_*$. Therefore, the simulation of $\mathcal{A}_{\mathrm{R}}$ on J, denoted by σ, lasts for l rounds, where $l = \min\{\text{length}(\hat{b}_*(\overset{*}{u})) : \overset{*}{u} \in \hat{V}_*\}$ is the length of the shortest bitstring assigned under $\hat{b}_*$ to the nodes in $\hat{V}_*$. If the simulation σ is successful (recall the definition of a successful simulation in Section 2.2), then `Update-Output` sets v's output to the value returned by node $\overset{*}{v}$ in σ.

`Update-Bits.`

The task of `Update-Bits` is to update the value of $b(v)$, extending it to a bitstring of length p. An assignment $\hat{b}'_* : \hat{V}_* \to \{0,1\}^p$ is said to be a *p-extension* of $\hat{b}_*$ if the bitstring $\hat{b}_*(\overset{*}{u})$ is a prefix of $\hat{b}'_*(\overset{*}{u})$ for every node $\overset{*}{u} \in \hat{V}_*$. Let $\mathcal{B}$ be the set of p-extensions of $\hat{b}_*$ that induce successful simulations of $\mathcal{A}_{\mathrm{R}}$ on $J = (\hat{V}_*, \hat{E}_*, \hat{\imath}_*)$.

If $\mathcal{B}$ is empty, then $b(v)$ remains unchanged. Otherwise, the predetermined total order on $\hat{V}_*$ implies a predetermined total order on $\mathcal{B}$ — let $b_{\min}$ be the smallest bitstring assignment in $\mathcal{B}$ according to this total order and update the bitsring $b(v)$ so that $b(v) \leftarrow b_{\min}(\overset{*}{v})$.

3.2 Analysis

In our effort to prove Theorem 1, we need to show two things: (1) algorithm $\mathcal{A}_*$ terminates; and (2) the output of $\mathcal{A}_*$ is valid. We use the same notation as in Section 3.1 to denote the various graphs involved with $\mathcal{A}_*$. Recall that the description of $\mathcal{A}_*$ in Section 3.1 is provided from the perspective of node v in phase p and when necessary, we explicitly mention p and/or v by adding them as a superscript.

Specifically, let

- $I^p_* = (V^p_*, E^p_*, i^p_*, c^p_*, b^p_*)$ be the finite view graph of I^p;
- $\mathcal{F}^{p,v}$ be the set of finite view graphs from Update-Graph;
- $\hat{G}^{p,v}_* = (\hat{V}^{p,v}_*, \hat{E}^{p,v}_*, \hat{i}^{p,v}_*, \hat{c}^{p,v}_*, \hat{b}^{p,v}_*) \in \mathcal{F}^{p,v}$ be the finite view graph selected by Update-Graph;
- $\overset{*}{v}{}^p$ be the node in $\hat{V}^{p,v}_*$ corresponding to v;
- $J^{p,v} = (\hat{V}^{p,v}_*, \hat{E}^{p,v}_*, \hat{i}^{p,v}_*)$ be the graph used to simulate $\mathcal{A}_R$ in Update-Output; and
- $\sigma^{p,v}$ be the corresponding simulation of $\mathcal{A}_R$ on $J^{p,v}$ induced by $\hat{b}^{p,v}_*$.

We further denote by $I^c_* = (V_*, E_*, i_*, c_*)$ the finite view graph of I^c and set $n = |V_*|$.

Termination.

Recall the node $\hat{v}$ in a candidate $\hat{G}$ promised by condition C2; we henceforth also refer to the node $\overset{*}{v}$ in the finite view graph of $\hat{G}$ that corresponds to $\hat{v}$ as being *promised* by condition C2. Our analysis of $\mathcal{A}_*$ begins with the following insight regarding the graphs in $\mathcal{F}^{p,v}$, which follows from Corollary 1 as $|\hat{V}^{p,v}_*| \leq p$.

COROLLARY 3. *Consider some $\hat{G}'_* = (\hat{V}'_*, \hat{E}'_*, \hat{i}'_*, \hat{c}'_*, \hat{b}'_*) \in \mathcal{F}^{p,v}$ and let $\overset{*}{v} \in \hat{V}'_*$ be the node promised by condition C2. Then, $L_p(\overset{*}{v}, \hat{G}_*) = L_p(v, I^p)$.*

Denote by $\hat{H}^{p,v}_* = (\hat{V}^{p,v}_*, \hat{E}^{p,v}_*, \hat{i}^{p,v}_*, \hat{c}^{p,v}_*)$ the graph obtained from $\hat{G}^{p,v}_*$ by ignoring the labeling $\hat{b}^{p,v}_*$. To establish that $\mathcal{A}_*$ terminates, we show that the graph $\hat{H}^{p,v}_*$ "converges" towards I^c_* as cast in the following lemma.

LEMMA 5. *There exists some q such that for every phase $p \geq q$, the graph $\hat{H}^{p,v}_*$ satisfies $\hat{H}^{p,v}_* \cong I^c_*$ for all nodes $v \in V$.*

The difficulty in proving Lemma 5 is that the finite view graphs $\hat{G}^{p,v}_*$ are constructed based on the local views in (V, E, i, c, b^p) rather than (V, E, i, c) — in particular, the labels $b^p(v)$ are constantly changing. Observe however that in $\mathcal{A}_*$, the value $b^{p+1}(v)$ depends solely on $L_p(v, I^p)$. This means that for every two nodes $u, v \in V$ and phase p, if $L_p(u, I^p) = L_p(v, I^p)$, then $b^{p+1}(u) = b^{p+1}(v)$. By induction on p, we conclude that $L_\infty(u, I^p) = L_\infty(v, I^p)$ if and only if $L_\infty(u, I^c) = L_\infty(v, I^c)$. In other words, nodes indistinguishable without the labeling b^p are also indistinguishable when the labeling b^p is included. This immediately implies that in every phase p, the graph obtained from I^p_∞ by ignoring the labeling b^p is isomorphic to I^c_∞, which derives the following observation due to Corollary 2.

OBSERVATION 1. *For every phase p under algorithm $\mathcal{A}_*$, it holds that $(V^p_*, E^p_*, i^p_*, c^p_*) \cong I^c_*$.*

Utilizing Observation 1, Lemma 5 can be established by showing that $\hat{G}^{p,v}_* = I^p_*$. The following Lemma 6 assures that I^p_* is among the candidates in all phases $p \geq n$.

LEMMA 6. *If $p \geq n$, then the set $\mathcal{F}^{p,v}$ contains I^p_* for every node $v \in V$.*

PROOF. We establish the assertion by showing that I^p_* (or a graph isomorphic to it) is a candidate for phase p, noticing that $(I^p_*)_* = I^p_*$. By Observation 1, we conclude that $|V^p_*| = |V^c_*| = n \leq p$, thus condition C1 holds. Since I^p_* is a factor of I^p, Fact 1 guarantees that node $\overset{*}{v} = L_n(v, I^p) \in V^p_*$ satisfies $L_p(\overset{*}{v}, I^p_*) = L_p(v, I^p)$, thus condition C2 holds as well. As already argued in Section 2.3.2, the lifting lemma guarantees that I^c_∞ is an instance of Π^c, therefore by Corollary 2, so is I^p_*, implying that condition C3 holds which completes the proof. □

Lemma 6 confirms that I^p_* *may* be selected by Update-Graph if $p \geq n$. It remains to show that there is a phase p in which I^p_* *will* be selected by Update-Graph. The following Lemma 7 confirms that the latter occurs if $p \geq 2n$, thus establishing Lemma 5.

LEMMA 7. *If $p \geq 2n$, then $\hat{G}^{p,v}_* = I^p_*$ for all nodes $v \in V$.*

PROOF. Lemma 6 guarantees that $I^p_* \in \mathcal{F}^{p,v}$ for every node $v \in V$. The assertion is established by showing that I^p_* is the smallest graph in $\mathcal{F}^{p,v}$ according to the total order used in Update-Graph.

Let $\hat{G}'_* = (\hat{V}'_*, \hat{E}'_*, \hat{i}'_*, \hat{c}'_*, \hat{b}'_*) \in \mathcal{F}^{p,v}$ be the finite view graph of some candidate $\hat{G}'$ and set $n' = |\hat{V}_*|$. Assume for the sake of contradiction that $\hat{G}_* < I^p_*$. This implies that either (1) $n' < n$; or (2) $n' = n$ and $s(\hat{G}'_*) < s(I^p_*)$. We will show that neither (1) nor (2) hold and thus, contradict $\hat{G}'_* < I^p_*$.

To that end, let $\overset{*}{v}{}' \in \hat{V}'_*$ and $\overset{*}{v} \in V^p_*$ be the nodes in $\hat{G}'_*$ and I^p_*, respectively, promised by property C2. Since $|V^p_*| = n$ and $|V'_*| = n' \leq n$, it follows that the diameter of both I^p_* and $\hat{G}'_*$ is at most $n - 1$. Since $p \geq 2n$, the local view $L_p(\overset{*}{v}{}', \hat{G}'_*)$ contains the sub-tree $\overset{*}{u}{}'$ for every $u' \in \hat{V}'_*$ and each distinct depth-n' sub-tree of $L_p(\overset{*}{v}{}', \hat{G}'_*)$ corresponds to a different node $\overset{*}{u}{}' \in \hat{V}'_*$. Similarly, the local view $L_p(\overset{*}{v}, I^p_*)$ contains the sub-tree $\overset{*}{u}$ for every $u \in V^p_*$ and each distinct depth-n sub-tree of $L_p(\overset{*}{v}, I^p_*)$ corresponds to a node $\overset{*}{u} \in V^p_*$.

Corollary 3 guarantees that $L_p(\overset{*}{v}{}', \hat{G}'_*) = L_p(v, I^p) = L_p(\overset{*}{v}, I^p_*)$. Therefore, the depth-$n'$ truncating function $f_{n'}$ maps every node $\overset{*}{u} \in V^p_*$ to a node in $\hat{V}'_*$. It follows by the definition of local view that $\hat{G}'_* \preceq_{f_{n'}} I^p_*$.

If $n' = n$, then $f_{n'}$ is the identity function, hence $\hat{G}'_* = I^p_*$, in contradiction to the assumption that $\hat{G}'_* < I^p_*$. If on the other hand $n' < n$, then $\hat{G}'_*$ is a non-trivial factor of I^p_*, contradicting the fact that the finite view graph I^p_* is prime. The assertion follows. □

Consider some node $v \in V$ and phase $p \geq 2n$. Lemma 7 guarantees that the graph $J^{p,v}$ on top of which the simulation $\sigma^{p,v}$ is carried out is in fact (V_*, E_*, i_*) — denote this graph by $\widetilde{J}$. The design of Update-Graph ensures that $\widetilde{J} \in I$ and the reasoning from Section 2.2 can be applied to show that all nodes $u \in V$ perform the same simulation $\sigma^{p,u}$ on $\widetilde{J}$ — denote this simulation by σ^p and let $b^p : V_* \to \{0,1\}^*$ be the bitstring assignment that induces σ^p.

Let z be the smallest integer $z \geq 2n$ so that there exists a z-extension of b^{2n} that induces a successful simulation on $\widetilde{J}$ and let b' be the smallest such z-extension according to the predetermined total order on the bitstring assignments. Notice that the integer z is well defined since $\mathcal{A}_R$ is guaranteed to produce a correct output with probability 1. The design of Update-Bits ensures that in phase z, every node $u \in V$ updates $b(u) \leftarrow b'(\overset{*}{u})$, where $\overset{*}{u}$ is the node in V_* that corresponds to u. The design of Update-Output then ensures that in phase $z + 1$, all nodes set their outputs according to the successful simulation σ^{z+1}, thus establishing the termination of $\mathcal{A}_*$ as cast in the following lemma.

LEMMA 8. *In phase $z+1$, all nodes $v \in V$ set their outputs $\mathcal{A}_*(v)$.*

Correctness.

It remains to show that the output produced by $\mathcal{A}_*$ is correct. Denote by $o^p(v)$ the output of node $v \in V$ in phase p of $\mathcal{A}_*$, where we use the designated symbol ε to indicate that v does not return any output in phase p, writing $o^p(v) = \varepsilon$. Intuitively, we establish the correctness of $\mathcal{A}_*$ by arguing that there exists an execution η of $\mathcal{A}_{\text{R}}$ on $I = (V, E, i)$ such that for every node $v \in V$ and integer $1 \leq p \leq z+1$, if $o^p(v) \neq \varepsilon$, then the output of node v in *round* p under η, denoted by $o^p_\eta(v)$, is $o^p_\eta(v) = o^p(v)$. (In fact, the execution η is obtained by lifting σ^{z+1} from V_* to V.) The correctness of $\mathcal{A}_*$ then follows from the correctness of $\mathcal{A}_{\text{R}}$.

LEMMA 9. *For any phase p, if node v returns an output $o^p(v) \neq \varepsilon$ in phase p, then $o^p(v) = o^p_\eta(v)$.*

PROOF. Let p be a phase, and suppose that node $v \in V$ sets its output in phase p to $o^p(v) \neq \varepsilon$. Since v sets $o^p(v)$ in phase p, the graph $\hat{G}^{p,v}_*$ is defined and the simulation $\sigma^{p,v}$ of the randomized algorithm $\mathcal{A}_{\text{R}}$ is successful. With that in mind, let t be the length of $\sigma^{p,v}$, and let η be the execution of $\mathcal{A}_{\text{R}}$ on $I = (V, E, i)$ obtained by lifting σ^{z+1} from V_* to V. The goal now is to show that $o^p(v) = o^p_\eta(v)$.

Note that for any $k > 0$, the first k rounds in η are fully determined by the first k random bits of each node $u \in V$ and their respective input values. More specifically, the first k rounds in η for a *single* node v are fully determined by $L_k(v, I)$ and the first $k - i$ bits replacing the random bits of each node $u \in \mathcal{H}^i(v)$, $0 \leq i \leq k$, where $\mathcal{H}^i(v)$ the set of all nodes at most i hops away from v, i.e, $\mathcal{H}^0(v) = \{v\}$ and $\mathcal{H}^{i+1}(v) = \mathcal{H}^i(v) \cup \Gamma(\mathcal{H}^i(v))$ for every $i \geq 0$.

By the construction of $J^{p,v}$ the equality $L_p(\overset{*}{v}^p, J^{p,v}) = L_p(v, I)$ holds. Moreover, for every $u \in \mathcal{H}^p(v)$, there exists a node $\overset{*}{u} \in \hat{V}^{p,v}_*$ such that the bitstring assigned to $\overset{*}{u}$ satisfies $\hat{b}^{p,v}_*(\overset{*}{u}) = b^p(u)$. Since v sets $o^p(v)$ in `Update-Output`, the simulation $\sigma^{p,v}$ is successful and thus, the length of $\hat{b}^{p,v}_*(\overset{*}{u})$ is at least t. The design of `Update-Bits` ensures that $b^p(u)$ is a prefix of $b^{p+1}(u)$ for every phase p and node $u \in V$. Therefore, the first $t - i$ bits assigned to node $u \in \mathcal{H}^i(v)$, $0 \leq i \leq t$ are the same $t - i$ bits that are used in the first t rounds of η. We conclude that in η node v returns the output $o^t_\eta(v) = o^p(v)$ at node v in round p. □

Lemma 9 is sufficient to establish the correctness of $\mathcal{A}_*$ as well: Using the same line of arguments as in Section 2.3.2, once more invoking the lifting lemma, one can show that the output obtained by lifting the output of simulation σ^{z+1} is valid for I (and I^c). By combining Lemmas 8 and 9, Theorem 1 now follows.

4. FIBRATIONS AND 2-HOP COLORINGS

Boldi and Vigna [13] extensively study the notion of fibrations, roughly speaking a generalization of factorizing maps to edge-colored directed graphs (refer to [13] for an exact definition). A special case the two authors study are *deterministic (edge) colorings* which require that for every node, all out-edges must be colored differently. In this section we wish to highlight a connection between our observations regarding 2-hop colored graphs in Section 2 and deterministically edge colored directed graphs. In the following, we write *undirected* as well as *directed* edges as tuples (u, v). It will be clear from the context whether we are referring to a directed or an undirected edge.

Let $G = (V, E, c)$ be a 2-hop colored undirected graph, and consider the edge colored directed graph $H = (V', E', c')$ obtained by (1) choosing $V' = V$; (2) adding two directed edges (u, v) and (v, u) to E' for every undirected edge $(u, v) \in E$; and (3) setting $c'(e) = \langle c(u), c(v) \rangle$ for every directed edge $e = (u, v) \in E'$. In the terminology of [13], the graph H is symmetric, since for every edge (u, v) a symmetric edge (v, u) is present. Moreover the edge coloring c' is deterministic, and c' respects the edge symmetries since for every edge $e = (u, v)$, colored $\langle c_1, c_2 \rangle$, the symmetric edge $\bar{e} = (v, u)$ is colored $\langle c_2, c_1 \rangle$. We call the graph H obtained from G in this manner as being G's *directed (edge colored) representation.* Note that reversing the construction, in hope to obtain a 2-hop colored graph, is not possible for general deterministically edge-colored symmetric directed graphs.

Observe that a fibration $\varphi : H \to H'$, where H and H' are directed representations of two graphs G and G', translates to a factorizing map $f : G \to G'$ as defined in Section 2, and vice versa. One can use this connection to derive the statements from Section 2 from the results presented in [13].

5. ACKNOWLEDGEMENTS

We would like to thank our anonymous reviewers for their invaluable comments.

6. REFERENCES

[1] K. R. Abrahamson, A. Adler, L. Higham, and D. G. Kirkpatrick. Probabilistic solitude verification on a ring. In J. Y. Halpern, editor, *PODC*, pages 161–173. ACM, 1986.

[2] Y. Afek and Y. Matias. Elections in anonymous networks. *Inf. Comput.*, 113(2):312–330, 1994.

[3] N. Alon, L. Babai, and A. Itai. A fast and simple randomized parallel algorithm for the maximal independent set problem. *J. Algorithms*, 7(4):567–583, 1986.

[4] A. Amit, N. Linial, J. Matousek, and E. Rozenman. Random lifts of graphs. In S. R. Kosaraju, editor, *SODA*, pages 883–894. ACM/SIAM, 2001.

[5] D. Angluin. Local and global properties in networks of processors (extended abstract). In R. E. Miller, S. Ginsburg, W. A. Burkhard, and R. J. Lipton, editors, *STOC*, pages 82–93. ACM, 1980.

[6] D. Angluin, J. Aspnes, M. Chan, M. J. Fischer, H. Jiang, and R. Peralta. Stably computable properties of network graphs. In V. K. Prasanna, S. S. Iyengar, P. G. Spirakis, and M. Welsh, editors, *DCOSS*, volume 3560 of *Lecture Notes in Computer Science*, pages 63–74. Springer, 2005.

[7] D. Angluin, J. Aspnes, Z. Diamadi, M. J. Fischer, and R. Peralta. Computation in networks of passively mobile finite-state sensors. In Chaudhuri and Kutten [15], pages 290–299.

[8] D. Angluin and A. Gardiner. Finite common coverings of pairs of regular graphs. *J. Comb. Theory, Ser. B*, 30(2):184–187, 1981.

[9] J. Beauquier, P. Blanchard, and J. Burman. Self-stabilizing leader election in population protocols over arbitrary communication graphs. In R. Baldoni,

N. Nisse, and M. van Steen, editors, *OPODIS*, volume 8304 of *Lecture Notes in Computer Science*, pages 38–52. Springer, 2013.

[10] J. Beauquier, M. Gradinariu, and C. Johnen. Memory space requirements for self-stabilizing leader election protocols. In Coan and Welch [16], pages 199–207.

[11] P. Boldi and S. Vigna. Computing anonymously with arbitrary knowledge. In Coan and Welch [16], pages 181–188.

[12] P. Boldi and S. Vigna. An effective characterization of computability in anonymous networks. In J. L. Welch, editor, *DISC*, volume 2180 of *Lecture Notes in Computer Science*, pages 33–47. Springer, 2001.

[13] P. Boldi and S. Vigna. Fibrations of graphs. *Discrete Mathematics*, 243(1-3):21–66, 2002. Using the author's version from `http://vigna.dsi.unimi.it/ftp/papers/FibrationsOfGraphs.pdf`.

[14] P. Boldi and S. Vigna. Universal dynamic synchronous self-stabilization. *Distributed Computing*, 15(3):137–153, 2002.

[15] S. Chaudhuri and S. Kutten, editors. *Proceedings of the Twenty-Third Annual ACM Symposium on Principles of Distributed Computing, PODC 2004, St. John's, Newfoundland, Canada, July 25-28, 2004*. ACM, 2004.

[16] B. A. Coan and J. L. Welch, editors. *Proceedings of the Eighteenth Annual ACM Symposium on Principles of Distributed Computing, PODC, '99Atlanta, Georgia, USA, May 3-6, 1999*. ACM, 1999.

[17] S. Dolev, A. Israeli, and S. Moran. Uniform dynamic self-stabilizing leader election. *IEEE Trans. Parallel Distrib. Syst.*, 8(4):424–440, 1997.

[18] S. Dolev, E. Schiller, and J. L. Welch. Random walk for self-stabilizing group communication in ad-hoc networks. In *SRDS*, pages 70–79. IEEE Computer Society, 2002.

[19] Y. Emek and R. Wattenhofer. Stone age distributed computing. In P. Fatourou and G. Taubenfeld, editors, *PODC*, pages 137–146. ACM, 2013.

[20] P. Fraigniaud, A. Korman, M. Parter, and D. Peleg. Randomized distributed decision. In M. K. Aguilera, editor, *DISC*, volume 7611 of *Lecture Notes in Computer Science*, pages 371–385. Springer, 2012.

[21] P. Fraigniaud, A. Korman, and D. Peleg. Local distributed decision. In R. Ostrovsky, editor, *FOCS*, pages 708–717. IEEE, 2011.

[22] A. H. Gebremedhin, F. Manne, and A. Pothen. Parallel distance-k coloring algorithms for numerical optimization. In B. Monien and R. Feldmann, editors, *Euro-Par*, volume 2400 of *Lecture Notes in Computer Science*, pages 912–921. Springer, 2002.

[23] E. Godard, Y. Métivier, and A. Muscholl. Characterizations of classes of graphs recognizable by local computations. *Theory Comput. Syst.*, 37(2):249–293, 2004.

[24] C. D. Godsil and G. Royle. *Algebraic Graph Theory*. Graduate Texts in Mathematics. Springer, 2001.

[25] M. Göös and J. Suomela. Locally checkable proofs. In C. Gavoille and P. Fraigniaud, editors, *PODC*, pages 159–168. ACM, 2011.

[26] A. Itai and M. Rodeh. Symmetry breaking in distributive networks. In *FOCS*, pages 150–158. IEEE Computer Society, 1981.

[27] A. Itai and M. Rodeh. Symmetry breaking in distributed networks. *Inf. Comput.*, 88(1):60–87, 1990.

[28] A. Korman, S. Kutten, and D. Peleg. Proof labeling schemes. In M. K. Aguilera and J. Aspnes, editors, *PODC*, pages 9–18. ACM, 2005.

[29] S. O. Krumke, M. V. Marathe, and S. S. Ravi. Models and approximation algorithms for channel assignment in radio networks. *Wireless Networks*, 7(6):575–584, 2001.

[30] F. Kuhn, T. Moscibroda, and R. Wattenhofer. What cannot be computed locally! In Chaudhuri and Kutten [15], pages 300–309.

[31] F. T. Leighton. Finite common coverings of graphs. *J. Comb. Theory, Ser. B*, 33(3):231–238, 1982.

[32] C. Lenzen, J. Suomela, and R. Wattenhofer. Local algorithms: Self-stabilization on speed. In R. Guerraoui and F. Petit, editors, *SSS*, volume 5873 of *Lecture Notes in Computer Science*, pages 17–34. Springer, 2009.

[33] N. Linial. Locality in distributed graph algorithms. *SIAM J. Comput.*, 21(1):193–201, 1992.

[34] M. Luby. A simple parallel algorithm for the maximal independent set problem. In R. Sedgewick, editor, *STOC*, pages 1–10. ACM, 1985.

[35] S. T. McCormick. Optimal approximation of sparse hessians and its equivalence to a graph coloring problem. *Mathematical Programming*, 26(2):153–171, 1983.

[36] Y. Métivier, J. M. Robson, and A. Zemmari. Analysis of fully distributed splitting and naming probabilistic procedures and applications - (extended abstract). In T. Moscibroda and A. A. Rescigno, editors, *SIROCCO*, volume 8179 of *Lecture Notes in Computer Science*, pages 153–164. Springer, 2013.

[37] Y. Métivier, N. Saheb, and A. Zemmari. Randomized local elections. *Inf. Process. Lett.*, 82(6):313–320, 2002.

[38] M. Naor and L. J. Stockmeyer. What can be computed locally? *SIAM J. Comput.*, 24(6):1259–1277, 1995.

[39] N. Norris. Universal covers of graphs: Isomorphism to depth $n-1$ implies isomorphism to all depths. *Discrete Applied Mathematics*, 56(1):61–74, 1995.

[40] D. Peleg. *Distributed Computing: A Locality-Sensitive Approach*. Society for Industrial and Applied Mathematics, 2000.

[41] M. K. Ramanathan, R. A. Ferreira, S. Jagannathan, A. Grama, and W. Szpankowski. Randomized leader election. *Distributed Computing*, 19(5-6):403–418, 2007.

[42] B. Schieber. Calling names in nameless networks. In P. Rudnicki, editor, *PODC*, pages 319–328. ACM, 1989.

[43] M. Yamashita and T. Kameda. Computing on anonymous networks: Part i-characterizing the solvable cases. *IEEE Trans. Parallel Distrib. Syst.*, 7(1):69–89, 1996.

Beyond Set Disjointness: The Communication Complexity of Finding the Intersection

Joshua Brody
Swarthmore College
brody@cs.swarthmore.edu

Amit Chakrabarti
Dartmouth College
ac@cs.dartmouth.edu

Ranganath Kondapally
Dartmouth College
rangak@cs.dartmouth.edu

David P. Woodruff
IBM Almaden
dpwoodru@us.ibm.com

Grigory Yaroslavtsev
Brown University, ICERM
grigory@grigory.us

ABSTRACT

We consider the following fundamental communication problem - there is data that is distributed among servers, and the servers want to compute the intersection of their data sets, e.g., the common records in a relational database. They want to do this with as little communication and as few messages (rounds) as possible. They are willing to use randomization, and fail with a tiny probability. Given a protocol for computing the intersection, it can also be used to compute the exact Jaccard similarity, the rarity, the number of distinct elements, and joins between databases. Computing the intersection is at least as hard as the set disjointness problem, which asks whether the intersection is empty.

Formally, in the two-server setting, the players hold subsets $S, T \subseteq [n]$. In many realistic scenarios, the sizes of S and T are significantly smaller than n, so we impose the constraint that $|S|, |T| \leq k$. We study the minimum number of bits the parties need to communicate in order to compute the intersection set $S \cap T$, given a certain number r of messages that are allowed to be exchanged. While $O(k \log(n/k))$ bits is achieved trivially and deterministically with a single message, we ask what is possible with more than one message and with randomization. We give a smooth communication/round tradeoff which shows that with $O(\log^* k)$ rounds, $O(k)$ bits of communication is possible, which improves upon the trivial protocol by an order of magnitude. This is in contrast to other basic problems such as computing the union or symmetric difference, for which $\Omega(k \log(n/k))$ bits of communication is required for any number of rounds. For two players, known lower bounds for the easier problem of set disjointness imply our algorithms are optimal up to constant factors in communication and number of rounds. We extend our protocols to m-player protocols, obtaining an optimal $O(mk)$ bits of communication with a similarly small number of rounds.

PODC'14, July 15–18, 2014, Paris, France.

http://dx.doi.org/10.1145/2611462.2611501 .

1. INTRODUCTION

Communication complexity [27] quantifies the communication necessary for two or more players to compute a function, where each player holds only a portion of the function's input. This model is widely studied, with applications in circuit complexity [24], combinatorial auctions [20], compressed sensing [2], data streams [1], and many other areas. We refer the reader to the book by Kushilevitz and Nisan [18] for a thorough treatment of the subject, which we only briefly describe here.

For randomized protocols, there are two well-studied and closely-related models. In the common random string model the players share an infinite string of independent unbiased coin tosses, and the players are otherwise deterministic. The correctness requirement is that for every input pair x, y, the output of Alice and Bob is equal to $f(x, y)$ with probability at least $1 - \delta$, for some specified $\delta > 0$, where the probability is taken over the shared random string. We let $R_\delta(f)$ be the minimum, over protocols in the common random string model satisfying the correctness protocol for f, of the maximum number of bits exchanged by the protocol over all inputs and shared random strings. For brevity, we let $R(f) = R_{1/3}(f)$. We note that a $2/3$ success probability can be amplified to $1 - \epsilon$ for an arbitrarily small constant $\epsilon > 0$ by incurring a constant factor overhead in communication.

In the private random string model, the players do not share a random string, but rather are allowed to be randomized using private randomness. By a result of Newman [19], any problem that can be solved in the common random string model can be solved in the private random string model, adding only $O(\log \log T)$ to the communication complexity, where T is the number of different inputs to the players. One unfortunate aspect of this reduction is that it is non-constructive in the sense that for each input length n, the protocol used is either hardwired an advice string that depends on n, or the players must search for the advice string, which doesn't require communication, but can result in unnecessary computation. We give our upper bounds in the common random string model, but describe how to translate them into constructive protocols in the private random string model, preserving optimality.

Besides the total communication, another well-studied resource is the total number of messages exchanged between the two players, known as the round complexity. In certain applications a server may not always be online, resulting in a significant delay between messages. There may also be undesirable overhead in the transmission of each message. Thus, it is important to not only achieve optimal communication, but also an optimal number of rounds for a given amount of communication. We use $D^{(r)}(f)$ and $R^{(r)}(f)$ to denote the deterministic and randomized communication complexity (in the common random string model) for protocols restricted to using at most r rounds.

One of the most well-studied problems in communication complexity is the disjointness function $\mathsf{DISJ}_k^n(S,T)$. In this problem, Alice has an input set $S \subseteq [n]$ of size at most k, Bob has an input set $T \subseteq [n]$ of size at most k, and $\mathsf{DISJ}_k^n(S,T) = 1$ iff $|S \cap T| = 0$. Håstad and Wigderson [15] showed that $R(\mathsf{DISJ}_k^n) = \Theta(k)$. The lower bound of $\Omega(k)$ follows by taking known lower bounds for set disjointness without a cardinality restriction on S and T, due to Kalysundaram and Schnitger [16], simplified by Razborov [25] and Bar-Yossef et al. [3], and combining them with a padding argument. The upper bound of $O(k)$ is due to a protocol given by Håstad and Wigderson, which they also remark was known and used many years ago [22].

In this paper we are interested in a seemingly much harder problem than the disjointness function. Namely, we are interested in recovering the *entire set intersection* $S \cap T$, rather than only deciding if $|S \cap T| = 0$. We call this problem the INT^k problem. Computing the intersection or the size of the intersection of two sets is a fundamental problem in computer science, with applications to distributed databases, including computing joins, finding duplicates, measuring Jaccard similarity, and computing rarity [9]; for more details on these applications, see below. We note that a recent work of Pagh et al. [21] studies approximating the size of the set intersection in the 1-way communication model, while we seek to recover the actual intersection and allow 2-way communication.

By the lower bound for the disjointness function, we have that $R(\mathrm{INT}^k) = \Omega(k)$, which holds for any number of rounds. Also, Alice and Bob can deterministically exchange their inputs using only $O(k \log(n/k))$ bits of communication, so $D^{(1)}(\mathrm{INT}^k) = O(k \log(n/k))$. They can also first hash the elements in their sets to $O(\log k)$-bit strings, and exchange the hashed values, from which they can decide which elements are in the intersection with probability $1 - 1/k^C$, for an arbitrarily large constant $C > 0$. This means that $R^{(1)}(\mathrm{INT}^k) = O(k \log k)$, which is optimal since $R^{(1)}\mathsf{DISJ}_k^n = \Omega(k \log k)$ [8, 7].

This was extended in [26] to interpolate between the one-round and unbounded-round situations, giving an r-round upper bound of $O(k \log^{(r)} k)$. Both [15] and [26] work by interpreting the public coin as a sequence of sets and having Alice or Bob send the index of the first set in this sequence containing her or his set. If $S \cap T = \emptyset$, then if the sets in the public coin were uniformly random and Alice sends the index of a set Z to Bob, w.h.p. $|Z \cap T| \approx |T|/2$, and so in $O(\log k)$ rounds they can solve k-DISJ. In [26] the public coin is instead interpreted as a list of random sparse sets, so now if $S \subseteq Z$, $|Z \cap T| \ll |T|/2$, and so in fewer rounds they can solve k-DISJ, at the cost of larger communication per round. These protocols seem specific to k-DISJ, and we do not know how to adapt them to the intersection problem, the main difficulty being in handling large $|S \cap T|$.

A somewhat related problem is that of computing k copies of the equality function EQ_k^n. In this problem, Alice has k strings $x^1, \ldots, x^k \in \{0,1\}^n$, Bob has k strings $y^1, \ldots, y^k \in \{0,1\}^n$ and they wish to compute $\mathsf{EQ}_k^n(x^1, \ldots, x^k, y^1, \ldots, y^k)$, a length-$k$ bit vector, where the i-th bit is 1 iff $x^i = y^i$. Feder, Kushilevitz, Naor, and Nisan [12] show that $R(\mathsf{EQ}_k^n) = \Theta(k)$. One unfortunate aspect of their protocol is that the number of rounds they achieve is $\Omega(\sqrt{k})$, as their protocol seems to be inherently sequential.

We observe in Section 3.1 below that by hashing into buckets, given a protocol for EQ_k^n, we can build a protocol for the INT^k problem. Plugging in the protocol of Feder et al., we obtain a randomized protocol for INT^k with the optimal $O(k)$ bits of communication in Theorem 3.1. However, the round complexity is $O(\sqrt{k})$. Another way of obtaining the optimal $O(k)$ bits of communication is to use a technique of Braverman and Rao to compress a protocol to its so-called internal information cost [5]. For the INT^k problem, the internal information cost is $O(k)$, and so this results in a protocol with the optimal $O(k)$ bits of communication, with a much smaller $O(\log k)$ number of rounds. It may seem plausible that one can combine the hashing technique we use in Section 3.1 together with $O(k)$ invocations of the recent round-optimal protocols for EQ^n [6], each with error probability $O(1/k)$. However, with such low error probability one invocation of the protocol of [6] requires $\Omega(\log k)$ communication for any number of rounds, even though the expected communication for the simpler task of verifying that two unequal inputs are indeed not equal with error probability $O(1/k)$, can be smaller.

Our Results: In this paper we give a new randomized protocol for INT^k which achieves the optimal $O(k)$ bits of communication, and simultaneously achieves $O(\log^* k)$ number of rounds, where $\log^* k$ is the iterated logarithm function, that is the number of times the logarithm function must be iteratively applied before the result is at most 1. Our number of rounds provides a significant improvement on the earlier $O(\log k)$ rounds needed to achieve the optimal $O(k)$ bits of communication given in previous work.

We also provide a more refined tradeoff, showing that with $O(r)$ rounds, one can achieve communication $O(k \log^{(r)} k)$, where $\log^{(r)} k$ is the function obtained by iteratively applying the logarithm function r times (e.g., $\log^{(0)} k = k, \log^{(1)} k = \log k$, $\log^{(2)} k = \log\log k$, etc.). Our protocols work in the common random string model, but can be turned into constructive protocols (i.e., without using Newman's theorem) in the private random string model, incurring an additive $O(\log\log n)$ bits of communication with no increase in the number of rounds.

Next we extend this to the setting in which there are m players in the private messages model [4, 23] and give a protocol with $O(k \log^{(r)} k)$ average communication per player, expected number of rounds $O(r \cdot \max(1, \frac{\log m}{k}))$, and error probability $1 - 1/2^k$. We give a similar guarantee with a worst-case communication bound ber player.

Our protocols for two players are communication-optimal, up to a constant factor in the number of rounds r, in light of a recent $\Omega(k \log^{(r)} k)$ communication lower bound for the DISJ_k^n problem [26]. For m players and $O(\log^* k \cdot \max(1, \frac{\log m}{k}))$ rounds, our $O(mk)$ communication is also optimal up to constant factors [4, 23].

Since EQ_k^n is also a special case of INT^k (Fact 2.1), we also significantly improve the round complexity of Feder et al. [12].

Applications: Set-intersection and list-intersection are very basic problems in databases, occurring in data mining applications, text analytics, and evaluation of conjunctive queries. They are also key operations in enterprise and web search. We refer the reader to a recent sample of database theory using the set-intersection primitive [10, 28, 13, 11]. While these papers focus on the computational costs of set-intersection, given the emergence of cloud computing and distributed databases, the communication cost is just as important. A quite basic problem, such as computing the join of two databases held by different servers, requires computing an intersection, which one would like to do with as little communication and as few messages as possible.

Prior to our work, it was not even known how to compute the size $|S \cap T|$ of the intersection with $O(k)$ communication and fewer than $O(\log k)$ rounds. Given our upper bound for set intersection, we significantly improve the communication/round tradeoffs for computing $|S \cap T|$. Since communicating $|S|$ and $|T|$ can be done in one-round, this gives the first protocol for computing the size $|S \cup T|$ of the union with our communication/round tradeoff. This in turn gives the first protocol for computing the exact Jaccard similarity $\frac{|S \cap T|}{|S \cup T|}$, exact Hamming distance, exact number of distinct elements, and exact 1-rarity and 2-rarity [9].

Our Technique: Our upper bound uses hashing and verification. First consider the following toy protocol: there is a hash function $h : [n] \to [k/\log k]$ that the two players share. For each $i \in [k/\log k]$, the players run a set intersection protocol on $S_i = \{x \in S \mid h(x) = i\}$ and $T_i = \{y \in T \mid h(y) = i\}$. To do so, note that with high probability, simultaneously for all $i \in [k/\log k]$, $|S_i| = O(\log k)$ and $|T_i| = O(\log k)$. Alice and Bob now agree on a hash function $g_i : [n] \to [\log^3 k]$. If Alice sends $g_i(x)$ to Bob for each $x \in S_i$, then Bob can compute $g_i(y)$ for each $y \in T_i$ and check if $g_i(y)$ is in the list of hashed elements that Alice sent. Bob can similary send the $g_i(y)$ values to Alice. Both parties therefore obtain candidate sets $I_A \subseteq S_i$ and $I_B \subseteq T_i$, respectively, for the intersection $S_i \cap T_i$. The communication for a given $i \in [k/\log k]$ is $O(\log k \log\log k)$ and the correctness probability is $1 - \frac{1}{\Omega(\log k)}$. An important observation now is that I_A and I_B contain $S_i \cap T_i$ with probability 1. Therefore, if $I_A = I_B$, then in fact $I_A = I_B = S_i \cap T_i$. By spending an additional $O(\log k)$ bits of communication, Alice and Bob can run an equality test on I_A and I_B, which one should think of as a "verification test", which succeeds with probability $1 - \frac{1}{k^C}$, for an arbitrarily large constant $C > 0$. Whenever the equality test succeeds, Alice and Bob can conclude $I_A = I_B = S_i \cap T_i$, since all such equality tests simultaneously succeed with very high probability. For the values of $i \in [k/\log k]$ for which the corresponding equality test detects that $I_A \neq I_B$, then the players re-run the set intersection protocol on S_i and T_i. The expected number of re-runs for each $i \in [k/\log k]$ is less than 1, and so the overall expected communication is at most $2k/\log k \cdot O(\log k \log\log k) = O(k \log\log k)$, which can be made worst-case by terminating the protocol if it consumes more than a constant factor times its expected communication cost.

To improve the communication futher, we instead hash into k buckets using a hash function h, and build a "verification tree" with these k buckets as the leaves. The tree has r levels, where r is the number of rounds we seek to achieve. For $2 \leq h \leq r$, the nodes with height h have $\log^{(r-h)} k / \log^{(r-h+1)} k$ children, while the nodes with height 1 (the parents of the leaves) have $\log^{(r-1)} k$ children. For a given $i \in [k]$, define S_i and T_i as before. For each $i \in [k]$, we run a set intersection protocol on S_i and T_i, now with only constant expected communication. For a node with height 1, we have a candidate set intersection for each of its $\log^{(r-1)} k$ children. We concatenate these $\log^{(r-1)} k$ candidate intersections as strings, and verify they are equal with a single equality test. If the equality test succeeds, then we proceed to the next level in the tree. At a node v in a given level of the tree, we perform a single equality test on all candidate intersections of leaves in the subtree $T(v)$ rooted at v. If the equality test fails at v, we re-run the set intersection protocol at all leaves in $T(v)$. By carefully choosing the correctness probabilty of the equality tests run at different levels in the tree, we are able to inductively show the expected communication until the root succeeds is $O(k)$, and the number of rounds is $O(r)$. Detailed description of the protocol and analysis is given in Section 3.3, which gives our main result:

THEOREM 1.1. *For $r > 0$ there exists an $6r$-round communication protocol for INT^k with total expected communication $O(k \log^{(r)} k)$ and success probability $1 - 1/poly(k)$.*

It remains open whether there exists an r-round protocol with communication $O(k \log^{(r)} k)$.

2. DEFINITIONS AND PRELIMINARIES

We will use the following definition of the iterated logarithm functions $\log^{(i)} z$. Let $\log^{(0)} z = z$ and for an integer $i \geq 1$ let $\log^{(i)} z = \log\left(\log^{(i-1)} z\right)$.

Let EQ^n denote the communication problem of solving EQUALITY on binary strings of length n. Let EQ^n_k denote the communication problem, corresponding to k independent instances of EQ^n. Let INT^k denote the communication problem of computing the intersection of two sets $S, T \subseteq [n]$, such that $|S|, |T| \leq k$.

A simple reduction from EQ^n_k to INT^k can be given as follows. For an instance $(x^1, \ldots, x^k, y^1, \ldots, y^k)$ of EQ^n_k an instance of INT^k is constructed by creating two sets of pairs $(1, x^1), \ldots (k, x^k)$ and $(1, y_1), \ldots (k, y^k)$. The size of the intersection between these two sets is exactly equal to the number of equal (x^i, y^i) pairs. This fact for DISJ^n_k can be also found in [6].

FACT 2.1 ([6]). *If there exists a protocol Π for INT^k, where the sets are drawn from a universe of size $N \geq k^c$ for $c > 2$ then there exists a protocol Π' for EQ^n_k with the same communication complexity and success probability for $n = \lfloor \log(\frac{N}{k}) \rfloor$.*

We will use the following fact about collision probability of a randomly chosen hash function.

FACT 2.2. *For any set $S \subseteq [n]$ of size $|S| \geq 2$ and $i \geq 0$ a random hash function $h \colon [n] \to [t]$, where $t = O(|S|^{i+2})$ has no collisions with probability at least $1 - 1/|S|^i$, namely for all $x, y \in S$ such that $x \neq y$ it holds that $h(x) \neq h(y)$. Moreover, a random hash function satisfying such guarantee can be constructed using only $O(\log n)$ random bits.*

3. TWO-PARTY SET INTERSECTION

In this section we give upper bounds in both private and public randomness model. In the private random string model, the players do not share a random string, but rather are allowed to be randomized using private randomness. By a result of Newman [19], any problem that can be solved in the common random string model can be solved in the private random string model, adding only $O(\log\log T)$ to the communication complexity, where T is the number of different inputs to the players. One unfortunate aspect of this reduction is that it is non-constructive in the sense that for each input length n, the protocol used is either hardwired an advice string that depends on n, or the players must search for the advice string, which doesn't require communication, but can result in unnecessary computation. We give our upper bounds in the common random string model, but describe how to translate them into constructive protocols in the private random string model, preserving optimality.

We start by describing a simple protocol with linear communication in Section 3.1 and then show how to achieve an optimum round vs. communication trade-off in Section 3.2 and Section 3.3.

3.1 $O(\sqrt{k})$-round protocol

THEOREM 3.1. *There exists an $O(\sqrt{k})$-round constructive randomized protocol for INT^k with success probability $1 - 1/poly(k)$. In the model of shared randomness the total expected communication is $O(k)$ and in the model of private randomness it is $O(k + \log\log n)$*

PROOF. Let $N = k^c$ for a constant $c > 2$. First, the parties pick a random hash function $H\colon [n] \to [N]$, which gives no collisions on the elements in $S \cup T$ with probability at least $1 - 1/\Omega(k^{c-2})$. Thus, for the rest of the analysis we can assume $S, T \subseteq [N]$.

The parties pick a random hash function $h\colon [N] \to [k]$. For a set $U \subseteq [N]$ we use notation $U_i = h^{-1}(i) \cap U$ for the preimage of i in U. Using preimages S_i and T_i the parties construct a collection of instances of EQUALITY, which contains an instance of EQUALITY(s,t) for every $(s,t) \in S_i \times T_i$ for every $i \in [k]$.

Formally, for two sets of instances of a communication problem C, say $C_1 = C(x_1, y_1), \dots, C(x_i, y_i)$ and $C_2 = C(x'_1, y'_1), \dots, C(x'_j, y'_j)$ let's denote their concatenation, which corresponds to solving C_1 and C_2 simultaneously as

$$C_1 \sqcup C_2 = (x_1, y_1), \dots, (x_i, y_i), (x'_1, y'_1), \dots (x'_j, y'_j).$$

Let's denote as $E_i = \bigsqcup_{(s,t)\in(S_i \times T_i)} \mathrm{Eq}(s,t)$ the collection of instances of equality corresponding to hash value i. The collection of all instances constructed by the parties is $E = \bigsqcup_{i=1}^{k} E_i$.

The expected number of instances $\mathbb{E}[|E|]$ is given as:

$$\mathbb{E}[|E|] = \mathbb{E}\left[\sum_{i=1}^{k} |S_i||T_i|\right] = \sum_{i=1}^{k} \mathbb{E}[|S_i||T_i|]$$

$$\leq \sum_{i=1}^{k} \mathbb{E}[|(S \cup T)_i|^2] = \sum_{i=1}^{k} Var[|(S \cup T)_i|] + \mathbb{E}[|(S \cup T)_i|]^2 \tag{1}$$

Given that for a set Z, the random variable $|Z_i|$ is distributed according to a binomial distribution $B(|Z|, 1/k)$, for each i we have $Var[|(S \cup T)_i|] \leq 2k \cdot (1/k)(1 - 1/k) \leq 2$ and $\mathbb{E}[|(S \cup T)_i|] \leq 2$ so $\mathbb{E}[|E|] \leq 6k$.

We use the following result of [12]:

THEOREM 3.2 ([12]). *There exists aconstructive randomized protocol for EQ_k^n with $O(\sqrt{k})$ rounds, which has success probability $2^{-\Omega(\sqrt{k})}$. In the public randomness model the expected total communication is $O(k)$ and in the private randomness model it is $O(k + \log n)$.*

In the shared randomness model the result now follows immediately. In the private randomness model the parties need to construct two random hash functions H and h, using Fact 2.2 with only $O(\log n) + O(\log k) = O(\log n)$ random bits. These bits are exchanged through the channel in the first round of the protocol and are added to the total communication, bringing it down to $O(k + \log n)$. To further reduce the communication we can use the hashing scheme of Fredman, Komlos and Szemeredi [14] as the first step of the protocol. In [14] it is shown that mapping elements $[n]$ by taking a remainder modulo a random prime $q = \tilde{O}(k^2 \log n)$ gives no collisions on a subset of size $O(k)$ with probability $1 - 1/poly(k)$. Applying this result to $S \cup T$ we can reduce the length of strings in the instances of equality down to $O(\log k + \log\log n)$. Thus, we can now specify the pairwise independent hash function using only $O(\log k + \log\log n)$ random bits. See Appendix A.1.1 in [17] for a detailed discussion.

3.2 Auxiliary protocols

We first describe auxiliary protocols BASIC-INTERSECTION (Lemma 3.3) and EQUALITY (Fact 3.5) that we use as building blocks in our main algorithm in Section 3.3. For a two-party communication protocol $\mathcal{P}$ we denote the output of the protocol for the first party as $\mathcal{P}_A(x,y)$ and for the second party as $\mathcal{P}_B(x,y)$.

LEMMA 3.3 (PROTOCOL BASIC-INTERSECTION(S,T)). *There exists a randomized protocol $\mathcal{P}$ (with shared randomness), such that for any $S, T \subset [n]$ and an integer $i \geq 1$, the sets $S' = \mathcal{P}_A(S,T)$ and $T' = \mathcal{P}_B(S,T)$ satisfy the following properties:*

1. *$S' \subseteq S, T' \subseteq T$.*
2. *If $S \cap T = \emptyset$ then $S' \cap T' = \emptyset$ with probability 1.*
3. *If $S \cap T \neq \emptyset$ then $(S \cap T) \subseteq (S' \cap T')$. Also, with probability $1 - 1/N^i$ it holds that $S' = T' = (S \cap T)$.*

The total communication in the protocol is

$$O\left(i \cdot (|S| + |T|)\log(|S| + |T|)\right)$$

and the protocol can be executed in 4 rounds.

Note that Lemma 3.3 guarantees that $S' \cap T'$ is always a superset of the intersection. Also, if the sets S' and T' are equal then each of them is exactly the intersection of S and T.

PROOF. The parties first exchange the sizes of their sets $|S|$ and $|T|$ and determine $m = |S| + |T|$. Using shared randomness they pick a random hash function $h\colon [n] \to [t]$, where $t = \Theta(m^{i+2})$. They exchange sets $h(S)$ and $h(T)$ using total communication $O(i \cdot N \log N)$. The outcome of the protocol is $\mathcal{P}_A(S,T) = h^{-1}(h(T)) \cap S$ and $\mathcal{P}_B(S,T) =$

$h^{-1}(h(S)) \cap T$. Since exchanging the sizes of the sets takes two rounds and another two rounds are required to exchange $h(S)$ and $h(T)$, the total number of rounds of communication is 4.

By construction we have $S' = h^{-1}(h(T)) \cap S \subseteq S$ and similarly $T' \subseteq T$ so the first property holds. If $S \cap T = \emptyset$ then $S' \cap T' = (h^{-1}(h(T)) \cap S) \cap (h^{-1}(h(S)) \cap T) \subseteq (S \cap T) = \emptyset$ and the second property holds. Because $S \subseteq h^{-1}(h(S))$ and $T \subseteq h^{-1}(h(T))$ we have

$$S \cap T \subseteq (h^{-1}(h(T)) \cap S) \cap (h^{-1}(h(S)) \cap T) = S' \cap T',$$

the first part of the third property. Moreover, if the hash function h has no collisions among $S \cup T$ then

$$S' = h^{-1}(h(T)) \cap S = T \cap S$$

and

$$T' = h^{-1}(h(S)) \cap T = S \cap T.$$

The proof is completed using the analysis of collision probability given by Fact 2.2. ∎

We have the following corollary.

COROLLARY 3.4. *If for the protocol $\mathcal{P}$ in Lemma 3.3 it holds that $\mathcal{P}_A(S,T) = \mathcal{P}_B(S,T)$ then*

$$\mathcal{P}_A(S,T) = \mathcal{P}_B(S,T) = S \cap T.$$

In our main protocol in Section 3.3 we will use an Eq_n test with the following guarantees to verify correctness of the protocol BASIC-INTERSECTION. The following guarantee is achieved by a protocol, which uses a random hash function h into k bits.

FACT 3.5. *There exists a randomized (with shared randomness) protocol $\mathcal{P}$ for Eq_n with the following properties.*

1. *If $x = y$ then $\mathcal{P}_A(x,y) = \mathcal{P}_B(x,y) = 1$ with probability 1.*
2. *If $x \neq y$ then $\mathcal{P}_A(x,y) = \mathcal{P}_B(x,y) = 0$ with probability at least $1 - 1/2^k$.*

The total communication in the protocol is $O(k)$ and it can be executed in two rounds.

3.3 Main protocol

THEOREM 3.6 (RESTATEMENT OF THEOREM 1.1). *For every integer $r > 0$ there exists an $6r$-round constructive randomized communication protocol (with shared randomness) for INT^k with total expected communication $O(k \log^{(r)} k)$ and success probability $1 - 1/poly(k)$.*

PROOF. For $r = 1$ the parties use shared randomness to pick a hash function $h\colon [n] \to [N]$ for $N = k^c$, where $c > 2$. Then each of the parties uses $ck \log k$ bits to exchange $h(S)$ and $h(T)$ respectively. By Fact 2.2 the probability that h has a collision on a set $S \cup T$ is at most $1 - 1/\Theta(k^{c-2})$.

For $r > 1$ consider a tree $\mathcal{T}$ of depth r with the set of nodes at the i-th level for $0 \le i \le r$ denoted as L_i (these are the nodes at distance i from the leaves). Let the degree at the i-th level for $2 \le i \le r$ be equal to $d_i = \log^{(r-i)} k / \log^{(r-i+1)} k$ and the degree at the first level is $d_1 = \log^{(r-1)} k$. Note that this guarantees that the total number of leaves in the tree is k. For a node $v \in \mathcal{T}$, let $c(v)$ denote the set of children of v. For a node $v \in \mathcal{T}$, let $\mathcal{C}(v)$ denote the set of all leaves in the subtree of v. Note that for a node $v \in L_i$ the number of such leaves is $|\mathcal{C}(v)| = \log^{(r-i)} k$.

DEFINITION 3.1 (SET ASSIGNMENT). *A set assignment $\mathcal{A}$ to the leaves of $\mathcal{T}$ is a vector $\mathcal{A} = (\mathcal{A}_1, \ldots, \mathcal{A}_k)$, consisting of k sets. We say that the set $\mathcal{A}_\ell$ is assigned to a corresponding leaf ℓ in $\mathcal{T}$.*

Every set assignment to the leaves of $\mathcal{T}$ naturally induces a set assignment on all internal vertices of $\mathcal{T}$. Let $\mathcal{A} = (\mathcal{A}_1, \ldots, \mathcal{A}_k)$ be a set assignment for the leaves of $\mathcal{T}$. For every internal node $v \in \mathcal{T}$ we denote an assignment induced at this vertex by $\mathcal{A}$ as $\mathcal{A}_v = \cup_{i \in \mathcal{C}(v)} \mathcal{A}_i$.

Now we describe the protocol used by the parties. First, Alice and Bob use shared randomness to pick a hash function $h\colon [n] \to [k]$. Using this hash function they define initial assignments of sets S^{-1} and T^{-1} respectively as follows. For a leaf $\ell \in [k]$ of $\mathcal{T}$, let $S_\ell^{-1} = h^{-1}(h(\ell)) \cap S$ and $T_\ell^{-1} = h^{-1}(h(\ell)) \cap T$.

Then the protocol proceeds in r stages. In stage i for $0 \le i < r$ the parties construct new assignments to the leaves of $\mathcal{T}$, which induce new assignments on the internal nodes. We will show that after r stages the parties obtain an assignment to the leaves, such that with high probability the set induced by this assignment in the root of $\mathcal{T}$ is exactly $S \cap T$. We use notation S^i and T^i respectively for the i-th assignment that the parties make to the leaves of the tree. The description of the i-th stage is given as Algorithm 1. This completes the description of the protocol.

Input: Sets $S, T \in [k]^k$, assignments S^{i-1}, T^{i-1}.

1: For every $v \in L_i$ run the protocol EQUALITY(S_v^{i-1}, T_v^{i-1}) with success probability $1 - 1/(\log^{(r-i-1)} k)^4$.
2: Let $\mathcal{F}$ be the set of vertices for which the equality protocol above returns $S_v^{i-1} \neq T_v^{i-1}$. We call these vertices *failed*.
3: For every $v \in \mathcal{F}$ and every leaf $u \in \mathcal{C}(v)$ run BASIC-INTERSECTION(S_u^{i-1}, T_u^{i-1}) with success probability $1 - 1/(\log^{(r-i-1)} k)^4$ and assign $S_u^i = \mathcal{P}_A(S_u^{i-1}, T_u^{i-1})$ and $T_u^i = \mathcal{P}_B(S_u^{i-1}, T_u^{i-1})$ respectively.
4: For every $v \notin \mathcal{F}$ and every leaf $u \in \mathcal{C}(v)$ assign $S_u^i = S_u^{i-1}$ and $T_u^i = T_u^{i-1}$.

Algorithm 1: Protocol for INT^k. Stage i.

In the rest of the proof we first analyze the correctness probability of the protocol above (the key lemma is Lemma 3.7) and then total communication (Lemma 3.10). The proof of Theorem 1.1 is completed by observing that the protocol can be executed in $O(r)$ rounds.

LEMMA 3.7. *After stage i for every leaf $u \in \mathcal{T}$ it holds that $S_u^i = T_u^i$ with probability at least $1 - 1/(\log^{(r-i-1)} k)^4$, taken over all the randomness of the protocol.*

PROOF. If u is in the subtree of a node v, which is not *failed* at level i then we know that $S_v = T_v$ and thus $S_u = T_u$ for each $u \in \mathcal{C}(v)$ with probability at least $1 - 1/(\log^{(r-i-1)} k)^4$ by the guarantee of the EQUALITY(S_v, T_v) test. Otherwise, u is in the subtree of a failed node v at level i. In this case the claim follows because we run BASIC-INTERSECTION protocol for this leaf with success probability at least $1 - 1/(\log^{(r-i-1)} k)^4$. ∎

We call a node $v \in L_i$ *correct* if after stage i it holds that $S_v^i = T_v^i$.

COROLLARY 3.8. *Every node $v \in L_i$ is correct with probability at least $1 - 1/(\log^{(r-i-1)} k)^3$. In particular, the root of the tree is correct with probability at least $1 - 1/k^3$.*

PROOF. From Lemma 3.7 applied to the level i it follows that after the execution of stage i for every leaf $u \in \mathcal{C}(v)$ it holds that $S_u^i = T_u^i$ with probability at least $1 - 1/(\log^{(r-i-1)} k)^4$. Hence, by a union bound over all $\log^{(r-i)} k$ such leaves with probability at least

$$1 - \log^{(r-i)} k/(\log^{(r-i-1)} k)^4 \geq 1 - 1/(\log^{(r-i-1)} k)^3$$

we have $S_v^i = T_v^i$. ∎

The correctness proof of the protocol now follows from Corollary 3.8 together with the following invariant applied to the root of the tree after round $r-1$.

PROPOSITION 3.9. *If for a node $v \in \mathcal{T}$ Alice and Bob assign S_v^i and T_v^i to it respectively then if $S_v^i = T_v^i$ then $S_v^i = T_v^i = S_v \cap T_v$.*

PROOF. Note that this invariant is maintained by BASIC-INTERSECTION (Corollary 3.4). During the execution of the protocol the sets S_v' and T_v' only change when we apply BASIC-INTERSECTION to the leaves in $\mathcal{T}$. Clearly, if the invariant is maintained for all leaves then it is also maintained for all internal nodes as well. ∎

Now we analyze the total communication in the protocol. For a leaf $u \in \mathcal{T}$ let n_u denote the expected number of times the BASIC-INTERSECTION protocol was run on the sets assigned to u.

LEMMA 3.10. *For every leaf $u \in \mathcal{T}$ it holds that $\mathbb{E}[n_u] = O(1)$.*

PROOF. For a leaf u let's denote it's unique predecessor in level i as $p_i(u)$. Formally, $p_i(u) = v$ if and only if $v \in L_i$ and u is in the subtree of v. We can express $\mathbb{E}[n_u]$ as:

$$\begin{aligned}
\mathbb{E}[n_u] &= \sum_{i=0}^{r-1} \Pr[p_i(u) \text{ is failed}] \cdot (4\log^{(r-i)} k) \\
&\leq \sum_{i=0}^{r-1} d_i \cdot \Pr[v \text{ is an incorrect child of } p_i(u)]\,(4\log^{(r-i)} k), \\
&\leq \sum_{i=0}^{r-1} \frac{\log^{(r-i)} k}{\log^{(r-i+1)} k} \cdot \frac{1}{(\log^{(r-i)} k)^3} \cdot (4\log^{(r-i)} k) = O(1)
\end{aligned}$$

where the first inequality holds by a union bound and the second by Corollary 3.8. ∎

The total expected communication in the protocol can be expressed as the sum of the total communication for EQUALITY and BASIC-INTERSECTION. The total communication for EQUALITY is:

$$\begin{aligned}
&\sum_{i=0}^{r-1} |L_i|(4\log^{(r-i)} k) \\
&= O(k\log^{(r)} k) + \sum_{i=1}^{r-1} (k/\log^{(r-i)} k) \cdot (4\log^{(r-i)} k) \\
&= O(k\log^{(r)} k) + O(rk) \\
&= O(k\log^{(r)} k).
\end{aligned}$$

The expected total communication for BASIC-INTERSECTION is by Lemma 3.3 equal to:

$$\mathbb{E}\left[\sum_{i=1}^{k} (|S_i| + |T_i|)\log(|S_i| + |T_i|) \cdot n_i\right] = \sum_{i=1}^{k} \mathbb{E}\left[(|S_i| + |T_i|)\log(|S_i| + |T_i|)\right]\mathbb{E}[n_i],$$

where the equality follows from the independence of the random variables. Because for every i we have $\mathbb{E}[n_i] = O(1)$ by Lemma 3.10, to complete the proof it is sufficient to show that $\mathbb{E}[(|S_i| + |T_i|)\log(|S_i| + |T_i|)] = O(1)$ and thus the total communication for BASIC-INTERSECTION is $O(k)$. We have $\mathbb{E}[(|S_i| + |T_i|)\log(|S_i| + |T_i|)] \leq \mathbb{E}[(|S_i| + |T_i|)^2]$, where the right-hand side is constant by the same argument as used to bound each term in (1). Finally, the bound on the number of rounds of communication follows from the fact the communication in each of the r stages for the EQUALITY tests can be done in parallel in two rounds (Fact 3.5). After in four more rounds we can perform all BASIC-INTERSECTION protocols in parallel (Lemma 3.3). This gives $6r$ rounds of communication. ∎

4. MULTI-PARTY SET INTERSECTION IN THE MESSAGE PASSING MODEL

In the multi-party case we have m players, each holding a set $S_i \subseteq [n]$ such that $|S_i| \leq k$. The goal of the parties is to output a set $S = \bigcap_{i=1}^{m} S_i$. We allow arbitrary communication between the parties (i.e. any player i can send a message to any player j). In each round of the protocol the parties first perform some local computation and then can exchange messages. This is known as the message passing model (see e.g. [4]). We consider two optimization goals: minimizing the total communication (or equivalently average communication per player) and minimizing the worst-case communication per player. In both cases we keep the number of rounds as small as possible.

First, observe that we can amplify the success probability of the two-party protocol in Theorem 1.1 to be $1-1/2^k$ while keeping the expected total communication $O(k\log^{(r)} k)$ and only incurring a penalty in the number of rounds: the protocol will have expected $O(r)$ rounds instead of worst-case $6r$ rounds. This follows by repeating the protocol if it hasn't succeeded. The latter condition can be checked by exchanging k-bit equality checks after the protocol terminates. With a total of $O(1)$ expected repetitions this gives expected $O(r)$ number of rounds and success probability which is only limited by the equality checks and is thus $1 - 1/2^k$ by Fact 3.5.

Using this observation we obtain a protocol with the following guarantee for the average-case multi-party setting.

COROLLARY 4.1. *(Average-case) For every $r > 0$ there exists a multi-party protocol in the message passing model with expected average communication per player $O(k\log^{(r)} k)$, expected number of rounds $O\left(r \cdot \max(1, \frac{\log m}{k})\right)$ and error probability $1 - 1/2^k$.*

PROOF. First, the set of m players is partitioned into groups of size at most 2^k. Consider one such group, which consists of players holding sets $S_1, \ldots, S_{2^k}$. The player holding S_1 is chosen as a coordinator. Within the group all players execute the modified version of the two-party protocol described above with the coordinator, who computes sets $T_i = S_1 \cap S_i$ for each $2 \le i \le 2^k$. This step is repeated until the coordinator succeeds in verifying that $\bigcap_{i=2}^{2^k} T_i = \bigcap_{i=1}^{2^k} S_i$ with probability at least $1 - 1/2^k$. This is done by using a $2k$-bit equality check with each of the players. By Fact 3.5 the equality check succeeds with probability $1 - 1/2^{2k}$ and hence by a union bound over the 2^k players in the group the desired success probability follows. Once all $m' = \lceil m/2^k \rceil$ coordinators succeed in verifying their sets the protocol is executed recursively among them for their respective sets.

The number of active players decreases exponentially between the levels and thus the total communication is dominated by the first level. The first level has average complexity $O(k \log^{(r)} k)$ per player and expected $O(r)$ rounds using the same reasoning as for the case of two-parties discussed above. The total number of levels of recursion is $\max(1, \log_{2^k} m) = \max\left(1, \frac{\log m}{k}\right)$, which gives the claimed bound on the total number of rounds. ∎

Taking $r = \log^* k$ in Corollary 4.1 we get average communication $O(k)$ per player, which matches the lower bounds of [23, 4] who show that average communication $\Omega(k)$ is necessary for solving SET INTERSECTION and SET DISJOINTNESS in the message passing model.

In the protocol from Corollary 4.1 every coordinator has to perform $O(2^k k \log^{(r)} k)$ communication per level. By increasing the number of rounds we can amortize this cost among the players.

COROLLARY 4.2. *(Worst-case) For every $r > 0$ there exists a multi-party protocol in the message passing model with worst-case communication $O\left(k^2 \log^{(r)} k \cdot \max\left(1, \frac{\log m}{k}\right)\right)$ per player, expected number of rounds $O\left(r \cdot k \cdot \max(1, \frac{\log m}{k})\right)$ and error probability $1 - 1/2^k$.*

PROOF. The protocol is executed recursively in $\max\left(1, \frac{\log m}{k}\right)$ levels and in each level the players are assigned to groups of size at most 2^k as in Corollary 4.1. Consider one such group. Instead of using a coordinator in each level the players are assigned to the leaves of a complete binary tree of depth k. They run the two-party protocol recursively in pairs. This gives expected number of rounds $O(rk)$ per level and the bound on the number of rounds follows. When the two-party protocol is executed for the top two nodes in the tree (the children of the root) the parties also perform a k-bit equality check in order to certify the correctness of the result with probability $1 - 1/2^k$. If this check fails then the entire computation in the tree is repeated, which gives $O(1)$ repetitions in expectation using the same reasoning as before. Finally, adding up over all nodes on a path of length k the worst-case communication per level is $O(k^2 \log^{(r)} k)$ which gives the bound on the desired worst-case communication per player. ∎

5. REFERENCES

[1] N. Alon, Y. Matias, and M. Szegedy. The space complexity of approximating the frequency moments. *J. Comput. Syst. Sci.*, 58(1):137–147, 1999.

[2] K. D. Ba, P. Indyk, E. Price, and D. P. Woodruff. Lower bounds for sparse recovery. In *SODA*, pages 1190–1197, 2010.

[3] Z. Bar-Yossef, T. S. Jayram, R. Kumar, and D. Sivakumar. An information statistics approach to data stream and communication complexity. *J. Comput. Syst. Sci.*, 68(4):702–732, 2004.

[4] M. Braverman, F. Ellen, R. Oshman, T. Pitassi, and V. Vaikuntanathan. A tight bound for set disjointness in the message-passing model. In *FOCS*, pages 668–677, 2013.

[5] M. Braverman and A. Rao. Information equals amortized communication. In *FOCS*, pages 748–757, 2011.

[6] J. Brody, A. Chakrabarti, R. Kondapally, D. P. Woodruff, and G. Yaroslavtsev. Certifying equality with limited interaction. *Manuscript.*

[7] H. Buhrman, D. García-Soriano, A. Matsliah, and R. de Wolf. The non-adaptive query complexity of testing k-parities. *CoRR*, abs/1209.3849, 2012.

[8] A. Dasgupta, R. Kumar, and D. Sivakumar. Sparse and lopsided set disjointness via information theory. In *APPROX-RANDOM*, pages 517–528, 2012.

[9] M. Datar and S. Muthukrishnan. Estimating rarity and similarity over data stream windows. In *ESA*, pages 323–334, 2002.

[10] B. Ding and A. C. König. Fast set intersection in memory. *PVLDB*, 4(4):255–266, 2011.

[11] B. Ding, H. Wang, R. Jin, J. Han, and Z. Wang. Optimizing index for taxonomy keyword search. In *SIGMOD Conference*, pages 493–504, 2012.

[12] T. Feder, E. Kushilevitz, M. Naor, and N. Nisan. Amortized communication complexity. *SIAM J. Comput.*, 24(4):736–750, 1995.

[13] M. Fontoura, M. Gurevich, V. Josifovski, and S. Vassilvitskii. Efficiently encoding term co-occurrences in inverted indexes. In *CIKM*, pages 307–316, 2011.

[14] M. L. Fredman, J. Komlós, and E. Szemerédi. Storing a sparse table with 0(1) worst case access time. *J. ACM*, 31(3):538–544, 1984.

[15] J. Håstad and A. Wigderson. The randomized communication complexity of set disjointness. *Theory of Computing*, 3(1):211–219, 2007.

[16] B. Kalyanasundaram and G. Schnitger. The probabilistic communication complexity of set intersection. *SIAM J. Discrete Math.*, 5(4):545–557, 1992.

[17] D. M. Kane, J. Nelson, and D. P. Woodruff. On the exact space complexity of sketching and streaming small norms. In *SODA*, pages 1161–1178, 2010.

[18] E. Kushilevitz and N. Nisan. *Communication complexity.* Cambridge University Press, 1997.

[19] I. Newman. Private vs. common random bits in communication complexity. *Inf. Process. Lett.*, 39(2):67–71, 1991.

[20] N. Nisan and I. Segal. The communication requirements of efficient allocations and supporting prices. *J. Economic Theory*, 129(1):192–224, 2006.

[21] R. Pagh, M. Stockel, and D. P. Woodruff. Is min-wise hashing optimal for summarizing set intersection? In *PODS*, 2014.

[22] I. Parnafes, R. Raz, and A. Wigderson. Direct product results and the gcd problem, in old and new communication models. In *STOC*, pages 363–372, 1997.

[23] J. M. Phillips, E. Verbin, and Q. Zhang. Lower bounds for number-in-hand multiparty communication complexity, made easy. In *SODA*, pages 486–501, 2012.

[24] R. Raz and A. Wigderson. Monotone circuits for matching require linear depth. *J. ACM*, 39(3):736–744, 1992.

[25] A. A. Razborov. On the distributional complexity of disjointness. *Theor. Comput. Sci.*, 106(2):385–390, 1992.

[26] M. Saglam and G. Tardos. On the communication complexity of sparse set disjointness and exists-equal problems. In *FOCS*, pages 678–687, 2013.

[27] A. C.-C. Yao. Some complexity questions related to distributive computing (preliminary report). In *STOC*, pages 209–213, 1979.

[28] J. Zhou, Z. Bao, W. Wang, T. W. Ling, Z. Chen, X. Lin, and J. Guo. Fast slca and elca computation for xml keyword queries based on set intersection. In *ICDE*, pages 905–916, 2012.

Breathe before Speaking: Efficient Information Dissemination Despite Noisy, Limited and Anonymous Communication

Ofer Feinerman *
Weizmann Institute
Rehovot, 76100, Israel
ofer.feinerman@weizmann.ac.il

Bernhard Haeupler
Microsoft Research
Mountain View, CA 94043, USA
haeupler@cs.cmu.edu

Amos Korman †
CNRS and Univ. Paris Diderot
Paris, 75013, France
amos.korman@liafa.univ-paris-diderot.fr

ABSTRACT

Distributed computing models typically assume reliable communication between processors. While such assumptions often hold for engineered networks, e.g., due to underlying error correction protocols, their relevance to biological systems, wherein messages are often distorted before reaching their destination, is quite limited. In this study we aim at bridging this gap by rigorously analyzing a model of communication in large anonymous populations composed of simple agents which interact through short and highly unreliable messages.

We focus on the rumor-spreading problem and the majority-consensus problem, two fundamental tasks in distributed computing, and initiate their study under communication noise. Our model for communication is extremely weak and follows the push gossip communication paradigm: In each synchronous round each agent that wishes to send information delivers a message to a random anonymous agent. This communication is further restricted to contain only one bit (essentially representing an opinion). Lastly, the system is assumed to be so noisy that the bit in each message sent is flipped independently with probability $1/2 - \epsilon$, for some small $\epsilon > 0$.

Even in this severely restricted, stochastic and noisy setting we give natural protocols that solve the noisy rumor-spreading and the noisy majority-consensus problems efficiently. Our protocols run in $O(\log n/\epsilon^2)$ rounds and use $O(n \log n/\epsilon^2)$ messages/bits in total, where n is the number of agents. These bounds are asymptotically optimal and, in fact, are as fast and message efficient as if each agent would have been simultaneously informed directly by the source. Our efficient, robust, and simple algorithms suggest balancing between silence and transmission, synchronization, and majority-based decisions as important ingredients towards understanding collective communication schemes in anonymous and noisy populations.

Categories and Subject Descriptors

F.2.2 [**Theory of Computation**]: ANALYSIS OF ALGORITHMS AND PROBLEM COMPLEXITY—*Nonnumerical Algorithms and Problems*; F.1.2 [**Theory of Computation**]: COMPUTATION BY ABSTRACT DEVICES—*Modes of Computation* Parallelism and concurrency

Keywords

gossip; information dissemination; noise; rumor spreading; consensus, reliability

1. INTRODUCTION

1.1 Background and motivation

Information theory originated as a search for methods to manage communication noise in engineered systems [49]. In many ways, this search has reached its goals. The existence of coding methods that reduce error rates to practically zero were proven to exist [49]. Not less important, such codes have been realized in a myriad of real-world systems [44]. In other words, given a large enough bandwidth, one can encode a message with a large number of error correcting bits in a way that makes communication noise essentially a non-issue. Fault-tolerance study in distributed computing focuses either on weak faults such as node *crashes* and message *failures*, or on very strong faults modeled as adversarial (*Byzantine*) interventions, but messages that are transmitted from one processor are, typically, assumed to reach their destination without distortion. Indeed, this perfect transmission relies on an implicit assumption that error-correcting is guaranteed by a lower level protocol that is responsible for implementing communication.

In contrast, communication in the natural world is inherently noisy. Biology, for one, is replete with communicating ensembles on all levels of organization: from molecules (e.g., the immune complement system [14]), and cells (e.g., bacterial populations [8]) to societies (e.g., a superorganism of

*Incumbent of the Shlomo and Michla Tomarin Career Development Chair. Supported by the Clore Foundation, the Israel Science Foundation (FIRST grant no. 1694/10), and the Minerva Foundation.

†Supported in part by the ANR project DISPLEXITY, and by the INRIA project GANG.

PODC'14, July 15–18, 2014, Paris, France.

http://dx.doi.org/10.1145/2611462.2611469.

social insects [52]). Whereas it is unrealistic to assume adversarial interventions, biological signals are extremely vulnerable to random distortion as they are being generated (e.g., probabilistic vesicle release in neuronal synapses [3]), transmitted over noisy media (e.g., acoustic communication in noisy environments [13]) and received (e.g., non-reliable measurements taken by immune cells [22].) Nevertheless, many studies show that, in practice, biological ensembles function reliably despite communication noise [23,47].

How biological systems overcome communication noise is a very basic and intriguing question. Indeed, for systems composed of simple and restricted individuals, as is often the case in biology, it may not be reasonable to assume sophisticated error-correcting at the level of an individual channel. Furthermore, when message size is highly restricted, redundancy drastically reduces the available alphabet and hence could not be used extensively. On the other hand, with only little redundancy, a random fault in the content of a transmitted message may lead to the reception of a meaningful message that is inconsistent with the original one [38].

1.2 Context and related work

Our paper falls within the scope of natural algorithms, a recent attempt to investigate biological phenomena from an algorithmic perspective [1,11,16,39]. Within this framework, many works in the computer science discipline have studied different computational aspects of abstract systems composed of simple and restrict individuals. This includes, in particular, the study of *population protocols* [4,5,7,10,40], which considers constant size individuals interacting in pairs (using constant size messages) in a communication pattern which is either uniformly at random or adversarial, and the *beeping* model [1,2,21], which assumes a fixed network with extremely restricted communication. However, despite interesting results obtained in such models, the understanding of their fault-tolerance aspects is still lacking [5,10]. Here, we study basic distributed tasks in a model that includes highly restricted *and* noisy communication.

Disseminating information to all the nodes of a network is one of the most fundamental communication primitives. In particular, the *rumor-spreading* problem, where a single piece of information initially residing at some source node is to be disseminated, and variants of it have received a lot of attention in the literature, see, e.g., [15,17,19,24,28–32,36]. Much of this research was devoted to bounding measures such as the number of rounds, and the total number of messages. Fault tolerant rumor-spreading algorithms have also been studied extensively, especially in complete networks and in synchronous environments, where the focus has been on weak types of failures such as (probabilistic) message failures and initial node crashes. Essentially, it has been shown that there exist rumor-spreading protocols that can overcome such faults with a relatively little penalty [18–20,30,33,36]. In the *majority-consensus* problem processors are required to agree on a common output value which is the majority input value [6,9]. In general, this problem has been studied under similar models to the ones used for studying the rumor-spreading problem, but, in comparison to the latter problem, has received much less attention in the literature.

Rumor-spreading related problems were studied in other contexts as well, often with settings where communication noise is inherent. Network information theory [27] discusses the problem of disseminating information from one or more sources to a large number of recipients over noisy information channels. The settings there are, however, different from those that interest us as they are non-distributed in nature and allow for complex coding schemes that may be computationally complex for simple agents [37]. Engineers have studied the related problem of sensor network consensus formation in the presence of communication noise and have demonstrated, for example, tradeoffs between consensus quality and running time [35]. Physicists have studied the spreading of epidemics [41] and the formation of consensus around a zealot in voter models [42,43] within probabilistic settings that include communication noise. These physically inspired studies often assume very simple algorithms and analyze their performance - this is different from a computer science approach which focuses on identifying the most efficient algorithms. Indeed, rumor spreading within a noisy voter model setting is expected to yield long convergence times, polynomial in the number agents.

Examples in biology: In the biological world, rumor-spreading is a common phenomenon which allows, for example, that a single receptor activate an entire cell [51], a small number of cells trigger large population responses [23], or a small number of vigilant individuals alert their herd [48]. There have been several direct experimental demonstrations of reliable rumor-spreading using unreliable messaging in biological systems. Examples include knowledgeable ants informing their nestmates regarding available food [47] and precise temporal codes achieved by coordinated neuronal populations [34]. Such examples serve as motivation for a more thorough theoretical understanding of how rumors spread through groups of simple individuals that communicate by noisy messages. Majority-consensus problems have also been shown to be relevant for several biological systems: Ants choosing between two alternative nesting sites and reach consensus on a nest that attracts a larger number of scouts [25] and a group of fish that reach consensus around the larger group of leaders [50] being two examples.

1.3 Model and Problems

1.3.1 Problem Definitions

As a first step into the study of noisy information dissemination, we study a very simple scenario in which there are only two possible states (or *opinions*) for the environment, namely, 0 and 1, one of which is the *correct* opinion, denoted by $\mathcal{B}$. We study two information dissemination problems both of which consider of n anonymous *agents*.

In the *noisy rumor-spreading* problem, we start the execution with one designated agent, called the *source* (representing the environment) that holds the correct opinion $\mathcal{B}$, while all other $n-1$ agents initially have no information regarding $\mathcal{B}$. Agents can propagate information and update their knowledge by using (noisy) interactions as specified below. The goal is that eventually, *with high probability*, all agents adopt $\mathcal{B}$ as their final opinion. Throughout we denote with high probability any probability of at least $1-1/n^c$, for some sufficiently large constant $c>2$.

In the *noisy majority-consensus* problem, we consider that initially we have a subset A of agents, each of which having an opinion in $\{0,1\}$ (all other agents do not have an opinion), where $\mathcal{B}$ is the majority opinion among the agents in A. The problem is parameterized by the extent to which

$\mathcal{B}$ is more common. That is, the *majority-bias* of A is defined as $\frac{1}{2}(A_{\mathcal{B}} - A_{\bar{\mathcal{B}}})/|A|$, where A_i is the number of agents in the initial opinionated group, A, with opinion i, for $i \in \{0,1\}$. As in the noisy rumor-spreading problem, the goal of the agents is to guarantee that with high probability, at the end of the execution, all agents hold the opinion $\mathcal{B}$.

1.3.2 The Flip model of communication

We assume a *synchronous* setting, in which all agents start the execution simultaneously and communication takes place in discrete rounds [45]. As mentioned, agents can use their (noisy) interactions to inform and update their opinion. In each round, each agent can choose to *wait*, i.e, do nothing, or to *send* a message.

The interaction pattern we study follows the standard *push* gossip model [17, 36, 46], where in each round each agent that chooses to send a message sends this message to another agent, chosen uniformly at random, without sender or receiver learning about each other's identity. If an agent receives several messages at the same round, it can only accept one of them (chosen uniformly at random), and all other messages are dropped. The message size is extremely restricted, specifically, each message sent consists of a single bit essentially encoding an opinion. Let $\epsilon > 0$ be a parameter. All messages are subject to noise, specifically, for each message sent by an agent, upon receiving it, the bit in the message is *flipped* independently with probability at most $1/2 - \epsilon$.

1.3.3 Symmetric algorithms

We view the two possible opinions $\{0,1\}$ as abstract symmetric opinions that cannot affect any decision made by individual agents, except for which message to transmit[1]. Accordingly, we consider only *symmetric* algorithms, in which the choices of individuals of whether or not to send a message at a given time are oblivious of the value of $\mathcal{B}$. That is, when fixing all random bits involved in an execution, the message-pattern (i.e., who sends who and at what time) in symmetric algorithms is the same regardless of whether $\mathcal{B}$ equals 1 or 0.

1.4 Lower Bounds

The restriction of the symmetric noisy rumor-spreading problem (or the majority-consensus problem) to two parties is, in some sense, classical for the area of information theory. Here, a source agent a wishes to deliver its bit opinion $\mathcal{B}$ to the second agent b through a binary symmetric channel with crossover probability $p = 1/2 - \epsilon$. The seminal result by Shannon [49] implies that using the channel $\Theta(1/\epsilon^2)$ times is both necessary and sufficient, for allowing b to possess the opinion $\mathcal{B}$ with sufficiently high constant probability. This immediately implies a $\Theta(1/\epsilon^2)$ bound for the number of rounds needed for the same confidence guarantee in the two-party noisy rumor-spreading problem, since each message here contains precisely one bit. When it comes to a population of n agents, the goal is to have each agent possess the opinion $\mathcal{B}$ with high probability (at least $1 - 1/n^c$). In this case, each agent would individually need to obtain $\Omega(\frac{1}{\epsilon^2}\log n)$ messages, even if all messages would come directly from the source node. These bounds immediately imply a lower bound of $\Omega(\frac{1}{\epsilon^2}n\log n)$ on the total bit complexity and hence also on the total number of messages sent. Moreover, since we assume that an agent can handle at most one message at a time, we get that $\Omega(\frac{1}{\epsilon^2}\log n)$ is also a lower bound on the number of rounds. All these bounds apply even if all messages would be as informative as those originated by the source agent. Hence, they apply in much stronger models of communication, such as ones that allow an agent to send messages to multiple destinations at the same round, and ones that consider non-anonymous populations, where an agent could direct a message to a desired destination. Note that the same arguments hold also for the noisy majority-consensus problem if the initial subset A of agents is small. On the other hand, without interacting with other agents and simply waiting to receive sufficiently many samples from the source agent, the noisy rumor-spreading problem could only be solved in $O(\frac{1}{\epsilon^2}n\log n)$ rounds.

1.5 Our results

We present a randomized symmetric algorithm that solves the noisy rumor-spreading problem in $O(\frac{1}{\epsilon^2}\log n)$ rounds and uses a total of $O(\frac{1}{\epsilon^2}n\log n)$ messages (or bits). These bounds are both asymptotically optimal and, in fact, are as fast and message efficient as if each agent would have been simultaneously informed by the environment directly. We also show that the same asymptotically tight bounds (for the running time and message complexity) hold also for solving the noisy majority-consensus problem with any initial subset A of agents of size $|A| = \Omega(\frac{1}{\epsilon^2}\log n)$ and whose majority-bias is $\Omega(\sqrt{\log n/|A|})$.

In this extended abstract, we assume that all nodes start the execution simultaneously at the same time. In the full version of this paper we show how to remove this assumption. This modification applies to both algorithms and comes at an additive cost of $O(\log^2 n)$ to the running time, while the message complexity remains the same.

Our results imply that even in severely restricted, stochastic and noisy settings one can still solve the noisy rumor-spreading and the noisy majority-consensus problems efficiently by applying simple protocols. Indeed, our basic algorithms employ very simple rules that can be implemented using restricted memory, specifically, using $O(\log\log n + \log(1/\epsilon))$ memory bits. Essentially, each agent has some waiting period (in which it does not send any message), and after which it starts sending its current opinion at each round until the protocol terminates. Furthermore, its opinion is occasionally updated following a majority-type procedure based on its recently received messages.

Our algorithms seem to rely on synchronization, at least to some extent. Although it is not realistic to assume that biological ensembles are highly synchronous, some degree of synchronicity may still exist [12, 34]. (For example, agents could potentially differentiate large enough windows of time considering each such window as a round.) Moreover, our algorithms do not actually employ synchronization in a strong sense, instead, they use synchronization mostly to ensure that propagation of local broadcasts are somewhat balanced. If this is guaranteed, it seems reasonable that algorithms in

[1] One could view this trait as a consequence of a symmetry of the world, in which an agent can decide if two opinions are the same or not but has no access to their actual values. For example, a flock of birds following a source (e.g., a bird that has spotted a predator) that travels either north or south can do this even in an environment where there is complete symmetry between these two directions. The only demand is that the escape direction of all birds agree with that of the source.

the spirit of what we propose may still work, even if the system is not highly synchronized. In this preliminary work, we assume synchronization to ease the mathematical analysis and presentation of our algorithms.

1.6 Insights on the Difficulty of the Problem

We first note that when the bias is small, solving the majority-consensus problem using small size messages is difficult even without accounting for noise, i.e., even assuming the communication is always reliable. Indeed, under reliable communication[2], this task was studied by Angluin et al. in the particular case of A being the set of all n agents [6]. The authors in [6] showed that in their model, the problem can be solved in $O(\log n)$ rounds.

We note that for our purposes, we could not use variants of the algorithm in [6] not only because it is not robust under communication noise, but also because it inherently uses *three* symbols in the communication, while we are restricted to only *two* symbols (a single opinion). Indeed, our construction is based on different principles.

Before we describe our algorithms, let us first highlight some of the complex features of the noisy rumor-spreading problem (the same difficulties arise also in the noisy majority-consensus problem). Consider an agent a that receives its first message. This agent now has several options for its actions. One option is to keep silent (wait) until receiving another message. This strategy would result in an algorithm that requires huge amount of time. Indeed, the first agent that hears two messages must hear both of them from the source (since all other agents are silent), and this would require waiting for $\Omega(\sqrt{n})$ rounds, by the birthday paradox. Another possible action for such an agent is to immediately forward the message it just received to others. This strategy would result in the typical agent hearing a very unreliable message for the first time. That is, the number of intermediate agents on the path between the source and the typical agent would be of size roughly $\log n$. Now, each time the message passes from an agent to an agent, the probability of preserving the original opinion drastically reduces. Specifically, it is not difficult to show that a message following a path of size c is correct with probability at most $1/2+(2\epsilon)^c$. This means that if ϵ is small, the probability that a typical agent receives the correct opinion on the first message it hears is at most $1/2 + 1/n$. If this is the case with all agents, it seems, again, almost impossible to recover and reconstruct the correct opinion $\mathcal{B}$. Another difficulty in the strategy of immediately forwarding messages, is that the execution seems to be dependent on the quality of messages received directly from the source by the first few agents, and these messages can be corrupted with non-negligible probability. Indeed, in the beginning of the execution, the pattern of meeting looks like a tree, rooted at the source agent. Moreover, the collection of subtrees hanging down from the children of the root (the agents directly informed by the source agent) do not have the same size, as the subtrees hanging down from the first informed children of the root grow much faster and dominate the population. Hence, the initial opinion of agents could not be more reliable than the initial opinions of the roots of the corresponding subtrees. At this point, with non-negligible probability, the majority of agents would have obtained the wrong opinion, from which is seems again almost impossible to recover.

To overcome these difficulties, we use a third option for the behavior of an agent, allowing it to wait for a prescribed number of rounds before sending a message. For doing so, we rely on synchronization, which we use to balance the sizes of the aforementioned subtrees and, therefore, constrain the deterioration of reliability.

[2]The algorithm in [6] is robust under a very small fraction of agents being Byzantine, but is not robust under communication noise.

2. ALGORITHMS

The interesting cases are when ϵ is a small constant, but we allow it to be much smaller. Specifically, let $\epsilon > 1/n^{1/2-\eta}$, for some arbitrarily small constant $\eta > 0$. We present symmetric and simple randomized algorithms that solve the noisy rumor-spreading and the majority-consensus problems. The running times and message complexities of both algorithms are asymptotically optimal, that is, they both terminate after $O(\frac{1}{\epsilon^2}\log n)$ rounds and use a total of $O(\frac{1}{\epsilon^2}n\log n)$ messages.

Although our algorithms are simple, their analysis is quite involved. Most of the technical ideas in this paper are used for the analysis of our noisy rumor-spreading algorithm, hence we focus on this algorithm. The algorithm consists of two stages. The first stage of the algorithm is intended to *activate* all agents (an agent is considered as activated upon receiving its first message), and to make sure that overall, the average initial opinion of activated agents has some non-negligible bias towards the correct opinion. Stage 2 of the algorithm is meant to boost the bias using repeated samplings until consensus is reached.

2.1 Stage 1: Spreading the Information

2.1.1 Intuition

For spreading the correct opinion $\mathcal{B}$ while controlling the deterioration of the average bias of informed agents towards $\mathcal{B}$, the first idea we employ is to delay propagation of messages, and synchronize them, by grouping the time slots into *phases*. That is, we propagate the information in layers, forming a tree, whose root is the source agent S (layer 0). To control the reliability deterioration of the messages, we synchronize the phases so that all activated agents broadcast in a phase at the same time (actually, we could allow some flexibility in these assumptions, and only require broadcasting in a phase at roughly the same time). In particular, in the first phase, called phase 0, only the source agent transmits messages (all non-source agents are waiting). Recall that every such message is correct with probability at least $1/2 + \epsilon$. Phase 0 lasts for $\beta_s := \Theta(\frac{1}{\epsilon^2}\log n)$ rounds, and is meant to allow the source agent to directly inform sufficiently many agents, and guarantee that with high probability the bias of these agents towards $\mathcal{B}$ is bounded away from zero, specifically, the bias is at least $\epsilon/2$. Note that at this point, we are left with solving the noisy majority-consensus problem with an initial set A of agents of size $\Theta(\frac{1}{\epsilon^2}\log n)$ whose majority-bias is $\Omega(\sqrt{\log n/|A|})$.

The general description of our algorithm in stage 1 is as follows: any agent receiving a message in some phase i (also including the case $i = 0$) sets the value of this message as its *initial opinion*, keeps *silent* (waits, and does not send messages) until phase i is completed and only then does it start sending messages. When the next phase $i + 1$ starts, each such agent will start to send its initial opinion repeatedly in every round until the whole of stage 1 is completed. Hence, phase i is responsible for passing information between all the already activated agents (these are the agents in layers $0, 1, \ldots i-1$) to the newly activated agents in phase i (forming layer i).

Because of the noise in the messages, the quality of information that propagates between layers deteriorates exponentially fast in ϵ. Specifically, if the fraction of correct agents at layer i is some $1/2+\delta_i$, then the expected fraction of correct messages reaching agents at layer $i+1$ is $1/2+2\epsilon\delta_i$. To guarantee that this controlled level of deterioration holds w.h.p., as well as to account for this already problematic phenomena, our phasing process makes sure that the number of agents informed in the next layer increases quadratically faster than the deterioration factor. Specifically, the number of newly informed agents increases by a factor larger than $1/\epsilon^2$. Maintaining this property throughout all phases allows us to guarantee that when x agents are activated (where x is sufficiently large), then, w.h.p., the bias towards the correct opinion is $\Omega(\sqrt{\log n/x})$. In particular, this implies that when all n agents are activated, the bias towards the correct opinion is $\Omega(\sqrt{\log n/n})$.

2.1.2 Formal Description of Stage 1

Choose parameters $f, \beta, s = \Theta(1/\epsilon^2)$ such that $f > c_1\beta > c_2 s > c_3/\epsilon^2$, for sufficiently large constants $c_1, c_2, c_3 > 0$. Let $\beta_s = s \log n$, and $\beta_f = f \log n$. In addition, let $T = \lfloor \log(n/2\beta_s)/\log(\beta+1) \rfloor$. Note that $\beta_s(\beta+1)^T \leq n/2$ and that $T = O(\frac{\log n}{\log(1/\epsilon)})$. We group the rounds of stage 1 into $T+2$ phases, such that for each $0 \leq i \leq T$, phase $i+1$ immediately follows phase i. Phase 0 takes β_s rounds, phase i, for $1 \leq i \leq T$, takes β rounds, and phase $T+1$ takes β_f rounds. Formally, letting $[x, y)$ denote the time period from round x until round $y-1$, we have: phase $0 = [0, \beta_s)$, for $1 \leq i \leq T$, phase $i = [\beta_s + (i-1)\beta, \beta_s + i\beta)$, and, phase $T+1 = [\beta_s + T\beta, \beta_s + T\beta + \beta_f)$.

At a given time, a non-source agent is called *activated* if it already heard a message by that time (the source agent is always considered activated). A non-activated agent is called *dormant*. For an agent a, let t_a denote the first time a was activated, and let its *initial opinion* $\mathcal{B}_0(a)$ be the opinion it heard at that time. An activated agent is called *initially correct* if the message it heard for the first time is correct, i.e., if $\mathcal{B}_0(a) = \mathcal{B}$. Let i_a be the integer i for which t_a belongs to phase i.

The rule of stage 1: An activated agent a acts as follows. If $i_a \leq T$ the agent sends its initial opinion $\mathcal{B}_0(a)$ in each round during the phases $i_a+1, i_a+2, \cdots, T+1$. (In other words, Agent a waits until phase i_a is completed and then it starts sending its initial opinion repeatedly in every round until the end of stage 1.)

Note first, that in particular, in phase 0, the source S is the only agent sending any messages. Let X_0 be the number of agents activated at phase 0.

CLAIM 2.1. *By choosing $s > c/\epsilon^2$ for a large enough constant c, it is guaranteed that at the end of phase 0, w.h.p., we have $\beta_s/3 \leq X_0 \leq \beta_s$ activated agents whose bias towards the correct opinion $\mathcal{B}$ is at least $\epsilon/2$.*

PROOF. Let Z_0 denote the number of initially correct agents among the Y_0 agents that were activated during phase 0 and let ϵ_0 be such that $Z_0 = (1/2+\epsilon_0)Y_0$. Our goal is to show that $\epsilon_0 \geq \epsilon/2$.

Recall that phase 0 lasts for $\beta_s = s \log n$ rounds, and that until the phase is completed only the source agent S is sending messages. Hence, during phase 0, there are always at most β_s activated agents, and in particular, at least $n/2$ dormant agents. Hence, each message sent during phase 0 has probability at least 1/2 to activate an agent. The expected number of activated agents at the end of phase 0 is thus at least $\beta_s/2$. By a simple generalization of Chernoff's inequality, we can choose the constant s (in the definition of β_s) to be a sufficiently large constant so that w.h.p., at the end of phase 0, we have at least $\beta_s/3$ activated agents, that is, $X_0 = Y_0 \geq \beta_s/3$.

Let us now focus on the random faults occurring in the messages sent during phase 0. Each of the Y_0 activated agents has probability at least $1/2 + \epsilon_s \geq 1/2 + \epsilon$ to be activated with the correct opinion $\mathcal{B}$. Hence, by linearity of expectation, the expected number of agents that were activated up with the correct opinion during phase 0 is at least $(1/2+\epsilon)Y_0$. Since $Y_0 \geq \beta_s/3 = (s/3)\log n$, it follows from Chernoff's inequality that by taking $s \gg 1/\epsilon^2$, we can ensure that w.h.p., the number of initially correct agents during phase 0 is $Z_0 > (1/2+\epsilon/2)Y_0$, that is, w.h.p., we have $\epsilon_0 \geq \epsilon/2$. This establishes the proof of the claim. □

Observe that by Claim 2.1, phase 0 essentially reduces the noisy rumor-spreading problem to an instance of the noisy majority-consensus problem, with an initial set of size $X_0 = \Theta(\beta_s) = \Theta(\frac{1}{\epsilon^2}\log n)$ and majority-bias of at least $\epsilon/2 = \Omega(\sqrt{\log n/|X_0|})$. What we shall show in the remainder of this subsection is that in general, phases $0, 1, \ldots i$, where $i \leq T+1$, take us to an instance of the noisy majority-consensus problem, with an initial set A_i of size $|A_i| = \Theta(\frac{1}{\epsilon^{2i+2}}\log n)$ and majority-bias of at least $\epsilon^{i+1}/2 = \Omega(\sqrt{\log n/|A_i|})$. For $T = \lfloor \log(n/2\beta_s)/\log(\beta+1) \rfloor$ this would lead to the following lemma summarizing the performances of stage 1.

LEMMA 2.2. *Stage 1 takes $O(\frac{1}{\epsilon^2}\log n)$ rounds. At the end of the stage the following event E holds w.h.p:*

1. *All agents are activated.*
2. *The fraction of initially correct agents is at least $1/2 + \Omega(\sqrt{\log n/n})$.*

The remainder of this subsection is devoted to the proof of Lemma 2.2. It is easy to verify that the number of rounds in stage 1 is $\beta_s + \beta T + \beta_f = O(\frac{1}{\epsilon^2}\log n)$. Our goal thus is to show that event E mentioned in the lemma holds with high probability. The proof considers a sequence of events $E_1, E_2, \cdots E_\tau$, for some $\tau = O(\log n)$, where $E_\tau = E$. We will show that event E_i occurs w.h.p., given E_{i-1}. This would imply that E occurs w.h.p., by repeatedly invoking the standard argument $|\Pr(E_{i+1} \mid E_i) - \Pr(E_{i+1})| \leq \Pr(\bar{E}_i)$.

Let i be a non-negative integer. Define X_i as the random variable indicating the number of agents that were activated at some time before the end of phase i. Let Y_i denote the random variable indicating the number of agents that were activated during phase i. Hence, we have: $X_i = \sum_{j=0}^{i} Y_j$. Let Z_i denote the number of initially correct agents among the Y_i agents that were activated during phase i and let ϵ_i be such that $Z_i = (1/2+\epsilon_i)Y_i$. Recall that Claim 2.1 asserts that w.h.p., we have $\beta_s/3 \leq X_0 \leq \beta_s$ and $\epsilon_0 \geq \epsilon/2$. In what follows, we assume that this highly likely event holds (see the paragraph above).

Analysis for phase i, where $1 \leq i \leq T$: It is easy to see that X_i, the number of activated agents at the end of phase i is at most $X_i \leq (\beta+1)^i X_0 = O\left(\frac{1}{\epsilon^{2i+2}} \log n\right)$. This follows trivially from the fact that $X_i = X_{i-1} + Y_i$, and from the fact that $Y_i \leq \beta X_{i-1}$ (because for $i \geq 1$, phase i is composed of β rounds and in each such round precisely X_{i-1} messages are being sent). The following claim states that w.h.p., the value of X_i is, in fact, very close to $(\beta+1)^i X_0$. Establishing this claim will enable us to show that up to phase T, the values Y_i are increasing exponentially and that at the beginning of phase T we already have $\Omega(\epsilon^2 n)$ activated agents. The proof of the claim extensively uses concentration properties given by Chernoff's inequality and is deferred to the full version:

CLAIM 2.3. *W.h.p., for every i, $1 \leq i \leq T$, we have: $(\beta+1)^i X_0/8 \leq X_i \leq (\beta+1)^i X_0$.*

Relying on the definition of T, the fact that $X_0 \geq \beta_s/3$ holds w.h.p., and taking $\beta = O(1/\epsilon^2)$ such that $\beta > 3s$, we ensure that $(\beta+1)^{T+1} X_0 \geq n/6$. Hence, Claim 2.3 implies the following lower bound on X_T, the number of activated agents at the beginning of the last phase in stage 1.

COROLLARY 2.4. *W.h.p., we have $X_T = \Omega((\beta+1)^T X_0) = \Omega(\epsilon^2 n)$.*

Recall that phase $T+1$ consists of $\beta_f = f \log n$ rounds, in which all X_T agents that were activated before the beginning of the phase are sending their initial opinion in each round of the phase. Hence, Corollary 2.4 implies that by setting f such that $f > c/\epsilon^2$ for large enough constant c, we obtain the first part of Lemma 2.2. That is, we have:

COROLLARY 2.5. *W.h.p., at the end of stage 1, all agents are activated.*

The next corollary gives a lower bound on the growth of Y_i, the number of newly activated agents in phase $i = 1 \ldots T+1$. This lower bound will be used for bounding the bias from below (see Claim 2.7). Note hat the duration of the last phase, $T+1$, is taken to be longer than that of phases $i = 1 \ldots T$ to guarantee a large number of newly activated agents even in this last phase. Indeed, continuing with phases of duration β would activate all agents relatively early, but would also restrict the number of newly activated agents at later phases.

COROLLARY 2.6. *W.h.p., for every phase i, where $1 \leq i \leq T+1$, we have $Y_i \geq \beta^{i-1} \log n$.*

Recall that $1/2+\epsilon_i$ is the fraction of initially correct agents among the Y_i agents that were activated in phase i, i.e., ϵ_i is the bias toward $\mathcal{B}$ among these Y_i agents. Corollary 2.6 will be useful for obtaining the following claim.

CLAIM 2.7. *W.h.p., for every phase i, where $0 \leq i \leq T+1$, we have $\epsilon_i \geq \epsilon^{i+1}/2$.*

We prove the claim by induction on i. The basis of the induction is $i = 0$, which has already been established in Claim 2.1. Consider now phase i, where $1 \leq i \leq T+1$. Fix the configuration at the end of phase $i-1$ and let $\phi = \epsilon_{i-1}$. By the induction hypothesis, we can assume that $\phi \geq \epsilon^i/2$. Moreover, we can assume that the faction of initially correct agents among the X_{i-1} activated agents in the beginning of phase i is at least $1/2+\phi \geq 1/2+\epsilon^i/2$. For any of the newly activated agents a in phase i, the probability that the initial opinion of a is correct is at least $(1/2+\phi)\cdot(1/2+\epsilon)+(1/2-\phi)\cdot(1/2-\epsilon) = 1/2+2\epsilon\phi$. By linearity of expectation, this equation implies that $E(Z_i) \geq (1/2+2\epsilon\phi)Y_i \geq (1/2+\epsilon^{i+1})Y_i$. Taking $\delta = \epsilon^{i+1}/2$ gives $(1-\delta)E(Z_i) > Y_i(1/2+\epsilon^{i+1}/2)$. We now apply Chernoff's inequality and rely on the fact that Y_i is large, as promised by Corollary 2.6. $\Pr[Z_i < Y_i(1/2+\epsilon^{i+1}/2)] \leq e^{-\delta^2 E(Z_i)/2} < e^{-\delta^2 Y_i/4} = e^{-\epsilon^{2i+2} Y_i/16} = 1/e^{\Omega(\epsilon^{2i}\beta^{i-1}\log n)}$. Taking $\beta > 3/\epsilon^2$ to be sufficiently large therefore implies that w.h.p., we have $Z_i \geq Y_i(1/2+\epsilon^{i+1}/2)$, or in other words, $\epsilon_i \geq \epsilon^{i+1}/2$. This establishes the proof of Claim 2.7, which implies that w.h.p., the fraction of initially correct agents at the end of stage 1 is at least $1/2+\epsilon^{T+2}/2 = 1/2+\Omega(\sqrt{\log n/n})$ (the equation follows by the definition of T, and the fact that $\beta > 1/\epsilon^2$). This completes the proof of Lemma 2.2.

2.2 Stage 2: Boosting the Bias

2.2.1 *Intuition*

We proved that, w.h.p., at the end of Stage 1 all agents are activated and the fraction of correct agents is at least δ_1, where $\delta_1 = \Omega(\sqrt{\log n/n})$. Stage 2 is meant to gradually boost the bias towards the correct opinion, so that, w.h.p., it will equal 1 (that is, all agents are correct) at the end of the stage. We note that since the initial bias of δ_1 is very close to 0, the task of boosting the majority opinion of a population is difficult even without accounting for noise, i.e., even assuming the communication is always reliable (see the discussion in Subsection 1.6 regarding the work in [6]).

Stage 2 is executed in $k+1$ phases, where $k = \lceil \log(1/\delta_1) \rceil = O(\log n)$. Informally, phase i, for $1 \leq i \leq k$, is associated with a parameter δ_i, such that it is guaranteed w.h.p., that when the phase starts, the fraction of correct agents is at least $1/2+\delta_i$. (Note that a sample from such a population is correct with strictly smaller probability than $1/2+\delta_i$, because of noise.) Essentially, in phase i, each agent takes $\gamma = O(1/\epsilon^2)$ samples from the population (during γ rounds) and then sets its opinion according to the majority opinion of these samples. Despite the noise in the samples, we will prove that, as long as δ_i is sufficiently small, this majority process increases the fraction of correct agents, w.h.p., from $1/2+\delta_i$ to at least $1/2+2\delta_i$. Moreover, we shall prove that if δ_i is large, then the majority process does not decrease δ_i too much. Hence, for the next phase, we can safely assume that either $\delta_{i+1} = 2\delta_i$ or that δ_{i+1} is already sufficiently large.

To establish the required boosting, the fact that δ_i may be very small prevented us from directly applying Chernoff's inequality and instead required us to come up with more involved arguments. To lower bound the probability that the majority opinion in the γ samples is correct, we perceive the samples as obtained by an imaginary process composed of two steps taken over γ players. In the first step, for each player we flip a *fair* coin which determines its opinion (i.e., probability 1/2 for having each opinion). Then, at the second step, each of the players with the wrong opinion, (independently) has a small probability (close to δ_i) of flipping its opinion to the correct one. The parameters are chosen such that at the end of this imaginary process, the probability that the majority opinion among the γ players is correct is the same as probability that the majority opinion in the original γ samples is correct. To bound the latter probability, we thus analyze the imaginary two-step process. Informally, the imaginary process allows us to understand the situation in a more modular manner. Indeed, the probability that the first step is successful (yielding a correct majority) is precisely $1/2$, and once the first-step is successful, the second step cannot harm the situation. If the first step turns out to be unsuccessful, then before the second step starts there are $\gamma/2 + x$ wrong players and $\gamma/2 - x$ correct ones, for some integer x. When x is small, Stirling's formula comes handy for bounding from below the probability that such a situation occurs after the first step. Specifically, this probability is $\Omega(x/\sqrt{\gamma})$. For such a situation to be fixed, we need that in the second step, at least $x+1$ wrong players flip their opinion. By carefully analyzing the probability of such a corrective event, we make sure that all together the majority is correct with probability $\min\{1/2 + 2^5\delta_i,\ 5/9\}$.

A direct application of Chernoff's inequality, relying on the fact that $\delta_i = \Omega(\sqrt{\log n/n})$, will then show that w.h.p., the bias increases from δ_i at phase i to at least $\min\{2^3\delta_i,\ 1/40\}$ at phase $i+1$. Hence, after invoking $k = \lceil\log(1/\delta_1)\rceil = O(\log n)$ phases, the fraction of correct agents becomes bounded away from $1/2$ by an additive constant. Hence, to achieve high probability that all agents are correct, it is sufficient that in the last phase, namely phase $k+1$, each agent takes $O(\frac{1}{\epsilon^2}\log n)$ samples of the population, and sets its opinion according to the majority opinion in these samples.

2.2.2 Formal description of Stage 2

As guaranteed by Lemma 2.2, at the end of stage 1, w.h.p., all agents are activated and the bias of their initial opinion towards $\mathcal{B}$ is $\Omega(\sqrt{\log n/n})$. Hence, stage 1 brings us to an instance of the majority-consensus problem, where the set A contains the whole population and the majority-bias is $\Omega(\sqrt{\log n/|A|})$. Stage 2 is meant to solve this problem.

Let $r = \lceil 2^{20}/\epsilon^2 \rceil$, and let $\gamma = 2r+1$ (no attempt has been made to minimize the constant factors). We define $k = O(\log n)$ and take stage 2 to be composed of $k+1$ phases. Each of the first k phases has $2\gamma = O(1/\epsilon^2)$ rounds, while phase $k+1$ is composed of $O(\frac{1}{\epsilon^2}\log n)$ rounds. Essentially, in each phase of the stage, agents repeatedly send their current opinion. At the end of the phase, agents may choose to update their opinion (essentially set to be the majority opinion among the opinions received in the phase). Since the opinion of an agent may be updated only at the end of a phase, all messages sent by an agent during any given phase are the same. For a phase i, let m_i denote the number of rounds in the phase (i.e., $m_i = 2\gamma$ for $i = 1, \ldots, k$, and $m_{k+1} = O(\frac{1}{\epsilon^2}\log n)$). During phase i, an agent that received at least $m_i/2$ messages is called *successful* and the messages it received are called *samples.* Since all agents are sending messages in each round then, w.h.p., at least half of the population will be successful in each phase. Only the successful agents in the phase will update their opinion at the end of the phase, while the rest will remain with their previous opinion.

The rule of stage 2: For each round in each phase i, where $1 \le i \le k+1$, each agent repeatedly sends its current opinion (each time to an arbitrary other agent). The opinion of an agent in phase 1 of stage 2 is its initial opinion. At the end of each phase, a successful agent in the phase will consider only the first $m_i/2$ samples it received and update its opinion according to the majority opinion in these samples.

LEMMA 2.8. *Consider taking $\gamma = 2r+1$ (noisy) samples from a population whose bias towards the correct opinion is at least δ. Then, the probability that the majority of these γ samples is correct is at least* $\min\{1/2 + 4\delta,\ 1/2 + 1/100\}$.

PROOF. Consider the $\gamma = 2r+1$ samples. We say that a sample is *correct* if it holds the correct opinion $\mathcal{B}$. The γ samples are chosen independently, and uniformly at random, among the population whose bias towards the correct opinion is at least δ. Let $b = 2\epsilon\delta$. Accounting for the noise in the samples, for each sample, the probability that the sample is correct is at least: $(1/2+\delta)\cdot(1/2+\epsilon) + (1/2-\delta)\cdot(1/2-\epsilon) = 1/2 + 2\epsilon\delta = 1/2 + b$. Note that b may be very small, so directly employing Chernoff's inequality over the γ samples would not imply the desired bound. Instead, let us look at the following imaginary two-step process that forms an equivalent view of the γ samplings.

The imaginary process is performed over a set S consisting of γ (boolean) players, namely, $S = \sigma_1, \sigma_2, \ldots, \sigma_\gamma$.

- **First step:** each player σ_j flips a fair coin to form an initial opinion (i.e., a bit in $\{0,1\}$).
- **Second step:** independently with probability $2b$, each player σ_j gets to see the correct opinion $\mathcal{B}$ and corrects its opinion if it was wrong initially (otherwise it remains with its correct opinion).

Note that after this two-step process, the probability that a player is correct is precisely $1 - \frac{1}{2}(1-2b) = 1/2 + b$. Thus, the probability that the majority opinion among the γ players is $\mathcal{B}$ bounds from below the probability that the majority of the original γ samples gathered by agent a is $\mathcal{B}$. To lower bound this latter probability, in what follows, we focus on the γ players, in the two-step process. Let x be a positive integer. Define the following events.

- C = at the end of the first step, the majority of players in S is correct.
- U_x = after the first step, the number w of wrong players in S satisfies $r+1 \le w \le r+x$.
- F_x = in the second step, the number of opinion flips is at least x.
- F = the majority opinion at the end of the two-steps is correct.

Our goal is to lower bound the probability that F occurs. Note first that $\Pr(C) = 1/2$. Assume now that C did not occur, hence U_x occurred for some x, that is, in S, the first step results in a set W of wrong players whose size w satisfies $r+1 \le w \le r+x$. In this case, for F to occur, it is sufficient that event F_x would occur in the second step. That is, for every positive integer x, we have:

$$\Pr(F) \ge \Pr(C) + \Pr(F_x \mid U_x)\cdot\Pr(U_x). \tag{1}$$

Stirling's formula can be used to lower bound the probability that U_x occurs, when x is a small integer. The bound is indicated by the following claim:

CLAIM 2.9. *For* $1 \leq x \leq \sqrt{r}$, *we have* $\Pr(U_x) > x/10\sqrt{r}$.

PROOF. For each j, let $P(j)$ denote the probability that precisely j players in S hold the wrong opinion after the first step. We rely on the fact that the coins tossed in the first step are fair, and on Stirling's formula to show that for $0 \leq i \leq \sqrt{r}$, we have $P(r+i) > 1/2\sqrt{r}$. This will establish the claim since for $x \leq \sqrt{r}$, the probability that Event U_x occurs is $\Pr(U_x) = \sum_{i=0}^{x} P(r+i) > x/2\sqrt{r}$.

For completeness, the bound on $P(r+1)$ can be obtained as follows:

$$P(r+i) = 2^{-2r}\binom{2r}{r+i} = 2^{-2r}\frac{2r!}{(r-i)!(r+i)!} \geq$$
$$\geq 2^{-2r}\frac{2r!}{(r-\sqrt{r})!(r+\sqrt{r})!}.$$

Applying Stirling's formula on the right side of the equation, we get as desired:

$$\begin{aligned} P(r+i) &> \frac{r^{2r}}{(r-\sqrt{r})^{r-\sqrt{r}}(r+\sqrt{r})^{r+\sqrt{r}}} \cdot \frac{1}{\sqrt{3\pi r}} \\ &= \frac{1}{\sqrt{3\pi r}} \cdot \frac{r^{r-\sqrt{r}}}{(r-\sqrt{r})^{r-\sqrt{r}}} \cdot \frac{r^{r+\sqrt{r}}}{(r+\sqrt{r})^{r+\sqrt{r}}} \\ &= \frac{1}{\sqrt{3\pi r}} \cdot \frac{1}{(1-\frac{\sqrt{r}}{r})^{r-\sqrt{r}}} \cdot \frac{1}{(1+\frac{\sqrt{r}}{r})^{r+\sqrt{r}}} \\ &= \frac{1}{\sqrt{3\pi r}} \cdot \frac{1}{(1-\frac{1}{r})^{r-\sqrt{r}}} \cdot \frac{1}{(1+\frac{1}{\sqrt{r}})^{2\sqrt{r}}} \\ &> \frac{1}{\sqrt{3\pi r}} \cdot \frac{1}{e^{-0.9}} \cdot \frac{1}{e^{2}} > \frac{1}{10\sqrt{r}}. \end{aligned}$$

□

To successfully use Equation 1, we need to bound from below the value of $\Pr(F_x \mid U_x)$, that is, the probability that given U_x, at least x players (in W) flip their opinion in the second step.

CLAIM 2.10. *(1) If* $r-1 \leq 2/b$ *then* $\Pr(F_1 \mid U_1) \geq 2rb/e^4$. *(2) If* $rb > 2$, *then for* $x \leq \lceil rb \rceil$, $\Pr(F_x \mid U_x) \geq 1/3$.

PROOF. Recall that in the second step, each of the wrong players flips its opinion with probability $2b$. Observe that $\Pr(F_1 \mid U_1)$ is bounded from below by the probability that precisely one of the first r wrong players in W flipped its opinion in the second step (note, $|W| = r+1$ since U_1 occurred). This latter probability is $r \cdot 2b(1-2b)^{r-1}$, which is at least $2rb/e^4$, if $r-1 \leq 2/b$. This establishes the first part of the claim. Let us now turn to prove the second part of the claim. Assume that $rb > 2$. Note that the expected number of flips in W is at least $2rb > 4$. Chernoff's inequality therefore implies that the probability that the number of flips in W is at most rb is bounded from above by $1/e^{1/2}$, implying that for integer $x \leq \lceil rb \rceil$, we have: $\Pr(F_x \mid U_x) \geq \Pr(F_{\lceil rb \rceil} \mid U_x) \geq 1 - 1/e^{1/2} > 1/3$. □

Finally, to establish Lemma 2.8, we combine Equation 1 with Claims 2.9 and 2.10 for different values of δ.

The case of small δ**:** Consider the case that $\delta \leq \epsilon/2^{20}$. This restriction on δ implies that $rb \leq 2$. In this case, Claim 2.10 tells us that $\Pr(F_1 \mid U_1) \geq 2rb/e^4$. Hence, by Claim 2.9 and Equation 1, we have: $\Pr(F) \geq \Pr(C) + \Pr(U_1)\Pr(F_1 \mid U_1) > 1/2 + (1/10\sqrt{r})(2rb/e^4) > 1/2 + 4\delta$.

The case of medium δ**:** Consider the case that $\epsilon/2^{20} < \delta < 1/2^{12}$. In this case, we have $4 < 2rb \leq 2(\sqrt{r}-1)$. Let us set $x := \lceil rb \rceil$. Hence, $1 \leq x \leq \sqrt{r}$, and we can employ Claim 2.9, yielding $\Pr(U_x) > x/10\sqrt{r}$. By the second part of Claim 2.10, we obtain: $\Pr(F) \geq \Pr(C) + \Pr(U_x) \cdot \Pr(F_x \mid U_x) \geq 1/2 + (x/10\sqrt{r})/3 \geq 1/2 + b\sqrt{r}/30 > 1/2 + 4\delta$.

The case of large δ**:** Consider the case that $\delta \geq 1/2^{12}$. In this case, we set $x := \lceil \sqrt{r}/3 \rceil$. Since $\lceil \sqrt{r}/3 \rceil < \lceil rb \rceil$, the second part of Claim 2.10 implies that $\Pr(F_x \mid U_x) \geq 1/3$. Hence, we get: $\Pr(F) \geq \Pr(C) + \Pr(U_x) \cdot \Pr(F_x \mid U_x) \geq 1/2 + x/30\sqrt{r} \geq 1/2 + 1/100$. This completes the proof of Lemma 2.8.

COROLLARY 2.11. *After the first* $k = \log(\sqrt{n/\log n})$ *phases, w.h.p., the fraction of correct agents is at least* $1/2 + 1/400$.

PROOF. Consider a phase i, for $1 \leq i \leq k$. Assume that phase i starts when the fraction of agents having the correct opinion is at least $1/2 + \delta_i$. The number of successful agents in the phase are w.h.p, at least $n/2$. Hence, by applying Chernoff bound, using Lemma 2.8 and relying on the fact that $\delta_i > \sqrt{\log n/n}$, we get that w.h.p., among the successful agents in the phase, the fraction of agents that correctly update their opinion at the end of the phase is at least

$$\min\{1/2 + 3\delta_i,\ 1/2 + 1/200\}.$$

Altogether, the number of correct agents at the end of the phase is at least: $\frac{n}{2}(1/2+\delta_i) + \frac{n}{2}(1/2+\min\{3\delta_i,\ 1/200\}) = n \cdot (1/2 + \min\{2\delta_i, 1/400\})$.

Hence, since $\delta_1 \geq \sqrt{\log n/n}$, then after applying $k = \log(\sqrt{n/\log n})$ phases, w.h.p., the fraction of correct agents becomes at least $1/2 + 1/400$, as desired. □

In the final phase, namely phase $k+1$, each agent collects $O(\frac{1}{\epsilon^2}\log n)$ independent samples, uniformly at random, from a population whose bias towards the correct opinion is at least $1/400$. Assuming the constant hiding behind the O-otation is sufficiently large, Chernoff's inequality guarantees that, w.h.p., the majority opinion of such samples is correct. Hence, a union bound argument guarantees that w.h.p, all agents are correct at the end of stage 2. Let us now analyze the running time of stage 2. Each of the first k phases takes $\gamma = O(1/\epsilon^2)$ rounds. Since $k = O(\log n)$, the number of rounds required to perform the first k phases is $O(\frac{1}{\epsilon^2}\log n)$. The running time of phase $k+1$ is $O(\frac{1}{\epsilon^2}\log n)$. Altogether, we obtain the following.

LEMMA 2.12. *Stage 2 takes* $O(\frac{1}{\epsilon^2}\log n)$ *rounds and at the end of the stage all agents are correct, with high probability.*

Lemmas 2.2 and 2.12 yield that our algorithm solves the noisy rumor-spreading problem in $O(\frac{1}{\epsilon^2}\log n)$ rounds. Since each message is composed of a single bit, and since in each round, each agent can send at most one message, we get the bound $O(\frac{1}{\epsilon^2}n\log n)$ on the total number of messages and bits sent. Altogether, we obtain the following.

THEOREM 2.13. *The noisy rumor-spreading problem can be solved using* $O(\frac{1}{\epsilon^2}\log n)$ *rounds, and a total of* $O(\frac{1}{\epsilon^2}n\log n)$ *messages (or bits).*

COROLLARY 2.14. *Consider the noisy majority-consensus problem with an initial set A of at least $\Omega(\frac{1}{\epsilon^2}\log n)$ agents and majority-bias of $\Omega(\sqrt{\log n/|A|})$. This problem can be solved in $O(\frac{1}{\epsilon^2}\log n)$ rounds, and using a total of $O(\frac{1}{\epsilon^2}n\log n)$ messages (or bits).*

PROOF. Recall that Claim 2.1 implies that after phase 0 is completed, we are left with solving the noisy majority-consensus problem with an initial set A_0 of agents of size $|A_0| = \Theta(\frac{1}{\epsilon^2}\log n)$ whose majority-bias is $\Omega(\sqrt{\log n/|A_0|})$. As we saw, this problem is solved by applying the remaining phases $i = 1, \ldots T+1$ of stage 1, and then applying stage 2. Specifically, as given by Claims 2.7 and 2.3, phase i of stage 1, for each $i \in \{1, \ldots T+1\}$, reduced the problem to the noisy majority-consensus problem with an initial set A_i of size $A_i = \Theta\left(\frac{1}{\epsilon^{2i+2}}\log n\right)$ and majority-bias of $\Omega(\sqrt{\log n/|A_i|})$. Hence, after applying stage 1, we were left with dealing with the noisy majority-consensus problem with an initial set X of agents composed of all n agents and majority-bias of $\Omega(\sqrt{\log n/n})$. Solving this latter problem is precisely the objective of stage 2.

In light of this, the general case of the noisy majority-consensus problem can be solved as follows. Recall, in this problem we consider an initial subset A of agents of size $|A| = \Omega(\frac{1}{\epsilon^2}\log n)$ and majority-bias of $\Omega(\sqrt{\log n/|A|})$. To solve this problem, we first set:

$$i_A := \frac{\log(|A|/\log n)}{2\log(1/\epsilon)},$$

and then execute phases $i_A, i_{A+1}\ldots T+1$ of stage 1, and subsequently execute stage 2. □

3. DISCUSSION

We have presented the Flip model, a basic model of communication wherein interactions are conveyed across noisy channels of limited capacity. This noisy communication can be expected to capture an important aspect of naturally occurring, biological interactions that is overlooked by the classical fault-tolerance models studied in distribute computing. We have then presented robust and simple algorithms that efficiently solve two basic information dissemination problems within the model's constraints. Besides the purely theoretical interest, we believe that the protocols presented in this paper provide valuable insights towards the understanding of communication schemes in nature. Indeed, our algorithms suggest balancing between silence and transmission, synchronization, and majority-based decisions as important ingredients towards understanding collective behavior in anonymous and noisy natural populations.

As this is a first attempt at analyzing randomly distorted messages with distributed computing tools, we did not attempt to describe a specific biological system or identify naturally occurring algorithms. Rather, our results indicate that to understand natural systems one must simultaneously consider communication noise, limited messaging alphabet, and algorithm. Typically, works in different fields take only subset of these three components into account.

Acknowledgments: The authors would like to thank Oded Goldreich, Kunal Talwar, James Aspnes, and George Giakkoupis for helpful discussions.

4. REFERENCES

[1] Yehuda Afek, Noga Alon, Omer Barad, Eran Hornstein, Naama Barkai, and Ziv Bar-Joseph. *A biological solution to a fundamental distributed computing problem.* Science 331:6014, 183–5, (2011).

[2] Yehuda Afek, Noga Alon, Ziv Bar-Joseph, Alejandro Cornejo, Bernhard Haeupler, Fabian Kuhn. *Beeping a maximal independent set.* Distributed Computing 26(4), 195–208, (2013).

[3] Christina Allen and Charles Stevens. *An evaluation of causes for unreliability of synaptic transmission.* Proceedings of the National Academy of Sciences 91, 10380–10383, (1994).

[4] Dana Angluin, James Aspnes, Zoë Diamadi, Michael J. Fischer, René Peralta. *Computation in networks of passively mobile finite-state sensors.* Distributed Computing 18(4), 235–253, (2006).

[5] Dana Angluin, James Aspnes, Michael J. Fischer, and Hong Jiang. *Self-stabilizing population protocols.* TAAS 3(4), (2008).

[6] Dana Angluin, James Aspnes, and David Eisenstat. *A simple population protocol for fast robust approximate majority.* Distributed Computing 21(2), 87–102, (2008).

[7] James Aspnes and Eric Ruppert. *An Introduction to Population Protocols.* Bulletin of the EATCS 93, 98–117, (2007).

[8] Bonnie L. Bassler and Christopher M. Waters. *Quorum Sensing: Cell-to-Cell Communication in Bacteria.* The Annual Review of Cell and Developmental Biology 21, 319–346, (2005).

[9] Reuven Bar-Yehuda and Shay Kutten. *Fault Tolerant Distributed Majority Commitment.* J. Algorithms 9(4), 568–582 (1988).

[10] Joffroy Beauquier, Janna Burman, and Shay Kutten. *Making Population Protocols Self-stabilizing.* SSS 2009: 90–104.

[11] Ohad Ben-Shahar, Shlomi Dolev, Andrey Dolgin, and Michael Segal. *Direction election in flocking swarms.* Ad Hoc Networks 12, 250–258 (2014)

[12] John Buck. *Synchronous Rhythmic Flashing of Fireflies. II.* The Quarterly Review of Biology 63(3), 265–289, (1988).

[13] Henrik Brumm and Hans Slabbekoorn. *Acoustic Communication in Noise.* Advances in the Study of Behavior 35, 151–209, (2005).

[14] Michael C. Carrol. *The complement system in regulation of adaptive immunity.* Nature Immunology 5, 981–986, (2004).

[15] Keren Censor-Hillel, Bernhard Haeupler, Jonathan A. Kelner, and Petar Maymounkov. *Global computation in a poorly connected world: fast rumor-spreading with no dependence on conductance.* Proc. of the ACM Symposium on Theory of Computing (STOC), 961–970, (2012).

[16] Bernard Chazelle. *Natural algorithms.* Proc. of the ACM-SIAM Symposium on Discrete Algorithms (SODA), 422–431, (2009).

[17] Alan J. Demers, Daniel H. Greene, Carl Hauser, Wes Irish, John Larson, Scott Shenker, Howard E. Sturgis, Daniel C. Swinehart, and Douglas B. Terry. *Epidemic algorithms for replicated database maintenance.* Operating Systems Review 22 no. 1, 8–32, (1988).

[18] Krzysztof Diks and Andrzej Pelc. *Optimal adaptive broadcasting with a bounded fraction of faulty nodes.* Algorithmica 28 no. 1, 37–50, (2000).

[19] Benjamin Doerr and Mahmoud Fouz. *Asymptotically optimal rumor-spreading.* Proc. of the International Colloquium on Automata, Languages, and Programming (ICALP), 502–513, (2011).

[20] Robert Elsässer and Thomas Sauerwald. *On the runtime and robustness of randomized broadcasting.* Theoretical Computer Science 410 no. 36, 3414– 3427, (2009).

[21] Yuval Emek and Roger Wattenhofer. *Stone age distributed computing.* Proc. of the ACM SIGACT-SIGOPS Symposium on Principles of Distributed Computing (PODC), 137–146, (2013).

[22] Ofer Feinerman, Joel Veiga, Jeffrey Dorfman, Ronald Germain, and Gregoire Altan-Bonnet. *Variability and robustness in T cell activation from regulated heterogeneity in protein levels.* Science 321(5892), 1081–1084, (2008).

[23] Ofer Feinerman, Garrit Jentsch, Karen Tkach, Jesse Coward, Matthew Hathorn, Michael Sneddon, Thierry Emonet, Kendall Smith, and Gregoire Altan-Bonnet. *Single-cell quantification of IL-2 response by effector and regulatory T cells reveals critical plasticity in immune response.*. Molecular systems biology 6, 437pp, (2010).

[24] Pierre Fraigniaud, and George Giakkoupis. *On the bit communication complexity of randomized rumor-spreading.* Proc. of the ACM Symposium on Parallelism in Algorithms and Architectures (SPAA), 134-143, (2010).

[25] Nigel R Franks, Stephen C Pratt, Eamonn B Mallon, Nicholas F Britton and David JT Sumpter. *Information flow, opinion polling and collective intelligence in houseï£¡hunting social insects.* The Royal Society B 537(1427), 1567–1583, (2002).

[26] Alan M. Frieze and Geoffrey R. Grimmett. *The shortest-path problem for graphs with random arc-lengths* Discrete Applied Mathematics 10, 57–77, (1985).

[27] Abbas El Gamal and Young-Han Kim. *Network Information Theory.* Cambridge University Press, 709pp, (2012).

[28] Chryssis Georgiou, Seth Gilbert, and Dariusz R. Kowalski. *Meeting the deadline: on the complexity of fault-tolerant continuous gossip.* Distributed Computing 24(5), 223–244 (2011).

[29] Chryssis Georgiou, Seth Gilbert, Rachid Guerraoui, and Dariusz R. Kowalski. *Asynchronous gossip.* J. ACM 60(2), 11 (2013).

[30] Leszek Gasieniec and Andrzej Pelc. *Adaptive broadcasting with faulty nodes.* Parallel Computing 22 no. 6, 903–912, (1996).

[31] George Giakkoupis and Thomas Sauerwald. *rumor-spreading and vertex expansion.* Proc. of the ACM-SIAM Symposium on Discrete Algorithms (SODA), 1623–1641, (2012).

[32] Bernhard Haeupler. *Analyzing Network Coding Gossip Made Easy.* Proc. of the ACM Symposium on Theory of Computing (STOC), 293–302, (2011).

[33] Bernhard Haeupler. *Simple, Fast, and Deterministic Gossip and rumor-spreading.* Proc. of the ACM-SIAM Symposium on Discrete Algorithms (SODA), 705–716, (2013).

[34] Yuji Ikegaya, Gloster Aaron, Rosa Cossart, Dmitriy Aronov, Ilan Lampl, David Ferster, and Rafael Yuste. *Synfire Chains and Cortical Songs: Temporal Modules of Cortical Activity.* Science 304(5670), 559–564, (2004).

[35] Soummya Kar and Jose MF Moura. *Distributed Consensus Algorithms in Sensor Networks With Imperfect Communication: Link Failures and Channel Noise* IEEE Transactions on SIgnal Processing 57(1), 355–369, (2009).

[36] Richard M. Karp, Christian Schindelhauer, Scott Shenker, and Berthold Vöcking. *Randomized rumor-spreading.* Proc. of the IEEE Symposium on Foundations of Computer Science (FOCS), 565–574, (2000)

[37] Ralf Koetter and Frank R. Kschischang. *Coding for errors and erasures in random network coding.* IEEE Transactions on Information Theory 54 no. 8, 3579–3591, (2008)

[38] Thierry Lengagne, Thierry Aubin, Jacques Lauga, and Pierre J.Jouventin. *How do king penguins (Aptenodytes patagonicus) apply the mathematical theory of information to communicate in windy conditions?* Proc. of the Royal Society B: Biological Sciences 266(1429), 1623–1628, (1999).

[39] George B. Mertzios, Sotiris E. Nikoletseas, Christoforos Raptopoulos, and Paul G. Spirakis. *Natural models for evolution on networks.* Theor. Comput. Sci. 477, 76–95 (2013).

[40] Othon Michail, Ioannis Chatzigiannakis, and Paul G. Spirakis. *Mediated population protocols. Theor. Comput. Sci.* 412(22), 2434–2450 (2011).

[41] Mauro Mobilia, A. Petersen, and Sidney Redner. *Spread of epidemic disease on networks.* Physical Review E 66(16128), (2002).

[42] Mauro Mobilia. *Does A Single Zealot Affect an Infinite Group of Voters* Physical Review Letters 91(028701), (2003)

[43] Mauro Mobilia, A. Petersen, and Sidney Redner. *On the role of zealotry in the voter model.* Journal of Statistical Mechanics, P08029, (2007).

[44] Todd Moon. *Error Correction Coding: Mathematical Methods and Algorithms.* Wiley-Interscience, 800pp, (2005).

[45] David Peleg. *Distributed Computing: A Locality-Sensitive Approach.* SIAM, (2000).

[46] Boris Pittel. *On spreading a rumor.* SIAM Journal on Applied Mathematics 47 no. 1, 213–223, (1987).

[47] Nitzan Razin, Jean-pierre Eckmann, and Ofer Feinerman. *Desert ants achieve reliable recruitment across noisy interactions.* Journal of the Royal Society Interface 10(20130079), (2013).

[48] Gilbert Roberts. *Why individual vigilance increases as group size increases.* Animal Behaviour 51, 1077–1086, (1996).

[49] Claude Shannon. *A Mathematical Theory of Communication.* Bell System Technical Journal 27(3), 379–423, (1948).

[50] David JT Sumpter, Jens Krause, Richard James, Iain D. Couzin, and Ashley JW Ward. *Consensus Decision Making by Fish.* Current Biology 22(25), 1773–1777, (2008).

[51] Yuri Sykulev, Michael Joo, Irina Vturina, Theodore J. Tsomides, and Herman N Eisen. *Evidence that a Single Peptide-MHC Complex on a Target Cell Can Elicit a Cytolytic T Cell Response.* Immunity 4(6), 565–571, (1996).

[52] Edward O. Wilson and Bert Holldobler. *The Superorganism: The Beauty, Elegance, and Strangeness of Insect Societies.* W. W. Norton & Company, 544pp, (2008).

Estimation for Monotone Sampling: Competitiveness and Customization

Edith Cohen
Microsoft Research
Mountain View, CA, USA
editco@microsoft.com

ABSTRACT

Random samples are lossy summaries which allow queries posed over the data to be approximated by applying an appropriate estimator to the sample. The effectiveness of sampling, however, hinges on estimator selection. The choice of estimators is subjected to global requirements, such as unbiasedness and range restrictions on the estimate value, and ideally, we seek estimators that are both efficient to derive and apply and *admissible* (not dominated, in terms of variance, by other estimators). Nevertheless, for a given data domain, sampling scheme, and query, there are many admissible estimators.

We define monotone sampling, which is implicit in many applications of massive data set analysis, and study the choice of admissible nonnegative and unbiased estimators. Our main contribution is general derivations of admissible estimators with desirable properties. We present a construction of *order-optimal* estimators, which minimize variance according to *any* specified priorities over the data domain. Order-optimality allows us to customize the derivation to common patterns that we can learn or observe in the data. When we prioritize lower values (e.g., more similar data sets when estimating difference), we obtain the L^* estimator, which is the unique monotone admissible estimator and dominates the classic Horvitz-Thompson estimator. We show that the L^* estimator is 4-competitive, meaning that the expectation of the square, on any data, is at most 4 times the minimum possible for that data. These properties make the L^* estimator a natural default choice. We also present the U^* estimator, which prioritizes large values (e.g., less similar data sets). Our estimator constructions are general, natural, and practical, allowing us to make the most from our summarized data.

1. INTRODUCTION

Random sampling is a common tool in the analysis of massive data. Sampling is highly suitable for parallel or distributed platforms. The samples facilitate scalable approximate processing of queries posed over the original data, when exact processing is too resource consuming or when the original data is no longer available. Random samples have a distinct advantage over other synopsis in their flexibility. In particular, they naturally support *domain* (subset) queries, which specify a selected set of records. Moreover, the same sample can be used for basic statistics, such as sums, moments, and averages, and more complex relations: distinct counts, size of set intersections, and difference norms.

The value of a sample hinges on the accuracy within which we can estimate query results. In turn, this boils down to the *estimators* we use, which are the functions we apply to the sample to produce the estimate. As a rule, we are interested in estimators that satisfy desirable *global* properties, which must hold for *all possible data* in our data domain. Common desirable properties are:

- *Unbiasedness*, which means that the expectation of the estimate is equal to the estimated value. Unbiasedness is particularly important when we are ultimately interested in estimating a sum aggregate, and our estimator is applied to each summand. Typically, the estimate for each summand has high variance, but with unbiasedness (and pairwise independence), the relative error decreases with aggregation.
- *Range restriction* of estimates: since the estimate is often used as a substitute of the true value, we would like it to be from the same domain as the query result. Often, the domain is *nonnegative* and we would like the estimate to be nonnegative as well. Another natural restriction is *boundedness* which means that for each given input, the set of possible estimate values is bounded.
- *Finite variance* (implied by boundedness but less restrictive)

Perhaps the most ubiquitous quality measure of an estimator is its variance. The variance, however, is a function of the input data. An important concept in estimation theory is a Uniform Minimum Variance Unbiased (UMVUE) estimator [30], that is, a single estimator which attains the minimum possible variance for all inputs in our data domain [27]. A UMVUE estimator, however, generally does not exist. We instead seek an *admissible* (Pareto variance optimal) estimator [30] – meaning that strict improvement is not possible without violating some global properties. More precisely, an estimator is admissible if there is no other estimator that satisfies the global properties with at most the variance of our estimator on all data and strictly lower variance on some data. A UMVUE must be admissible, but when one does not exist, there is typically a full Pareto front of admissible estimators. We recently proposed *variance competitiveness* [16], as a robust "worst-case" performance measure when there is no UMVUE. The variance competitive ratio is the maximum, over data, of the ratio of the expectation of the square of our estimator to the minimum possible for the data subject to the global properties. A small ratio means that variance on each input in the data domain is not too far off the minimum variance attainable on this data by an estimator which satisfies the global properties. In particular, the UMVUE, when it exists, is 1-competitive.

We propose the following definition of a sampling scheme. In the sequel we show how it incorporates common sampling schemes.

> A *monotone sampling scheme* $(\mathbf{V}, S^*)$ is specified by a *data domain* $\mathbf{V}$ and a mapping $S^* : \mathbf{V} \times (0, 1] \to 2^{\mathbf{V}}$. The mapping is such that the set $S^*(\boldsymbol{v}, u)$ for a fixed v is monotone non-decreasing with u.

PODC'14, July 15–18, 2014, Paris, France.

http://dx.doi.org/10.1145/2611462.2611485.

The sampling interpretation is that a *sample* $S(\boldsymbol{v}, u)$ of the *input* $\boldsymbol{v}$ (which we also refer to as the *data vector*) is obtained by drawing a *seed* $u \sim U[0, 1]$, uniformly at random from $[0, 1]$. The sample deterministically depends on $\boldsymbol{v}$ and the (random) *seed* u. The mapping $S^*(\boldsymbol{v}, u)$ is the set of all data vectors that are consistent with S (which we assume includes the seed value u). It represents all the information we can glean from the sample on the input. In particular, we must have $\boldsymbol{v} \in S^*(\boldsymbol{v}, u)$ for all $\boldsymbol{v}$ and u. The sampling scheme is monotone in the randomization: When fixing $\boldsymbol{v}$, the set $S^*(\boldsymbol{v}, u)$ is non-decreasing with u, that is, the smaller u is, the more information we have on the data $\boldsymbol{v}$.

In the applications we consider, the (expected) representation size of the sample $S(\boldsymbol{v}, u)$ is typically much smaller size than $\boldsymbol{v}$. The set S^* can be very large (or infinite), and our estimators will only depend on performing certain operations on it, such as obtaining the infimum of some function. Monotone sampling can also be interpreted as obtaining a "measurement" $S(\boldsymbol{v}, u)$ of the data $\boldsymbol{v}$, where u determines the granularity of our measuring instrument. Ultimately, the goal is to recover some function of the data from the sample (the outcome of our measurement):

> A *monotone estimation* problem is specified by a monotone sampling scheme and a nonnegative function $f : \mathbf{V} \geq 0$. The goal is to specify an *estimator*, which is a function of all possible outcomes $\hat{f} : \mathcal{S} \geq 0$, where $\mathcal{S} = \{S(\boldsymbol{v}, u) | \boldsymbol{v} \in \mathbf{V}, u \in (0, 1]$. The estimator should be unbiased $\forall \boldsymbol{v}$, $\mathsf{E}_{u \sim U[0,1]} \hat{f}(S(\boldsymbol{v}, u)) = f(\boldsymbol{v})$ and satisfy some other desirable properties.

The interpretation is that we obtain a query, specified in the form of a nonnegative function $f : \mathbf{V} \geq 0$ on all possible data vectors $\boldsymbol{v}$. We are interested in knowing $f(\boldsymbol{v})$, but we can not see $\boldsymbol{v}$ and only have access to the sample S. The sample provides us with little information on $\boldsymbol{v}$, and thus on $f(\boldsymbol{v})$. We approximate $f(\boldsymbol{v})$ by applying an *estimator*, $\hat{f}(S) \geq 0$ to the sample. The monotone estimation problem is a bundling of a function f and a monotone sampling scheme. We are interested in estimators $\hat{f}$ that satisfy properties. We always require nonnegativity and unbiasedness and consider admissibilitiy, variance competitiveness, and what we call customization (lower variance on some data patterns).

Our formulation departs from traditional estimation theory. We view the data vectors in the domain as the possible inputs to the sampling scheme, and we treat estimator derivation as an optimization problem. The variance of the estimator parallels the "performance" we obtain on a certain input. The work horse of estimation theory, the maximum likelihood estimator, is not even applicable here as it does not distiguish between the different data vectors in S^*. Instead, the random "coin flips," in the form of the seed u, that are available to the estimator are used to restrict the set S^* and obtain meaningful estimates.

We next show how monotone sampling relates to the well-studied model of coordinated sampling, that has extensive applications in massive data analysis. In particular, estimator constructions for monotone estimation can be applied to estimate functions over coordinated samples.

Coordinated shared-seed sampling

In this framework our data has a matrix form of two or more ($r > 1$) *instances*, where each instance (row) has the form of a weight assignment to the (same) set of items (columns). Different instances may correspond to snapshots, activity logs, measurements, or repeated surveys that are taken at different times or locations. When instances correspond to documents, items can correspond to features. When instances are network neighborhoods, items can correspond to members or objects they store.

Over such data, we are interested in queries which depend on two or more of the instances and a subset D of the items. Some examples are Jaccard similarity, distance norms, or the number of distinct items with positive entry in at least one instance (distinct count).

Such queries often can be expressed, or can be well approximated, by a sum over items in D of an *item function* that is applied to the tuple containing the values of the item in the different instances. Distinct count is a sum aggregate of logical OR and the L_p difference is the pth root of L_p^p, which sum-aggregates $|v_1 - v_2|^p$. For $r \geq 2$ instances, we can consider sum aggregates of the exponentiated range functions $\mathrm{RG}_p(\boldsymbol{v}) = (\max(\boldsymbol{v}) - \min(\boldsymbol{v}))^p$, where $p > 0$. This is made concrete in Example 1 which illustrates a data set of 3 instances over 8 items, example queries, specified over a selected set of items, and the corresponding item functions.

Example 1 Dataset with 3 instances and queries

Instances $i \in \{1, 2, 3\}$ *and items* $k \in \{a, b, c, d, e, f, g, h\}$:

	a	b	c	d	e	f	g	h
v_1	0.95	0	0.23	0.70	0.10	0.42	0	0.32
v_2	0.15	0.44	0	0.80	0.05	0.50	0.20	0
v_3	0.25	0	0	0.10	0	0.22	0	0

Example queries over $D \subset [a\text{-}h]$. L_p difference, L_p^p: the pth power of L_p difference and a sum aggregate, L_{p+}^p: asymmetric (increase only) L_p^p. G: example "arbitrary" sum aggregate.

$$L_p^p(D) = \sum_{k \in D} |v_1^{(k)} - v_2^{(k)}|^p \qquad L_p(D) = (L_p^p(D))^{1/p}$$
$$L_{p+}^p(D) = \sum_{k \in D} \max\{0, v_1^{(k)} - v_2^{(k)}\}^p$$
$$G(D) = \sum_{k \in D} |v_1^{(k)} - 2v_2^{(k)} + v_3^{(k)}|^2$$

sum aggregate	*item function*
L_p^p	$\mathrm{RG}_p(\boldsymbol{v}) = (\max(\boldsymbol{v}) - \min(\boldsymbol{v}))^p$
L_{p+}^p	$\mathrm{RG}_{p+}(v_1, v_2) = \max\{0, v_1 - v_2\}^p$
G	$g(v_1, v_2, v_3) = \lvert v_1 + v_3 - 2v_2 \rvert^2$

$$L_1(\{b, c, e\}) = |0 - 0.44| + |0.23 - 0| + |0.10 - 0.05| = 0.71$$
$$L_2^2(\{c, f, h\}) = (0.23 - 0)^2 + (0.50 - 0.42)^2 + (0.32 - 0)^2 \approx 0.16$$
$$L_2(\{c, f, h\}) = \sqrt{L_2^2(\{c, f, h\})} \approx 0.40$$
$$L_{1+}(\{b, c, e\}) = \max\{0, 0 - 0.44\} + \max\{0, 0.23 - 0\} + \max\{0, 0.10 - 0.05\} = 0.235$$
$$G(\{b, d\}) = |0 - 2 * 0.44 + 0|^2 + |0.7 - 2 * 0.8 + 0.1|^2 \approx 1.18$$

We now assume that each instance is sampled and the sample of each instance contains a subset of the items that were active in the instance (had a positive weight). Common sampling schemes for a single instance are Probability Proportional to Size (PPS) [24] or bottom-k sampling which includes Reservoir sampling [26, 36], Priority (Sequential Poisson) [31, 20], or Successive weighted sample without replacement [33, 12]. The sampling of items in each instance can be completely independent or slightly dependent (as with Reservoir or bottom-k sampling, which samples exactly k items).

Coordinated sampling is a way of specifying the randomization so that the sampling of different instances utilizes the same "randomization" [2, 35, 6, 32, 34, 4, 3, 14, 28, 17]. That is, the sampling of the same item in different instances is highly correlated. This is in contrast to independent sampling. Alternative term used in the survey sampling literature is Permanent Random Numbers (PRN). Coordinated sampling is also a form of locality sensitive hashing (LSH): When the weights in two instances (rows) are similar, the samples we obtain are similar.

The method of coordinating samples had been rediscovered many times, for different applications, in both statistics and computer science. The main reason for its consideration by computer scientists is that it allows for more accurate estimates of queries that span multiple instances such as distinct counts and similarity measures [4, 3, 6, 18, 29, 21, 22, 5, 19, 1, 23, 28, 14, 17]. In some cases, such as all-distances sketches [6, 11, 29, 12, 13, 8] of neighborhoods of nodes in a graph, coordinated samples are obtained much more efficiently than independent samples. Coordination can be efficiently achieved by using a random hash function, applied to the item key k, to generate the seed $u^{(k)}$, in conjunction with the single-instance scheme of our choice (PPS or Reservoir). The use of hashing allows the sampling of different instances to be performed independently with very small shared state.

Coordinated PPS sampling of the instances in Example 1 is demonstrated in Example 2. The same random seed $u^{(k)}$ is used to determine the sampling of item k across instances.

Sum aggregates $\sum_{i\in D} f(\boldsymbol{v}^{(i)})$, such as L_p^p, over a domain of items D are estimated by summing up item function estimators over the selected items, that is $\sum_{i\in D} \hat{f}(S(\boldsymbol{v}^{(i)}, u^{(i)})$. The sampling of each item tuple is generally very sparse, with no entries or almost no entries sampled, and we therefore expect zero estimates $\hat{f} = 0$ for most items and a high variance. We therefore insist on unbiasedness and pairwise independence of the single-item estimates. That way, the variance of the sum estimate is the sum over items in $i \in D$ of the variance of $\hat{f}$ for $\boldsymbol{v}^{(i)}$. Thus (assuming variance is balanced) we can expect the relative error to decrease $\propto 1/\sqrt{|D|}$. Lastly, since the functions we are interested in are nonnegative, we also require the estimates to be nonnegative.

Coordinated sampling, when projected on the tuple $\boldsymbol{v}$ of the weights of the item on the different instances (a column in our matrix) is a monotone sampling scheme [1] and the estimation problem of an item-function is a corresponding monotone estimation problem.

More precisely, the data domain in the monotone estimation problem we obtain is a subset of $r \geq 1$ dimensional vectors $\mathbf{V} \subset \mathbb{R}^r_{\geq 0}$ (where r is the number of instances in the query specification). The sampling is specified by r continuous non-decreasing functions on $(0, 1]$: $\boldsymbol{\tau} = \tau_1, \ldots, \tau_r$. The sample S includes the ith entry of $\boldsymbol{v}$ with its value v_i if and only $v_i \geq \tau_i(u)$. Note that when entry i is not sampled, we also have some information, as we know that $v_i < \tau_i(u)$. Therefore the set S^* of data vectors consistent with our sample (which we do not explicitly compute) includes the exact values of some entries and upper bounds on other entries. Since the functions τ_i are non-decreasing, the sampling scheme is monotone. In particular, PPS sampling of different instances, restricted to a single item, is expressed with $\tau_i(u)$ that are linear functions: There is a fixed vector $\boldsymbol{\tau}^*$ such that $\tau_i(u) \equiv u\tau_i^*$.

Therefore, the estimation of the sum-aggregate over coordinated samples is reduced to monotone estimation.

In [16] we provided a complete characterization of item-function estimation problems over coordinated samples for which estimators with desirable global properties exist. This characterization can be extended to monotone estimation. The properties considered were unbiasedness and nonnegativity, and together with finite variances or boundedness. We also showed that for any coordinated estimation problem for which an unbiased nonnegative estimator with finite variances exists, we can construct an estimator, which we named the J estimator, that is 84-competitive. The J estimator, however, is generally not admissible, and also, the construction was geared to establish $O(1)$ competitiveness rather than obtain a "natural" estimator or to minimize the constant.

[1]Bottom-k samples select exactly k items in each instance, hence inclusions of items are dependent. We obtain a single-item restriction by considering the sampling scheme for the item conditioned on fixing the seed values of other items. A similar situation is with all-distances sketches, where we can use the HIP inclusion probabilities [8], which are conditioned on fixing the randomization of all closer nodes.

Contributions

Our main technical contributions are the derivation of estimators for general monotone estimation problems. Our estimators are admissible, easy to apply, and satisfy desirable properties. We state and explain our results and provide pointers to examples and to the appropriate sections in the body of the paper. Due to page limitations, many proofs and details are omitted and can be found in [9].

The optimal range: We start by studying the admissibility playing field for unbiased nonnegative estimators. We define the *optimal range* of estimates (Section 3) for each particular outcome, *conditioned* on the aggregate estimate over all "less-informative" outcomes (outcomes which correspond to larger seed value u). The range includes all estimate values that are "locally" optimal with respect to at least one data vector that is consistent with the outcome. We show that being "in range" almost everywhere is necessary for admissibility and is sufficient for unbiasedness and nonnegativity, when an unbiased nonnegative estimator exists.

The L* estimator: We study the estimator obtained when requiring the estimate on each outcome to be equal to the infimum of the optimal range. We name it the *L* estimator* and study it extensively in Section 4. The L* estimator can be expressed as the solution of a respective integral equation, which we solve to obtain a convenient form:

$$\hat{f}^{(L)}(S, \rho) = \frac{\underline{f}^{(\boldsymbol{v})}(\rho)}{\rho} - \int_\rho^1 \frac{\underline{f}^{(\boldsymbol{v})}(u)}{u^2} du \,, \qquad (1)$$

where ρ is the seed value used to obtain the sample S, $\boldsymbol{v} \in S^*$ is any (arbitrary) data vector consistent with S and ρ, and the *lower bound* function $\underline{f}^{(\boldsymbol{v})}(u)$ is defined as the infimum of $f(\boldsymbol{z})$ over all vectors $\boldsymbol{z} \in S^*(\boldsymbol{v}, u)$ that are consistent with the sample obtained for data $\boldsymbol{v}$ with seed u. Note that the right hand side is the same for any choice of $\boldsymbol{v} \in S^*$ and can be computed from the information in S and ρ. Therefore, the estimate is well defined and we can compute it by numeric integration or a closed form (when a respective definite integral has a closed form). The lower bound function is presented more precisely in Section 2 and an example is provided in Example 3. An example derivation of the L* estimator for the functions RG_{p+} is provided in Example 4.

We show that the L* estimator has a natural and compelling combination of properties. It satisfies both our quality measures, being both admissible and 4-competitive for any instance of the monotone estimation problem for which a bounded variance estimator exists. The competitive ratio of 4 improves over the previous upper bound of 84 [16]. We show that the ratio of 4 of the L* estimator is tight in the sense that there is a family of functions on which the supremum of the ratio, over functions and data vectors, is 4. We note however that the L* estimator has lower ratio for specific functions. For example, we computed ratios of 2 and 2.5, respectively, for exponentiated range with $p = 1, 2$ (Which facilitates estimation of L_p differences, see Example 1).

Moreover, the L* estimator is *monotone*, meaning that when fixing the data vector, the estimate value is monotone non-decreasing with the information in the outcome (the set S^* of data vectors that are consistent with our sample). In terms of our monotone sampling formulation, estimator monotonicity means that when we fix the data $\boldsymbol{v}$, the estimate is non-increasing with the seed u. Furthermore, the L* estimator is the *unique* admissible monotone estimator and thus dominates (has at most the variance on every data vector) the Horvitz-Thompson (HT) estimator [25] (which is also unbiased, nonnegative, and monotone).

To further illustrate comparison with HT, recall that the HT estimate is positive only on outcomes that reveal $f(\boldsymbol{v})$. In this case, the inverse probability estimate $f(\boldsymbol{v})/p$, where p is the probability of an outcome which reveals $f(\boldsymbol{v})$. When we have partial information on $f(\boldsymbol{v})$, the HT estimate does not utilize that and is 0 whereas admissible estimators, such as the L* estimators, must use this information. It is also possible that the probability of an outcome that reveals $f(\boldsymbol{v})$ is 0. In this case, the HT estimator is not even applicable. One natural such example is the range $|v_1 - v_2|$ with coordinated PPS sampling using $\boldsymbol{\tau}^* = (1, 1)$. When the input is $(0.5, 0)$, the range is 0.5, but there is 0 probability of revealing $v_2 = 0$. We can obtain informative lower (and upper) bounds on the range: When $u \in (0, 0.5)$, we have a lower bound of $0.5 - u$. Nonetheless, the probability of knowing the exact value ($u = 0$) is 0. In contrast to the HT estimate, our L* estimator is defined for any monotone estimation instance for which a nonnegative unbiased estimator with finite variance exists.

Order-optimal estimators: In many situations we have information on data patterns. For example, if our data consists of hourly temperature measurements across locations or daily summaries of Wikipedia, we expect it to be fairly stable. That is, we expect instances to be very similar. That is, most tuples of values , each corresponding to a particular geographic location or Wikipedia article, would have most entries being very similar. In other cases, such as IP traffic, differences are typically larger. Since there is a choice, a Pareto front of admissible estimators, we would like to be able to select an estimator that would have lower variance on more likely patterns of data vectors, this while still providing some weaker "worst case" guarantees for all applicable data vectors in our domain.

Customization of estimators to data patterns can be facilitated through *order optimality* [15]. More precisely, an estimator is $\prec^+$-optimal with respect to some partial order $\prec$ on data vectors if any other (nonnegative unbiased) estimator with lower variance on some data $\boldsymbol{v}$ must have strictly higher variance on some data that precedes $\boldsymbol{v}$. Order-optimality implies admissibility, but not vice versa. By specifying an order which prioritizes more likely patterns in the data, we can customize the estimator to these patterns.

We show (Section 5) how to construct a $\prec^+$-optimal nonnegative unbiased estimators for *any* function and order $\prec$ for which such estimator exists. We show that when the data domain is discrete, such estimators always exist whereas continuous domains require some natural convergence properties of $\prec$.

We also show that the L* estimator is $\prec^+$-optimal with respect to the order $\prec$ such that $\boldsymbol{z} \prec \boldsymbol{v} \iff f(\boldsymbol{z}) < f(\boldsymbol{v})$. This means that when estimating the exponentiated range function, the L* estimator is optimized for high similarity (this while providing a strong 4-competitiveness guarantee even for highly dissimilar data).

The U* estimator: We also explore the upper extreme of the optimal range, that is, the solution obtained by aiming for the supremum of the range. We call this solution the *U* estimator* and we study it in Section 6. This estimator is unbiased, nonnegative, and has finite variances. We formulate some conditions on the monotone estimation problem which are satisfied by natural functions including the exponentiated range with coordinated PPS sampling , under which the estimator is admissible. The U* estimator, under some conditions, is $\prec^+$-optimal with respect to the order $\boldsymbol{z} \prec \boldsymbol{v} \iff f(\boldsymbol{z}) > f(\boldsymbol{v})$. In the context of the exponentiated range, it means that it is optimized for highly dissimilar instances.

Lastly, in Section 7 we conclude with a discussion of future work and of follow-up applications of our estimators.

2. PRELIMINARIES

Consider monotone sampling, as defined in the introduction.

LEMMA 2.1. *For any two outcomes, $S_1^* = S^*(u, \boldsymbol{v})$ and $S_2^* = S^*(u', \boldsymbol{v}')$, the sets S_1^* and S_2^* must be either disjoint or one is contained in the other.*

PROOF. If there is a common data vector $\boldsymbol{z} \in S_1^* \cap S_2^*$, then $S_1^* = S^*(u, \boldsymbol{z})$ and $S_2^* = S^*(u', \boldsymbol{z})$. From definition, if $u' > u$ then $S_1^* \subseteq S_2^*$ and vice versa. □

LEMMA 2.2. *For any $\boldsymbol{v}, \boldsymbol{z} \in \mathbf{V}$, the set of u values which satisfy $S^*(u, \boldsymbol{v}) = S^*(u, \boldsymbol{z})$ is a suffix of the interval $(0, 1]$.*

PROOF. $S^*(u, \boldsymbol{v}) = S^*(u, \boldsymbol{z})$ implies $S^*(u', \boldsymbol{v}) = S^*(u', \boldsymbol{z})$ for all $u' > u$. □

For convenience, we assume without loss of generality that this interval is open to the left: [2]

$$\forall \rho \in (0, 1]\ \forall \boldsymbol{v}, \qquad (2)$$
$$\boldsymbol{z} \in S^*(\rho, \boldsymbol{v}) \implies \exists \epsilon > 0,\ \forall x \in (\rho - \epsilon, 1],\ \boldsymbol{z} \in S^*(x, \boldsymbol{v})$$

Example 2 Coordinated PPS sampling for Example 1

We show shared-seed coordinated sampling, where each of the instances 1,2,3 is PPS sampled with $\tau^* = 1$. Therefore, each entry is sampled with probability equal to its value. We draw $u^{(k)} \in U[0, 1]$, independently for different items. An item k is sampled in instance i if and only if $v_i^{(k)} \geq u^{(k)}$. $S^{*(k)}$ contains all vectors consistent with the sampled entries and with value at most $u^{(k)}$ in unsampled entries.

item	a	b	c	d	e	f	g	h
v_1	0.95	0	0.23	0.70	0.10	0.42	0	0.32
v_2	0.15	0.44	0	0.80	0.05	0.50	0.20	0
v_3	0.25	0	0	0.10	0	0.22	0	0
$u^{(k)}$	0.32	0.21	0.04	0.23	0.84	0.70	0.15	0.64

The outcomes for the different items are: $S^{(a)} = (0.95, *, *)$, $S^{(b)} = (*, 0.44, *)$, $S^{(c)} = (0.23, *, *)$, $S^{(d)} = (0.7, 0.8, *)$, $S^{(e)} = S^{(f)} = S^{(h)} = (*, *, *)$, $S^{(g)} = (*, 0.2, *)$. The sets of vectors consistent with the outcomes are $S^{*(a)} = \{0.95\} \times [0, 0.32)^2$ and $S^{*(h)} = [0, 0.64)^3$.

Estimators: Given a monotone estimation problem, we are interested in estimating $f(\boldsymbol{v})$. An estimator $\hat{f}$ is a function of the outcome (including the seed) $S(u, \boldsymbol{v})$. We use the notation $\hat{f}(u, \boldsymbol{v}) \equiv \hat{f}(S(u, \boldsymbol{v}))$. When the domain is continuous, we only consider $\hat{f}$ that are (Lebesgue) integrable. Two estimators $\hat{f}_1$ and $\hat{f}_2$ are *equivalent* if for all data $\boldsymbol{v}$, $\hat{f}_1(u, \boldsymbol{v}) = \hat{f}_2(u, \boldsymbol{v})$ with probability 1.

[2]This assumption can be integrated while affecting at most a "zero measure" set of outcomes for any data point.

An estimator $\hat{f}$ is *nonnegative* if $\forall S,\ \hat{f}(S) \geq 0$ and is *unbiased* if $\forall \boldsymbol{v},\ \mathsf{E}_{u \sim U[0,1]}[\hat{f}(u, \boldsymbol{v})] = f(\boldsymbol{v})$. An estimator has *finite variance* on $\boldsymbol{v}$ if $\int_0^1 \hat{f}(u, \boldsymbol{v})^2 du < \infty$ (the expectation of the square is finite) and is *bounded* on $\boldsymbol{v}$ if $\sup_{u \in (0,1]} \hat{f}(u, \boldsymbol{v}) < \infty$. If a nonnegative estimator is bounded on $\boldsymbol{v}$, it also has finite variance for $\boldsymbol{v}$. An estimator is *monotone* on $\boldsymbol{v}$ if when fixing $\boldsymbol{v}$ and considering outcomes consistent with $\boldsymbol{v}$, the estimate value is non decreasing with the information on the data that we can glean from the outcome, that is, $\hat{f}(u, \boldsymbol{v})$ is non-increasing with u. We say that an estimator is bounded, has finite variances, or is monotone, if the respective property holds for all $\boldsymbol{v} \in \mathbf{V}$.

The lower bound function. For $Z \subset \mathbf{V}$, we define $\underline{f}(Z) = \inf\{f(v) \mid v \in Z\}$ as the infimum of f on Z. We use the notation $\underline{f}(S) \equiv \underline{f}(S^*)$, $\underline{f}(\rho, \boldsymbol{v}) \equiv \underline{f}(S^*(\rho, \boldsymbol{v}))$. When $\boldsymbol{v}$ is fixed, we use $\underline{f}^{(\boldsymbol{v})}(u) \equiv \underline{f}(u, \boldsymbol{v})$. Some properties which we need in the sequel are [16]:

$$\bullet \forall \boldsymbol{v},\ \underline{f}^{(\boldsymbol{v})}(u) \text{ is monotone non increasing and left-continuous.} \tag{3}$$

$$\bullet \hat{f} \text{ is unbiased and nonnegative } \Longrightarrow \tag{4}$$

$$\forall \boldsymbol{v}, \forall \rho,\ \int_\rho^1 \hat{f}(u, \boldsymbol{v}) du \leq \underline{f}^{(\boldsymbol{v})}(\rho)\,. \tag{5}$$

The lower bound function $\underline{f}^{(\boldsymbol{v})}$, and its lower hull $H_f^{(\boldsymbol{v})}$, are used to characterize existence of estimators with desirable properties [16]:

$$\bullet \exists \text{ unbiased nonnegative } f \text{ estimator } \Longleftrightarrow \tag{6}$$

$$\forall \boldsymbol{v} \in \mathbf{V},\ \lim_{u \to 0+} \underline{f}^{(\boldsymbol{v})}(u) = f(\boldsymbol{v})\,. \tag{7}$$

$\bullet$If f satisfies (7),

$\exists$ unbiased nonnegative estimator with finite variance for $\boldsymbol{v}$

$$\Longleftrightarrow \int_0^1 \left(\frac{dH_f^{(\boldsymbol{v})}(u)}{du}\right)^2 du < \infty\,. \tag{8}$$

$\exists$ unbiased nonnegative estimator that is bounded on $\boldsymbol{v}$

$$\Longleftrightarrow \lim_{u \to 0+} \frac{f(\boldsymbol{v}) - \underline{f}^{(\boldsymbol{v})}(u)}{u} < \infty\,. \tag{9}$$

Example 3 illustrates lower bound functions and respective lower hulls for RG_{p+}. **Partially specified estimators.** We use *partial specifications* $\hat{f}$ of (nonnegative and unbiased) estimators, which are specified on a set of outcomes $\mathcal{S}$ so that

$$\forall \boldsymbol{v}\ \exists \rho_v \in [0,1],\ S(u, \boldsymbol{v}) \in \mathcal{S} \textit{ almost everywhere} \text{ for } u > \rho_v \ \wedge$$
$$S(u, \boldsymbol{v}) \notin \mathcal{S} \textit{ almost everywhere} \text{ for } u \leq \rho_v\,.$$

When $\rho_v = 0$, we say that the estimator is *fully specified* for $\boldsymbol{v}$. We also require that $\hat{f}$ is nonnegative where specified and satisfies

$$\forall \boldsymbol{v},\ \rho_v > 0 \implies \int_{\rho_v}^1 \hat{f}(u, \boldsymbol{v}) du \leq f(\boldsymbol{v}) \tag{10a}$$

$$\forall \boldsymbol{v},\ \rho_v = 0 \implies \int_{\rho_v}^1 \hat{f}(u, \boldsymbol{v}) du = f(\boldsymbol{v})\,. \tag{10b}$$

LEMMA 2.3. *[16] If f satisfies* (7) *(has a nonnegative unbiased estimator), then any partially specified estimator can be extended to an unbiased nonnegative estimator.*

$\boldsymbol{v}$-optimal extensions and estimators. Given a partially specified estimator $\hat{f}$ so that $\rho_v > 0$ and $M = \int_{\rho_v}^1 \hat{f}(u, \boldsymbol{v}) du$, a *$\boldsymbol{v}$-optimal extension* is an extension which is fully specified for $\boldsymbol{v}$ and minimizes variance for $\boldsymbol{v}$ (amongst all such extensions). The $\boldsymbol{v}$-optimal extension is defined on outcomes $S(u, \boldsymbol{v})$ for $u \in (0, \rho_v]$ and satisfies

$$\begin{aligned} \min & \int_0^{\rho_v} \hat{f}(u, \boldsymbol{v})^2 du \\ \text{s.t.} & \int_0^{\rho_v} \hat{f}(u, \boldsymbol{v}) du = f(\boldsymbol{v}) - M \\ \forall u, & \int_u^{\rho_v} \hat{f}(x, \boldsymbol{v}) dx \leq \underline{f}^{(\boldsymbol{v})}(u) - M \\ \forall u, & \hat{f}(u, \boldsymbol{v}) \geq 0 \end{aligned} \tag{11}$$

For $\rho_v \in (0,1]$ and $M \in [0, \underline{f}^{(\boldsymbol{v})}(\rho_v)]$, we define the function $\hat{f}^{(\boldsymbol{v},\rho_v,M)} : (0, \rho_v] \to R_+$ as the solution of

$$\hat{f}^{(\boldsymbol{v},\rho_v,M)}(u) = \inf_{0 \leq \eta < u} \frac{\underline{f}^{(\boldsymbol{v})}(\eta) - M - \int_u^{\rho_v} \hat{f}^{(\boldsymbol{v},\rho_v,M)}(u) du}{\rho - \eta}\,. \tag{12}$$

Geometrically, the function $\hat{f}^{(\boldsymbol{v},\rho_v,M)}$ is the negated derivative of the lower hull of the lower bound function $\underline{f}^{(\boldsymbol{v})}$ on $(0, \rho_v)$ and the point (ρ_v, M).

THEOREM 2.1. *[16] Given a partially specified estimator $\hat{f}$ so that $\rho_v > 0$ and $M = \int_{\rho_v}^1 \hat{f}(u, \boldsymbol{v}) du$, then $\hat{f}^{(\boldsymbol{v},\rho_v,M)}$ is the unique (up to equivalence) $\boldsymbol{v}$-optimal extension of $\hat{f}$.*

The *$\boldsymbol{v}$-optimal* estimates are the minimum variance extension of the empty specification. We use $\rho_v = 1$ and $M = 0$ and obtain $\hat{f}^{(\boldsymbol{v})} \equiv \hat{f}^{(\boldsymbol{v},1,0)}$. $\hat{f}^{(\boldsymbol{v})}$ is the solution of

$$\hat{f}^{(\boldsymbol{v})}(u) = \inf_{0 \leq \eta < u} \frac{\underline{f}^{(\boldsymbol{v})}(\eta) - \int_u^1 \hat{f}^{(\boldsymbol{v})}(u) du}{\rho - \eta}\,, \tag{13}$$

which is the negated slope of the lower hull of the lower bound function $\underline{f}^{(\boldsymbol{v})}$. This is illustrated in Example 3.

Admissibility and order optimality. An estimator is *admissible* if there is no (nonnegative unbiased) estimator with same or lower variance on all data and strictly lower on some data. We also consider *order optimality*, specified with respect to a partial order $\prec$ on $\mathbf{V}$: An estimator $\hat{f}$ is *$\prec^+$-optimal* if there is no other nonnegative unbiased estimator with strictly lower variance on some data $\boldsymbol{v}$ and at most the variance of $\hat{f}$ on all vectors that precede $\boldsymbol{v}$. Order-optimality (with respect to some $\prec$) implies admissibility but the converse is not true in general [15].

Variance competitiveness [16] An estimator $\hat{f}$ is *c-competitive* if

$$\forall \boldsymbol{v},\ \int_0^1 \left(\hat{f}(u, \boldsymbol{v})\right)^2 du \leq c \inf_{\hat{f}'} \int_0^1 \left(\hat{f}'(u, \boldsymbol{v})\right)^2 du,$$

where the infimum is over all unbiased nonnegative estimators of f. When the estimator is unbiased, the expectation of the square is closely related to variance, and an estimator that minimizes one also minimizes the other.

$$\text{VAR}[\hat{f}|\boldsymbol{v}] = \int_0^1 \hat{f}(u, \boldsymbol{v})^2 du - f(\boldsymbol{v})^2 \tag{14}$$

3. THE OPTIMAL RANGE

We say that an estimator $\hat{f}$ is $\boldsymbol{v}$-optimal *at an outcome* $S(u, \boldsymbol{v})$ if it satisfies (13). For an outcome $S(\rho, \boldsymbol{v})$, we are interested in the *range* of $\boldsymbol{z}$-optimal estimates at S for all $\boldsymbol{z} \in S^*$, with respect to a value M, which captures the contribution to the expectation of the estimator made by outcomes which are less informative than S.

Example 3 Lower bound function and its lower hull

Consider $\text{RG}_{p+}(v_1, v_2) = \max\{0, v_1 - v_2\}^p$ (see Example 1) over the domain $\mathbf{V} = [0,1]^2$ and PPS sampling with $\tau_1^* = \tau_2^* = 1$ (as in Example 2). The lower bound function for data $\boldsymbol{v} = (v_1, v_2)$ is

$$\underline{\text{RG}_{p+}}(u, \boldsymbol{v}) = \max\{0, v_1 - \max\{v_2, u\}\}^p .$$

The figures below illustrate $\underline{\text{RG}_{p+}}^{(\boldsymbol{v})}(u)$ (LB) and its lower hull (CH) for the data vectors $(0.6, 0.2)$ and $(0.6, 0)$ and $p = \{0.5, 1, 2\}$. For $u > 0.2$, the outcome when sampling both vectors is the same, and thus the lower bound function is the same. For $u \le 0.2$, the outcomes diverge. For $p \le 1$, $\underline{\text{RG}_{p+}}^{(\boldsymbol{v})}(u)$ is concave and the lower hull is linear on $(0, v_1]$. For $p > 1$, the lower hull coincides with $\underline{\text{RG}_{p+}}^{(\boldsymbol{v})}(u)$ on some interval $(a, v_1]$ and is linear on $(0, a]$. When $v_2 = 0$, $\underline{\text{RG}_{p+}}^{(\boldsymbol{v})}(u)$ is equal to its lower hull.

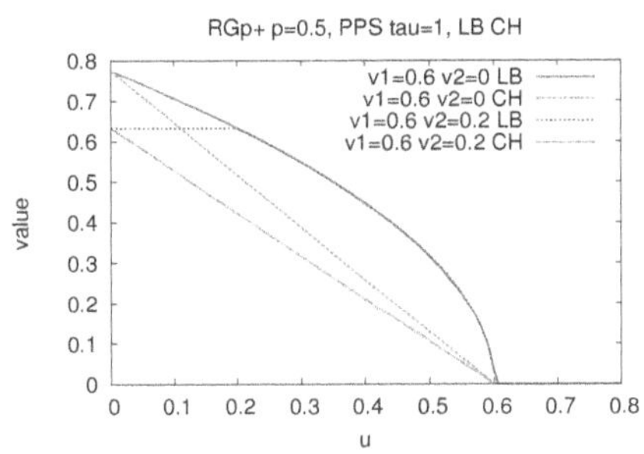

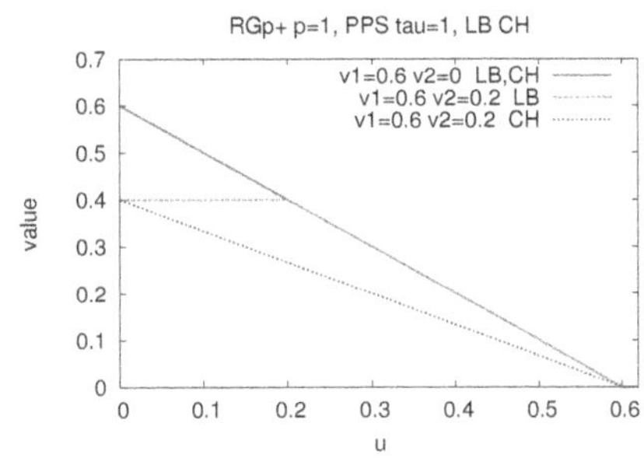

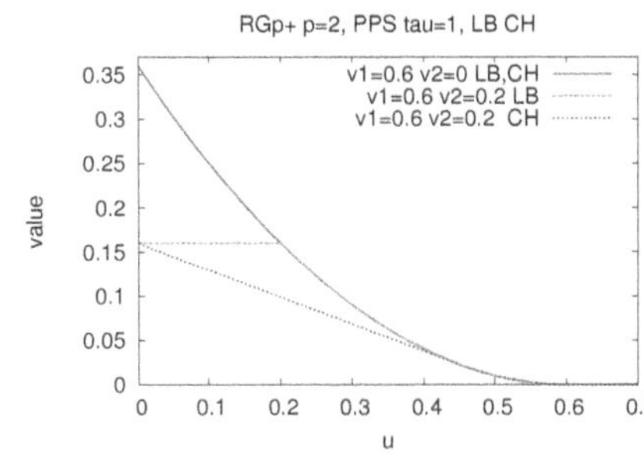

The $\boldsymbol{v}$-optimal estimates are the negated slopes of the lower hulls. They are 0 when $u \in (0.6, 1]$, since these outcomes are consistent with data on which $\underline{\text{RG}_{p+}} = 0$. They are constant for $u \in (0, v_1]$ when $p \le 1$. Observe that for $u \in (0.2, 0.6]$, the $\boldsymbol{v}$-optimal estimates are different even though the outcome of sampling the two vectors are the same – demonstrating that it is not possible to simultaneously minimize the variance of the two vectors.

$$\lambda(\rho, \boldsymbol{v}, M) = \inf_{0 \le \eta < \rho} \frac{\underline{f}(\eta, \boldsymbol{v}) - M}{\rho - \eta} \tag{15}$$

$$\lambda_U(\rho, \boldsymbol{v}, M) \equiv \lambda_U(S, M) = \sup_{\boldsymbol{z} \in S^*(\rho, \boldsymbol{v})} \lambda(\rho, \boldsymbol{z}, M) \tag{16}$$

$$\begin{aligned} \lambda_L(\rho, \boldsymbol{v}, M) \equiv \lambda_L(S, M) &= \inf_{\boldsymbol{z} \in S^*(\rho, \boldsymbol{v})} \lambda(\rho, \boldsymbol{z}, M) \\ &= \inf_{\boldsymbol{z} \in S^*(\rho, \boldsymbol{v})} \inf_{0 \le \eta < \rho} \frac{\underline{f}(\eta, \boldsymbol{z}) - M}{\rho - \eta} \\ &= \frac{\underline{f}(\rho, \boldsymbol{v}) - M}{\rho} \end{aligned} \tag{17}$$

To verify equality (17), observe that from left continuity of $\underline{f}(u, \boldsymbol{z})$,

$$\inf_{\eta < \rho,\ \boldsymbol{z} \in S^*} \underline{f}(\eta, \boldsymbol{z}) = \underline{f}(\rho, \boldsymbol{v})$$

and that the denominator $\rho - \eta$ is maximized at $\eta = 0$. $\lambda(\rho, \boldsymbol{v}, M)$ is the $\boldsymbol{v}$-optimal estimate at ρ, given a specification of the estimator $\hat{f}(u, \boldsymbol{v})$ for $u \in (\rho, 1]$ with $\int_\rho^1 \hat{f}(u, \boldsymbol{v}) du = M$. In short, we refer to $\lambda(\rho, \boldsymbol{v}, M)$ as the $\boldsymbol{v}$-optimal estimate at ρ given M. Geometrically, $\lambda(\rho, \boldsymbol{v}, M)$ is the negated slope of the lower hull of $\underline{f}^{(\boldsymbol{v})}$ and the point (ρ, M). $\lambda_U(S, M)$ and $\lambda_L(S, M)$, respectively, are the supremum and infimum of the *range* of $\boldsymbol{z}$-optimal estimates at S given M. Figure 1 illustrates an outcome S and the optimal range at S given M. We can see how the lower endpoint of the range is realized by a vector with f value equal to the lower bound at S, as in equality (17).

When $\hat{f}$ is provided for seed values $u \in (\rho, 1]$, we use $M = \int_\rho^1 \hat{f}(u, \boldsymbol{v}) du$. We then abbreviate the notations (we remove M) to $\lambda(\rho, \boldsymbol{v})$, $\lambda_U(S)$, and $\lambda_L(S)$.

We say that the estimator $\hat{f}$ is *in-range* (in the optimal range) at outcome $S(\rho, \boldsymbol{v})$ if

$$\lambda_L(S) \le \hat{f}(S) \le \lambda_U(S) . \tag{18}$$

Writing (18) explicitly, we obtain

$$\hat{f}(\rho, \boldsymbol{v}) \ \ge\ \lambda_L(\rho, \boldsymbol{v}) = \frac{\underline{f}(\rho, \boldsymbol{v}) - \int_\rho^1 \hat{f}(u, \boldsymbol{v}) du}{\rho} \tag{19a}$$

$$\begin{aligned} \hat{f}(\rho, \boldsymbol{v}) &\le \lambda_U(\rho, \boldsymbol{v}) \\ &= \sup_{\boldsymbol{z} \in S^*} \inf_{0 \le \eta < \rho} \frac{\underline{f}(\eta, \boldsymbol{z}) - \int_\rho^1 \hat{f}(u, \boldsymbol{v}) du}{\rho - \eta} \end{aligned} \tag{19b}$$

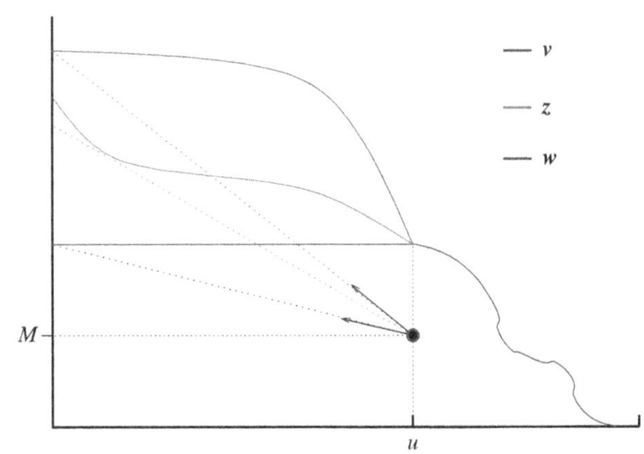

Figure 1: Lower bound functions for vectors $\boldsymbol{v}, \boldsymbol{z}, \boldsymbol{w}$. Outcomes are consistent for all $x \ge u$: $S(x, \boldsymbol{v}) = S(x, \boldsymbol{z}) = S(x, \boldsymbol{w}) \equiv S_x$. The figure illustrates the $\boldsymbol{y}$-optimal estimates $\lambda(u, \boldsymbol{y}, M)$ at u given M for $\mathbf{y} \in \{\boldsymbol{v}, \boldsymbol{z}, \boldsymbol{w}\}$. The estimates are the negated slopes of the lower hull of the point (u, M) and the lower bound function $\underline{f}^{(\boldsymbol{y})}$. The optimal range at S_u given M is lower-bounded by $\boldsymbol{w}$, that is $\lambda_L(S_u, M) = \lambda(u, \boldsymbol{w}, M)$, and upper-bounded by $\boldsymbol{v}$, $\lambda_U(S_u, M) = \lambda(u, \boldsymbol{v}, M)$. The figure illustrates the general property that the optimal range is lower bounded by the w which satisfies $f(\boldsymbol{w}) = \underline{f}(\boldsymbol{w}, u)$.

Two special solutions that we study are the *L^* estimator* ($\hat{f}^{(L)}$, see Section 4) and the *U^* estimator* ($\hat{f}^{(U)}$, see Section 6), which respectively solve (19a) and (19b) with equalities. For all $\rho \in (0,1]$ and $\boldsymbol{v}$, $\hat{f}^{(L)}$ minimizes and $\hat{f}^{(U)}$ maximizes $\int_\rho^1 \hat{f}(u,\boldsymbol{v})du$ among all solutions of (18).

We show that being in-range (satisfying (18) for all outcomes S) is sufficient for nonnegativity and unbiasedness. The proof can be found in [9].

LEMMA 3.1. *If f satisfies* (7) *then any in-range estimator is unbiased and nonnegative.*

We next show that being in-range is necessary for optimality. For our analysis of order-optimality (Section 5), we need to slightly refine the notion of admissibility to be with respect to a partially specified estimator $\hat{f}$ and a subset of data vectors $Z \subset \mathbf{V}$.

An extension of $\hat{f}$ that is fully specified for all vectors in Z is admissible on Z if any other extension with strictly lower variance on at least one $\boldsymbol{v} \in Z$ has a strictly higher variance on at least one $\boldsymbol{z} \in Z$. We say that a partial specification is in-range *with respect to Z* if:

$$\forall \boldsymbol{v} \in Z, \text{ for } \rho \in (0, \rho_v] \text{ almost everywhere},$$
$$\inf_{\boldsymbol{z}\in Z\cap S^*(\rho,\boldsymbol{v})} \lambda(\rho,\boldsymbol{z}) \le \hat{f}(\rho,\boldsymbol{v}) \le \sup_{\boldsymbol{z}\in Z\cap S^*(\rho,\boldsymbol{v})} \lambda(\rho,\boldsymbol{z}) \quad (20)$$

We show that a necessary condition for admissibility with respect to a partial specification and Z is that almost everywhere, estimates for outcomes consistent with vectors in Z are in-range for Z. Formally: (The proof can be found in [9].)

THEOREM 3.1. *An extension is admissible on Z only if* (20) *holds.*

4. THE L* ESTIMATOR

The L* estimator, $\hat{f}^{(L)}$, is the solution of (19a) with equalities, obtaining values that are minimum in the optimal range. Formally, it is the solution of the integral equation $\forall \boldsymbol{v} \in \mathbf{V}, \forall \rho \in (0,1]$:

$$\hat{f}^{(L)}(\rho,\boldsymbol{v}) = \frac{\underline{f}^{(\boldsymbol{v})}(\rho) - \int_\rho^1 \hat{f}^{(L)}(u,\boldsymbol{v})du}{\rho} \quad (21)$$

Geometrically, as visualized in Figure 2, the L* estimate on an outcome $S(\rho,\boldsymbol{v})$ is exactly the slope value that if maintained for outcomes $S(u,\boldsymbol{v})$ ($u \in (0,\rho]$), would yield an expected estimate of $\underline{f}(S)$. We derive a convenient expression for the L* estimator, which enables us to derive explicit forms or compute it for any function f. We show that the L* estimator is 4-competitive and that it is the unique admissible monotone estimator. We also show it is order-optimal with respect to the natural order that prioritizes data vectors with lower $f(\boldsymbol{v})$.

Fixing $\boldsymbol{v}$, (21) is a first-order differential equation for $F(\rho) \equiv \int_\rho^1 \hat{f}^{(L)}(u,\boldsymbol{v})du$ and the initial condition $F(1) = 0$. Since the lower bound function $\underline{f}^{(\boldsymbol{v})}$ is monotonic and bounded, it is continuous (and differentiable) almost everywhere. Therefore, the equation with the initial condition has a unique solution:

LEMMA 4.1.

$$\hat{f}^{(L)}(\rho,\boldsymbol{v}) = \frac{\underline{f}^{(\boldsymbol{v})}(\rho)}{\rho} - \int_\rho^1 \frac{\underline{f}^{(\boldsymbol{v})}(u)}{u^2}du \quad (22)$$

(23)

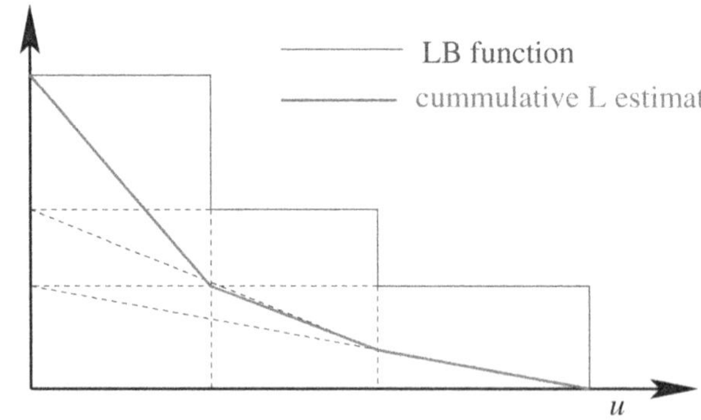

Figure 2: An example lower bound function $\underline{f}^{(\boldsymbol{v})}(u)$ with 3 steps and the respective cummulative L estimate $\int_u^1 \hat{f}^{(L)}(u,\boldsymbol{v})du$. The estimate $\hat{f}^{(L)}$ is the negated slope and in this case is also a step function with 3 steps.

When $\underline{f}^{(\boldsymbol{v})}(1) = 0$, which we can assume without loss of generality[3]*, the solution has the simpler form:*

$$\hat{f}^{(L)}(\rho,\boldsymbol{v}) = -\int_\rho^1 \frac{\frac{d\underline{f}^{(\boldsymbol{v})}(u)}{du}}{u}du \quad (24)$$

We show a tight bound of 4 for the competitive ratio for $\hat{f}^{(L)}$, meaning that it is at most 4 for all functions f and for any $\epsilon > 0$, there exists a function f on which the ratio is no less than $4-\epsilon$.

THEOREM 4.1.

$$\sup_{f,\boldsymbol{v}\,|\,\int_0^1 \hat{f}^{(\boldsymbol{v})}(u)^2du<\infty} \frac{\int_0^1 \hat{f}^{(L)}(u,\boldsymbol{v})^2du}{\int_0^1 \hat{f}^{(\boldsymbol{v})}(u)^2du} = 4\,,$$

We present a family of functions for which the supermum of this ratio is 4. We use the domain $\mathbf{V} = [0,1]$, a PPS sampling scheme with $\tau(u) = u$, and the function $f(v) = \frac{1}{1-p} - \frac{v^{1-p}}{1-p}$ for $p \in [0, 0.5)$. For the data $v = 0$ we have the following convex lower bound function

$$\underline{f}(u,0) = \frac{1}{1-p} - \frac{u^{1-p}}{1-p}\,.$$

Being convex, this lower bound function is equal to its lower hull. Therefore, by taking its negated derivative, we get $\hat{f}^{(0)}(u) = 1/u^p$. The function $\hat{f}^{(0)}$ is square integrable when $p < 0.5$:

$$\int_0^1 \hat{f}^{(0)}(u)^2du = \int_0^1 1/u^{2p}du = \frac{1}{1-2p}\,.$$

From (24), the L* estimator on outcomes consistent with $v = 0$ for $p \in (0, 0.5)$ is

$$\hat{f}^{(L)}(x,0) = \int_x^1 \frac{1}{u^{1+p}} = \frac{1}{p}\left(\frac{1}{x^p} - 1\right).$$

Hence,

$$\int_0^1 \hat{f}^{(L)}(u,0)^2du = \frac{1}{p^2}\int_0^1 \left(\frac{1}{u^{2p}} - \frac{2}{u^p} + 1\right)du$$
$$= \frac{1}{p^2}\left(\frac{1}{1-2p} - \frac{2}{1-p} + 1\right) = \frac{2}{(1-2p)(1-p)}\,.$$

[3]Otherwise, we can instead estimate the function $f(\boldsymbol{v}) - \underline{f}^{(\boldsymbol{v})}(1)$, which satisfies this assumption, and then add a fixed value of $\underline{f}^{(\boldsymbol{v})}(1)$ to the resulting estimate.

We obtain the ratio

$$\frac{\int_0^1 \hat{f}^{(L)}(u,0)^2 du}{\int_0^1 \hat{f}^{(0)}(u)^2 du} = \frac{2}{1-p} \leq 4 \, .$$

The ratio approaches 4 when $p \to 0.5^-$.

We conclude the proof of Theorem 4.1 using the following lemma that shows that if $\hat{f}^{(\boldsymbol{v})}(u)$ is square integrable, that is, (8) holds, then $\hat{f}^{(L)}(u,\boldsymbol{v})$ is also square integrable and the ratio between these integrals is at most 4.

LEMMA 4.2.

$$\forall \boldsymbol{v}, \int_0^1 \hat{f}^{(\boldsymbol{v})}(u)^2 du < \infty \implies \frac{\int_0^1 \hat{f}^{(L)}(u,\boldsymbol{v})^2 du}{\int_0^1 \hat{f}^{(\boldsymbol{v})}(u)^2 du} \leq 4 \, .$$

PROOF. Fixing $\boldsymbol{v}$, the function $\hat{f}^{(\boldsymbol{v})}$ only depends on the lower hull of the lower bound function $\underline{f}^{(\boldsymbol{v})}(u)$. The estimator $\hat{f}^{(L)}$ depends on the lower bound function $\underline{f}$ and can be different for different lower bound functions with the same lower hull. Fixing the lower hull, the variance of the L* estimator is maximized for f such that $\underline{f}^{(\boldsymbol{v})} \equiv H_{\underline{f}}^{(\boldsymbol{v})}$. It therefore suffices to consider convex $\underline{f}^{(\boldsymbol{v})}(u)$, that is, $\frac{d^2 \underline{f}^{(\boldsymbol{v})}(u)}{d^2 u} > 0$ for which we have $\hat{f}^{(\boldsymbol{v})}(u) = -\frac{d\underline{f}^{(\boldsymbol{v})}(u)}{du}$.

Recall that $\hat{f}^{(\boldsymbol{v})}(u)$ is monotone non-increasing. From (24), we have $\hat{f}^{(L)}(\rho,\boldsymbol{v}) = -\int_\rho^1 \frac{\frac{d\underline{f}^{(\boldsymbol{v})}(u)}{du}}{u} du$.

To establish our claim, it suffices to show that for all monotone, non increasing, square integrable functions $g : (0, 1]$,

$$\frac{\int_0^1 (\int_x^1 \frac{g(u)}{u} du)^2 dx}{\int_0^1 g(x)^2 dx} \leq 4 \qquad (25)$$

Define $h(x) = \int_x^1 \frac{g(u)}{u} du$.

$$\int_0^1 h^2(x)dx = -\int_0^1 \int_x^1 2h(y)h'(y)dydx$$
$$= -\int_0^1 \int_0^y 2h(y)h'(y)dxdy = -2\int_0^1 h(y)h'(y)\int_0^y dxdy$$
$$= -2\int_0^1 h(y)h'(y)ydy = 2\int_0^1 h(y)\frac{g(y)}{y}ydy$$
$$= 2\int_0^1 h(y)g(y)dy \leq 2\sqrt{\int_0^1 h^2(y)dy}\sqrt{\int_0^1 g^2(y)dy}$$

The first equality uses $h(1) = 0$. The third uses $h'(x) = -g(x)/x$. The inequality uses Cauchy-Schwartz. Finally, to obtain (25), we divide both sides by $\sqrt{\int_0^1 h^2(y)dy}$.

□

THEOREM 4.2. *The estimator $\hat{f}^{(L)}$ is monotone. Moreover, it is the unique admissible monotone estimator and dominates all monotone estimators.*

PROOF. Recall that an estimator $\hat{f}$ is monotone if and only if, for any data $\boldsymbol{v}$, the estimate $\hat{f}(\rho,\boldsymbol{v})$ is non-increasing with ρ. To show monotonicity of the L* estimator, we rewrite (22) to obtain

$$\hat{f}^{(L)}(\rho,\boldsymbol{v}) = \underline{f}^{(\boldsymbol{v})}(\rho) + \int_\rho^1 \frac{\underline{f}^{(\boldsymbol{v})}(\rho) - \underline{f}^{(\boldsymbol{v})}(x)}{x^2} dx \, , \qquad (26)$$

which is clearly non-increasing with ρ.

We now show that $\hat{f}^{(L)}$ dominates all monotone estimators (and hence is the unique admissible monotone estimator). By definition, a monotone estimator $\hat{f}$ can not exceed λ_L on any outcome, that is, it must satisfy the inequalities $\forall \boldsymbol{v}$, $\forall \rho \in [0,1]$:

$$\rho\hat{f}(\rho,\boldsymbol{v}) + \int_\rho^1 \hat{f}(u,\boldsymbol{v})du \leq \inf_{\boldsymbol{z}\in S^*(\rho,\boldsymbol{v})} \int_0^1 \hat{f}(u,\boldsymbol{z})du =$$
$$\inf_{\boldsymbol{z}\in S^*(\rho,\boldsymbol{v})} f(\boldsymbol{z}) = \underline{f}^{(\boldsymbol{v})}(\rho) \, . \qquad (27)$$

Estimator $\hat{f}^{(L)}$ satisfies (27) with equalities. If there is a monotone estimator $\hat{f}$ which is not equivalent to $\hat{f}^{(L)}$, that is, for some $\boldsymbol{v}$, the integral is strictly smaller than the integral of $\hat{f}^{(L)}$ on some interval $(\rho-\epsilon,\rho)$ ($\epsilon > 0$ may depend on $\boldsymbol{v}$), we can obtain a monotone estimator that strictly dominates $\hat{f}$ by decreasing the estimate for $u \leq \rho - \epsilon$ and increasing it for $u > \rho - \epsilon$. The variance decreases because we decrease the estimate on higher values and increase on lower values. □

Example 4 contains an example derivation of the L* estimator. See [9] for a proof of the order-optimality of L* with respect to $\prec$ which prioritizes vectors with lower $f(\boldsymbol{v})$.

5. ORDER-OPTIMALITY

We identify conditions on f and $\prec$ under which a $\prec^+$-optimal estimator exists and specify this estimator as a solution of a set of equations. Our derivations of $\prec^+$-optimal estimators follow the intuition to require the estimate on an outcome S to be $\boldsymbol{v}$-optimal with respect to the $\prec$-minimal vector that is consistent with the outcome:

$$\forall S = S(\rho,\boldsymbol{v}), \; \hat{f}(S) = \lambda(\rho, \min_\prec(S^*)) \, . \qquad (28)$$

When $\prec$ is a total order and V is finite, $\min_\prec(S^*)$ is unique and (28) is well defined. Moreover, as long as f has a nonnegative unbiased estimator, a solution (28) always exists and is $\prec^+$-optimal. We preview a simple construction of the solution: Process vectors in increasing $\prec$ order, iteratively building a partially defined nonnegative estimator. When processing $\boldsymbol{v}$, the estimator is already defined for $S(u,\boldsymbol{v})$ for $u \geq \rho_v$, for some $\rho_v \in (0,1]$. We extend it to the outcomes $S(u,\boldsymbol{v})$ for $u \leq \rho_v$ using the $\boldsymbol{v}$-optimal extension $\hat{f}^{(\boldsymbol{v},\rho_v,M)}(u)$, where $M = \int_{\rho_v}^1 \hat{f}(u,\boldsymbol{v})du$ (see Theorem 2.1).

We now formulate conditions that will allow us to establish $\prec^+$-optimality of a solution of (28) in more general settings. These conditions always hold when $\prec$ is a total order and V is finite. Generally,

$$\min_\prec(S^*) = \{\boldsymbol{z} \in S^* | \neg\exists \boldsymbol{w} \in S^*, \; \boldsymbol{w} \prec \boldsymbol{z}\}$$

is a *set* and (28) is well defined when $\forall S$, this set is not empty and $\lambda(\rho, \min_\prec(S^*))$ is unique, that is, the value $\lambda(\rho,\boldsymbol{z})$ is the same for all $\prec$-minimal vectors $\boldsymbol{z} \in \min_\prec(S^*)$. A sufficient condition for this is that

$$\forall\rho\,\forall\boldsymbol{v}\,\forall x \in (0, \underline{f}(\rho,\boldsymbol{v})]\;\forall \boldsymbol{z},\boldsymbol{w} \in \min_\prec(S^*(\rho,\boldsymbol{v})),$$
$$\inf_{\eta<\rho} \frac{f(\eta,\boldsymbol{z}) - x}{\rho - \eta} = \inf_{\eta<\rho} \frac{f(\eta,\boldsymbol{w}) - x}{\rho - \eta} \qquad (29)$$

In this case, the respective Equation (28) on $u \in (0,\rho]$ are the same for all $\boldsymbol{z} \in \min_\prec(S^*)$ and thus so are the estimate values $\hat{f}(u,\boldsymbol{z})$.

We say that $Z \subset V$ is *$\prec$-bounded* if

$$\forall \boldsymbol{v} \in Z \; \exists \boldsymbol{z} \in \min_\prec(Z), \; \boldsymbol{z} \preceq \boldsymbol{v} \qquad (30)$$

That is, for all $\boldsymbol{z} \in Z$, $\boldsymbol{z}$ is $\prec$-minimal or is preceded by some vector that is $\prec$-minimal in Z.

Example 4 L* and U* estimates for Example 3

We compute the L* and U* estimators for RG_{p+} for the sampling scheme and data in Example 3. For the two vectors $(0.6, 0.2)$ and $(0.6, 0)$, both the L* and U* estimates are 0 when $u \geq 0.6$, this is necessary from unbiasedness and nonnegativity because for these outcomes $\exists \boldsymbol{v} \in S^*, \text{RG}_{p+}(\boldsymbol{v}) = 0$. Otherwise, the L* estimate is $\hat{\text{RG}}^{(L)}_{p+}(S) = (v_1 - v'_2)^p / v'_2 - \int_{v'_2}^{v_1} \frac{(v_1 - x)^p}{x^2} dx$, where $v'_2 = u$ when $S = \{1\}$ and $v'_2 = v_2$ when $S = \{1, 2\}$. When $p \geq 1$, the U* estimate is $\hat{\text{RG}}^{(U)}_{p+}(S) = p(v_1 - u)^{p-1}$ when $u \in (v_2, v_1]$ and 0 when $u \leq v_2 < v_1$. When $p \leq 1$ the U* estimate is v_1^{p-1} when $u \in (v_2, v_1]$ and $\frac{(v_1 - v_2)^p - v_1^{p-1}(v_1 - v_2)}{v_2}$ when $u \leq v_2 < v_1$.
The figure also include the $\boldsymbol{v}$-optimal estimates, discussed in Example 3. When $v_2 = 0$, the U* estimates are $\boldsymbol{v}$-optimal. The L* estimate is not bounded when $v_2 = 0$ (but has bounded variance and is competitive).

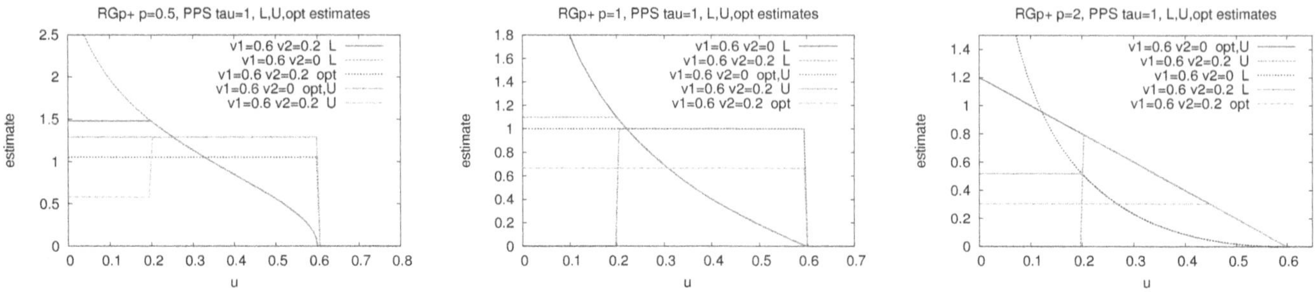

We say that an outcome S is $\prec$-bounded if S^* is $\prec$-bounded, that is,

$$\forall \boldsymbol{v} \in S^* \; \exists \boldsymbol{z} \in \min_{\prec}(S^*), \; \boldsymbol{z} \preceq \boldsymbol{v} \tag{31}$$

When all outcomes $S(u, \boldsymbol{v})$ are $\prec$-bounded, we say that a set of vectors R *represents* $\boldsymbol{v}$ if any outcome consistent with $\boldsymbol{v}$ has a $\prec$-minimal vector in R:

$$\forall u \in (0, 1], \exists \boldsymbol{z} \in R, \; \boldsymbol{z} \in \min_{\prec}(S^*(u, \boldsymbol{v})) \, .$$

We now show that we can obtain a $\prec^+$-optimal estimator if every vector $\boldsymbol{v}$ has a set of finite size that represents it. Exampe derivation and the treatment of continuous domains can be found in [9].

LEMMA 5.1. *If f satisfies* (7), (29), (31) *and*

$$\forall \boldsymbol{v}, \; \min\{|R| \mid \forall u \in (0, 1], \exists \boldsymbol{z} \in R, \; \boldsymbol{z} \in \min_{\prec} S^*(u, \boldsymbol{v})\} < \infty \, ,$$

then a $\prec^+$-optimal estimator exists and must be equivalent to a solution of (28).

PROOF. We provide an explicit construction of a $\prec^+$-optimal estimator for f.

Fixing $\boldsymbol{v}$, we select a finite set of representatives. We can map the representatives (or a subset of them) to distinct subintervals covering $(0, 1]$. The subintervals have the form $(a_i, a_{i-1}]$ where $0 = a_n < \cdots a_1 < a_0 = 1$ such that a representative $\boldsymbol{z}$ that is minimal for $(a_i, a_{i-1}]$ is not minimal for $u \leq a_i$. Such a mapping can always be obtained since from (2), each vector is consistent with an open interval of the form $(a, 1]$, and thus if $\prec$-minimum at $S^*(u, \boldsymbol{v})$ (we must have $u > a$) it must be $\prec$-minimum for $S^*(x, \boldsymbol{v})$ for $x \in (a, u]$. Thus, the region on which $\boldsymbol{z}$ is in $\min_{\prec} S^*(u, \boldsymbol{v})$ is open to the left. We can always choose a mapping such that the left boundary of this region corresponds to a_i.

Let $\boldsymbol{z}^{(i)}$ ($i \in [n]$) be the representative mapped to outcomes $S(u, \boldsymbol{v})$ where $u \in (a_i, a_{i-1}]$. Since $S^*(u, \boldsymbol{v})$ is monotone non-decreasing with u, $i < j$ implies that $\boldsymbol{z}^{(i)} \prec \boldsymbol{z}^{(j)}$ or that they are incomparable in the partial order.

We construct a partially specified nonnegative estimator in steps, by solving (28) iteratively for the vectors $\boldsymbol{z}^{(i)}$. Initially we invoke Theorem 2.1 to obtain estimate values for $S(u, \boldsymbol{z}^{(1)})$ $u \in (0, 1]$ that minimize the variance for $\boldsymbol{z}^{(1)}$. The result is a partially specified nonnegative estimator. In particular for $\boldsymbol{v}$, the estimator is now specified for outcomes $S(u, \boldsymbol{v})$ where $u \in (a_1, 1]$. Any modification of this estimator on a subinterval of $(a_1, 1]$ with positive measure will strictly increase the variance for $\boldsymbol{z}^{(1)}$ (or result in an estimator that can not be completed to a nonnegative unbiased one).

After step i, we have a partially specified nonnegative estimator that is specified for $S(u, \boldsymbol{v})$ for $u \in (a_i, 1]$. The estimator is fully specified for $\boldsymbol{z}^{(j)}$ $j \leq i$ and is $\prec^+$-optimal on these vectors in the sense that any other partially specified nonnegative estimator that is fully specified for $\boldsymbol{z}^{(j)}$ $j \leq i$ and has strictly lower variance on some $\boldsymbol{z}^{(j)}$ ($j \leq i$) must have strictly higher variance on some $\boldsymbol{z}^{(h)}$ such that $h < j$.

We now invoke Theorem 2.1 with respect to the vector $\boldsymbol{z}^{(i+1)}$. The estimator is partially specified for $S(u, \boldsymbol{z}^{(i+1)})$ on $u > a_i$ and we obtain estimate values for the outcomes $S(u, \boldsymbol{z}^{(i+1)})$ for $u \in (0, a_i]$ that constitute a partially specified nonnegative estimator with minimum variance for $\boldsymbol{z}^{(i+1)}$. Note again that this completion is unique (up to equivalence). This extension now defines $S(u, \boldsymbol{v})$ for $u \in (a_{i+1}, 1]$.

Lastly, we must have $f(\boldsymbol{z}^{(n)}) = f(\boldsymbol{v})$ because $f(\boldsymbol{z}^{(n)}) < f(\boldsymbol{v})$ implies that (7) is violated for $\boldsymbol{v}$ whereas the reverse inequality implies that (7) is violated for $\boldsymbol{z}^{(n)}$. Since at step n the estimator is specified for all outcomes $S(u, \boldsymbol{z}^{(n)})$ and unbiased, it is unbiased for $\boldsymbol{v}$.

The estimator is invariant to the choice of the representative sets $R_{\boldsymbol{v}}$ for $\boldsymbol{v} \in V$ and also remains the same if we restrict $\prec$ so that it includes only relations between $\boldsymbol{v}$ and $R_{\boldsymbol{v}}$.

We so far showed that there is a unique, up to equivalence, partially specified nonnegative estimator that is $\prec^+$ optimal with respect to a vector $\boldsymbol{v}$ and all vectors it depends on. Consider now all outcomes $S(u, \boldsymbol{v})$, for all u and $\boldsymbol{v}$, arranged according to the containment order on $S^*(u, \boldsymbol{v})$ according to decreasing u values with branching points when $S^*(u, \boldsymbol{v})$ changes. If for two vectors $\boldsymbol{v}$ and $\boldsymbol{z}$, the sets of outcomes $S(u, \boldsymbol{v}), u \in (0, 1]$ and $S(u, \boldsymbol{z}), u \in (0, 1]$ intersect, the intersection must be equal for $u > \rho$ for some $\rho < 1$. In this case the estimator values computed with respect to either $\boldsymbol{z}$ or $\boldsymbol{v}$ would be identical for $u \in (\rho, 1]$. Also note that partially specified nonnegative solutions on different branches are independent. Therefore, solutions with respect to different vectors $\boldsymbol{v}$ can be consistently combined to a fully specified estimator. □

6. THE U* ESTIMATOR

The estimator $\hat{f}^{(U)}$ satisfies (19b) with equality.

$$\forall S(\rho, \boldsymbol{v}),\ \hat{f}(\rho, \boldsymbol{v}) = \sup_{\boldsymbol{z}\in S^*} \inf_{0\leq\eta<\rho} \frac{\underline{f}(\eta, \boldsymbol{z}) - \int_\rho^1 \hat{f}(u, \boldsymbol{v})du}{\rho - \eta} \quad (32)$$

The U* estimator is not always admissible. We do show, however, that under a natural condition, it is order-optimal with respect to an order that prioritizes vectors with higher f values (and hence also admissible). The condition states that for all $S(\rho, \boldsymbol{v})$ and $\eta < \rho$, the supremum of the lower bound function $\underline{f}(\eta, \boldsymbol{z})$ over $\boldsymbol{z} \in S^*$ is attained (in the limiting sense) at vectors that maximize f on S^*. Formally:

$$\forall \eta < \rho,\ \lim_{x\to\overline{f}(S)} \sup_{\boldsymbol{z}\in S^* | f(\boldsymbol{z})\geq x} \underline{f}(\eta, \boldsymbol{z}) = \sup_{\boldsymbol{z}\in S^*} \underline{f}(\eta, \boldsymbol{z}) , \quad (33)$$

where $\overline{f}(S) = \sup_{\boldsymbol{z}\in S^*} f(\boldsymbol{z})$.

LEMMA 6.1. *If f satisfies* (33), *then the U* estimator is $\prec^+$-optimal with respect to the order $\boldsymbol{z} \prec \boldsymbol{v} \iff f(\boldsymbol{z}) > f(\boldsymbol{v})$.*

The condition (33) is satisfied by RG_p and RG_{p+}. In this case, the conditions of Lemma 5.1 are also satisfied and thus the U* estimator is $\prec^+$ optimal.

7. CONCLUSION

We define monotone sampling, and discuss its applications as a summarization tool of massive data. We propose general derivations of estimators with worst-case (competitiveness) or common-case (customization) guarantees.

Some interesting future research directions are (i) bounding the *universal ratio* for monotone sampling: the lowest ratio we can guarantee when an estimator with finite variances exists. Our L* estimator implies an upper bound of 4, and we have examples where the ratio is at least 1.4. (ii) Efficient constructions of estimators with *instance optimal* competitive ratio. (iii) Study monotone sampling with several independent seeds, which captures independent sampling [15].

Finally, we mention applications of our estimator constructions which include estimating L_p difference from sampled data [7] and sktech-based similarity estimation in social networks [10].

Acknowledgement

We thank Micha Sharir for his help in the proof of Lemma 4.2 and Haim Kaplan for many comments and helpful feedback.

8. REFERENCES

[1] K. S. Beyer, P. J. Haas, B. Reinwald, Y. Sismanis, and R. Gemulla. On synopses for distinct-value estimation under multiset operations. In *SIGMOD*, pages 199–210. ACM, 2007.

[2] K. R. W. Brewer, L. J. Early, and S. F. Joyce. Selecting several samples from a single population. *Australian Journal of Statistics*, 14(3):231–239, 1972.

[3] A. Z. Broder. On the resemblance and containment of documents. In *Proceedings of the Compression and Complexity of Sequences*, pages 21–29. IEEE, 1997.

[4] A. Z. Broder. Identifying and filtering near-duplicate documents. In *Proc.of the 11th Annual Symposium on Combinatorial Pattern Matching*, volume 1848 of *LNCS*, pages 1–10. Springer, 2000.

[5] J. W. Byers, J. Considine, M. Mitzenmacher, and S. Rost. Informed content delivery across adaptive overlay networks. *IEEE/ACM Trans. Netw.*, 12(5):767–780, October 2004.

[6] E. Cohen. Size-estimation framework with applications to transitive closure and reachability. *J. Comput. System Sci.*, 55:441–453, 1997.

[7] E. Cohen. Distance queries from sampled data: Accurate and efficient. Technical Report cs.DS/1203.4903, arXiv, 2012.

[8] E. Cohen. All-distances sketches, revisited: Hip estimators for massive graphs analysis. In *PODS*. ACM, 2014.

[9] E. Cohen. Estimation for monotone sampling: Competitiveness and customization. Technical Report cs.ST/1212.0243, arXiv, 2014.

[10] E. Cohen, D. Delling, F. Fuchs, A. Goldberg, M. Goldszmidt, and R. Werneck. Scalable similarity estimation in social networks: Closeness, node labels, and random edge lengths. In *COSN*, 2013.

[11] E. Cohen and H. Kaplan. Spatially-decaying aggregation over a network: model and algorithms. *JCSS.*, 73:265–288, 2007. Full version of a SIGMOD 2004 paper.

[12] E. Cohen and H. Kaplan. Summarizing data using bottom-k sketches. In *ACM PODC*, 2007.

[13] E. Cohen and H. Kaplan. Tighter estimation using bottom-k sketches. In *Proceedings of the 34th VLDB Conference*, 2008.

[14] E. Cohen and H. Kaplan. Leveraging discarded samples for tighter estimation of multiple-set aggregates. In *ACM SIGMETRICS*, 2009.

[15] E. Cohen and H. Kaplan. Get the most out of your sample: Optimal unbiased estimators using partial information. In ACM PODS, 2011. `http://arxiv.org/abs/1203.4903`.

[16] E. Cohen and H. Kaplan. What you can do with coordinated samples. In RANDOM, 2013. `http://arxiv.org/abs/1206.5637`.

[17] E. Cohen, H. Kaplan, and S. Sen. Coordinated weighted sampling for estimating aggregates over multiple weight assignments. VLDB 2009. full version: `http://arxiv.org/abs/0906.4560`.

[18] E. Cohen, Y.-M. Wang, and G. Suri. When piecewise determinism is almost true. In *Proc. Pacific Rim International Symposium on Fault-Tolerant Systems*, pages 66–71, December 1995.

[19] A. Das, M. Datar, A. Garg, and S. Rajaram. Google news personalization: scalable online collaborative filtering. In *WWW*, 2007.

[20] N. Duffield, M. Thorup, and C. Lund. Priority sampling for estimating arbitrary subset sums. *J. ACM*, 54(6), 2007.

[21] P. Gibbons and S. Tirthapura. Estimating simple functions on the union of data streams. In ACM SPAA 2001.

[22] P. B. Gibbons. Distinct sampling for highly-accurate answers to distinct values queries and event reports. In VLDB 2001.

[23] M. Hadjieleftheriou, X. Yu, N. Koudas, and D. Srivastava. Hashed samples: Selectivity estimators for set similarity selection queries. In VLDB 2008.

[24] J. Hájek. *Sampling from a finite population*. Marcel Dekker, New York, 1981.

[25] D. G. Horvitz and D. J. Thompson. A generalization of sampling without replacement from a finite universe. *Journal of the American Statistical Association*, 47(260):663–685, 1952.

[26] D. E. Knuth. *The Art of Computer Programming, Vol 2, Seminumerical Algorithms*. Addison-Wesley, 1st edition, 1968.

[27] J. Lanke. On UMV-estimators in survey sampling. *Metrika*, 20(1):196–202, 1973.

[28] P. Li, , K. W. Church, and T. Hastie. One sketch for all: Theory and application of conditional random sampling. In *NIPS*, 2008.

[29] D. Mosk-Aoyama and D. Shah. Computing separable functions via gossip. In *ACM PODC*, 2006.

[30] P. Mukhopandhyay. *Theory and Methods of Survey Sampling*. PHI learning, New Delhi, 2 edition, 2008.

[31] E. Ohlsson. Sequential poisson sampling. *J. Official Statistics*, 14(2):149–162, 1998.

[32] E. Ohlsson. Coordination of pps samples over time. In *The 2nd International Conference on Establishment Surveys*, pages 255–264. American Statistical Association, 2000.

[33] B. Rosén. Asymptotic theory for successive sampling with varying probabilities without replacement, I. *The Annals of Mathematical Statistics*, 43(2):373–397, 1972.

[34] B. Rosén. Asymptotic theory for order sampling. *J. Statistical Planning and Inference*, 62(2):135–158, 1997.

[35] P. J. Saavedra. Fixed sample size pps approximations with a permanent random number. In *Proc. of the Section on Survey Research Methods, Alexandria VA*, pages 697–700. American Statistical Association, 1995.

[36] J.S. Vitter. Random sampling with a reservoir. *ACM Trans. Math. Softw.*, 11(1):37–57, 1985.

Distributed Algorithms for the Lovász Local Lemma and Graph Coloring*

Kai-Min Chung
Academia Sinica
Taipei, Taiwan
kmchung@iis.sinica.edu.tw

Seth Pettie
University of Michigan
Ann Arbor, MI
pettie@umich.edu

Hsin-Hao Su
University of Michigan
Ann Arbor, MI
hsinhao@umich.edu

ABSTRACT

The Lovász Local Lemma (LLL), introduced by Erdős and Lovász in 1975, is a powerful tool of the probabilistic method that allows one to prove that a set of n "bad" events do not happen with non-zero probability, provided that the events have limited dependence. However, the LLL itself does not suggest how to find a point avoiding all bad events. Since the work of Beck (1991) there has been a sustained effort to find a constructive proof (i.e. an algorithm) for the LLL or weaker versions of it. In a major breakthrough Moser and Tardos (2010) showed that a point avoiding all bad events can be found efficiently. They also proposed a distributed/parallel version of their algorithm that requires $O(\log^2 n)$ rounds of communication in a distributed network.

In this paper we provide two new distributed algorithms for the LLL that improve on both the efficiency and simplicity of the Moser-Tardos algorithm. For clarity we express our results in terms of the symmetric LLL though both algorithms deal with the asymmetric version as well. Let p bound the probability of any bad event and d be the maximum degree in the dependency graph of the bad events. When $epd^2 < 1$ we give a truly simple LLL algorithm running in $O(\log_{1/epd^2} n)$ rounds. Under the tighter condition $ep(d+1) < 1$, we give a slightly slower algorithm running in $O(\log^2 d \cdot \log_{1/ep(d+1)} n)$ rounds. Furthermore, we give an algorithm that runs in *sublogarithmic* rounds under the condition $p \cdot f(d) < 1$, where $f(d)$ is an exponential function of d. Although the conditions of the LLL are locally verifiable, we prove that any distributed LLL algorithm requires $\Omega(\log^* n)$ rounds.

In many graph coloring problems the existence of a valid coloring is established by one or more applications of the LLL. Using our LLL algorithms, we give logarithmic-time distributed algorithms for frugal coloring, defective coloring, coloring girth-4 (triangle-free) and girth-5 graphs, edge coloring, and list coloring.

*The last two authors are supported by NSF grants CCF-0746673, CCF-1217338, and CNS-1318294 and a grant from the US-Israel Binational Science Foundation. Part of the work was done while visiting MADALGO at Aarhus University, supported by Danish National Research Foundation grant DNRF84.

PODC'14 July 15–18, 2014, Paris, France
Copyright 2014 ACM 978-1-4503-2944-6/14/07 ...$15.00.
http://dx.doi.org/10.1145/2611462.2611465.

Categories and Subject Descriptors

F.2.2 [**Analysis of Algorithms and Problem Complexity**]: Nonnumerical Algorithms and Problems—*computations on discrete structures*; G.2.2 [**Discrete Mathematics**]: Graph Theory—*network problems*

Keywords

Lovász Local Lemma; distributed graph coloring; constructive algorithm; probabilistic method; locality

1. INTRODUCTION

Consider a system $\mathcal{P}$ of independent random variables and a set $\mathcal{A}$ of n *bad* events, where each $A \in \mathcal{A}$ depends solely on some subset $\text{vbl}(A) \subseteq \mathcal{P}$. For example, in a hypergraph 2-coloring instance, $\mathcal{P}$ represents the vertex colors and $\mathcal{A}$ the events in which an edge is monochromatic. The dependency graph $G_{\mathcal{A}} = (\mathcal{A}, \{(A,B) \mid \text{vbl}(A) \cap \text{vbl}(B) \neq \emptyset\})$ includes edges between events if and only if they depend on at least one common variable. Let $\Gamma(A)$ be A's neighborhood in $G_{\mathcal{A}}$ and $\Gamma^+(A) = \Gamma(A) \cup \{A\}$ be its inclusive neighborhood. The (general, asymmetric) LLL states [11, 31] that if there is a function $x : \mathcal{A} \to (0,1)$ such that

$$\Pr(A) \leq x(A) \cdot \prod_{B \in \Gamma(A)} (1 - x(B))$$

then $\Pr(\bigcap_{A \in \mathcal{A}} \overline{A}) > 0$, that is, there is a *satisfying assignment* to the underlying variables in which no bad events occur. The symmetric LLL is a useful corollary of the general LLL. If p and d are such that $\Pr(A) \leq p$ and $|\Gamma(A)| \leq d$ for all A, and $ep(d+1) < 1$, then $\Pr(\bigcap_{A \in \mathcal{A}} \overline{A}) > 0$. For example, consider a hypergraph in which each edge contains k vertices and intersects at most $d < 2^{k-1}/e - 1$ other edges. Under a uniformly random color assignment $\mathcal{P} \to \{\text{red,blue}\}$ the probability an edge is monochromatic is $p = 2^{-(k-1)}$, so $ep(d+1) < 1$. The symmetric LLL proves the *existence* of a satisfying color assignment but does not yield an efficient algorithm to find one. Beginning with Beck [7], a long line of research has sought to find efficient (and ideally deterministic) algorithms for computing satisfying assignments [7, 1, 19, 9, 32, 22, 23, 24, 8, 12, 14, 25]. Most of these results required a major weakening of the standard symmetric LLL constraint $ep(d+1) < 1$. In many applications we consider, the bad events are that the sum of $d^{\Theta(1)}$ random variables deviates away from its expectation. So the probability they are violated is often bounded by Chernoff-type tail bounds, e.g. $\exp(-d^{\Theta(1)})$.

In a relatively recent breakthrough, Moser and Tardos [24] gave an *algorithmic* proof of the general asymmetric LLL, with no weakening of the parameters. Their algorithm is simple though the analysis is not trivial. At initialization the algorithm chooses a random assignment to the variables $\mathcal{P}$. Call an event $A \in \mathcal{A}$ *violated* if it occurs under the current assignment to the variables. Let $\mathcal{F} \subseteq \mathcal{A}$ be the set of violated events. The algorithm repeatedly chooses some $A \in \mathcal{F}$ and *resamples* the variables in $\text{vbl}(A)$, until $\mathcal{F} = \emptyset$.

The Distributed LLL Problem.

We consider Linial's LOCAL model [26] of distributed computation in which the distributed network is identical to the dependency graph. In other words, each node $A \in \mathcal{A}$ hosts a processor, which is aware of n, the degree bound d, and its neighborhood $\Gamma(A)$. Computation proceeds in synchronized rounds in which each node may send an unbounded message to its neighbors. *Time* is measured by the number of rounds; computation local to each node is free. Upon termination each node A must commit to an assignment to its variables $\text{vbl}(A)$ that is consistent with its neighbors, i.e., the nodes must collectively agree on a satisfying assignment to $\mathcal{P}$ avoiding all bad events. We consider the LOCAL model because we will need to send the assignment of $\text{vbl}(A)$ in one message, which can be large.

Moser and Tardos proposed a parallel version of their resampling algorithm (Algorithm 1), which can easily be implemented in the LOCAL model. Let $G_\mathcal{F}$ be the graph induced by the violated events $\mathcal{F}$ under the current variable assignment. They proved that $O(\log_{1/ep(d+1)} n)$ iterations of Algorithm 1 suffice to avoid all bad events with probability $1 - 1/\text{poly}(n)$, i.e., $O(\log n)$ iterations suffice if $ep(d+1)$ is bounded away from 1[1]. (For the sake of a simpler presentation we shall state many results in the symmetric LLL language. Our algorithms and Moser-Tardos work for the asymmetric LLL as well.) Moser and Tardos suggested using Luby's randomized MIS algorithm [18], which runs in $\Theta(\log n)$ rounds w.h.p. (which can also be achieved by [2]), for a total running time of $\Theta(\log n \cdot \log_{1/ep(d+1)} n)$. This is, intuitively, a very wasteful LLL algorithm since nodes spend nearly all their time computing MISs rather than performing resampling steps. For certain values of d the running time can be improved by plugging in an MIS algorithm running in $O(d + \log^* n)$ time [5] or $O(\log d \cdot \sqrt{\log n})$ time w.h.p. [6].[2] However, it is not possible to find an MIS in constant time. Kuhn et al. [15] gave an $\Omega(\min\{\log d, \sqrt{\log n}\})$ lower bound on the complexity of MIS and other symmetry-breaking problems.

New Results.

We give a new distributed LLL algorithm in the Moser-Tardos resampling framework that avoids the computation of MISs altogether. Due to its simplicity we are happy to display the algorithm in its entirety. We assume that nodes possess unique IDs, which could be assigned in an adversarial manner. Let $\Gamma_\mathcal{F}(A)$ be A's neighborhood in $G_\mathcal{F}$.

```
Initialize a random assignment to the variables P.
while F ≠ ∅ do
  Compute a maximal independent set I in G_F.
  Resample each variable in vbl(I) = ∪_{A∈I} vbl(A).
end while
```

Algorithm 1: The Moser-Tardos Parallel Resampling Algorithm. Here $\mathcal{F}$ is the set of bad events occurring under the current variable assignment and $G_\mathcal{F}$ is the dependency graph induced by $\mathcal{F}$.

```
Initialize a random assignment to the variables P

while F ≠ ∅ do
  Let I = {A ∈ F | ID(A) = min{ID(B) | B ∈ Γ_F^+(A)}}
  Resample vbl(I) = ∪_{A∈I} vbl(A).
end while
```

Algorithm 2: A Simple Distributed LLL Algorithm

One can see that $\mathcal{I}$ is computed in one round: each node A tells its neighbors whether $A \in \mathcal{F}$ under the current variable assignment. Once A receives messages from all neighbors it can determine if $\text{ID}(A)$ is a local minimum in $G_\mathcal{F}$. We prove that under the slightly stronger criterion $epd^2 < 1$, this algorithm halts in $O(\log_{1/epd^2} n)$ steps w.h.p. Most applications of the LLL satisfy the $epd^2 < 1$ criterion, though not all. We give another distributed LLL algorithm in the resampling framework that finds a satisfying assignment in $O(\log^2 d \cdot \log_{1/ep(d+1)} n)$ time under the usual $ep(d+1) < 1$ criterion.

We show that faster algorithms exist when the condition $ep(d+1) < 1$ is replaced by a stronger condition $p \cdot f(d) < 1$, where $f(d)$ is a faster growing function than $e(d+1)$. However, it is not clear whether there exists $f(d)$ so that the LLL can be solved in sublogarithmic time in n, independent of d. Moser and Tardos observed that any parallel algorithm in the resampling framework requires $\Omega(\log_{1/p} n)$ resampling steps, even if the dependency graph has no edges. We combine the resampling framework with a locality approach to give an $O(\log n/\log\log n)$ algorithm for an exponential function $f(d)$. On the other hand, we prove that no constant time distributed LLL algorithm exists and that the LLL for any $f(d)$ requires $\Omega(\log^* n)$ time.

New Applications.

Existential results in graph coloring [20] (those taking the *Rödl nibble* approach) can often be phrased as distributed algorithms in which each step succeeds with some tiny but non-zero probability, as guaranteed by the LLL. By using our distributed LLL algorithms we are able to solve a number of graph coloring problems in $O(\log n)$ time or faster.[3] Some of these applications require minor changes to existing

[1]Note that $\log_{1/ep(d+1)} n$ could be sublogarithmic or superlogarithmic depending on how close $ep(d+1)$ is to 0 or 1.

[2]These MIS algorithms are significantly more complex than Luby's and use larger messages.

[3]Suppose H is both the distributed network and the graph to be colored. When invoking the LLL, the dependency graph $G_\mathcal{A}$ is not *identical* to H. Typically bad events in $\mathcal{A}$ are associated with H-vertices and two bad events are adjacent in $G_\mathcal{A}$ only if the corresponding vertices are at distance $O(1)$ in H. Thus, a distributed LLL algorithm for $G_\mathcal{A}$ can be simulated in H with an $O(1)$ slowdown.

algorithms while others are quite involved. Below Δ is the maximum degree, and $\epsilon > 0$ an arbitrarily small parameter.

Frugal Coloring A k-frugal vertex coloring is one in which each color appears at most k times in the neighborhood of any vertex. Pemmaraju and Srinivasan [27] showed the existence of $(\Delta + 1)$-colorings that are $O(\log^2 \Delta / \log\log \Delta)$-frugal, and proved that $(\log \Delta \cdot \log n / \log\log n)$-frugal colorings could be computed in $O(\log n)$ time. With some modifications to their proof we show that a $O(\log^2 \Delta / \log\log \Delta)$-frugal $(\Delta + 1)$-coloring can be computed in $O(\log n)$ time. Notice that the best existential bound on the frugality for $(\Delta + 1)$-coloring is $O(\log \Delta / \log\log \Delta)$ by Molloy and Reed [21].

Hind et al. [13] showed there exist β-frugal, $O(\Delta^{1+\frac{1}{\beta}})$-colorings by using the asymmetric LLL. We show how to turn their proof into a distributed algorithm that runs in $O(\log n \cdot \log^2 \Delta)$ time.

Girth 4 and 5 In prior work [28] we proved that triangle-free graphs have $(4 + \epsilon)\Delta / \ln \Delta$-colorings and gave $O(\log^{1+o(1)} n)$ time algorithms for $(4 + \epsilon)\Delta / \ln \Delta$-coloring triangle-free graphs and $(1 + \epsilon)\Delta / \ln \Delta$-coloring girth-5 graphs. Here we prove that both problems can be solved in $O(\log n)$ time.

Edge Coloring Dubhashi et al. [10] gave a $(1+\epsilon)\Delta$ edge-coloring algorithm running in $O(\log n)$ time, provided that $\Delta = (\log n)^{1+\Omega(1)}$ is sufficiently large relative to n. We give a logarithmic time algorithm for the same problem that works for any $\Delta > \Delta_\epsilon$, where Δ_ϵ is a sufficiently large constant depending on ϵ.

List-Coloring Suppose each vertex is issued a list of $(1 + \epsilon)D > D_\epsilon$ colors such that each color appears in at most D lists in the neighborhood of any vertex, where D_ϵ is a sufficiently large constant depending on ϵ. (D need not be close to the degree Δ.) Reed and Sudakov [29] proved that $(1+\epsilon)D$-list-colorings exist. We show how to construct them in $O(\log D + \log_D n + \log\log D \cdot \log n / D^{1/2}) = O(\log n)$ time. Significant modifications are needed to adapt their approach to a distributed network. Furthermore, for *any* D and any constant $\epsilon > 0$, we show that $(2e + \epsilon)D$ list coloring can be solved in $O(\log n)$ time.

Defective Coloring An f-defective coloring is one in which a vertex may share its color with up to f neighbors. Barenboim and Elkin [4], and implicitly, Kuhn and Wattenhofer [16] gave an $O(1)$ time procedure to compute a $O(\log n)$-defective $O(\Delta / \log n)$-coloring. We prove that for any $f = \Omega(\log \Delta)$, an f-defective $O(\Delta / f)$-coloring can be computed in $O((\log n)/f)$ time.

2. PRELIMINARIES

Let $\Gamma^r(A)$ be the r-neighborhood of A (the set of nodes at distance at most r from A, excluding A) and $\Gamma^{r+}(A) = \Gamma^r(A) \cup \{A\}$ be its inclusive r-neighborhood. A node set in the subscript indicates a restriction of the neighborhood to that set, e.g., $\Gamma^{2+}_{\mathcal{F}}(A) = \Gamma^{2+}(A) \cap \mathcal{F}$.

Consider an execution of a Moser-Tardos-type resampling algorithm. Let $C : \mathbb{N} \to \mathcal{A}$ be such that $C(i)$ is the ith event selected by the algorithm for resampling; C is called the *record* of the execution. (If the algorithm selects events in independent batches then the events in each batch can be listed arbitrarily.) A *witness tree* $\tau = (T, \sigma_T)$ is a finite rooted tree where $\sigma_T : V(T) \to \mathcal{A}$ labels each vertex in T with an event such that the children of $u \in T$ receive labels from $\Gamma^+(\sigma_T(u))$. A *2-witness tree* $\tau = (T, \sigma_T)$ is defined in the same way except that the children of $u \in T$ may receive labels from $\Gamma^{2+}(\sigma_T(u))$. A witness tree (or 2-witness tree) is *proper* if the children of a vertex receive distinct labels.

Given a record C, the witness tree $\tau_C(t)$ is constructed as follows. First, create a root node labelled $C(t)$. Looking backward in time, for each $i = t-1, t-2, \ldots, 1$, check if an existing node is labeled with an event from $\Gamma^+(C(i))$. If so, let u be one of the *deepest* such nodes. Create a new node v labeled $C(i)$ and make it a child of u. Given a witness tree τ, we say τ *occurs in* C if there exists an index t such that $\tau_C(t) = \tau$. Moser and Tardos proved the following lemma:

LEMMA 2.1. *Let τ be a fixed witness tree and C be the record produced by the algorithm.*

1. If τ occurs in C, then τ is proper.
2. The probability that τ appears in C is at most $\prod_{v \in V(\tau)} \Pr(\sigma_T(v))$.

Similarly, for $r \geq 2$, we can define an r-witness tree $\tau^r_C(t)$ in the same way except that in each step we attach a node labelled $C(i)$ to the deepest node among nodes labelled $\Gamma^{r+}(C(i))$. Also, we say τ r-occurs in C if there exists $t \in \mathbb{N}$ such that $\tau^r_C(t) = \tau$. Then Lemma 2.1 holds analogously:

LEMMA 2.2. *Let τ be a fixed r-witness tree and C be the record produced by the algorithm.*

1. If τ r-occurs in C, then τ is proper.
2. The probability that τ appears in C is at most $\prod_{v \in V(\tau)} \Pr(\sigma_T(v))$.

3. DISTRIBUTED CONSTRUCTIVE LOVÁSZ LOCAL LEMMA

Recall that the parallel/distributed Moser-Tardos algorithm iteratively selects maximal independent sets (MIS) of violated events for resampling. They proved that if there is some slack in the general LLL preconditions then the algorithm terminates in $O(\log n)$ rounds of MIS.

THEOREM 3.1. *(Moser and Tardos) Let $\mathcal{P}$ be a finite set of mutually independent random variables in a probability space. Let $\mathcal{A}$ be a finite set of events determined by these variables. If there exists an assignment of reals $x : \mathcal{A} \to (0,1)$ such that*

$$\forall A \in \mathcal{A} : \Pr(A) \leq (1-\epsilon)x(A) \prod_{B \in \Gamma(A)} (1 - x(B)),$$

then the probability any bad event occurs after k resampling rounds of Algorithm 1 is at most $(1-\epsilon)^k \sum_{A \in \mathcal{A}} \frac{x(A)}{1-x(A)}$.

In other words, if $x(A)$ is bounded away from 1 then $O(\log_{\frac{1}{1-\epsilon}} n)$ resampling rounds suffice, w.h.p. A distributed implementation of this algorithm takes $O(\log_{\frac{1}{1-\epsilon}} n \cdot \mathrm{MIS}(n,d))$, where d is the maximum degree of $G_{\mathcal{A}}$ and $\mathrm{MIS}(n,d)$ is the time needed to find an MIS in an n-vertex degree-d graph. It is known that $\mathrm{MIS}(n,d) =$

$\Omega(\min\{\sqrt{\log n}, \log d\})$ [15]. Our algorithms avoid the computation of MISs. In Section 3.1 we analyze the simple distributed LLL algorithm presented in the introduction, which requires slightly weakening the general LLL conditions. In Section 3.2 we present an algorithm that works for the standard LLL conditions but is slower by a $O(\log^2 d)$ factor.

3.1 A Simple Distributed Algorithm

Recall that in each round of Algorithm 2, a violated event $A \in \mathcal{F}$ is selected for resampling if $\text{ID}(A)$ is a local minimum in the violated subgraph $G_{\mathcal{F}}$. In order to analyze this algorithm in the witness-tree framework we must establish some connection between the depth of witness trees and the number of rounds of resampling. Lemma 3.2 will let us make such a connection.

LEMMA 3.2. *Suppose an event A is resampled in round $j > 1$ of Algorithm 2. There must exist some $B \in \Gamma^{2+}(A)$ resampled in round $j-1$.*

PROOF. Let $\mathcal{F}'$ and $\mathcal{F}$ be the violated event sets just before and after the resampling step at round $j-1$. If A is not in $\mathcal{F}'$ but is in $\mathcal{F}$ then its variables $\text{vbl}(A)$ must have been changed in round $j-1$, which could only occur if some $B \in \Gamma(A)$ were resampled. Now suppose A is in both $\mathcal{F}'$ and $\mathcal{F}$. It was not resampled in round $j-1$ but was in round j, meaning $\text{ID}(A)$ is not a local minimum in $\Gamma_{\mathcal{F}'}(A)$ but is a local minimum in $\Gamma_{\mathcal{F}}(A)$. This implies that some neighbor $B \in \Gamma(A)$ with $\text{ID}(B) < \text{ID}(A)$ is in $\mathcal{F}'$ but not $\mathcal{F}$, which could only occur if some $C \in \Gamma^+(B) \subseteq \Gamma^{2+}(A)$ were resampled in round $j-1$. □

We can now proceed to bound the number of rounds of Algorithm 2 needed to find a satisfying assignment.

THEOREM 3.3. *(Asymmetric LLL) Let $\mathcal{P}$ be a finite set of mutually independent random variables in a probability space. Let $\mathcal{A}$ be a finite set of events determined by these variables. If there exists an assignment of reals $x : \mathcal{A} \to (0,1)$ such that*

$$\forall A \in \mathcal{A} : \Pr(A) \leq (1-\epsilon)x(A) \prod_{B \in \Gamma^2(A)} (1 - x(B)),$$

then the probability any bad event occurs after k resampling rounds of Algorithm 2 is at most $(1-\epsilon)^k \sum_{A \in \mathcal{A}} \frac{x(A)}{1-x(A)}$.

Note the difference with Theorem 3.1 is that the product is over all $B \in \Gamma^2(A)$ not $B \in \Gamma(A)$.

COROLLARY 3.4. *(Symmetric LLL) Let $\mathcal{P}$ be a finite set of mutually independent random variables in a probability space. Let $\mathcal{A}$ be a finite set of events determined by these variables, such that for $\forall A \in \mathcal{A}$*

1. *$Pr(A) \leq p < 1$, and*
2. *A shares variables with at most d of the other events.*

If $epd^2 < 1$, then w.h.p. none of the bad events occur after $O(\log_{\frac{1}{epd^2}} n)$ rounds of Algorithm 2.

PROOF. Setting $x(A) = 1/d^2$ and $\epsilon = 1 - epd^2$ in Theorem 3.3, we have

$$(1-\epsilon)x(A) \prod_{B \in \Gamma^2(A)} (1 - x(B)) \geq \frac{1-\epsilon}{d^2}(1 - 1/d^2)^{|\Gamma^2(A)|}$$
$$\geq \frac{1-\epsilon}{d^2}(1-1/d^2)^{(d^2-1)} \geq \frac{1-\epsilon}{ed^2} \geq p \geq \Pr(A).$$

Therefore, the probability a bad event occur after k rounds of resampling is at most $(1-\epsilon)^k \sum_{A \in \mathcal{A}} \frac{x(A)}{1-x(A)} = (1-\epsilon)^k n/(d^2-1)$, which is $1/\text{poly}(n)$ if $k = O(\log_{\frac{1}{1-\epsilon}} n) = O(\log_{\frac{1}{epd^2}} n)$. □

Following Moser and Tardos [24], we analyze the following Galton-Watson process for generating an r-witness tree and prove the following lemma. See Appendix B for the proof.

LEMMA 3.5. *If for all $A \in \mathcal{A}$, we have $\Pr(A) \leq (1-\epsilon)x(A) \cdot \prod_{B \in \Gamma^r(A)}(1 - x(B))$, then the probability that any r-witness tree of size at least k occurs is at most $(1-\epsilon)^k \cdot \sum_{A \in \mathcal{A}} \frac{x(A)}{1-x(A)}$.*

Let C be the record of Algorithm 2 and S_j be the segment of the record corresponding to resamplings in round j. The following lemma relates the number of resampling rounds with the occurence of 2-witness trees.

LEMMA 3.6. *If there is still a violated event after k resampling rounds in Algorithm 2 then some 2-witness tree of size at least k occurs in C.*

PROOF. Let A_k be any event in S_k and t be its position in the record C. By Lemma 3.2 there exist events $A_{k-1}, \ldots, A_1$ in $S_{k-1}, \cdots, S_1$ such that for all $j < k$, $A_j \in \Gamma^{2+}(A_{j+1})$. This implies that $A_{k-1}, \ldots, A_1$ are mapped to distinct nodes in the 2-witness tree $\tau_C(t)$, whose root is labeled A_k. □

Therefore, by Lemma 3.6, if there is a violated event after k resampling rounds, then a 2-witness tree of size at least k occurs. However, by Lemma 3.5, it happens with probability at most $(1-\epsilon)^k \cdot \sum_{A \in \mathcal{A}} \frac{x(A)}{1-x(A)}$. Thus, Theorem 3.3 holds. Note that if $x(A)$ is bounded away from 1, then after $O(\log_{\frac{1}{1-\epsilon}} n)$ rounds, w.h.p. no bad event occurs.

3.2 Resampling by Weak MIS

In this section we analyze the efficiency of Moser and Tardos's Algorithm 1 when a new *weak MIS* procedure (Algorithm 3) is used in lieu of an actual MIS. The Weak-MIS procedure produces, in $O(\log^2 d)$ time, an independent set S such that the probability that a node is *not* in $\Gamma^+(S) = S \cup \Gamma(S)$ is $1/\text{poly}(d)$. The procedure consists of $O(\log d)$ iterations where the probability that a vertex avoids $\Gamma^+(S)$ is constant per iteration. Each iteration consists of $\log d$ phases where, roughly speaking, the goal of phase i is to eliminate vertices with degree at least $d/2^i$ with constant probability. Each phase is essentially one step of Luby's MIS algorithm, though applied only to a judiciously chosen subset of the vertices. See Algoirthm 3.

Our main results are as follows.

THEOREM 3.7. *(Assymmetric LLL) Let $\mathcal{P}$ be a finite set of mutually independent random variables in a probability space. Let $\mathcal{A}$ be a finite set of events determined by these variables. If there exists an assignment of reals $x : \mathcal{A} \to (0,1)$ such that*

$$\forall A \in \mathcal{A} : \Pr(A) \leq (1-\epsilon)x(A) \prod_{B \in \Gamma(A)} (1 - x(B)),$$

then the probability any bad event occurs after k resampling rounds using the Weak-MIS algorithm is at most $n(\frac{1}{d+1})^k + (1-\epsilon)^{k/2} \sum_{A \in \mathcal{A}} \frac{x(A)}{1-x(A)}$.

COROLLARY 3.8. *(Symmetric LLL) Let $\mathcal{P}$ be a finite set of mutually independent random variables in a probability space. Let $\mathcal{A}$ be a finite set of events determined by these variables, such that for $\forall A \in \mathcal{A}$,*

1. *$Pr(A) \leq p < 1$, and*

2. *A shares variables with at most d of the other events.*

If $ep(d+1) < 1$, then w.h.p. none of the bad events occur after $O(\max(\log_{d+1} n, \log_{\frac{1}{ep(d+1)}} n))$ Weak-MIS resampling rounds.

Corollary 3.8 follows directly by plugging in $x(A) = 1/(d+1)$ for all $A \in \mathcal{A}$ and $k = O(\max(\log_{d+1} n, \log_{\frac{1}{ep(d+1)}} n))$. Notice that if $\frac{1}{ep(d+1)} > d+1$, we can apply the faster simple distributed algorithm, so the running time in Corollary 3.8 will be dominated by $O(\log_{\frac{1}{ep(d+1)}} n \cdot \log^2 d)$.

```
S ← ∅
for iteration 1 ..., t = 4e² ln(2e(d+1)⁴) do
  G' ← G_F \ Γ⁺(S)
  for phase i = 1 ... ⌈log d⌉ do
    V_i ← {v ∈ G' | deg_G'(v) ≥ d/2^i}.
    For each vertex v ∈ G', set b(v) = 1 with probability
        p_i = 1/(d/2^(i-1) + 1) and 0 otherwise.
    For each vertex v ∈ G', if b(v) = 1 and b(w) = 0 for all
        w ∈ Γ_G'(v), then set S ← S ∪ {v}.
    G' ← G' \ (Γ⁺(S) ∪ V_i) (i.e., remove both Γ⁺(S) and V_i
        from G'.)
  end for
  Let S' be the (isolated) vertices that remain in G'.
  Set S ← S ∪ S'
end for
return S
```

Algorithm 3: Weak-MIS

Consider the first iteration of the Weak-MIS algorithm. For each phase i, G' is the subgraph of $G_{\mathcal{F}}$ containing vertices with degree at most $d/2^i$ and not adjacent to the independent set S. Let $V_i = \{v \in G' \mid \deg_{G'}(v) \geq d/2^i\}$. Note that every vertex in $G_{\mathcal{F}}$ must end up isolated in S' or one of the V_i's. Let (u, v) be an edge in G'. Following Peleg's analysis [26], define $\mathcal{E}(u, w)$ to be the event that at phase i, $b(u) = 0$ and $b(w) = 1$ and for all other neighbors x of u and w, $b(x) = 0$. Define $\mathcal{E}(u) = \bigcup_{w \in \Gamma_{G'}(u)} \mathcal{E}(u, w)$ to be the event that exactly one neighbor joins S in this phase. Since these events are disjoint, we have $\Pr(\mathcal{E}(u)) = \sum_{w \in \Gamma_{G'}(u)} \Pr(\mathcal{E}(u, w))$.

LEMMA 3.9. *If $v \in V_i$, then $\Pr(\mathcal{E}(u)) \geq \frac{1}{4e^2}$.*

PROOF. $\Pr(\mathcal{E}(u,w)) \geq p_i(1-p_i)^{\deg_{G'}(u)+\deg_{G'}(w)} \geq p_i(1-p_i)^{2d/2^{i-1}} \geq p_i e^{-2}$. Since $\deg_{G'}(u) \geq d/2^i$, $Pr(\mathcal{E}(u)) \geq \frac{d}{2^i} p_i e^{-2} \geq \frac{1}{4e^2}$ □

Therefore, if $v \in G_{\mathcal{F}} \setminus \Gamma^+(S)$ at the beginning of iteration l, the probability that $v \in \Gamma^+(S)$ at the end of iteration l is at least $1/(4e^2)$. We say a vertex in $G_{\mathcal{F}}$ *fails* if, after all $t = 4e^2 \ln(2e(d+1)^4)$ iterations, it is still not in $\Gamma^+(S)$.

LEMMA 3.10. *Let S be an independent set selected by Weak-MIS. If $v \in \mathcal{F}$ then $\Pr(\Gamma^+(v) \cap S = \emptyset) \leq \frac{1}{2e(d+1)^4}$.*

PROOF. By Lemma 3.9, the probability that v survives iteration ℓ conditioned on it surviving iterations 1 through $\ell - 1$ is at most $1 - 1/(4e^2)$. Over $t = 4e^2 \ln(2e(d+1)^4$ iterations the probability of failure is at most $(1 - 1/(4e^2))^t \leq e^{-\ln(2e(d+1)^4)} = \frac{1}{2e(d+1)^4}$. □

The next step is to relate the number of rounds of Weak-MIS resampling with the size of witness trees.

LEMMA 3.11. *Suppose a bad event is violated after k rounds of Weak-MIS resampling and the maximum depth of the witness trees is t, then there exists a sequence of not necessarily distinct vertices $v_1, \ldots, v_k$ such that the following hold:*

(1) $v_i \in G_i$, where G_i is the violated subgraph $G_{\mathcal{F}}$ the beginning of round i.

(2) $v_{i+1} \in \Gamma^+(v_i)$ for $1 \leq i \leq k-1$.

(3) For at least $k - t$ indices $1 < l \leq k$, v_l failed in the call to Weak-MIS in round $l - 1$.

PROOF. For $1 \leq i \leq k$, let S_i be the segment of the record C corresponding to events resampled at round i. Suppose that an event A is violated after k resampling rounds. Build a witness tree τ with root labeled A, adding nodes in the usual fashion, by scanning the record C in time-reversed order. For each j, in decreasing order, attach a node labelled $C(j)$ to the deepest node in τ whose label is in $\Gamma^+(C(j))$, if such a node in τ exists. Let $v_{k+1} = A$. We will build $v_k, v_{k-1}, \ldots, v_1$ in backward manner. For $k \geq i \geq 1$, we claim there is an event $v_i \in \Gamma^+(v_{i+1})$ such that either $v_i \in S_i$ or $v_i \in G_i$ and v_i failed at round i. If $v_{i+1} \notin G_i$ is not violated at the beginning of round i, then it must be the case that there exists an event $v_i \in \Gamma^+(v_{i+1})$ resampled at round i to cause $v_{i+1} \in G_{i+1}$. On the other hand, if $v_{i+1} \in G_i$ *is* violated at the beginning of round i, then either there exists $v_i \in \Gamma^+(v_{i+1})$ resampled at round i or v_{i+1} failed at round i. In the latter case, we let $v_i = v_{i+1}$. Notice that τ (excluding its artificial root labeled A) is a witness that occured and thus has depth at most t. Since in each of the k rounds, either the depth of our witness tree grows or a vertex is failed, at least $k - t$ vertices must have failed in their respective rounds. □

Notice that the total possible number of sequences satisfying (2) in Lemma 3.11 is at most $n(d+1)^{k-1}$. Given a sequence of vertices $P = (v_1, \ldots, v_k)$ satisfying (2), define $X_P^{(i)}$ to be 1 if $v_i \in G_i$ and v_i failed, 0 otherwise. Let $X_P = \sum_{i=1}^k X_P^{(i)}$. If a sequence satisfying (1–3) occured, then there exists P such that $X_P \geq k - t$. Since $X_P^{(1)}, \ldots, X_P^{(i-1)}$ are determined by $S_1, \ldots, S_{i-1}$ and $G_1, \ldots, G_{i-1}$, $\mathrm{E}(X_P^i \mid X_1, \ldots, X_{i-1}) = \mathrm{E}(X_P^i \mid S_1, \ldots, S_{i-1}, G_1, \ldots, G_{i-1}) \leq q \stackrel{\text{def}}{=} \frac{1}{2e(d+1)^4}$ by Lemma 3.10. Fixing $t = k/2$, we have $k - t = k/2 = kq \cdot e(d+1)^4 \leq \mathrm{E}[X_P] \cdot e(d+1)^4$. By Corollary A.4 (Conditional Chernoff Bound):

$$\Pr(X_P \geq k/2) \leq \left(\frac{e^{e(d+1)^4 - 1}}{(e(d+1)^4)^{e(d+1)^4}}\right)^{\frac{k}{2e(d+1)^4}} \leq \left(\frac{1}{(d+1)^2}\right)^k.$$

By the union bound over all possible P satsfying (2), the probability that any such sequence in Lemma 3.11 occurs is at most

$$n\,(d+1)^{k-1}\cdot\left(\frac{1}{(d+1)^2}\right)^k \le n\cdot\left(\frac{1}{d+1}\right)^k.$$

Moser and Tardos showed that the probability that any witness tree of size at least t occurs is at most $(1-\epsilon)^t\sum_{A\in\mathcal{A}}\frac{x(A)}{1-x(A)}$. Thus, either a witness tree of depth at least $t=k/2$ occurs or there exists a sequence of vertices (as in Lemma 3.11) such that $t-k=k/2$ of them failed. The probability either of these occurs is at most $n\cdot\left(\frac{1}{d+1}\right)^k+(1-\epsilon)^{k/2}\sum_{A\in\mathcal{A}}\frac{x(A)}{1-x(A)}$ by the union bound.

3.3 A Sublogarithmic Algorithm

We have seen a faster algorithm for LLL when the general condition $ep(d+1)<1$ is replaced by a stronger condition $p\cdot f(d)<1$, where $f(d)$ is a faster growing function than $e(d+1)$. The question of how fast we can do for a stronger condition arises. Does there exists a sublogarithmic algorithm for faster growing $f(d)$, independent of n? We answer this affirmatively for an exponential function of d.

Inspired by [3], our approach is a two-stage approach. In the first stage, we run Algorithm 2 for k rounds. Then we identify the *dangerous* events, who are likely to become violated if some subset of its neighbors are resampled. We will show there is a feasible solution by re-assigning the variables belonging to dangerous events. Moreover, we show the components induced by the dangerous events are likely to have *weak diameter* at most k. The weak diameter of a component is the maximum distance w.r.t. the original graph of any pair in the component. In the second stage, each component computes the answer independent of others in time proportional to its weak diameter.

Consider an event A. Let $P_1(A), P_2(A)$ be probabilities such that $P_1(A)P_2(A)=2^d\cdot\Pr(A)$. Given an assignment of the random variables, we say A is dangerous w.r.t. the current assignment if resampling of some subset of neighbors causes A to become violated with probability more than $P_2(A)$. We will show that the probability for A to become dangerous is at most $P_1(A)$.

Given that $P_2(A)$ is small enough for all $A\in\mathcal{A}$, we can find a feasible solution by resassiging the variables belonging to the dangerous vertices. Also, given that $P_1(A)$ is small enough, we will show that the weak diameter of each component after the first stage is at most k w.h.p. We explain the idea roughly. If we build a 2-witness tree rooted at a dangerous vertex after the first stage, the 2-witness tree has size at least k. If there exists a path consisting of dangerous vertices of length k after the first stage, we will show the union of the witness trees rooted at these vertices has size at least $\Omega(k\log k)$. Then, we will glue them together into a 3-witness tree. By choosing $k=\Theta(\log n/\log\log n)$, we would have a 3-witness tree with size $\Theta(\log n)$, which does not occur w.h.p. We defer the proof for the following theorem and corollary to the full version.

THEOREM 3.12 (ASYMMETRIC LLL). *Let $\Pr(A)\le P_2(A)\le 1$ and $P_1(A)=2^d\cdot\frac{\Pr(A)}{P_2(A)}$, where d is the maximum degree of the dependency graph. If there exists an assgiments of reals $x_1,x_2:\mathcal{A}\to(0,0.99)$ such that for all $A\in\mathcal{A}$*

1. $P_1(A)\le(1-\epsilon)x_1(A)\prod_{B\in\Gamma^3(A)}(1-x_1(B))$
2. $P_2(A)\le x_2(A)\prod_{B\in\Gamma(A)}(1-x_2(B))$

then the LLL problem can be solved in $O\left(\log_{1/(1-\epsilon)}n/\log\log_{1/(1-\epsilon)}n\right)$ rounds.

COROLLARY 3.13 (SYMMETRIC LLL). *Suppose that for all $A\in\mathcal{A}$, $\Pr(A)\le p$ and A is dependent with at most d other events in $\mathcal{A}$. Let $z=4ep2^dd^4$. If $z<1$, then a satisfying assignment can be found in $O(\log_{1/z}n/\log\log_{1/z}n)$ rounds.*

3.4 Lower Bound

Linial [17] proved that in an n-vertex ring, any distributed $(\log^{(k)}n)$-coloring algorithm requires $\Omega(k)$ rounds of communication, even if randomization is used. In particular, $O(1)$-coloring a ring requires $\Omega(\log^* n)$ time. We prove that Linial's lower bound implies that even weak versions of the Lovász Local Lemma cannot be computed in constant time.

THEOREM 3.14. *Let $\mathcal{P}$, $\mathcal{A}$, and $G_{\mathcal{A}}$ be defined as usual. Let d be the maximum degree of any vertex in $G_{\mathcal{A}}$, $p=\max_{A\in\mathcal{A}}\Pr(A)$ be the maximum probability of any bad event, and $f:\mathbb{N}\to\mathbb{N}$ be an arbitrarily quickly growing function, where $f(d)\ge e(d+1)$. If $p\cdot f(d)<1$ then $\Pr(\bigcap_{A\in\mathcal{A}}\overline{A})>0$. However, $\Omega(\log^*|\mathcal{A}|)$ rounds of communication are required for the vertices of $G_{\mathcal{A}}$ to agree on a point in $\bigcap_{A\in\mathcal{A}}\overline{A}$.*

The purpose of the function f is to show that our lower bound is insensitive to significant weakening of the standard criterion "$ep(d+1)<1$." We could just as easily substitute $e^{e^d}p<1$ or any similar criterion, for example.

PROOF. Consider the following coloring procedure. Each vertex in an n-vertex ring selects a color from $\{1,\ldots,c\}$ uniformly at random. An edge is *bad* if it is monochromatic, an event that holds with probability $p=1/c$. Let $\mathcal{A}$ be the dependency graph for these events having maximum degree $d=2$ and choose c to be (the constant) $f(2)+1$, for any quickly growing function f. It follows from the LLL that a good c-coloring exists since $p\cdot f(2)<1$. However, by [17], the vertices of $G_{\mathcal{A}}$ require $\Omega(\log^* n-\log^* c)=\Omega(\log^* n)$ time to find a good c-coloring. □

It is also possible to obtain *conditional* lower bounds on distributed versions of the LLL. For example, the best known randomized $O(\Delta)$-coloring algorithm takes $\exp(O(\sqrt{\log\log n}))$ time [6], though better bounds are possible if $\Delta\gg\log n$ [30]. If LLL could be solved in less than $\exp(O(\sqrt{\log\log n}))$ time then we could improve on [6], as follows. Each vertex in G selects a color from a palette of size $c\ge 2e\Delta$ uniformly at random. As usual, an edge is bad if it is monochromatic. The dependency graph of these bad events corresponds to the line graph of G, which has maximum degree $d=2\Delta-2$. Since $e(1/c)(d+1)<1$, a valid coloring can be found with one invocation of an LLL algorithm.

4. APPLICATIONS

The Lovász Local Lemma has applications in many coloring problems, such as list coloring, frugal coloring, total coloring and coloring triangle-free graphs [20]. We give a few examples of constructing these colorings distributively. In these applications, the existential bounds are usually achieved by the so called "Rödl Nibble" method or the semi-random method. The method consists of one or more iterations. Each iteration is a random process and some local properties are maintained in the graph. The properties depend on the randomness within a constant radius. Each property is associated with a bad event, which is the event that the property fails to hold. The Lovász Local Lemma can then be used to show the probability none of the bad events hold is positive, though it may be exponentially small in the size of the graph. This probability can then be amplified in a distributed fashion using a Moser-Tardos-type resampling algorithm. Notice that we will need to find an independent set (e.g., an MIS or Weak-MIS or set of events with locally minimal IDs) *in the dependency graph* induced by the violated local properties. Since we assumed the LOCAL model, the violated local properties can be identified in constant time and the algorithms for MIS/Weak-MIS can be simulated with a constant factor overhead, where each property is taken care by one of the processors nearby (within constant distance). The important point here is that the dependency graph and the underlying distributed network are sufficiently similar so that distributed algorithms on one topology can be simulated on the other with $O(1)$ slowdown.

Most applications of the LLL demand $epd^2 < 1$ or even weaker bounds. In this case, the efficient simple distributed algorithm can be applied. (The local properties are often that some quantities do not deviate too much from their expectations. Thus, the the failure probability of each local property is often bounded via standard Chernoff-type concentration inequalities.)

In the following, we present the distributed defective coloring and the frugal coloring algorithms. The other applications mentioned in the introduction will be deferred to the full version due to the page limit.

4.1 Distributed Defective Coloring

We begin with a simple single-iteration application that uses the local lemma. Given a k-coloring $\phi : V \to \{1, 2, \ldots, k\}$. Define $\mathrm{def}_\phi(v)$ to be the number of neighbors $w \in N(v)$ such that $\phi(v) = \phi(w)$. ϕ is said to be f-defective if $\max_v \mathrm{def}_\phi(v) \le f$. Barenboim and Elkin ([4], Open Problem 10.7) raised the problem of devising an efficient distributed algorithm for computing an f-defective $O(\Delta/f)$-coloring. Here we extend one of their procedures for obtaining a $O(\log n)$-defective $O(\Delta/\log n)$-coloring to obtaining an f-defective $O(\Delta/f)$-coloring in $O(\log n/f)$ time w.h.p., for $f \ge 7 + 28\ln\Delta$. Suppose each vertex colors itself with a color selected from $\{1, 2, \ldots, \lceil 2\Delta/f \rceil\}$ uniformly at random. For every $v \in N(u)$, let X_v be 1 if v is colored the same as u, 0 otherwise. Let $X = \sum_{v\in\Gamma(u)} X_v$ denote the number of neighbors colored the same as v. Let A_u denote the bad event that $X > f$ at u. Clearly, whether A_u occurs is locally checkable by u in a constant number of rounds. Moreover, the event A_u only depends on the the random choices of u's neighbors. If A_u occured and is selected for resampling, the colors chosen by A_u and its neighbors will be resampled. The dependency graph $G_{\mathcal{A}}$ has maximum degree $d = \Delta^2$, because two events share variables only if they are within distance two. Now we will calculate the probability that A_u occurs. If we expose the choice of u first, then $\Pr(X_v = 1) \le f/(2\Delta)$ and it is independent among other $v \in N(u)$. Letting $M = f/2$, we have $E[X] \le f/2 = M$. By Corollary A.3 (a useful form of the Chernoff Bound), $\Pr(X > f) \le e^{-f/6}$. Let A_u denote the bad event that $X > f$ at u. Therefore, $epd^2 \le e^{-(f/6-1-4\ln\Delta)} \le e^{-(f/42)}$, since $f \ge 7 + 28\ln\Delta$. By using the simple distributed algorithm, it takes $O(\log_{1/epd^2} n) = O(\log n/f)$ rounds to avoid the bad events w.h.p.

4.2 Distributed Frugal Coloring

A *β-frugal coloring* of a graph G is a proper vertex-coloring of G such that no color appears more than β times in any neighborhood. Molloy and Reed [20] showed the following by using an asymmetric version of the local lemma:

THEOREM 4.1. *For any constant integer $\beta \ge 1$, if G has maximum degree $\Delta \ge \beta^\beta$ then G has a β-frugal proper vertex coloring using at most $16\Delta^{1+\frac{1}{\beta}}$ colors.*

Here we outline their proof and show how to turn it into a distributed algorithm that finds such a coloring in $O(\log n \cdot \log^2\Delta)$ rounds. If $\beta = 1$, then simply consider the square graph of G, which is obtained by adding the edges between vertices whose distance is 2. A proper coloring in the square graph is a 1-frugal coloring in G. Since the square graph has maximum degree Δ^2, it can be (Δ^2+1)-colored by simulating distributed algorithms for $(\Delta+1)$-coloring.

For $\beta \ge 2$, let $k = 16\Delta^{1+\frac{1}{\beta}}$. Suppose that each vertex colors itself with one of the k colors uniformly at random. Consider two types of bad events. For each edge uv, the Type I event $A_{u,v}$ denotes that u and v are colored the same. For each subset $\{u_1, \ldots, u_{\beta+1}\}$ of the neighborhood of a vertex, Type II event $A_{u_1,\ldots,u_{\beta+1}}$ denotes that $u_1, \ldots, u_{\beta+1}$ are colored the same. If none of the events occur, then the random coloring is a β-frugal coloring. For each Type I event $A_{u,v}$, $\Pr(A_{u,v})$ is at most $1/k$. For each Type II event $A_{u_1,\ldots,u_{\beta+1}}$, $\Pr(A_{u_1,\ldots,u_{\beta+1}}) \le 1/k^\beta$. For each bad event A, let $x(A) = 2\Pr(A)$. Notice that $x(A) \le 1/2$, we have:

$$
\begin{aligned}
x(A) \prod_{B\in\Gamma(A)} (1 - x(B)) &\ge x(A) \prod_{B\in\Gamma(A)} \exp\left(-x(B)\cdot 2\ln 2\right) \\
&\qquad \{(1-x) \ge e^{-x\cdot 2\ln 2} \text{ for } x \le 1/2\} \\
&= x(A)\exp\left(-2\ln 2 \cdot \sum_{B\in\Gamma(A)} 2\Pr(B)\right)
\end{aligned}
$$

Since A shares variables with at most $(\beta+1)\Delta$ Type I events and $(\beta+1)\Delta\binom{\Delta}{\beta}$ Type II events,

$$
\begin{aligned}
\sum_{B\in\Gamma(A)} \Pr(B) &\le (\beta+1)\Delta \cdot \frac{1}{k} + (\beta+1)\Delta\binom{\Delta}{\beta} \cdot \frac{1}{k^\beta} \\
&< \frac{(\beta+1)\Delta}{k} + \frac{(\beta+1)\Delta^{\beta+1}}{\beta! k^\beta} \\
&= \frac{\beta+1}{16\Delta^{\frac{1}{\beta}}} + \frac{\beta+1}{\beta!(16)^\beta} \\
&< 1/8 \qquad (\text{for } \Delta \ge \beta^\beta \text{ and } \beta \ge 2)
\end{aligned}
$$

Therefore,

$$
\begin{aligned}
x(A) \prod_{B\in\Gamma(A)} (1 - x(B)) &\ge x(A)\exp\left(-\frac{\ln 2}{2}\right) \\
&= \sqrt{2}\Pr(A).
\end{aligned}
$$

By letting $1 - \epsilon = 1/\sqrt{2}$ in Theorem 3.7, we need at most $O(\log_{\sqrt{2}} n)$ rounds of weak MIS resampling. In each resampling round, we have to identify the bad events first.

Type I events $A_{u,v}$ can be identified by either u or v in constant rounds, where ties can be broken by letting the node with smaller ID check it. If $\{u_1, \ldots, u_{\beta+1}\}$ is in the neighborhood of u, then the Type II event $A_{u_1,\ldots,u_{\beta+1}}$ will be checked by u. If $\{u_1, \ldots, u_{\beta+1}\}$ is in the neighborhood of multiple nodes, we can break ties by letting the one having the smallest ID to check it. All Type II events in the neighborhood of u can be identified from the colors selected by the neighbors of u. Next we will find a weak MIS induced by the bad events in the dependency graph. Each node will simulate the weak MIS algorithm on the events it is responsible to check. Each round of the weak MIS algorithm in the dependency graph can be simulated with constant rounds. The maximum degree d of the dependency graph is $O((\beta+1)\Delta\binom{\Delta}{\beta})$. Therefore, we need at most $O(\log n \cdot \log^2 d) = O(\log n \cdot \log^2 \Delta)$ rounds, since β is a constant and $(\beta+1)\Delta\binom{\Delta}{\beta} \leq (\beta+1)\Delta^{\beta+1} = \text{poly}(\Delta)$.

4.2.1 β-frugal, $(\Delta+1)$-coloring

The frugal $(\Delta+1)$-coloring problem for general graphs is studied by Hind et al. [13], Pemmaraju and Srinivasan [27], and Molloy and Reed [21]. In particular, the last one gave an upper bound of $O(\log\Delta/\log\log\Delta)$ on the frugality of $(\Delta+1)$-coloring. This is optimal up to a constant factor, because it matches lower bound of $\Omega(\log\Delta/\log\log\Delta)$ given by Hind et al. [21]. However, it is not obvious whether it can be implemented efficiently in a distributed fashion, because they used a structural decomposition computed by a sequential algorithm. Pemmaraju and Srinivasan [27] showed an existential upper bound of $O(\log^2\Delta/\log\log\Delta)$. Furthermore, they gave a distributed algorithm that computes an $O(\log\Delta\cdot\frac{\log n}{\log\log n})$-frugal, $(\Delta+1)$-coloring in $O(\log n)$ rounds. We show how to improve it to find a $O(\log^2\Delta/\log\log\Delta)$-frugal, $(\Delta+1)$-coloring also in $O(\log n)$ rounds. They proved the following theorem:

THEOREM 4.2. *Let G be a graph with maximum vertex degree Δ. Suppose that associated with each vertex $v \in V$, there is a palette $P(v)$ of colors, where $|P(v)| \geq \deg(v)+1$. Furthermore, suppose $|P(v)| \geq \Delta/4$ for all vertices v in G. Then, for some subset $C \subseteq V$, there is a list coloring of the vertices in C such that:*

(a) $G[C]$ is properly colored.

(b) For every vertex $v \in V$ and for every color x, there are at most $9\cdot\frac{\ln\Delta}{\ln\ln\Delta}$ neighbors of v colored x.

(c) For every vertex $v \in V$, the number of neighbors of v not in C is at most $\Delta(1-\frac{1}{e^5}) + 27\sqrt{\Delta\ln\Delta}$.

(d) For every vertex $v \in V$, the number of neighbors of v in C is at most $\frac{\Delta}{e^5} + 27\sqrt{\Delta\ln\Delta}$.

They showed by iteratively applying the theorem for $O(\log\Delta)$ iterations, an $O(\log^2\Delta/\log\log\Delta)$-frugal, $(\Delta+1)$-coloring can be obtained. Let G_i be the graph after round i obtained by deleting already colored vertices and Δ_i be the maximum degree of G_i. The palette $P(u)$ for each vertex u contains colors that have not been used by its neighbors. It is always true that $|P(v)| \geq \deg(v)+1$. Notice that to apply Theorem 4.2, we also need the condition $|P(v)| \geq \Delta/4$. The worst case behavior of Δ_i and p_i is captured by the recurrences:

$$\Delta_{i+1} = \Delta_i(1-\frac{1}{e^5}) + 27\sqrt{\Delta_i\ln\Delta_i}$$
$$p_{i+1} = p_i - \frac{\Delta_i}{e^5} - 27\sqrt{\Delta_i\ln\Delta_i}. \quad (1)$$

They showed the above recurrence can be solved to obtain the following bounds on Δ_i and p_i:

LEMMA 4.3. *Let $\alpha = (1-1/e^5)$. There is a constant C such that for all i for which $\Delta_i \geq C$, $\Delta_i \leq 2\Delta_0\alpha^i$ and $p_i \geq \frac{\Delta_0}{2}\alpha^i$.*

Therefore, $|P(v)| \geq \Delta/4$ always holds. The two assumptions of Theorem 4.2 are always satisfied and so it can be applied iteratively until $\Delta_i < C$, which takes at most $\log_{1/\alpha}\left(\frac{2\Delta_0}{C}\right) = O(\log\Delta)$ iterations. Since each iteration introduces at most $O(\log\Delta/\log\log\Delta)$ neighbors of the same color to each vertex, the frugality will be at most $O(\log^2\Delta/\log\log\Delta)$. In the end, when $\Delta_i < C$, one can color the remaining graph in $O(\Delta_i + \log^* n)$ time using existing (Δ_i+1)-coloring algorithms [5]. This will only add $O(1)$ copies of each color to the neighborhood, yielding a $O(\log^2\Delta/\log\log\Delta)$-frugal, $(\Delta+1)$-coloring. In order to make it suitable for our simple distributed algorithm and achieve the running time of $O(\log n)$, we will relax the criteria of (b),(c),(d) in Theorem 4.2:

(b') For every vertex $v \in V$ and for every color x, there are at most $18\cdot\frac{\ln\Delta_0}{\ln\ln\Delta_0}$ neighbors of v colored x.

(c') For every vertex $v \in V$, the number of neighbors of v not in C is at most $\Delta(1-\frac{1}{e^5}) + 40\sqrt{\Delta}\ln\Delta$.

(d') For every vertex $v \in V$, the number of neighbors of v in C is at most $\frac{\Delta}{e^5} + 40\sqrt{\Delta}\ln\Delta$.

In (b'), Δ is replaced by Δ_0, which is the maximum degree of the initial graph. Also, the constant 9 is replaced by 18. In (c') and (d'), the constant 27 is replaced by 40 and $\sqrt{\ln\Delta}$ is replaced by $\ln\Delta$. It is not hard to see that Lemma 4.3 still holds and an $O(\log^2\Delta/\log\log\Delta)$-frugal coloring is still obtainable. Originally, by Chernoff Bound and Azuma's Inequality, they showed

$$\Pr\left(\#\text{ neighbors of } v \text{ colored } x \text{ exceeds } 9\cdot\tfrac{\ln\Delta}{\ln\ln\Delta}\right) < \frac{1}{\Delta^6} \quad (2)$$

and

$$\Pr\left(\left|P_v - \frac{\deg(v)}{e^5}\right| > 27\sqrt{\Delta\ln\Delta}\right) < \frac{2}{\Delta^{4.5}} \quad (3)$$

where P_v is the number of colored neighbors of v. Theorem 4.2 can be derived from (2) and (3). The relaxed version (b'), (c'), and (d') can be shown to fail with a lower probability.

$$\Pr\left(\#\text{ neighbors of } v \text{ colored } x \text{ exceeds } 18\cdot\tfrac{\ln\Delta_0}{\ln\ln\Delta_0}\right) < \frac{1}{\Delta_0^{12}} \quad (4)$$

and

$$\Pr\left(\left|P_v - \frac{\deg(v)}{e^5}\right| > 40\sqrt{\Delta}\ln\Delta\right) < \frac{2}{\Delta^{9\ln\Delta}} \quad (5)$$

The bad event A_v is when the neighbors of v colored x exceeds $18\cdot\frac{\ln\Delta_0}{\ln\ln\Delta_0}$ for some color x or $|P_v - \frac{\deg(v)}{e^5}| > 40\sqrt{\Delta}\ln\Delta$ happens. By (4), (5), and the union bound, $\Pr(A_v) \leq (\Delta+1)/\Delta_0^{12} + 2/\Delta^{9\ln\Delta}$. In their random process, they showed A_v depends on variables up to distance two. Thus, the dependency graph $G_{\mathcal{A}}$ has maximum degree d less than Δ^4. Note that $epd^2 = e\Delta^8((\Delta+1)/(2\Delta_0^{12}) + 2/\Delta^{9\ln\Delta}) \leq 1/(2\Delta_0) + 1/(2\Delta^{\ln\Delta}) < 2\cdot\max(1/(2\Delta_0), 1/(2\Delta^{\ln\Delta})) = \max(1/\Delta_0, 1/\Delta^{\ln\Delta})$. The number of resampling rounds needed is at most $O(\log_{\frac{1}{epd^2}} n)$, which is at most $\frac{\ln n}{\min(\ln\Delta_0, \ln^2\Delta)} \leq \frac{\ln n}{\ln\Delta_0} + \frac{\ln n}{\ln^2\Delta}$. Therefore, the total number of rounds needed is at most:

$$\begin{aligned}
&\sum_{i=1}^{c\ln\Delta_0}\left(\frac{\ln n}{\ln\Delta_0} + \frac{\ln n}{\ln^2\Delta_i}\right)\\
&\leq \sum_{i=1}^{c\ln\Delta_0}\left(\frac{\ln n}{\ln\Delta_0} + \frac{\ln n}{\ln^2(2\Delta_0\alpha^i)}\right)\\
&= c\ln\Delta_0\cdot\frac{\ln n}{\ln\Delta_0} + \ln n\sum_{i=1}^{c\ln\Delta_0}\frac{1}{(\ln\Delta_0 - i\ln\frac{1}{\alpha} + \ln 2)^2}\\
&\leq c\ln n + \ln n\cdot O\left(\sum_{i=1}^{\infty}\frac{1}{i^2}\right) = O(\log n)
\end{aligned}$$

where $c > 0$ is some constant, and $\alpha = (1 - 1/e^5)$.

5. REFERENCES

[1] N. Alon. A parallel algorithmic version of the local lemma. *Random Structures & Algorithms*, 2(4):367–378, 1991.

[2] N. Alon, L. Babai, and A. Itai. A fast and simple randomized parallel algorithm for the maximal independent set problem. *Journal of Algorithms*, 7(4):567 – 583, 1986.

[3] N. Alon, M. Krivelevich, and B. Sudakov. Coloring graphs with sparse neighborhoods. *Journal of Combinatorial Theory, Series B*, 77(1):73 – 82, 1999.

[4] L. Barenboim and M. Elkin. *Distributed Graph Coloring: Fundamentals and Recent Developments.* Synthesis Lectures on Distributed Computing Theory. Morgan & Claypool Publishers, 2013.

[5] L. Barenboim, M. Elkin, and F. Kuhn. Distributed $(\Delta+1)$-coloring in linear (in Δ) time. *SIAM Journal on Computing*, 43(1):72–95, 2014.

[6] L. Barenboim, M. Elkin, S. Pettie, and J. Schneider. The locality of distributed symmetry breaking. In *Proc. IEEE 53rd Symposium on Foundations of Computer Science (FOCS)*, pages 321 – 330, oct. 2012.

[7] J. Beck. An algorithmic approach to the Lovász local lemma. I. *Random Structures & Algorithms*, 2(4):343–365, 1991.

[8] K. Chandrasekaran, N. Goyal, and B. Haeupler. Deterministic algorithms for the Lovász local lemma. *SIAM Journal on Computing*, 42(6):2132–2155, 2013.

[9] A. Czumaj and C. Scheideler. A new algorithm approach to the general Lovász local lemma with applications to scheduling and satisfiability problems (extended abstract). In *Proc. 32nd ACM Symposium on Theory of Computing (STOC)*, pages 38–47, 2000.

[10] D. Dubhashi, D. A. Grable, and A. Panconesi. Near-optimal, distributed edge colouring via the nibble method. *Theor. Comput. Sci.*, 203(2):225–251, August 1998.

[11] P. Erdős and L. Lovász. Problems and results on 3-chromatic hypergraphs and some related questions. In A. Hanjal, R. Rado, and V. T. Sós, editors, *Infinite and Finite Sets*, volume 11, pages 609–627. North-Holland, 1975.

[12] B. Haeupler, B. Saha, and A. Srinivasan. New constructive aspects of the Lovász local lemma. *J. ACM*, 58(6):28, 2011.

[13] H. Hind, M. Molloy, and B. Reed. Colouring a graph frugally. *Combinatorica*, 17(4):469–482, 1997.

[14] K. Kolipaka and M. Szegedy. Moser and Tardos meet Lovász. In *Proceedings 43rd ACM Symposium on Theory of Computing (STOC)*, pages 235–244, 2011.

[15] F. Kuhn, T. Moscibroda, and R. Wattenhofer. Local computation: Lower and upper bounds. *CoRR*, abs/1011.5470, 2010.

[16] F. Kuhn and R. Wattenhofer. On the complexity of distributed graph coloring. In *Proc. 25th Annual ACM Symposium on Principles of Distributed Computing (PODC)*, pages 7–15, 2006.

[17] N. Linial. Locality in distributed graph algorithms. *SIAM J. Comput.*, 21(1):193–201, February 1992.

[18] M. Luby. A simple parallel algorithm for the maximal independent set problem. *SIAM Journal on Computing*, 15(4):1036–1053, 1986.

[19] M. Molloy and B. Reed. Further algorithmic aspects of the local lemma. In *Proc. 30th ACM Symposium on Theory of Computing (STOC)*, pages 524–529, 1998.

[20] M. Molloy and B. Reed. *Graph Colouring and the Probabilistic Method.* Algorithms and Combinatorics. Springer, 2001.

[21] M. Molloy and B. Reed. Asymptotically optimal frugal colouring. *J. Comb. Theory Ser. B*, 100(2):226–246, March 2010.

[22] R. A. Moser. Derandomizing the Lovász local lemma more effectively. *CoRR*, abs/0807.2120, 2008.

[23] R. A. Moser. A constructive proof of the Lovász local lemma. In *Proc. 41st ACM symposium on Theory of computing (STOC)*, pages 343–350, 2009.

[24] R. A. Moser and G. Tardos. A constructive proof of the general Lovász local lemma. *J. ACM*, 57(2):11, 2010.

[25] W. Pegden. An extension of the Moser-Tardos algorithmic local lemma. *CoRR*, abs/1102.2853, 2011.

[26] D. Peleg. *Distributed Computing: A Locality-Sensitive Approach.* Monographs on Discrete Mathematics and Applications. Society for Industrial and Applied Mathematics, 2000.

[27] S. Pemmaraju and A. Srinivasan. The randomized coloring procedure with symmetry-breaking. In *Proc. 35th Int'l Colloq. on Automata, Languages, and Programming (ICALP)*, volume 5125 of *LNCS*, pages 306–319. 2008.

[28] S. Pettie and H.-H. Su. Fast distributed coloring algorithms for triangle-free graphs. In *Proc. 40th Int'l Colloq. on Automata, Languages, and Programming (ICALP)*, volume 7966 of *LNCS*, pages 687–699, 2013.

[29] B. Reed and B. Sudakov. Asymptotically the list colouring constants are 1. *Journal of Combinatorial Theory, Series B*, 86(1):27 – 37, 2002.

[30] J. Schneider and R. Wattenhofer. A new technique for distributed symmetry breaking. In *Proc. 29th ACM Symposium on Principles of Distributed Computing (PODC)*, pages 257–266, 2010.
[31] J. Spencer. Asymptotic lower bounds for Ramsey functions. *Discrete Mathematics*, 20:69–76, 1977.
[32] A. Srinivasan. Improved algorithmic versions of the Lovász local lemma. In *Proc. 19th ACM-SIAM Symposium on Discrete Algorithms (SODA)*, pages 611–620, 2008.

APPENDIX

A. TOOLS

The following lemma shows when conditioning on a very likely event B, the probability of an event can only be affected by a small amount.

LEMMA A.1. *Let A, B be two events,* $|\Pr(A) - \Pr(A|B)| \le \Pr(\overline{B})$.

PROOF. $\Pr(A) = \Pr(B)\Pr(A|B) + \Pr(\overline{B})\Pr(A|\overline{B}) = \Pr(A|B) + \Pr(\overline{B})(\Pr(A|\overline{B}) - \Pr(A|B))$. Therefore, $|\Pr(A) - \Pr(A|B)| \le \Pr(\overline{B})$. □

LEMMA A.2. (Chernoff Bound) *Let $X_1, \ldots, X_n$ be independent trials such that $\Pr(X_i) = p$. Let $X = \sum_{i=1}^n X_i$. Then, for $\delta > 0$:*

$$\Pr(X > (1+\delta)\,\mathrm{E}[X]) \le \left[\frac{e^\delta}{(1+\delta)^{(1+\delta)}}\right]^{\mathrm{E}[X]}$$

$$\Pr(X < (1-\delta)\,\mathrm{E}[X]) \le \left[\frac{e^\delta}{(1-\delta)^{(1-\delta)}}\right]^{\mathrm{E}[X]}$$

The two bounds above imply that for $0 < \delta < 1$, we have:

$$\Pr(X > (1+\delta)\,\mathrm{E}[X]) \le e^{-\delta^2\,\mathrm{E}[X]/3}$$

$$\Pr(X < (1-\delta)\,\mathrm{E}[X]) \le e^{-\delta^2\,\mathrm{E}[X]/2}.$$

The proof for the following corollaries will be included in the full version.

COROLLARY A.3. *Let $X_1, \ldots, X_n$ be independent trials such that $\Pr(X_i) = p_i$. Let $X = \sum_{i=1}^n X_i$. If $M \ge \mathrm{E}[X]$ and $0 < \delta \le 1$, then*

$$\Pr(X > \mathrm{E}[X] + \delta M) \le e^{-\delta^2 M/3}$$

COROLLARY A.4. *Let $X_1, \ldots, X_n$ be trials such that for each $1 \le i \le n$,*

$$\Pr(X_i \mid X_1, \ldots, X_{i-1}) \le p$$

Then the upper tail of $X = \sum_{i=1}^n X_i$ can be bounded by the upper tail Chernoff estimate for an independent set of variables $X_1', X_2', \ldots, X_n'$ with $\mathrm{E}[X_i'] = p$. In particular, for $\delta > 0$:

$$\Pr(X > (1+\delta)np) \le \left[\frac{e^\delta}{(1+\delta)^{(1+\delta)}}\right]^{np}$$

B. PROOF OF LEMMA 3.5

LEMMA 3.5. *If for all $A \in \mathcal{A}$, we have $\Pr(A) \le (1-\epsilon)x(A) \cdot \prod_{B \in \Gamma^r(A)}(1 - x(B))$, then the probability that any r-witness tree of size at least k occurs is at most $(1-\epsilon)^k \cdot \sum_{A \in \mathcal{A}} \frac{x(A)}{1-x(A)}$.*

Following Moser and Tardos [24] we analyze the following Galton-Watson process for generating a r-witness tree T. Fix an event $A \in \mathcal{A}$. Begin by creating a root for T labelled A. To shorten the notation, we let $[v] := \sigma_T(v)$. In each subsequent step, consider each vertex v created in the previous step. For each $B \in \Gamma^{r+}([v])$, independently, attach a child labelled B with probability $x(B)$ or skip it with probability $1 - x(B)$. Continue the process until no new vertices are born. We prove a lemma analogous to one in [24].

LEMMA B.1. *Let τ be a fixed proper r-witness tree with its root vertex labelled A. The probability p_τ that the Galton-Watson process yields exactly the tree τ is*

$$p_\tau = \frac{1-x(A)}{x(A)} \prod_{v \in V(\tau)} x'([v])$$

where $x'(B) = x(B) \cdot \Pi_{C \in \Gamma^r(B)}(1 - x(C))$.

PROOF. Let $W_v \subseteq \Gamma^{r+}([v])$ denote the set of inclusive r-neighbors of $[v]$ that do not occur as a label of some child node of v. Then,

$$\begin{aligned}
p_\tau &= \frac{1}{x(A)} \cdot \prod_{v \in V(\tau)} \left(x([v]) \cdot \prod_{u \in W_v} (1 - x([u])) \right) \\
&= \frac{1-x(A)}{x(A)} \cdot \prod_{v \in V(\tau)} \left(\frac{x([v])}{1 - x([v])} \cdot \prod_{u \in \Gamma^{r+}([v])} (1 - x([u])) \right) \\
&= \frac{1-x(A)}{x(A)} \cdot \prod_{v \in V(\tau)} \left(x([v]) \cdot \prod_{u \in \Gamma^{r}([v])} (1 - x([u])) \right) \\
&= \frac{1-x(A)}{x(A)} \cdot \prod_{v \in V(\tau)} x'([v])
\end{aligned}$$

□

Let $\mathcal{T}_A^r(k)$ denote the infinite set of r-witness trees having root labelled A and containing at least k vertices. By Lemma 3.6 and the union bound, the probability there exists a violated event after k resampling rounds is at most

$$\begin{aligned}
&\sum_{A \in \mathcal{A}} \sum_{\tau \in \mathcal{T}_A^r(k)} \Pr(\tau \text{ } r\text{-occurs in } C) \\
&\le \sum_{A \in \mathcal{A}} \sum_{\tau \in \mathcal{T}_A^r(k)} \prod_{v \in V(\tau)} \Pr([v]) && \text{by Lemma 2.2} \\
&\le \sum_{A \in \mathcal{A}} \sum_{\tau \in \mathcal{T}_A^r(k)} \prod_{v \in V(\tau)} (1-\epsilon) x'([v]) && \text{cond. of Thm 3.3} \\
&\le (1-\epsilon)^k \sum_{A \in \mathcal{A}} \frac{x(A)}{1-x(A)} \sum_{\tau \in \mathcal{T}_A^r(k)} p_\tau && \text{by Lemma B.1} \\
&\le (1-\epsilon)^k \sum_{A \in \mathcal{A}} \frac{x(A)}{1-x(A)}
\end{aligned}$$

The last inequality follows since the Galton-Watson process grows exactly one tree.

Brief Announcement: Towards Security and Privacy for Outsourced Data in the Multi-Party Setting

Matteo Maffei Giulio Malavolta Manuel Reinert Dominique Schröder
Saarland University & CISPA
Saarbrücken, Germany
{maffei, malavolta, reinert, schroeder}@cs.uni-saarland.de

ABSTRACT

Cloud storage has rapidly acquired popularity among users, constituting a seamless solution for the backup, synchronization, and sharing of large amounts of data. This technology, however, puts user data in the direct control of cloud service providers, which raises increasing security and privacy concerns related to the integrity of outsourced data, the accidental or intentional leakage of sensitive information, the profiling of user activities and so on.

We present GORAM, a cryptographic system that protects the secrecy and integrity of the data outsourced to an untrusted server and guarantees the anonymity and unlinkability of consecutive accesses to such data. GORAM allows the database owner to share outsourced data with other clients, selectively granting them read and write permissions. GORAM is the first system to achieve such a wide range of security and privacy properties for outsourced storage. Technically, GORAM builds on a combination of ORAM to conceal data accesses, attribute-based encryption to rule the access to outsourced data, and zero-knowledge proofs to prove read and write permissions in a privacy-preserving manner. We implemented GORAM and conducted an experimental evaluation to demonstrate its feasibility.

Categories and Subject Descriptors

K.6.5 [**Management of Computing and Information Systems**]: Security and Protection

Keywords

Oblivious RAM; ORAM; GORAM; Cloud Storage; Privacy-enhancing Technologies

1. INTRODUCTION

Cloud storage has rapidly acquired a central role in the digital society. It is convenient for users, who can smoothly backup their data, access them from computationally limited devices, synchronize them across multiple locations, and share them with other parties. Typical examples are data storage services such as Dropbox, Microsoft SkyDrive, and Google Drive, or music and app synchronization services such as iCloud or Amazon. Despite its convenience, cloud storage poses a number of security and privacy issues.

The first problem is related to the *integrity* of user data. The server has the possibility to modify client's data, which can be harmful for several reasons: for instance, a storage provider could charge the client for space it is not using by adding fake data, or save on storage space by deleting old backup copies of large files, which are likely not to be accessed by the user.

A second problem is related to the *secrecy* of user data, which are often sensitive and, thus, should be concealed from the server. For instance, a client accessing a medical database in search for symptoms of and remedies against a certain disease would probably like to keep both the queried documents private. As shown in the literature [10, 12], even the capability to link consecutive accesses to the same file can be exploited by the server to learn sensitive information: hence the *obliviousness* of data accesses is another fundamental property for cloud storage services.

Furthermore, modern cloud storage services (e.g., Google Docs) offer the database owner the possibility to share some of the documents with other clients, yet in a controlled manner, i.e., selectively granting them read and write permissions. *Data sharing* complicates the enforcement of integrity properties, since clients might be malicious and try themselves to break the integrity of the user data. Additionally, *access control* is in seeming contradiction with the obliviousness property: how can the server check if the client is authorized to read or write a certain file if the server is not supposed to learn which file the client is accessing?

Related Work. Oblivious RAM (ORAM) [5] has recently proved an effective technique to hide the data as well as the access patterns of a client from an untrusted server in storage outsourcing services [3, 12, 1, 6]. Some of these protocols further guarantee the integrity of user data against a malicious server [16, 13]. Standard constructions, however, are not suitable for a multi-client setting, since clients would need to hold the ORAM key, a top-level key used to encrypt data on the server's side, which would allow them to read and also potentially disrupt the entire database.

A few recent works have started to tackle this problem. Franz *et al.* introduced the concept of delegated ORAM [4]. The idea is to encrypt and sign each entry with a unique set of keys, initially only known to the database owner: giving a client the decryption key (resp. the decryption and signing

PODC'14, July 15–18, 2014, Paris, France.
ACM 978-1-4503-2944-6/14/07.
http://dx.doi.org/10.1145/2611462.2611508.

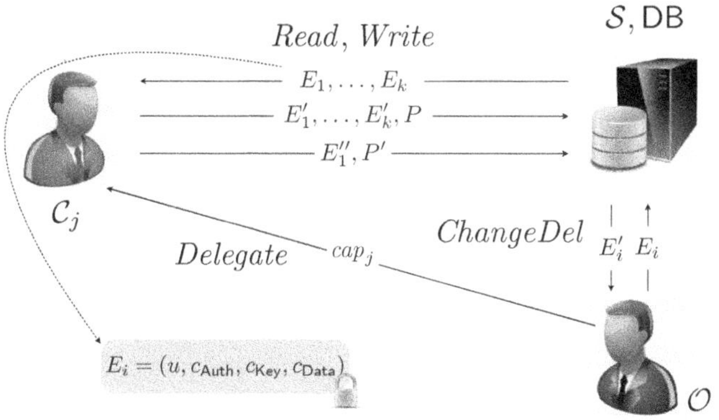

Figure 1: The overview of our construction.

keys) suffices to grant read (resp. write) access to that entry. This solution, however, has the drawback of forcing the database owner to track the individual client accesses and to come back periodically to reshuffle the ORAM according to the access history in order to enable further unlinkable ORAM accesses. Furthermore, revoking access for a single client requires to change (and distribute) the capabilities of all other users that have access to that file. Goodrich *et al.* [7] developed an ORAM construction for the multi-client setting, but their scheme considers only trusted clients and does not allow clients to verify the integrity of outsourced data. Huang and Goldberg presented a protocol for outsourced private information retrieval (PIR) [9], which is obtained by layering a PIR scheme on top of an ORAM data layout. This solution is efficient and conceals client accesses from the database owner, but it does not give clients the possibility to update data, as required in collaborative applications. Furthermore, it assumes ℓ non-colluding servers, due to the information theoretic multi-server PIR. Despite the significant progress in this field, none of the existing approaches constitutes a practical solution to the problem of sharing data stored on the cloud with potentially distrustful clients.

Our Contributions. We tackle this long-standing problem by presenting GORAM (Group ORAM), the first ORAM construction that allows the database owner to verify the integrity of outsourced data and, at the same time, to share these data with other clients, selectively granting them read as well as write permissions, without the need for the database owner to manage the consistency of the database. Data accesses are oblivious and the server does not learn any information about them. The fundamental idea is to combine ORAM [14] to conceal data accesses, attribute-based encryption [11] to rule the access to outsourced data, and zero-knowledge proofs [8, 2] to prove read and write permissions in a privacy-preserving manner; finally, we demonstrate the feasibility of our approach with an experimental evaluation.

2. OVERVIEW OF GORAM

Cryptographic Construction. We consider the following storage outsourcing scenario. A database owner $\mathcal{O}$ stores her data DB on an untrusted server $\mathcal{S}$. Moreover, she wants to share data with other clients $\mathcal{C}_1, \ldots, \mathcal{C}_n$. In order to operate on the server, the clients should not synchronize with $\mathcal{O}$, since this would require $\mathcal{O}$ to be always online, which is not a realistic assumption. In order to manage the database, $\mathcal{O}$ has several functions at her disposal. She can read and write entries from and to the database, she can grant other clients access, and she can change the access permissions for single entries in the database. GORAM provides three different access modes: read access, read and write access, and no access. Clients which $\mathcal{O}$ shares data with can read and write database entries according to their access permissions.

The protocols supported by GORAM are depicted in Figure 1 and explained below. The database of size $O(N)$ is a binary tree of depth $O(\log N)$. An entry E_i has four components, which are all secured by a top-level public-key encryption layer: (1) a unique resource identifier u, (2) an attribute-based encryption ciphertext c_{Auth} that regulates write access, (3) an attribute-based encryption ciphertext c_{Key} that contains a symmetric key and regulates the read access, and (4) the actual data c_{Data} that is secured by a symmetric-key encryption scheme. Attribute-based encryption (see, e.g., [11]) is a cryptographic primitive that encodes access policies in ciphertexts and secret keys. Intuitively, a user can only decrypt a ciphertext c if her secret key fulfills the policy encoded in c. For the structure of E_i, this means that, if the client has read access, she is able to decrypt c_{Key} and can extract the symmetric key that allows her to decrypt c_{Data}.

In order to grant client $\mathcal{C}_j$ access, $\mathcal{O}$ hands over a capability cap_j that contains the top-level private key and two attribute-based secret keys, for read and write access control. Furthermore, $\mathcal{O}$ can set for each entry E_i in the database the access permissions separately. If she wants to give $\mathcal{C}_j$ read (resp. write) access to index i, she sets c_{Key} (resp. c_{Auth}) such that $\mathcal{C}_j$ can decrypt it.

In order to read or write data from the database, a client downloads a path $E_1, \ldots, E_k$ in the tree from the root to a leaf. After the client has read the entry that she was interested in (by inspecting the resource identifiers), she shuffles and re-randomizes the entries such that the entry that she read is in the top position. She then sends the shuffled and re-randomized path $E'_1, \ldots, E'_k$ together with a proof P to the server. P is a zero-knowledge proof showing that the new path's content has not changed except for the applied permutation and the randomness used in the encryption. $\mathcal{S}$ verifies P with respect to the new and the old path and replaces the entries accordingly. If, additionally, the client wants to write an entry that she has access to (which is now in the top position, i.e., E'_1), she encrypts the new data with the key that she extracted from c_{Key}. She then creates E''_1 by re-randomizing c_{Auth} and the top-level encryption of E'_1. Finally, she sends E''_1 and P' to $\mathcal{S}$. P' is a zero-knowledge proof showing that the client is able to decrypt c_{Auth} in E'_1 (this proves that she possesses a valid decryption key). $\mathcal{S}$ verifies P' and replaces E'_1 by E''_1.

Security and Privacy Properties. GORAM achieves the following properties:

Secrecy. The attribute-based encryption scheme ensures that only clients holding read permissions on a certain file can learn any information about its content.

Integrity. The zero-knowledge (ZK) proofs ensure that every database entry can be modified only by clients holding write permissions on it, as long as $\mathcal{S}$ is honest but curious. If $\mathcal{S}$ is malicious and colludes with a subset of users, our model still guarantees honest clients to notice whenever a data is

(a) 8KB block size, 3 groups of clients.

(b) 1GB storage, 3 groups of clients.

Figure 2: The results for a computer with 8 cores and a multi-threaded Java implementation.

tampered, as long as corrupted clients have neither read nor write permissions on that data.

Anonymity. The ZK proofs further ensure that nobody can link a read or write operation to a particular client, within the set of users having access to the target entry.

Obliviousness. The ORAM scheme along with the ZK proofs ensures that the pattern of two subsequent accesses is uniformly distributed over the database entries, independent of the processed data and the performed operation.

3. EXPERIMENTAL EVALUATION

The computational complexity of our construction both on the client and on the server as well as the space needed on the client's side is $O((G+B)\log N)$ where B is the block size of entries in the database, N is the size of the database, and G is the number of client groups that have access to the database. Hence, our construction only adds G to the original ORAM complexity. Our experimental results for the read and write protocols are depicted in Figure 2. Figure 2a shows the logarithmic growth in the client and server time while we increase the storage size N. Figure 2b shows the linear increase in client and server time while we grow the block size B. Interestingly enough, multi-threading keeps the time almost constant from 8KB to 64KB. Overall, the computation overhead is dominated by the re-randomization of the top-level public-key encryption and the computation of the zero-knowledge proofs. In order to optimize our implementation, we envision the usage of GPUs, which can speed up the computation time by a factor of 20 [17, 15].

4. ACKNOWLEDGEMENTS

This work was supported by the German research foundation (DFG) through the Emmy Noether program and by the German Federal Ministry of Education and Research (BMBF) through the Center for IT-Security, Privacy and Accountability (CISPA). Finally, we thank the reviewers for their helpful comments.

5. REFERENCES

[1] M. Ajtai. Oblivious RAMs Without Cryptogrpahic Assumptions. In *STOC'10*, pages 181–190. ACM, 2010.

[2] S. Bayer and J. Groth. Efficient Zero-Knowledge Argument for Correctness of a Shuffle. In *EUROCRYPT'12*, LNCS, pages 263–280. Springer, 2012.

[3] B. Carbunar and R. Sion. Regulatory Compliant Oblivious RAM. In *ACNS'10*, LNCS, pages 456–474. Springer, 2010.

[4] M. Franz, C. Carbunar, R. Sion, S. Katzenbeisser, M. Sotakova, P. Williams, and A. Peter. Oblivious Outsourced Storage with Delegation. In *FC'11*, pages 127–140. Springer, 2011.

[5] O. Goldreich and R. Ostrovsky. Software Protection and Simulation on Oblivious RAMs. *J. ACM*, 43(3):431–473, May 1996.

[6] M. T. Goodrich and M. Mitzenmacher. Privacy-Preserving Access of Outsourced Data Via Oblivious RAM Simulation. In *ICALP'11*, LNCS, pages 576–587. Springer, 2011.

[7] M. T. Goodrich, M. Mitzenmacher, O. Ohrimenko, and R. Tamassia. Privacy-Preserving Group Data Access via Stateless Oblivious RAM Simulation. In *SODA'12*, pages 157–167. SIAM, 2012.

[8] J. Groth and A. Sahai. Efficient Noninteractive Proof Systems for Bilinear Groups. *SIAM J. Comp.*, 41(5):1193–1232, 2012.

[9] Y. Huang and I. Goldberg. Outsourced Private Information Retrieval with Pricing and Access Control. In *WPES'13*. ACM, 2013.

[10] M. Islam, M. Kuzu, and M. Kantarcioglu. Access Pattern Disclosure on Searchable Encryption: Ramification, Attack and Mitigation. In *NDSS'12*. Internet Society, 2012.

[11] J. Katz, A. Sahai, and B. Waters. Predicate Encryption Supporting Disjunctions, Polynomial Equations, and Inner Products. In *EUROCRYPT'08*, pages 146–162. Springer, 2008.

[12] B. Pinkas and T. Reinman. Oblivious RAM Revisited. In *CRYPTO'10*, LNCS, pages 502–519. Springer, 2010.

[13] E. Stefanov, E. Shi, , and D. Song. Towards Practical Oblivious RAM. In *NDSS'12*. Internet Society, 2012.

[14] E. Stefanov, M. van Dijk, E. Shi, C. Fletcher, L. Ren, X. Yu, and S. Devadas. Path ORAM: An Extremely Simple Oblivious RAM Protocol. In *CCS'13*. ACM, 2013.

[15] R. Szerwinski and T. Güneysu. Exploiting the Power of GPUs for Asymmetric Cryptography. In *CHES'08*, LNCS, pages 79–99. Springer, 2008.

[16] P. Williams, R. Sion, and B. Carbunar. Building Castles out of Mud: Practical Access Pattern Privacy and Correctness on Untrusted Storage. In *CCS'08*, pages 139–148. ACM, 2008.

[17] Y. Zhang, C. J. Xue, D. S. Wong, N. Mamoulis, and S. M. Yiu. Acceleration of Composite Order Bilinear Pairing on Graphics Hardware. In *ICICS'12*, LNCS, pages 341–348. Springer, 2012.

Brief Announcement: Game Theoretical Approach for Energy-Delay Balancing in Distributed Duty-Cycled MAC Protocols of Wireless Networks

Messaoud Doudou
CERIST Research Center
Algiers, Algeria
doudou@cerist.dz

Jose M. Barcelo Ordinas
Universitat Politecnica de Catalunya (UPC)
Barcelona, Spain
joseb@ac.upc.edu

Djamel Djenouri
CERIST Research Center
Algiers, Algeria
ddjenouri@acm.org

Jorge Garcia Vidal
Universitat Politecnica de Catalunya (UPC)
Barcelona, Spain
jorge@ac.upc.edu

Nadjib Badache
USTHB university
Algiers, Algeria
badache@cerist.dz

ABSTRACT

Optimizing energy consumption and end-to-end (e2e) packet delay in energy constrained distributed wireless networks is a conflicting multi-objective optimization problem. This paper investigates this trade-off from a game-theoretic perspective, where the two optimization objectives are considered as virtual game players that attempt to optimize their utility values. The cost model of each player is mapped through a generalized optimization framework onto protocol specific MAC parameters. A cooperative game is then defined, in which the Nash Bargaining solution assures the balance between energy consumption and e2e packet delay. For illustration, this formulation is applied to three state-of-the-art wireless sensor network MAC protocols; X-MAC, DMAC, and LMAC as representatives of preamble sampling, slotted contention-based, and frame-based MAC categories, respectively. The paper shows the effectiveness of such framework in optimizing protocol parameters for achieving a fair energy-delay performance trade-off, under the application requirements in terms of initial energy budget and maximum e2e packet delay. The proposed framework is scalable with the increase in the number of nodes, as the players represent the optimization metrics instead of nodes.

Categories and Subject Descriptors

C.2.2 [**Network Protocols**]; C.2.4 [**Distributed System**]; G.1.6 [**Mathematics of computing**]: Optimization—*Convex programming*

Keywords

Wireless Networks; Game Theory; Duty-Cycling; MAC; Energy; Delay.

1. INTRODUCTION

Maximizing the network lifetime while assuring the application requirements in terms of e2e delay is challenging in distributed energy-constrained wireless networks, such as wireless sensor networks (WSN). Energy saving is achieved at the MAC protocol by duty-cycling the radio, which necessitates multiple operational cycles in forwarding data packets. This mechanism can violate the e2e delay bound required in multi-hop networks. Given the application constraints in terms of initial energy budget devoted to each individual node and the maximum e2e packet delay tolerated, the choice of MAC protocol's parameters is of great importance; yet their choice is currently done by system designers based on repeated real experiences [2], or on optimizing one objective subject to other objectives as constraints [12]. These solutions achieve the optimal running performance for one objective that is not necessarily optimal for the other, which yields a performance far off the application requirements.

Contribution: We investigate the inherent trade-off between the two metrics from a game-theoretic perspective. We propose a game-theory framework that permits to determine optimal values for tunable MAC parameters to achieve a fair energy-delay trade-off for design considerations. These tunable parameters, related to application sampling and MAC duty-cycle operations, allow to find an equilibrium point in which the system operates. In the proposed framework, the virtual players are the performance metrics (energy and delay), instead of the individual nodes that is common in the state-of-the-art models. The cost model of each player is then mapped onto a protocol specific MAC parameters that are system wide optimal. The following steps are followed in order to find the optimal operation that balances energy consumption and latency: (i) Energy and Latency are characterized in duty-cycle MAC protocols according to sampling rate and duty-cycle operation parameters. (ii) Energy consumption optimization is achieved by deriving optimal parameters that minimize energy consumption subject to latency constraints. (iii) Latency optimization is achieved by deriving optimal parameters that minimize latency subject to to energy budget constraints. Finally, (iv) a Nash Bargaining solution model is used to find a cooperative optimal point between players that represent energy consumption and latency.

Related Work: While most of the energy-efficient MAC protocols for wireless networks followed pure experimental approaches, some works have attempted to model and analyze these protocols. Langendoen and Meier, [3] consider traffic and network models for very low data rate applications, and they analyze energy consumption and average latency of well known MAC protocols. Protocol optimization have been investigated by Ye et al. [10], notably for energy minimization of SCP-MAC protocol. While most models consider single- objective optimization, protocol optimization under application needs in terms of both energy and e2e delay have been considered in [12]. However, their approaches are based on optimizing energy subject to constraints on the delay. Lately, numerous efforts have been devoted to address MAC optimization in wireless networks using game theory. First, Nuggehalli et al [7] use game-theory to address the QoS support in 802.11 networks that enables users with high-priority or low-priority traffic to fairly negotiate channel access. Energy-efficiency is also addressed by Voulkidis et al. [9], using game-theory-based coalition formation between spatial correlated sensors to reduce the amount of transmitted packets. The energy-delay tradeoff is considered by Nahir et al, [5], where multiple cost models (power level, direct/indirect transmissions) are used by each node to determine the Nash equilibrium point. All these works consider nodes as players

PODC'14, July 15–18, 2014, Paris, France.
ACM 978-1-4503-2944-6/14/07.
http://dx.doi.org/10.1145/2611462.2611509.

in the game and attempt to maximize the defined utility function. These approaches lack of scalability and do not apply to large networks. Last but not the least, Zhao et al. [11] propose a game-theoretical solution to achieve a trade-off between load-balancing and energy-efficiency in traffic engineering, where the performance goals are considered as peers (players) of the game. The proposed framework is based on the energy model derived in [3], and it uses of the Nash Bargaining solution to balance objectives modeled as virtual players, which is inspired by the model proposed in [11]. To the best of our knowledge, this work is the first that considers the energy/delay trade-off in duty-cycled MAC protocols using game-theory.

2. GAME THEORY FRAMEWORK

In the proposed framework, the key performance metrics are the energy consumption $\boldsymbol{E}$ and the maximum end-to-end (e2e) packet delay $\boldsymbol{L}$. The application requirements expressed as the maximum energy budget per node, E_{budget}, and the maximum allowed end-to-end delay per node, L_{max}, are used as inputs for the framework. The framework builds then a system-wide model for energy and delay based on, (i) the specified MAC model defined by its operating modes: idle, transmission, reception, and sleep modes, and (ii), the network and traffic models that permit to determine the topology information and the traffic load at each node.

Energy Consumption, E^n, is defined as the amount of energy consumed by the radio of node, $n \in V$ (V a set of nodes in the network), according to its position and the amount of traffic it handles. Thus, the Energy Consumption depends on node density and data sampling rate. It is calculated as a function of the operating modes the sensor node runs, and the MAC intrinsic parameters. In general, the energy consumed in any MAC protocol is due to: carrier sensing E_{cs}, data transmission E_{tx}, data reception E_{rx}, overhearing E_{ovr}, and sending/receiving synchronization frames (resp. E_{stx} and E_{srx}) in the case of synchronous protocols. Given that the network lifetime can be expressed as the expected shortest node-lifetime [12], we define the system wide Energy Consumption, $\boldsymbol{E}$, as the maximum consumed energy in the network,

$$\boldsymbol{E} = \max_{n \in V} \left(E^n = E^n_{cs} + E^n_{tx} + E^n_{rx} + E^n_{ovr} + E^n_{stx} + E^n_{srx} \right)$$

End-to-end (e2e) Delay, L^n, is defined as the expected time between the first transmission of a packet at node, $n \in V$, and its reception at the sink. It is then a per-topology parameter, in the sense that it depends on the position of the node that generates the data. L^n denotes the sum of per-hop latencies of the shortest path $\mathcal{P}^n$ from node n to the sink, where L^n_l is the one-hop latency on link $l \in \mathcal{P}^n$. The maximum end-to-end latency, $\boldsymbol{L}$, is defined as the maximum latency from all nodes to the sink as follows:

$$\boldsymbol{L} = \max_{n \in V} \left(L^n = \sum_{l \in \mathcal{P}^n} L^n_l \right)$$

Network and Traffic Model. Let us consider an unsaturated network with low traffic, which is typical in energy-constrained networks, e.g., WSN applications. For the sake of simplicity, a ring topology is adopted following the same analysis as in [3]. A spanning tree is constructed, where nodes are static and maintain a unique path to the sink and use the shortest path routing with a maximum length of D hops; the depth or number of rings of the tree. Assume a network with uniform node density on the plane, and a unit disk graph communication model with density, C, i.e., unit disks contain C+1 nodes. The nodes are layered into levels according to their distance to the static sink in terms of minimal hop count, d (d=1,...,D), where d =0 is reserved for the sink. Periodic traffic generation is considered, where every source node generates traffic with frequency F_s. Consequently, the same input F^d_I, output F^d_{out}, background F^d_B traffic and input links I^d equations for every node are similar to those derived in [3].

Eenrgy-Delay Optimization. Let Θ denote the set of parameters that can be optimized in the system for a given application. Given a specific MAC protocol, let $X \in \Theta$ be the vector of system parameters that can be optimized. The following optimization problems are defined for energy consumption and e2e delay minimization:

$(\boldsymbol{P1})$		$(\boldsymbol{P2})$	
Minimize	$\boldsymbol{E}(X)$	Minimize	$\boldsymbol{L}(X)$
S.t.	$\boldsymbol{L}(X) \leqslant L_{max}$	S.t.	$\boldsymbol{E}(X) \leqslant E_{budget}$
Var.	X,	Var.	X,

The pairs (E_{best}, L_{worst}) and (E_{worst}, L_{best}) are the optimal solutions of problems $(\boldsymbol{P1})$ and $(\boldsymbol{P2})$ respectively, where, E_{best}=$E(X^*_E)$ and L_{worst}=$L(X^*_E)$, while E_{worst}=$E(X^*_L)$ and L_{best}=$L(X^*_L)$.

Nash Bargaining Solution. In order to find the optimal trade-off, we use the Nash Bargaining solution where every optimization problem represents a player, i.e., player *Energy* and player *Latency*. A bargaining game with two players selects one of the possible player's outcomes of a joint collaboration [6]. Let $A \in R^2$ be the set of alternatives the players face, S={$s = (u_1(a), u_2(a)) | a \in A$} be the set of feasible utility payoffs u, and $v \in S$ be a disagreement or *threat* point. Each point in S corresponds to the outcome of the bargaining and specifies the utility for this outcome. The disagreement point, $v = (v_1, v_2)$, represents the value that each player expects to receive if the negotiation breaks down. The goal of the bargaining is to choose a feasible agreement $\Phi : (S, v) \rightarrow S$ that results from the negotiation. The Nash Bargaining solution considers that S is convex, compact, and there exists an s∈S such that, s>v for both players. Players have complete information over S, v. The Nash Bargaining solution deals with the bargaining game by solving optimization problem $(\boldsymbol{NBS})$:

$(\boldsymbol{NBS})$		$(\boldsymbol{P3})$	
Maximize	$(s_1 - v_1)(s_2 - v_2)$	Maximize	$\left(E_{worst}\text{-}\boldsymbol{E}\right)\left(L_{worst}\text{-}\boldsymbol{L}\right)$
S.t.	$s \in S$	S.t.	$(E_{budget}, L_{max}) \geq (\boldsymbol{E}, \boldsymbol{L})$
	$(s_1, s_2) \geq (v_1, v_2)$		$(E_{worst}, L_{worst}) \geq (\boldsymbol{E}, \boldsymbol{L})$
Var.	s,	Var.	$\boldsymbol{E}, \boldsymbol{L}$,

The Nash Bargaining solution has the following axioms, [6], (i) *Pareto Optimality*, (ii) *Symmetry*, (iii) *Scale Independence*, and (iv) *Independence of Irrelevant Alternatives*. It specifies that there exists an optimal solution since S is compact, the objective function is continuous. The uniqueness of the optimal solution is guaranteed when the objective function is quasi-concave. The Nash Bargaining solution $\Phi(S, v)$ is the unique bargaining solution that satisfies the previous four axioms. Let X^*_E and X^*_L be the point values obtained by both players, Energy and Delay, if the agreement for problems $(\boldsymbol{P1})$ and $(\boldsymbol{P2})$ fails. Noting that $\boldsymbol{E}$ and $\boldsymbol{L}$ are cost functions instead of utility functions, and that the pair (E_{best}, L_{best}) is an infeasible solution in both problems $(\boldsymbol{P1})$ and $(\boldsymbol{P2})$. The Nash Bargaining Solution to the Duty-Cycled MAC problem is given by problem $(\boldsymbol{P3})$. Each player can prevent the agreement threatening with his best value and the other's worst value, or it can reduce its threat, looking for a feasible point that satisfies both players. The solution $\left(E^*, L^*\right)$ of the optimization problem $(\boldsymbol{P3})$ will be the optimal cost for both players under the agreement.

3. APPLICATION TO DUTY-CYCLED MAC PROTOCOLS

We apply the optimization framework to three state-of-the-art energy-delay efficient MAC protocols, X-MAC [1], DMAC [4], and LMAC [8] as representatives of the main categories of duty-cycled MAC protocols, asynchronous preamble sampling, slotted contention-based, and frame-based respectively. The application to these protocols exemplify the framework and show its usefulness to optimize different MAC parameters that permit to achieve a fair energy-delay trade-off. The per-node energy consumption based on the protocol operation modes, the e2e packet delay, and the bottleneck constraint are provided in [3].

Energy Optimization: Given the application requirements in terms of e2e packet delay bound L_{max}, energy optimization derives optimal MAC parameters that give the minimal network energy consumption subject to maximum e2e packet delay. Let X^*_i be the optimal point of problem $(\boldsymbol{P1})$ with i={$XMAC, DMAC, LMAC$}. Then, the optimal values of problem $(\boldsymbol{P1})$ are E^i_{best}= $E^i(X^*_i)$. The corresponding e2e packet delays are obviously non-optimal, L^i_{worst}= $L^i(X^*_i)$.

Delay Optimization: Given the application constraints in terms of initial energy budget E_{budget}, the delay optimization problems can be solved similarly to the energy optimization models, except the fact that the largest delay occurs at the outer ring nodes, d=D. Let Y^*_i denotes the optimal point of problem $(\boldsymbol{P2})$ with i={$XMAC, DMAC, LMAC$}. The optimal delay values of problem $(\boldsymbol{P2})$ are denoted L^i_{best}= $L^i(Y^*_i)$. The network energy consumption is non-optimal for this point, and it is denoted by: E^i_{worst}= $E^i(Y^*_i)$.

Energy-Delay Tradeoff: The Nash Bargaining solution $(\boldsymbol{P3})$ is applied in the following to the three protocols. Let the point $(E^i_{worst}, L^i_{worst})$ be the disagreement point[1] with i={$XMAC, DMAC, LMAC$}. Both

[1] Note that although the energy is considered at nodes at ring d=1, and latency at nodes d=D, the game is not played by the nodes, but it is played later at the system level.

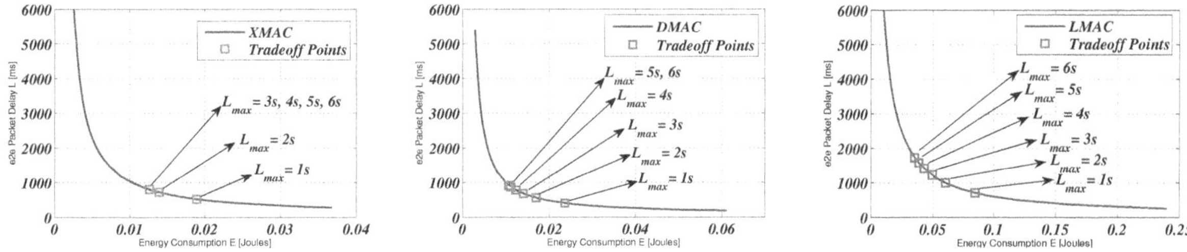

(a) (b) (c)

Figure 1: E-L trade-off when fixing E_{budget}=0.06 J for (a) X-MAC, (b) DMAC, and (c) LMAC.

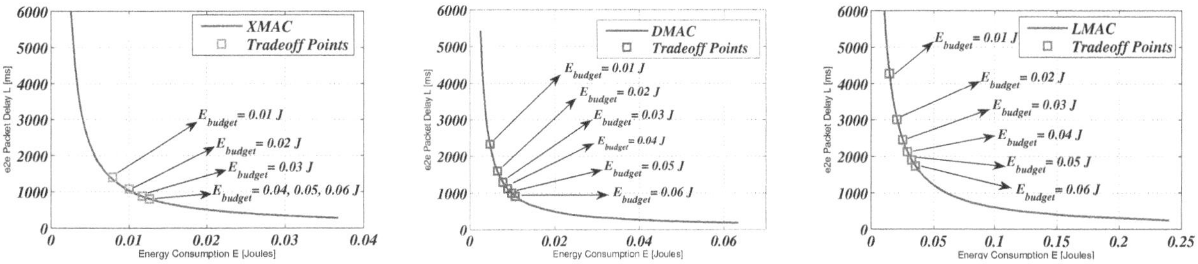

(a) (b) (c)

Figure 2: E-L trade-off when fixing L_{max}=6 s for (a) X-MAC, (b) DMAC, and (c) LMAC.

players can threat with their optimal values E^i_{best} and L^i_{best}. The problem $(\boldsymbol{P3})$ is non-linear non-convex. The authors of [11] show how to transform similar problems into a standard convex optimization problem without changing its solution. The idea is to define auxiliary variables E_1 and L_1 such that E_1=$E^i(X)$ and L_1=$L^i(X)$, which should be satisfied by the optimal solution. Whenever the problem $(\boldsymbol{P3})$ is feasible, $E^i(X) \leq E^i_{worst}$, $L^i(X) \leq L^i_{worst}$, and application of $(\boldsymbol{P3})$ to the MAC protocols yields a concave problem $(\boldsymbol{P4})$ with i=$\{XMAC, DMAC, LMAC\}$.

$$
\begin{array}{lll}
(\boldsymbol{P4}) & Maximize & log(E^i_{worst} - E_1) + log(L^i_{worst} - L_1), \\
 & s.t. & (E^i_{worst}, L^i_{worst}) \geqslant (E^i(X), L^i(X)) \\
 & & (E_1, L_1) \geqslant (E^i(X), L^i(X)) \\
 & s.t. & (E_1, L_1) \leq (E_{budget}, L_{max}) \\
 & Var. & E_1, L_1, X
\end{array}
$$

Optimal values of the parameters that ensure the Nash bargaining are obtained by resolving (P4) for every protocol (each with its specific formulas of energy and latency that yields the parameters). Results are analyzed in the following. Fig. 1.a (XMAC), Fig. 1.b (DMAC), and Fig. 1.c (LMAC) plots the results obtained by fixing E_{budget} to $0.06J$, and L_{max} has been varied in $[1sec, 6sec]$. Fig. 2.a (XMAC). Fig. 2.b (DMAC) and Fig. 2.c (LMAC) plots the results obtained by when fixing L_{max} to $6sec$ and varying the E_{budget} in $[0.01J, 0.06J]$. As it can be observed from Fig. 1, relaxing the e2e packet delay bound (L_{max}) for every protocol leads to an agreement in favor to the energy consumption player, while rising the energy initial budget, E_{budget}, leads to an agreement in favor to the e2e packet delay player (as depicted in Fig. 2). As it is proved in [11], choosing the pair (E_{worst},L_{worst}) in the Nash Bargaining Solution, leads to a solution that is proportional fair, i.e., that fulfills the following condition:

$$\frac{E^* - E_{worst}}{E_{best} - E_{worst}} = \frac{L^* - L_{worst}}{L_{best} - L_{worst}}$$

where (E^*, L^*) is the optimal point obtained by solving problem $(\boldsymbol{P3})$.

Acknowledgments

This works is partly supported by Algerian Ministry of Higher Education through the DGRSDT, and the national Spanish funding TIN2010-21378-C02-01.

4. REFERENCES

[1] M. Buettner, G. V. Yee, E. Anderson, and R. Han. X-mac: a short preamble mac protocol for duty-cycled wireless sensor networks. In *ACM SenSys*, pages 307–320, 2006.

[2] M. Ceriotti, M. Corrà, L. D'Orazio, R. Doriguzzi, D. Facchin, S. Guna, G. P. Jesi, R. L. Cigno, L. Mottola, A. L. Murphy, M. Pescalli, G. P. Picco, D. Pregnolato, and C. Torghele. Is there light at the ends of the tunnel? wireless sensor networks for adaptive lighting in road tunnels. In *IPSN*, pages 187–198, 2011.

[3] K. Langendoen and A. Meier. Analyzing mac protocols for low data-rate applications. *ACM TOSN*, 7(2), 2010.

[4] G. Lu, B. Krishnamachari, and C. S. Raghavendra. An adaptive energy-efficient and low-latency mac for tree-based data gathering in sensor networks. *Wireless Communications and Mobile Computing*, 7(7):863–875, 2007.

[5] A. Nahir and A. Orda. The energy-delay tradeoff in wireless networks - system-wide optimization and game-theoretic perspectives. In *Tech. Report*. Technion University., 2007.

[6] N. Nissan, T. Roughgarden, E. Tardos, and V. Vazirani. *Algorithmic Game Theory*. Cambridge University Press.

[7] P. Nuggehalli, M. Sarkar, K. Kulkarni, and R. Rao. A game-theoretic analysis of qos in wireless mac. In *INFOCOM, IEEE*, pages 1903–1911, 2008.

[8] L. van Hoesel and P. Havinga. A lightweight medium access protocol (lmac) for wireless sensor networks: Reducing preamble transmissions and transceiver state switches. In *INSS*, pages 205–208, Tokio, Japan, 2004.

[9] A. C. Voulkidis, M. P. Anastasopoulos, and P. G. Cottis. Energy efficiency in wireless sensor networks: A game-theoretic approach based on coalition formation. *ACM TOSN*, 9(4):1–27, July 2013.

[10] W. Ye, F. Silva, and J. Heidemann. Ultra-low duty cycle mac with scheduled channel polling. In *SenSys*, pages 321–334, 2006.

[11] Y. Zhao, S. Wang, S. Xu, X. Wang, X. Gao, and C. Qiao. Load balance vs energy efficiency in traffic engineering: A game theoretical perspective. In *INFOCOM, IEEE*, pages 530–534, 2013.

[12] M. Zimmerling, F. Ferrari, L. Mottola, T. Voigt, and L. Thiele. Ptunes: runtime parameter adaptation for low-power mac protocols. In *IEEE IPSN*, pages 173–184, 2012.

Coding Theory for Scalable Media Delivery

Michael Luby
Qualcomm Technologies, Inc.
Berkeley CA, USA
luby@qti.qualcomm.com

ABSTRACT

A review of a collaborative body of work focused on coding theory with applications to scalable media delivery.

Categories and Subject Descriptors

[**General and reference - Surveys and overviews**]: ; [**Mathematics of computing-Coding theory**]: Mathematics of computing-Random graphs; [**Theory of computation-Design and analysis of algorithms**]; [**Theory of computation-Error-correcting codes**]: Theory of computation-Sublinear and near linear time algorithms; Information systems-Multimedia streaming; Human-centered computing-Smartphones; Human-centered computing-Mobile devices

General Terms

Coding theory; erasure codes; streaming; file delivery; broadcast; scalability; reliability

1. INTRODUCTION

This paper reviews my collaborative body of work focused on design, implementation and usage of erasure codes.

One of the primary initiatives has been to design state of the art erasure codes that can be used in a variety of applications. The most advanced erasure code currently available, the result of years of collaborative coding theory research, is the RaptorQ code [9], [24]. The RaptorQ code has the most sophisticated theoretical foundations, supports the widest range of use cases, and is the most advanced among available standardized erasure codes.

2. CODING THEORY

Theoretical design work on scalable erasure codes started back in the mid-1990's, for example [1].

PODC'14, July 15–18, 2014, Paris, France.
ACM 978-1-4503-2944-6/14/07.
http://dx.doi.org/10.1145/2611462.2611515.

The first breakthrough was erasure and error-correcting code constructions based on the design and analysis of irregular random graphs [2], [3], [4], [5], [6]. This breakthrough resulted in design and analysis tools that show how to construct erasure codes and error-correcting codes based on random graphs where nodes have different degrees according to a well-designed degree distribution. A code based on such a design has almost optimal recovery and linear time encoding and decoding. This breakthrough is the basis for many of the modern codes used today, i.e., erasure codes applied at the application and transport layers, and error-correcting codes applied at the physical layer.

A second breakthrough was erasure code constructions with almost optimal recovery and fast encoding and decoding that have the *fountain property* [7], i.e., as many encoded symbols can be generated on the fly as needed. Fountain codes provide previously unheard of application flexibility: a fountain code can be incorporated into many interesting applications for which it is difficult to use traditional codes.

A third breakthrough was fountain codes with almost optimal recovery and linear time encoding and decoding [8]. The culmination of this many years of design, analysis, implementation, testing and deployment is the RaptorQ code [9]. The RaptorQ code has the following properties:

- The encoding and decoding speed is linear time independent of the size of the source block or number of encoded symbols to be generated. Practically, software-based encoding and decoding is orders of magnitude faster than required by even the most demanding applications on standard servers, laptops, and mobile devices.

- It is is a *fountain code*. Theoretically, as many encoded symbols as desired can be generated on the fly. Practically, the number of encoded symbols that can be generated is many times that needed by applications.

- It is essentially *Maximum Distance Separable*, abbreviated to *MDS*. A code is MDS if a source block with K source symbols can be recovered from any K encoded symbols. The RaptorQ code has the property that a source block can be recovered from K, $K+1$, or $K+2$ encoded symbols with reliability 99%, 99.99%, and 99.9999%, respectively. Practically, this means that there is essentially no difference between the RaptorQ code and an MDS code in terms of recovery properties when used in applications.

3. APPLICATIONS AND USAGE

The RaptorQ code, as well as earlier generations of Raptor codes, have been used in a multitude of applications. Examples include IPTV streaming deployments around the world, streaming and file delivery applications in the defense industry, delivering digital dailies for movie production studios around the world, satellite distribution of movies, video advertisements, and large datasets related to postal delivery, and streaming and multimedia file delivery to mobile devices over cellular broadcast networks.

Furthermore, a variety of interesting use cases are starting to arise as more and more content is delivered to mobile devices, including peer-to-peer applications, distributed storage applications, and live streaming applications.

The RaptorQ code is particularly suitable for these applications due to its flexibilty, scalability and efficiency:

- The excellent recovery properties allow scalable and efficient delivery of multimedia content concurrently to millions of receivers over broadcast channels.
- Encoding and decoding in linear time allows application to very small objects, such as fragments of a video stream, or very large objects, such as high quality video files.
- The fountain code properties allow flexible handling of a wide variety of different applications that have requirements for different amount of repair, and in some cases dynamically varying amounts of repair data.

The papers [10]-[23] describe some of the possible applications and usages of erasure codes such as the RaptorQ code.

4. STANDARDIZATION

Erasure codes, and in particular Raptor codes and the RaptorQ code, have been specified as the reliable streaming and file delivery solution by a variety of commercial standards bodies. In addition, frameworks for usage of erasure codes for streaming and file delivery has also been specified. Examples of these specifications include [24]-[37].

5. ACKNOWLEDGMENTS

I would like to thank my many collaborators who helped create and support this body of work over the years. Although many deserve mention, those whose contributions are especially notable include Amin Shokrollahi, Mark Watson, Thomas Stockhammer, Lorenz Minder, Valerie Wentworth and Roberto Padovani.

6. REFERENCES

[1] N. Alon, M. Luby. A Linear Time Erasure-Resilient Code With Nearly Optimal Recovery. *IEEE Transactions on Information Theory*, Special issue devoted to coding theory, Vol. 42, No. 6, November 1996.

[2] M. Luby, M. Mitzenmacher, A. Shokrollahi, D. Spielman. Efficient Erasure Correcting Codes. *IEEE Transactions on Information Theory*, Special Issue: Codes on Graphs and Iterative Algorithms, pp. 569-584, Vol. 47, No. 2, February 2001.

[3] M. Luby, M. Mitzenmacher, A. Shokrollahi, D. Spielman. Improved Low-Density Parity-Check Codes Using Irregular Graphs. *IEEE Transactions on Information Theory*, Special Issue: Codes on Graphs and Iterative Algorithms, pp. 585-598, Vol. 47, No. 2, February 2001.

[4] M. Luby, M. Mitzenmacher, A. Shokrollahi. Analysis of Random Processes via And-Or Tree Evaluation. *ACM-SIAM Symposium on Discrete Algorithms*, San Francisco, California, January 25–27, 1998.

[5] M. Luby, M. Mitzenmacher, A. Shokrollahi, D. Spielman. Improved Low-Density Parity-Check Codes Using Irregular Graphs and Belief Propagation. *IEEE Symposium on Information Theory*, 1998.

[6] M. Luby, M. Mitzenmacher, A. Shokrollahi, D. Spielman. Analysis of Low Density Codes and Improved Designs Using Irregular Graphs. *ACM Symposium on Theory of Computing*, 1998.

[7] M. Luby. LT Codes. *IEEE Symposium on Foundations of Computer Science*, November 16-19 2002, pp. 271-282.

[8] A. Shokrollahi. Raptor codes. *IEEE Transaction on Information Theory*, Vol. 52, No. 6, June 2006, pp. 2551-2567.

[9] A. Shokrollai, M. Luby. Raptor Codes. *Foundations and Trends in Communications and Information Theory*, 2011, Vol. 6: No 3-4, pp 213-322.

[10] J. Byers, M. Luby, M. Mitzenmacher, A. Rege. A digital fountain approach to reliable distribution of bulk data. Proceedings of the ACM SIGCOMM, pp. 56-67, 1998.

[11] M. Luby. Best practices for mobile broadcast delivery and playback of multimedia content. *IEEE International Symposium on Broadband Multimedia Systems and Broadcasting*, Seoul, South Korea, June 2012

[12] T. Stockhammer, A. Shokrollahi, M. Watson, M. Luby, T. Gasiba. Application Layer Forward Error Correction for Mobile Multimedia Broadcasting. *Handbook of Mobile Broadcasting: DVB-H, DMB, ISDB-T and Media FLO*, March 2008, CRC Press, Taylor and Francis Group, Borko Furht, Syed Ahson

[13] T. Stockhammer, M. Luby, M. Watson. Application Layer FEC in IPTV Services. *IEEE Communications Magazine*, Vol. 45, No. 5, May 2008, p. 94-101

[14] M. Luby, T. Gasiba, T. Stockhammer, M. Watson. Reliable Multimedia Download Delivery in Cellular Broadcast Networks. *IEEE Transactions on Broadcasting*, Vol. 53, Issue 1, March 2007, p. 235-246

[15] J.W. Byers, M. Luby, M. Mitzenmacher. A Digital Fountain Approach to Asynchronous Reliable Multicast. *IEEE J. on Selected Areas in Communications*, Special Issue on Network Support for Multicast Communication, Vol. 20, No. 8, October 2002, pp. 1528 – 1540.

[16] J.W. Byers, G. Horn, M. Luby, M. Mitzenmacher, W. Shaver. FLID-DL: Congestion control for layered multicast. *IEEE J. on Selected Areas in Communications*, Special Issue on Network Support for Multicast Communication, Vol. 20, No. 8, October 2002, pp. 1558 – 1570.

[17] T. Stockhammer, M. Watson, M. Luby. DVB Application Layer FEC in IPTV Services. *SMPTE and VSF 2008 Joint Conference*, Houston, TX, USA, February 2008

[18] T. Stockhammer, M. Watson, M. Luby, T. Gasiba. High-Quality Video Distribution using Power Line Communication and Application Layer Forward Error Correction. *IEEE International Symposium on Power Line Communications and its Applications*, Pisa, Italy, March 2007

[19] M. Luby, M. Watson, T. Gasiba, T.Stockhammer, W. Xu. Raptor Codes for Reliable Download Delivery in Wireless Broadcast Systems. *IEEE Consumer Communications and Networking Conference*, Las Vegas, Nevada, USA, January 2006

[20] M. Luby, V. K Goyal, S. Skaria, G. Horn. Wave and Equation Based Rate Control using Multicast Round-trip Time. *ACM SIGCOMM 2002*, Pittsburgh PA, August 19 – 23, 2002.

[21] J.W. Byers, M. Frumin, G. Horn, M. Luby, M. Mitzenmacher, A. Roetter, W. Shaver. FLID-DL: Congestion control for layered multicast. *2nd Int. Workshop Network Group Comm.*, pages 71–81, Stanford, California, November 2000.

[22] J.W. Byers, M. Luby, M. Mitzenmacher. Accessing Multiple Mirror Sites in Parallel: Using Tornado Codes to Speed Up Downloads. *IEEE INFOCOM*, New York, NY, pp. 275 – 283, 1999.

[23] M. Adler, Y. Bartal, J.W. Byers, M. Luby, D. Raz. A Modular Analysis of Network Transmission Protocols. *Israeli Symposium on Theory of Computing and Systems*, June 1997.

[24] IETF RFC6330. RaptorQ Forward Error Correction Scheme for Object Delivery. M. Luby, A. Shokrollahi, M. Watson, T. Stockhammer, L. Minder. Internet Engineering Task Force, August 2011.

[25] IETF RFC6681. Raptor Forward Error Correction Schemes for FECFRAME. M. Watson, T. Stockhammer, M. Luby. Internet Engineering Task Force, August 2012.

[26] OMA Mobile Broadcast Services V1.0 - Broadcast Distribution System Adaptation 3GPP/MBMS Specification. Open Mobile Alliance technical specification, Ver. 1.0, October 2008.

[27] IPTV (DVB-IPTV) (DVB A086r7) Content Download. Digital Video Broadcasting Project technical specification, DVB Bluebook A086r7, September 2008.

[28] IPTV (DVB-IPTV) (ETSI TS 102 034) Streaming. Digital Video Broadcasting Project technical specification, Ver. 1.3.1, October 2007.

[29] IETF RFC5053. Raptor Forward Error Correction Scheme for Object Delivery. M. Luby, A. Shokrollahi, M. Watson, T. Stockhammer. Internet Engineering Task Force, October 2007.

[30] IETF RFC5052. Forward Error Correction (FEC) Building Block. M. Watson, M. Luby, L. Vicisano. Internet Engineering Task Force, August 2007.

[31] IP Datacast (DVB-IPDC) (ETSI TS 102 472) for DVB-H and DVB-SH. Digital Video Broadcasting Project technical specification, Ver. 1.1.1 June 2006.

[32] Multimedia Broadcast Multicast Service (3GPP TS 26.346). 3rd Generation Partnership Program technical specification, Ver. 6.0.0, April 2005.

[33] IETF RFC6726. FLUTE - File Delivery over Unidirectional Transport. T. Paila, M. Luby, R. Lehtonen, V. Roca, R. Walsh. Internet Engineering Task Force, November 2012.

[34] IETF RFC3738. Wave and equation based rate control building block. M. Luby, V. K Goyal. Internet Engineering Task Force, April 2004.

[35] IETF RFC5775. Asynchronous Layered Coding (ALC) Protocol Instantiation. M. Luby, J. Gemmell, L. Vicisano, L. Rizzo, J. Crowcroft. Internet Engineering Task Force RFC5775, April 2010.

[36] IETF RFC5651. Layered Coding Transport (LCT) Building Block. M. Luby, J. Gemmell, L. Vicisano, L. Rizzo, M. Handley, J. Crowcroft. Internet Engineering Task Force RFC5651, October 2009.

[37] IETF RFC3453. The Use of Forward Error Correction (FEC) in Reliable Multicast. M. Luby, L. Vicisano, J. Gemmell, L. Rizzo, M. Handley, J. Crowcroft. Internet Engineering Task Force RFC3453, December 2002.

Distributed Connectivity Decomposition

Keren Censor-Hillel
Technion, Israel
ckeren@cs.technion.ac.il

Mohsen Ghaffari
MIT, USA
ghaffari@mit.edu

Fabian Kuhn
U. of Freiburg, Germany
kuhn@cs.uni-freiburg.de

ABSTRACT

A fundamental problem in distributed network algorithms is to manage congestion and obtain information flow matching the graph's connectivity. In this paper, we present time-efficient distributed algorithms for decomposing graphs with large edge or vertex connectivity into multiple spanning or dominating trees, respectively. These decompositions allow us to achieve a flow with size close to the connectivity by parallelizing it along the trees. More specifically, our distributed decomposition algorithms are as follows:

(I) A decomposition of each undirected graph with *vertex-connectivity* k into (fractionally) *vertex-disjoint* weighted *dominating trees* with total weight $\Omega(\frac{k}{\log n})$, in $\widetilde{O}(D+\sqrt{n})$ rounds in networks, where each node can send a total of at most $O(\log n)$ bits per round.

(II) A decomposition of each undirected graph with *edge-connectivity* λ into (fractionally) *edge-disjoint* weighted *spanning trees* with total weight $\lceil\frac{\lambda-1}{2}\rceil(1-\varepsilon)$, in $\widetilde{O}(D+\sqrt{n\lambda})$ rounds, if in each round, each edge can carry at most $O(\log n)$ bits of information.

We also show round complexity lower bounds of $\tilde{\Omega}(D+\sqrt{\frac{n}{k}})$ and $\tilde{\Omega}(D+\sqrt{\frac{n}{\lambda}})$ for the above two decompositions, using techniques of [Das Sarma et al., STOC'11]. Moreover, our vertex-connectivity decomposition extends to centralized algorithms and improves the time complexity of [Censor-Hillel et al., SODA'14] from $O(n^3)$ to near-optimal $\tilde{O}(m)$.

Additional implications of our results are: a near-linear time centralized approximation of vertex connectivity (which can be seen as a step towards a conjecture of Aho, Hopcroft and Ullman), the first distributed approximating of vertex connectivity, and distributed algorithms with near-optimal competitiveness for *oblivious broadcast routing*.

PODC'14, July 15–18, 2014, Paris, France.
Copyright is held by the owner/author(s). Publication rights licensed to ACM.
ACM 978-1-4503-2944-6/14/07 ...$15.00.
http://dx.doi.org/10.1145/2611462.2611491.

A full version of this paper can be found in [10].

Categories and Subject Descriptors

F.2.2 [**Analysis of Algorithms and Problem Complexity**]: Non-numerical Algorithms and Problems—*Computations on Discrete Structures*; G.2.2 [**Discrete Mathematics**]: Graph Theory—*Network Problems; Graph Algorithms*

Keywords

Graph Connectivity, Decomposition, Distributed Algorithm

1. INTRODUCTION AND RELATED WORK

Edge and vertex connectivity are two basic graph-theoretic concepts. As an important application, they characterize limits on how well information can be transferred among nodes of a network; one of the central goals of any communication network and also a core issue in distributed computing [46, Section 1.3.1]. This is because each edge or vertex cut defines an upper bound on the flow across the cut. Naturally, we expect networks with larger connectivity to provide a better communication medium and support larger information flow. However, designing distributed algorithms that leverage large connectivity remains challenging.

This paper provides a distributed solution for exploiting large connectivity towards the goal of obtaining a large flow of information. We use a rather natural approach, which we call *connectivity decomposition*, of decomposing connectivity into smaller and more manageable units. We present distributed algorithms that decompose a graph with large connectivity into many (essentially) "disjoint" trees, while almost preserving the total connectivity through the trees. This decomposition will be into edge-disjoint spanning-trees when we are interested in edge connectivity and into vertex-disjoint dominating trees[1] when we are interested in vertex connectivity. These decompositions allow us to easily parallelize the flow of information along the trees and thus achieve a total flow value close to the connectivity of the network.

An interesting comparison of our approach of handling *congestion* is to that of addressing *locality*, as these are two core issues in distributed network algorithms [46, Section 2.3]. Classically, locality has received significantly more attention and many general techniques are known for dealing

[1] A tree $H = (V_T, E_T)$ is a *dominating tree* of $G = (V_G, E_G)$ if $V_T \subseteq V_G$, $E_T \subseteq E_G$, and each node in $V_G \setminus V_T$ has a G-neighbor in V_T. Note that if we want to have many vertex-disjoint subgraph, unavoidably we have to relax the *"spanning"* property and the *"dominating"* condition is the natural requirement.

with it. Congestion on the other hand is less understood, but the recent years have seen a surge in focus on solving various problems while taking congestion into account (see e.g., [14, 15, 19, 23, 30, 40, 42, 43]). However, the methods used for handling congestion in different problems appear to be rather ad hoc, each being well-suited for a particular problem. A fundamental and generic technique centered around locality are *locality-based decompositions* [46], which group nodes in small-diameter clusters with certain properties; classical examples include [2–4, 39, 45]. We feel that connectivity decompositions can be viewed as a direction essentially orthogonal to that of *locality-based* decompositions, and we hope they are a first step towards systematically addressing congestion.

The rest of this section is organized as follows: We first briefly explain the relation between tree packings and connectivity in Section 1.1. Then, we present our decomposition results and their applications in Sections 1.2 and 1.3, respectively. We review some other related work and particularly the corresponding centralized connectivity decompositions results in Section 1.4.

1.1 Connectivity and Tree Packings

Menger's theorem (see [8, Chapter 9])—which is the most basic result regarding graph connectivity—states that in each graph with edge connectivity λ or vertex connectivity k, each pair of vertices are connected via λ edge-disjoint paths or k internally vertex-disjoint paths, respectively. However, when we have to deal with more than two nodes, the theorem is insufficient especially because it does not provide any information about the structure of overlaps between paths of different vertex pairs.

Spanning and dominating tree packings allow us to manage this overlap and provide a medium for decomposing edge and vertex connectivity, respectively, into their single units: If we find a collection of λ' edge-disjoint spanning trees—which we call a *spanning tree packing of size* λ'—then for each pair of vertices we get λ' edge-disjoint paths, one through each tree. More importantly, for any number of vertex pairs, the paths going through different trees are edge-disjoint. Similarly, if we have k' vertex-disjoint dominating trees[1]—which we call a *dominating tree packing* of size k'— then for each vertex pair we get k' internally vertex-disjoint paths, one through each tree. More importantly, for any number of pairs, the paths going through different trees are internally vertex-disjoint.

In both spanning and dominating tree packings, we can relax the disjointness requirement to *fractional disjointness*. That is, we allow the trees to overlap but now each tree τ has a weight $\omega_\tau \in [0, 1]$ and the total weight in each edge or vertex, respectively, has to be at most 1. This naturally corresponds to sharing the edge or vertex between the trees proportional to their weights (e.g., for time-sharing in information dissemination).

Edge connectivity decompositions have been well-known[2] for a long time, thanks to beautiful and highly non-trivial (existential) results of Tutte [52] and Nash-Williams [44] from 1960. These results show that each graph with edge-connectivity λ contains a spanning tree packing of size $\lceil \frac{\lambda-1}{2} \rceil$ (see [38]). This bound is existentially tight even for the fractional version and has numerous important applications.

Vertex connectivity decompositions were addressed only recently: [11] shows that each graph with vertex-connectivity k contains a dominating tree packing of size $\Omega(\kappa/\log^2 n)$ and a fractional dominating tree packing of size $\Omega(k/\log n)$. Here, κ is the vertex-connectivity of the sampled graph when each vertex is sampled with probability 1/2, where $\kappa = \Omega(k/\log^3 n)$ is currently the best known bound. The paper also shows that the $\Omega(k/\log n)$ fractional packing bound is existentially best possible.

1.2 Our Results

We present distributed algorithms that provide edge and vertex connectivity decompositions, which are comparable to their centralized counterparts, while having efficient (or near-optimal) round complexity.

We note that, although our edge-connectivity decomposition builds on a number of standard techniques and known results, our vertex connectivity decomposition algorithm is the main technical novelty of this paper and interestingly, it achieves near-optimal time complexities in both distributed and centralized settings (Theorem 1.1 and Theorem 1.2).

For distributed algorithms, we consider two synchronous message passing models: V-CONGEST, where in each round, each node can send one $O(\log n)$-bit message to *all* of its neighbors, and E-CONGEST, where in each round, one $O(\log n)$-bit message can be sent in each direction of each edge. As the names suggest, the congestion in the V-CONGEST model is in the vertices whereas in E-CONGEST, it is in the edges. We note that E-CONGEST, often just called CONGEST, is the more classical distributed model to consider *congestion* and bounded size messages [46]. Considering congestion on vertices is however also not new and for example appears in [25, 26, 37]. Also, notice that V-CONGEST is considerably more restrictive than E-CONGEST and clearly any algorithm working in the V-CONGEST model, also works in the E-CONGEST model. However, obviously there is no relation in the other direction.

In all our results, we assume a connected undirected network with n nodes, m edges, and diameter D. Moreover, we usually use k to denote the vertex connectivity and λ for the edge connectivity.

Theorem 1.1. *There is an $\tilde{O}(\min\{D + \sqrt{n}, \frac{n}{k}\})$-rounds randomized distributed algorithm in the* V-CONGEST *model that w.h.p.*[3] *finds a fractional dominating tree packing of size $\Omega(\frac{k}{\log n})$, where k is the vertex connectivity of the graph. More specifically, this algorithm finds $\Omega(k)$ dominating trees, each of diameter $\tilde{O}(\frac{n}{k})$, such that each node is included in $O(\log n)$ trees.*

Note that diameter $\Omega(n/k)$ for all except very few of the dominating trees is unavoidable, even in graphs of diameter 2. Just consider a graph consisting of sequence of n/k cliques of size k, where subsequent cliques are connected by matchings of size k. Adding a single node u and connecting u to all other nodes creates a graph with diameter 2 and vertex connectivity $k+1$, where any dominating tree that does not include u needs to have diameter at least n/k. Also,

[2]Although we remark that they were not called "edge-connectivity decomposition". Often, the phrase "edge-disjoint spanning trees" was used to refer to the related concept. A simpler proof follows from the *Matroid intersection theorem.*

[3]We use the phrase with high probability (w.h.p.) to indicate a probability at least $1-\frac{1}{n^c}$ for some constant $c \geq 1$.

notice that this issue is not particular to the tree-packing approaches but rather any algorithm faces a similar barrier: for achieving super-constant throughput (e.g., for concurrent broadcasts), almost all messages have to travers paths of length $\Omega(n/k)$.

Theorem 1.2. *There is an $\tilde{O}(m)$ time randomized centralized algorithm that w.h.p. finds a fractional dominating tree packing of size $\Omega(\frac{k}{\log n})$, where k is the vertex connectivity of the graph. More specifically, this algorithm finds $\Omega(k)$ dominating trees, each of diameter $\tilde{O}(\frac{n}{k})$, such that each node is included in $O(\log n)$ trees.*

Theorem 1.2 improves over the $\Omega(n^3)$ algorithms of [11] and [16]. Regarding Theorem 1.1, we note that the algorithm of [16] does not appear to admit a distributed implementation as it is based on a number of centralized tools and techniques such as the ellipsoid method for linear programming, the meta-rounding of [9], and the Min-Cost-CDS approximation result of [24]. The algorithm of [11] has a similar problem which seems essential and unavoidable. See the last part of Section 4.1 for an explanation of why the algorithm of [11] does not extend to a distributed setting and for how it compares with the approach in this paper.

Theorem 1.3. *There is an $\tilde{O}(D+\sqrt{\lambda n})$-rounds randomized distributed algorithm in the* E-CONGEST *model that w.h.p. finds a fractional spanning tree packing of size $\lceil\frac{\lambda-1}{2}\rceil(1-\varepsilon)$, where λ is the edge connectivity of the graph. Furthermore, each edge is included in at most $O(\log^3 n)$ trees.*

Integral Tree Packings Both algorithms of Theorem 1.1 and Theorem 1.2 can be adapted to produce a dominating tree packing of size $\Omega(\frac{\kappa}{\log^2 n})$, in similar time-complexities, using the random layering technique of the (proof of) [11, Theorem 1.2]. Here, κ is the remaining vertex-connectivity when each vertex is sampled with probability 1/2, for which currently the best known bound is $\kappa = \Omega(\frac{k}{\log^3 n})$ [11]. Also, a considerably simpler variant of the algorithm of Theorem 1.3 can be adapted to produce a spanning tree packing of size $\Omega(\frac{\lambda}{\log n})$, with a similar $\tilde{O}(D+\sqrt{\lambda n})$ round complexity.

We note that for information dissemination purposes—which is the primary application of our decompositions—fractional packings usually are as useful as integral packings. We can typically timeshare each node or edge among the trees that use (proportionally to the weights of the trees). Since our fractional packing results have better sizes, our main focus will be on describing the fractional versions.

Lower Bounds While $\Omega(m)$ is a trivial lower bound on the time complexity of the centralized decompositions, by extending results of [13], we show lower bounds of $\tilde{\Omega}(D+\sqrt{\frac{n}{k}})$ and $\tilde{\Omega}(D+\sqrt{\frac{n}{\lambda}})$ on the round complexities of the distributed decompositions of Theorem 1.1 and Theorem 1.3. See Appendix G of the full version [10] for the formal statements and the proofs.

1.3 Applications

1.3.1 Information Dissemination

As their primary application, our decompositions provide time-efficient distributed constructions for broadcast algorithms (based on routing, i.e., without using network coding) with existentially optimal throughput. See Section 3 for a simple example. Note that in the V-CONGEST model, vertex cuts characterize the main limits on the information flow, and k messages per round is the clear information-theoretic limit on the broadcast throughput (even with network coding) in each graph with vertex connectivity k. Similarly, in the E-CONGEST model, edge cuts characterize the main limits on the information flow, and λ messages per round is the information-theoretic limit on the broadcast throughput (even with network coding) in each graph with edge connectivity λ. Our optimal-throughput broadcast algorithms are as follows:

Corollary 1.4. *In the* V-CONGEST *model, using the $\tilde{O}(D+\sqrt{n})$-rounds construction of Theorem 1.1, and then broadcasting each message along a random tree, we get a broadcast algorithm with throughput of $\Omega(\frac{k}{\log n})$ messages per round. [11] shows this throughput to be existentially optimal.*

See Section 3 for an explanation and a simple example of how one can use dominating tree packings to broadcast messages by routing them along different trees.

Corollary 1.5. *In the* E-CONGEST *model, using the $\tilde{O}(D+\sqrt{\lambda n})$-rounds construction of Theorem 1.3, and then broadcasting each message along a random tree, we get a broadcast algorithm with throughput of $\lceil\frac{\lambda-1}{2}\rceil(1-\varepsilon)$ messages per round.*

We emphasize that the above broadcast algorithms provide *oblivious broadcast routing* (see [48]). In an *oblivious routing* algorithm, the path taken by each message is determined (deterministically or probabilistically) independent of the current load on the graph; that is, particularly independent of how many other messages exist in the graph and how they are routed. Note that this is in stark contrast to adaptive algorithms which can tailor the route of each message, while knowing the current (or future) load on the graph, in order to minimize congestion. Oblivious routing algorithms appear to be a much more restricted family and a priori, it is somewhat unclear whether they can have a performance close to the of the optimal adaptive algorithms. Interestingly, a beautiful line of work [5,7,27,48,49] shows this to be possible: These papers present centralized oblivious routing algorithms with successively improved edge-congestion competitiveness ratios. This line ends in the algorithm of Racke [49] which achieves the optimal $O(\log n)$-competitive edge-congestion. That is, in this algorithm, the expected maximum congestion over all edges is at most $O(\log n)$ times the maximum congestion of the offline optimal algorithm. The problem of designing distributed oblivious routing algorithms achieving this performance remains open. Furthermore, it is known that no *point-to-point* oblivious routing can have vertex-congestion competitiveness better than $\Theta(\sqrt{n})$ [26].

Our results address *oblivious routing for broadcast:*

Corollary 1.6. *By routing each message along a random one of the trees generated by Theorem 1.1 and Theorem 1.3, we get distributed oblivious routing broadcast algorithms that respectively have vertex-congestion competitiveness of $O(\log n)$ and edge-congestion competitiveness of $O(1)$.*

1.3.2 Vertex Connectivity Approximation

Vertex connectivity is a central concept in graph theory and extensive attention has been paid to developing algorithms that compute or approximate it. In 1974, Aho, Hopcraft and Ulman [1, Problem 5.30] conjectured that there should be an $O(m)$ time algorithm for computing the vertex connectivity. Despite many interesting works in this direction—e.g., [17,20,22,28,29,51]—finding $O(m)$ time algorithms for vertex connectivity has yet to succeed. The current state of the art is an $O(\min\{n^2k+nk^{3.5}, n^2k+n^{1.75}k^2\})$ time exact algorithm by Gabow [20] and an $O(\min\{n^{2.5}, n^2k\})$ time 2-approximation by Henzinger [28]. The situation is considerably worse in distributed settings and the problem of upper bounds has remained widely open, while we show in the full version [10] that an $\Omega(D+\sqrt{\frac{n}{k}})$ round complexity lower bound follows from techniques of [13].

Since Theorem 1.1 and Theorem 1.2 work without a priori knowledge of vertex connectivity and as the size of the achieved dominating trees packing is in the range $[\Omega(\frac{k}{\log n}), k]$, our dominating tree packing algorithm provides the following implication:

Corollary 1.7. *We can compute an $O(\log n)$ approximation of vertex connectivity, centralized in $\tilde{O}(m)$ time, and distributed in $\tilde{O}(D+\sqrt{n})$ rounds of the* V-CONGEST *model.*

Note that it is widely known that in undirected graphs, vertex connectivity and vertex cuts are significantly more complex than edge connectivity and edge cuts, for which currently the following result are known: an $\tilde{O}(m)$ time centralized exact algorithm [34], an $O(m)$ time centralized $(1+\varepsilon)$-approximation [33], and a quite recent $\tilde{O}(D+\sqrt{n})$ rounds distributed $(2+\varepsilon)$-approximation [23].

1.4 Other Related Work

1.4.1 Independent Trees

Dominating tree packings have some resemblance to *vertex independent trees* [35,53] and are in fact a strictly stronger concept. In a graph $G=(V,E)$, k' trees are called *vertex independent* if they are spanning trees all rooted in a node $r \in V$ and for each vertex $v \in V$, the paths between r and v in different trees are internally vertex-disjoint. We emphasize that these trees are not vertex disjoint.

Zehavi and Itai conjectured in 1989 [53] that each graph with vertex connectivity k contains k vertex independent trees. Finding such trees, if they exist, is also of interest. The conjecture remains open and is confirmed only for cases $k \in \{2,3\}$. Itai and Rodeh [31] present an $O(m)$ time centralized algorithm for finding 2 vertex independent trees, when the graph is 2-vertex-connected and Cheriyan and Maheshvari [12] present an $O(n^2)$ time centralized algorithm for finding 3 vertex independent trees, when the graph is 3-vertex-connected.

Vertex disjoint dominating trees are a strictly stronger notion[4]: Given k' vertex-disjoint dominating trees, we get k' vertex independent trees, for *any* root $r \in V$. This is by adding all the other nodes to each dominating tree as leaves to make it spanning. Then, for each vertex $v \in V$, the path from r to v in each (now spanning) tree uses only internal vertices from the related dominating tree.

In this regard, one can view [11, Theorem 1.2] as providing a poly-logarithmic approximation of the Zehavi and Itai's conjecture. Furthermore, the vertex connectivity algorithm presented here (formally, its extension to integral dominating tree packing, mentioned in Section 1.1) makes this approximation algorithmic with near-optimal complexities $\tilde{O}(m)$ centralized and $\tilde{O}(D+\sqrt{n})$ distributed.

1.4.2 A Review of Centralized Connectivity Decompositions

Edge Connectivity Edge connectivity decompositions into spanning tree packings of $\lceil\frac{\lambda-1}{2}\rceil$ have been known due to results of Tutte [52] and NashWilliams [44] from 1960, and they have found many important applications: the best known centralized minimum edge cut algorithm [34], the network coding advantage in edge-capactitated networks [41], and tight analysis of the number of minimum cuts of a graph and random edge-sampling [34]. Centralized algorithms for finding such a spanning tree packing include: an $\tilde{O}(\min\{mn, \frac{m^2}{\sqrt{n}}\})$ time algorithm for unweighted graphs by Gabow and Westermann [21], an $\tilde{O}(mn)$ time algorithm for weighted graphs by Barahona [6], and an $\tilde{O}(m\lambda)$ time algorithm for a fractional packing via the general technique of Plotkin et al. [47] (see [34]).

Vertex Connectivity As mentioned before, the case of vertex connectivity decompositions was addressed only recently [11], and it was shown to have applications on analyzing vertex connectivity under vertex sampling and also network coding gap in node-capacitated networks. Consequent to (a preliminary version of) [11], Ene et al. [16] presented a nice alternative proof for obtaining fractional dominating tree packing of size $\Omega(\frac{k}{\log n})$, which uses metarounding results of Carr and Vempala [9] and the Min-Cost-CDS approximation result of Guha and Khuller [24]. That proof does not extend to integral packing. Even though the proofs presented in [11] and [16] are based on polynomial time algorithms, neither of the algorithms seems to admit a distributed implementation and even their centralized complexities are at least $\Omega(n^3)$.

We also note that finding many *dominating sets* (particularly algorithmic inapproximability of it) was addressed in the beautiful work of Feige et al. [18]. Although, as we will see in Section 4.1 (and can also be seen in [11]), from an algorithmic viewpoint, finding many dominating sets is significantly simpler than finding many connected dominating sets, and in fact, getting just the domination part in our results is rather a triviality (see Lemma 5.1).

2. NOTATIONS AND PROB. STATEMENTS

Given an undirected graph $G=(V,E)$ and a set $S \subseteq V$, we use the notation $G[S]$ to indicate the subgraph of G induced by S. A set $S \subseteq V$ is called a *connected dominating set (CDS)* iff $G[S]$ is connected and for each node $u \in V \setminus S$, u has a neighbor $v \in S$. A subgraph $T=(V_T, E_T)$ of graph $G=(V_G, E_G)$ is a *dominating tree* of graph G if T is a tree and V_T is a dominating subset of V_G.

Dominating Tree Packing Let $DT(G)$ be the set of all dominating trees of G. A κ-size dominating tree packing of G is a collection of κ *vertex-disjoint dominating* trees in G.

[4]The relation is strict as e.g., the following graph with vertex connectivity 3 does not admit more than 1 vertex-disjoint dominating trees while [12] implies that this graph has 3 vertex independent trees: A graph with a clique of size $n^{1/3}$, plus one additional node for each subset of three nodes of the clique, connected exactly to those three clique nodes.

A κ-size fractional dominating tree packing of G assigns a weight $x_\tau \in [0,1]$ to each $\tau \in DT(G)$ s.t. $\sum_{\tau \in DT(G)} x_\tau = \kappa$ and $\forall v \in V$, $\sum_{\tau, v \in \tau} x_\tau \leq 1$.

Spanning Tree Packing Let $ST(G)$ be the set of all spanning trees of G. A κ-size dominating tree packing of G is a collection of κ *edge-disjoint spanning* trees in G. A κ-size fractional spanning tree packing of G assigns a weight $x_\tau \in [0,1]$ to each $\tau \in ST(G)$ s.t. $\sum_{\tau \in ST(G)} x_\tau = \kappa$ and $\forall e \in E$, $\sum_{\tau, e \in \tau} x_\tau \leq 1$.

Distributed Problem Requirements In the distributed versions of dominating or spanning tree packing problems, we consider each tree τ as one class with a unique identifier ID_τ and a weight x_τ. In the spanning tree packing problem, for each node v and each edge e incident to v, for each spanning tree τ that contains e, node v should know ID_τ and x_τ. In the dominating tree packing problem, for each node v and each dominating tree τ that contains v, node v should know ID_τ, x_τ, and the edges of τ incident to v.

Distributed Model Details See Section 1.2 for the definitions of our communication models. Note that as we work with randomized algorithms, nodes can generate random ids by each taking random binary strings of $4 \log n$ bits and delivering it to their neighbors. Moreover, we assume no initial knowledge about the graph. Note that in our models, by using a simple and standard BFS tree approach, in $O(D)$ rounds, nodes can learn the number of nodes in the network n, and also a 2-approximation of the diameter of the graph D, which is enough for our applications. Our algorithms assume this knowledge to be ready for them.

3. A SIMPLE APPLICATION EXAMPLE: GOSSIPING

Here, we explain a simple and crisp example which shows how our connectivity decompositions can be used in information dissemination. We study the classical *gossiping* problem (aka *all-to-all broadcast*): Each node of the network has one $O(\log n)$-bit message and the goal is for each node to receive all the messages. In the following, we study this problem in the V-CONGEST model. To make the discussion more intuitive, we first explain the approach for a particular value of connectivity and then state how it extends to other connectivity values.

If the network is merely connected, solving the gossiping problem in $O(n)$ rounds is trivial. Now suppose that the network has in fact a vertex connectivity of $\sqrt{n}$. Despite this extremely good connectivity, prior to this work, the aforementioned $O(n)$ rounds solution remained the best known bound[5]. The main difficulty is that, even though we know that each vertex cut of the network admits a flow of $\sqrt{n}$ messages per round, it is not clear how to organize the transmissions such that a flow of $\Omega(\sqrt{n})$ (distinct) messages per round passes through each cut. As a side note, it is worth mentioning that a graph with vertex connectivity k can have up to $\Theta(2^k \cdot (\frac{n}{k})^2)$ vertex-cuts of size k [32].

Our vertex connectivity decomposition, claimed in Theorem 1.1, runs in $\tilde{O}(\sqrt{n})$ rounds in this example. Note that in a graph with vertex connectivity k, the diameter is at most $O(n/k)$ and thus here we have $D = O(\sqrt{n})$. This construction generates $O(\sqrt{n})$ dominating trees, each of diameter $\tilde{O}(\sqrt{n})$, where each node is contained in $O(\log n)$ trees. Then, to use this decomposition for gossiping, we do as follows: first each node gives its message to (one node in) a random one of the trees. Note that this is easy as each node has neighbors in all of the trees and it can easily learn the ids of those trees in just one round. Then, w.h.p, we have $O(\sqrt{n})$ messages in each tree, ready to be broadcast. We can broadcast all the messages just inside the dominating trees in $\tilde{O}(\sqrt{n})$ rounds. Furthermore, by a small change, we can make sure that each node transmits the messages assigned to its dominating trees and thus, each node in the network receives all the messages (because of domination). Overall, this method solves the problem in $\tilde{O}(\sqrt{n})$ rounds.

We now state how this bound generalizes:

Corollary 3.1. *Suppose that there are N messages in arbitrary nodes of the network such that each node has at most η messages. Using our vertex connectivity decomposition, we can broadcast all messages to all nodes in $\tilde{O}(\eta + \frac{N+n}{k})$ rounds of the* V-CONGEST *model.*

Proof Sketch. This approach is exactly as explained above. Each node gives its messages to random dominating trees of the decomposition and then we broadcast each message only using the nodes in its designated dominating tree. The vertex connectivity decomposition runs in $\tilde{O}(\min\{D+\sqrt{n}, \frac{n}{k}\})$. Then, delivering messages to the trees takes at most η rounds. Finally, broadcasting messages using their designated trees takes $\tilde{O}(\frac{n}{k} + \frac{N}{k})$ rounds because the diameter of each tree is $O(\frac{n \log n}{k})$ and each tree w.h.p is responsible for broadcasting at most $O(\frac{N}{k} + \log n)$ messages. □

Note that the bound in Corollary 3.1 is optimal, modulo logarithmic factors, because, (1) $\frac{N}{k}$ is a clear information theoretic lower bound as per round only $O(k \log n)$ bits can cross each vertex cut of size k, (2) similarly, if a node has η messages, it takes at least η rounds to send them, (3) in graphs with vertex connectivity k, the diameter can be up to $\frac{n}{k}$. In fact, the diameter of the original graph is a measure that is rather irrelevant because even if the diameter is smaller, achieving a flow of size $\tilde{\Theta}(k)$ messages per round unavoidably requires routing messages along routes that are longer than the shortest path (for any algorithm). See Appendix G of [10] for more discussion about this last point.

4. DOMINATING TREE PACKING ALGORITHM

In this section, we present the main technical contribution of the paper, which is introducing a new algorithm for vertex connectivity decomposition that has near optimal time complexities for both centralized and distributed implementations. In this decomposition, we construct a collection of $\Omega(k)$ classes, each of which is a dominating tree w.h.p., such that each vertex is included in at most $O(\log n)$ classes. This gives a fractional dominating tree packing[6] of size $\Omega(\frac{k}{\log n})$ and lets us achieve Theorems 1.1 and 1.2. The analysis is presented in Section 5.

[5] We note that one can achieve an $O(\sqrt{n})$-round solution using network coding. Our focus in this paper is on routing based algorithms where messages are viewed as atomic tokens and they are never mixed.

[6] The approach of this algorithm can be also used to get an $\Omega(\frac{k}{\log^5 n})$ dominating tree packing, see [11, Section 4].

4.1 The Algorithm Outline

For the construction, we first assume that we have a 2-approximation of k, and then explain how to remove this assumption. We construct $t = \Theta(k)$ connected dominating sets (CDS) such that each node is included in $O(\log n)$ CDSs. We work with CDSs, since it is simply enough to determine their vertices. To get dominating trees, at the end of the CDS packing algorithm, we remove the cycles in each CDS using a simple application of a minimum spanning tree algorithm.

We transform the graph $G = (V, E)$ into a graph $\mathcal{G} = (\mathcal{V}, \mathcal{E})$, which is called the *virtual graph* [7], and is constructed as follows: Each node $v \in V$ simulates $\Theta(\log n)$ *virtual* nodes $\nu_1, \nu_2, \ldots, \nu_{\Theta(\log n)} \in \mathcal{V}$ and two virtual nodes are connected if they are simulated by the same real node or by two G-adjacent real nodes. To get the promised CDS Packing, we partition the virtual nodes $\mathcal{V}$ into t disjoint *classes*, each of which is a CDS of $\mathcal{G}$, w.h.p. Each CDS $\mathcal{S}$ on $\mathcal{G}$ defines a CDS S on G in a natural way: S includes all real nodes v for which at least one virtual node of v is in $\mathcal{S}$. Thus, the t classes of virtual nodes w.h.p. give t CDSs on G and clearly each real node is included in $O(\log n)$ CDSs.

For the construction, we organize the virtual nodes by giving them two attributes: each virtual node has a *layer number* in $\{1, 2, \ldots, L\}$, where $L = \Theta(\log n)$, and a *type number* in $\{1, 2, 3\}$. For each real node $v \in V$, the $3L = \Theta(\log n)$ virtual nodes simulated by v are divided such that, for each layer number in $\{1, 2, \ldots, L\}$ and each *type number* in $\{1, 2, 3\}$, there is exactly one virtual node. For the communication purposes in the distributed setting, note that each communication round on $\mathcal{G}$ can be simulated via $\Theta(\log n)$ communication rounds on G. Thus, to simplify discussions, we divide the rounds into groups of $\Theta(\log n)$ consecutive rounds and call each group one *meta-round.*

As explained, we assign each virtual node to a class. This class assignment is performed in a recursive manner based on the layer numbers. First, with a jump-start, we assign each virtual node of layers 1 to $L/2$ to a random class in classes 1 to t. This step gives us that each class dominates $\mathcal{G}$, w.h.p. The interesting and challenging part is to achieve connectivity for all classes. For this purpose, we go over the layers one by one and for each layer $\ell \in [L/2, L-1]$, we assign class numbers to the virtual nodes of layer $\ell + 1$ based on the assignments to the virtual nodes of layers 1 to ℓ. The goal is to connect the components of each class such that the total number of connected components (summed up over all classes) decreases (in expectation) by a constant factor, with the addition of each layer. This would give us that after $\Theta(\log n)$ layers, all classes are connected, w.h.p. We next explain the outline of this step, after presenting some notations.

Let $\mathcal{V}_\ell^i$ be the set of virtual nodes of layers 1 to ℓ assigned to class i (note that $\mathcal{V}_\ell^i \subseteq \mathcal{V}_{\ell+1}^i$). Let N_ℓ^i be the number of connected components of $\mathcal{G}[\mathcal{V}_\ell^i]$ and let $M_\ell := \sum_{i=1}^{t}(N_\ell^i - 1)$ be the total number of excess components after considering layers $1, \ldots, \ell$, compared to the ideal case where each class is connected. Initially $M_1 \leq n - t$, and as soon as $M_\ell = 0$, each class induces a connected subgraph.

[7]The virtual graph $\mathcal{G}$ is nothing but using $\Theta(\log n)$ copies of G, or simply reusing each node of G for $\Theta(\log n)$ times, $\Theta(1)$ times per *layer* (described later). We find it more formal to use $\mathcal{G}$ instead of directly talking about G.

Recursive Class Assignment Suppose that we are at the step of assigning classes to virtual nodes of layer $\ell + 1$. We call virtual nodes of layer $\ell + 1$ *new nodes* and the virtual nodes of layers 1 to ℓ are called *old nodes.* Also, in the sequel, our focus is on the virtual nodes and thus, unless we specifically use the phrase "real node", we are talking about a virtual node. First, each new node of type 1 or type 3 joins a random class. It then remains to assign classes to type-2 new nodes, which is the key part of the algorithm. The outline of this procedure is as follows:

Recursive Class Assignment Outline:

(1) ***Identify the connected components of old nodes***, i.e., those of $\mathcal{G}[\mathcal{V}_\ell^i]$ for each class i.

(2) ***Create the bridging graph***, a bipartite graph between the connected components of old nodes and type-2 new nodes defined as follows: We view each connected component of old nodes as one node on one side of the bipartite graph, by assuming all its vertices are contracted into one node. Each type-2 new node v is adjacent to a connected component $\mathcal{C}$ of $\mathcal{G}[\mathcal{V}_\ell^i]$ if all the following conditions hold: (a) v has a neighbor in $\mathcal{C}$, (b) $\mathcal{C}$ does not have a type-1 new node neighbor u such that u joined class i and that u has a neighbor in a component $\mathcal{C}' \neq \mathcal{C}$ of $\mathcal{G}[\mathcal{V}_\ell^i]$, and (c) v has a type-3 new node neighbor w such that w has joined class i and w has a neighbor in a connected component $\mathcal{C}'' \neq \mathcal{C}$ of $\mathcal{G}[\mathcal{V}_\ell^i]$.

(3) ***Find a maximal matching $\mathcal{M}$ in the bridging graph***, i.e., between components and type-2 new nodes. For each type-2 new node v, if it is matched in $\mathcal{M}$, then it joins the class of its matched component and otherwise, it joins a random class.

Intuitively, the rule described in step (2) means the following: v is a neighbor of $\mathcal{C}$ in the bridging graph if component $\mathcal{C}$ is not (already) connected to another component of $\mathcal{G}[\mathcal{V}_\ell^i]$ via one type-1 new node, but if v joins class i, then with the help of v and w, the component $\mathcal{C}$ will be merged with some other component $\mathcal{C}'' \neq \mathcal{C}$ of $\mathcal{G}[\mathcal{V}_\ell^i]$. See Figure 1.

This recursive class assignment outline can be implemented distributed in $\tilde{O}(\min\{D+\sqrt{n}, \frac{n}{k}\})$ rounds of the V-CONGEST model, and centralized in $\tilde{O}(m)$ steps, thus proving respectively Theorems 1.1 and 1.2. We present the details of the distributed implementation in Appendix B of the full version [10]. The centralized implementation is presented in Appendix C of the full version [10].

We show in the analysis that the above algorithm indeed constructs k CDSs, w.h.p., and clearly each real node is contained in at most $O(\log n)$ CDSs, at most one for each of its virtual nodes. To turn these CDSs into dominating trees, we simply remove some of the edges of each class so as to make it a tree. We do this by an application of a MST algorithm on the virtual graph $\mathcal{G}$: We give weight of 0 to the edges between virtual nodes of the same class and weight 1 to other edges. Then, the edges with weight 0 that are included in the MST of $\mathcal{G}$ form our dominating trees, exactly one for each CDS.

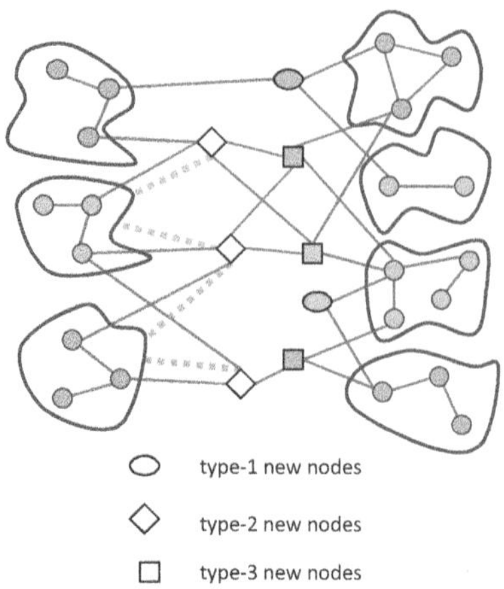

Figure 1: Bridging graph edges are presented by dotted lines; each color is one class.

Remark 4.1. *The assumption of knowing a 2-approximation of k can be removed at the cost of at most an $O(\log n)$ increase in the time complexities.*

To remove the assumption, we use a classical try and error approach: we simply try exponentially decreasing guesses about k, in the form $\frac{n}{2^j}$, and we test the outcome of the dominating tree packing obtained for each guess (particularly its domination and connectivity) using a randomized testing algorithm , presented in the full version [10], on the virtual graph $\mathcal{G}$. For this case, this test runs in a distributed setting in $O(\min\{\frac{n\log^2 n}{k}, (D+\sqrt{n\log n}\log^* n)\log^2 n\})$ round of the V-CONGEST model, and in a centralized setting with step complexity of $O(m\log^3 n)$.

An intuitive comparison with the approach of [11] We note that the approach of the above algorithm is significantly different than that of [11]. Mainly, the key part in [11] is that it finds short paths between connected components of the same class, called *connector paths.* The high-level idea is that, by adding the nodes on the connector paths of a class to this class, we can merge the connected components at the endpoints of this path. However, unavoidably, each node of each path might be on connector paths of many classes. Thus, the class assignment of this node is not clear. [11] cleverly allocates the nodes on the connector paths to different classes so as to make sure that the number of connected components goes down by a constant factor in each layer (in expectation).

Finding the connector paths does not seem to admit an efficient distributed algorithm and it is also slow in a centralized setting. The algorithm presented in this paper does not find connector paths or use them explicitly. However, it is designed such that it enjoys the existence of connector paths and its performance gains implicitly from the abundance of the connector paths. While this is the key part that allows us to make the algorithm distributed and also makes it simpler and faster centralized, the analysis becomes more involved. The main challenging part in the analysis is to show that the the size of the maximal matching found in the bridging graph is large enough so that in each layer, the number of connected components (summed up over all classes) goes down by a constant factor, with at least a constant probability. This is addressed in Section 5.2.

5. DOMINATING TREE PACKING ANALYSIS

In this section, we present the analysis for the algorithm explained in Section 4. We note that this analysis is regardless of whether we implement the algorithm in a distributed or a centralized setting. In a first simple step, we show that each class is a dominating set. Then, proving the connectivity of all classes, which is the core technical part, is divided into two subsections: We first present the concept of connector paths in Section 5.1 and then use this concept in Section 5.2 to achieve the key point of the connectivity analysis, i.e., the Fast Merger Lemma (Lemma 5.4). Some simpler proofs are deferred to the full version [10] .

Lemma 5.1 (Domination Lemma). *W.h.p., for each class i, $\mathcal{V}^i_{L/2}$ is a dominating set.*

Note that since $\mathcal{V}^i_\ell \subseteq \mathcal{V}^i_{\ell'}$ for $\ell \leq \ell'$, the domination of each class follows directly from this lemma. For the rest of this section, we assume that for each class i, $\mathcal{V}^i_{L/2}$ is a dominating set.

5.1 Connector Paths

The concept of connector paths is a simple toolbox that we developed in [11]. For completeness, we present a considerably simpler version here:

Consider a class i, suppose $N^i_\ell \geq 2$, and consider a component $\mathcal{C}$ of $\mathcal{G}[\mathcal{V}^i_\ell]$. For each set of virtual vertices $\mathcal{W} \subseteq \mathcal{V}$, define the projection $\Psi(\mathcal{W})$ of $\mathcal{W}$ onto G as the set $W \subseteq V$ of real vertices w, for which at least one virtual node of w is in $\mathcal{W}$.

A path P in the real graph G is called a *potential connector* for $\mathcal{C}$ if it satisfies the following three conditions: (A) P has one endpoint in $\Psi(\mathcal{C})$ and the other in $\Psi(\mathcal{V}^i_\ell \setminus \mathcal{C})$, (B) P has at most two internal vertices, (C) if P has exactly two internal vertices and has the form s, u, w, t where $s \in \Psi(\mathcal{C})$ and $t \in \Psi(\mathcal{V}^i_\ell \setminus \mathcal{C})$, then w does not have a neighbor in $\Psi(\mathcal{C})$ and u does not have a neighbor in $\Psi(\mathcal{V}^i_\ell \setminus \mathcal{C})$.

Intuitively, condition (C) requires *minimality* of each potential connector path. That is, there is no potential connector path connecting $\Psi(\mathcal{C})$ to another component of $\Psi(\mathcal{V}^i_\ell)$ via only u or only w.

From a potential connector path P on graph G, we derive a connector path $\mathcal{P}$ on virtual graph $\mathcal{G}$ by determining the types of the related internal virtual vertices as follows: (D) If P has one internal real vertex w, then for $\mathcal{P}$ we choose the virtual vertex of w in layer $\ell+1$ in $\mathcal{G}$ with type 1. (E) If P has two internal real vertices w_1 and w_2, where w_1 is adjacent to $\Psi(\mathcal{C})$ and w_2 is adjacent to $\Psi(\mathcal{V}^i_\ell \setminus \mathcal{C})$, then for $\mathcal{P}$ we choose the virtual vertices of w_1 and w_2 in layer $\ell+1$ with types 2 and 3, respectively. Finally, for each endpoint w of P we add the copy of w in $\mathcal{V}^i_\ell$ to $\mathcal{P}$. We call a connector path that has one internal vertex a *short connector path*, whereas a connector path with two internal vertices is called a *long connector path.* Because of condition (C), and rules (D) and (E) above, we get the following fact:

Proposition 5.2. *For each class i, each type-2 virtual vertex u of layer $\ell+1$ is on connector paths of at most one connected component of $\mathcal{G}[\mathcal{V}^i_\ell]$.*

We next show that each component that is not single in its class has k connector paths.

Lemma 5.3 (Connector Abundance Lemma). *Consider a layer $\ell \geq L/2+1$ and a class i such that $\mathcal{V}^i_{L/2} \subseteq \mathcal{V}^i_\ell$ is a dominating set of $\mathcal{G}$ and $N^i_\ell \geq 2$. Further consider an arbitrary connected component $\mathcal{C}$ of $\mathcal{G}[\mathcal{V}^i_\ell]$. Then, $\mathcal{C}$ has at least k internally vertex-disjoint connector paths.*

The proof is based on a simple application of Menger's theorem [8, Theorem 9.1] and crucially uses the domination of each class, Lemma 5.1. The proof can also be viewed as a simplified version of that of [11, Lemma 3.4] and appears in Appendix D of the full version [10].

5.2 The Fast Merger Lemma

We next show that the described algorithms will make the number of connected components go down by a constant factor in each layer. The formal statement is as follows:

Lemma 5.4 (Fast Merger Lemma). *For each layer $\ell \in [\frac{L}{2}, L-1]$, $M_{\ell+1} \leq M_\ell$, and moreover, there are constants $\delta, \rho > 0$ such that $\Pr[M_{\ell+1} \leq (1-\delta)\cdot M_\ell] \geq \rho$ with independence between layers.*

Proof. Let ℓ be a layer in $[\frac{L}{2}, L-1]$. For the first part note that since from Lemma 5.1 we know that $\mathcal{V}^i_{L/2}$ is a dominating, and as $\mathcal{V}^i_\ell \subseteq \mathcal{V}^i_{\ell'}$ for $\ell \leq \ell'$, each new node of layer $\ell+1$ that is added to class i has a neighbor in the old components of this class and thus, the new nodes do not increase the number of connected components.

For the second part, let i be a class for which $N^i_\ell \geq 2$ and consider a component $\mathcal{C}$ of $\mathcal{G}[\mathcal{V}^i_\ell]$. We say that $\mathcal{C}$ is *good* if one of the following two conditions is satisfied: (I) There is a type-1 new node v that has a neighbor in $\mathcal{C}$ and a neighbor in a component $\mathcal{C}' \neq \mathcal{C}$ of G^i_ℓ and v joins class i. (II) There are two neighboring new nodes, w and u, with types 2 and 3, respectively, such that w has a neighbor in $\mathcal{C}$, u has a neighbor in a component $\mathcal{C}' \neq \mathcal{C}$ of $\mathcal{G}[\mathcal{V}^i_\ell]$, and both u and w join class i. Otherwise, we say that $\mathcal{C}$ is *bad*. By definition, if a connected component of old nodes is good, then at the next layer it is merged with another component of its class.

Let X^i_ℓ be the number of bad connected components of class i if $N^i_\ell \geq 2$ and $X^i_\ell = 0$ otherwise. Also, define $Y_\ell = \sum_{i=1}^t X^i_\ell$, which gives $M_{\ell+1} \leq \frac{M_\ell - Y_\ell}{2} + Y_\ell$. To prove the lemma, we show that $\mathbb{E}[Y_\ell] \leq (1-3\delta)\cdot M_\ell$ for some constant $\delta > 0$. Then, using Markov's inequality we get that $\Pr[Y_\ell \leq (1-2\delta)\cdot M_\ell] \geq 1-\frac{1-3\delta}{1-2\delta}$ and therefore $\Pr[M_{\ell+1} \leq (1-\delta)M_\ell] \geq 1-\frac{1-3\delta}{1-2\delta}$ and thus the lemma follows.

Hence, it remains to prove that $\mathbb{E}[Y_\ell] \leq (1-3\delta)\cdot M_\ell$ for some $\delta > 0$. For this, we divide the connected components of old nodes into two groups of *fast* and *slow* components, as follows: Consider a class i such that $N^i_\ell \geq 2$. A connected component $\mathcal{C}$ of $\mathcal{G}[\mathcal{V}^i_\ell]$ is called *fast* if it has at least $\Omega(k)$ short connector paths, and *slow* otherwise. Note that by Lemma 5.3, w.h.p., each slow component has at least $\Omega(k)$ long connector paths.

Let M^F_ℓ and M^S_ℓ be the total number of fast and slow connected components, respectively, of graphs $\mathcal{G}[\mathcal{V}^i_\ell]$ as i ranges over all classes. Note that $M^F_\ell + M^S_\ell = M_\ell$. We say that a short connector path p for $\mathcal{C}$ is *good* if its internal node is in the same class as $\mathcal{C}$. Let Y^F_ℓ be the total number of fast connected components for which none of the short paths is good. Because every type-1 new node picks its class number randomly, each of the $\Omega(k)$ short paths (independently) has probability at least $1/k$ to be in the right class. The expected number of short paths in the right class is therefore constant and hence, there exists a constant $\delta > 0$ such that $\mathbb{E}[Y^F_\ell] \leq (1-3\delta)\cdot M^F_\ell$.

Moreover, let $\mathcal{K}$ be set of the slow connected components of the graphs $\mathcal{G}[\mathcal{V}^i_\ell]$ (for all classes $i \in [1,t]$) for which none of the short paths is good and let $K := |\mathcal{K}|$. Let $\mathcal{M}$ be the maximal matching the algorithm computes for the bridging graph. In order to complete the proof, we show that the expected size of $\mathcal{M}$ is at least $3\delta \cdot K$ for some $\delta > 0$. Given this, we get that

$$\begin{aligned}\mathbb{E}[Y_\ell] &= \mathbb{E}[Y^F_\ell] + \big(\mathbb{E}[K] - \mathbb{E}[|\mathcal{M}|]\big)\\ &\leq (1-3\delta)\cdot(M^F_\ell + K)\\ &\leq (1-3\delta)\cdot(M^F_\ell + M^S_\ell) = (1-3\delta)\cdot M_\ell,\end{aligned}$$

which would complete the proof.

To show that the expected size of the maximal matching is at least $3\delta\cdot K$ for some $\delta > 0$, it is sufficient to prove that the expected size of a maximum matching is at least $\Omega(K)$. It is easy to see that the size of any maximal matching is at least half of the size of a maximum matching. Hence, we just need to show that the expected size of the maximum matching is at least $\Omega(K)$. We do this in Lemma 5.5. □

Lemma 5.5. *The expected size of the maximum matching in the bridging graph is at least $\Omega(K)$.*

This lemma is the key part of the analysis. As the proof has many technical details, we defer it to full version [10] and only mention a rough outline here: The bridging graph might have a complex structure and thus, we do not know how to work with it directly. However, the saving grace is that we know more about the connector paths, thanks to Lemma 5.3. Using long connector paths, we algorithmically identify a (random) subgraph $\mathcal{H}$ of the bridging graph and show that just this subgraph $\mathcal{H}$ contains a matching of size $\Omega(K)$. The analysis of this algorithm uses a simple probability tail bound inequality that we develop for our specific problem.

Lemma 5.6. *W.h.p., for each i, the number of virtual nodes in class i is $O(\frac{n \log n}{k})$.*

6. DISTRIBUTED FRACTIONAL SPANNING-TREE PACKING

Recall that the celebrated results of Tutte [52] and Nash-Williams [44] show that each graph with edge connectivity λ contains $\lceil\frac{\lambda-1}{2}\rceil$ edge-disjoint spanning trees. Here we explain how one can find a fractional spanning tree packing with almost the same size. We particularly explain only the algorithm for the case where $\lambda = O(\log n)$. In the full version [10], we explain how to extend this algorithm to the general case. The analysis are also deferred to [10].

The algorithm follows a classical approach, which can be viewed as an adaptation of the Lagrangian relaxation method of optimization theory (see e.g. [34,36,47,50]). Tailored to tree packing, this approach means we maintain a collection of weighted trees and we iteratively improve this collection by penalizing the edges with large load, which pushes the collection to take some weight away from the edges with larger load and distribute it over those with smaller loads.

Algorithm Outline We will always maintain a collection T of weighted trees—where each tree $\tau \in T$ has weight $w_\tau \in [0,1]$—such that the total weight of the trees in the collection is 1. That is $\sum_{\tau \in T} w_\tau = 1$. We start with a collection containing only one (arbitrary) tree with initial weight 1 and iteratively improve this collection for $\Theta(\log^3 n)$ iterations: During each iteration, for each edge $e \in E$, let x_e be the *weighted load* on edge e, that is $x_e = \sum_{\tau, e \in \tau} w_\tau$ and also, let $z_e = x_e \lceil \frac{\lambda-1}{2} \rceil$. Our goal is that at the end, we have $\max_{e \in E} z_e \leq 1 + O(\varepsilon)$.

In each iteration, for each edge e, we define a cost $c_e = exp(\alpha \cdot z_e)$, where $\alpha = \Theta(\log n)$. Then, we find the Minimum Spanning Tree (MST) with respect to these costs. If $Cost(MST) = \sum_{e \in MST} c_e > (1-\varepsilon) \sum_{e \in E} c_e \cdot x_e$, then the algorithm terminates. On the other hand, if $Cost(MST) = \sum_{e \in MST} c_e \leq (1-\varepsilon) \sum_{e \in E} c_e \cdot x_e$, then we add this MST to our weighted tree collection T, with weight $\beta = \Theta(\frac{1}{\alpha \log n})$, and to maintain condition $\sum_{\tau \in T} w_\tau = 1$, we multiply the weight of the old trees in T by $1 - \beta$.

Distributed Implementation Using the distributed MST algorithm of Kutten and Peleg [39], we can perform one iteration in $O(D + \sqrt{n} \log^* n)$ rounds of the V-CONGEST model. Hence, the $\Theta(\log^3 n)$ iterations of the above algorithm can be performed in $O((D + \sqrt{n} \log^* n) \log^3 n)$ rounds. Note that in these iterations, each node v simply needs to know the weight on edges incident on v and whether another iteration will be used or not. The latter decision can be made centrally—in a leader node, e.g., the node with the largest id—by gathering the total cost of the minimum spanning tree over a breadth first search tree rooted at this leader and then propagating the decision of whether to continue to next iteration or not to all nodes.

Acknowledgement

We thank Noga Alon for bringing to our attention the resemblance between dominating tree packing and vertex independent trees (see Section 1.4.1). We also thank David Karger for discussions in the preliminary stages of this work and Bernhard Haeupler, Stephan Holzer, Christoph Lenzen, and Nancy Lynch for helpful comments about the write up.

7. REFERENCES

[1] A. V. Aho, J. E. Hopcroft, and J. D. Ullman. *The Design & Analysis of Computer Algorithms.* Addison-Wesley, 1974.

[2] B. Awerbuch, B. Berger, L. Cowen, and D. Peleg. Fast network decomposition. In *Proc. 11th ACM Symp. on Principles of Distributed Computing (PODC)*, pages 169–177, 1992.

[3] B. Awerbuch, B. Berger, L. Cowen, and D. Peleg. Fast distributed network decompositions and covers. *Journal of Parallel and Distributed Computing*, 39(2):105–114, 1996.

[4] B. Awerbuch, M. Luby, A. Goldberg, and S. A. Plotkin. Network decomposition and locality in distributed computation. In *Proc. 30th IEEE Symp. Foundations of Computer Science (FOCS)*, pages 364–369, 1989.

[5] Y. Azar, E. Cohen, A. Fiat, H. Kaplan, and H. Racke. Optimal oblivious routing in polynomial time. In *Proc. 35th ACM Symp. on Theory of Computing (STOC)*, pages 383–388, 2003.

[6] F. Barahona. Packing spanning trees. *Mathematics of Operations Research*, 20(1):104–115, 1995.

[7] M. Bienkowski, M. Korzeniowski, and H. Räcke. A practical algorithm for constructing oblivious routing schemes. In *Proc. 15th ACM Symp. on Parallel Algorithms and Architectures (SPAA)*, pages 24–33, 2003.

[8] J. Bondy and U. Murty. Graph theory (graduate texts in mathematics, vol. 244), 2008.

[9] R. Carr and S. Vempala. Randomized metarounding (extended abstract). In *Proc. 32nd ACM Symp. on Theory of Computing (STOC)*, pages 58–62, 2000.

[10] K. Censor-Hillel, M. Ghaffari, and F. Kuhn. Distributed connectivity decomposition. *CoRR*, abs/1311.5317, 2013.

[11] K. Censor-Hillel, M. Ghaffari, and F. Kuhn. A new perspective on vertex connectivity. In *Proc. 25th ACM-SIAM Symp. on Discrete Algorithms (SODA)*, 2014.

[12] J. Cheriyan and S. Maheshwari. Finding nonseparating induced cycles and independent spanning trees in 3-connected graphs. *Journal of Algorithms*, 9(4):507–537, 1988.

[13] A. Das Sarma, S. Holzer, L. Kor, A. Korman, D. Nanongkai, G. Pandurangan, D. Peleg, and R. Wattenhofer. Distributed verification and hardness of distributed approximation. *SIAM J. on Comp.*, 41(5):1235–1265, 2012.

[14] A. Das Sarma, D. Nanongkai, and G. Pandurangan. Fast distributed random walks. In *The Proceedings of the International Symposium on Principles of Distributed Computing (PODC)*, pages 161–170, 2009.

[15] A. Das Sarma, D. Nanongkai, G. Pandurangan, and P. Tetali. Efficient distributed random walks with applications. In *The Proceedings of the International Symposium on Principles of Distributed Computing (PODC)*, pages 201–210, 2010.

[16] A. Ene, N. Korula, and A. Vakilian. Connected domatic packings in node-capacitated graphs. *http://arxiv.org/abs/1305.4308/v2*, 2013.

[17] S. Even. An algorithm for determining whether the connectivity of a graph is at least k. *SIAM Journal on Computing*, 4(3):393–396, 1975.

[18] U. Feige, M. M. Halldórsson, and G. Kortsarz. Approximating the domatic number. In *The Proceedings of the Symposium on Theory of Computing (STOC)*, pages 134–143, 2000.

[19] S. Frischknecht, S. Holzer, and R. Wattenhofer. Networks cannot compute their diameter in sublinear time. In *The Proceedings of ACM-SIAM Symposium on Discrete Algorithms (SODA)*, pages 1150–1162, 2012.

[20] H. Gabow. Using expander graphs to find vertex connectivity. In *Proc. 41st IEEE Symp. Foundations of Computer Science (FOCS)*, pages 410–420, 2000.

[21] H. Gabow and H. Westermann. Forests, frames, and games: algorithms for matroid sums and applications. In *Proc. 20th ACM Symp. on Theory of Computing (STOC)*, pages 407–421, 1988.

[22] Z. Galil. Finding the vertex connectivity of graphs. *SIAM Journal on Computing*, 9(1):197–199, 1980.

[23] M. Ghaffari and F. Kuhn. Distributed minimum cut approximation. In *Proc. 27th Symp. on Distributed Computing (DISC)*, pages 1–15, 2013.

[24] S. Guha and S. Khuller. Approximation algorithms for connected dominating sets. *Algorithmica*, 20(4):374–387, Apr. 1998.

[25] B. Haeupler and F. Kuhn. Lower bounds on information dissemination in dynamic networks. In *Distributed Computing*, pages 166–180. Springer, 2012.

[26] M. T. Hajiaghayi, R. D. Kleinberg, H. Räcke, and T. Leighton. Oblivious routing on node-capacitated and directed graphs. *ACM Trans. Algorithms*, 3(4), Nov. 2007.

[27] C. Harrelson, K. Hildrum, and S. Rao. A polynomial-time tree decomposition to minimize congestion. In *Proc. 15th ACM Symp. on Parallel Algorithms and Architectures (SPAA)*, pages 34–43, 2003.

[28] M. R. Henzinger. A static 2-approximation algorithm for vertex connectivity and incremental approximation algorithms for edge and vertex connectivity. *J. Algorithms*, 24(1):194–220, 1997.

[29] M. R. Henzinger, S. Rao, and H. N. Gabow. Computing vertex connectivity: new bounds from old techniques. In *Proc. 37th IEEE Symp. Foundations of Computer Science (FOCS)*, pages 462–471. IEEE, 1996.

[30] S. Holzer and R. Wattenhofer. Optimal distributed all pairs shortest paths and applications. In *The Proceedings of the International Symposium on Principles of Distributed Computing (PODC)*, pages 355–364, 2012.

[31] A. Itai and M. Rodeh. The multi-tree approach to reliability in distributed networks. *Information and Computation*, 79(1):43–59, 1988.

[32] A. Kanevsky. On the number of minimum size separating vertex sets in a graph and how to find all of them. In *Proc. 1st ACM-SIAM Symp. on Discrete Algorithm (SODA)*, pages 411–421, 1990.

[33] D. R. Karger. Using randomized sparsification to approximate minimum cuts. In *Proc. 5th ACM-SIAM Symp. on Discrete Algorithms (SODA)*, pages 424–432, 1994.

[34] D. R. Karger. Minimum cuts in near-linear time. In *Proc. 28th ACM Symp. on Theory of Computing (STOC)*, STOC'96, pages 56–63, 1996.

[35] S. Khuller and B. Schieber. On independent spanning trees. *Information Processing Letters*, 42(6):321–323, 1992.

[36] P. Klein, S. Plotkin, C. Stein, and E. Tardos. Faster approximation algorithms for the unit capacity concurrent flow problem with applications to routing and finding sparse cuts. *SIAM Journal on Computing*, 23(3):466–487, 1994.

[37] F. Kuhn, N. Lynch, and R. Oshman. Distributed computation in dynamic networks. In *The Proceedings of the Symposium on Theory of Computing (STOC)*, pages 513–522, 2010.

[38] S. Kundu. Bounds on the number of disjoint spanning trees. *J. of Comb. Theory, Series B*, 17(2):199 – 203, 1974.

[39] S. Kutten and D. Peleg. Fast distributed construction of k-dominating sets and applications. In *Proc. 14th ACM Symp. on Principles of Distributed Computing (PODC)*, pages 238–251, 1995.

[40] C. Lenzen and B. Patt-Shamir. Fast routing table construction using small messages: Extended abstract. In *The Proceedings of the Symposium on Theory of Computing (STOC)*, pages 381–390, 2013.

[41] Z. Li, B. Li, and L. C. Lau. A constant bound on throughput improvement of multicast network coding in undirected networks. *IEEE Trans. Inf. Theory*, 55(3):1016–1026, 2009.

[42] D. Nanogkai. Distributed approximation algorithms for weighted shortest paths. In *The Proceedings of the Symposium on Theory of Computing (STOC)*, 2014, to appear.

[43] D. Nanongkai, A. Das Sarma, and G. Pandurangan. A tight unconditional lower bound on distributed randomwalk computation. In *The Proceedings of the International Symposium on Principles of Distributed Computing (PODC)*, pages 257–266, 2011.

[44] C. Nash-Williams. Edge-disjoint spanning trees of finite graphs. *J. of the London Math. Society*, 36:445–450, 1961.

[45] A. Panconesi and A. Srinivasan. Improved distributed algorithms for coloring and network decomposition problems. In *Proc. 24th ACM Symp. on Theory of Computing (STOC)*, STOC '92, pages 581–592, 1992.

[46] D. Peleg. *Distributed computing: a locality-sensitive approach*, volume 5. SIAM, 2000.

[47] S. A. Plotkin, D. B. Shmoys, and E. Tardos. Fast approximation algorithms for fractional packing and covering problems. In *Proc. 32nd IEEE Symp. Foundations of Computer Science (FOCS)*, pages 495–504, 1991.

[48] H. Räcke. Minimizing congestion in general networks. In *Proc. 43rd IEEE Symp. Foundations of Computer Science (FOCS)*, pages 43–52, 2002.

[49] H. Räcke. Optimal hierarchical decompositions for congestion minimization in networks. In *Proc. 35th ACM Symp. on Theory of Computing (STOC)*, pages 255–264, 2008.

[50] F. Shahrokhi and D. W. Matula. The maximum concurrent flow problem. *Journal of the ACM (JACM)*, 37(2):318–334, 1990.

[51] R. E. Tarjan. Testing graph connectivity. In *Proc. 6th ACM Symp. on Theory of Computing (STOC)*, STOC '74, pages 185–193, 1974.

[52] W. T. Tutte. On the problem of decomposing a graph into n connected factors. *J. of the London Math. Society*, 36:221–230, 1961.

[53] A. Zehavi and A. Itai. Three tree-paths. *Journal of Graph Theory*, 13(2):175–188, 1989.

Can Quantum Communication Speed Up Distributed Computation?*

Michael Elkin[†]
Department of Computer Science Ben-Gurion University, Israel
elkinm@cs.bgu.ac.il

Hartmut Klauck[‡]
Nanyang Technological University & Centre for Quantum Technologies, Singapore
hklauck@gmail.com

Danupon Nanongkai[§]
Faculty of Computer Science University of Vienna, Austria
danupon@gmail.com

Gopal Pandurangan[¶]
Nanyang Technological University, Singapore & Brown University, Providence, USA.
gopalpandurangan@gmail.com

ABSTRACT

The focus of this paper is on *quantum distributed* computation, where we investigate whether quantum communication can help in *speeding up* distributed network algorithms. Our main result is that for certain fundamental network problems such as minimum spanning tree, minimum cut, and shortest paths, quantum communication *does not* help in substantially speeding up distributed algorithms for these problems compared to the classical setting.

In order to obtain this result, we extend the technique of Das Sarma et al. [SICOMP 2012] to obtain a uniform approach to prove non-trivial lower bounds for quantum distributed algorithms for several graph optimization (both exact and approximate versions) as well as verification problems, some of which are new even in the classical setting, e.g. tight randomized lower bounds for Hamiltonian cycle and spanning tree verification, answering an open problem of Das Sarma et al., and a lower bound in terms of the weight aspect ratio, matching the upper bounds of Elkin [STOC 2004]. Our approach introduces the *Server model* and *Quantum Simulation Theorem* which together provide a connection between distributed algorithms and communication complexity. The Server model is the standard two-party communication complexity model augmented with additional power; yet, most of the hardness in the two-party model is carried over to this new model. The Quantum Simulation Theorem carries this hardness further to quantum distributed computing. Our techniques, except the proof of the hardness in the Server model, require very little knowledge in quantum computing, and this can help overcoming a usual impediment in proving bounds on quantum distributed algorithms. In particular, if one can prove a lower bound for distributed algorithms for a certain problem using the technique of Das Sarma et al., it is likely that such lower bound can be extended to the quantum setting using tools provided in this paper and without the need of knowledge in quantum computing.

*The full version of this paper is available at `http://arxiv.org/abs/1207.5211`

[†]Supported by the Israeli Academy of Science, grant 593/11, and by the Binational Science Foundation, grant 2008390.

[‡]This work is funded by the Singapore Ministry of Education (partly through the Academic Research Fund Tier 3 MOE2012-T3-1-009) and by the Singapore National Research Foundation.

[§]Work done while at Nanyang Technological University, Singapore, and Brown University, USA.

[¶]Supported in part by the following research grants: Nanyang Technological University grant M58110000, Singapore Ministry of Education (MOE) Academic Research Fund (AcRF) Tier 2 grant MOE2010-T2-2-082, Singapore MOE AcRF Tier 1 grant MOE2012-T1-001-094, and a grant from the US-Israel Binational Science Foundation (BSF).

PODC'14, July 15–18, 2014, Paris, France.

http://dx.doi.org/10.1145/2611462.2611488.

Categories and Subject Descriptors

C.2.4 [**Computer Systems Organization**]: Computer Communication Networks — *Distributed Systems*; F.2.0 [**Analysis of Algorithms and Problem Complexity**]: General; G.2.2 [**Mathematics of Computing**]: Discrete Mathematics — *Graph Theory*

General Terms

Algorithms,Theory

Keywords

distributed computing; graph algorithms; quantum communication; time complexity; lower bound, CONGEST model

1. INTRODUCTION

The power and limitations of distributed (network) computation have been studied extensively over the last three decades or so. In a distributed network, each individual node can communicate only with its neighboring nodes. Some distributed problems can be solved entirely via local communication, e.g., maximal independent set, maximal matching, coloring, dominating set, vertex cover, or approximations thereof. These are considered "local" problems, as they can be shown to be solved using *small (i.e., polylogarithmic)* communication (e.g., see [44, 53, 61]). For example, a maximal independent set can be computed in $O(\log n)$ time [45]. However, many important problems are "global" problems (which are the focus of this paper) from the distributed computation point of view. For example, to count the total number of nodes, to elect a leader, to compute a spanning tree (ST) or a minimum spanning tree (MST) or a shortest path tree (SPT), information necessarily must travel to the farthest nodes in a system. If exchanging a message over a single edge costs one time unit, one needs $\Omega(D)$ time units to compute the result, where D is the network diameter [53]. If message size was unbounded, one can simply collect all the information in $O(D)$ time, and then compute the result. However, in many applications, there is *bandwidth restriction* on the size of the message (or the number of bits) that can be exchanged over a communication link in one time unit. This motivates studying global problems in the CONGEST model [53], where each node can exchange at most B bits (typically B is small, say $O(\log n)$) among its neighbors in one time step. This is one of the central models in the study of distributed computation. The design of efficient algorithms for the CONGEST model, as well as establishing lower bounds on the time complexity of various fundamental distributed computing problems, has been the subject of an active area of research called (locality-sensitive) *distributed computing* for the last three decades (e.g., [53, 20, 18, 32, 61, 13]). In particular, it is now established that $\tilde{\Omega}(D+\sqrt{n})$ [1] is a fundamental lower bound on the running time of many important graph optimization (both exact and approximate versions) and verification problems such as MST, ST, shortest paths, minimum cut, ST verification etc [13].

The main focus of this paper is studying the power of distributed network computation in the *quantum setting*. More precisely, we consider the CONGEST model in the quantum setting, where nodes can use quantum processing, communicate over quantum links using quantum bits, and use exclusively quantum phenomena such as *entanglement* (e.g., see [17, 6, 25]). A fundamental question that we would like to investigate is whether quantumness can help in speeding up distributed computation for graph optimization problems; in particular, whether the above mentioned lower bound of $\tilde{\Omega}(D+\sqrt{n})$ (that applies to many important problems in the classical setting) also applies to the quantum setting.

Lower bounds for local problems (where the running time is $O(\text{poly}\log n)$) in the quantum setting usually follow directly from the same arguments as in the classical setting. This is because these lower bounds are proved using the "limited sight" argument: The nodes do not have time to get the information of the entire network. Since entanglement *cannot be used to replace communication* (by, e.g., Holevo's theorem [28] (also see [51, 50])), the same argument holds in the quantum setting with prior entanglement. This argument is captured by the notion of *physical locality* defined by Gavoille et al. [25], where it is shown that for many *local* problems, quantumness does not give any significant speedup in time compared to the classical setting.

The above limited sight argument, however, does not seem to be extendible to *global* problems where the running time is usually $\Omega(D)$, since nodes have enough time to see the whole network in this case. In this setting, the argument developed in [13] (which follows the line of work in [54, 43, 21, 36]) can be used to show tight lower bounds for many problems in the classical setting. However, this argument does not always hold in the quantum setting because it essentially relies on network "congestion": Nodes cannot communicate fast enough (due to limited bandwidth) to get important information to solve the problem. However, we know that the quantum communication and entanglement can potentially *decrease the amount of communication* and thus there might be some problems that can be solved faster. One example that illustrates this point is the following *distributed verification of disjointness function* defined in [13, Section 2.3].

EXAMPLE 1.1. *Suppose we give b-bit string x and y to node u and v in the network, respectively, where $b = \sqrt{n}$. We want to check whether the inner product $\langle x, y\rangle$ is zero or not. This is called the* Set Disjointness *problem (*Disj*). It is easy to show that it is impossible to solve this problem in less than $D/2$ rounds since there will be no node having the information from both u and v if u and v are of distance D apart. (This is the very basic idea of the limited sight argument.) This argument holds for both classical and quantum setting and thus we have a lower bound of $\Omega(D)$ on both settings. [13, Lemma 4.1] shows that this lower bound can be significantly improved to $\tilde{\Omega}(b) = \tilde{\Omega}(\sqrt{n})$ in the classical setting, even when the network has diameter $O(\log n)$. This follows from the communication complexity of $\Omega(b)$ of* Disj *[2, 31, 3, 57] and the* Simulation Theorem *of [13]. This lower bound, however, does not hold in the quantum setting since we can simulate the known $O(\sqrt{b})$-communication quantum protocol of [1] in $O(\sqrt{b}D) = O(n^{1/4}D)$ rounds.* □

Thus we have an example of a global problem that quantum communication gives an advantage over classical communication. This example also shows that the previous techniques and results from [13] does not apply to the quantum setting since [13] heavily relies on the hardness of the above distributed disjointness verification problem. A fundamental question is: *"Does this phenomenon occur for natural global distributed network problems?"*

Our paper answers the above question where we show that this phenomenon does not occur for many global graph problems. Our main result is that for fundamental global problems such as minimum spanning tree, minimum cut, and shortest paths, quantum communication *does not* help significantly in speeding up distributed algorithms for these problems compared to the classical setting. More precisely, we show that $\tilde{\Omega}(D+\sqrt{n})$ is a lower bound for these problems in the quantum setting as well. An $\tilde{O}(D+\sqrt{n})$ time algorithm for MST problem in the classical setting is well-known [38]. Recently, it has been shown that minimum cut also admits a distributed $(1+\epsilon)$-approximation algorithm in the same time in the classical setting [27, 60, 46, 49]. Also, recently it has been shown that shortest paths admits an $\tilde{O}(D+\sqrt{n}D^{1/4})$-time $(1+\epsilon)$-approximation and

[1] $\tilde{\Omega}$ and $\tilde{O}$ notations hide polylogarithmic factors.

$\tilde{O}(\sqrt{n} + D)$-time $O(\log n)$-approximation distributed classical algorithms [41, 47]. Thus, our quantum lower bound shows that quantum communication does not speed up distributed algorithms for MST and minimum cut, while for shortest paths the speed up, if any, is bounded by $O(D^{1/4})$ (which is small for small diameter graphs).

In order to obtain our quantum lower bound results, we develop a uniform approach to prove non-trivial lower bounds for quantum distributed algorithms. This approach leads us to several non-trivial quantum distributed lower bounds (which are the first-known quantum bounds for problems such as minimum spanning tree, shortest paths etc.), some of which are new even in the classical setting. Our approach introduces the *Server model* and *Quantum Simulation Theorem* which together provide a connection between distributed algorithms and communication complexity. The Server model is simply the standard two-party communication complexity model augmented with a powerful *Server* who can communicate for free but receives no input (cf. Def. 3.1). It is more powerful than the two-party model, yet captures most of the hardness obtained by the current quantum communication complexity techniques. The Quantum Simulation Theorem (cf. Theorem 3.5) is an extension of the Simulation Theorem of Das Sarma et al. [13] from the classical setting to the quantum one. It carries this hardness from the Server model further to quantum distributed computing. Most of our techniques require very little knowledge in quantum computing, and this can help overcoming a usual impediment in proving bounds on quantum distributed algorithms. In particular, if one can prove a lower bound for distributed algorithms in the classical setting using the technique of Das Sarma et al., then it is possible that one can also prove the same lower bound in the quantum setting in essentially the same way – the only change needed is that the proof has to start from problems that are hard on the server model that we provide in this paper.

2. THE SETTING

2.1 Quantum Distributed Computing Model

We study problems in a natural quantum version of the CONGEST(B) model [53] (or, in short, the B-model), where each node can exchange at most B bits (typically B is small, say $O(\log n)$) among its neighbors in one time step. The main focus of the current work is to understand the time complexity of fundamental graph problems in the B-model in the *quantum setting*. We now explain the model. We refer the readers to full version for a more rigorous and formal definition of our model.

Consider a synchronous network of processors modeled by an undirected n-node graph, where nodes model the processors and edges model the links between the processors. The processors (henceforth, nodes) are assumed to have unique IDs. Each node has limited topological knowledge; in particular, it only knows the IDs of its neighbors and knows no other topological information (e.g., whether its neighbors are linked by an edge or not). The node may also accept some additional inputs as specified by the problem at hand.

The communication is synchronous, and occurs in discrete pulses, called *rounds*. All the nodes wake up simultaneously at the beginning of each round. In each round each node u is allowed to send an arbitrary message of B bits through each edge $e = (u, v)$ incident to u, and the message will arrive at v at the end of the current round. Nodes then perform an internal computation, which finishes instantly since nodes have infinite computation power. There are several measures to analyze the performance of distributed algorithms, a fundamental one being the *running time*, defined as the worst-case number of rounds of distributed communication.

In the quantum setting, a distributed network could be augmented with two additional resources: *quantum communication* and *shared entanglement* (see e.g., [17]). Quantum communication allows nodes to communicate with each other using *quantum bits (qubits)*; i.e., in each round at most B qubits can be sent through each edge in each direction. Shared entanglement allows nodes to possess qubits that are entangled with qubits of other nodes[2]. Quantum distributed networks can be categorized based on which resources are assumed (see, e.g., [25]). In this paper, we are interested in the *most powerful model*, where both quantum communication and the *most general form of shared entanglement* are assumed: in a technical term, we allow nodes to share an arbitrary n-partite entangled state as long as it does not depend on the input (thus, does not reveal any input information). Throughout the paper, we simply refer to this model as quantum distributed network (or just distributed network, if the context is clear). All lower bounds we show in this paper hold in this model, and thus also imply lower bounds in weaker models.

2.2 Distributed Graph Problems

We focus on solving graph problems on distributed networks. We are interested in two types of graph problems: optimization and verification problems. In both types of problems, we are given a distributed network N modeled by a graph and some property $\mathcal{P}$ such as "Hamiltonian cycle", "spanning tree" or "connected component".

In optimization problems, we are additionally given a (positive) weight function $w : E(N) \to \mathbb{R}_+$ where every node in the network knows weights of edges incident to it. Our goal is to find a subnetwork M of N of minimum weight that satisfies $\mathcal{P}$ (e.g. minimum Hamiltonian cycle or MST) where every node knows which edges incident to it are in M in the end of computation. Algorithms can sometimes depend on the *weight aspect ratio* W defined as $W = \frac{\max_{e \in E(N)} w(e)}{\min_{e \in E(N)} w(e)}$.

In verification problems, we are additionally given a subnetwork M of N as the problem input (each node knows which edges incident to it are in M). We want to determine whether M has some property, e.g., M is a Hamiltonian cycle ($\mathsf{Ham}(N)$), a spanning tree ($\mathsf{ST}(N)$), or a connected component ($\mathsf{Conn}(N)$), where every node knows the answer in the end of computation.

[2]Roughly speaking, one can think of shared entanglement as a "quantum version" of shared randomness. For example, a well-known entangled state on two qubits is the *EPR* pair [19, 4] which is a pair of qubits that, when measured, will either both be zero or both be one, with probability 1/2 each. An EPR pair shared by two nodes can hence be used to, among other things, generate a shared random bit for the two nodes. Assuming entanglement implies shared randomness (even among all nodes), but also allows for other operations such as quantum teleportation [51], which replaces quantum communication by classical communication plus entanglement.

We use[3] $Q^{*,N}_{\epsilon_0,\epsilon_1}(\mathsf{Ham}(N))$ to refer to the quantum time complexity of Hamiltonian cycle verification problem on network N where for any 0-input M (i.e. M is not a Hamiltonian cycle), the algorithm has to output zero with probability at least $1-\epsilon_0$ and for any 1-input M (i.e. M is a Hamiltonian cycle), the algorithm has to output one with probability at least $1-\epsilon_1$. (We call this type of algorithm (ϵ_0, ϵ_1)*-error.*) When $\epsilon_0 = \epsilon_1 = \epsilon$, we simply write $Q^{*,N}_{\epsilon}(\mathsf{Ham}(N))$. Define $Q^{*,N}_{\epsilon_0,\epsilon_1}(\mathsf{ST}(N)))$ and $Q^{*,N}_{\epsilon_0,\epsilon_1}(\mathsf{Conn}(N))$ similarly.

We also study the *gap versions* of verification problems. For any integer $\delta \geq 0$, property $\mathcal{P}$ and a subnetwork M of N, we say that M is δ*-far*[4] from $\mathcal{P}$ if we have to add at least δ edges *from* N and remove any number of edges in order to make M satisfy $\mathcal{P}$. We denote the problem of distinguishing between the case where the subnetwork M satisfies $\mathcal{P}$ and is δ-far from satisfying $\mathcal{P}$ *the* δ-$\mathcal{P}$ *problem* (it is promised that the input is in one of these two cases). When we do not want to specify δ, we write Gap-$\mathcal{P}$. Other graph problems that we are interested in are those in [13] and their gap versions. See full version for precise definitions.

3. OUR CONTRIBUTIONS

Our first contribution is lower bounds for various fundamental verification and optimization graph problems, some of which are new even in the classical setting and answers some previous open problems (e.g. [13]). We explain these lower bounds in detail in Section 3.2. The main implication of these lower bounds is that quantum communication does *not* help in substantially speeding up distributed algorithms for many of these problems compared to the classical setting. Notable examples are MST, minimum cut, s-source distance, shortest path tree, and shortest s-t paths. In Corollary 3.9, we show a lower bound of $\Omega(\sqrt{\frac{n}{B \log n}})$ for these problems which holds against any quantum distributed algorithm with any approximation guarantee. Due to the seminal paper of Kutten and Peleg [38], we know that MST can be computed exactly in $\tilde{O}(\sqrt{n}+D)$ time in the classical setting, and thus we cannot hope to use quantum communication to get a significant speed up for MST. Recently, Ghaffari and Kuhn [27] showed that minimum cut can be $(2+\epsilon)$-approximated in $\tilde{O}(\sqrt{n}+D)$ time in the classical setting, and Su [60] and Nanongkai [46] independently improved the approximation ratio to $(1+\epsilon)$; this implies that, again, quantum communication does not help. More recently, Nanongkai [47] showed that s-source distance, shortest path tree, and shortest s-t paths, can be $(1+o(1))$-approximated in $\tilde{O}(\sqrt{n}D^{1/4}+D)$ time in the classical setting; thus, the speedup that quantum communication can provide for these problems, if any, is bounded by $O(D^{1/4})$. Moreover, if we allow higher approximation factor, the result of Lenzen and Patt-Shamir [41] implies that we can $O(\log n)$-approximate these problems in $\tilde{O}(\sqrt{n}+D)$ time; this upper bound together with our lower bound leaves no room for quantum algorithms to improve the time complexity. Besides the above lower bounds for optimization problems, we show the same lower bound of $\Omega(\sqrt{\frac{n}{B \log n}})$ for verification problems in Corollary 3.7. Das Sarma et al. [13] showed that these problems, except least-element list verification, can be solved in $\tilde{O}(\sqrt{n}+D)$ time in the classical setting; thus, once again, quantum communication does not help.

Our second contribution is the systematic way to prove lower bounds of quantum distributed algorithms. The high-level idea behind our lower bound proofs is by establishing a connection between quantum communication complexity and quantum distributed network computing. Our work is inspired by [13] (following a line of work in [54, 43, 21, 36]) which shows lower bounds for many graph verification and optimization problems in the classical distributed computing model. The main technique used to show the classical lower bounds in [13] is the *Simulation Theorem* (Theorem 3.1 in [13]) which shows how one can use lower bounds in the standard two-party classical communication complexity model [37] to derive lower bounds in the "distributed" version of communication complexity. We provide techniques of the same flavor for proving quantum lower bounds. In particular, we develop the *Quantum Simulation Theorem.* However, due to some difficulties in handling quantum computation (especially the entanglement) we need to introduce one more concept: instead of applying the Quantum Simulation Theorem to the standard two-party communication complexity model, we have to apply it to a slightly stronger model called *Server model.* We show that working with this stronger model does not make us lose much: several hard problems in two-party communication complexity remain hard in this model, so we can still prove hardness results using these problems. Quantum Simulation Theorem together with the Server model give us a tool to bring the hardness in the quantum two-party setting to the distributed setting. In Section 3.1, we give a more comprehensive overview of our techniques. Along the way, we also obtain new results in the standard communication complexity model, which we explain in Section 3.3.

3.1 Lower Bound Techniques for Quantum Distributed Computing

The high-level idea behind our lower bound proofs is establishing a connection between quantum communication complexity and quantum distributed network computing via a new communication model called the *Server model,* as shown in two middle columns of Fig. 1. This model is a generalization of the standard two-party communication complexity model in the sense that the Server model can simulate the two-party model; thus, lower bounds on this model imply lower bounds on the two-party network models. More importantly, we show that lower bounds on this model imply lower bounds on the quantum distributed model as well. This is depicted by the rightmost arrows in Fig. 1. In addition, we prove quantum lower bounds in the server model, some of which also imply *new* lower bounds in the two-party model for problems such as Hamiltonian cycle and spanning tree, even in the classical setting. This is done by

[3] We mention the reason behind our complexity notations. First, we use $*$ as in Q^* in order to emphasize that our lower bounds hold even when there is a shared entanglement, as usually done in the literature. Since we deal with different models in this paper, we put the model name after $*$. Thus, we have $Q^{*,N}$ for the case of distributed algorithm on a distributed network N, and $Q^{*,cc}$ and $Q^{*,sv}$ for the case of the standard communication complexity and the Server model (cf. Subsection 3.1), respectively.

[4] We note that the notion of δ-far should not be confused with the notion of ϵ*-far* usually used in property testing literature where we need to add and remove at least ϵ *fraction* of edges in order to achieve a desired property. The two notions are closely related. The notion that we chose makes it more convenient to reduce between problems on different models.

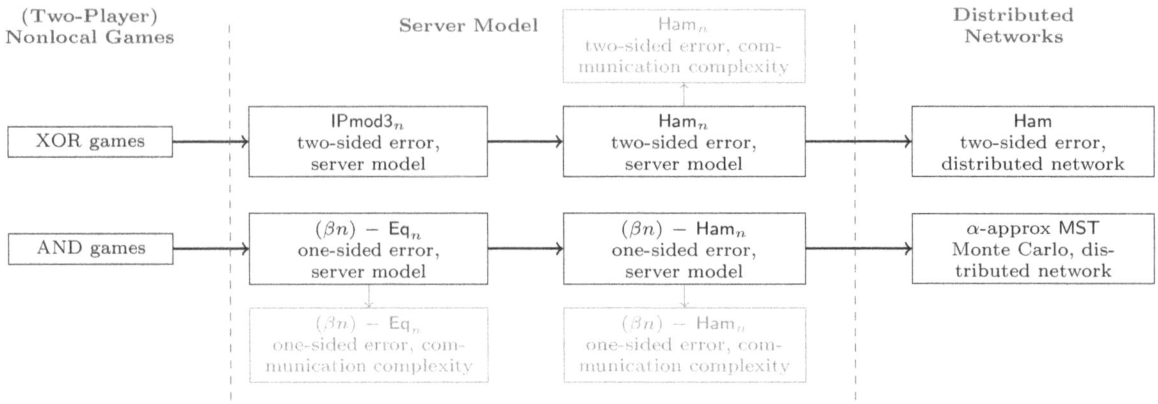

Figure 1: *Our proof structure. Lines in gray show the implications of our results in communication complexity.*

showing that certain techniques based on *nonlocal games* can be extended to prove lower bounds on the Server model as depicted by leftmost arrows in Fig. 1, and by reductions between problems in the Server models (cf. Section 5) as depicted by middle arrows in Fig. 1.

DEFINITION 3.1 (SERVER MODEL). *There are three players in the server model: Carol, David and the server. Carol and David receive the inputs x and y, respectively, and want to compute $f(x,y)$ for some function f. (Observe that the server receives no input.) Carol and David can talk to each other. Additionally, they can talk to the server. The catch here is that the server can send messages for* free. *Thus, the communication complexity in the server model counts only messages sent by Carol and David.*

We let $Q^{*,sv}_{\epsilon_0,\epsilon_1}(f)$ denote the communication complexity — in the quantum setting with entanglement — of computing function f where for any i-input (an input whose correct output is $i \in \{0,1\}$) the algorithm must output i with probability at least $1-\epsilon_i$. We will write $Q^{*,sv}_{\epsilon}(f)$ instead of $Q^{*,sv}_{\epsilon,\epsilon}(f)$. For the standard two-party communication complexity model [37], we use $Q^{*,cc}_{\epsilon_0,\epsilon_1}(f)$ to denote the communication complexity in the quantum setting with entanglement.

To the best of our knowledge, the Server model is different from other known models in communication complexity. Clearly, it is different from multi-party communication complexity since the server receives no input and can send information for *free*. Moreover, it is easy to see that the Server model, even without prior entanglement, is at least as strong as the standard quantum communication complexity model with shared entanglement, since the server can dispense any entangled state to Carol and David. Interestingly, it turns out that the Server model is *equivalent* to the standard two-party model in the classical communication setting, while it is not clear if this is the case in the quantum communication setting. This is the main reason that proving lower bounds in the quantum setting is more challenging in its classical counterpart.

To explain some issues in the quantum setting, let us sketch the proof of the fact that the two models are *equivalent* in the classical setting. Let us first consider the deterministic setting. The proof is by the following "simulation" argument. Alice will simulate Carol and the server. Bob will simulate David and the server. In each round, Alice will see all messages sent from the server to Carol and thus she can keep simulating Carol. However, she does not see the message sent from David to the server which she needs to simulate the server. So, she must get this message from Bob. Similarly, Bob will get from Alice the message sent from Carol to the server. These are the only messages we need in each round in order to be able to simulate the protocol. Observe that the total number of bits sent between Alice and Bob is exactly the number of bits sent by Carol and David to the server. Thus, the complexities of both models are exactly the same in the deterministic case. We can conclude the same thing for the public coin setting (where all parties share a random string) since Alice and Bob can use their shared coin to simulate the shared coin of Carol, David and the server.

The above argument, however, does not seem to work in the quantum setting. The main issue with a simulation along the lines of the one sketched above is that Alice and Bob cannot simulate a "copy" of the server each. For instance one could try to simulate the server's state in a distributed way by maintaining the state that results by applying CNOT to every qubit of the server and a fresh qubit, and distribute these qubits to Alice and Bob. But then if the server sends a message to Carol, Bob would have to disentangle the corresponding qubits in his copy, which would require a message to Alice.

While we leave as an open question whether the two models are equivalent in the quantum setting, we prove that many lower bounds in the two-party model extend to the server model, via a technique called nonlocal games.

Lower Bound Techniques on the Server Model. We show that many hardness results in the two-party model (where there is no server) carry over to the Server model. This is the only part that the readers need some background in quantum computing. The main difficulty in showing this is that, the Server model, even *without* prior entanglement, is clearly at least *as strong as* the standard quantum communication complexity model (where there is no server) *with* shared entanglement, since the server can dispense any entangled state to Carol and David. Thus, it is a challenging problem, which could be of an independent interest, whether *all* hard problems in the standard model remain hard in the server model.

While we do not fully answer the above problem, we identify a set of lower bound techniques in the standard quantum communication complexity model that can be carried over to the Server model, and use them to show that *many* problems remain hard. Specifically, we show that techniques based on the (two-player) *nonlocal* games (see, e.g., [39, 40, 33]) can be extended to show lower bounds on the Server model.

Nonlocal games are games where two players, Alice and Bob, receive an input x and y from some distribution that is known to them and want to compute $f(x, y)$. Players cannot talk to each other; instead, they output one bit, say a and b, which are then combined to be an output. For example, in *XOR games* and *AND games*, these bits are combined as $a \oplus b$ and $a \wedge b$, respectively. The players' goal is to maximize the probability that the output is $f(x, y)$. We relate nonlocal games to the server model by showing that the XOR- and AND-game players can use an efficient server-model protocol to guarantee a good winning chance:

LEMMA 3.2. (SERVER MODEL LOWER BOUNDS VIA NONLOCAL GAMES) *For any boolean function f and $\epsilon_0, \epsilon_1 \geq 0$, there is an (two-player nonlocal) XOR-game strategy $\mathcal{A}'$ (respectively, AND-game strategy $\mathcal{A}''$) such that, for any input (x, y), with probability $4^{-2Q^{*,sv}_{\epsilon_0,\epsilon_1}(f)}$, $\mathcal{A}'$ (respectively, $\mathcal{A}''$) outputs $f(x, y)$ with probability at least $1 - \epsilon_{f(x,y)}$ (i.e. it outputs 1 with probability at least $1-\epsilon_1$ and 0 with probability at least $1 - \epsilon_0$); otherwise (with probability $1 - 4^{-2Q^{*,sv}_{\epsilon_0,\epsilon_1}(f)}$), $\mathcal{A}'$ outputs 0 and 1 with probability 1/2 each (respectively, $\mathcal{A}''$ outputs 0 with probability 1).*

Roughly speaking, the above lemma compares two cases: in the "good" case $\mathcal{A}'$ outputs the correct vaue of $f(x, y)$ with high probability (the probability controlled by ϵ_0 and ϵ_1) and in the "bad case" $\mathcal{A}'$ simply outputs a random bit. It shows that if $Q^{*,sv}_{\epsilon_0,\epsilon_1}(f)$ is small, then the "good" case will happen with a non-negligible probability. In other words, the lemma says that if $Q^{*,sv}_{\epsilon_0,\epsilon_1}(f)$ is small, then the probability that the nonlocal game players win the game will be high.

This lemma gives us an access to several lower bound techniques via nonlocal games. For example, following the γ_2-norm techniques in [42, 59, 40] and the recent method of [33], we show one- and two-sided error lower bounds for many problems on the server model (in particular, we can obtain lower bounds in general forms as in [58, 59, 40]). These lower bounds match the two-party model lower bounds.

Graph Problems and Reductions between Server-Model Problems (Details in Section 5). To bring the hardness in the Server model to the distributed setting, we have to prepare hardness for the right problems in the Server model so that it is easy to translate to the distributed setting. In particular, the problems that we need are the following graph problems.

DEFINITION 3.3 (SERVER-MODEL GRAPH PROBLEMS). *Let G be a graph of n nodes[5]. We partition edges of G to $E_C(G)$ and $E_D(G)$, which are given to David and Carol, respectively. The two players have to determine whether G has some property, e.g., G is a Hamiltonian cycle (Ham_n)[6], a spanning tree (ST_n), or is connected (Conn_n). For the purpose of this paper in proving lower bounds for distributed algorithms, we restrict the problem and assume that in the case of the Hamiltonian cycle problem $E_G(C)$ and $E_D(C)$ are both perfect matchings.*

We also consider the gap version in the case of communication complexity. The notion of δ-far is slightly different from the distributed setting (cf. Section 2.2) in that we can add *any* edges to G instead of adding *only* edges in N to M. The *main challenge* in showing hardness results for these graph problems is that some of them, e.g. Hamiltonian cycle and spanning tree verification, are not known to be hard, even in the classical two-party model (they are left as open problems in [13]). To get through this, we derive several new reductions (using novel gadgets) to obtain this:

THEOREM 3.4. (SERVER-MODEL LOWER BOUNDS FOR Ham_n) *There exist some constants $\epsilon, \beta > 0$ such that for any n, $Q^{*,sv}_{\epsilon,\epsilon}(\mathsf{Ham}_n)$ and $Q^{*,sv}_{0,\epsilon}((\beta n)\text{-}\mathsf{Ham}_n)$ are $\Omega(n)$.*

We prove Theorem 3.4 using elementary (but intricate) gadget-based reductions. Thus, no knowledge in quantum computing is required to understand this proof. Theorem 3.4 also leads to lower bounds that are new even in the classical two-party model. We discuss this in Section 3.3.

Quantum Simulation Theorem: From Server Model to Distributed Algorithms. To show the role of the Server model in proving distributed algorithm lower bounds, we prove a *quantum version* of the *Simulation Theorem* of [13] which shows that the hardness of graph problems of our interest in the Server model implies the hardness of these problems in the quantum distributed setting (the theorem below holds for several graph problems but we state it only for the Hamiltonian Cycle verification problem since it is sufficient for our purpose):

THEOREM 3.5 (QUANTUM SIMULATION THEOREM). *For any B, L, $\Gamma \geq \log L$, $\beta \geq 0$ and $\epsilon_0, \epsilon_1 > 0$, there exists a B-model quantum network N of diameter $\Theta(\log L)$ and $\Theta(\Gamma L)$ nodes such that if $Q^{*,N}_{\epsilon_0,\epsilon_1}((\beta\Gamma)\text{-}\mathsf{Ham}(N)) \leq \frac{L}{2} - 2$ then $Q^{*,sv}_{\epsilon_0,\epsilon_1}((\beta\Gamma)\text{-}\mathsf{Ham}_\Gamma) = O((B \log L) Q^{*,N}_{\epsilon_0,\epsilon_1}((\beta\Gamma)\text{-}\mathsf{Ham}(N)))$.*

In words, the above theorem states that if there is an (ϵ_0, ϵ_1)-error quantum distributed algorithm that solves the Hamiltonian cycle verification problem on N in at most $(L/2) - 2$ time, i.e. $Q^{*,N}_{\epsilon_0,\epsilon_1}(\mathsf{Ham}(N)) \leq (L/2) - 2$, then the (ϵ_0, ϵ_1)-error communication complexity in the Server model of the Hamiltonian cycle problem on Γ-node graphs is $Q^{*,sv}_{\epsilon_0,\epsilon_1}(\mathsf{Ham}_\Gamma) = O((B \log L) Q^{*,N}_{\epsilon_0,\epsilon_1}(\mathsf{Ham}(N)))$. The same statement also holds for its gap version $((\beta\Gamma)\text{-}\mathsf{Ham}(N))$. We note that the above theorem can be extended to a large class of graph problems. The proof of the above theorem does not need any knowledge in quantum computing to follow. In fact, it can be viewed as a simple modification of the Simulation Theorem in the classical setting [13]. The main difference, and the most difficult part to get our Quantum Simulation Theorem to work, is to realize that we must start from the Server model instead of the two-party model.

[5]To avoid confusion, throughout the paper we use G to denote the input graph in the Server model and N and M to denote the distributed network and its subnetwork, respectively, unless specified otherwise. For any graph H, we use $V(H)$ and $E(H)$ to denote the set of nodes and edges in H, respectively.

[6]Ham_n is used for the Hamiltonian cycle verification problem in the Server models, where n denotes the size of input graphs, and $\mathsf{Ham}(N)$ is used for the Hamiltonian cycle verification problem on a distributed network N (defined in Section 2.2).

	Problems	Previous results	Our results
B-model distributed network	Ham, ST, MST verification	$\Omega(\sqrt{n/B\log n})$ deterministic, classical communication [13, 36]	$\Omega(\sqrt{n/B\log n})$ two-sided error, quantum communication with entanglement
	Conn and other verification problems from [13]	$\Omega(\sqrt{n/B\log n})$ two-sided error, classical communication [13]	
	α-approx MST and other optimization problems from [13]	$\Omega(\sqrt{n/B\log n})$ Monte Carlo, classical communication for $W=\Omega(\alpha n)$ [13]	$\Omega(\min(\sqrt{n}, W/\alpha)/\sqrt{B\log n})$ Monte Carlo, quantum communication with entanglement
Communication Complexity	Ham, ST, and other verification problems	$\Omega(n)$ one-sided error, classical communication [56]	$\Omega(n)$ two-sided error, quantum communication with entanglement
	Gap-Ham, Gap-ST, Gap-Conn, and other gap problems for $\Omega(n)$ gap	unknown	$\Omega(n)$ one-sided error, quantum communication with entanglement

Figure 2: *Previous and our new lower bounds. We note that n is the number of nodes in the network in the case of distributed network and the number of nodes in the input graph in the case of communication complexity.*

3.2 Quantum Distributed Lower Bounds

We present specific lower bounds for various fundamental verification and optimization graph problems. Some of these bounds are new even in the classical setting. To the best of our knowledge, our bounds are the first non-trivial lower bounds for fundamental global problems.

1. Verification problems. We prove a *tight* two-sided error quantum lower bound of $\tilde{\Omega}(\sqrt{n})$ time, where n is the number of nodes in the distributed network and $\tilde{\Theta}(x)$ hides poly $\log x$, for the *Hamiltonian cycle* and *spanning tree verification problems*. Our lower bound holds even in a network of small ($O(\log n)$) diameter.

THEOREM 3.6 (VERIFICATION LOWER BOUNDS). *For any B and large n, there exists $\epsilon > 0$ and a B-model n-node network N of diameter $\Theta(\log n)$ such that any (ϵ, ϵ)-error quantum algorithm with prior entanglement for Hamiltonian cycle and spanning tree verification on N requires $\Omega(\sqrt{\frac{n}{B\log n}})$ time. That is, $Q^{*,N}_{\epsilon,\epsilon}(\mathsf{Ham}(N))$ and $Q^{*,N}_{\epsilon,\epsilon}(\mathsf{ST}(N))$ are $\Omega(\sqrt{\frac{n}{B\log n}})$.*

Our bound implies a new bound on the classical setting which answers the open problem in [13], and is the *first randomized lower bound* for both graph problems, subsuming the deterministic lower bounds for Hamiltonian cycle verification [13], spanning tree verification [13] and minimum spanning tree verification [36]. It is also shown in [13] that Ham can be reduced to several problems via deterministic classical-communication reductions. Since these reductions can be simulated by quantum protocols, we can use these reductions straightforwardly to show that all lower bounds in [13] hold even in the quantum setting.

COROLLARY 3.7. *The statement in Theorem 3.6 holds for the following verification problems: Connected component, spanning connected subgraph, cycle containment, e-cycle containment, bipartiteness, s-t connectivity, connectivity, cut, edge on all paths, s-t cut and least-element list. (See [13] and the full version for definitions.)*

Fig. 2 compares our results with previous results for verification problems.

2. Optimization problems. We show a *tight* $\tilde{\Omega}(\min(W/\alpha, \sqrt{n}))$-time lower bound for any α-approximation quantum randomized (Monte Carlo and Las Vegas) distributed algorithm for the MST problem.

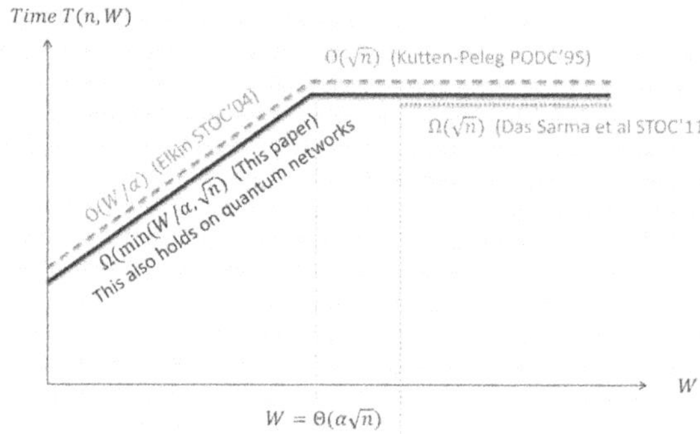

Figure 3: *Previous and our new bounds (cf. Theorem 3.8 and Corollary 3.9) for approximating the MST problem in distributed networks when N and α are fixed. The dashed line (in blue) represents the deterministic upper bounds (Algorithms). The dotted line (in red) is the previous lower bound for randomized algorithms. The solid line (in black) represents the bounds shown in this paper. Note that the previous lower bounds hold only in the classical setting while the new lower bounds hold in the quantum setting even when entanglement is allowed.*

THEOREM 3.8 (OPTIMIZATION LOWER BOUNDS). *For any n, B, W and $\alpha < W$ there exists $\epsilon > 0$ and a B-model $\Theta(n)$-node network N of diameter $\Theta(\log n)$ and weight aspect ratio W such that any ϵ-error α-approximation quantum algorithm with prior entanglement for computing the minimum spanning tree problem on N requires $\Omega(\frac{1}{\sqrt{B\log n}}\min(W/\alpha, \sqrt{n}))$ time.*

This result generalizes the bounds in [13] to the quantum setting. Moreover, this lower bound implies the same bound in the classical model, which improves [13] (see Fig. 3) and matches the deterministic upper bound of $O(\min(W/\alpha, \sqrt{n}))$ resulting from a combination of Elkin's α-approximation $O(W/\alpha)$-time deterministic algorithm [21] and Peleg and Rubinovich's $O(\sqrt{n})$-time exact deterministic algorithm [24, 38] in the classical communication model. Thus this bound is tight up to a $\Theta(\sqrt{B\log n})$ factor. It is the first bound that is *tight for all values of the aspect ratio W*. Fig. 3 compares our lower bounds with previous bounds. By using the same reduction as in [13], our bound also implies that all lower bounds in [13] hold even in the quantum setting.

COROLLARY 3.9. *The statement in Theorem 3.8 also holds for the following problems: minimum spanning tree, shallow-light tree, s-source distance, shortest path tree, minimum routing cost spanning tree, minimum cut, minimum s-t cut, shortest s-t path and generalized Steiner forest. (See [13] and the full version for definitions.)*

3.3 Additional Results: Lower Bounds on Communication Complexity

In proving the results in previous subsections, we prove several bounds on the Server model. Since the Server model is stronger than the standard communication complexity model (as discussed in Subsection 3.1), we obtain lower bounds in the communication complexity model as well. Some of these lower bounds are new even in the classical setting. In particular, our bounds in Theorem 3.4 lead to the following corollary. (Note that we use $Q^{*,cc}_{\epsilon_0,\epsilon_1}(\mathcal{P}_n)$ to denote the communication complexity of verifying property $\mathcal{P}$ of n-node graphs on the standard quantum communication complexity model with entanglement.)

COROLLARY 3.10. *For any n and some constants $\epsilon, \beta > 0$, $Q^{*,cc}_{\epsilon,\epsilon}(\mathsf{P}_n) = \Omega(n)$, and $Q^{*,cc}_{0,\epsilon}((\beta n) - \mathsf{P}_n) \geq Q^{*,sv}_{0,\epsilon}((\beta n) - \mathsf{P}_n) = \Omega(n)$, where P_n can be any of the following verification problems: Hamiltonian cycle, spanning tree, connectivity, s-t connectivity, and bipartiteness.*

To the best of our knowledge, the lower bounds for Hamiltonian cycle and spanning tree verification problems are the first two-sided error lower bounds for these problems, even in the classical two-party setting (only nondeterministic, thus one-sided error, lower bounds are previously known [56]). The bounds for Bipartiteness and s-t connectivity follow from a reduction from Inner Product given in [2], and a lower bound for Connectivity was recently shown in [30]. We note that we prove the gap versions via a reduction from recent lower bounds in [33] and observe new lower bounds for the gap versions of Set Disjointness and Equality.

4. OTHER RELATED WORK

While our work focuses on solving graph problems in quantum distributed networks, there are several prior works focusing on other distributed computing problems (including communication complexity in the two-party or multiparty communication model) using quantum effects. We note that fundamental distributed computing problems such as leader election and byzantine agreement have been shown to solved better using quantum phenomena (see e.g., [17, 63, 5]). Entanglement has been used to reduce the amount of communication of a specific function of input data distributed among 3 parties [12] (see also the work of [9, 16, 62] on multiparty quantum communication complexity).

There are several results showing that quantum communication complexity in the two-player model can be more efficient than classical randomized communication complexity (e.g. [7, 55]). These results also easily extend to the so-called number-in-hand multiparty model (in which players have separate inputs). As of now no separation between quantum and randomized communication complexity is known in the number-on-the-forehead multiparty model, in which players' inputs overlap. Other papers concerning quantum distributed computing include [8, 11, 34, 35, 52, 23].

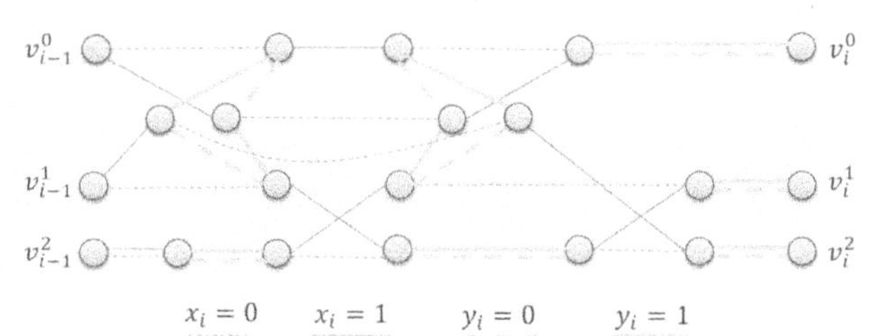

Figure 4: The construction of gadget G_i. If $x_i = 0$ then Alice adds dashed thin edges (in red); otherwise she adds solid thin edges (in red). If $y_i = 0$ then Bob adds dashed thick edges (in blue); otherwise he adds solid thick edges (in blue).

5. SERVER-MODEL LOWER BOUNDS FOR Ham_n (THEOREM 3.4)

In this section, we prove Theorem 3.4, which leads to new lower bounds for several graph problems as discussed in Section 3.3. The proof uses gadget-based reductions between problems on the Server model. This illustrates our point that no knowledge in quantum computing is needed after a lower bound in the Server model is obtained. We will reduce from the $\mathsf{IPmod3}_n$: two players, Carol and David, are given n-bit strings x and y, respectively, and they have to output 1 if $(\sum_{i=1}^n x_i y_i) \mod 3 = 0$ and 0 otherwise. We use the following lower bound, which is proved in the full version.

THEOREM 5.1. *For some $\beta, \epsilon > 0$ and any large n,*

$$Q^{*,sv}_{\epsilon,\epsilon}(\mathsf{IPmod3}_n) = \Omega(n).$$

We first sketch the lower bound proof of $Q^{*,sv}_{\epsilon,\epsilon}(\mathsf{Ham}_n)$ and show later how to extend to the gap version. We will show that for any $0 \leq \epsilon \leq 1$ and some constant c, $Q^{*,sv}_{\epsilon,\epsilon}(\mathsf{IPmod3}_n) = O(Q^{*,sv}_{\epsilon,\epsilon}(\mathsf{Ham}_{cn}))$. The theorem then immediately follows from the fact that $Q^{*,sv}_{\epsilon,\epsilon}(\mathsf{IPmod3}_n) = \Omega(n)$.

Let $x = x_1 \dots x_n$ and $y = y_1 \dots y_n$ be the input of $\mathsf{IPmod3}_n$. We construct a graph G which is an input of Ham_{cn} as follows. The graph G consists of n gadgets, denoted by $G_1, \dots, G_n$. For any $1 \leq i \leq n-1$, gadgets G_i and G_{i+1} share exactly three nodes denoted by v_i^0, v_i^1, v_i^2. Each gadget G_i is constructed based on the values of x_i and y_i as outlined in Fig. 4. The following observation can be checked by drawing G_i for all cases of x_i and y_i (as in Fig. 5).

OBSERVATION 5.2. *For any value of (x_i, y_i), G_i consists of three paths where v_{i-1}^j is connected by a path to $v_i^{(j+x_i \cdot y_i) \mod 3}$, for any $0 \leq j \leq 2$. Moreover, Alice's (respectively Bob's) edges, i.e. thin (red) lines (respectively thick (blue) lines) in Fig. 4, form a matching that covers all nodes except v_i^j (respectively v_{i-1}^j) for all $0 \leq j \leq 2$.*

Thus, when we put all gadgets together, graph G will consist of three paths connecting between nodes in $\{v_0^j\}_{0 \leq j \leq 2}$ on one side and nodes in $\{v_n^j\}_{0 \leq j \leq 2}$ on the other. How these paths look like depends on the structure of each gadget G_i which depends on the value of $x_i \cdot y_i$. The following lemma follows trivially from Observation 5.2.

LEMMA 5.3. *G consists of three paths P^0, P^1 and P^2 where for any $0 \leq j \leq 2$, P^j has v_0^j as one end vertex and $v_n^{(j+\sum_{1 \leq i \leq n} x_i \cdot y_i) \mod 3}$ as the other.*

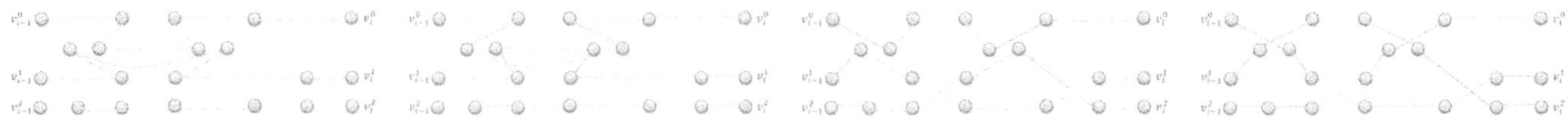

(a) $x_i y_i = 00$ (b) $x_i y_i = 01$ (c) $x_i y_i = 10$ (d) $x_i y_i = 11$

Figure 5: Gadget G_i for different values of x_i and y_i. The main observation is that if $x_i \cdot y_i = 0$ then G_i consists of paths from v_{i-1}^j to v_i^j for all $0 \le j \le 2$. Otherwise, it consists of paths from v_{i-1}^j to $v_i^{(j+1) \bmod 3}$.

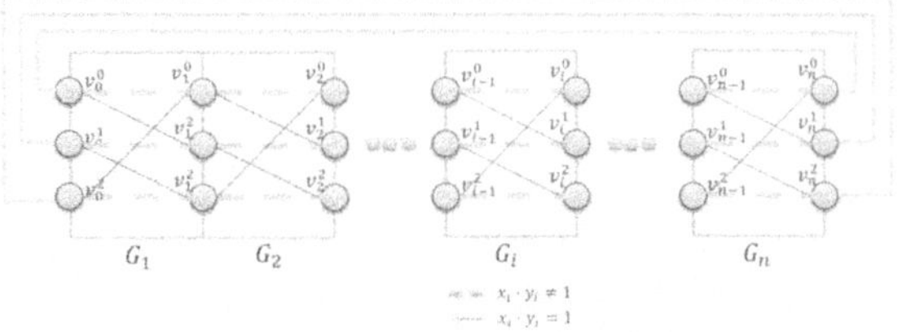

Figure 6: The graph G consists of gadgets $G_1, \ldots G_n$. The solid thick edges (in gray) linking between v_0^j and v_n^j, for $0 \le j \le 2$ represent the fact that $v_0^j = v_n^j$. Lines that appear in each gadget G_i depicts what we observe in Observation 5.2: solid thin lines (in red) represent paths that will appear in G_i if $x_i \cdot y_i = 0$, and dashed thick lines (in blue) represent paths that will appear in G_i if $x_i \cdot y_i = 1$.

Now, we complete the description of G by letting $v_0^j = v_n^j$ for all $0 \le j \le 2$. It then follows that G is a Hamiltonian cycle if and only if $\sum_{1 \le i \le n} x_i \cdot y_i \mod 3 \neq 0$ (see Fig. 6). Thus we can check that $\sum_{1 \le i \le n} x_i \cdot y_i \mod 3$ is zero or not by checking whether G is a Hamiltonian cycle or not. Theorem 3.4 now follows from Theorem 5.1.

6. CONCLUSION AND OPEN PROBLEMS

In this paper, we derive several lower bounds for important network problems in a quantum distributed network. We show that quantumness does not really help in obtaining faster distributed algorithms for fundamental problems such as minimum spanning tree, minimum cut, and shortest paths. Our approach gives a uniform way to prove lower bounds for various problems. Our technique closely follows the Simulation Theorem introduced by Das Sarma et al. [13], which shows how to use the two-party communication complexity to prove lower bounds for distributed algorithms. The main difference of our approach is the use of the Server model. We show that many problems that are hard in the quantum two-party communication setting (e.g. IPmod3) are also hard in the Server model, and show new reductions from these problems to graph verification problems of our interest. Some of these reductions give tighter lower bounds even in the classical setting.

Since the technique of Das Sarma et al. can be used to show lower bounds of many problems that are not covered in this paper (e.g. [22, 29, 48, 41, 14, 26, 10]), it is interesting to see if these lower bounds remain valid in the quantum setting. Since most of these problems rely on a reduction from the set disjointness problem, the main challenge is to obtain new reductions that start from problems that are proved hard on the Server model such as IPmod3. One problem that seems to be harder than others is the random walk problem [48, 15] since the previous lower bound in the classical setting requires a *bounded-round* communication complexity [48]. Proving lower bounds for the random walk problem thus requires proving a bounded-round communication complexity in the Server model as the first step. This requires different techniques since the nonlocal games used in this paper destroy the round structure of protocols.

It is also interesting to better understand the role of the Server model: Can we derive a quantum two-party version of the Simulation Theorem, thus eliminating the need of the Server model? Is the Server model *strictly* stronger than the two-party quantum communication complexity model? Also, it will be interesting to explore *upper* bounds in the quantum setting: Do quantum distributed algorithms help in solving other fundamental graph problems ?

References

[1] S. Aaronson and A. Ambainis. Quantum search of spatial regions. *Theory of Computing*, 1(1):47–79, 2005. Also in FOCS'03.

[2] L. Babai, P. Frankl, and J. Simon. Complexity classes in communication complexity theory. In *FOCS*, pages 337–347, 1986.

[3] Z. Bar-Yossef, T. S. Jayram, R. Kumar, and D. Sivakumar. An information statistics approach to data stream and communication complexity. *J. Comput. Syst. Sci.*, 68(4):702–732, 2004. Also in FOCS'02.

[4] J. S. Bell. On the Einstein-Podolsky-Rosen paradox. *Physics*, 1:195–200, 1964.

[5] M. Ben-Or and A. Hassidim. Fast quantum byzantine agreement. In *STOC*, pages 481–485, 2005.

[6] A. Broadbent and A. Tapp. Can quantum mechanics help distributed computing? *SIGACT News*, 39(3):67–76, 2008.

[7] H. Buhrman, R. Cleve, and A. Wigderson. Quantum vs. classical communication and computation. In *STOC*, pages 63–68, 1998.

[8] H. Buhrman and H. Röhrig. Distributed quantum computing. In *MFCS*, pages 1–20, 2003.

[9] H. Buhrman, W. van Dam, P. Hoyer, and A. Tapp. Quantum multiparty communication complexity. *Physical Review A*, 60:2737–2741, 1999.

[10] K. Censor-Hillel, M. Ghaffari, and F. Kuhn. Distributed connectivity decomposition. In *PODC*, 2014.

[11] B. S. Chlebus, D. R. Kowalski, and M. Strojnowski. Scalable quantum consensus for crash failures. In *DISC*, pages 236–250, 2010.

[12] R. Cleve and H. Buhrman. Substituting quantum entanglement for communication. *Physical Review A*, 56(2):1201–1204, 1997.

[13] A. Das Sarma, S. Holzer, L. Kor, A. Korman, D. Nanongkai, G. Pandurangan, D. Peleg, and R. Wattenhofer. Distributed verification and hardness of distributed approximation. *SIAM J. Comput.*, 41(5):1235–1265, 2012.

[14] A. Das Sarma, A. R. Molla, and G. Pandurangan. Distributed computation of sparse cuts. *CoRR*, abs/1310.5407, 2013.

[15] A. Das Sarma, D. Nanongkai, G. Pandurangan, and P. Tetali. Distributed random walks. *J. ACM*, 60(1):2, 2013.

[16] R. de Wolf. Quantum communication and complexity. *Theoretical Computer Science*, 287(1):337–352, 2002.

[17] V. S. Denchev and G. Pandurangan. Distributed quantum computing: a new frontier in distributed systems or science fiction? *SIGACT News*, 39(3):77–95, 2008.

[18] D. P. Dubhashi, F. Grandioni, and A. Panconesi. Distributed Algorithms via LP Duality and Randomization. In *Handbook of Approximation Algorithms and Metaheuristics*. Chapman and Hall/CRC, 2007.

[19] A. Einstein, B. Podolsky, and N. Rosen. Can quantum-mechanical description of physical reality be considered complete? *Phys. Rev.*, 47(10):777–780, May 1935.

[20] M. Elkin. Distributed approximation: a survey. *SIGACT News*, 35(4):40–57, 2004.

[21] M. Elkin. An Unconditional Lower Bound on the Time-Approximation Trade-off for the Distributed Minimum Spanning Tree Problem. *SIAM J. Comput.*, 36(2):433–456, 2006. Also in STOC'04.

[22] S. Frischknecht, S. Holzer, and R. Wattenhofer. Networks cannot compute their diameter in sublinear time. In *SODA*, pages 1150–1162, 2012.

[23] S. Gaertner, M. Bourennane, C. Kurtsiefer, A. Cabello, and H. Weinfurter. Experimental demonstration of a quantum protocol for byzantine agreement and liar detection. *PHYS.REV.LETT.*, 100:070504, 2008.

[24] J. Garay, S. Kutten, and D. Peleg. A sublinear time distributed algorithm for minimum-weight spanning trees. *SIAM J. on Computing*, 27:302–316, 1998. Also in FOCS'93.

[25] C. Gavoille, A. Kosowski, and M. Markiewicz. What can be observed locally? In *DISC*, pages 243–257, 2009.

[26] M. Ghaffari. Near-optimal distributed approximation of minimum-weight connected dominating set. In *ICALP (2)*, 2014.

[27] M. Ghaffari and F. Kuhn. Distributed minimum cut approximation. In *DISC*, pages 1–15, 2013.

[28] A. S. Holevo. Bounds for the quantity of information transmitted by a quantum communication channel. *Problemy Peredachi Informatsii*, 9(3):3–11, 1973. English translation in *Problems of Information Transmission*, 9:177–183, 1973.

[29] S. Holzer and R. Wattenhofer. Optimal distributed all pairs shortest paths and applications. In *PODC*, pages 355–364, 2012.

[30] G. Ivanyos, H. Klauck, T. Lee, M. Santha, and R. de Wolf. New bounds on the classical and quantum communication complexity of some graph properties. In *FSTTCS*, pages 148–159, 2012.

[31] B. Kalyanasundaram and G. Schnitger. The Probabilistic Communication Complexity of Set Intersection. *SIAM J. Discrete Math.*, 5(4):545–557, 1992.

[32] M. Khan, F. Kuhn, D. Malkhi, G. Pandurangan, and K. Talwar. Efficient distributed approximation algorithms via probabilistic tree embeddings. In *PODC*, pages 263–272, 2008.

[33] H. Klauck and R. de Wolf. Fooling one-sided quantum protocols. *Manuscript*, 2012.

[34] H. Kobayashi, K. Matsumoto, and S. Tani. Ba: Exactly electing a unique leader is not harder than computing symmetric functions on anonymous quantum networks. In *PODC*, pages 334–335, 2009.

[35] H. Kobayashi, K. Matsumoto, and S. Tani. Computing on anonymous quantum network. *CoRR*, abs/1001.5307, 2010.

[36] L. Kor, A. Korman, and D. Peleg. Tight bounds for distributed mst verification. In *STACS*, pages 69–80, 2011.

[37] E. Kushilevitz and N. Nisan. *Communication complexity*. Cambridge University Press, New York, NY, USA, 1997.

[38] S. Kutten and D. Peleg. Fast Distributed Construction of Small k-Dominating Sets and Applications. *J. Algorithms*, 28(1):40–66, 1998. Also in PODC'95.

[39] T. Lee and A. Shraibman. Lower bounds in communication complexity. *Foundations and Trends in Theoretical Computer Science*, 3(4):263–398, 2009.

[40] T. Lee and S. Zhang. Composition theorems in communication complexity. In *ICALP (1)*, pages 475–489, 2010.

[41] C. Lenzen and B. Patt-Shamir. Fast routing table construction using small messages: extended abstract. In *STOC*, pages 381–390, 2013.

[42] N. Linial and A. Shraibman. Lower bounds in communication complexity based on factorization norms. *Random Struct. Algorithms*, 34(3):368–394, 2009. Also in STOC'07.

[43] Z. Lotker, B. Patt-Shamir, and D. Peleg. Distributed MST for constant diameter graphs. *Distributed Computing*, 18(6):453–460, 2006. Also in PODC'01.

[44] M. Luby. A simple parallel algorithm for the maximal independent set problem. *SIAM J. Comput.*, 15(4):1036–1053, 1986.

[45] M. Luby. A simple parallel algorithm for the maximal independent set problem. *SIAM J. Comput.*, 15(4):1036–1053, 1986. Also in STOC'85.

[46] D. Nanongkai. Brief announcement: Almost-tight approximation distributed algorithm for minimum cut. In *PODC*, 2014.

[47] D. Nanongkai. Distributed Approximation Algorithms for Weighted Shortest Paths. In *STOC*, 2014.

[48] D. Nanongkai, A. Das Sarma, and G. Pandurangan. A tight unconditional lower bound on distributed randomwalk computation. In *PODC*, pages 257–266, 2011.

[49] D. Nanongkai and H. Su. Almost-tight distributed minimum cut algorithms. Manuscript, 2014.

[50] A. Nayak. Optimal lower bounds for quantum automata and random access codes. In *FOCS*, pages 369–377, 1999.

[51] M. A. Nielsen and I. L. Chuang. *Quantum Computation and Quantum Information (Cambridge Series on Information and the Natural Sciences)*. Cambridge University Press, 1 edition, Jan. 2004.

[52] S. P. Pal, S. K. Singh, and S. Kumar. Multi-partite quantum entanglement versus randomization: Fair and unbiased leader election in networks, 2003.

[53] D. Peleg. *Distributed computing: a locality-sensitive approach*. Society for Industrial and Applied Mathematics, Philadelphia, PA, USA, 2000.

[54] D. Peleg and V. Rubinovich. A Near-Tight Lower Bound on the Time Complexity of Distributed Minimum-Weight Spanning Tree Construction. *SIAM J. Comput.*, 30(5):1427–1442, 2000. Also in FOCS'99.

[55] R. Raz. Exponential separation of quantum and classical communication complexity. In *STOC*, pages 358–369, 1999.

[56] R. Raz and B. Spieker. On the "log rank"-conjecture in communication complexity. *Combinatorica*, 15(4):567–588, 1995. Also in FOCS'93.

[57] A. A. Razborov. On the Distributional Complexity of Disjointness. *Theor. Comput. Sci.*, 106(2):385–390, 1992. Also in ICALP'90.

[58] A. A. Razborov. Quantum communication complexity of symmetric predicates. *Izvestiya: Mathematics*, 67(1):145, 2003.

[59] A. A. Sherstov. The pattern matrix method. *SIAM J. Comput.*, 40(6):1969–2000, 2011. Also in STOC'08.

[60] H. Su. Brief announcement: A distributed minimum cut approximation scheme. In *SPAA*, 2014.

[61] J. Suomela. Survey of local algorithms. *ACM Computing Surveys*, to appear.

[62] A. Ta-Shma. Classical versus quantum communication complexity. *SIGACT News*, 30(3):25–34, 1999.

[63] S. Tani, H. Kobayashi, and K. Matsumoto. Exact quantum algorithms for the leader election problem. In *STACS*, pages 581–592, 2005.

Optimal Gossip with Direct Addressing

Bernhard Haeupler
Microsoft Research
1065 La Avenida, Mountain View
Mountain View, CA 94043
haeupler@cs.cmu.edu

Dahlia Malkhi
Microsoft Research
1065 La Avenida, Mountain View
Mountain View, CA 94043
dalia@microsoft.com

ABSTRACT

Gossip algorithms spread information in distributed networks by nodes repeatedly forwarding information to a few random contacts. By their very nature, gossip algorithms tend to be *distributed* and *fault tolerant*. If done right, they can also be *fast* and *message-efficient*. A common model for gossip communication is the random phone call model, in which in each synchronous round each node can PUSH or PULL information to or from a random other node. For example, Karp et al. [FOCS 2000] gave algorithms in this model that spread a message to all nodes in $\Theta(\log n)$ rounds while sending only $O(\log \log n)$ messages per node on average. They also showed that at least $\Theta(\log n)$ rounds are necessary in this model and that algorithms achieving this round-complexity need to send $\omega(1)$ messages per node on average.

Recently, Avin and Elsässer [DISC 2013], studied the random phone call model with the natural and commonly used assumption of *direct addressing*. Direct addressing allows nodes to directly contact nodes whose ID (e.g., IP address) was learned before. They show that in this setting, one can "break the $\log n$ barrier" and achieve a gossip algorithm running in $O(\sqrt{\log n})$ rounds, albeit while using $O(\sqrt{\log n})$ messages per node.

In this paper we study the same model and give a simple gossip algorithm which spreads a message in only $O(\log \log n)$ rounds. We furthermore prove a matching $\Omega(\log \log n)$ lower bound which shows that this running time is best possible. In particular we show that any gossip algorithm takes with high probability at least $0.99 \log \log n$ rounds to terminate. Lastly, our algorithm can be tweaked to send only $O(1)$ messages per node on average with only $O(\log n)$ bits per message. Our algorithm therefore simultaneously achieves the optimal round-, message-, and bit-complexity for this setting. As all prior gossip algorithms, our algorithm is also robust against failures. In particular, if in the beginning an oblivious adversary fails any F nodes our algorithm still, with high probability, informs all but $o(F)$ surviving nodes.

PODC'14, July 15–18, 2014, Paris, France.

ACM 978-1-4503-2944-6/14/07 ...$15.00.
http://dx.doi.org/10.1145/2611462.2611489.

Categories and Subject Descriptors

F.2.2 [**Theory of Computation**]: ANALYSIS OF ALGORITHMS AND PROBLEM COMPLEXITY—*Nonnumerical Algorithms and Problems*; F.1.2 [**Theory of Computation**]: COMPUTATION BY ABSTRACT DEVICES—*Modes of Computation* Parallelism and concurrency

General Terms

Algorithms, Theory, Performance, Reliability

Keywords

direct addressing, gossip, information dissemination, peer-to-peer (P2P), pointer jumping, rumor spreading

1. INTRODUCTION

Gossip algorithms, also called rumor spreading protocols, spread information in a network by having nodes repeatedly forward (limited amounts of) information to a few, often randomly selected, contacts. They have found countless applications in solving coordination and information dissemination tasks in large distributed systems or networks. Their advantages in this setting over alternative approaches is manifold: They are naturally distributed and due to their randomized nature often very *fault tolerant* with respect to many kinds of failures, such as, permanent or transient link-failures or node crashes. If done right, they can also be very efficient in their round-, message-, and bit-complexity.

Two models for gossip communication that have been considered and intensely studied in the literature are the *random phone call model* and *direct addressing*.

The *random phone call model* assumes a complete network and synchronous rounds in which each node is able to PUSH or PULL information to or from a random other node. Both variants spread a message in $O(\log n)$ rounds with $O(\log n)$ messages sent per node [12] if every node communicates in every round. While the logarithmic running time is best possible for this setting, Karp et al. showed in an influential paper [10], that the message-complexity could be reduced to $O(\log \log n)$ message per node on average. They also proved that any address-oblivious algorithm with logarithmic running time needs to send at least $\Omega(\log \log n)$ messages per node on average. Here *address-oblivious* means that the decision of if and what a node sends is independent of the ID of its communication partner(s) this round (see also [1]). Lastly, they demonstrated the *fault-tolerance* of their gossip algorithm. In particular, they remarked that any oblivious F

node failures still lead to all but $O(F)$ nodes being informed in the end, with high probability. Since then the random phone call model has been generalized in many directions, most notably to non-complete network topologies. For example, in [4–6] arbitrary topologies are assumed and the stopping time of the uniform PUSH-PULL gossip is studied where in each round each node initializes a communication with a uniformly random neighbor.

Direct addressing is another natural assumption that has been intensely studied. Direct addressing assumes that nodes have *unique IDs* (e.g., IP addresses) and that in each synchronous round a node can contact any node (or neighbor) whose ID (or IP address) is known to it. Since nodes do not know the topology and are only able to initiate one communication at a time, many algorithms for this setting let nodes contact a random node known to them. For example, in the famous Name-Dropper algorithm of Harchol-Balter et al. [9], nodes repeatedly forward all IDs they know to a random node known to them. They show that this simple algorithm terminates in $O(\log^2 n)$ rounds (using $O(\log^2 n)$ messages per node) if started from any (weakly) connected initial topology. Recently, [11] gave an improved deterministic algorithm which achieves $O(\log n)$ rounds for the same setting. A similar setting but restricting a message to only contain one contact was considered in [8]. Lastly, direct addressing has also been extensively studied in general topologies. For example in [2, 3, 7] it is assumed that all possible communications are given by an arbitrary unknown topology in which nodes only know their neighbors.

Recently Avin and Elsässer [1] showed that adding the natural direct addressing assumption in the random phone call model allows for gossip algorithms that "break the $\log n$ barrier". Their algorithm runs in $O(\sqrt{\log n})$ rounds however at the cost of having a larger message-complexity of $\Theta(\sqrt{\log n})$ messages per node and also a larger bit-complexity of $O(n \log^{3/2} n + nb \log\log n)$ (compared to the $O(nb \log\log n)$ bit-complexity of [10]). Their algorithm is fault-tolerant in the same way as discussed for [10] above:

THEOREM 1 (THEOREM 1 OF [1]).
In the random phone call model with direct addressing there is a randomized fault-tolerant gossip algorithm that, with high probability, spreads a message of $b = \Omega(\log n)$ bits in $O(\sqrt{\log n})$ rounds using $O(\sqrt{\log n})$ messages per node and a total bit-complexity of $O(n \log^{3/2} n + nb \log\log n)$ bits.

1.1 Our Results

In this paper we study the same setting and improve upon the state of the art by providing a drastically faster algorithm with simultaneously improved message- and bit-complexity:

THEOREM 2.
In the random phone call model with direct addressing there is a randomized fault-tolerant gossip algorithm that, with high probability, spreads a message of $b = \Omega(\log n)$ bits in $O(\log\log n)$ rounds using $O(1)$ messages per node on average and a total bit-complexity of $O(nb)$ bits.

In addition to the faster running time, it is easy to see that the $O(1)$ message-complexity per node and the total $O(nb)$ bit-complexity are optimal. In contrast to [1], which performed worse than [10] on these complexity measures, our algorithm actually improves on the bounds of [10] and even breaks both message-complexity lower bounds given in [10] for the random phone call model without direct addressing. Lastly, we also prove a matching $\Omega(\log\log n)$ lower bound on the running time of any gossip algorithm in the random phone call model with direct addressing. This shows that our gossip algorithm achieves the optimal round-, message-, and bit-complexity simultaneously.

Our lower bound is particularly strong in the following sense: Instead of showing that any algorithm that takes $c \log\log n$ rounds for a sufficiently small constant c fails with non-negligible probability we prove that any algorithm that takes $0.99 \log\log n$ rounds or less fails with high probability. Our lower bound furthermore holds irrespectively of many model assumptions and even applies to non-gossip algorithms which can contact more than one known node per round:

THEOREM 3. *In the random phone call model with direct addressing any (randomized) gossip algorithm fails to spread a message to all nodes with high probability if less than $0.99 \log\log n$ rounds are used. This remains true if nodes are allowed to use arbitrarily large messages, communicate non address-obliviously and even contact an unbounded number of known nodes per round instead of just one.*

As a last contribution we consider bounds on the number of communications done by a node per round. While in a gossip algorithm each node initializes only one communication per round, nodes might have to respond to multiple requests. In fact, the number of simultaneous requests Δ can be as large as $n-1$. While this asymmetry is crucially used in essentially all algorithms that use direct addressing, it is unfortunately a questionable assumption for at least some systems and applications (see Section 7 for a more detailed discussion). In this regard, we discuss the easy to prove fact that a sub-logarithmic running time inherently requires $\Delta = \omega(1)$ and show that the best running time possible for any given Δ is $\log n / \log \Delta$. We then give a general framework for working efficiently in a setting with bounded Δ. In particular, we show how our gossip algorithm can efficiently compute a Δ-clustering which can then be used to achieve any point on this trade-off curve between running time and round complexity (subject only to our $\Omega(\log\log n)$ lower bound from Theorem 3). This shows, for example, that one can still have gossip algorithms with an optimal $\Theta(\log\log n)$ running-time while keeping Δ smaller than any polynomial in n, that is, $\Delta = n^{o(1)}$. We believe this to be a useful setting of parameters which seems realistic in many settings.

THEOREM 4. *For any $\Delta = \log^{\omega(1)} n$ there is a randomized gossip algorithm that, with high probability, computes a Δ-clustering in $O(\log\log n)$ rounds using $O(1)$-messages per node on average but having no node respond to more than Δ requests per round. Given such a Δ-clustering a message broadcast can then be performed easily with an optimal round-, message-, and bit-complexity.*

Organization.

The rest of the paper is organized as follows: In Section 3 we introduce *clusterings*, which are the main abstraction used to design our gossip algorithms. In Section 4 we give the simplest version of our algorithm which demonstrates the main ideas needed to achieve the $\Theta(\log \log n)$ round complexity. In Section 5 we then explain how to reduce the number of messages sent to $O(1)$ per node on average and achieve an optimal bit-complexity which proves our main theorem. In Section 6 we prove Theorem 3, i.e., our $\Omega(\log \log n)$ round lower bound. In Section 7 we provide our results on gossip algorithms with a bounded amount of communications per node. We defer the discussion of the fault-tolerance of our algorithms to the full version.

2. THE RANDOM PHONE CALL MODEL AND DIRECT ADDRESSING

In this section we give the formal definitions for the random phone call model and the direct addressing assumption used throughout this paper.

The Network.

The random phone call model assumes a complete network consisting of n nodes. Each node has a unique *address* or *ID* consisting of $O(\log n)$ bits, that is, we assume a polynomially large ID space. Initially nodes know their own ID but not the ID of any other node in the system. For convenience we assume that nodes know the number of nodes n. This assumption is without loss of generality since for all problems considered in this paper it is easy to test with high probability whether the algorithm succeeded. This allows for determining the parameter n using the classical guess-test-and-double strategy without increasing the running times by more than a constant factor.

Communication.

Communication takes place in synchronous rounds. In each round a node can choose to initialize one communication. In particular, it can either choose to contact a random node or use direct addressing to contact a node whose ID it knows. Each such contact from a node u to a node v consists of either node u PUSHing a message to v or of node u PULLing a message from v. A message can in principle contain any number of bits but all[1] algorithms throughout this paper only use messages of (minimal) size containing $O(\log n)$ bits. In particular, every message carries either the information to be broadcast, a node count, or $O(1)$ node IDs. Following [1] (and [10]) we say a gossip algorithm is *address-oblivious* if the decision whether to send or not and if so what to send (or respond with) is independent of the communication partner(s) in this round. In particular this means that for every node u the messages PUSHed by u does not depend on the ID of the communication partner and all responses u gives to a PULL are the same in one round. All algorithms presented in this paper are address-oblivious.

Round-, Message-, and Bit-Complexity.

The important figures of efficiency for such a gossip algorithm are the round-complexity, that is, the number of synchronous rounds needed, the message-complexity, that is, the number of messages sent per node on average throughout the execution, and the bit-complexity, that is, the total number of bits communicated in all messages throughput the execution. We only consider and present randomized protocols which complete their task with high probability in the round-, bit-, and message-complexity stated, that is, with probability at least $1 - \frac{1}{n^C}$ for some large chosen constant $C > 1$.

The (Fault-Tolerant) Broadcast Task.

Gossip algorithms can be used for a multitude of different communication and coordination tasks. The algorithms in this paper compute a cluster containing all nodes or, in the case of Theorem 4, a Δ-clustering which can then be used to perform any of these tasks easily and efficiently. To be consistent with prior work we focus on one specific task, namely, broadcasting. In this task there is a message, often also called rumor, consisting of b bits with $b = \Omega(\log n)$ which is initially known to one node (or multiple nodes). The goal is to inform all nodes in the network. In the full version we also address the setting of node-failures. In this setting an oblivious adversary fails any F nodes at the beginning of the execution. Follow [10] and [1], the desired guarantee in this setting is that all but $o(F)$ surviving nodes are clustered/informed. We call an algorithm achieving this *fault-tolerant*.

3. CLUSTERINGS

In this section we introduce clusterings, the main tool used in this paper to achieve efficient gossip.

First, in Section 3.1, we define the concept and implementation of a clustering. In Section 3.2 we then explain how these clustering support efficient implementations of several primitives allowing for coordination and communication between clusters. These primitives are extensively used throughout this paper to implement our fast and message efficient gossip communication algorithms.

3.1 Clustering Definition and Implementation

A *clustering* is a partition of all nodes $v \in V$ in a network into disjoint *clusters* $C_1, C_2, \ldots, C_k$ and the set $U = V \setminus \bigcup_i C_i$ of *unclustered nodes*. Each cluster C has one *cluster leader* $l_C \in C$ known to all nodes in C. We call all clustered nodes that are not leaders *cluster followers*. We define the *ID of a cluster* to be the ID of its leader and the *size of a cluster* C to be the number of nodes $|C|$ it contains.

Clusterings are implemented by each node $v \in V$ containing a variable $follow_v$. For any clustered node $v \in C$ this variable contains the ID of the cluster leader $ID(l_c)$ while for all unclustered nodes $v' \in U$ it is set to ∞. This also allows nodes to determine whether they are a cluster leader of follower by simply comparing their own ID to their $follow$ variable.

3.2 Cluster Coordination Primitives

Having a central leader which is known to all nodes in a cluster allows a cluster to coordinate using only a constant number of communication rounds. In one communication round, followers may PUSH information to the leader and thus have the leader collect inputs from the entire cluster. In a second round, followers may PULL a response from the leader. Below, we omit the details concerning PUSHing and PULLing messages, and briefly refer to exchanges such as

[1]The only exceptions are when we share a b-bit message (via a ClusterShare) and for resizing clusters in the Algorithm CLUSTER1, which demonstrates the ideas for achieving the optimal $\Theta(\log \log n)$ round complexity while ignoring message counts and message sizes for simplicity.

above as followers sending information (if any) to the leader and pulling one directive from it.

Following is a list of cluster-macros that make use of the power of clusters, and will be used later in our constructions. All these cluster primitives require only a constant number of rounds and therefore also a constant number of messages per node.

- ClusterActivate(p): This primitive allows clusters to be activated independently with probability p by having followers pull the outcome of a p-biased coin flipped by their leader. Each cluster stays activated until the next call of ClusterActivate or until it is explicitly deactivated.
- ClusterSize: Each cluster can determine its size in two rounds by each cluster follower sending its ID to the cluster leader, the cluster leader counting the received IDs and all followers pulling this count from the leader.
- ClusterDissolve(s): This primitive ensures that all clusters are at least of the given size s and runs in two rounds: In the first round each cluster follower pushes their ID to the leader. The cluster leader uses these messages to determine the cluster size s'. In the second round followers pull a value indicating their new clustering status from their current leader and set their $follow$ variable to this value. If $s' \geq s$ the cluster leader responds with its own ID and otherwise responds with ∞ to dissolve the cluster. It also sets its own $follow$ variable the same way.
- ClusterResize(s): This primitive ensures that all clusters are of size at most $2s$. It runs in two rounds. In the first round each cluster follower pushes their ID to the leader. This allows the leader of any cluster to determine the size s' of its cluster. In the second round followers pull a message from their current leader and update their $follow$ variable as follows: The cluster leader (in his mind) re-clusters its followers into $\lfloor \frac{s'}{s} \rfloor$ clusters of equal size (up to one) declaring for each new cluster the node with the largest ID its leader. To announce[2] and establish this clustering the leader responds to each node's pull request with the IDs of the $\lfloor \frac{s'}{s} \rfloor$ new leaders. Each follower then sets its $follow$ variable to the largest leader ID that is at least as large as its own ID. It is easy to see that after a cluster resizing step all clusters have size at most $2s - 1$.
- ClusterPUSH(msg)/ClusterPULL(msg): This is a similar primitive to a random PUSH or PULL of a node except on a cluster level. Each cluster leader decides on whether a push or pull is to be performed and what message msg to send or with what message msg to respond if pulled. This decision is then shared within each cluster by followers pulling it from the leader. All nodes in clusters instructed to do now contact a random node and either relay the message of the cluster leader via a PUSH or request a message via a PULL. All messages received by a node through either a PULL or PUSH get then relayed to their cluster leader (if there is one).
- ClusterMerge(new leader ID): This primitive allows to merge clusters in one round. For this all followers simply request the ID of the new leader from their current leader to update their $follow$ variable. In addition to answering these pulls the leader also sets its own $follow$ variable to the new leader.
- ClusterShare(.): This primitive allows clusters to share information within a cluster in two rounds. In the first round, followers who have relevant information send this information to the leader, who aggregates the information. In a second round, followers pull the aggregated information from the leader.

[2]The messages used in this primitive are of size $O(\frac{s'}{s} \log n)$ bits. This calls for ensuring that $\frac{s'}{s} = \Theta(1)$ if a small bit complexity is desired. We note that this complication arises only for address-oblivious algorithms as a non address-oblivious algorithm could simply respond to each follower separately with the ID of its new leader.

4. GOSSIP IN $O(\log \log N)$ ROUNDS

In this section we present the simplest version of our algorithm to demonstrate the principal ideas needed achieve the optimal $O(\log \log n)$ round-complexity. The resulting algorithm CLUSTER1 is, for sake of simplicity, not tuned to have a good message- or bit-complexity. In particular, a constant fraction of the nodes is sending during most of the $\Theta(\log \log n)$ rounds and the message sizes occurring in the first ClusterResize call is hard to analyze.

4.1 Overview

The idea of CLUSTER1 is simple, and a general outline can be inferred from the procedure calls and comments at the top of Algorithm 1: To obtain an initial clustering, Procedure GROWINITIALCLUSTERS samples a small logarithmic fraction of the nodes to active singleton-clusters. Then a standard PUSH gossip is performed for $\Theta(\log \log n)$ rounds in which these clusters recruit unclustered nodes. The usual exponential growth behavior of the PUSH gossip protocol leads to clusters of size at least $s = C' \log n$ while also ensuring that all but a small constant fraction of the nodes are recruited into some cluster. In the main phase of the algorithm, namely Procedure SQUARECLUSTERS, we repeatedly square this cluster size by merging clusters in the following manner: We start by using ClusterDissolve(s) and ClusterResize(s) to ensure that clusters have sizes between s and $2s$. Next, we determine the new cluster leaders by activating each cluster with probability $1/s$. The inactive clusters are then prompted to join one of the new active clusters via two ClusterPUSHes. This results in each new cluster recruiting $\Theta(s)$ inactive clusters which leads to the desired new cluster size of $\Theta(s^2)$. In particular, the first such PUSH guarantees that each new cluster grows by a factor of $\Theta(s)$, while the second iteration ensures that all old inactive clusters are merged into some new, larger active cluster. The doubly exponential growth of squaring the cluster size with every iteration guarantees that $\Theta(\log \log n)$ iterations are sufficient to obtain clusters of size $\frac{\sqrt{n}}{\log n}$. Procedure MERGEALLCLUSTERS uses two ClusterPUSHes to merge all clusters into the cluster with the smallest ID. With one cluster comprising most of the nodes in the network, Procedure UNCLUSTEREDNODESPULL uses a standard PULL gossip to have the remaining unclustered nodes join the cluster which is known to require only $\Theta(\log \log n)$ rounds. Lastly, with all nodes in one cluster spreading any desired message can be done via one ClusterShare.

A breakdown of the various steps is given in the detailed procedures of Algorithm 1, using the cluster communication primitives from Section 3.2.

Algorithm 1 CLUSTER1

```
1: GROWINITIALCLUSTERS                      ▷ cluster most nodes
2: SQUARECLUSTERS                    ▷ repeatedly merge clusters
3: MERGEALLCLUSTERS                      ▷ merge clusters to one
4: UNCLUSTEREDNODESPULL              ▷ unclustered nodes join
5: ClusterShare(message)

6: procedure GROWINITIALCLUSTERS
7:     follow ← ∞
8:     With probability 1/C log n set follow ← ownID
9:     for Θ(log log n) times do
10:        ClusterPUSH(clusterID)
11:        unclustered nodes: follow ← received ID (if any)

12: procedure SQUARECLUSTERS
13:    s = C' log n
14:    ClusterDissolve(s)
15:    repeat
16:        ClusterResize(s)
17:        ClusterActivate(1/s)
18:        for two repetitions do
19:            active: ClusterPUSH(follow)
20:            inactive: ClusterMerge(smallest received ID)
21:        s ← Θ(s^2)
22:    until s > √n / log n

23: procedure MERGEALLCLUSTERS
24:    for two repetitions do
25:        ClusterPUSH(follow)
26:        ClusterMerge(smallest received ID)

27: procedure UNCLUSTEREDNODESPULL
28:    for Θ(log log n) times do
29:        unclustered nodes PULL follow value
```

4.2 Correctness Proof

In this section we prove the correctness and efficiency of CLUSTER1, which is described in Section 4.1 and Algorithm 1. We break the proof down to several lemmas, which then lead to the main result.

LEMMA 5. *At the end of Procedure* GROWINITIALCLUSTERS *in* CLUSTER1, *at least* $0.9n$ *nodes are contained in clusters of size* $C' \log n$ *with high probability.*

PROOF. The clustering at the end of the procedure is created by $\Theta(\log\log n)$ rounds of random PUSH gossip starting from cluster centers that were obtained by sampling nodes independently with probability $p = \frac{1}{C \log n}$. By a Chernoff bound, we initially have the expected $\Theta\left(\frac{n}{C\log n}\right)$ cluster centers occur with high probability. By standard gossip analysis, the set containing all clustered nodes grows by a constant factor in each round, so long as some constant fraction of the system remains unclustered. Furthermore, by choosing $C' \ll C$ at most an arbitrary small constant fraction of nodes account for clusters that are smaller than $C' \log n$, namely about $\frac{n}{C \log n} \cdot C' \log n$ many. In total, one can guarantee that at least a 90% fraction of nodes are good, that is, contained in a large cluster. □

LEMMA 6. *Every iteration inside Procedure* SQUARECLUSTERS *in* CLUSTER1 *squares the cluster size* s *while ensuring that all clustered nodes are contained in clusters of the new size, with high probability.*

PROOF. Initially, due to Theorem 5 which is followed by ClusterDissolve(s), we can assume that at least $0.9n$ nodes are clustered and divided into clusters of size between s and two $2s$ after the ClusterResize(s) in Line 16 is performed. The same holds from there on by induction. These $\Theta(n/s)$ clusters then get independently activated with probability $1/s$. Since $s \le \frac{\sqrt{n}}{\log n}$ the expected number of activated clusters is $\Theta(n/s^2) = \omega(\log n)$ and a Chernoff bound shows that indeed $\Theta(n/s^2)$ clusters are activated with high probability. Now, in the first ClusterPUSH/ClusterMerge iteration of Procedure SQUARECLUSTERS, these active clusters PUSH $\Theta(s)$ messages each for a total of $\Theta(n/s)$ messages in order to recruit the $\Theta(n/s)$ inactive clusters. By standard balls and bins analysis, a linear fraction of every set of $s = \Omega(\log n)$ PUSHes of each cluster lands in a unique cluster and result in a merge. Therefore, after the first iteration all active clusters will recruit $\Theta(s)$ inactive clusters and thus grow to size $\Theta(s^2)$. However, there is also a constant fraction of inactive clusters that did not get recruited. The second ClusterPUSH/ClusterMerge iteration ensures that these clusters merge with some active cluster to ensure that all clustered nodes remain clustered. This is indeed the case since there are $\Theta(n)$ total number of nodes contained in the active clusters which PUSH out in the second iteration. Every inactive cluster of size $s = \Omega(\log n)$ is therefore reached and merged into an active cluster with high probability. □

LEMMA 7. *After Procedure* MERGEALLCLUSTERS *in Algorithm* CLUSTER1, *with high probability, there is a single cluster which contains at least* $0.9n$ *nodes.*

PROOF. Theorem 6 shows that before Procedure MERGEALLCLUSTERS is invoked at least $0.9n$ nodes are contained in clusters of size $\Theta(s)$ with $s \ge \frac{\sqrt{n}}{\log n}$. We now consider the cluster with the smallest ID. The first ClusterPUSH/ClusterMerge iteration of Procedure MERGEALLCLUSTERS will, with high probability, grow this cluster to size $\Omega(\frac{n}{\log^2 n})$. The second iteration then recruits all remaining clusters, with high probability. □

Lastly, it is well known (see, e.g., [10]) that the standard PULL gossip takes only $O(\log\log n)$ rounds to inform the remaining constant or even $1 - 1/\log^{\Theta(1)} n$ fraction of nodes. This is exactly what is used in Procedure UNCLUSTEREDNODESPULL to have all unclustered nodes join the single cluster in the end:

LEMMA 8. *The PULL gossip given in Algorithm* CLUSTER1 *as Procedure* UNCLUSTEREDNODESPULL *results in all* *nodes joining the single cluster, with high probability, in $O(\log\log n)$ rounds.*

PROOF. It is well known that the standard uniform PULL gossip terminates with high probability in $\Theta(\log\log n)$ if one starts with at least $n/\log^{\Theta(1)} n$ nodes being informed. For completeness we include the analysis here: We look at the fraction x of unclustered nodes and note that in one round any unclustered node (pulling a random node) remains unclustered with probability x. As long as the number of unclustered nodes is still at least $\Theta(\log n)$ a Chernoff bound shows that the quantity x shrinks to at most $2x^2$ with high probability after each pull. This can happen at most for $2\log\log n$ rounds. Lastly, with high probability, it takes at most a constant number of rounds until each remaining node pulls from a clustered node. This shows that the $\Theta(\log\log n)$ rounds of PULL gossip indeed, with high probability, lead to one cluster containing all nodes. □

The correctness and efficiency of CLUSTER1 now follows immediately:

THEOREM 9. *Algorithm* CLUSTER1 *runs for $O(\log\log n)$ rounds and, with high probability, spreads any message to all nodes.*

PROOF. The ClusterShare(message) performed at the end of CLUSTER1 correctly spreads any message to all nodes since according to Theorem 8 all nodes are contained in one single cluster. The running time of CLUSTER1 is furthermore easily seen to be $O(\log\log n)$ rounds. In particular, the loops inside Procedures GROWINITIALCLUSTERS and UNCLUSTEREDNODESPULL run explicitly for $O(\log\log n)$ iterations, while the loop inside Procedure SQUARECLUSTERS squares the parameter s in each iteration, and therefore runs for at most $\Theta(\log\log n)$ iterations as well. To complete the proof, we refer to Section 3.2 for the fact that all cluster primitives performed in these loops can be performed in a constant number of rounds. □

5. LINEAR MESSAGE COMPLEXITY

In this section we prove Theorem 2 by explaining how the CLUSTER1 algorithm can be tweaked to also have optimal message- and bit-complexity without compromising its optimal $O(\log\log n)$ round-complexity. We call the resulting algorithm CLUSTER2.

5.1 Overview

First, we give the intuition behind achieving a linear message complexity and describe in which aspects CLUSTER2 is different from CLUSTER1. The high-level recipe of CLUSTER2 is the same as CLUSTER1. The key idea for achieving the optimal message-complexity is in modifying Procedures GROWINITIALCLUSTERS and SQUARECLUSTERS to work with only $\Theta(n/\log n)$ clustered nodes. This guarantees that even if all clustered nodes actively transmit in these rounds, only $o(n)$ messages are used for these parts. After merging all clusters, we are left with one large cluster of size $\Theta(n/\log n)$. While the standard PULL gossip would still finish in $O(\log\log n)$ rounds this would again take to many messages (of unclustered nodes PULLing unclustered nodes). We therefore PUSH the cluster ID to $\Theta(n)$ nodes first before doing the final PULL phase. With so many informed nodes each node expects to PULL at most a constant number of times and it is easy to see that in total at most $O(n)$ messages are used with high probability.

All in all a much more delicate control on the number of clusters, their size and the number of clustered nodes is required. This is also important to provably guarantee an optimal bit-complexity. The subtle problem here is that a ClusterResize(s) on a cluster of size $\omega(s)$ leads to messages of size $\omega(\log n)$ (see footnote in Section 3.2). This control is achieved as follows:

To control the number of nodes clustered in the Procedures GROWINITIALCLUSTERS we have clusters measure their growth. More precisely before and after each PUSH in the initial recruiting phase each cluster checks its size. If a cluster has size at least $\Omega(\log^3 n)$ but grew by less than a factor of $2-\frac{1}{\log n}$ then it stops recruiting. A Chernoff Bound shows that no cluster will stop recruiting if less than $n/2\log n$ nodes are clustered. On the other hand, similar arguments as for CLUSTER1 show that indeed $\Theta(n/\log n)$ nodes will get recruited of which most lie in clusters of size $s=\Omega(\log^3 n)$. A ClusterResize($C'\log n$) called for every large cluster in every iteration furthermore ensures that no individual cluster gets too big. For the ProcedureSQUARECLUSTERS we then again merge clusters. Due to the smaller number of clustered nodes most cluster requests now go to unclustered nodes and get ignored. Still, any iteration starting with clusters of size s ends up with larger clusters of size $\Theta(s^2/\log n)=\omega(s^{1.5})$. Growing the cluster sizes from $s=\Theta(\log^3 n)$ to $\Omega(n/\log^2 n)$ therefore still takes only $O(\log\log n)$ rounds. Chernoff bounds over the larger $\Omega(\log^3 n)$ sized clusters still guarantee that the new cluster size can be predicted up to a constant with high probability which ensures that no ClusterResize(s) is applied to a too large (or too small) cluster.

The formal description of CLUSTER2 is given as Algorithm 2.

5.2 Correctness Proof

In this section we prove Theorem 2 by showing that CLUSTER2 spreads a message with the desired optimal round-, message- and bit-complexity.

The proof follows along the same line as Theorem 9 while including the extra arguments given in Section 5.1. We again break the proof into several lemmas, which then lead to the main result.

LEMMA 10. *If at most $n/f(n)$ nodes are clustered, then a ClusterPUSH by some cluster X, where $|X|\geq\Omega(\log n)$, grows X by factor at least $(2-\Theta(1/f(n)))$ with high probability.*

PROOF. Each PUSH request of one of the $|X|$ nodes is hits a unique unclustered node with probability of approximately $(1-\frac{1}{f(n)})$. The expected number of nodes recruited for cluster X is therefore $(1-\frac{1}{2f(n)})|X|$ for a total number of $|X|+(1-\frac{1}{2f(n)})|X|$ and a growth factor of $(2-\Theta(1/2f(n)))$. Since the recruitment success of different nodes are essentially independent of each other applying a Chernoff type bound shows that the growth factor is close to the expected and in particular is $(2-\Theta(1/f(n)))$, with high probability. □

LEMMA 11. *Procedure* GROWINITIALCLUSTERS *of* CLUSTER2 *leads to $\Theta(n/\log n)$ clustered nodes that are contained*

Algorithm 2 CLUSTER2

GROWINITIALCLUSTERS
SQUARECLUSTERS
MERGEALLCLUSTERS ▷ as in Algorithm 1
BOUNDEDCLUSTERPUSH
UNCLUSTEREDNODESPULL ▷ as in Algorithm 1
ClusterShare(message)

procedure GROWINITIALCLUSTERS
  $follow \leftarrow \infty$
  With probability $1/C\log^4 n$ set $follow \leftarrow ownID$
  ClusterActivate(1)
  for $\Theta(\log\log n)$ times **do**
    active clusters: ClusterPUSH($follow$)
    unclustered nodes: $follow \leftarrow$ any received ID
    if ClusterSize $\geq C'\log^3 n$ **then**
      if cluster growth factor $< (2 - 1/\log n)$ **then**
        deactivate cluster
      else
        ClusterResize($C'\log^3 n$)

procedure SQUARECLUSTERS
  $s = C'\log^3 n$
  ClusterDissolve(s)
  repeat
    ClusterResize(s)
    ClusterActivate($1/s$)
    for two repetitions **do**
      active: ClusterPUSH($follow$)
      inactive: ClusterMerge(random received ID)
    $s \leftarrow \Theta(s^2/\log n)$
  until $s > \frac{\sqrt{n}}{\log^2 n}$

procedure BOUNDEDCLUSTERPUSH
  ClusterActivate(1)
  for $\Theta(\log\log n)$ rounds **do**
    ClusterPUSH($follow$)
    unclustered nodes: $follow \leftarrow$ any received ID
    ClusterSize
    if cluster growth factor < 1.1 **then**
      deactivate cluster

in clusters of size $(1+\Theta(1))(C'\log n)$, with high probability, while at most $O(n)$ messages of $\Theta(\log n)$ bits each are sent.

PROOF. For the initial sampling of singleton clusters, for which the sampling probability is $1/C\log^4 n$, a Chernoff bound shows that $\Theta(\frac{n}{C\log^4 n})$ such singleton clusters are created, with high probability. We would like to argue as in Theorem 5 that the growth of the set of clustered nodes is exponential until at least $\Omega(n/\log n)$ nodes are clustered. We need to show that the newly introduced size-control does not prevent this exponential growth. By Theorem 10, as long as at least $n(1-O(1/\log n))$ nodes are unclustered each cluster will grow by a factor of at least $2-1/\log n$, with high probability. Hence, the size control mechanism does not inhibit the exponential growth until at least $\Theta(n/\log n)$ nodes are clustered. Since at most about $\frac{n}{C\log^4 n}\cdot(C'\log^3 n)$ nodes account for clusters that are smaller than $C'\log^3 n$, indeed at least $\Theta(n/\log n)$ nodes are contained in large clusters.

To guarantee that the message complexity incurred by the initialization is small we note that only clustered nodes are transmitting. This leads to at most $O(n\log\log n/\log n) = O(n)$ messages sent. Since every cluster can grow by at most a factor of two in each iteration it is furthermore clear that all message sizes used in a ClusterResize contain at most two IDs. This results in messages of size $\Theta(\log n)$, as claimed. □

LEMMA 12. *Before and after every iteration inside Procedure* SQUARECLUSTERS *in* CLUSTER2, *$\Theta(n/\log n)$ nodes are contained in clusters of size at least s, with high probability. Furthermore, the total number of messages sent during Procedure* SQUARECLUSTERS *is $O(n)$, each containing $\Theta(\log n)$ bits.*

PROOF. We prove the lemma by induction. The base case is already given by Theorem 11. Here, we show that each iteration of the loop increases the cluster size from s to $s' = \Theta(\frac{s^2}{\log n})$ while keeping all clustered nodes clustered. In the first iteration each active cluster PUSHes to $\Theta(s)$ random nodes and hits with high probability $\Theta(s/\log n)$ inactive clusters (alone). Once these clusters merge, any active cluster therefore grows to $s' = \Theta(\frac{s^2}{\log n})$ as desired. The second PUSH, performed by the larger clusters which cover $\Theta(n/\log n)$ nodes, guarantees that no inactive cluster of size s is left behind without merging to a new larger cluster of size at least s'. Furthermore, since inactive clusters randomly join the large active clusters during this second iteration no active cluster grows by more than a constant factor. The new clusters are therefore all of the desired size $s' = \Theta(\frac{s^2}{\log n})$ while all clustered nodes remain clustered. Lastly, since $s > \log^3 n$ we have that $s' = \omega(s^{1.5})$ which shows that the number of iterations until the final cluster size of $\Omega(\frac{\sqrt{n}}{\log^2 n})$ is reached is at most $\Theta(\log\log n)$.

All in all, only $\Theta(n/\log n)$ nodes are communicating in each of the $O(\log\log n)$ rounds, which leads to the desired $O(n)$ messages-complexity. Regarding the bit-size of these messages, the only thing to worry about is the calls to ClusterResize(s). However, since the cluster sizes are, up to constants, exactly what they are resized to, ClusterResize(s) produces only $\Theta(\log n)$ bit messages containing $\Theta(1)$ IDs. □

Theorem 7 applies without change to CLUSTER2 and we do not repeat it.

LEMMA 13. *Procedure* BOUNDEDPUSHCLUSTER *expands the single large cluster to $\Theta(n)$ nodes in $O(\log\log n)$ rounds, with high probability, while at most $O(n)$ messages are sent.*

PROOF. At the beginning of the procedure, we have from Theorem 7 that $\Theta(n/\log n)$ belong to a single giant cluster. From here, we use a standard analysis of PUSH-PULL gossip: So long as at least $.1n$ nodes are unclustered, during each iteration the number of clustered nodes grows exponentially (and therefore for at most $O(\log\log n)$ rounds) until a large constant fraction of the nodes is clustered. By Theorem 10, the cluster detects this event successfully. Since the number of messages sent out in every round is exponentially increasing until it stops the total number of messages form a geometric sum which sums to $O(n)$ messages sent in total. □

Putting these claims together, it follows that CLUSTER2 has a bit-complexity of $O(n\log n + nb) = O(nb)$ and message complexity of $O(1)$ messages per node on average while maintaining the optimal $O(\log\log n)$ round complexity of CLUSTER1. This proves Theorem 2.

6. THE $\Omega(\log\log N)$ ROUND LOWER BOUND

This section is dedicated to prove the $\Omega(\log\log n)$ round-complexity lower bound of Theorem 3.

We first remark that the simple lower bound provided in Section 7 as Theorem 16 does not give any super constant number of rounds for the most interesting setting of $\Delta = n^{\Theta(1)}$. Here we show that the round-complexity of broadcasting a message has to be at least $0.99\log\log n$ with high probability. This holds for any Δ and remains true even if one ignores many restrictions of the model regarding message sizes, address-obliviousness, or the number of known nodes that can be contacted per round. The main implication of this lower bound is that both CLUSTER1 and CLUSTER2 achieve the optimal asymptotic running time.

We need some notation: Instead of each node sampling (up to) one random contact in each round we assume that these nodes are sampled in advance. In particular, let $u_{v,t}$ be the uniformly random node given to node v if it samples an node at time t. Based on these samples we define G_t to be the union of all edges (node-pairs) that are potentially sampled at time t, that is, $G_t = (V, E_t)$ with $E_t = \{\{u,v\} \mid \exists v : u = u_{v,t}\}$.

LEMMA 14. *For every $t = 0, 1, \ldots$ let K_t be the graph indicating which node knows whom at the beginning of round t. It holds that: $K_0 = \emptyset$; $K_{t+1} \subseteq (K_t \cup G_{t+1})^2$, and therefore also that:*

$$K_t \subseteq \left(\bigcup_{i=1}^{t} G_i\right)^{2^t}.$$

Here G^j is the graph that connects a node u to any node for which there is a path of length at most j in G.

PROOF. The first equation is simply stating that nodes do not know each other initially. To see the second equation we note that there are two ways nodes can learn about new nodes. The first one is by contacting a random node. This only adds edges in G_{t+1} to the knowledge graph K_t. By initiating a contact along an edge in G_{t+1} or along an edge in K_t corresponding to a node known from previous rounds, nodes can also indirectly learn about nodes known to nodes they know. Even if all such "neighbors" are contacted and every node responds with everything they know (which would result in many message of very large size), a nodes does not learn about more nodes than its 2-hop neighborhood. This is exactly what is stated in the second equation. The last equation now follows from the other two by induction and taking into account that for any two graphs G, G' and any $j, j' > 1$ we have $G^i \cup G' \subseteq (G \cup G')^i$ and of course $(G^j)^{j'} = G^{jj'}$. □

We can now prove Theorem 3:

THEOREM 15 (THEOREM 3 RESTATED). *Suppose we allow unlimited messages sizes, non address-oblivious communication, and have no restriction on how many communications a node can be involved in or even to how many known nodes a node contact in one round. Still, any algorithm running in less than $T = \log\log n - \log\log\log n - \omega(1)$ rounds fails to spread a message that starts at one node u to all nodes with high probability.*

PROOF. First we note that spreading a message starting at one node u can be used to elect u as a cluster leader by simply attaching its ID to the message spread. This could then be used to make K_T the complete graph by informing all nodes about each other in at most two additional rounds, at least if the message size is unbounded. We show that this is, with high probability, impossible in less than T rounds by using Theorem 14. In particular, it certainly holds that $K_T \subseteq K'^{2^T}$ where $K' = (\bigcup_{i=1}^{T} G_i)$. Note that K' is simply a random graph that is created by each node sampling T neighbors independently and adding an undirected edge to those neighbors. It is clear that K_T is a complete graph if and only if the diameter of K' is at most 2^T. It is easy to see that for $T = \log\log n - \log\log\log n - \omega(1)$ the probability that such a random graph has diameter $o(\log n/\log\log n)$ is extremely small which completes the proof. An easy way to get such a high probability result is to say that the probability that there is a node in K' with degree $\Delta = \omega(\log n)$ is at most $n^{-\omega(1)}$ and any graph with maximum degree $\Theta(\log n)$ necessarily has a diameter of $\Omega(\log n/\log\log n)$. □

7. BOUNDED COMMUNICATIONS

In this section we discuss and prove tradeoffs between the running time of any gossip algorithm and the maximum number of communications a node can be involved in per round.

In the standard gossip model which is also employed in this paper, each node can only initiate one PUSH or PULL communication per round. Still, a node might be involved in multiple communications initiated by other nodes. The possibility of this happening is present in the models of *all* prior gossip works (discussed in Section 1). In few cases, in particular the random phone call model with an underlying complete graph, having a large number of communications per round in one node is not crucial. For example, the running time of the uniformly random gossip on the complete graph remains $O(\log n)$ even if each node only accepts one communication per round (but the result of [12] which concentrates on the leading constants and lower order terms change). For most gossip works however such a concentration of communications is unavoidable. For example the works [4–6] which generalize the random phone call model to arbitrary topologies show that gossip is fast on any topology with good vertex or edge expansion. In particular, they imply that gossip completes in $\log^{O(1)} n$ rounds on a star graph because the star graph has a constant edge expansion $\Phi = O(1)$ and constant vertex expansion $\alpha = O(1)$. This is obviously not possible without the center node talking to at least $\Delta = n/\log^{O(1)} n$ nodes per round on average. Similarly, all results that use direct addressing crucially rely on each node being able to respond to many nodes and many of them can have one node communicate with (almost) all other nodes in the network in one round. This is also the case for CLUSTER1 and CLUSTER2. In fact our entire set of cluster-operations are based on having a cluster-center coordinating $\omega(1)$ cluster-followers in a single communication step.

While in some settings having $\Delta = n$ may be acceptable, in other settings one would like to have Δ to be not much more than a small polynomial or even (significantly) less. In what follows we explicitly address this parameter and design optimal algorithms for any Δ.

We first remark that having a super-constant Δ is unavoidable if one wants to achieve a sub-logarithmic round complexity. In particular, it is easy to see that any global communication with the restriction that no node responds to more than Δ requests per round takes at least $\log n/\log \Delta$ rounds:

LEMMA 16. *Any algorithm in which no node participates in more than Δ communications per round requires at least $\log n/\log \Delta$ rounds to inform all nodes of a message.*

PROOF. Since each informed node can participate in at most Δ communications the number of informed nodes cannot grow by more than a Δ factor per round. Inductively the the number of informed nodes in round r is therefore at most Δ^{r-1} and $\log n/\Delta$ rounds are needed to bring this quantity to n. □

In the remainder of this section we will show that the algorithmic ideas developed in this paper can be used to achieve any point on the this tradeoff curve between Δ and the required number of rounds while also maintaining the optimal message- and bit-complexity. We do this in two steps. We first define a Δ-clustering and show that any such clustering easily allows Δ-bounded communications in the desired $\log n/\log \Delta$ round complexity by running simple and robust gossip algorithms on top of this clustering. We then show that a Δ-clustering can be computed in $\Theta(\log\log n)$ rounds:

DEFINITION 1. *A Δ-clustering is a clustering in which every node is clustered and all clusters have a size between Δ and 2Δ.*

We will show in Theorem 17 that such a Δ-clustering indeed allows to efficiently spread information in the desired $O(\log n/\log \Delta)$ rounds using the CLUSTERPUSH-PULL protocol given in Algorithm 3. For sake of simplicity we focus on the case $\Delta = \log^{\omega(1)} n$ since for smaller Δ the improvement of $\log \Delta$ is at most $O(\log\log n)$ and therefore essentially negligible. Similarly, in this section we assume for convenience that $\Delta < n^{0.9}$ as otherwise one can might as well set $\Delta = n$ and run CLUSTER2.

LEMMA 17. *For any bound $\Delta = \log^{\omega(1)} n$ the algorithm CLUSTERPUSH-PULL(Δ) given in Algorithm 3 spreads a message to all nodes, with high probability. It furthermore uses only $O(\frac{\log n}{\log \Delta})$ rounds and $O(n)$ messages once the Δ-clustering is computed.*

Algorithm 3 CLUSTERPUSH-PULL(Δ)

1: Compute Δ-Clustering
2: ClusterShare(message)
3: **for** $\Theta(\frac{\log n}{\log \Delta})$ iterations **do**
4:     **if** newly informed clusters **then**
5:         ClusterPUSH(message), ClusterShare(message)
6: uninformed nodes: PULL message from a random node
7: ClusterShare(message)

PROOF. We first address the round and message complexity and then prove correctness:

The claimed round complexity of $O(\frac{\log n}{\log \Delta})$ is easily verified since the only loop of the algorithm in Line 3 takes 3 rounds per iteration and runs for $\Theta(\frac{\log n}{\log \Delta})$ iterations. All other instructions take only $O(1)$ rounds. It is also easy to see that each node processes at most $O(1)$ messages over the course of the algorithm.

Next we prove correctness, that is, that CLUSTERPUSH-PULL spreads any message to all nodes with high probability. The first ClusterShare (Line 5) spreads the message to $\Delta = \omega(\log n)$ nodes. From there on, so long as at most $n/\Omega(\Delta)$ nodes are informed, each ClusterPUSH and ClusterShare in the main loop (of Line 3) increases the number of informed nodes with high probability by a $\Delta/O(1)$ factor. Hence, the set of informed nodes grows exponentially until it reaches $n/\Delta > (\Delta/O(1))^{\Theta(\frac{\log n}{\log \Delta})}$ nodes.

To see that this suffices for the ClusterPULL/ClusterShare in Lines 6–7 to inform all remaining nodes with high probability we focus on one uninformed node. This node gets informed during the ClusterPULL if at least one of the nodes in its cluster PULLs the message from a node in Line 6. Since there are at least $\Delta = \log^{\omega(1)} n$ such nodes of which each has an independent chance of $1/\Delta$ to PULL from an informed node this happens with high probability.

This shows that CLUSTERPUSH-PULL indeed informs all nodes about the message with high probability using only $O(\frac{\log n}{\log \Delta})$ rounds and $O(n)$ messages. □

What remains to show is that a $\Theta(\Delta)$-clustering can be computed efficiently. The process for generating the clustering is essentially a generalization of the CLUSTER2 algorithm, where we stop growing clusters at around size Δ. Then for additional $O(\log\log n)$ rounds, we join all unclustered nodes to existing clusters. All the while, we never connect any leader to more than Δ followers, nor transmit more than $O(n)$ messages. The detailed pseudo-code description of the resulting algorithm CLUSTER3(Δ) is given in Algorithm 4.

THEOREM 18. *For any given $\Delta = \log^{\omega(1)} n$ the algorithm CLUSTER3(Δ), with high probability, computes a $\Theta(\Delta)$-clustering using $O(\log\log n)$-rounds and $O(n)$ messages while no node communicates with more than Δ nodes in any round.*

PROOF. As before, the Procedures GROWINITIALCLUSTERS and SQUARECLUSTERS result in $\Theta(n/\log n)$ clustered nodes grouped into clusters of size $\Theta(s)$. Here the cluster

Algorithm 4 CLUSTER3(Δ) with $\Delta = \log^{\omega(1)} n$

GROWINITIALCLUSTERS ▷ as in Algorithm 2
SQUARECLUSTERS(to size $s \geq \sqrt{\Delta \log n}/C''$) ▷ as in Algorithm 2
MERGECLUSTERS
BOUNDEDCLUSTERPUSH
UNCLUSTEREDNODESPULL ▷ as in Algorithm 1
ClusterResize(Δ/C'')

procedure MERGECLUSTERS
    ClusterActivate($10\frac{s}{\Delta/C''}$)
    active: ClusterPUSH(clusterID)
    inactive: ClusterMerge(random received ID)

procedure BOUNDEDCLUSTERPUSH
    ClusterActivate(1)
    for $\Theta(\log\log n)$ rounds **do**
        ClusterResize(Δ/C'')
        ClusterPUSH(*follow*)
        unclustered nodes: *follow* $\leftarrow$ any received ID
        ClusterSize
        if cluster growth factor < 1.1 **then**
            deactivate cluster

size is $s = \Omega(\sqrt{\Delta \log n}/C'')$. The proof for this follows the same way as for CLUSTER2, and we do not repeat the arguments here.

Procedure MERGECLUSTERS of CLUSTER3 is a bit different from CLUSTER2, though the techniques are similar. It activates every cluster with probability $10\frac{s}{\Delta/C''}$ followed by a ClusterPUSH of the active clusters. Since Δ is small enough a Chernoff bound shows that roughly a $\frac{10C''}{\Delta}$ fraction of clusters is activated. Since $\Delta = \log^{\omega(1)} n$ each inactive cluster gets furthermore PUSHed by multiple active clusters to merge. Importantly, and differently to other merging phases, inactive clusters choose one to merge with among these clusters uniformly at random. A Chernoff type-bound shows that this way inactive clusters get assigned to active clusters evenly, i.e., each active cluster gets chosen by $\Theta(\frac{\Delta/C''}{s})$ inactive clusters and will therefore grow to size about $\Delta/10C''$.

Subsequently, these clusters then recruit unclustered nodes in the BOUNDEDCLUSTERPUSH call. After each recruiting step clusters measure whether they grew by at least a factor of 1.1 and resize. As before this guarantees that all but a small constant fraction of the nodes joins a cluster while the number of messages is $O(n)$. Resizing active clusters guarantees that no cluster gets too big and no leader has to communicate too much.

As a last step, we run UNCLUSTEREDNODESPULL on the unclustered nodes and make them join the first cluster they PULL from. Up to constants every unclustered node joins a uniformly random cluster. Even without any size control every cluster grows by at most a small constant in this round. The final ClusterResize(Δ/C'') ensures that all clusters have the same size (up to a factor of two) as desired by a $\Theta(\Delta)$-clustering. □

Acknowledgments

We thank Chen Avin and Robert Elsässer for sharing an early version of [1] and for interesting discussions.

8. REFERENCES

[1] C. Avin and R. Elsässer. Faster Rumor Spreading: Breaking the $\log n$ Barrier. In *Proceedings of the International Symposium on Distributed Computing*, DISC '13, pages 209–223, 2013.

[2] K. Censor-Hillel, B. Haeupler, J. Kelner, and P. Maymounkov. Global Computation in a Poorly Connected World: Fast Rumor Spreading with no Dependence on Conductance. In *Proceedings of the ACM Symposium on Theory of Computing*, STOC '12, pages 961–970, 2012.

[3] K. Censor-Hillel and H. Shachnai. Fast information spreading in graphs with large weak conductance. In *Proceedings of the 22nd ACM-SIAM Symposium on Discrete Algorithms (SODA)*, pages 440–448, 2011.

[4] G. Giakkoupis. Tight bounds for rumor spreading in graphs of a given conductance. In *Proceedings of the 28th International Symposium on Theoretical Aspects of Computer Science*, STACS, pages 57–68, 2011.

[5] G. Giakkoupis and T. Sauerwald. Rumor spreading and vertex expansion. In *Proceedings of the ACM-SIAM Symposium on Discrete Algorithms*, SODA '12, pages 1623–1641, 2012.

[6] B. Haeupler. Analyzing network coding gossip made easy. In *Proceedings of the ACM Symposium on Theory of Computing*, STOC, pages 293–302, 2011.

[7] B. Haeupler. Simple, fast and deterministic gossip and rumor spreading. In *Proceedings of the ACM-SIAM Symposium on Discrete Algorithms*, SODA '13, pages 705–716, 2013.

[8] B. Haeupler, G. Pandurangan, D. Peleg, R. Rajaraman, and Z. Sun. Discovery through gossip. In *Proceedings of the 24th ACM Symposium on Parallelism in Algorithms and Architectures*, SPAA, pages 140–149, 2012.

[9] M. Harchol-Balter, T. Leighton, and D. Lewin. Resource discovery in distributed networks. In *Proceedings of the ACM Symposium on Principles of Distributed Computing*, PODC'99, pages 229–237, 1999.

[10] R. Karp, C. Schindelhauer, S. Shenker, and B. Vocking. Randomized rumor spreading. In *Proceedings of the 41st Annual Symposium on Foundations of Computer Science*, FOCS, pages 565–574, 2000.

[11] S. Kutten, D. Peleg, and U. Vishkin. Deterministic resource discovery in distributed networks. *Theory of Computing Systems*, 36(5):479–495, 2003.

[12] B. Pittel. On spreading a rumor. *SIAM Journal on Applied Mathematics*, pages 213–223, 1987.

Complexity Tradeoffs for Read and Update Operations*

Danny Hendler
Department of Computer-Science
Ben-Gurion University
hendlerd@cs.bgu.ac.il

Vitaly Khait
Department of Computer-Science
Ben-Gurion University
khvitaly@gmail.com

ABSTRACT

Recent work established that some restricted-use objects, such as max registers, counters and atomic snapshots, admit polylogarithmic step-complexity wait-free implementations using only reads and writes: when only polynomially-many updates are allowed, reading the object (by performing a `ReadMax`, `CounterRead` or `Scan` operation, depending on the object's type) incurs $O(\log N)$ steps (where N is the number of processes), which was shown to be optimal.

But what about the step-complexity of update operations? With these implementations, updating the object's state (by performing a `WriteMax`, `CounterIncrement` or `Update` operation, depending on the object's type) requires $\Omega(\log N)$ steps. The question that we address in this work is the following: are there read-optimal implementations of these restricted-use objects for which the asymptotic step-complexity of update operations is sub-logarithmic?

We present tradeoffs between the step-complexity of read and update operations on these objects, establishing that updating a read-optimal counter or snapshot incurs $\Omega(\log N)$ steps. These tradeoffs hold also if compare-and-swap (CAS) operations may be used, in addition to reads and writes.

We also derive a tradeoff between the step-complexities of read and update operations of M-bounded max registers: if the step-complexity of the `ReadMax` operation is $O\big(f(min(N,M))\big)$, then the step-complexity of the `WriteMax` operation is $\Omega(\log \frac{\log min(N,M)}{\log f(min(N,M))})$. It follows from this tradeoff that the step-complexity of `WriteMax` in any read-optimal implementation of a max register from read, write and CAS is $\Omega\big(\log\log min(N,M)\big)$. On the positive side, we present a wait-free implementation of an M-bounded max register from read, write and CAS for which the step complexities of `ReadMax` and `WriteMax` operations are $O(1)$ and $O\big(\log min(N,M)\big)$, respectively.

*Partially supported by the Israel Science Foundation (grant number 1227/10) and by the Lynne and William Frankel Center for Computing Science at Ben-Gurion University.

PODC'14, July 15–18, 2014, Paris, France.
Copyright 2014 ACM 978-1-4503-2944-6/14/07 ...$15.00.
http://dx.doi.org/10.1145/2611462.2611472.

Categories and Subject Descriptors

D.1.3 [**Software**]: Programming Techniques—*Concurrent Programming*

Keywords

Counter, max register, snapshot, restricted-use objects.

1. INTRODUCTION

Concurrent objects are often constructed only for a restricted use. Their use can be restricted either by limiting the number of operations applied to them (e.g., an *atomic snapshot* object that only supports a limited number of `Update` operations), or by passing bounded arguments to the operations applied to them (e.g., a *max register* that supports only writes of values below some threshold).

Recent work established that some restricted-use objects admit polylogarithmic step-complexity wait-free [10] implementations using only reads and writes. Aspnes, Attiya and Censor-Hillel [2] presented a wait-free implementation of an M-bounded max register that supports a `WriteMax` operation that writes a value to the max register, and a `ReadMax` operation that returns the largest value previously written. Both these operations have step-complexity of $O(\log M)$. By using max register as a building block, they constructed an efficient wait-free counter. `CounterRead` operations on the counter incur a number of steps logarithmic in N, the number of processes sharing the implementation. If the counter is required to support only a limited number of `CounterIncrement` operations (polynomial in N), then the step complexity of `CounterIncrement` operations is $O(\log^2 N)$. Restricted-use max registers and counters have already been used for devising efficient randomized consensus [5] and mutual exclusion algorithms [7].

More recently, Aspnes et al. [3] presented an implementation of restricted-use atomic snapshots. For polynomially-many updates, the step-complexities of the `Scan` and `Update` operations in their implementation are $O(\log N)$ and $O(\log^3 N)$, respectively.

Are the step-complexities of these implementations asymptotically optimal? For read operations, it was shown that they are. Assuming (as we do in the rest of this paper) polynomially-many updates, Aspnes et al. [2] proved an $\Omega(\log M)$ step lower bound on `ReadMax` operations for obstruction-free implementations of M-bounded max registers. They also proved an $\Omega(\log N)$ step-complexity lower bound on `CounterRead` operations for obstruction-free counter implementations. This result was later generalized by Aspnes et al. [4] for a class of objects that includes atomic snapshots, establishing an $\Omega(\log N)$ step-complexity lower bound on **Scan** operations for obstruction-free implementations of snapshots.

But what about the step-complexity of update operations on these objects? The **WriteMax** operation of the max register algorithm presented in [2] has logarithmic step-complexity, and the counter **CounterIncrement** and snapshot **Update** operations of the algorithms presented in [2, 3] have poly-logarithmic step-complexities. Can we do better? *Are there read-optimal implementations of these restricted-use objects for which the asymptotic step-complexity of update operations is sub-logarithmic or even constant?* This is the question that we address in this paper.

Our Contributions:
We prove the following tradeoff for counters and atomic snapshots: if the step-complexity of the read operation is $O(f(N))$, then the step-complexity of the update operation is $\Omega(\log \frac{N}{f(N)})$. The tradeoff holds for obstruction-free implementations, even if CAS may be used in addition to reads and writes. Setting $f(N) = \log N$ establishes that for any read-optimal implementation of a counter or snapshot object from reads and writes, the step-complexity of update operations is $\Omega(\log N)$.

For M-bounded max registers, we were only able to obtain a weaker tradeoff: if the step-complexity of the **ReadMax** operation is $O(f(min(N, M)))$, then the step-complexity of the **WriteMax** operation is $\Omega(\log \frac{\log min(N,M)}{\log f(min(N,M))})$. It follows from this tradeoff that the step-complexity of **WriteMax** in any read-optimal implementation of a max register from read, write and CAS is $\Omega(\log\log min(N, M))$. On the positive side, we present a wait-free implementation of an M-bounded max register from read, write and CAS for which the step complexities of **ReadMax** and **WriteMax** operations are $O(1)$ and $O(\log min(N, M))$, respectively.

2. PRELIMINARIES

We consider a standard model of an asynchronous shared memory system, in which processes communicate by applying operations to shared objects. An object is characterized by a domain of possible values and by a set of *operations* that provide the only means to manipulate it. An *implementation* of an object shared by a set $\mathbf{P}= \{p_1, \cdots, p_N\}$ of N processes provides a specific data-representation for the object from a set $\mathbf{B}$ of shared *base objects*, each of which is assigned an initial value; the implementation also provides algorithms for each process in $\mathbf{P}$ to apply each operation to the object being implemented.

A *wait-free* implementation of a concurrent object guarantees that any process can complete an operation in a finite number of its own steps. An *obstruction-free* [11] implementation guarantees only that if a process eventually runs by itself then it completes its operation within a finite number of its own steps. Each *step* consists of some local computation and one shared memory *event*, which is a *primitive operation* (or simply *primitive*) applied atomically to an object in $\mathbf{B}$ that may return a response value. We say that the event *accesses* the object and that it *applies* the primitive to it. We say that an event is *trivial*, if it does not change the value of the base object to which it is applied.

An *execution fragment* is a (finite or infinite) sequence of events. An *execution* is an execution fragment that starts from the *initial configuration*, resulting when processes apply operations to the implemented object as they execute the implementation's algorithm. We let $\perp$ denote the empty execution. For any finite execution fragment E and any execution fragment E', the execution fragment EE' denotes the concatenation of E and E'. Let E and F be two executions. We say that F is *an extension of* E if $F = EE'$ for some execution fragment E'. We say that executions E, E' are *indistinguishable* to process p, if p performs the same events and receives the same responses to these events in both executions. For an execution E and a set of processes P, we let E^{-P} denote the sequence of events obtained by removing all the events issued by the processes of P from E.

If a process has not completed its operation, it has exactly one *enabled* event, which is the next event it will issue, as specified by the algorithm it is using to apply its operation to the implemented object. We say that a process p is *active* after E if p has not completed its operation in E. Operation Φ_1 *precedes* operation Φ_2 in execution E, if Φ_1 completes in E before the first event of Φ_2 has been issued in E.

The *compare-and-swap* (CAS) operation is defined as follows: *CAS(v,expected,new)* changes the value of variable v to *new* only if its value just before CAS is applied is *expected*; in this case, the *CAS* operation returns *true* and we say it is *successful*. Otherwise, CAS does not change the value of v and returns *false*; in this case, we say that the *CAS* was *unsuccessful*. We assume that base objects support only the read, write, and CAS primitives.

A *max register* supports a **WriteMax**(v) operation, which writes the value v to the object, and a **ReadMax** operation; in its sequential specification, **ReadMax** returns the maximum value written by a **WriteMax** operation instance preceding it. In the bounded version of these objects, the max register is only required to satisfy its specification if its associated value does not exceed a certain threshold M. A *counter* object supports a **CounterIncrement** operation and a **CounterRead** operation; the sequential specification of a counter requires that a **CounterRead** operation instance returns the number of **CounterIncrement** operation instances that precede it. An (atomic) *single-writer snapshot* object consist of an array of N *segments*. An **Update** operation by process p_i atomically sets the value of segment i. The **Scan** operation atomically reads the values of all segments.

3. TRADEOFF FOR COUNTERS AND SNAPSHOT OBJECTS

In this section, we prove the following theorem.

THEOREM 1. *Let I be an N-process obstruction-free implementation of a counter from the* read, write *and* CAS *primitives. If the step-complexity of **CounterRead** is $O(f(N))$, then the step-complexity of **CounterIncrement** is $\Omega\left(\log \frac{N}{f(N)}\right)$.*

By way of reduction, we show a similar result for single-writer snapshot objects. A key idea underlying our proofs, previously used by [13], is that the rate at which processes become aware of the existence of others is not too rapid. Our proofs extend a technique presented in [6], based on the following definitions which allow quantifying the extent of inter-process communication.

DEFINITION 1. *Let e be an event applied by process p to a base object o in an execution E, where $E = E_1eE_2$. We say* *that e is* invisible in E, *if either the value of o is not changed by e or if $E_2 = E'e'E''$, e' is a write event to o, p does not take steps in E', and no event in E' is applied to o.*

Informally, an *invisible* event is an event by some process that cannot be observed by other processes. If an event e applied to some object o in an execution E is not *invisible*, we say that *e is visible in E on o.*

We next capture the extent by which processes are aware of the participation of other processes in an execution. Intuitively, a process p is aware of the participation of another process q in an execution if there is (either direct or indirect) information flow from q to p in that execution via shared memory. The following definitions formalize this notion.

DEFINITION 2. *Let e_q be an event by process q in an execution E, which applies a write or a CAS primitive to a base object o. We say that an event e_p in E by process p is* aware *of e_q, if e_p accesses o and at least one of the following holds: 1) There is a prefix E' of E such that e_q is visible on o in E' and e_p is a read or CAS event that follows e_q in E', or 2) there is an event e_r that is aware of e_q in E and e_p is aware of e_r in E. If an event e_p of process p is aware of an event e_q of process q in E, we say that p is* aware *of e_q and that e_p is* aware *of q in E.*

DEFINITION 3. *Process p is* aware *of process q after an execution E if either $p = q$ or if p is aware of an event of q in E. The* awareness set *of p after E, denoted $AW(p, E)$, is the set of processes that p is aware of after E.*

DEFINITION 4. *Let E be an execution, o be a base object, and q be a process. We say that o* is familiar *with q after E if there is an event e, visible on o in E, such that $E = E_1eE_2$ and e is an application of a write or a CAS primitive to o by some process r such that $q \in AW(r, E_1e)$. The* familiarity set *of o after E, denoted $F(o, E)$, contains all processes that o is familiar with after E.*

A more general version of the following lemma for implementations that use *read*, *write* and *k-CAS* primitives appears in [6]. For the sake of presentation completeness, we provide here a simpler proof for our model.

LEMMA 1. *Let E be an execution. Let $\mathcal{M}(E) = \max_{p,o}(\{|AW(p, E)||p \in P\} \cup \{|F(o, E)||o \in B\})$ be the maximum size of all familiarity and awareness sets after E. Let S be a set of enabled events by processes that are active after E, each about to apply a read, write or CAS primitive. Then there is a schedule $\sigma(E, S)$ of these events such that $\mathcal{M}(E\sigma(E, S)) \leq 3 \cdot \mathcal{M}(E)$.*

PROOF. First, we schedule all *read*, trivial *CAS* and trivial *write* events in an arbitrary order. Let σ_1 denote the resulting execution fragment. No event in σ_1 is visible, hence $\forall o \in B : F(o, E\sigma_1) = F(o, E) \leq \mathcal{M}(E)$. Moreover, for every $p \in P$ that takes a step in σ_1: $AW(p, E\sigma) \leq AW(p, E) + \max_o(\{|F(o, E)||o \in B\}) \leq 2 \cdot \mathcal{M}(E)$.

We next schedule all remaining *write* events (in an arbitrary order) and let σ_2 denote the resulting execution fragment. Consider all the events of σ_2 that access a specific base object o, if there are any. Only the last of them, denoted by e_l, is visible in $E\sigma_1\sigma_2$; let p_l be the process that issues e_l. Consequently, $F(o, E\sigma_1\sigma_2) = F(o, E) + AW(p_l, E) \leq 2 \cdot \mathcal{M}(E)$. Moreover, for every $p \in P$ that takes a step in σ_2: $AW(p, E\sigma) = AW(p, E) \leq \mathcal{M}(E)$.

Finally, we schedule all remaining *CAS* events (in an arbitrary order) and denote the resulting execution fragment by σ_3. Consider all events of σ_3 that access a specific base object o, if there are any. Let e_f be the first of these events and let p_f be a process that issues e_f. We consider two cases.

1. If o was written in σ_2, then its value after $E\sigma_1\sigma_2$ differs from the *expected* parameter of e_f and of all the other *CAS* events of σ_3. Thus, all these events are trivial, hence: $F(o, E\sigma_1\sigma_2\sigma_3) = F(o, E\sigma_1\sigma_2) \leq 2 \cdot \mathcal{M}(E)$. Moreover, for every $p \in P$ that takes a step in σ_3, $AW(p, E\sigma) \leq AW(p, E) + F(o, E\sigma_1\sigma_2) \leq 3 \cdot \mathcal{M}(E)$.

2. If o was not written in σ_2, then e_f is non-trivial and does changes the value of o, making all consequent *CAS* events in σ_3 trivial. Hence $F(o, E\sigma_1\sigma_2\sigma_3) = F(o, E\sigma_1) + AW(p_f, E) \leq 2 \cdot \mathcal{M}(E)$. Moreover, for every $p \in P$ that takes a step in σ_3: $AW(p, E\sigma) \leq AW(p, E) + F(o, E) + AW(p_f, E) \leq 3 \cdot \mathcal{M}(E)$. □

LEMMA 2. *Let E be an execution and let $p \in P$ be a process that issues events in E. Let E' be an execution obtained from E in the following manner. First, all the events issued by p are removed from E. Then, for every process $q \neq p$, all the events of q that are aware of p are removed. Then E' is an execution.*

PROOF. Let $e_q \in E'$ be an event by process q such that $E' = E'_1e_qE'_2$. Since $e_q \in E$ we can write $E = E_1e_qE_2$. If $|E'_1| = k$ we denote E_1 by σ_k and E'_1 by σ'_k. By induction on $k = 1, \cdots |E'|$ we prove that σ'_k is an execution.
<u>Base</u>: σ'_0 is empty and is obviously an execution.
<u>Hypothesis</u>: σ'_k is an execution.
<u>Step</u>: $\sigma'_{k+1} = \sigma'_ke_q$. From induction hypothesis, σ_k is an execution. Assume towards a contradiction that σ_ke_q is not an execution, i.e. e_q returns different responses when scheduled after σ_k and after σ'_k. Then e_q is aware of some event e_1 that was removed from σ_k. However, from Definition 2 and from the way E' is constructed from E, it follows that there is a finite sequence of events $e_q, e_1, \ldots, e_j$, each of which is aware of its successor, such that e_j is an event of p. It follows from Definition 2 that e_q is aware of p and cannot appear in σ'_{k+1}. This is a contradiction. □

LEMMA 3. *Let I be a linearizable obstruction-free implementation of a counter and let EE_1 be an execution of I such that each of the processes of $P' = \{p_1, \ldots, p_{N-1}\}$ completes a `CounterIncrement` operation in E, and E_1 is an extension of E, in which p_N performs to completion a single `CounterRead` operation. Then $|AW(p_N, EE_1)| = N$.*

PROOF. Assume towards a contradiction that $|AW(p_N, EE_1)| < N$. Hence, p_N is not aware of some process $p_i \in P'$. We construct from EE_1 a new execution E' in the following manner. First, we remove from EE_1 all the events of p_i. Then, for each $p_k \in P', p_k \neq p_i$, if any of p_k's events in E is aware of p_i, then we remove all the events of p_k starting from the first event of p_k that is aware of p_i. Since p_N is unaware of p_i, all its events are preserved in E'. From Lemma 2, E' is an execution.

From Definitions 2-3, since p_N is unaware of p_i in EE_1, EE_1 and E' are indistinguishable to p_N. From linearizability, p_N'th `CounterRead` operation returns $N - 1$ in EE_1 but must return a smaller value in E', since at most $N-2$ CounterIncrement operations were completed in E'. This is a contradiction. □

PROOF OF THEOREM 1. We iteratively construct an execution $E = \sigma_1\sigma_2, \ldots, \sigma_r$, in which each of the processes of $P' = \{p_1, \ldots, p_{N-1}\}$ completes a CounterIncrement operation. For $j \in \{1, \ldots, r\}$, we let $E_j = \sigma_1\sigma_2, \ldots, \sigma_j$. Our construction maintains the invariant that for all $j \in \{1, \ldots, r\}$ and $o \in \mathbf{B}$, $|F(o, E_j)| \leq 3^j$.

In the initial configuration, the familiarity set of all base objects is empty, the awareness set of each process contains only itself, and each of the processes of P' has an enabled event. Let S denote the set of these events. From Lemma 1, there is a schedule $\sigma_1 = \sigma(\perp, S)$ such that $\mathcal{M}(\sigma_1) = \mathcal{M}(E_1) \leq 3$.

Assume we have constructed execution E_i. If a subset $Q \subseteq P'$ of processes did not complete their CounterIncrement operations in E_i, then we construct execution $E_{i+1} = E_i\sigma_{i+1}$ as follows. Let S denote the set of the events of the processes of Q that are enabled after E_i. From Lemma 1, there is a schedule $\sigma_{i+1} = \sigma(E_i, S)$ such that $\mathcal{M}(E_{i+1}) \leq 3\mathcal{M}(E_i) \leq 3^{i+1}$. We proceed in this manner until all the processes of P' complete their operations or until we complete $\lceil \log_3 \frac{N}{f(N)} \rceil$ iterations, whatever occurs first.

Let p_l be a process that does not terminate its CounterIncrement operation in E_{r-1}. There must be such a process, as otherwise the construction of E would have stopped after the $(r-1)$'th iteration. Clearly from our construction, p_l issues r events in E. To prove the theorem, we will show that $r = \Omega\left(\log_3 \frac{N}{f(N)}\right)$.

Assume towards a contradiction that $r = o\left(\log_3 \frac{N}{f(N)}\right)$, implying that all the processes of P' completed their CounterIncrement operations in E. From our construction, the following holds:

$$\forall o \in \mathbf{B} : |F(o, E)| \leq 3^r = o(\frac{N}{f(N)}). \quad (1)$$

Let E_1 be an extension of E in which p_N performs a CounterRead operation. Since p_N performs $O(f(N))$ steps in E_1, it accesses at most $O(f(N))$ base objects. Therefore, it follows from Equation 1 that $|AW(p_N, EE_1)| = o(N)$. This is a contradiction to Lemma 3. □

Given an N-component single-writer snapshot object, it is straightforward to implement a counter as follows. To perform a CounterIncrement operation, process p_i increments the value of the i'th component by performing a single Update operation. To read the counter, a process performs a single Scan operation and returns the sum of all components. We get the following:

COROLLARY 1. *Let I be an N-process obstruction-free implementation of a single-writer snapshot object from the* read, write *and* CAS *primitives. If the step-complexity of Scan is $O(f(N))$, then the step-complexity of Update is $\Omega\left(\log \frac{N}{f(N)}\right)$.*

Jayanti presented an *f-arrays*-based [14] construction of counters and snapshots where CounterRead and Scan operations have constant step complexity, and CounterIncrement and Update operations have logarithmic step complexity. His construction uses the *load-link/store-conditional* primitives in addition to reads and writes, but can be made to work also using CAS instead.

It follows from Theorem 1 and Corollary 1 that no constant-read implementation for these objects from read, write and CAS can have update operations with sub-logarithmic step complexity. This follows also from another work of Jayanti [13] where he shows that the sum of steps performed by a CounterIncrement operation followed by a CounterRead operation (or an Update operation followed by a Scan operation) is logarithmic. The following theorem, however, does not follow from [13].

THEOREM 2. *Let I be a obstruction-free N-process implementation of a counter (respectively single-writer snapshot) object from reads and writes that supports only a limited (polynomial in N) number of CounterIncrement (respectively Update) operations. If the worst-case step complexity of I's CounterRead (respectively Scan) operations is optimal (that is, $O(\log N)$), then the worst-case step-complexity of its CounterIncrement (respectively Update) operations is $\Omega(\log N)$.*

PROOF. Immediate from Theorem 1 and Corollary 1. □

4. TRADEOFF FOR MAX REGISTERS

In this section, we prove the following tradeoff.

THEOREM 3. *Let I be an N-process obstruction-free implementation of an M-bounded* maxRegister *from the* read, write *and* CAS *primitives. Let $K = min(M, N)$. If the step complexity of ReadMax is $O(f(K))$, then there is an execution of I in which each of $\Omega(f(K))$ processes takes $\Omega(\log \frac{\log K}{\log f(K)})$ steps as it performs a single WriteMax operation.*

Our proofs combine and extend techniques from [1, 6, 15]. We start by describing our proof strategy. This is followed by formal proofs.

We construct an execution involving $\Theta(f(K))$ processes, each performing $\Omega(\log \frac{\log K}{\log f(K)})$ steps. The construction proceeds iteratively, where iteration i constructs execution E_i. Initially, we have a set $P' = \{p_1, \cdots, p_{K-1}\}$ of $K-1$ processes such that, for $i \in \{1, \ldots, K-1\}$, p_i is about to perform a WriteMax (i) operation.

A key concept in our construction is that of an *essential set*. Each execution E_i is associated with an essential set $\mathcal{E}_i \subseteq P'$ (the *essential set of* E_i) of size $\Omega(\sqrt[2^i]{K})$ that satisfies the following properties: 1) Each process in $\mathcal{E}_i$ performs exactly i steps in E_i. 2) If p is in $\mathcal{E}_i$, then no $q \neq p$ is aware of p after E_i. 3) No base object is familiar with more than a single process in $\mathcal{E}_i$ after E_i. 4) The identifiers of the processes of $\mathcal{E}_i$ are larger than those of all other processes that issue events in E_i.

The properties stated above guarantee that not too many of the processes of $\mathcal{E}_i$ may complete their operations in E_i. To see why, consider a set $F \subseteq \mathcal{E}_i$ of m such processes. As we prove, a ReadMax operation Φ by p_K, scheduled after E_i, must access m distinct base objects in the course of its execution - those base objects that are familiar with the processes of F. If Φ fails to read even one such base object (say, the one familiar with p_j), then we can remove all the events issued by $\mathcal{E}_i \backslash \{p_j\}$ from $E_i\Phi$. In this case, Φ will fail to return j, which is the largest value written prior to Φ's execution. It follows that at most $O(f(n))$ processes of $\mathcal{E}_i$ can terminate in E_i.

Let us denote by $\mathcal{E}_i^e$ the set of those processes of $\mathcal{E}_i$ that remain active after E_i. Our goal is to pick a relatively large subset $\mathcal{E}_{i+1} \subseteq \mathcal{E}_i^e$, each of whose processes can perform an additional step, while limiting information flow so that properties 1)-4) above hold for $\mathcal{E}_{i+1}$. We now describe how we select $\mathcal{E}_{i+1}$ and construct E_{i+1}.

First, all the events of the processes of $\mathcal{E}_i \setminus \mathcal{E}_i^e$ are removed. We say that these processes are *erased from the execution* (or simply *erased*). Then, we consider the next event that will be issued by the processes of $\mathcal{E}_i^e$. Specifically, we consider the number j of distinct base-objects that these events will access. The following two cases exist.

Case 1 (Low Contention): If $j > \sqrt{|\mathcal{E}_i^e|}$, we pick an arbitrary set A' of $\sqrt{|\mathcal{E}_i^e|}$ processes accessing *distinct* base objects. We then pick a subset $A \subseteq A'$ such that no step by a process of A is about to access a base object that has another process of A in its familiarity set. As we show, a constant fraction of the processes of A' remain in A. The set A is defined as $\mathcal{E}_{i+1}$.

To construct E_{i+1}, the processes of $\mathcal{E}_i^e \setminus A$ are also erased. E_{i+1} is obtained by extending the remaining execution by allowing each of the processes of $\mathcal{E}_{i+1}$ to perform an additional step. We refer to this case as the *low-contention scenario.* Figure 1 illustrates the construction of $\mathcal{E}_{i+1}$ in the low-contention scenario.

Figure 1: Low contention case for iteration i

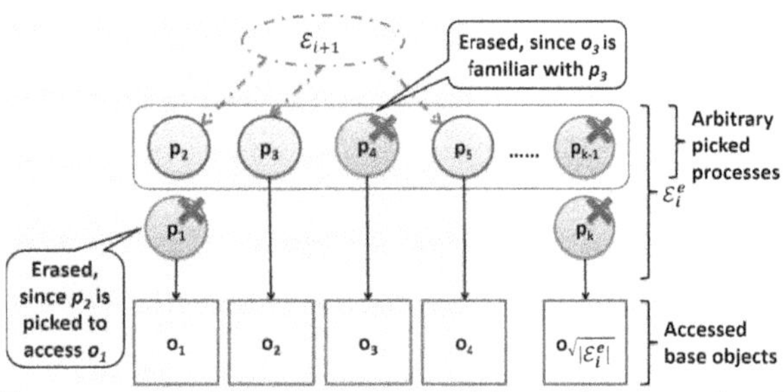

The processes that are not *erased* from the execution form the *essential set* $\mathcal{E}_{i+1}$.

Case 2 (High Contention): Otherwise $(j \leq \sqrt{|\mathcal{E}^e|})$, we pick an arbitrary base object o accessed by a subset (denoted P^o) of at least $\sqrt{|\mathcal{E}^e|}$ processes from $\mathcal{E}_i^e$. We erase all the processes of $\mathcal{E}_i \setminus P^o$ from the execution. As for the processes of P^o, there are two possibilities. Either we can schedule their steps so that none of them becomes visible on o (in which case they will all belong to $\mathcal{E}_{i+1}$); or we schedule them so that a *single* process, say p_k, becomes visible and a constant fraction of the processes of P^o have bigger identifiers. These are the processes that will form $\mathcal{E}_{i+1}$. As for p_k, we say that it is *halted.* It will not issue additional events in later iterations, nor will it be a part of essential sets of later iterations. The rest of the processes of P^o are erased from the execution. We refer to this case as the *high contention* scenario. Figure 2 illustrates the construction of $\mathcal{E}_{i+1}$ in the high-contention scenario.

The high-level structure of our construction is depicted in Figure 3. As we show, the construction may proceed for $\Omega(\log \frac{\log K}{\log f(K)})$ iterations. Before providing the formal proofs, we give a few required definitions. In the following, we let E denote an execution of a max register implementation I and we let P be the set of processes taking steps in E.

Figure 2: High contention case for iteration i

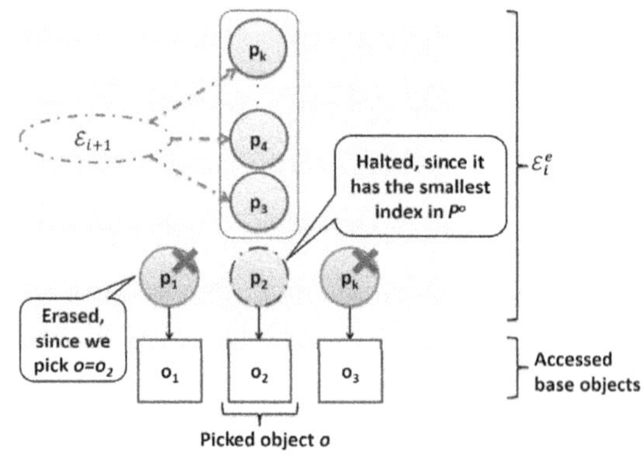

The processes not in P^o are *erased* from the execution. Process p_2 becomes *halted.* The rest of the processes in P^o form the *essential set* $\mathcal{E}_{i+1}$.

Figure 3: The construction of execution E

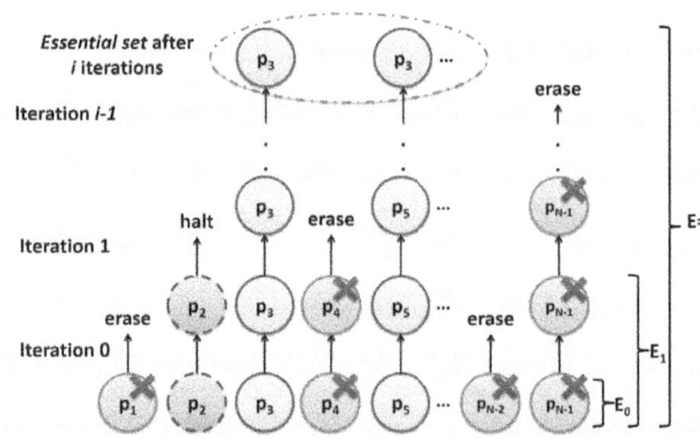

Erased processes do not appear in E. *Halted* processes issue an event in each construction iteration until they become halted. *Essential set* processes issue an event in every construction iteration.

DEFINITION 5. *Let O be the set of all base objects used by I. We say that a process $p \in P$ is* hidden *after E, if $\forall p' \in P : p \in AW(p', E) \rightarrow p = p'$ (informally, no process except p is aware of p after E). We say that $P' \subseteq P$ is a* hidden set *after E, if the processes of P' are* hidden *after E and if $\forall o \in O : |F(o, E) \cap P| \leq 1$ (informally, each base object in O is familiar with at most a single process in P after E).*

CLAIM 1. *Let P' be a set of processes hidden after E, then $E' = E^{-P'}$ is an execution.*

PROOF. From Definition 5, for all $p \in P'$, no process but p is aware of p after E, hence the claim follows from Lemma 2. □

DEFINITION 6. *We say that $P' \subseteq P$ is a* supreme *set, if $\forall p_i \in P', \forall p_j \in P \setminus P' : i > j$ holds (informally, the processes of P' have the highest indices out of all processes that issue events in the execution).*

DEFINITION 7. *We say that $P' \subseteq P$ is an i-step* essential set *of E, if P' is a supreme set hidden after E, such that every process in it issues exactly i events in E.*

LEMMA 4. *Let E_i be an execution and let $\mathcal{E}_i$ be an i-step essential set of E_i. Let $\mathcal{E}^e \subseteq \mathcal{E}_i$ be the set of those processes of $\mathcal{E}_i$ that have an enabled event after E_i and let $m = |\mathcal{E}^e|$ denote its size. If $m \geq 81$, then there exists an execution E_{i+1} with an $(i+1)$-step essential set of size at least $\frac{\sqrt{m}}{3} - 2$.*

PROOF. Let $S = \{e_1 \ldots e_m\}$ be the set of events that the processes of $\mathcal{E}^e$ are about to issue after E_i. Let O denote the set of all base objects accessed by the events of S. Also, for $o \in O$, let $P^o \subseteq \mathcal{E}^e$ denote the set of all processes from $\mathcal{E}^e$ that are about to access o. There are two cases to consider.

Case 1 (Low Contention): For each base object $o \in O$: $|P^o| \leq \sqrt{m}$. In this case the steps by $\mathcal{E}^e$ access $k \geq \sqrt{m}$ distinct base objects. For every accessed object o we arbitrary pick a process $p^o \in P^o$ and denote the resulting set by P". We build an undirected graph $G =< V, E >$ such that $V = \{v^o | p^o \in P"\}$ and $E = \{< v^o, v^{o'} > | p^{o'} \in F(o, E_i)\}$. It follows immediately from the construction that $|V| = |P"| = k$.

$P" \subseteq \mathcal{E}_i$, hence from Definitions 5 and 7, $\forall o \in O$: $|F(o, E_i) \cap P"| \leq 1$, i.e $|E| \leq k$. Consequently, the average degree of G is $d \leq 2$. From Turán's theorem [9], there is an independent set $V' \subseteq V$ such that $|V'| = \lceil \frac{k}{3} \rceil$. Let $\mathcal{E}_{i+1} = \{p^o | v^o \in V'\}$ and let σ be a sequence of events in which we schedule all the events by the processes of $\mathcal{E}_{i+1}$ (in some arbitrary order). Let $K = \mathcal{E}_i \backslash \mathcal{E}_{i+1}$. From Claim 1, $E_{i+1} = E_i{}^{-K}\sigma$ is an execution. We now show that $\mathcal{E}_{i+1}$ is an $(i+1)$-step essential set of E_{i+1}.

No process $p^o \in \mathcal{E}_{i+1}$ becomes aware of $p^{o'} \in \mathcal{E}_{i+1}$ in σ, otherwise $p^{o'} \in F(o, E_i)$, i.e $< v^o, v^{o'} > \in E$ in contradiction to the fact that V' is an independent set. Moreover, every process in σ accesses a distinct object, i.e. $F(o, E_i\sigma) \subseteq F(o, E_i) \cup AW(p^o, E_i)$. If $p^{o'} \in \mathcal{E}_{i+1} \cap F(o, E_i\sigma)$, then $p^{o'} \in F(o, E_i)$, i.e $< v^o, v^{o'} > \in E$ in contradiction to the fact that V' is an independent set. Consequently, o is familiar with at most a single process of $\mathcal{E}_{i+1}$ after E_{i+1}. It follows from Definition 5 that $\mathcal{E}_{i+1}$ is hidden after E_{i+1}.

$\mathcal{E}_i$ is an essential set of E_i, $\mathcal{E}_{i+1} \subset \mathcal{E}_i$ and all the processes of $\mathcal{E}_i \backslash \mathcal{E}_{i+1}$ are erased, hence $\mathcal{E}_{i+1}$ is a supreme set of E_{i+1}. Since $\mathcal{E}_i$ is an i-step essential set of E_i, every process of $\mathcal{E}_i$ issues exactly i events in E_i. It follows immediately from our construction of E_{i+1} that every process of $\mathcal{E}_{i+1}$ issues exactly $i+1$ events in E_{i+1}. Thus, $\mathcal{E}_{i+1}$ is an $(i+1)$-step essential set. Finally, it is immediate from our construction that $|\mathcal{E}_{i+1}| \geq \frac{\sqrt{m}}{3} - 1$.

Case 2 (High Contention): There is a base object $o \in O$ such that $|P^o| \geq \sqrt{m} + 1$. We consider the processes of P^o according to the type of operation they are about to apply to o after E_i: we let $P^o{}_C \subseteq P^o$ denote those processes about to apply a CAS event that will change the value of o (if applied immediately after E_i); we let $P^o{}_W \subseteq P^o$ denote those processes about to apply a *write* event, and we let $P^o{}_T \subseteq P^o$ denote those processes about to apply a *read* or a CAS event that will not change the value of o. We need to consider the following three sub-cases.

Sub-case 1: $|P^o{}_C| \geq \frac{\sqrt{m}}{3}$. Let $S = F(o, E_i) \cap \mathcal{E}^e$. After execution E_i, object o is familiar with at most a single process of $\mathcal{E}^e$, thus $|S| \leq 1$. Let p_l be the process with the smallest identifier of all the processes of $P^o{}_C$ and let $\mathcal{E}_{i+1} = P^o{}_C \backslash (\{p_l\} \cup S\})$ (since $m \geq 81$, $\mathcal{E}_{i+1}$ is non-empty). Let σ be a sequence of events in which we schedule all the CAS events by the processes of $\mathcal{E}_{i+1}$ (in some arbitrary order), preceded by the non-trivial CAS by p_l. Let $K = (\mathcal{E}_i \backslash P^o{}_C) \cup S$. From Claim 4, $E_{i+1} = E_i{}^{-K}\sigma$ is an execution. We now show that $\mathcal{E}_{i+1}$ is an $(i+1)$-step essential set of E_{i+1}.

Since the CAS event by p_l changes the value of o, the CAS events by the processes of $\mathcal{E}_{i+1}$ are trivial and invisible on o after σ. Hence, all the processes of $\mathcal{E}_{i+1}$ become aware in σ only of processes of $F = (F(o_i, E_i) \backslash K) \cup \{p_l\}$. Since $F \cap \mathcal{E}_{i+1} = \emptyset$, these processes do not become aware of one another in σ. Moreover, no base object except o becomes familiar with a new process, and o's familiarity set may only be extended by $AW(p_l, E_i)$, hence o is familiar with no process of $\mathcal{E}_{i+1}$ after E_{i+1}. It follows from Definition 5 that $\mathcal{E}_{i+1}$ is hidden after E_{i+1}.

$\mathcal{E}_i$ is an essential set of E_i, $\mathcal{E}_{i+1} \subset \mathcal{E}_i$, all the processes of $\mathcal{E}_i \backslash \mathcal{E}_{i+1}$ except for p_l are erased and p_l's identifier is smaller than the identifiers of the processes of $\mathcal{E}_{i+1}$, hence $\mathcal{E}_{i+1}$ is a supreme set of E_{i+1}. Since $\mathcal{E}_i$ is an i-step essential set of E_i, every process of $\mathcal{E}_i$ issues exactly i events in E_i. It follows immediately from our construction of E_{i+1} that every process of $\mathcal{E}_{i+1}$ issues exactly $i+1$ events in E_{i+1}. Thus, $\mathcal{E}_{i+1}$ is an $(i+1)$-step essential set. Finally, it is immediate from our construction that $|\mathcal{E}_{i+1}| \geq \frac{\sqrt{m}}{3} - 2$.

Sub-case 2: $|P^o{}_W| \geq \frac{\sqrt{m}}{3}$. Let p_l be the process with the smallest identifier of all the processes of $P^o{}_W$ and let $\mathcal{E}_{i+1} = P^o{}_W \backslash \{p_l\}$ (since $m \geq 81$, $\mathcal{E}_{i+1}$ is non-empty). Let σ be a sequence of events in which we schedule all *write* events (in some arbitrary order) by the processes of $\mathcal{E}_{i+1}$ followed by the *write* by p_l. Let $K = \mathcal{E}_i \backslash P^o{}_W$. Since $\mathcal{E}_i$ is hidden after E_i, it follows from Claim 4 that $E_{i+1} = E_i{}^{-K}\sigma$ is an execution. We now show that $\mathcal{E}_{i+1}$ is an $(i+1)$-step essential set of E_{i+1}.

Since σ consists of write events, no process becomes aware of another process in σ. Moreover, no base object except o becomes familiar with a new process, and o's familiarity set may only be extended by $p_l \notin \mathcal{E}_{i+1}$, hence o is familiar with at most a single process of $\mathcal{E}_{i+1}$ after E_{i+1}. It follows from Definition 5 that $\mathcal{E}_{i+1}$ is hidden after E_{i+1}.

$\mathcal{E}_i$ is an essential set of E_i, $\mathcal{E}_{i+1} \subset \mathcal{E}_i$ and p_l's identifier is smaller than the identifiers of the processes of $\mathcal{E}_{i+1}$, hence $\mathcal{E}_{i+1}$ is a supreme set of E_{i+1}. Since $\mathcal{E}_i$ is an i-step essential set of E_i, every process of $\mathcal{E}_i$ issues exactly i events in E_i. It follows immediately from our construction of E_{i+1} that every process of $\mathcal{E}_{i+1}$ issues exactly $i+1$ events in E_{i+1}. Thus, $\mathcal{E}_{i+1}$ is an $(i+1)$-step essential set.

Sub-case 3: $|P^o{}_T| \geq \frac{\sqrt{m}}{3}$. Let $S = F(o, E_i) \cap \mathcal{E}^e$. After execution E_i, object o is familiar with at most a single process of $\mathcal{E}^e$, thus $|S| \leq 1$. Let $\mathcal{E}_{i+1} = P^o{}_T \backslash S$ (since $m \geq 81$, $\mathcal{E}_{i+1}$ is non-empty) and let σ be a sequence of events in which we schedule all *read* and trivial CAS events by the processes of $\mathcal{E}_{i+1}$ in some arbitrary order. Let $K = (\mathcal{E}_i \backslash P^o{}_T) \cup S$. Since $\mathcal{E}_i$ is hidden after E_i, it follows from Claim 4 that $E_{i+1} = E_i{}^{-K}\sigma$ is an execution. We now show that $\mathcal{E}_{i+1}$ is an $(i+1)$-step essential set of E_{i+1}.

All the processes of $\mathcal{E}_{i+1}$ become aware in σ only of processes in $F = F(o_i, E_i) \backslash K$. Since $F \cap \mathcal{E}_{i+1} = \emptyset$, these processes do not become aware of one another in σ. Moreover, all events in σ are trivial, thus the familiarity set of o (or any other object) is not changed. It follows from Definition 5 that $\mathcal{E}_{i+1}$ is hidden after E_{i+1}.

$\mathcal{E}_i$ is an essential set of E_i, $\mathcal{E}_{i+1} \subset \mathcal{E}_i$ and all the processes of $\mathcal{E}_i \backslash \mathcal{E}_{i+1}$ are erased, hence $\mathcal{E}_{i+1}$ is a supreme set of E_{i+1}. Since $\mathcal{E}_i$ is an i-step essential set of E_i, every process of $\mathcal{E}_i$ issues exactly i events in E_i. It follows immediately from our construction of E_{i+1} that every process of $\mathcal{E}_{i+1}$ issues exactly $i+1$ events in E_{i+1}. Thus, $\mathcal{E}_{i+1}$ is an $(i+1)$-step essential set. Finally, it is immediate from our construction that $|\mathcal{E}_{i+1}| \geq \frac{\sqrt{m}}{3} - 1$. □

LEMMA 5. *Let E be an execution in which a process p_i that is hidden after E completes its WriteMax operation. Assume also that p_i wrote a (unique) maximum value in E. Let p_j be a process that issued no events in E and let Φ be an execution of a ReadMax operation by p_j immediately after E. Then p_j must access in Φ an object familiar with p_i.*

PROOF. Assume towards a contradiction that p_j accesses no such object. Consider execution E' obtained from E by removing all the events by p_i from E. From Claim 1, E' is an execution. Since p_i is hidden in E, E' is indistinguishable from E for p_j. Consequently, p_j performs Φ also after E' and returns the same response in both $E\Phi$ and $E'\Phi$. This is a contradiction since the maximum values written in E and E' differ. □

LEMMA 6. *Let E be an execution in which each process $p_i \in P \subseteq \{p_1, \cdots, p_{K-1}\}$ performs a WriteMax(i) operation. Let A be a a hidden and supreme set of E and let $\mathcal{E}^c \subseteq A$ denote the set of those processes of A that complete their operation in E. If the step complexity of ReadMax operations is at most m, then $|\mathcal{E}^c| \leq m$.*

PROOF. We iteratively construct an execution E' such that, if $|\mathcal{E}^c| > m$, then process p_K must miss the maximum value written to the max object when it performs its `ReadMax` operation after E'. We denote the execution obtained after r iterations as E'_r. Our construction starts with $E'_0 = E^{-A \backslash \mathcal{E}^c}$. From Claim 1, E'_0 is an execution.

We construct E'_r from E'_{r-1} as follows. Let e_r be the r-th event about to be issued by p_K after E'_{r-1} and let o be the object it will access. We let $I = F(o, E'_{r-1}) \cap \mathcal{E}^c$ and $E'_r = {E'_{r-1}}^{-I} e_r$. Since $\mathcal{E}^c$ is a hidden set, $|I| \leq 1$, hence E'_r is either $E'_{r-1} e_r$ or ${E'_{r-1}}^{-\{p_i\}} e_r$ for some $p_i \in \mathcal{E}^c$. Since E'_{r-1} is an execution and since p_i (if it exists) is hidden, it follows from Claim 1 that E'_r is an execution. Since none of the events of p_K access an object that is familiar with a process of A, $E'_r e_1 \cdots e_r$ is an execution as well. The construction stops after p_K takes its last step, hence it stops after at most m iterations.

Assume towards a contradiction that $|\mathcal{E}^c| > m$. Let K be the set of processes erased in the course of the construction of E'. Since $|K| \leq m$, the set $\mathcal{E}^c \backslash K$ is non-empty. Let p_{max} be the process in $\mathcal{E}^c \backslash K$ with maximum ID. Since $p_{max} \in \mathcal{E}^c \subseteq A$ and from construction, p_{max} is the process that performed in E' the `WriteMax` operation with the maximum operand. Moreover, p_{max} completed its operation in E'.

From Lemma 5, p_K must access an object familiar with p_{max}. However, our construction of E' ensures that none of the objects accessed by p_K is familiar with a process of $\mathcal{E}^c$. This is a contradiction. □

PROOF OF THEOREM 3. We construct an execution E with the required properties. The construction proceeds in iterations. In iteration i, we construct an execution E_i that has an i-step essential set $\mathcal{E}_i$ of size $\Omega(K^{1/3^i})$. Initially, we have a set $P' = \{p_1, \cdots, p_{K-1}\}$ of $K-1$ processes such that, for $i \in \{1, \ldots, K-1\}$, p_i is about to perform a `WriteMax` (i) operation.

For the base case, we let E_0 be the empty execution and claim that P' is a 0-step essential set. In the initial configuration, all processes are aware only of themselves and all base objects have empty familiarity sets. Hence, all processes are hidden after the empty execution . Moreover, P' is supreme and all processes in it issue 0 events in E_0. It follows from Definition 7 that P' is a 0-step essential set of E_0.

The construction stops after the first iteration i^*, such that at least half of the processes of $\mathcal{E}_{i^*}$ terminate in E_{i^*}, or $|\mathcal{E}_{i^*+1}| < f(K)$, whichever happens first. In the first case, from Lemma 6:

$$|\mathcal{E}_{i^*}| \leq 2 \cdot f(K). \quad (2)$$

In the second case, we get from Lemma 4 and from our construction:

$$|\mathcal{E}_{i^*}| = O(|\mathcal{E}_{i^*+1}|)^2 = O(f(K))^2. \quad (3)$$

On the other hand, from Lemma 4, we have:

$$\forall i \in \{1, \ldots, i^*\} : |\mathcal{E}_i| \geq \frac{1}{2}(|\mathcal{E}_{i-1}|)^{1/2} - 2 = \Omega(|\mathcal{E}_{i-1}|)^{1/3} \implies |\mathcal{E}_i| = \Omega(K^{1/3^i}). \quad (4)$$

Combining Equations 2, 3 and the right-hand equality of Equation 4, we get $i^* = \Omega(\log \frac{\log K}{\log f(K)})$. The theorem now follows from the fact that each process in $\mathcal{E}_{i^*}$ issues i^* events in E_{i^*} and the fact that, from our construction, $|\mathcal{E}_{i^*}| \geq f(K)$. □

The following is immediate from Theorem 3.

THEOREM 4. *Let I be a obstruction-free N-process implementation of an M-bounded max register from read, write and CAS. If the worst-case step complexity of I's ReadMax operation is $O(\log M)$, then the worst-case step-complexity of its WriteMax operation is $\Omega(\log\log min(N, M))$.*

5. MAX REGISTER IMPLEMENTATIONS USING READ/WRITE/CAS

We now present a wait-free *maxRegister* algorithm, using *read*, *write* and *CAS* primitives. The step-complexity of `ReadMax` operations is constant and the step complexity of a `WriteMax`(v) operation is $O(\log min(N, v))$. The algorithm uses a binary tree T, every node of which stores an integer *value* (initialized to $-\infty$) and pointers to its child nodes and parent node. The left sub-tree of T, denoted as T_L, is an unbalanced binary tree with $N-1$ leaves such that its i-th leaf is at depth $O(\log i)$ (the construction of such a tree, referred to as a B_1 tree, is introduced in [8]). The right sub-tree of T, denoted as T_R, is a complete binary tree with N leaves. An illustration of the data structure for $N = 4$ processes is depicted in Figure 4.

The pseudo-code appears in Algorithm A. To perform a `ReadMax`, a process simply reads the *value* stored in the root. To perform a `WriteMax` (v) operation, process p_i writes v to a leaf $\mathcal{L}$ and attempts to propagate it up to the root of T in a manner we soon explain. $\mathcal{L}$ is selected as follows: if $v < N$

Figure 4: The data structure for *maxRegister* shared by $N = 4$ processes

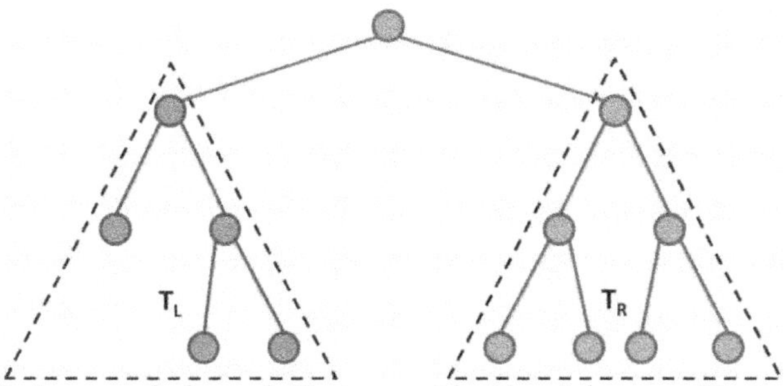

T_L is an unbalanced B_1 tree with $N-1$ leaves. T_R is a complete binary tree with N leaves.

Algorithm A Max Register

```
1:  function READ
2:      return T.root.value
3:  procedure PROPAGATE(n)
4:      while n.parent ≠ nil do
5:          n ← node.parent
6:          for i = 1 to 2 do
7:              old_value ← n.value
8:              new_value ← max(n.left_child.value,
                                 n.right_child.value)
9:              CAS(n.value, old_value, new_value)
10: procedure Write_i(value)
11:     if value < N then
12:         L ← T_L.leaves[value]
13:     else
14:         L ← T_R.leaves[i]
15:         old_value ← L.value
16:         if value ≤ old_value then return
17:     L.value ← value
18:     PROPAGATE(L)
```

then $\mathcal{L}$ is the v-th leaf of T_L, otherwise it is the i-th leaf of T_R.

Propagating a value given as operand to a `WriteMax` operation up the tree is implemented by the *Propagate* procedure, which works similarly to the *Tree Algorithm* of Jayanti [14]. At each level of the tree along the path from the leaf to the root, a process computes the maximum of the value of its current node and its sibling and attempts to write this maximum to the parent node by using *CAS*. Since the *CAS* may fail, the computation of the maximum value and the *CAS* are performed twice at each level. This ensures that if the *CAS* failed, then a *CAS* by another process must have succeeded in updating the parent node based on the new value.

Now we prove that Algorithm A is correct and wait-free, that the step-complexity of the `ReadMax` operation is constant and that the step complexity of the `WriteMax(v)` operation is $O(\min(\log N, \log v))$.

Linearizability.

In the following, we prove that Algorithm A is *linearizable* [12]. For every operation Φ_i in an execution E of A, we uniquely identify a *linearization point*, i.e. an event $e_i \in E$ within the time interval of Φ_i. For simplicity and WLOG, we assume that no process tries to write a value which is smaller than the values it has written earlier.

DEFINITION 8. *We say that a node $\mathcal{N}$* counts *an operation Φ after E, if $E = E'eE''$, e is a* visible *event on $\mathcal{N}.value$ and either e is issued in Φ or it was issued by some process p such that*

1. *$E' = E_1e'E_2$, where e' is a* read *by p of $\mathcal{N}'.value$.*
2. *$\mathcal{N}'$ is a child of $\mathcal{N}$ and $\mathcal{N}'$* counts *Φ after E_1.*

We denote the set of all operations counted by $\mathcal{N}$ after E as $\mathcal{C}(N, E)$.

Clearly, if $\mathcal{N}$ counts Φ after E, then it counts Φ in all extensions of E; and if $\mathcal{N}$ does not count Φ after E, then it does not count Φ in any prefix of E.

DEFINITION 9. *For **ReadMax** operation Φ_r in E we define the* linearization point *as the* read *event on $T.root.value$ (line 2). For **WriteMax** operation Φ_w in E we define the* linearization point *as the first event e after which $T.root$ counts Φ_w, i.e. if $E = E_1eE_2$ then $\Phi_w \notin \mathcal{C}(T.root, E_1)$ and $\Phi_w \in \mathcal{C}(T.root, E_1e)$.*

Note that a `WriteMax` operation may be linearized by an event of another `WriteMax` operation.

We let H be the sequential history obtained from E according to the linearization points specified above. We let $e_1 \overset{E}{\prec} e_2$ denote that event e_1 *precedes* event e_2 in E. Moreover, we say that event e *precedes* (is *preceded* by) operation Φ in E if it is issued before the first (after the last) event of Φ and denote this by $e \overset{E}{\prec} \Phi$ ($\Phi \overset{E}{\prec} e$). We now prove the following:

1. H preserves the partial order of operations in E. It is sufficient to prove that the *linearization point* e of every operation Φ is defined uniquely within the time interval of Φ, i.e $\neg(e \overset{E}{\prec} \Phi)$ and $\neg(\Phi \overset{E}{\prec} e)$.
2. H is legal sequential history of *maxRegister*. It is sufficient to prove that every `ReadMax` operation in H returns the maximum value written before it in H.

OBSERVATION 1. *By Definition 9, the* linearization point *e of **ReadMax** operation Φ is a* read *issued by Φ on $T.root.value$. Obviously, e is within the time interval of Φ and is defined uniquely.*

OBSERVATION 2. *By Definition 9, the* linearization point *e of **WriteMax** operation Φ is the first and thus unique event, after which Φ is counted by $T.root$.*

LEMMA 7. *Let Φ be a **WriteMax** operation in E such that its* linearization point *e, as specified by Definition 9, is also in E. Then e does not precede Φ in E.*

PROOF. Assume towards a contradiction that $e \overset{E}{\prec} \Phi$, i.e. $\Phi \in \mathcal{C}(T.root, E'e)$, where $E'e$ is a prefix of E. Since no events of Φ are issued in $E'e$, from Definition 8, some child of $T.root$ counts Φ in $E'e$. We apply this argument recursively until it implies that some leaf $\mathcal{L}$ should count Φ in $E'e$. Consequently, from Definition 8, $\mathcal{L}$ must be written by Φ in $E'e$. On the other hand, Φ issues no events in $E'e$. This is a contradiction. □

Let $\mathcal{N}$ be some internal node of T and let p_j be a process that accesses $\mathcal{N}$ when executing a `WriteMax` operation Φ. For $i \in \{1,2\}$ we denote the i-th *read* of $\mathcal{N}.value$ by p_j in line 7 as $read_j^i(\mathcal{N},\Phi)$, the i-th *read* of $\mathcal{N}.left\_child.value$ by p_j in line 8 as $read\_lc_j^i(\mathcal{N},\Phi)$, the i-th *read* of $\mathcal{N}.right\_child.value$ by p_j in line 8 as $read\_rc_j^i(\mathcal{N},\Phi)$ and the i-th *CAS* of $\mathcal{N}.value$ by p_j in line 9 as $cas_j^i(\mathcal{N},\Phi)$. The following lemma will help us prove that a `WriteMax` operation does not precede its *linearization point.*

LEMMA 8. *In execution E, the sequence of values stored in every node of T is non-decreasing.*

PROOF. First, we consider values stored in the leaves of T. The v-th leaf of T_L stores either $-\infty$ (initial vale) or $v \geq 0$ (when written in line 17), hence its values are non-decreasing. The i-th leaf of T_R is written only by p_i, hence it only stores the operands of `WriteMax` operations by p_i, that are always non-decreasing.

We now consider the internal nodes of T. Assume towards a contradiction that the claim of the lemma is violated in E and let event e, issued by some process p_i, be the first event violating the claim, by changing $\mathcal{N}.value$, for some node $\mathcal{N}$, from value x to a smaller value y. Obviously e is a non-trivial *CAS* event issued by p_i when executing some `WriteMax` operation Φ_i. WLOG, e is a $cas_i^1(\mathcal{N},\Phi_i)$ and y is the maximum of values obtained by $read\_lc_i^1(\mathcal{N},\Phi_i)$ and $read\_rc_i^1(\mathcal{N},\Phi_i)$.

Since e changes the value of $\mathcal{N}.value$, according to the algorithm A, x is the value obtained by $read_i^1(\mathcal{N},\Phi_i)$. Let p_j be the process that wrote x to $\mathcal{N}.value$, when executing a `WriteMax` operation Φ_j. WLOG, p_j obtained x from $read\_lc_j^1(\mathcal{N},\Phi_j)$ and wrote it to $N.value$ in $cas_j^1(\mathcal{N},\Phi_j)$. It holds that,

$$\begin{aligned} read\_lc_j^1(\mathcal{N},\Phi_j) &\overset{E}{\prec} cas_j^1(\mathcal{N},\Phi_j) \overset{E}{\prec} read_i^1(\mathcal{N},\Phi_i) \\ &\overset{E}{\prec} read\_lc_i^1(\mathcal{N},\Phi_i) \overset{E}{\prec} read\_rc_i^1(\mathcal{N},\Phi_i). \end{aligned}$$

On the other hand, $read\_lc_j^1(\mathcal{N},\Phi_j)$ returns x, while $read\_lc_i^1(\mathcal{N},\Phi_i)$ returns $y' \leq y < x$. Hence the maximal value stored in $\mathcal{N}$'s left child has decreased in the execution prior to E. Thus e is not the first event violating the claim. This is a contradiction. $\square$

LEMMA 9. *Let Φ be a `WriteMax` operation in E such that its* linearization point *e, as specified by Definition 9, is also in E. Then Φ does not precede e in E.*

PROOF. If Φ does not complete in E then obviously $\neg(e \overset{E}{\prec} \Phi)$. Hence we only consider operations that complete in E. Let E' be a prefix of E such that Φ completes in E'. We prove that $\Phi \in \mathcal{C}(T.root, E')$. We consider this claim as a special case of the following invariant.

INVARIANT 1. *Let $e^{\mathcal{N}}$ be the last* write *or* CAS *event of Φ that accesses some node $\mathcal{N}$ in E. Let $E = E_1^{\mathcal{N}} e^{\mathcal{N}} E_2^{\mathcal{N}}$. Then $\Phi \in \mathcal{C}(\mathcal{N}, E_1^{\mathcal{N}} e^{\mathcal{N}})$*

Let $\mathcal{N}_1, \cdots, \mathcal{N}_d$, where d is the depth of the leaf $\mathcal{L}$ written by Φ, denote the nodes in the propagation path of Φ, such that $\mathcal{N}_1$ is $\mathcal{L}$ and $\mathcal{N}_d$ is $T.root$. We prove by induction on $r = 1, \cdots, d$ that the invariant holds for every node $\mathcal{N}_r$.

For the induction base, note that $\mathcal{N}_1$ is a leaf and thus $\mathcal{N}_1.value$ is written by the event $e^{\mathcal{L}}$ of Φ in line 17. Immediately after $e^{\mathcal{L}}$ the operation Φ is counted by $\mathcal{N}_1$. Since $e^{\mathcal{N}_1} = e^{\mathcal{L}}$ the invariant holds for $\mathcal{N}_1$.

For the induction step, assume that the invariant holds for $\mathcal{N}_r$. WLOG, $\mathcal{N}_r$ is the left child of $\mathcal{N}_{r+1}$. Let p_i be the process that executes Φ.

If either $cas_i^1(\mathcal{N}_{r+1},\Phi)$ or $cas_i^2(\mathcal{N}_{r+1},\Phi)$ (if it is ever issued) change the value of $\mathcal{N}_{r+1}$, then $\mathcal{N}_{r+1}$ starts counting Φ in $E_1^{\mathcal{N}_{r+1}} e^{\mathcal{N}_{r+1}}$ and the invariant holds. Hence, we consider the case in which both of these *CAS* events are trivial. This case occurs when $\mathcal{N}_{r+1}.value$ is changed by some process $p_j \neq p_i$ (executing a `WriteMax` operation Φ_j) between $read_i^1(\mathcal{N}_{r+1},\Phi)$ and $cas_i^1(\mathcal{N}_{r+1},\Phi)$, and by some process $p_k \neq p_i$ (executing a `WriteMax` operation Φ_k) between $read_i^2(\mathcal{N}_{r+1},\Phi)$ and $cas_i^2(\mathcal{N}_{r+1},\Phi)$.

WLOG, assume that the value of $\mathcal{N}_{r+1}.value$ is updated by $cas_j^1(\mathcal{N}_{r+1},\Phi_j)$ and $cas_k^1(\mathcal{N}_{r+1},\Phi_k)$, that

$cas_j^1(\mathcal{N}_{r+1},\Phi_j) \overset{E}{\prec} cas_k^1(\mathcal{N}_{r+1},\Phi_k)$ and that

$read\_lc_j^1(\mathcal{N}_{r+1},\Phi_j) \overset{E}{\prec} read\_lc_k^1(\mathcal{N}_{r+1},\Phi_k)$

If prior to $read\_lc_k^1(\mathcal{N}_{r+1},\Phi_k)$ the node $\mathcal{N}_r$ counts Φ then after $cas_k^1(\mathcal{N}_{r+1},\Phi_k)$, $\mathcal{N}_{r+1}$ starts counting Φ in $E_1^{\mathcal{N}_{r+1}} e^{\mathcal{N}_{r+1}}$ and the invariant holds.

The only case left to consider is that $\mathcal{N}_r$ does not count Φ in the execution prefix prior to $read\_lc_k^1(\mathcal{N}_{r+1},\Phi_k)$. We prove that this case is impossible. Assume towards a contradiction, that $read\_lc_k^1(\mathcal{N}_{r+1},\Phi_k)$ occurs before the event after which $\mathcal{N}_r$ counts Φ. Hence, by induction hypothesis, $read\_lc_k^1(\mathcal{N}_{r+1},\Phi_k) \overset{E}{\prec} e^{\mathcal{N}_r} \overset{E}{\prec} read_i^1(\mathcal{N}_{r+1},\Phi)$.

Since $read\_lc_k^1(\mathcal{N}_{r+1},\Phi_k) \overset{E}{\prec} cas_j^1(\mathcal{N}_{r+1},\Phi_j) \overset{E}{\prec} cas_k^1(\mathcal{N}_{r+1},\Phi_k)$, it is obvious that $p_j \neq p_k$. We denote the value stored in $\mathcal{N}_{r+1}.value$ as x upon $read_k^1(\mathcal{N}_{r+1},\Phi_k)$, as y upon $read_i^1(\mathcal{N}_{r+1},\Phi)$, as z upon $cas_i^1(\mathcal{N}_{r+1},\Phi)$ and as t upon $cas_k^1(\mathcal{N}_{r+1},\Phi_k)$. From Lemma 8, $x \leq y \leq z \leq t$. Since $cas_i^1(\mathcal{N}_{r+1},\Phi)$ does not update $\mathcal{N}_{r+1}.value$ then $y != z$ and, consequently $x < t$. On the other hand, $cas_k^1(\mathcal{N}_{r+1},\Phi_k)$ is non-trivial, yielding $x = t$. This is a contradiction. $\square$

LEMMA 10. *Let E' be a prefix of E and let $W(E') = \{\Phi_1, \cdots, \Phi_w\}$ denote the set of all `WriteMax` operations such that for $i = 1, \cdots, w$ the linearization point e_i of Φ_i appears in E'. If for each $i = 1, \cdots, w$ the operand of $\Phi_i \leq v$, then $T.root.value \leq v$ after E'.*

PROOF. Assume towards a contradiction, that $T.root.value = v' > v$ after E'. Obviously, the value v' is written by some `WriteMax` operation $\Phi \notin W(E')$ on some leaf $\mathcal{L}$ and then propagated to $T.root$. Let $\mathcal{N}_1, \cdots, \mathcal{N}_d$, where d is the depth of $\mathcal{L}$, denote the nodes in the propagation path of value v', such that $\mathcal{N}_1$ is $\mathcal{L}$ and $\mathcal{N}_d$ is $T.root$. For $r = 1, \cdots, d$, let $e^{\mathcal{N}_r}$ denote the event that writes the value v' to $\mathcal{N}_r$ such that $E' = E_1^{\mathcal{N}_r} e^{\mathcal{N}_r} E_2^{\mathcal{N}_r}$.

To obtain a contradiction we prove that $T.root$ counts Φ after $E_1^{\mathcal{N}_d} e^{\mathcal{N}_d}$ and thus $\Phi \in W(E')$. We consider this claim as a special case of the following invariant: for $r = 1, \cdots, d$, $\mathcal{N}_r$ counts Φ after $E_1^{\mathcal{N}_r} e^{\mathcal{N}_r}$. The proof is by induction on r.

For the induction base, we note that $\mathcal{N}_1$ is a leaf and thus $e^{\mathcal{N}_1}$ is a *write* issued by Φ. Hence, $\Phi \in \mathcal{C}(\mathcal{N}_1, E_1^{\mathcal{N}_1} e^{\mathcal{N}_1})$ and the invariant holds for $\mathcal{N}_1$.

For the induction step, assume that $\Phi \in \mathcal{C}(\mathcal{N}_r, E_1^{\mathcal{N}_r} e^{\mathcal{N}_r})$. Let Φ' be an operation by p_j that issues $e^{\mathcal{N}_{r+1}}$. WLOG, $\mathcal{N}_r$ is the left child of $\mathcal{N}_{r+1}$ and $e^{\mathcal{N}_{r+1}}$ is $cas_j^1(\mathcal{N}_{r+1},\Phi')$.

According to Algorithm A, $e^{\mathcal{N}_r} \overset{E}{\prec} read\_lc^1_j(\mathcal{N}_{r+1}, \Phi')$ $\overset{E}{\prec} cas^1_j(\mathcal{N}_{r+1}, \Phi') \equiv e^{\mathcal{N}_{r+1}}$. Since $\Phi \in \mathcal{C}(\mathcal{N}_r, E_1^{\mathcal{N}_r} e^{\mathcal{N}_r})$, from Definition 8, $\Phi \in \mathcal{C}(\mathcal{N}_{r+1}, E_1^{\mathcal{N}_{r+1}} e^{\mathcal{N}_{r+1}})$ and the invariant holds for $\mathcal{N}_{r+1}$. This is a contradiction. □

LEMMA 11. *Let Φ be a* **WriteMax** *operation by p_i with operand v. Let event e be the* linearization point *of Φ in E. If $E = E'eE''$, then $T.root.value \geq v$ after $E'e$.*

PROOF. From Definition 9, $\Phi \in \mathcal{C}(T.root, E'e)$.

Let $\mathcal{L}$ be the leaf accessed by Φ. Let $\mathcal{N}_1, \cdots, \mathcal{N}_d$, where d is the depth of $\mathcal{L}$, denote the nodes in the path of Φ, such that $\mathcal{N}_1$ is $\mathcal{L}$ and $\mathcal{N}_d$ is $T.root$. For $r = 1, \cdots, d$, let $e^{\mathcal{N}_r}$ denote the first event in E such that $E' = E_1^{\mathcal{N}_r} e^{\mathcal{N}_r} E_2^{\mathcal{N}_r}$ and $\Phi \in \mathcal{C}(\mathcal{N}_r, E_1^{\mathcal{N}_r} e^{\mathcal{N}_r})$.

From Definition 9, $E'e \equiv E_1^{\mathcal{N}_d} e^{\mathcal{N}_d}$. We prove that after $E_1^{\mathcal{N}_d} e^{\mathcal{N}_d}$ the value of $T.root \geq v$, considering this as a special case of the following invariant: for $r = 1, \cdots, d$, $\mathcal{N}_r.value \geq v$ after $E_1^{\mathcal{N}_r} e^{\mathcal{N}_r}$. The proof is by induction on r.

For induction base, note that $\mathcal{N}_1$ is a leaf and thus $e^{\mathcal{N}_1}$ is the *write* of value v on $\mathcal{N}_1.value$ (in line 17). Hence $\mathcal{N}_1.value = v$ after $E_1^{\mathcal{N}_1} e^{\mathcal{N}_1}$ and the invariant holds for $\mathcal{N}_1$.

For induction step, assume that $\mathcal{N}_r.value \geq v$ after $E_1^{\mathcal{N}_r} e^{\mathcal{N}_r}$. Let Φ' be a **WriteMax** operation by p_j that issues $e^{\mathcal{N}_{r+1}}$. WLOG, $\mathcal{N}_r$ is the left child of $\mathcal{N}_{r+1}$ and $e^{\mathcal{N}_{r+1}}$ is $cas^1_j(\mathcal{N}_{r+1}, \Phi')$. We consider the following cases.

1. if $\Phi = \Phi'$, then by Invariant 1, $\mathcal{N}_r$ counts Φ in execution prior to $read\_lc^1_i(\mathcal{N}_{r+1}, \Phi) \equiv read\_lc^1_j(\mathcal{N}_{r+1}, \Phi')$.
2. if $\Phi \neq \Phi'$, then obviously $p_i \neq p_j$ and from Definition 9, $\mathcal{N}_r$ counts Φ in the execution prefix prior to $read\_lc^1_j(\mathcal{N}_{r+1}, \Phi')$.

According to Algorithm A, the value v' written by $cas^1_j(\mathcal{N}_{r+1}, \Phi') \equiv e^{\mathcal{N}_{r+1}}$ is greater than or equal to the value read by $read\_lc^1_j(\mathcal{N}_{r+1}, \Phi')$. Since $e^{\mathcal{N}_r} \overset{E}{\prec} read\_lc^1_j(\mathcal{N}_{r+1}, \Phi')$, $\mathcal{N}_r.value \geq v$ prior to $read\_lc^1_j(\mathcal{N}_{r+1}, \Phi')$ and thus $v' \geq v$. Consequently, $\mathcal{N}_{r+1}.value \geq v$ after $E_1^{\mathcal{N}_{r+1}} e^{\mathcal{N}_{r+1}}$ and the invariant holds for $\mathcal{N}_{r+1}$. □

LEMMA 12. *Let Φ be a* **ReadMax** *operation in H, such that $H = H_1 \Phi H_2$. Then Φ returns the largest value written in H_1 (or $-\infty$, if no* **WriteMax** *appears in H_1).*

PROOF. Let e be the linearization point of Φ in E, such that $E = E_1 e E_2$. From Definition 9, e is a *read* of $T.root.value$ and according to Algorithm A, Φ returns the value obtained by e.

If no **WriteMax** appears in H_1, then no event is visible on $T.root.value$ after E_1. Hence e reads the initial value of $T.root.value$, which is $-\infty$.

Let v be the largest value written in H_1 and let Φ_w be the **WriteMax** operation that wrote v. We prove that $T.root.value = v$ after E_1. Let e_w be the *linearization point* of Φ_w such that $E_1 = E'_1 e_w E'_2$. From Lemma 11, $T.root.value \geq v$ after $E'_1 e_w$ and thus after E_1. Moreover, from Lemma 10, $T.root.value \leq v$ after E_1, otherwise v was not the largest value written in H_1. □

From Observations 1 - 2 and from Lemmas 7 - 9, for every operation Φ in E its *linearization point* is uniquely defined within the time interval of Φ, and thus H preserves a partial precedence order of operations in E. Moreover, from Lemma 12, H is a legal sequential history of *maxRegister*. This immediately leads us to the following theorem.

THEOREM 5. *Algorithm A is a linearizable implementation of N-process unbounded* maxRegister.

Wait-freedom and Complexity.

Clearly, Algorithm A is wait-free. The number of events issued by **ReadMax** is constant. The number of events issued by **WriteMax**(v) is proportional to the depth d of leaf $\mathcal{L}$:

1. if $v < N$, then $\mathcal{L} \in T_L$ and from the definition of B_1 tree, $d = O(\log v) = O(\min(\log N, \log v))$.
2. if $v \geq N$, then $\mathcal{L} \in T_R$ and from the definition of complete binary tree, $d = O(\log N) = O(\min(\log N, \log v))$

THEOREM 6. *Algorithm A is wait-free; the step-complexity of the* **ReadMax** *operation is $O(1)$ and the step-complexity of the* **WriteMax**(v) *is $O(\min(\log N, \log v))$.*

6. REFERENCES

[1] J. H. Anderson and Y.-J. Kim. An improved lower bound for the time complexity of mutual exclusion. *Distributed Computing*, 15(4):221–253, 2002.

[2] J. Aspnes, H. Attiya, and K. Censor. Polylogarithmic concurrent data structures from monotone circuits. *J. ACM*, 59(1), Feb. 2012. Previous version in *PODC*, pages 36–45, 2009.

[3] J. Aspnes, H. Attiya, K. Censor-Hillel, and F. Ellen. Faster than optimal snapshots (for a while): preliminary version. In *PODC*, pages 375–384, 2012.

[4] J. Aspnes, H. Attiya, K. Censor-Hillel, and D. Hendler. Lower bounds for restricted-use objects: extended abstract. In *SPAA*, pages 172–181, 2012.

[5] J. Aspnes and K. Censor. Approximate shared-memory counting despite a strong adversary. *ACM Transactions on Algorithms*, 6(2), 2010.

[6] H. Attiya and D. Hendler. Time and space lower bounds for implementations using k-cas. *IEEE Trans. Parallel Distrib. Syst.*, 21(2):162–173, 2010.

[7] M. A. Bender and S. Gilbert. Mutual exclusion with $O(\log \log n)$ amortized work. In *FOCS*, pages 728–737, 2011.

[8] J. L. Bentley and A. C. chih Yao. An almost optimal algorithm for unbounded searching, 1975.

[9] B. Bollobas. *Extremal Graph Theory*. Dover Publications, Incorporated, 2004.

[10] M. Herlihy. Wait-free synchronization. *ACM Trans. Prog. Lang. Syst.*, 13(1):124–149, January 1991.

[11] M. Herlihy, V. Luchangco, and M. Moir. Obstruction-free synchronization: Double-ended queues as an example. In *Proceedings of the 23rd IEEE International Conference on Distributed Computing Systems (ICDCS'03)*, pages 522–529, 2003.

[12] M. Herlihy and J. M. Wing. Linearizability: a correctness condition for concurrent objects. *ACM Trans. Prog. Lang. Syst.*, 12(3):463–492, June 1990.

[13] P. Jayanti. A time complexity lower bound for randomized implementations of some shared objects. In *PODC*, pages 201–210, 1998.

[14] P. Jayanti. *f*-arrays: implementation and applications. In *PODC*, pages 270–279, 2002.

[15] Y.-J. Kim and J. H. Anderson. A time complexity bound for adaptive mutual exclusion. In *DISC*, pages 1–15, 2001.

Concurrent Updates with RCU: Search Tree as an Example*

Maya Arbel
Department of Computer Science
Technion
mayaarl@cs.technion.ac.il

Hagit Attiya
Department of Computer Science
Technion
hagit@cs.technion.ac.il

ABSTRACT

Read copy update (RCU) is a novel synchronization mechanism, in which the burden of synchronization falls completely on the updaters, by having them wait for all pre-existing readers to finish their read-side critical section. This paper presents CITRUS, a concurrent binary search tree (BST) with a wait-free contains operation, using RCU synchronization and fine-grained locking for synchronization among updaters. This is the first RCU-based data structure that allows concurrent updaters. While there are methodologies for using RCU to coordinate between readers and updaters, they do not address the issue of coordination among updaters, and indeed, all existing RCU-based data structures rely on coarse-grained synchronization between updaters.

Experimental evaluation shows that CITRUS beats previous RCU-based search trees, even under mild update contention, and compares well with the best-known concurrent dictionaries.

Categories and Subject Descriptors

D.1.3 [**Programming Techniques**]: Concurrent Programming—*Concurrent programming*; F.1.2 [**Computation By Abstract Devices**]: Modes of Computation—*Parallelism and concurrency*

General Terms

Algorithms, Architecture

Keywords

Shared memory; internal search tree; read-copy-update

1. INTRODUCTION

The traditional approach to synchronization between readers and writers allows concurrency among readers, but excludes readers when a writer is executing, e.g., through a *readers/writer lock*. An alternative, contemporary approach is presented by *read copy update (RCU)* [22], a distinctive synchronization mechanism favoring read-only operations even further, by allowing them to proceed even while writers are modifying the data they are reading. Instead, the *read-side critical section* is wrapped by the rcu_read_lock and rcu_read_unlock functions; an additional synchronize_rcu function can be used by a writer as a barrier ensuring that all preceding read-side critical sections complete. In typical RCU usage, the burden of synchronization is placed on updates, who can wait for all pre-existing readers to finish their read-side critical section.

RCU is used extensively within the Linux kernel [20], mostly to facilitate memory reclamation [12, 21]. However, its potential for concurrent programming remained unexploited. Although several RCU-based data structures have been proposed, for example, search trees and hash tables [6, 18, 25, 26], they all do not allow concurrent updates, either pessimistically, using a coarse-grained lock [6], or optimistically, using transactional memory [18]. At best, the data structure is partitioned into segments, e.g., buckets in a hash table [25, 26], each guarded by a single lock.

This leaves unanswered the question of coordination *between concurrent updates* to the data structure, while using RCU, which is the topic of this paper.

A natural approach for supporting concurrent updates is to employ fine-grained locks, acquired and released according to some locking policy, e.g., *two-phase* locking or *hand-over-hand* locking. We found that these fine-grained approaches fail to ensure consistent views for read-only operations that access several items in the data structure, e.g., partial snapshots [2] or other iterators [24]. Figure 1 shows an example in which two readers, r_1 and r_2, attempt to collect the leaves, by in-order traversal, while two updates delete leaves 9 and 12. In (a), r_2 already traversed the left sub-tree while r_1 has not yet started its traversal. After 9 is deleted (b), r_1 finishes traversing the tree while r_2 did not take additional steps, and 12 is deleted before both readers complete (c). Since each reader may observe a different permutation of the writes to the data structure, the values returned by r_1 and r_2 are such that they observed the updates in different order. This means that without additional iterations or interaction, there is no consistent way to order the updates and the readers, complicating the task of designing a concurrent data structure.

Nevertheless, this example (and others that we found) hints that the difficulty is in having read-only operations that need to atomically access several locations. The counter-examples do not hold when the read-only operation only searches for a particular data item, e.g., in a dictionary.

This observation led to the design of CITRUS, a binary search tree implementing a dictionary with concurrent updates (insert and delete) and contains queries. Updates synchronize using fine-

*This research is supported by Yad-HaNadiv foundation and the Israel Science Foundation (grant number 1227/10).

PODC'14, July 15–18, 2014, Paris, France.
Copyright 2014 ACM 978-1-4503-2944-6/14/07 ...$15.00.
http://dx.doi.org/10.1145/2611462.2611471.

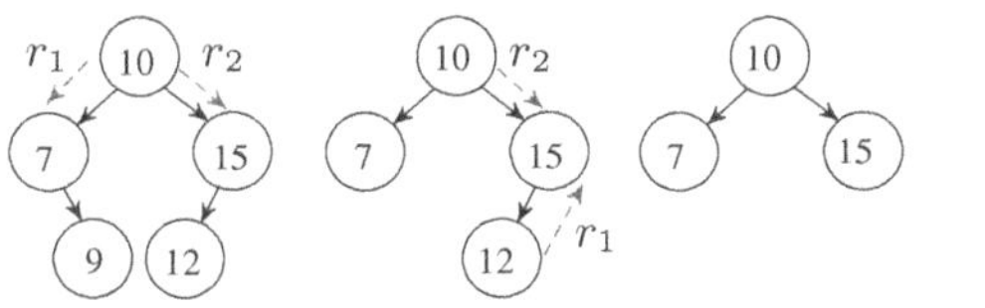

(a) $r_1 = \{\}$ $r_2 = \{9\}$

(b) $r_1 = \{7, 12\}$ $r_2 = \{9\}$

(c) $r_1 = \{7, 12\}$ $r_2 = \{9, 15\}$

Figure 1: An example in which RCU readers may observe a different permutation of the writes to the data structure.

grained locks, while contains proceeds in a wait-free manner, in parallel with updates, relying on RCU to ensure correctness. The combination of RCU synchronization with fine-grained locking of modified nodes yields a simple design, greatly resembling the sequential algorithm, and leading to a (relatively) simple proof of correctness, only several pages long.

CITRUS implements an *internal* search tree, with keys stored in all nodes, and it is *unbalanced*. Searching for a key, either in a contains operation or at the beginning of an update, is done in a wait-free manner, as in the sequential data structure, but inside an *RCU read-side critical section*.

Updates start by searching for their key, in a manner similar to contains. An unsuccessful update (insert that finds its key or delete that does not find its key), returns immediately. Otherwise, the update is located where the change should be done.

A new node is inserted as a leaf, requiring little synchronization, but delete may need to remove an internal node. When the node has two children, this is done by replacing the node with its *successor* in the tree. This scenario requires coordination with concurrent searches that could miss the successor in both its previous location and in its new location, necessitating delicate synchronization in some concurrent search trees [4, 7, 9, 19]. CITRUS easily circumvents this pitfall by copying the successor to the new location, and using the RCU synchronization mechanism to wait for on-going searches, before removing the successor from its previous location.

Experimental evaluation of CITRUS shows that its performance beats previous RCU-based search trees [6, 18], even under mild update contention. It also compares well with the best-available concurrent dictionaries, e.g., [4, 15, 23].

The evaluation also reveals that the user-level RCU implementation [8] is ill-suited for workloads in which many updates concurrently synchronize through it. We sketch a new implementation that avoids these pitfalls and scales better with growing number of updates. In the new implementation, a thread indicates that it starts a read-side critical section by incrementing a counter and setting a flag to true; the flag is set to false at the end of the section. To synchronize, an update waits until every other thread either increases its counter or sets its flag to false.

2. PRELIMINARIES

A concurrent system consists of a set of threads, communicating by applying *primitives* to shared variables. A shared data structure *implementation* provides a set of operations, each invoked with possible parameters and returning with a response. The invocation of an operation is a local step of a thread, leading to the execution of an *algorithm*, directing the thread to execute a sequence of *atomic* steps. Each atomic step is either an instance of a shared memory primitive or computation on variables that are local to the thread. Returning from an operation is a local computation step.

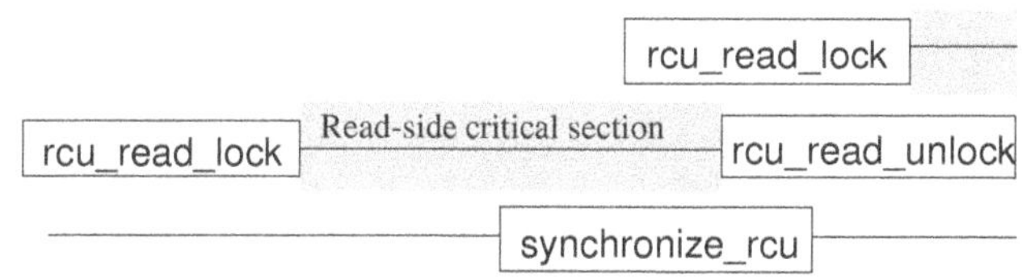

Figure 2: The semantics of synchronize_rcu

A *configuration* is an instantaneous snapshot of the system describing the state of all local and shared variables. In the *initial* configuration, all variables hold an initial value.

An *execution* π is an alternating sequence of configurations and steps, $C_0, s_1, ..., s_i, C_i, ...$, where C_0 is the initial configuration, and each configuration C_i is the result of executing the step s_i in configuration C_{i-1}. A *prefix* σ of π is a sub-sequence of π starting in C_0 and ending with a configuration. An *interval* of π is a subsequence that starts with a step and ends with a configuration. The *interval of an operation* op starts with the invocation step of op and ends with the configuration following the response of op or the end of π, if there is no such response.

The API for *read copy update* (RCU) provides several functions, three of which are used in CITRUS to synchronize between readers and updates: rcu_read_lock, rcu_read_unlock and synchronize_rcu. A *read-side critical section* is the interval starting with the step returning from rcu_read_lock and ending with the configuration after the invocation of rcu_read_unlock. The implementations of rcu_read_lock and rcu_read_unlock must be wait-free. The *RCU property* (Figure 2) ensures that if a step of a read-side critical section precedes the invocation of synchronize_rcu, then all steps of this critical section precede the return from synchronize_rcu [12, 13].

A *dictionary* is a set of key-value pairs, with totally ordered keys, with the following operations:

insert(*k,val*) adds (k, val) to the set; returns true if k is not in the set and false otherwise.

delete(*k*) removes (k, val) from the set; returns true if k is in the set and false otherwise.

contains(*k*) returns val if (k, val) is in the set; otherwise, it returns false.

An *update* is either an insert or a delete.

A binary search tree implements a dictionary; it is *internal* if key-value pairs are stored in all nodes. A node v of the tree stores a key, *Key*(v), which never changes. Two dummy key values $-1, \infty$ are used to avoid corner cases, when the tree has fewer than two nodes; for every key k, $-1 < k < \infty$. The root of the tree always points to a node with key -1, this node has a right child with key ∞; all other nodes are in the left sub-tree of ∞.

In a *binary search tree* (BST), all descendants in the left sub-tree of v have keys smaller than the key of v, and all descendants in the right sub-tree of v have keys larger than the key of v.

The *successor* of node v is the node u with the smallest key among the nodes with keys larger than or equal to *Key*(v). In a BST, u is the leftmost node in the right sub-tree of v.

3. THE CITRUS TREE ALGORITHM

Overview. A primary goal of CITRUS is to avoid locking when searching for a node, either in contains or at the beginning of

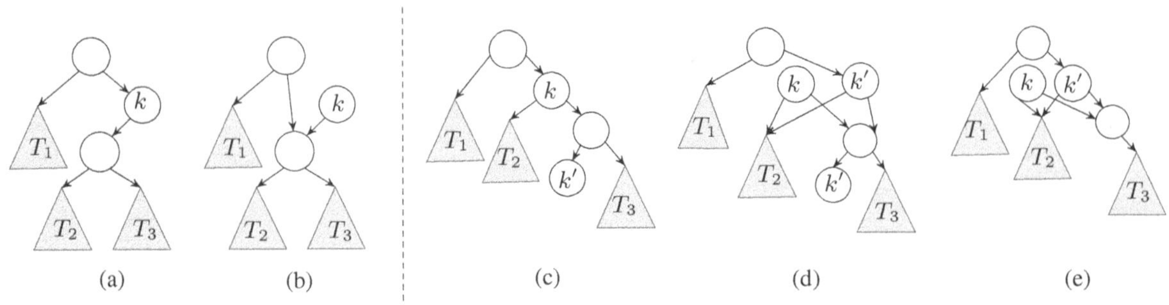

Figure 3: (a) and (b) show delete(k) when a node has one child. (c)-(e) show delete(k) that replaces a node with two children with its successor; synchronize_rcu is invoked between (d) and (e).

an update. This is implemented in an auxiliary procedure get, which starts at the root and searches down the tree in a manner similar to the sequential algorithm, except that it is performed inside a read-side critical section, wrapped with rcu_read_lock and rcu_read_unlock.

A contains simply invokes get to find the key; if the key is found, it returns the value stored in the node returned by get; otherwise, it returns false.

An insert invokes get, and returns false if get finds the key. Otherwise, a new node with the key is inserted as a leaf, added to the tree as the child of the last node in get's search.

A delete invokes get, and returns false if get does not find the key. If the key is found in node v, then there are two cases. If v has at most one child, the node is removed by redirecting the child field of v's parent to point to v's child (see Figure 3(a) and (b)); later in the proof this is called *bypassing*. Otherwise, v has two children and it is replaced with its successor in the tree, which is stored in the leftmost node in the right sub-tree of v.

Moving the successor, when v has two children, requires coordination with a concurrent get searching for the successor, which may return a false negative response (Figure 4). To overcome this problem, delete first inserts a copy of the successor node in the deleted key's location. Then the delete waits for concurrent searches by executing synchronize_rcu, and only then, removes the old successor node. Searches that start before synchronize_rcu starts, find the successor in its previous location, where it remains until they complete (Figure 3(c)-(e)). Searches that start after synchronize_rcu starts, find the new copy of the successor.

Note that during a delete, there might be two copies of the successor—in the original and in the new locations. This motivates the following *weak BST* (WBST) property (formally defined in Definition 1): all descendants in the left sub-tree of v have keys smaller than the key of v, and all descendants in the right sub-tree of v have keys larger than or equal to the key of v.

The WBST property allows multiple nodes with the same key. If all nodes with the same key hold the same value, preserving the WBST property ensures that contains is correct, as it may return the value of some duplicate node, and ignore the others.

Updates synchronize among themselves by acquiring locks on nodes returned by get. To avoid RCU deadlocks, locks are acquired outside the read-side critical section. This creates a region of uncertainty, for example, if an insert reaches the node with key k, but an overlapping delete operation removes this node from the tree before insert locks it (see Figure 5). If insert continues its operation, the new key will not be part of the tree.

We overcome this problem by *validating* the nodes after locking them, and restarting the operation if validation fails. An update restarts either because the locked nodes no longer have a parent-child relation or because one (or both) of the two nodes was deleted from the tree. Validating the parent-child relation is done locally by checking the child pointer of the parent node. When the operation validating is an insert, the child pointer of the parent should be $\perp$ (null pointer). A *tag* is added to each child field, in order to avoid an ABA problem (a child pointer changed to non-$\perp$ when a leaf is inserted, then back to $\perp$, when the leaf is moved by a delete). (A total of two tag fields in each node, one for each child.) A tag field is initialized to zero, and incremented every time the corresponding child field is set to $\perp$. Validating that a node was not removed is also done locally, using a *marked* field indicating that the node was deleted (in a manner similar to [14]). If validation fails, the operation releases all locks and restarts from the root.

Detailed description. All operations use procedure get to search for a key k, which starts from the root, and returns two nodes, curr and prev, which is the parent of curr (Line 15). The procedure also returns a *direction*, indicating whether curr is the left or right child of prev, and the tag of prev that is associated with direction. If the key k exists in the tree, then curr is the node containing k. If the key does not exist, curr $=\perp$ and prev is the last node found in the search. All operations executed by get are wrapped with rcu_read_lock and rcu_read_unlock creating a read-side critical section (Lines 2 and 14).

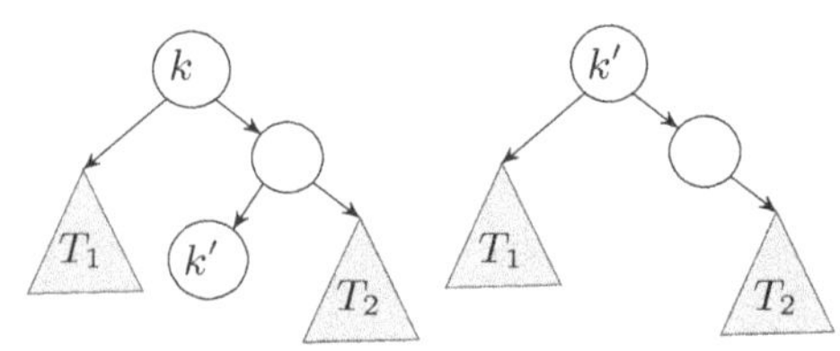

Figure 4: Search for key k' returns a false negative response due to an overlapping delete.

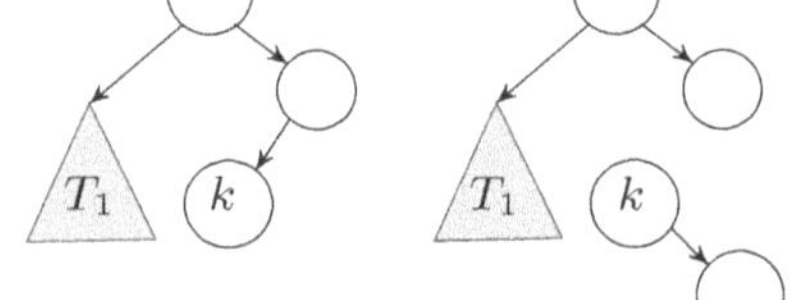

Figure 5: insert can add a node to an incorrect location due to an overlapping delete.

CITRUS get function

```
1  function get(key)
2    rcu_read_lock
3    prev ← root
4    curr ← prev.child[right]                    ▷ root is never ⊥
5    currentKey ← curr.key          ▷ root's right child is never ⊥
6    direction ← right
7    while curr ≠⊥ and currentKey ≠ key do
8      prev ← curr
9      direction ← (currentKey > key ? left : right)
10     curr ← prev.child[direction]
11     if curr ≠⊥ then
12       currentKey ← curr.key
13   tag = prev.tag[direction]
                         ▷ Save tag inside read-side critical section
14   rcu_read_unlock
15   return (prev,tag,curr,direction)
```

The contains operation simply invokes get. If the key is not in the tree, it returns false (Line 19). If the key is found, it returns the value associated with it (Line 20).

CITRUS contains function

```
16 function contains(key)
17   (-,-,curr,-) ← get(key)
18   if curr =⊥ then                      ▷ The key was not found
19     return false
20   return curr.value
```

The insert operation invokes get, if the key is found, it returns false (Line 25). If the key is not in the tree, insert locks prev (Line 26) and then validates it (Line 27). If validation fails, the operation starts over; otherwise, the new node is created (Line 28) and added to the tree (Line 29).

CITRUS insert function

```
21 function insert(key,value)
22   loop
23     (prev,tag,curr,direction) ← get(key)
24     if curr ≠⊥ then                         ▷ The key was found
25       return false
26     lock(prev)
27     if validate(prev,tag,⊥,direction) then
28       node ← new(key,value,⊥,⊥) ▷ Create a new leaf node
29       prev.child[direction] ← node
30       unlock(prev)
31       return true
32     unlock(prev)   ▷ Validation failed, release locks and retry
```

The validate procedure is a simple check of local properties of the given nodes.

CITRUS validate function

```
33 function validate(prev,tag,curr,direction)
34   if prev.marked or prev.child[direction]≠curr then
35     return false
36   if curr ≠⊥ then       ▷ If curr ≠⊥ validate curr's marked bit
37     return !curr.marked
38   return prev.tag[direction] = tag      ▷ Otherwise validate tag
```

The incrementTag procedure receives a node and a direction, if the child of node in this direction is ⊥, it increments the tag associated with this direction.

CITRUS incrementTag function

```
39 function incrementTag(node,direction)
40   if node.child[direction] = ⊥ then
41     node.tag[direction] ← node.tag[direction]+1
```

The delete operation invokes get. If the key is not found, it returns false (Line 46). If the key is found, prev and curr are locked (Lines 47, 48) and validated (Line 49). If validation fails, the operation unlocks prev and curr and starts over. If curr has only one child, delete does not use the successor (Line 50), curr is marked (Line 51) and deleted (Line 53).

If curr has two children (Line 57), the operation tries to delete curr by using a successor. It finds the successor succ and its parent prevSucc, by traversing the leftmost branch of the sub-tree rooted at curr (Lines 58-64). This traversal does not need a read-side critical section since the keys of nodes traversed do not impact the direction. Once found, prevSucc and succ are locked (Lines 67, 68) and validated (Line 69). If validation fails, all nodes are unlocked and the operation starts over; otherwise, a deletion using a successor is executed (Lines 72 - 83). A new node with succ's key and curr's children is created (Line 70) and locked (Line 71). Then, curr is marked (Line 72) and replaced by node (Line 73). Next, the operation waits for all pre-existing readers, by invoking synchronize_rcu (Line 74). When the operation returns, it removes the old successor from the tree (Lines 75-80); note that succ might be the right child of curr (Line 76). The operation completes by unlocking all the nodes and returning true (Line 83). After removing a node from the tree (in one of Lines 53, 77 or 80), incrementTag is called in case the tag should be updated.

4. LINEARIZABILITY OF CITRUS

Fix an execution π of the CITRUS algorithm. Roughly speaking, an implementation is *linearizable* [17] if it is possible to identify, for each operation, a *linearization point*, inside its interval, so that the responses of the operations are *consistent*: that is, they are the same as if the operations were performed sequentially in their linearization points.

The following notation is used in the proof. Let u, v be two nodes in the tree, $v \rightarrow u$ indicates that u is a child of v, $v \overset{left}{\rightarrow} u$ when u is the left child of v and $v \overset{right}{\rightarrow} u$ when u is the right child of v; generally, $v \overset{d}{\rightarrow} u$, $d = left$ means that u is the left child of v, and analogously if $d = right$. There is a *path* from node v to node u in configuration C, if there is a sequence of nodes $v = v_0, v_1, ..., v_m = u$, $m > 0$, such that for every $i, 0 \leq i < m$, $v_i \rightarrow v_{i+1}$ in C. We denote $\rho_C(v,u)$=$v_0, ..., v_m$. A node v is *reachable* in configuration C if there is a path from the root to v in C. A key k is reachable in configuration C if there is a reachable node v such that k =*Key*(v); recall that *Key*(v) never changes. The set of reachable keys stored in the sub-tree rooted at v, in a configuration C, is denoted $Set_C(v)$; $Set_C(root)$ is the set of reachable keys in the whole tree. We define the WBST property:

DEFINITION 1. The weak BST (*WBST*) property holds *in configuration C if for every internal node v, if u is a node such that $v \overset{left}{\rightarrow} u$ and $k \in Set_C(u)$ then $k <$Key(v) and if $v \overset{right}{\rightarrow} u$ and $k \in Set_C(u)$ then $k \geq$Key(v).* The WBST property holds in *an execution prefix σ if it holds in every configuration C in σ.*

```
CITRUS delete function
42 function delete(key)
43   loop
44     (prev,-,curr,direction) ← get(key)
45     if curr=⊥ then                                  ▷ The key was not found
46       return false
47     lock(prev)
48     lock(curr)
49     if validate(prev,-,curr,direction) then
50       if curr.child[left] =⊥ or curr.child[right] =⊥ then
                                                       ▷ curr has a single child
51         curr.marked ← true
52         notNoneChild ← (curr.child[left] ≠⊥ ? left : right)
53         prev.child[direction] ← curr.child[notNoneChild]
54         incrementTag(prev,direction)
55         release all locks
56         return true
57       else                                          ▷ curr has two children
58         prevSucc ← curr                 ▷ Searching for the successor
59         succ ← curr.child[right]
60         next ← succ.child[left]                              ▷ succ ≠⊥
61         while next ≠⊥ do
62           prevSucc ← succ
63           succ ← next
64           next ← next.child[left]
65         succDirection ← (curr = prevSucc ? right : left)
66         if curr ≠ prevSucc then                   ▷ Do not lock twice
67           lock(prevSucc)
68         lock(succ)
69         if validate(prevSucc,-,succ,succDirection) and
                     validate(succ,succ.tag[left],⊥,left) then
70           node ← new(succ.key,succ.value,curr.child[left],
                                                      curr.child[right])
71           lock(node)
72           curr.marked ← true
73           prev.child[direction] ← node
74           synchronize_rcu                         ▷ Wait for readers
75           succ.marked ← true  ▷ Remove the old successor
76           if prevSucc = curr then
                                        ▷ succ is the right child of curr
77             node.child[right] ← succ.child[right]
78             incrementTag(node,right)
79           else
80             prevSucc.child[left] ← succ.child[right]
81             incrementTag(prevSucc,left)
82           release all locks
83           return true
84     release all locks ▷ Validation failed, release locks and retry
```

If the WBST property holds in an execution prefix σ that ends in configuration C, then the range of keys in the sub-tree of node v, denoted $Range_C(v)$, can be defined by induction on $\rho_C(root, v)$: $Range_C(root) = (-\infty, \infty)$; if the parent of v is node u with $k = Key(u)$ and $Range_C(u) = [min_u, max_u)$ or $Range_C(u) = (min_u, max_u)$, then $Range_C(v) = [min_u, k)$ or $Range_C(v) = (min_u, k)$ if $u \overset{left}{\to} v$, and $Range_C(v) = [k, max_u)$ if $u \overset{right}{\to} v$.

Let u, v, w be nodes such that $u \overset{d}{\to} v \to w$, $d \in \{left, right\}$, and node v has only one child, in configuration $C \in \pi$. A primitive write operation s that immediately follows C is a *bypass* of node v if $u \overset{d}{\to} w$ in the configuration that follows s in π (Figure 3(a) and (b)). The write in Line 53 is a bypass of the node curr, and the writes in Line 77 and Line 80 are a bypass of the node succ.

In order to distinguish between variables of different operations, we denote by $\mathsf{var}_{\mathsf{op}}$ the variable var of operation op; the operation is omitted when it is clear from the context. An operation op *accesses* a node v when op reads one of v's fields. Only updates execute primitive writes, and when an update op writes to a field of node v, v is locked by op. Therefore, the fields of node v cannot be modified by another operation until the lock on v is released.

Updates use validate to ensure that they operate on nodes in the tree. The next lemma argues that if a node is not reachable in a configuration, then its marked bit is true. Note that a node is unmarked when it is added to the tree, and marked before it is removed. Since updates operate on locked nodes, this suffices to prove the lemma, even though marking and removing a node are not performed atomically.

LEMMA 1. *If a node v is reachable in configuration $C \in \pi$ and v is unmarked in configuration $C' \in \pi$ that follows C, then v is reachable in C'.*

PROOF. Assume, by way of contradiction, that the property does not hold and let C be the last configuration in π in which the property holds. Let s be the step by operation op immediately following C; s must be a primitive write to a child field of a locked node, in an update.

Case 1: insert. Line 29: By the validation in Line 27, prev has no child in direction d (where d is the value of direction), hence, s does not make an unmarked node unreachable. Since node was created by op, it is unreachable in the configuration immediately following the step in Line 28. If s makes node reachable, then node is unmarked, as required.

Case 2: delete. By the validation in Line 49, prev $\overset{d}{\to}$ curr (where d is the value of direction).

Bypassing (Lines 53, 77, 80) makes only curr or succ unreachable. The lemma holds since curr is marked before Line 53 and succ is marked before Lines 77 and 80.

Line 73: By Line 72, curr is marked and can become unreachable. Both children of curr become the children of node in Line 70. Since s adds node to the tree as a left or right child of prev (depending on d), curr is the only node that becomes unreachable. Since node is created by op, it is unreachable in the configuration immediately following the step in Line 70. If node becomes reachable by s, then it is unmarked, as required. □

To ensure that get with key k is correct, we prove that all nodes accessed by get are in the tree at some point during its interval (Lemma 2) and that if k is in the tree throughout a search from the root, then it is found (Lemma 8). Recall that an operation op accesses a node v when op reads one of v's fields.

LEMMA 2. *Let π' be the interval of operation op. If op accesses a node v in step s, then v is reachable in some configuration $C \in \pi'$ that precedes s.*

PROOF. By induction on the length of the path taken by op from the root to node v. In the base case, the root is always reachable.

For the induction step, assume that the lemma holds for paths of length $< \ell$. Let v be the ℓ'th node in the path taken by op and let u be the $(\ell - 1)$'th node in this path. Suppose, without loss of generality, that op read $u \overset{right}{\to} v$ in step s'.

By the induction hypothesis, u is reachable in some configuration during π'; let C be the last such configuration. If s' precedes C, then v is reachable in the configuration C' that immediately follow s'. Since the pointer read in step s' precedes any access to v, C' precedes s (Figure 6(a)).

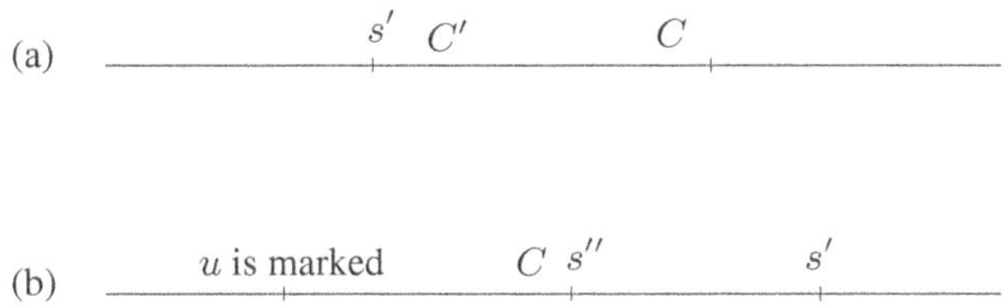

Figure 6: The proof of Lemma 2. Case (a) u is reachable when $u \rightarrow v$ is read. Case (b) u is unreachable when $u \rightarrow v$ is read

If s' does not precede C, we argue that v is the right child of u when u is removed from the tree. Suppose, by way of contradiction, that u has some other right child $w \neq v$ in C and s'' is the step removing u from the tree, i.e., the step that immediately follows C. Since op read $u \xrightarrow{right} v$, there is an update that sets the right child of u to v before s'. Since u is reachable in C and unreachable in the configuration following s'', Lemma 1 implies that u is marked before s''. The update removing u does not change u's children fields (by the code, no operation writes to child fields of curr or succ). Any other update validates all locked nodes to check that they are not marked. Since u is marked, any update that tries to write to u restarts without changing u, which is a contradiction.

When u is removed from the tree, v is the right child of u. Since C is the last configuration in π' in which u is reachable, both v and u are reachable in $C \in \pi'$, C precedes s' that precedes s, as required. □

The next lemma shows the correctness of tag validation. It shows that if a child pointer is set to $\perp$, by another operation, after the tag is read and before the node is locked, then the tag is incremented during this interval. Due to space constraints, the proof appears in the full version.

LEMMA 3. *Let π' be the interval starting with the step of Line 13 by* op *and ending with the configuration that immediately follows the lock acquisition by* op*. If* $prev_{op}$*.child[*$direction_{op}$*] was set to $\perp$ during the interval π' then* $prev_{op}$*.tag[*$direction_{op}$*]* $\neq tag_{op}$ *in every configuration in the interval of* op *that follows π'.*

Searches, implemented in get, follow the sequential algorithm, so it is critical to show that the tree maintains the WBST property. This is proved by induction on the prefixes of the execution π. A critical step in the proof is to show that an insert adds a node in the right location. This relies on the following lemma (Lemma 4), showing that the RCU mechanism of waiting for all pre-existing readers guarantees that if the search of an insert ends up in the wrong location, due to overlapping delete, then its validation fails.

LEMMA 4. *Let* op *be an* insert *operation with key k that successfully validates* prev *and* curr*, and let σ be the execution prefix that ends in configuration C that immediately follows the return from* validate*. If the WBST property holds in σ, then $k \in Range_C($*prev*$)$.*

PROOF. If the path traversed by op is the same as $\rho_C(root, \text{prev})$, then, by the WBST property, $k \in Range_C(\text{prev})$. The path traversed by op is different from $\rho_C(root, \text{prev})$, if it was changed by an overlapping update op'. Consider every possible write to a child field, during π', the interval of op.

Case 1: insert. Line 29: By the validation in Line 27, $prev_{op'}$ has no child in direction d (where d is the value of direction), Thus, op' adds a leaf to the tree, without changing the range of $prev_{op}$.

Case 2: delete. By the validation in Line 49, prev $\xrightarrow{d}$ curr (where d is the value of direction).

Bypassing (Lines 53, 77, 80) only increases the ranges of other nodes and $k \in Range_C(\text{prev}_{op})$ is maintained.

Line 73: Both children of $curr_{op'}$ become the children of $node_{op'}$ in Line 70. Hence, $curr_{op'}$ is replaced with $node_{op'}$ that has the key of $succ_{op'}$. The node $succ_{op'}$ is found by traversing the leftmost branch of the sub-tree rooted at $curr_{op'}$. Since the WBST property holds in σ, this traversal starting at $curr_{op'}$ finishes at the location of the successor of $curr_{op'}$. Since op' accesses $succ_{op'}$, Lemma 2 implies that $succ_{op'}$ is reachable after some prefix of π ending before Line 69. By the validation in Line 69 and Lemma 1, $succ_{op'}$ is reachable and it has no left child, implying that $succ_{op'}$ is the successor of $curr_{op'}$. Therefore, $Key(\text{succ}_{op}) = k'' \geq k'$.

If $k < k'$ or $k \geq k''$, then $k \in Range_C(\text{prev}_{op})$ still holds.

Suppose otherwise that $k' \leq k < k''$ and $k \notin Range_C(\text{prev}_{op})$. If the step of line 73 by op' precedes or is in the read-side critical section of op then before removing the successor $succ_{op'}$ from the tree, op' invokes synchronize_rcu and waits until the end of op's read side critical section, by the RCU property. Since the WBST property holds during the get of op, its search ends in $succ_{op'}$ ($succ_{op'}$ equals $prev_{op}$ and $curr_{op}$ equals $\perp$). Since op is an insert, it invokes rcu_read_unlock and locks $prev_{op}$ prior to validation. On the other hand, op' unlocks $succ_{op'}$ only after marking it in Line 75. Therefore, the validation of $prev_{op}$ by op finds that it is marked, and fails (Figure 7).

Otherwise, the step of Line 73 by op' is executed after the read side critical section of op and before op locks $prev_{op}$. If $prev_{op}$ equals $succ_{op'}$ then op' marks $prev_{op}$ before releasing its lock, and the validation of op fails. If not then by the WBST property the change was in the left sub-tree of $prev_{op}$. In this case, validation fails, because either $prev_{op}$.child[left] $\neq \perp$ or $prev_{op}$.tag[left] $\neq tag_{op}$ (Lemma 3). □

The WBST property now follows by a simple induction. Lemmas 1 and 2 show that the correct successor replaces a deleted node with two children (bypassing a node with one child clearly preserves the WBST property), while Lemma 4 shows that new nodes are correctly inserted. Due to space constraints, the proof appears in the full version.

LEMMA 5. *The WBST property holds after every prefix σ of π.*

The next lemma shows that each node has a single parent, and thus, delete makes a node unreachable in a single write to a child field. It is proved by way of contradiction, considering the first time when the property is violated. Due to space constraints, the proof appears in the full version.

LEMMA 6. *A node that is reachable in a configuration $C \in \pi$ has one reachable parent in C.*

The following lemma is used to prove that if a node v with key k remains in the tree during a get, then v can be found. The reason is that the path to v never gets longer, and that even if a node u, that used to be on the path from the root to v, is read, there is still a path from u to v.

LEMMA 7. *If there is a path from u to v in configuration $C \in \pi$ and v is reachable in a configuration $C' \in \pi$ that follows C, then there is a path from u to v in C' and $|\rho_{C'}(u,v)| \leq |\rho_C(u,v)|$.*

PROOF. Assume, by way of contradiction, that v is reachable in some configuration that follows C, but the properties are not maintained. Let C' be the last configuration in which both propertied

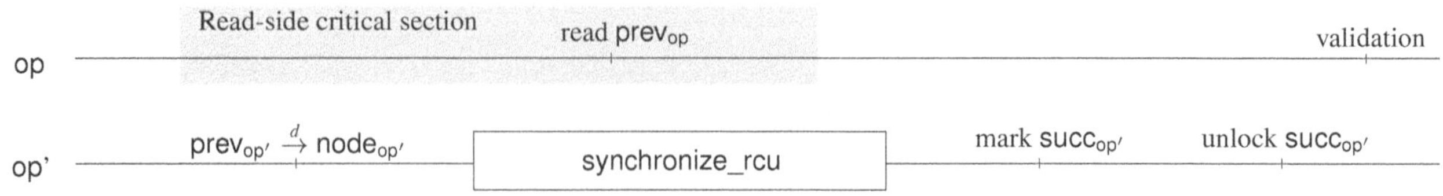

Figure 7: The execution considered in the proof of Lemma 4

hold. Let s be the step immediately following C'; s must be a write to a child field of a locked node, by an update op. We consider all possible cases:

Case 1: insert. Line 29: By the validation in Line 27, prev has no child in direction d (where d is the value of direction), thus, op adds a leaf to the tree, which does not change the reachability of v from u nor the length of existing paths in the tree.

Case 2: delete. By the validation in Line 49, prev $\xrightarrow{d}$ curr (where d is the value of direction).

Bypassing (Lines 53, 77, 80): By the conditions of the lemma and Lemma 6, the node being bypassed is not v (bypassing a node with a single reachable parent makes it unreachable). If the node being bypassed is u, then s does not change any child field on the path from u to v, and the path and its length are maintained. If the node being bypassed is any other node in $\rho_{C'}(u,v)$, then s only shortens the path and the lemma holds.

Line 73: Both children of curr become the children of node, in Line 70, and curr is replaced with node. Therefore, only curr may become unreachable. By Lemma 6 curr becomes unreachable, and by the conditions of the lemma $v \neq$curr. If curr $= u$, then s does not change any child field on the path from u to v, and the path and its length are maintained. If curr is any other node in $\rho_{C'}(u,v)$, and C'' is the configuration immediately following s, then node $\in \rho_{C''}(u,v)$, the path exists and its length remains the same. □

We linearize the successful updates, as follows:

- A successful insert is linearized with its primitive write in Line 29.
- A successful delete is linearized with its primitive write in Line 53 or 73. (At most one of these lines is executed.)

Let $s_1, s_2, \ldots$ be the primitive writes in π, in which successful updates are linearized, in their order in π. For every $i \geq 1$, let C_i be the configuration immediately preceding s_i and let C_i' be the configuration immediately following s_i. A successful insert linearized at s_i is *consistent* if $k \notin Set_{C_i}(root)$ and $k \in Set_{C_i'}(root)$, and a successful delete linearized at s_i is *consistent* if $k \in Set_{C_i}(root)$ and $k \notin Set_{C_i'}(root)$.

The next lemma is important for proving the consistency of successful inserts. It shows that if the key was inserted, by another operation, during the get of an insert then either (i) get finds the key or (ii) the key is inserted as a child of the last node in the search. Later, the first case of this lemma is used to linearize unsuccessful contains and delete.

LEMMA 8. *Let π' be read-side critical section of get(k), and suppose that every successful update linearized before the last configuration of π' is consistent. Let C be the first configuration in π' such that $k \in Set_C(root)$ and assume that $k \in Set_{C'}(root)$, for every configuration $C' \in \pi'$ that follows C. If C precedes the last access to a child field by get then, (i) get returns curr such that $k =Key($curr$)$. Otherwise, (ii) get returns prev such that prev $\xrightarrow{d} v$ and $k =Key(v)$ where d is the value of direction.*

PROOF. Let v be the closest reachable node to the root in C such that $k =Key(v)$, and let v' be the value of prev$_{op}$ in C or the root if C precedes Line 3 of get. since the WBST property holds in π and insert adds leaves, $v' \in \rho_C(root,v)$.

If C does not precedes the last access to a child field by get, then prev $= v' \xrightarrow{d} v$ as required.

If C precedes the last access to a child field by get, then get must reach a node with key k. Suppose otherwise that get does not reach a node with key k. If v is reachable in the last configuration of π', then the path from v' to v does not get longer (Lemma 7). Since the WBST property holds in π, get traverses this path, and hence, if a node with key k is not found, then v is unreachable in the last configuration of π'.

Let $s \in \pi'$ be the primitive write by operation op' that makes v unreachable. Let C_s be the configuration immediately preceding s in π' and let C_s' be the configuration immediately following s in π'; v is reachable in C_s and unreachable in C_s'. By the validation in Line 27, insert does not make a node unreachable, and hence, only delete can make v unreachable. Since $k \in Set_{C_s'}(root)$, op' has key $k' \neq k$. The only other way a delete makes a node unreachable is when $v =$succ$_{op'}$ and s is the primitive write of either Line 77 or Line 80.

Let $s' \in \pi'$ be the primitive write by operation op' that adds node$_{op'}$ to the tree. Let $C_{s'}$ be the configuration immediately preceding s' in π' and let $C_{s'}'$ be the configuration immediately following s' in π'; Since succ$_{op'}$ is found by traversing the left-most branch of the sub-tree rooted at curr$_{op'}$, there is a path from curr$_{op'}$ to v in a configuration that precedes $C_{s'}$, there is a path from curr$_{op'}$ to v in $C_{s'}$ (Lemma 7). By Line 70, node$_{op'}$ has the same children as curr$_{op'}$, and therefore, there is a path from node$_{op'}$ to v in $C_{s'}'$. This means that node$_{op'}$ $\in \rho_{C_{s'}'}(root,v)$, and by the choice of v, node$_{op'}$ is not in the tree in C. Therefore, synchronize_rcu is invoked by op' after get is invoked by op, and by the RCU property, op' executes Line 77 or Line 80 after the last configuration of π', contradicting the assumption that v is unreachable in the last configuration of π'. □

The next lemma proves that there is only one node with key k, and thus, only one node should be made unreachable in order for delete to be consistent. Due to space constraints, the proof appears in the full version.

LEMMA 9. *Let v be a node that is successfully validated by an operation op. Let σ be the prefix ending with the configuration C that immediately follows the return from validate. If all successful updates linearized in σ are consistent, then there is no other reachable node v' such that $Key(v)$=$Key(v')$.*

LEMMA 10. *All successful updates are consistent.*

PROOF. By induction on the linearization points, $s_1, s_2, \ldots$. For every $j \geq 1$, let C_j be the configuration immediately preceding s_j and C_j' be the configuration immediately following s_j.

Base: A successful update op is linearized at its first primitive write, hence, there is no write before s_1. Let k be the key of op, and note that $k \notin Set_C(root)$ for every configuration C preceding s_1, and by Lemma 2, op cannot access a node with key k, hence, op is a successful insert. Since op accesses prev, by Lemma 2, prev is reachable in some configuration preceding the step of Line 27. Since prev is validated in Line 27 and is unmarked, Lemma 1 implies that prev is reachable in C_1 and $k \in Set_{C'_1}(root)$.

For the induction step, assume that the successful updates linearized at $s_1, s_2, ..., s_{i-1}$ are consistent, and consider the successful update op linearized at s_i.

Case 1: op is delete(k). The if statement in Line 45 implies that $k = Key$(curr). By the validation in Line 49, curr and prev are both unmarked and prev $\xrightarrow{d}$curr (where d is the value of direction). Since op accesses prev and curr, Lemma 2 implies that they are reachable in some configuration preceding the step of Line 49. Furthermore, Lemma 1 implies that prev and curr are reachable in C_i. Since prev is the only reachable parent of curr (Lemma 6) curr is unreachable in C'_i. By the induction hypothesis, all successful updates linearized at $s_1, s_2, ..., s_{i-1}$ are consistent. Together with the fact that op validates curr, this implies that curr is the only reachable node with key k in C_i (Lemma 9) Therefore, $k \notin Set_{C'_i}(root)$.

Case 2: op is insert(k): Since op accesses prev_{op}, Lemma 2 implies that prev_{op} is reachable in some configuration preceding the step of Line 27. Since prev_{op} is validated in Line 27, it is unmarked, and Lemma 1 implies that it is reachable in C_i. Since $k = Key(\text{node}_{\text{op}})$, $k \in Set_{C'_i}(root)$.

Assume, by way of contradiction, that $k \in Set_{C_i}(root)$. Let $s_j, j < i$ be the last linearization point of a successful insert with key k. By the induction hypothesis, and since $k \in Set_{C_i}(root)$, no delete(k) is linearized between s_j and s_i, and for every configuration C that follows C_j and precedes C_i, $k \in Set_C(root)$.

If C'_j precedes or is in the read-side critical section of op then Lemma 8 implies that either $k = Key(\text{curr}_{\text{op}})$ or $\text{prev}_{\text{op}} \xrightarrow{d} v$ and $k = Key(v)$ (where d is the value of direction). If $k = Key(\text{curr}_{\text{op}})$ then $\text{curr}_{\text{op}} \neq \perp$ and op returns false in contradiction to op being a successful update. If $\text{prev}_{\text{op}} \xrightarrow{d} v$ then the validation in Line 27 fails, in contradiction to the linearization of op.

Otherwise, since the WBST property holds in π, s_j inserts the new node as the child of prev_{op} in direction d, and the validation of op fails, because either $\text{prev}_{\text{op}}.\text{child}[d] \neq \perp$ or $\text{prev}_{\text{op}}.\text{tag}[d] \neq \text{tag}_{\text{op}}$ (Lemma 3) □

An operation op with interval π', of the remaining types, is linearized as follows:

- If op is a failed contains or a failed delete, then curr $= \perp$.

  If $k \in Set_C(root)$ for every configuration $C \in \pi'$, then $k \in Set_C(root)$ for every configuration $C \in \pi''$, where π'' is the read-side critical section of op. By Lemma 8(i), op reaches a node with key k, which is a contradiction. Therefore, $k \notin Set_C(root)$, for some configuration $C \in \pi'$. The linearization point of op is after last $C' \in \pi'$ such that $k \notin Set_{C'}(root)$, and before the successful insert with the same linearization point, if such insert exists. This linearization point is clearly consistent.

- If op is a successful contains that returns a node v's value or a failed insert that reached node v with key k, then it is linearized after the last configuration $C \in \pi'$ such that v is reachable in C, and before the successful delete with the same linearization point, if such delete exists.

  In op, curr $= v$, and by condition of the while loop in get (Line 7), $k = Key(v)$. By Lemma 2, curr is reachable in some configuration $C' \in \pi'$, and the linearization point exists. This linearization point is consistent since $k \in Set_C(root)$ and if op is a successful contains, it returns $v.value$.

Together with Lemma 10, this proves the linearizability of CITRUS. Furthermore, if there is only a finite number of keys, then every path from the root is finite, and contains is wait-free.

THEOREM 11. *The* CITRUS *algorithm is a linearizable implementation of a binary search tree, supporting wait-free* contains.

5. EVALUATION

Setup. We implemented CITRUS in C since both the RCU implementation and the RCU-based trees are implemented in C. We considered two RCU-based trees, the *red-black* tree [18] and *Bonsai*, a balanced search tree [6], both using a global lock to synchronize among updates.[1] We also compared CITRUS to three concurrent dictionary data structures, which have C implementations: The optimistic *AVL* tree[2] [4], the lock-free search tree [23] and the lock-based lazy *skiplist*[3] [15].

The experiments were run on a machine with four AMD Opteron 6376 Processors, each with 16 cores, for a total of 64 cores. All memory allocation used the `jemalloc` library, to avoid synchronization bottlenecks during memory allocation.

Experiment sets were run with two key ranges, $[0, 2 \cdot 10^5]$ and $[0, 2 \cdot 10^6]$; in both sets, the tree was pre-filled to the size of half the key range. During pre-filling memory was reclaimed. For every test, each thread ran for five seconds, continuously executing randomly chosen operations with a randomly chosen key, without performing any memory reclamation. We show the overall throughput (total number of executed operations divided by the running time). Each experiment was run five times for each configuration of operation distribution, key range and thread count; we report the arithmetic average as the final result.

Running experiments in the unmanaged C environment revealed that memory management, and in particular cache usage, has a significant impact on performance. The size of nodes, order of fields, and their alignment inside cache lines, often influences the results much more than the algorithmic aspects of the implementation.

New RCU. During our initial evaluation of CITRUS, we identified that the user-space RCU implementation [8] does not scale for workloads with many concurrent updates, due to expensive synchronization among them, which include acquiring a global lock. The left side of Figure 8 shows representative results; similar behaviour was observed under different update contention and key ranges. To show that the drop in throughput is just an implementation issue, we re-implemented the subset of the RCU API used in CITRUS, in a manner similar to *epoch-based reclamation* [11]. In our implementation, each thread has a counter and flag, the counter counts the number of critical sections executed by the thread and a flag indicates if the thread is currently inside its read-side critical section. The rcu_read_lock operation increments the counter and sets the flag to true, while the rcu_read_unlock operation sets the flag to false. When a thread executes a synchronize_rcu operation, it waits for every other thread, until one of two things occurs:

[1] We were unable to run the red-black tree variant [18] using transactional memory to optimistically handle conflicting updates.

[2] Implemented in C by Philip W. Howard, `https://github.com/philip-w-howard/RP-Red-Black-Tree`.

[3] Implemented in C by Vincent Gramoli, `https://github.com/gramoli/synchrobench`.

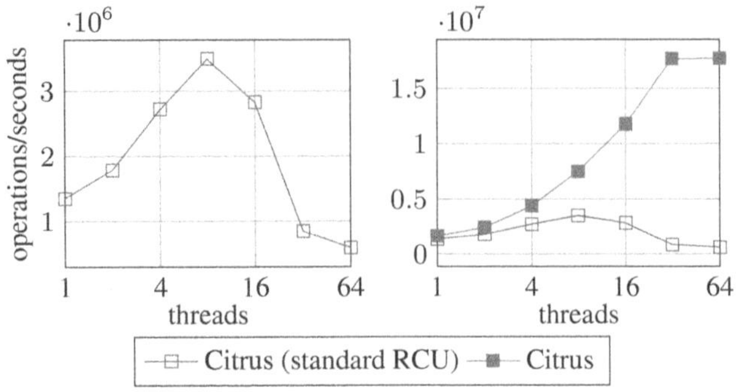

Figure 8: Impact of concurrent updates on the standard RCU implementation compared to our scalable implementation: example with operation distribution of 50% contains and key range $[0, 2 \cdot 10^5]$. Left side is a detailed view of the behaviour of the original implementation.

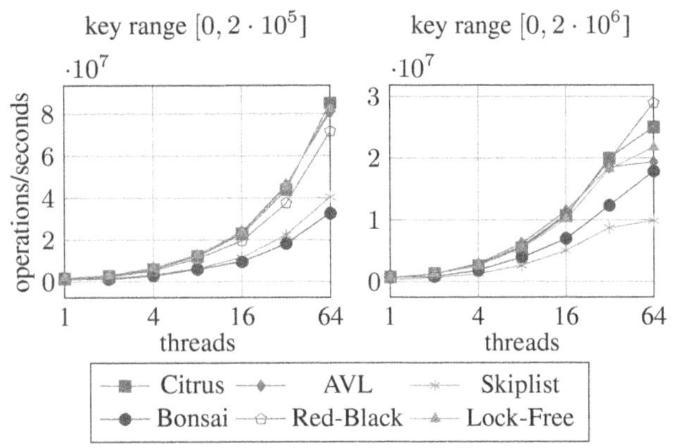

Figure 9: Throughput of the different algorithms with a single writer.

either the thread has increased its counter or the thread's flag is set to false. The main advantage of this implementation is that multiple threads executing synchronize_rcu need not coordinate among themselves, and they do not acquire any locks. The right side of Figure 8 shows the throughput of CITRUS with the new RCU implementation. All other experiments were run with the new RCU implementation.

Single writer. The throughput results of the single-writer workload appear in Figure 9. This set of experiments was designed to favor the RCU-based trees, red-black tree and Bonsai: they all include a single thread executing updates (50% insert and 50% delete). Though this set favors the RCU-based trees, Bonsai does not perform well, possibly due to its functional programming style, which reconstruct parts of the tree after every update.

Other results. Figure 10 shows the results for key ranges $[0, 2 \cdot 10^5]$ and $[0, 2 \cdot 10^6]$. Experiments with 100% contains distribution (on the left) are supposed to favor the RCU-based trees. As expected, the RCU-based trees show good performance, which is more visible in large key ranges.

The shortcomings of RCU-based trees with coarse-grained locks are seen already with 98% contains distribution. Both red-black and Bonsai do not scale even with a low update contention, while CITRUS has similar performance to other trees. In heavy update workload of 50% contains distribution, CITRUS continues to scale, though the cost of synchronize_rcu is evident. Note that unlike the AVL tree, CITRUS and the lock-free tree do not pay a cost for tree balancing, which is not cost-effective when considering a uniform distribution of keys.

6. RELATED WORK

Read copy update (RCU) was introduced [22] as a solution to lock contention and synchronization overhead in read-intensive workloads. RCU can be used for explicit memory reclamation [21]. A formal semantics for RCU appears in [12, 13].

Relativistic programing is a methodology for concurrent programming using RCU, which does not assume sequentially consistent memory. It instructs readers to access items in the data structure in an order that is reverse to the order that updates modify them, but it does not deal with concurrent updates. Relativistic programming was employed in a concurrent *hash table* [25, 26] in which a lock protects each bucket. Relativistic programming was also used in a *red-black tree* [18], which allows only one concurrent writer to the tree, optimistically enforced by transactional memory [16]. RCU was used in a different way in Bonsai, a balanced tree algorithm [6]. Inspired by functional programming, Bonsai never modifies the tree in place, creating instead a new instance for the changed data structure.

Many concurrent search trees were presented in recent years, several of them using fine-grained locks, e.g., [1, 4, 7, 9]. The AVL tree of Bronson et al. [4] uses fine-grained locks, and it is partially external and relaxed balanced. Other trees are *nonblocking*, e.g., [3, 5, 10, 11, 19, 23]. These algorithms typically use *compare&swap* primitives, and in some cases, even stronger primitives on several shared variables, like *multi-word* compare&swap [11] or the customized LLX, SCX and VLX primitives [5].

Several of these implementations [5, 3, 7, 9, 10, 23] also provides wait-free contains.

7. DISCUSSION

We have shown that it is possible, and even relatively simple, to design RCU-based concurrent search trees with concurrent updates. This opens up many interesting directions for future research. The obvious question is to extend CITRUS to a *balanced* search tree. It is also important to integrate into CITRUS two primary aspects of RCU usage, namely, efficient memory reclamation and out-of-order execution of memory instructions. A broader topic is to employ RCU in lock-free algorithms, using primitives such as *compare-and-swap* instead of locks. This will necessitate more refined mechanisms for synchronization among readers and updates, since synchronize_rcu is inherently blocking.

Acknowledgements. We would like to thank Hongseok Yang for suggesting that we look at concurrent algorithms using RCU, Noam Rinetzky for discussions of the correctness proof, Adam Morrison for his help with understanding the performance of the implementation and many insightful discussions, and finally, Yehonatan Rubin, Dana Drachsler, Alexander Libov and Eran Yahav for their help with the evaluation.

8. REFERENCES

[1] Y. Afek, H. Kaplan, B. Korenfeld, A. Morrison, and R. E. Tarjan. CBTree: A practical concurrent self-adjusting search tree. *DISC* 2012, pp. 1–15.

[2] H. Attiya, R. Guerraoui, and E. Ruppert. Partial snapshot objects. *SPAA* 2008, pp. 336–343.

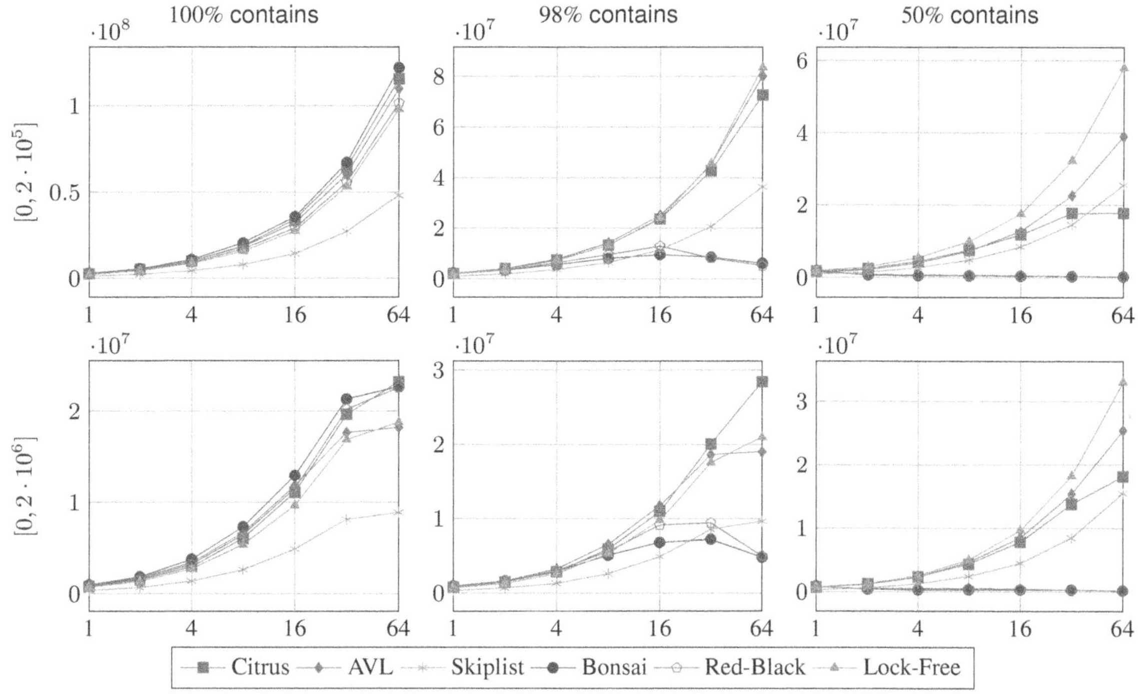

Figure 10: Throughput of the different algorithms with key range $[0, 2 \cdot 10^5]$ and $[0, 2 \cdot 10^6]$ under different operation distribution; y-axis show the throughput (operations/sec), and x-axis show the number of threads.

[3] A. Braginsky and E. Petrank. A lock-free B+tree. *SPAA* 2012, pp. 58–67, 2012.

[4] N. G. Bronson, J. Casper, H. Chafi, and K. Olukotun. A practical concurrent binary search tree. *PPoPP* 2010, pp. 257–268.

[5] T. Brown, F. Ellen, and E. Ruppert. A general technique for non-blocking trees. *PPoPP* 2014, pp. 329–342.

[6] A. T. Clements, M. F. Kaashoek, and N. Zeldovich. Scalable address spaces using RCU balanced trees. *ASPLOS* 2012, pp. 199–210.

[7] T. Crain, V. Gramoli, and M. Raynal. A contention-friendly binary search tree. *Euro-Par* 2010, pp. 229–240.

[8] M. Desnoyers, P. McKenney, A. Stern, M. Dagenais, and J. Walpole. User-level implementations of Read-Copy Update. *IEEE Transactions on Parallel and Distributed Systems*, 23(2):375–382, 2012.

[9] D. Drachsler, M. Vechev, and E. Yahav. Practical concurrent binary search trees via logical ordering. *PPoPP* 2014, pp. 343–356.

[10] F. Ellen, P. Fatourou, E. Ruppert, and F. van Breugel. Non-blocking binary search trees. *PODC* 2010, pp. 131–140.

[11] K. Fraser. *Practical lock-freedom*. PhD thesis, University of Cambridge, 2003.

[12] A. Gotsman, N. Rinetzky, and H. Yang. Verifying concurrent memory reclamation algorithms with grace. *ESOP* 2013, pp. 249–269.

[13] D. Guniguntala, P. E. McKenney, J. Triplett, and J. Walpole. The read-copy-update mechanism for supporting real-time applications on shared-memory multiprocessor systems with Linux. *IBM Systems Journal*, 47(2):221–236, May 2008.

[14] S. Heller, M. Herlihy, V. Luchangco, M. Moir, W. N. Scherer III, and N. Shavit. A lazy concurrent list-based set algorithm. *OPODIS* 2006, pp. 3–16.

[15] M. Herlihy, Y. Lev, V. Luchangco, and N. Shavit. A simple optimistic skiplist algorithm. *SIROCCO* 2007, pp. 124–138.

[16] M. Herlihy and J. E. B. Moss. Transactional memory: architectural support for lock-free data structures. *SIGARCH Comput. Archit. News*, 21(2):289–300, May 1993.

[17] M. P. Herlihy and J. M. Wing. Linearizability: a correctness condition for concurrent objects. *ACM Trans. Program. Lang. Syst.*, 12(3):463–492, July 1990.

[18] P. W. Howard and J. Walpole. Relativistic red-black trees. *Concurrency & Computation: Practice & Experience*, 2013.

[19] S. V. Howley and J. Jones. A non-blocking internal binary search tree. *SPAA* 2012, pp. 161–171.

[20] P. E. McKenney. RCU Linux usage. `http://www.rdrop.com/users/paulmck/RCU/linuxusage.html`.

[21] P. E. McKenney. *Exploiting Deferred Destruction: An Analysis of Read-Copy-Update Techniques in Operating System kernels*. PhD thesis, Oregon State University, 2004.

[22] P. E. McKenney and J. D. Slingwine. Read-copy update: Using execution history to solve concurrency problems. *Parallel and Distributed Computing and Systems*, pp. 509–518, 1998.

[23] A. Natarajan and N. Mittal. Fast concurrent lock-free binary search trees. *PPoPP* 2014, pp. 317–328.

[24] E. Petrank and S. Timnat. Lock-free data-structure iterators. *DISC* 2013, pp. 224–238.

[25] J. Triplett, P. E. McKenney, and J. Walpole. Scalable concurrent hash tables via relativistic programming. *SIGOPS Oper. Syst. Rev.*, 44(3):102–109, Aug. 2010.

[26] J. Triplett, P. E. McKenney, and J. Walpole. Resizable, scalable, concurrent hash tables. *USENIX Annual Technical Conference*, 2011.

Brief Announcement: Distributed Universality Contention-Awareness; Wait-freedom; Object Progress, and Other Properties

Michel Raynal
Institut Universitaire de France
IRISA, Université de Rennes
35042 Rennes Cedex, France
raynal@irisa.fr

Julien Stainer
IRISA, Université de Rennes
35042 Rennes Cedex, France
julien.stainer@irisa.fr

Gadi Taubenfeld
The Interdisciplinary Center
Herzliya 46150, Israel
tgadi@idc.ac.il

ABSTRACT

A notion of a *universal construction* suited to distributed computing has been introduced by M. Herlihy in his celebrated paper "*Wait-free synchronization*" (ACM TOPLAS, 1991). A universal construction is an algorithm that can be used to wait-free implement any object defined by a sequential specification. Herlihy's paper shows that the basic system model, which supports only atomic read/write registers, has to be enriched with consensus objects to allow the design of universal constructions. The generalized notion of a *k-universal* construction has been recently introduced by Gafni and Guerraoui (CONCUR, 2011). A k-universal construction is an algorithm that can be used to simultaneously implement k objects (instead of just one object), with the guarantee that at least one of the k constructed objects progresses forever. While Herlihy's universal construction relies on atomic registers and consensus objects, a k-universal construction relies on atomic registers and k-simultaneous consensus objects (which have been shown to be computationally equivalent to k-set agreement objects in the read/write system model where any number of processes may crash).

This paper significantly extends the universality results introduced by Herlihy and Gafni-Guerraoui. In particular, we present a k-universal construction which satisfies the following five desired properties, which are not satisfied by the previous k-universal construction: (1) among the k objects that are constructed, *at least* ℓ objects (and not just one) are guaranteed to progress forever; (2) the progress condition for processes is *wait-freedom*, which means that each correct process executes an infinite number of operations on each object that progresses forever; (3) if one of the k constructed objects stops progressing, it stops in the *same* state at each process; (4) the proposed construction is *contention-aware*, which means that it uses only read/write registers in the absence of contention; and (5) it is *indulgent* with respect to the *obstruction-freedom* progress condition, which means that each process is able to complete any one of its pending operations on the k objects if all the other process hold still long enough. The proposed construction, which is based on new design principles, is called a (k, ℓ)-universal construction. It uses a natural extension of k-simultaneous consensus objects, called (k, ℓ)-simultaneous consensus objects ((k, ℓ)-SC). Together with atomic registers, (k, ℓ)-SC objects are shown to be necessary and sufficient for building a (k, ℓ)-universal construction, and, in that sense, (k, ℓ)-SC objects are *(k, ℓ)-universal*.

PODC'14, July 15–18, 2014, Paris, France.
ACM 978-1-4503-2944-6/14/07.
http://dx.doi.org/10.1145/2611462.2611503 .

Categories and Subject Descriptors

C.2.4 [**Computer-Communication Networks**]: Distributed Systems—*distributed applications*; D.4.1 [**Operating Systems**]: Process Management—*concurrency, synchronization*; D.4.5 [**Operating Systems**]: Reliability—*fault-tolerance*; F.1.1 [**Computation by Abstract Devices**]: Models of Computation—*computability theory*

Keywords

asynchronous read/write system, universal construction, k-set agreement, k-simultaneous consensus, wait-freedom, non-blocking, obstruction-freedom, crash failures, state machine replication

Asynchronous crash-prone read/write systems and the notion of a universal construction.

This paper considers systems made up of n sequential asynchronous processes that communicate by reading and writing atomic registers. Up to $n-1$ processes may crash unexpectedly. This is the basic $(n-1)$-resilient model, which is also called the read/write *wait-free model*, and is denoted here $\mathcal{ARW}_{n,n-1}[\emptyset]$. A fundamental problem encountered in this kind of systems consists in implementing any object, defined by a sequential specification, in such a way that the object behaves reliably despite any pattern of process crashes. It has been shown in [10, 13, 19] that such a general implementation, of *any* object, is impossible in $\mathcal{ARW}_{n,n-1}[\emptyset]$. Thus, in order to be able to implement any object, the model has to be enriched with basic objects whose computational power is stronger than atomic read/write registers [13].

Several progress conditions have been proposed for concurrent objects. The strongest, and most extensively studied condition, is wait-freedom. Wait-freedom guarantees that *every* process will always be able to complete its pending operations in a finite number of its own steps [13]. Thus, a *wait-*

free implementation of an object guarantees that an invocation of an object operation may fail to terminate only when the invoking process crashes. Non-blocking (which is sometimes also called lock-freedom) guarantees that *some* process will always be able to complete its pending operations in a finite number of its own steps [18]. Obstruction-freedom guarantees that a process will be able to complete its pending operations in a finite number of its own steps, if all the other processes "hold still" long enough [14]. Obstruction-freedom does not guarantee progress under contention.

Objects that can be used, together with registers, to implement any other object which satisfies a given progress condition *PC*, are called universal objects with respect to *PC*. Previous work provided methods, called *universal constructions*, to transform sequential specifications of arbitrary objects into wait-free concurrent implementations that use universal objects. It is shown in [13] that the *consensus* object is universal with respect to wait-freedom. A consensus object allows all the correct processes to reach a common decision based on their initial inputs. A consensus object is used in a universal construction to allow processes to agree –despite concurrency– on a total order on the operations they invoke on the constructed object.

In addition to the universal construction of [13], several other wait-free universal constructions were proposed, which address additional properties. As an example, a universal construction is presented in [8], where "processes operating on different parts of an implemented object do not interfere with each other by accessing common base objects". Several additional properties have been addressed in [2, 9]. The notion of a universal construction has also been investigated in the context of transactional memories (e.g., [6, 7, 15, 16, 23] to cite a few).

From consensus to k-set agreement.

k-Set agreement is a simple generalization of consensus, namely, at most k different values can be decided on when using a k-set agreement object [5] ($k = 1$ corresponds to consensus). While the impossibility proof (e.g., [13, 19]) of building a wait-free consensus object in $\mathcal{ARW}_{n,n-1}[\emptyset]$ relies on the notion of valence introduced in [10], due to its inherent strong combinatorics, the impossibility to build a wait-free k-set agreement object in $\mathcal{ARW}_{n,n-1}[\emptyset]$ relies on algebraic topology notions [3, 17, 22]. It is nevertheless possible to consider system models, stronger than the basic wait-free read/write model, enriched with consensus or k-set agreement objects. It follows that these enriched system models, denoted $\mathcal{ARW}_{n,n-1}[CONS]$ and $\mathcal{ARW}_{n,n-1}[k\text{-}SA]$, respectively, are computationally strictly stronger than the basic model $\mathcal{ARW}_{n,n-1}[\emptyset]$.

k-Set agreement vs. k-simultaneous consensus.

k-Simultaneous consensus has been introduced in [1]. Its definition is close to that of k-set agreement. Each process proposes a value to k independent consensus instances, and decides on a pair (x, v) such that x is a consensus instance, and v is a value proposed to that consensus instance. Hence, if the pairs (x, v) and (x, v') are decided by two processes, then $v = v'$.

It is shown in [1] that, in $\mathcal{ARW}_{n,n-1}[\emptyset]$, k-set agreement and k-simultaneous consensus have the same computational power. That is, each one of them can be solved in $\mathcal{ARW}_{n,n-1}[\emptyset]$ enriched with the other. This is no longer the case in asynchronous message-passing systems, namely k-simultaneous consensus is then strictly stronger than k-set agreement (as shown using different techniques in [4, 20]).

Universal construction for k objects.

An interesting question introduced in [11] by Gafni and Guerraoui is the following: what happens if, when considering the design of a universal construction, k-set agreement (or equivalently, k-simultaneous consensus) objects are considered instead of consensus objects? The authors claim that k-simultaneous consensus objects are k-*universal* in the sense that they allow to implement k deterministic concurrent objects, each defined by a sequential specification "with the guarantee that *at least one* machine remains highly available to all processes" [11]. In their paper, Gafni and Guerraoui focus on the replication of k state machines. They present a k-universal construction, based on the replication –at every process– of each of the k state machines.

Our contributions.

This paper is focused on *distributed universality*, namely it presents a very general universal construction for a set of n processes that access k concurrent objects, each defined by a sequential specification on total operations. An operation on an object is "total" if, when executed alone, it always returns [18]. The noteworthy features of this construction are the following.

- At least ℓ among the k objects progress forever, $1 \leq \ell \leq k$. This means that an infinite number of operations is applied to each of these ℓ objects. This set of ℓ objects is not predetermined, and depends on the current execution.
- The progress condition associated with the processes is wait-freedom. That is, a process that does not crash executes an infinite number of operations on each object that progresses forever.
- Objects may stop progressing when no more operations are being applied to them. The construction guarantees that when an object stops progressing, it always stops at the same state in each of the participating process. That is, *all* the processes must have the *same* view of what is the last state of an object on which no more operations are being executed.
- The construction is *contention-aware*. This means that the overhead introduced by using synchronization objects other than atomic read/write registers is eliminated where there is no contention. In the absence of contention, a process completes its operations by accessing only read/write registers.
- The construction is *indulgent* [12] with respect to the *obstruction-freedom* progress condition [14]. This means that each process is able to complete its pending operations on the k objects if all the other processes hold still long enough. That is, if once and again all the processes except one hold still long enough, all the k objects, and not just ℓ objects, are guaranteed to always progress.

This new universal construction is consequently called a *contention-aware indulgent wait-free* (k, ℓ)*-universal construction*. Differently, the universal construction presented in [11] is a $(k, 1)$-universal construction and is neither contention-aware, nor indulgent with respect to obstruction-freedom.

Moreover, the construction presented in [11] suffers from the following limitations: (a) it does not satisfy the wait-freedom progress condition, but only satisfies non-blocking (i.e., infinite progress is guaranteed for only one process); (b) in some scenarios, an operation that has been invoked by a process can (incorrectly) be applied twice, instead of just once; and (c) the view of the last state of an object on which no more operations are being executed can be different at distinct processes. While issue (b) can be fixed, we do not see how to modify the construction from [11] to overcome drawback (c).

We point out that for the special case of $k = \ell = 1$, in [13], Herlihy has implemented a wait-free $(1,1)$-universal construction. While our construction is also contention-aware, Herlihy's construction is not.

To ensure the progress of at least ℓ of the k implemented objects, the proposed construction uses a new synchronization object, that we call (k,ℓ)-simultaneous consensus object, which is a simple generalization of the k-simultaneous consensus object. This object type is such that its $(k,1)$ instance is equivalent to k-simultaneous consensus, while its (k,k) instance is equivalent to consensus. Thus, when added to the basic $\mathcal{ARW}_{n,n-1}[\emptyset]$ system model, (k,ℓ)-simultaneous consensus objects add computational power. The paper shows that (k,ℓ)-simultaneous consensus objects are necessary and sufficient to ensure that, in the universal construction, at least ℓ among the k objects progress forever. Differently, the wait-freedom progress condition is obtained on top of a non-blocking solution, with the help of atomic registers only.

From a software engineering point of view, the proposed (k,ℓ)-universal construction is built in a modular way. First a non-blocking $(k,1)$-universal construction is designed, using k-simultaneous consensus objects and atomic register. Interestingly, its design principles are different from all the other universal constructions we are aware of. Then, this basic construction is extended to obtain a contention-aware $(k,1)$-universal construction, and then a wait-free contention-aware $(k,1)$-universal construction. Finally, assuming that the system is enriched with (k,ℓ)-simultaneous consensus objects instead of k-simultaneous consensus objects, we obtain a contention-aware wait-free (k,ℓ)-universal construction. During the modular construction, we make sure that the universal construction implemented at each stage is also indulgent with respect to obstruction-freedom.

1. REFERENCES

[1] Afek Y., Gafni E., Rajsbaum S., Raynal M., and Travers C., The k-simultaneous consensus problem. *Distributed Computing*, 22(3):185-195, 2010.

[2] Anderson J.H. and Moir M., Universal constructions for large objects. *IEEE Trans. of Parallel and Distributed Systems*, 10(12):1317-1332, 1999.

[3] Borowsky E. and Gafni E., Generalized FLP impossibility results for t-resilient asynchronous computations. *Proc. 25th ACM Symp. on Theory of Computing (STOC'93)*, ACM Press, pp. 91-100, 1993.

[4] Bouzid Z. and Travers C., Simultaneous consensus is harder than set agreement in message-passing. *Proc. 33rd Int'l IEEE Conference on Distributed Computing Systems (ICDCS'13)*, IEEE Press, pp. 611-620, 2013.

[5] Chaudhuri S., More choices allow more faults: set consensus problems in totally asynchronous systems. *Information and Computation*, 105(1):132-158, 1993.

[6] Chuong Ph., Ellen F. and Ramachandran V., A Universal construction for wait-free transaction friendly data structures. *Proc. 22th Int'l ACM Symp. on Parallelism in Algorithms and Architectures (SPAA'10)*, ACM Press, pp. 335-344, 2010.

[7] Crain T., Imbs D., and Raynal M., Towards a universal construction for transaction-based multiprocess programs. *Theoretical Computer Science*, 496:154-169, 2013.

[8] Ellen F., Fatourou P., Kosmas E., Milani A., and Travers C., Universal construction that ensure disjoint-access parallelism and wait-freedom. *Proc. 31th ACM Symp. on Principles of Distributed Computing (PODC)*, ACM Press, pp. 115-124, 2012.

[9] Fatourou P. and Kallimanis N.D., A highly-efficient wait-free universal construction. *Proc. 23th ACM Symp. on Parallel Algorithms and Architectures (SPAA)*, ACM Press, pp. 325-334, 2012.

[10] Fischer M.J., Lynch N.A., and Paterson M.S., Impossibility of distributed consensus with one faulty process. *Journal of the ACM*, 32(2):374-382, 1985.

[11] Gafni E. and Guerraoui R., Generalizing universality. *Proc. 22nd Int'l Conference on Concurrency Theory (CONCUR'11)*, Springer, LNCS 6901, pp. 17-27, 2011.

[12] Guerraoui R. and Lynch N.A., A general characterization of indulgence. *ACM Trans. on Autonomous and Adaptive Systems*, 3(4), Article 20, 2008.

[13] Herlihy M.P., Wait-free synchronization. *ACM Trans. on Programming Languages and Systems*, 13(1):124-149, 1991.

[14] Herlihy M.P., Luchangco V., and Moir M., Obstruction-free synchronization: double-ended queues as an example. *Proc. 23th Int'l IEEE Conference on Distributed Computing Systems (ICDCS'03)*, IEEE Press, pp. 522-529, 2003.

[15] Herlihy M., Luchangco V., Moir M., and Scherer III W.M., Software transactional memory for dynamic-sized data structures. *Proc. 22nd Int'l ACM Symp. on Principles of Distributed Computing (PODC'03)*, ACM Press, pp. 92-101, 2003.

[16] Herlihy M.P. and Moss J.E.B., Transactional memory: architectural support for lock-free data structures. *Proc. 20th ACM Int'l Symp. on Computer Architecture (ISCA'93)*, ACM Press, pp. 289-300, 1993.

[17] Herlihy M.P. and Shavit N., The topological structure of asynchronous computability. *Journal of the ACM*, 46(6):858-923, 1999.

[18] Herlihy M.P. and Wing J.M, Linearizability: a correctness condition for concurrent objects. *ACM Trans. on Programming Languages and Systems*, 12(3):463-492, 1990.

[19] Loui M. and Abu-Amara H., Memory requirements for agreement among unreliable asynchronous processes. *Advances in Computing Research*, 4:163-183, JAI Press, 1987.

[20] Raynal M. and Stainer J., Simultaneous consensus vs set agreement: a message-passing-sensitive hierarchy of agreement problems. *Proc. 20th Int'l Colloquium on Structural Information and Communication Complexity (SIROCCO 2013)*, Springer LNCS 8179, pp. 298-309, 2013.

[21] Raynal M., Stainer J., and Taubenfeld G., Distributed universality: contention-awareness, wait-freedom, object Progress, and other properties. *Tech Report*, pages, IRISA, Université de Rennes, France, 2014.

[22] Saks M. and Zaharoglou F., Wait-free k-set agreement is impossible: the topology of public knowledge. *SIAM Journal on Computing*, 29(5):1449-1483, 2000.

[23] Shavit N. and Touitou D., Software transactional memory. *Distributed Computing*, 10(2):99-116, 1997.

Brief Announcement: Concurrency-Aware Linearizability

Nir Hemed
Tel Aviv University
nirh@mail.tau.ac.il

Noam Rinetzky
Tel Aviv University
maon@cs.tau.ac.il

ABSTRACT

Linearizabilty allows to describe the behaviour of concurrent objects using sequential specifications. Unfortunately, as we show in this paper, sequential specifications cannot be used for concurrent objects whose *observable behaviour* in the presence of concurrent operations *should* be different than their behaviour in the sequential setting. As a result, such *concurrency-aware objects* do not have formal specifications, which, in turn, precludes formal verification.

In this paper we present *Concurrency Aware Linearizability* (CAL), a new correctness condition which allows to formally specify the behaviour of a certain class of concurrency-aware objects. Technically, CAL is formalized as a strict extension of linearizability, where *concurrency-aware specifications* are used instead of sequential ones. We believe that CAL can be used as a basis for modular formal verification techniques for concurrency-aware objects.

Categories and Subject Descriptors

D.1.3 [**Programming Techniques**]: Concurrent Programming; D.2.4 [**Software Engineering**]: Software/Program Verification

Keywords

Linearizability; sequential specification; concurrent specification

1. INTRODUCTION

Linearizability [4] is a property of the externally-observable behaviour of concurrent objects [4]. Intuitively, a concurrent object is linearizable if in every execution each operation seems to take effect instantaneously between its invocation and response, and the resulting sequence of (seemingly instantaneous) operations respects a given sequential specification. Unfortunately, as we show below, for some concurrent objects it is *impossible* to provide a sequential specification: their behaviour in the presence of concurrent (overlapping) operations is, and should be, *observably different* from their behaviour in the sequential setting. For these objects, which we refer to as *Concurrency-Aware Concurrent Objects (CA-objects)*, the traditional notion of linearizability is simply not expressive enough to allow for describing all desired behaviours without introducing undesired ones. As a result, CA-objects are not given a formal specification. The lack of formal specifications is problematic as it precludes formal proofs.

Concurrency-Aware Linearizabilty (CAL) is a correctness condition which addresses the aforementioned problem. CAL enables programmers to provide natural and intuitive specifications for an important class of CA-objects. Technically, CAL is an extension of linearizabilty where *Concurrency-Aware specifications* are used to describe concurrency-dependent behaviours. Sequential specifications are a special case of concurrency-aware specifications in which concurrent behaviours can be explained by sequential ones.

Running Example. `Exchanger` objects (as found, e.g., in `java.util.concurrent.Exchanger`) serve as a synchronization point at which threads can pair up and *atomically swap* elements. `Exchangers` are useful in applications such as genetic algorithms and pipeline designs, and are embedded in practice in thread-pool implementations as well as other higher-level data structures [5, 6].

Figure 1(`E`) shows a simplified version of the wait-free exchanger of [5] in which retires are omitted. Intuitively, a client thread uses the `Exchanger` by invoking the `exchange()` method with a value that it offers to swap (in our case a positive `int`). `exchange()` attempts to find a partner thread and, if successful, instantaneously exchanges the offered value with the one offered by the partner. If a partner thread is not found, `exchange()` returns `-1`, indicating that the operation has failed. More technically, the exchange is performed by using `Offer` objects, consisting of the `data` offered for exchange and a `hole` pointer. A successful swap occurs when the `hole` pointer in the `Offer` of one thread points to the `Offer` of another thread. This can be achieved in two ways: A thread that finds that the value of `g` is null can set it to its `Offer` (line 10) and wait for a partner thread to match with (`sleep` in line 11). Upon awakening, it checks whether it was paired with another thread by executing a CAS on its own `hole` (line 12). If the CAS succeeds, then a match did not occur, and setting the `hole` pointer to point to the `fail` sentinel signals that the thread is no longer interested in the exchange. If the CAS fails then some other thread has already matched the `Offer` and the exchange can complete successfully. If `g` is not null, then the thread attempts to update the `hole` field of the `Offer` pointed to by `g` from its initial null value to its own `Offer` (line 16). An additional CAS (line 17) sets `g` back to null. By doing so, it helps to remove already-matched offers from the global pointer; hence, the CAS in line 17 is unconditional.

`Exchanger` objects do not have a formal specification. This is not surprising; describing the concurrent behaviour that requires that `exchange()` succeeds only if *two* threads invoke the method simultaneously is, as we show below, impossible using the form of sequential specifications suggested in [4]. As a result, correctness proofs of concurrent objects that utilize `Exchanger`-like ob-

PODC'14, July 15–18, 2014, Paris, France.
ACM 978-1-4503-2944-6/14/07.
http://dx.doi.org/10.1145/2611462.2611513.

(E)

```
class Offer {
  int data;
  Offer hole;
  Offer(int d){data = d; hole = null;}
}
Offer g = null;
Offer fail = new Offer(-1);
int exchange(int d){ // we assume 0 ≤ d
  Offer n = new Offer(d);
  if (CAS(g, null, n)){
    sleep(50);
    CAS(n.hole, null, fail)
    return n.hole.data;
  }
  Offer cur = g;
  bool success = CAS(cur.hole, null, n);
  CAS(g, cur, null);
  if (success)
    return cur.data;
  else return -1;
}
```

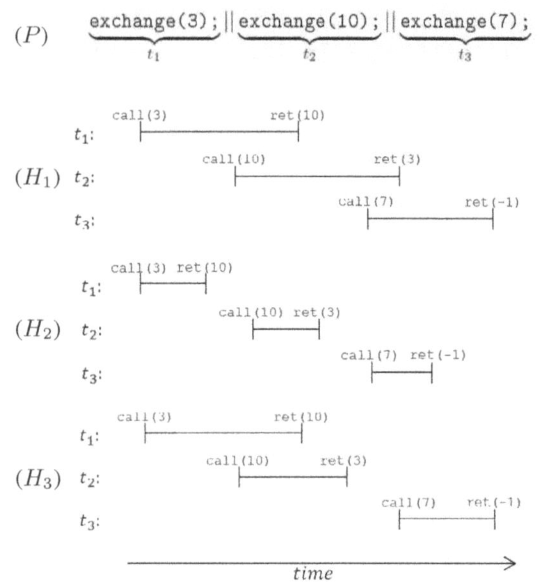

Figure 1: (E) a simplified Exchanger, (P) a client program, (H_1) a concurrent history, (H_2) an undesired sequential history, (H_3) a CA-history, a graphical depiction of a (SH) sequential history, a (CAH) CA-history, and a (CH) concurrent history.

jects are not modular. For example, the proof of the HSY-stack [3] mixes reasoning about the implementation of an (`Exchanger`-like) elimination array with its particular usage by the stack.

2. CONCURRENCY-AWARE LINEARIZABILITY (CAL)

Linearizability relates an implementation of a concurrent object with a sequential specification. Both the implementation and the specification are formalized as *prefix-closed sets of histories*. A history $H = \psi_1\psi_2\ldots$ is a sequence of methods invocations and responses. Specifications are given using *sequential histories* in which every response is immediately preceded by its matching invocation. Implementations, on the other hand, allow for arbitrary interleaving of actions by different threads, as long as the subsequence of actions of every thread is sequential. Informally, a concurrent object OS_C is linearizable with respect to a specification OS_A if every history H in OS_C can be *explained* by a history S in OS_A that "looks similar" to H. The similarity is formalized by a real-time relation $H \sqsubseteq_{RT} S$, which requires S to be a permutation of H preserving the per-thread order of actions and the order of non-overlapping operations.[1]

Why it is *impossible* to provide a sequential specification for `Exchangers`? Consider the client program P shown in Figure 1(P) which uses an `Exchanger` object. Figures 1(H_1-H_3) show three histories, where an `exchange(n)` operation returning value `n'` is depicted using an interval bounded by a "`call(n)`" and a "`ret(n')`" actions. Note that histories H_1 and H_3 might occur when P executes, but H_2 cannot.

History H_1 corresponds to the case where threads t_1 and t_2 exchange items 3 and 10 respectively and t_3 fails to pair-up. History H_2 is one possible sequential explanation of H_1. Using H_2 to explain H_1 raises the following problem: if H_2 is allowed by the specification then every prefix of H_2 must be allowed as-well. In particular, history H_2' in which only t_1 performs its operation should be allowed. Note that in H_2' a thread exchanges an item without finding a partner. Clearly, H_2' is an *undesired* behaviour. In fact, any sequential history that attempts to explain H_1 would allow for similar undesired behaviours. (In general, only executions in which all `exchange()` operations fail can be explained by sequential histories.) We conclude that any sequential specification of the `Exchanger` is either too restrictive or too loose.

We now turn to the definition of *concurrency-aware linearizability*. A key notion here is that of *concurrency-aware histories*. A history H is **concurrency-aware** (**CA-History**) if for any history H_1 such that $H = H_1\psi'\psi H_2$ if ψ' is a response and ψ is an invocation then the matching response of any invocation in $H_1\psi'$ is also in $H_1\psi'$. Note that a CA-history may contain concurrent operations. However, it ensures that such operations overlap pairwise. This provides the illusion that *all* concurrent operations are performed instantaneously at the same point in time. Figure 1 illustrates a sequential history (SH), a CA-history (CAH), and a concurrent history (CH). Note that every sequential history is a CA-history and every CA-history is a concurrent history, but not vice-versa. CAL extends linearizability by allowing specifications to be a (prefix-closed) set of CA-histories: A concurrent object OS_C is *CA-linearizable* with respect to a specification OS_A, if every history H in OS_C has a "similar-looking" *CA-history* S in OS_A. The "similar-looking" relation used in CAL is the same real-time order relation used to define linearizability [4]; the term *Concurrency-Aware Linearizability* emphasizes that the specification is comprised of **concurrency-aware** histories rather than a sequential ones.

Note that history H_3, depicted in Figure 1, is a *concurrency-aware history*. It describes the observable behavior as in H_1 while maintaining the same real-time order of operations and requiring

[1]For brevity, formal details, e.g., the treatment of *history completions*, are deferred to the Appendix.

that exchange(3) and exchange(10) execute concurrently and, seemingly, at the same point in time. Also note that every prefix of H_3 describes a behavior which is allowed by the implementation. Indeed, the behaviour of Exchanger objects can be specified precisely using CA-histories.

3. CONCLUSIONS AND FUTURE WORK

We present Concurrency-Aware Linearizabilty (CAL), a new correctness condition for an important class of CA-objects, concurrent objects whose behaviour does not have a sequential explanation. CA-objects exist in practice but currently do not have formal specifications. CAL allows providing accurate formal specifications for CA-objects using CA-histories, a restricted generalization of sequential histories. We believe that CAL can form the semantical basis for modular and reusable correctness proofs for CA-objects.

Acknowledgements. This research was supported by the EU project ADVENT.

References

[1] Abstraction for concurrent objects. *TCS*, 411(51-52), 2010.

[2] Y. Afek, M. Hakimi, and A. Morrison. Fast and scalable rendezvousing. In *Distributed Computing*. 2011.

[3] D. Hendler, N. Shavit, and L. Yerushalmi. A scalable lock-free stack algorithm. In *SPAA*, 2004.

[4] M. P. Herlihy and J. M. Wing. Linearizability: A correctness condition for concurrent objects. *TOPLAS*, 1990.

[5] W. N. Scherer III, D. Lea, and M. L. Scott. A scalable elimination-based exchange channel. *SCOOL*, 2005.

[6] W. N. Scherer III, D. Lea, and M. L. Scott. Scalable synchronous queues. In *PPoPP*, 2006.

[7] W. N. Scherer III and M. L. Scott. Nonblocking concurrent data structures with condition synchronization. In *Distributed Computing*. 2004.

APPENDIX

In this section we formalize the notion of *contentaion-aware linearizability* (CAL). We assume infinite sets of object names $o \in \mathcal{O}$, method names $f \in \mathcal{F}$, and threads identifiers $t \in \mathcal{T}$.

DEFINITION 1. *An **object action** is either an **inocation** $\psi = (t, \mathrm{inv}\, o.f(n))$ or a **response** $\psi' = (t', \mathrm{res}(n')o'.f')$.*

Intuitively, an invocation $\psi = (t, \mathrm{inv}\, o.f(n))$ means transfer of control from the client to the library, and response $\psi' = (t', \mathrm{res}(n')o'.f')$ means the return of control to the invoking client. As in [4], the observable behaviour of a concurrent object is represented by a set of histories, which are sequences of *invocations* and *responses* of methods calls.

DEFINITION 2. *A **history** H is a finite sequence of invocations and responses. We use H_i to denote the ith action of H and $H|_t$ to denote the projection of H onto actions of thread t. We denote by _ an expression that is irrelevant and implicitly existentially quantified. A history is **sequential** if every response action is immediately preceded by a matching invocation. A history H is **well-formed** if invocations and responses are properly matched: for every thread t, $H|_t$ is sequential. A history is **complete** if it is well-formed and every invocation has a matching response (i.e, for every thread t, if $H|_t = \_\psi$ then ψ is a response). History H^c is a **completion** of a well-formed history H if it is complete and can be obtained from H by (possibly) extending H with some response actions and (possibly) removing some invocation actions. We denote by **complete(H)** the set of all completions of H.*

Linearizability is a relation between **object systems**, prefix-closed sets of well-formed histories. Following [4], we define it using the notion of real-time order.

DEFINITION 3. *The **real-time order** between actions of a well-formed history H is an irreflexive partial order $\prec_H$ on (indices of) object actions:*

$$
\begin{aligned}
&H_i \prec_H H_j \iff \\
&\quad \exists i \le i' < j' \le j.\, tid(H_i) = tid(H_{i'}) \wedge tid(H_j) = tid(H_{j'}) \wedge \\
&\qquad (tid(H_i) = tid(H_j) \vee H_{i'} = (\_, \mathrm{res}\_) \wedge H_{j'} = (\_, \mathrm{inv}\,\_))
\end{aligned}
$$

*A history H **agrees** with the real-time order of a history S, denoted by $H \sqsubseteq_{RT} S$, if (i) for every thread t, $H|_t = S|_t$ and (ii) there is a bijection $\pi : \{1, \cdots, |H|\} \to \{1, \cdots, |S|\}$ such that*

$$\forall i.(H_i = S_{\pi(i)}) \wedge (\forall i, j. H_i \prec_H H_j \implies S_{\pi(i)} \prec_S S_{\pi(j)})\,.$$

Intuitively, history S "agrees" with H if in both histories every thread performs the same sequence of actions and the real-time order induced by H is a subset of that of S, i.e. $\prec_H \subseteq \prec_S$.

DEFINITION 4 (LINEARIZABILITY [4]). *Let OS_C and OS_A be object systems. We say that OS_C is **linearizable** with respect to OS_A if every history $H \in OS$ is* sequential *and*

$$\forall H \in OS_C.\, \exists H^c \in complete(H).\, \exists S \in OS_A.\, H^c \sqsubseteq_{RT} S\,.$$

We now turn on to formally define *CAL*. The key aspect is the notion of *CA-History*, which is the building block of new class of specifications which strictly extend sequential specifications. We use the notion of complete histories to provide an alternative definition for CA-histories.

DEFINITION 5 (CONCURRENCY-AWARE HISTORY). *A history H is **concurrency-aware (CA-History)** if for any history H_1 such that $H = H_1\psi'\psi H_2$ if ψ' is a response and ψ is an invocation then $H_1\psi'$ is a complete history. An object system is OS **concurrency-aware** if each $H \in OS$ is a concurrency-aware history.*

A concurrency-aware history allows for some operations to be executed concurrently by multiple threads. Moreover, it ensures that out of the set of threads that are operating concurrently, no thread will return before all other threads have invoked the operation (i.e. all operations must overlap pairwise). Figure 1 illustrates sequential history (SH), concurrency-aware history (CAH) and concurrent history (CH). Note that while every sequential history is CA, the opposite does not hold.

Extending Definition 4, Concurrency-aware linearizabilty of an object system is described using the $\sqsubseteq_{RT}$ relation to a concurrency-aware object system:

DEFINITION 6 (CONCURRENCY AWARE LINEARIZABILITY). *Let OS_C and OS_A be object systems. We say that OS_C is **concurrency-aware linearizable (CAL)** with respect to OS_A if*

$$\forall H \in OS_C.\, \exists H^c \in complete(H).\, \exists S \in OS_A.\, H^c \sqsubseteq_{RT} S$$

and every history $H \in OS_A$ is concurrency-aware.

Thus, CA-linearizable object is such that every interaction with it can be "explained" by a CA-history of some concurrency-aware object system OS_A.

Note that the same real-time order $\sqsubseteq_{RT}$ and notion of completions are used in the definitions of linearizability and concurrency-aware linearizability; the term concurrency-aware linearizability emphasizes that the specification is comprised of *concurrency-aware* histories, rather than a *sequential* ones.

Software-Improved Hardware Lock Elision

Yehuda Afek
Tel Aviv University

Amir Levy
Tel Aviv University

Adam Morrison*
Technion

ABSTRACT

With hardware transactional memory (HTM) becoming available in mainstream processors, lock-based critical sections may now initiate a hardware transaction instead of taking the lock, enabling their concurrent execution unless a real data conflict occurs. However, just a few transactional aborts can cause the lock to be acquired non-transactionally resulting in the serialization of all the threads, severely degrading the amount of speedup obtained.

In this paper we provide two software extension mechanisms that considerably improve the concurrency and speedup levels attained by lock based programs using HTM-based lock elision. The first sacrifices opacity to achieve higher levels of concurrency, and the second retains opacity while reaching slightly lower levels of concurrency.

Evaluation on STAMP and on data structure benchmarks on an Intel Haswell processor shows that these techniques improve the speedup by up to 3.5 times and 10 times respectively, compared to using Haswell's hardware lock elision as is.

Categories and Subject Descriptors

D.1.3 [**Software**]: Programming Techniques—*concurrent programming*

Keywords

Lock elision; Lock removal

1. INTRODUCTION

Hardware transactional memory (HTM) [16] is now available on mainstream mass-market processors (e.g., Intel's latest Haswell microarchitecture, IBM POWER architecture [2, 8]), and programmers are expected to use the offered hardware-based *lock elision* [21] to improve the performance of their (legacy) coarse-grained lock-based programs [1]. However, naively using hardware lock elision can lead to disappointing performance results. We therefore provide software techniques for *assisting* the hardware's lock elision, to get around the limitations which introduce excessive serialization in an otherwise potentially concurrent application. Our techniques significantly improve the performance of concurrent applications when using lock elision.

In HLE, lock protected code segments are executed speculatively by starting a transaction and "taking" the lock without actually taking it. That is, the lock is read, and if its state is unlocked then it is placed in the transaction read set as locked without affecting the state of the lock, that remains unlocked. However, when a transaction aborts (e.g., due to a conflict) it rolls back to acquire the lock non-speculatively, writing the lock as taken. The globally visible lock acquisition by the aborted thread conflicts with the speculative loads of the lock that has been performed by the speculatively running HLE transactions, and *causes all of them to abort* because of this conflict on the lock location. In addition, *new threads arriving at the critical section see that the lock is taken* and thus they do not start their transaction. In the case of fair locks this conflict on the lock serializes the run until a quiescent period in which no thread tries to access the lock. This *lemming effect* [12] which causes unnecessary serialization limits the concurrency exposed. To mitigate this effect, Intel recommends retrying an aborted transaction several times [1]. However, our experiments (Section 7) reveal that this simple technique does not completely alleviate the problem, especially when the lemming effect is severe such as with fair locks or with a high degree of concurrency.

Software-assisted lock removal (SLR): Our first software technique to overcome this lemming effect can be viewed as a software hardware hybrid implementation of the Rajwar Goodman hardware lock removal technique [22]. They observed that one can simply execute transactions with the same scope of the critical section (i.e., start a transaction instead of acquiring the lock and commit instead of releasing the lock) *without accessing the lock at all*, provided the TM offers some progress guarantee for conflicting transactions. (Otherwise, livelock situations, in which transactions repeatedly abort each other, can occur.) However, Haswell's HTM has a simple "requestor wins" conflict resolution policy [1] which is prone to livelock [7]. Our *software-assisted lock removal* SLR scheme guarantees progress despite this by doing the following. It uses the HTM to transactionally execute critical sections without accessing the lock until it is ready to commit. Then it reads the lock and commits if the lock is not taken; otherwise, it aborts and retries. If it fails a few times it gives up and executes non speculatively, by acquiring the lock. In SLR a thread acquiring the lock does not automatically conflict with running transactions nor does it prevent an arriving thread from starting its transaction speculatively. Since in SLR a speculative transaction may run concurrently to a transaction that holds the lock, the speculative transaction may see an inconsistent state (which guarantees that it will fail to commit and

*Work done while a PhD student at Tel Aviv University.

PODC'14, July 15–18, 2014, Paris, France.
Copyright 2014 ACM 978-1-4503-2944-6/14/07 ...$15.00.
http://dx.doi.org/10.1145/2611462.2611482.

abort). In many cases this loss of opacity [14] is safe because of the transactions sand boxing.

Software-assisted conflict management (SCM): To prevent the lemming effect in HLE transactions without resorting to lock removal, and without losing the opacity property, we propose a simple *conflict management* technique that allows the non-conflicting threads to continue their speculative HLE-based run *without any interference* from conflicting threads. To do this we add a *serializing path* to the lock implementation, in which an aborted thread has to acquire a distinct *auxiliary lock* (without using lock elision) in order to rejoin the speculative execution with the other threads. Using this approach conflicting threads are serialized among themselves and do not interfere with other threads. Only if the thread fails due to a conflict many times it must give up and acquire the original lock.

While SCM provides the most benefits when employed with HLE, the two schemes, SCM and SLR can be combined together to further reduce any progress problems caused when SLR threads give up and acquire the lock non-transactionally. Furthermore, to the best of our knowledge, SCM is the only scheme that enables HLE-based fair locks, with starvation freedom and progress guarantees and with no performance degradation.

We implemented our software-assisted methods in a library that uses the standard `pthreads` lock interface. This allows using our methods without requiring changing or recompiling the program.

This paper's contributions are therefore:

- Analyzing the performance dynamics of Haswell's HLE and quantifying the impact of the lemming effect on it (Section 4).
- Introducing software assisted lock removal (SLR) that regains the concurrency and speedup that were lost due to the HLE lemming effect (Section 5). SLR achieves higher levels of concurrency while sacrificing opacity.
- Introducing the software assisted conflict management (SCM) an alternative scheme that overcomes the lemming effect that works well with fair locks, such as MCS, Ticket or CLH locks (Section 6). SCM retains opacity while reaching slightly lower levels of concurrency (compared to SLR).
- Evaluating the two schemes showing that they improve performance by up to 3.5 times in the STAMP application benchmarks and up to 10 times in data structures benchmarks as compared to using Haswell's HLE as is (Section 7).

2. RELATED WORK

Rajwar and Goodman [21] introduced the concept of speculative lock elision (SLE). They subsequently proposed transactional lock removal [22], which uses hardware-based conflict management to serialize conflicting transactions. Our approaches achieve a similar goal, but using software to assist the hardware implementation.

Dice et al. [12] studied transactional lock elision (TLE) using Sun's Rock processor and mentioned the lemming effect. In response, they sketch a non-backoff software mechanism to speedup *recovery* from the lemming effect. In contrast to their technique, our conflict management scheme prevents the problem in the first place and manages to prevent the continuous zigzag between speculative and standard executions altogether.

Implementing elision-friendly locks using Intel's Haswell processor is discussed in [1]. However Intel's optimization guidelines essentially turn fair locks into TTAS locks. This has two disadvantages: (1) wasting time when arriving while the lock is taken (as our experiments on STAMP show, this is significant), and (2) the lock no longer guarantees starvation-freedom and loses its fairness.

```
shared variable:
  lock : 1 bit (boolean),   initially   FALSE

lock() {
  while (TRUE) {
    while (lock = TRUE) {
      // busy wait
    }
    ret := XACQUIRE test&set(lock)
    if ( ret = FALSE)
      return
} }

unlock() {
  XRELEASE lock := FALSE
}
```

Figure 1: Applying hardware lock elision to a TTAS (Test&Test&Set) lock.

Roy et al. [23] and Afek et al. [5] implement lock elision completely in software, using specialized software transactional memory algorithms. These implementations instrument the critical sections to track read and written memory locations. In contrast, our algorithms are based on hardware TM and thus do not require such instrumentation.

We have sketched the software-assisted conflict management in a previous poster publication [3]. Concurrently to the current work, Calciu et al. [9] proposed using a mechanism similar to software-assisted lock removal as a fallback for transactional memory systems.

3. BACKGROUND: INTEL'S HASWELL HTM

Intel's transactional synchronization extensions (TSX) [2] defines two interfaces to designate the scope of a transaction:

Hardware lock elision (HLE): In HLE, the scope of a lock-protected critical section defines a transaction's scope. HLE is implemented as a backward-compatible instruction set extension of two new prefixes, XACQUIRE and XRELEASE. Upon executing an XACQUIRE-prefixed instruction that writes to memory (e.g., a store or `compare-and-swap`) (see Figure 1), the processor starts a transaction and *elides* the actual store, treating it as a transactional read instead (i.e., placing the lock in the read set). Internally, however, the processor maintains an illusion that the lock was acquired: if the transaction reads the lock, it sees the value stored locally. Upon executing an XRELEASE store, the transaction commits. HLE requires that an XRELEASE store restores the lock to its original state; otherwise, it aborts the transaction. If an HLE transaction aborts, the XACQUIRE store is re-executed non-transactionally to acquire the lock in order to ensure progress. Notice that such a non-transactional store conflicts with every concurrent HLE transaction eliding the same lock, since such a transaction has the lock's cache line in its read set. This is the root cause for the lemming effect.

Restricted transactional memory (RTM): RTM is Haswell's generic TM interface with three new instructions: XBEGIN, XEND, and XABORT. XBEGIN begins a transaction, XEND commits, and XABORT allows a transaction to abort itself. Upon an abort a fallback code that is pointed by an operand of the XBEGIN instruction is executed and uses an *abort status* register in which the processor records the cause for the abort, whether due to an XABORT, a data conflict, or an "internal buffer overflow" [2].

RTM can be used to implement custom lock elision algorithms [1] by replacing the lock acquisition code with custom code that begins a transaction and reads from the lock's cache line. However, such a lock elision scheme fails to maintain the illusion that the thread wrote to the lock, as the lock's cache line is indistinguishable from any other line in the read-set.

3.1 Haswell's TSX Implementation

Haswell appears to use a *requestor wins* conflict management policy. A transaction aborts if either a coherency message (read or write) arrives for a cache line in its write set, or if an eviction due to a write arrives for a cache line in its read set.

Experiments we conducted (described in [4]) show that transactions are prone to *spurious aborts* that are not explained by data conflicts or read/write set overflow. Spurious aborts imply that even in a perfect conflict free workload, degradation such as the lemming effect, described below, is possible.

HLE compatible locks Haswell's HLE mechanism conservatively requires that the store releasing the lock restores the lock to its original state prior to the acquisition [2]. Unfortunately, the popular (fair) ticket lock [18] (used in the Linux kernel [20]) and CLH lock [17, 11] do not meet this requirement. As an additional contribution, we adapt these locks for use under HLE, thus enabling HLE-based code to maintain the progress guarantees fair locks provide, and making HLE applicable to programs that use ticket locks or CLH locks.

We adjust both locks in a way that guarantees that a thread running alone (which is the illusion given by HLE) restores the lock to its original state when it releases the lock. The idea is that a thread releasing the lock first tries to optimistically restore the original state using a `compare-and-swap` instruction. If this fails the thread reverts to using the standard lock algorithm. But if the CAS succeeds, the lock's state is restored, which is exactly what HLE requires. The algorithms appear in Appendix A and (due to space constraints) their correctness proofs appear in [4].

4. LEMMING EFFECT IN HASWELL HLE

In this section we experimentally quantify the serialization penalty due to transactional aborts during an HLE execution. We focus our analysis on the HLE-based test-and-test-and-set (TTAS) lock (Figure 1) and the fair HLE-based MCS [18] lock. We use the MCS lock as the representative of the class of fair locks because it is compatible with HLE, unlike other fair locks such as ticket locks or CLH locks. However, we have verified that both these locks suffer from the same problems reported below for the MCS lock.

We use a red-black tree data structure protected by a single global lock. Varying the number of threads, the operation mix, and the tree size allows us to control the conflict level and the length and amount of data accessed in the critical section. Small tree and/or many mutating `insert/delete` threads result in higher conflict levels. Increasing the size of the tree reduces the chance that two operations' data accesses conflict, as the elements accessed are more sparsely distributed. For a given size, s, we initially fill the tree with random elements from a domain of size $2s$. Then, we run for a period of 3 seconds in which each thread continuously performs random `insert`, `delete` and `lookup` operations, according to a specified distribution. (We use an equal rate of `insert`s and `delete`s so that on average the tree size does not change.)

Experiments were performed on a Core i7-4770 3.4 GHz Haswell processor, with 4 cores, each with 2 hyperthreads. Each core has private L1 and L2 caches, whose sizes are 32 KB and 256 KB respectively. There is also an 8 MB L3 cache shared by all cores. Each test point is the average on 10 runs (with little observed variance). We measured: (1) the total number of operations completed, (2) S, the number of successful speculative operations, (3) A, the number of aborted speculative operations and (4) N, the number of

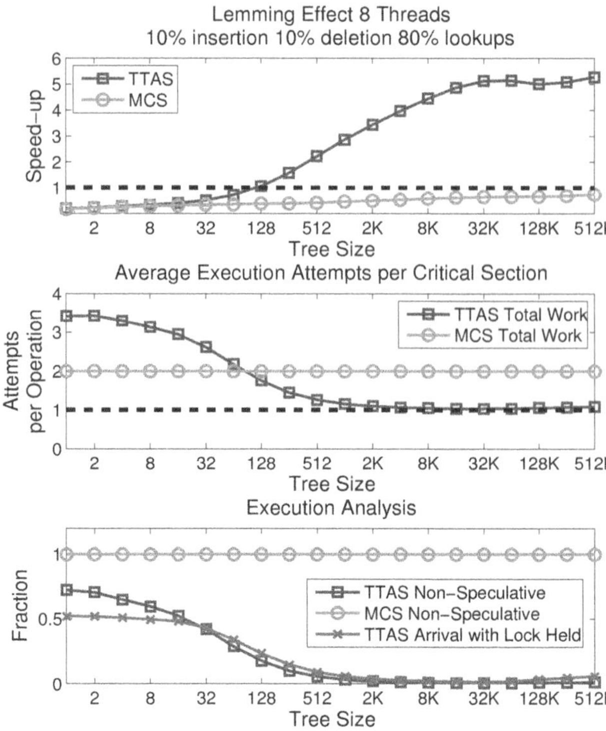

Figure 2: Impact of aborts on executions under different lock implementations. For each tree size we show the average number of times a thread attempts to execute the critical section until successfully completing a tree operation, and the fraction of operations that complete non-speculatively. CLH and ticket results are omitted, as they are similar to the MCS lock results.

operations that complete via a non-speculative execution. The total number of operations performed is $S+N$. In some lock implementations an operation can start and abort several speculation attempts before completing, so there is no formula relating A to S and N.

Figure 2 shows the amount of serialization caused by aborts, as a function of the tree size, for a moderate level of tree modifications (20%). In addition to the fraction of operations that complete non-speculatively (i.e., $\frac{N}{N+S}$), we report the amount of *work* required to complete an operation, i.e., $\frac{A+N+S}{N+S}$, the number of times a thread tries to complete the critical section before succeeding.

As Figure 2 shows, the serialization dynamics for each lock type are quite different. With an MCS lock, the benchmark executes virtually all operations non-speculatively after an initial speculative section aborts. As a result, an HLE MCS lock offers little if any speedup over a standard MCS lock, even when there is little underlying contention.

The TTAS lock, on the other hand, manages to recover from aborts. At high conflict levels (on small trees) it requires $2-3.5$ attempts to complete a single operation, but nevertheless a fraction of 30% to 70% of the operations complete speculatively. As the tree size increases and conflict levels decrease, HLE shines and nearly all operations complete speculatively. We now turn to analyze the causes for these differences.

TTAS spinlock (the boxed line in Figure 2) The first thread to abort acquires the lock non-speculatively. As for the remaining threads, we distinguish between two behaviors. First, a thread that aborts because of this lock acquisition re-executes its acquiring TAS instruction, which returns 1 because the lock is held. The thread then spins, and once it observes the lock free re-issues its

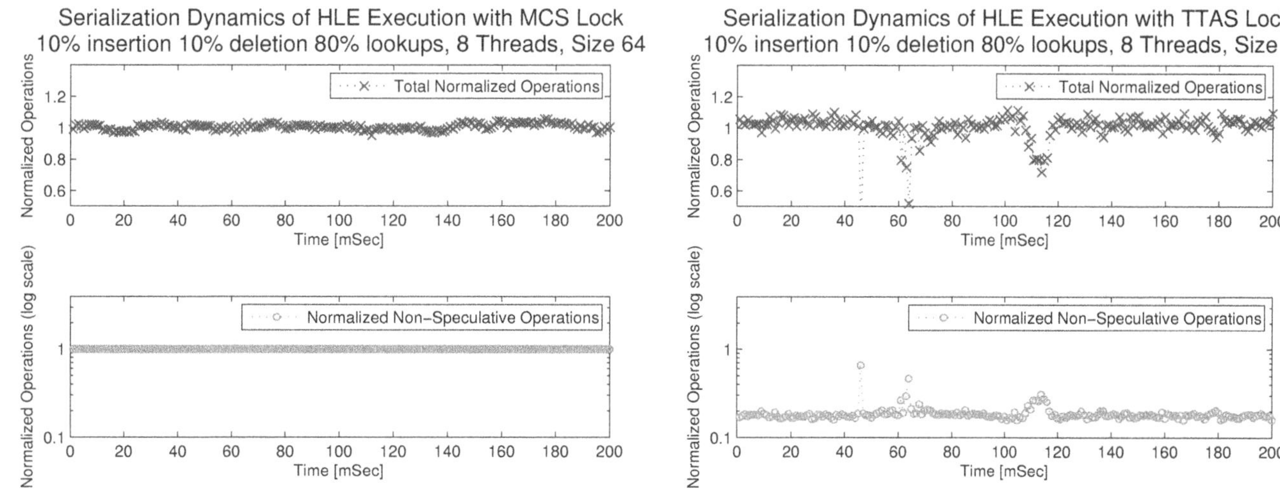

MCS lock: All operations complete non-speculatively.

TTAS lock: Most operations complete speculatively but there are periods of serialization.

Figure 3: Normalized throughput and serialization dynamics over time. We divide the execution into 1 millisecond time slots. **Top:** Throughput obtained in each time slot, normalized to the average throughput over the entire execution. **Bottom:** Fraction of operations that complete non-speculatively in each time slot.

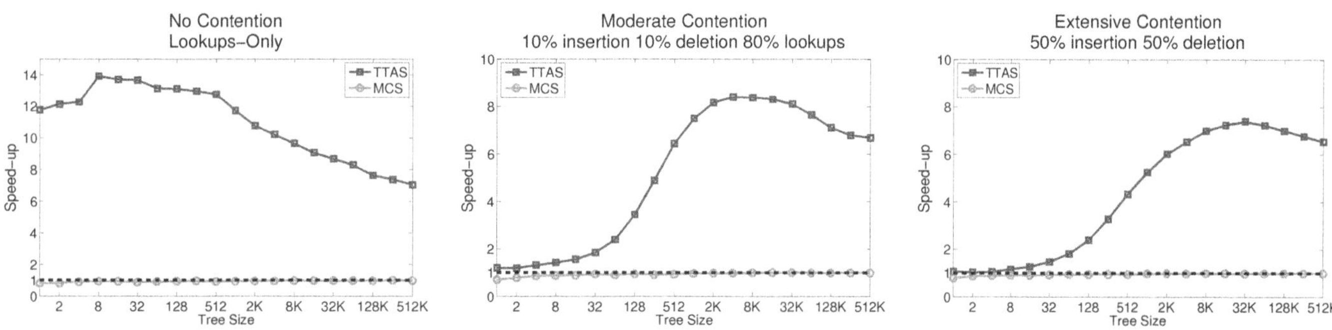

Figure 4: The HLE speedup of 8 threads with different types of locks. The base-line of each speedup line is the standard version of that specific lock (the horizontal dotted black line at y=1). By mixing different access operations we vary the amount of contention: (i) lookups only – no contention, (ii) moderate contention – 10% of the tree accesses are insertions and 10% are deletions and (iii) extensive contention – all the accesses are insertions or deletions.

XACQUIRE TAS and re-enters a speculative execution. Second, a newly arriving thread initially observes the lock as taken and spins. Once the thread in the critical section releases the lock, the waiting thread issues an XACQUIRE TAS as in the first case. The bottom line is that all threads are blocked from entering a speculative execution until the initial aborted thread exits the critical section, but then all the threads resume execution speculatively. The flip side of this behavior is that a thread may thus abort several times before successfully completing its operation, either speculatively or non-speculatively.

MCS Fair lock (the circled line in Figure 2) The MCS lock represents the lock as a linked list of nodes, where each node represents a thread waiting to acquire the lock. An arriving thread uses an atomic SWAP [15] to atomically append its own node to the tail of the queue, and in the process retrieves a pointer to its predecessor in the queue. It then spins on the *locked* field of its node, waiting for its predecessor to set this field to false.

In the case of the HLE-based MCS lock the lemming effect is much worse because all the threads that were aborted form a chain, each spinning on a different location waiting for the predecessor to release the lock. Neither an aborted thread nor newly arriving thread can now enter the critical section speculatively. In either case the thread spins and once its turn arrives enters the critical section *non-speculatively*. Thus, a single abort causes the serialization of all concurrent critical sections, as well as newly arriving threads, all of which will now execute non-speculatively. Essentially, because of the fairness guarantees provided by the MCS lock, it "remembers" conflict events and makes it harder to resume a speculative execution. Even when the original lock holder releases the lock, it moves it into a state that does not allow new threads to speculatively execute. The MCS lock requires a *quiescence period*, in which no new threads arrive, so that all waiting threads acquire the lock, execute the critical section and leave. Only then does the MCS lock return to a state that allows the next arriving threads execute speculatively.

Performance impact In Figure 3 we divide the benchmark's execution into 1 millisecond time slots and show the throughput obtained in each slot, normalized to the throughput over the entire execution. We also show the fraction of operations that completed via a non-speculative execution in each time slot. As can be seen, TTAS performance can fluctuate severely, sometimes falling by as much as 2.5×. These throughput drops are correlated with periods in which more critical sections finish non-speculatively, i.e., after serialization caused by an abort. The MCS performance reinforces the results of the previous benchmark (Figure 2): the benchmark executes virtually all operations non-speculatively due to serialization caused by an abort. Finally, Figure 4 depicts the performance advantage of the lock elision usage with different types of locks.

As observed, MCS lock gains no benefit with HLE usage. On the other hand the TTAS lock gains performance boost while using the HLE mechanism.

5. SOFTWARE-ASSISTED LOCK REMOVAL

The lemming effect demonstrated in the previous section arises because an HLE transaction runs with the lock in its read set. That is, although HLE only pretends to hold a lock without globally locking, still the lock creates an abort chain effect once one thread aborts. One then wonders why bother touching the lock: if the hardware already detects conflicts (through the coherency protocol), how about starting the transaction without touching the lock at all? Two problems are created when we naively eliminate any reference to the lock, first the threads may easily get into a live-lock scenario, where they keep aborting each other due to data conflicts without any thread making progress. Second, if concurrently to the transactional threads another thread runs non-transactionally with the lock, some transactions may observe an inconsistent state (in which partial writes of the non-transactional thread are observed). In this section we take this approach of trying to eliminate any usage of the lock, sacrificing opacity but ensuring there is no live-lock.

Rajwar and Goodman observed [22] that given transactional capabilities, one can simply run transactions with the same scope as the critical section without accessing the lock. They relied on a hardware conflict management scheme that guarantees *starvation freedom* to prevent the live-lock problem. Unfortunately, Haswell's TM "requestor wins" conflict management policy guarantees neither starvation freedom nor livelock freedom [7].

Our solution to this progress problem is to go back to using the lock, as a progress-guaranteeing mechanism, but only at commit time. However, simply having an aborted thread acquire the lock (to avoid starvation) can lead to an incorrect execution due to the *non-atomicity* of a thread running in the critical section in a non-speculative manner, as depicted in the following *erroneous* example. Memory updates performed by such a thread are made globally visible one at a time, making it possible for concurrent transactions to observe an inconsistent state.

Erroneous Example: Consider two code segments protected by the same lock L, as depicted on the right. Suppose now that thread T_1 transactionally executes C_1 without accessing L and reads $X = 0$. Now another thread, T_2, executes C_2 non-transactionally, acquiring L and then storing 1 to Y. Following this T_1 reads Y from memory. Since Y is not in T_1's read set, there is no conflict with T_2's previous store and T_1 observes $Y = 1$. T_1 then commits. Thus T_1 observes an inconsistent state, $X = 0$ and $Y = 1$. (Had thread T_2 run transactionally in the above example, T_1 would observe either both or none of T_2's stores.)

C_1:	C_2:
`lock(L)`	`lock(L)`
`load(X)`	`store(Y,1)`
`load(Y)`	`store(X,1)`
`unlock(L)`	`unlock(L)`

Software-assisted lock removal (SLR, Figure 5) Our solution to the non-atomicity problem uses the lock to verify that a transaction commits only if it has observed a consistent state. A transaction starts without accessing the lock. Once it reaches the end of the critical section, it reads the lock. If the lock is free, the transaction commits (no transaction wrote on a value read by it); otherwise, there is a concurrent non-speculative transaction, and the transaction aborts itself using XABORT. Returning to our example, the scenarios depicted in Figure 6 demonstrate how SLR enforces correct executions, though sometimes the transaction can observe an inconsistent state. This is usually not a problem, as the transaction

```
shared variables:
  lock : speculative lock

thread local variables:
  retries : int

lock() {
  retries := 0
  // speculative path
  XBEGIN (Line 14) // jump to Line 14 on abort
  return

  // fallback path
  retries ++
  if ( retries < MAX_RETRIES)
    goto Line 10
  else
    lock.lock() // standard lock acquire
}

unlock() {
  if (XTEST()) { // returns TRUE if the run is speculative
    if (lock is locked)
      XABORT // aborts the speculative run
    else
      XEND
  } else {
    lock.unlock() // standard lock release
  }
}
```

Figure 5: Software-Assisted Lock Removal

is sandboxed by the TM, but program correctness may be violated if inconsistent reads cause the transaction to compromise the lock check. For example, this can happen if the transaction erroneously writes to the lock itself, or jumps directly to an XEND instruction without checking the lock first, and so on. Therefore, to use SLR one must verify that the observable inconsistent states a transaction might encounter cannot cause the transaction to misbehave in such ways. Most common transaction types, such as those used in data structures and STAMP, are safe for SLR.

Performance impact SLR alleviates the two problems that lead to the HLE lemming effect. First, with SLR a thread that non-transactionally acquires the lock does not automatically cause all running transactions to abort. If it manages to complete the critical section before these transactions try to commit, they may successfully commit, given they do not conflict on the data. Second, while a thread is executing non-transactionally in the critical section, arriving threads continue to enter speculative transactional execution and are not forced to wait.

Correctness Haswell's TM conflict detection checks guarantee that once a transaction accesses a cache line, a conflicting access by a lock holding thread will abort the transaction. In the other direction, if the transaction accesses a memory location following a lock holder's access and yet successfully commits, then the lock was released before the transaction ended. Thus the transaction's execution is indistinguishable from the case in which the entire critical section (of the lock holder) ran before the transaction.

6. SOFTWARE-ASSISTED CONFLICT MANAGEMENT

In this section we propose a *software-assisted conflict management* (SCM) scheme which serializes conflicting threads that cannot run concurrently, but does this *without acquiring the lock* to

Scenarios ending in abort

T_1	T_2
begin SLR txn	
`load(X)`	
	`lock(L)`
	`store(Y)`
`load(Y)`	
`load(L)`	
L is locked: ABORT	

T_1	T_2
begin SLR txn	
`load(X)`	
	`lock(L)`
	`store(Y)`
	`store(X)`
ABORT: conflict on X	

Successfully committing scenario

T_1	T_2
begin SLR txn	
	`lock(L)`
	`store(Y)`
	`store(X)`
`load(X)`	
	`unlock(L)`
`load(Y)`	
`load(L)`	
COMMIT	

Figure 6: How SLR enforces correct executions in different scenarios.

avoid impact on the other speculatively running threads in the system. This scheme is compatible with any lock implementation, and resolves the lemming effect problem in HLE transactions without resorting to using lock removal, and without sacrificing opacity.

For example, when using lock removal in highly contended workloads with lots of aborts, new threads keep starting transactions and causing more aborts and wasted work. Here HLE's ability to grab the lock and stop newly arriving threads from entering speculative execution turns out to be extremely helpful and greatly improves performance (as shown in Section 7). Our conflict management scheme thus maintains this ability of HLE, and prevents the lemming effect in less contended scenarios.

Preventing livelock, the SCM scheme: Our scheme uses two locks, the original *main* lock which is taken using the HLE/SLR mechanism and an *auxiliary* standard lock which is only acquired in a standard non-transactional manner. The auxiliary lock groups all the threads that are involved in a conflict and serializes them (see Figure 8). When a transaction is aborted, the aborted thread non-transactionally acquires the auxiliary lock and then rejoins the speculative execution of the original critical section. The process of acquiring the auxiliary lock in order to rejoin the speculative run is called the *serializing path*. As with previous schemes, the thread may retry its transaction before going to the serializing path.

To see why this scheme prevents livelock, consider two transactions, T_1 and T_2, which repeatedly abort each other. Once T_1 acquires the auxiliary lock and re-joins the speculative execution, one of the following can happen: (1) T_1 aborts again, but T_2 commits, or (2) T_2 aborts and thus tries to acquire the auxiliary lock, where it must wait for T_1 to commit and release the auxiliary lock. Generalizing this, once a thread T acquires the auxiliary lock any transaction that conflicts with T either commits or gets serialized to run after T. Thus the system makes progress.

Preventing starvation In the above scheme starvation remains possible due to one of two scenarios: (1) a thread fails to acquire the auxiliary lock (as can happen with a TTAS lock), or (2) a thread holding the auxiliary lock fails to commit. To solve issue (1) we require that the auxiliary lock be a starvation-free (or "fair") lock, such as an MCS lock. Our scheme then inherits any fairness properties of the auxiliary lock. To solve issue (2), the auxiliary lock holder non-transactionally acquires the main lock after failing to commit a given number of times. If all accesses to the main lock go through the HLE/SLR mechanism, then *only* the auxiliary lock holder can ever try to acquire the main lock and is therefore guaranteed to succeed. Otherwise (i.e., if the program sometimes explicitly acquires the lock non-transactionally), the main lock must be starvation-free as well.

While SCM provides the most benefits when employed with HLE, the two schemes, SCM and SLR can be combined together to further reduce any progress problems caused when SLR threads give up and acquire the lock non-transactionally.

```
1  shared variables:
2    main_lock : elided main lock
3    aux_lock : auxiliary standard lock
4
5  thread local variables:
6    retries : int
7    aux_lock_owner : boolean, initially FALSE
8
9  lock() {
10   retries := 0
11   // primary path
12   XBEGIN (Line 17) // jump to Line 17 on abort
13   | call HLE or SLR lock() as appropriate |
14   return
15
16   // serializing path
17   if (aux_lock_owner = FALSE) {
18     retries ++
19   } else {
20     aux_lock.lock() // standard lock acquire
21     aux_lock_owner := TRUE
22   }
23   if ( retries < MAX_RETRIES)
24     goto Line 12
25   else
26     main_lock.lock() // standard lock acquire
27 }
28
29 unlock() {
30   if (XTEST()) { // returns TRUE if the run is speculative
31     | call HLE or SLR unlock() as appropriate |
32     XEND
33   } else {
34     main_lock.unlock() // standard lock release
35   }
36   if (aux_lock_owner = TRUE) {
37     aux_lock.unlock() // standard lock release
38     aux_lock_owner := FALSE
39   }
40 }
```

Figure 7: Software-Assisted Conflict Management

Implementation and HLE compatibility (Figure 7) Our scheme maintains HLE-compatibility by *nesting* an HLE transaction within an RTM transaction. When used with HLE, we first start an RTM transaction which "acquires" the lock with an XACQUIRE store. Because TSX provides a flat nesting model [2], an abort will abort the parent RTM transaction and execute the fall-back code instead of re-issuing the XACQUIRE store and aborting all the running transactions.

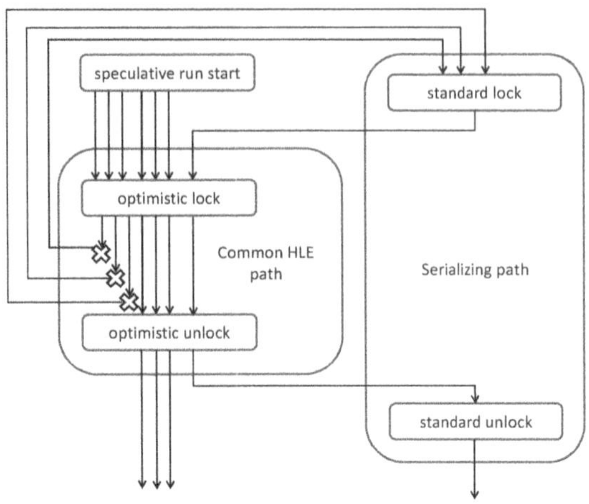

Figure 8: A block diagram of a run using our software scheme. The entry point of a speculative section is the 'speculative run' rectangle. All threads acquire the original main lock using the lock-elision mechanism. If a conflict occurs (described by 'x'), the conflicting threads are sent to the serializing path. Once a thread acquires the auxiliary standard lock in a non-speculative manner, it rejoins the speculative run.

Unfortunately, the initial implementation of TSX in Haswell does not support nesting of HLE within RTM. Therefore, in our experiments we use RTM to implement lock elision (by reading the lock address), which does not provide the self-illusion that the lock is taken. More precisely, in our current implementation we omit Line 31 of the Unlock() function in Figure 7, and perform the following at Line 12 of the Lock():

```
// put the main_lock in the read set
// and check that it is free
if (main_lock is locked) then
    XABORT('non-speculative run')
end if
```

Remark In principle, grouping the conflicting threads in one group may be too strict since a single conflicting thread does not have to conflict with the entire group. A natural extension (left for future work) to explore is dividing the conflicting threads to different groups, each containing only threads that conflict among themselves.

7. EVALUATION

In this section we evaluate the benefit provided by our lock elision schemes using two data structure benchmarks and applications from the STAMP suite (commonly used for evaluating hardware TM implementations [12, 24, 19]), which consists of eight applications that cover a variety of domains and exhibit different characteristics in terms of transaction lengths, read and write set sizes and amounts of contention. The premise of HLE is to enable simple coarse-grained programming with the performance of fine-grained locks, thus obviating the need for fine-grained locking. Therefore, we deliberately use coarse-grained benchmarks. Our experience with fine-grained benchmarks, such as those in the PARSEC [6] suite, is that in general applying HLE there shows little performance impact because the benchmarks are already optimized to avoid contention (see [4]).

Methodology We evaluate our methods on both the MCS lock and the TTAS lock. For each lock type we test the following six schemes: (1) Standard (non-speculative) version of the lock, (2) HLE version of the lock, (3) *HLE-retries* version, based on Intel's recommendations [1], in which a thread acquires the lock non-speculatively only after retrying speculatively 10 times, (4) HLE version of the lock with conflict management (*HLE-SCM*), (5) Optimistic SLR version, in which a thread only acquires the lock non-speculatively after retrying speculatively 10 times (*Opt SLR*), and (6) Optimistic SLR version with conflict management applied (*SLR-SCM*). As in Section 4, we use a Core i7-4770 3.4 GHz processor with 4 cores, each with 2 hyperthreads. We run the benchmarks on an otherwise idle machine using the `jemalloc` memory allocator which is tuned for multi-threaded programs.

Conflict management tuning Because SLR and HLE behave differently when the main lock is taken non-speculatively, we tune the conflict management as appropriate for each technique. Taking the lock non-speculatively in an HLE-based execution has large performance impact, and so the thread holding the auxiliary lock retries to complete its operation speculatively 10 times before giving up and acquiring the main lock. In contrast, SLR is much less sensitive to the main lock being taken and so if the bits in the abort status register indicate the transaction is unlikely to succeed, we switch to a non-speculative execution. We have verified that using other tuning options only degrade the schemes' performance.

7.1 Red-black Tree Data Structure Benchmark

We evaluate our methods using two data structure benchmarks, the red-black tree (described in Section 4) and a hash table. In each test, we measure the average number of operations per second (throughput) when running the benchmark 20 times on an otherwise idle machine. The results of the two data structure benchmarks are comparable, as hash table transactions are always short and therefore "zoom in" on the short transaction portion of the red-black workload spectrum. We therefore discuss only the red-black tree.

Red-black tree Figure 9 shows the *speedup* (relative to a single thread with no locking) obtained by the various methods on a 128-node tree under moderate contention (20% updates). With HLE the MCS lock does not scale at all, and even the TTAS does not scale past 4 threads. Simply adding speculative retries allows HLE-TTAS to scale, but when the lemming effect is more severe—as with HLE-MCS at 8 threads—merely retrying the transactions no longer works. We believe that with higher amounts of concurrency, the simple retry policy will not be effective even with TTAS. In contrast, using our schemes, the throughput always scales with the number of threads.

Figure 10 depicts the *speedup* that our methods obtain (relative to the HLE version of the specific lock) across the full spectrum of workloads. Notice that increasing the tree size also increases the size of the critical section, resulting in a lower conflict probability but also lower throughput. Our software schemes improve the speedup compared to the plain HLE version of the specific lock (especially on fair locks).

TTAS lock On the lookup only (no contention) workload, the HLE-based TTAS is good enough, and none of the software-assisted methods improve on its performance. However, as we increase the level of contention by increasing the fraction of mutating operations, our methods outperform the plain HLE-based TTAS by up to 3.5×. This is the result of letting new arriving threads immediately enter the critical section speculatively, instead of waiting for the aborted thread currently in the critical section to leave.

In general, the HLE-SCM and SLR versions of TTAS give comparable performance, which is also similar to the simple HLE-retries policy. The exception is short transactions, where HLE-SCM out-

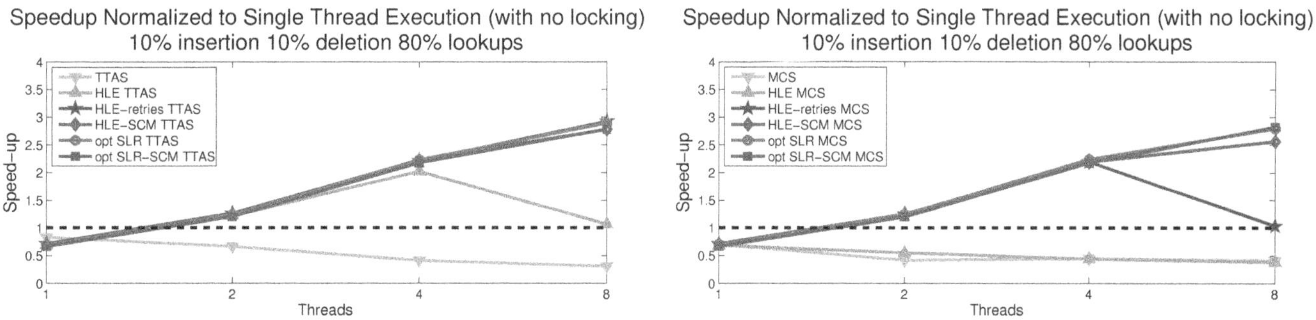

(a) TTAS lock (b) MCS lock

Figure 9: The execution results on a small tree size (128 nodes) under moderate contention. The two graphs are normalized to the throughput of a single thread with no locking (the horizontal dotted black line at y=1). The software assisted schemes scale well and the performance gap between MCS and TTAS is closed.

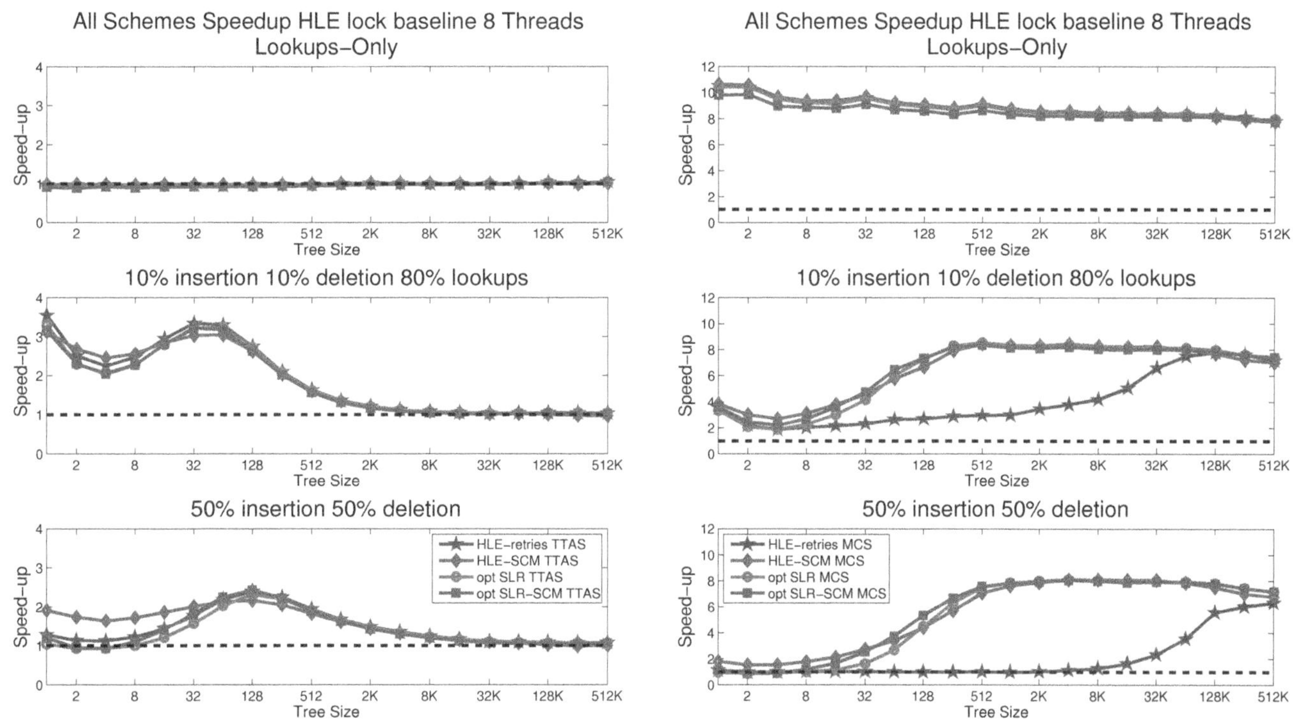

(a) TTAS lock (b) MCS lock

Figure 10: The speedup of our generic software lock elision schemes compared to Haswell HLE. The base-line of each speedup line is the HLE version of that specific lock (the horizontal dotted black line at y=1): on the left – TTAS lock and on the right – MCS lock. Since the performances are scaled using different base lines, the reader can not compare between the performance of the different lock types.

performs SLR, SLR-SCM and HLE-retries by up to 2×, exactly because of the serialization it induces.

MCS lock Our software-assisted schemes increase throughput by $2-10\times$ in every MCS workload (even in a read-only workload, the MCS lock experiences a severe lemming effect behavior due to spurious aborts). We again see comparable results for HLE-SCM and SLR, with a 50% advantage to HLE-SCM in short transactions. In contrast to the TTAS case, here the HLE-retires policy does not alleviate the lemming effect. In fact, under high contention HLE-retries does not do better than the plain HLE. Our software-assisted methods thus outperform HLE-retries significantly, by 4× under moderate contention (20% updates) and $2-10\times$ under high contention.

Analysis Detailed analysis of the number of attempts per successful operation and fraction of operations that complete in a speculative execution is deferred to [4], due to space constraints.

7.2 STAMP

To apply our methods to the STAMP suite of benchmark programs [10], we replace the transactions with critical sections that use the same global lock. Figure 11 shows the runtime of the STAMP programs at maximum concurrency (8 threads) with the various lock elision methods, normalized to the execution time using the plain non-speculative lock. (We exclude the `bayes` benchmark due to its non-deterministic behavior, as done in prior work using STAMP [13].)

As with the red-black tree data structure benchmark, MCS lock gains no benefit from HLE usage. But, MCS lock provides considerable benefit when used with HLE combined with our conflict management scheme. The HLE-SCM scheme typically improves the performance by up to 2.5×.

On the other hand, TTAS lock gains some benefit of HLE usage (up to 2× in `intruder`) but the HLE-SCM scheme with TTAS gives modest improvement with the exception of `genome` (up to

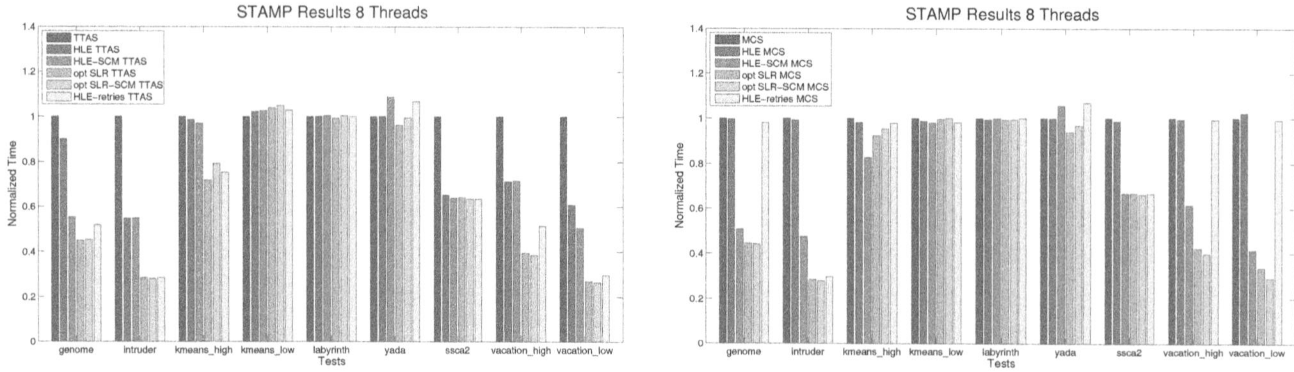

(a) Relative execution time over non-speculative TTAS lock

(b) Relative execution time over non-speculative MCS lock

Figure 11: Normalized run time of STAMP applications (**lower is better**) using standard locking, HLE, and our software-assisted methods.

1.5×). Here too we see that the benefit of HLE usage in TTAS depends on the workload's characteristics.

Both locks benefit considerably from lock removal usage. In most of the tests, the optimistic SLR scheme gives the highest improvement (with one exception of `kmeans-high` MCS HLE-SCM lock), sometimes up to 2× compared to the HLE-based scheme and up to 4× compare to the plain non-speculative version of the lock. The HLE-retries scheme generally performs comparable to SLR, except on `genome`, `yada` and `vacation` where it is slower: marginally so on TTAS (about 10%-30%), but drastically slower when using MCS, where HLE-retries obtains almost no speedup over the standard MCS lock.

For the most part, when the SCM scheme is used with SLR, the performance gain is negligible with only one exception. In the `vacation-low` test, the SLR-SCM gives 15% improvement over the Opt-SLR.

Summary: Our SCM scheme improves the performance of HLE-based locks in both data structure benchmarks and STAMP no matter what the contention level is. MCS lock (or any other fair lock) gains the highest performance boost since these locks need quiescence period in order to overcome the lemming effect and return to speculative execution. The impact of our SCM method on the SLR is more modest and depends on the characteristics of the execution (such as transaction length and contention level).

8. CONCLUSION

We have described several lightweight software techniques to considerably improve the performance of lock-based code when executed over HTM. Moreover, our techniques, enable HLE-based fair locks with starvation freedom and progress guarantee and with no performance degradation. Our evaluation on a Haswell processor is encouraging, improving the run time of applications from the STAMP suite by up to 3.5 times and of data structure benchmarks by up to 10 times.

As we show, even very few aborts are enough to trigger the lemming effect for some lock implementations. Hence, any processor that may cause the HLE to abort and acquire the lock non-speculatively is likely to benefit from our techniques.

In the future, we plan to explore more refined conflict management policies. In particular, utilizing abort information provided by the hardware (such as the location in which a conflict occurs, and/or the identify of the conflicting thread) appears to be a promising direction.

Availability

Our implementation is available on Tel Aviv University's Multicore Algorithmics group web site at `http://mcg.cs.tau.ac.il/`.

Acknowledgments

This work was supported by the Israel Science Foundation (grants 1386/11 and 1227/10) and by Yad-HaNadiv foundation. Adam Morrison is supported in part at the Technion by an Aly Kaufman Fellowship.

9. REFERENCES

[1] Intel 64 and IA-32 Architectures Optimization Reference Manual.

[2] Intel Architecture Instruction Set Extensions Programming Reference.

[3] Y. Afek, A. Levy, and A. Morrison. Programming with hardware lock elision. In *PPoPP 2013*.

[4] Y. Afek, A. Levy, and A. Morrison. Software-Improved Hardware Lock Elision. Technical report, Tel Aviv University.

[5] Y. Afek, A. Matveev, and N. Shavit. Pessimistic software lock-elision. In *DISC 2012*.

[6] C. Bienia. *Benchmarking Modern Multiprocessors*. PhD thesis, Princeton University, January 2011.

[7] J. Bobba, K. E. Moore, H. Volos, L. Yen, M. D. Hill, M. M. Swift, and D. A. Wood. Performance pathologies in hardware transactional memory. In *ISCA 2007*.

[8] H. W. Cain, M. M. Michael, B. Frey, C. May, D. Williams, and H. Le. Robust architectural support for transactional memory in the power architecture. In *ISCA 2013*.

[9] I. Calciu, T. Shpeisman, G. Pokam, and M. Herlihy. Improved Single Global Lock Fallback for Best-effort Hardware Transactional Memory. In *TRANSACT 2014*.

[10] C. Cao Minh, J. Chung, C. Kozyrakis, and K. Olukotun. STAMP: Stanford transactional applications for multi-processing. In *IISWC 2008*.

[11] T. S. Craig. Building FIFO and priority-queuing spin locks from atomic swap. Technical Report 93-02-02, Department of Computer Science and Engineering, University of Washington, 1993.

[12] D. Dice, Y. Lev, M. Moir, D. Nussbaum, and M. Olszewski. Early experience with a commercial hardware transactional memory implementation. Technical Report TR-2009-180, Sun Microsystems, 2009.

[13] N. Diegues and P. Romano. Time-warp: Lightweight Abort Minimization in Transactional Memory. In *PPoPP 2014*.

[14] R. Guerraoui and M. Kapalka. On the correctness of transactional memory. In *PPoPP 2008*.

[15] M. Herlihy. Wait-free synchronization. *ACM TOPLAS*, 13:124–149, January 1991.

[16] M. Herlihy and J. E. B. Moss. Transactional memory: architectural support for lock-free data structures. In *ISCA 1993*.

[17] P. S. Magnusson, A. Landin, and E. Hagersten. Queue locks on cache coherent multiprocessors. In *ISPP '94*.

[18] J. M. Mellor-Crummey and M. L. Scott. Algorithms for scalable synchronization on shared-memory multiprocessors. *ACM TOCS*, 9(1):21–65, Feb. 1991.

[19] D. Papagiannopoulou, G. Capodanno, R. I. Bahar, T. Moreshet, A. Holla, and M. Herlihy. Energy-Efficient and High-Performance Lock Speculation Hardware for Embedded Multicore Systems. In *TRANSACT 2013*.

[20] N. Piggin. x86: FIFO ticket spinlocks. `http://lkml.org/lkml/2007/11/1/125`, 2007.

[21] R. Rajwar and J. R. Goodman. Speculative Lock Elision: enabling highly concurrent multithreaded execution. In *MICRO 2001*.

[22] R. Rajwar and J. R. Goodman. Transactional lock-free execution of lock-based programs. In *ASPLOS 2002*.

[23] A. Roy, S. Hand, and T. Harris. A runtime system for software lock elision. In *EuroSys 2009*.

[24] A. Wang, M. Gaudet, P. Wu, J. N. Amaral, M. Ohmacht, C. Barton, R. Silvera, and M. Michael. Evaluation of Blue Gene/Q hardware support for transactional memories. In *PACT 2012*.

APPENDIX

A. ADJUSTING LOCKS TO WORK WITH HLE: DETAILS

Ticket Lock (Figure 12) Adjustments The new implementation (Figure 13) handles both speculative and standard (non-speculative) runs. We use a compare-and-swap (CAS) primitive [15] in order to distinguish between the two cases: the release attempts to CAS the lock back to its original value, i.e., decrement the *next* counter instead of incrementing the *owner*. If successful, it removes all traces of the lock acquisition; this occurs in either a speculative execution or a non-speculative single-thread execution. An unsuccessful CAS indicates a standard run with multiple requesters.

The only difference in the lock acquiring function is the XACQUIRE usage. In the adjusted unlock function (Figure 13), if Line 8 is successfully executed, either: (1) the lock is taken in a standard manner and the lock owner is the only running thread (no other requesters) or (2) the lock is taken in speculative manner and the lock owner (can be one of many) removes all traces of its run. Line 9 is used to release the lock when the lock is taken in a standard manner and the lock owner is not the only requester. This behavior is identical to the original implementation.

CLH Lock (Figure 14) Adjustments The pseudo-code of the CLH lock implementation, adjusted to the HLE mechanism, is depicted in Figure 15. As in the ticket lock, we need to adjust the CLH lock so that the lock reverts to its original state when released in a solo run. Again, we use a CAS to do this, in an attempt to place *pred* at the tail of the queue, effectively erasing the presence of our node.

```
shared variables:
  next : integer, initially 0
  owner : integer, initially 0

lock() {
  current := F&A(&next, 1)
  while (owner ≠ current) {
    // busy wait
} }

unlock() {
  owner := owner + 1
}
```

Figure 12: Ticket lock.

```
1  lock() {
2    current := XACQUIRE F&A(&next, 1)
3    while (owner ≠ current) {
4      // busy wait
5  } }
6
7  unlock() {
8    if (!XRELEASE CAS(&next, owner+1, owner)) {
9      owner := owner + 1
10 } }
```

Figure 13: Lock elision adjusted ticket lock.

```
shared variable:
  struct Node {
    locked : 1 bit (boolean)
    next : pointer to Node
  }
  tail : pointer to Node, initially points to T =< FALSE, NULL >

thread-local variables:
  myNode : pointer to Node, initially points to thread-local Node
  pred : pointer to Node

lock() {
  myNode.locked := TRUE
  pred := SWAP(&tail, myNode)
  while (pred.locked) {
    // busy wait
} }

unlock() {
  myNode.locked := FALSE
  myNode := pred
}
```

Figure 14: CLH lock.

```
lock() {
  myNode.locked := TRUE
  pred := XACQUIRE SWAP(&tail, myNode)
  while (pred.locked) {
    // busy wait
} }

unlock() {
  if (!XRELEASE CAS(&tail, myNode, pred)) {
    myNode.locked := FALSE
    myNode := pred
} }
```

Figure 15: Lock elision adjusted CLH lock.

A Generalized Asynchronous Computability Theorem

Eli Gafni
Computer Science Department, UCLA
eli@ucla.edu

Petr Kuznetsov
Télécom ParisTech
petr.kuznetsov@telecom-paristech.fr

Ciprian Manolescu *
Department of Mathematics, UCLA
cm@math.ucla.edu

ABSTRACT

We consider the models of distributed computation defined as subsets of the runs of the iterated immediate snapshot model. Given a task T and a model M, we provide topological conditions for T to be solvable in M.

When applied to the wait-free model, our conditions result in the celebrated Asynchronous Computability Theorem (ACT) of Herlihy and Shavit.

To demonstrate the utility of our characterization, we consider a task that has been shown earlier to admit only a very complex t-resilient solution. In contrast, our generalized computability theorem confirms its t-resilient solvability in a straightforward manner.

Categories and Subject Descriptors

C.2.4 [**Computer-Communication Networks**]: Distributed Systems; F.1.1 [**Computation by Abstract Devices**]: Models of Computation—*relations between models*

Keywords

asynchronous computability, iterated models, characterization, topology

1. INTRODUCTION

This paper characterizes task solvablility in models of distributed computing, where processes communicate via reading from and writing to a shared memory. We treat a model as a set of *runs*, i.e., interleaving of read and write steps issued by different processes.

What do we mean by a characterization? We say that a task T is solvable in a model M, if there exists a *protocol* by which, in every run of M, each process taking sufficiently many steps eventually *outputs*, so that the outputs satisfy the task's specification with respect to the provided inputs. The conventional definition of solvability is therefore *operational*, based on the existence of a protocol. A topological characterization replaces the operational definition with the existence of a continuous map between topological spaces, capturing the sets of possible inputs and outputs of the task. This topological characterization may provide insights about the (in)solvability of the task that are not easy to grasp operationally [1, 21, 32].

In 1993, Herlihy and Shavit [21, 22] characterized read-write communication with no restrictions on the runs; this is referred to as the *wait-free* model. They formulated the Asynchronous Computability Theorem (ACT) stating that a task T is wait-free solvable *if and only if* there exists a simplicial, chromatic map from a subdivision of simplexes of an appropriately defined input simplicial complex to an appropriately defined output simplicial complex, satisfying the specification of T.

The original proof of ACT is given in [22] directly for the conventional read-write shared-memory model (referred to as the *standard shared-memory* and denoted SM), where memory consists of persistent objects which can be written and read by a given process arbitrarily often. However, the original proof can be simplified by casting the problem to the *iterated immediate-snapshots* (IIS) [3] shared memory model, in which processes march through a sequence of Immediate-snapshots (IS) tasks invoking the next one with their output from the previous one.

The IIS model can be thought of as convenient mathematical tool to analyze and understand distributed computing, contrasting with the more realistic but less convenient standard shared-memory model (SM). Casting distributed computation in SM to IIS is not unlike analyzing electromagnetic communication in the complex-number domain. We start with the real-world, we move the reasoning to an abstract mathematical world, and then we translate the results back to reality.

The proof of ACT in [22] can thus be simplified along the following lines:

(1) The wait-free runs in standard shared-memory can be simulated in the IIS model [3, 13], and the IIS model can be simulated by the standard shared-memory model [1]. Thus all we need is to characterize task solvability in IIS.

(2) If a task T is wait-free solvable in the IIS model, then there exists an integer k_T such that after the first k_T invocations of immediate snapshots, each process can output in T. This can be shown by a compactness argument or König's lemma (cf., e.g., [3]).

*CM was supported by NSF grant DMS-1104406.

PODC'14, July 15–18, 2014, Paris, France.

ACM 978-1-4503-2944-6/14/07 ...$15.00..

(3) Solving a task by k_T immediate snapshots can be interpreted topologically as constructing a simplicial map from the k_T-th standard chromatic subdivision of the input complex to the output complex. This is because each immediate snapshot can be represented by a standard subdivision [23, 25].

(4) A chromatic map from an arbitrary subdivision of a complex can be approximated by a chromatic map from an iterated standard chromatic subdivision. This is a chromatic version of the standard simplicial approximation theorem, and a proof can be found in Section 5 of [22]. It also follows from an operational argument in [3].

In this paper we extend this method of proof to models representing proper subsets of the runs of the wait-free standard shared-memory model.

To this end, we start with a formal definition of the very notion of solving a task in IIS. Surprisingly, no such definition appeared in the literature until now.[1] In particular, we introduce the notions of *participating* (taking at least one step) and *infinitely participating* (taking infinitely many steps) processes in an IIS run.

Further, to benefit from Step (1) in the list above, we need a mapping between SM and IIS, that preserves the notions of participating and infinitely participating sets. Furthermore, in addition to this forward simulation $F:$ SM $\to$ IIS we need a backward simulation $B:$ IIS $\to$ SM, such that for all $M \subseteq$ SM we have $B(F(M)) \subseteq M$. We also ask for the restriction of B to the image of F to preserve the notions of participating and infinitely participating sets. Given that the standard simulations [2, 3] do not meet these requirements, we employ a new two-way simulation presented in [4]. This applies to a large set of *adversarial* SM models [7,24], specified by sets of processes that can be infinitely participating in a model run.

Thus, we can cast an adversarial SM model to its equivalent model in IIS. Moreover, the IIS model is, in a strict sense, richer than SM: multiple IIS runs collapse into a single SM run by the simulation [4]. Our characterization of IIS task solvability applies to any *sub-IIS model* (that is, a subset of the runs in the IIS model), including those that have no equivalents in SM.

Imitating Step (2) in sub-IIS models is in general impossible. For example, in the 1-resilient 3-process model, the task of 2-set agreement can be easily solved. However, every such solution has a run in which two processes fail and the remaining process never outputs [1, 21, 32]. In every 1-resilient extension of a finite prefix of this run, all infinitely participating processes output. Since such a prefix may have an arbitrary length, a uniform bound k_T on the number of steps sufficient to output in a run of the 1-resilient sub-IIS model does not exist. This observation is related to the fact that the model is *non-compact*, with respect to a metric that will be defined in Section 5.

Therefore, our main theorem, which we call the *generalized* asynchronous computability theorem (GACT), is a generalization of Step (3) in the outline above, without relying on Step (2). Instead, the characterization proposes to "approximate" a non-compact model by a sequence of compact models. The sequence converges to a superset of the target model. Thus, if the task is solvable by each compact model in the sequence, it is solvable by the target model. Each compact model is represented as subcomplex of a subdivided simplex. Hence GACT deals with a sub-complex of a subdivided simplex instead of a subdivided simplex (as ACT does), and instead of saying that there exists a single subdivision (as in ACT) it requires the existence of a sequence of sub-complexes.

Step (4) now applies individually to each subdivision in the sequence. In this paper we do not deal with this step, because the formulation would be too cumbersome, and because it is not necessary for our examples. Nevertheless, we believe that our theorem can be extended to arbitrary rather than standard chromatic subdivisions.

ACT turned out to be an essential tool in distributed computing [6,12,17–20]. We show that our GACT holds that promise too. We consider a task T, solvable t-resiliently, but (to our knowledge) only with a very involved algorithm [8]. In contrast, by applying the methods developed in this paper, we show that determining the t-resilient solvability of T is relatively simple.

The paper is organized as follows: In Section 2 we describe the IIS model and give some examples of sub-IIS models. In Section 3 we review some notions from combinatorial topology. In Section 4 we review the topological definition of a task, and explain what it means for a task to be solvable in a model. In Section 5 we describe sub-IIS models topologically. In Section 6 we prove our main result, GACT. In Section 7 we explain how GACT gives back the well-known ACT in the wait-free case. In Section 8 we introduce a new topological tool: a version of the simplicial approximation for infinite chromatic complexes. Using this tool, in Section 9 we show how GACT can be applied to a class of tasks called link connected; in particular, we use GACT to prove that a particular task can be solved in the t-resilient model. In Section 10 we recall some related work, and in Section 11 we draw the conclusions.

2. SUB-IIS MODELS

In this section, we describe our perspective on the *Iterated Immediate Snapshot* (IIS) model [3] and give examples of sub-IIS models.

2.1 The IIS model

Suppose we have $n+1$ processes $p_0, p_1, \ldots, p_n$. A run r in IIS is a sequence of *non-empty* sets of processes $S_1 \supseteq S_2 \supseteq \ldots$, with each $S_k \subseteq \{p_0, \ldots, p_n\}$ consisting of those processes that participate in the kth iteration of immediate snapshot (IS). Furthermore, each S_k is equipped with an ordered partition: $S_k = S_k^1 \cup \cdots \cup S_k^{n_k}$ (for some $n_k \leq n$), corresponding to the order in which processes are invoked in the respective IS.

Let $\mathcal{R}$ be the set of runs in IIS. Fix a run $r \in \mathcal{R}$, with $r = S_1, S_2, \ldots$ as above. The processes $p_i \in S_1$ are called *participating.* If p_j appears in all the sets S_k, we say that p_j is *infinitely participating* in r. The sets of participating and infinitely participating processes in a run r are denoted $part(r)$ and ∞-$part(r)$, respectively.

If either $k=0$ or $p_i \in S_k$ for some $k \geq 1$, then we define a set called the *kth view of p_i in the run r*, $view(p_i, k)$, recursively, as follows:

1. $view(p_i, 0) = \{p_i\}$;

[1]Some specific *compact* subsets of IIS runs were formally treated in [29].

2. For $k \geq 1$, the view of $p_i \in S_k^j \subseteq S_k$ is $view(p_i, k) = \{view(p_s, k-1) \mid p_s \in S_k^1 \cup \cdots \cup S_k^j\}$.

Our definitions can be interpreted operationally as follows. Every process proceeds through an infinite series of one-shot immediate snapshot (IS) instances [2]: $IS_1, IS_2 \ldots$. Then S_k is interpreted as the set of processes accessing memory IS_k, and each S_k^j is the set of processes obtaining the same *view* after accessing IS_k. Recall that in IS, the view of a process $p_i \in S_k^j$ is defined by the values written by the processes in $S_k^1 \cup \cdots \cup S_k^j$.

The original definition of IIS [3] can be thought of as the variant of our model, in which we impose the condition $S_1 = S_2 = \cdots = \{p_0, \ldots, p_n\}$, i.e., every process is infinitely participating. What is the advantage of our new, more refined, definition of IIS? It allows a run to be extended to more processes without changing the views of the already existing processes. For instance, in the run $r = \{\{p_0\}\}, \{\{p_0\}\}, \ldots$ we have $part(r) = \infty\text{-}part(r) = \{p_0\}$. In the run $r' = \{\{p_0\}, \{p_1\}\}, \{\{p_0\}, \{p_1\}\}, \{\{p_0\}, \{p_1\}\}, \ldots$ we have $part(r') = \infty\text{-}part(r') = \{p_0, p_1\}$. However, p_0 cannot tell whether it is in r or in r', because the corresponding views of p_0 are the same in both runs. In this situation, we say that r' is an extension of r.

Formally, we say that a run $r' = S'_1, S'_2, \ldots$ is an *extension* of a run $r = S_1, S_2, \ldots$, and we write $r \leq r'$, if (i) $S_j \subseteq S'_j$ for all j, and (ii) the views of the processes in $part(r)$ are the same in r' as in r. This defines a partial order on $\mathcal{R}$.

If r is a run, let $minimal(r)$ be the smallest run r_0 such that $r_0 \leq r$ (that is, for all $r' \leq r$, we have $r_0 \leq r'$). It is not difficult to see that $minimal(r)$ exists and is unique. We then define $fast(r) = \infty\text{-}part(minimal(r))$. We define $slow(r)$ to be the complement set of $fast(r)$.

Intuitively, $fast(r)$ is the largest set of processes that "see" each other (appear in each other's view) infinitely often in r. In other words, for all $p_i, p_j \in fast(r)$ and all $k \geq 0$, there exists $\ell \geq k$ such that $view(p_i, k)$ appears in $view(p_j, \ell)$.

2.2 Examples of models

We define a *sub-IIS model* M to be any subset of $\mathcal{R}$.

EXAMPLE 2.1. *The* wait-free *(or* completely asynchronous*) model WF is the set $\mathcal{R}$ itself. The interpretation of WF is that anything can happen (all sorts of step interleavings are allowed).*

EXAMPLE 2.2. *For $t \leq n$, the* t-resilient model Res_t *consists of the runs $r \in \mathcal{R}$ such that $|fast(r)| \geq n + 1 - t$. This is the model in which at most t processes are slow.*

EXAMPLE 2.3. *For $k \leq n+1$, the* k-obstruction-free model OF_k *consists of all the runs r in which no more than k processes are fast, i.e., $|fast(r)| \leq k$. This model was previously discussed in [11], following a suggestion of Guerraoui.*

EXAMPLE 2.4. *More generally, consider the* model with adversary $\mathbb{A}$ *[7], which we denote by $M^{\text{adv}}(\mathbb{A})$. Here, $\mathbb{A}$ is any subset of the power set of $\{0, 1, \ldots, n\}$. We then define $M^{\text{adv}}(\mathbb{A})$ to consist of all runs r such that $slow(r) \in \mathbb{A}$.*

3. TOPOLOGICAL DEFINITIONS

Before moving forward, we need to review several notions from topology. We will assume that the reader has a basic knowledge of metric spaces (open sets, continuity, compactness), as in [31, Chapter 7].

3.1 Simplicial complexes

A good reference for the material in this section is Chapter 3 in [33].

A *simplicial complex* is a set V, together with a collection C of finite nonempty subsets of V such that:

(a) For any $v \in V$, the one-element set $\{v\}$ is in C;

(b) If $\sigma \in C$ and $\sigma' \subseteq \sigma$, then $\sigma' \in C$.

The elements of V are called *vertices*, and the elements of C are called a *simplices*. We usually drop V from the notation, and refer to the simplicial complex as C.

A simplicial complex C is called *finite* if the collection C is finite. A weaker notion is *locally finite*: C is said to be locally finite if every vertex of C belongs to only finitely many simplices in C. For simplicity, we will assume that our complexes are locally finite.

A subset of a simplex is called a *face* of that simplex.

A *subcomplex* of C is a subset of C that is also a simplicial complex.

The *dimension* of a simplex $\sigma \in C$ is its cardinality minus one. The k-skeleton of a complex C, denoted $\text{Skel}^k C$, is the subcomplex formed of all simplices of C of dimension k or less.

A simplicial complex C is called *pure* of dimension n if C has no simplices of dimension $> n$, and every k-dimensional simplex of C (for $k < n$) is a face of an n-dimensional simplex of C.

Given a simplex $\sigma \in C$, we denote by $\text{st}\,\sigma$ the *open star* of σ, that is, the set of all simplices in C that have σ as a face. The *closed star* of σ, denoted $\text{St}\,\sigma$, is the smallest simplicial complex that contains $\text{st}\,\sigma$. The difference $(\text{St}\,\sigma) \setminus (\text{st}\,\sigma)$ is called the *link* of σ.

Let A and B be simplicial complexes. A map $f : A \to B$ is called *simplicial* if it is induced by a map on vertices; that is, f maps vertices to vertices, and for any $\sigma \in A$, we have

$$f(\sigma) = \bigcup_{v \in \sigma} f(\{v\}).$$

A simplicial map f is called *noncollapsing* (or *dimension-preserving*) if $\dim f(\sigma) = \dim \sigma$ for all $\sigma \in A$.

Any simplicial complex C has an associated *geometric realization* $|C|$, defined as follows. Let V be the set of vertices in C. As a set, we let C be the subset of $[0,1]^V = \{\alpha : V \to [0,1]\}$ consisting of all functions α such that $\{v \in V \mid \alpha(v) > 0\} \in C$ and $\sum_{v \in V} \alpha(v) = 1$. For each $\sigma \in C$, we set $|\sigma| = \{\alpha \in |C| \mid \alpha(v) \neq 0 \Rightarrow v \in \sigma\}$. Each $|\sigma|$ is in one-to-one correspondence to a subset of $\mathbb{R}^n$ of the form $\{(x_1, \ldots, x_n) \in [0,1]^n \mid \sum x_i = 1\}$. We put a metric on $|C|$ by $d(\alpha, \beta) = \sum_{v \in V} |\alpha(v) - \beta(v)|$.

Given a simplicial map $f : A \to B$, there is an associated continuous, piecewise linear map $|f| : |A| \to |B|$, defined by the formula

$$|f|(\alpha)(v') = \sum_{f(v)=v'} \alpha(v).$$

A nonempty complex C is called k-*connected* if, for each $m \leq k$, any continuous map of the m-sphere into $|C|$ can be extended to a continuous map over the $(m+1)$-disk.

A *subdivision* of a simplicial complex C is a simplicial complex C' such that:

1. The vertices of C' are points of $|C|$.
2. For any $\sigma' \in C'$, there exists $\sigma \in C$ such that $\sigma' \subset |\sigma|$.
3. The piecewise linear map $|C'| \to |C|$ mapping each vertex of C' to the corresponding point of C is a homeomorphism.

In particular, every complex C admits a *barycentric subdivision* $\operatorname{Bary}(C)$, defined as follows. The vertices of $\operatorname{Bary}(K)$ are the barycenters of the simplices of C (in the geometric realization). The simplices of $\operatorname{Bary}(K)$ correspond to ordered sequences $(\sigma_0, \dots, \sigma_m)$ of simplices of C, where σ_i is a face of σ_{i+1}; the barycenters of σ_i are then the vertices of the corresponding simplex in $\operatorname{Bary}(K)$.

By iterating this construction k times we obtain the kth barycentric subdivision, $\operatorname{Bary}^k(C)$.

3.2 Chromatic complexes

We now turn to the chromatic complexes used in distributed computing, and recall some notions from [22].

Fix $n \geq 0$. The *standard n-simplex* $\mathbf{s}$ has $n+1$ vertices, in one-to-one correspondence with $n+1$ *colors* $0, 1, \dots, n$. A face $\mathbf{t}$ of $\mathbf{s}$ is specified by a collection of vertices from $\{0, \dots, n\}$. We view $\mathbf{s}$ as a complex, with its simplices being all possible faces $\mathbf{t}$. Note that the open star of a face $\mathbf{t}$ is $\operatorname{st} \mathbf{t} = \{\mathbf{t}' \mid \mathbf{t} \subseteq \mathbf{t}'\}$, while the closed star of any face is the whole simplex $\mathbf{s}$.

A *chromatic complex* is a simplicial complex C together with a noncollapsing simplicial map $\chi : C \to \mathbf{s}$. Note that C can have dimension at most n. We usually drop χ from the notation. We write $\chi(C)$ for the union of $\chi(v)$ over all vertices $v \in C$. Note that if $C' \subseteq C$ is a subcomplex of a chromatic complex, it inherits a chromatic structure by restriction.

In particular, the standard n-simplex $\mathbf{s}$ is a chromatic complex, with χ being the identity.

Every chromatic complex C has a *standard chromatic subdivision* $\operatorname{Chr} C$. Let us first define $\operatorname{Chr} \mathbf{s}$ for the standard simplex $\mathbf{s}$. The vertices of $\operatorname{Chr} \mathbf{s}$ are pairs $(i, \mathbf{t})$, where $i \in \{0, 1, \dots, n\}$ and $\mathbf{t}$ is a face of $\mathbf{s}$ containing i. We let $\chi(i, \mathbf{t}) = i$. Further, $\operatorname{Chr} s$ is characterized by its n-simplices; these are the $(n+1)$-tuples $((0, \mathbf{t}_0), \dots, (n, \mathbf{t}_n))$ such that:

(a) For all $\mathbf{t}_i$ and $\mathbf{t}_j$, one is a face of the other;

(b) If $j \in \mathbf{t}_i$, then $\mathbf{t}_j \subseteq \mathbf{t}_i$.

The geometric realization of $\mathbf{s}$ can be taken to be the set $\{\mathbf{x} = (x_0, \dots, x_n) \in [0,1]^{n+1} \mid \sum x_i = 1\}$, with the vertex i corresponding to the point $\mathbf{x}^i$ with i coordinate 1 and all other coordinates 0. Then, we can identify a vertex $(i, \mathbf{t})$ of $\operatorname{Chr} \mathbf{s}$ with the point

$$\frac{1}{2k-1}\mathbf{x}_i + \frac{2}{2k-1}\Big(\sum_{\{j \in \mathbf{t} | j \neq i\}} \mathbf{x}_j \Big) \in |\mathbf{s}| \subset \mathbb{R}^{n+1},$$

where k is the cardinality of $\mathbf{t}$. (Compare [22, Definition 5.7].) Thus, $\operatorname{Chr} \mathbf{s}$ becomes a subdivision of $\mathbf{s}$ and the geometric realizations are identical: $|\mathbf{s}| = |\operatorname{Chr} \mathbf{s}|$.

Next, given a chromatic complex C, we let $\operatorname{Chr} C$ be the subdivision of C obtained by replacing each simplex in C with its chromatic subdivision. Thus, the vertices of $\operatorname{Chr} C$ are pairs (p, σ), where p is a vertex of C and σ is a simplex of C containing p. If we iterate process this m times we obtain the mth chromatic subdivision, $\operatorname{Chr}^m C$.

Let A and B be chromatic complexes. A simplicial map $f : A \to B$ is called a *chromatic map* if for all vertices $v \in A$, we have $\chi(v) = \chi(f(v))$. Note that chromatic map is automatically noncollapsing. A chromatic map has chromatic subdivisions $\operatorname{Chr}^m f : \operatorname{Chr}^m A \to \operatorname{Chr}^m B$. Under the identifications of topological spaces $|A| \cong |\operatorname{Chr}^m A|, |B| \cong |\operatorname{Chr}^m B|$, the continuous maps $|f|$ and $|\operatorname{Chr}^m f|$ are identical.

A *chromatic multi-map* between A and B is a map $\Delta : A \to 2^B$ that, for any $m \leq n$, takes every m-simplex of A to a pure m-dimensional subcomplex of B, such that: (i) For every simplex σ of A, we have $\chi(\sigma) = \chi(\Delta(\sigma))$, and (ii) For all simplices $\sigma, \tau \in A$, we have $\Delta(\sigma \cap \tau) \subseteq \Delta(\sigma) \cap \Delta(\tau)$. In particular, if σ' is a face of σ, then $\Delta(\sigma') \subseteq \Delta(\sigma)$.

4. TASKS

4.1 Definitions

A *task* $T = (\mathcal{I}, \mathcal{O}, \Delta)$ on $n+1$ processes $\{p_0, \dots, p_n\}$ consist of two finite, pure n-dimensional chromatic complexes $\mathcal{I}$ and $\mathcal{O}$, together with a chromatic multi-map $\Delta : \mathcal{I} \to 2^{\mathcal{O}}$. The *input complex* $\mathcal{I}$ specifies the possible input values, the *output complex* $\mathcal{O}$ specifies the possible output values, and Δ describes which output values are allowed for a given input. The colors specify to which process each input or output value corresponds.

A task is called *input-less* if the input complex is the standard simplex $\mathbf{s}$, colored by the identity. Then each process starts with input only its own id.[2]

4.2 Affine tasks

Many examples of input-less tasks can be constructed as follows. Let $L \subseteq \operatorname{Chr}^k \mathbf{s}$ be a pure n-dimensional subcomplex of the kth chromatic subdivision of $\mathbf{s}$, for some k. For each face $\mathbf{t} \subseteq \mathbf{s}$, the intersection $L \cap \operatorname{Chr}^k \mathbf{t}$ is a subcomplex of $\operatorname{Chr}^k \mathbf{s}$; we assume that this subcomplex is pure of the same dimension as $\mathbf{t}$ (and possibly empty).

We define an input-less task $(\mathbf{s}, L, \Delta)$ by setting $\Delta(\mathbf{t}) = L \cap \operatorname{Chr}^k \mathbf{t}$ for any face $\mathbf{t} \subseteq \mathbf{s}$. Tasks constructed like this are called *affine*. To depict an affine task, we can simply draw the corresponding complex L.

By abuse of notation, we will usually write L for the affine task $(\mathbf{s}, L, \Delta)$. We chose the name *affine* because if we have a task L as above, the geometric realizations of the simplices of L can be depicted as lying on affine subspaces of $\mathbb{R}^n$. Similar terminology appears in algebraic geometry, where one talks about affine varieties.

For example, consider the task of *total order* L^{ord}, defined as follows. For each permutation α of $\{0, 1, \dots, n\}$, there is a unique n-simplex σ_α in the second chromatic subdivision $\operatorname{Chr}^2 \mathbf{s}$ with the property that the vertex of σ_α colored i is in the interior of an i-dimensional face of $\mathbf{s}$. For example, for 3

[2]Note that in the definition of a multi-map we allowed images to be empty. This is somewhat non-standard, as it means that processes in a task do not have to output. If one prefers to avoid that, for every task $T = (\mathcal{I}, \mathcal{O}, \Delta)$ we can construct a new, equivalent task $T^+ = (\mathcal{I}^+, \mathcal{O}^+, \Delta^+)$ as follows. We let $\mathcal{I}^+ = \mathcal{I}$. The output complex $\mathcal{O}^+$ is obtained from $\mathcal{O}$ by adding extra vertices $v_0, \dots, v_n$ (with v_i corresponding to "no output" for the process i); moreover, for each simplex σ in $\mathcal{O}$, we add an n-simplex σ^+ in $\mathcal{O}^+$ by adjoining vertices v_i for the colors i not represented in σ. Finally, we let $\Delta^+(\tau) = (\Delta(\tau))^+$.

processes, the six simplices of the form σ_α are those shown here:

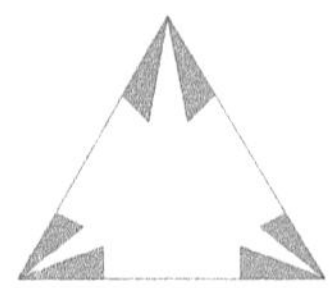

The total order task is the affine task associated to the complex $L^{\text{ord}} \subseteq \text{Chr}^2 \mathbf{s}$ is the union of all the $(n+1)!$ simplices of the form σ_α. The name total order refers to the fact that the possible outputs (when all $n+1$ processes are running) are in one-to-one correspondence with the total orderings (i.e., permutations) of the set of processes $\{0, 1, \ldots, n\}$, similar to *one-shot total-order broadcast* [15] where every process proposes broadcasts its identifier and the processes agree on the order in which the identifiers are delivered.

4.3 Views with input

Let $r = S_1, S_2, \ldots$ be a run in IIS. Recall that in Section 2.1 we defined the kth view of a process in the run, $view(p_i, k)$. We now generalize this to allow arbitrary inputs.

Let $\mathcal{I}$ be a pure n-dimensional chromatic complex, and let $\omega \in \mathcal{I}$ be an n-dimensional simplex. The kth view of p_i in the run r starting with input ω is denoted $view(p_i, \omega, k)$ and defined recursively as follows:

1. $view(p_i, \omega, 0) = \{(p_i, v)\}$, where v is the vertex colored i in the simplex ω;
2. For $k \geq 1$, the view of $p_i \in S_k^j \subseteq S_k$ is $view(p_i, \omega, k) = \{view(p_s, \omega, k-1) \mid p_s \in S_k^1 \cup \cdots \cup S_k^j\}$.

4.4 Task Solvability

In a sub-IIS model, informally, a task $T = (\mathcal{I}, \mathcal{O}, \Delta)$ is solvable in M if for all runs $r \in M$, the infinitely participating processes output, and their output is a subsimplex of the allowed outputs for the participating processes. An output is the result of a *protocol*. For us, when dealing with solvability rather than complexity, a protocol is just a partial map from views to outputs. Thus, requiring an infinitely participating process to output means requiring that eventually it will have a view that is mapped by the protocol to an output value.

We define the set $\mathcal{V} = \mathcal{V}(\mathcal{I})$ to consist of all possible $view(p_i, \omega, k)$ in all runs $r \in \mathcal{R}$, for all processes p_i, simplices $\omega \in \mathcal{I}$, and integers $k \geq 0$. Formally, a protocol Π for the task T is a map from a subset of $\mathcal{V}$ to the set of vertices in the output complex $\mathcal{O}$.

Definition 4.1. *A task $T = (\mathcal{I}, \mathcal{O}, \Delta)$ is* solvable *in a sub-IIS model M if there exists a protocol Π for T such that for all $r \in M$ (with $r = S_1, S_2, \ldots$ as before):*

1. *For each p_i, and for each n-dimensional simplex $\omega \in \mathcal{I}$, there exist k_0 and a vertex v of $\mathcal{O}$ colored i, such that:*
   - *For all $k < k_0$, $view(p_i, \omega, k) \notin domain(\Pi)$;*
   - *For all $k \geq k_0$ such that $p_i \in S_k$ exists, we have $\Pi(view(p_i, \omega, k)) = v$.*

   (This condition is satisfied vacuously if p_i is not infinitely participating, because we can find k_0 such that p_i did not take k_0 steps in r, so $p_i \notin S_k$ for $k \geq k_0$.)
2. *For all k, $\{\Pi(view(p_i, \omega, k)) \mid view(p_i, \omega, k) \in domain(\Pi)\}$ is a sub-simplex of a simplex in $\Delta(\omega \cap \chi^{-1}(part(r)))$.*

In every run $r \in M$, condition (1) above requires every infinitely participating to eventually produce an output, and condition (2) requires the produced output to respect the task specification Δ given the inputs of participating processes.

4.5 Example: solving tasks in sub-IIS

Note that our definition of task solvability in sub-IIS models brings illuminating subtleties that were not observed in the conventional SM model. Consider a sub-IIS model M and the corresponding model $M_{fast} = \{r \mid \exists r' \in M, r = minimal(r')\}$. If a task T is solvable in M then it is obviously solvable in M_{fast}, but not necessarily vice-versa. Indeed, consider the obstruction-free model $OF = OF_1$, consisting of runs with a single fast process. Obviously, the total order task L^{ord} cannot be solved in OF, because in runs r where the process in $fast(r)$ is always ahead of the rest ($S_k = fast(r)$ for all k), the rest of the processes essentially proceed *wait-free*. In contrast, we can easily solve L^{ord} in OF_{fast} using commit-adopt [9] (implemented in IIS).

5. TOPOLOGICAL INTERPRETATION

Recall that $\mathcal{R}$ denotes the set of runs in IIS. We put a metric on $\mathcal{R}$ as follows. Given runs $r, r' \in \mathcal{R}$, we let $k = k(r, r')$ denote the largest $k \geq 0$ such that the first k steps of r and r' are identical. (In particular, we let $k = \infty$ when $r = r'$.) We set the distance between r and r' to be $d(r, r') = 1/(1+k)$. It is easy to see that $d(r, r')$ is a metric that captures how "close" the two runs are.

Recall that a metric space is compact if every open cover has a finite subcover; or, equivalently, if any infinite sequence has a convergent subsequence. (See [31, Section 7.7], for example.) For future reference, we mention:

Lemma 5.1. *The metric space $\mathcal{R}$ is compact.*

Proof. Let $r[1] = (S[1]_1, S[1]_2, \ldots), r[2] = (S[2]_1, S[2]_2, \ldots), \ldots$ be an infinite sequence of runs. (Each $S[i]_k$ is a set equipped with an ordered partition.) There are only finitely many possibilities for the first step S_1^j, so we can find a subsequence $(r[1,1], r[1,2], \ldots)$ of $(r[1], r[2], \ldots)$ such that the first step in each $r[1,i]_q$ is a constant choice S_1, with a constant partition $S_1 = S_1^1 \cup \cdots \cup S_1^{n_1}$. From the subsequence $(r[1,1], r[1,2], \ldots)$ we can extract a further subsequence $(r[2,1], r[2,2], \ldots)$ such that the second step is a constant choice $S_2 = S_2^1 \cup \cdots \cup S_2^{n_2}$, and so on. Hence, the diagonal subsequence $(r[1,1], r[2,2], r[3,3], \ldots)$ converges to $r = (S_1, S_2, \ldots)$. Thus, every sequence in $\mathcal{R}$ has a converging subsequence. □

The metric space $\mathcal{R}$ is not easy to visualize. We can however get a partial understanding by focusing on the views of the fast processes in each run.

Consider the standard chromatic subdivisions of the n-simplex $\mathbf{s}$. Recall that a run in IIS can be identified with a sequence of simplices $\sigma_0, \sigma_1, \sigma_2, \ldots$, with $\sigma_k \in \text{Chr}^k \mathbf{s}$ and $|\sigma_{k+1}| \subset |\sigma_k|$ [23, 25].

Note that every run converges to a point of the geometric realization $|\mathbf{s}|$, so there is a natural, continuous map $\pi : \mathcal{R} \to |\mathbf{s}|$, which we call the *affine projection*. The information captured in $p = \pi(r)$ exactly consists of the views of the fast processes in r. In fact, each point $\pi(r) \in |\mathbf{s}|$ can be identified with the minimal run *minimal*(r).

There is a canonical coloring map $\chi : |\mathbf{s}| \to 2^{\{0,1,\ldots,n\}}$ that extends the colorings on all chromatic subdivisions $\mathrm{Chr}^m\, \mathbf{s}$ to $|\mathbf{s}|$. Precisely, given a point $p \in |\mathbf{s}|$, we let $\chi(p)$ be the minimal subset $A \subseteq \{0,1,\ldots,n\}$ such that p lies in a simplex σ of a chromatic subdivision $\mathrm{Chr}^k\, \mathbf{s}$ with $\chi(\sigma) = A$. It is easy to see that $\chi(p) = \mathit{fast}(r)$, for any r such that $\pi(r) = p$.

A special case of a sub-IIS model is a set of runs of the form $\pi^{-1}(S)$, where $S \subseteq |\mathbf{s}|$. We call such models *geometric*, because they can be easily visualized as associated subsets of $|\mathbf{s}|$. Notice that all models in Examples 2.1-2.4 are geometric. However, our main results will apply equally well to *all* (not necessarily geometric) sub-IIS models.

6. THE GENERALIZED ASYNCHRONOUS COMPUTABILITY THEOREM

6.1 Terminating subdivisions

Let C be a chromatic complex. Consider standard chromatic subdivisions $\mathrm{Chr}^m\, C$ for $m > 0$ (Section 4), and recall that the vertices of $\mathrm{Chr}^m\, C$ can be identified with a subset of the vertices in $\mathrm{Chr}^{m+1}\, C$.

A *terminating subdivision* $\mathscr{T}$ of C is specified by a sequence of chromatic complexes $C_0, C_1, C_2, \ldots$, and a sequence of subcomplexes $\Sigma_0 \subseteq \Sigma_1 \subseteq \Sigma_2 \subseteq \ldots$ such that for all $k \geq 0$:

(i) Σ_k is a subcomplex of C_k;

(ii) $C_0 = C$, and C_{k+1} is obtained from C_k by taking the partial chromatic subdivision in which the simplices in Σ_k are "terminated", i.e., not further subdivided. Precisely, we replace a simplex σ in C_k by a coarser subdivision than $\mathrm{Chr}(\sigma)$. Whereas the vertices of $\mathrm{Chr}(\sigma)$ are pairs (p, τ) with τ being a face of σ and p a vertex of τ, in C_{k+1} we consider the pairs (p, τ) of that form such that either $\tau \notin \Sigma_k$, or τ consists of a single vertex in Σ_k. For example, if Σ_k is zero-dimensional, then $C_{k+1} = \mathrm{Chr}^1\, C_k$; if C_k is the standard 2-dimensional simplex and Σ_k is one of its 1-dimensional faces, we have:

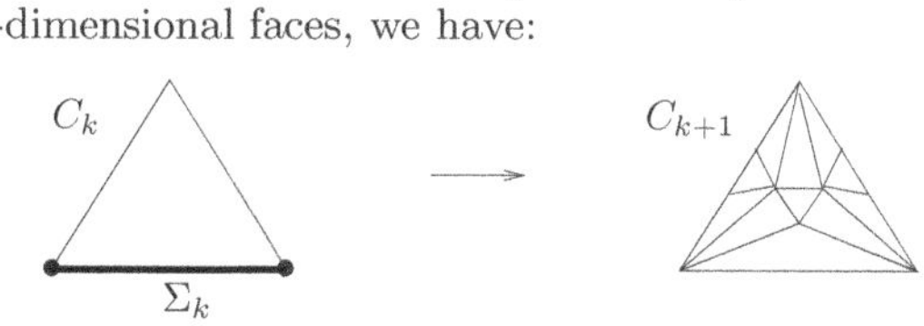

A simplex of Σ_k for some k is called a *stable simplex* in the subdivision $\mathscr{T}$; such a simplex remains unchanged in all further complexes $C_{k+1}, C_{k+2}, \ldots$. The union $\cup_k \Sigma_k$ of stable simplices in $\mathscr{T}$ forms a chromatic complex, which we denote by $K(\mathscr{T})$; it usually has infinitely many vertices. Observe that the geometric realization $|K(\mathscr{T})|$ can be identified with a subset of $|C|$.

In particular, if there exists k such that $\Sigma_k = C_k$, then we must have $C_k = C_{k+1} = \ldots$, and $\mathscr{T}$ is just a finite subdivision of C; in this case, all the simplices in C_k are stable, and $|K(\mathscr{T})| = |C|$. At the other extreme, if Σ_k is empty for all k, then $\mathscr{T}$ consists of the kth chromatic subdivisions of C for all k; in this case, no simplices are stable, and $K(\mathscr{T})$ is empty.

Stable simplices intend to model processes that have produced outputs and thus, intuitively, do not need to communicate among themselves any longer. Therefore, stable simplices are not further subdivided. However, processes with outputs keep participating in the computation: simplices that contain non-stabilized vertices continue to be subdivided. This will allow us to formulate the conditions of task solvability in non-compact sub-IIS models.

6.2 The main result

We are now ready to formulate and prove our main result: a characterization of taks solvability in sub-IIS models.

Let $M \subseteq \mathcal{R}$ be a sub-IIS model on $n+1$ processes. Let $\mathscr{T}$ be a terminating subdivision of a pure n-dimensional chromatic complex $\mathcal{I}$, and let $\chi : \mathcal{I} \to \mathbf{s}$ be the coloring map. Let $\rho : |\mathcal{I}| \to |\mathbf{s}|$ be the geometric realization (piecewise linear extension) of the map χ. Note that ρ maps vertices of $\mathrm{Chr}^k\, \mathcal{I}$ to vertices of $\mathrm{Chr}^k\, \mathbf{s}$ of the same color.

Recall that each vertex v in $\mathscr{T}$ belongs to $\mathrm{Chr}^k(\sigma)$ for some $k \geq 0$ and some n-dimensional simplex σ of $\mathcal{I}$. Thus, $\rho(v)$ is a vertex of $\mathrm{Chr}^k(\mathbf{s})$. If we have a simplex $\tau \in K(\mathscr{T})$, then $\rho(|\tau|)$ is the convex hull of $\rho(v)$ for $v \in \tau$.

We say that $\mathscr{T}$ is *admissible* for M if for any run $r \in M$ (viewed as a sequence of simplices $\sigma_0, \sigma_1, \ldots$ in $\mathbf{s}$) and for every n-dimensional simplex ω in $\mathcal{I}$, there exists $k > 0$ and a stable simplex $\tau \in K(\mathscr{T})$ such that $|\tau| \subseteq |\omega|$ and $|\sigma_k| \subseteq \rho(|\tau|)$. The intuition here is that every run of M with inputs ω should eventually land in a simplex of $\mathscr{T}$.

THEOREM 6.1 (GACT). *A sub-IIS model M solves a task $T = (\mathcal{I}, \mathcal{O}, \Delta)$ if and only if there exists a terminating subdivision $\mathscr{T}$ of $\mathcal{I}$ and a chromatic map $\delta : K(\mathscr{T}) \to \mathcal{O}$ such that:*

(a) $\mathscr{T}$ is admissible for the model M;

(b) For any simplex σ of $\mathcal{I}$, if τ is a stable simplex of $\mathscr{T}$ such that $|\tau| \subseteq |\sigma|$, then $\delta(\tau) \in \Delta(\sigma)$.

PROOF. "$\Rightarrow$" : Suppose M solves T using a protocol Π. By induction on the recursion that defines $\mathit{view}(p_i, \omega, k)$, it is easy to see that the kth view of p_i in a run $r \in M$ (with input ω) corresponds to a vertex $v \in \mathrm{Chr}^k(\omega) \subseteq \mathrm{Chr}^k(\mathcal{I})$ with $\chi(v) = \{p_i\}$.

We construct a terminating subdivision $\mathscr{T}$ with desirable properties as follows. We proceed with the standard subdivisions $\mathrm{Chr}^k(\mathcal{I})$ for $k = 0, 1, 2, \ldots$, and we examine all runs $r \in M$. At the kth stage we take the inductively constructed C_k, whose vertices are a subset of the vertices of $\mathrm{Chr}^k(\mathcal{I})$. We then terminate those simplices for which Π has given an output: A simplex σ of C_k (with $|\sigma| \subseteq |\omega|$) is included in Σ_k if there exists a run $r \in M$ such that the vertices of σ are of the form $v_i = \mathit{view}(p_i, \omega, k)$ for that run, and the outputs $\Pi(v_i)$ exist (that is, $v_i \in \mathit{domain}(\Pi)$). Then Σ_k determines C_{k+1}.

Given a simplex $\sigma \in \Sigma_k$ with vertices v_i, we set $\delta(\sigma)$ be the simplex with vertices $\Pi(v_i)$.

Part (a) (admissibility of $\mathscr{T}$) follows from the construction: Given any run $r \in M$ and a top-dimensional simplex ω in $\mathcal{I}$, pick k such that all the processes infinitely participating in r have produced output at the kth step when they are given input from ω. Let σ_k be the corresponding simplex of $\mathrm{Chr}^k\, \mathbf{s}$. If $\rho^{-1}(|\sigma_k|) \cap |\omega|$ is an embedded simplex of C_k, then it is necessarily a stable simplex (because all the processes have output), and we are done. If $\rho^{-1}(|\sigma_k|) \cap |\omega|$

is not an embedded simplex of C_k, then, by construction, it is contained in a simplex of C_k that was terminated before (because some of the processes have produced outputs at an earlier time).

Part (b) follows from the fact that M solves T using Π.

"$\Leftarrow$" : Conversely, suppose there exists a terminating subdivision $\mathscr{T}$ and a map $\delta : K(\mathscr{T}) \to \mathcal{O}$ as in the statement of the theorem. We construct a protocol Π by which M solves T. Suppose we have a run $r \in M$, corresponding to a sequence of simplices $\sigma_0 \subseteq \sigma_1 \subseteq \sigma_2 \subset \dots$ Since $\mathscr{T}$ is admissible for M, for each input ω there exists a stable simplex τ such that $|\tau| \subseteq |\omega|$ and $|\sigma_k| \subseteq \rho(|\tau|)$ for all $k \gg 0$. Given a process $p_i \in \infty$-$part(r)$, we can assign it as output value the vertex of $\delta(\tau)$ that has color p_i. Now, p_i may obtain an output value (necessarily the same as before) through another run, at a different step k. We take the minimum over all such k, to obtain the value k_0 needed in the definition of Π. Condition (b) implies that Π solves T. □

7. THE WAIT-FREE MODEL

For the wait-free model WF, let us see how we can derive the original Asynchronous Computability Theorem of [22]. Indeed, Theorem 6.1 has the following:

COROLLARY 7.1. *A task $T = (\mathcal{I}, \mathcal{O}, \Delta)$ is solvable in the wait-free model if and only if there exists $k \geq 0$ and a chromatic map $\eta : \mathrm{Chr}^k \mathcal{I} \to \mathcal{O}$ such that, for any simplex $\tau \subseteq \mathcal{I}$ and any subsimplex σ of $\mathrm{Chr}^k \tau \subset \mathrm{Chr}^k \mathcal{I}$, we have $\eta(\sigma) \in \Delta(\tau)$.*

PROOF. If $\eta : \mathrm{Chr}^k \mathcal{I} \to C$ exists, solvability of T follows from GACT because $\mathrm{Chr}^k \mathcal{I}$ (with all the vertices terminated at the kth step) is a terminating subdivision that is admissible for WF.

Conversely, suppose that T is wait-free solvable. GACT provides a terminating subdivision $\mathscr{T}$ that is admissible for WF, and a map $\delta : K(\mathscr{T}) \to \mathcal{O}$. For each run $r \in WF = \mathcal{R}$ and top-dimensional input simplex $\omega \in I$, there is a k such that $|\sigma_k|$ is contained in a stable simplex τ of $\mathscr{T}$ with $|\tau| \subseteq |\omega|$. Since there are finitely many possibilities for ω, we can find a $k = k(r)$ that works for all ω. Let $\mathcal{R}_k$ be the set of runs r for which $k(r) \leq k$. We have inclusions $\mathcal{R}_0 \subseteq \mathcal{R}_1 \subseteq \mathcal{R}_2 \subseteq \dots$, and each $\mathcal{R}_k$ is open in the metric on $\mathcal{R}$ introduced in Section 5. We know from Lemma 5.1 that the set $\mathcal{R}$ is compact. Hence, the open cover $\mathcal{R}_k$ of $\mathcal{R}$ admits a finite subcover; i.e., there exists k such that $\mathcal{R}_k = \mathcal{R}$. We now define the desired map $\eta : \mathrm{Chr}^k \mathcal{I} \to \mathcal{O}$ by setting $\eta(\sigma) = \delta(\tau)$, where $\tau \in K(\mathscr{T})$ is the minimal simplex with $|\sigma| \subseteq |\tau|$. □

As stated in [22], ACT characterizes solvability in terms of a map from an arbitrary colored subdivision of $\mathcal{I}$ to the output complex. That any colored subdivided simplex can be approximated by $\mathrm{Chr}^k(\mathcal{I})$ for some k large enough is a purely topological result, proved in [22], and which can be used here verbatim. (This corresponds to Step 4 in the outline of the proof of ACT from the Introduction.)

8. SIMPLICIAL APPROXIMATION

To be able to apply GACT, we need a tool for constructing chromatic maps between two chromatic complexes A and B (subject to some boundary conditions). In many cases, it is easier to first construct a continuous map $f : |A| \to |B|$. Standard results in algebraic topology (reviewed in Subsection 8.1 below) say that after replacing A by a fine enough subdivision, we can deform f into a geometric realization of a simplicial map. Such a map may collapse the dimension of simplices, so it is not always clear how to turn it into a chromatic map. However, if we impose an additional condition (link-connectedness for the target), we will show in Subsection 8.2 that one can do the approximation using chromatic maps.

8.1 Classical results

Let A and B be simplicial complexes and let $f : |A| \to |B|$ be a continuous map between their geometric realizations. If A' is a subdivision of A, a simplicial map $\phi : A' \to B$ is called a *simplicial approximation* to f if for every $x \in |A| = |A'|$ and $\sigma \in B$ we have

$$f(x) \in |\sigma| \;\Rightarrow\; |\phi|(x) \in |\sigma|.$$

Roughly, the simplicial approximation theorem says that every continuous map between simplicial complexes can be approximated by a simplicial map. There are several versions of this in the literature. For finite simplicial complexes, we have:

THEOREM 8.1. *Let A and B be simplicial complexes such that A is finite, and let $f : |A| \to |B|$ be a continuous map. Then:*

(a) There exists an integer N such that for all $n \geq N$, the map f admits a simplicial approximation $\phi : \mathrm{Bary}^n(A) \to B$.

(b) Furthermore, if we have a subcomplex $C \subseteq A$ such that the restriction of f to C is the geometric realization of a simplicial map $g : C \to B$, then the approximation ϕ can be taken so that the restriction of ϕ to $|C|$ equals $|g|$.

Part (a) of this result is a special case of Theorem 8 in [33, p.128]. The theorem is stated in [33] in more generality, for pairs of simplicial complexes. Part (b) above follows from this more statement, taking into account Lemma 1 in [33, p.126].

In this paper we will need a different variant of the simplicial approximation theorem, one that applies without the hypothesis that A is finite:

THEOREM 8.2. *Let A and B be simplicial complexes, and let $f : |A| \to |B|$ be a continuous map. Then:*

(a) There exists a subdivision A' of A such that the map f admits a simplicial approximation $\phi : A' \to B$.

(b) Furthermore, if we have a subcomplex $C \subseteq A$ such that the restriction of f to C is the geometric realization of a simplicial map $g : C \to B$, then the approximation ϕ can be taken so that the restriction of ϕ to $|C|$ equals $|g|$.

Theorem 8.2 is mentioned in the remarks at the bottom of p.128 in [33]; see [34] or [28] for a more complete treatment.

Note that, in the case when A is countable and locally finite, we can deduce Theorem 8.2 from Theorem 8.1 as follows. Let us write A as a union of finite simplicial complexes $A_1 \subseteq A_2 \subseteq \dots$ We construct the subdivision A' and the map ϕ inductively. Suppose we found a simplicial approximation

ϕ_k : $\mathrm{Bary}^{n_k}(A_k) \to B$ for the restriction of f to A_k. Consider the restriction of f to $|A_{k+1}| = |\mathrm{Bary}^{n_k}(A_{k+1})|$. We extend the approximation ϕ_k to A_{k+1} by using part (b) of Theorem 8.1, applied to $\mathrm{Bary}^{n_k}(A_{k+1})$ and B. The result is a simplicial approximation $\phi_{k+1} : \mathrm{Bary}^{n_{k+1}}(A_{k+1}) \to B$ for some $n_{k+1} \geq n_k$, such that $|\phi_k| = |\phi_{k+1}|$ on $|A_k|$. The desired approximation $\phi : A' \to B$ has $|\phi| = |\phi_k|$ on each $|A_k|$. A subtle point here is the construction of the subdivision A', which is getting finer and finer as we go towards infinity. In principle, we would like A' to be $\mathrm{Bary}^{n_k}(A_k)$ on each $|A_k| \setminus |A_{k-1}|$. This is not a simplicial complex, but we can turn it into one by introducing additional simplices, as shown in the figure:

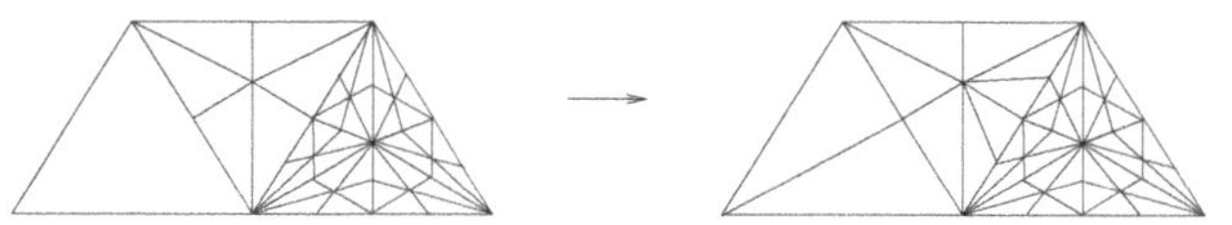

The local finiteness of A ensures that there is an upper bound on the number of times we have to subdivide each simplex.

8.2 Chromatic approximations

Let us go back to Theorem 8.1. Note that if A is a chromatic complex, then instead of the barycentric subdivisions $\mathrm{Bary}^n(A)$, one could take standard chromatic subdivisions $\mathrm{Chr}^n(A)$. (The same proof applies.) However, we cannot a priori conclude that the simplicial approximation is a chromatic simplicial map. For example, if the continuous map f collapses a simplex of A to a single vertex in B, then any simplicial approximation would do the same, but on the other hand chromatic maps are non-collapsing.

Nevertheless, we can avoid collapsing by assuming that the following property (for the target complex B):

DEFINITION 8.3 (DEFINITION 4.14 IN [22]). *A pure n-dimensional complex B is called* link-connected *if for all simplices $\sigma \in B$, the link of σ in B is $(n-\dim(\sigma)-2)$-connected.*

For example, the output complex L^{ord} for the total order task on three processes is not link-connected, because the link (in L^{ord}) of a vertex of $\mathbf{s}$ is not connected.

A variant of Theorem 8.2 for chromatic maps is proved in [22, Lemma 4.21] under the assumptions that A and B are chromatic complexes, B is link-connected, A is a finite subdivision of the standard simplex, and C is the boundary of A. The conclusion is that the map g can be taken to be chromatic. Furthermore, Theorem 5.29 in [22] shows that, under the same assumptions, the subdivision A' of A can be taken to be a standard chromatic subdivision; this yields a chromatic variant of Theorem 8.1.

One can generalize the results of Herlihy and Shavit to the setting of infinite complexes:

THEOREM 8.4. *Let A and B be chromatic simplicial complexes, and let $f : |A| \to |B|$ be a continuous map. Suppose that A is countable and locally finite, and that B is link-connected. Then:*

(a) There exists a subdivision A' of A such that the map f admits a chromatic simplicial approximation $\phi : A' \to B$.

(b) Furthermore, if we have a subcomplex $C \subseteq A$ such that the restriction of f to C is the geometric realization of a chromatic simplicial map $g : C \to B$, then the approximation ϕ can be taken so that the restriction of ϕ to $|C|$ equals $|g|$.

PROOF. We do this inductively on the skeleta of A. Suppose we have defined the map ϕ on a subdivision the k-skeleton $\mathrm{Skel}^k(A)$. We apply [22, Lemma 4.21] to the restriction of f to each $(k+1)$-simplex σ of A, mapped to the $(k+1)$-skeleton of B. (Observe that if B is link-connected, then so are its skeleta.) We obtain a simplicial approximation to f on σ, agreeing with the already constructed approximation on the boundary of σ. In the process we have to subdivide the simplices σ' in $\mathrm{Skel}^k(A)$, and each σ' is on the boundary of several $(k+1)$-simplices σ. However, by local finiteness, we can find a sufficiently fine subdivision that works for all $\sigma \supset \sigma'$. By continuing this ad infinitum, we obtain the approximation ϕ. Furthermore, if we have a subcomplex C as in part (b), then at each step we arrange so that the approximation agrees with the one defined on the corresponding skeleton of C. □

9. LINK-CONNECTED TASKS

9.1 A general result

The following proposition is an extension of the work of Herlihy and Shavit from [22] to the case of *infinite* chromatic complexes.

PROPOSITION 9.1. *Let M be a sub-IIS model, and $\mathscr{T}$ a terminating subdivision of $\mathcal{I}$ that is admissible for M. Suppose we have a task $T = (\mathcal{I}, \mathcal{O}, \Delta)$ such that the complexes $\Delta(\tau)$ are link-connected, for any $\tau \in \mathcal{I}$. Then, the task T is solvable in M if and only if there exists a continuous map $f : |K(\mathscr{T})| \to |\mathcal{O}|$ such that $f(|K(\mathscr{T})| \cap |\tau|) \subseteq |\Delta(\tau)|$ for all $\tau \in \mathcal{I}$.*

PROOF. If $\mathscr{T}$ and $\mathscr{T}'$ are terminating subdivisions of $\mathbf{s}$, we say that $\mathscr{T}'$ is a *stable refinement* of $\mathscr{T}$ if $|K(\mathscr{T})| = |K(\mathscr{T}')|$, and every simplex of $\mathscr{T}'$ is contained in a simplex of $\mathscr{T}$; i.e., $K(\mathscr{T}')$ should be a subdivision of $K(\mathscr{T})$. Note that if $\mathscr{T}$ is admissible for a model M, then so is $\mathscr{T}'$.

Given the continuous map f, we shall construct a simplicial, chromatic approximation $\delta : K(\mathscr{T}') \to \mathcal{O}$ as needed to apply GACT; here, $\mathscr{T}'$ is a stable refinement of $\mathscr{T}$.

We first construct a chromatic subdivision K' of $K(\mathscr{T})$, whose vertices are not necessarily in the standard chromatic subdivisions of $\mathcal{I}$, and a chromatic map $\delta' : K' \to \mathcal{O}$ (an approximation to f) such that δ' is carrier-preserving: $\delta'(\sigma) \in \Delta(\tau)$ when $|\sigma| \subseteq |\tau|$. We do this inductively on $d \geq 0$: For each d, we define the values of δ' on the simplices that are contained in d-dimensional faces of $|\mathcal{I}|$. Suppose we have defined δ' for $d-1$, and pick a d-dimensional face τ of $|\mathcal{I}|$. The restriction of f to $|K(\mathscr{T})| \cap |\tau|$ can be approximated by a simplicial map from a subdivision of $K(\mathscr{T})$, extending the already constructed δ' on the $(d-1)$-dimensional boundary. Further, since $K(\mathscr{T})$ is locally finite (by definition) and $\Delta(\tau)$ is link-connected, it follows from Theorem 8.4 that we can arrange for δ' to preserve colors.

Thus, we find a sufficiently fine stable refinement $\mathscr{T}'$ of $\mathscr{T}$ and a chromatic, carrier-preserving map $g : K(\mathscr{T}') \to K'$. We then set $\delta = \delta' \circ g$ and apply Theorem 6.1.

Conversely, if T is solvable in M, we can apply GACT and obtain a terminating subdivision $\mathscr{T}$ and a chromatic map $\delta : K(\mathscr{T}) \to \mathcal{O}$. The desired continuous map f is the geometric realization of δ. □

9.2 An example of GACT in action

Consider the t-resilient model Res_t from Example 2.2. Let L_t be the affine task with output complex consisting of all the simplices σ in the second chromatic subdivision $\mathrm{Chr}^2\,\mathbf{s}$ such that no vertex of σ is on an $(n-t-1)$-dimensional face of $\mathbf{s}$. For example, when $n=2$ and $t=1$, the output complex for L_1 looks like:

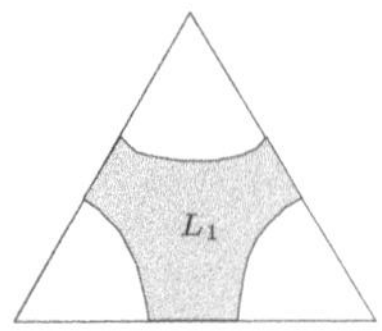

PROPOSITION 9.2. *The task L_t is solvable in the model Res_t.*

PROOF. Note that for each face $\mathbf{t} \subseteq \mathbf{s} = \mathcal{I}$, the complex $\Delta(\mathbf{t})$ for the task L_t is link-connected. Therefore, it suffices to find a terminating subdivision $\mathscr{T}$ and a continuous map f with the properties required in Proposition 9.1.

For $n \geq 0$, let $\tilde{R}_n \subset |\mathbf{s}|$ be the union of (the geometric realizations of) all the simplices $\sigma \subset \mathrm{Chr}^{n+2}\,\mathbf{s}$ such that no vertex of σ is on an $(n-t-1)$-dimensional face of $\mathbf{s}$. Let $R_0 = |L_t|$ and, for $n > 0$, let R_n be the closure of $\tilde{R}_n - \tilde{R}_{n-1}$. The union of all R_n's is the complement of the $(n-t-1)$-skeleton of $\mathbf{s}$:

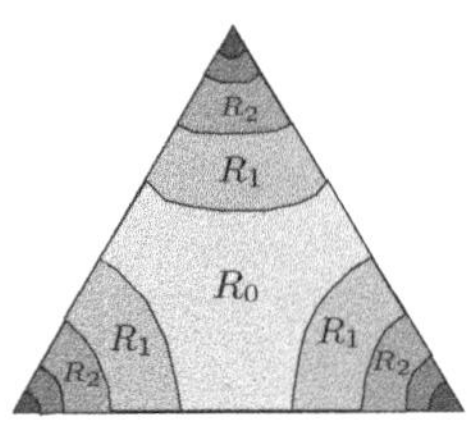

The terminating subdivision $\mathscr{T}$ is as follows: It starts with $\Sigma_0 = \Sigma_1 = \emptyset$, so that $C_0 = \mathbf{s}, C_1 = \mathrm{Chr}^1\,\mathbf{s}, C_2 = \mathrm{Chr}^2\,\mathbf{s}$. We then let Σ_2 be the subcomplex of $\mathrm{Chr}^2\,\mathbf{s}$ supported in the region R_0. This defines C_2 so that on the complement of R_0 it consists of the simplices in $\mathrm{Chr}^3\,\mathbf{s}$. After this, we terminate all the simplices in R_1. Now on the complement of $R_0 \cup R_1$ we have the fourth chromatic subdivision. We then terminate the simplices in R_2, and so on. By construction, eventually, every simplex contained in any R_k is stable in this terminating subdivision. Since the affine projection $\pi(Res_t)$ is contained in the union $|K(\mathscr{T})|$ of all the R_k's, we deduce that $\mathscr{T}$ is admissible for Res_t.

It remains to construct the continuous map $f : |K(\mathscr{T})| \to |L_t| = R_0$. We let the restriction of f to R_0 be the identity, and map everything else onto the boundary $R_0 \cap R_1$ using radial projection away from the $(n-t-1)$-skeleton of $\mathbf{s}$:

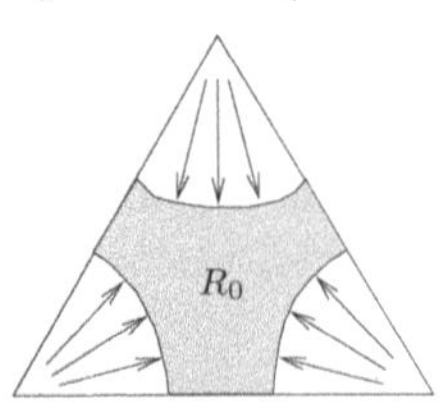

Observe that radial projection preserves boundaries, so Proposition 9.1 applies. □

REMARK 9.3. *An alternative, operational solution of task L_t via t-resilient atomic-snapshots was given by the first author in [8]. More precisely, the Red-Yellow-Green algorithm in [8, Section 4] specifies an intricate simulation scheme that allows for solving L_t.*

10. RELATED WORK

The topological conditions of wait-free task solvability were expressed by Herlihy and Shavit [21,22] in the form of ACT. In the restricted case of *colorless* tasks that, roughly, can be defined without taking process identifiers in mind, Herlihy and Rajsbaum [19,20] derived task solvability conditions in adversarial shared-memory models [7]. This paper proposes a characterization of generic (not necessarily colorless) tasks in any (not necessarily adversarial) sub-IIS model.

The IIS model was introduced by Borowsky and Gafni [3] and shown to precisely capture the standard chromatic subdivision of the input complex [23,25]. Due to the elegance of its topological representation, IIS has been widely used topological reasoning about distributed computing [1,3,16, 21,22]. In [3,13], IIS has been shown equivalent to SM in terms of task solvability. Rajsbaum et al. [29] and, more recently, Raynal and Stainer [30] relate proper subsets of sub-IIS and sub-SM models restricted using specific failure detectors. A recent paper [4] extends these equivalences to arbitrary sub-SM and sub-IIS models, thus justifying the choice of IIS as a model of study.

The difficulty of dealing with certain problems in certain non-compact models, such as consensus and t-resilience, has been studied before by Lubitsch and Moran [26], Brit and Moran [5], Moses and Rajsbaum [27]. By deriving topological solvability conditions for any task and any sub-IIS model, this paper brings this work to a higher level of generality. The continuous space $|\mathbf{s}|$ has appeared previously in the work of Saks and Zaharoglou [32] where it was used to derive the impossibility wait-free set agreement.

11. CONCLUDING REMARKS

We presented a version of a generalization of ACT. Other versions may be possible through the relation between simplicial and continuous maps, as well as through defining terminating subdivisions not necessarily with respect to $\mathrm{Chr}^m(\mathbf{s})$, in analogy to the sufficiency condition of ACT [22]. We chose the simplest version which still provides us with the benefit of producing a "topological solution" to the given task.

The main technical challenge we faced was to define and view the IIS model directly, rather than just through the prism of the simulations from the standard (non-iterated) model [3,13]. This brought forth a coherent view of IIS, as well as exposed the richness of the model.

The generic IIS models considered in this paper are just arbitrary subsets of the various possible interleaving of reads and writes, which is an extension with respect to the previous attempts to model sub-IIS computations [29,30]. Yet, distributed computing refers also to the availability of one-shot objects, e.g., consensus, k-set agreement, etc. Of course, we can produce a sub-IIS model which is equivalent to having consensus, or any other simple object. An open question is whether our framework embedded in a large enough dimension can capture "all of distributed computing," at least with respect to terminating computations. In particular, what will be the sets of runs that correspond to the availability of the Möbius task [14] or a task from the family of 0-1 exclusion [10]? We know that, for instance, the "symmetric" task on n processes from [14] can also be formulated as a regular task on $2n-1$ processes, hence increasing the task dimension does help here. Our speculation is that any computability question for a "reasonable" one-shot problem in distributed computing is equivalent to a question of task solvability in a sub-IIS model.

Acknowledgement

We are in debt to Robert F. Brown for helpful discussions in the very early stages of this research.

12. REFERENCES

[1] E. Borowsky and E. Gafni. Generalized FLP impossibility result for t-resilient asynchronous computations. In *STOC*, pages 91–100, May 1993.

[2] E. Borowsky and E. Gafni. Immediate atomic snapshots and fast renaming. In *PODC*, pages 41–51, 1993.

[3] E. Borowsky and E. Gafni. A simple algorithmically reasoned characterization of wait-free computation (extended abstract). In *PODC*, pages 189–198, 1997.

[4] Z. Bouzid, E. Gafni, and P. Kuznetsov. Live equals fast in iterated models. *CoRR*, abs/1402.2446, 2014. http://arxiv.org/abs/1402.2446.

[5] H. Brit and S. Moran. Wait-freedom vs. bounded-freedom in public data structures. *J. UCS*, 2(1):2–19, 1996.

[6] A. Castañeda, M. Herlihy, and S. Rajsbaum. An equivariance theorem with applications to renaming. In *LATIN*, pages 133–144, 2012.

[7] C. Delporte-Gallet, H. Fauconnier, R. Guerraoui, and A. Tielmann. The disagreement power of an adversary. *Distributed Computing*, 24(3-4):137–147, 2011.

[8] E. Gafni. On the wait-free power of iterated-immediate-snapshots. Unpublished manuscript, online at `http://www.cs.ucla.edu/~eli/eli/wfiis.ps`, 1998.

[9] E. Gafni. Round-by-round fault detectors (extended abstract): Unifying synchrony and asynchrony. In *PODC*, 1998.

[10] E. Gafni. The 0-1-exclusion families of tasks. In *OPODIS*, pages 246–258, 2008.

[11] E. Gafni. Free-for-all execution: Unifying resiliency, set-consensus, and concurrency. Unpublished manuscript, online at `http://www.cs.ucla.edu/~eli/eli/concurrency25.pdf`, 2008.

[12] E. Gafni and E. Koutsoupias. Three-processor tasks are undecidable. *SIAM J. Comput.*, 28(3):970–983, 1999.

[13] E. Gafni and S. Rajsbaum. Distributed programming with tasks. In *OPODIS*, pages 205–218, 2010.

[14] E. Gafni, S. Rajsbaum, and M. Herlihy. Subconsensus tasks: Renaming is weaker than set agreement. In *DISC*, pages 329–338, 2006.

[15] V. Hadzilacos and S. Toueg. A modular approach to fault-tolerant broadcasts and related problems. Technical Report TR 94-1425, Department of Computer Science, Cornell University, May 1994.

[16] M. Herlihy, D. N. Kozlov, and S. Rajsbaum. *Distributed Computing Through Combinatorial Topology*. Morgan Kaufmann, 2014.

[17] M. Herlihy and S. Rajsbaum. The decidability of distributed decision tasks (extended abstract). In *STOC*, pages 589–598, 1997.

[18] M. Herlihy and S. Rajsbaum. Algebraic spans. *Mathematical Structures in Computer Science*, 10(4):549–573, 2000.

[19] M. Herlihy and S. Rajsbaum. Concurrent computing and shellable complexes. In *DISC*, pages 109–123, 2010.

[20] M. Herlihy and S. Rajsbaum. The topology of distributed adversaries. *Distributed Computing*, 26(3):173–192, 2013.

[21] M. Herlihy and N. Shavit. The asynchronous computability theorem for t-resilient tasks. In *STOC*, pages 111–120, May 1993.

[22] M. Herlihy and N. Shavit. The topological structure of asynchronous computability. *J. ACM*, 46(2):858–923, 1999.

[23] D. N. Kozlov. Chromatic subdivision of a simplicial complex. *Homology, Homotopy and Applications*, 14(1):1–13, 2012.

[24] P. Kuznetsov. Understanding non-uniform failure models. *Bulletin of the EATCS*, 106:53–77, 2012.

[25] N. Linial. Doing the IIS. Unpublished manuscript, 2010.

[26] R. Lubitch and S. Moran. Closed schedulers: A novel technique for analyzing asynchronous protocols. *Distributed Computing*, 8(4):203–210, 1995.

[27] Y. Moses and S. Rajsbaum. A layered analysis of consensus. *SIAM J. Comput.*, 31(4):989–1021, 2002.

[28] J. R. Munkres. *Elements of algebraic topology*. Addison-Wesley Publishing Company, Menlo Park, CA, 1984.

[29] S. Rajsbaum, M. Raynal, and C. Travers. The iterated restricted immediate snapshot model. In *COCOON*, pages 487–497, 2008.

[30] M. Raynal and J. Stainer. Increasing the power of the iterated immediate snapshot model with failure detectors. In *SIROCCO*, pages 231–242, 2012.

[31] H. L. Royden. *Real analysis*. Macmillan Publishing Company, New York, third edition, 1988.

[32] M. Saks and F. Zaharoglou. Wait-free k-set agreement is impossible: The topology of public knowledge. *SIAM J. on Computing*, 29:1449–1483, 2000.

[33] E. H. Spanier. *Algebraic topology*. McGraw-Hill Book Co., New York, 1966.

[34] J. H. C. Whitehead. Simplicial Spaces, Nuclei and m-Groups. *Proc. London Math. Soc.*, S2-45(1):243, 1939.

Balls-into-Leaves: Sub-logarithmic Renaming in Synchronous Message-Passing Systems

Dan Alistarh
Microsoft Research
Cambridge, UK
dan.alistarh@microsoft.com

Oksana Denysyuk
INESC-ID,
Instituto Superior Técnico,
Universidade de Lisboa
oksana@gsd.inesc-id.pt

Luís Rodrigues
INESC-ID,
Instituto Superior Técnico,
Universidade de Lisboa
ler@ist.utl.pt

Nir Shavit
MIT & Tel-Aviv University
shanir@csail.mit.edu

ABSTRACT

We consider the following natural problem: n failure-prone servers, communicating synchronously through message passing, must assign themselves one-to-one to n distinct items. Existing literature suggests two possible approaches to this problem. First, model it as an instance of *tight renaming* in synchronous message-passing systems; for deterministic solutions, a tight bound of $\Theta(\log n)$ communication rounds is known. Second, model the scenario as an instance of randomized load-balancing, for which elegant sub-logarithmic solutions exist. However, careful examination reveals that known load-balancing schemes do not apply to our scenario, because they either do not tolerate faults or do not ensure one-to-one allocation. It is thus natural to ask if sub-logarithmic solutions exist for this apparently simple but intriguing problem.

In this paper, we combine the two approaches to provide a new randomized solution for tight renaming, which terminates in $O(\log \log n)$ communication rounds with high probability, against a strong adaptive adversary. Our solution, called Balls-into-Leaves, combines the deterministic approach with a new randomized scheme to obtain perfectly balanced allocations. The algorithm arranges the items as leaves of a tree, and participants repeatedly perform random choices among the leaves. The algorithm exchanges information in each round to split the participants into progressively smaller groups whose random choices do not conflict. We then extend the algorithm to terminate early in $O(\log \log f)$ rounds w.h.p., where f is the actual number of failures. These results imply an exponential separation between deterministic and randomized algorithms for the tight renaming problem in message-passing systems.

PODC'14, July 15–18, 2014, Paris, France.

http://dx.doi.org/10.1145/2611462.2611499.

Categories and Subject Descriptors

F.2.2 [**Analysis of Algorithms and Problem Complexity**]: *Nonnumerical Algorithms and Problems*

General Terms

Theory, Algorithms

Keywords

Randomized algorithms; synchronous message-passing model; renaming problem.

1. INTRODUCTION

We study the following assignment problem: n fault-prone servers must assign themselves one-to-one to n distinct items in an efficient distributed manner. This natural problem has received considerable research attention, and is an instance of the fundamental *renaming* problem that has been extensively studied in both shared-memory and message-passing systems, e.g. [2, 3, 4, 7, 8, 16]. In renaming, n processes start with distinct identifiers taken from an unbounded *original namespace*, and output distinct names from a smaller *target namespace*. If the size of the target namespace is exactly n, then the problem is known as *tight* (or *strong/perfect*) renaming.

In this paper, we assume that the servers are arranged in a fully connected network and communicate by synchronous messages. Therefore, the above formulation is an instance of tight renaming in a synchronous message-passing system where $t < n$ processes may crash. Previous work by Chaudhuri, Herlihy, and Tuttle [8] gave an elegant algorithm in this setting with $O(\log n)$ round complexity, and showed this to be optimal for algorithms which distinguish state through comparisons. These results concern only deterministic algorithms, and we are interested in studying whether randomization can yield better, sub-logarithmic algorithms.

Randomization is a natural approach for renaming, and has been used to achieve low-complexity solutions in the related shared-memory model, e.g. [2]. Moreover, seen as an assignment problem, renaming is related to the extensive line of work on randomized load balancing, e.g. [1, 5, 14, 15], for which different sub-logarithmic solutions have been proposed. Surprisingly, a careful analysis of such sub-logarithmic solutions reveals that none of them can be used to achieve tight renaming, since they either are designed for a fault-free setting, or relax the one-to-one allocation requirement. It is therefore tempting to ask whether randomization can in fact be used to obtain fault-tolerant, perfectly-balanced allocation in sub-logarithmic time.

In this paper, we answer this question in the affirmative. We present a new algorithm to solve tight renaming in $O(\log\log n)$ communication rounds, with high probability, exponentially faster than the optimal deterministic counterpart. The algorithm, which we call *Balls-into-Leaves*, is based on the idea of arranging the target names as leaves of a binary tree; processes start at the root of the tree, and perform repeated random choices in order to disperse themselves towards leaves, while minimizing contention. We also present an early-terminating variant, which terminates in $O(\log\log f)$ rounds, where f is the actual number of failures in the execution, which is again exponentially faster than the best known deterministic version [3].

More precisely, our algorithm works as follows: processes (balls) start at the root of a virtual binary tree, whose n leaves correspond to the target names. In each iteration, each ball picks a random available leaf and broadcasts its choice; in case of collisions, a deterministic rule is used to select a winner. The remaining balls backtrack towards the root, stopping at the lowest node at which the ball can still find an available leaf within the corresponding subtree. (Please see Figures 1 and 2 for an illustration.) Balls then iterate this procedure, exchanging information and progressively descending in the tree.

Our main technical contribution is to show that this natural strategy is fault-tolerant, and in fact converges extremely quickly to a perfectly balanced allocation. Our argument has two parts: we first exploit the concentration properties of the binomial distribution to bound the maximum contention on a leaf after $\Theta(\log\log n)$ communication rounds to be $O(\text{polylog } n)$, with high probability (w.h.p). Second, we fix a root-to-leaf path, and prove via a technical argument that all $O(\text{polylog } n)$ balls, except at most one, will disperse themselves off the path within the next $O(\log\log n)$ rounds, again w.h.p. Therefore, each ball reaches a leaf within $O(\log\log n)$ rounds w.h.p.

Since the number of leaves matches the number of balls, Balls-into-Leaves solves *tight renaming*. Given that comparison based deterministic algorithms take $\Omega(\log n)$ rounds [8], this result establishes an exponential separation between such algorithms and their randomized counterparts. (Our algorithm is also comparison-based.) Moreover, Balls-into-Leaves guarantees deterministic termination; in particular, it will complete in a linear number of rounds, even in unlucky runs.

We then extend the Balls-into-Leaves algorithm to ensure *early termination*. Roughly, an early-terminating algorithm terminates faster when there are fewer failures, as its running time is a function of the number f of failures rather than n. We do so by introducing an initial phase that ensures that balls take advantage of a small number of failures in this round, descending deeply into the tree. With this modification, the algorithm terminates in $O(\log\log f)$ rounds w.h.p., where f is the actual number of crashes. Furthermore, in a fault-free execution, it terminates in constant time.

An examination of the argument (in particular, the concentration properties of the binomial distribution) suggests that our complexity upper bound for Balls-into-Leaves is in fact tight. The main open question is therefore whether the Balls-into-Leaves strategy is optimal for this problem. We conjecture that answering this question will require a new lower bound technique for randomized renaming.

Roadmap. The rest of the paper is organized as follows. In Section 2 we review the related work. In Section 3 we describe the system model and in Section 4 we define the renaming problem. In Section 5 we describe our Balls-into-Leaves algorithm and Section 6 analyzes its complexity. In Section 7 we discuss an early terminating extension. We conclude in Section 8.

2. RELATED WORK

Renaming was first introduced in [4], for an asynchronous message-passing system where $t < n/2$ processes may crash. The authors show that tight renaming is impossible in this model, and give an algorithm for $(n+t-1)$-renaming. Subsequently, the problem has been extensively studied in both message passing and shared memory. We limit the related work discussion to the synchronous message-passing model considered in this paper, and we direct the reader to [2, 7] for a survey of renaming in other models.

In synchronous systems, wait-free tight renaming can be solved using reliable broadcast [6] or consensus [12] to agree on the set of existing ids. This approach requires linear round complexity [10].

Tight renaming in synchronous message-passing is first studied by Chaudhuri, Herlihy, and Tuttle [8]. They define *comparison-based* algorithms, which distinguish states only through comparisons, and show such algorithms are vulnerable to a "sandwich" failure pattern, which forces processes to continue in indistinguishable (*order-equivalent*) states for $\Omega(\log n)$ rounds. This yields an $\Omega(\log n)$-round lower bound for deterministic comparison-based algorithms, which the authors match via an elegant wait-free algorithm [8].

Order-preserving renaming (where decided names preserve the order of their original ids) was considered by Okun [16]. The author finds a new connection between the problems of renaming and *approximate agreement*, and shows that this approach also has round complexity of $O(\log n)$. This approach was extended by [3] to provide *early termination*. The round complexity of this extension is $O(\log f)$. Interestingly, the authors also observed that the algorithm in [16] terminates in constant number of rounds if the number of actual faults is bounded by $n > 2f^2$. This is because with few faults approximate agreement can be solved in a constant time.

The algorithms surveyed above are deterministic. On the other hand, randomization has been employed as a tool to improve *resilience* in a synchronous system prone to Byzantine failures. The authors of [9] give a tight renaming algorithm with round complexity of $O(\log n)$, which tolerates $n-1$ Byzantine failures under an oblivious adversary. By contrast, the present work uses randomization to improve the *round complexity* in a system with crash failures against an adaptive adversary.

Tight renaming can be seen as a balls-into-bins load balancing problem, where n balls must be randomly placed into n distinct bins. Early work on this problem addressed a scenario in which balls are placed into bins by trying randomly

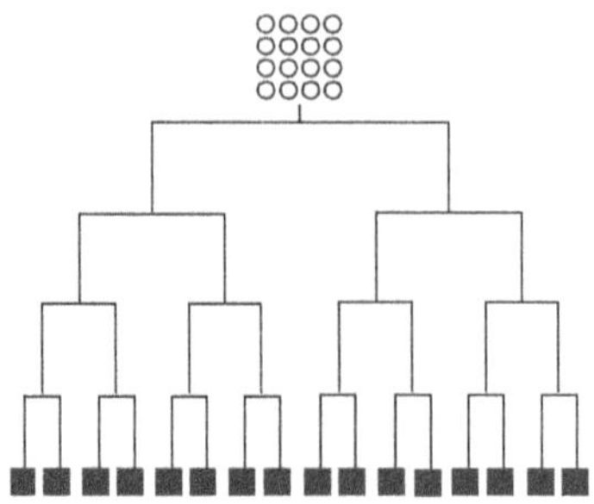

(a) All balls at the root

Figure 1: Initial configuration

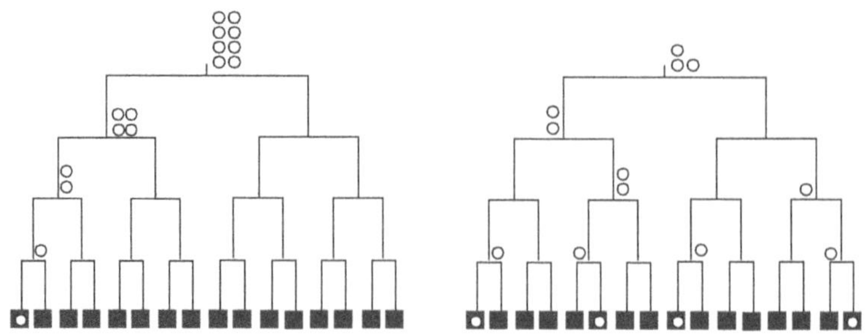

(a) All balls choose the first leaf (b) Choices are well distributed

Figure 2: After one phase

in sequential order, e.g. [11]. Since then, the problem has been extensively studied in different scenarios, e.g. [1, 5, 15]. In particular, the closest model to ours is the one where balls are placed by contacting bins in parallel, motivated by distributed load-balancing with bandwidth limitations.

Several algorithms have been proposed for this setting, e.g. [1, 14], which show that significant complexity gains can be achieved over the naive random balls-into-bins strategy. For a complete survey of existing results on parallel load-balancing, we refer the reader to [13]. To the best of our knowledge, none of the known sub-logarithmic parallel load-balancing techniques can be used to obtain wait-free tight renaming. The existing work either relaxes the exact one-ball-per-bin requirement [14], or requires balls to always have consistent views when making their choice (which cannot be guaranteed under crash faults).

3. SYSTEM MODEL

We consider the standard round-based synchronous message-passing model with a fully-connected network and n processes, where n is known a priori. Each process has a unique id, originally known only to itself. Computation proceeds in lock-step rounds. In each round, each process can send messages to its neighbors, receive a message from each neighbor, obtain a finite number of random bits, and change state.

Up to $t < n$ processes may fail by crashing. Crashed processes stop executing and do not recover.

4. RENAMING PROBLEM

The renaming problem is defined as follows. Each process starts with *initial id* in some *original namespace*, and it must decide on a new name in some *target namespace* $1 \ldots m$, where $m \geq n$ is a parameter of the problem, such that the following conditions must hold [4]:

- *Termination:* Each correct process eventually decides on a new name.
- *Validity:* If a correct process decides, it decides on a new name in $1 \ldots m$.
- *Uniqueness:* No two correct processes decide on the same new name.

When $m = n$, the problem is called *tight* renaming.

5. BALLS-INTO-LEAVES ALGORITHM

The algorithm treats processes as *balls* and target names as *bins*, where each ball wants to find an exclusive bin for it. The algorithm ensures that the correct balls terminate in distinct bins.

The algorithm organizes the n bins as leaves of a binary tree of depth $\log n$[1]. Balls have unique labels (the processes' initial ids), and they communicate by broadcasting messages.

The algorithm at a high level. Each ball starts at the root of the tree and descends the tree along a random path. As balls descend, they communicate with each other to determine if there are collisions. Collisions occur if many balls try to go to the same leaf or, more generally, if many balls try to enter a subtree without enough capacity for them. For example, if all n balls at the root tried to enter the left subtree, they would collide since the subtree has capacity for only $n/2$ balls. When balls collide, the algorithm assigns priorities to them based in part on their unique labels; balls with higher priorities keep descending, while the others stop. Because balls pick random paths, very few collide at higher levels, so balls quickly disperse within the tree and soon after find an exclusive leaf for them.

Local tree, candidate path, remaining capacity. The binary tree has $\log n$ levels. To finish in $O(\log \log n)$ rounds w.h.p., balls must descend many levels with each round of communication. To do so, each ball b_i keeps a *local tree*, containing the current position of every ball, including itself. Initially, all balls in the local tree of b_i are at the root (Fig. 1). In a single round, a ball b_i picks a random *candidate path* in its local tree: starting with its current position, b_i successively chooses the left or right subtree to follow for each level, until the leaf is reached. The choice between left and right subtree is weighted by the *remaining capacity* of each subtree (within b_i's local tree). The remaining capacity is the number of leafs of the subtree minus the number of balls in the subtree. Say, if one subtree has no remaining capacity, b_i chooses the other with probability 1.

In this way, b_i picks the entire candidate path to the leaf *locally*, without communication with other balls and without regard to collisions. Ball b_i does not yet go down its path (this will happen later). Rather, b_i broadcasts its path and waits for the paths of others; this requires a round of communication.

Collisions, priority. Once ball b_i has received the candidate paths of other balls, b_i can calculate new positions of these balls. Ideally, a ball just follows its candidate path.

[1]To simplify exposition, we assume n is a power of two.

Algorithm 1 Balls-into-Leaves Algorithm

Local Data Structures and Functions

Data Structures

- binary tree with n leaves;
- path$_i$: an ordered set of nodes of the tree;

Operations over the tree

- Remove(b_j): removes b_j from the tree;
- CurrentNode(b_j): current position of b_j in the tree;
- UpdateNode(b_j,η): removes b_j from its current position and places it at node η;
- OrderedBalls(): returns a set of all balls in the tree, ordered by $<_R$ (first by depth in the tree, then by ids);
- RemainingCapacity(η): number of leaves in the subtree rooted at node η minus number of balls in that subtree;
- η.LeftChild(), η.RightChild(), η.isLeaf() are operation over nodes of the tree.

Additional Functions

- First(): first element in a set;
- Next(): iterator over a set (returns the next element in a set, advancing to the next position);
- RandomCoin(p): returns *heads* with prob. p, or *tails* with prob. $(1 - p)$.

Code for Ball b_i

```
1: Initialize: broadcast ⟨b_i⟩;
2:         ∀b_j received: insert b_j at the root;
3: repeat
                                   ▷ begin Phase φ ← 1, 2, 3, ...
                                   ▷ begin Round 1 of Phase φ
4:     η ← CurrentNode(b_i);
5:     path_i ← {η};
6:     while not η.IsLeaf() do
                                   ▷ choose path randomly
7:         coin ← RandomCoin( RemainingCapacity(η.LeftChild()) / RemainingCapacity(η) );
8:         if coin = heads then η ← η.LeftChild();
9:         else η ← η.RightChild();
10:        path_i ← path_i ⊔ {η};
11:    end while
12:    broadcast ⟨b_i,path_i⟩;            ▷ exchange paths
13:    for all b_j ∈ OrderedBalls() do
                                   ▷ move balls in the priority order
14:        if ⟨b_j,path_j⟩ has been received then
15:            η ← path_j.First();
16:            while remainingCapacity(η)> 0 do
17:                η ← path_j.Next();
18:            end while
19:            UpdateNode(b_j,η);
20:        else
21:            Remove(b_j);
22:    end for
                                   ▷ begin Round 2 of Phase φ
                                   ▷ synchronize
23:    broadcast ⟨b_i, CurrentNode(b_i)⟩;
24:    for all b_j ∈ OrderedBalls() do
25:        if ⟨b_j,η_j⟩ has been received then
26:            UpdateNode(b_j ,η_j);
27:        else
28:            Remove(b_j);
29:    end for
30: until ∀b_j ∈ OrderedBalls(): CurrentNode(b_j).IsLeaf();
```

But b_i may find that different candidate paths collide: more balls may try to enter a subtree than the subtree's remaining capacity. In this case, b_i allows balls with higher priority to proceed, while others must stop where the collision occurs (and the rest of their candidate path is discarded). The priority is determined by an order $<_R$ where smaller balls under $<_R$ have higher priority.

Definition 1 (Priority Order $<_R$). *Let η_i and η_j be the current nodes of balls b_i and b_j. Then,*

$$b_i <_R b_j \iff (depth(\eta_i) > depth(\eta_j)) \\ \vee ((depth(\eta_i) = depth(\eta_j)) \wedge (b_i < b_j)).$$

Under $<_R$, balls are ordered by their depth in the tree (balls downstream ordered first), breaking ties by their unique labels. To implement these priorities, b_i iterates over all balls $\bar{b}$ in $<_R$ order; for each $\bar{b}$, b_i lets $\bar{b}$ follow its candidate path until $\bar{b}$ reaches a *full* subtree—one with no remaining capacity. If $\bar{b}$ is lucky, it ends up at a leaf in b_i's local tree; otherwise, it stops at a higher level. Irrespective of where $\bar{b}$ stops, the algorithm ensures that there is enough space below to accommodate it. Because balls lower in the tree have a higher priority, this space cannot be displaced subsequently by balls higher in the tree. Figures 1 and 2 show the local tree before and after new positions are calculated.

Failures, synchronization, termination. A ball may crash while broadcasting its candidate path; some balls may receive this broadcast, while others do not. The result is that the local trees of the surviving balls may diverge. To resynchronize, after b_i has updated its local tree using the candidate path, b_i broadcasts its current position, and waits to learn the positions of other balls; this requires another round of communication. Based on the received information, if necessary b_i corrects the positions of balls in its local tree; if b_i does not hear from a ball in its tree, b_i removes it (the ball has crashed). If b_i finds that every ball is at a leaf, it terminates. Otherwise, it repeats the entire procedure.

Detailed pseudocode. Algorithm 1 gives the detailed pseudocode. Initially, each ball b_i broadcasts its label, receives labels from other balls, and inserts them at the root of its local tree (Lines 1–2). Then, b_i repeatedly executes the main loop (Lines 3–30); each iteration is called a *phase*, and each phase has two communication rounds. In round one, b_i first chooses its candidate path (Lines 6–11) one edge at a time, where the probability of each child is the ratio of remaining slots in either subtree (Line 7). Then b_i broadcasts its candidate path (Line 12). After receiving the candidate paths of others, b_i iterates over the balls $\bar{b}$ in $<_R$ order, to compute their new positions. Each ball $\bar{b}$ moves down its path as long as the subtree has remaining capacity (Lines 13–19). Balls that do not announce their paths have crashed and are removed from the local tree (Lines 20–21). In the second round (Lines 23–29), b_i sends its position, receives positions of other balls, and updates its local tree, again removing balls which fail to send their positions. If all balls in the local tree have reached leaves, b_i terminates. It is easy to change the algorithm to allow a ball to terminate as soon as it reaches a leaf. Such modification requires additional checks that have been left out in favor of clarity.

5.1 Tight Renaming using Balls-into-Leaves

We now prove that the Balls-into-Leaves algorithm solves tight renaming in $O(\log \log n)$ communication rounds w.h.p.

$B(n,p)$ is the binomial distribution with parameters n and p. By abuse of notation, $B(n,p)$ also denotes a random variable that follows the binomial distribution.

FACT 1. *If $X \sim B(M,p)$, $Y \sim B(M',p)$, and $M \leq M'$, then* $\Pr(|E[X] - X| > x) \leq \Pr(|E[Y] - Y| > x)$.

FACT 2. *If $0 \leq p \leq 1$, $X \sim B(M,p)$, $Y \sim B(M, \frac{1}{2})$, then* $\Pr(|E[X] - X| > x) \leq \Pr(|E[Y] - Y)| > x)$.

FACT 3 (CHERNOFF BOUND). *If $X \sim B(m,p)$, then* $\Pr(|E[X] - X| > x) < e^{-\frac{x^2}{2mp(1-p)}}$.

Figure 3: Notation and facts from probability theory used in the proofs.

The process with original identifier id_i runs Balls-into-Leaves for the ball labeled id_i. It then returns the (left-to-right) index of the leaf where the ball terminates, and outputs this rank as its name.

Name uniqueness follows from the fact that no two correct balls terminate at the same leaf (see Theorem 1 below). *Validity* follows because the number of leaves is n. Termination and complexity follow from the complexity analysis of the Balls-into-Leaves algorithm.

5.2 Correctness

We show that in our algorithm correct balls terminate at distinct leaves. This follows mainly from ensuring that, in every view, the subtrees never exceed their remaining capacities.

LEMMA 1. *For any phase $\phi \geq 1$, in any local view, the number of correct balls in each subtree $\leq$ the number of leaves in that subtree.*

THEOREM 1. *In the Balls-into-Leaves algorithm, correct balls terminate at distinct leaves.*

The proofs of correctness are intuitive and have been moved to Appendix A.

6. COMPLEXITY ANALYSIS

In this section, we prove that Balls-into-Leaves terminates in $O(\log\log n)$ rounds with high probability.

For clarity, we first consider a failure-free execution. We then show that faults do not slow down the progress of the algorithm. (Intuitively, collisions are less likely as the number of surviving balls decreases).

Without crashes, local views of the tree are always identical, and we therefore focus on one local view. The analysis consists of two parts. In the first part, we show that, after $O(\log\log n)$ phases, the number of balls at each node decreases to $O(\log^2 n)$. In the second part, we consider an arbitrary path from the root to the parent of a leaf. We use the fact that there are $O(\log^2 n)$ balls at each node, and show that the path becomes completely empty within the next $O(\log\log n)$ rounds, with high probability. By a union bound over all such paths, we obtain that the tree is empty w.h.p.

We first prove a useful invariant of Balls-into-Leaves algorithm that we call *Path Isolation Property*. Informally stated, this says that no new balls appear on any path from the root.

LEMMA 2 (PATH ISOLATION PROPERTY). *For any phase $\phi \geq 1$ and path π from the root, the set of balls on π in ϕ is a superset of balls on π in ϕ+1.*

PROOF. By construction, balls can only move down the tree. Fix some node η on path π. The only way new ball b_i, located at some node μ in phase ϕ, reaches η in phase $\phi+1$ is by constructing in ϕ a path from μ that contains η. Thus, by construction of a binary tree, μ is on π. □

In our proofs, we use some notation and facts from theory of probability, shown in Figure 3.

6.1 Part 1 - Bounding the Number of Balls at a Node

We now give a lower bound on how fast the number of balls at each node decreases. Consider some node η, and let pM and $(1-p)M$ be the remaining capacities of its left and right subtrees, respectively, for some integer M and $0 \leq p \leq 1$ in phase ϕ. By construction, at most M balls reach η. The balls that get stuck at η in phase $\phi+1$ are those which had η on their paths in ϕ, but did not fit in a subtree below η. By Lemma 1, these balls have enough space in the sibling subtree of η. We use the notation $balls(\eta, \phi)$ to denote the number of balls at node η in phase ϕ. We denote by $b_{max}(\phi)$ the most populated node in phase ϕ.

LEMMA 3. *For some node η, let pM and $(1-p)M$ denote remaining capacities of its left and right subtrees respectively, in some phase ϕ. If $M' \leq M$ balls choose between the left and right subtrees of η in ϕ, then, for any $x > 0$,* $\Pr(balls(\eta, \phi+1) > x) \leq \Pr(|\frac{M}{2} - B(M, \frac{1}{2})| > x)$.

PROOF. Choosing between the left and right subtrees of η can be seen as choosing between two bins with capacities pM and $(1-p)M$. Each of the $M' \leq M$ balls chooses independently between the two bins with probabilities p and $(1-p)$ respectively. If there is space in the chosen bin, then the ball is accepted; if the bin is full, then the ball is rejected. Since $M' \leq M$, there are three cases: either both bins are filled (perfect split), no bin has been filled, or exactly one bin has been filled, and there is some overflow. Note that, in the first two cases, η is empty in phase $\phi+1$.

If one bin has filled, then, w.l.o.g., assume it is the left bin. Let Y be a random variable that counts the number of balls that have chosen left. Clearly, $Y \sim B(M',p)$. Then, the number of rejected balls is $Y - Mp$. Since $Mp \geq M'p = E[Y]$, then $Y - Mp \leq Y - E[Y]$.
From Fact 2, we obtain that,

$$\Pr(|Y - E[Y]| > x) \leq \Pr(|\tfrac{M}{2} - B(M, \tfrac{1}{2})| > x). \quad \square$$

Let us now consider what happens after the first phase.

LEMMA 4. *Let i be the depth of node η. Then, for some constant $c > 0$, we have that*

$$\Pr\left(balls(\eta, 2) > c(\tfrac{n}{2^i}\log n)^{\frac{1}{2}}\right) < \tfrac{1}{n^c}.$$

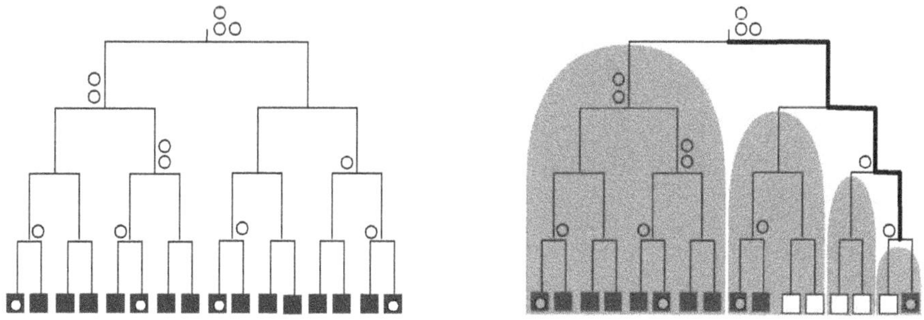

(a) entire tree

(b) 5 balls on the rightmost path and 5 empty leaves reachable from the path

Figure 4: Closer look at a path in a possible configuration

PROOF. Initially n balls start at the root.
The initial capacity of the subtree rooted at η is $\frac{n}{2^i}$. Then, at most $\frac{n}{2^i}$ balls reach η. Define $Y_\eta \sim B(\frac{n}{2^i}, \frac{1}{2})$.
Applying Lemma 3 and the Chernoff bound (Fact 3),

$$\Pr(balls(\eta,2)>x) < \Pr\left(|E[Y_\eta]-Y_\eta| > c(\frac{n}{2^i}\log n)^{\frac{1}{2}}\right)$$
$$< \frac{1}{n^c}. \quad \square$$

The analysis of the next phases is more involved, since we do not know the exact remaining capacities of each subtree. Therefore, we consider the worst case scenario by assuming that any node η has enough capacity to accommodate all balls on the path from the root to η.

LEMMA 5. *For any $\phi > 1$, node η, and some const. $c > 0$,* $\Pr\left(balls(\eta,\phi+1) > c(b_{max}(\phi))^{\frac{1}{2}}\log n\right) < \frac{1}{n^c}$.

PROOF. By the path isolation property (Lemma 2), the only balls that may attempt to choose between subtrees of η are those on the path from the root to η. Let i be the depth of η. The total number of balls on path π is at most $i \times b_{max}(\phi)$. By Fact 1, the probability to have more rejected balls is the highest if we inflate the remaining capacity of the subtrees of η to $i \times b_{max}(\phi)$.

Thus, by Lemma 3, the probability that at least x balls get stuck at η can be bounded as follows,

$$\Pr(balls(\eta,\phi+1)>x)$$
$$\leq \Pr\left(\left|\frac{i \times b_{max}(\phi)}{2} - B(i \times b_{max}(\phi), \frac{1}{2})\right| > c\right).$$

By the Chernoff Bound (Fact 3),

$$\Pr\left(\left|\frac{i \times b_{max}(\phi)}{2} - B(i \times b_{max}(\phi), \frac{1}{2})\right| > c(i \times b_{max}(\phi)\log n)^{\frac{1}{2}}\right)$$
$$< \frac{1}{n^c}.$$

Since $i \leq \log n$, the claim follows. $\square$

LEMMA 6. *For some const. $c' > 0$, after $\phi = O(\log\log n)$ phases,* $\Pr(balls(\eta,\phi) > O(1)\log^2 n) < \frac{1}{n^{c'}}$.

PROOF. Fix some constant $c > 0$. By Lemma 4,

$$\Pr\left(balls(\eta,2) > c(n\log n)^{\frac{1}{2}}\right) < \frac{1}{n^c}.$$

By Lemma 5, $\Pr\left(balls(\eta,\phi+1) > c(b_{max}(\phi))^{\frac{1}{2}}\log n\right) < \frac{1}{n^c}$.
Since $n^{\frac{1}{2}^{\log\log n}} = O(1)$, we pick some constant γ such that $n^{\frac{1}{2}^{\gamma\log\log n}} = 1$.
Let $f(x) = x^{\frac{1}{2}} c\log n$. Taking $x = c(n\log n)^{\frac{1}{2}}$,

$$f^{\gamma\log\log n}(x) = c^2\log^2 n.$$

Applying Lemma 4 and Lemma 5 iteratively for $\gamma\log\log n$ phases, we obtain that

$$\Pr\left(b_{max}(\eta,\gamma\log\log n) > c^2\log^2 n\right) < \frac{\gamma\log\log c}{n^c}.$$

Therefore, there exists some small constant $\epsilon < 1$, such that $\frac{\gamma\log\log n}{n^c} < \frac{1}{n^{(c-\epsilon)}}$, and the claim follows. $\square$

6.2 Part 2 - Bounding the Number of Balls on a Path

Lemma 6 shows that, after $O(\log\log n)$ phases, the number of balls at each node is at most $O(\log^2 n)$ w.h.p., which means that there are at most $O(\log^3 n)$ balls on each path w.h.p. In the following, we complete the argument by showing that all inner nodes of the tree are empty after another $O(\log\log n)$ phases.

To show this, instead of looking at nodes, we focus on paths from the root to a parent of a leaf (there are $n/2$ such paths). By the path isolation property (Lemma 2), new balls never appear on a path. (In other words, new balls arriving at a node can only come from nodes higher on the same path.) We show that at least a constant fraction of balls escapes from each path once every two phases. Intuitively, this analysis captures how fast balls disperse within the tree.

Formally, let us fix a phase ϕ and a path π from the root to a parent of a leaf. Let $\eta_1, \eta_2, \ldots, \eta_{\log n}$ be the nodes on π, ordered by depth. A *gateway* node (or simply a gateway) is a child of η_i that is not on π. For uniformity, we combine both children of the last node on π (tree leaves) into one gateway meta-child [2]. For instance, in the sample configuration from Figure 4a, consider the rightmost path (highlighted in Figure 4b); all the left children of nodes on π are gateways.

By construction, the sum of remaining capacities of all gateway subtrees (corresponding to empty leaves reachable from π) is equal to the total number of balls on π. In phase

[2]Obviously, a collision in a subtree with 2 leaves is solved within one phase.

ϕ, all balls on the path propose paths going through these gateways.

We now show that, if ball b_i is among the highest priority balls that have chosen the same gateway, then b_i will escape from path π either in phase ϕ or ϕ+1.

LEMMA 7. *Consider node η_i on π and let c_i be the remaining capacity of its gateway subtree. If m balls choose that subtree in ϕ, then at least $\min(m, c_i)$ balls escape π in ϕ and ϕ+1.*

PROOF. Let ball b_k be among $\min(m, c_i)$ highest priority balls that have chosen the gateway at η_i. Then, b_k is in one of the following scenarios.

Case 1: b_k attempts to move down towards η_i, and stops at some node η_j above η_i. This happens because the subtree down on π has exceeded its capacity. In this case, in ϕ+1, b_k tries the gateway subtree at η_j and, by Lemma 1, that subtree has enough space to accommodate b_k.

Case 2: b_k reaches η_i. By assumption, ball b_k is among $\min(m, c_i)$ highest priority balls that have chosen the same gateway. Thus, b_k escapes π into the gateway subtree of node η_i.[3]

If b_k is in Case 1, it escapes path π in phase ϕ+1. If b_k is in Case 2, it escapes π in phase ϕ. There are at least $\min(m, c_i)$ such balls, and the claim follows. □

We now bound the probabilities with which balls try each gateway on π.

LEMMA 8. *Let $M_i = \sum_{1\leq j\leq i} balls(\eta_j, \phi)$ be the number of balls on the subpath of π from the root to η_i. If c_i is the remaining capacity of the gateway subtree of η_i, then M_i balls try this gateway in ϕ with probability at least c_i/M_i.*

PROOF. (Sketch) Recall that balls construct paths trying between the children of each node with probabilities indexed by their remaining capacities (Lines 6–10 of Algorthim 1).

Intuitively, each ball competes on a subtree with every other ball that can reach the same subtree. And, by construction, the remaining capacity of all subtrees reachable from some path from the root is equal to the number of balls on this path. Note that the total remaining capacity of the subpath from the root to η_i (i.e., all gateway subtrees and the non-gateway subtree at η_i) is M_i. Thus, every ball tries the gateway at η_i with prob. at least c_i/M_i. □

In the following, we show that at least a constant fraction of balls escape π in every two phases.

LEMMA 9. *Let M be the total number of balls on π in phase ϕ. For some const. $c > 1$, less than M/c balls have escaped π after ϕ+1 with probability $< e^{\frac{-M}{c}}$.*

PROOF. By Lemma 8, M_i balls try the gateway at η_i with prob. at least c_i/M_i.

By Lemma 7, for any $\gamma > 1$, $\frac{c_i}{\gamma} \leq c_i$ highest priority balls that choose the gateway at η_i, escape π in ϕ or ϕ+1. Define as success the event that some ball chooses the gateway at η_i. By Lemma 8, such an event occurs with prob. at least c_i/M_i among M_i tries. Thus, the number of successes follows $\mathrm{B}(M_i, c_i/M_i)$. From the Chernoff Bound (Fact 3),

$$\Pr\left(\mathrm{B}(M_i, c_i/M_i) < c_i - \tfrac{c_i}{\gamma}\right) < e^{-\frac{M_i}{\gamma}}.$$

Recall that $\sum_{1\leq i\leq \log n} c_i = M$. Considering all η_i, $1 \leq i \leq \log n$ on π, the sum of successes is less than $M - \frac{M}{\gamma}$ with prob. $< e^{-\frac{M}{\gamma}}$. Since γ is arbitrary, the claim follows. □

From the above lemma, it follows that all M balls on π escape the path within $O(\log M)$ phases, with probability at least $1 - (1/e)^{\Theta(M)}$.

LEMMA 10. *Consider a path π containing M balls. After $O(\log M)$ phases, the probability that π remains non-empty is less than $e^{-\frac{M}{c'}}$, for some constant $c' > 0$.*

PROOF. Fix some constant c. By Lemma 9, at least M/c balls have escaped from π after phase ϕ+1, with probability at least $1 - e^{-\frac{M}{c}}$. Starting with M balls, and iterating in Lemma 9 over the remaining balls for $2c \log M$ phases, we obtain that the probability that π is not empty after $2c \log M$ phases is at most $2c \log M e^{-\frac{M}{c'}} < e^{-\frac{M}{(c-\epsilon)}}$ for some small constant $\epsilon < 1$. □

Finally, we combine the two parts of the proof in the following theorem.

THEOREM 2. *Balls-into-Leaves terminates in $O(\log \log n)$ rounds with probability at least $\left(1 - \frac{1}{n^c}\right)$, where $c > 0$ is a constant.*

PROOF. From Lemma 6, after $O(\log \log n)$ phases, the probability there is a path with more than $O(\log^3 n)$ balls, is less than $\frac{1}{n^{c'}}$, for some const. $c' > 0$. Taking $M = O(\log^3 n)$ balls on path π from the root to a parent of some leaf, by Lemma 10 and a union bound over all such $n/2$ paths, the probability that some path is not empty is less than $\frac{1}{n^{c'}}$, for some constant $c' > 0$. Putting together the above results, we get the probability that the tree still has a populated inner node is at most $\frac{1}{n^{c'+c''}}$ where c', c'' are constants. By construction, the algorithm terminates when all balls have reached leaves. Choosing some constant $c > c' + c''$, the algorithm terminates in $O(\log \log n)$ phases with probability at least $1 - \frac{1}{n^c}$.

Since each phase consists of 2 rounds, the claim follows. □

6.3 Crashes

To show that crashes do not slow down termination, we continue the analysis of some path π that starts at the root. By construction, at the end of each phase, in every local view, the position of each surviving ball b_i is updated according to b_i's local view. We thus focus on the progress of b_i in its local view.

Iterating on each phase ϕ that contains at least one failure, we compare the local view V of ball b_i in ϕ with its hypothetical view V' in an execution with a failure-free ϕ. First, note that views V and V' are equivalent if b_i has not seen a failure. Now, assume b_i has seen a failure in V.

We show that b_i is at least as likely to escape from π in V, as it is in V'. First, we note that if b_i has seen a failure in some disjoint subtree, or the crashed ball had lower priority than b_i, then, by construction, such a failure does not affect the progress of b_i. Consider now a failure that occurs in a subtree of b_i. Such a failure implies that, in V, the total capacity of all gateways on π is larger than the number of balls on π. Thus, b_i is at least as likely to be among the first

[3] In Case 2, ball b_k can stop somewhere else deeper in the tree, but this no longer affects the analysis of π.

highest priority balls that have chosen the same gateway in ϕ. Since the choice of b_i and π is arbitrary, the argument applies to every ball in every view.

6.4 Experimental Evaluation

We complement with simulations the analytical analysis of the round complexity of Balls-into-Leaves. The results are depicted in Table 1 (the number of rounds was obtained by averaging over 200 failure-free runs of the algorithm).

Number of balls	Number of rounds
2^5	2,76
2^{10}	4,00
2^{15}	4,92
2^{20}	5,24
2^{25}	6,00

Table 1: Experimental evaluation of Balls-into-Bins

Our simulations confirm that the running time grows very slowly with n: e.g., for 2^{25} balls the algorithm takes only 6 rounds to terminate. These results are consistent with our $O(\log\log n)$ bound. Moreover, the simulations show that the hidden constants are small.

7. EARLY TERMINATING EXTENSION

We now extend the algorithm to terminate faster in executions with fewer crashes. Without failures, balls can use their unique labels to pick distinct leaves in one round: balls exchange their labels, and each ball chooses a leaf indexed by the rank of its label in the ordered set of all labels. But collisions may occur due to failures. A single crash can cause up to $n/2$ collisions: the ball with the lowest label b_{lowest} sends to every second ball (by label order) and then crashes, so that all other balls collide in pairs.

On the other hand, if balls use this scheme to deterministically pick paths in the Balls-into-Leaves algorithm, it is easy to see that the paths are well distributed; in the first phase, the tree collapses into small subtrees of depth 2 in every local tree. But the balls cannot use deterministic paths in every phase, otherwise the algorithm's round complexity would be no better than $\Omega(\log n)$, due to the lower bound of [8].

We combine the deterministic and randomized approaches, by first deterministically collapsing the tree into disjoint subtrees of depth $O(\log f)$ (where f is a number of failures that have occurred in an execution), and then resorting to randomization. The modified Balls-into-Leaves algorithm works as follows. In Round 1 of phase 1, replace Lines 6–11 in Algorithm 1 with the following: ball b_i constructs path deterministically towards the leaf ranked by b_i in OrderedBalls(); the rest of phase 1 is executed as in the original algorithm. In the remaining phases, b_i executes the code of the original algorithm.

It is easy to see that, in a failure-free execution, the modified algorithm terminates in one phase.

THEOREM 3. *In a failure-free execution, the modified Balls-into-Leaves algorithm terminates in $O(1)$ rounds.*

In an execution with f failures, we show that the algorithm terminates in $O(\log\log f)$ rounds w.h.p. (the proof can be found in Appendix B).

THEOREM 4. *The modified Balls-into-Leaves algorithm terminates in $O(\log\log f)$ rounds with prob. at least $\left(1 - \frac{1}{n^c}\right)$, where $c > 0$ is a constant.*

8. DISCUSSION

Extending the classical balls-into-bins technique, we have proposed Balls-into-Leaves, a randomized algorithm that places n balls into n leaves of a binary tree in $O(\log\log n)$ rounds w.h.p. Our simulations confirm that, in fact, the algorithm terminates in few rounds even for very large values of n. However, we do not optimize the algorithm for the message complexity—in each round Balls-into-Leaves employs all-to-all communication. Therefore, the total message complexity is $O(n^2 \log\log n)$. It is possible to reduce it to $O(n^2)$ by eliminating communication between balls in disjoint subtrees. However, to overcome the $O(n^2)$ barrier ($O(n)$ messages per ball) would require a different approach.

We have also presented an extension of the algorithm that provides early termination in $O(\log\log f)$ rounds w.h.p. when there are f failures, and deterministic termination in $O(1)$ rounds in failure-free executions.

Our results imply an exponential separation between deterministic and randomized algorithms for tight renaming. An open question is whether the Balls-into-Leaves algorithm is optimal for this problem. Answering this question requires new lower bounds for randomized renaming. We conjecture that obtaining such lower bounds will be challenging, given that lower bounds for other variants of renaming have required subtle topological or reduction techniques.

Acknowledgements

Dan Alistarh was partially supported by the SNF Postdoctoral Fellows Program, NSF grant CCF-1217921, DoE ASCR grant ER26116/DE-SC0008923, and by grants from the Oracle and Intel corporations.

Oksana Denysyuk and Luís Rodrigues were partially supported by Fundação para a Ciência e Tecnologia (FCT) via the project PEPITA (PTDC/EEI-SCR/2776/2012) and via the INESC-ID multi-annual funding through the PIDDAC Program fund grant, under project PEst-OE/EEI/LA0021/2013.

Nir Shavit was supported in part by NSF grants CCF-1217921 and CCF-1301926, DoE ASCR grant ER26116/DE-SC0008923, and by grants from the Oracle and Intel corporations.

9. REFERENCES

[1] Micah Adler, Soumen Chakrabarti, Michael Mitzenmacher, and Lars Rasmussen. Parallel randomized load balancing. In *Proceedings of the Twenty-seventh Annual ACM Symposium on Theory of Computing*, STOC '95, pages 238–247, New York, NY, USA, 1995.

[2] Dan Alistarh, James Aspnes, Keren Censor-Hillel, Seth Gilbert, and Rachid Guerraoui. Tight bounds for asynchronous renaming. *J. ACM*, page to appear, 2014.

[3] Dan Alistarh, Hagit Attiya, Rachid Guerraoui, and Corentin Travers. Early deciding synchronous renaming in O(log f) rounds or less. In *Proceedings of the 19th International Colloquium on Structural*

Information and Communication Complexity, SIROCCO '12, Reykjavik, Iceland, June 2012.

[4] Hagit Attiya, Amotz Bar-Noy, Danny Dolev, David Peleg, and Rüdiger Reischuk. Renaming in an asynchronous environment. *J. ACM*, 37(3):524–548, July 1990.

[5] Petra Berenbrink, Kamyar Khodamoradi, Thomas Sauerwald, and Alexandre Stauffer. Balls-into-bins with nearly optimal load distribution. In *Proceedings of the 25th ACM Symposium on Parallelism in Algorithms and Architectures*, SPAA '13, pages 326–335, Montreal, Canada, 2013.

[6] Gabriel Bracha and Sam Toueg. Asynchronous consensus and broadcast protocols. *J. ACM*, 32(4):824–840, October 1985.

[7] Alex Brodsky, Faith Ellen, and Philipp Woelfel. Fully-adaptive algorithms for long-lived renaming. *Distributed Computing*, 24(2):119–134, 2011.

[8] Soma Chaudhuri, Maurice Herlihy, and Mark Tuttle. Wait-free implementations in message-passing systems. *Theoretical Computer Science*, 220(1):211–245, June 1999.

[9] Oksana Denysyuk and Luís Rodrigues. Byzantine renaming in synchronous systems with $t < N$. In *Proceedings of the 32nd ACM Symposium on Principles of Distributed Computing*, PODC '13, pages 210–219, Montreal, Canada, 2013.

[10] Danny Dolev and Raymond Strong. Polynomial algorithms for multiple processor agreement. In *Proceedings of the 14th Annual ACM Symposium on Theory of Computing*, STOC '82, pages 401–407, San Francisco (CA), USA, 1982.

[11] Gaston Gonnet. Expected length of the longest probe sequence in hash code searching. *J. ACM*, 28(2):289–304, April 1981.

[12] Leslie Lamport, Robert Shostak, and Michael Pease. The byzantine generals problem. *ACM Trans. Program. Lang. Syst.*, 4(3):382–401, July 1982.

[13] Christoph Lenzen and Roger Wattenhofer. Tight bounds for parallel randomized load balancing. *CoRR*, abs/1102.5425, 2011.

[14] Christoph Lenzen and Roger Wattenhofer. Tight bounds for parallel randomized load balancing: Extended abstract. In *Proceedings of the 43rd Annual ACM Symposium on Theory of Computing*, STOC '11, pages 11–20, San Jose, CA, USA, 2011.

[15] Michael Mitzenmacher. The power of two choices in randomized load balancing. *IEEE Transactions on Parallel and Distributed Systems*, 12(10):1094–1104, Oct 2001.

[16] Michael Okun. Strong order-preserving renaming in the synchronous message passing model. *Theoretical Computer Science*, 411(40-42):3787 – 3794, 2010.

APPENDIX

We now present the omitted proofs.

A. CORRECTNESS

We prove that in the Balls-into-Leaves algorithm correct balls terminate at distinct leaves.

We first notice that, at the beginning of each phase, the positions of all correct balls are synchronized across the views. Positions are considered at the beginning of a phase.

PROPOSITION 1. *For any phase $\phi \geq 1$, if balls b_i and b_j are correct, then the tree position of b_i in the view of ball b_i is the same as the position of b_i in the view of ball b_j.*

PROOF. We proceed by induction on the phase index. At the beginning of phase 1, this holds since all n correct balls have broadcasted their labels and have been placed at the root in local views of all correct balls (Lines 1–2).

For the induction step, assume by contradiction that the claim holds in $\phi \geq 1$, but not in $\phi+1$. This is only possible if b_j has not sent its position to b_i in ϕ (Line 23 of Algorithm 1). However, since b_j is correct, b_j must have executed Line 23 in phase ϕ. Contradiction. □

This implies the following.

PROPOSITION 2. *For any phase $\phi \geq 1$ and any local view, the number of correct balls in each subtree is $\leq$ the total number of balls in that subtree.*

The priority order $<_R$ ensures that the descent of correct balls is simulated consistently across views.

PROPOSITION 3. *For any phase $\phi \geq 1$, if b_i and b_j are correct, then either $b_i <_R b_j$ in every view, or $b_i >_R b_j$ in every view.*

PROOF. By Proposition 1, the positions of correct balls are synchronized across the views. Assume, w.l.o.g., $b_i < b_j$. Thus, by definition of order $<_R$, $b_i <_R b_j$ in each view. □

Below we restate and prove Lemma 1.

Lemma 1 *For any phase $\phi \geq 1$, in any local view, the number of correct balls in each subtree $\leq$ the number of leaves in that subtree.*

PROOF. We prove the claim by induction over the phase index ϕ. For $\phi = 1$, the claim holds since all n balls are at the root of the tree.

Assume the claim is true for $\phi \geq 1$. Since each subtree contains at least all correct balls (Proposition 2), and (Proposition 3), balls simulate the descent of correct balls in a consistent order (if $b_j <_R b_k$, then b_j is moved before b_k), when b_i simulates the descent of each ball locally, every ball (including b_i) stops in a subtree where it still fits among at least all correct balls. □

We now prove Theorem 1.

PROOF OF THEOREM 1. By Proposition 1 and Lemma 1, after correct ball b_i reaches a leaf and announces its position, all correct balls have b_j at the same leaf in their local views and thus never propose a path to that leaf. By algorithmic construction, balls do not move once they have reached the bottom. □

Finite Deterministic Termination

We now prove the algorithm terminates always in a finite number of rounds.

LEMMA 11. *If no failures occur in some phase ϕ, then at least one ball at an inner node reaches a leaf in its local view of the tree.*

PROOF. Let b_j be the highest priority correct ball among the balls at inner nodes (not leaves) at the beginning of ϕ. By algorithmic construction, b_i chooses in Round 1 a path to an empty leaf in its local view of the tree. Since by assumption no crashes occur, balls receive identical sets of paths and move balls down in the same order. By algorithmic construction, balls at the leaves are not moved. So, b_j is the first to move down in its own view and thus it will reach the leaf chosen by its path. □

By Lemma 11 balls require at most n fault-free phases to reach the bottom; since there are at most $t<n$ faults in total, the algorithm terminates in $O(n)$ phases deterministically.

B. EARLY TERMINATION

In the following, we restate and prove Theorem 4.

Theorem 4 *The modified Balls-into-Leaves algorithm terminates in $O(\log\log f)$ rounds with prob. at least $\left(1 - \frac{1}{n^c}\right)$, where $c > 0$ is a constant.*

PROOF. Let i be rank of ball b_i among the surviving balls. Assume b_i has not seen $k \leq f$ failures. The rank in its local view has shifted right by at most k with regard to other views. Since all survivors have each other, including b_i, in their local views, at most $f-1$ other survivors see their ranks in the interval $i..(i+f)$.

Consider binary representation of leaf ranks. We note that each subtree that contains some leaf is indexed by the binary prefix of the leaf rank. From the previous discussion, the surviving balls collide on at most $\lceil \log f \rceil$ least significant bits. Thus, in every local view, collisions occur at the depth at least $\log n - \lceil \log f \rceil$ in phase 1.

In the subsequent phases, balls in disjoint subtrees propose non-overlapping paths. Therefore, the rest of the execution is equivalent to running at most $\frac{n}{2^{\log n - \lceil \log f \rceil}} \leq n$ parallel instances of Balls into Leaves with at most f balls each. From Theorem 2, and for a sufficiently large const. $c > 0$, the claim follows. □

Dynamic-Sized Nonblocking Hash Tables*

Yujie Liu
Lehigh University
lyj@lehigh.edu

Kunlong Zhang
Tianjin University
zhangkl@tju.edu.cn

Michael Spear
Lehigh University
spear@cse.lehigh.edu

ABSTRACT

This paper presents nonblocking hash table algorithms that support resizing in both directions: shrinking and growing. The heart of the table is a freezable set abstraction, which greatly simplifies the task of moving elements among buckets during a resize. Furthermore, the freezable set abstraction makes possible the use of highly optimized implementations of individual buckets, including implementations in which a single flat array is used for each bucket, which improves cache locality.

We present lock-free and wait-free variants of our hash table, to include fast adaptive wait-free variants based on the Fastpath/Slowpath methodology. In evaluation on SPARC and x86 architectures, we find that performance of our lock-free implementation is consistently better than the current state-of-the-art split-ordered list, and that performance for the adaptive wait-free algorithm is compelling across microbenchmark configurations.

Categories and Subject Descriptors

D.1.3 [**Programming Techniques**]: Concurrent Programming—*Parallel Programming*; E.2 [**Data Storage Representations**]: Hash-table representations

Keywords

Hash Table, Concurrent Data Structures, Nonblocking

1. INTRODUCTION

Hash tables are often chosen as the data structure to implement set and map objects, because they offer constant time insert, remove and lookup operations. Typically, a hash table consists of a static *bucket array*, where each bucket is a pointer to a dynamic set object, and a *hash function* that directs operations to buckets according to the values of the operations' operands. To preserve constant time complexity when the number of elements grows, a *resize* operation (or rehash) must be performed on the hash table to extend the size of the bucket array. However, resizing a hash table in the presence of concurrent operations in a nonblocking manner is a difficult problem. For example, Shalev and Shavit [17] state:

> *THE LOCK-FREE RESIZING PROBLEM.* What is it that makes lock-free extensible hashing hard to achieve? The core problem is that even if individual buckets are lock-free, when resizing the table, several items from each of the "old" buckets must be relocated to a bucket among "new" ones. However, in a single CAS operation, it seems impossible to atomically move even a single item, as this requires one to remove the item from one linked list and insert it in another. If this move is not done atomically, elements might be lost, or to prevent loss, will have to be replicated, introducing the overhead of "replication management". The lock-free techniques for providing the broader atomicity required to overcome these difficulties imply that processes will have to "help" others complete their operations. Unfortunately, "helping" requires processes to store state and repeatedly monitor other processes' progress, leading to redundancies and overheads that are unacceptable if one wants to maintain the constant time performance of hashing algorithms.

In their paper, Shalev and Shavit proposed the split-ordered list [17], which circumvents explicit migration of keys between buckets. However, their algorithm has several limitations. A "shrinking" feature is missing in the resizing mechanism: the bucket array can only extend when the size of the set grows, during which "marker" nodes are permanently inserted into the underlying linked list; it is unclear how these marker nodes can be reclaimed when the set shrinks. Furthermore, the implementation leverages the assumption that memory size is bounded and known, and relies on a tree-based indexing structure with predetermined configurations.

We introduce new resizable hash table implementations that eliminate the above limitations, by solving the resizing problem with a direct and more efficient approach. In contrast to the split-ordered list, our implementations achieve three new properties. First, they are **dynamic**: the bucket array can adjust its size both upward *and downward*, according to the size of the set. Second, the bucket array is **unbounded** and we make no assumption about the size of memory. Third, our algorithm admits **wait-free** variants, where every insert, remove, and lookup operation completes in a bounded number of steps, even in the presence of resizing.

The major technical novelty of our implementations stems from the definition and use of freezable set objects. In addition to canonical set operations (i.e., insert, lookup, and remove), a freezable set

*This work was supported in part by the National Science Foundation under grants CNS-1016828, CCF-1218530, and CAREER-1253362.

PODC'14, July 15–18, 2014, Paris, France.
Copyright 2014 ACM 978-1-4503-2944-6/14/07 ...$15.00.
http://dx.doi.org/10.1145/2611462.2611495.

provides a "freeze" operation that makes the object immutable. In our algorithms, each bucket is implemented using a freezable set. To resize a hash table, buckets in the old bucket array are frozen before their key values are copied to the new table. The migration of keys during resizing is incrementally performed in a *lazy* manner, and more importantly, the logical state of the set is never changed by migration. This ensures that every insert, remove, and lookup operation is linearizable [9].

Practical lock-free and wait-free implementations of freezable sets can be derived from a recent unordered list algorithm [20]. In this paper, we introduce two new implementations, both of which are specialized and streamlined for use in our hash table algorithms to achieve better performance. Of particular interest is the fact that bounds on the size of freezable sets allow an array-based implementation, which increases locality and decreases space overhead relative to linked lists.

In experimental evaluation, we show that our hash table achieves both high scalability and low latency. In particular, our lock-free implementation significantly outperforms the state-of-the-art split ordered list. Although our implementation does not lower the asymptotic time complexity over prior work, it gains a performance benefit by reducing the number of memory indirections, which in turn translates to improved cache utilization on modern processors. The performance benefit, coupled with the dynamic feature and the possibility of wait-freedom, makes our algorithms ideal candidates for use in applications requiring progress and performance.

The remainder of this paper is organized as follows. In Section 2, we discuss related work. We briefly introduce freezable set objects in Section 3, and discuss the implementations in Sections 6 and 7. The lock-free and wait-free hash set algorithms are discussed in Section 4 and Section 5. We evaluate performance in Section 8, and conclude in Section 9.

2. RELATED WORK

While there are many types of sequential hash tables, only a few concurrent hash tables exist. Hash tables using fine-grained locks have been known for decades [1, 2, 10, 12], but continue to see new innovations [7, 8, 18]. More recently, several nontrivial nonblocking implementations [3–5, 15–17, 19] have been discovered.

The first practical nonblocking hash table was designed by Michael [15], which uses a fixed-size bucket array of lock-free linked lists. The lists are a streamlined version of the lock-free ordered list by Harris [6]. Independently, Greenwald [5] implemented a lock-free closed addressing hash table. Greenwald's hash table is resizable, but relies on a DCAS (double-compare-and-swap) operation. Unfortunately, simulating DCAS in a lock-free manner is expensive [14], requiring at least 5 CAS operations, and implementing it via hardware transactional memory can only achieve obstruction-freedom.

Shalev and Shavit [17] presented a lock-free extendible hash table using the recursive split-ordering technique. Their hash table consists of two substructures: an ordered linked list based on the work of Michael [15], and a static tree-based directory structure. The ordered list contains both data and marker nodes, where marker nodes roughly partition the list into constant-size contiguous sub-lists. To find an element (or its predecessor), threads first perform a constant-time traversal of the directory to locate the closest preceding "marker" node, and then inspect the sub-list that follows. A clever bit-reversal technique used on the hash value of an element ensures that as buckets are split, and new marker nodes added, the order of elements within the list need not change. Thus while resizing may require a large number of updates to the directory, the relative position of elements in the list does not change. Zhang and Larson [19] announced that they had implemented a lock-free linear hash table, also using the recursive split-ordering technique.

Gao, Groote, and Hesselink [4] proposed a resizable, lock-free, open addressing hash table. They maintain a second table during resizing; to migrate a key, they first mark the key as being moved, then copy it to the second table, and finally update the original key's mark to indicate that it has moved. Whenever an operation finds a marked key, it must help finish resizing the entire table, and then resume its execution on the second table. Purcell and Harris [16] proposed another lock-free open addressing hash table that is not resizable, but is space-efficient. In particular, their hash table can reuse the space occupied by deleted keys.

Feldman, LaBorde, and Dechev [3] demonstrated that with perfect hashing, it is possible to implement a wait-free hash table. Their implementation makes use of a tree-like array-of-arrays structure, with data stored in single-element leaf arrays.

abstract states of FSET
  set : Set of **integer**
  ok : **boolean**

abstract states of FSETOP
  $type$: $\{INS, REM\}$
  key : **integer**
  $done$: **boolean**
  $resp$: **boolean**

```
GETRESPONSE(op : FSETOP) : boolean
  atomic
    return op.resp

HASMEMBER(b : FSET, k : integer) : boolean
  atomic
    return k ∈ b.set

INVOKE(b : FSET, op : FSETOP) : boolean
  atomic
    if b.ok ∧ ¬op.done then
      if op.type = INS then
        op.resp ← op.key ∉ b.set
        b.set ← b.set ∪ {op.key}
      else if op.type = REM then
        op.resp ← op.key ∈ b.set
        b.set ← b.set \ {op.key}
      op.done ← true
    return op.done

FREEZE(b : FSET) : Set of integer
  atomic
    if b.ok then
      b.ok ← false
    return b.set
```

Figure 1: Specification of FSET and FSETOP Objects

3. FREEZABLE SETS

In this section, we briefly introduce FSET, a freezable set object that serves as the common building block of our lock-free and wait-free hash table algorithms. Figure 1 presents the FSET specification. Discussion of nonblocking implementations of FSET appears in Section 6 and Section 7.

An FSET object implements an integer set with insert, remove, and lookup operations, and in addition, provides a special FREEZE operation. The abstract states consist of a set of integers, and an *ok* bit indicating whether the set is mutable. Modification of an FSET object can be either insertion or removal of a key. Logically, an insert returns true if the key was not in the set, and a remove returns true if the key was in the set; otherwise, the modification operation returns false. However, we encode insert and remove operations as FSETOP objects. The states of an FSETOP object include the operation type (*INS* or *REM*), the key value, a boolean *done* field that indicates whether the operation was ever applied, and a boolean *resp* field that holds the return value.

The INVOKE operation attempts to apply an insert or a remove operation *op* on an FSET object b. The operation *op* is executed only if b is mutable ($b.ok$) and *op* was not applied before ($\neg op.done$). In case *op* is successfully applied, it is marked as done, with the return value written in its *resp* field. The INVOKE operation returns true if *op* is (or was already) applied; otherwise, the operation returns false, in which case b is immutable and *op* was not applied.

The HASMEMBER operation tests whether the given key is in the FSET object. The FREEZE operation marks the given FSET object as immutable by setting its *ok* bit to false, and returns all elements of the set. The GETRESPONSE operation returns the *resp* field of the given FSETOP object.

FREEZE renders an FSET permanently immutable, and also returns the final state of an FSET object. This plays prominently in a nonblocking resize operations: when resizing, a thread first freezes the buckets (which are implemented using FSET objects) that will be merged or split; thereafter, keys in the frozen buckets can be safely migrated into new buckets without loss or duplication.

The role of the FSETOP's *done* bit is to ensure that every modification is applied *at most* once. This is critical to our wait-free hash set design, where threads announce operations and help each other to make progress. Using *done*, we can be sure that helping does not cause an operation to execute multiple times.

Instead of letting threads invoke insert or remove operations on an FSET object, we adopt an alternative style where modifications are performed via the INVOKE and GETRESPONSE interface. This simplifies discussion of linearization points. The linearization of every modification is within INVOKE. However, linearization and subsequent pre-response computation can occur in different phases, which facilitates the wait-free helping mechanism. Details of the wait-free FSET appear in Section 7.

4. A LOCK-FREE, DYNAMIC-SIZED HASH SET ALGORITHM

Figure 2 presents a lock-free hash set algorithm. The hash set object provides three operations: INSERT adds a key value to the set and returns true if the key was not in the set, REMOVE removes a key value from the set and returns true if the key was in the set, and CONTAINS returns whether the given key is in the set.

Our algorithm assumes the availability of a nonblocking implementation of the FSET object. In particular, all INVOKE, FREEZE, and HASMEMBER operations performed on an FSET object must be lock-free with respect to the object. We also require the implementation of GETRESPONSE to be wait-free.

4.1 Implementation

Our hash set is a linked list of HNODE (Hash Table Node) objects, where an HNODE represents a version of the set (a new version is installed during a RESIZE operation). An HNODE consists of an array of FSETs (*buckets*), with the array length stored in the *size* field, and a *pred* pointer that points to a predecessor HNODE object. A shared pointer *head* points to the head of the HNODE list. For simplicity, we make the following assumptions:

(1) A RESIZE operation either doubles (grows) or halves (shrinks) the size of the bucket array.

(2) The use of modular arithmetic ($index = k$ **mod** $size$) for the hash function is acceptable.

The key challenge in our algorithm is to coordinate the resizing mechanism (embodied in the RESIZE operation) with the set operations (INSERT, REMOVE, and CONTAINS).

A RESIZE operation takes a boolean parameter that indicates whether the caller intends to grow or shrink the hash table. The thread must first ensure that all the logical key values of the set are *physically* stored in the buckets of the head HNODE. This is achieved by invoking INITBUCKET on each bucket (line 23), which migrates to t those key values stored in t's predecessor but not yet in t. After the migration is complete, we set $t.pred$ to **nil** (line 24) to allow the predecessor (which is now immutable) and its buckets to be garbage collected. The thread then allocates a new HNODE t' with t as the predecessor, and uses a CAS instruction to make t' the new head HNODE (line 28). The operation does *not* initialize entries of the new bucket array: these entries are initialized lazily as they are later accessed by INSERT and REMOVE operations.

The INITBUCKET operation initializes the i-th bucket of a given HNODE t, by merging or splitting the corresponding buckets of t's predecessor HNODE s, if s exists. The operation compares the sizes of t and s to determine whether t is growing or shrinking with respect to s, and then freezes the corresponding bucket(s) of s before copying the elements to t. If t doubles the size of s, then (roughly) half of the elements in the (i **mod** $s.size$)-th bucket of s migrate to the i-th bucket of t (line 44). Otherwise, t halves the size of s, in which case the i-th and $(i + t.size)$-th buckets of s are merged to form the i-th bucket of t (line 48). Note that a new FSET object is allocated to store the merged or split bucket (line 49), and a CAS instruction is used to prevent races with helping threads (line 50).

Both INSERT and REMOVE operations delegate their work to the APPLY operation (lines 2 and 7), which applies the modification to the appropriate bucket. APPLY first allocates an FSETOP object to represent the modification request (line 30), and then repeatedly attempts to apply the request to the corresponding bucket b (line 36). If b is **nil**, the thread must invoke INITBUCKET to initialize the bucket (line 35) before applying the modification. After the modification is successfully applied (line 36 returns true), the operation receives its return value via GETRESPONSE (line 37).

A modification may trigger the resizing mechanism according to heuristic policies. Since the choice of policy is orthogonal to the algorithm, we leave it unspecified in our presentation (lines 3 and 8). As typical heuristics, INSERT might approximate the bucket size by the number of elements it visits, and grow the hash table if the cost exceeds some threshold; upon completing a REMOVE, the thread may sample the sizes of randomly selected buckets and shrink the hash table if their sizes all fall below some threshold.

A CONTAINS operation starts by searching for the given key value in the corresponding bucket b of the head HNODE. If b is not **nil**, the thread simply searches the bucket (line 18) to determine if the key value is in the set. Otherwise, the thread must trace back to t's predecessor HNODE(s) (line 15) and perform the search in s. There is one troublesome interleaving, which occurs when s is resized concurrently with the CONTAINS. Thus we must double-check (line 16) if s has become **nil** between lines 13 and 15,

```
record HNODE
  buckets  : FSET[ ]
  size     : integer
  pred     : HNODE

shared variables
  head  : HNODE

initially
  head ← new HNODE⟨new FSET[1], 1, nil⟩
  head.buckets[0] ← new FSET⟨∅, true⟩

1  INSERT(k : integer) : boolean
2     resp ← APPLY(INS, k)
3     if ⟨heuristic-policy⟩ then
4        RESIZE(true)
5     return resp

6  REMOVE(k : integer) : boolean
7     resp ← APPLY(REM, k)
8     if ⟨heuristic-policy⟩ then
9        RESIZE(false)
10    return resp

11 CONTAINS(k : integer) : boolean
12    t ← head
13    b ← t.buckets[k mod t.size]
14    if b = nil then
15       s ← t.pred
16       if s ≠ nil then b ← s.buckets[k mod s.size]
17       else b ← t.buckets[k mod t.size]
18    return HASMEMBER(b, k)

19 RESIZE(grow : boolean)
20    t ← head
21    if t.size > 1 ∨ grow then
22       for i from 0 to t.size − 1 do
23          INITBUCKET(t, i)
24       t.pred ← nil
25       size ← grow ? t.size ∗ 2 : t.size/2
26       buckets ← new FSET[size]
27       t′ ← new HNODE⟨buckets, size, t⟩
28       CAS(&head, t, t′)

29 APPLY(type : {INS, REM}, k : integer) : boolean
30    op ← new FSETOP(type, k, false, −)
31    while true do
32       t ← head
33       b ← t.buckets[k mod t.size]
34       if b = nil then
35          b ← INITBUCKET(t, k mod t.size)
36       if INVOKE(b, op) then
37          return GETRESPONSE(op)

38 INITBUCKET(t : HNODE, i : integer) : FSET
39    b ← t.buckets[i]
40    s ← t.pred
41    if b = nil ∧ s ≠ nil then
42       if t.size = s.size ∗ 2 then
43          m ← s.buckets[i mod s.size]
44          set ← FREEZE(m) ∩ {x | x mod t.size = i}
45       else
46          m ← s.buckets[i]
47          n ← s.buckets[i + t.size]
48          set ← FREEZE(m) ∪ FREEZE(n)
49       b′ ← new FSET⟨set, true⟩
50       CAS(&t.buckets[i], nil, b′)
51    return t.buckets[i]
```

Figure 2: A Lock-free Dynamic-Sized Hash Set Implementation

in which case we re-read the corresponding bucket of t (line 17), which must have become initialized during prior to s becoming **nil**, and perform the search in it.

4.2 Linearizability

We sketch a proof of linearizability of the lock-free hash set object by showing that every INSERT, REMOVE, and CONTAINS operation happens at its linearization point, defined as follows:

An INSERT or a REMOVE operation by thread p linearizes at an INVOKE operation (line 36) that returns true (which logically sets $op_p.done$ to true). A CONTAINS operation linearizes at the HASMEMBER operation (line 18) if b is mutable ($b.ok$ is true) when the operation is performed; otherwise, b must have been made immutable by some FREEZE operation, in which case we let the CONTAINS operation linearize at the FREEZE operation that sets $b.ok$ to false, or at p's step at line 12, whichever happens later.

The major obligation of the proof is to show that a concrete hash set object refines an abstract set object (AbsSet), with respect to the mapping function in Figure 3. Intuitively, the abstract set object is defined as the union of all bucket sets of the head HNODE. A bucket set (BuckSet(t, i)) is defined as the elements of the bucket (Elems(t, i)) if the bucket pointer is not **nil**, or otherwise, the union (Merge(t, i)) or intersection (Split(t, i)) of the corresponding buckets of the predecessor HNODE.

For convenience, we say an FSET object X is *mutable* if $X.ok$, and *immutable* otherwise. We say an HNODE object X is *growing* if $X.pred \neq$ **nil** and $X.size = X.pred.size * 2$, and *shrinking* if $X.pred \neq$ **nil** and $X.size = X.pred.size\ /\ 2$.

For HNODE object X and bucket index i, we define the *predecessor buckets* of $X.buckets[i]$ as follows: if X is growing, then $X.pred.buckets[i \textbf{ mod } X.pred.size]$ is the only predecessor bucket of $X.buckets[i]$; if X is shrinking, both $X.pred.buckets[i]$ and $X.pred.buckets[i + X.size]$ are predecessor buckets of $X.buckets[i]$.

The following observations can be verified from the pseudo-code and do not require proof.

OBSERVATION 1. *head* $\neq$ **nil**.

OBSERVATION 2. *The pred field of an* HNODE *does not change unless it is set to* **nil** *by a step at line 24.*

OBSERVATION 3. *The size field of a* HNODE *does not change and always equals the size of the buckets array.*

OBSERVATION 4. *For every* HNODE *object* X*, if* $X.pred \neq$ **nil**, *then* X *is either growing or shrinking.*

$$\text{AbsSet} \equiv \text{NodeSet}(head)$$

$$\text{NodeSet}(t) \equiv \bigcup_{i=0}^{t.size-1} \text{BuckSet}(t,i)$$

$$\text{BuckSet}(t,i) \equiv \begin{cases} \text{Elems}(t,i) & \text{if } t.buckets[i] \neq \textbf{nil} \\ \text{Split}(t,i) & \text{if } t.buckets[i] = \textbf{nil} \wedge t.pred.size * 2 = t.size \\ \text{Merge}(i) & \text{if } t.buckets[i] = \textbf{nil} \wedge t.pred.size \; / \; 2 = t.size \end{cases}$$

$$\begin{aligned} \text{Elems}(t,i) &\equiv t.buckets[i].set \\ \text{Split}(t,i) &\equiv \text{Elems}(t.pred,\; i \textbf{ mod } t.pred.size) \cap \{x \mid x \textbf{ mod } t.size = i\} \\ \text{Merge}(t,i) &\equiv \text{Elems}(t.pred,\; i) \cup \text{Elems}(t.pred,\; i + t.size) \end{aligned}$$

Figure 3: Refinement Mapping Function from Concrete Hash Sets to Abstract Sets

OBSERVATION 5. *For every* HNODE *object* X, $X.buckets[i]$ *never changes after it is initialized on line 50.*

The following invariants are mutually dependent on each other, and we prove them together in a conjunction.

INVARIANT 6. *If p is at lines 24 - 28, then* $t.buckets[i] \neq \textbf{nil}$.

INVARIANT 7. *If p is at line 24 and* $t.pred \neq \textbf{nil}$, *then* $t = head$, *and* $t.pred.buckets[k]$ *is immutable for every valid index k.*

INVARIANT 8. *If p is at lines 39 - 50 and* $t.buckets[i] = \textbf{nil} \vee t.pred \neq \textbf{nil}$, *then* $t = head$.

INVARIANT 9. *If p is at lines 39 - 50 and* $t.buckets[i] \neq \textbf{nil} \wedge t.pred \neq \textbf{nil}$, *then every predecessor bucket of* $t.buckets[i]$ *is immutable.*

INVARIANT 10. *If p is at line 50 and* $t.buckets[i] = \textbf{nil}$, *then every predecessor bucket of* $t.buckets[i]$ *is immutable.*

INVARIANT 11. *For every* HNODE *object* X, *if exists* i *such that* $X.buckets[i] = \textbf{nil}$, *then* $X.pred \neq \textbf{nil}$.

INVARIANT 12. *For every* HNODE *object* X, *if* $X.pred \neq \textbf{nil}$, *then* $X.pred.buckets[k] \neq \textbf{nil}$ *for every valid index k.*

INVARIANT 13. *For every* HNODE *object* X, *if* $X.buckets[i] \neq \textbf{nil} \wedge X.pred \neq \textbf{nil}$, *then every predecessor bucket of* $X.buckets[i]$ *is immutable.*

The following lemma ensures that the resizing mechanism cannot change the abstract states of the set object defined by the refinement mapping function.

LEMMA 14. *AbsSet does not change between the pre-state and post-state of a step* α, *if* α *is a CAS at line 28 or line 50.*

We say an HNODE object X is *reachable* if $head = X$, or $head.pred \neq \textbf{nil}$ and $head.pred = X$. Otherwise, we say the node is *unreachable*.

LEMMA 15. *For every* HNODE *object* X *that is unreachable,* $X.buckets[k]$ *is* **nil** *or immutable for every valid index k.*

We say a thread p is *viable* if p is at the INVOKE(b, op) operation at line 36 and b is mutable.

The following lemma captures the key insight of the algorithm: for an insert or remove operation with key value k, there is always a *unique* FSET object to which the operation can be applied (The FSET dictates the corresponding subset of the abstract set). If two threads p and q both attempt to insert or remove the same key value (after modulo arithmetic), and both are at the INVOKE operation, they either invoke on the *same* bucket b, or at least one of them is invoked on an immutable bucket. This property precludes the possibility that multiple INVOKE operations concurrently insert or remove the same key value at different buckets, and hence, prevents the violation of linearizability (e.g., two INSERT operations both insert the same key values to the set and return true).

LEMMA 16. *For any viable thread p, exactly one of the following claims holds:*

(1) $b_p = head.buckets[op_p.key \textbf{ mod } head.size]$;

(2) $b_p = head.pred.buckets[op_p.key \textbf{ mod } head.pred.size]$, *and* $head.buckets[j] = \textbf{nil}$ *for all j such that* b_p *is a predecessor bucket of* $head.buckets[j]$.

THEOREM 17. *The algorithm in Figure 2 is a linearizable implementation of a set object.*

4.3 Lock Freedom

We show that from any reachable configuration, some INSERT, REMOVE or CONTAINS operation completes in finite number of steps. First, note that a CONTAINS operation cannot delay indefinitely between lines 12 and 17, and the final call to HASMEMBER is lock-free by definition. An INSERT or a REMOVE operation consists of a call to APPLY and a potential call to RESIZE. We show that an APPLY operation takes the back edge of the while loop at line 31 only if another RESIZE operation (called by an INSERT or REMOVE) completes. Since we maintain the invariant that every bucket of the head HNODE is mutable, for an INVOKE operation of thread p to fail, p must encounter an immutable bucket. Since a bucket is made immutable only by a RESIZE, then for T threads, if p's APPLY fails more than T times, then it means that even if $T-1$ threads were all in RESIZE when APPLY was called, the T-th failure of p's APPLY indicates that some thread must have finished its RESIZE, then called APPLY again, indicating that it succeeded in another INSERT or REMOVE.

Suppose S is the maximum size of the head HNODE during execution. Then a RESIZE operation contains at most $2S$ FSET operations. Each iteration of the while loop in APPLY includes at most 3 FSET operations (at most 2 in INITBUCKET, and one in INVOKE). Therefore, at least one INSERT, REMOVE or CONTAINS operation must complete upon the completion of $(3T + 2S) \cdot T$ FSET operations, and hence, the hash set implementation is lock-free by the assumption that the FSET operations are lock-free.

5. A WAIT-FREE ALGORITHM

In this section, we extend the lock-free implementation to obtain a wait-free hash set algorithm. Our wait-free hash set algorithm assumes that a *wait-free* FSET implementation is available. We start with an illustration of the main challenge of achieving wait-freedom. Recall that in our lock-free hash set algorithm, FSET objects are only required to be lock-free. Now suppose a wait-free FSET implementation is given. Does the algorithm immediately become wait-free? The answer is negative: as demonstrated in the following example, an APPLY operation may take an infinite number of steps to complete, due to concurrent RESIZE operations performed on the hash set object.

Let thread p attempt to insert some key value k into the hash set, and stall at the INVOKE operation at line 36. Let t be the head of the HNODE list and let b be the corresponding bucket where p wishes to perform the insertion. Now let another thread q complete an INSERT operation that triggers a RESIZE operation on the hash set, after which a new object t' becomes the head of the HNODE list. Now suppose q inserts the same key value k into the hash set, and since all buckets of t' are **nil**, q invokes INITBUCKET to initialize the corresponding bucket of t', which freezes b, the corresponding bucket of its predecessor t. When thread p resumes, its INVOKE operation will fail since b is frozen (immutable), and p will repeat the while loop in the APPLY operation. The above process can repeat forever, by alternating removals and insertions of k by q, so that p's APPLY operation never completes.

5.1 A Wait-free Implementation of Apply

We present a wait-free implementation of the APPLY operation in Figure 4. The basic idea is to let threads help each other to complete their APPLY operations instead of constantly competing to change and/or freeze the buckets. Our helping mechanism is similar to the doorway stage of Lamport's bakery algorithm [13].

In the wait-free algorithm, an insert or remove operation is represented using a WFOP object which adds a $prio$ field to the FSETOP object. The $prio$ field represents the "priority" of an operation, which dictates the operation's precedence in the helping mechanism: an operation with smaller $prio$ has the precedence over one with larger $prio$. The priorities of operations are generated from a strictly increasing counter (initially 0), implemented using an atomic fetch-and-increment instruction (line 53).

In APPLY, thread p first allocates an WFOP object for its modification operation, associated with a unique priority, and then announces the object (line 55) in a shared array A, indexed by p's thread id. Then p iterates through A and for any operation op announced by thread q (including p itself), if $op.prio$ is smaller than (or equal to) p's most recent priority, p helps q complete (lines 59 to 64). Finally, p invokes GETRESPONSE to get the return value of its own operation (line 65).

5.2 Wait Freedom

First, observe that CONTAINS is wait-free, as it does not have any loops, and the call to HASMEMBER is wait-free. To demonstrate that INSERT and REMOVE are wait-free, we show that for T threads, the inner while loop at line 58 executes at most T iterations. For thread p whose INVOKE at line 63 returns false, the head HNODE must be changed between p's line 59 and line 63, since no bucket of head can be in a frozen state. The change of head must be made by a step at line 28 of some RESIZE, indicating the completion of the outer INSERT or REMOVE operation. After T iterations of the while loop, some thread must have completed at least 2 INSERT or REMOVE operations, where the second one must have a lower priority (larger $prio$) than the priority of op_p. Thus, $op_p.done$ must have been set to true, and p's INVOKE will return true in the next iteration. Therefore, APPLY operations are wait-free, since each contains at most $O(T^2)$ FSET operations, which are wait-free by assumption.

```
record WFOp extends FSetOp
  prio    : integer

additional shared variables
  A        : WFOp[THREADS]
  counter  : integer

initially
  counter ← 0
  for tid ← 0 to (THREADS − 1) do
    A[tid] ← new WFOp⟨−, −, −, −, ∞⟩

52 Apply(type : {INS, REM}, k : integer) : boolean
53   prio ← F&I(&counter)
54   myop ← new WFOp⟨type, k, false, −, prio⟩
55   A[threadid] ← myop
56   for tid ← 0 to (THREADS − 1) do
57     op ← A[tid]
58     while op.prio <= prio do
59       t ← head
60       b ← t.buckets[op.key mod t.size]
61       if b = nil then
62         b ← InitBucket(t, op.key mod t.size)
63       if Invoke(b, op) then
64         break
65   return GetResponse(myop)
```

Figure 4: A Wait-free Implementation of APPLY

6. A SPECIALIZED LOCK-FREE FSET IMPLEMENTATION

Figure 5 presents a lock-free FSET implementation specialized for the lock-free hash set in Figure 2. It exploits the property that in the lock-free hash set algorithm, every FSETOP object can only be applied to a bucket FSET by the allocating thread, due to absence of helping, and thus, we need not keep an actual *done* field in an FSETOP object.

The idea of the implementation is straightforward: we keep the underlying FSET objects (namely FSETNODEs) immutable, and let all updates be performed in a copy-on-write manner. We maintain a pointer $node$ that points to the current FSETNODE object, which consists of the elements of the set (set) and a bit (ok) indicating whether the set is mutable. Any update to an FSET, either via an INVOKE or an FREEZE operation, must first allocate a new

```
record FSetNode
    set  : Set of integer
    ok   : boolean

record FSet
    node  : FSetNode

record FSetOp
    type  : {INS, REM}
    key   : integer
    resp  : boolean

Freeze(b : FSet) : Set of integer
    o ← b.node
    while o.ok do
        n ← new FSetNode⟨o.set, false⟩
        if CAS(&b.node, o, n) then
            break
        o ← b.node
    return o.set

Invoke(b : FSet, op : FSetOp) : boolean
    o ← b.node
    while o.ok do
        if op.type = INS then
            resp ← op.key ∉ o.set
            set ← o.set ∪ {op.key}
        else if op.type = REM then
            resp ← op.key ∈ o.set
            set ← o.set \ {op.key}
        n ← new FSetNode⟨set, true⟩
        if CAS(&b.node, o, n) then
            op.resp ← resp
            return true
        o ← b.node
    return false

HasMember(b : FSet, k : integer) : boolean
    o ← b.node
    return k ∈ o.set

GetResponse(op : FSetOp) : boolean
    return op.resp
```

Figure 5: A Specialized Lock-free FSet Implementation

FSetNode object (cloned from the current FSetNode), then apply its change, and then finalize the modification with a CAS instruction that points *node* to the new FSetNode.

The immutable nature of FSetNode objects allows us to implement the inner set using any sequential algorithm. Since each bucket of a hash table tends to contain only a small number of elements, one appealing option is an unsorted array: it exploits better cache locality than list-based alternatives, and affords the compiler an opportunity to employ wide "vector" operations.

We also note that some simple (but useful) optimizations are elided in the pseudo code to avoid clutter. In particular, it would be wise to let an insert (or remove) operation exit early if the key value is (or is not) in the set, thereby avoiding an unnecessary update (allocation, CAS).

7. A COOPERATIVE WAIT-FREE FSET IMPLEMENTATION

Figure 6 presents an FSet implementation designed for our wait-free hash set algorithm. The FSet implementation "cooperates" with the helping mechanism (Figure 4) to achieve wait-freedom[1]. We inherit the immutable design of the underlying set objects as in the previous lock-free FSet implementation. Now, however, the wait-free implementation must prevent duplicate execution of operations due to the presence of helping. This is achieved by leveraging the *prio* field: for any FSetOp object *op*, its abstract *done* field is **true** if *op.prio* is set to ∞, and we maintain an invariant that *op* is performed only if *op.prio* is *not* ∞.

The crux of the protocol is to let contending threads synchronize at the *op* field of an FSetNode object. To perform an FSetOp (*op*), a thread first attempts to change *node.op* from **nil** using CAS. Subsequently, the thread invokes HelpFinish to compute the return value of *op*, marks *op* as done, and replaces the current FSetNode with the result set (a new object) using CAS.

A Freeze operation first announces its intention by setting *flag* to **true**, and invokes DoFreeze to set *node.op* to $\perp$. To show a Freeze operation is wait-free, it is sufficient to show that DoFreeze completes in a finite number of steps. For any thread p in a DoFreeze operation, we notice that the CAS at line 123 can fail only because *node.op* is changed by a concurrent CAS at line 123 or line 102. In the former case, *node.op* is set to $\perp$ and p's while loop will terminate in the next iteration. In the latter case, any subsequent Invoke operation will see that *flag* is set, and invoke DoFreeze. Thus, either p succeeds in the CAS in its next iteration, or a concurrent DoFreeze sets *node.op* to $\perp$, which forces p to terminate its while loop in the following iteration.

A HasMember operation must first check if there exists a linearized insert or remove operation by inspecting the *op* field. This is necessary because an Invoke operation on an FSet object b may return **true** without invoking HelpFinish on b (in cases where *op* is performed by a concurrent thread), leaving b in an intermediate state. Neglecting to check the *op* field can cause a subsequent Contains operation to erroneously miss the immediately preceding insert or remove operation, which violates linearizability.

8. PERFORMANCE EVALUATION

We evaluate the performance of our hash tables via a stress-test microbenchmark. The experiments were run on a Niagara2 system with one 1.165 GHz, 64-way Sun UltraSPARC T2 CPU with 32 GB of RAM, running Solaris 10. The Niagara2 has eight cores, each eight-way multi-threaded, for a total of 64 threads. We used the Oracle JDK version 1.7.0_13. We also run experiments on an x86 system with one 2.66GHz Intel Xeon X5650 processor and 6GB of RAM, running Linux kernel 3.11. The processor has six cores, each two-way multi-threaded, for a total of 12 threads. On the x86, we used OpenJDK version 1.7.0_51. Due to space limitations, we elide the x86 performance charts.

We compare eight implementations. We use the Shalev and Shavit split ordered list [17] (**SplitOrder**) as our baseline. Our Java implementation of SplitOrder used the latest C++ version as a reference, to ensure a faithful implementation. To the best of our knowledge, this is the best-performing algorithm for implementing an extensible (but not shrinkable) hash table. Furthermore, the implemen-

[1]The implementation is lock-free by itself.

```
record FSetNode
  set  : Set of integer
  op   : FSetOp ∪ {⊥}

record FSet
  node : FSetNode
  flag : boolean

record FSetOp
  type : {INS, REM}
  key  : integer
  resp : boolean
  prio : integer

Invoke(b : FSet, op : FSetOp) : boolean
  while b.node.op ≠ ⊥ ∧ op.prio ≠ ∞ do
    if b.flag then
      DoFreeze(b)
      break
    o ← b.node
    if o.op = nil then
      if op.prio ≠ ∞ then
        if CAS(&o.op, nil, op) then
          HelpFinish(b)
          return true
    else
      HelpFinish(b)
  return op.prio = ∞

Freeze(b : FSet) : Set of integer
  b.flag ← true
  return DoFreeze(b)

HasMember(b : FSet, k : integer) : boolean
  o ← b.node
  op ← o.op
  if op ≠ nil ∧ op ≠ ⊥ ∧ op.key = k then
    return op.type = INS
  return k ∈ o.set

GetResponse(op : FSetOp) : boolean
  return op.resp

DoFreeze(b : FSet) : Set of integer
  while b.node.op ≠ ⊥ do
    o ← b.node
    if o.op = nil then
      if CAS(&o.op, nil, ⊥) then
        break
    else
      HelpFinish(b)
  return b.node.set

HelpFinish(b : FSet)
  o ← b.node
  op ← o.op
  if op ≠ nil ∧ op ≠ ⊥ then
    if op.type = INS then
      resp ← op.key ∉ o.set
      set ← o.set ∪ {op.key}
    else if op.type = REM then
      resp ← op.key ∈ o.set
      set ← o.set \ {op.key}
    op.resp ← resp
    op.prio ← ∞
    CAS(&b.node, o, new FSetNode⟨set, nil⟩)
```

Figure 6: A Cooperative Wait-free FSet Implementation

tation optimized its configuration of the directory structure (using a two-level tree) for the size of each experiment. This ensures a minimal bucket size for the duration of each experiment.

Unlike the baseline, the remaining seven algorithms were run with support for dynamic resizing. **LFArray** is our lock-free hash table, in which per-bucket freezable sets are implemented as arrays of unsorted elements (Section 6). **LFArrayOpt** removes a level of indirection from LFArray by pointing buckets directly to array elements, rather than FSet markers. **LFList** is similar to **LFArray**, except it uses an unsorted list implementation [20] for its freezable sets. In addition to the above lock-free implementations, we consider four wait-free implementations, which use a wait-free FSet (Section 7). **WFArray** and **WFList** employ the straightforward wait-free Apply from Figure 4 to make the LFArray and LFList algorithms wait-free. **Adaptive** applies the Fastpath/Slowpath technique [11] to reduce the overhead of WFArray, and **AdaptiveOpt** applies the optimizations from LFArrayOpt to Adaptive. All adaptive algorithms used a threshold of 256 consecutive failures to trigger a switch to the slow path. All implementations (to include SplitOrder) were optimized using techniques from the `java.util.concurrent` package.

Our main focus is performance in the absence of resizing operations. To this end, for a given experiment we begin by prepopulating each hash table to hold half of the experiment's key range. For a lookup ratio L, we randomly select operations such that insert and remove are chosen with equal probability $(1-L)/2$. Thus while operations and keys are randomly selected, the number of elements in the table remains steady. We report the average of five 5-second trials. Variance was negligible.

8.1 SPARC Performance

Figure 7 presents performance on the Niagara2. The Niagara2 has simple in-order cores with per-core L1 caches and a shared L2 cache. While memory access latencies are low, there is no out-of-order execution to hide the latency of memory accesses: during a cache miss, another hardware thread is scheduled. For all but the smallest key range, the random distribution of keys ensures that every access will incur an L1 cache miss to dereference the bucket, regardless of the implementation. Since SplitOrder uses a sorted list, whereas LFList uses an unsorted list, SplitOrder should traverse half as many pointers, on average. However, our efficient mechanism for finding buckets keeps the gap below 2×.

When we implement each per-bucket FSet as an array, a new trade-off is introduced. On the one hand, all pointer chasing within a bucket is eliminated; on the other, insert and remove operations must copy the entire array. The high memory bandwidth of the Niagara2, coupled with the absence of pointer chasing within each bucket, result in superior performance for LFArray and LFArrayOpt. The most important factor in hash table performance on Niagara2 appears to be pointer chasing.

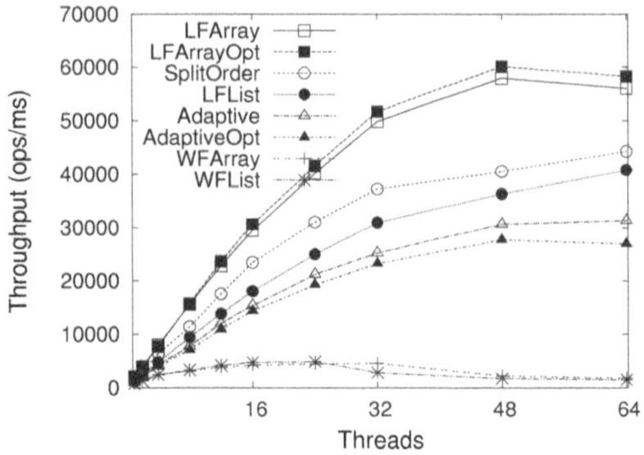

(a) Lookup=0% Range=256

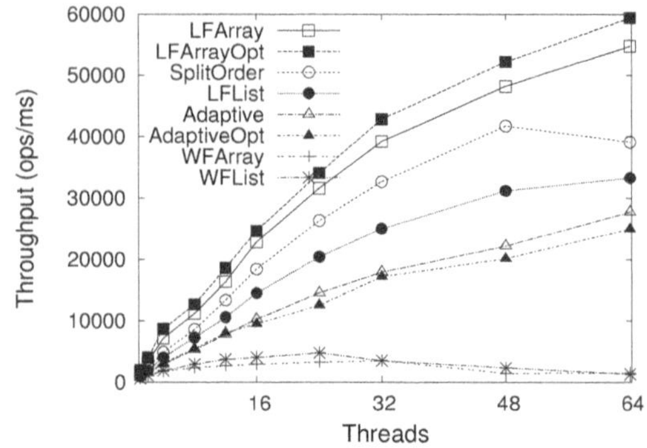

(b) Lookup=0% Range=64K

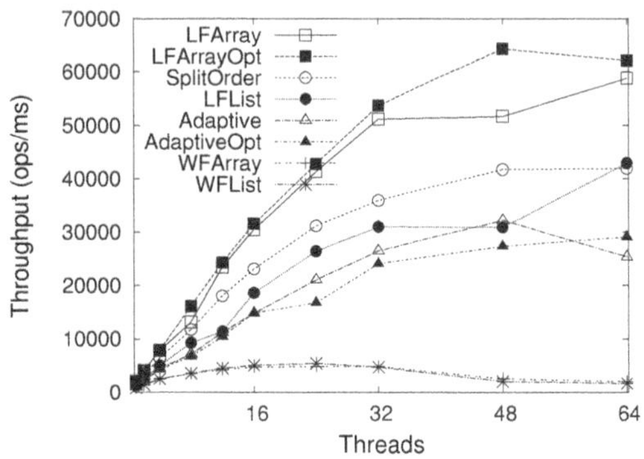

(c) Lookup=10% Range=256

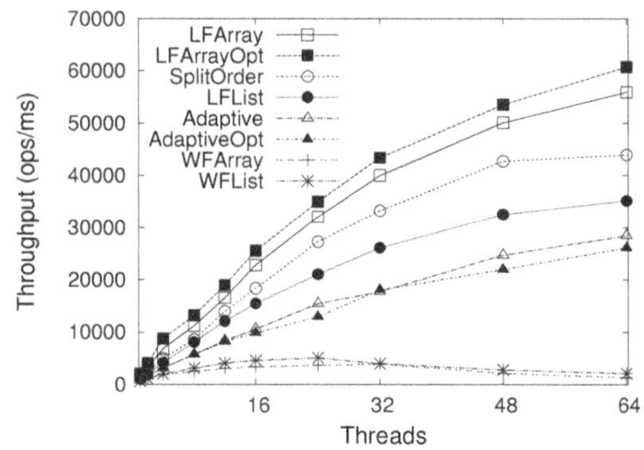

(d) Lookup=10% Range=64K

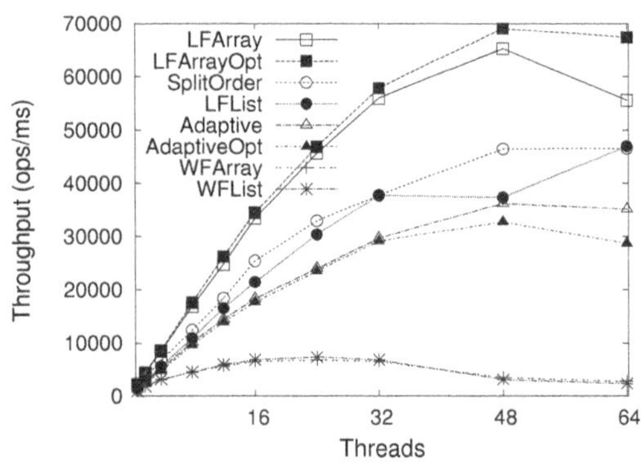

(e) Lookup=34% Range=256

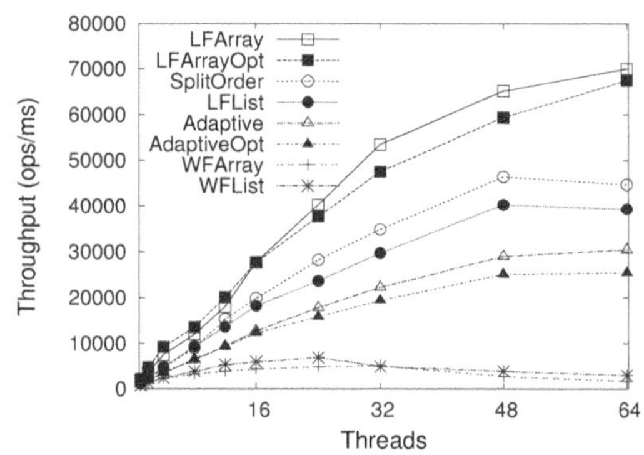

(f) Lookup=34% Range=64K

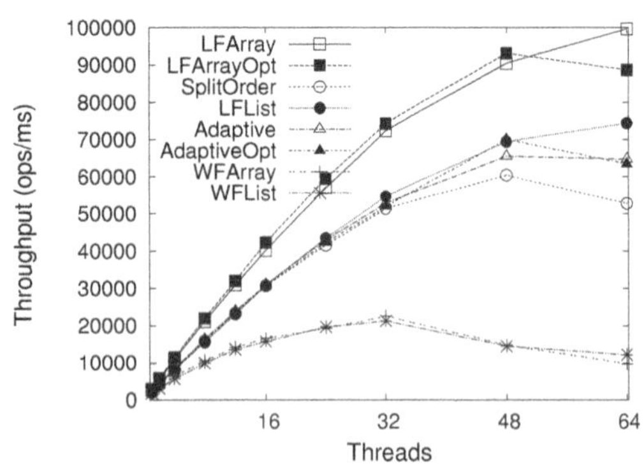

(g) Lookup=80% Range=256

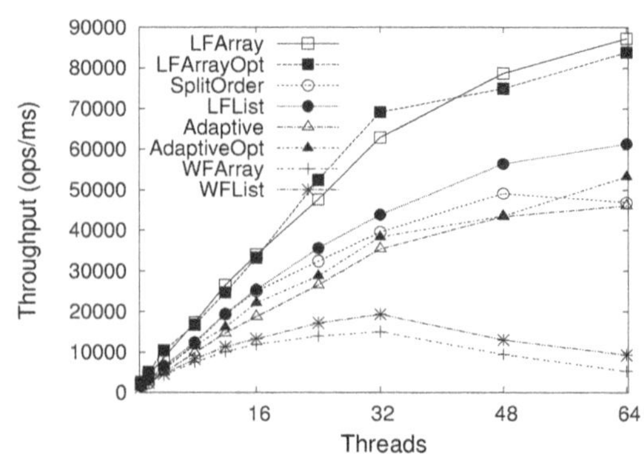

(h) Lookup=80% Range=64K

Figure 7: Microbenchmark Performance on Niagara2

The WFArray and WFList implementations show limited scaling, except when lookups dominate. The poor performance is due to the cost of announcing every operation: incrementing a single global shared counter is a bottleneck, as is the use of the WFOP array for announcing operations and finding threads to help. The Fastpath/Slowpath technique does much to recover this cost. However, even though our threshold of 256 failures virtually guarantees no fallbacks to the slow path, wait-free FSET operations still carry a cost due to extra memory indirection and allocation.

8.2 x86 Performance

In experiments on a 6-core/12-thread Intel Xeon 5650, our algorithms behaved similarly to the Niagara2. The key differences were that there was little difference between LFArray and LFArray-Opt, and that, at high lookup ratios, the adaptive algorithms were able to close much of the gap with LFList. Given the much different microarchitecture of the X5650, the lack of significant difference between these results and those reported for the Niagara2 give confidence that the behaviors we observed were consequences of the fundamental characteristics of our algorithms, rather than architecture-specific anomalies. In particular, the locality afforded by implementing each bucket as an array enables LFArray to outperform SplitOrder in most cases.

9. CONCLUSIONS AND FUTURE WORK

In this paper, we introduced new lock-free and wait-free hash tables, which differ from prior efforts in that they allow keys to be moved among buckets during a resize, without sacrificing throughput or progress. Our technique allows the hash table's buckets to be implemented as arrays, which increases locality and reduces pointer chasing. Our practical wait-free algorithms also demonstrate the resilience of the Fastpath/Slowpath technique [11]: it took little effort to make our lock-free algorithms wait-free, and the result was dramatically faster than a naive wait-free solution.

The interaction between the FSET objects used within the table and the implementation of scaffolding of the hash table leaves some opportunity for improvement. Most significantly, the copy-on-write algorithm we use might be replaced by hardware transactions, if it were possible to still guarantee progress. Another question involves extending the set to a map: in this case, again, the copy-on-write technique is likely to prove valuable, since it avoids the need to atomically modify distinct key and value fields.

Acknowledgments

We thank Alex Kogan, Victor Luchangco, and our anonymous reviewers, whose detailed suggestions greatly improved this paper.

10. REFERENCES

[1] C. S. Ellis. Extendible Hashing for Concurrent Operations and Distributed Data. In *Proceedings of the Second ACM SIGACT-SIGMOD Symposium on Principles of Database Systems*, Atlanta, GA, Mar. 1983.

[2] C. S. Ellis. Concurrency in Linear Hashing. *ACM Transactions on Database Systems*, 12(2):195–217, 1987.

[3] S. Feldman, P. LaBorde, and D. Dechev. Concurrent Multi-Level Arrays: Wait-Free Extensible Hash Maps. In *Proceedings of the 13th International Conference on Embedded Computer Systems: Architectures, Modeling, and Simulation*, Samos Island, Greece, July 2013.

[4] H. Gao, J. F. Groote, and W. H. Hesselink. Almost Wait-Free Resizable Hashtable. In *Proceedings of the 18th International Parallel and Distributed Processing Symposium*, Santa Fe, NM, Apr. 2004.

[5] M. Greenwald. Two-Handed Emulation: How to Build Non-Blocking Implementation of Complex Data-Structures using DCAS. In *Proceedings of the 21st ACM Symposium on Principles of Distributed Computing*, Monterey, California, July 2002.

[6] T. Harris. A Pragmatic Implementation of Non-Blocking Linked Lists. In *Proceedings of the 15th International Symposium on Distributed Computing*, Lisbon, Portugal, Oct. 2001.

[7] M. Herlihy and N. Shavit. *The Art of Multiprocessor Programming*. Morgan Kaufmann, 2008.

[8] M. Herlihy, N. Shavit, and M. Tzafrir. Hopscotch Hashing. In *Proceedings of the 22nd International Symposium on Distributed Computing*, Arcachon, France, Sept. 2008.

[9] M. P. Herlihy and J. M. Wing. Linearizability: a Correctness Condition for Concurrent Objects. *ACM Transactions on Programming Languages and Systems*, 12(3):463–492, 1990.

[10] M. Hsu and W.-P. Yang. Concurrent Operations in Extendible Hashing. In *Proceedings of the 12th International Conference on Very Large Data Bases*, Kyoto, Japan, Aug. 1986.

[11] A. Kogan and E. Petrank. A Methodology for Creating Fast Wait-Free Data Structures. In *Proceedings of the 16th ACM Symposium on Principles and Practice of Parallel Programming*, New Orleans, LA, Feb. 2012.

[12] V. Kumar. Concurrent Operations on Extendible Hashing and its Performance. *Communications of the ACM*, 33(6):681–694, 1990.

[13] L. Lamport. A New Solution of Dijkstra's Concurrent Programming Problem. *Communications of the ACM*, 17(8):453–455, 1974.

[14] V. Luchangco, M. Moir, and N. Shavit. Nonblocking k-compare-single-swap. In *Proceedings of the 15th ACM Symposium on Parallel Algorithms and Architectures*, San Diego, CA, June 2003.

[15] M. Michael. High Performance Dynamic Lock-Free Hash Tables and List-Based Sets. In *Proceedings of the 14th ACM Symposium on Parallel Algorithms and Architectures*, Winnipeg, Manitoba, Canada, Aug. 2002.

[16] C. Purcell and T. Harris. Non-blocking Hashtables with Open Addressing. In *Proceedings of the 19th International Symposium on Distributed Computing*, Cracow, Poland, Sept. 2005.

[17] O. Shalev and N. Shavit. Split-Ordered Lists: Lock-Free Extensible Hash Tables. *Journal of the ACM*, 53(3):379–405, 2006.

[18] J. Triplett, P. McKenney, and J. Walpole. Resizable, Scalable, Concurrent Hash Tables via Relativistic Programming. In *Proceedings of the USENIX Annual Technical Conference*, Portland, OR, June 2011.

[19] D. Zhang and P.-Å. Larson. LHlf: Lock-Free Linear Hashing (Poster Paper). In *Proceedings of the 16th ACM Symposium on Principles and Practice of Parallel Programming*, New Orleans, LA, Feb. 2012.

[20] K. Zhang, Y. Zhao, Y. Yang, Y. Liu, and M. Spear. Practical Non-Blocking Unordered Lists. In *Proceedings of the 27th International Symposium on Distributed Computing*, Jerusalem, Israel, Oct. 2013.

Trade-offs between Selection Complexity and Performance when Searching the Plane without Communication*

Christoph Lenzen
MIT
Cambridge, MA, USA
clenzen@csail.mit.edu

Nancy Lynch
MIT
Cambridge, MA, USA
lynch@csail.mit.edu

Calvin Newport
Georgetown University
Washington D.C., USA
cnewport@cs.georgetown.edu

Tsvetomira Radeva
MIT
Cambridge, MA, USA
radeva@csail.mit.edu

ABSTRACT

We argue that in the context of biology-inspired problems in computer science, in addition to studying the *time complexity* of solutions it is also important to study the *selection complexity*, a measure of how likely a given algorithmic strategy is to arise in nature. In this spirit, we propose a selection complexity metric χ for the ANTS problem [Feinerman et al.]. For algorithm $\mathcal{A}$, we define $\chi(\mathcal{A}) = b + \log \ell$, where b is the number of memory bits used by each agent and ℓ bounds the fineness of available probabilities (agents use probabilities of at least $1/2^{\ell}$).

We consider n agents searching for a target in the plane, within an (unknown) distance D from the origin. We identify $\log\log D$ as a crucial threshold for our selection complexity metric. We prove a new upper bound that achieves near-optimal speed-up of $(D^2/n + D) \cdot 2^{\mathcal{O}(\ell)}$ for $\chi(\mathcal{A}) \leq 3\log\log D + \mathcal{O}(1)$, which is asymptotically optimal if $\ell \in \mathcal{O}(1)$. By comparison, previous algorithms achieving similar speed-up require $\chi(\mathcal{A}) = \Omega(\log D)$. We show that this threshold is tight by proving that if $\chi(\mathcal{A}) < \log\log D - \omega(1)$, then with high probability the target is not found if each agent performs $D^{2-o(1)}$ moves. This constitutes a sizable gap to the straightforward $\Omega(D^2/n + D)$ lower bound.

Categories and Subject Descriptors

F.2.3 [**Analysis of Algorithms and Problem Complexity**]: Tradeoffs between Complexity Measures; G.3 [**Probability and Statistics**]: Markov processes; G.2.2 [**Graph Theory**]: Graph algorithms

*This work is supported in part by AFOSR Contract Number FA9550-13-1-0042, NSF Award numbers: 0939370-CCF, CCF-1217506, CCF-AF-0937274, CCF 1320279, the DFG under reference number Le 3107/1-1., and the Ford University Research Program.

PODC'14, July 15–18, 2014, Paris, France.

ACM 978-1-4503-2944-6/14/07 ...$15.00.
http://dx.doi.org/10.1145/2611462.2611463 .

Keywords

distributed algorithms; biology-inspired algorithms; search algorithms; Markov chains; mobile agents

1. INTRODUCTION

It is increasingly accepted by biologists and computer scientists that the tools of distributed computation can improve our understanding of distributed biological processes. Examples include problems inspired by social insects: foraging for food [11, 12, 13], deciding on a location for a new nest [22], collectively carrying a large object [6]. A standard approach is to translate a biological process of interest (e.g., ant foraging [11, 13] or sensory organ pre-cursor selection [1]) into a formal problem in a distributed computing model, and then prove upper and lower bounds on the problem. The aim is to use these bounds to gain insight into the behavior of the motivating biological process.

A recognized pitfall of this approach is *incongruous analysis*, in which theoreticians focus on metrics relevant to computation but not biology, or ignore metrics relevant to biology but not to computation. Motivated by this pitfall, we promote the use of *selection complexity* metrics for studying biology-inspired distributed problems. Unlike standard metrics from computation, which tend to focus only on performance, selection complexity metrics attempt to measure the difficulty of a given algorithmic strategy arising in nature as the result of selective pressures. Roughly speaking, a solution with low selection complexity should be more likely to arise in nature than one with high selection complexity.

We argue that theoreticians who study biology-inspired problems should evaluate solutions in terms of selection complexity in addition to focusing on standard performance metrics; perhaps even measuring the trade-off between the two classes of metrics. This paper provides a case study of this approach by fixing a standard biology-inspired problem and new selection complexity metric, and then bounding the trade-off between performance and selection complexity with respect to this metric. In doing so, we also obtain results regarding concurrent non-uniform random walks that are of independent mathematical interest.

We recognize that most papers on biology-inspired distributed problems implicitly address selection complexity in their fixed model constraints. Restricting agents to not have access to communication in the search problem, for example, is a constraint that likely lowers the selection complexity of solutions in the model. What is new about our approach is that we are capturing such complexity in a variable metric, allowing us to study the trade-offs between algorithmic power and performance more generally. This can provide insights beyond those gained by characterizing the capabilities of a given static set of constraints.

In this paper, we focus on the problem of n probabilistic non-communicating agents collaboratively searching for a target placed in a two-dimensional grid at (unknown) distance D from the origin. For our lower bound, we assume that n is polynomial in D.[1] This problem is described and analyzed in recent work by Feinerman et al. [13] (referred to as the ANTS problem), who argue that it provides a good approximation of insect foraging and represents a useful intersection between biological behavior and distributed computation. The analysis in [13] focuses on the *speed-up* performance metric, which measures how the expected time to find the target improves with n. The authors describe and analyze search algorithms that closely approximate the straightforward $\Omega(D+D^2/n)$ lower bound for finding a target placed at distance D from the origin.

1.1 Selection Metric Motivation

We consider the selection complexity metric χ, which captures the bits of memory and probabilistic range used by a given algorithm. This metric is motivated by the fact that memory can be used to simulate small probability values, and such values give more power to algorithms, e.g. permitting longer directed walks with a given amount of memory. In more detail, for algorithm $\mathcal{A}$, we define $\chi(\mathcal{A}) = b + \log \ell$, where b is the number of bits of memory required by the algorithm and ℓ is the smallest value such that all probabilities used in $\mathcal{A}$ are bounded from below by $1/2^\ell$. In Section 3 and Section 4, we show that the choice of the selection metric arises naturally from the analysis of our algorithms and the lower bound.

We conjecture that, from a biological perspective, it is reasonable to assume that large values of ℓ imply higher selection complexity. Clearly, algorithms relying on small probabilities are more sensitive to additive disturbances of the probability values. Hence, a small probability based on a single event is harder to create, since the event must not only have a strong bias towards one outcome, but also be well-protected against influencing factors (like temperature, noise, etc.). On the other hand, using multiple independent events to simulate one with larger bias (also known as probability boosting) constitutes a hidden cost. Our model and algorithms make this cost explicit, by accounting for it in terms of the memory needed for counting such events.

1.2 Results

In this paper, we generalize the problem of [13] by also considering the selection complexity metric χ. We identify $\log\log D$, for target within distance D, as a crucial threshold for the χ metric when studying the achievable speed-up in the foraging problem. In more detail, our lower bound proves that for any algorithm $\mathcal{A}$ such that $\chi(\mathcal{A}) \leq \log\log D - \omega(1)$, there is a placement of the target within distance D such that the probability that $\mathcal{A}$ finds the target in fewer than $D^{2-o(1)}$ moves of each agent is polynomially small in D, and the probability of finding a target placed randomly within this distance is $o(1)$. The *speed-up* in this case is bounded from above by $\min\{n, D^{o(1)}\}$, as opposed to the optimal speed-up of $\min\{n, D\}$. At the core of our lower bound is a novel analysis of recurrence behavior of small Markov chains with probabilities of at least $1/2^\ell$.

Concerning upper bounds, we note that the foraging algorithms in [13] achieve near-optimal speed-up in n, but their selection complexity, as measured by $\chi(\mathcal{A})$, is higher than the $\log\log D$ threshold identified by our lower bound: these algorithms require sufficiently fine-grained probabilities and enough memory to randomly generate and store, respectively, coordinates up to distance at least D from the origin; this entails $\chi(\mathcal{A}) \geq \log D$. In this paper, we seek upper bounds that work for $\chi(\mathcal{A}) \approx \log\log D$, the minimum value for which good speed-up is possible. With this in mind, we begin by describing and analyzing a very simple algorithm that is non-uniform in D (agents know the value of D) and has asymptotically optimal expected running time. It illustrates our main ideas of walking up to certain points in the plane while counting approximately, thus using little memory, and showing that this is sufficient for searching the plane efficiently. This algorithm uses a value of $\chi = \log\log D + \mathcal{O}(1)$, which matches our lower bound result for χ up to factor $1 + o(1)$.

We generalize the ideas used in our simple algorithm to derive a solution that is uniform in D. The main idea is to start with some estimate of D and keep increasing it while executing a corresponding version of the simple search algorithm described above for each such estimate. Our uniform algorithm solves the problem after $\mathcal{O}(D^2/n+D)\cdot 2^{\mathcal{O}(\ell)}$ moves of each agent in expectation (if $\ell = \mathcal{O}(1)$, the algorithm matches the $\Omega(D^2/n + D)$ lower bound), for $\chi(\mathcal{A}) \leq 3\log\log D + \mathcal{O}(1)$. We remark that the increased running time is due to the fact that in order to keep the value of χ small, we increase our estimate of D by a factor of $2^{\mathcal{O}(\ell)}$ each time, which may result in "overshooting" the correct distance by factor $2^{\mathcal{O}(\ell)}$. Also, this suboptimal expected running time arises from enforcing $o(\log\log D)$ memory bits; otherwise, one is always free to use only constant probabilities.

1.3 Discussion

An interesting question that arises from our results is the relationship between b and ℓ in the definition of $\chi(\mathcal{A})$: roughly speaking, more bits of memory might be of greater utility than having access to smaller probabilities. This seems intuitive given that smaller probability values can be simulated using additional memory (e.g., to simulate a coin that returns heads with probability $1/2^k$, flip a uniform coin k times while storing the number of coin tosses in the additional memory), but in general more precise probabilities cannot be used to simulate additional memory.

From a biological perspective, we do not claim that χ is necessarily the *right* selection metric to use in studying such problems. We chose it because b and ℓ seem to be important factors in search, and they are potentially difficult to increase in nature. However, we recognize that the refinement and validation of such metrics require close collaboration with evolutionary biologists. In this paper, our main goal is to advertise the selection complexity approach as a promising tool for studying biology-inspired problems.

From a mathematical perspective, we emphasize that our lower bound result is of independent interest. It is known

[1] Note that an exponential number of agents finds the target quickly even if they employ simple random walks.

that uniform random walks do not provide substantial speed-up in searching the plane [3]; the speed-up is bounded by $\min\{\log n, D\}$. Our lower bound generalizes this observation from uniform random walks to probabilistic processes with bounded probabilities and small state complexities.

1.4 Related Work

This work was initially inspired by the results in [11] and [13], which originally introduced the ANTS problem. More precisely, [13] presents an algorithm to find the target in optimal expected time $\mathcal{O}(D^2/n+D)$, assuming that each agent in the algorithm knows the number of agents n (but not D). For unknown n, [13] shows that for every constant $\epsilon > 0$, there exists a uniform search algorithm that is $\mathcal{O}(\log^{1+\epsilon} k)$-competitive, but there is no uniform search algorithm that is $\mathcal{O}(\log k)$-competitive. In [11], Feinerman et al. provide multiple lower bounds on the advice size (number of bits of information the agents are given prior to the search), which can be used to store the value n, some approximation of it, or any other information. In particular, they show that in order for an algorithm to be $\mathcal{O}(\log^{1-\epsilon} n)$-competitive, the agents need advice size of $\Omega(\log\log n)$ bits. Note that this result also implies a lower bound of $\Omega(\log\log n)$ bits on the total size of the memory of the agents, but only under the condition that optimal speed-up is required. Our lower bound is stronger in that we show that there is an exponential gap of $D^{1-o(1)}$ to the maximum speed-up if $\chi(\mathcal{A})$ is too small (and n is polynomial in D). Also, the algorithms in [13] require $\Omega(\log D)$ bits of memory, as contrasted with our algorithm that uses $b \leq 3\log\log D + \mathcal{O}(1)$ bits of memory.

Searching and exploration of various types of graphs by single and multiple agents are widely studied. Several works study the case of a single agent exploring directed graphs [2, 5, 7], undirected graphs [21, 23], or trees [8, 16]. Out of these, the following papers have restrictions on the memory used in the search: [16] uses $\mathcal{O}(\log n)$ bits to explore an n-node tree, [5] studies the power of a pebble placed on a vertex so that the vertex can later be identified, [8] shows that $\Omega(\log\log n)$ bits of memory are needed to explore some n-node trees, and [23] presents a log-space algorithm for *st*-connectivity. There have been works on graph exploration with multiple agents [3, 9, 15]; while [3] and [15] do not include any memory bounds, [9] presents an optimal algorithm for searching in a grid with constant memory and constant-sized messages in a model [10] of very limited computation and communication capabilities. Note that even though these models restrict the agents' memory, the fact that the models allow communication makes it possible to simulate larger memory.

In the above papers, we have seen that the metrics typically considered by computer scientists in graph search algorithms are usually the amount of memory used and the running time. In contrast, biologists look at a much wider range of models and metrics, more closely related to the physical capabilities of the agents. For example, in [4] the focus is on the capabilities of foragers to learn about different new environments, [17] considers the physical fitness of agents and the abundance and quality of the food sources, [18] considers interesting navigational capabilities of ants and assumes no communication between them, [19] measures the efficiency of foraging in terms of the energy over time spent per agent, and [24] explores the use of different chemicals used by ants to communicate with one another.

2. MODEL

Our model is similar to the models considered in [11, 13]. We consider an infinite two-dimensional square grid with coordinates in $\mathbb{Z}^2$. The grid is to be explored by $n \in \mathbb{N}$ identical, non-communicating, probabilistic agents. Each agent is always located at a point on the grid. Agents can move in one of four directions, to one of the four adjacent grid points, but they have no information about their current location in the grid. Initially all agents are positioned at the origin. We also assume that an agent can return to the origin, and for the purposes of this paper, we assume this action is based on information provided by an oracle. We also assume the agent returns on a shortest path in the grid that keeps closest to the straight line connecting the origin to its current position. Note that the return path is no longer than the path of the agent away from the origin; therefore, since we are interested in asymptotic complexity, we ignore the lengths of the return paths in our analysis.

Agents. Each agent is modeled as a probabilistic finite state automaton; since agents are identical, so are their state automata. Each automaton is a tuple (S, s_0, δ), where S is a set of states, state $s_0 \in S$ is the unique starting state, and δ is a transition function $\delta : S \to \Pi$, where Π is a set of discrete probability distributions. Thus, δ maps each state $s \in S$ to a discrete probability distribution $\delta(s) = \pi_s$ on S, which denotes the probability of moving from state s to any other state in S. For our lower bound in Section 4, it is convenient to use a Markov chain representation of each agent. We can express each agent as a Markov chain with transition matrix P, such that for each $s_1, s_2 \in S$, $P[s_1][s_2] = \pi_{s_1}(s_2)$, and start state $s_0 \in S$.

In addition to the Markov chain that describes the evolution of an agent's state, we also need to characterize its movement on the grid. We define the labeling function $M : S \to \{\text{up, down, right, left, origin, none}\}$ mapping each state $s \in S$ to an action the agent performs on the grid. For simplicity, we require $M(s_0) = \text{origin}$. Using this labeling function, any sequence of states $(s_i \in S)_{i\in\mathbb{N}}$ is mapped to a sequence of moves in the grid $(M(s_i))_{i\in\mathbb{N}}$ where $M(s_i) = $ none denotes no move in the grid (i.e., s_i does not contribute to the derived sequence of moves) and $M(s_i) = \text{origin}$ means that the agent returns to the origin, as described above.

Executions. An execution of a single agent is defined as a sequence $(s_0, s_1, \cdots)$ of states that an agent visits while executing some algorithm, where s_0 is the start state. An execution of an algorithm with n agents is just an n-tuple of executions of single agents. For our analysis of the lower bound, it is useful to assume a synchronous model. So, we define a *round* of an execution to consist of one transition of each agent in its Markov chain. Note that we do not use such synchrony for our algorithms. In order to consider probabilistic executions, note that the Markov chain (S, P) induces a probability distribution of executions in a natural way, by performing an independent random walk on S with transition probabilities given by P for each of the n agents. For probabilistic executions of all n agents, we consider the product distribution of the agents' individual distributions.

Problem Statement. The goal is to find a target located at some vertex at distance (measured in terms of the max-norm) at most D from the origin. Note that measuring paths in terms of the max-norm gives is a constant-factor approximation of the actual hop distance. We will consider both uniform and non-uniform algorithms with respect to

D; that is, the agents may or may not know the value of D. For simplicity, throughout this paper we will consider algorithms that are non-uniform in n, i.e., the agents' state machine depends on n.[2]

Metrics. We consider both a performance and a selection metric and study the trade-off between the two. We will use the term *step* of an agent interchangeably with a transition of the agent in the Markov chain. We define a *move* of the agent to be a step that the agent performs in its Markov chain resulting in a state labeled up, down, left, or right. We do not count states labeled "none" for our performance metric as we consider them to be part of an agent's local processing. We also ignore the states labeled "origin" because, as we already mentioned, returning back to the origin increases the total number of moves by at most a factor of two and does not affect the asymptotic performance of the algorithm.

For our performance metric, we focus on the asymptotic running time in terms of D and n; more precisely, we are interested in the expected value of the metric M_{moves}: the minimum over all agents of the number of moves of the agent until it finds the target. We define the metric M_{steps} to be the minimum over all agents of the number of steps of the agent until it finds the target.

The selection metric of a state automaton (and thus a corresponding algorithm) is defined as $\chi(\mathcal{A}) = b + \log \ell$, where $b := \lceil \log |S| \rceil$ is the number of bits required to encode all states from S and $\ell \in \mathbb{N}$ is minimal with the property that $1/2^{\ell} \leq \min\{P[s,s'] \mid s,s' \in S \wedge P[s,s'] \neq 0\}$, the smallest non-zero probability value used by the algorithm.

3. ALGORITHMS

In this section, we begin by describing a non-uniform algorithm in D that finds the target in asymptotically optimal time. The main purpose for presenting this algorithm is to illustrate our main techniques in a very simple setting. This algorithm uses probability values of the form $1/D$, which can easily be simulated using only biased coins that show heads with probability $1/2^{\ell}$ for any ℓ such that $\log D$ is an integer multiple of ℓ. We show that the target can be found in asymptotically optimal time using $b = \log\log D - \log \ell + 3$ bits of memory.

We then generalize this algorithm to work for the case of unknown D. This ensures that closer targets are found faster by the algorithm than targets that are far away. The way we achieve this is by starting with an estimate of D equal to 2 and repeatedly increasing it until the target is found. For each such estimate we execute the non-uniform algorithm. Since D is not known by the algorithm anymore, we cannot easily pick fixed values for some of the parameters we use in the algorithm in order to guarantee asymptotically optimal results for all possible values of D. Therefore, in our general algorithm the expected number of moves for the first agent to find the target becomes $(D^2/n + D) \cdot 2^{\mathcal{O}(\ell)}$ for $\chi = 3 \log\log D + \mathcal{O}(1)$. Hence, for $\ell = \mathcal{O}(1)$ the algorithm is asymptotically optimal with respect to both metrics, and we achieve non-trivial speed-up of $\min\{n, D\}/D^{o(1)}$ for any $\ell \in o(\log D)$ (i.e., $\omega(1)$ bits of memory).

[2]We remark that it is possible to apply a technique from [13] in order to generalize our results and obtain an algorithm that is uniform in both D and n.

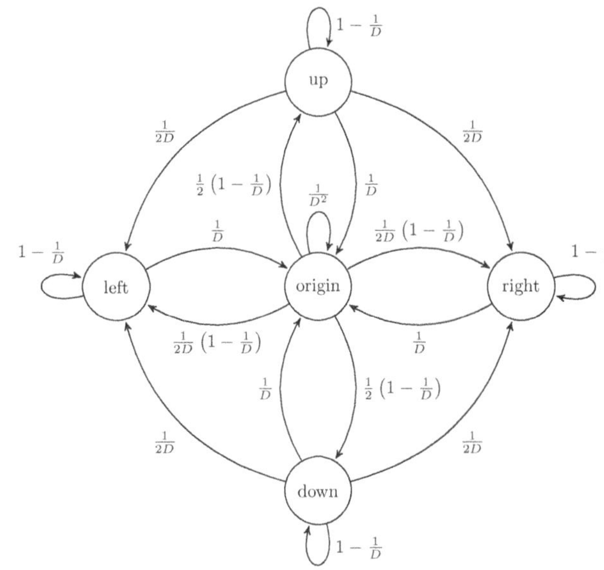

State machine representation of Algorithm 1. State names match the values of the labeling function.

3.1 Non-uniform Algorithm

Our general approach is the following: each agent chooses a vertical direction (up or down) with probability 1/2, walks in that direction for a random number of steps that depends on D, then does the same for the horizontal direction, and finally returns to the origin and repeats this process. We show that the expected number of moves for the first agent to find a target at distance up to D from the origin is at most $\mathcal{O}(D^2/n + D)$. We assume that $D > 1$; the cases of $D = 0$ and $D = 1$ are straightforward.

Let coin C_p denote a coin that shows tails with probability p. Using this convention, the pseudocode of this simple routine is given in Algorithm 1, accompanied by a state machine representation showing that the algorithm can be implemented using only three bits of memory. Later in this section we show that a slightly modified version of the algorithm guarantees that $\chi = \log\log D + 3$.

Algorithm 1: Non-uniform search.

```
while true do
    if coin C_{1/2} shows heads then
        while coin C_{1/D} shows heads do
            move up
    else
        while coin C_{1/D} shows heads do
            move down
    if coin C_{1/2} shows heads then
        while coin C_{1/D} shows heads do
            move left
    else
        while coin C_{1/D} shows heads do
            move right
    return to the origin
```

Next, we state the main performance complexity result and give a brief proof overview. We omit the complete proof of Theorem 3.1 below, since it is a special case of the proof of our uniform algorithm in Theorem 3.6; for additional details, refer to the full version of the paper [20].

THEOREM 3.1. *Let each of n agents execute Algorithm 1. For a target located within distance $D > 1$ from the origin, $\mathbb{E}[M_{moves}] = \mathcal{O}(D^2/n + D)$.*

Proof Sketch. First, we calculate the expected number of moves R for a single agent to complete an iteration of the main loop; by the properties of the geometric distribution $R \leq 2D$. Note that the time to complete an iteration is not independent of whether the target is found or not, so we also compute the value of R conditioning on the event that the agent does *not* find the target in the given iteration; we call this value $\hat{R}$ and we show that $\hat{R} \leq 2R$. Using the value of $\hat{R}$ and the fact that in the iteration in which an agent finds the target this takes at most $2D$ moves, we show that the expected number of moves $R_{i,a}$, for a fixed agent a to complete iteration i if i is the earliest iteration in which agent a finds the target, is at most $4iD$.

Next, we move on to considering all n agents; we calculate the probability q that no agent finds the target after each agent executes one iteration of the main loop. Since the probability for a single agent to find the target in a given iteration is at least $1/(64D)$, we can show $q \leq (1-1/(64D))^n \leq \max\{1 - \Omega(n/D), 1/2\}$, where the first value is for the case $n \leq D$, and the second one for the case $n > D$.

Finally, we calculate $\mathbb{E}[M_{\text{moves}}]$. Let event $\mathcal{E}_i$ denote the event that iteration i is the earliest iteration in which some agent finds the target. Then, $\mathbb{E}[M_{\text{moves}}] = \sum_{i=1}^{\infty} P[\mathcal{E}_i] \cdot \mathbb{E}[M_{\text{moves}}|\mathcal{E}_i]$. The value of $\mathbb{E}[M_{\text{moves}}|\mathcal{E}_i]$ can be calculated using the Law of Total Expectation, by partitioning event $\mathcal{E}_i$ based on which agent finds the target (see Theorem 3.6 for a similar argument). We can then show that

$$\mathbb{E}[M_{\text{moves}}] \leq \sum_{i=1}^{\infty}(1-q)q^{i-1} \cdot \hat{R} = \mathcal{O}(D^2/n + D). \quad \square$$

We now generalize this algorithm to one that uses probabilities lower-bounded by $1/2^\ell$ for some given $\ell \geq 1$. This is achieved by the following subroutine, which implements a coin that shows tails with probability $1/2^{k\ell}$ using a biased coin that shows tails with probability $1/2^\ell$, for $\ell \geq 1$.

Algorithm 2: coin(k,ℓ): Biased coin flip showing tails with probability $1/2^{k\ell}$.

```
for i = 0 ··· k do
 | if C_{1/2^ℓ} shows heads then
 |  | return heads
return tails
```

LEMMA 3.2. *Algorithm 2 returns tails with probability $1/2^{k\ell}$ and uses $\lceil \log k \rceil$ bits of memory.*

Next, we construct Algorithm Non-Uniform-Search by replacing the lines where coin $C_{1/D}$ is tossed in Algorithm 1 with a copy of Algorithm 2, with parameters $k = \lceil \log D/\ell \rceil$ and ℓ. Since Algorithm 2 does not generate any moves on the grid, the complexity bound in Theorem 3.1 holds.

THEOREM 3.3. *Let each of n agents execute Algorithm Non-Uniform-Search. For a target located within distance $D > 1$ from the origin $\mathbb{E}[M_{moves}] = \mathcal{O}(D^2/n + D)$. Moreover, χ(Algorithm Non-Uniform-Search) $= \log\log D + \mathcal{O}(1)$.*

3.2 Uniform Algorithm

In this section, we generalize the results from Section 3.1 to derive an algorithm that is uniform in D. The main difference is that now each agent maintains an estimate of D that it increases until the target is found. For each estimate, an agent simply executes the corresponding variant of Algorithm Non-Uniform-Search. We show that for the algorithm in this section, the expected number of moves for the first agent to find a target at distance at most D from the origin is $(D^2/n + D)2^{\mathcal{O}(\ell)}$. Also, the algorithm uses only $b = 3\log\log D - 3\log \ell + \mathcal{O}(1)$ bits of memory.

To simplify the presentation, we break up the main algorithm into subroutines. We begin by showing how to move in a given direction by a random number of moves that depends on the current estimate $\hat{D}$ of D. In the following algorithm, recall that ℓ is used to bound from below the smallest probability available to each agent by $1/2^\ell$. We use an integer k as a parameter in order to generate different distance estimates $\hat{D} = 2^{k\ell}$.

Algorithm 3: walk(k,ℓ,dir): Move by a random number of moves in direction dir.

```
while coin(k, ℓ) = heads do
 | move one step in direction dir
```

LEMMA 3.4. *For $i \in \{0, \ldots, 2^{k\ell}\}$, the probability that an agent executing Algorithm 3 makes exactly i moves is at least $1/2^{k\ell+2}$. The probability that it makes at least $2^{k\ell}$ moves is at least $1/4$. The expected number of moves is smaller than $2^{k\ell}$. The algorithm uses $\lceil \log k \rceil$ bits of memory.*

This lemma follows from basic properties of the geometric distribution.

Using the subroutines above, Algorithm 4 visits each grid point of a square of side length $2^{k\ell}$ centered at the origin with probability $\Omega(1/2^{2k\ell})$.

Algorithm 4: search(k,ℓ): Visit each grid point of a square of side length $2^{k\ell}$ centered at the origin with probability $\Omega(1/2^{2k\ell})$.

```
if if C_{1/2} shows heads then
 | walk(k, ℓ,up)
else
 | walk(k, ℓ,down)
if C_{1/2} shows heads then
 | walk(k, ℓ,right)
else
 | walk(k, ℓ,left)
```

LEMMA 3.5. *An agent executing Algorithm 4 from the origin visits each point $(x, y) \in \{0, \ldots, 2^{k\ell}\}^2$ with probability at least $1/2^{k\ell+6}$. Algorithm 4 uses $\lceil \log k \rceil + 2$ bits of memory.*

The lemma follows by observing that to move to a specific point (x, y) in the grid an agent needs (i) two specific outcomes of the unbiased coins (probability 1/2 each), (ii) exactly $|y|$ steps up/down (probability $1/2^{k\ell+2}$ by Lemma 3.4), and (iii) at least $|x|$ steps left/right (probability 1/4 by Lemma 3.4).

Finally, in Algorithm 5, we use Algorithm 4 to efficiently search an area of $\mathcal{O}(D^2)$ with n agents. The algorithm iterates through different values of the outer-loop parameter i, which correspond to the different estimates of D, increasing by approximately a factor of 2^ℓ in each iteration. For each such estimate, the algorithm needs to execute a number of calls to the search subroutine with parameter i. However, since agents have limited memory and limited probability values, we can only count the number of such calls to the search routine approximately. We do so similarly to Algorithm 3, by repeatedly tossing a biased coin and calling the search algorithm as long as the coin shows heads.

Algorithm 5: Search Algorithm for n agents. K is a sufficiently large constant.

```
for i = 1, ... do
    while coin(K + max{i − ⌊(log n)/ℓ⌋, 0}, ℓ) = heads do
        search(i, ℓ)
        return to the origin
```

Throughout the rest of the proofs, we refer to an iteration of the outer-most loop of Algorithm 5 as a phase.

THEOREM 3.6. *Let each of n agents execute Algorithm 5. For a target located within distance $D > 1$ from the origin, $\mathbb{E}[M_{moves}] \leq 2^{\mathcal{O}(\ell)}(D + D^2/n)$.*

Proof Overview. First, in Lemma 3.7, we calculate the expected number of moves R_i for an agent to complete phase i. Then, we determine the expected number of moves $\tilde{R}_{i,a}$ for an agent a to complete phase i (past some initial number of $\lceil \log_{2^\ell} D \rceil$ phases), conditioning on agent a finding the target in phase i, but not earlier. Next, we move on to reasoning about all n agents, instead of a single agent. In Lemma 3.9, we bound the probability that in each phase i, at least $\Omega(2^{i\ell})$ calls to the subroutine search(i, ℓ) are executed by all agents together. In Lemma 3.10, we use this result to calculate the probability that at least one of the n agents finds the target in some phase i. Finally, we use these intermediate results to prove the main result of this section, Theorem 3.6, which shows that the expected number of moves for the first agent to find a target within distance D from the origin is $(D + D^2/n) \cdot 2^{\mathcal{O}(\ell)}$.

Denote by R_i the expected number of moves until an agent completes phase i. Let $\rho_i := 2^{(K+\max\{i-\lfloor(\log n)/\ell\rfloor,0\})\ell}$.

LEMMA 3.7. $R_i \leq 4\rho_i 2^{i\ell}$.

PROOF. Using linearity of expectation and independence of coin flips, R_i is the nested sum over all phases $i' \leq i$, of the number j of calls to the search subroutine times the probability that j such calls are executed, and the number of moves k for an agent to complete a given call to the search subroutine times the respective probability: $\sum_{i'=1}^{i}(\sum_{j=0}^{\infty} 1/\rho_{i'}(1-1/\rho_{i'})^j \sum_{k=0}^{\infty} 1/2^{i'\ell}(1-1/2^{i'\ell})^k \cdot 2k) < 4\rho_i 2^{i\ell}$. □

Denote by $\tilde{R}_{i,a}$ the expected number of moves until a given agent a finds the target, conditioning on the fact that agent a finds the target in phase $i \in \mathbb{N}$, but no earlier phase.

COROLLARY 3.8. *If $i \geq i_0 = \lceil \log_{2^\ell} D \rceil$, then it holds that $\tilde{R}_{i,a} \leq 8\rho_i 2^{i\ell} + 2D = 2^{\max\{2i\ell - \log n, i\ell\}} \cdot 2^{\mathcal{O}(\ell)}$.*

PROOF. In the (first) call to the search subroutine in which agent a finds the target, it walks directly to the target, which takes at most $2D$ moves. Hence[3] $\tilde{R}_{i,a} \leq \tilde{R}'_{i,a} + 2D$, where $\tilde{R}'_{i,a}$ is the random variable counting all moves of a up to and including phase i, conditioning on a *not* finding the target in any of these phases. By the pseudocode, it is clear that the probability for an agent to miss the target in a given call to the search subroutine is at least $1/2$. We partition the probability space according to the events that (1) the target is found during a given call to search, and (2) the target is not found during a given call to search. From the law of total expectation, it follows that $R_i \leq 1/2 \cdot \tilde{R}'_{i,a}$, so $\tilde{R}_{i,a} \leq \tilde{R}'_{i,a} + 2D \leq 2R_i + 2D$. The claim now follows from Lemma 3.7 and the fact that $2^{i\ell} \geq 2^{i_0\ell} \geq D$. □

At this point, we start considering a probability distribution for all n agents, as opposed to a single agent. Denote by $\mathcal{E}_1(i)$ the event that in total at least $2^{(K/2+i)\ell}$ calls to search(i, ℓ) are executed in phase i.

LEMMA 3.9. $P[\mathcal{E}_1(i)] \geq 1 - 1/2^{2\ell+2}$.

PROOF. By Lemma 3.2 and linearity of expectation, the expected number of calls to search(ℓ, i) performed by all agents during phase i is:

$$n \sum_{j=1}^{\infty} 1/\rho_i \cdot (1 - 1/\rho_i)^j \cdot j \geq n/2 \cdot \rho_i \geq 2^{(K+i-1)\ell}.$$

Since the coin flips are independent, we can apply a Chernoff bound to show that the probability that fewer than $2^{(K/2+i)\ell}$ searches are executed in total is at most $e^{-\Omega(K\ell)}$. The claim follows since K is a sufficiently large constant. □

Denote by $\mathcal{E}_2(i)$ the event that the target is found by some agent in phase i. Let $i_0 = \lceil \log_{2^\ell} D \rceil$.

LEMMA 3.10. *For $i \geq i_0$, $P[\mathcal{E}_2(i)] \geq 1 - 1/2^{2\ell+1}$.*

PROOF. By Lemma 3.9, with probability at least $1 - 1/2^{2\ell+2}$, at least $2^{(K/2+i)\ell}$ iterations of the while loop are executed in total. Because $i \geq i_0 \geq \log_{2^\ell} D$, i.e., $2^{i\ell} \geq D$, Lemma 3.5 shows that in each iteration, the probability to find the target is at least $1/2^{i\ell+6}$. Therefore, the probability to miss the target in all calls is at most $(1 - 1/2^{i\ell+6})^{2^{(K/2+i)\ell}} = 2^{-\Omega(K\ell)}$.

Because K is sufficiently large, we may assume that this is at most $1/2^{2\ell+2}$. We infer that $P[\mathcal{E}_2(i)] \geq P[\mathcal{E}_2(i) \mid \mathcal{E}_1(i)] \cdot P[\mathcal{E}_1(i)] \geq (1 - 1/2^{2\ell+2})^2 \geq 1 - 1/2^{2\ell+1}$. □

PROOF OF THEOREM 3.6. Let $\mathcal{E}_3(i)$ denote the event that the target is found for the first time in phase i. Observe that because the probability to find the target in phase i is independent of all coin flips in earlier phases, by Lemma 3.10 it follows that for $i \geq i_0$:

$$P[\mathcal{E}_3(i)] \leq \prod_{i'=i_0}^{i-1} (1 - P[\mathcal{E}_2(i')]) \leq 1/2^{(2\ell+1)(i-i_0)}.$$

Let random variable X denote the number of moves until the first agent finds the target.

$$\mathbb{E}[X] = \sum_{i=1}^{\infty} P[\mathcal{E}_3(i)] \cdot \mathbb{E}[X|\mathcal{E}_3(i)].$$

[3]This inequality is to be read as probabilistic domination.

Fix an arbitrary order of the agents (independently of the execution). We partition event $\mathcal{E}_3(i)$ into disjoint events $\mathcal{E}_3(i,a)$, where $\mathcal{E}_3(i,a)$ denotes the event that agent a is the minimal agent w.r.t. the chosen order that finds the target in phase i (by the definition of $\mathcal{E}_3(i)$, we know that such an agent exists). By the law of total expectation applied to the partition of event $\mathcal{E}_3(i)$, it follows that:

$$\mathbb{E}[X|\mathcal{E}_3(i)] = \sum_a P[\mathcal{E}_3(i,a)|\mathcal{E}_3(i)] \cdot \mathbb{E}[X|\mathcal{E}_3(i,a)].$$

Let random variable $X_{i,a}$ denote the number of moves agent a takes to complete iteration i. Note that because we condition on event $\mathcal{E}_3(i,a)$, we know that the expected number of moves until the target is found by *some* agent is at most the expected number of moves for the fixed agent a to find the target and complete iteration i. Therefore, it follows that $\mathbb{E}[X|\mathcal{E}_3(i,a)] \leq \mathbb{E}[X_{i,a}|\mathcal{E}_3(i,a)]$.

By definition, we have $\mathbb{E}[X_{i,a}|\mathcal{E}_3(i,a)] = \tilde{R}_{i,a}$. We conclude that $\mathbb{E}[X|\mathcal{E}_3(i)]$ is upper-bounded by:

$$\sum_a P[\mathcal{E}_3(i,a)|\mathcal{E}_3(i)] \cdot \tilde{R}_{i,a} = \tilde{R}_{i,a} \cdot \sum_a P[\mathcal{E}_3(i,a)|\mathcal{E}_3(i)] = \tilde{R}_{i,a}$$

Finally, we sum over all phases to calculate the value of $\mathbb{E}[X]$. Using Corollary 3.8, we bound $\mathbb{E}[X]$ by.

$$\begin{aligned} &\sum_{i=1}^{i_0} P[\mathcal{E}_3(i)] \cdot \tilde{R}_{i,a} + \sum_{i=i_0+1}^{\infty} P[\mathcal{E}_3(i)] \cdot \tilde{R}_{i,a} \\ \leq\ & \tilde{R}_{i_0,a} + \sum_{i=i_0+1}^{\infty} \frac{1}{2^{(2\ell+1)(i-i_0)}} \cdot 2^{\max\{2i\ell - \log n, i\ell\}} \cdot 2^{\mathcal{O}(\ell)}. \end{aligned}$$

Simple calculations bound this by $\max\{D^2/n, D\} \cdot 2^{\mathcal{O}(\ell)}$. □

4. LOWER BOUND

In this section, we present a lower bound showing that any algorithm $\mathcal{A}$ satisfying $\chi(\mathcal{A}) \leq \log\log D - \omega(1)$ with high probability (w.h.p.) does *not* find a target placed adversarially within distance D from the origin in $D^{2-o(1)}$ rounds. For uniform placement, this holds with probability $1-o(1)$.

Let $c > 1$ be a arbitrary predefined constant. Throughout this section, we say that an event occurs with high probability iff the probability of the event occurring is at least $1 - 1/D^c$ for $D \in \mathbb{N}$. We say that two probability distributions π_1 and π_2 are *approximately equivalent* iff $\|\pi_1 - \pi_2\| = \mathcal{O}(1/D^c)$. By $\|\cdot\|$ we denote the max-norm on the respective space.

First, we state the main theorem of the section in terms of the performance metric M_{steps}. Note that, by the definition of a round, this is equivalent to counting the expected number of rounds until the first agent finds the target. At the end of the section, in Corollary 4.10, we generalize the main result to apply to metric M_{moves}.

THEOREM 4.1. *Let $\mathcal{A}$ be an algorithm with $\chi(\mathcal{A}) = b + \log\ell \leq \log\log D - \omega(1)$ and let each of $n \in poly(D)$ agents execute algorithm $\mathcal{A}$. There is a placement of the target within distance D from the origin for which w.h.p. $M_{steps} \geq D^{2-o(1)}$. Moreover, if the target is placed uniformly at random in the square of side $2D$ centered at the origin, then $M_{steps} = D^{2-o(1)}$ with probability $o(1)$.*

4.1 Proof Overview

Here we provide a high-level overview of our main proof argument. We fix an algorithm $\mathcal{A}$ and focus on executions of this algorithm of $D^{2-o(1)}$ rounds. We prove that since agents have $o(\log D)$ states, they "forget" about past events too fast to behave substantially different from a biased random walk.

More concretely, first we show, in Corollary 4.3, that after $D^{o(1)}$ initial rounds each agent a is located in some recurrent class $C(a)$ of the Markov chain. We use this corollary to prove, in Corollary 4.4, that after the initial $D^{o(1)}$ rounds each agent a does not return to the origin (or it keeps returning every $D^{o(1)}$ rounds, so it does not explore much of the grid). Therefore, throughout the rest of the proof we can essentially ignore the states labeled "origin".

Assume there is a unique stationary distribution of $C(a)$[4]. Since the number of states is bounded from above and non-zero transition probabilities are bounded from below, standard results on Markov chains imply that taking $D^{o(1)}$ steps from any state in the recurrent class will result in a distribution on the class's states that is (almost) indistinguishable from the stationary distribution (Corollary 4.5); in other words, any information agents try to preserve in their state is lost quickly with respect to D.

Next, we split up the rounds in the execution into groups such that within each group, rounds are sufficiently far apart from one another for the above "forgetting" to take place. For each group, we show that drawing states independently from the stationary distribution introduces a negligible error (Lemma 4.6 and Corollary 4.7). Thus, we can apply a Chernoff bound to each group, yielding that agents will not deviate substantially from the expected path they take when, in each round, they draw a state according to the stationary distribution and execute the corresponding move on the grid (Lemma 4.8 and Corollary 4.9). Taking a union bound over all groups, we show that, w.h.p., each agent will not deviate from a straight line (the expected path associated with its recurrent class) by more than distance $o(D/|S|)$, where S is the number of states of the Markov chain. It is crucial that the corresponding region in the grid, restricted to distance D from the origin, has size $o(D^2/|S|)$ and depends only on the agent's recurrent class. Therefore, since there are at most $|S|$ components, taking a union bound over all agents shows that w.h.p. together they visit an area of $o(D^2)$.

4.2 Proof

Without loss of generality, we assume that values like $\ln D$ are integers; for the general case, we can round up. Also, since we are interested in asymptotics with respect to D, we may always assume that D is larger than any given constant.

Fix any algorithm $\mathcal{A}$, some $D \in \mathbb{N}$, and let $b + \log\ell \leq \log\log D - \omega(1)$. Consider the probability distribution of executions of $\mathcal{A}$ of length $\Delta = D^{2-o(1)}$ rounds; we will fix the $o(1)$-term in the exponent later, in Lemma 4.8.

We break the proof down into three main parts. First, in Section 4.2.1, we show that after a certain number of initial rounds each agent is in a recurrent class and, for simplicity, we can ignore the states labeled "origin". Next, in Section 4.2.2, we show that if we break down the execution into large enough blocks of rounds, we can assume that the steps associated with rounds in different blocks do not depend on

[4]The general case of $C(a)$ potentially being periodic is discussed in Section 4.2

each other, within a small error. Finally, in Section 4.2.3, we focus on the movement of the agents in the grid, derived from these "almost" independent steps, and show that w.h.p. the agents do not explore any points outside of an area of size $o(D^2)$ around the origin.

4.2.1 Initial steps in the Markov chain

Let random variable $C(a,r)$ denote the recurrent class of the Markov chain in which agent a is located at the end of round r; if a is in a transient state at the end of round r, we set $C(a,r) := \perp$. Also, by p_0 we denote the smallest non-zero probability in the Markov chain. By assumption, we know that $p_0 \geq 1/2^{\ell}$.

First we show that for any agent a and any state s, if state s is always reachable by agent a, then agent a visits state s within $D^{o(1)}$ rounds. Let $R_0 = p_0^{-2^b} 2^b c \log D = D^{o(1)}$ where the constant $c > 0$ will be specified later.

Lemma 4.2. *For some agent a, round r, state s, condition on the event that during rounds $r, \ldots, r + R_0$ agent a never visits a state s' such that s is not reachable from s'. Then, w.h.p. a visits s in some round $r' \in \{r, \ldots, r + R_0\}$.*

Proof. Since state s remains reachable, there is always a path of length at most $|S| - 1$ from the state in which agent a is in round $r' \in \{r, \ldots, r + R_0\}$ to state s. Therefore, the probability that the agent visits state s within R_0 rounds is bounded from below by the probability that a (biased) random walk on a line of $2^b \geq |S| - 1$ nodes starting at the leftmost node reaches the rightmost node within R_0 rounds. In the following expression we bound this probability from below by observing that the probability for an agent to visit all nodes in the line in one try is $p_0^{2^b}$ and within R_0 rounds the agent can try at most $R_0/2^b$ times. Therefore,

$$1 - (1 - p_0^{2^b})^{R_0/2^b} \geq 1 - 1/2^{\Omega(c \log(D+n))} = 1 - 1/D^{\Omega(c)},$$

where we use the fact that $p_0 \leq 1/2$; otherwise, each state has only one outgoing transition, in which case the claim of the lemma is trivial. Thus, for an appropriate choice of c, w.h.p. agent a visits state s within R_0 rounds. □

In the following corollary we show that for a given agent and any round $r \geq R_0$, w.h.p. the agent is located in some recurrent class of the Markov chain.

Corollary 4.3. *For any agent a and any round $r \geq R_0$, w.h.p. $C(a,r) = C(a, r+1) \neq \perp$.*

The corollary follows from the fact that from any state in the Markov chain, there is always a reachable recurrent state. By Lemma 4.2, w.h.p. the agent reaches such a recurrent state in $D^{o(1)}$ rounds and never subsequently leaves the associated recurrent class.

Since the recurrent class $C(a,r)$ in which agent a is located is the same for all rounds $r \geq R_0$, we will refer to it by $C(a)$. Next, we show that the recurrent class $C(a)$ in which agent a is located does not contain any states labeled "origin", or otherwise, the agent keeps returning to the origin too often and makes no progress exploring the grid.

Corollary 4.4. *W.h.p., at least one of the following is true for any agent a and each round $R_0 \leq r \leq \Delta$: (1) agent a never visits a point in the grid at distance more than $D^{o(1)}$ from the origin, or (2) agent a is located in a recurrent class in which none of the states are labeled "origin".*

The idea of the proof is that if $C(a)$ contains a state labeled "origin", then we can show, by applying Lemma 4.2, that w.h.p. the agent visits that state every $D^{o(1)}$ rounds.

Throughout the rest of the proof, we consider executions after round R_0; since, $R_0 = D^{o(1)}$ and we consider executions of length $\Delta = D^{2-o(1)}$, we can just ignore these initial rounds. Therefore, from Corollary 4.3 and Corollary 4.4, we can assume for the rest of the proof that each agent a is in a recurrent class $C(a)$ and it does not return to the origin.

4.2.2 Moves drawn from the stationary distribution

Consider $C := C(a)$ for a fixed agent a. For the rest of the proof, we assume that C is aperiodic, and thus, has a unique stationary distribution π. In the general case, C applying standard results from Markov chain theory [14, Chapter XV.9] shows that by considering the Markov chain induced by P^t, where P is the probability matrix of the original Markov chain and t is its period, a unique stationary distribution exists for some subset of states of C. For the general case, refer to the full version of the paper [20].

Consider blocks of rounds of size $\beta = c|S| \ln D/p_0^{|S|} = D^{o(1)}$, where $c > 0$ is a sufficiently large constant. We define groups of rounds such that each group contains one round from each block. Formally, for $1 \leq i \leq \beta$ and $j \in \mathbb{N}_0$, group B_i contains round numbers $i + j\beta \leq \Delta$.

Let $\pi_{r+\beta,s}$ denote the probability distribution on C of possible states agent a may be in at the end of round $r + \beta$, conditional on its state being $s \in C$ at the end of round r. Note that this distribution is, in fact, independent of r. We obtain the following corollary of Lemma 2 in [25] applied to the Markov chain restricted to class C.

Recall that two probability distributions π_1 and π_2 are defined to be *approximately equivalent* iff $\|\pi_1 - \pi_2\| = \mathcal{O}(1/D^c)$ for an arbitrary predefined constant $c > 0$.

Corollary 4.5. *There is a unique stationary distribution π of the Markov chain on C. For any state $s \in C$ and any round r, $\pi_{r+\beta,s}$ and π are approximately equivalent.*

From this corollary, we know that probability distributions π and $\pi_{r+\beta,s}$ are close to each other. Next, we identify the probability distribution that constitutes the "gap" between π and $\pi_{r+\beta,s}$.

Lemma 4.6. *Let $1 \leq i \leq \beta$. Then, for any state $s \in C$ and any constant $c > 0$, there exists a probability distribution π_s such that $\forall r \in B_i, r \leq \Delta - \beta:\ \pi_s/D^c + (1 - 1/D^c)\pi = \pi_{r+\beta,s}$, where π is the unique stationary distribution of C.*

Proof Sketch. First, we bound the value of $\pi(s')$ for each $s' \in C$. We can show that $\pi(s') \geq p_0^{|S|}$ because p_0 is the minimum transition probability of getting to state s' from any other state, and we can do this at most $|S|$ times. Since $b + \log \ell \leq \log\log D - \omega(1)$, it follows that $p_0^{|S|} \geq 1/D^{o(1)}$. This also implies that $\pi(s') \leq 1 - 1/D^{o(1)}$ (assuming $|C| > 1$). Using the above equation involving π_s as definition, we can show that π_s is a probability distribution, i.e., for each $s' \in C$, $0 \leq \pi_s(s') \leq 1$ and $\sum_{s' \in C} \pi_s(s') = 1$. Here, we leverage that by, Corollary 4.5, π and $\pi_{r+\beta,s}$ are approximately equivalent. □

We now show that within each class B_i, approximating the random walk of an agent in the Markov chain by drawing its state for each round $r \in B_i$ *independently* from the stationary distribution π does not introduce a substantial error. To this end, consider the following random experiment E_i. For each round $r + \beta \le \Delta$, $r \in B_i$, we toss an independent biased coin such that it shows heads w.h.p. In this case, we draw the state at the end of round r independently from π. Otherwise, we draw it from the distribution π_s, where s is the state the agent was in β steps ago and π_s is the distribution given by Lemma 4.6. Since each time the coin shows heads w.h.p., a union bound shows that it holds that w.h.p. the coin shows head in *all* rounds $r \in B_i$.

COROLLARY 4.7. *If the experiment E_i described above is executed with probability of heads being $1 - 1/D^{c+2}$, where c is the constant fixed in the beginning of the section (in the definition of "approximately equivalent"), w.h.p. no coin flip shows tail. In other words, for each round r, the state of the agent at the end of round $r + \beta \le \Delta$, $r \in B_i$, is drawn independently from the stationary distribution π.*

4.2.3 Movement on the grid

Having established that an agent's state can essentially be understood as a (sufficiently small) collection of sets of independent random variables, we focus on the implications on the agents' movement in the grid. Let the random variable $X_r^\uparrow$ have value 1 if the state of the agent at the end of round r is labeled up, and 0 otherwise. Note that these random variables depend only on the state transitions the agent performs in the Markov chain. Also let $X_{\le r}^\uparrow = \sum_{r'=1}^{r} X_{r'}^\uparrow$.

LEMMA 4.8. *Suppose an agent is initially in a state from the recurrent class C. Then there is a real number $p^\uparrow \in [0,1]$ depending only on C, such that for each round $r \le \Delta$ it holds that $\left|X_{\le r}^\uparrow - rp^\uparrow\right| = o(D/|S|)$ w.h.p.*

PROOF SKETCH. First, we consider the special case of $r = \Delta$. Because $\beta = o(D/|S|)$ (follows from the assumptions for the value of χ), it suffices to show that, for a suitable choice of $p^\uparrow$, $\sum_{r'=\beta+1}^{\Delta} \left|X_{r'}^\uparrow - (r-\beta)p^\uparrow\right| = o(D/|S|)$. We break this sum down into β sums, each considering only the round numbers from the same class B_i.

For each such class B_i, we condition on the event that experiment E_i results in all coin flips showing heads, and so each subsequent state within class B_i is drawn independently from the stationary distribution. Now, we apply a Chernoff bound to show that w.h.p. the number of moves up in the grid that occur in rounds $r' \in B_i$ does not differ from the expected number of such moves by more than $o(D/(|S|\beta))$. Finally, we show by a union bound that w.h.p. both (1) all coin flips from experiment E_i indeed show heads, and (2) for all i it is true that the number of moves up in the grid that occur in rounds $r' \in B_i$ does not differ from the expected number of such moves by more than $o(D/(|S|\beta))$. The value of $p^\uparrow$ now is simply the sum over i of the expectation for class B_i divided by its size.

For the general case of $r < \Delta$, observe that decreasing r by an integer multiple of β decreases the computed expectation by exactly $p^\uparrow$ (as long as $r > \beta + 1 = o(D/|S|)$). Also, decreasing the number of rounds only decreases the probability of large deviations from the expectation of the random variable. Since $\beta = o(D/|S|)$, the general statement hence follows analogously to the special case. □

Repeating these arguments for the other directions (right, down, and left), we see that overall, each agent behaves fairly predictably. Define $X_{\le r} \in \mathbb{Z}^2$ to be the random variable describing the sum of all moves the agent performs in the grid up to round r, i.e., its position in the grid (in each dimension) at the end of round r. For this random variable, the following statement holds.

COROLLARY 4.9. *Suppose an agent is initially in a state of the recurrent class C. Then there is a real number $\vec{p} \in [0,1]^2$ depending only on C such that for each $r \le \Delta$, it holds that $\|X_{\le r} - r\vec{p}\| = o(D/|S|)$ w.h.p.*

We now resume the proof of Theorem 4.1.

PROOF OF THEOREM 4.1. Denote by $\mathcal{C}$ the set of recurrent classes of the Markov chain representing the state machine of each agent. By Corollary 4.3, it holds for each agent a that, after each round $r \ge R_0 = D^{o(1)}$, w.h.p. the agent is located in recurrent class $C(a) \in \mathcal{C}$. Since Lemma 4.8, and therefore Corollary 4.9, do not depend on the initial state from $C(a)$ the agent is in, the same reasoning shows that, at the end of round r, w.h.p. the position of a will not deviate by more than distance $o(D/|S|)$ from a straight line in the grid. By a union bound, this holds for all agents jointly w.h.p (recall that by assumption n is polynomial in D). Hence, w.h.p., it holds for each agent a and each round $r \ge R_0$ that a never ventures further away from the origin than distance $o(D/|S|)$, or its position does not deviate by more than distance $o(D/|S|)$ from one of at most $|\mathcal{C}|$ straight lines. Since for any straight line only a segment of length $\mathcal{O}(D)$ is in distance $\mathcal{O}(D)$ from the origin, the union of all grid points that are (i) in distance at most D from the origin and (ii) in distance at most $o(D/|S|)$ from one of the straight lines has cardinality $\mathcal{O}(D) \cdot o(D/|S|) \cdot |\mathcal{C}| \le o(D^2/|S|) \cdot |S| = o(D^2)$. Hence, there is a set $G \subset \mathbb{Z}^2$ of $o(D^2)$ grid points that only depends on the algorithm $\mathcal{A}$, D, and n, with the following property: w.h.p., all grid points in distance D from the origin that are visited within the first Δ steps of an execution of $\mathcal{A}$ are in G. Since there are $\Theta(D^2)$ grid points in distance D from the origin, this implies that the target can be placed in such a way that w.h.p. no agent will find it within $\Delta = D^{2-o(1)}$ rounds, and a uniformly placed target is found in this amount of time with probability $o(1)$. □

Finally, we show that Theorem 4.1 also holds with respect to the metric M_{moves}. In the following corollary, we show that each move of an agent on the grid corresponds to at most $D^{o(1)}$ transitions in its Markov chain, or otherwise, the agent does not move on the grid after some point.

COROLLARY 4.10. *Let $\mathcal{A}$ be an algorithm with $\chi(\mathcal{A}) = b + \log \ell \le \log\log D - \omega(1)$ and let each of $n \in poly(D)$ agents execute algorithm $\mathcal{A}$. There is a placement of the target within distance D from the origin such that w.h.p. $M_{moves} \ge D^{2-o(1)}$. Moreover, if the target is placed uniformly at random in the square of side $2D$ centered at the origin, then $M_{moves} = D^{2-o(1)}$ with probability $o(1)$.*

The proof proceeds by showing that w.h.p., at least one of the following is true about any agent a in any round $r \ge R_0$: (1) a is located in a recurrent class in which all states are labeled "none", or (2) each move on the grid performed by a corresponds to at most $D^{o(1)}$ steps in its Markov chain. In the first case, the agent does not make much progress exploring the grid; in the second case, it follows that $D^{2-o(1)}$ moves in the grid correspond to $D^{2-o(1)}$ transitions in the Markov chain and the result is implied by Theorem 4.1.

5. DISCUSSION AND CONCLUSION

We have presented an algorithm and a lower bound for the problem of n agents searching in a grid for a target placed at distance at most D from the origin. Our lower bound shows that if $\chi(\mathcal{A}) < \log\log D - \omega(1)$ and n is polynomial in D, w.h.p. no agent finds the target within its first $D^{2-o(1)}$ moves. In fact, it is straightforward to generalize the result to $n \in 2^{D^{o(1)}}$. For the remaining case of an exponential number of agents, just performing independent unbiased random walks results in finding the target quickly. We also present an algorithm $\mathcal{A}$ with $\chi(\mathcal{A}) \leq 3\log\log D$ that finds the target in $(D + D^2/n) \cdot 2^{\mathcal{O}(\ell)}$ rounds in expectation, proving our lower bound to be near-tight.

For the upper bound we get stronger results if we consider a fixed search area of radius D centered at the origin, as opposed to aiming at a time complexity that is a function of the actual distance of the target from the origin. In this case, $\chi(\mathcal{A}) = \log\log D + \mathcal{O}(1)$ suffices to find the target in $(D + D^2/n) \cdot 2^{\mathcal{O}(\ell)}$ rounds in expectation.

Concerning open problems, note that there is a gap of $2^{\mathcal{O}(\ell)}$ between the running time of our uniform algorithm and the lower bound. Also, for our lower bound we assume that $\chi(\mathcal{A}) = b + \log \ell < \log\log D - \omega(1)$, but our algorithm requires $b = 3(\log\log D - \log \ell) + O(1)$ bits of memory.

6. REFERENCES

[1] Y. Afek, N. Alon, O. Barad, E. Hornstein, N. Barkai, and Z. Bar-Joseph. A biological solution to a fundamental distributed computing problem. *Science*, 331(6014):183–185, 2011.

[2] S. Albers and M. Henzinger. Exploring unknown environments. *SIAM Journal on Computing*, 29(4):1164–1188, 2000.

[3] N. Alon, C. Avin, M. Koucky, G. Kozma, Z. Lotker, and M. R. Tuttle. Many random walks are faster than one. In *Proceedings of the Twentieth Annual Symposium on Parallelism in Algorithms and Architectures*, SPAA '08, pages 119–128, New York, NY, USA, 2008. ACM.

[4] M. Arbilly, U. Motro, M. W. Feldman, and A. Lotem. Co-evolution of learning complexity and social foraging strategies. *Journal of Theoretical Biology*, 267(4):573 – 581, 2010.

[5] M. A. Bender, A. Fernández, D. Ron, A. Sahai, and S. Vadhan. The power of a pebble: Exploring and mapping directed graphs. In *Proceedings of the Thirtieth Annual ACM Symposium on Theory of Computing*, STOC '98, pages 269–278, New York, NY, USA, 1998. ACM.

[6] S. Berman, Á. Halász, V. Kumar, and S. Pratt. Algorithms for the analysis and synthesis of a bio-inspired swarm robotic system. In *Swarm Robotics*, pages 56–70. Springer, 2007.

[7] X. Deng and C. H. Papadimitriou. Exploring an unknown graph. In *Foundations of Computer Science, 1990. Proceedings., 31st Annual Symposium on*, pages 355–361 vol. 1, Oct 1990.

[8] K. Diks, P. Fraigniaud, E. Kranakis, and A. Pelc. Tree exploration with little memory. In *Proceedings of the Thirteenth Annual ACM-SIAM Symposium on Discrete Algorithms*, SODA '02, pages 588–597, Philadelphia, PA, USA, 2002. Society for Industrial and Applied Mathematics.

[9] Y. Emek, T. Langner, J. Uitto, and R. Wattenhofer. Ants: Mobile finite state machines. *arXiv preprint arXiv:1311.3062*, 2013.

[10] Y. Emek and R. Wattenhofer. Stone Age Distributed Computing. In *ACM Symposium on Principles of Distributed Computing (PODC), Montreal, Quebec, Canada*, July 2013.

[11] O. Feinerman and A. Korman. Memory lower bounds for randomized collaborative search and implications for biology. In *Distributed Computing*, volume 7611 of *Lecture Notes in Computer Science*, pages 61–75. Springer Berlin Heidelberg, 2012.

[12] O. Feinerman and A. Korman. Theoretical distributed computing meets biology: A review. In *ICDCIT*, pages 1–18, 2013.

[13] O. Feinerman, A. Korman, Z. Lotker, and J.-S. Sereni. Collaborative Search on the Plane without Communication. In *Proc. 31st Symposium on Principles of Distributed Computing (PODC)*, pages 77–86, 2012.

[14] W. Feller. *An introduction to probability theory and its applications*, volume 2. John Wiley & Sons, 2008.

[15] P. Fraigniaud, L. Gasieniec, D. R. Kowalski, and A. Pelc. Collective tree exploration. *Networks*, 48(3):166–177, 2006.

[16] L. Gasieniec, A. Pelc, T. Radzik, and X. Zhang. Tree exploration with logarithmic memory. In *Proceedings of the Eighteenth Annual ACM-SIAM Symposium on Discrete Algorithms*, SODA '07, pages 585–594, 2007.

[17] L.-A. Giraldeau and T. Caraco. *Social foraging theory.* Princeton University Press, 2000.

[18] R. Harkness and N. Maroudas. Central place foraging by an ant (cataglyphis bicolor fab.): a model of searching. *Animal Behaviour*, 33(3):916 – 928, 1985.

[19] K. Holder and G. Polis. Optimal and central-place foraging theory applied to a desert harvester ant, pogonomyrmex californicus. *Oecologia*, 72(3):440–448, 1987.

[20] C. Lenzen, N. Lynch, C. Newport, and T. Radeva. Trade-offs between selection complexity and performance when searching the plane without communication. *arXiv preprint arXiv:1405.1688*, 2014.

[21] P. Panaite and A. Pelc. Exploring unknown undirected graphs. *Journal of Algorithms*, 33(2):281 – 295, 1999.

[22] S. C. Pratt and D. J. Sumpter. A tunable algorithm for collective decision-making. *Proceedings of the National Academy of Sciences*, 103(43):15906–15910, 2006.

[23] O. Reingold. Undirected st-connectivity in log-space. In *Proceedings of the Thirty-seventh Annual ACM Symposium on Theory of Computing*, STOC '05, pages 376–385, New York, NY, USA, 2005. ACM.

[24] E. J. Robinson, D. E. Jackson, M. Holcombe, and F. L. Ratnieks. Insect communication: No entry signal in ant foraging. *Nature*, 438(7067):442–442, 2005.

[25] J. S. Rosenthal. Rates of convergence for data augmentation on finite sample spaces. *The Annals of Applied Probability*, pages 819–839, 1993.

Improved Distributed Steiner Forest Construction

Extended Abstract

Christoph Lenzen*
Massachusetts Institute of Technology
32 Vassar Street, 02139 Cambridge, USA
clenzen@csail.mit.edu

Boaz Patt-Shamir†
Tel Aviv University
Tel Aviv 69978, Israel
boaz@eng.tau.ac.il

ABSTRACT

We present new distributed algorithms for constructing a Steiner Forest in the CONGEST model. Our deterministic algorithm finds, for any given constant $\varepsilon > 0$, a $(2+\varepsilon)$-approximation in $\tilde{\mathcal{O}}(sk + \sqrt{\min\{st, n\}})$ rounds, where s is the shortest path diameter, t is the number of terminals, k is the number of terminal components in the input, and n is the number of nodes. Our randomized algorithm finds, with high probability, an $\mathcal{O}(\log n)$-approximation in time $\tilde{\mathcal{O}}(k + \min\{s, \sqrt{n}\} + D)$, where D is the unweighted diameter of the network. We also prove a matching lower bound of $\tilde{\Omega}(k + \min\{s, \sqrt{n}\} + D)$ on the running time of any distributed approximation algorithm for the Steiner Forest problem. Previous algorithms were randomized, and obtained either an $\mathcal{O}(\log n)$-approximation in $\tilde{\mathcal{O}}(sk)$ time, or an $\mathcal{O}(1/\varepsilon)$-approximation in $\tilde{\mathcal{O}}((\sqrt{n} + t)^{1+\varepsilon} + D)$ time.

1. INTRODUCTION

Ever since the celebrated paper of Gallager, Humblet, and Spira [12], the task of constructing a minimum-weight spanning tree (MST) continues to be a rich source of difficulties and ideas that drive network algorithmics (see, e.g., [10, 13, 21, 23]). The *Steiner Forest* (SF) problem is a strict generalization of MST: We are given a network with edge weights and some disjoint node subsets called *input components*; the task is to find a minimum-weight edge set which makes each component connected. MST is a special case of SF, and so are the Steiner Tree and shortest s-t path problems. The general SF problem is well motivated by many practical situations involving the design of networks, be it physical (it was famously posed as a problem of railroad design), or virtual (e.g., VPNs or streaming multicast). The problem has attracted much attention in the classic algorithms community, as detailed on the dedicated website [14].

The first network algorithm for SF in the CONGEST model (where a link can deliver $\mathcal{O}(\log n)$ bits in a time unit—precise definitions in Section 2) was presented by Khan *et al.* [16]. It provides $\mathcal{O}(\log n)$-approximate solutions in time $\tilde{\mathcal{O}}(sk)$, where n is the number of nodes, k is the number of components, and s the *shortest path diameter* of the network, which is (see Section 2) the maximal number of edges in a weighted shortest path. Subsequently, in [19], it was shown that for any given $0 < \varepsilon \leq 1/2$, an $\mathcal{O}(\varepsilon^{-1})$-approximate solution to SF can be found in time $\tilde{\mathcal{O}}((\sqrt{n} + t)^{1+\varepsilon} + D)$, where D is the diameter of the unweighted version of the network, and t is the number of *terminals*, i.e., the total number of nodes in all input components. The algorithms in [16, 19] are both randomized.

Our Results. In this paper we improve the results for SF in the CONGEST model in two ways. First, we show that for any given constant $\varepsilon > 0$, a $(2+\varepsilon)$-approximate solution to SF can be computed by a deterministic network algorithm in time $\tilde{\mathcal{O}}(sk + \sqrt{\min\{st, n\}})$. Second, we show that an $\mathcal{O}(\log n)$-approximation can be attained by a randomized algorithm in time $\tilde{\mathcal{O}}(k + \min\{s, \sqrt{n}\} + D) \subseteq \tilde{\mathcal{O}}(s + k)$. On the other hand, we show that any algorithm in the CONGEST model that computes a solution to SF with non-trivial approximation ratio has running time in $\tilde{\Omega}(k + \min\{s, \sqrt{n}\} + D)$. If the input is not given by indicating to each terminal its input component, but rather by *connection requests* between terminal pairs, i.e., informing each terminal which terminals it must be connected to, an $\tilde{\Omega}(t + \min\{s, \sqrt{n}\} + D)$ lower bound holds. (It is easy to distributively transform connection requests into equivalent input components in $\mathcal{O}(t + D)$ rounds.)

Related work. The Steiner Tree problem (the special case of SF where there is one input component) has a remarkable history, starting with Fermat, who posed the geometric 3-point on a plane problem circa 1643, including Gauss (1836), and culminating with a popularization in 1941 by Courant and Robbins in their book "What is Mathematics" [8]. An interesting account of these early developments is given in [3]. The contribution of Computer Science to the history of the problem apparently started with the inclusion of Steiner Tree as one of the original 21 problems proved NP-complete by Karp [15]. There are quite a few variants of the SF problem which are algorithmically interesting, such as Directed Steiner Tree, Prize-Collecting Steiner Tree,

*Supported in part by the National Science Foundation under Grant Nos. CCF-AF-0937274, 0939370-CCF, and CCF-1217506, the AFOSR under Contract No. AFOSR Award number FA9550-13-1-0042, the German Research Foundation (DFG, reference number Le 3107/1-1).

†Supported in part by a grant from the Israel Ministry of Science, Technology and Space and the French Ministry of Higher Education and Research.

PODC'14, July 15–18, 2014, Paris, France.

ACM 978-1-4503-2944-6/14/07 ...$15.00.
http://dx.doi.org/10.1145/2611462.2611464.

Group Steiner Tree, and more. The site [14] gives a continuously updated state of the art results for many variants. Let us mention results for the most common variants: For the Steiner Tree problem, the best (polynomial-time) approximation ratio known is $\ln 4 + \varepsilon \approx 1.386 + \varepsilon$ for any constant $\varepsilon > 0$ [4]. For Steiner Forest, the best approximation ratio known is $2 - 1/(t-k)$ [1]. It is also known that the approximation ratio of the Steiner Tree (or Forest) problem is at least 96/95, unless P=NP [6].

Regarding distributed algorithms, there are a few relevant results. First, the special case of minimum-weight spanning tree (MST) is known to have time complexity of $\tilde{\Theta}(D+\sqrt{n})$ in the CONGEST model [9, 10, 13, 18, 23]. In [5], a 2-approximation for the special case of Steiner Tree is presented, with time complexity $\tilde{\mathcal{O}}(n)$. The first distributed solution to the Steiner Forest problem was presented by Khan *et al.* [16], where a randomized algorithm is used to embed the instance in a virtual tree with $\mathcal{O}(\log n)$ distortion, then finding the optimal solution on the tree (which is just the minimal subforest connecting each input component), and finally mapping the selected tree edges back to corresponding paths in the original graph. The result is an $\mathcal{O}(\log n)$-approximation in time $\tilde{\mathcal{O}}(sk)$. Intuitively, s is the time required by the Bellman-Ford algorithm to compute distributed single-source shortest paths, and the virtual tree of [16] is computed in $\tilde{\mathcal{O}}(s)$ rounds. A second distributed algorithm for Steiner Forest is presented in [19]. Here, a sparse spanner for the metric induced on the set of terminals and a random sample of $\tilde{\Theta}(\sqrt{n})$ nodes is computed, on which the instance then is solved centrally. To get an $\mathcal{O}(\varepsilon^{-1})$-approximation, the algorithm runs for $\tilde{\mathcal{O}}(D + (\sqrt{n}+t)^{1+\varepsilon})$ rounds. For approximation ratio $\mathcal{O}(\log n)$, the running time is $\tilde{\mathcal{O}}(D+\sqrt{n}+t)$.

Main Techniques. Our lower bounds are derived by the standard technique of reduction from results on 2-party communication complexity. Our deterministic algorithm is an adaptation of the "moat growing" algorithm of Agrawal, Klein, and Ravi [1] to the CONGEST model. It involves determining the times in which "significant events" occur (e.g., all terminals in an input component becoming connected by the currently selected edges) and extensive usage of pipelining. The algorithm generalizes the MST algorithm from [18]: for the special case of a Steiner Tree (i.e., $k=1$), one can interpret the output as the edge set induced by an MST of the complete graph on the terminals with edge weights given by the terminal-terminal distances, yielding a factor-2 approximation; specializing further to the MST problem, the result is an exact MST and the running time becomes $\tilde{\mathcal{O}}(\sqrt{n}+D)$.

Our randomized algorithm is based on the embedding of the graph into a tree metric from [16], but we improve the complexity of finding a Steiner Forest. A key insight is that while the least-weight paths in the original graph corresponding to virtual tree edges might intersect, no node participates in more than $\mathcal{O}(\log n)$ distinct paths. Since the union of all least-weight paths ending at a specific node induces a tree, letting each node serve routing requests corresponding to different destinations in a round-robin fashion achieves a pipelining effect reducing the complexity to $\tilde{\mathcal{O}}(s+k)$. If $s > \sqrt{n}$, the virtual tree and the corresponding solution are constructed only partially, in time $\tilde{\mathcal{O}}(\sqrt{n}+k+D)$, and the partial result is used to create another instance with $\mathcal{O}(\sqrt{n})$ terminals that captures the remaining connectivity demands; we solve it using the algorithm from [19], obtaining an $\mathcal{O}(\log n)$-approximation.

Paper style. Due to the insufficient space allocated in the proceedings, we defer most details to the full paper, available online [20]. Here we give a high level description of algorithms and arguments used, together with precise definitions and statements to make the paper mathematically meaningful. In Section 2 we define the model, problem and basic concepts. Section 3 contains our lower bounds. In Section 4 and Section 5 we present our deterministic and randomized algorithms, respectively.

2. MODEL AND NOTATION

System Model. We consider the CONGEST($\log n$) or simply the CONGEST model as specified in [22], briefly described as follows. The distributed system is represented by a weighted graph $G = (V, E, W)$ of $n := |V|$ nodes. The weights $W : E \to \mathbb{N}$ are polynomially bounded in n (and therefore polynomial sums of weights can be encoded with $\mathcal{O}(\log n)$ bits). Each node initially knows its unique identifier of $\mathcal{O}(\log n)$ bits, the identifiers of its neighbors, the weight of its incident edges, and the local problem-specific input specified below. Algorithms proceed in synchronous rounds, where in each round, (i) nodes perform arbitrary, finite local computations,[1] (ii) may send, to each neighbor, a possibly distinct message of $\mathcal{O}(\log n)$ bits, and (iii) receive the messages sent by their neighbors. For randomized algorithms, each node has access to an unlimited supply of unbiased, independent random bits. Time complexity is measured by the number of rounds until all nodes (explicitly) terminate.

Notation. We use the following conventions and graph-theoretic notions.

- The number of *hops* of a path $p = (v_0, \dots, v_{\ell(p)})$ in G is $\ell(p)$.
- The weight of path p is $W(p) := \sum_{i=1}^{\ell(p)} W(v_i, v_{i-1})$. For notational convenience, we assume w.l.o.g. that different paths have different weight (ties broken lexicographically).
- By $\mathcal{P}(v,w)$ we denote the set of all paths between $v, w \in V$ in G, i.e., $v_0 = v$ and $v_{\ell(p)} = w$.
- The (unweighted) *diameter* of G is defined as $D := \max_{v,w\in V}\{\min_{p\in\mathcal{P}(v,w)}\{\ell(p)\}\}$.
- The (weighted) *distance* of v and w in G is $\mathrm{wd}(v,w) := \min_{p\in\mathcal{P}(v,w)}\{W(p)\}$.
- $\mathrm{WD} := \max_{v,w\in V}\{\mathrm{wd}(v,w)\}$ is the *weighted diameter* of G.
- The *shortest-path-diameter* of G is defined as $s := \max_{v,w\in V}\{\min\{\ell(p) \,|\, p \in \mathcal{P}(v,w) \wedge W(p) = \mathrm{wd}(v,w)\}\}$.
- For $v \in V$ and $r \in \mathbb{R}_0^+$, we use $B_G(v,r)$ to denote the ball of radius r around v in G, which includes all nodes and edges at weighted distance at most r from v. The ball may contain edge fractions: for an edge $\{w,u\}$ for which only w is in $B_G(v,r)$, the $(r - \mathrm{wd}(v,w))/\mathrm{wd}(v,w)$ fraction of the edge closer to w is considered to be within $B_G(v,r)$, and the remainder is considered outside $B_G(v,r)$.

We use "soft" asymptotic notation. Formally, given functions f and g, define (i) $f \in \tilde{\mathcal{O}}(g)$ iff there is some $h \in \operatorname{polylog} n$ so that $f \in \mathcal{O}(gh)$; (ii) $f \in \tilde{\Omega}(g)$ iff $g \in \tilde{\mathcal{O}}(f)$; and (iii) $f \in \tilde{\Theta}(g)$ iff $f \in \tilde{\mathcal{O}}(g) \cap \tilde{\Omega}(g)$.

The abbreviation *w.h.p.* means *with probability* $1-n^{-\Omega(1)}$, for a sufficiently large constant in the $\Omega(1)$ term.

[1] All our algorithms require polynomial computations only.

The Distributed Steiner Forest Problem (SF). In the Steiner Forest problem, the output is a set of edges. We require that the output edge set F is represented distributively, i.e., each node can locally answer which of its adjacent edges are in the output. The input may be represented by two alternative methods, which are both justified and common in the literature. We give the two definitions.

DEFINITION 2.1 (SF CONNECTION REQ. (DSF-CR)).
Input: *At each* $v \in V$, *a set of* connection requests $R_v \subseteq V$.
Output: *An edge set* $F \subseteq E$ *such that for each connection request* $w \in R_v$, v *and* w *are connected by* F.
Goal: *Minimize* $W(F) = \sum_{e \in F} W(e)$.

The set of *terminals* is $T = \{w \mid w \in R_v \text{ for some } v \in V\} \cup \{v \mid R_v \neq \emptyset\}$, i.e., the set of nodes v for which there is some connection request $\{v, w\}$.

DEFINITION 2.2 (SF INPUT COMPONENTS (DSF-IC)).
Input: *At each node* v, $\lambda(v) \in \Lambda \cup \{\bot\}$, *where* Λ *is the set of* component identifiers. *The set of* terminals *is* $T := \{v \in V \mid \lambda(v) \neq \bot\}$. *An* input component C_λ *for* $\lambda \neq \bot$ *is the set of terminals with label* λ.
Output: *An edge set* $F \subseteq E$ *such that all terminals in each input component are connected by* F.
Goal: *Minimize* $W(F) = \sum_{e \in F} W(e)$.

An instance of DSF-IC is *minimal*, if $|C_\lambda| \neq 1$ for all $\lambda \in \Lambda$. We assume that the labels $\lambda \in \Lambda$ are encoded using $\mathcal{O}(\log n)$ bits. We define $t := |T|$ and $k := |\Lambda| \leq t$, i.e., the number of terminals and input components, respectively.

We say that any two instances of the above problems on the same weighted graph, regardless of the way the input is given, are *equivalent* if the set of feasible outputs for the two instances is identical.

LEMMA 2.3. *Any instance of* DSF-CR *can be transformed into an equivalent instance of* DSF-IC *in* $\mathcal{O}(D + t)$ *rounds.*

LEMMA 2.4. *Any instance of* DSF-IC *can be transformed into an equivalent minimal instance of* DSF-IC *in* $\mathcal{O}(D + k)$ *rounds.*

3. LOWER BOUNDS

As our first result, we show that applying Lemma 2.3 to instances of DSF-CR comes at no penalty in asymptotic running time (a lower bound of $\Omega(D)$ is trivial).

LEMMA 3.1. *Any distributed algorithm for* DSF-CR *with finite approximation ratio has time complexity* $\Omega(t/\log n)$. *This is true even in graphs with diameter at most* 4 *and no more than* 2 *input components.*

The main result of this section is the following theorem.

THEOREM 3.2. *Any algorithm for the Steiner Forest problem with non-trivial approximation ratio has worst-case expected time complexity in* $\tilde{\Omega}(\min\{s, \sqrt{n}\} + k + D)$.

The proof of Theorem 3.2 in fact consists of proving the following two separate lower bounds.

LEMMA 3.3. *Any distributed algorithm for* DSF-IC *with finite approximation ratio has time complexity* $\Omega(k/\log n)$. *This is true even for unweighted graphs of diameter 3.*

LEMMA 3.4. *For* $s \in \mathcal{O}(\sqrt{n})$, *any distributed algorithm for* DSF-IC *or* DSF-CR *with finite approximation ratio requires* $\Omega(s/\log n)$ *rounds. This holds even for instances with* $t = 2$, $k = 1$, *and* $D \in \mathcal{O}(\log n)$.

We remark that the proofs of Lemmas 3.1, 3.3, and 3.4 are by reductions from Set Disjointness (see, e.g., [17]). In Lemmas 3.1 and 3.3, it is trivial to increase the other parameters, i.e., D, s, t, or n, so we may apply Lemmas 2.3 and 2.4 to obtain a minimal instance of DSF-IC without affecting the asymptotic time complexity.

4. DETERMINISTIC ALGORITHM

We start the description of our algorithm with a quick survey of known results that we shall use.

The "red" and "blue" rules. Tarjan [25] was the first to formulate the dual rules for MST construction in the following way. Define a *cut* to be a partition of the node set.

- An edge which is the lightest edge across *some* cut of the graph is called *blue*. An edge known to be blue is a part of the MST.
- An edge which is the heaviest edge in *some* cycle of the graph is called *red*. An edge proved to be red is not a part of the MST.

Kruskal's algorithm. Kruskal's algorithm constructs an MST by scanning the edge set in order of ascending weight and selecting each edge that does not close a cycle. The correctness of this procedure follows from the red rule.

A distributed version of this idea is presented in [13]. The edges are convergecast over a BFS tree, where each tree node sends them to its parent in ascending order and discards heavy cycle-closing edges. They show that nice pipelining is achieved: the root learns the first l MST edges in $l + \mathcal{O}(D)$ rounds; by broadcasting them over the BFS tree, these edges become common knowledge at the same asymptotic time complexity (instead of the trivial $\mathcal{O}(|E|)$ complexity).

Prim's/GHS algorithm. Prim's algorithm constructs an MST by, starting from an arbitrary node, adding in each step the lightest edge leaving the so far connected node set to the tree. The correctness of this algorithm follows from the blue rule.

Prim's algorithm can be parallelized as follows: starting with no selected edges, in each step, each connected component (initially just isolated nodes) selects its least-weight outgoing edge, until there is a single connected component, which is the MST. Using the selected edges for communication within the components, one obtains the Gallager-Humblet-Spira algorithm [12]. Since in each step the minimum size of a connected component at least doubles, the running time is $\mathcal{O}(\mu \log n)$, where $\mu < n$ is the hop diameter of the MST. In [12], this bound is, in fact, derived in the asynchronous setting using few messages. For the synchronous case, one can reduce the time complexity to $\mathcal{O}(\mu)$ by allowing only components of strong diameter at most 2^i to select edges. Note, however, that possibly $\mu = n - 1$, irrespective of other parameters like D or s.

GKP algorithm. Garay, Kutten, and Peleg [13, 18] show how to combine the distributed variants of Kruskal's and Prim's algorithm to obtain an algorithm of running time $\mathcal{O}(\sqrt{n \log^* n} + D)$, which is optimal up to a factor of $\mathcal{O}(\sqrt{\log n \log^* n})$, even for approximate solutions [9, 23]. The key idea is to first apply the GHS approach until components contain at least $\kappa := \sqrt{n/\log^* n}$ nodes, and then connect the remaining at most $n/\kappa = \sqrt{n \log^* n}$ components by the pipelined variant of Kruskal's algorithm, taking $\mathcal{O}(\sqrt{n \log^* n} + D)$ rounds.

A central challenge in realizing this approach is that, for the second stage of the algorithm, two nodes must be able to determine whether they belong to the same component. In [18], this is solved efficiently by breaking down the components from the first stage into $\mathcal{O}(n/\kappa)$ smaller pieces of strong diameter $\mathcal{O}(\kappa)$ using a recursive procedure determining $\mathcal{O}(\kappa)$-hop dominating sets of size $\mathcal{O}(n/\kappa)$.

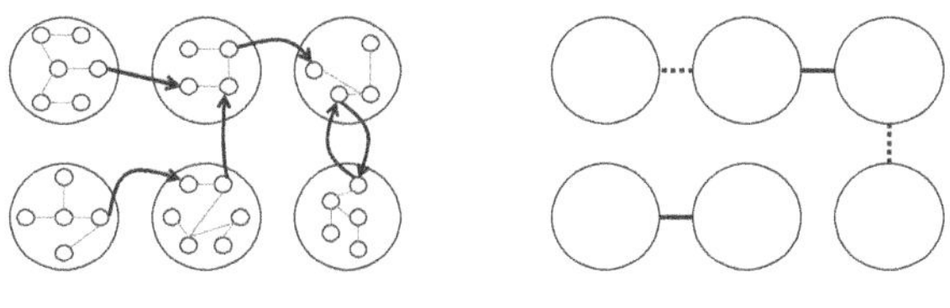

Figure 1: *Example for component growing. Left: each component is a big circle, arrows represent proposed edges. Right: Thick lines represent matching edges, dashed lines represent edges from isolated components.*

As a secondary contribution, in this work we propose a simple solution to this problem, avoiding to grow components too much in the first place. Instead of adding all proposed edges (i.e., least-weight outgoing edges of small components) in each step, we build a graph whose nodes are components and whose edges are the proposed edges; we then emulate a maximal matching algorithm on this graph, and add only the matching edges and those proposed by components which were not matched (see Figure 1). This ensures that small components are still guaranteed to be merged, but the longest "merging paths" in the component graph have at most 3 hops. Since each component proposes at most one edge, a maximal matching can be computed efficiently by simulating the Cole-Vishkin algorithm [7] on the component graph. We note that this variant has the same asymptotic time complexity as the original GKP algorithm.

SF Approximation via the Terminal Graph. The *terminal graph* G_T is the complete graph on the node set T with edge weights of $\mathrm{wd}(v, w)$, i.e., the terminal-terminal distances in G. Mapping an optimal solution to the Steiner Forest problem on G_T to G by mapping an edge in G_T to a shortest path in G yields a 2-approximation in G [19, 24].

The Bellman-Ford Algorithm (BF). "Finding" a terminal graph edge amounts to determining the distance between its terminals in G. Having a canonical interpretation as distributed algorithm, the Bellman-Ford (henceforth, "BF") algorithm is an obvious choice for this task. The single-source version of BF runs for at most s rounds and, by maintaining a pointer to the node whose message gave rise to the most recent distance update, constructs a distributed representation of a shortest-path-tree rooted at the source.

Moat Growing Algorithm. For the Steiner Forest problem, the best known polynomial-time approximation ratio is, essentially, 2. It is achieved by the centralized *moat growing* algorithm proposed by Agrawal, Ravi, and Klein [1]. The algorithm proceeds as follows.

1. Grow weighted balls around each terminal up to the radius where a pair of balls centered at v and w touch.[2]

2. Contract each ball to a node. This merges v and w into a single terminal u.

3. Add the edges of a shortest path from v to w to the solution (if v or w are contracted balls, connect the pair of original terminals $v' \in v$ and $w' \in w$ closest to each other).

4. Merge the input components of v and w, if they are different (they are now connected anyway).

5. If the input component of u contains a single terminal (u), delete that component (i.e., its terminals become regular nodes).

6. If terminals remain, go to Step 1.

Note that in the special case of a Steiner Tree, the only deletion terminates the algorithm. The algorithm thus simulates Kruskal's algorithm on the terminal graph and maps the computed MST back to G as a 2-approximation. In general, such an analogy does not hold in a straightforward way, as the combination of deletion and contraction operation changes distances in the terminal graph; refraining from contractions and simply deleting connected components whose terminals are unions of a subset of the input components yields different results.

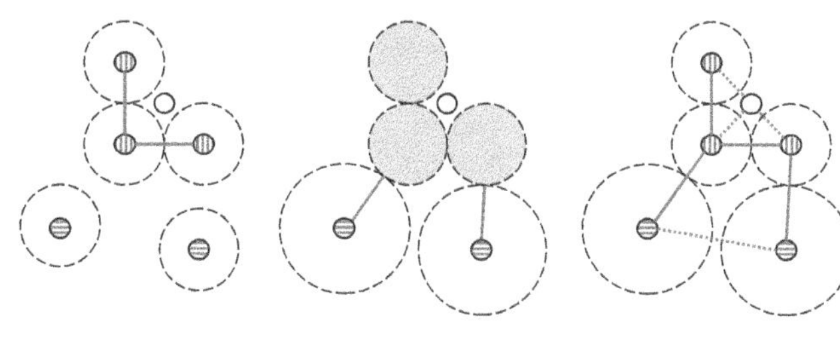

Figure 2: *Example for moat growing. circles with horizontal lines are terminals of Input Component (IC) 1, and vertical lines indicate IC 2. The white circle is a non-terminal node. Left: after growing moats, moats of IC 1 meet, path corresponding to the think lines are chosen, and the new moat is inactivated. Middle: the moats of terminals from IC 2 grow and meet with the inactive moat, adding the new thick lines. Right: The solution of the algorithm (thick lines) and the optimal solution (dotted lines).*

The proof that the algorithm yields a 2-approximation for the general case, i.e., arbitrary number of input components k, is an elegant primal-dual argument based on the observation that, in each step, the weight of the intersection of an optimal solution with the balls is at least the number of (current) balls times their radius (see Fig. 2): the center of each ball must be connected to *some* other terminal outside the ball. On the other hand, terminals are connected by shortest paths, whose intersection with the two terminal's balls they connect weighs at most twice the balls' radius. The ingenuity of the argument lies in the fact that it allows for using contracted balls whose centers have been deleted to be used as shortcuts—the respective path weights inside the contracted balls have been accounted for, as *any* forest connecting the ball centers by shortest paths intersecting only two balls each requires less than twice the budget of an optimal solution.

4.1 Key Ideas and Main Results

Voronoi Decompositions and the Terminal Graph. The key observation underlying our algorithm is that certain Voronoi (or closely related) decompositions of G yield

[2]Recall that we assume w.l.o.g. that different paths have different weights.

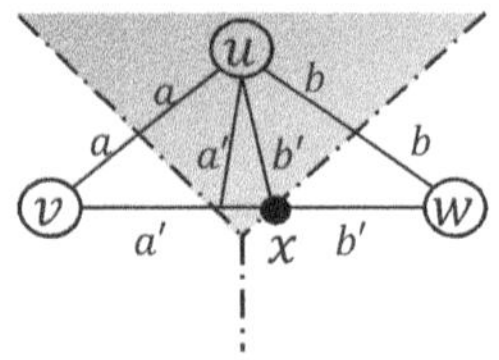

Figure 3: *v, u, w are terminals and dashed lines are borders between Voronoi regions. If a shortest path between v and w crosses the region of u (shaded), then* $\text{wd}(v, w) = \text{wd}(v, x) + \text{wd}(x, w) > 2b' \geq 2b$. *Similarly,* $\text{wd}(v, w) > 2a$.

crucial information on the terminal graph. A Voronoi decomposition of G w.r.t. the terminals T is a partition of the graph into regions so that $u \in \text{Vor}_v$ (for some $u \in V$ and $v \in T$) iff $v = \text{argmin}_{w \in T}\{\text{wd}(w, u)\}$. Such a decomposition and the corresponding distances $\text{wd}(u, v)$ for $u \in \text{Vor}_v$ can be computed in $\mathcal{O}(s)$ rounds using the Bellman-Ford algorithm. To see this, connect all terminals to a virtual source node by edges of weight 0 and piggy-back on all messages (and store) the identifier of the terminal through which the indicated path to the virtual node passes.

The utility of the resulting distributed data structure is illustrated by the special case of a Steiner Tree. Recall that an MST of the terminal graph induces a 2-approximate solution. let $\{v, w\}$ be an MST edge in the terminal graph, and consider any shortest path p from v to w in G. The salient point is that p must be contained in $\text{Vor}_v \cup \text{Vor}_w$. Otherwise, p would pass through Vor_u for some $u \in T$, implying that $\text{wd}(v, u) < \text{wd}(v, w)$ and $\text{wd}(w, u) < \text{wd}(v, w)$ (see Fig. 3). In other words, the terminal graph edge $\{v, w\}$ is the heaviest edge of the cycle (v, w, u, v) in the terminal graph, contradicting the red rule.

This basic insight already gives us the tools to derive an efficient distributed algorithm for 2-approximating a Steiner Tree based on the GKP algorithm:

1. Compute the Voronoi decomposition of G w.r.t. T.
2. Simulate GHS on the terminal graph up to components of at least $\sqrt{n}$ nodes and strong diameter at most $\mathcal{O}(\sqrt{n} + s)$ *in* G (each step does not only merge components, but also add a path of up to s hops). Note that nodes on the selected paths learn that respective edges in G are selected, as communication is routed via them.
3. Simulate Kruskal's algorithm on the terminal graph, starting from the already selected edge set.
4. For each terminal edge $\{v, w\}$ selected in the previous stage, notify the nodes on the corresponding path that the path's edges have been selected. This is done by sending tokens from the nodes of the path edge crossing the boundary between Vor_v and Vor_w to v and w, respectively, using the pointers inducing the shortest-path-trees constructed in the first step.

Note that in the last step, it suffices that each node in the shortest-path-tree of, e.g., node $v \in T$, sends only the first received token to its parent—we do not care how many paths use a specific edge in G. Hence, the overall running time becomes $\tilde{\mathcal{O}}(s + \sqrt{n})$.

One can refine the approach slightly by capping component's growth in the GHS phase of the algorithm at the following strong diameter value.

NOTATION 4.1. *We use* $\sigma \stackrel{\text{def}}{=} \sqrt{\min\{st, n\}}$.

The point is that the constructed solution will consist of the union of $t-1$ paths of at most s hops. Capping component's growth at σ improves the running time to $\tilde{\mathcal{O}}(s + \sigma)$. Our algorithm generalizes this idea.

COROLLARY 4.2. *For $k = 1$, a solution to* DSF-IC *that is optimal up to factor 2 can be computed deterministically in* $\tilde{\mathcal{O}}(s + \sigma)$ *rounds.*

Note that if $s > t$, the first term dominates the complexity. Hence this bound is always better than plain application of Kruskal's selection scheme, which would yield running time $\mathcal{O}(s + t)$.

Moat Growing without Contraction. In light of the above and the aforementioned fact that for $k = 1$ the moat growing algorithm also constructs an MST of the terminal graph, it is natural to seek to extend the existing distributed techniques in order to implement the moat growing algorithm. The main obstacle to an efficient implementation is the contraction of moats. Simulating operations on a graph in which we recursively contract long paths directly will be very slow: a single round of the Bellmann-Ford algorithm would require to route communication through a contracted region whose strong diameter satisfies only trivial upper bounds; on the other hand, trying to route communication through a BFS tree will result in high congestion.

Instead, we take a different point of view, avoiding contractions (this can be seen as a simulation argument). A considerable part of our technical contribution consists of rephrasing the centralized moat growing algorithm, adapting the proof of its approximation ratio to this formulation, and finally deriving and proving equivalent the distributed version of the algorithm. In a nutshell, we replace the contraction operation by electing a leader of each *moat*, a set of terminals that are connected by the currently selected edges. A moat can be *active*, corresponding to a non-deleted merged terminal in the original algorithm, or *inactive*. The latter state is attained when the moat is a union of whole input components and therefore would be deleted; we simply "halt" the growth of its surrounding "ball". Such a "ball" now is the *union* of weighted balls around the terminals, and when any two balls of terminals from different moats touch, the respective moats are *merged* and a shortest path connecting the centers of the touching balls is added.

Note that this differs from the original algorithm in that we may merge an active moat M_1 with inactive moat M_2 into an active moat M_{12}. In contrast, the original algorithm would have deleted the terminal representing the contracted region of M_2. The crucial observations are that with this modification,

(i) M_2 interferes only *twice* with "distances", when it is formed (the balls of its terminals stop growing) and when it gets merged (the balls start growing again); and

(ii) if later M_{12} gets merged with a moat M_3 so that the respective path connects a (formerly inactive) terminal of M_2 with one of M_3, we constructed a path that the original moat growing algorithm would have selected as well: the original algorithm would have grown the ball of M_1 "through" the contracted region associated with M_2 (represented by the corresponding merge operation), and once the balls of M_1 and M_3 touched, the selected shortest path would pass via the contracted region of M_2 that became part of $M_1 \cup M_2$ in our approach.

Observation (i) shows why we can implement the algorithm efficiently with this modification: for each input component, at most once a moat becomes inactive (stopping to grow its balls) and at most one inactive moat merges with an active moat (causing an "instantaneous" extension of the active moat); in both cases we recompute a suitable Voronoi decomposition of the graph, requiring in total $\mathcal{O}(sk)$ rounds throughout the entire algorithm.

Observation (ii) explains why forming connections to inactive moats does not render the algorithm useless. While the resulting forest may very well not be a 2-approximate solution, (ii) says that it *contains* a subforest that solves the problem and has cost at most twice the optimum. Therefore, to "fix" this issue, it suffices to postprocess the computed forest, leaving only the edges required to satisfy the requested connectivity.

The moat growing mechanism can be viewed as Kruskal's algorithm on the terminal graph, *but with the terminal graph changing up to* $2k$ *times* during the execution of the algorithm. On each such event, we recompute a suitably adapted Voronoi decomposition and recommence executing the pipelined version of Kruskal's edge selection scheme until the next such change is encountered. When this procedure is done, the root of the BFS tree knows all selected terminal graph edges. Hence the root can compute the minimal subset satisfying all constraints (learning each terminal's input label takes $\mathcal{O}(t + D)$ rounds over the BFS tree), and broadcast the result to all nodes. Finally, the underlying edges in G can be marked in $\mathcal{O}(s)$ rounds as before. The result is a 2-approximation of SF with running time $\tilde{\mathcal{O}}(sk + t)$, as at most $t - 1$ terminal graph edges are to be selected.

THEOREM 4.3. DSF-IC *can be solved deterministically with approximation factor* 2 *in* $\mathcal{O}(sk + t)$ *rounds.*

Combining Moat Growing and Prim's Approach. Interpreting the moat growing algorithm as a generalization of Kruskal's algorithm raises the question of whether we can also here combine it with the GHS approach to achieve a time complexity that is sublinear in the number of terminals. This is possible, but it is more involved than the special cases of MST and Steiner Tree. Intuitively, this is because edge weights in the terminal graph are dynamic. More concretely, while scanning edges in ascending order of weight (as in Kruskal's and the moat growing algorithm), we also need to recompute distance information on every merge in which a participating or the resulting moat is inactive. In contrast, naive application of Prim's selection scheme may merge two moats under the assumption that they remain active up to the ball radii corresponding to the respective path weight, but this assumption may turn out to be wrong due to merges for smaller radii the algorithm has not determined yet (see Fig. 4).

The distance information available from the Voronoi decomposition can be invalidated due to an inactive moat either forming, or being merged. We handle these cases differently. First, we defer moats inactivation to ball radii that are integral powers of $1 + \varepsilon$, for a given constant $\varepsilon > 0$. Since the maximal ball radius required to merge all moats is polynomial in n, it follows that there at most $i_{\max} \stackrel{\text{def}}{=} \lfloor \log_{1+\varepsilon} \text{WD} \rfloor + 1 \in \mathcal{O}(\log n/\varepsilon)$ different radii at which we need to recompute the Voronoi decomposition due to inactivation of moats: for each power $i \in \{1, \ldots, i_{\max}\}$, we determine all merges that correspond to moat radius in

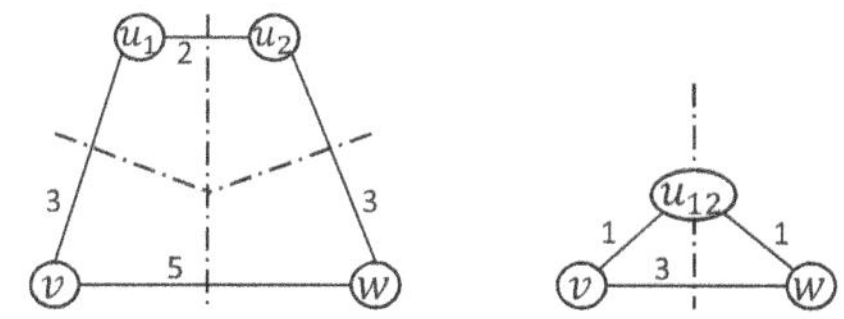

Figure 4: *Example for moat order-changing contraction. Left: numbers indicate terminal-terminal distance and dashed lines represent region borders. Right: after growing the radius to* 1*,* u_1 *and* u_2 *merge into a single inactive moat which is a shortcut between* v *and* w*.*

$\big[(1 + \varepsilon)^{i-1}/2, (1 + \varepsilon)^i/2\big)$. It is not hard to show that the approximation ratio remains bounded by $2(1 + \varepsilon)$.

The second issue is when an inactive moat is merged with an active one, resulting in resumed moat growing. This is solved within a *growth phase* (i.e., a range of radii as above) as follows. Since all balls around active terminals grow at the same rate, we determine the minimal increase in radius to see when an active terminal's moat touches a an inactive moat v. We then repeat distance calculations from the corresponding radius on, where all terminals in the moat of v are now active, find the next inactive moat that is merged, and so on, until the maximal radius of balls reaches the next power of $1 + \varepsilon$. This allows us to collect all the information on terminal graph edges that we need for the current growth phase.

Using this process, we can iteratively compute *all* the decompositions needed to provide correct distance information between moats throughout the growth phase. Based on this knowledge, we first grow moats locally and concurrently as in the GHS algorithm, until components either contain σ nodes, or have no further outgoing edges that may be selected during the current growth phase (this happens in phase i if all outgoing edges have weight at least $(1 + \varepsilon)^i/2$). Subsequently, we apply the pipelined variant of Kruskal's algorithm to the edges connecting different components that have weight at most $(1 + \varepsilon)^i/2$. Note that, as before, it is essential that all terminals in a component refer to it by the same identifier in order to avoid closing cycles by choosing edges that connect terminals of the same component. Due to the iterative approach switching back and forth between Prim and Kruskal type edge selection, there can be no guarantee that components are small. However, there are at most $\min\{st, n\}/\sigma = \sigma$ components of strong diameter larger than σ; for the purpose of selecting an identifier (e.g., the largest node identifier in the component), we simply pipeline their communication over a single BFS tree, taking $\mathcal{O}(\sigma + D)$ rounds in each of the $\mathcal{O}(\log n)$ growth phases.

COROLLARY 4.4. *For any instance of* DSF-IC*, a solving forest* F *with the property that its minimal subforest solving the instance is optimal up to factor* $2 + \varepsilon$ *can be computed in* $\tilde{\mathcal{O}}(sk + \sigma)$ *rounds.*

Fast Pruning of Unneeded Edges. By Corollary 4.4, we now face the following setting. We have a forest of edges that connect any two terminals in the same component by a unique path, but some edges are superfluous. We are guaranteed that the minimal subforest that is a solution is a $(2 + \varepsilon)$-approximation. Discarding the unnecessary edges is trivial centrally, but may be costly distributively: e.g., collecting the information at a single node may result in $\Omega(t)$ time; also, the tree depths could be as large as $\Omega(n)$.

Our approach is to decompose the problem into a few subproblems; we first solve the high-level problem and then, in parallel, all subproblems. Specifically, we first decompose the forest into clusters of strong diameter $\tilde{\mathcal{O}}(\sigma)$ that contain at least σ nodes each (see Fig. 5). This can be done, say, by running the first stage of the GKP algorithm up to size σ, in $\tilde{\mathcal{O}}(\sigma)$ rounds. Note that there are at most σ clusters. We then focus on the *cluster forest* graph, denoted FC, in which each cluster is a node, and two nodes are connected iff the corresponding clusters are connected by an edge (at most $\sigma - 1$ edges). FC is broadcast to all nodes at the cost of $\mathcal{O}(\sigma + D)$ rounds.

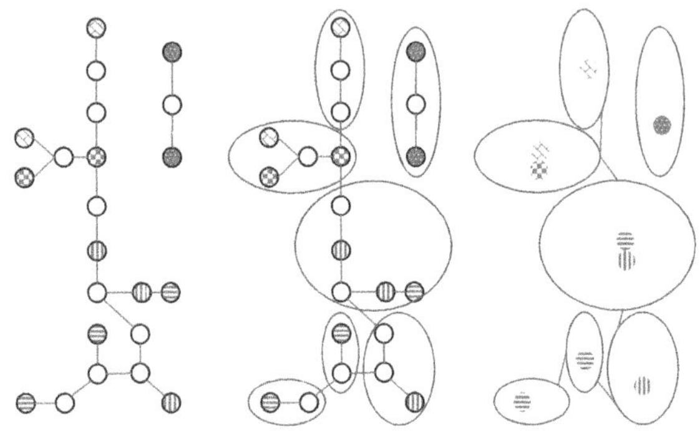

Figure 5: *First steps of pruning. left: the initial forest. The pattern in the circles indicate the input component (empty circles are non-terminals). Middle: clustering. Right: The cluster forest FC before the label merging.*

Next, we collect the label information of FC over the global BFS tree. A naïve implementation may cost $\Omega(k\sigma)$ time, because each of the clusters may be labeled by $\Omega(k)$ labels. Instead, we use the following rule for disseminating the necessary information to all nodes. Nodes send up the BFS tree messages of the form (C, λ), meaning "Cluster C contains a terminal with label λ." Terminals have the base information. When a node v receives a message (C, λ), it applies the following changes to its local copy of FC:

(a) Label C by λ.

(b) If there is another cluster C' labeled λ, label by λ all clusters and edges along the unique path connecting C to C' in FC.

(c) If there is now some edge of FC labeled both λ and λ', then these labels are merged in the sense that any cluster or edge labeled either λ or λ' is relabeled by both λ and λ'.

(d) If the local copy of FC has changed, enqueue the (C, λ) message for forwarding it to the parent.

Step c is justified by the observation that in the solution we seek, the input component set is divided into equivalence classes defined by the connected components of the solution: if two input components λ and λ' are connected in the solution, they are in the same equivalence class, and it is these classes that we need.

The important advantage of this approach is that for any given node, there can be at most $\mathcal{O}(\sigma + k)$ messages that pass the filter of Step d. To see this, observe that whenever the local copy of FC changes, it holds that either (i) a new label $\lambda \in \Lambda$ is added that was not present before, or (ii) an edge receives its first label, or (iii) at least two (current) equivalence classes of labels are merged. Clearly, (i) and (ii) can apply at most k times each, while (ii) may happen no more than $\sigma - 1$ times. It follows that every node sends $\mathcal{O}(\sigma + k)$ messages, and thus, after $\mathcal{O}(\sigma + k + D)$ rounds, the root knows the full (new) labeling of FC; this information then is disseminated to all nodes in the same asymptotic running time, by the root broadcasting the non-filtered labels over the BFS tree.

This information allows the nodes to identify the inter-cluster edges that are required in the output. Inside each cluster, we can solve the problem directly: Each node needs to know what labels are at the other end of each of its incident edges (a terminal has its original label, and the labels of inter-cluster edges are known by the previous stage). Selecting intra-cluster edges takes $\mathcal{O}(\sigma + k)$ rounds, because the cluster diameter is $\mathcal{O}(\sigma)$ and there are at most k labels to propagate. Thus, the pruning procedure yields the main result of this section.

THEOREM 4.5. *For any constant $\varepsilon > 0$, a deterministic distributed algorithm can compute a solution for problem* DSF-IC *that is optimal up to factor $(2 + \varepsilon)$ in $\tilde{\mathcal{O}}(sk + \sqrt{\min\{st, n\}})$ rounds.*

Finally, we preprocess the input to make the instance minimal using Lemma 2.4 and note that, because weights are integer, there can be at most 2 WD different moat radii at which moats are merged and thus recomputation of the Voronoi decomposition may be required.

COROLLARY 4.6. *For any constant $\varepsilon > 0$, a deterministic distributed algorithm can compute a $(2+\varepsilon)$-optimal solution for problem* DSF-IC *in $\tilde{\mathcal{O}}(s \min\{k_0, WD\} + \sqrt{\min\{st, n\}} + k + D)$ rounds, where k_0 is the number of input components with at least two terminals.*

5. RANDOMIZED ALGORITHM

Again, we start by describing the known results and techniques our randomized algorithm makes use of.

Probabilistic Tree Embedding. A *metric embedding* of a metric space (X, d_X) is an injective mapping $\iota : X \to Y$, where (Y, d_Y) is a metric space and for all $x, x' \in X$ it holds that $d_X(x, x') \leq d_Y(\iota(x), \iota(y))$. A *tree embedding* is a metric embedding for which d_Y is the distance metric of a weighted tree on Y. A *probabilistic tree embedding of expected stretch* ρ is a distribution of metric tree embeddings satisfying that $\mathbb{E}[d_Y(\iota(x), \iota(y))] \leq \rho \cdot d_X(x, x')$ for all $x, x' \in X$.

Probabilistic tree embeddings have proven to be an excellent tool for deriving probabilistic approximation algorithms to hard problems, granted that the cost function is the sum of edge weights of the solution. Instead of solving the problem on (X, d_X), one solves the problem on the instance on (Y, d_Y) sampled from the distribution, translating the instance by means of ι. Since (Y, d_Y) is a tree, the problem is much simpler to solve, yet in expectation the cost of an optimal solution increases by at most ρ. This strategy lies at the heart of our randomized algorithm.

FRT Embedding. The FRT algorithm [11] produces a probabilistic tree embedding of G (i.e., $(X, d_x) = (V, \mathrm{wd})$) with expected stretch $\mathcal{O}(\log n)$. It works as follows.

1. Select uniformly at random: a permutation $r : V \to [n]$, and a real $\beta \in [1, 2)$.

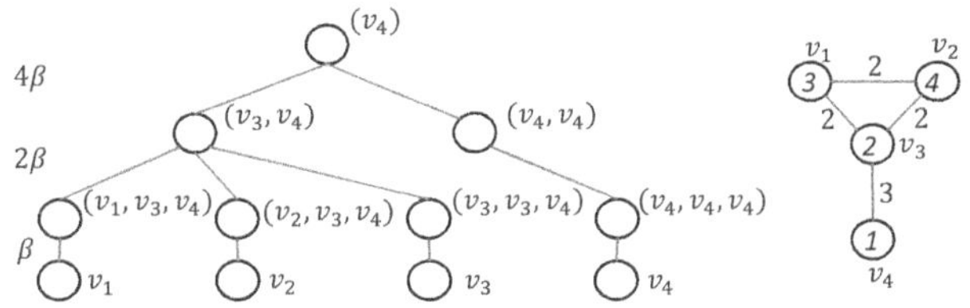

Figure 6: *FRT embedding example, with $n = 4$ and $L = 2$. Right: original graph, permutation values inside circles. Left: tree, edge weights indicated at the left hand side.*

2. Set $L := \lceil \log W \rceil \in \mathcal{O}(\log n)$. For each $v \in V$ and $i \in \{0, \ldots, L\}$, define $v_i := \text{argmin}_{v \in B_G(v, \beta 2^i)}\{r(v)\}$.

3. Set $Y := V \cup \{(v_i, \ldots, v_L) \,|\, v \in V \wedge i \in \{0, \ldots, L\}\}$ and $\iota(v) := v$ for all $v \in V$.

4. For each $v \in V$, there is an edge $\{v, (v_0, \ldots, v_L)\}$ of weight β and, for each $v \in V$ and $i \in \{1, \ldots, L\}$, there are edges $\{(v_{i-1}, \ldots, v_L), (v_i, \ldots, v_L)\}$ of weight $\beta 2^i$ (see Fig. 6). The metric d_Y is the distance metric of the weighted tree on Y defined by these edges and weights.

SF Approximation Based on FRT Embedding. We can solve DSF-IC as follows. (1) Map an instance of DSF-IC to the virtual tree (Y, d_Y), (2) solve the instance optimally on (Y, d_Y) by selecting, for each label λ, the minimal subtree containing all $v \in T$ with $\lambda(v) = \lambda$ (rooted at their least common ancestor), and (3) map the solution back to G by selecting, for each solution edge between child c and parent $p = (v_i, \ldots, v_L)$, an arbitrary terminal t in c's subtree, and outputting the edges of a shortest path from t to v_i in G.

Now, the solution is optimal in (Y, d_Y), and hence its image in G has weight $\mathcal{O}(\log n)$ times the optimum in G.

Khan et al. [16] give a distributed implementation of this scheme running in time $\tilde{\mathcal{O}}(sk)$ w.h.p., based on *LE lists.*

LE Lists: definition and computation. Given a uniformly random permutation of the nodes, the *Least Elements (LE)* list L_v of node $v \in V$ is the list of pairs $(w, \text{wd}(v, w))$ for all $w \in V$, ordered in increasing distance $\text{wd}(v, w)$, after deleting all nodes whose rank is larger than the rank of some prior (closer) node. Given β and its LE list, v can easily find $v_0, \ldots, v_L$ and a neighbor w which is the next hop on a shortest path from v to v_i (for a given i) such that $(v_i, \text{wd}(w, v_i)) \in L_w$. LE lists therefore provide a distributed data structure representing the virtual tree, and the aforementioned distributed $\mathcal{O}(\log n)$-approximation in $\tilde{\mathcal{O}}(sk)$ time is straightforward to find, given these lists.

We now sketch the algorithm computing LE lists from [16]. First, each node v selects a uniformly random number $r(v)$ of $c \log n$ bits (c is large enough to ensure that all $r(v)$ are distinct w.h.p.). Then, after initializing $L_v := \{(v, 0, r(v))\}$, the following is repeated until no L_v variable is modified:

1. Each node v sends L_v to all neighbors.

2. For each $(u, d, r(u))$ received from neighbor w, each node v sets $L_v \cup \{(u, d + W(v, w), r(u))\}$.

3. Each node scans L_v in increasing weight order (second entries), deleting tuples whose rank (third entry) is not larger than all previous ones.

This algorithm terminates after at most s iterations. One can show that w.h.p., the LE lists at each node, at any time, have $\mathcal{O}(\log n)$ entries, and therefore the algorithm terminates in $\tilde{\mathcal{O}}(s)$ rounds w.h.p.

Spanner Construction. A *ρ-spanner* of a graph is a graph obtained by deleting edges so that distance increase at most by factor ρ. Typically one is interested in sparse spanners, i.e., those that have few edges. A distributed randomized spanner construction that can be directly run in the CONGEST model was given by Baswana and Sen [2]. It computes a $(2\kappa - 1)$-spanner with $\mathcal{O}(n^{1+1/\kappa})$ expected edges in $\mathcal{O}(\kappa)$ rounds, for $\kappa \in \mathbb{N}$.

Skeleton Graph and Skeleton Spanner. We use a technique introduced in [19], the construction of a spanner of a *skeleton graph.* A skeleton graph is defined similarly to the terminal graph, with some important variations. Given a subset $\mathcal{S} \subseteq V$ and a parameter $h \in \mathbb{N}$, the skeleton graph has nodes $\mathcal{S}$ and edges $\{\{v, w\} \,|\, \exists p \in \mathcal{P}(v, w) : \ell(p) \leq h\}$, where an edge $\{v, w\}$ has weight $\min_{p \in \mathcal{P}(v,w): \ell(p) \leq h}\{W(p)\}$.

Now, let $\mathcal{S}$ be a random set, where each node is included independently with probability $1/\sqrt{n}$. Then any node set (including paths) with $\Omega(\sqrt{n} \log n)$ nodes contains a node from $\mathcal{S}$ w.h.p. Hence, taking such a random $\mathcal{S}$ and setting $h = \sqrt{n} \log n$, we obtain a skeleton graph in which the distances are, w.h.p., identical to the corresponding distances (between nodes of $\mathcal{S}$) in G.

The number of edges in the skeleton graph may be as large as $\Theta(|\mathcal{S}|^2) = \Theta(n)$. In [19], we show how to simulate the Baswana-Sen algorithm on the skeleton graph to obtain a $(2\kappa - 1)$-spanner of the skeleton graph with $\tilde{\mathcal{O}}(n^{1/2+1/(2\kappa)})$ edges w.h.p., within $\tilde{\mathcal{O}}(n^{1/2+1/(2\kappa)} + D)$ rounds. This edge set can be made known to all nodes in the same asymptotic time, and nodes on the corresponding paths in G will know the respective next hops on the paths.

SF Approximation Using Skeleton Spanner. For a given instance of DSF-IC, if we add the set of terminals T to $\mathcal{S}$ (in addition to the random sample), the above algorithm determines and makes known to all nodes a $(2\kappa - 1)$-spanner of the skeleton graph with $\tilde{\mathcal{O}}((n^{1/2} + t)^{1+1/\kappa})$ edges in time $\tilde{\mathcal{O}}((n^{1/2} + t)^{1+1/\kappa} + D)$ w.h.p. In other words, all nodes obtain knowledge of a metric embedding of the terminal graph of (worst-case) stretch $2\kappa - 1$.

After broadcasting the labels $\lambda(v)$, $v \in T$, over a BFS tree to all nodes in $\mathcal{O}(t + D)$ rounds, each node deterministically solves the instance of DSF-IC on the skeleton spanner locally by a centralized α-approximation algorithm.[3] The result is interpreted as an $\alpha(2\kappa - 1)$-approximate solution on the terminal graph. As discussed in Section 4, this in turn induces a $2\alpha(2\kappa - 1)$-approximate solution of the original instance on G. Mapping the locally computed solution back to G is trivial, as the nodes on the corresponding paths know their incident edges on such paths. Overall, for $\alpha \in \mathcal{O}(1)$, we obtain a randomized $\mathcal{O}(\kappa)$-approximation to DSF-IC in $\tilde{\mathcal{O}}((n^{1/2} + t)^{1+1/\kappa} + D)$ rounds w.h.p.

5.1 Key Ideas and Main Results

Pipelining of FRT Edge Selection. Our first observation is that it is possible to exploit the fact that LE lists have $\mathcal{O}(\log n)$ entries w.h.p. to improve on the construction from [16]. From a high-level perspective, our algorithm proceeds as follows. Initially, each terminal v has label $\{\lambda(v)\}$. Then, for $i = 0, \ldots, L$, all nodes execute:

1. Each active terminal v *moves* (i.e., sends and subsequently deletes) its label to v_i. These messages are routed in G according to the LE lists, and all traversed edges are

[3] Finding an exact solution is NP-hard.

added to the solution in G (this corresponds to selecting and mapping back to G the virtual tree edge between $(v_i, \dots, v_L)$ and $(v_{i-1}, \dots, v_L)$ or, if $i = 0$, v).

2. Delete any label which is received by a single node v_i (because $(v_i, \dots, v_L)$ is the least common ancestor of all terminals with that label).

3. For each label that v_i received and did not delete, it picks a terminal v that sent the label to v_i and moves the label back to v; here all labels sent by terminals in the same subtree of the virtual tree are sent to the same terminal. This is done by backtracking sending routes.

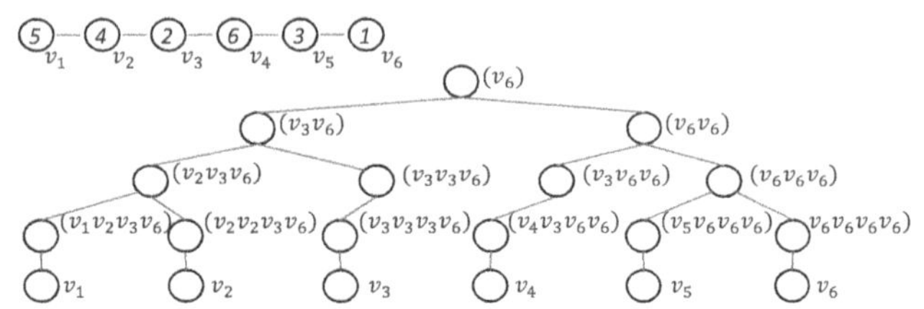

Figure 7: *Another FRT embedding example. Top Left: original graph, permutation values inside circles. In the tree,* v_3 *appears in both* $(v_3v_3v_6)$ *and* $(v_3v_6v_6)$.

Given as local inputs the LE lists and β (i.e., the distributed representation of the FRT embedding), this *almost* implements the strategy for deriving an expected $\mathcal{O}(\log n)$-approximation outlined earlier (see Fig. 7). The difference is that on the virtual tree, v_i may correspond to multiple nodes $(v_i, \dots, v_L)$, $(w_i = v_i, \dots, w_L)$, etc. However, v_i picks only a single terminal u so that $u_i = v_i$ to send a given received (non-deleted) label to. Hence, the algorithm will only select paths corresponding to a subset of the edges of the virtual tree solution. Nonetheless, we obtain a valid solution: Since all terminals that sent a label to v_i are already connected by the selected edge set, for the purpose of the Steiner Forest problem, there is no need to uphold the distinction that they are in different subtrees of the virtual tree.

This procedure enables pipelining, thus avoiding the multiplicative complexity of $\tilde{\mathcal{O}}(sk)$ of [16]. Since the messages are routed on least-weight paths, all messages destined at a node v_i are sent over a shortest-paths tree rooted at v_i. This tree has depth at most s by definition. Because it does not matter from which particular terminal v_i receives a given label λ, it suffices if each node forwards only the *first* message λ destined to v_i to its parent in the tree. Hence, if there was a single tree only and each node transmitted a single label in each round (guaranteeing message size $\mathcal{O}(\log n)$), all labels would be delivered to v_i within at most $s + k$ rounds.

In general, however, each node participates in multiple trees, and if the same neighbor serves as its parent in a few of them, congestion occurs. Fortunately (w.h.p.) the LE lists contain only $\mathcal{O}(\log n)$ entries, and therefore, each node participates in at most $\mathcal{O}(\log n)$ shortest-paths trees used for routing. It follows that by using time-multiplexing, we can guarantee that for each of the trees it participates in, each node sends at least one message every $\mathcal{O}(\log n)$ rounds. Since we can determine in $\mathcal{O}(k + D)$ rounds whether a label is held by a single node only, we conclude that each loop iteration can be completed within $\mathcal{O}((s + k)\log n + D) \subseteq \tilde{\mathcal{O}}(s + k)$ rounds w.h.p., and since $L \in \mathcal{O}(\log n)$, the entire procedure completes within $\tilde{\mathcal{O}}(s + k)$ rounds.

THEOREM 5.1. *An* $\mathcal{O}(\log n)$*-optimal solution to problem* DSF-IC *can be computed in* $\tilde{\mathcal{O}}(s + k)$ *rounds w.h.p.*

Partial FRT Construction plus Skeleton Spanner. If $s > \sqrt{n}$, the above bound does not match the lower bound of Theorem 3.2. The problem is that in the FRT construction information travels long routes. We can avoid this issue by performing the construction only partially and leveraging the spanner construction for the top levels. The key is that the $\sqrt{n}$ nodes of largest rank are a random subset of V. Therefore we do the following.

1. Let $\mathcal{S}$ be the set consisting of the $\sqrt{n}$ nodes of highest rank. Delete $\mathcal{S}$ from the FRT tree.

2. For each node v, let i_v be such that $(v_{i_v}, \dots, v_L)$ is the first deleted ancestor. Replace $(v_{i_v}, \dots, v_L)$ by $\tilde{v}_{i_v} := \text{argmin}_{w \in \mathcal{S}}\{\text{wd}(v, w)\}$, the node from $\mathcal{S}$ closest to v.

3. Run the FRT-based algorithm from above on the resulting (virtual) forest.

As on each path a sampled node is encountered within $\mathcal{O}(\sqrt{n}\log n)$ hops w.h.p., this routine can be executed within $\tilde{\mathcal{O}}(\sqrt{n} + k + D)$ rounds w.h.p.—the maximal depth of the shortest-path-trees used for routing becomes $\tilde{\mathcal{O}}(\sqrt{n})$ w.h.p., replacing the additive s in the complexity. We note the following crucial properties of the selected edge set:

- The total cost of all selected edges is bounded from above by the cost of the optimal solution on the virtual tree: abstractly speaking, we deleted all edges between nodes in $\mathcal{S}$, and replaced edges between nodes in $\mathcal{S}$ and $V \setminus \mathcal{S}$ by "lighter" ones (terminals connect to the closer $\tilde{v}_{i_v}$ instead of $(v_{i_v}, \dots, v_L)$). Thus we selected edges of weight $\mathcal{O}(\log n)$ times the optimum in expectation.
- Recall that the optimal solution on the virtual tree is the union, over all λ, of the minimal trees spanning all terminals v with $\lambda(v) = \lambda$. If such a tree is still present in the forest resulting from deleting $\mathcal{S}$, the selected edge set connects all terminals v with $\lambda(v) = \lambda$.
- Conversely, if terminal v is *not* connected to all terminals w with $\lambda(v) = \lambda(w)$, it must be connected to *some* node from $\mathcal{S}$ that received its label, by a path of $\mathcal{O}(L\sqrt{n}\log n) \subset \tilde{\mathcal{O}}(\sqrt{n})$ hops.

Hence, if we decide that nodes in $\mathcal{S}$ simply hold on to received labels instead of pushing them back to some terminal, when the above routine terminates, all that is left is to connect nodes from $\mathcal{S}$ that share a label.

To this end, we use the spanner-based algorithm of [19]. Since $|\mathcal{S}| = \sqrt{n}$, setting $\kappa = \log n$ results in time complexity $\tilde{\mathcal{O}}(n^{1/2} + D)$, which is our target. However, this may cause the approximation ratio to deteriorate to $\mathcal{O}(\log^2 n)$: Since $\mathcal{S}$ is not the original set of terminals, but only connected to it by edges of total (expected) weight $\mathcal{O}(\log n)$ times the optimum, the weight of an optimal solution on the derived instance on terminal set $\mathcal{S}$ may grow by this factor.

Component Contraction. We resolve this issue as follows. We associate each unsatisfied terminal with a node from $\mathcal{S}$ to which it is already connected. Since unsatisfied terminals are within $\tilde{\mathcal{O}}(\sqrt{n})$ hops from $\mathcal{S}$ using only selected edges, this can be done in $\tilde{\mathcal{O}}(\sqrt{n})$ rounds.

Next, we contract the constructed clusters, associating with each resulting cluster the labels of all terminals it contains. Leveraging pipelining techniques similar to those used earlier, in $\mathcal{O}(|\mathcal{S}| + k + D)$ rounds we can assign to each cluster a single label so that the connectivity requirements are identical to those given by the terminal labels. The key observation here is that whenever two terminals in different clusters are to be connected, it suffices to connect *any* pair of nodes from the clusters, because all nodes within each cluster are already connected. Finally, we run the spanner-based algorithm from [19] on this instance; conveniently, the technique trivially extends to the modified setting with nodes that are, in fact, contracted sets of nodes in G.

Because we constructed the new instance by means of contraction, an optimal solution of the original instance induces a solution of at most the same weight for the new instance. Therefore, the computed solution has weight within factor $\mathcal{O}(\log n)$ of the optimum, but this weight contributes *additively* to the weight of the complete solution. And as the new instance has at most $|\mathcal{S}| = \sqrt{n}$ terminals, the algorithm completes within $\tilde{\mathcal{O}}(\sqrt{n} + D)$ rounds.

THEOREM 5.2. *There is an algorithm that solves* DSF-IC *in $\tilde{\mathcal{O}}(\sqrt{n} + k + D)$ rounds w.h.p. within factor $\mathcal{O}(\log n)$ of the optimum in expectation.*

By combining this algorithm and the one from the previous section of running time $\tilde{\mathcal{O}}(s+k)$, we obtain an $\mathcal{O}(\log n)$-approximation whose running time is optimal up to a polylogarithmic factor. Applying the algorithm $\mathcal{O}(\log n)$ times and choosing the solution of minimum weight ensures that the approximation guarantee holds w.h.p.

COROLLARY 5.3. *There is an algorithm that solves* DSF-IC *in $\tilde{\mathcal{O}}(\min\{s, \sqrt{n}\} + k + D)$ rounds within factor $\mathcal{O}(\log n)$ of the optimum w.h.p.*

Acknowledgements

We thank Fabian Kuhn for valuable discussions.

6. REFERENCES

[1] A. Agrawal, P. Klein, and R. Ravi. When trees collide: An approximation algorithm for the generalized Steiner tree problem on networks. *SIAM Journal of Computing*, 24:440–456, 1995.

[2] S. Baswana and S. Sen. A simple and linear time randomized algorithm for computing sparse spanners in weighted graphs. *Random Structures and Algorithms*, 30(4):532–563, 2007.

[3] M. Brazil, R. Graham, D. Thomas, and M. Zachariasen. On the history of the Euclidean Steiner tree problem. *Archive for History of Exact Sciences*, pages 1–28, 2013.

[4] J. Byrka, F. Grandoni, T. Rothvoß, and L. Sanità. An improved LP-based Approximation for Steiner Tree. In *Proc. 42nd ACM Symp. on Theory of Computing*, pages 583–592, 2010.

[5] P. Chalermsook and J. Fakcharoenphol. Simple Distributed Algorithms for Approximating Minimum Steiner Trees. In *Proc. 11th Conf. on Computing and Combinatorics*, volume 3595 of *LNCS*, pages 380–389, 2005.

[6] M. Chlebík and J. Chlebíková. The Steiner tree problem on graphs: Inapproximability results. *Theoretical Computer Science*, 406(3):207–214, 2008.

[7] R. Cole and U. Vishkin. Deterministic Coin Tossing and Accelerating Cascades: Micro and Macro Techniques for Designing Parallel Algorithms. In *Proc. 18th ACM Symp. on Theory of Computing*, pages 206–219, 1986.

[8] R. Courant and H. Robbins. *What is Mathematics? An Elementary Approach to Ideas and Methods.* London. Oxford University Press, 1941.

[9] A. Das Sarma, S. Holzer, L. Kor, A. Korman, D. Nanongkai, G. Pandurangan, D. Peleg, and R. Wattenhofer. Distributed Verification and Hardness of Distributed Approximation. In *Proc. 43th ACM Symp. on Theory of Computing*, pages 363–372, 2011.

[10] M. Elkin. An Unconditional Lower Bound on the Time-Approximation Tradeoff for the Minimum Spanning Tree Problem. *SIAM Journal of Computing*, 36(2):463–501, 2006.

[11] J. Fakcharoenphol, S. Rao, and K. Talwar. A Tight Bound on Approximating Arbitrary Metrics by Tree Metrics. *J. Comput. System Sci.*, 69(3):485–497, 2004.

[12] R. G. Gallager, P. A. Humblet, and P. M. Spira. A Distributed Algorithm for Minimum-Weight Spanning Trees. *ACM Trans. on Comp. Syst.*, 5(1):66–77, Jan. 1983.

[13] J. Garay, S. Kutten, and D. Peleg. A sub-linear time distributed algorithm for minimum-weight spanning trees. *SIAM Journal of Computing*, 27:302–316, 1998.

[14] M. Hauptmann and M. Karpinski. A Compendium on Steiner Tree Problems. `http://theory.cs.uni-bonn.de/info5/steinerkompendium/netcompendium.html`. Retreived January 2014.

[15] R. M. Karp. Reducibility among combinatorial problems. In R. E. Miller and J. W. Thatcher, editors, *Complexity of Computer Computations*, pages 85–103. Plenum, New York, 1972.

[16] M. Khan, F. Kuhn, D. Malkhi, G. Pandurangan, and K. Talwar. Efficient Distributed Approximation Algorithms via Probabilistic Tree Embeddings. *Distributed Computing*, 25:189–205, 2012.

[17] E. Kushilevitz and N. Nisan. *Communication Complexity.* Cambridge University Press, 1997.

[18] S. Kutten and D. Peleg. Fast Distributed Construction of Small k-Dominating Sets and Applications. *J. Algorithms*, 28(1):40–66, 1998.

[19] C. Lenzen and B. Patt-Shamir. Fast Routing Table Construction Using Small Messages: Extended Abstract. In *Proc. 45th Ann. ACM Symp. on Theory of Computing*, pages 381–390, 2013.

[20] C. Lenzen and B. Patt-Shamir. Improved Distributed Steiner Forest Construction. *CoRR*, abs/1405.2011, 2014.

[21] Z. Lotker, B. Patt-Shamir, and D. Peleg. Distributed MST for constant diameter graphs. *Distributed Computing*, 18(6):453–460, 2006.

[22] D. Peleg. *Distributed Computing: A Locality-Sensitive Approach.* SIAM, Philadelphia, PA, 2000.

[23] D. Peleg and V. Rubinovich. Near-tight Lower Bound on the Time Complexity of Distributed MST Construction. *SIAM J. Computing*, 30:1427–1442, 2000.

[24] H. Takahashi and A. Matsuyama. An Approximate Solution for the Steiner Problem in Graphs. *Mathematica Japonica*, 6:573–577, 1980.

[25] R. E. Tarjan. *Data Structures and network Algorithms*, chapter 6. Society for Industrial and Applied Mathematics, Philadelphia, PA, USA, 1983.

Spanners and Sparsifiers in Dynamic Streams

Michael Kapralov*
MIT

David P. Woodruff
IBM Almaden

ABSTRACT

Linear sketching is a popular technique for computing in dynamic streams, where one needs to handle both insertions and deletions of elements. The underlying idea of taking randomized linear measurements of input data has been extremely successful in providing space-efficient algorithms for classical problems such as frequency moment estimation and computing heavy hitters, and was very recently shown to be a powerful technique for solving graph problems in dynamic streams [AGM'12]. Ideally, one would like to obtain algorithms that use one or a small constant number of passes over the data and a small amount of space (i.e. sketching dimension) to preserve some useful properties of the input graph presented as a sequence of edge insertions and edge deletions.

In this paper, we concentrate on the problem of constructing linear sketches of graphs that (approximately) preserve the spectral information of the graph in a few passes over the stream. We do so by giving the first sketch-based algorithm for constructing multiplicative graph spanners in only *two passes* over the stream. Our spanners use $\tilde{O}(n^{1+1/k})$ bits of space and have stretch 2^k. While this stretch is larger than the conjectured optimal $2k-1$ for this amount of space, we show for an appropriate k that it implies the first 2-pass spectral sparsifier with $n^{1+o(1)}$ bits of space. Previous constructions of spectral sparsifiers in this model with a constant number of passes would require n^{1+c} bits of space for a constant $c > 0$. We also give an algorithm for constructing spanners that provides an *additive* approximation to the shortest path metric using *a single pass* over the data stream, also achieving an essentially best possible space/approximation tradeoff.

1. INTRODUCTION

Massive graphs are now a common way of representing real world data. Search engines and social networks require supporting various queries on large-scale graphs efficiently, and in particular, without having to store the entire graph in memory. An important type of query is a distance query between nodes in the graph. Various notions of distance can be used depending on the application, e.g., shortest path distances, minimum cuts, and effective resistances.

For each of these notions of distance it is known how to *compress* a graph to a small representation that allows for computing distance queries approximately given only the compressed representation. For shortest path distances this is achieved by the spanner construction algorithms of Thorup and Zwick[TZ01] (see also [TZ06, MN06, Bas08, BKMP10, BS03, BS06]), for cuts this is provided by the sparsifiers of Benczúr and Karger[BK96] (see also [FHHP11]) and for effective resistances this is given by the spectral sparsifiers of Spielman and Srivastava [SS08] (see also [BSS09]).

While these compression schemes have been quite successful, when processing massive graphs the data is often distributed and presented online as a long stream of insertions and deletions to its edges on multiple servers. The servers would like to determine aggregate properties of the underlying graph with low communication. Existing compression methods no longer apply, and this has motivated techniques for developing short synopses which are efficiently updatable in these settings. Linear sketching provides such a tool for compressing an object, represented as a vector x, where one chooses a random, succinctly representable matrix S and projects x to a vector $S \cdot x$. If S has fewer rows than columns, this can provide a significant compression. Moreover, given a positive or negative update to the i-th coordinate of x, denoted (i, Δ) and indicating that $x_i \leftarrow x_i + \Delta$, one can add $\Delta \cdot S_i$ to the current sketch $S \cdot x$ to efficiently update the sketch of the underlying vector. Here S_i denotes the i-th column of S. In the distributed setting, the servers can agree upon a sketching matrix S, which is often efficient to communicate if the entries of S are pseudorandom, and then locally compute Sx^i, where $x = x^1 + x^2 + \cdots x^s$ and x^i is the vector held by the i-th server, for $i = 1, 2, \ldots, s$. Communicating Sx^i rather than x^i itself can lead to significant savings.

Linear sketching has only recently emerged as a powerful technique for compressing graphs, pioneered in the work of Ahn, Guha, and McGregor [AGM12a]. In this setting, one views an underlying multigraph on n vertices as an $\binom{n}{2}$-dimensional vector x, indicating the multiplicity of each edge. A stream $\mathcal{S} = a_1, \ldots, a_t$ is given where each $a_k \in [n] \times [n] \times \{-1, 1\}$, and where $x_{i,j} = |\{k : a_k = (i,j,+)\}| - |\{k : a_k = (i,j,-)\}|$ for $i < j$. We assume that the edge multiplicity is non-negative and that the multigraph has no self-loops. This model is known as the dynamic streaming model. In a sequence of work [AGM12a, AGM12b, AGM13], Ahn, Guha, and McGregor show that it is possible to evaluate properties such as bipartiteness, connectivity, k-connectivity, dense subgraphs, maximum weighted matchings, minimum spanning trees, spanners and

*This research was supported by NSF award CCF-1065125, MADALGO center and Simons Foundation. We also acknowledge financial support from grant #FA9550-12-1-0411 from the U.S. Air Force Office of Scientific Research (AFOSR) and the Defense Advanced Research Projects Agency (DARPA).

PODC'14, July 15–18, 2014, Paris, France.

http://dx.doi.org/10.1145/2611462.2611497.

sparsifiers with near linear space in n (as opposed to n^2, which one can do simply by storing each of the edge multiplicities). See also the survey by Guha and McGregor [GM12].

Despite this progress, several important open questions remain. For instance, for multiplicative graph spanners, one seeks to find a sparse subgraph H of a graph G such that for all pairs of vertices u, v one has $d_G(u, v) \leq d_H(u, v) \leq t \cdot d_G(u, v)$, where $d_G(u, v)$ denotes the shortest path distance in G, and $t \geq 1$ is known as the distortion factor. One of the main applications of multiplicative graph spanners is to building spectral sparsifiers. If L_G is the Laplacian of a graph G (see Section 2 for background), a weighted graph H on the same vertex set is said to be a spectral sparsifier of G if $x^T L_H x = (1 \pm \epsilon) x^T L_G x$ simultaneously for all unit vectors x. Spectral sparsifiers approximately preserve the value of all cuts in a graph, by restricting x to binary vectors, but in fact preserve the entire quadratic form associated with the Laplacian of G, and are the focus of a very active line of research [ST04, SS08, BSS09, ST11, AGM12b, AGM13]. They have been instrumental in obtaining the first near-linear time algorithm for solving SDD linear systems [ST11], and have led to many other beautiful ideas [KMP10, KMP11].

Recently, it was shown how to find a spectral sparsifier in a single pass in the dynamic streaming model using $\tilde{O}(n^{5/3})$ bits of space. By combining work of [AGM12b] with the connection between multiplicative spanners and spectral sparsifiers in [KP12], it is possible to construct a spectral sparsifier in the dynamic streaming model with $\tilde{O}(n^{1+1/k})$ bits of space using $O(\log k)$ passes, for any $k \geq 2$. Note that if one wants a constant number of passes, this approach would require at least n^{1+c} bits of space for some positive constant $c > 0$. A natural question is if a sparsifier can be constructed in less space in a constant number of passes.

While multiplicative spanners are well-studied in the dynamic streaming model, another natural question is whether it is possible to design additive spanners in this model. For an additive spanner, one seeks to find a sparse subgraph H of a graph G such that for all pairs of vertices u, v one has $d_G(u, v) \leq d_H(u, v) \leq d_G(u, v) + t$, where t is the distortion factor. Note that additive spanners provide a much stronger guarantee on the distortion than multiplicative spanners. Compression schemes for these spanners have been extensively studied in the algorithms community, where surprisingly, one can achieve $\tilde{O}(n^{4/3})$ space and $O(1)$ distortion (see, e.g. [ACIM99, BKMP10, Che13] and references therein). A natural question is if such results are possible in the dynamic streaming model.

Our results.

In this paper we study the same dynamic streaming model defined above, as in [AGM12a, AGM12b, AGM13]. Note that the edge multiplicity in this model should not to be confused with the *weight* of an edge, in the case that we consider algorithms for weighted graphs. In the case of weighted graphs, the underlying stream can either add a weighted edge or completely remove the weighted edge that has already been added (i.e., set its weight to 0), that is, we do not allow turnstile updates which increment and decrement the weights [1].

[1]This is consistent with the algorithms in [AGM12b], e.g., in Section 3.5 of that paper in their proof of Theorem 3.8 for sparsifiers the authors assume the weights are given beforehand (otherwise they cannot perform the partitioning into weights given after their Lemma 3.7), while in Section 5 of that paper their algorithm for spanners is only for unweighted graphs.

First, for multiplicative spanners we show that for any $k \geq 1$ a 2^k-spanner can be constructed in $\tilde{O}(n^{1+1/k})$ space in the dynamic streaming model if only *two passes* over the stream are allowed:

THEOREM 1. *There exists an algorithm for constructing a 2^k-spanner of a weighted graph G using $\tilde{O}(n^{1+1/k})$ bits of space and two passes in the dynamic streaming model.*

This gives a different tradeoff than the multiplicative spanner constructions of [AGM12b], who show how to achieve $\tilde{O}(n^{1+1/k})$ bits of space using either $O(k)$ passes and $O(k)$ distortion, or $O(\log k)$ passes and poly(k) distortion. Our result shows that $O(1)$ passes and 2^k distortion are also possible. Unlike the algorithms in [AGM12b], our algorithm does not seem to be a less adaptive implementation of a non-streaming algorithm of Baswana and Sen [BS07]. Rather, it requires a different way of growing clusters, based on connecting clusters via randomly sampled vertices chosen ahead of time, which causes the diameter of our clusters to grow exponentially. The algorithm and its analysis are given in Section 3. While the distortion is rather large, we show that it is sufficient in order to use the reduction from spectral sparsification to spanner construction presented in [KP12]. By doing so we obtain the first algorithm for constructing ϵ-spectral sparsifiers in two passes over the input stream and $O(n^{1+o(1)}/\epsilon^4)$ space, for any $\epsilon > 0$:

COROLLARY 2. *For any $\epsilon > 0$ there exists an algorithm for constructing an ϵ-spectral sparsifier of a graph G presented in the dynamic streaming model using $\frac{1}{\epsilon^4} n 2^{O(\sqrt{\log n})} \log(w_{max}/w_{min})$ space and two passes over the stream (here w_{min}, w_{max} are the minimum and maximum edge weights in the input graph).*

We also consider the related problem of constructing additive spanners. For this problem, we present a single pass algorithm:

THEOREM 3. *For each $d \geq 1$ there exists an $\tilde{O}(nd)$-space algorithm for constructing an n/d-additive spanner of an unweighted undirected graph G in a single pass in the dynamic streaming model.*

This space versus approximation tradeoff is optimal even for the insertion-only model, in which each edge is inserted only once and there are no deletions:

THEOREM 4. *In the insertion-only model, any 1-pass streaming algorithm returning a spanner with additive distortion at most n/d with probability at least $6/7$ requires $\Omega(nd)$ bits of space.*

All our algorithms are randomized and succeed with high probability.

Organization.

We start with preliminaries and notation in section 2. Our two-pass spanner construction is presented in section 3. Section 4 gives the algorithm for additive spanner construction in a single pass, and section 5 shows that our approximation versus space tradeoff for this problem is near-optimal even for the insertion-only model. Finally, the spectral sparsification algorithm that we obtain from our multiplicative spanner construction is discussed in Appendix 6.

2. PRELIMINARIES

DEFINITION 5 (t-SPANNER). *A t-spanner of a weighted undirected graph G is a subgraph H of G such that the distances in H are stretch t estimates of the distances in G, i.e. for all $u, v \in V$ one has $d_G(u, v) \leq d_H(u, v) \leq t \cdot d_G(u, v)$.*

For a weighted undirected graph $G = (V, E, w)$ the Laplacian matrix of G is the matrix defined as $L_G(i, j) = -w_{(i,j)}$ and $L_G(i, i) = \sum_{j \neq i} w_{ij}$.

DEFINITION 6 (SPECTRAL ORDERING OF GRAPHS). *We define a partial ordering $\prec$ on graphs by letting $G \prec H$ if and only if $x^T L_G x \leq x^T L_H x \; \forall x \in \mathbb{R}^{|V|}$.*

A weighted undirected graph G can be associated with an electrical network with link e having conductance w_e (i.e. corresponding to a resistor of resistance $1/w_e$). Then the effective resistance R_e across an edge e is the potential difference induced across it when a unit of current is injected at one end of e and extracted at the other end of e. The best known parameters for spectral sparsification are achieved by the algorithm of Spielman and Srivastava:

THEOREM 7 (SPECTRAL SPARSIFICATION, [SS08]). *Let H be obtained by sampling edges of G independently with probability $p_e = \Theta(w_e R_e \log n/\epsilon^2)$ for some $\epsilon > 1/\sqrt{n}$ and giving each sampled edge weight $1/p_e$. Then whp $(1-\epsilon)G \prec H \prec (1+\epsilon)G$.*

For a graph $G = (V, E)$ and a set $S \subseteq V$ we let $N(S) = \{v \in V : (u, v) \in E$ for some $u \in S\}$ denote the vertex neighborhood of S. We will use the following results from sparse recovery and sketching distinct elements:

THEOREM 8 ([CM06]). *We can construct a randomized $0/1$ matrix T of dimension $O(ck \log^3 n) \times n$ such that for any k-sparse signal A of dimension N, given the transformation TA we can reconstruct A exactly with probability at least $1 - n^{-c}$ in time $O(c^2 k \log^3 n)$. The matrix T is constructed using $O(1)$-wise independent hash functions, and individual entries can be queried efficiently.*

We note that we could also use other sketches, such as CountSketch instead of Theorem 8, improving upon the logarithmic factors in the space, though the reconstruction time will be larger.

THEOREM 9 ([KNW10]). *There is a linear sketch-based algorithm using $O(\epsilon^{-2} \log^2 n \log 1/\delta)$ bits of space that can estimate the number of distinct elements of an n-dimensional vector with integer entries bounded by a polynomial in n to within a factor of $(1 \pm \epsilon)$ with probability $1 - \delta$.*

Theorem 9 follows by repeating the algorithm of [KNW10] $O(\log 1/\delta)$ times and taking the median (note also, one can implement that algorithm as a linear sketch over the integers rather than over a finite field if desired, incurring the above space bound).

It is convenient to introduce notation for the linear sketches guaranteed by Theorem 8. In what follows, we assume that we have a (randomized) linear function $\text{SKETCH}_B : \mathbb{R}^n \to \mathbb{R}^r$ with $r = O(B \log^3 n)$ and a function $\text{DECODE} : \mathbb{R}^r \to \mathbb{R}^n$ such that for every $x \in \mathbb{R}^n$ with $||x||_\infty \leq \text{poly}(n)$ and $||x||_0 \leq B$ one has $\text{DECODE}(\text{SKETCH}_B(x)) = x$ with probability at least $1 - 1/\text{poly}(n)$. In general, most primitives that we use have a $1/\text{poly}(n)$ failure probability that can be made arbitrarily small at the expense of increased constants in space bounds, so we will always condition on the failure event not happening. In what follows we assume that we always know if a $\text{SKETCH}_B(x)$ can be decoded. This is easily achieved by maintaining a distinct elements sketch for each instantiation of $\text{SKETCH}_B(x)$, and declaring the sketch to be not decodable when the number of distinct elements is estimated to be above $2B$, for example. This involves an $O(\log^3 n)$ overhead for each instantiation of $\text{SKETCH}_B(x)$ by Theorem 9, and hence does not influence the asymptotic space requirement of $\text{SKETCH}_B(x)$.

AGM sketches.

In [AGM12a] Ahn et al gave an algorithm for constructing connectivity certificates from linear sketches of graphs. We will need

THEOREM 10 (AGM SKETCH, [AGM12A]). *There is a single-pass, linear sketch-based algorithm supporting edge additions and deletions that uses $O(n \log^3 n)$ space and returns a spanning forest of the graph with high probability.*

It will be very useful for our application that the sketches are linear. In particular, we will maintain AGM sketches as in Theorem 10 for a graph G and use them for finding a spanning forest of a graph G' obtained by subtracting a set of edges from G. Besides linearity, AGM sketches have the following property, which we use in our additive spanner construction. The AGM sketch is in fact a collection of vertex neighborhood sketches, and if a graph H is obtained from G by collapsing some sets of nodes into supernodes, an AGM sketch for H can be obtained from an AGM sketch for G (by adding sketches of vertex neighborhoods appropriately).

3. TWO PASSES: BASIC ALGORITHM

In this section we first describe a simple algorithm for constructing spanners in unweighted graphs, and then implement it in the dynamic streaming model using two passes over the stream. Our algorithm extends trivially to weighted graphs by partitioning edges into a geometric sequence of weight classes (this can be done since we are assuming that edges are either added or completely deleted, i.e. the weight of the edge is known during each update).

3.1 Basic algorithm.

Let $\mathcal{C}_i, i = 0, \ldots, k-1$ be a subset of V where nodes are present independently with probability $n^{-i/k}$. In what follows $C > 0$ is a sufficiently large constant. Our algorithm runs in two phases. In the *first phase* for each $i = 0, \ldots, k-2$ we cluster vertices in $\mathcal{C}_i$ around vertices in $\mathcal{C}_{i+1}$. The clusters will be defined by a forest $F \subseteq E$ on V, with the edges of each tree in F always connecting a node in $u \in \mathcal{C}_i$ to at most one node in $v \in \mathcal{C}_{i+1}$[2], $i = 0, \ldots, k-2$. Then v is a parent of u in F. For a node $u \in V$ we denote the subtree of u in F by T_u. For a node $u \in V$ we let $p(u)$ denote the parent of u in F ($p(u) = \perp$ if u is the root of its subtree). For each $u \in \mathcal{C}_i$ we either make u a child of a node $v \in \mathcal{C}_{i+1}$ if $N(T_u) \cap \mathcal{C}_{i+1} \neq \emptyset$ and make u the root of its own component otherwise. As we will show below, if u ends up a root of its own component, then the vertex expansion of its subtree T_u cannot be large (in particular, it cannot be that $|N(T_u)| \gg n^{(i+1)/k}$). We note that the forest F is only a logical construction. Its edges may not necessarily be a subset of the graph G. However, each edge e in the forest F will be associated with an edge $\eta(e)$ of G (which we refer to as the *witness edge* for e; see below for formal definition). For each sutree T_u of F, the set of corresponding witness edges will provide connectivity to nodes in T_u using edges of the graph G.

The *second phase* selects a set of edges to be added to the spanner: we include a set of edges F' determined by F, and a sufficient number of edges to preserve the vertex neighborhood $N(T_u)$ for each $u \in V$ (namely one edge from each $v \in N(T_u) \setminus T_u$ to some $w \in T_u$). We now describe both phases formally, specify parameters and prove correctness and space bounds.

First phase – constructing the clusters.

We start with $F = (V, \emptyset)$, i.e. $T_u = \{u\}$ for all $u \in V$. Then for each $i = 0, \ldots, k-1$ and for each $u \in \mathcal{C}_i$ **(1)** if $i = k-1$ or $\mathcal{C}_{i+1} \cap N(T_u) = \emptyset$, mark u as a *terminal* node; **(2)** otherwise make an arbitrary $w \in \mathcal{C}_{i+1} \cap N(T_u)$ the parent of u, i.e. add

[2] In fact, a node u could belong to multiple sets $\mathcal{C}_i$, so F is not necessarily a forest on V, but a forest on $V \times \{0, \ldots, k-1\}$, where each node $u \in V$ is present via its k copies. We do not make this explicit in the interest of keeping notation simple.

the edge (u, w) to F. Let $v \in T_u$ denote an arbitrary vertex such that $(v, w) \in E$. Define $\eta((u, w)) = (v, w)$ (we say that the edge $\eta((u, w))$ is the edge that *witnesses* the connection of T_u to w).

Second phase – adding edges to the spanner.

In the second phase we construct the set E' of edges of the spanner. We start by setting $E' := \emptyset$. Then for each $u \in V$ **(1)** if u is non-terminal, add the edge $\eta((u, p(u)))$ to E'; **(2)** if u is terminal, for each $v \in N(T_u) \setminus T_u$ add exactly one edge (v, w) to E', where w is an arbitrary node in T_u. First, we have

CLAIM 11. *For every $i = 0, \ldots, k-1$ and every non-terminal node in $\mathcal{C}_i$ one has $|N(T_u)| \leq (C \log n)n^{(i+1)/k}$ with high probability as long as $C > 0$ is a sufficiently large constant.*

PROOF. Suppose that for a node $u \in \mathcal{C}_i$ one has $|N(T_u)| \leq (C \log n)n^{(i+1)/k}$. Then $\mathbf{E}[|N(T_u) \cap \mathcal{C}_{i+1}|] \geq (C \log n)n^{(i+1)/k} \cdot n^{-(i+1)/k} \geq C \log n$. Furthermore, the construction of T_u only depends on the random choices made for $\mathcal{C}_j, j = 0, \ldots, i$, and $\mathcal{C}_{i+1}$ is independent of $\mathcal{C}_j, j = 0, \ldots, i$, so by Chernoff bounds $N(T_u) \cap \mathcal{C}_{i+1} \neq \emptyset$ with probability $1 - n^{-10}$, say, whenever $C > 0$ is a sufficiently large constant, so such a node u would not be terminal. Thus, for every terminal node in $\mathcal{C}_i$ one has $|N(T_u)| \leq (C \log n)n^{(i+1)/k}$ with high probability, as required. □

The number of edges added to the spanner is small:

LEMMA 12. *One has $|E'| = O(kn^{1+1/k} \log n)$.*

PROOF. The set E' is a union of the witness edges $\eta(F)$ and the edges added in step 2 of the second phase, where for each terminal node we add exactly one edge to each $v \in N(T_u) \setminus T_u$.

It remains to bound the number of edges added to the spanner in the second step of the algorithm. By Claim 11 for every non-terminal node in $\mathcal{C}_i$ one has $|N(T_u)| \leq (C \log n)n^{(i+1)/k}$, and hence the total number of edges is bounded by $|\eta(F)| + \sum_{i=0}^{k-1} |\mathcal{C}_i| \cdot O(n^{(i+1)/k} \log n) \leq k(n-1) + \sum_{i=0}^{k-1} O(n^{1-i/k} \cdot n^{(i+1)/k} \log n) = O(kn^{1+1/k} \log n)$. □

Approximation quality is guaranteed by

LEMMA 13. *$H = (V, E')$ is a 2^k-spanner of $G = (V, E)$.*

PROOF. In what follows we abuse notation somewhat by writing, for a node $u \in \bigcup_{i \geq 0} \mathcal{C}_i$, $\eta(T_u)$ to denote the subgraph formed by edges in $\bigcup_{e \in T_u} \eta(e)$. We prove by induction on $j \geq 1$ that for every $u \in \mathcal{C}_j$ the diameter of $\eta(T_u)$ is bounded by $2^{j+1} - 2$.

Base:$j = 1$ The tree $\eta(T_u)$ is a star when $u \in \mathcal{C}_1$, so the diameter is $2 = 2^{1+1} - 2$.

Inductive step:$j \to j + 1$ Consider $u \in \mathcal{C}_{j+1}$. We need to show that any two vertices $a, b \in T_u$ are connected by a path of length at most $2^{j+2} - 2$. Let w be the least common ancestor of a and b in F. If $w \neq u$, then we are done since the diameter of $\eta(T_w)$ is bounded by $2^{j+1} - 2 \leq 2^{j+2} - 2$ by the inductive hypothesis (since w is necessarily at level no higher than i).

Now suppose that u is the least common ancestor of a and b. Let (u, q_a) (resp. (u, q_b)) denote the edges connecting u to the subtrees that a and b belong to. By the inductive hypothesis the distance from q_a to a and the distance from q_b to b is bounded by $2^{j+1} - 2$. Thus, the distance from a to b is bounded by $2(2^{j+1} - 2) + 2 \leq 2^{j+2} - 2$ as required.

We now show that each edge of G is stretched by at most a factor of 2^k. Consider an edge $(u, v) \in E$. Let u' denote the terminal parent of u and v' denote the terminal parent of v. If $u' = v'$, then u and v are connected by a path of length at most $2^k - 2$ since the highest level that $u' = v'$ could be at is $k - 1$, so we are done. Now suppose that $u' \neq v'$. Let (w, v) denote the edge from $w \in T_u$ to v that was added to E' by our algorithm (such an edge exists since the edge (u, v) is in E). Then the path $v \to w \to u$ has length at most $(2^k - 2) + 1 \leq 2^k$, yielding the result. □

REMARK 14. *We note that our algorithm extends to weighted graphs by the simple reduction: round weights to the nearest power of $1 + \epsilon$ for some $\epsilon > 0$, and run the unweighted spanner construction on each weight class. This requires at most a factor of $O(\frac{1}{\epsilon} \log(w_{max}/w_{min}))$ more space.*

In the next section we give a two-pass dynamic streaming implementation of our algorithm.

3.2 Streaming implementation using two passes

Our streaming implementation uses two passes, one for each phase of the algorithm above.

First pass – constructing the clusters.

Recall that in the first phase we construct the forest F bottom up. For each $i = 0, \ldots, k-2$ and $u \in \mathcal{C}_i$ one makes an arbitrary node $v \in N(T_u) \cap \mathcal{C}_{i+1}$ the parent of u if this intersection is non-empty. Otherwise u is declared to be a terminal node, i.e. the root of its own component in F. Since later we will also need to recover an edge $e = (v, w)$ for a node $w \in T_u$, a natural approach to implementing this in small space as follows. We sample random subsets $E_j, j = 0, \ldots, \log_2 n^2$ by including each pair $(a, b) \in \binom{V}{2}$ into E_j independently with probability 2^{-j} and sketch the vector $E_j \cap E \cap (\mathcal{C}_{i+1} \times T_u)$. We assume that the input graph does not have multiple edges to simplify notation, even though the same analysis holds if edges can have multiplicities (one needs to replace sets by multisets in this case, but this does not affect the performance of our sketches since they can handle vectors with polynomially large entries).

We accomplish the first task by keeping linear sketches for $E_j \cap E \cap (\mathcal{C}_r \times T_u)$ for $r = 1, \ldots, k-1$, $j = 0, \ldots, \log_2 n^2$, i.e. by maintaining $\text{SKETCH}_B(E_j \cap E \cap (\mathcal{C}_r \times T_u))$ for $B = O(\log n)$. That way we can keep decoding sketches starting from the largest $j = \log_2 n^2$ until one of the sketches gives us a nonempty set of edges. We will abuse notation somewhat by using $\text{SKETCH}_B(A)$ to denote the sketch of the indicator vector of $A \subset \binom{V}{2}$, i.e. the vector in $\mathbb{R}^{\binom{V}{2}}$ with ones in positions that belong to A and zeros everywhere else.

We now give formal definitions. Let $E_j, j = 0, \ldots, \log_2 n^2$ denote random subsets of $\binom{V}{2}$ where each pair of nodes is present with probability 2^{-j}. Now each node $u \in \mathcal{C}_i$ computes

$$S_j^r(u) \leftarrow \text{SKETCH}_{O(\log n)}^{r,j}((\{u\} \times \mathcal{C}_r) \cap E \cap E_j)$$

for all $j = 0, \ldots, \log_2 n^2$ and $r \in [0 : k-1]$. The superscript r, j corresponds to the fact that the random bits used by SKETCH are a function of r, j, and independent for different (r, j). To construct the forest, for each $i = 0, \ldots, k-2$ each $u \in \mathcal{C}_i$ computes $Q_j^{i+1}(u) := \sum_{v \in T_u} S_j^{i+1}(v)$ for each $j = 0, \ldots, \log_2 n^2$. By linearity, this is a sketch for $(T_u \times \mathcal{C}_{i+1}) \cap E \cap E_j$, so we can detemine if there exists an edge from T_u to $\mathcal{C}_{i+1}$ by decoding this sketch for at least one value of j between 0 and $\log_2 n^2$. We note that it is sufficient to use $O(\log n)$-wise independent random variables to generate the sets E_j. We summarize this in Algorithm 1.

We have

LEMMA 15. *Algorithm 1 constructs the forest F together with witness edges whp. The space requirement is $\tilde{O}(kn)$.*

PROOF. The space complexity is immediate. We now argue correctness. Recall that to construct the forest, for each $i = 0, \ldots, k-2$ each $u \in \mathcal{C}_i$ computes $Q_j^{i+1}(u) := \sum_{v \in T_u} S_j^{i+1}(v)$, for j from $\log_2 n^2$ down to 1 until one of the sketches gives a nonempty set of edges or j reaches 0. By linearity, this is a sketch for $(T_u \times \mathcal{C}_{i+1}) \cap E \cap E_j$, so we can detemine if there exists an edge from T_u to $\mathcal{C}_{i+1}$ by decoding this sketch for at least one value of j between $\log_2 n^2$ and 0 unless decoding of a sketch fails (which happens with probability at most $1/\text{poly}(n)$). The edge recovered from the sketch serves as the witness for $(u, p(u))$. Thus, Algorithm 1 correctly emulates the first phase of our basic algorithm whp. □

Note that our algorithm runs the DECODE procedure on various sketches. The decoding procedure is guaranteed to succeed with $1 - 1/\text{poly}(n)$ probability as long as the sparsity of the sketched signal is smaller than the budget and its entries are properly bounded. In what follows we condition on the event that all such invocations of the decoding procedure succeed. We will need the following claim in section 6.

CLAIM 16. *Consider the execution of Algorithm 1 on a graph $G = (V, E)$. Let R denote the random seed used by the algorithm, and let $\Lambda_1(R) \subset \binom{V}{2}$ denote the set of locations of the adjacency matrix of G whose content the execution path of the algorithm depends on. Then Algorithm 1 can be augmented to output the set of all edges of G that belong to $\Lambda_1(R)$ with high probability.*

PROOF. The algorithm accesses sketches starting from small samples of the adjacency matrix and stops as soon as one of the sketches is nonzero. Thus, it is able to decode all sketches that its execution depends on, and output the corresponding edges. □

Second pass – recovering spanner edges.

We recover the edges of the spanner in the second pass. Recall that in order to do that, we need to recover: **(1)** for each non-terminal node $u \in V$ an edge $(w, p(u)) \in E$, for an arbitrary node $w \in T_u$ (such witness edges have been constructed in our implementation of the first phase already); **(2)** for each terminal node $u \in V$ and each node $v \in V \setminus T_u$ at least one edge from v to T_u.

We only need to show how to achieve (2). For each terminal node $u \in \mathcal{C}_i$ one has $|N(T_u)| \le Cn^{(i+1)/k} \log n$, so it is sufficient to keep a *linear* hash table with $\tilde{O}(n^{(i+1)/k})$ cells such that each cell can hold for each $v \in N(T_u)$ a $O(\text{poly}(\log n))$-size sketch of $N(v) \cap T_u$ (we define the properties of the desired hash table and give an implementation below). Note that sketches are only maintained at terminal nodes, and whenever an update to an edge incident on $w \in T_u$ for a *terminal* node u is received, this update is added directly to the sketch maintained by u. We now give formal definitions (the algorithm as given as Algorithm 2).

First, for each $j = 0, \ldots, \log_2 n$ let Y_j contain each node in V independently with probability 2^{-j}. For each $i \in [0 : k-1]$, each j, terminal node $u \in \mathcal{C}_i$ and $v \in V \setminus T_u$ we store $\text{SKETCH}_{O(\log n)}(N(v) \cap T_u \cap Y_j)$ in a linear hash table H_j^u of size $\tilde{O}(n^{(i+1)/k})$ using v as the key. We will be able to retrieve the contents of H_j^u since for a terminal node $u \in \mathcal{C}_i$ we have $|N(T_u)| = O(n^{(i+1)/k} \log n)$ with high probability. Then edges of the spanner are reconstructed as in the offline algorithm. We summarize this in Algorithm 2. We note that the use of the sets Y_j could be eliminated by using L0-SAMPLER in a similar way as [AGM12a] does, but we find it notationally simpler to present the algorithm in this way.

Algorithm 1 First pass (constructing clusters)

```
procedure ConstructClusters(k)
    F ← (V, ∅)
    Let E_j contain each (a,b) ∈ (V choose 2) independently with probability 2^{-j}, for j = 0,...,log_2 n^2
    Let C_r contain each v ∈ V independently with probability n^{-r/k}, for r = 0,...,k-1
    for u ∈ V do                                        ▷ During the first pass
        Maintain S_j^r(u) ← SKETCH^{r,j}_{O(log n)}(({u} × C_r) ∩ E ∩ E_j), j = 0,...,log_2 n^2, r ∈ [0 : k-1]
    end for
    for i = 0 to k-2 do                                 ▷ After the first pass
        for u ∈ C_i do
            Q_j^{i+1}(u) ← Σ_{v∈T_u} S_j^{i+1}(v) for j = 0,...,log_2 n^2    ▷ Sketch for (T_u × C_{i+1}) ∩ E ∩ E_j
            for j = log_2 n^2 down to 0 do
                x_u ← Decode(Q_j^{i+1}(u))
                if DECODE succeeded and x_u ≠ 0 then
                    (a,b) ← an arbitrary element in the support of x_u, a ∈ T_u, b ∈ C_{i+1}
                    Make b parent of u in F,
                    and let η((u,b)) := (a,b)
                end if
            end for
        end for
    end for
    return F
end procedure
```

We now also provide an outline of an implementation of such a linear hash table H_j^u in space $\tilde{O}(n^{(i+1)/k})$. Recall that the hash table H_j^u needs to support recovery of $\tilde{O}(n^{(i+1)/k})$ values indexed by elements of V, where each value is a string of $\text{poly}(\log n)$ bits (this is the amount of space that $\text{SKETCH}_{O(\log n)}$ needs). The hash table can be implemented by treating the sketches associated with nodes $v \in V$ as $\text{poly}(\log n)$-length bit numbers and sketching this vector $x \in \mathbb{R}^V$ using $\text{SKETCH}_{\tilde{O}(n^{(i+1)/k})}(x)$. It remains to note that we can recover the contents of this hash table whenever the number of inserted elements is $\tilde{O}(n^{(i+1)/k})$, and this is the case by Claim 11 because we only need to decode the table for terminal nodes.

LEMMA 17. *Algorithm 2 correctly executes the second phase of spanner construction whp using $\tilde{O}(kn^{1+1/k})$ space.*

PROOF. Recall that the algorithm needs to recover for each terminal node u and each $v \in V \setminus T_u$ that is connected to T_u at least one edge $(w, v), w \in T_u$. Algorithm 2 for each $j = 0, \ldots, \log_2 n$ stores sketches of neighborhoods of each $v \in V \setminus T_u$ sampled at rate 2^{-j} in the hash table H_j^u. Since u is a terminal node, at most $O(n^{(i+1)/k} \log n)$ nodes $v \in V \setminus T_u$ are connected to T_u at the end of the stream. Thus, each table H_j^u contains $O(n^{(i+1)/k} \log n)$ keys at the end of the stream and hence can be decoded. Now consider $v \in \text{keys}(H_j^u)$. Since $N(v) \cap T_u \cap Y_j$ is sketched to allow reconstruction of $O(\log n)$ sparse vectors, there exists at least one j such that reconstruction is possible whp, and it provides the necessary edge (w, v). The space complexity follows since a hash table of size $\tilde{O}(n^{(i+1)/k})$ is stored for each node in $\mathcal{C}_i$, for a total space of $\sum_{i=0}^{k-1} \tilde{O}(n^{(i+1)/k}) \cdot n^{1-i/k} = \tilde{O}(kn^{1+1/k})$. □

We will need the following claim in section 6.

CLAIM 18. *Consider the execution of Algorithm 2 on a graph $G = (V, E)$. Let R denote the random seed used by the algorithm, and let $\Lambda_2(R) \subset \binom{V}{2}$ denote the set of locations of the adjacency matrix of G whose content the execution path of the algorithm depends on. Then Algorithm 1 can be augmented to output the set of all edges of G that belong to $\Lambda_2(R)$ with high probability.*

PROOF. Algorithm 2 stores for each terminal node $u \in V$ hash tables $H_j^u, j = 0, \ldots, \log_2 n$. For a terminal node u each hash table is guaranteed to be decodable whp. For each key $v \in V$ of hash table H_j^u the entry stored is a sketch of $N(v) \cap T_u \cap Y_j$, where Y_j is a random sample of V at rate 2^{-j}. Our algorithm for each $v \in \text{keys}(H_j^u)$ starts with the largest j and decreases j until it gets a nonempty sketch (say, when $j = j^*$). This sketch can be decoded whp. Crucially, for each v the algorithm ignores the sketches $N(v) \cap T_u \cap Y_j$ for $j < j^*$, and hence its execution path only depends on the sketches that it can completely decode (we condition on the failures not happening for sketches that are guaranteed to be decoded with $1 - 1/\text{poly}(n)$ probability, and thus treat invocations of the decoding procedure as a black box). □

Proof of Theorem 1: Follows by putting together Lemma 13, Lemma 15 and Lemma 17. □

4. $O(N/D)$-ADDITIVE SPANNERS IN $\tilde{O}(ND)$ SPACE IN A SINGLE PASS

In this section we give an algorithm for constructing additive spanners in the dynamic stream model. The algorithm is similar in spirit to the multiplicative spanner construction in section 3, with the important distinction that it samples just one set of centers instead of a hierarchy, like in section 3, and, most importantly, uses the approach of [AGM12a] to connect the sampled centers by a spanning tree.

In particular, we start by choosing a set of $O(n/d)$ centers $\mathcal{C} \subseteq V$ uniformly at random, so that each node of degree above $O(d \log n)$ will have a neighbor in $\mathcal{C}$ with high probability, and let such nodes $u \in V \setminus \mathcal{C}$ select a neighbor in $\mathcal{C}$ as their parent. This way we construct a forest F such that all subtrees of F are stars with nodes in $\mathcal{C}$ at their center. Constructing such a forest is easy – it is sufficient to sketch for every $u \in V \setminus \mathcal{C}$ the set of neighbors of u in (a subsampled version of) $\mathcal{C}$, taking polylogarithmic space per node.

Further, for each node $u \in V$ we maintain a sketch of the set of edges incident on u so that we can reconstruct all edges incident on u if there are at most d of them. Finally, we also store a polylogarithmic number of independent AGM sketches. The edges of the spanner are constructed as follows. First, we let E_{low} denote the set of edges incident on low degree nodes of G (i.e. nodes whose degree was $O(d \log n)$). Then we associate each node with degree above $Cd \log n$ with a neighbor in $\mathcal{C}$ (such a neighbor exists whp by our choice of parameters). This yields $O(n/d)$ clusters $T_u, u \in \mathcal{C}$. We now let G' be the graph obtained from G by subtracting all edges in E_{low}. We then collapse all clusters $T_u, u \in \mathcal{C}$, into supernodes in the new graph G'; let F' denote a spanning forest in the contracted G'. Note that the spanning forest in G' can be computed using Theorem 10 since, starting with AGM sketches for G, we can first subtract all edges in E_{low}, and then invoke Theorem 10 on G'. Finally, we output $E_{low} \cup F \cup F'$. We formalize this in Algorithm 3. Note that as before, we introduce auxiliary sets $Z^r \subseteq V, r = 0, \ldots, \log_2 n$, and then maintain a sketch of $N(u) \cap \mathcal{C} \cap Z^r$ for each $r = 0, \ldots, \log_2 n$ in order to be able to recover a neighbor in $\mathcal{C}$ for each u with degree $\Omega(d)$. We formalize this in Algorithm 3. The guarantees provided by the algorithm are summarized in

THEOREM 19. *Algorithm 3 outputs an $O(n/d)$-additive spanner using space $\tilde{O}(nd)$.*

PROOF. The space bound follows immediately from the definition of Algorithm 3. Let $P = (u = p_0 \to p_1 \to \ldots \to p_t = v)$ be a shortest path between u and v in G. Let H denote the spanner output by Algorithm 3. We show that there exists a path of length at most $t + O(n/d)$ in H.

We first show that P visits every cluster $T_w, w \in \mathcal{C}$ at most once, i.e. there are no two indices $0 \le t_1, t_2 \le t, t_1 < t_2 - 1$ such that $p_{t_1}, p_{t_2} \in T_w$ and $p_{t_1+1} \notin T_w$. Indeed, in that case we can construct the path P' by removing the edges (p_i, p_{i+1}) for $i \in [t_1 : t_2 - 1]$(of which there are at least two) and replace it with two edges $(p_{t_1}, w), (w, p_{t_2})$, preserving (and possibly reducing) path length.

Algorithm 2 Second pass (constructing spanner edges)

procedure CONSTRUCTSPANNER($\{\mathcal{C}_r\}_{r=0}^{k-1}, F, k$)
  $E' \leftarrow \emptyset$
  $Y_j \leftarrow$ sample of V at rate $2^{-j}, j = 0, \ldots, \log_2 n$
  for $u \in \mathcal{C}_i$, u a terminal node, $i \in [0 : k-1]$ **do**
    for $j = 0$ to $\log_2 n$ **do**
      $H_j^u \leftarrow$ hash table with $\tilde{O}(n^{(i+1)/k})$ cells of size $O(\text{poly}(\log n))$ ▷ Create empty hash table
    end for
  end for
  ▷ During the second pass
  for each update $\delta \cdot (a, b)$ **do** ▷ $\delta \in \{-1, 1\}$ is the sign of the update, $a, b \in V$
    $u \leftarrow$ terminal parent of a, $v \leftarrow$ terminal parent of b
    for $j = 0$ to $\log_2 n$ **do**
      If $a \in T_u \cap Y_j, b \in V \setminus T_u$,
        add SKETCH$_{O(\log n)}(\delta \cdot a)$ to b-th entry of H_j^u
      If $b \in T_v \cap Y_j, a \in V \setminus T_v$,
        add SKETCH$_{O(\log n)}(\delta \cdot b)$ to a-th entry of H_j^v
    end for
  end for
  ▷ After the second pass
  for $u \in \mathcal{C}_i$, u a non-terminal node, $i \in [0 : k-1]$ **do**
    Add $\eta((u, p(u)))$ to E' ▷ The edge $\eta((u, p(u)))$ was constructed in first pass
  end for
  for $u \in \mathcal{C}_i$, u a terminal node, $i \in [0 : k-1]$ **do**
    for $v \in V \setminus T_u$ **do**
      for $j = \log_2 n$ down to 0 **do**
        If $v \notin \text{keys}(H_j^u)$ **continue**
        $S \leftarrow H_j^u(v)$ ▷ retrieve sketch with key v
        $w \leftarrow$ DECODE(S)
        If $w \neq \mathbf{0}$ **then** $E' \leftarrow E' \cup \{(w, v)\}$, **break**
          ▷ w is an arbitrary decoded neighbor of v
      end for
    end for
  end for
  return E'
end procedure

We now assume that P visits every cluster at most once and show how to construct a path P' between u and v that has length at most $t + O(n/d)$. We consider edges $e = (a, b) \in P$ of types:
Type 1. e is incident on a low degree node, or belongs to F. Then the edge is available in E^*;
Type 2. $a, b \in T_u \setminus \{u\}$ for some $u \in \mathcal{C}$. Then we can replace the edge by a pair of edges $(a, u), (u, b)$, since they are available in

$F \subseteq E^*$. Since by the argument above P contains $O(n/d)$ such edges, (a, b), in total, this only increases the path length by an additive $O(n/d)$ term;

Type 3. $a \in T_u, b \in T_v$ for some $u, v \in \mathcal{C}, u \neq v$. We call such pairs (u, v) *cross-edges* arising from P (note that (u, v) may not belong to P, only the edge (a, b) is guaranteed to). We now consider the graph $G' = (V, E')$ defined above, i.e. the graph obtained by removing edges in E_{low}. Let G'' be obtained by collapsing all clusters $T_x, x \in \mathcal{C}$ into supernodes. Consider paths P_{uv} from u to v in the spanning forest F'' of G'' for all cross-edges arising from P. We can assume that these paths do not overlap, since otherwise they can be shortcut to provide the same connectivity. It remains to note that the union of these paths contains $O(n/d)$ edges, and can be extended to paths in E^* by using edges of F.

We have shown how to construct a path P' in E^* that has length $t + O(n/d)$, which completes the proof. □

5. LOWER BOUNDS FOR ADDITIVE SPANNERS

In this section we prove Theorem 4, which we restate here for convenience of the reader.

Theorem 4 *In the insertion-only model, any* 1*-pass streaming algorithm returning a spanner with additive distortion at most* n/d *with probability at least* $6/7$ *requires* $\Omega(nd)$ *bits of space.*

PROOF. We use a 2-player *distributional* communication game to prove this. We reduce from the distributional version of the indexing problem IND, in which Alice is given a bit string X of length r, while Bob is given an index $I \in \{1, 2, \ldots, r\}$, and Bob's goal is to output X_I. We endow X with the uniform distribution on $\{0, 1\}^r$, and I with the uniform distribution on $\{1, 2, \ldots, r\}$. Further, X and I are independent. It is known that in any, possibly randomized, protocol in which Alice sends a single message $M(X)$ to Bob, and Bob succeeds in outputting X_I with probability at least $2/3$, where the probability is taken both over Alice's coin tosses and the random choice of X and I, that in expectation Alice's message $M(X)$ must be $\Omega(r)$ bits long [KNR99].

Set $r = Cnd$, for an appropriate constant $C > 0$ to be determined. Let us interpret Alice's input X as $s = 18n/d$ disjoint and independent random graphs $G_1, \ldots, G_s$ each drawn from $G(d, 1/2)$, that is, each G_ℓ has exactly d vertices and each edge is present independently in each G_ℓ with probability $1/2$. Note that each G_ℓ requires $\binom{d}{2} = \Theta(d^2)$ bits to specify, each bit indicating the presence or absence of each potential edge. For $C > 0$ a suitable constant, it is indeed possible to interpret Alice's string in this way.

Suppose we have a 1-pass streaming algorithm returing a spanner with additive distortion n/d. Alice runs this algorithm on the disjoint union of $G_1, \ldots, G_s$, and sends the state of the algorithm to Bob.

Suppose Bob is interested in the bit X_I, which can be interpreted as a specific pair of verices $\{U, V\}$ in a specific graph G_J, for some $J \in [1 : s]$. Note that with our choice of input distribution for IND, J is uniformly random, and U, V are uniformly random distinct vertices in G_J.

For each $\ell \in [1 : s]$, Bob chooses a uniformly random pair $\{U_\ell, V_\ell\}$ of distinct vertices in G_ℓ, with the exception that in G_J, Bob sets $\{U_J, V_J\} = \{U, V\}$. Bob then inserts the edges $\{V_1, U_2\}$, $\{V_2, U_3\}, \ldots, \{V_{s-1}, U_s\}$ into the input stream, and continues the computation of the streaming algorithm on this input stream, starting with the state of the streaming algorithm that Alice sent him. Suppose that with probability at least $6/7$, the output of the streaming algorithm is an additive spanner H with additive distortion at most n/d between all pairs of vertices.

The shortest path from U_1 to V_s follows the edges that Bob inserted into the stream, together with as many of the pairs $\{U_\ell, V_\ell\}$ as possible which correspond to actual edges in G_ℓ. For those G_ℓ for which $\{U_\ell, V_\ell\}$ is not an edge, then the path length is at least 2 inside of G_ℓ.

By Chernoff bounds (over the choice of edges in the different G_ℓ), with probability at least $1 - \exp(-\Theta(n/d))$, at least $s/3$ of the different $\{U_\ell, V_\ell\}$ pairs occur in the stream, as we range over $\ell \in \{1, 2, \ldots, s\}$. Hence, to achieve additive distortion at most n/d, since $s/3 = 6n/d$, at least a $5/6$ fraction of the different $\{U_\ell, V_\ell\}$ which occur in the stream must also occur in H. Since J is uniformly random, $\{U_J, V_J\} = \{U, V\}$ is uniformly random in G_J, and all other $\{U_\ell, V_\ell\}$ are uniformly random edges in G_ℓ for $\ell \neq J$, it follows that the algorithm has no information about J, and therefore if $\{U, V\}$ is an edge in G_J then with probability at least $1 - 1/6 - 1/7 - \exp(-\Theta(n/d)) > 2/3$ it occurs in H, while if $\{U, V\}$ is not an edge in G_J, then it occurs in H with probability at most $1/7$, i.e., if the streaming algorithm fails.

Algorithm 3 Construction of an $O(n/d)$-additive spanner

---

procedure ADDITIVESPANNER(d)
    $F \leftarrow (V, \emptyset)$
    $\mathcal{C} \leftarrow$ sample of V at rate $O(\frac{1}{d})$
    $Z^r \leftarrow$ sample of V at rate 2^{-r}, $r = 0, \ldots, \log_2 n$
        ▷ Auxiliary variables for recovering a node in $N(u) \cap \mathcal{C}$
    For each $u \in V$ maintain:
    $S(u) \leftarrow$ SKETCH$_{\tilde{O}(d)}(N(u))$ ▷ Sketching neighborhood of all nodes $u \in V$
    $A^r(u) \leftarrow$ SKETCH$_{O(\log n)}(N(u) \cap \mathcal{C} \cap Z^r)$ for $r = 0, \ldots, \log_2 n$
    Sketch $\hat{d}_u$ to degree of u (using Theorem 9)
    AGM sketches as per Theorem 10
    $E_{low} \leftarrow \emptyset$
    for $u \in V$ **do**
        if $\hat{d}_u \leq O(d \log n)$ **then**
            $W \leftarrow$ DECODE($S(u)$)
            $E_{low} \leftarrow E_{low} \cup \{(u, v)\}_{v \in W}$
        else
            for $r = 0$ to $\log_2 n$ **do**▷ Associate u with a node in $\mathcal{C}$
                $w \leftarrow$ DECODE($A^r(u)$)
                If $w \neq \perp$ **then** make (an arbitrary element of) w parent of u in F, **break**
            end for
        end if
    end for
    $E' \leftarrow E \setminus E_{low}$ ▷ Subtract edges incident on low-degree nodes from E
    $F' \leftarrow$ SPANNINGFOREST($E', \{T_u\}_{u \in \mathcal{C}}$) ▷ Spanning forest on clusters $T_u, u \in \mathcal{C}$ using AGM sketches
    $E^* \leftarrow E_{low} \cup F \cup F'$
    return E^*
end procedure

It follows that if Bob outputs 1 iff $\{U, V\}$ occurs in H, he will have solved IND with probability at least $2/3$. By the abovementioned communication lower bound for IND, it follows that the space complexity of the streaming algorithm is $\Omega(r) = \Omega(nd)$. In the above lower bound the graph is on $sd = 18n$ vertices; rescaling n by a factor of 18 establishes the theorem. □

6. SPECTRAL SPARSIFIERS

In this section we show that Algorithm 3 of [KP12] can be easily implemented in the dynamic stream model using our multiplicative spanner construction in place of the Thorup-Zwick distance oracles used in [KP12]. The oracle required by [KP12] needs to output, given a pair of nodes $u, v \in V$, an estimate $\hat{d}(u, v)$ that satisfies $d(u, v) \leq \hat{d}(u, v) \leq \kappa d(u, v)$. Note that our multiplicative spanner construction provides such an estimate with $\kappa \leq 2^k$ when $\tilde{O}(n^{1+1/k})$ space is used, by our analysis in section 3.

There is an omission in the proof of a sampling lemma in [KP12] (Lemma 21), so we reprove this lemma here for our application. Also, we outline small space implementation details for other subroutines in [KP12] since [KP12] does not stress the small space requirement. We state the algorithms of [KP12] here for completeness. First, we round all edge weights to the nearest power of $(1+\epsilon)$ (our algorithm will produce a $(1 + O(\epsilon))$-sparsifier, which is fine by rescaling variables). Thus, it is sufficient to construct sparsifiers of unweighted graphs (at the expense of a loss of a factor of $\frac{1}{\epsilon} \log(w_{max}/w_{min})$ in runtime and space complexity).

6.1 Estimating connectivities

We first give a version of the ESTIMATE algorithm from [KP12] that we can use to estimate robust connectivities in the dynamic streaming model. Note that we cannot execute this algorithm directly in the dynamic streaming model since we do not have access to the edge set E of the graph explicitly. This, however, is not necessary, since we can perform estimates for any pair $(u, v) \in \binom{V}{2}$ on demand, i.e. we obtain an oracle for computing estimates of robust connectivities $\hat{q}_{\kappa,\delta}$. This version of the ESTIMATE algorithm of [KP12] is given as Algorithm 4 below.

Algorithm 4 Estimation of robust connectivities

```
procedure ESTIMATE(G, κ, δ)
                                                  ▷ Preprocessing
    for j = 1 to J do                             ▷ J = O(log n/δ^2)
        Set E_t^j ← ∅ for t ∈ [1 : T].            ▷ T = log n^4
        For each e ∈ E add e to E_1^j.
        for t = 1 to T − 1 do
            Add each e ∈ E_t^j to E_{t+1}^j independently with probability 1/2.
        end for
    end for
    for t = 1 to T do
        Construct a distance oracle O_t^j for E_t^j, j ∈ [1 : J].
    end for
                                     ▷ Query time, on input (u, v)
    for t = 1 to T do
        for j = 1 to J do                         ▷ J = O(log n/δ^2)
            If O_t^j(u, v) > κ^2 then η^j(t) ← 1
            else η^j(t) ← 0
        end for
    end for
    q̂_{κ,δ}(e) ← 2^{−t}, where t is the smallest such that |{j : η^j(t) = 1}| ≥ (1 − δ)J
    return q̂_{κ,δ}
end procedure
```

These estimates can be used for sampling as shown in Algorithm 5. Algorithm 5 uses a sequence of subsets of edges of G. Let $E_j, j = 0, \ldots, H = \log_2 n^2$ contain edges of G sampled independently at rate 2^{-j}. Let $q(e) = \hat{q}_{\kappa,\epsilon}(e), e \in E$ be the vector of sampling parameters obtained from ESTIMATE(G, κ, ϵ). We now show how to use the spanner construction primitive to sample edges $e \in E$ with probability proportional to $q(e)$. Since we use the spanner construction algorithm to sample, the sampling is imperfect. However, we show that the quality of our sampling procedure is sufficient to produce a spectral sparsifier.

6.2 Sampling using augmented spanners

Consider an execution of our 2-pass spanner construction algorithm (Algorithms 1 and 2) and let $\Lambda(R) \subseteq \binom{V}{2}$ define the set of locations in the adjacency matrix of the graph accessed by the algorithm, where R is the random seed. Recall that $\Lambda(R) = \Lambda_1(R) \cup \Lambda_2(R)$ as defined in Claims 16 and 18.

CLAIM 20. *Algorithms 1 and 2 can be augmented to output all edges in the set of locations $\Lambda(R)$ that their execution path depends on with probability $1 - 1/poly(n)$ over the choice of the random seed.*

PROOF. Follows by Claim 16 and Claim 18. □

We denote this augmented construction by AUGMENTEDSPANNER(E, κ), where E is the input set of edges, and κ is the stretch parameter. (note that this algorithm outputs all edges of G that belong to $\Lambda(R)$). As in [KP12], our sampling procedure is given by

Algorithm 5 Sampling using an augmented spanner construction

```
procedure SAMPLE-AUGMENTED-SPANNER(G, q, κ)
    for j = 1, ..., H do                          ▷ H ← log_2 n^2
        E_j ← random sample of edges of G at rate 2^{−j}
    end for
    for j = 1, ..., H do
        S_j ← AUGMENTED-SPANNER(V, E_j, κ)    ▷ κ is the stretch parameter
        For each e ∈ S_j, assign weight 0 to e if q(e) ≠ 2^{−j}, otherwise assign weight 2^j.
    end for
    Return the weighted collection S_1 ∪ ... ∪ S_H.
end procedure
```

The sampling process is then given by Algorithm 6. Note that Algorithm 6 differs from the corresponding algorithm in [KP12] in that parameter Z is chosen as $Z \leftarrow \Theta(\kappa^2 \log n/((1-\epsilon)\epsilon^3))$ as opposed to $Z \leftarrow \Theta(\log^3 n/((1-\epsilon)\epsilon^3))$. This is because κ was instantiated to $\log n$ for this algorithm in [KP12].

Algorithm 6 Sparsification via spanners

```
procedure AUGMENTED-SPANNER-SPARSIFY(G, q, ε, κ)
    q ← ESTIMATE(G, κ, ε).
    Z ← Θ(κ^2 log n/((1 − ε)ε^3))
    for t = 1, ..., Z do
        X_t ← SAMPLE-AUGMENTED-SPANNER(G, q, κ)
    end for
    return (1/Z)(X_1 + ... + X_H)
        ▷ Addition above refers to taking a union of X_1, ..., X_H and scaling weights by 1/Z
end procedure
```

We now prove that AUGMENTED-SPANNER-SPARSIFY(G, q, ϵ, Z) produces a spectral sparsifier whp. We will use the following

THEOREM 21. *Let $G = (V, E)$ be an unweighted graph, $\epsilon > 0$ a precision parameter. Let sampling parameters τ_e satisfy $\tau_e \geq R_e/M$ for a parameter M. Let $C > 0$ be a sufficiently large* *constant, and for $j = 1, \ldots, (C/\epsilon^2)M \log n$, $e \in E$ let Y_e^j be independent random variables that equal $1/\tau_e$ with probability τ_e and 0 otherwise. Let G' contain each edge $e \in E$ with weight $\sum_{j=1}^{(C/\epsilon^2)M \log n} Y_e^j$. Then $(1-\epsilon)G \prec G' \prec (1+\epsilon)G$ whp.*

A proof of this theorem follows easily using concentration inequalities for positive semidefinite matrix-valued random variables proved in [Tro12]. We now show that our sampling procedure works nearly as well as independent sampling analyzed in Theorem 21.

LEMMA 22. *Algorithm 6 produces a $(1 \pm O(\epsilon))$-spectral sparsifier of the input graph G whp.*

PROOF. Set $Z = O(\kappa^2 \log n/((1-\epsilon)\epsilon^3))$, as in line 3 of Algorithm 6. By Lemma 19 of [KP12] we have that

$$\hat{q}_{\kappa,\epsilon}(e) = \Omega(\epsilon R_e/\kappa^2) \tag{1}$$

for all $e \in E$. The complication is that in an invocation of SAMPLE-AUGMENTED-SPANNER(G, q, κ) the function AUGMENTED-SPANNER(E_j, κ) may not necessarily output all edges $e \in E_j$ such that $\hat{q}_{\kappa,e} = 2^{-j}$. It is, however, guaranteed to output at least an $1-\epsilon$ fraction of such edges in expectation by the definition of $\hat{q}_{\kappa,e}$ (which we denote by $q(e)$ in what follows). More precisely, for each $e = (u, v)$ such that $q(e) = 2^{-j}$ the set E_j contains no path between u and v of length less than κ with probability at least $1 - 2\epsilon$. Indeed, since the estimation procedure invokes the spanner construction algorithm with stretch κ, the pair (u, v) would not have been assigned $q(e) = 2^{-j}$ otherwise. Thus, the set $E_j \setminus \{e\}$ contains no path between u and v of length less than κ with probability at least $1 - 2\epsilon$, and hence our κ-stretch spanner outputs e with probability at least $1 - 2\epsilon$ over the choice of $E_j \setminus \{e\}$. We now introduce relevant notation and show that this implies that our algorithm outputs a spectral sparsifier.

For each $s = 1, \ldots, Z$ and each $j = 1, \ldots, H = \log_2 n^2$ let $E_{s,j}$ denote the sets sampled in the s-th invocation of AUGMENTED-SPANNER in line 5 of Algorithm 6. For $e \in E$ let $j(e)$ be such that $q(e) = 2^{-j(e)}$. Recall that each invocation of AUGMENTED-SPANNER outputs all edges e in $E_{s,j} \cap \Lambda(R_{s,j})$, where $R_{s,j}$ is the random seed used. Let $X_e^s = 1$ if $e \in E_{s,j(e)}$ and 0 otherwise. First, we have

CLAIM 23. *Fix j. Conditional on $\Lambda(R)$ the random variables $\{X_e^j\}_{e \in E \setminus \Lambda(R)}$ are statistically n^{-C}-close to independent Bernoulli $0/1$ with expectation 2^{-j}, where the choice of $C > 0$ only affects the space requirement of our algorithm by a constant factor.*

PROOF. Recall that $\Lambda_1(R)$ and $\Lambda_2(R)$ are the locations in the adjacency matrix that affect the execution path of our algorithm, conditional on our sketches succeeding. The probability of at least one sketch failing can be chosen to be n^{-C} by choosing parameters appropriately (and the choice of C only affects space complexity by constant factors). □

For each s, j and $\{u, v\} \in \binom{V}{2}$ let $c_{uv}^{s,j} = 1$ if $\{u, v\} \in \binom{V}{2} \setminus \Lambda(R_{s,j})$ and 0 otherwise. We say that a pair $\{u, v\}$ is *covered* in invocation (s, j) if $c_{uv}^{s,j} = 1$. Note that if an edge $e = (u, v)$ is covered, then the constructed spanner must contain a path of length bounded by κ between u and v. Thus, we have $\mathbf{Pr}[c_{uv}^{s,j} = 1] \leq 2\epsilon$ for any $e = (u, v)$ with $q(e) = 2^{-j}$ whp.

Since samples are independent for different $s = 1, \ldots, Z$ and $Z \geq (C/\epsilon) \log n$ for a sufficiently large constant $C > 0$, one has for any $e = (u, v)$ that

$$\sum_{s=1}^{Z} c_e^{s,j(e)} \leq 4\epsilon Z \tag{2}$$

with probability at least $1 - n^{-20}$.

The Laplacian of the sampled graph G' output by AUGMENTED-SPANNER-SPARSIFY is given by

$$L_{G'} = \frac{1}{Z} \sum_{s=1}^{Z} \sum_{e \in E} (1 - c_e^{s,j(e)}) \frac{1}{q(e)} X_e^s \cdot \mathbf{e} \cdot \mathbf{e}^T, \tag{3}$$

where for an edge $e = (u, v)$ we denote the vector in $\mathbb{R}^V$ with -1 at u and $+1$ at v by $\mathbf{e}$. Let

$$L_{\tilde{G}} = \frac{1}{Z} \sum_{s=1}^{Z} \sum_{e \in E} \frac{1}{q(e)} X_e^s \cdot \mathbf{e} \cdot \mathbf{e}^T. \tag{4}$$

By Theorem 21 we have with high probability

$$(1 - O(\epsilon))L_G \prec L_{\tilde{G}} \prec (1 + O(\epsilon))L_G. \tag{5}$$

Let $L_H = \frac{1}{Z} \sum_{s=1}^{Z} \sum_{e \in E} c_e^{s,j(e)} \frac{1}{q(e)} X_e^s \cdot \mathbf{e} \cdot \mathbf{e}^T$. By Claim 23 conditional on $\Lambda(R_{s,j})$ and failure events for our sketching primitives not happening, the random variables $\{X_e^j\}$ for $e \in E \setminus \Lambda(R_{s,j})$ are statistically $n^{-C'}$-close to independent Bernoulli $0/1$ with expectation 2^{-j} (where the choice of constant C' only affects our space requirements by constant factors). Let $\widetilde{X}_e^s$, $s = 1, \ldots, Z, e \in E$ be such Bernoulli $0/1$ random variables coupled with X_e^s on a $1 - n^{-C'}$ fraction of probability space. Letting $L_{\widetilde{H}} = \frac{1}{Z} \sum_{s=1}^{Z} \sum_{e \in E} c_e^{s,j(e)} \frac{1}{q(e)} \widetilde{X}_e^s \cdot \mathbf{e} \cdot \mathbf{e}^T$, we have that $\mathbf{Pr}[L_H \neq L_{\widetilde{H}}] \leq n^{-C'}$. Let R' denote the random bits (random seed R of our algorithm and random choices made in sampling edges that belong to $\Lambda(R)$) that determine the values of $c_e^{s,j}$. By (2) with probability at least $1 - n^{-20}$ one has $\sum_{s=1}^{Z} c_e^{s,j(e)} \leq 4\epsilon Z$ for each $e \in E$ (call this event $\mathcal{E}$). Without loss of generality (and to simplify notation) we assume that conditional on this event one has $c_e^{s,j} = 0$ for all $s > 4\epsilon Z$ and all e (note that this does not change the distribution of $L_{\widetilde{H}}$ since all $\widetilde{X}_e^s$ are iid for fixed e and different s).

Thus, conditional on $\mathcal{E}$, $L_{\widetilde{H}}$ is stochastically dominated by $L_{H,*} := \frac{1}{Z} \sum_{s=1}^{4\epsilon Z} \sum_{e \in E} \frac{1}{q(e)} W_e^s \cdot \mathbf{e} \cdot \mathbf{e}^T$, where $W_e^s = 1$ independently with probability $2^{-j(e)}$ and 0 otherwise. This is because for each fixed $R' \in \mathcal{E}$ and each $e \in E$ the random variable $c_e^{s,j(e)} \widetilde{X}_e^s$ is either 0 or independent Bernoulli $0/1$ with expectation $2^{-j(e)}$, and hence W_e^s and $c_e^{s,j(e)} \widetilde{X}_e^s$ can be coupled so that $c_e^{s,j(e)} \widetilde{X}_e^s \leq W_e^s$. Under this coupling we have that for each $R' \in \mathcal{E}$ the difference $L_{H,*} - L_{\widetilde{H}} = \frac{1}{Z} \sum_{s=1}^{4\epsilon Z} \sum_{e \in E} \frac{1}{q(e)} (W_e^s - c_e^{s,j(e)} \widetilde{X}_e^s) \cdot \mathbf{e} \cdot \mathbf{e}^T$ is a positive semidefinite matrix with probability 1 (since it is a sum of positive semidefinite rank-1 matrices).

By Theorem 21 together with (1) we have that $L_{\widetilde{H}} \prec L_{H,*} \prec O(\epsilon) \cdot L_G$ with high probability (we are using the fact that $\mathbf{Pr}[\mathcal{E}] \geq 1 - n^{-20}$). We also have $\mathbf{Pr}[L_H \neq L_{\widetilde{H}}] < n^{-C'}$, so $L_H \prec O(\epsilon) \cdot L_G$ with high probability. Finally, since $L_{G'} = L_{\tilde{G}} - L_H$ by (3) and (4), this implies by (5) that $(1 - O(\epsilon))L_G \prec L_{G'} \prec (1 + O(\epsilon))L_G$ with high probability, as required.

6.3 Randomness in small space and setting parameters

Note that in order to implement our algorithm in the dynamic stream model it is sufficient to implement the partitioning of the set E of edges of G into classes $E_j, j = 1, \ldots, H$ needed in Algorithm 5 and into sets $E_j^t, j = 1, \ldots, J, t = 1, \ldots, T$ needed in Algorithm 4 (recall that $J = O(\log n/\epsilon^2)$ and $T = \log n^4$). We show how to generate the first sequence of sets in the dynamic streaming model. The second is analogous. We choose uniformly random numbers $h^j_{uv}, u, v \in V, j = 1, \ldots, H$ such that h^j_{uv} are independent and uniform in $[0, 1]$ (rather, a sufficiently fine discretization of $[0, 1]$ with step size $1/\text{poly}(n)$, say). Then a potential edge (u, v) belongs to E_j iff $h^j_{uv} \leq 2^{-j}$. This yields a filtered input stream for each $j = 1, \ldots, H$, which is given as input to our 2-pass distance oracle. Since the approximation guarantees provided by our oracle satisfy the requirements of [KP12], the same analysis holds, and hence calls to ESTIMATE give the same guarantees. It remains to verify that SAMPLE-AUGMENTED-SPANNER and AUGMENTED-SPANNER-SPARSIFY can be implemented in the dynamic stream model with small space. Note that the sequence of sets E_j used in SAMPLE-AUGMENTED-SPANNER can be emulated as we just described. Finally, note that we assumed perfect randomness in the choice of the subsets E^t_j, as required by [KP12], which results in $\Omega(n^2)$ space requirement for the random bits. Since our algorithm works in space $S = O(n^{1+o(1)}/\epsilon^4)$ (after setting parametes appropriately, as we do below), we can replace this perfect randomness with Nisan's pseudoradom generator, taking space $O(n^{1+o(1)}/\epsilon^4)$, in the same way as in [AGM12b] (see section 3.4; the argument is identical, so we do not repeat it here).

It remains to set parameters. Let $\kappa = 2^k$ denote the upper bound on the stretch provided by our algorithm with $\tilde{O}(n^{1+1/k})$ space. Then Algorithm 6 requires $Z = O(\kappa^2(\log n)/\epsilon^3)$ invocations of SAMPLE-AUGMENTED-SPANNER, each of which requires $H = \log_2 n^2$ copies of our spanner construction algorithm, for a total space of $\tilde{O}(\kappa^2 n^{1+1/k}/\epsilon^3) = \tilde{O}(2^{2k} n^{1+1/k}/\epsilon^3)$. A similar calculation shows that the space complexity of ESTIMATE is $\tilde{O}(n^{1+1/k}(\log n^4)/\epsilon^2)$. We now choose $k = \sqrt{\log n}$ to obtain space complexity $\tilde{O}(2^{2\sqrt{\log n}} n^{1+1/\sqrt{\log n}}/\epsilon^4) = n \cdot 2^{O(\sqrt{\log n})}/\epsilon^4$ as desired (an extra factor of $\frac{1}{\epsilon} \log \frac{w_{max}}{w_{min}}$ appears for weighted graphs).

Corollary 2 *For any $\epsilon > 0$ there exists an algorithm for constructing an ϵ-spectral sparsifier of a graph G presented in the dynamic streaming model using $O(n 2^{O(\sqrt{\log n})}(\log(w_{max}/w_{min}))/\epsilon^4)$ space and two passes over the stream.*

7. REFERENCES

[ACIM99] Donald Aingworth, Chandra Chekuri, Piotr Indyk, and Rajeev Motwani. Fast estimation of diameter and shortest paths (without matrix multiplication). *SIAM J. Comput.*, 28(4):1167–1181, 1999.

[AGM12a] Kook Jin Ahn, Sudipto Guha, and Andrew McGregor. Analyzing graph structure via linear measurements. *SODA*, pages 459–467, 2012.

[AGM12b] Kook Jin Ahn, Sudipto Guha, and Andrew McGregor. Graph sketches: sparsification, spanners, and subgraphs. *PODS*, pages 5–14, 2012.

[AGM13] Kook Jin Ahn, Sudipto Guha, and Andrew McGregor. Spectral sparsification in dynamic graph streams. *APPROX-RANDOM*, pages 1–10, 2013.

[Bas08] Surender Baswana. Streaming algorithm for graph spanners - single pass and constant processing time per edge. *Inf. Process. Lett.*, 106(3):110–114, 2008.

[BK96] András A. Benczúr and David R. Karger. Approximating *s-t* minimum cuts in $\tilde{O}(n^2)$ time. *STOC*, pages 47–55, 1996.

[BKMP10] Surender Baswana, Telikepalli Kavitha, Kurt Mehlhorn, and Seth Pettie. Additive spanners and (alpha, beta)-spanners. *ACM Transactions on Algorithms*, 7(1), 2010.

[BS03] Surender Baswana and Sandeep Sen. A simple linear time algorithm for computing a (2k-1)-spanner of $o(n^{1+1/k})$ size in weighted graphs. *ICALP*, pages 384–296, 2003.

[BS06] Surender Baswana and Sandeep Sen. Approximate distance oracles for unweighted graphs in expected $o(n^2)$ time. *ACM Transactions on Algorithms*, 2(4):557–577, 2006.

[BS07] Surender Baswana and Sandeep Sen. A simple and linear time randomized algorithm for computing sparse spanners in weighted graphs. *Random Struct. Algorithms*, 30(4):532–563, 2007.

[BSS09] Joshua D. Batson, Daniel A. Spielman, and Nikhil Srivastava. Twice-ramanujan sparsifiers. *STOC*, pages 255–262, 2009.

[Che13] Shiri Chechik. New additive spanners. In *SODA*, pages 498–512, 2013.

[CM06] G. Cormode and S. Muthukrishnan. Combinatorial algorithms for compressed sensing. *Structural Information and Communication Complexity*, 4056:280–294, 2006.

[FHHP11] Wai Shing Fung, Ramesh Hariharan, Nicholas J. A. Harvey, and Debmalya Panigrahi. A general framework for graph sparsification. *STOC*, pages 71–80, 2011.

[GM12] Sudipto Guha and Andrew McGregor. Graph synopses, sketches, and streams: A survey. *PVLDB*, 5(12):2030–2031, 2012.

[KMP10] Ioannis Koutis, Gary L. Miller, and Richard Peng. Approaching optimality for solving sdd linear systems. In *FOCS*, pages 235–244, 2010.

[KMP11] Ioannis Koutis, Gary L. Miller, and Richard Peng. A nearly-m log n time solver for sdd linear systems. In *FOCS*, pages 590–598, 2011.

[KNR99] Ilan Kremer, Noam Nisan, and Dana Ron. On randomized one-round communication complexity. *Computational Complexity*, 8(1):21–49, 1999.

[KNW10] Daniel M. Kane, Jelani Nelson, and David P. Woodruff. An optimal algorithm for the distinct elements problem. In *PODS*, pages 41–52, 2010.

[KP12] Michael Kapralov and Rina Panigrahy. Spectral sparsification via random spanners. *ITCS*, pages 393–398, 2012.

[MN06] Manor Mendel and Assaf Naor. Ramsey partitions and proximity data structures. *FOCS*, pages 109–118, 2006.

[SS08] D.A. Spielman and N. Srivastava. Graph sparsification by effective resistances. *STOC*, pages 563–568, 2008.

[ST04] D.A. Spielman and S.-H. Teng. Nearly-linear time algorithms for graph partitioning, graph sparsification, and solving linear systems. *STOC*, pages 81–90, 2004.

[ST11] D. Spielman and S. Teng. Spectral sparsification of graphs. *SIAM Journal on Computing*, 40(4):981–1025, 2011.

[Tro12] Joel A. Tropp. User-friendly tail bounds for sums of random matrices. *Found. Comput. Math.*, 12(4):389–434, August 2012.

[TZ01] M. Thorup and U. Zwick. Approximate distance oracles. *STOC*, 2001.

[TZ06] Mikkel Thorup and Uri Zwick. Spanners and emulators with sublinear distance errors. *SODA*, pages 802–809, 2006.

Time Versus Cost Tradeoffs for Deterministic Rendezvous in Networks

Avery Miller
Université du Québec en Outaouais
Gatineau, Canada
avery.miller@utoronto.ca

Andrzej Pelc*
Université du Québec en Outaouais
Gatineau, Canada
pelc@uqo.ca

ABSTRACT

Two mobile agents, starting from different nodes of a network at possibly different times, have to meet at the same node. This problem is known as *rendezvous*. Agents move in synchronous rounds using a deterministic algorithm. In each round, an agent decides to either remain idle or to move to one of the adjacent nodes. Each agent has a distinct integer label from the set $\{1, \ldots, L\}$, which it can use in the execution of the algorithm, but it does not know the label of the other agent.

Two main efficiency measures of a rendezvous algorithm's performance are its *time* (the number of rounds until the meeting) and its *cost* (the combined number of edge traversals by both agents). We investigate tradeoffs between these two measures. A natural benchmark for both time and cost of rendezvous in a network is the number of edge traversals needed for visiting all nodes of the network, called the exploration time. Indeed, this is a lower bound on both the time and the cost of rendezvous. Hence we express the time and cost of rendezvous as functions of an upper bound E on the time of exploration (known to both agents) and the size L of the label space. We present two natural rendezvous algorithms. Algorithm `Cheap` has cost $O(E)$ (and, in fact, a version of this algorithm for the model where the agents start simultaneously has cost exactly E) and time $O(EL)$. Algorithm `Fast` has both time and cost $O(E \log L)$. Our main contributions are lower bounds showing that, perhaps surprisingly, these two algorithms capture the tradeoffs between time and cost of rendezvous almost tightly. We show that any rendezvous algorithm of cost asymptotically E (i.e., of cost $E+o(E)$) must have time $\Omega(EL)$. On the other hand, we show that any rendezvous algorithm with time complexity $O(E \log L)$ must have cost $\Omega(E \log L)$. Moreover, while our algorithms work for arbitrary connected graphs and arbitrary starting times of the agents, these lower bounds hold even in a scenario that is very favorable for potential rendezvous algorithms, i.e., for oriented rings of known size and with simultaneous start.

*Partially supported by NSERC discovery grant and by the Research Chair in Distributed Computing at the Université du Québec en Outaouais.

PODC'14, July 15–18, 2014, Paris, France.

http://dx.doi.org/10.1145/2611462.2611473.

Categories and subject descriptors: F.2.2 [Analysis of Algorithms and Problem Complexity]: Nonnumerical Algorithms and Problems—Computations on discrete structures

Keywords: rendezvous; deterministic algorithm; mobile agent; cost; time.

1. INTRODUCTION

Background. Two autonomous mobile agents, starting from different nodes of a network, have to meet at the same node. This well-researched distributed task is known as *rendezvous.* These mobile entities might represent human-made objects, such as software agents in computer networks or mobile robots navigating in a network of corridors in a mine. They might also be natural, such as migrating birds flying to distant destinations or people who want to meet in an unknown city whose streets form a network. The purpose of meeting might be to exchange data previously collected by the agents, or to coordinate future network maintenance tasks, for example checking functionality of websites or of sensors forming a network.

Model and Problem Description. The network is modeled as an undirected connected graph with n nodes. We seek deterministic rendezvous algorithms that do not rely on perceiving node identifiers, and therefore can work in anonymous graphs as well (cf. [5]). The reason for designing such algorithms is that, even when nodes have distinct identifiers, agents may be unable to perceive them because of limited sensory capabilities (e.g., a mobile robot may be unable to read signs at corridor crossings), or nodes may be reluctant to reveal their identifiers to software agents, e.g., due to security or privacy reasons. Note that, if nodes had distinct identifiers visible to the agents, the agents might explore the graph and meet at the node with the smallest identifier, hence rendezvous would reduce to graph exploration.

On the other hand, we assume that, at each node v, each edge incident to v has a distinct *port number* from $\{0, \ldots, d-1\}$, where d is the degree of v. These port numbers are visible to the agents. Port numbering is *local* to each node, i.e., there is no relation between port numbers at the two endpoints of an edge. Note that in the absence of port numbers, edges incident to a node would be undistinguishable for agents and thus rendezvous would be often impossible, as an adversary could prevent an agent from taking some edge incident to the current node, and this edge could be a bridge to the part of the network where the other agent is located. Security and privacy reasons for not revealing node identifiers to software agents are irrelevant in the case of port numbers, and port numbers in the case of a mine or labyrinth can be made implicit, e.g., by marking one edge at each intersection (using a simple mark legible even by a mobile robot with very limited vision), considering it as corresponding to port 0, and all other port numbers increasing clockwise.

Agents are initially located at different nodes of the graph and traverse its edges in synchronous rounds. They cannot mark visited nodes or traversed edges in any way, and they cannot communicate before meeting. The adversary wakes up each of the agents, possibly in different rounds. Each agent starts executing the algorithm in the round of its wake-up. It has a clock that ticks at each round and starts at the wake-up round of the agent. In each round, each agent decides to either remain at the current node, or to choose a port in order to move to one of the adjacent nodes. When an agent enters a node, it learns the node's degree and the port of entry. When agents cross each other on an edge while traversing it simultaneously in different directions, they do not notice this fact.

Each agent has a distinct integer label from a fixed *label space* $\{1, \ldots, L\}$, which it can use in its execution of the deterministic algorithm that both agents execute. It does not know the label nor the starting round of the other agent. Notice that, since we study deterministic rendezvous, the absence of distinct labels precludes the possibility of meeting in highly symmetric networks, such as rings or tori, for which there exist non-trivial port-preserving automorphisms. Indeed, in such networks, identical agents starting simultaneously and executing the same deterministic algorithm in a distributed way will never meet, since they will be at different nodes in every round. In other words, assigning different labels to agents is the only way to break symmetry, as is needed to meet in every network using a deterministic algorithm. On the other hand, if agents knew each other's identities, then the smaller-labelled agent could stay idle, while the other agent would try to find it. In this case rendezvous reduces to graph exploration. Assuming such knowledge, however, is not realistic, as agents are often created independently in different parts of the network and they know nothing about each other prior to meeting.

The rendezvous is defined as both agents being at the same node in the same round. Two main efficiency measures of a rendezvous algorithm are its *time* (the number of rounds from the start of the earlier agent until the meeting) and its *cost* (the total number of edge traversals by both agents before rendezvous) [1]. We investigate tradeoffs between these measures of rendezvous performance. A natural benchmark for both time and cost of rendezvous in a network is the time of exploration of this network by a single agent, i.e., the worst-case number of edge traversals needed for visiting all nodes of the network, taken over all starting nodes. Indeed, this is a lower bound on both the time and the cost of rendezvous: an adversary can impose a large delay on one of the agents and place it at the node last explored by the other agent. Even for simultaneous start, there are many networks for which the best exploration time is a lower bound on rendezvous time and cost. (One such example is oriented rings.) Hence we assume that some upper bound E on the time of exploration starting at any node of the graph is known to the agents, and that an agent is able to explore the graph in time at most E, starting at any node of the graph.

We express the time and cost of rendezvous as functions of E and the size L of the label space. In the Conclusion, we comment on the situation when no upper bound E is known to the agents. For given parameters E and L, we say that a deterministic rendezvous algorithm works at a cost at most C and in time at most T, if, for any two agents whose distinct labels are from the label space $\{1, \ldots, L\}$ and whose initial positions are arbitrary distinct nodes in a graph that can be explored by a single agent in time E, the agents meet after a total of at most C edge traversals and after at most T rounds since the start of the earlier agent.

A remark is in order about the value of E and how it is calculated. If only an upper bound m on the size of the network is known, then the best known estimate of the time of a (log-space constructible) exploration is Reingold's [44] polynomial estimate $R(m)$ based on Universal Exploration Sequences (UXS); see also [2, 19] for solutions not log-space constructible. The situation improves significantly if each agent has a map of the graph with unlabeled nodes, labeled ports, and the agent's starting position marked. In this case, Depth-First-Search can be performed in time at most $2n-3$, so E can be taken as $2n-3$, which is the optimal exploration time in networks such as the star (a tree of diameter 2). However, for some graphs a better bound E can be found. For example, if the graph has a Hamiltonian cycle, then E can be taken as $n-1$. If the graph has an Eulerian cycle, then E can be taken as $e-1$, where e is the number of edges. Next, suppose that each agent has a port-labeled map, but without a marked starting position. In this case the agent can "try" DFS from all hypothetical starting nodes. In each attempt, the agent aborts the exploration if a prescribed port is not available at the current node, and returns to the starting node. Within n attempts the DFS will succeed, so E can be taken to be $2n(n-2)$. In our study we consider E to be a parameter available to both agents, together with the corresponding exploration procedure, regardless of the particular scenario and of the sharpness of this bound.

As far as the memory of the agent is concerned, the most demanding part of our algorithms is the underlying graph exploration. Hence, the way in which an exploration of time at most E is performed has a decisive impact on the size of the memory required. If the agent knows only an upper bound m on the size of the graph and relies on a UXS to make the exploration, then exploration requires only $O(\log m)$ bits of memory (this is the main result of [44]) but the upper bound E is then fairly large, i.e., a high-degree polynomial in m. If the agent is given as input a DFS walk, coded as a sequence of port numbers, starting and ending at its starting node, then the memory required to record this walk is of size $O(n \log n)$, but the bound E is then sharper. If, given a port-labeled map of the graph with a marked starting node, the agent has to discover an efficient exploration walk by itself, then recording this map is memory-consuming, i.e., up to $O(n^2 \log n)$ bits. In particular cases, e.g., when the underlying graph is a ring of size n, only $\lceil \log n \rceil$ bits of memory are needed to record n, and E can be made as tight as possible, i.e., $n-1$. However, apart

[1] A different way of counting time and cost (under which our results still hold) is discussed in the Conclusion.

from what is needed to perform the underlying graph exploration, our algorithms do not require much memory: as will be seen, it is enough to have simple counters that can be implemented with $O(\log E + \log L)$ memory bits.

Our results. First, recall that the cost of every rendezvous algorithm is at least E and the time is at least $\Omega(E \log L)$, even for the class of rings [26] (for which $E = n - 1$). We present two natural rendezvous algorithms that achieve optimal cost and time, respectively. Algorithm `Cheap` has cost $O(E)$ (and, in fact, a version of this algorithm for the model where the agents start simultaneously has cost exactly E) and time $O(EL)$. Algorithm `Fast` has both time and cost $O(E \log L)$. Our main contributions are lower bounds showing that, perhaps surprisingly, these two algorithms achieve optimal tradeoffs between the time and cost of rendezvous. We show that any rendezvous algorithm of cost asymptotically E (i.e., of cost $E + o(E)$) must have time $\Omega(EL)$. Hence, if we want to be as cheap as `Cheap`, we cannot be faster. On the other hand, we show that any rendezvous algorithm with time complexity $O(E \log L)$ must have cost $\Omega(E \log L)$. Hence, if we want to be as fast as `Fast`, we cannot be cheaper. Moreover, while our algorithms work for arbitrary connected graphs and arbitrary starting times of the agents, these lower bounds hold even in a scenario very favourable for potential rendezvous algorithms, i.e., for oriented rings of known size and when the agents start simultaneously.

It is natural to ask if it is possible to solve rendezvous both at cost $o(E \log L)$, i.e., beating the cost of Algorithm `Fast`, and in time $o(EL)$, i.e., beating the time of Algorithm `Cheap`. It turns out that the answer to this question is "yes". We present a family of algorithms called `Hybrid`(s), for any function $s(L) \leq L$. These algorithms are a combination of Algorithm `Cheap` and Algorithm `Fast`, and solve rendezvous at cost $O(E \log s)$ and in time $O(EL\frac{\log s}{s})$. For $s \in O(1)$ and for $s = L$, Algorithm `Hybrid`(s) is equivalent to Algorithm `Cheap` and to Algorithm `Fast`, respectively. However, for s polylogarithmic in L, it has cost $o(E \log L)$ and time $o(EL)$. Moreover, if we choose as s a function $\varphi(L)$ that grows arbitrarily slowly (but diverges to infinity as L grows), `Hybrid`(s) solves rendezvous at cost $O(E\varphi(L))$ and in time $o(EL)$. The question of whether it is possible to achieve cost $O(E)$ and time $o(EL)$ is an intriguing open problem.

Several proofs are omitted and will appear in the full version of the paper.

Related work. Exploration and rendezvous are the two main tasks accomplished by mobile agents in networks modeled as graphs. Algorithms for graph exploration by mobile agents (often called robots) have been intensely studied in recent literature. A lot of research is concerned with the case of a single agent exploring a labeled graph. In [1, 16, 17, 23, 31] the agent explores strongly-connected directed graphs. In a directed graph, an agent can move only in the direction from tail to head of an edge, not vice-versa. In particular, [23] investigates the minimum time of exploration of directed graphs, and [1, 31] give improved algorithms for this problem in terms of the deficiency of the graph (i.e., the minimum number of edges to be added to make the graph Eulerian). Many papers, e.g., [6, 27, 30, 41] study the scenario where the explored graph is labeled and undirected, and the agent can traverse edges in both directions. In [41], it is shown that a graph with n nodes and e edges can be explored in time $e+O(n)$. In some papers, additional restrictions on the moves of the agent are imposed. It is assumed that the agent has either a restricted tank [12, 18], forcing it to periodically return to the base for refueling, or that it is tethered, i.e., attached to the base by a rope or cable of restricted length [30]. In [27], the authors investigate the problem of how the availability of a map influences the efficiency of exploration. In [2], the authors proved the existence of a polynomial-time deterministic exploration for all graphs with a given bound on size. In [44], a log-space construction of such an exploration was shown.

In all the above papers, except [17], exploration is performed by a single agent. Deterministic exploration by many agents has been investigated mostly in the context when the moves of the agents are centrally coordinated. In [35], approximation algorithms are given for the collective exploration problem in arbitrary graphs. In [10, 11], the authors construct approximation algorithms for the collective exploration problem in weighted trees. On the other hand, in [33], the authors study the problem of distributed collective exploration of trees of unknown topology. In [28], exploration of arbitrary networks by many anonymous agents is investigated, while in [25], this task is studied for labeled agents and labeled nodes.

The problem of rendezvous has been studied both under randomized and deterministic scenarios. An extensive survey of randomized rendezvous in various models can be found in [5], cf. also [3, 4, 7, 14, 36]. Deterministic rendezvous in networks has been surveyed in [42]. Several authors considered geometric scenarios (rendezvous in an interval of the real line, e.g., [14, 15], or in the plane, e.g., [8, 9]). Gathering more than two agents was studied, e.g., in [32, 36, 40, 46].

For the deterministic setting many authors studied the feasibility and time complexity of rendezvous. For instance, deterministic rendezvous of agents equipped with tokens that are used to mark nodes was considered, e.g., in [39]. Deterministic rendezvous in rings by labeled agents, without the ability to mark nodes, was investigated, e.g., in [26, 37]. In [26], the authors gave tight upper and lower bounds of $\Theta(D \log \ell)$ on the time of rendezvous when agents start simultaneously, where D is the initial distance between agents and ℓ is the smaller label. They also gave a lower bound of $\Omega(n + D \log \ell)$ on the time of rendezvous with arbitrary delay in n-node rings. In [37] an upper bound $O(n \log \ell)$ on the time of rendezvous was given, even without knowledge of n. Most relevant to our work are the results about deterministic rendezvous in arbitrary graphs, when the two agents cannot mark nodes, but have unique labels [26, 37, 45]. In [26], the authors present a rendezvous algorithm whose running time is polynomial in the size of the graph, in the length of the shorter label and in the delay between the starting times of the agents. In [37, 45], rendezvous time is polynomial in the first two of these parameters and independent of the delay.

The amount of memory required by the agents to achieve deterministic rendezvous was studied in [34] for trees and in [21] for general graphs. Memory requirements for randomized rendezvous in the ring is discussed, e.g., in [38].

Apart from the synchronous model used in this paper, several authors investigated asynchronous rendezvous in the plane [20, 32] and in network environments [13, 22, 24, 29]. In the latter scenario, the agent chooses the edge to traverse, but the adversary controls the speed of the agent. Under this assumption, rendezvous at a node cannot be guaranteed even in very simple graphs. Hence the rendezvous requirement is relaxed to permit the agents to meet inside an edge.

2. ALGORITHMS

In this section we present three rendezvous algorithms: Algorithm **Cheap**, Algorithm **Fast** and Algorithm **Hybrid**(s), for any function $s(L) \leq L$. In each case, we first describe the algorithm in the easier case of simultaneous start, give a general formulation for arbitrary starting times of the agents, prove its correctness, and establish its time and cost complexities.

Assume that each agent X is given a unique label ℓ_X from the set $\{1, \ldots, L\}$. Let EXPLORE be a procedure that, for every possible starting node, takes E rounds to perform an exploration of the entire input graph. If the exploration is completed earlier, the agent waits after finishing it until a total of E rounds have elapsed. Upon meeting, both agents stop.

We start with the description of a version of Algorithm Cheap for the model where the agents start simultaneously. Agent X waits $(\ell_X - 1)E$ rounds and then explores the graph once. To see why this works, assume, without loss of generality, that $\ell_A < \ell_B$. Then, agent B waits at its starting node in rounds $\{1, \ldots, (\ell_B - 1)E\} \supseteq \{1, \ldots, \ell_A E\}$, and agent A explores the entire graph in rounds $\{(\ell_A - 1)E + 1, \ldots, \ell_A E\}$. Therefore, agent A meets agent B at its starting node by round $\ell_A E$. Thus, rendezvous is achieved in at most ℓE rounds, where ℓ is the smaller label. In the worst case this is $(L-1)E$. Since at most one exploration is performed, the cost is at most E.

In the general case of arbitrary starting times, Algorithm Cheap is described as follows.

Algorithm 1 Cheap(ℓ,EXPLORE)

Execute EXPLORE once
Wait $2\ell E$ rounds
Execute EXPLORE once

PROPOSITION 2.1. *Algorithm* Cheap *completes rendezvous at cost $O(E)$ and in time $O(LE)$.*

Next, in order to describe Algorithm Fast, we recall the label transformation from [29]. If $x = (c_1 \cdots c_r)$ is the binary representation of the label ℓ of an agent, define its *modified label* to be the sequence $M(\ell) = (c_1 c_1 c_2 c_2 \cdots c_r c_r 01)$. Note that, for any x and y, the sequence $M(x)$ is never a prefix of $M(y)$. Also, $M(x) \neq M(y)$ if $x \neq y$. Since the (original) labels of the agents are different, there exists an index for which their transformed labels differ. Note that if $z = 1 + \lfloor \log \ell \rfloor$ is the length of the binary representation of the label ℓ of the agent, then $m = 2z + 2$ is the length of its modified label.

We describe Algorithm Fast, first in the case of simultaneous start. Suppose that $(b_1 \cdots b_m)$ is the transformed label of an agent. In the time segment $[(i-1)E + 1, iE]$, the agent executes EXPLORE if $b_i = 1$, and, otherwise, the agent stays idle.

To see why this works, consider any two agents A and B, and let S_A and S_B denote their transformed labels, respectively. Consider the smallest index j such that $S_A[j] \neq S_B[j]$. Without loss of generality, assume that $S_A[j] = 1$ and $S_B[j] = 0$. It follows that, during the time segment $[(j-1)E + 1, \ldots, jE]$, agent A explores the entire graph while B is idle. Therefore, agent A meets agent B by round jE. Hence the worst possible time is $(2\lfloor \log(L-1) \rfloor + 4)E = O(E \log L)$. The cost is bounded above by twice the time, hence it is also $O(E \log L)$.

In the general case of arbitrary starting times Algorithm Fast is described as follows.

Algorithm 2 Fast(ℓ,EXPLORE)

$S[1 \ldots m] \leftarrow M(\ell)$
$T[1 \ldots 2m+1] \leftarrow (1, S[1], S[1], S[2], S[2], \ldots, S[m], S[m])$
for $i = 1$ to $2m + 1$ **do**
  if $(T[i] = 1)$ **then**
    execute EXPLORE once
  else
    wait E rounds
  end if
end for

PROPOSITION 2.2. *Algorithm* Fast *completes rendezvous at cost $O(E \log L)$ and in time $O(E \log L)$.*

Next, we describe Algorithm Hybrid, which combines Algorithm Cheap and Algorithm Fast. The high-level idea is to partition the set of all possible agent labels into buckets of size $s \in \{1, \ldots, L\}$, where s is provided as an input to the algorithm. Each agent uses its bucket number as its label for executing a modified version of Algorithm Cheap in which all executions of the EXPLORE procedure are replaced by executions of Algorithm Fast with a modified label. In particular, each agent uses its original label ℓ to calculate two labels: $\ell_{\texttt{Cheap}} = \lceil \ell / s \rceil$ which serves as its bucket number, and $\ell_{\texttt{Fast}} = (\ell \mod s) + 1$ which serves as its modified label for Algorithm Fast. Let $T_{\texttt{Fast}}(s)$ be the upper bound on the number of rounds used by Algorithm Fast, given that the labels used by agents running the algorithm come from the set $\{1, \ldots, s\}$. The agents can calculate $T_{\texttt{Fast}}(s)$ knowing s.

We first present the algorithm in the easier case of simultaneous start. An agent with label ℓ waits for $(\ell_{\texttt{Cheap}} - 1)T_{\texttt{Fast}}(s)$ rounds, then executes Algorithm Fast using $\ell_{\texttt{Fast}}$ as its label. To see why this works, first consider the case where the two agents have different values for $\ell_{\texttt{Cheap}}$. In this case, the agent with the smaller label performs an entire execution of Algorithm Fast (and thus explores the entire graph) during the time segment $[(\ell_{\texttt{Cheap}} - 1)T_{\texttt{Fast}}(s) + 1, \ldots, \ell_{\texttt{Cheap}} T_{\texttt{Fast}}(s)]$, while the agent with the larger label is idle; this implies rendezvous. Otherwise, if both agents have the same value for $\ell_{\texttt{Cheap}}$, then they both execute Algorithm Fast starting in round $(\ell_{\texttt{Cheap}} - 1)T_{\texttt{Fast}}(s) + 1$. However, since the two agents have different values for ℓ, they have different values for $\ell_{\texttt{Fast}}$ from the range $\{1, \ldots, s\}$. Thus, by the correctness of Algorithm Fast, the two agents will meet by round $\ell_{\texttt{Cheap}} T_{\texttt{Fast}}(s)$. Since $\ell_{\texttt{Cheap}} \leq \lceil L/s \rceil$ and $T_{\texttt{Fast}}(s) \in O(E \log s)$, the worst-case meeting time is $O(\frac{EL \log s}{s})$. Further, since the two agents meet during the first execution of Algorithm Fast, the total cost is $O(E \log s)$.

In the general case of arbitrary starting times, Algorithm Hybrid is described as follows.

Algorithm 3 Hybrid(s,ℓ,EXPLORE)

1: $\ell_{\texttt{Cheap}} \leftarrow \lceil \ell/s \rceil$
2: $\ell_{\texttt{Fast}} \leftarrow (\ell \mod s) + 1$
3: Execute **Fast**($\ell_{\texttt{Fast}}$, **EXPLORE**) once
4: Wait $2\ell_{\texttt{Cheap}}T_{\texttt{Fast}}(s)$ rounds
5: Execute **Fast**($\ell_{\texttt{Fast}}$, **EXPLORE**) once

PROPOSITION 2.3. *For arbitrary $s \in \{1, \ldots, L\}$, Algorithm* **Hybrid**(s) *completes rendezvous at cost $O(E \log s)$ and in time $O(\frac{EL \log s}{s})$.*

3. LOWER BOUNDS

In order to make our lower bounds as strong as possible, we show that they hold even in a very restricted situation: when the underlying graph is particularly simple and the agents have full knowledge of it. A ring is *oriented* if every edge has port labels 0 and 1 at the two end-points. Such a port labeling induces orientation of the ring: at each node, we will say that taking port 0 is going clockwise and taking port 1 is going counterclockwise. Throughout this section, we assume that agents operate in an oriented ring of size n known to the agents. Hence, in this case, E is taken as $n-1$: starting from any node an agent can explore the ring going $n-1$ steps clockwise. This is, of course, an optimal exploration. Moreover, we assume that both agents start simultaneously, i.e., their clock values are equal in each round. Even in this scenario, which is very favourable to potential rendezvous algorithms, we establish lower bounds proving that our algorithms **Cheap** and **Fast** capture the time vs. cost tradeoffs for rendezvous almost tightly.

In our lower bound proofs, we use the following terminology. For simplicity, an agent with label x will be called agent x. Consider a rendezvous algorithm $\mathcal{A}$. Consider two arbitrary agents x, y and two arbitrary nodes p_x, p_y in the oriented ring of size n. We denote by $\alpha(x, p_x, y, p_y)$ the execution of algorithm $\mathcal{A}$ in which x starts at node p_x and y starts at node p_y. The final round of $\alpha(x, p_x, y, p_y)$, denoted by $|\alpha(x, p_x, y, p_y)|$, is the first round in which x and y meet. In a slight abuse of notation, we denote by $\alpha(x, p_x, \perp, \perp)$ the *solo* execution of $\mathcal{A}$, i.e., when x executes the algorithm alone, starting at node p_x. Note that the behaviour of agent x in an execution $\alpha(x, p_x, y, p_y)$ is the same as its behaviour in execution $\alpha(x, p_x, \perp, \perp)$ until round $|\alpha(x, p_x, y, p_y)|$.

For each label $x \in \{1, \ldots, L\}$, algorithm $\mathcal{A}$ specifies a *behaviour vector* V_x. In particular, V_x is a sequence with terms from $\{-1, 0, 1\}$ that specifies, for each round i of the solo execution of agent x, whether agent x moves clockwise (denoted by -1), remains idle (denoted by 0), or moves counterclockwise (denoted by 1). Note that an agent's behaviour vector is independent of its starting position, since an agent cannot determine where on the ring it is initially positioned.

We now describe a procedure Trim($\mathcal{A}$) which modifies the behaviour vectors specified by $\mathcal{A}$. At a high level, we are zeroing the entries that the algorithm never uses so that, if we show the existence of a non-zero entry in round number i of some behaviour vector, then there is an execution of the algorithm that takes at least i rounds. Specifically, for each $x \in \{1, \ldots, L\}$:

1. Find the maximum value of $|\alpha(x, p_x, y, p_y)|$, taken over all $y \in \{1, \ldots, L\} \setminus \{x\}$ and nodes p_x, p_y.
   Denote this maximum by m_x.
2. For all $j > m_x$, set $V_x[j] = 0$.

Note that this does not change any non-solo execution of $\mathcal{A}$: any modified entry in V_x corresponds to a round that occurs after x has met with any other agent. Also, after performing this trimming operation, for any non-zero entry $V_x[i]$, there exists an agent y and there exist starting positions for x and y such that x and y have not met by round i and agent x moves during round i. We obtain lower bounds on the running time (or cost) of $\mathcal{A}$ by proving lower bounds on the length (or weight) of behaviour vectors resulting from procedure Trim($\mathcal{A}$).

Our first lower bound shows that no rendezvous algorithm of cost asymptotically E (i.e., of cost $E + o(E)$), can beat the time $\Theta(EL)$ of Algorithm **Cheap**. (Recall that Algorithm **Cheap** always has cost $O(E)$ and it has cost exactly E in a model with simultaneous start.)

THEOREM 3.1. *Any rendezvous algorithm of cost $E+o(E)$ must have time $\Omega(EL)$.*

PROOF. Let $\mathcal{A}$ be a rendezvous algorithm such that, for some $\varphi \in o(E)$, for every pair of agent labels, and for every pair of starting positions of the agents, rendezvous is completed at cost at most $E + \varphi$. As previously explained, instead of behaviour vectors of algorithm $\mathcal{A}$, we consider behaviour vectors resulting from procedure Trim($\mathcal{A}$).

Starting with an arbitrary node, label the nodes of the ring using the integers $0, \ldots, n-1$, ascending in the counterclockwise direction. This is for analysis only: the agents do not have access to any node labeling.

During any round of an execution α, we can determine on which 'side' of its starting position an agent is currently situated. Specifically, in any round i of α, if the prefix of an agent's behaviour vector up to round i has at least as many (resp. at most as many) -1's as 1's, then we say that the agent is on its *clockwise side* (resp. *counter-clockwise side*) in round i. For any agent x, let $back(x)$ be the number of distinct edges that x traverses on its clockwise side, and let $forward(x)$ be the number of distinct edges that x traverses on its counter-clockwise side. Without loss of generality, we assume that, for at least half of the agents x, $back(x) \leq forward(x)$. We call these agents *counter-clockwise-heavy*, and we proceed by considering only the counter-clockwise-heavy agents.

FACT 3.1. *For any agent A, $back(A) \leq \varphi$.*

For any execution α involving an agent A, let $disp(A, \alpha) = \sum_{j=1}^{|\alpha|} V_A[j]$. In other words, $disp(A, \alpha)$ is the displacement of agent A in the counter-clockwise direction at the end of execution α. The following fact follows from this definition.

FACT 3.2. *For any execution α involving an agent A, $-back(A) \leq disp(A, \alpha) \leq forward(A)$.*

Let $F = \lceil E/2 \rceil$. For any execution α involving agents A and B, we say that a node A is *eager* if $disp(A, \alpha) \geq disp(B, \alpha) + F$.

FACT 3.3. *Consider any two agents A, B. In the execution $\alpha(A, 0, B, F)$, exactly one of A or B is eager.*

A directed graph G is a *tournament* if, for each pair of distinct vertices $a, b \in V(G)$, exactly one of (a, b) or (b, a) is an edge in $E(G)$. We construct a tournament graph T with $\lfloor \frac{L}{2} \rfloor$ vertices, as follows. First, assign to each vertex in T a unique label from the set of counter-clockwise-heavy agents. Next, for each pair of vertices A, B in T, with $A < B$, we add a directed edge whose tail is the eager agent in $\alpha(A, 0, B, F)$. By Fact 3.3, this operation is well-defined. Every tournament graph has a directed Hamiltonian path [43]. Let $(A_1, \ldots, A_{\lfloor \frac{L}{2} \rfloor})$ be the sequence of agent labels encountered along one such path. For each $i \in \{1, \ldots, \lfloor \frac{L}{2} \rfloor - 1\}$, let $\alpha_i = \alpha(A_i, 0, A_{i+1}, F)$.

FACT 3.4. *For each $i \in \{1, \ldots, \lfloor \frac{L}{2} \rfloor - 1\}$, $disp(A_{i+1}, \alpha_i) \leq (F + \varphi)/2$.*

FACT 3.5. *For each $i \in \{1, \ldots, \lfloor \frac{L}{2} \rfloor - 1\}$, $|\alpha_{i+1}| > |\alpha_i|$.*

In order to prove this fact, first note that, by Fact 3.4, $disp(A_{i+1}, \alpha_i) \leq (F+\varphi)/2$. It follows from Fact 3.1 that for each $k \in \{1, \ldots, |\alpha_i|\}$ we have $\sum_{j=1}^{k} V_{A_{i+1}}[j] \leq (F + 3\varphi)/2$. Since A_{i+1} is eager in execution α_{i+1} and $\varphi \in o(F)$, we have $\sum_{j=1}^{|\alpha_{i+1}|} V_{A_{i+1}}[j] = disp(A_{i+1}, \alpha_{i+1}) \geq F - \varphi > (F + 3\varphi)/2 \geq \sum_{j=1}^{k} V_{A_{i+1}}[j]$, for each $k \in \{1, \ldots, |\alpha_i|\}$. This implies that $|\alpha_{i+1}| \notin \{1, \ldots, |\alpha_i|\}$, which proves the fact.

FACT 3.6. *For each $i \in \{1, \ldots, \lfloor \frac{L}{2} \rfloor - 1\}$, $|\alpha_i| \geq i\left(\frac{F-3\varphi}{2}\right)$.*

We prove this fact by induction on i. For the base case, note that, in execution α_1, the time needed for rendezvous is at least $F/2$, hence $|\alpha_1| \geq F/2 \geq \frac{F-3\varphi}{2}$.

Next, as induction hypothesis, assume that for some $i \in \{1, \ldots, \lfloor \frac{L}{2} \rfloor - 2\}$, $|\alpha_i| \geq i\left(\frac{F-3\varphi}{2}\right)$. Consider the execution α_{i+1}. From Fact 3.4, $disp(A_{i+1}, \alpha_i) = \sum_{j=1}^{|\alpha_i|} V_{A_{i+1}}[j] \leq (F+\varphi)/2$. However, in execution α_{i+1}, agent A_{i+1} is eager, so $\sum_{j=1}^{|\alpha_{i+1}|} V_{A_{i+1}}[j] = disp(A_{i+1}, \alpha_{i+1}) \geq disp(A_{i+2}, \alpha_{i+1}) + F$. By Facts 3.1 and 3.2, $disp(A_{i+2}, \alpha_{i+1}) + F \geq F - \varphi$. So, we have shown that

$$F - \varphi \leq \sum_{j=1}^{|\alpha_{i+1}|} V_{A_{i+1}}[j] = \left[\sum_{j=1}^{|\alpha_i|} V_{A_{i+1}}[j]\right] + \left[\sum_{j=|\alpha_i|+1}^{|\alpha_{i+1}|} V_{A_{i+1}}[j]\right]$$

$$\leq [(F+\varphi)/2] + \left[\sum_{j=|\alpha_i|+1}^{|\alpha_{i+1}|} V_{A_{i+1}}[j]\right].$$

(Note that the above decomposition of the sum into two sub-sums is possible in view of Fact 3.5). It follows that $\sum_{j=|\alpha_i|+1}^{|\alpha_{i+1}|} V_{A_{i+1}}[j] \geq \frac{F-3\varphi}{2}$, so $|\alpha_{i+1}| - |\alpha_i| \geq \frac{F-3\varphi}{2}$. Finally, by the induction hypothesis, we get that $|\alpha_{i+1}| = (|\alpha_{i+1}| - |\alpha_i|) + |\alpha_i| \geq (i+1)\left(\frac{F-3\varphi}{2}\right)$. This proves Fact 3.6 by induction.

Fact 3.6 implies that the length of execution $\alpha_{\lfloor \frac{L}{2} \rfloor - 1}$ is at least $(\lfloor \frac{L}{2} \rfloor - 1)\left(\frac{F-3\varphi}{2}\right) \in \Omega(EL)$ rounds. $\square$

Our second lower bound shows that no rendezvous algorithm of time complexity of Algorithm `Fast` can beat the cost complexity of this algorithm.

THEOREM 3.2. *Any rendezvous algorithm that has time $O(E \log L)$ must have cost $\Omega(E \log L)$.*

PROOF. Let $\mathcal{A}$ be a rendezvous algorithm such that for every pair of agent labels, and for every pair of starting positions of the agents, rendezvous is completed in at most $cE \log L$ rounds, for some constant $c > 0$. Our goal is to prove that there exists an execution in which the total combined cost incurred by the agents is in $\Omega(E \log L)$.

Instead of behaviour vectors of algorithm $\mathcal{A}$, we consider behaviour vectors resulting from procedure `Trim`($\mathcal{A}$). Recall, from the trimming of algorithm $\mathcal{A}$, that m_x is defined to be the maximum value of $|\alpha(x, p_x, y, p_y)|$, taken over all $y \in \{1, \ldots, L\} \setminus \{x\}$ and all nodes p_x, p_y. Further, in agent x's trimmed behaviour vector, all entries after m_x have value 0.

Starting with an arbitrary node, label the nodes of the ring using the integers $0, \ldots, n-1$, ascending in the counter-clockwise direction. This is for analysis only: the agents do not have access to any node labeling. For simplicity, assume that n is divisible by 6. The proof can be modified in the general case. Partition the set of nodes into 6 equal-sized *sectors*: for each $j \in \{0, \ldots, 5\}$, let P_j be $\{j(\frac{n}{6}), \ldots, (j+1)(\frac{n}{6}) - 1\}$. For ease of notation, it will be assumed that all subscripts of sectors are taken modulo 6. Next, let $L' = \lceil 6c \log L \rceil$, and, for each integer $i \in \{1, \ldots, L'\}$, we define *block* B_i to be the time interval $[(i-1)(\frac{n}{6})+1, \ldots, i(\frac{n}{6})]$. For each agent x, let $B(x)$ be the block that contains round m_x. Since there are L distinct agent labels and $L' < L$ blocks, it follows from the Pigeonhole Principle that there exist at least $\ell = \lceil L/L' \rceil$ agents $x_1, \ldots, x_\ell$ such that $B(x_1) = \cdots = B(x_\ell)$. Let $M \leq L'$ be the index of the block that contains $m_{x_1}, \ldots, m_{x_\ell}$. In what follows, we only consider agents from the set $\{x_1, \ldots, x_\ell\}$.

Since the number of nodes in a sector is equal to the number of rounds in a block, we observe that the segment of the ring explored by an agent during a single block cannot contain nodes from 3 different sectors. This implies the following fact about which nodes an agent may visit during a given block.

FACT 3.7. *If agent x is located in a sector P_j at the beginning of a block B_i, then, in all rounds from the beginning of block B_i until the beginning of block B_{i+1}, x is never located at a node outside of $P_{j-1} \cup P_j \cup P_{j+1}$.*

We now define an *aggregate behaviour vector* for x, denoted by Agg_{x,p_x}, that describes x's movement in execution $\alpha(x, p_x, \bot, \bot)$ during each of the blocks $B_1, \ldots, B_M$. At the beginning of an arbitrary block B_i, suppose that agent x is located at a node in P_j for some $j \in \{0, \ldots, 5\}$. By Fact 3.7, at the beginning of block B_{i+1}, agent x is located at a node in $P_{j-1} \cup P_j \cup P_{j+1}$. For each $i \in \{1, \ldots, M\}$, we define $Agg_{x,p_x}[i]$ to be $z \in \{-1, 0, 1\}$ if x is located at a node in P_{j+z} at the beginning of block B_{i+1}. Note that, for any choice of nodes p_x, p'_x such that $p_x \equiv p'_x (\mod \frac{n}{6})$, we get $Agg_{x,p_x} = Agg_{x,p'_x}$.

For any integer-valued vector V, define $surplus(V) = \sum_{i=1}^{length(V)} V[i]$. For a vector V, we write $V[a \ldots b]$ to denote the part of the vector V between positions a and b, inclusive.

We now define a *progress vector* for each agent x, denoted by $Prog_{x,p_x}$. At a high level, an agent x's progress vector keeps track of each time that x takes a "significant" number of steps more in one direction than in the other. Essentially, our goal is to zero out the entries of x's aggregate behaviour vector that amount to x oscillating back and forth on the ring without making sufficient progress towards the other agent. More formally, a node x's progress vector $Prog_{x,p_x}$ is obtained from its aggregate behaviour vector Agg_{x,p_x} in the following way. First, if every prefix of Agg_{x,p_x} has surplus of absolute value at most 1, then $Prog_{x,p_x}$ is defined to be the zero-vector of length M. This means that x is essentially idle and waiting for the other agent to come meet it. Otherwise, when there is a prefix of Agg_{x,p_x} that has surplus of absolute value 2, then the smallest such prefix *pre* is chosen. Next, the 'significant' non-zero entries are found, i.e., entries that actually contribute to the large surplus. More formally, consider the case where $surplus(pre) = 2$ (the case where $surplus(pre) = -2$ is symmetric) and suppose that x is initially located at a node in P_j. We determine the last block B_a during which x moves from P_j to P_{j+1}, and, the first block B_b during which x moves from P_{j+1} to P_{j+2}. Note that, by definition, $b = length(pre)$. Then, we set $Prog_{x,p_x}[i] = Agg_{x,p_x}[i]$ for each $i \in \{a, b\}$, and set $Prog_{x,p_x}[i] = 0$ for each $i \in \{1, \ldots, length(pre)\} \setminus \{a, b\}$. The rest of $Prog_{x,p_x}$ is calculated by repeating the above process on the remaining part of the aggregate behaviour vector, i.e., on $Agg_{x,p_x}[length(pre) + 1 \ldots M]$.

Our next goal is to show that progress vectors of different agents that meet in every execution, must be distinct. This is not immediately clear because, in the construction of progress vectors, distinct aggregate behaviour vectors can be mapped to equal progress vectors.

FACT 3.8. *For any agents $x \neq y$, if $Prog_{x,0} = Prog_{y,0}$, then x and y do not meet in execution $\alpha(x, 0, y, \frac{n}{2})$.*

Using the fact that the progress vectors must all be distinct (cf. Fact 3.8), we now show that there must be a progress vector of large weight.

FACT 3.9. *Consider the $\ell = \lceil \frac{L}{\lceil 6c \log L \rceil} \rceil$ distinct progress vectors $Prog_{x_1}, \ldots, Prog_{x_\ell}$. There exists $j \in \{1, \ldots, \ell\}$ such that $Prog_{x_j,0}$ contains $\Omega(\log L)$ non-zero entries.*

We now set out to prove that there exists an agent incurring cost $\Omega(E \log L)$ in some execution of the algorithm. Using the complete description of progress vectors, we can show that, for each agent x, there exists a positive integer k_x, such that there are k_x pairwise disjoint time segments during which x makes progress in the same direction twice. These time segments correspond to pairs of equal non-zero entries in the progress vector. During each such time segment, agent x traverses an entire sector, which implies the following fact.

FACT 3.10. *During execution $\alpha(x, 0, \perp, \perp)$, agent x performs at least $k_x E/6$ edge traversals.*

By Fact 3.9 there exists an agent x_j such that $Prog_{x_j,0}$ has at least $\Omega(\log L)$ non-zero entries. Applying Fact 3.10 to this agent implies that it incurs cost $\Omega(E \log L)$ in its solo execution of the trimmed version of algorithm $\mathcal{A}$. Hence, there exists an agent y and nodes p_{x_j} and p_y, such that agent x_j incurs the same cost in execution $\alpha(x_j, p_{x_j}, y, p_y)$. This completes the proof. □

4. CONCLUSION

Our results show that Algorithm **Cheap** is the fastest of all rendezvous algorithms that have the lowest possible cost, and Algorithm **Fast** is the cheapest of all rendezvous algorithms that run in shortest possible time. Hence, we established tight tradeoffs at both ends of the time/cost tradeoff curve, up to multiplicative constants. A challenging open problem yielded by our work is establishing the entire precise tradeoff curve, i.e., finding, for each cost value between $\Theta(E)$ and $\Theta(E \log L)$, the minimum time of rendezvous that can be performed at this cost. In particular, it is natural to ask if the performance of our Algorithm **Hybrid**(s) is on, or close to, this optimal tradeoff curve. By varying s from constant to L, the cost of Algorithm **Hybrid**(s) varies from $\Theta(E)$ to $\Theta(E \log L)$, and for these extreme values, Algorithm **Hybrid**(s) is equivalent to Algorithm **Cheap** and Algorithm **Fast**, respectively. Hence its performance is on the optimal curve at the extremities of the cost interval. Is it on this curve inside this interval as well?

In this paper, we adopted a model in which both agents are located at their starting positions from the beginning, and the adversary wakes them up possibly at different times. Hence, if the delay is sufficiently large, it is possible that the earlier agent finds the later agent before it even starts executing the algorithm. Consequently, both time and cost are counted from the wake-up of the earlier agent. Such an approach is natural, since we are interested in both the time and cost of the algorithm, and the cost is defined as the combined number of edge traversals by both agents. An alternative model, used in papers dealing only with time of rendezvous (cf. [26, 45]), assumes that agents are "parachuted" onto their respective starting positions at the time of their wake-up. In this model, the earlier agent cannot find the later agent before its wake-up because the later agent is not yet present. Hence, in [26, 45], time was counted from the wake-up of the *later* agent, since otherwise rendezvous time can be made arbitrarily large by an adversary. Similarly, in our case, we would have to count both the time and the cost since the wake-up of the later agent. This does not seem natural as far as cost is concerned, because it is often the case that incurring cost results in consuming a limited resource, such as energy. So ignoring the cost incurred by the earlier agent until the wake-up of the later agent is unrealistic. Nevertheless, the time and cost complexities of our algorithms do not change in this alternative model (although the proofs have to be slightly modified). Our lower bounds are not affected either, as they work even for simultaneous start.

Finally, we address our assumption that an exploration procedure and its cost E are known. As we argued in the introduction, the exploration time is a benchmark for the cost of rendezvous. Further, this knowledge can be deduced by the agents from an upper bound on the size of the graph. What if agents do not have any such upper bound? It turns out that our algorithms can be slightly modified to preserve their time and cost complexities in this case as well. Recall that a Universal Exploration Sequence (UXS) is a sequence of integers that can be used to explore any graph of size at most m at cost $R(m)$, (for some fixed polynomial R), starting at any node of the graph. Let **EXPLORE**$_i$ be the the UXS-based exploration procedure for the class of graphs of size at most 2^i, and let E_i be the time of **EXPLORE**$_i$. Each of our algorithms can be modified by iterating the original algorithm using **EXPLORE** = **EXPLORE**$_i$ and $E = E_i$ in the i-th iteration. Iterations proceed until rendezvous, which will occur when 2^i is at least the actual size of the graph. Due to telescoping, the time and cost complexities will not change. Again, our lower bounds remain unaffected, since they work even when the graph size is known.

5. REFERENCES

[1] S. Albers and M. R. Henzinger, Exploring unknown environments, SIAM J. Comput. 29 (2000), 1164-1188.

[2] R. Aleliunas, R.M. Karp, R.J. Lipton, L. Lovasz, and C. Rackoff, Random walks, universal traversal sequences, and the complexity of maze problems, Proc. 20th Annual Symposium on Foundations of Computer Science (FOCS 1979), 218-223.

[3] S. Alpern, The rendezvous search problem, SIAM J. on Control and Optimization 33 (1995), 673-683.

[4] S. Alpern, Rendezvous search on labelled networks, Naval Reaserch Logistics 49 (2002), 256-274.

[5] S. Alpern and S. Gal, The theory of search games and rendezvous. Int. Series in Operations research and Management Science, Kluwer Academic Publisher, 2002.

[6] C. Ambuehl, L. Gasieniec, A. Pelc, T. Radzik, X. Zhang, Tree exploration with logarithmic memory, ACM Transactions on Algorithms 7 (2011), article 17.

[7] E. Anderson and R. Weber, The rendezvous problem on discrete locations, Journal of Applied Probability 28 (1990), 839-851.

[8] E. Anderson and S. Fekete, Asymmetric rendezvous on the plane, Proc. 14th Annual ACM Symp. on Computational Geometry (1998), 365-373.

[9] E. Anderson and S. Fekete, Two-dimensional rendezvous search, Operations Research 49 (2001), 107-118.

[10] I. Averbakh and O. Berman, A heuristic with worst-case analysis for minimax routing of two traveling salesmen on a tree, Discr. Appl. Math. 68 (1996), 17-32.

[11] I. Averbakh and O. Berman, $(p-1)/(p+1)$-approximate algorithms for p-traveling salesmen problems on a tree with minmax objective, Discr. Appl. Mathematics 75 (1997), 201-216.

[12] B. Awerbuch, M. Betke, R. Rivest and M. Singh, Piecemeal graph learning by a mobile robot, Proc. 8th Conf. on Comput. Learning Theory (1995), 321-328.

[13] E. Bampas, J. Czyzowicz, L. Gasieniec, D. Ilcinkas, A. Labourel, Almost optimal asynchronous rendezvous in infinite multidimensional grids, Proc. 24th International Symposium on Distributed Computing (DISC 2010), 297-311.

[14] V. Baston and S. Gal, Rendezvous on the line when the players' initial distance is given by an unknown probability distribution, SIAM J. on Control and Opt. 36 (1998), 1880-1889.

[15] V. Baston and S. Gal, Rendezvous search when marks are left at the starting points, Naval Reaserch Logistics 48 (2001), 722-731.

[16] M.A. Bender, A. Fernandez, D. Ron, A. Sahai and S. Vadhan, The power of a pebble: exploring and mapping directed graphs, Proc. 30th Ann. Symp. on Theory of Computing (STOC 1998), 269-278.

[17] M.A. Bender and D. Slonim, The power of team exploration: Two robots can learn unlabeled directed graphs, Proc. 35th Ann. Symp. on Foundations of Computer Science (FOCS 1994), 75-85.

[18] M. Betke, R. Rivest and M. Singh, Piecemeal learning of an unknown environment, Machine Learning 18 (1995), 231-254.

[19] J. Chalopin, S. Das, A. Kosowski, Constructing a map of an anonymous graph: Applications of universal sequences, Proc. 14th International Conference on Principles of Distributed Systems (OPODIS 2010), 119-134.

[20] M. Cieliebak, P. Flocchini, G. Prencipe, N. Santoro, Distributed computing by mobile robots: Gathering, SIAM J. Comput. 41 (2012), 829-879.

[21] J. Czyzowicz, A. Kosowski, A. Pelc, How to meet when you forget: Log-space rendezvous in arbitrary graphs, Distributed Computing 25 (2012), 165-178.

[22] J. Czyzowicz, A. Labourel, A. Pelc, How to meet asynchronously (almost) everywhere, ACM Transactions on Algorithms 8 (2012), article 37.

[23] X. Deng and C. H. Papadimitriou, Exploring an unknown graph, Journal of Graph Theory 32 (1999), 265-297.

[24] G. De Marco, L. Gargano, E. Kranakis, D. Krizanc, A. Pelc, U. Vaccaro, Asynchronous deterministic rendezvous in graphs, Theoretical Computer Science 355 (2006), 315-326.

[25] D. Dereniowski, Y. Disser, A. Kosowski, D. Pajak, P. Uznanski, Fast collaborative graph exploration, Proc. 40th International Colloquium on Automata, Languages and Programming (ICALP 2013), 520-532.

[26] A. Dessmark, P. Fraigniaud, D. Kowalski, A. Pelc. Deterministic rendezvous in graphs. Algorithmica 46 (2006), 69-96.

[27] A. Dessmark and A. Pelc, Optimal graph exploration without good maps, Theoretical Computer Science 326 (2004), 343-362.

[28] Y. Dieudonné, A. Pelc, Deterministic network exploration by anonymous silent agents with local traffic reports, Proc. 39th International Colloquium on Automata, Languages and Programming (ICALP 2012), 500-512.

[29] Y. Dieudonné, A. Pelc, V. Villain, How to meet asynchronously at polynomial cost, Proc. 32nd Annual ACM Symposium on Principles of Distributed Computing (PODC 2013), 92-99.

[30] C.A. Duncan, S.G. Kobourov and V.S.A. Kumar, Optimal constrained graph exploration, Proc. 12th Ann. ACM-SIAM Symp. on Discrete Algorithms (SODA 2001), 807-814.

[31] R. Fleischer, G. Trippen, Exploring an unknown graph efficiently, Proc. 13th European Symp. on Algorithms (ESA 2005), 11-22.

[32] P. Flocchini, G. Prencipe, N. Santoro, P. Widmayer, Gathering of asynchronous robots with limited visibility, Theoretical Computer Science 337 (2005), 147-168.

[33] P. Fraigniaud, L. Gasieniec, D. Kowalski, A. Pelc, Collective tree exploration, Networks 48 (2006), 166-177.

[34] P. Fraigniaud, A. Pelc, Delays induce an exponential memory gap for rendezvous in trees, ACM Transactions on Algorithms 9 (2013), article 17.

[35] G. N. Frederickson, M. S. Hecht and C. E. Kim, Approximation algorithms for some routing problems. SIAM J. Comput. 7 (1978), 178-193.

[36] A. Israeli and M. Jalfon, Token management schemes and random walks yield self stabilizing mutual exclusion, Proc. 9th Annual ACM Symposium on Principles of Distributed Computing (PODC 1990), 119-131.

[37] D. Kowalski, A. Malinowski, How to meet in anonymous network, Theoretical Computer Science 399 (2008), 141-156.

[38] E. Kranakis, D. Krizanc, and P. Morin, Randomized Rendez-Vous with Limited Memory, Proc. 8th Latin American Theoretical Informatics (LATIN 2008), 605-616.

[39] E. Kranakis, D. Krizanc, N. Santoro and C. Sawchuk, Mobile agent rendezvous in a ring, Proc. 23rd Int. Conference on Distributed Computing Systems (ICDCS 2003), 592-599.

[40] W. Lim and S. Alpern, Minimax rendezvous on the line, SIAM J. on Control and Optimization 34 (1996), 1650-1665.

[41] P. Panaite and A. Pelc, Exploring unknown undirected graphs, Journal of Algorithms 33 (1999), 281-295.

[42] A. Pelc, Deterministic rendezvous in networks: A comprehensive survey, Networks 59 (2012), 331-347.

[43] L. Redei, Ein kombinatorischer Satz, Acta Litteraria Szeged 7 (1934), 39-43.

[44] O. Reingold, Undirected connectivity in log-space, Journal of the ACM 55 (2008).

[45] A. Ta-Shma and U. Zwick. Deterministic rendezvous, treasure hunts and strongly universal exploration sequences. Proc. 18th ACM-SIAM Symposium on Discrete Algorithms (SODA 2007), 599-608.

[46] L. Thomas, Finding your kids when they are lost, Journal on Operational Res. Soc. 43 (1992), 637-639.

An Incomplete History of Concurrency
Chapter 1. 1965–1977

Leslie Lamport
Microsoft Research

It is insufficiently considered that men more often require to be reminded than informed.
~Samuel Johnson

Abstract
A personal view of the first dozen years of the modern field of concurrent and distributed computing, viewed from the perspective of 2014. Further chapters are left for others to write.

Categories and Subject Descriptors:
K.2 [**Computing Milieux**]: History of Computing - *Theory*

Keywords
Concurrent computing; Distributed computing

PODC'14, July 15–18, 2014, Paris, France.
ACM 978-1-4503-2944-6/14/07.
http://dx.doi.org/10.1145/2611462.2611514

Rigorous System Design

Joseph Sifakis
RiSD Laboratory
INJ 341, Station 14
CH-1015 Lausanne
SWITZERLAND
joseph.sifakis@epfl.ch

ABSTRACT

We advocate rigorous system design as a coherent and accountable model-based process leading from requirements to implementations. We present the state of the art in system design, discuss its current limitations, and identify possible avenues for overcoming them.

A rigorous system design flow [3] is defined as a formal accountable and iterative process composed of steps, and based on four principles: (1) separation of concerns; (2) component-based construction; (3) semantic coherency; and (4) correctness-by-construction. We show that the combined application of these principles allows the definition of rigorous design flows clearly identifying where human intervention and ingenuity are needed to resolve design choices, as well as activities that can be supported by tools to automate tedious and error-prone tasks. An implementable system model is progressively derived by source-to-source automated transformations in a single host component-based language rooted in well-defined semantics. Using a single modeling language throughout the design flow enforces semantic coherency. Correct-by-construction techniques allow well-known limitations of a posteriori verification to be overcome and ensure accountability. It is possible to explain, at each design step, which among the requirements are satisfied and which may not be satisfied.

The presented view has been amply implemented in the BIP (Behavior, Interaction, Priority) component framework and substantiated by numerous experimental results showing both its relevance and feasibility [1]. We show in particular, how distributed implementations can be generated from BIP models with multiparty interactions by application of correct-by-construction transformations [2].

We conclude with a discussion advocating a system-centric vision for computing, identifying possible links with other disciplines, and emphasizing centrality of system design.

Categories and Subject Descriptors

D.1.3 [**Programming Techniques**]: Distributed Programming; D.2.2 [**Software Engineering**]: Design Tools and Techniques

Keywords

System design; Design methodology; Correctness by construction; Component-based systems; Distributed code generation

1. REFERENCES

[1] Ananda Basu, Saddek Bensalem, Marius Bozga, Jacques Combaz, Mohamad Jaber, Thanh-Hung Nguyen, and Joseph Sifakis. Rigorous component-based system design using the BIP framework. *IEEE Software*, 28(3):41–48, 2011.

[2] Borzoo Bonakdarpour, Marius Bozga, Mohamad Jaber, Jean Quilbeuf, and Joseph Sifakis. A framework for automated distributed implementation of component-based models. *Distributed Computing*, 25(5):383–409, 2012.

[3] Joseph Sifakis. Rigorous system design. *Foundations and Trends in Electronic Design Automation*, 6(4):293–362, 2013.

PODC'14, July 15–18, 2014, Paris, France.
ACM 978-1-4503-2944-6/14/07.

How to Withstand Mobile Virus Attacks, Revisited

Joshua Baron*
RAND Corporation
1776 Main Street
Santa Monica, CA 90407
jbaron@rand.org

Karim El Defrawy
HRL Laboratories
3011 Malibu Canyon Rd
Malibu, CA 90265
kmeldefrawy@hrl.com

Joshua Lampkins†
Department of Mathematics, UCLA
Box 951555
Los Angeles, CA 90095
jlampkins@math.ucla.edu

Rafail Ostrovsky
Department of Computer Science and Department of Mathematics, UCLA
4732 Boelter Hall
Los Angeles, CA 90095
rafail@cs.ucla.edu

ABSTRACT

In PODC 1991 Ostrovsky and Yung [35] introduced the proactive security model, where corruptions spread throughout the network, analogous to the spread of a virus or a worm. PODC 2006 distinguished lecture by Danny Dolev, that also appears in the PODC06 proceedings, lists the above work as one of PODC's "Century Papers at the First Quarter-Century Milestone" [22]. At the very center of this work is the notion of proactive secret sharing schemes. Secret sharing schemes allow a dealer to distribute a secret among a group of parties such that while the group of parties jointly possess the secret, no sufficiently small subset of the parties can learn any information about the secret. The secret can be reconstructed only when a sufficient number of shares are combined together. Most secret sharing schemes assume that an adversary can only corrupt some fixed number of the parties over the entire lifetime of the secret; such a model is unrealistic in the case where over a long enough period of time, an adversary can eventually corrupt all parties or a large enough fraction that exceeds such a threshold. More specifically, in the proactive security model, the adversary is not limited in the number of parties it can corrupt, but rather in the rate of corruption with respect to a "rebooting" rate. Ostrovsky and Yung proposed the first proactive secret sharing scheme, which received a lot of follow-up attention. In the same paper, Ostrovsky and Yung also showed that constructing a general purpose secure multiparty computation (MPC) protocol in the proactive security model is feasible as long as the rate of corruption is a constant fraction of the parties. Their result, however, was shown only for stand-alone security and incurred a large polynomial communication overhead for each gate of the computation. Following the initial work defining the proactive security model, numerous cryptographic primitives and distributed protocols have been adapted to the proactive security model, such as proactively secure threshold encryption, proactive Byzantine agreement, proactive key management, proactive digital signatures, and many others. All these results use proactive secret sharing schemes. In this paper, we introduce a new "packed" proactive secret sharing (PPSS) scheme, where the amortized communication and the amortized computational cost of maintaining each individual secret is optimal (e.g., a constant rate), resolving a long standing problem in this area. Assuming secure point-to-point channels and authenticated, reliable broadcast over a synchronous network, our PPSS scheme can tolerate a $1/3-\epsilon$ (resp. $1/2-\epsilon$) corruption rate against a malicious adversary, and is perfectly (resp. statistically) UC-secure, whereas all previous proactive secret sharing schemes have been secure under cryptographic assumptions only. As an application of our PPSS scheme, we show how to construct a proactive multiparty computation (PMPC) protocol with the same threshold as the PPSS scheme and near-linear communication complexity. PMPC problem is very general and implies, for example, proactive Byzantine Agreement. Our PMPC result also matches the asymptotic communication complexity of the best known MPC results in the "classical" model of stationary faults [19].

*The work of this author was performed while at HRL Laboratories.

†The work of this author was performed while at HRL Laboratories.

PODC'14, July 15–18, 2014, Paris, France.

http://dx.doi.org/10.1145/2611462.2611474.

Categories and Subject Descriptors

C.2.4 [**Computer-Communication Networks**]: Distributed Systems—*Distributed applications*; H.3.4 [**Information Storage and Retrieval**]: Systems and Software—*Distributed systems*

Keywords

Proactive security; secure multiparty computation; secret sharing

1. INTRODUCTION

Secret sharing schemes allow a dealer to distribute *shares* of a secret among a set of parties such that a coalition of parties is needed in order to reconstruct the secret. The notion of secret sharing was introduced independently by Shamir [39] and Blakley [8]. Most secret sharing schemes provide threshold security, in which an adversary must corrupt more than a threshold number of parties over the lifetime of the secret in order to learn the secret. However, fixed bounds on adversary's corruption limit can be unrealistic for applications in which secrets are stored over long periods of time; indeed, a sophisticated adversary may be able to corrupt all parties given enough time.

Typically based on secret sharing schemes, secure multiparty computation (MPC) protocols allow a set of distrusting parties $P_1, ..., P_n$, with private inputs $x_1, ..., x_n$, to jointly compute a function f while guaranteeing correctness of its evaluation and privacy of inputs for honest parties. The study of secure computation was initiated by [42] for two parties and [29] for many parties. The information-theoretic setting was introduced by [4] and [18], where assuming private channels MPC protocols were shown to tolerate less than 1/3 of malicious parties. Assuming a broadcast channel, [36] shows how protocols can tolerate less than 1/2 of malicious parties. Fixed bounds on adversary's corruption limit are unrealistic for protocols that have very long execution times, especially when considering so-called "reactive" functionalities that never stop executing, e.g., continuously running control loops. Constructing MPC protocols that guarantee security against stronger adversary models and at the same time satisfy low communication and computational complexity bounds has been an important program in cryptography, and has seen significant progress, e.g., [31, 20, 19, 5].

One approach to modeling security in secret sharing and secure computation settings where an adversary is able to eventually corrupt *all* parties is the so-called proactive security model [35], which introduces the notion of a *mobile adversary*. A mobile adversary is one that can corrupt all parties in a distributed protocol during the execution but with the following limitations: (1) a fixed number of parties can be corrupted during any round; (2) parties periodically get rebooted to a clean initial state, where all previous state information is also erased[1]. The idea of such rebooting is to guarantee that only a small fraction of parties will be corrupted at any one time, though this guarantee depends on the rates of corruption and rebooting. We remark that we model rebooting to a clean initial state including global computation information (e.g., the circuit to be computed, the identities of the other parties in the computation, access to perfectly secure point-to-point channels and to a broadcast channel).

This paper consider two questions: (1) can we construct efficient, proactive, *UC-secure* secret sharing schemes and MPC protocols, and (2) how much can we improve the communication complexity of previous proactive protocols, both for secret sharing and MPC? The paper answers the former question positively by designing such a proactive, *UC-secure* secret sharing scheme and using it to construct a proactive, *UC-secure* MPC protocol. In addressing the latter question, we show that the constructed proactive secret sharing scheme has constant amortized communication thus improving significantly (by a factor of n^2) on all previously know proactive secret sharing schemes (see Table 1 for a comparison). The constructed proactive MPC protocol matches the asymptotic communication complexity of the best known MPC results in the "classical" model of stationary faults [19].

[1]Methods for deciding which parties to reboot are discussed in the full version of this paper [2].

1.1 Related Work

Ostrovsky and Yung introduced the proactive security model in [35]. The same paper also contains the first proactive secret sharing (PSS) scheme and proactive MPC (PMPC) protocol.

The central tool introduced in [35] is Proactive Secret sharing (PSS) and there has been significant follow up work on PSS schemes, both in the synchronous and asynchronous network models (see Table 1 for a comparison). The most efficient PSS scheme is [30], which has $O(n^2)$ communication complexity per secret share. By contrast, our work has $O(1)$ (amortized) communication complexity per secret share. Further, we are not aware of any previous UC-secure PSS scheme. We note that our work is in the synchronous model; extending our work to the asynchronous model is an interesting open problem.

In addition to proactive secret sharing, proactive security has played a fundamental role in several areas, including proactively secure threshold encryption and signature schemes [23, 24, 37, 14, 25, 9, 34, 33] (and in particular [1], which also sketches a definition of UC security in the proactive framework), intrusion-resilient signatures [32], eavesdropping games [26], pseudorandomness [15], and state-machine replication [16, 17].

The only known general PMPC protocol is due to [35]. The protocol is proven secure in the stand-alone corruption model and requires at least $O(Cn^3)$ communication complexity. By contrast, the PMPC protocol in this paper is UC-secure and has near-linear communication complexity.

1.2 Main Ideas Behind Our Protocols

We construct the first UC-secure proactive secret sharing scheme and MPC protocol with near-linear communication complexity using the following new ideas.

Packed Proactive Secret Sharing (PPSS). We construct the UC-secure packed proactive secret sharing (PPSS) scheme by extending techniques presented in [19, 27] to the proactive security model. The new scheme allows one to share *many* secrets with constant (amortized) communication complexity per secret. In order to renew, i.e., rerandomize, sharings of secrets, the parties generate random masking polynomials. To renew a polynomial f that stores a block of secrets via the evaluation points $(f(\beta^1), \ldots, f(\beta^\ell))$, parties generate a random polynomial R which evaluates to zero at $\beta^1, \ldots, \beta^\ell$ and set the renewed polynomial to be $f+R$. In contrast to previous schemes (such as [30] and [38]), our scheme amortizes random polynomial generation by using hyper-invertible matrices to more efficiently construct batches of random polynomials.

Paper	Network	Security	Threshold	Communication Complexity
[41]	synch.	cryptographic	$t/n < 1/2$	$\exp(n)$
[43]	asynch.	cryptographic	$t/n < 1/3$	$\exp(n)$
[11]	asynch.	cryptographic	$t/n < 1/3$	$O(n^4)$
[38]	asynch.	cryptographic	$t/n < 1/3$	$O(n^4)$
[30]	synch.	cryptographic	$t/n < 1/2$	$O(n^2)$
This Paper	synch.	perfect	$t/n < 1/3-\epsilon$	$O(1)$
This Paper	synch.	statistical	$t/n < 1/2-\epsilon$	$O(1)$

Table 1: Comparison of Proactive Secret Sharing (PSS) Schemes. Threshold is for each reboot phase. Our communication complexity is amortized per bit.

The process of reconstructing new shares for rebooted parties, who no longer hold secret shares, is a major communication bottleneck in previous work [38, 30]. Our new reconstruction protocol combines, for the first time, double sharing with packed sharing to achieve $O(1)$ per-secret amortized communication complexity, improving upon previous protocols by a factor of n^2. In order to use these double sharings, it is necessary to verify that the players shared their shares correctly. This is accomplished using hyper-invertible matrices in a novel way, which we now sketch. Previous protocols [3, 20] have used hyper-invertible matrices for error correction by multiplying a vector of data structures by a hyper-invertible matrix and having each party check one entry/data structure in the resultant vector for errors. In [20], the data structures are packed sharings; in [3], the data structures are pairs of Shamir-sharings that share the same value. In our protocol, each data structure is a collection of sharings and corresponding double sharings[2]. After multiplication by a hyper-invertible matrix, each player checks one entry in the resultant vector to make sure that the double sharings contain the correct shares. By using hyper-invertible matrices with these larger data structures, a technique introduced for the first time in this paper, we are able to check the correctness of the double sharings without asymptotically increasing the communication complexity of the protocol.

Proactive MPC (PMPC) Techniques. The main approach for our PMPC protocol is to compute the circuit layer by layer, while proactively redistributing the parties' secret shares after each layer. Therefore, if each layer is computed using subprotocols that are secure in the *non-proactive* setting up to a threshold t, and our PPSS share redistribution protocol is also secure up to threshold t, then the overall PMPC protocol is *proactively* secure up to a threshold t between proactive refreshes. The approach to construct our PMPC protocol is realized as follows:

During initialization of the protocol, the circuit is transformed as in [19] so that each layer contains either only addition gates or only multiplication gates; each gate has two inputs, multiplication gates have one output, and addition gates have either one or two outputs. This transformation is necessary in order to do arithmetic with block-shared secrets, and it does not asymptotically increase the size of the circuit (measured as the number of gates plus the number of wires).

Each party then shares their inputs using the PPSS scheme. The circuit is then evaluated layer by layer. Before each layer, the secrets are permuted so that they are in the correct order for performing the arithmetic operations for that layer. For an addition layer, the gates are computed by locally adding shares. For a multiplication layer, the gates are computed using a standard technique.

After each circuit layer and after each permutation, the parties execute the new redistribution protocol[3]. This rerandomizes the sharings of the secrets so that old shares are erased and leak no information about current sharings to an adversary that obtained them. Redistribution also allows parties that have been rebooted to recover the required shares to continue the computation. This is where our new PPSS scheme is critically utilized.

Once all the layers of the circuit have been evaluated, the parties reconstruct the shares to obtain their outputs.

The initial PMPC protocol that is constructed has a corruption rate threshold less than $(1/3-\epsilon)n$ and subsequently uses Bracha committees [10] to obtain a protocol with the desired threshold, with each committee simulating one player. However, one must overcome an additional difficulty because using Bracha committees might violate the need to have a constant number of rounds between share redistributions. More specifically, we construct a new multiparty protocol that is executed within each committee, allowing the committee to perform the Berlekamp-Welch algorithm in a constant number of communication rounds (whereas performing the Berlekamp-Welch algorithm in a "straightforward" manner would lead to $\Omega(n)$ communication rounds).

We remark that our techniques can be used to also construct a proactive, *statistically* UC-secure MPC protocol with similar communication and computational complexity that tolerates up to $(1/2-\epsilon)n$ corruptions between refreshments. See the full version [2] for further discussion.

1.3 Contributions

The main contribution of this paper is the construction of the first UC-secure packed proactive secret sharing (PPSS) scheme. The PPSS scheme has an amortized communication complexity of $O(1)$ per shared secret and is perfectly UC-secure in the synchronous model with secure point-to-point channels and authenticated, reliable broadcast against a malicious adversary that can corrupt up to $(1/3-\epsilon)n$ parties per fixed period of time for any constant $\epsilon > 0$. The PPSS protocol can also be modified to be statistically UC-

[2]We note that [3] uses the phrase "double sharing" differently than in this paper.

[3]Alternatively, one could construct a protocol that computes multiple circuits in succession and redistributes secrets only at the end of each circuit. However, this would lead to a non-constant number of rounds between redistributions, and would violate the assumption that the adversary corrupts a constant number of players per communication round. One could also redistribute secrets after each gate, but this would cause an increase in communication and computational complexity.

secure and tolerate up to $(1/2-\epsilon)n$ corruptions between refreshments.

A second contribution of this paper is a new proactive MPC (PMPC) protocol with communication complexity on par with the most efficient non-proactive MPC protocol in the literature today [19]. The constructed PMPC protocol greatly improves on the communication complexity of the only other known PMPC protocol in [35].

Our PMPC protocol has communication and computational complexity

$$O(DC\log^2(C)\text{polylog}(n) + D\,\text{poly}(n)\log^2(C)),$$

where C is the number of gates plus the number of wires in the circuit, D is the depth of the circuit, and n is the number of parties (see Section 4.3 for an explanation of the PMPC protocol complexity). Our protocol is perfectly UC-secure in the synchronous network model against a malicious adversary that can corrupt up to $(1/3-\epsilon)n$ parties between refreshments for any constant $\epsilon > 0$. The most efficient non-proactive MPC protocol under the same assumptions ([19]) has communication and computational complexity

$$O(C\log(C)\log^2(n) + D^2\text{poly}(n,\log(C))).$$

Our PMPC protocol can also be modified to be statistically UC-secure and tolerate up to $(1/2-\epsilon)n$ corruptions between refreshments with similar communication and computational complexity as in the perfectly secure case.

2. DEFINITIONS AND PRELIMINARIES

This section outlines the main techniques required for constructing the proactive secret sharing scheme and MPC protocol. It also contains a brief discussion of the proactive security model under the UC framework (for further details, see the full version [2]).

2.1 The Proactive Model under the UC Framework

Security of the proactively-secure protocols in this paper is proven in the Universal Composability (UC) framework introduced in [12] and revised in [13]. Specifically, the proactive UC model considered in this paper considers parties that can perform erasures; in the proactive model, parties must be able to erase their states so that when they are compromised, an adversary only learns their current state and not all their previous ones. Parties communicate synchronously and have access to secure point-to-point channels and a broadcast channel; how this would be implemented is beyond the scope of this paper.[4] Similar to the definition of proactive UC security in [1], the execution of a *proactive protocol*, π, proceeds in communication *rounds*, denoted by $\mathsf{r}_{i,l}$, and the initial round is round $\mathsf{r}_{0,0}$. A *phase*, denoted ph consists of a number of consecutive rounds $\mathsf{r}_{i,l},\ldots,\mathsf{r}_{i+j,l}$, and every round $\mathsf{r}_{j,l}$ belongs to exactly one phase ph_l. Each phase of π is either a *refreshment* or an *operation* phase. The phases of π alternate between *refreshment* and *operation* phases. Each *refreshment* phase ph_l consists of rounds $\mathsf{r}_{i,l},\ldots,\mathsf{r}_{i+j,l}$, such that there exists a k, $0\le k<j$ where rounds $\mathsf{r}_{i,l},\ldots,\mathsf{r}_{i+k,l}$ are denoted the *closing* period of refreshment phase ph_l while $\mathsf{r}_{i+k+1,l},\ldots,\mathsf{r}_{i+j,l}$ denote the *opening* period of refreshment phase ph_l. Finally, a *stage* st (starting at stage 0) consists of an *opening* refreshment period, an operation phase and then a *closing* refreshment period, therefore including a full (operation) phase and two sequences of two refreshment stages; each refreshment is the closing of one stage and the opening of the other. An adversary in the proactive model is limited to corrupting a certain threshold of parties per *stage*. At the end of each stage (i.e., at the refreshment phase) corrupted parties are rebooted to a pristine state and sent the shares to continue the computation. We note that, as in [1], a party corrupted during the refreshment phase is considered to be corrupted in both stages associated with that phase. We refer the reader to Section 1 for a discussion of rebooting and to the full version [2] for a discussion of an oblivious resetting strategy. The full version contains the exact details of the the proactive UC model as well as definitions of security.

[4]This could be implemented using proactive PKI or by using a TPM to perform encryption/decryption.

2.2 Preliminaries

Packed Secret Sharing. Our proactive secret sharing scheme relies on a generalization of Shamir's polynomial-based secret sharing scheme [39]. In particular, we start with a variant of the *packed secret sharing scheme* due to [27] which was utilized in an MPC protocol by [20, 19]. The scheme works as follows: for n parties and $d\in\mathbb{N}$, fix a finite field $\mathbb{F}=\mathbb{Z}_q$ for $q>2n$ as well as a generator $\alpha\in\mathbb{F}^*$. Set $\beta=\alpha^{-1}$; the field $\mathbb{F}$ is large enough so that $\beta^1,\ldots,\beta^d,\alpha,\ldots,\alpha^n$ are distinct for $d\le n$. A vector $(x_1,\ldots,x_\ell)$ of secrets is shared simultaneously as a *block* by extending the vector to $(x_1,\ldots,x_\ell,r_{\ell+1},\ldots,r_{d+1})$ for $r_{\ell+1},\ldots,r_{d+1}$ chosen uniformly and independently at random and constructing the unique degree d polynomial p such that $p(\beta^i)=x_i$ for $1\le i\le\ell$ and $p(\beta^j)=r_j$ for $\ell+1\le j\le d+1$. Each party P_i receives the share $p(\alpha^i)$. We denote the sharing in this fashion of $x=(x_1,\ldots,x_\ell)$ as $[x]_d$, where $[x]_d$ is the ordered n-length vector consisting of the respective shares for each P_i. The reader can verify that $c[x]_d=[cx]_d$ for any $c\in\mathbb{F}$, $[x]_d+[y]_d=[x+y]_d$, and $[x]_d[y]_d=[xy]_{2d}$, where addition and multiplication here are element-wise. We refer the reader to [20, 19] for further details.

We use two different thresholds and batch sizes in the construction of our protocols. For constructing the perfectly secure PPSS scheme, we use a threshold of $t<(1/3-\epsilon)n$ and a batch size of $\ell=n-3t$. For constructing the statistically secure PPSS scheme and for constructing the PMPC protocol (either perfect or statistical), we will require that ℓ is the highest power of 2 not greater than $n/4$, that the maximal corruption rate[5] is $t<n/8$ and that $d=t+\ell-1$. We will rely on the constant-round protocol RobustShare in [20] to implement this sharing; it is perfectly UC-secure with the above parameters. We stress, however, that the techniques above have never been adopted to the proactive setting before; in particular, one of the main contributions of this paper is to perform a new proactive packed secret share redistribution with low amortized overhead.

When a party is accused of being corrupt during secret sharing or redistribution, the parties make a worst-case assumption that both the accuser and the accused are corrupt.

[5]Our PMPC protocol without additional party virtualization will therefore have a maximal per-stage corruption rate of $t=n/8$. Only after using Bracha committee-based techniques [10] will our protocol have a corruption rate of $t=(1/3-\epsilon)n$ for perfect security and $t=(1/2-\epsilon)n$ for statistical security.

Thus both are added to the set $Corr$, which is initialized to be empty. Note that security is maintained because the initial threshold of corruption is either $t < (1/3 - \epsilon)n$ or $t < n/8$. In the case that the threshold is $t < n/8$, the threshold is later raised to $t < (1/3 - \epsilon)n$ with perfect security ($t < (1/2 - \epsilon)n$ with statistical security) using party virtualization [10]; see the full version [2] for further details. For the perfectly secure PPSS scheme, the initial threshold of $t < (1/3 - \epsilon)n$ is never raised, and hence we do not use player virtualization. It is only in the PMPC protocol and the statistically secure PPSS scheme that player virtualization is employed. In the proactive model, the set of corrupt parties may change over time, so in addition to initializing $Corr = \emptyset$ at the beginning of the PPSS protocol, $Corr$ is also reset to $\emptyset$ after each redistribution.

Hyper-Invertible Matrices. Many of the subprotocols that we use require a publicly agreed upon hyper-invertible matrix [3]. A hyper-invertible matrix is a matrix where any square sub-matrix formed by removing rows and columns is invertible. It is shown in [3] that one can construct an $a \times b$ hyper-invertible matrix M as follows: Pick $a+b$ distinct field elements $\theta_1, \ldots, \theta_a, \phi_1, \ldots, \phi_b \in \mathbb{F}$, and let M be the matrix be such that if $(y_1, \ldots, y_a)^T = M(x_1, \ldots, x_b)^T$; then the points $(\theta_1, y_1), \ldots, (\theta_a, y_a)$ lie on the polynomial of degree $\leq b-1$ which evaluates to x_j at ϕ_j for each $j = 1, \ldots, b$. (In other words, M interpolates the points $\theta_1, \ldots, \theta_a$ on a polynomial given the points $\phi_1, \ldots, \phi_b$ on that polynomial.) Many of the sub-protocols assume the existence of a publicly known hyper-invertible matrix, and these may be efficiently constructed during pre-processing.

Polynomial Interpolation. One algorithm relied upon for our proactive share redistribution protocol is the classic Berlekamp-Welch algorithm [7]. If a party is given points on a polynomial (such as shares of a block of secrets) and some of the points have been corrupted (such as when corrupted parties alter their shares), the Berlekamp-Welch algorithm allows correct interpolation of the polynomial despite the corrupted points.

Required Subprotocols To perform basic operations such as secret sharing, generating random sharings, and multiplying shared secrets, we use three protocols from [20] (RobustShare, RanDouSha, and Reco) and three from [19] (RandomPairs, PermuteWithinBlocks, and Multiply). We refer the reader to those works for protocol specifications and corresponding ideal functionalities. Each of these protocols is constant-round and is proven secure in their respective papers, though in the *standard*, non-proactive model with a corruption threshold of at least $n/8$. The sharings used in these protocols are all block sharings.

- RobustShare(d):[6] Allows a set of parties to verifiably share $\Theta(n)$ secrets in blocks with polynomials of degree d.
- RanDouSha(d): Generates random sharings of blocks of secrets $r^{(i)}$ and shares each of them with a degree d sharing $[r^{(i)}]_d$ and a degree $2d$ sharing $[r^{(i)}]_{2d}$.
- RandomPairs(L,π,d): For a permutation π, this protocol generates L pairs of random block-sharings $([r^{(i)}]_d, [\pi(r^{(i)})]_d)$ for $1 \leq i \leq L$ such that the secret stored in location j in the sharing $[r^{(i)}]_d$ is stored in location $\pi(j)$ in $[\pi(r^{(i)})]_d$.
- PermuteWithinBlocks: Using random masks ($[r]_d$, $[\pi(r)]_d$) generated with RandomPairs, this protocol applies a permutation to a block $[x]_d$ of already-shared secrets, resulting in a sharing $[\pi(x)]_d$.
- Multiply($[x]_d, [y]_d, ([r]_d, [r]_{2d})$): Multiplies two blocks of secrets $[x]_d$ and $[y]_d$ element-wise using the random pair $([r]_d, [r]_{2d})$. In the output sharing, the secret in location j is the product of the secret in location j in $[x]_d$ and the secret in location j in $[y]_d$.
- Reco(P_i, d): Reveals an already-shared block of secrets $[x]_d$ to a party P_i.

[6]For the case in which the initial threshold is $t < (1/3-\epsilon)n$, we require a modification of RobustShare in which the set H in that protocol has size $n - 2t$ instead of $n - 3t$ as stated in [20]. The authors state in footnote b of RobustShare that up to $2t$ players can be eliminated due to disputes and up to t may be corrupt, so that there are at least $n-3t$ honest, un-eliminated players. However, it is clear that for every honest eliminated player, there is a corrupt eliminated player, so we are actually guaranteed at least $n-2t$ honest, un-eliminated players.

3. DETAILS OF THE PACKED PROACTIVE SECRET SHARING (PPSS) SCHEME

In this section we construct our efficient PPSS scheme. We do so using the packed secret sharing subprotocol RobustShare, which shares packed secrets in the non-proactive model [20, 19]. We construct a new subprotocol Block-Redistribute, that only requires constant amortized communication, to perform proactive secret redistribution to complete the PPSS scheme.

3.1 Proactive Share Redistribution

The share redistribution protocol Block-Redistribute forms the core of our PPSS scheme, and forms the redistribution phase of PMPC. It is constructed to redistribute shares for W secrets shared among the parties $\mathcal{P}$ (some of whom may be recently rebooted and do not actually have any shares). The subprotocol consists of three consecutive phases. First, the parties *rerandomize* their shares so that secret shares in the next proactive stage are independently distributed from previous stages. The parties then perform *verifiable double sharing* in order to correctly and privately distribute party share information to all parties without actually revealing the shares. Finally, the parties perform *share reconstruction* to restore the current state of the computation to newly rebooted parties who do not have shares to continue the computation. We will give an overview of each phase in Section 3.1.1 and then specify Block-Redistribute in Section 3.1.2. The ideal functionality $\mathcal{F}_{BR}$ that the protocol is designed to emulate and the security proof for Block-Redistribute are given in the full version [2].

3.1.1 *Outline of* Block-Redistribute

We refer the reader to Section 2 for the notation used in this section. For simplicity, we assume that the number of secrets, W, to be used as input for Block-Redistribute is a multiple of $\ell^2(n-3t)$ (e.g., $W = B\ell^2(n-3t)$ for some B), where secrets are shared[7] in blocks of size ℓ. We can then

[7]If W is not a multiple of $\ell^2(n-3t)$, we can generate random sharings of blocks to make it so; using RanDouSha, this can

arrange the polynomials $\widehat{H}$ corresponding to these shares as

$$\left\{\widehat{H}_a^{(k,m)}\right\}_{\substack{m=1,\dots,B\\ k=1,\dots,n-3t\\ a=1,\dots,\ell}}. \quad (1)$$

We think of B as the number of groupings of secret shares, and operations will be performed on each group in parallel throughout the protocol. We first provide some intuition for this arrangement of polynomials as well as for the parameters a, k, and m, before further outlining Block-Redistribute.

We will require a particular structure of secrets in order to perform share reconstruction in an efficient fashion. The idea is that we want to be able to allow rebooted parties to reconstruct their shares in such a way that corrupt parties cannot learn any information about honest parties' shares. We accomplish this by having parties distribute shares of their shares. The parameter a is bounded by ℓ because every ℓ shares (each corresponding to ℓ secrets) will form the basis for a single polynomial for the double sharing. One can perform computations on these double sharings using Lagrange coefficients to perform share reconstruction for the rebooted parties.

In order to verify that these double sharings are correct, the parties arrange their shares and double shares in B vectors of length $n-3t$, with an additional t elements chosen at random to further mask the inputs; this is why k is bounded by $n-3t$. A hyper-invertible matrix M will be applied to each of these B vectors to obtain B vectors of length n, corresponding to the n parties. Each party P_i will check the double sharings by each checking the ith entry of the B output vectors; in this fashion, we completely distribute double sharing verification. Because M is hyper-invertible, the outputs that each party checks will be immune from corrupt parties trying to skew the verification. We now explain the three phases of Block-Redistribute in more detail.

Share Rerandomization. This component comprises the *closing period* of the redistribution phase (see Section 2.1). We mask the shares by constructing $\ell(n-3t)B$ polynomials $Q_a^{(k,m)}$ that correspond to $[0^\ell]_d$, using a slight variant of RanDouSha and then computing $H_a^{(k,m)} \leftarrow \widehat{H}_a^{(k,m)} + Q_a^{(k,m)}$. All parties then erase all their shares for $\widehat{H}_a^{(k,m)}$ and $Q_a^{(k,m)}$. By the additive property of our secret sharing scheme, the new shares correspond to the same secrets but are now distributed uniformly at random from all past shares.

Verifiable Double Sharing. This component together with Share Reconstruction below comprises the *opening period* of the redistribution phase. Let M be a (publicly agreed upon) hyper-invertible matrix with n rows and $n-2t$ columns. As was noted in [21], if $\boldsymbol{y} = M\boldsymbol{x}$, then we can also use Berlekamp-Welch to "interpolate" $\boldsymbol{x}$ from $\boldsymbol{y}$ if no more than t coordinates of $\boldsymbol{y}$ are in error (via adversarial corruption in this context).

The first step is to construct random padding in the form of additional polynomials $\left\{H_a^{(k,m)}\right\}_{\substack{m=1,\dots,B\\ k=n-3t+1,\dots,n-2t\\ a=1,\dots,\ell}}$ using RanDouSha. Now all parties hold shares for the set of polynomials $\left\{H_a^{(k,m)}\right\}_{\substack{m=1,\dots,B\\ k=1,\dots,n-2t\\ a=1,\dots,\ell}}$. Each party P_i then shares all of their shares; that is, each P_i constructs polynomials $U^{(i,k,m)}$ for $1 \le k \le n-2t$, $1 \le m \le B$ such that $U^{(i,k,m)}(\beta^a) = H_a^{(k,m)}(\alpha^i)$. Note that for each i and m, the last t polynomials of the $U^{(i,k,m)}$ correspond with the t random padding polynomials. Each P_i then secret shares the $U^{(i,k,m)}$ with $\mathcal{P}$. Therefore, every party has their own share of every $U^{(j,k,m)}$.

Next, for each m, each party uses their local shares of the group of polynomials $H_a^{k,m}$ and $U^{(i,k,m)}$ (each of length $n-2t$) to construct shares for new polynomials $\widetilde{H}_a^{(\tilde{k},m)}$ and $\widetilde{U}^{(i,\tilde{k},m)}$ for $\tilde{k} = 1,\dots,n$ by applying M to each group, respectively (see step 2.3 in the full specification of Block-Redistribute below). Each P_i then sends their share for $\widetilde{H}_a^{(\tilde{k},m)}$ and $\widetilde{U}^{(i,\tilde{k},m)}$ to $P_{\tilde{k}}$, who can interpolate the polynomials via Berlekamp-Welch.

The new polynomials $\widetilde{H}$ and $\widetilde{U}$ perfectly hide the values of H and U used to construct them because of the t random padding inputs used to construct the polynomials via M; in other words, there is a degree of freedom in the random padding for each potential corruption that can occur. Further, since at most t shares of the $\widetilde{H}_a^{(\tilde{k},m)}$ and $\widetilde{U}^{(i,\tilde{k},m)}$ can be corrupted, by the error correction properties of polynomials, $P_{\tilde{k}}$ is able to reconstruct $\widetilde{H}_a^{(\tilde{k},m)}$ and $\widetilde{U}^{(i,\tilde{k},m)}$.

Therefore, $P_{\tilde{k}}$ can verify that $\widetilde{U}^{(i,\tilde{k},m)}(\beta^a) = \widetilde{H}_a^{(\tilde{k},m)}(\alpha^i)$; if not, $P_{\tilde{k}}$ broadcasts an accusation of P_i and *both* parties are viewed as corrupted. While this strategy lowers the corruption threshold from $n/4$ to $n/8$, it is an efficient way to handle dispute resolution, and increasing the threshold later can be accomplished using Bracha committees (see [19] and the full version of this paper [2]).

Share Reconstruction. Now that each party has verified double shares of all the other parties' shares, share reconstruction for a newly rebooted[8] party P_j can be accomplished by applying the appropriate Lagrange coefficients $\lambda_{j,i}$ to the double sharings $U^{(i,k,m)}$ and then having P_j apply Berlekamp-Welch to interpolate her own share. This is because, for indices $z_1, \dots, z_{n-2t}$ of parties with correct double shares, $\lambda_{j,1}U^{(z_1,k,m)}(\beta^a) + \cdots + \lambda_{j,n-2t}U^{(z_{n-2t},k,m)}(\beta^a) = \lambda_{j,1}H_a^{(k,m)}(\alpha^{z_1}) + \cdots + \lambda_{j,n-2t}H_a^{(k,m)}(\alpha^{z_{n-2t}}) = H_a^{(k,m)}(\alpha^j)$.

3.1.2 Specification of Block-Redistribute

Our protocol requires a slightly altered version of RanDouSha for the first step. In [20], RanDouSha calls on a subprotocol SemiRobustShare, and in that protocol, step 2(a) (see page 6 in [20]) is altered so that the parties check that the polynomials evaluate to zero at β^j for $j = 1,\dots,\ell$, and an accusation is broadcast if they do not. Security for this slightly modified protocol easily follows.

> **Block-Redistribute**
>
> We assume that the secrets have been stored in blocks of size ℓ (as described in Section 2) using polynomials $\left\{\widehat{H}_a^{(k,m)}\right\}_{\substack{m=1,\dots,B\\ k=1,\dots,n-3t\\ a=1,\dots,\ell}}$.
>
> *1. Share Rerandomization*
>
> *1.1* The parties in $\mathcal{P}$ invoke RanDouSha to generate polynomials $Q_a^{(k,m)}$ for $1 \le a \le \ell$, $1 \le k \le n-3t$

be done with poly(n) communication complexity, and since it adds only a poly(n) amount of data to W, this does not asymptotically affect the overall communication complexity of redistributing W secrets.

[8]Asymptotically, there is no cost to executing share redistribution for all, rather than rebooted, parties.

and $1 \le m \le B$, satisfying $Q_a^{(k,m)}(\beta^j) = 0$ for $j = 1, \ldots, \ell$.

1.2 The parties locally compute $H_a^{(k,m)} \leftarrow \widehat{H}_a^{(k,m)} + Q_a^{(k,m)}$.

1.3 All parties erase their shares of each $\widehat{H}_a^{(k,m)}$ and $Q_a^{(k,m)}$.

2. *Verifiable Double Sharing*

2.1 The parties use RanDouSha to generate polynomials $H_a^{(k,m)}$ for $1 \le a \le \ell$, $1 \le m \le B$ and $k = n - 3t + 1, \ldots, n - 2t$.

2.2 Each P_i selects polynomials $U^{(i,1,m)}, \ldots, U^{(i,(n-2t),m)}$ of degree $\le d$ such that $U^{(i,k,m)}(\beta^a) = H_a^{(k,m)}(\alpha^i)$ for $a = 1, \ldots, \ell$, $k = 1, \ldots, n - 2t$, and $m = 1, \ldots, B$ and shares them via RobustShare.

2.3 Define $\widetilde{H}_a^{(\widetilde{k},m)}$ and $\widetilde{U}^{(i,\widetilde{k},m)}$ for $\widetilde{k} = 1, \ldots, n$ by

$$\left(\widetilde{H}_a^{(1,m)}, \ldots, \widetilde{H}_a^{(n,m)}\right)^T = M\left(H_a^{(1,m)}, \ldots, H_a^{(n-2t,m)}\right)^T$$

and

$$\left(\widetilde{U}^{(i,1,m)}, .., \widetilde{U}^{(i,n,m)}\right)^T = M\left(U^{(i,1,m)}, .., U^{(i,n-2t,m)}\right)^T$$

Each party in $\mathcal{P}$ locally computes their shares of these polynomials.

2.4 Each party in $\mathcal{P}$ sends *all* their shares of $\widetilde{H}_a^{(\widetilde{k},m)}$ and $\widetilde{U}^{(i,\widetilde{k},m)}$ to party $P_{\widetilde{k}}$ for each a, i, and m.

2.5 Each $P_{\widetilde{k}}$ uses Berlekamp-Welch on the shares of each $\widetilde{U}^{(i,\widetilde{k},m)}$ to interpolate $\widetilde{U}^{(i,\widetilde{k},m)}(\beta^a)$ for each $a = 1, \ldots, \ell$.

2.6 Each $P_{\widetilde{k}}$ uses Berlekamp-Welch on the shares of each $\widetilde{H}_a^{(\widetilde{k},m)}$ to interpolate $\widetilde{H}^{(\widetilde{k},m)}(\alpha^i)$ for each $i = 1, \ldots, n$.

2.7 Each $P_{\widetilde{k}}$ checks if $\widetilde{U}^{(i,\widetilde{k},m)}(\beta^a) = \widetilde{H}_a^{(\widetilde{k},m)}(\alpha^i)$ for each $a = 1, \ldots, \ell$. If not for some $\widetilde{U}^{(i,\widetilde{k},m)}$, then $P_{\widetilde{k}}$ broadcasts ($P_{\widetilde{k}}$, `J'accuse`, P_i). All parties add P_i and $P_{\widetilde{k}}$ to *Corr*. (After a party is added to set of nodes marked as corrupted, *Corr*, any further accusations from that party are ignored.)

2.8 Each party erases all their shares of each $\widetilde{H}_a^{(\widetilde{k},m)}$ and $\widetilde{U}^{(i,\widetilde{k},m)}$ for $\widetilde{k} = 1, \ldots, n$ and $H_a^{(k,m)}$ and $U^{(i,k,m)}$ for $k = n - 3t + 1, \ldots, n - 2t$.

3. *Share Reconstruction*

3.1 P_j: Define G to be the set of the first $n - 2t$ parties in $\mathcal{P} - Corr$. Let $\{z_1, \ldots, z_{n-2t}\}$ denote the set of indices of parties in G. Let $\lambda_{j,i}$ denote the Lagrange coefficients for interpolating P_j's share of a secret from the shares of parties in G (i.e., for a polynomial f of degree $\le d$, $f(\alpha^j) = \lambda_{j,1} f(\alpha^{z_1}) + \cdots + \lambda_{j,n-2t} f(\alpha^{z_{n-2t}})$.)

3.2 For each $k = 1, \ldots, n - 3t$, each $m = 1, \ldots, B$, and each $j = 1, \ldots, n$, each party in G sends their share of $\lambda_{j,1} U^{(z_1,k,m)} + \cdots + \lambda_{j,n-2t} U^{(z_{n-2t},k,m)}$ to P_j.

3.3 Each P_j uses Berlekamp-Welch to interpolate the polynomials received in the previous step to obtain all $H_a^{(k,m)}(\alpha^j)$.

3.4 Each party erases all their shares of each $U^{(i,k,m)}$ (retaining the shares of $H_a^{(k,m)}$).

3.5 Set $Corr = \emptyset$.

The protocol Block-Redistribute has communication complexity $O(W + \text{poly}(n))$ and computational complexity $O(W \text{polylog}(n)) + \text{poly}(n))$ for redistributing W secrets[9].

THEOREM 1. *Assuming perfectly secure point-to-point channels and a secure broadcast channel, protocol* Block-Redistribute *perfectly UC-realizes block redistibution (corresponding ideal functionality $\mathcal{F}_{BR}$ in [2]) in the synchronous, adaptive corruption model with corruption threshold $t < (1/3 - \epsilon)n$.*

We note that this theorem is in the standard, rather than proactive, security model. For the proof of Theorem 1, see the full version [2].

4. DETAILS OF THE PROACTIVE MPC (PMPC) PROTOCOL

This section describes the details of our efficient proactively secure MPC protocol. We first give a more detailed overview of the protocol construction and the techniques and subprotocols required. Next, we discuss the circuit transformations that are required to perform required operations on packed secret shares (further details are given in the full version [2]). Finally, we construct the full protocol secure with per-stage corruption threshold $n/8$. In order to obtain a corruption threshold of $(1/3 - \epsilon)n$ for perfect security or $(1/2 - \epsilon)n$ for statistical security, we use a Bracha committee construction; due to lack of space, we discuss the construction in the full version [2].

4.1 PMPC Protocol Overview

We first provide an overview of how we construct the PMPC protocol. As discussed in Section 2.2, we rely upon several subprotocols already in the MPC literature.

We stress that each of the subprotocols that we use, including Block-Redistribute, are proven secure individually in the *non-proactive* security model. However, by composing them properly, namely by applying Block-Redistribute after each layer of the computation, we obtain proactive security. This is because by construction at each stage, the number of corrupted parties is at most the stage corruption threshold; executing Block-Redistribute ensures that corruptions in one stage cannot be carried over to break security of another future stage.

During initialization of the PMPC protocol, the circuit is transformed so that all addition and multiplication gates have only two inputs and either one or two outputs and

[9]See the full version [2] for more details about the polynomial terms.

are arranged in such a way that each layer consists of only addition gates or multiplication gates. This increases the circuit size (measured as the number of wires) by a constant factor, and increases circuit depth by a $\log C$ multiplicative factor.

In the first step of the PMPC protocol, parties share their inputs using RobustShare. Over the course of the protocol, whenever random shares are needed, either by RanDouSha or RandomPairs, they are generated within a constant number of circuit layers from use; this "dynamic" preprocessing is so that Block-Redistribute does not have to be executed unnecessarily to maintain these shares, thereby increasing the asymptotic communication complexity.

Before each layer of the circuit is computed, the secrets are permuted (or re-arranged) to facilitate the process of computation. This is because the secrets are shared in blocks and they must be rearranged to compute on them per circuit specification. This rearrangement is performed by decomposing the required permutation into sub-permutations and then performing each of the sub-permutations in succession; this adds another $\log C$ multiplicative factor to the communication complexity. See Section 4.2 for details.

After the permutation has been executed, addition gates are evaluated via locally adding shares, while multiplication gates are evaluated by creating pairs of random sharings using RanDouSha (through dynamic preprocessing) and then executing Multiply.

After each layer of the circuit is evaluated, where we now include each sub-permutation execution to constitute a layer, the parties run Block-Redistribute to re-randomize all stored secrets, thereby preserving proactive privacy of all stored values.

Once a sharing for an output gate has been computed, the parties invoke Reco to reveal it to the intended recipient. Once all the outputs have been revealed, the protocol is complete.

4.2 Circuit Transformation and Share Permutation

Since the circuit computes on individual values but secrets are shared in blocks, care must be taken to actually implement the circuit on secret-shared blocks of data because addition and multiplication of blocks occurs element-wise according to position within the blocks, which therefore must be rearranged to perform arbitrary addition and multiplication of the shares per the circuit instructions. To remedy this, we first transform the circuit itself in the same manner as [19]. Again, this increases the circuit size by a constant factor, and increases circuit depth by a $\log C$ multiplicative factor. Then, at each layer of computation of the circuit we will perform a permutation on *all* the secrets to make sure that the secrets are arranged in the correct order for whatever arithmetic operations that layer requires.

In order to perform the permutations, we use Beneš networks [6], also known as Waksman networks [40]. These networks were used in the context of multiparty computation in [19], and also in the context of fully homomorphic encryption in [28]. Let the layer of the circuit have width w, where each gate has fan-in 2. The main idea is that an arbitrary permutation on the $O(w/\ell)$ blocks of secrets needed to compute the layer can be performed using $O(\log(w))$ constant-round subprotocols that execute the decomposition of the permutation into $O(\log(w))$ sub-permutations. We denote this protocol PermuteLayer, which has as inputs the permutation π as well as all the secret shares of each of the parties. We defer the construction of PermuteLayer to the the full version [2] due to lack of space.

4.3 The Full PMPC Protocol

Figure 1 outlines the protocol that uses all the sub-protocols described above to securely compute the circuit. We note that step 4.1 below is abbreviated; in the full implementation, we invoke RanDouSha to pad to a multiple of $\ell^2(n-3t)$ sharings.

PMPC:

1. The circuit is transformed so that each layer of computation contains only one type of gate (addition or multiplication) and each gate has fan-in 2 and fan-out 1 or 2.
2. Each party shares their inputs using RobustShare.
3. Execute Block-Redistribute to redistribute all the currently stored secrets.
4. For each layer of the circuit, the following steps are performed.
   - 4.1 Suppose we have W input secrets for this layer where W is a multiple of $\ell^2(n-3t)$. Let σ denote the permutation to be performed on the first W secrets before the computation for this layer. Execute PermuteLayer using σ on the W secrets.
   - 4.2 If this is an addition layer, then compute the additions locally. If this is a multiplication layer, then the parties invoke RanDouSha to generate random sharings, and then use these random sharings to invoke Multiply for each block to multiply.
   - 4.3 All secrets no longer needed for the rest of the computation are erased.
   - 4.4 Invoke Block-Redistribute to redistribute all W secrets.
5. For the output layer, invoke Reco to reconstruct all the outputs toward the intended recipients.

Figure 1: PMPC Protocol Outline

To analyze the communication complexity[10] of PMPC, note that the communication complexity of performing multiplications on a layer, performing additions on a layer, permuting a layer, and redistributing a layer are all the same, namely $O(W + \text{poly}(n))$ if the circuit width is W. In the worst case, $W = C$, so it is $O(C + \text{poly}(n))$. The number of layers is initially D, the depth of the circuit. After the circuit is transformed so that no gate has fan-in or fan-out more than 2, the depth is $D\log(C)$. Furthermore, if there are C secrets to permute at each layer, than this would take $\log(C)$ permutations. So if we think of the operation of permutation as a layer in the circuit, the final depth of the circuit would be $D\log^2(C)$. Thus the communication complexity is $O((C + \text{poly}(n)) \cdot D\log^2(C))$, or $O(DC\log^2(C) + D\text{poly}(n)\log^2(C))$. The same reasoning

[10]See the full version [2] for more details about the polynomial terms.

shows that the computational complexity is $O(DC\log^2(C)\text{polylog}(n) + D\text{poly}(n)\log^2(C))$.

For circuits that are "layered" in such a way that each output from a gate is used in the next layer and no other layers, we no longer assume that $W = C$; instead, we denote the widths of layers 1 through $D' := D\log^2(C)$ by $W_1, \ldots, W_{D'}$, and we have $C\log^2(C) = \sum_{i=1}^{D'} W_i$. The communication complexity is therefore $\sum_{i=1}^{D'}[W_i + \text{poly}(n)] = O(C\log^2 C + D\text{poly}(n)\log^2 C)$ with a computational complexity of $O(C\log^2 C\text{polylog}(n) + D\text{poly}(n)\log^2 C)$.

In terms of broadcast complexity, our protocol uses $O(1)$ broadcasts per dispute. Since the number of disputes that can arise between secret redistributions is at most t, the total number of broadcasts is $O(Dn)$.

THEOREM 2. *For n parties and an arithmetic circuit C that is at least $\Omega(n)$ gates wide, the protocol* PMPC *realizes proactive multiparty computation (corresponding ideal functionality $\mathcal{F}_C$ in [2]) with perfect security in the proactive UC model against an active and adaptive adversary corrupting up to $t < n/8$ parties per stage.*

Using the party virtualization techniques of [10] (see [19] and the full version of this paper [2]), we can increase the corruption threshold as to $t < (1/3-\epsilon)n$. We denote PMPC-pv as the protocol that executes PMPC using player virtualization. The communication complexity of PMPC-pv is $O(C\log^2 C\text{polylog}n + D\text{poly}(n)\log^2 C)$, which is sum of the communication complexity and the computation complexity of PMPC. However, the communication complexity of Block-Redistribute is *not* affected by player virtualization.

THEOREM 3. *For any $0 < \delta < 1/3$, for n parties and an arithmetic circuit C that is at least $\Omega(n)$ gates wide, the protocol* PMPC-pv *realizes proactive multiparty computation (corresponding ideal functionality $\mathcal{F}_C$ in [2]) with perfect security in the proactive UC model against an active and adaptive adversary corrupting up to $t < \delta n$ parties per stage.*

Theorem 3 can also be extended so that, with statistical security, $0 < \delta < 1/2$; see the full version [2] for further details.

Acknowledgements

The authors thank Ivan Damgård, Yuval Ishai and Jonathan Katz for helpful discussions about this work, as well as the anonymous referees for their comments.

The fourth author's work is supported in part by NSF grants 09165174, 1065276, 1118126 and 1136174, US-Israel BSF grant 2008411, OKAWA Foundation Research Award, IBM Faculty Research Award, Xerox Faculty Research Award, B. John Garrick Foundation Award, Teradata Research Award, and Lockheed-Martin Corporation Research Award. The fourth author's work is also supported by the Defense Advanced Research Projects Agency through the U.S. Office of Naval Research under Contract N00014 -11 - 1-0392. The views expressed are those of the author and do not reflect the official policy or position of the Department of Defense or the U.S. Government.

5. REFERENCES

[1] Jesús F. Almansa, Ivan Damgård, and Jesper Buus Nielsen. Simplified threshold rsa with adaptive and proactive security. In *Proceedings of the 24th annual international conference on The Theory and Applications of Cryptographic Techniques*, EUROCRYPT'06, pages 593–611, Berlin, Heidelberg, 2006. Springer-Verlag.

[2] Joshua Baron, Karim El Defrawy, Joshua Lampkins, and Rafail Ostrovsky. How to withstand mobile virus attacks, revisited. Cryptology ePrint Archive, Report 2013/529, 2013. http://eprint.iacr.org/2013/529.

[3] Zuzana Beerliová-Trubíniová and Martin Hirt. Perfectly-secure mpc with linear communication complexity. In *TCC*, pages 213–230, 2008.

[4] Michael Ben-Or, Shafi Goldwasser, and Avi Wigderson. Completeness theorems for non-cryptographic fault-tolerant distributed computation (extended abstract). In *STOC*, pages 1–10, 1988.

[5] Eli Ben-Sasson, Serge Fehr, and Rafail Ostrovsky. Near-linear unconditionally-secure multiparty computation with a dishonest minority. In *CRYPTO*, pages 663–680, 2012.

[6] Václav E. Beneš. Optimal rearrangeable multistage connecting networks. *The Bell System Technical Journal*, 43(4):1641–1656, July, 1964.

[7] Elwyn R. Berlekamp. *Algebraic Coding Theory.* Aegean Park Press, 1984.

[8] G. R. Blakley. Safeguarding cryptographic keys. *Proc. of AFIPS National Computer Conference*, 48:313–317, 1979.

[9] Alexandra Boldyreva. Threshold signatures, multisignatures and blind signatures based on the gap-diffie-hellman-group signature scheme. In *Proceedings of the 6th International Workshop on Theory and Practice in Public Key Cryptography: Public Key Cryptography*, PKC '03, pages 31–46, London, UK, UK, 2003. Springer-Verlag.

[10] Gabriel Bracha. An o(log n) expected rounds randomized byzantine generals protocol. *J. ACM*, 34(4):910–920, 1987.

[11] Christian Cachin, Klaus Kursawe, Anna Lysyanskaya, and Reto Strobl. Asynchronous verifiable secret sharing and proactive cryptosystems. In *ACM Conference on Computer and Communications Security*, pages 88–97, 2002.

[12] Ran Canetti. Universally composable security: A new paradigm for cryptographic protocols. In *FOCS*, pages 136–145, 2001.

[13] Ran Canetti. Universally composable security: A new paradigm for cryptographic protocols. Cryptology ePrint Archive, Report 2000/067, 2005.

[14] Ran Canetti, Rosario Gennaro, Stanislaw Jarecki, Hugo Krawczyk, and Tal Rabin. Adaptive security for threshold cryptosystems. In *Proceedings of the 19th Annual International Cryptology Conference on Advances in Cryptology*, CRYPTO '99, pages 98–115, London, UK, UK, 1999. Springer-Verlag.

[15] Ran Canetti and Amir Herzberg. Maintaining security in the presence of transient faults. In *CRYPTO*, pages 425–438, 1994.

[16] Miguel Castro and Barbara Liskov. Proactive recovery in a byzantine-fault-tolerant system. In *OSDI*, pages 273–288, 2000.

[17] Miguel Castro and Barbara Liskov. Practical byzantine fault tolerance and proactive recovery. *ACM Trans. Comput. Syst.*, 20(4):398–461, 2002.

[18] David Chaum, Claude Crépeau, and Ivan Damgard. Multiparty unconditionally secure protocols. In *Proceedings of the twentieth annual ACM symposium on Theory of computing*, STOC '88, pages 11–19, New York, NY, USA, 1988. ACM.

[19] Ivan Damgård, Yuval Ishai, and Mikkel Krøigaard. Perfectly secure multiparty computation and the computational overhead of cryptography. In *EUROCRYPT*, pages 445–465, 2010.

[20] Ivan Damgård, Yuval Ishai, Mikkel Krøigaard, Jesper Buus Nielsen, and Adam Smith. Scalable multiparty computation with nearly optimal work and resilience. In *CRYPTO*, pages 241–261, 2008.

[21] Ivan Damgård and Jesper Buus Nielsen. Scalable and unconditionally secure multiparty computation. In *CRYPTO*, pages 572–590, 2007.

[22] Danny Dolev. Century papers at the first quarter-century milestone. In *Proceedings of the Twenty-fifth Annual ACM Symposium on Principles of Distributed Computing*, PODC '06, pages 3–4, New York, NY, USA, 2006. ACM.

[23] Y. Frankel, P. Gemmell, P. D. MacKenzie, and Moti Yung. Optimal-resilience proactive public-key cryptosystems. In *Proceedings of the 38th Annual Symposium on Foundations of Computer Science*, FOCS '97, pages 384–, Washington, DC, USA, 1997. IEEE Computer Society.

[24] Yair Frankel, Peter Gemmell, Philip D. MacKenzie, and Moti Yung. Proactive rsa. In *Proceedings of the 17th Annual International Cryptology Conference on Advances in Cryptology*, CRYPTO '97, pages 440–454, London, UK, UK, 1997. Springer-Verlag.

[25] Yair Frankel, Philip D. MacKenzie, and Moti Yung. Adaptive security for the additive-sharing based proactive rsa. In *Proceedings of the 4th International Workshop on Practice and Theory in Public Key Cryptography: Public Key Cryptography*, PKC '01, pages 240–263, London, UK, UK, 2001. Springer-Verlag.

[26] Matthew K. Franklin, Zvi Galil, and Moti Yung. Eavesdropping games: A graph-theoretic approach to privacy in distributed systems. In *FOCS*, pages 670–679, 1993.

[27] Matthew K. Franklin and Moti Yung. Communication complexity of secure computation (extended abstract). In *STOC*, pages 699–710, 1992.

[28] Craig Gentry, Shai Halevi, and Nigel P. Smart. Fully homomorphic encryption with polylog overhead. In *EUROCRYPT*, pages 465–482, 2012.

[29] O. Goldreich, S. Micali, and A. Wigderson. How to play any mental game. In *Proceedings of the Nineteenth Annual ACM Symposium on Theory of Computing*, STOC '87, pages 218–229, New York, NY, USA, 1987. ACM.

[30] Amir Herzberg, Stanislaw Jarecki, Hugo Krawczyk, and Moti Yung. Proactive secret sharing or: How to cope with perpetual leakage. In *CRYPTO*, pages 339–352, 1995.

[31] Yuval Ishai, Eyal Kushilevitz, Rafail Ostrovsky, and Amit Sahai. Cryptography with constant computational overhead. In *STOC*, pages 433–442, 2008.

[32] Gene Itkis and Leonid Reyzin. Sibir: Signer-base intrusion-resilient signatures. In *CRYPTO*, pages 499–514, 2002.

[33] Stanislaw Jarecki and Josh Olsen. Proactive rsa with non-interactive signing. In Gene Tsudik, editor, *Financial Cryptography and Data Security*, pages 215–230. Springer-Verlag, Berlin, Heidelberg, 2008.

[34] Stanislaw Jarecki and Nitesh Saxena. Further simplifications in proactive rsa signatures. In *Proceedings of the Second international conference on Theory of Cryptography*, TCC'05, pages 510–528, Berlin, Heidelberg, 2005. Springer-Verlag.

[35] Rafail Ostrovsky and Moti Yung. How to withstand mobile virus attacks (extended abstract). In *PODC*, pages 51–59, 1991.

[36] T. Rabin and M. Ben-Or. Verifiable secret sharing and multiparty protocols with honest majority. In *Proceedings of the twenty-first annual ACM symposium on Theory of computing*, STOC '89, pages 73–85, New York, NY, USA, 1989. ACM.

[37] Tal Rabin. A simplified approach to threshold and proactive rsa. In *Proceedings of the 18th Annual International Cryptology Conference on Advances in Cryptology*, CRYPTO '98, pages 89–104, London, UK, UK, 1998. Springer-Verlag.

[38] David Schultz. *Mobile Proactive Secret Sharing*. PhD thesis, Massachusetts Institute of Technology, 2007.

[39] Adi Shamir. How to share a secret. *Commun. ACM*, 22(11):612–613, 1979.

[40] Abraham Waksman. A permutation network. *J. ACM*, 15(1):159–163, 1968.

[41] Theodore M. Wong, Chenxi Wang, and Jeannette M. Wing. Verifiable secret redistribution for archive system. In *IEEE Security in Storage Workshop*, pages 94–106, 2002.

[42] Andrew C. Yao. Protocols for secure computations. In *Proceedings of the 23rd Annual Symposium on Foundations of Computer Science*, FOCS '82, pages 160–164, Washington, DC, USA, 1982. IEEE Computer Society.

[43] Lidong Zhou, Fred B. Schneider, and Robbert van Renesse. Apss: proactive secret sharing in asynchronous systems. *ACM Trans. Inf. Syst. Secur.*, 8(3):259–286, 2005.

Born and Raised Distributively: Fully Distributed Non-Interactive Adaptively-Secure Threshold Signatures with Short Shares

Benoît Libert*
ENS Lyon, LIP
Lyon, France
benoit.libert@ens-lyon.fr

Marc Joye
Technicolor
Palo Alto, CA, USA
marc.joye@technicolor.com

Moti Yung
Google Inc. and Columbia U.
New York, NY, USA
moti@cs.columbia.edu

ABSTRACT

Threshold cryptography is a fundamental distributed computational paradigm for enhancing the availability and the security of cryptographic public-key schemes. It does it by dividing private keys into n shares handed out to distinct servers. In threshold signature schemes, a set of at least $t+1 \leq n$ servers is needed to produce a valid digital signature. Availability is assured by the fact that any subset of $t+1$ servers can produce a signature when authorized. At the same time, the scheme should remain robust (in the fault tolerance sense) and unforgeable (cryptographically) against up to t corrupted servers; *i.e.*, it adds quorum control to traditional cryptographic services and introduces redundancy. Originally, most practical threshold signatures have a number of demerits: They have been analyzed in a static corruption model (where the set of corrupted servers is fixed at the very beginning of the attack), they require interaction, they assume a trusted dealer in the key generation phase (so that the system is not fully distributed), or they suffer from certain overheads in terms of storage (large share sizes). In this paper, we construct practical *fully distributed* (the private key is born distributed), non-interactive schemes —where the servers can compute their partial signatures without communication with other servers— with adaptive security (*i.e.*, the adversary corrupts servers dynamically based on its full view of the history of the system). Our schemes are very efficient in terms of computation, communication, and scalable storage (with private key shares of size $O(1)$, where certain solutions incur $O(n)$ storage costs at each server). Unlike other adaptively secure schemes, our schemes are erasure-free (reliable erasure is a hard to assure and hard to administer property in actual systems). To the best of our knowledge, such a fully distributed highly constrained scheme has been an open problem in the area. In particular, and of special interest, is the fact that Pedersen's traditional distributed key generation (DKG) protocol can be safely employed in the initial key generation phase when the system is born —although it is well-known not to ensure uniformly distributed public keys. An advantage of this is that this protocol only takes one round optimistically (in the absence of faulty player).

*This research was done while this author was at Technicolor, France.

PODC'14, July 15–18, 2014, Paris, France.

http://dx.doi.org/10.1145/2611462.2611498.

Categories and Subject Descriptors

E.3 [**Data**]: Data encryption; H.4 [**Information Systems Applications**]: Miscellaneous; C.2.4 [**Computer Systems Organization**]: Distributed systems

General Terms

Theory, Security

Keywords

Threshold signature schemes, fully distributed systems, non-interactivity, adaptive security, efficiency, availability, fault tolerance, distributed key generation, erasure-free schemes

1. INTRODUCTION

Threshold cryptography [29, 30, 15, 28] is a paradigm where cryptographic keys are divided into $n > 1$ shares to be stored by distinct servers, which increases the system's availability and resilience to failures. In (t, n)-threshold cryptosystems, private-key operations require the cooperation of at least $t+1$ out of n servers (any subset is good). By doing so, the system remains secure against adversaries that break into up to t servers. (The mechanism can be viewed as extending Shamir's secret sharing of one value [67] to sharing of the capability to apply cryptographic function efficiently). The public-key portion of the function (*e.g.*, signature verification key) does not change from its usual format.

Threshold primitives are widely used in distributed protocols. Threshold homomorphic encryption schemes are utilized in voting systems (see, *e.g.*, [22, 23]) and multiparty computation protocols [24]. Threshold signatures enhance the security of highly sensitive private keys, like those of certification authorities (*e.g.*, [18]). They can also serve as tools for distributed storage systems [48, 65]. RSA and Elgamal-type constructions have been at the core of many threshold protocols the last two decades (see, *e.g.*, [28, 39, 40, 47]). A *fully distributed* public-key system is one where the public (and the distributed private) key are jointly generated by the same servers which end up holding the private key's shares (*e.g.*, via a threshold secret sharing [67]). Efficient distributed key generation (DKG) protocols were put forth for both RSA [12, 34, 33, 26] and discrete-logarithm-based systems [62, 41, 35, 16, 43].

NON-INTERACTIVE THRESHOLD SIGNATURES. For a long time, RSA-based threshold signatures have been the only solutions to enable non-interactive distributed signature generation. By "non-interactive", we mean that each server can compute its own partial signature without any online conversation with other servers: each server should send a single message to an entity, called *combiner*, which gathers the signature shares so as to obtain a full signature. Unlike threshold versions of Schnorr and DSA signatures [42, 39], threshold RSA signatures are well-suited to non-interactive signing protocols as they are deterministic. Hence, they do not require the servers to jointly generate a randomized signature component in a first round before starting a second round. Practical robust non-interactive threshold signatures were described by Shoup [68] under the RSA assumption and by Katz and Yung [50] assuming the hardness of factoring. Boldyreva [10] showed a threshold version of Boneh-Lynn-Shacham signatures [14], which provided an alternative non-interactive scheme with robustness and short signatures. The latter construction [10] was subsequently generalized by Wee [69]. These solutions are only known to resist static attacks, where the set of corrupted servers is chosen by the adversary at the very beginning of the attack, before even seeing the public key.

ADAPTIVE CORRUPTIONS. More realistically than the static model, the adaptive corruption model allows adversaries to choose whom to corrupt at any time, based on their entire view so far. Adaptive adversaries are known to be strictly (see, *e.g.*, [25]) stronger. The first adaptively secure threshold signatures were independently described in 1999 by Canetti *et al.* [16] and by Frankel *et al.* [35, 36]. These constructions rely on a technique, called "single inconsistent player" (SIP), which inherently requires interaction. The SIP technique basically consists in converting a t-out-of-n secret sharing into an t-out-of-t secret sharing in such a way that, in the latter case, there is only one server whose internal state cannot be consistently revealed to the adversary. Since this player is chosen at random by the simulator among the n severs, it is only corrupted with probability less than $1/2$ and, upon this undesirable event, the simulator can simply rewind the adversary back to one of its previous states. After this backtracking operation, the simulator uses different random coins to simulate the view of the adversary, hoping that the inconsistent player will not be corrupted again (and the expected number of rewinding-s is bounded by 2).

Jarecki and Lysyanskaya [49] extended the SIP technique in order to eliminate the need for servers to reliably erase intermediate computation results. However, their adaptively secure version of the Canetti-Goldwasser threshold cryptosystem [17] requires a substantial amount of interaction at each private-key operation. The same holds for the adaptively secure threshold signatures of Lysyanskaya and Peikert [57] and the universally composable protocols of Abe and Fehr [1].

In 2006, Almansa, Damgård and Nielsen [4] showed a variant of Rabin's threshold RSA signatures [64] and proved them adaptively secure using the SIP technique and ideas from [35, 36]. Similar techniques were used in [70] to construct adaptively secure threshold Waters signatures [71]. While the SIP technique provides adaptively secure threshold signatures based on RSA or the Diffie-Hellman assumption, these fall short of minimizing the amount of interaction. The constructions of [35, 36] proceed by turning a (t, n) polynomial secret sharing into a (t, t) additive secret sharing by first selecting a pool of at least t participants. However, if only one of these fails to provide a valid contribution to the signing process, the whole protocol must be restarted from scratch. The protocol of Almansa *et al.* [4] is slightly different in that; like [64], it proceeds by sharing an RSA private key in an additive (n, n) fashion (*i.e.*, the private RSA exponent d is split into shares $d_1, \ldots, d_n$ such that $d = \sum_{i=1}^{n} d_i$). In turn, each additive share d_i is shared in a (t, n) fashion using a polynomial verifiable secret sharing and each share $d_{i,j}$ of d_i is distributed to another server j. This is done in such a way that, if one participant fails to provide a valid RSA signature share $H(M)^{d_i}$, the missing signature share can be re-constructed by running the reconstruction algorithm of the verifiable secret sharing scheme that was used to share d_i. The first drawback of this approach is that it is only non-interactive when all players are honest as a second round is needed to reconstruct missing multiplicative signature shares $H(M)^{d_i}$. Another disadvantage is that players have to store $\Theta(n)$ values, where n is the number of servers, as each player has to store a polynomial share of other players' additive share. Ideally, we would like a solution where each player only stores $O(1)$ elements, regardless of the number of players.

Recently, Libert and Yung [55, 56] gave several constructions of adaptively secure threshold encryption schemes with chosen-ciphertext security. They also suggested an adaptively secure and non-interactive threshold variant [55] of a signature scheme due to Lewko and Waters [51]. The use of bilinear maps in composite order groups makes the scheme of [55] expensive when it comes to verifying signatures: as discussed by Freeman [38], computing a bilinear map in composite order groups is at least 50 times slower than evaluating the same bilinear map in prime-order groups at the 80-bit security level (things can only get worse at higher security levels). The techniques of Lewko [52] can be used to adapt the construction of [55] to the setting of prime-order groups. In the resulting construction, each signature consists of 6 group elements. The use of asymmetric bilinear maps (see [19]) allows reducing the signature size to 4 group elements. Unfortunately, the techniques of [52, 19] assume a trusted dealer and, if implemented in a distributed manner, their key generation phase is likely to be communication-expensive (resorting to generic multiparty secure computations). In particular, they seem hardly compatible with a round-optimal DKG protocol. The reason is that [19] requires to generate public keys containing pairs of matrices of the form $g^{\mathbf{A}} \in \mathbb{G}^{n \times n}$ and $g^{\mathbf{A}^{-1}} \in \mathbb{G}^{n \times n}$, for some matrix $\mathbf{A} \in \mathbb{Z}_p^{n \times n}$, and it is not clear how these non-linear operations can be achieved in a round-optimal distributed manner (let alone with adaptive security). Finally, the solutions of [55] require reliable erasures due to the use of the dual system encryption technique [72, 51] and the existence of several distributions of partial signatures.

OUR CONTRIBUTIONS. We consider the problem of devising a fully distributed, non-interactive, robust, and adaptively secure construction which is as efficient as the centralized schemes obtained from [55, 19] and does not rely on erasures. In particular, we want to retain private-key shares of $O(1)$ size, no matter how many players are involved in the protocol. Here, "fully distributed" implies that the public key is jointly generated by all players —so that no trusted dealer is needed— while guaranteeing the security of the scheme against an adaptive adversary. As mentioned above, we wish to avoid the costly and hard-to-control use of reliable erasures. This means that, whenever the adversary corrupts a player, it learns the entire history of that player.

At the same time, the distributed key generation phase should be as communication-efficient as possible. Ideally, a single communication round should be needed when the players follow the protocol. Finally, we would like to avoid interaction during the distributed signing process. To the best of our knowledge, no existing solution combines all the aforementioned highly constraining properties. We thus provide the first candidates.

Our constructions are derived from linearly homomorphic structure-preserving signatures (LHSPS). As defined by Abe *et al.* [2, 3], structure-preserving signatures (SPS) are signature schemes where messages and public keys live in an abelian group over which a bilinear map is efficiently computable. Recently, Libert *et al.* [54] considered SPS schemes with additive homomorphic properties: given signatures on linearly independent vectors of group elements, anyone can publicly compute a signature on any linear combination of these vectors. In order to sign a message $M \in \{0,1\}^*$ in a distributed manner, our idea is to hash M onto a vector of group elements which is signed using the LHSPS scheme of [54]. In the random oracle model, we prove that the resulting system is a secure digital signature even if the underlying LHSPS scheme satisfies a weak security definition. Since the LHSPS signing algorithm is deterministic and further presents certain homomorphic properties over the key space, the resulting signature is also amenable for non-interactive distributed signature generation. In the threshold setting, we take advantage of specific properties of the LHSPS scheme of [54] to prove that the scheme provides security against adaptive corruptions in the absence of secure erasures.

More surprisingly, we prove that the scheme remains adaptively secure if the public key is generated using Pedersen's DKG protocol [62]. The latter basically consists in having all players verifiably share a random value using Feldman's verifiable secret sharing (VSS) [32] before computing the shared secret as the sum of all well-behaved players' contributions. While very efficient (as only one round is needed in the absence of faulty players), this protocol is known [41] *not* to guarantee the uniformity of the resulting public key. Indeed, even a static adversary can bias the distribution by corrupting only two players. Nonetheless, the adversary does not have much control on the distribution of the public key and Pedersen's protocol can still be safely used in some applications, as noted by Gennaro *et al.* [42, 43]. For example, it was recently utilized by Cortier *et al.* [21] in the context of voting protocols. However, these safe uses of Pedersen's protocol were in the static corruption setting and our scheme turns out to be its first application in an adaptive corruption model. To our knowledge, it is also the first adaptively secure threshold signature where the DKG phase takes only one round when all players follow the specification.

As an extension of our first scheme, we describe a variant supporting signature aggregation: as suggested by Boneh *et al.* [13], a set of n signatures for distinct public keys $PK_1, \ldots, PK_s$ on messages $M_1, \ldots, M_s$ can be aggregated into a single signature σ which convinces a verifier that, for each i, M_i was signing by the private key underlying PK_i. In the threshold setting, this property allows for de-centralized certification authorities while enabling the compression of certification chains.

As a final contribution, we give a non-interactive adaptively secure threshold signature scheme in the standard model that retains all the useful properties (including the erasure-freeness) of our first realization. In particular, Pedersen's protocol can still be used in the key generation phase if a set of uniformly random common parameters —which can be shared by many public keys— is set up beforehand. As is natural for standard-model constructions, this scheme is somewhat less efficient than its random-oracle-based counterpart but it remains sufficiently efficient for practical applications.

Like Gennaro *et al.* [43] and Cortier *et al.* [21], we prove security via a direct reduction from the underlying number theoretic assumption instead of reducing the security of our schemes to that of their centralized version. We emphasize that our proof technique is different from those of [43, 21], where the reduction runs Pedersen's DKG protocol on behalf of honest players and embeds a discrete logarithm instance in the contribution of honest players to the public key, using a proper simulation of Feldman's verifiable secret sharing. In the adaptive corruption setting, this would at least require an adaptively secure variant of Feldman's VSS, such as [1], and thus extra communications. Instead, our reduction always faithfully runs the protocol on behalf of honest players, and thus always knows their internal state so as to perfectly answer corruption queries. Yet, we can use the adversary's forgery to break the underlying hardness assumption by taking advantage of key homomorphic properties of the scheme, which allow us to turn a forgery for the jointly generated public key —of possibly skewed distribution— into a forgery for some uniformly random key.

2. BACKGROUND

2.1 Definitions for Threshold Signatures

A non-interactive (t,n)-threshold signature scheme consists of a tuple $\Sigma = (\mathsf{Dist\text{-}Keygen}, \mathsf{Share\text{-}Sign}, \mathsf{Share\text{-}Verify}, \mathsf{Verify}, \mathsf{Combine})$ of efficient algorithms or protocols such that:

$\mathsf{Dist\text{-}Keygen}(\mathsf{params}, \lambda, t, n)$: This is an interactive protocol involving n players $P_1, \ldots, P_n$, which all take as input common public parameters params, a security parameter $\lambda \in \mathbb{N}$ as well as a pair of integers $t, n \in \mathsf{poly}(\lambda)$ such that $1 \leq t \leq n$. The outcome of the protocol is the generation of a public key PK, a vector of private key shares $\mathbf{SK} = (SK_1, \ldots, SK_n)$ where P_i only obtains SK_i for each $i \in \{1, \ldots, n\}$, and a public vector of verification keys $\mathbf{VK} = (VK_1, \ldots, VK_n)$.

$\mathsf{Share\text{-}Sign}(SK_i, M)$: is a possibly randomized algorithm that takes in a message M and a private key share SK_i. It outputs a signature share σ_i.

$\mathsf{Share\text{-}Verify}(PK, \mathbf{VK}, M, (i, \sigma_i))$: is a deterministic algorithm that takes as input a message M, the public key PK, the verification key $\mathbf{VK}$ and a pair (i, σ_i) consisting of an index $i \in \{1, \ldots, n\}$ and signature share σ_i. It outputs 1 or 0 depending on whether σ_i is deemed as a valid signature share or not.

$\mathsf{Combine}(PK, \mathbf{VK}, M, \{(i, \sigma_i)\}_{i \in S})$: takes as input a public key PK, a message M and a subset $S \subset \{1, \ldots, n\}$ of size $|S| = t + 1$ with pairs $\{(i, \sigma_i)\}_{i \in S}$ such that $i \in \{1, \ldots, n\}$ and σ_i is a signature share. This algorithm outputs either a full signature σ or $\perp$ if $\{(i, \sigma_i)\}_{i \in S}$ contains ill-formed partial signatures.

$\mathsf{Verify}(PK, M, \sigma)$: is a deterministic algorithm that takes as input a message M, the public key PK and a signature σ. It outputs 1 or 0 depending on whether σ is deemed valid share or not.

We shall use the same communication model as in, *e.g.*, [41, 42, 43], which is partially synchronous. Namely, communications proceed in synchronized rounds and sent messages are always received within some time bound in the same round. All players have access to a public broadcast channel, which the adversary can use as a sender and a receiver. However, the adversary cannot modify messages sent over this channel, nor prevent their delivery. In addition, we assume private and authenticated channels between all pairs of players.

In the adaptive corruption setting, the security of non-interactive threshold signatures can be defined as follows.

DEFINITION 1. *A non-interactive threshold signature scheme Σ is adaptively secure against chosen-message attacks if no PPT adversary $\mathcal{A}$ has non-negligible advantage in the game hereunder. At any time, we denote by $\mathcal{C} \subset \{1, \ldots, n\}$ and $\mathcal{G} := \{1, \ldots, n\} \setminus \mathcal{C}$ the dynamically evolving subsets of corrupted and honest players, respectively. Initially, we set $\mathcal{C} = \emptyset$.*

1. *The game begins with an execution of the DKG protocol* $\mathsf{Dist\text{-}Keygen}(\mathsf{params}, \lambda, t, N)$ *during which the challenger plays the role of honest players P_i and the adversary $\mathcal{A}$ is allowed to corrupt players at any time. When $\mathcal{A}$ chooses to corrupt a player P_i, the challenger sets $\mathcal{G} = \mathcal{G} \setminus \{i\}$, $\mathcal{C} = \mathcal{C} \cup \{i\}$ and returns the internal state of P_i. Moreover, $\mathcal{A}$ is allowed to act on behalf of P_i from this point forward. The protocol ends with the generation of a public key PK, a vector of private key shares $\mathbf{SK} = (SK_1, \ldots, SK_n)$ and the corresponding verification keys $\mathbf{VK} = (VK_1, \ldots, VK_n)$. At the end of this phase, the public key PK and $\{SK_i\}_{i \in \mathcal{C}}$ are available to the adversary $\mathcal{A}$.*

2. *On polynomially many occasions, $\mathcal{A}$ adaptively interleaves two kinds of queries.*

   - *Corruption query: At any time, $\mathcal{A}$ can choose to corrupt a server. To this end, $\mathcal{A}$ chooses $i \in \{1, \ldots, n\}$ and the challenge returns SK_i before setting $\mathcal{G} = \mathcal{G} \setminus \{i\}$ and $\mathcal{C} = \mathcal{C} \cup \{i\}$.*
   - *Signing query: For any $i \in \mathcal{G}$, $\mathcal{A}$ can also submit a pair (i, M) and ask for a signature share on an arbitrary message M on behalf of player P_i. The challenger responds by computing $\sigma_i \leftarrow$* $\mathsf{Share\text{-}Sign}(SK_i, M)$ *and returning σ to $\mathcal{A}$.*

3. *$\mathcal{A}$ outputs a message $M^\star$ and a signature $\sigma^\star$. We define $\mathcal{V} = \mathcal{C} \cup \mathcal{S}$, where $\mathcal{S} \subset \{1, \ldots, n\}$ is the subset of players for which $\mathcal{A}$ made a signing query of the form $(i, M^\star)$. The adversary wins if the following conditions hold: (i) $|\mathcal{V}| < t + 1$; (ii)* $\mathsf{Verify}(PK, M^\star, \sigma^\star) = 1$.

$\mathcal{A}$'s advantage is defined as its probability of success, taken over all coin tosses.

Since we focus on non-interactive schemes, Definition 1 allows the adversary to individually query each partial signing oracle whereas usual definitions only provide the adversary with an oracle that runs the distributed signing protocol on behalf of all honest players. We also remark that Definition 1 allows the adversary to obtain some partial signatures on the forgery message $M^\star$ as long as its output remains a non-trivial forgery. In a weaker (but still compelling) definition, partial signing queries for $M^\star$ would be completely disallowed. In the following, we will stick to the stronger definition.

2.2 Hardness Assumptions

We first recall the definition of the Decision Diffie-Hellman problem.

DEFINITION 2. *In a cyclic group $\mathbb{G}$ of prime order p, the* Decision Diffie-Hellman Problem *(DDH) in $\mathbb{G}$, is to distinguish the distributions (g, g^a, g^b, g^{ab}) and (g, g^a, g^b, g^c), with $a, b, c \xleftarrow{R} \mathbb{Z}_p$. The Decision Diffie-Hellman assumption is the intractability of DDH for any PPT distinguisher.*

We use bilinear maps $e : \mathbb{G} \times \hat{\mathbb{G}} \to \mathbb{G}_T$ over groups of prime order p. We will work in asymmetric pairings, where we have $\mathbb{G} \neq \hat{\mathbb{G}}$ so as to allow the DDH assumption to hold in $\mathbb{G}$ (see, *e.g.*, [66]). In certain asymmetric pairing configurations, DDH is even believed to hold in both $\mathbb{G}$ and $\hat{\mathbb{G}}$. This assumption is called *Symmetric eXternal Diffie-Hellman* (SXDH) assumption and it implies that no isomorphism between $\hat{\mathbb{G}}$ and $\mathbb{G}$ be efficiently computable.

For convenience, we also use the following problem in asymmetric pairing configurations.

DEFINITION 3 ([3]). *The* Double Pairing problem *(DP) in $(\mathbb{G}, \hat{\mathbb{G}}, \mathbb{G}_T)$ is, given $(\hat{g_z}, \hat{g_r}) \in_R \hat{\mathbb{G}}^2$, to find a pair $(z, r) \in \mathbb{G}^2 \setminus \{(1_{\mathbb{G}}, 1_{\mathbb{G}})\}$ that satisfies $e(z, \hat{g_z}) \cdot e(r, \hat{g_r}) = 1_{\mathbb{G}_T}$. The Double Pairing assumption asserts that the DP problem is infeasible for any PPT algorithm.*

The DP problem is known [3] to be at least as hard as DDH in $\hat{\mathbb{G}}$. Given $(\hat{g_z}, \hat{g_r}, \hat{g_z}^{\theta_1}, \hat{g_r}^{\theta_2})$, a solution (z, r) allows deciding whether $\theta_1 = \theta_2$ or not by testing if the equality $e(z, \hat{g_z}^{\theta_1}) \cdot e(r, \hat{g_r}^{\theta_2}) = 1_{\mathbb{G}_T}$ holds.

2.3 Linearly Homomorphic Structure-Preserving Signatures

Structure-preserving signatures [2, 3] are signature schemes that allow signing elements of an abelian group while preserving their algebraic structure, without hashing them first. In [54], Libert *et al.* described structure-preserving signatures with linearly homomorphic properties. Given signatures on several vectors $\vec{M}_1, \ldots, \vec{M}_n$ of group elements, anyone can publicly derive a signature on any linear combination of $\vec{M}_1, \ldots, \vec{M}_n$. They suggested the following scheme, which is a one-time LHSPS (namely, it only allows signing one linear subspace) based on the DP assumption.

Keygen(λ, N): Given a security parameter λ and the dimension $N \in \mathbb{N}$ of the subspace to be signed, choose bilinear group $(\mathbb{G}, \hat{\mathbb{G}}, \mathbb{G}_T)$ of prime order $p > 2^\lambda$. Then, choose $\hat{g}_z, \hat{g}_r \xleftarrow{R} \hat{\mathbb{G}}$. For $k = 1$ to N, pick $\chi_k, \gamma_k \xleftarrow{R} \mathbb{Z}_p$ and compute $\hat{g}_k = \hat{g}_z{}^{\chi_k} \hat{g}_r{}^{\gamma_k}$. The private key is $\mathsf{sk} = \{\chi_k, \gamma_k\}_{i=1}^N$ while the public key consists of $\mathsf{pk} = \big(\hat{g}_z,\ \hat{g}_r,\ \{\hat{g}_k\}_{k=1}^N\big)$.

Sign$(\mathsf{sk}, (M_1, \ldots, M_N))$: To sign $(M_1, \ldots, M_N) \in \mathbb{G}^N$ using $\mathsf{sk} = \{\chi_k, \gamma_k\}_{k=1}^N$, compute $z = \prod_{k=1}^N M_k^{-\chi_k}$ and $r = \prod_{k=1}^N M_k^{-\gamma_k}$. Return $\sigma = (z, r) \in \mathbb{G}^2$.

SignDerive$(\mathsf{pk}, \{(\omega_i, \sigma^{(i)})\}_{i=1}^\ell)$: Given the public key pk and ℓ tuples $(\omega_i, \sigma^{(i)})$, parse $\sigma^{(i)}$ as $\sigma^{(i)} = (z_i, r_i) \in \mathbb{G}^3$ for $i = 1$ to ℓ. Then, compute and return $\sigma = (z, r)$, where $z = \prod_{i=1}^\ell z_i^{\omega_i}$ and $r = \prod_{i=1}^\ell r_i^{\omega_i}$.

Verify$(\mathsf{pk}, \sigma, (M_1, \ldots, M_N))$: Given a purported signature $\sigma = (z, r) \in \mathbb{G}^2$ and a vector $(M_1, \ldots, M_N)$, return 1 if and only if $(M_1, \ldots, M_N) \neq (1_{\mathbb{G}}, \ldots, 1_{\mathbb{G}})$ and (z, r) satisfies $1_{\mathbb{G}_T} = e(z, \hat{g}_z) \cdot e(r, \hat{g}_r) \cdot \prod_{k=1}^N e(M_k, \hat{g}_k)$.

A useful property of the scheme is that, if the DP assumption holds, it is computationally hard to come up with two distinct signatures on the same vector, *even* if the private key is available.

3. A PRACTICAL ADAPTIVELY SECURE NON-INTERACTIVE THRESHOLD SIGNATURE

The construction notably relies on the observation that, as shown in the full version of the paper [53], any one-time linearly homomorphic SPS can be turned into a fully secure ordinary signature by introducing a random oracle. The public key is simply that of a linearly homomorphic SPS for vectors of dimension $n > 1$. Messages are signed by hashing them to a vector $\vec{H} \in \mathbb{G}^n$ and generating a one-time homomorphic signature on $\vec{H}$. The security reduction programs the random oracle in such a way that all signed messages are hashed into a proper subspace of $\mathbb{G}^n$ whereas, with some probability, the adversary forges a signature on a message which is hashed outside this subspace. Hence, a forgery for this message translates into an attack against the underlying linearly homomorphic SPS.

In the threshold setting, our system can be seen as an adaptively secure variant of Boldyreva's threshold signature [10], which builds on the short signatures of Boneh, Lynn, and Shacham [14].

The DKG phase uses Pedersen's protocol [62] (or, more precisely, a variant with two generators). Each player verifiably shares a random secret using Pedersen's verifiable secret sharing [63] —where verification is enabled by having all parties broadcast commitments to their secret polynomials— and the final secret key is obtained by summing up the shares of non-disqualified players. When all parties follow the protocol, a single communication round is needed. Moreover, we do not need to rely on zero-knowledge proofs or reliable erasures at any time.

In order to sign a message using his private key share, each player first hashes the message M to obtain a vector $(H_1, H_2) \in \mathbb{G}^2$ of two group elements, which can be signed using the linearly homomorphic structure-preserving signature of Section 2.3. We actually build on the observation that any one-time linearly homomorphic SPS implies a fully secure digital signature in the random oracle model. In the threshold setting, we take advantage of two specific properties in the underlying homomorphic signature. First, it is also key homomorphic[1] and thus amenable for non-interactively distributing the signing process. Second, in the security proof of [54], the reduction always knows the private key, which allows consistently answering adaptive corruption queries.

3.1 Description

In the description below, we assume that all players agree on public parameters params consisting of asymmetric bilinear groups $(\mathbb{G}, \hat{\mathbb{G}}, \mathbb{G}_T)$ of prime order $p > 2^\lambda$ with generators $\hat{g}_z, \hat{g}_r \in_R \hat{\mathbb{G}}$ and a hash function $H : \{0,1\}^* \to \mathbb{G}^2$ that ranges over $\mathbb{G} \times \mathbb{G}$. This hash function is modeled as a random oracle in the security analysis. While no party should know $\log_{\hat{g}_z}(\hat{g}_r)$, we do not need an extra round to generate $\hat{g}_r$ in a distributed manner as it can simply be derived from a random oracle.

Dist-Keygen$(\mathsf{params}, \lambda, t, n)$: Given common public parameters $\mathsf{params} = \{(\mathbb{G}, \hat{\mathbb{G}}, \mathbb{G}_T), \hat{g}_z, \hat{g}_r, H\}$, a security parameter λ and integers $t, n \in \mathbb{N}$ such that $n \geq 2t + 1$, each player P_i conducts the following steps.

1. Each player P_i shares two pairs $\{(a_{ik0}, b_{ik0})\}_{k=1}^2$. To this end, he does the following:
   (a) For each $k \in \{1, 2\}$, choose random polynomials $A_{ik}[X] = a_{ik0} + a_{ik1}X + \cdots + a_{ikt}X^t$, $B_{ik}[X] = b_{ik0} + b_{ik1}X + \cdots + b_{ikt}X^t \in \mathbb{Z}_p[X]$ of degree t and broadcast
   $$\hat{W}_{ik\ell} = \hat{g}_z{}^{a_{ik\ell}} \hat{g}_r{}^{b_{ik\ell}} \qquad \forall \ell \in \{0, \ldots, t\} \ .$$
   (b) For $j = 1$ to n, send $\{(A_{ik}(j), B_{ik}(j))\}_{k=1}^2$ to P_j.
2. For each set of shares $\{(A_{jk}(i), B_{jk}(i))\}_{k=1}^2$ received from another player P_j, P_i verifies that
   $$\hat{g}_z{}^{A_{jk}(i)} \hat{g}_r{}^{B_{jk}(i)} = \prod_{\ell=0}^{t} \hat{W}_{jk\ell}{}^{i^\ell} \qquad \text{for } k = 1, 2 \ . \quad (1)$$
   If these equalities do not both hold, P_i broadcasts a complaint against the faulty sender P_j.
3. Any player who received strictly more than t complaints from other players is immediately disqualified. Each player P_i who received a complaint from another player P_j responds by returning the correct shares $\{(A_{ik}(j), B_{ik}(j))\}_{k=1}^2$. If any of these new shares does not satisfy (1), P_i is disqualified. Let $\mathcal{Q} \subset \{1, \ldots, n\}$ be the set of non-disqualified players at the end of step 3.
4. The public key is obtained as $PK = \{\hat{g}_k\}_{k=1}^2$, where $\hat{g}_k = \prod_{i \in \mathcal{Q}} \hat{W}_{ik0} = \hat{g}_z^{\sum_{i \in \mathcal{Q}} a_{ik0}} \hat{g}_r^{\sum_{i \in \mathcal{Q}} b_{ik0}}$.

[1] Namely, the private key space forms an additive group such that, for any message M, given any two signatures $\sigma_1 \leftarrow \mathsf{Sign}(sk_1, M)$ and $\sigma_2 \leftarrow \mathsf{Sign}(sk_2, M)$, anyone can compute a valid signature on M for the private key $sk_1 + sk_2$.

Each P_i locally defines his private key share

$$SK_i = \{(A_k(i), B_k(i))\}_{k=1}^2 = \{(\sum_{j\in\mathcal{Q}} A_{jk}(i), \sum_{j\in\mathcal{Q}} B_{jk}(i))\}_{k=1}^2$$

and anyone can publicly compute his verification key $VK_i = (\hat{V}_{1,i}, \hat{V}_{2,i})$ as

$$VK_i = (\hat{g}_z{}^{A_1(i)} \hat{g}_r{}^{B_1(i)}, \hat{g}_z{}^{A_2(i)} \hat{g}_r{}^{B_2(i)}) = \Big(\prod_{j\in\mathcal{Q}}\prod_{\ell=0}^{t} \hat{W}_{j1\ell}^{i^\ell}, \prod_{j\in\mathcal{Q}}\prod_{\ell=0}^{t} \hat{W}_{j2\ell}^{i^\ell}\Big) .$$

For any disqualified player $i \in \{1, \ldots, n\} \setminus \mathcal{Q}$, the i-th private key share is implicitly set as $SK_i = \{(0,0)\}_{k=1}^2$ and the corresponding verification key is $VK_i = (1_{\hat{\mathbb{G}}}, 1_{\hat{\mathbb{G}}})$.

This completes the generation of the private key shares $\mathbf{SK} = (SK_1, \ldots, SK_n)$, the vector of verification keys $\mathbf{VK} = (VK_1, \ldots, VK_n)$ and the public key, which consists of $PK = \big(\mathsf{params}, (\hat{g}_1, \hat{g}_2)\big)$.

When the protocol ends, the obtained private key shares $\{A_k(i)\}_{k=1}^2$ and $\{B_k(i)\}_{k=1}^2$ all lie on t-degree polynomials $A_k[X] = \sum_{j\in\mathcal{Q}} A_{jk}[X]$ and $B_k[X] = \sum_{j\in\mathcal{Q}} B_{jk}[X]$. Each player also holds an additive share $\{(a_{ik0}, b_{ik0})\}_{k=1}^2$ of the secret key $\{(A_k(0), B_k(0)) = (\sum_{i\in\mathcal{Q}} a_{ik0}, \sum_{i\in\mathcal{Q}} b_{ik0})\}_{k=1}^2$ but these shares will not be used in the scheme.

Share-Sign(i, SK_i, M): To generate a partial signature on a message $M \in \{0,1\}^*$ using his private key share $SK_i = \{(A_k(i), B_k(i))\}_{k=1}^2$, P_i first computes the hash value $(H_1, H_2) = H(M) \in \mathbb{G} \times \mathbb{G}$ and generates the partial signature $\sigma_i = (z_i, r_i) \in \mathbb{G}^2$ as

$$z_i = \prod_{k=1}^{2} H_k^{-A_k(i)}, \qquad r_i = \prod_{k=1}^{2} H_k^{-B_k(i)} .$$

Share-Verify$(PK, \mathbf{VK}, M, (i, \sigma_i))$: Given a candidate partial signature $\sigma_i = (z_i, r_i) \in \mathbb{G}^2$ and the verification key $VK_i = (\hat{V}_{1,i}, \hat{V}_{2,i})$, the partial verification algorithm first computes $(H_1, H_2) = H(M) \in \mathbb{G}^2$. It returns 1 if the equality $e(z_i, \hat{g}_z) \cdot e(r_i, \hat{g}_r) \cdot \prod_{k=1}^2 e(H_k, \hat{V}_{k,i}) = 1_{\mathbb{G}_T}$ holds and 0 otherwise.

Combine$(PK, \mathbf{VK}, M, \{(i, \sigma_i)\}_{i\in S})$: Given a $(t+1)$-set with valid shares $\{(i, \sigma_i)\}_{i\in S}$, parse the signature share σ_i as $(z_i, r_i) \in \mathbb{G}^2$ for each $i \in S$. Then, compute

$$(z, r) = \Big(\prod_{i\in S} z_i^{\Delta_{i,S}(0)}, \prod_{i\in S} r_i^{\Delta_{i,S}(0)}\Big)$$

by Lagrange interpolation in the exponent. Return the pair $(z, r) \in \mathbb{G}^2$.

Verify(PK, M, σ): Given a purported signature $\sigma = (z, r) \in \mathbb{G}^2$, compute $(H_1, H_2) = H(M) \in \mathbb{G} \times \mathbb{G}$ and return 1 if and only if the following equality holds:

$$e(z, \hat{g}_z) \cdot e(r, \hat{g}_r) \cdot e(H_1, \hat{g}_1) \cdot e(H_2, \hat{g}_2) = 1_{\mathbb{G}_T} .$$

If the scheme is instantiated using Barreto-Naehrig curves [5] at the 128-bit security level, each signature consists of 512 bits. For the same security level, RSA-based threshold signatures like [68, 4] require 3076 bits. The scheme is also very efficient from a computational standpoint. Each server only has to compute two multi-exponentiations with two base elements and two "hash-on-curve" operations. The verifier has to compute a product of four pairings.

At the end of the key generation phase, each player only needs to store a private key share $SK_i = \{(A_k(i), B_k(i))\}_{k=1}^2$ of constant-size —whereas solutions like [4] incur the storage of $O(n)$ elements at each player— and can erase all intermediate values, including the polynomials $A_{ik}[X]$ and $B_{ik}[X]$. However, we insist that the security analysis does not require reliable erasures. When a player is corrupted, we assume that the adversary learns the entire history of this player.

3.2 Security

Although the public key is not guaranteed to be uniform due to the use of Pedersen's DKG protocol, the key homomorphic property allows the reduction to turn the adversary's forgery into a valid signature with respect to some uniformly random public key obtained by multiplying honest users' contributions to the public key. This is sufficient for solving a given Double Pairing instance.

THEOREM 3.1. *The scheme provides adaptive security under the SXDH assumption in the random oracle model. For any PPT adversary $\mathcal{A}$, there exist DDH distinguishers $\mathcal{B}_1$ and $\mathcal{B}_2$ with comparable running time in the groups $\mathbb{G}$ and $\hat{\mathbb{G}}$, respectively.*

A detailed proof of Theorem 3.1 is available in the full version of the paper [53]. It proceeds with a sequence of games which can be outlined as follows.

The first game is the real game where the challenger assumes the role of all honest players in the distributed key generation phase. Since it controls a majority of players, the challenger knows $\{A_{jk}[X], B_{jk}[X]\}_{j\in\mathcal{Q},k\in\{1,2\}}$ and the private key shares $\{SK_j\}_{j\in\mathcal{Q}}$ of all non-disqualified players —either because it obtained at least $t+1$ polynomial shares $\{(A_{jk}(i), B_{jk}(i))\}_{i\in\mathcal{G},k\in\{1,2\}}$ for each $j \in \mathcal{Q}$ or because it chose the polynomials itself— at the end of Dist-Keygen.

In subsequent games, the challenger applies Coron's proof technique for Full Domain Hash signatures [20]. At each random oracle query $H(M)$, it flips a coin $\vartheta_M \in \{0,1\}$ that takes the value 0 with probability $1/q_s$ and the value 1 with probability $1/(q_s+1)$, where q_s is the number of signing queries. If $\vartheta_M = 1$, the challenger defines $H(M)$ to be a random vector of $\mathbb{G}^2$. If $\vartheta_M = 0$, the message M is hashed to a subspace of dimension 1. We prove that, although H does no longer behave as an actual random oracle, this change should not affect the adversary's view if the DDH assumption holds in $\mathbb{G}$. Coron's analysis [20] shows that, with probability $\Omega(1/q_s)$, the following conditions are fulfilled: (i) The adversary only obtains partial signatures on messages $M_1, \ldots, M_{q_s}$ that are hashed in a one-dimensional subspace; (ii) The adversary's forgery involves a message $M^\star$ such that $(H_1^\star, H_2^\star) = H(M^\star)$ is linearly independent of the vectors $\{(H_{1,i}, H_{2,i}) = H(M_i)\}_{i=1}^{q_s}$. Condition (i) ensures that the adversary obtains little information about the private key shares $\{SK_i\}_{i\in\mathcal{G}}$ and the additive shares $\{a_{ik0}, b_{ik0}\}_{i\in\mathcal{G},k\in\{1,2\}}$ of honest players. Hence, if the challenger computes the additive contribution of honest players to a signature on the vector $(H_1^\star, H_2^\star) = H(M^\star)$, this contribution is completely unpredictable by the adversary due to condition (ii). With overwhelming probability, this contribution does *not* coincide with the one that can be extracted (using the additive shares $\{a_{jk0}, b_{jk0}\}_{j \in \mathcal{Q} \setminus \mathcal{G},\ k \in \{1,2\}}$ that the reduction knows from the key generation phase) from the adversary's forgery $(z^\star, r^\star)$ using the key homomorphic property of the scheme. The challenger thus obtains two distinct linearly homomorphic signatures on the vector $(H_1^\star, H_2^\star)$, which allows solving an instance of the Double Pairing problem.

The proof of Theorem 3.1 goes through if, during the DKG phase, each player P_i additionally publicizes the pair $(Z_{i0}, R_{i0}) = (g^{-a_{i10}} h^{-a_{i20}}, g^{-b_{i10}} h^{-b_{i20}})$, for public generators $g, h \in \mathbb{G}$, which satisfies

$$e(Z_{i0}, \hat{g_z}) \cdot e(R_{i0}, \hat{g_r}) \cdot e(h, \hat{W}_{i10}) \cdot e(g, \hat{W}_{i20}) = 1_{\mathbb{G}_T}$$

and forms a LHSPS on (g, h) for the public key $\{\hat{W}_{ik0}\}_{k=1}^2$. Based on this observation, we describe a simple modification of the scheme that supports signature aggregation in the full version of the paper [53].

3.3 Adding Proactive Security

The scheme readily extends to provide proactive security [61, 47, 37] against mobile adversaries that can potentially corrupt all the players at some point as long as it never controls more than t players at any time. By having the players refreshing all shares (without changing the secret) at discrete time intervals, the scheme remains secure against an adversary corrupting up to t players during the same period. This is achieved by having all players run a new instance of Pedersen's DKG protocol where the shared secret is $\{(0,0)\}_{k=1}^2$ and locally add the resulting shares to their local shares before updating $\{VK_i\}_{i=1}^n$ accordingly.

The techniques of [46, Section 4] can also be applied to detect parties holding a corrupted share (due to a crash during an update phase or an adversarial behavior) and restore the correct share if necessary.

4. A CONSTRUCTION IN THE STANDARD MODEL

This section gives a round-optimal construction in the standard model. We remark that, under the Decision Linear assumption [11], any one-time LHSPS in symmetric bilinear groups can be turned into a full-fledged digital signature, as shown in the full version of the paper. In the threshold setting, we need to rely on specific properties of the underlying LHSPS in order to achieve adaptive security without relying on a trusted dealer.

The scheme relies on the Groth-Sahai non-interactive witness indistinguishable (NIWI) proof systems [45], which are recalled in Appendix A. In its centralized version, a signature consists of a NIWI proof of knowledge —somewhat in the spirit of Okamoto's signature scheme [60]— of a one-time linearly homomorphic signature on a fixed vector $g \in \mathbb{G}$ of dimension $n = 1$. To generate this proof, the signer forms a Groth-Sahai [45] common reference string (CRS) $(\vec{f}, \vec{f}_M)$ using the bits of the message M, according to a technique suggested by Malkin *et al.* [58]. Due to the witness indistinguishability property of Groth-Sahai proofs, no information leaks about the private key of the underlying one-time homomorphic signature. For this reason, when the adversary creates a fake signature, the reduction is able to extract a different homomorphic signature than the one it can compute. Hence, it obtains two distinct signatures on the same vector, which allows solving an instance of the DP problem.

The scheme can also be seen as a threshold version of (a variant of) the signature presented in [58]. In order to distribute the signing process, we take advantage of the homomorphic properties of Groth-Sahai proofs. More precisely, we use the fact that linear pairing product equations and their proofs can be linearly combined in order to obtain a valid proof for the desired statement when performing a Lagrange interpolation in the exponent. In order to avoid interaction during the signing process, we leverage the property that the centralized signature scheme is key homomorphic.

However, we have to prove that the scheme remains adaptively secure when the DKG phase uses Pedersen's protocol [62]. To this end, we take further advantage of the key homomorphic property. In the security proof, we show that, if the adversary can forge a signature for a non-uniform public key PK, we can turn this forgery into one for another public key PK', which is uniformly distributed.

In the following notations, for each $h \in \mathbb{G}$ and any vector $\vec{g} = (g_1, g_2) \in \mathbb{G}^2$, we denote by $E(\vec{g}, \hat{h})$ the vector $(e(g_1, \hat{h}), e(g_2, \hat{g})) \in \mathbb{G}_T^2$.

Here, we assume public parameters params made of asymmetric bilinear groups $(\mathbb{G}, \hat{\mathbb{G}}, \mathbb{G}_T)$ of prime order $p > 2^\lambda$ with generators $g \in_R \mathbb{G}$, $\hat{g_z}, \hat{g_r} \in_R \hat{\mathbb{G}}$ and vectors $\vec{f} = (f, h) \in \mathbb{G}^2$ and $\vec{f_i} = (f_i, h_i) \stackrel{R}{\leftarrow} \mathbb{G}^2$ for $i = 0$ to L, where $L \in \mathsf{poly}(\lambda)$.

$\mathsf{Dist\text{-}Keygen}(\mathsf{params}, \lambda, t, n)$: This protocol proceeds as in the scheme of Section 3. Namely, given common parameters $\mathsf{params} = \{(\mathbb{G}, \hat{\mathbb{G}}, \mathbb{G}_T), g, \hat{g_z}, \hat{g_r}, \vec{f}, \{\vec{f_i}\}_{i=0}^L\}$, a security parameter λ and integers $t, n \in \mathbb{N}$ such that $n \geq 2t+1$, each player P_i conducts the following steps.

1. Each player P_i shares a random pair (a_{i0}, b_{i0}) according to the following step:
   (a) Pick random polynomials $A_i[X] = a_{i0} + a_{i1}X + \cdots + a_{it}X^t$, $B_i[X] = b_{i0} + b_{i1}X + \cdots + b_{it}X^t$ of degree t and broadcast $\hat{W}_{i\ell} = \hat{g_z}^{a_{i\ell}} \hat{g_r}^{b_{i\ell}}$ for all $\ell \in \{0, \ldots, t\}$.
   (b) For $j = 1$ to n, send $(A_i(j), B_i(j))$ to P_j.
2. For each received shares $(A_j(i), B_j(i))$, player P_i verifies that
$$\hat{g_z}^{A_j(i)} \hat{g_r}^{B_j(i)} = \prod_{\ell=0}^{t} \hat{W}_{j\ell}^{\,i^\ell}. \qquad (2)$$
   If the latter equality does not hold, P_i broadcasts a complaint against P_j.
3. Any player receiving more than t complaints is disqualified. Each player P_i who received a complaint from another player P_j responds by returning the correct shares $(A_i(j), B_i(j))$. If any of these new shares fails to satisfy (2), the faulty P_i is expelled. Let $\mathcal{Q} \subset \{1, \ldots, n\}$ be the set of non-disqualified players at the end of step 3.
4. The public key PK is obtained as $PK = \hat{g}_1$, where $\hat{g}_1 = \prod_{i \in \mathcal{Q}} \hat{W}_{i0} = \hat{g_z}^{\sum_{i \in \mathcal{Q}} a_{i0}} \hat{g_r}^{\sum_{i \in \mathcal{Q}} b_{i0}}$. Each player P_i locally defines his private key share as $SK_i = (A(i), B(i)) = (\sum_{j \in \mathcal{Q}} A_j(i), \sum_{j \in \mathcal{Q}} B_j(i))$ and anyone can publicly compute his verification key as

$VK_i = \hat{V}_i = \hat{g_z}^{A(i)} \hat{g_r}^{B(i)} = \prod_{j \in \mathcal{Q}} \prod_{\ell=0}^{t} \hat{W}_{j\ell}^{i^\ell}$. Any disqualified player $i \in \{1, \dots, n\} \setminus \mathcal{Q}$ is implicitly assigned the share $SK_i = (0, 0)$ and the matching verification key $VK_i = 1_{\hat{\mathbb{G}}}$.

At the end of the protocol, the vector of private key shares is $\mathbf{SK} = (SK_1, \dots, SK_n)$ and the corresponding vector of verification keys $\mathbf{VK} = (VK_1, \dots, VK_n)$. The public key consists of $PK = (\mathsf{params}, \hat{g}_1)$.

Share-Sign(SK_i, M): To generate a partial signature on a L-bit message $M = M[1] \dots M[L] \in \{0,1\}^L$ using $SK_i = (A(i), B(i))$, define $(z_i, r_i) = (g^{-A(i)}, g^{-B(i)})$.

1. Using the bits $M[1] \dots M[L]$ of $M \in \{0,1\}^L$, define the vector $\vec{f}_M = \vec{f}_0 \cdot \prod_{i=1}^{L} \vec{f}_i^{M[i]}$ so as to assemble a Groth-Sahai CRS $\mathbf{f}_M = (\vec{f}, \vec{f}_M)$.
2. Using the CRS $\mathbf{f}_M = (\vec{f}, \vec{f}_M)$, compute Groth-Sahai commitments $\vec{C}_{z,i} = (1_{\mathbb{G}}, z_i) \cdot \vec{f}_1^{\nu_{z,1}} \cdot \vec{f}_M^{\nu_{z,2}}$ and $\vec{C}_{r,i} = (1_{\mathbb{G}}, r_i) \cdot \vec{f}^{\nu_{r,1,i}} \cdot \vec{f}_M^{\nu_{r,2,i}}$ to the group elements z_i and r_i, respectively. Then, generate a NIWI proof $\vec{\hat{\pi}}_i = (\hat{\pi}_{1,i}, \hat{\pi}_{2,i}) \in \hat{\mathbb{G}}^2$ that committed elements $(z_i, r_i) \in \mathbb{G}^2$ satisfy the verification equation $1_{\mathbb{G}_T} = e(z_i, \hat{g}_z) \cdot e(r_i, \hat{g}_r) \cdot e(g, \hat{V}_i)$. This proof is obtained as

$$\vec{\hat{\pi}}_i = (\hat{\pi}_{1,i}, \hat{\pi}_{2,i}) = \left(\hat{g_z}^{-\nu_{z,1,i}} \cdot \hat{g_r}^{-\nu_{r,1,i}},\ \hat{g_z}^{-\nu_{z,2,i}} \cdot \hat{g_r}^{-\nu_{r,2,i}}\right)$$

Return $\sigma_i = (\vec{C}_{z,i}, \vec{C}_{r,i}, \vec{\hat{\pi}}_i) \in \mathbb{G}^4 \times \hat{\mathbb{G}}^2$.

Share-Verify$(PK, \mathbf{VK}, M, (i, \sigma_i))$: Given $M \in \{0,1\}^L$ and a candidate σ_i, parse σ_i as $\sigma_i = (\vec{C}_{z,i}, \vec{C}_{r,i}, \vec{\hat{\pi}}_i)$. Define $\vec{f}_M = \vec{f}_0 \cdot \prod_{i=1}^{L} \vec{f}_i^{M[i]}$ and return 1 if $\vec{\hat{\pi}}_i = (\hat{\pi}_{1,i}, \hat{\pi}_{2,i})$ satisfies

$$E\big((1_{\mathbb{G}}, g), \hat{V}_i\big)^{-1} = E(\vec{C}_{z,i}, \hat{g}_z) \cdot E(\vec{C}_{r,i}, \hat{g}_r) \cdot E(\vec{f}, \hat{\pi}_{1,i}) \cdot E(\vec{f}_M, \hat{\pi}_{2,i})$$

and 0 otherwise.

Combine$(PK, \mathbf{VK}, M, \{(i, \sigma_i)\}_{i \in S})$: Given a $(t+1)$-set with valid shares $\{(i, \sigma_i)\}_{i \in S}$, parse each signature share σ_i as $(\vec{C}_{z,i}, \vec{C}_{r,i}, \vec{\hat{\pi}}_i) \in \mathbb{G}^4 \times \hat{\mathbb{G}}^2$, where $\vec{\hat{\pi}}_i = (\hat{\pi}_{1,i}, \hat{\pi}_{2,i})$, for all $i \in S$. Then, compute $(\vec{C}'_z, \vec{C}'_r, \hat{\pi}'_1, \hat{\pi}'_2)$ as

$$\Big(\prod_{i \in S} \vec{C}_{z,i}^{\Delta_{i,S}(0)},\ \prod_{i \in S} \vec{C}_{r,i}^{\Delta_{i,S}(0)},\ \prod_{i \in S} \hat{\pi}_{1,i}^{\Delta_{i,S}(0)},\ \prod_{i \in S} \hat{\pi}_{2,i}^{\Delta_{i,S}(0)}\Big)$$

by Lagrange interpolation in the exponent. Finally, re-randomize $(\vec{C}'_z, \vec{C}'_r, \hat{\pi}'_1, \hat{\pi}'_2)$ and output the resulting re-randomized full signature $\sigma = (\vec{C}_z, \vec{C}_r, \hat{\pi}_1, \hat{\pi}_2)$.

Verify(PK, M, σ): Given a message $M \in \{0,1\}^L$ and a purported signature σ, parse σ as $(\vec{C}_z, \vec{C}_r, \vec{\hat{\pi}}) \in \mathbb{G}^4 \times \hat{\mathbb{G}}^2$. Define $\vec{f}_M = \vec{f}_0 \cdot \prod_{i=1}^{L} \vec{f}_i^{M[i]}$ and return 1 if and only if $\vec{\hat{\pi}} = (\hat{\pi}_1, \hat{\pi}_2)$ satisfies

$$E\big((1_{\mathbb{G}}, g), \hat{g}_1\big)^{-1} = E(\vec{C}_z, \hat{g}_z) \cdot E(\vec{C}_r, \hat{g}_r) \cdot E(\vec{f}, \hat{\pi}_1) \cdot E(\vec{f}_M, \hat{\pi}_2) \ .$$

The scheme can be simplified by having each player set his private key share as $SK_i = (g^{-A(i)}, g^{-B(i)})$ so as to spare two exponentiations in the signing phase. In the description, we defined SK_i as $(A(i), B(i))$ to insist that no reliable erasures are needed. At each corruption query, the adversary obtains $(A(i), B(i))$ and, not only $(g^{-A(i)}, g^{-B(i)})$. In any case, each player only needs to store two elements of $\mathbb{Z}_p$.

At the 128-bit security level, if each element of $\mathbb{G}$ (resp. $\hat{\mathbb{G}}$) has a 256-bit (resp. 512 bit) representation on Barreto-Naehrig curves [5], we only need 2048 bits per signature.

THEOREM 4.1. *The scheme provides adaptive security under the SXDH assumption in the standard model. For any PPT adversary $\mathcal{A}$, there exist DDH distinguishers $\mathcal{B}_1$ and $\mathcal{B}_2$ with comparable running time in $\mathbb{G}$ and $\hat{\mathbb{G}}$, respectively.* (The proof is available in the full version of the paper).

Acknowledgements

The first author's work has been supported in part by the ERC Starting Grant ERC-2013-StG-335086-LATTAC.

5. REFERENCES

[1] M. Abe, S. Fehr. Adaptively secure Feldman VSS and applications to universally-composable threshold cryptography. In *Crypto '04*, *LNCS* 3152, pp. 317–334, 2004.

[2] M. Abe, G. Fuchsbauer, J. Groth, K. Haralambiev, M. Ohkubo. Structure-preserving signatures and commitments to group elements. In *Crypto '10*, *LNCS* 6223, pp. 209–236, 2010.

[3] M.Abe, K. Haralambiev, M. Ohkubo. Signing on elements in bilinear groups for modular protocol design. In Cryptology ePrint Archive: Report 2010/133, 2010.

[4] J. Almansa, I. Damgård, J.-B. Nielsen. Simplified threshold RSA with adaptive and proactive security. In *Eurocrypt '06*, *LNCS* 4004, pp. 593–611, 2006.

[5] P. Barreto, M. Naehrig. Pairing-friendly elliptic curves of prime order. In *SAC '05*, *LNCS* 3897, pp. 319–331, 2005.

[6] M. Belenkiy, J. Camenisch, M. Chase, M. Kohlweiss, A. Lysyanskaya, H. Shacham. Randomizable proofs and delegatable anonymous credentials. In *Crypto '09*, *LNCS* 5677, pp. 108–125, 2009.

[7] M. Bellare, C. Namprempre, G. Neven. Unrestricted aggregate signatures. In *ICALP '07*, *LNCS* 4596, pp. 411–422, 2007.

[8] M. Bellare, T. Ristenpart. Simulation without the artificial abort: Simplified proof and improved concrete security for Waters' IBE scheme. In *Eurocrypt '09*, *LNCS* 5479, pp. 407–424, 2009.

[9] M. Bellare, P. Rogaway. Random oracles are practical: A paradigm for designing efficient protocols. In *ACM CCS '93*, pp. 62–73, 1993.

[10] A. Boldyreva. Threshold signatures, multisignatures and blind signatures based on the Gap-Diffie-Hellman-group signature scheme. In *Public-Key Cryptography 2003 (PKC '03)*, *LNCS* 2567, pp. 31–46, 2003.

[11] D. Boneh, X. Boyen, H. Shacham. Short group signatures. In *Crypto '04*, *LNCS* 3152, pp. 41–55, 2004.

[12] D. Boneh, M. Franklin. Efficient Generation of Shared RSA Keys. In *Crypto '97*, *LNCS* 1924, pp. 425–439, 1997.

[13] D. Boneh, C. Gentry, B. Lynn, H. Shacham. Aggregate and verifiably encrypted signatures from bilinear maps. In *Eurocrypt '03*, *LNCS* 2656, pp. 416–432, 2003.

[14] D. Boneh, B. Lynn, H. Shacham. Short signatures from the Weil pairing. *J. Cryptology* 17(4), pp. 297–319, 2004. Earlier version in *Asiacrypt '01*, *LNCS* 2248, pp. 514–532, 2001.

[15] C. Boyd. Digital Multisignatures. In *Cryptography and Coding*, Oxford University Press, pp. 241–246, 1989.

[16] R. Canetti, R. Gennaro, S. Jarecki, H. Krawczyk, T. Rabin. Adaptive security for threshold cryptosystems. In *Crypto '99*, *LNCS* 1666, pp. 98–115, 1999.

[17] R. Canetti, S. Goldwasser. An efficient threshold public key cryptosystem secure against adaptive chosen ciphertext attack. In *Eurocrypt '99*, *LNCS* 1592, pp. 90–106, 1999.

[18] Distributed CA for Visa-MC SET Infrastructure announcement, 1997 see: `http://www.geocities.ws/rayvaneng/w0597_09.htm`

[19] J. Chen, H.-W. Lim, S. Ling, H. Wang, H. Wee. Shorter IBE and signatures via asymmetric pairings. In *Pairing '12*, *LNCS* 7708, pp. 122–140, 2012.

[20] J.-S. Coron. On the exact security of full domain hash. In *Crypto '00*, *LNCS* 1880, pp. 229–235, 2000.

[21] V. Cortier, D. Galindo, S. Glondu, M. Izabachène. Distributed ElGamal à la Pedersen: Application to Helios. In *WPES '13*, pp. 131–142, 2013.

[22] R. Cramer, M. Franklin, B. Schoenmakers, M. Yung. Multi-autority secret-ballot elections with linear work. In *Eurocrypt '96*, *LNCS* 1070, pp. 72–83, 1996.

[23] R. Cramer, R. Gennaro, B. Schoenmakers. A secure and optimally efficient multi-authority election scheme. In *Eurocrypt '97*, *LNCS* 1233, pp. 103–118, 1997.

[24] R. Cramer, I. Damgård, J.-B. Nielsen. Multiparty computation from threshold homomorphic encryption. In *Eurocrypt '01*, *LNCS* 2045, pp. 280–299, 2001.

[25] R. Cramer, I. Damgård, S. Dziembowski, M. Hirt, T. Rabin. Efficient multi-party computations secure against an adaptive adversary. In *Eurocrypt '99*, *LNCS* 1592, pp. 311–326, 1999.

[26] I. Damgård, G. Mikkelsen. Efficient, robust and constant-round distributed RSA key generation. In *TCC '10*, *LNCS* 5978, pp. 183–200, 2010.

[27] A. Dent. A Note On Game-Hopping Proofs. Cryptology ePrint Archive: Report 2006/260.

[28] A. De Santis, Y. Desmedt, Y. Frankel, M. Yung. How to share a function securely. In *STOC '94*, pp. 522-533, 1994.

[29] Y. Desmedt. Society and group oriented cryptography: A new concept. In *Crypto '87*, *LNCS* 293, pp. 120–127, 1987.

[30] Y. Desmedt, Y. Frankel. Threshold cryptosystems. In *Crypto '89*, *LNCS* 435, pp. 307–315, Springer, 1990.

[31] T. El Gamal. A public key cryptosystem and a signature scheme based on discrete logarithms. In *Crypto '84*, *LNCS* 196, pp. 10–18, 1984.

[32] P. Feldman. A practical scheme for non-interactive verifiable secret sharing. In *FOCS '87*, pp. 427–437, 1987.

[33] P.-A. Fouque, J. Stern. Fully Distributed Threshold RSA under standard assumptions. In *Asiacrypt '01*, *LNCS* 2248, pp. 310–330, Springer, 2001.

[34] Y. Frankel, P. MacKenzie, M. Yung. Robust efficient distributed RSA-key generation. In *STOC '98*, pp. 663–672, 1998.

[35] Y. Frankel, P. MacKenzie, M. Yung. Adaptively-secure distributed public-key systems. In *ESA '99*, *LNCS* 1643, pp. 4–27, 1999.

[36] Y. Frankel, P. MacKenzie, M. Yung. Adaptively-secure optimal-resilience proactive RSA. In *Asiacrypt '99*, *LNCS* 1716, pp. 180–194, 1999.

[37] Y. Frankel, P. Gemmell, P. MacKenzie, M. Yung. Optimal resilience proactive public-key cryptosystems. In *FOCS '97*, pp. 384–393, 1997.

[38] D. Freeman. Converting pairing-based cryptosystems from composite-order groups to prime-order groups. In *Eurocrypt '10*, *LNCS* 6110, pp. 44-61, 2010.

[39] R. Gennaro, S. Jarecki, H. Krawczyk, T. Rabin. Robust threshold DSS signatures. In *Eurocrypt '96*, *LNCS* 1070, pp. 354–371, 1996.

[40] R. Gennaro, S. Jarecki, H. Krawczyk, T. Rabin. Robust and efficient sharing of RSA functions. In *Crypto '96*, *LNCS* 1109, pp. 157–172, 1996.

[41] R. Gennaro, S. Jarecki, H. Krawczyk, T. Rabin. Secure distributed key generation for discrete-log based cryptosystems. In *Eurocrypt '99*, *LNCS* 1592, pp. 295–310, 1999.

[42] R. Gennaro, S. Jarecki, H. Krawczyk, T. Rabin. Secure applications of Pedersen's distributed key generation protocol. In *CT-RSA '03*, *LNCS* 2612, pp. 373–390, 2003.

[43] R. Gennaro, S. Jarecki, H. Krawczyk, T. Rabin. Secure distributed key generation for discrete-log based cryptosystems. In *J. Cryptology* 20(1), pp. 51–83, 2007.

[44] R. Gennaro, S. Halevi, H. Krawczyk, T. Rabin. Threshold RSA for dynamic and ad-hoc groups. In *Eurocrypt '08*, *LNCS* 4965, pp. 88–107, 2008.

[45] J. Groth, A. Sahai. Efficient non-interactive proof systems for bilinear groups. In *Eurocrypt '08*, *LNCS* 4965, pp. 415–432, 2008.

[46] A. Herzberg, S. Jarecki, H. Krawczyk, M. Yung. Proactive Secret Sharing Or: How to Cope With Perpetual Leakage. In *Crypto '95*, *LNCS* 963, pp. 339-352, 1995.

[47] A. Herzberg, M. Jakobsson, S. Jarecki, H. Krawczyk, M. Yung. Proactive public key and signature systems. In *ACM-CCS '97*, pp. 100–110, 1997.

[48] J. Kubiatowicz, D. Bindel, Y. Chen, S. Czerwinski, P. Eaton, D. Geels, R. Gummadi, S. Rhea, H. Weatherspoon, W. Weimer, C. Wells, B. Zhao. OceanStore: An architecture for global-scale persistent storage. In *ASPLOS '00*, pp. 190-201, 2000.

[49] S. Jarecki, A. Lysyanskaya. Adaptively secure threshold cryptography: Introducing concurrency, removing erasures. In *Eurocrypt '00*, *LNCS* 1807, pp. 221–242, 2000.

[50] J. Katz, M. Yung. Threshold cryptosystems based on factoring. In *Asiacrypt '02*, *LNCS* 2501, pp. 199-205, 2002.

[51] A. Lewko, B. Waters. New techniques for dual system encryption and fully secure HIBE with short ciphertexts. In *TCC '10*, *LNCS* 5978, pp. 455–479, 2010.

[52] A. Lewko. Tools for simulating features of composite order bilinear groups in the prime order setting. In *Eurocrypt '12*, *LNCS* 5978, pp. 318–33, 2012.

[53] B. Libert, M. Joye, M. Yung. Born and raised distributively: fully distributed non-interactive adaptively-secure threshold signatures with short shares. Full version. Available from `http://hal.inria.fr/hal-00983149`.

[54] B. Libert, T. Peters, M. Joye, M. Yung. Linearly homomorphic structure-preserving signatures and their applications. In *Crypto '13*, *LNCS* 8043, pp. 289–307, 2013.

[55] B. Libert, M. Yung. Adaptively secure non-interactive threshold cryptosystems. *Theoretical Computer Science*, vol. 478, pp. 76–100, March 2013. Extended abstract in *ICALP 2011*, *LNCS* 6756, pp. 588–600, 2011.

[56] B. Libert, M. Yung. Non-interactive CCA2-secure threshold cryptosystems with adaptive security: New framework and constructions. In *TCC '12*, *LNCS* 7194, pp. 75–93, Springer, 2012.

[57] A. Lysyanskaya, C. Peikert. Adaptive security in the threshold setting: From cryptosystems to signature schemes. In *Asiacrypt '01*, *LNCS* 2248, pp. 331–350, 2001.

[58] T. Malkin, I. Teranishi, Y. Vahlis, M. Yung. Signatures resilient to continual leakage on memory and computation. In *TCC '11*, *LNCS* 6597, pp. 89–106, 2011.

[59] M. Naor, O. Reingold. Number-theoretic constructions of efficient pseudo-random functions. In *FOCS '97*, pp. 458–467, 1997.

[60] T. Okamoto. Provably secure and practical identification schemes and corresponding signature schemes. In *Crypto '92*, *LNCS* 740, pp. 31–53, 2011.

[61] R. Ostrovksy, M. Yung. How to withstand mobile virus attacks. In *PODC '91*, pp. 51–59, 1991.

[62] T. Pedersen. A threshold cryptosystem without a trusted party. *Eurocrypt '91*, *LNCS* 547, pp. 522–526, 1991.

[63] T. Pedersen. Non-interactive and information-theoretic secure verifiable secret sharing. *Crypto '91*, *LNCS* 576, pp. 129–140, 1991.

[64] T. Rabin. A simplified approach to threshold and proactive RSA. In *Crypto '98*, *LNCS* 1462, pp. 89–104, 1998.

[65] S. Rhea, P. Eaton, D. Geels, H. Weatherspoon, B. Zhao, J. Kubiatowicz. Pond: The OceanStore prototype. In *2003 USENIX Workshop on File and Storage Technologies*, 2003.

[66] M. Scott. Authenticated ID-based key exchange and remote log-in with simple token and PIN number. Cryptology ePrint Archive: Report 2002/164.

[67] A. Shamir. How to share a secret. In *Commun. ACM* 22(11), pp. 612–613, 1979.

[68] V. Shoup. Practical threshold signatures. In *Eurocrypt 2000*, *LNCS* 1807, pp. 207–220, 2000.

[69] H. Wee. Threshold and revocation cryptosystems via extractable hash proofs. In *Eurocrypt '11*, *LNCS* 6632, pp. 589–609, 2011.

[70] Z. Wang, H. Qian, Z. Li. Adaptively secure threshold signature scheme in the standard model. In *Informatica* 20(4), pp. 591-612, 2009.

[71] B. Waters. Efficient identity-based encryption without random oracles. In *Eurocrypt '05*, *LNCS* 3494, 2005.

[72] B. Waters. Dual system encryption: Realizing fully secure IBE and HIBE under simple assumptions. In *Crypto '09*, *LNCS* 5677, pp. 619–636, 2009.

APPENDIX

A. GROTH-SAHAI NON-INTERACTIVE PROOF SYSTEMS

In [45], Groth and Sahai described efficient non-interactive witness indistinguishable (NIWI) proof systems of which one instantiation relies on the SXDH assumption. This instantiation uses prime order groups and a common reference string containing three vectors $\vec{f_1}, \vec{f_2} \in \mathbb{G}^2$, where $\vec{f_1} = (g, f_1)$, $\vec{f_2} = (h, f_2)$, for some $g, h, f_1, f_2 \in \mathbb{G}$. To commit to a group element $X \in \mathbb{G}$, the prover chooses $r, s \stackrel{R}{\leftarrow} \mathbb{Z}_p$ and computes $\vec{C} = (1, X) \cdot \vec{f_1}^{\,r} \cdot \vec{f_2}^{\,s}$. On a perfectly sound common reference string, we have $\vec{f_2} = \vec{f_1}^{\,\xi}$, for some $\xi \in \mathbb{Z}_p$. Commitments $\vec{C} = (g^{r+\xi s}, f_1^{r+\xi s} \cdot X)$ are extractable as their distribution coincides with that of an Elgamal ciphertexts [31] and the committed X can be extracted using $\beta = \log_g(f_1)$. In the witness indistinguishability (WI) setting, the vector $\vec{f_2}$ is chosen so that $(\vec{f_1}, \vec{f_2})$ are linearly independent vectors and $\vec{C}$ is a perfectly hiding commitment. Under the DDH assumption in $\mathbb{G}$, the two kinds of CRS can be exchanged for one another without the adversary noticing.

To convince the verifier that committed variables satisfy a set of relations, the prover computes one commitment per variable and one proof element per equation. Such NIWI proofs can be efficiently generated for linear pairing-product equations, which are relations of the type

$$\prod_{i=1}^{n} e(\mathcal{X}_i, \mathcal{A}_i) = t_T \,, \qquad (3)$$

for variables $\mathcal{X}_1, \ldots, \mathcal{X}_n \in \mathbb{G}$ and constants $\mathcal{A}_1, \ldots, \mathcal{A}_n \in \hat{\mathbb{G}}$, $t_T \in \mathbb{G}_T$, $a_{ij} \in \mathbb{Z}_p$, for $i, j \in \{1, \ldots, n\}$.

Under the SXDH assumption, proving a linear pairing product equation like (3) requires two elements of $\hat{\mathbb{G}}$.

In [6], Belenkiy *et al.* showed that Groth-Sahai proofs are perfectly randomizable. Given commitments $\{\vec{C}_{\mathcal{X}_i}\}_{i=1}^n$ and a NIWI proof $\vec{\pi}_{\mathrm{PPE}}$ that committed $\{\mathcal{X}\}_{i=1}^n$ satisfy (3), anyone can publicly compute re-randomized commitments $\{\vec{C}_{\mathcal{X}_i'}\}_{i=1}^n$ and a re-randomized proof $\vec{\pi}'_{\mathrm{PPE}}$ of the same statement. Moreover, $\{\vec{C}_{\mathcal{X}_i'}\}_{i=1}^n$ and $\vec{\pi}'_{\mathrm{PPE}}$ are distributed as freshly generated commitments and proof.

Fast and Unconditionally Secure Anonymous Channel

Juan Garay
Yahoo Labs
701 First Ave.
Sunnyvale, CA 94089, USA
garay@yahoo-inc.com

Clint Givens
Maine School of Science and Mathematics
Limestone, MN, USA
cgivens@gmail.com

Rafail Ostrovsky*
Department of Computer Science and Department of Mathematics
UCLA, Los Angeles, CA, USA
rafail@cs.ucla.edu

Pavel Raykov
ETH Zurich
Zurich, Switzerland
pavel.raykov@inf.ethz.ch

ABSTRACT

In this paper we focus on sender-anonymous channels (a.k.a. *Dining Cryptographers networks*) and present a construction requiring a very low (constant) number of rounds of interaction while tolerating actively malicious behavior by some of the participants (up to less than half of them). Our construction is unconditionally secure (meaning that no bounds are placed on the computational power of the adversary), makes black-box use of a verifiable secret sharing (VSS) protocol, and is based on a special-purpose secure multiparty computation protocol implementing the method of "throwing darts;" its round complexity is essentially equal to that of the VSS protocol.

In addition, since broadcast *cannot* be simulated in a point-to-point network when a third or more of the participants are corrupt, it is impossible to construct VSS (and, more generally, any other basic multiparty protocol) in this setting without using a "physical broadcast channel," and a recent line of research has sought to minimize the use of this expensive resource. Our anonymous channel protocol's reduction to VSS is broadcast-round-preserving, thus making the fewest (known to date) calls to the broadcast channel while running in an overall constant number of rounds.

Finally, anonymous channels play an important role in the setup phase of an authentication technique known as *pseudosignatures*, which then may be used to simulate *authenticated* Byzantine agreement protocols in the information-theoretic setting. Plugging in our anonymous channel translates into a fast (and broadcast-efficient) pseudosignature construction.

Categories and Subject Descriptors

F.0 [**Theory of Computation**]: General

Keywords

Anonymous message transmission; DC-nets; pseudosignatures; Byzantine agreement

1. INTRODUCTION

Anonymous (or untraceable) message transmission is a powerful privacy-preserving tool, both in theory and in practice (see, non-exhaustively, [A14]; see also [IKOS06] for a glance at its power). In this paper we consider the seminal technique introduced by Chaum known as *Dining Cryptographers networks* (a.k.a. DC-nets, or, plainly, "anonymous channel") [Cha88], where the responsibility of providing "anonymization" lies on the same participants providing the input to the computation. This is in contrast to Chaum's alternative anonymity technique known as *mixnets* [Cha81], which operates by "proxy."

Now, while the latter has been extensively studied in the literature and serves as the basis of multiple deployed systems (e.g., [GRS99, RR99, BSG00, DDM03, DMS04]), this is considerably less the case for the former. Indeed, only a handful of anonymous-channel constructions exist, both in the information-theoretic (a.k.a. "unconditional," where no bounds are placed on the computational power of an adversary) and cryptographic settings ([Cha88, BdB89, Wai89, PW96] and, more recently, [Zha11], and [vABH03, GJ04], respectively), all of which perform poorly in terms of running time (specifically, rounds of interaction) when having to cope with disruptive behavior by some of the participants.

*Supported in part by NSF grants 0830803, 09165174, 1065276, 1118126 and 1136174, US-Israel BSF grant 2008411, OKAWA Foundation Research Award, IBM Faculty Research Award, Xerox Faculty Research Award, B. John Garrick Foundation Award, Teradata Research Award, and Lockheed-Martin Corporation Research Award. This material is based upon work supported by the Defense Advanced Research Projects Agency through the U.S. Office of Naval Research under Contract N00014-11-1-0392. The views expressed are those of the author and do not reflect the official policy or position of the Department of Defense or the U.S. Government.

PODC'14, July 15–18, 2014, Paris, France.
Copyright 2014 ACM 978-1-4503-2944-6/14/07 ...$15.00.
http://dx.doi.org/10.1145/2611462.2611494.

This is unsatisfactory, not only because of scalability reasons, but also because anonymous channels play a powerful role in the pre-processing and setup stages of secure multiparty protocols (an application also treated in this paper), and where a speedy execution is of utmost importance.

1.1 Our results

In this work we present and unconditionally secure sender-anonymous channel construction requiring a very low (constant) number of rounds of interaction. Our protocol tolerates actively malicious parties, relies on the standard resources of secure pairwise channels and broadcast, and works in the case the number of such parties $t < n/2$, where n is the total number of participants. For a long time, the best unconditional anonymous channel construction, due to Pfitzmann and Waidner [PW96], required $\Omega(n^2)$ rounds[1]. Recently, a constant-round construction was proposed by Zhang [Zha11] with a value however in the hundreds. In constrast, the round complexity of the protocol presented here is essentially equal to that of the used VSS protocol (e.g., 7 rounds in the case of [RB89]). Constant-round anonymous channel protocols were not considered in the cryptographic setting (see Related work below).

As mentioned above, our protocol makes black-box use of a (linear) *verifiable secret sharing* (VSS) [CGMA85] protocol, and is based on a special-purpose secure multiparty computation (MPC) [GMW87, BGW88, CCD88, RB89] protocol implementing the method of "throwing darts" (e.g., [Hag91]). (See next section for a description of the method and comparison to its previous use.) In addition, because broadcast *cannot* be simulated in the information-theoretic setting on a point-to-point network when a third or more of the parties are corrupt [LSP82], it is impossible to construct VSS, and more generally, any basic MPC protocol in this setting without using a "physical broadcast channel" (that is, a black box which securely implements broadcast), or some equivalent addition to the model. Consequently, a recent line of research [GGOR13] has sought to minimize the use of this expensive resource. Our anonymous channel protocol's reduction to VSS is broadcast-round-preserving, thus making the fewest (known to-date) calls to the broadcast channel (namely, *two*) while running in an overall constant number of rounds. The protocol is presented in Section 3.

As already discussed above, anonymous message transmission is a fundamental privacy-preserving tool, both in theory and in practice. In particular, many-to-one anonymous channels play an important role in the construction of *pseudosignatures*, an information-theoretic authentication technique for multiparty protocols introduced by Pfitzmann and Waidner [PW96], as an extension of and improvement to a scheme by Chaum and Roijakkers [CR90]. Suppose there is a setup phase during which the parties enjoy access to a physical broadcast channel (but need not know their future inputs), in a setting where $t \geq n/3$. The parties may use such a setup phase to implement pseudosignatures; then, using the pseudosignatures for authentication, they may simulate future invocations of broadcast by running an *authenticated* Byzantine agreement protocol (e.g., [DS83, KK06]), thus avoiding any need for a physical broadcast channel during the main phase of the protocol.

The pseudosignatures of [PW96] rely on a subprotocol implementing a secure, many-to-one anonymous channel. Thus, "plugging in" our constant-round anonymous channel construction translates into a very fast and broadcast-efficient pseudosignature construction. We recall the [PW96] approach and further elaborate on this application in Section 4.

1.2 Related work

We already mentioned the introduction by Chaum of his seminal *Dining Cryptographers networks* (DC-nets) technique for anonymous message publication [Cha88]. DC-nets' major obstacle, namely, being subject to "jamming" by actively malicious players, was subsequently overcome by Waidner and Pfitzmann and Waidner [Wai89, PW96], by means of a somewhat complicated procedure of setting "traps" during a "slot reservation" phase, resulting in protocols running in $\Omega(n^2)$ rounds, as pointed out above. These constructions (as well as other, cryptography-based constructions [GJ04]—see below) rely on a special algebraic technique, wherein after players have shared pair-wise secret keys (called "DC-keys" or "pads") plus some other secret information which specifies, for example, a sender's turn to send a message, the receiver is only able to reconstruct the *sum* of the real message with the shared pads; as the pads cancel each other out, the receiver retrieves the message, but is unable to establish the identity of the sender.

In [Zha11], the author presents a sorting algorithm that enjoys unconditional security in the setting of a malicious adversary corrupting $t < n/2$ players (the setting considered in the current paper). Based on this sorting algorithm, [Zha11] gives a protocol for the "obfuscated shuffle" problem that can be directly translated into an anonymous channel protocol. The resulting protocol employs four functionalities: VSS, comparison, equality testing and multiplication. Its total round complexity is $r_{\mathsf{VSS\text{-}share}} + r_{\mathsf{comp}} + r_{\mathsf{eq}} + r_{\mathsf{mult}}$, where $r_{\mathsf{VSS\text{-}share}}, r_{\mathsf{comp}}, r_{\mathsf{eq}}, r_{\mathsf{mult}}$ are the round complexities of the corresponding functionalities. If all r's are constant (e.g., VSS is implemented as in [RB89, GGOR13] and comparison, equality testing and multiplication as in [DFK$^+$06]), then the overall round complexity of the protocol is constant. In contrast, the round complexity of the anonymous channel protocol presented in this paper is essentially equal to $r_{\mathsf{VSS\text{-}share}}$, which currently is significantly faster than the [Zha11] construction given that comparison and equality testing functionalities require bit decomposition of the shared values, whose round costs are significantly larger than that of a single VSS execution—i.e., 114 rounds for bit decomposition [DFK$^+$06] vs. 7 rounds for VSS sharing [RB89].

While in the cryptographic setting the anonymous message transmission functionality can in principle be realized in constant rounds by a generic MPC protocol (e.g., [DI05]), that has not been the case by existing non-generic constructions [vABH03, GJ04], which we now briefly review. The work by Golle and Juels [GJ04], in particular, employs bilinear maps [BF03] and achieves what the authors call "non-interactivity," in the sense that subsequently to key estab-

[1]The anonymous channel protocol in [PW96] in fact tolerates an arbitrary number of corruptions. The protocol uses fault detection and localization: any failed invocation leads to public identification of either a single corrupt player, or a pair of players at least one of whom is corrupt. Thus, even with an honest majority, there are $\Omega(n^2)$ pairs of players with one of them corrupt; therefore the adversary can force the protocol to run for $\Omega(n^2)$ rounds. (Potentially, this could be reduced to $\Omega(n)$ rounds by making use of more recent "player elimination" techniques [HMP00].)

lishment, players may publish their messages in a single broadcast round (while detecting and identifying cheating players with high probability). "Collisions," namely, a common problem which arises in DC-nets in the selection of message positions, even when all the players are honest, are not considered. The suggestion to plainly repeat the execution of the protocol until the messages get delivered, however, is a bit problematic, as it also allows the adversary to introduce additional spurious values; thus, in addition to being unreliable the construction becomes *malleable* (see security properties in Section 2).

While the work of von Ahn *et al.* [vABH03] focuses on the weaker goal of "k-anonymity" (as opposed to full anonymity, for k a constant smaller than but otherwise not related to n), in the sense that the adversary is able to learn something about the origin (as well as destination) of a particular message, but cannot narrow down its guess to a set of less than k participants, technique-wise it is related to ours, as it also follows the "dart-throwing" method mentioned above. In some detail, in order to anonymously publish a message (or send it to a specific receiver) the method consists of each player randomly choosing a few indices in a long vector, and that player's message appears at these indices. (Some collisions between different messages, of course, may occur.) Then, the long vector is revealed (to the receiver) with an outcome corresponding to the multiset of messages appearing sufficiently many times in the vector. Provided the players can correctly simulate the dart-throwing in such a way that each player's choice of indices remains private from the receiver, and so that only the long vector with the messages is revealed, the channel will be anonymous. In our construction, a careful choice of parameters guarantees the channel's security properties (cf. Section 2) except with negligible probability. In contrast, the construction in [vABH03] guarantees success (specifically, the Reliability property[2]) with probability 1/2 only, bringing us back to the challenge pointed out above of achieving $(1-\epsilon)$-reliability, for negligible ϵ, just by repetition without sacrificing non-malleability.

An approach similar to the "dart-throwing" technique has also been recently used in [AIKW13] for a different problem, namely, the randomized encoding of the subset function. There the authors encrypt each of the sparse vectors under a separate key. Then, if an additive homomorphic encryption is employed, it is guaranteed that, for any set of indices I, the partial sum of vectors' encryptions with indices in I is an encryption of the corresponding partial sum of plain vectors (with indices in I) under the corresponding partial sum of the keys (with indices in I).

Regarding pseudosignatures, an interesting alternative construction to [PW96]'s was proposed by Shikata *et al.* [SHZI02], relying on the evaluation of random low-degree multivariate polynomials in the setup phase. In [BTHR07] it is shown how to compute these polynomials using a special type of MPC protocol, which can also be made in a constant number of rounds. A salient difference of the approach is that pseudosignatures obtained this way can only be applied to messages drawn from the underlying field where the MPC computation takes place, whereas the [PW96] approach is domain-independent, as the generated setup can be used to sign messages from domains that are not known during the setup phase. On the flip side, the [SHZI02]-[BTHR07] realization is more communication-efficient than [PW96]'s with our anonymous channel, thus presenting a tradeoff between versatility and speed on one hand and communication efficiency on the other. (Further details in Section 4.)

[2]Called "Robustness" in [vABH03].

In that sense, we finally remark that since the focus of this paper is on the feasibility of *fast* (i.e., constant-round) anonymous channels, we forgo explicit treatment of communication complexity. We do however note that the protocols described herein can be compiled via generic techniques (see, for example, [BFO12]) into more communication-efficient versions.

2. MODEL, DEFINITIONS AND TOOLS

We consider a complete, synchronous network of n players $P_1, \ldots, P_n$ who are pairwise connected by secure (private and authenticated) channels, and who additionally have access to a broadcast channel. Some of these players, up to $t < n/2$, are corrupted by a centralized adversary $\mathcal{A}$ with *unbounded computing power*. The adversary is *active*, directing players under his control to deviate from the protocol in arbitrary ways, and may be *static* or *adaptive*, depending on whether he chooses which players to corrupt prior to the start of the protocol execution or on the fly, respectively; the type of adversary tolerated by our protocol will in turn depend on the security properties of the underlying VSS protocol[3].

The network computation evolves as a series of rounds. In a given round, honest players' messages depend only on information available to them from prior rounds; $\mathcal{A}$, however, is *rushing*, and receives all messages (and broadcasts) sent by honest players before deciding on the messages (and broadcasts) of corrupted players. Sometimes we refer to $\mathcal{A}$ thus defined as a *t-adversary*. Messages are drawn from and computations are carried out in a fixed finite field $\mathbb{F}$, $|\mathbb{F}| > n$. We consider statistical security (i.e., protocols are subject to some [negligibly small] probability of error), as perfect security is possible only when $t < n/3$ [CCD88, DDWY93][4], and let $\kappa \in \mathbb{N}$ denote the error parameter, $\kappa \geq 2n$. As usual, we say a function $f : \mathbb{N} \to \mathbb{R}$ is *negligible* if for all polynomials p, $f \leq 1/p$.

For the sake of simplicity, we adopt in all our protocols the usual convention that whenever a party fails to send an expected message, or sends a syntactically incorrect message, it is replaced with some default message. Thus we do not deal separately with the case of missing or improper messages.

2.1 Many-to-one anonymous channel

As mentioned above, *Dining Cryptographers networks* (or DC-nets) are a privacy-preserving primitive introduced by Chaum [Cha81, Cha88] for anonymous message publication. Here we formally define a *secure, many-to-one anonymous channel* which allows n players to simultaneously transmit messages to any single player P^*. Let X denote the multiset of honest senders' messages and Y denote the multiset output by P^*. Then the following conditions are satisfied in the presence of a t-adversary $\mathcal{A}$:

[3]Our constant-round, most broadcast-efficient construction, based on [GGOR13], will only be statically secure, for example.

[4]This result is mentioned also in [BGW88, RB89]; [CCD88] give an informal argument and [DDWY93] a formal proof.

ANONYMITY: Even if P^* is corrupt, $\mathcal{A}$ learns no more than X (and in particular gains no information on which messages came from which honest players).

PRIVACY: If P^* is honest, then $\mathcal{A}$ learns no information on X.

RELIABILITY: If P^* is honest, then $X \subseteq Y$.

NON-MALLEABILITY: If P^* is honest, then $|Y| \leq n$ and the probability distribution of $Y \setminus X$ is independent from X.

Some of these properties (in particular, Reliability—cf. our comment on statistical security above) may hold except with a negligible error probability in the security parameter. In addition, these security properties are required to hold under parallel composition of the anonymous channel. We now turn to the definition of the main building block used by the anonymous channel construction.

2.2 Verifiable secret sharing

An (n,t)-*verifiable secret sharing scheme* [CGMA85] is a pair of protocols (VSS-Share, VSS-Rec) for a set of players $\mathcal{P} = \{P_1, \ldots, P_n\}$, one of whom, the *dealer* D, holds input $s \in \mathbb{F}$. It must satisfy the following guarantees in the presence of a t-adversary $\mathcal{A}$:

COMMITMENT: With high probability (w.h.p.), at the end of VSS-Share there exists a fixed value $s^* \in \mathbb{F}$, defined by the joint view of the honest parties, such that all honest parties will output s^* in VSS-Rec. If D is honest, then $s^* = s$. On the other hand, if D is dishonest, then the value of s^* is efficiently computable given the sharing-phase views (messages sent and received) of all correct parties.[5]

PRIVACY: If D is honest, then w.h.p. prior to VSS-Rec the adversary gains no information on s (i.e., his view is statistically independent of s).

We say that the parties *verifiably share* a secret s if each (honest) party maintains some state such that, when the honest parties invoke VSS-Rec on that joint state, they will reconstruct the value s (w.h.p.). Clearly, if a dealer D has just completed VSS-Share with effective input s, then the parties verifiably share s.

LINEARITY: If the parties verifiably share secrets $\{s^{(k)}\}$, then they also (without further interaction) verifiably share any (public) linear combination of the secrets.

In this paper we are interested in *fast* (i.e., constant-round) anonymous channel constructions. Linear, constant-round VSS protocols for the $t < n/2$ regime are presented in [RB89, Rab94, CDD+01, GGOR13][6]; the protocol presented in [GGOR13], in particular, only requires the use of the broadcast channel twice in the sharing phase and none in reconstruction, although is not as round-efficient[7].

[5]Combined with Privacy, this latter property guarantees malicious dealers' inputs are independent of honest dealers' inputs when several copies of VSS are run in parallel.

[6]The VSS protocols presented in [KPC10] are also constant-round, but not (apparently) linear.

[7]21 rounds in [GGOR13] vs. 9 in [Rab94], for example.

3. FAST AND UNCONDITIONAL ANONYMOUS CHANNEL

We first give a high-level description of the protocol. We instantiate the anonymous channel using a special-purpose MPC protocol. As mentioned in Section 1, our special-purpose MPC protocol can be characterized by the method of "throwing darts" [Hag91]. To wit, each player randomly chooses a few indices in a long vector, and that player's message appears at these indices. (Some collisions between different messages, of course, may occur.) Then, the long vector is revealed to the receiver who delivers the multiset of messages appearing sufficiently many times in the vector. Provided the players can correctly simulate the dart-throwing in such a way that each player's choice of indices remains private from the receiver, and so that the long vector with the messages is revealed only to the receiver, the channel will be anonymous. A careful choice of parameters guarantees the channel's security properties (cf. Section 2) except with negligible probability.

Security against maliciously active adversaries requires that dishonest players *commit* to and are not able to change their original inputs, and provide a proof of good behavior throughout the computation. For the former, our construction makes use of a (constant-round, broadcast-efficient) VSS protocol, the distributed analogue of a commitment functionality. The latter is achieved through the traditional "cut-and-choose" approach of preparing many instances and then collectively deciding on which ones to open while maintaining the privacy and anonymity of the construction. However, while in the cryptographic setting a variety of zero-knowledge proofs exists for this type of task, the design of such a mechanism in our (unconditional) setting requires some additional care.

We now present the protocol, AnonChan, which implements an anonymous channel for $t < n/2$ using secure point-to-point channels and black-box access to a linear VSS protocol. Although the VSS itself must rely on physical broadcast when $t \geq n/3$, our construction uses no additional broadcast rounds beyond those required by the calls to VSS.

First of all we ensure that the messages the honest players send are all unique and non-zero. This is achieved by players appending non-zero random tags to them, which P^* strips off upon receipt—this decreases reliability by at most a negligible amount (the probability that two honest tags collide).

We now explain how the "throwing darts" paradigm described above is implemented. Each player P_i commits, by invoking the VSS sharing phase in many parallel executions, to a sufficiently long and sparse vector $\mathbf{v}^{(i)}$ in which the few nonzero entries are set equal to P_i's input. If all players do so correctly, then the sum of the vectors will have relatively few collisions among nonzero entries—in particular, it will preserve enough instances of each input value with high probability. Then the players use the linearity of the VSS scheme to locally compute shares of the sum of the $\mathbf{v}^{(i)}$'s, and send the resulting shares to the receiver P^* (privately). P^* then simulates the VSS reconstruction function internally to recover the sum, which contains at least one copy of each player's input (along with some additional garbage arising from collisions, which we can tolerate).

Of course, dishonest players may not prepare their $\mathbf{v}^{(i)}$'s properly—if a cheater were to commit to (say) a vector full of random entries, then including it in the sum would destroy all information about honest players' inputs. Therefore we require that, after committing to his vector, each player must *prove* that it is indeed sparse, and that nonzero entries are equal. A simple cut-and-choose proof suffices: The prover P_i prepares many additional vectors $\mathbf{w}_j^{(i)}$, $1 \le j \le \kappa$, in the same manner as the original $\mathbf{v}^{(i)}$, except that he rerandomizes the locations of nonzero entries. He also commits, for each $\mathbf{w}_j^{(i)}$, to both the list of locations of nonzero entries, and to a permutation on vector entries which sends nonzero locations of $\mathbf{v}^{(i)}$ to nonzero locations of $\mathbf{w}_j^{(i)}$.

The parties then jointly generate a random challenge r: For each $\mathbf{w}_j^{(i)}$, P_i is challenged to reveal either (a) the permutation, in which case the parties reconstruct the *difference* of the permuted $\mathbf{v}^{(i)}$ and $\mathbf{w}_j^{(i)}$, to verify it is the zero vector; or (b) the nonzero entries of $\mathbf{w}_j^{(i)}$, in which case the parties reconstruct the alleged *zero* entries to verify they are all zero, and reconstruct the *differences* of nonzero entries, which should be zero to verify that all nonzero entries are equal. Vectors which fail this check are excluded, and with overwhelming probability all accepted vectors are indeed sparse, with nonzero entries equal. Finally, the players randomly permute each of the accepted vectors in order to ensure that their nonzero entries appear at random indices. (If a random permutation is not applied, then the non-zero entries of accepted vectors belonging to malicious players appear at the indices chosen by the adversary and hence are not random.)

The protocol parameters are the player set $\mathcal{P} = \{P_1, \dots, P_n\}$, a designated receiver $P^* \in \mathcal{P}$, and error parameter κ. All computations are done over a finite field $\mathbb{F} = GF(2^\kappa)$, where we assume that $\kappa \ge 2n$. The length of vectors ℓ and their sparseness d used in the protocol are polynomial in n and κ (both ℓ and d are given explicitly in the proof). Protocol AnonChan is shown in Figure 1. Constant number of rounds can easily be verified by inspection, and the fact that the invoked VSS protocol is also constant-round.

THEOREM 1. *Let* (VSS-Share, VSS-Rec) *be a linear verifiable secret sharing scheme which fails with probability at most* $2^{-\Omega(\kappa)}$ *in the presence of an unbounded adversary corrupting up to* $t < n/2$ *parties. Then protocol* AnonChan *implements a many-to-one anonymous channel, except with probability* $2^{-\Omega(\kappa)}$.

PROOF. We now show each of the security properties of a many-to-one anonymous channel (cf. Section 2):

ANONYMITY. Without loss of generality consider an adversary corrupting P^*. By the privacy of VSS, $\mathcal{A}$'s view of the VSS sharing phases at the end of step 1 reveals only negligible information on the honest players' inputs. The random value r, reconstructed in step 2, is independent of the honest players' inputs.

Each honest player P_i will have correctly shared sparse vectors $\mathbf{v}^{(i)}, \mathbf{w}_j^{(i)}$. Consequently, in step 3 $\mathcal{A}$ can predict beforehand, the outcome of all reconstructions associated with honest players' vectors (namely, they will be zero), and so $\mathcal{A}$ learns negligible information on honest inputs. Also, w.h.p. all honest players will be included in PASS.

In step 4, P^* receives shares of $\mathbf{v} = \sum_{P_i \in \mathsf{PASS}} g_i(\mathbf{v}^{(i)})$. Because $\mathcal{A}$ knows the value of $\mathbf{v}^{(j)}$ for each dishonest player P_j in PASS, he may subtract these from $\mathbf{v}$ and get $\mathbf{v}_{\mathsf{honest}} = \sum_{P_i \text{ honest}} g_i(\mathbf{v}^{(i)})$. Which is to say, $\mathcal{A}$ learns no more information from $\mathbf{v}$ than he would from learning $\mathbf{v}_{\mathsf{honest}}$ directly. But since each honest P_i chose his d indices of $\mathbf{v}^{(i)}$ independently at random, the distribution of $\mathbf{v}_{\mathsf{honest}}$ is a function only of the *set* of honest players' (unique) values. Hence $\mathcal{A}$ gains no information from seeing $\mathbf{v}_{\mathsf{honest}}$ other than what he could learn from seeing the set of honest players' values.

PRIVACY. Assume P^* is honest. As above, by the privacy of VSS, $\mathcal{A}$ learns at most a negligible amount of information about honest players' inputs from the VSS sharing phases in step 1; no information from the reconstruction of r in step 2, which is independent of the x_i's; and a negligible amount from the step 3 proof of sparseness, the outcome of which he can predict with all but negligible probability. Then statistical privacy is ensured since all communication in step 4 is on the private channels to P^*.

RELIABILITY. We must show that Y output by an honest P^* at step 4 contains a copy of each honest input x_i, with overwhelming probability. As noted in the proof of Anonymity, each honest player is included in PASS with high probability. Call a vector *proper* if it is d-sparse, and all its non-zero entries are equal (if not, we call it *improper*). First we prove the following claim showing that all vectors used in step 4 are proper.

CLAIM 1. *If a dishonest P_i shares in step 1 an improper vector $\mathbf{v}^{(i)}$, he will be disqualified w.h.p. at step 3.*

PROOF. P_i must commit to $\mathbf{v}^{(i)}$ and to all $\mathbf{w}_j^{(i)}$'s in step 1, before $\mathcal{A}$ has any information on the value of the challenge r, which will be uniformly distributed over $\mathbb{F}$.

For each j: If $\mathbf{w}_j^{(i)}$ is proper, then no permutation will map the entries of an improper $\mathbf{v}^{(i)}$ onto matching entries of $\mathbf{w}_j^{(i)}$; hence the vector $\mathbf{u} := \pi_j^{(i)}(\mathbf{v}^{(i)}) - \mathbf{w}_j^{(i)}$ will be nonzero and P_i will be disqualified w.h.p. provided $b_j = 0$. Alternatively, if $\mathbf{w}_j^{(i)}$ is improper, then either the alleged zero entries will actually contain some non-zero value, or the alleged *non-zero* entries will contain unequal values (or both). In either case, opening the alleged zero entries, and the differences of alleged non-zero entries, will reveal an error and P_i will be disqualified w.h.p. provided $b_j = 1$.[8]

Since each b_j is uniformly random, P_i will be disqualified with probability $\ge 1 - 2^{-\Omega(\kappa)}$, and with probability $\ge 1 - t \cdot 2^{-\Omega(\kappa)} = 1 - 2^{-\Omega(\kappa)}$, *every* dishonest P_i who commits to an improper $\mathbf{v}^{(i)}$ will be disqualified. □

Now we know that w.h.p. all the vectors $\mathbf{v}^{(i)}$ used in step 4 are proper. Since P^* is honest we have that each $\mathbf{v}^{(i)}$ used in step 4 is randomly permuted with g_i. Let I_i denote the non-zero indices of permuted $\mathbf{v}^{(i)}$. In the following claim we estimate how many indices in $I_1, \dots, I_n$ may coincide.

CLAIM 2. *Let $I_1, \dots, I_n$ be random subsets of size d chosen from $[\ell]$. Let $X_{ij} = |I_i \cap I_j|$. Then for any $C \ge 0$ holds:*

$$\Pr\left[\sum_{i \ne j} X_{ij} \ge n^2(d^2/\ell + C \cdot d)\right] \le n^2 \exp\left(-C^2 \cdot d\right)$$

[8]The reason P_i will only be disqualified "with high probability" is that, with negligible probability, the adversary may succeed in causing incorrect values to be reconstructed for one or more of the VSS sharings.

Protocol $\mathsf{AnonChan}(\mathcal{P}, P^*, \kappa)$

Input: Each $P_i \in \mathcal{P}$ has as input a message $x_i \in \mathbb{F}$.
Output: P^* outputs a multiset Y.

0. Each P_i creates a random non-zero κ-bit tag $a_i \in \mathbb{F}$.

1. Each P_i constructs a random d-sparse vector $\mathbf{v}^{(i)} \in (\mathbb{F} \times \mathbb{F})^\ell$ whose d nonzero entries are (x_i, a_i). At the same time, P_i constructs κ random permutations $\pi_j^{(i)} : [\ell] \to [\ell]$. For each $\pi_j^{(i)}$ let $\mathbf{w}_j^{(i)}$ be a vector $\mathbf{v}^{(i)}$ permuted with $\pi_j^{(i)}$, i.e., $\mathbf{w}_j^{(i)}[k] = \mathbf{v}^{(i)}[\pi_j^{(i)}(k)]$ for all $k \in [\ell]$.
   P_i invokes $\mathsf{VSS\text{-}Share}$ $O(\ell\kappa)$ times in parallel to share each of the following values:
   - Each coordinate of $\mathbf{v}^{(i)}$ and of the $\mathbf{w}_j^{(i)}$'s;
   - each of the permutations $\pi_j^{(i)}$;
   - for each $\mathbf{w}_j^{(i)}$, its list of nonzero indices;
   - a random element $r^{(i)} \in \mathbb{F}$.

   At the same time P^* generates n random permutations $g_i : [\ell] \to [\ell]$ and shares them using $\mathsf{VSS\text{-}Share}$.

2. The players invoke $\mathsf{VSS\text{-}Rec}$ to reconstruct the sum $r := \sum r^{(i)}$, and interpret it as a random bit-string of length κ.

3. For each bit $b_j \in r$ (in parallel):

   $b_j = 0$:
   1. The players invoke n instances of $\mathsf{VSS\text{-}Rec}$ to reconstruct the permutations $\pi_j^{(i)}$, for all P_i. (If the result is not a valid permutation, P_i is disqualified.)
   2. For each $\mathbf{w}_j^{(i)}$, the players invoke ℓ instances of $\mathsf{VSS\text{-}Rec}$ to reconstruct the vector $\mathbf{u} := \pi_j^{(i)}(\mathbf{v}^{(i)}) - \mathbf{w}_j^{(i)}$. If $\mathbf{u} \neq (0,0)^\ell$, P_i is disqualified. ($\pi_j^{(i)}$ acts on a vector by permuting its components.)

   $b_j = 1$:
   1. The players invoke n instances of $\mathsf{VSS\text{-}Rec}$ to reconstruct the list of nonzero indices for $\mathbf{w}_j^{(i)}$, for all P_i. (If the result is not a valid list of d distinct indices in $[\ell]$, P_i is disqualified.)
   2. For each $\mathbf{w}_j^{(i)}$, invoke $\ell - d$ instances of $\mathsf{VSS\text{-}Rec}$ to reconstruct the values at (alleged) zero-indices of $\mathbf{w}_j^{(i)}$. If any are actually nonzero, P_i is disqualified. Also invoke $d-1$ instances of $\mathsf{VSS\text{-}Rec}$ to reconstruct consecutive *differences* of (alleged) nonzero entries of $\mathbf{w}_j^{(i)}$. If any such differences are nonzero, P_i is disqualified.

4. Let PASS denote the set of players who are not disqualified. Players use $\mathsf{VSS\text{-}Rec}$ to reconstruct P^*'s permutations $g_1, \ldots, g_n$ globally. Each player locally computes his shares of the vector $\mathbf{v} := \sum_{P_i \in \mathsf{PASS}} g_i(\mathbf{v}^{(i)})$. He sends the shares, over private channel, to the receiver P^*. P^* uses the received shares to internally simulate $\mathsf{VSS\text{-}Rec}$ and recover the vector $\mathbf{v}$. Let T denote the set of nonzero pairs which appear $\geq d/2$ times in $\mathbf{v}$. Let Y be an empty multiset; then, for each $(x_i, a_i) \in T$, include x_i in Y. P^* outputs Y.

Figure 1: *A secure anonymous channel protocol using black-box VSS.*

PROOF. Consider X_{ij} for any fixed i and j. There are d fixed indices in I_i and ℓ indices in total. The intersection of I_j and these fixed indices follows a hypergeometric distribution. We have that $\mathbb{E}[X_{ij}] = d^2/\ell$. We use a tail bound on the hypergeometric distribution appearing in [Chv79, Ska13] to conclude that, for any $C \geq 0$:

$$\Pr\left[X_{ij} \geq d^2/\ell + C \cdot d\right] \leq \exp\left(-C^2 \cdot d\right).$$

We trivially have that

$$\Pr\left[\sum_{i \neq j} X_{ij} \geq n^2(d^2/\ell + C \cdot d)\right] \leq \Pr\left[\bigvee_{i \neq j} (X_{ij} \geq d^2/\ell + C \cdot d)\right].$$

Using the union bound we upper bound the latter probability with $n^2 \exp(-C^2 \cdot d)$. $\square$

Now we choose ℓ, C and d such that the following holds: $n^2(d^2/\ell + C \cdot d) = d/2$ and $C^2 \cdot d \in \Omega(\kappa)$. This will ensure that w.h.p. in total $< d/2$ indices coincide in $I_1, \ldots, I_n$. This requirement is satisfied for $C = 1/(4n^2)$, $d = n^4\kappa$ and $\ell = 4n^6\kappa$.

Hence, among d indices I_i of any honest P_i at least $d/2$ are untouched in $\mathbf{v}$ implying that $(x_i, a_i) \in T$ at Step 4. Finally, since a_i are chosen uniformly at random from $\mathbb{F} \setminus \{0\}$ the probability that a_i collides with any other a_j is at most $2^{-\Omega(\kappa)}$. So P^* will include a copy of x_i sent by P_i in Y.

NON-MALLEABILITY. By independence of inputs for the VSS, all the values which dishonest players commit to in step 1 are independent of those which honest players commit to in step 1.

Consider any value $x \in Y$. Since $x \in Y$ this implies that for some $a \in \mathbb{F}$ it holds that $(x, a) \in T$ at step 4. We know that (x, a) is included in T only if it appears at least $d/2$ times in $\mathbf{v}$. Due to Claim 1 and Claim 2 this implies that (x, a) must have been a non-zero value in some vector $\mathbf{v}^{(i)}$ with $P_i \in \mathsf{PASS}$. The vector $\mathbf{v}^{(i)}$ originates either from an honest player or from a dishonest. In the latter case since adversary learns no information about inputs of the honest players, the value (x, a) is generated by $\mathcal{A}$ independently of all honest players' messages. Hence, Y can be split into two subsets: X—multiset with honest players' messages, and $Y \setminus X$—multiset with the messages independent of X. Finally, since each value in Y originates from some $\mathbf{v}^{(i)}$ we have that $|Y| \leq n$. $\square$

4. APPLICATIONS: PSEUDOSIGNATURES

As mentioned in Section 1, *pseudosignatures* [PW96] are an information-theoretic authentication technique for multiparty protocols. They require a setup phase during which the parties enjoy access to a physical broadcast channel (recall that we are in the $t \geq n/3$, information-theoretic regime, where broadcast cannot be simulated on a point-to-point network); during this phase the parties need not know their future inputs. After the setup phase, using the pseudosignatures for authentication, the parties are able to simulate future invocations of broadcast by running an authenticated Byzantine agreement protocol [DS83, KK06], thus avoiding any need for a physical broadcast channel during the main phase of the protocol.

One does pay a price for not relying on cryptographic assumptions—in the case of pseudosignatures, the price is *limited transferability*: The integrity of a pseudosignature "degrades" each time it is passed from one party to another, so that it only remains valid for an *a priori* bounded number of transfers[9]. In the case of deterministic Byzantine agreement, for example, $O(t)$-transferability would suffice, given the number of rounds lower bound [LSP82] and protocols matching it (e.g., [DS83]).

The pseudosignatures of [PW96] rely on a subprotocol implementing a many-to-one anonymous channel, as defined above. Assuming such a channel, the pseudosignature scheme is roughly as follows. (For simplicity, let us consider a one-time signature.) Each player chooses a large number of random keys, which will function as information-theoretic message authentication codes. The players invoke the anonymous channel many times in parallel, each sending one key per invocation to the signer P^*. Hence, for each invocation of the channel, P^* receives an associated *signature block* containing $n-1$ anonymous keys. Now, in order to (pseudo-) sign a message M, P^* simply signs it—i.e., computes the message authentication code on the message—using every authentication key, in every block; these individual signatures are referred to as *minisignatures*, and the collection of all of them, arranged in blocks, is P^*'s *pseudosignature* on M.

Verification is more involved. The *first* verifier V_1 (i.e., the player to whom P^* originally sends M with pseudosignature) accepts the signature provided that, in *every* signature block, one of the minisignatures matches the key V_1 sent for that block. The second verifier V_2 accepts the signature provided that, in *most* of the signature blocks, one of the minisignatures matches the key V_2 sent for that block. The third verifier accepts the signature provided *a fair number* of minisignatures check out, and so on, where each new verifier has a lower acceptance threshold than the previous one.

The rationale for the increasingly tolerant verifiers is the fear that a cheating signer P^*, even though he does not know whose keys are whose in any given block, could (for example) correctly sign M with every key except for half the keys in a certain block. There is a good chance then that V_1 will find a correct minisignature in every block, but will pass it on to V_2 who will *not* find a correct minisignature in the half-signed block. If V_1 accepts the signature while V_2 rejects, P^* has successfully broken the signature scheme.

By having the parties simply invoke protocol AnonChan (Figure 1) for each P_i, $1 \leq i \leq n$, acting as receiver for many sessions in parallel, the duration of the setup phase is reduced from $\Omega(n^2)$ to constant—the number of rounds that AnonChan takes. Further, by using the broadcast-efficient VSS protocol in [GGOR13], the use of the physical broadcast channel is reduced to 2 (also from $\Omega(n^2)$ in [PW96]). On the other hand, we should note that the pseudosignature setup in [PW96] works for any $t < n$, while ours is limited to $t < n/2$. This would not impose additional limitations, as we consider an important application of pseudosignatures to simulate broadcast in unconditional honest-majority MPC protocols.

To conclude, we mentioned in Section 1 that an alternative pseudosignature construction has been proposed by Shikata *et al.* [SHZI02], relying on the evaluation of random low-degree multivariate polynomials in the setup phase. In [BTHR07] it is shown how to compute these polynomials using a special type of MPC protocol. This MPC computation uses a generic VSS scheme, and thus it can also be made in a constant number of rounds. (In [BTHR07] this is not the case as the goal is communication efficiency.) In addition to pseudosignatures being confined to messages drawn from the underlying field, as pointed out in Section 1, the MPC protocol, in contrast to ours, requires to compute multiplication of the shared values, which translates into additional interaction. On the flip side, the type of computation enjoys lower communication costs, thus presenting a versatility and speed versus communication efficiency tradeoff.

[9]Another price is finite, fixed-in-advance player set!

5. REFERENCES

[A14] Selected papers in anonymity. The Free Haven Project. `http://freehaven.net/anonbib/full/date.html`, 2014.

[AIKW13] B. Applebaum, Y. Ishai, E. Kushilevitz, and B. Waters. Encoding functions with constant online rate or how to compress garbled circuits keys. In R. Canetti and J. A. Garay, editors, *CRYPTO (2)*, volume 8043 of *Lecture Notes in Computer Science*, pages 166–184. Springer, 2013.

[BdB89] J. N. Bos and B. den Boer. Detection of disrupters in the dc protocol. In J.-J. Quisquater and J. Vandewalle, editors, *EUROCRYPT*, volume 434 of *Lecture Notes in Computer Science*, pages 320–327. Springer, 1989.

[BF03] D. Boneh and M. Franklin. Identity-based encryption from the weil pairing. *SIAM J. Comput.*, 32(3):586–615, 2003.

[BFO12] E. Ben-Sasson, S. Fehr, and R. Ostrovsky. Near-linear unconditionally-secure multiparty computation with a dishonest minority. In R. Safavi-Naini and R. Canetti, editors, *CRYPTO*, volume 7417 of *Lecture Notes in Computer Science*, pages 663–680. Springer, 2012.

[BGW88] M. Ben-Or, S. Goldwasser, and A. Wigderson. Completeness theorems for non-cryptographic fault-tolerant distributed computation. In *Proc. 20th Annual ACM Symposium of the Theory of Computation*, pages 1–10, May 1988.

[BIB89] J. Bar-Ilan and D. Beaver. Non-cryptographic fault-tolerant computing in constant number of rounds of interaction. In P. Rudnicki, editor, *PODC*, pages 201–209. ACM, 1989.

[BSG00] P. Boucher, A. Shostack, and I. Goldberg. Freedom systems 2.0 architecture. White paper, Zero Knowledge Systems, Inc., December 2000.

[BTHR07] Z. Beerliová-Trubíniová, M. Hirt, and M. Riser. Efficient byzantine agreement with faulty minority. In K. Kurosawa, editor, *ASIACRYPT*, volume 4833 of *Lecture Notes in Computer Science*, pages 393–409. Springer, 2007.

[CCD88] D. Chaum, C. Crépeau, and I. Damgård. Multiparty unconditionally secure protocols. In *Proceedings 20th Annual Symposium on Theory of Computing, STOC*. Association for Computing Machinery, May 1988.

[CDD+01] R. Cramer, I. Damgård, S. Dziembowski, M. Hirt, and T. Rabin. Efficient multiparty computations secure against an adaptive adversary. In *Advances in Cryptology–EUROCRYPT'01*, Lecture Notes in Computer Science. Springer Verlag, May 2001.

[CGMA85] B. Chor, S. Goldwasser, S. Micali, and B. Awerbuch. Verifiable secret sharing and achieving simultaneity in the presence of faults. In *Proceedings of Twenty Sixth IEEE Symposium in Foundations of Computer Science*, pages 383–395, 1985.

[Cha81] D. Chaum. Untraceable electronic mail, return addresses, and digital pseudonyms. *Commun. ACM*, 24(2):84–88, 1981.

[Cha88] D. Chaum. The dining cryptographers problem: Unconditional sender and recipient untraceability. *J. Cryptology*, 1(1):65–75, 1988.

[Chv79] V. Chvátal. The tail of the hypergeometric distribution. *Discrete Mathematics*, 25(3):285 – 287, 1979.

[CR90] D. Chaum and S. Roijakkers. Unconditionally secure digital signatures. In A. Menezes and S. Vanstone, editors, *CRYPTO*, volume 537 of *Lecture Notes in Computer Science*, pages 206–214. Springer, 1990.

[DDM03] G. Danezis, R. Dingledine, and N. Mathewson. Mixminion: Design of a Type III Anonymous Remailer Protocol. In *Proceedings of the 2003 IEEE Symposium on Security and Privacy*, pages 2–15, May 2003.

[DDWY93] D. Dolev, C. Dwork, O. Waarts, and M. Yung. Perfectly secure message transmission. *Journal of ACM*, 1(40):17–47, 1993.

[DFK+06] I. Damgård, M. Fitzi, E. Kiltz, J. B. Nielsen, and T. Toft. Unconditionally secure constant-rounds multi-party computation for equality, comparison, bits and exponentiation. In S. Halevi and T. Rabin, editors, *TCC*, volume 3876 of *Lecture Notes in Computer Science*, pages 285–304. Springer, 2006.

[DI05] I. Damgård and Y. Ishai. Constant-round multiparty computation using a black-box pseudorandom generator. In V. Shoup, editor, *CRYPTO*, volume 3621 of *Lecture Notes in Computer Science*, pages 378–394. Springer, 2005.

[DMS04] R. Dingledine, N. Mathewson, and P. Syverson. Tor: The second-generation onion router. In *Proceedings of the 13th Conference on USENIX Security Symposium - Volume 13*, SSYM'04, pages 21–21, Berkeley, CA, USA, 2004. USENIX Association.

[DS83] D. Dolev and H. Strong. Authenticated algorithms for Byzantine agreement. *SIAM Journal on Computing*, 12(4):656–666, 1983.

[GGOR13] J. Garay, C. Givens, R. Ostrovsky, and P. Raykov. Broadcast (and round) efficient verifiable secret sharing. In C. Padro, editor, *ICITS*, volume 8317 of *Lecture Notes in Computer Science*, pages 200–219. Springer, 2013.

[GJ04] P. Golle and A. Juels. Dining cryptographers revisited. In C. Cachin and J. Camenisch, editors, *EUROCRYPT*, volume 3027 of *Lecture Notes in Computer Science*, pages 456–473. Springer, 2004.

[GMW87] O. Goldreich, S. Micali, and A. Wigderson. How to play any mental game or a completeness theorem for protocols with honest majority. In *Proc. 19th Annual ACM Symposium on Theory of Computation*, pages 218–229, May 1987.

[GRS99] D. M. Goldschlag, M. G. Reed, and P. F. Syverson. Onion routing. *Commun. ACM*, 42(2):39–41, 1999.

[Hag91] T. Hagerup. Fast parallel generation of random permutations. In J. Albert, B. Monien, and M. Rodríguez-Artalejo, editors, *ICALP*, volume 510 of *Lecture Notes in Computer Science*, pages 405–416. Springer, 1991.

[HMP00] M. Hirt, U. Maurer, and B. Przydatek. Efficient secure multi-party computation. In *Advances in Cryptology, ASIACRYPT*, Lecture Notes in Computer Science, 2000.

[IKOS06] Y. Ishai, E. Kushilevitz, R. Ostrovsky, and A. Sahai. Cryptography from anonymity. In *FOCS*, pages 239–248. IEEE Computer Society, 2006.

[KK06] J. Katz and C. Koo. On expected constant-round protocols for Byzantine agreement. In *Advances in Cryptology – CRYPTO 2006*, volume 4117 of *Lecture Notes in Computer Science*, pages 445–462. Springer, 2006.

[KPC10] R. Kumaresan, A. Patra, and C. Pandu Rangan. The round complexity of verifiable secret sharing: The statistical case. In M. Abe, editor, *ASIACRYPT*, volume 6477 of *Lecture Notes in Computer Science*, pages 431–447. Springer, 2010.

[LSP82] L. Lamport, R. Shostak, and M. Pease. The Byzantine generals problem. *ACM Transactions on Programming Languages and Systems*, pages 382–401, July 1982.

[PW96] B. Pfitzmann and M. Waidner. Information-theoretic pseudosignatures and byzantine agreement for $t \geq n/3$. Technical Report RZ 2882 (#90830), IBM Research, 1996.

[Rab94] T. Rabin. Robust sharing of secrets when the dealer is honest or cheating. *J. ACM*, 41(6):1089–1109, 1994.

[RB89] T. Rabin and M. Ben-Or. Verifiable secret sharing and multiparty protocols with honest majority. In *Proc. 21st ACM Symposium on the Theory of Computing*, pages 73–85, 1989.

[RR99] M. K. Reiter and A. D. Rubin. Anonymous web transactions with crowds. *Commun. ACM*, 42(2):32–38, 1999.

[SHZI02] J. Shikata, G. Hanaoka, Y. Zheng, and H. Imai. Security notions for unconditionally secure signature schemes. In L. R. Knudsen, editor, *EUROCRYPT*, volume 2332 of *Lecture Notes in Computer Science*, pages 434–449. Springer, 2002.

[Ska13] M. Skala. Hypergeometric tail inequalities: ending the insanity. *ArXiv e-prints*, November 2013.

[vABH03] L. von Ahn, A. Bortz, and N. Hopper. K-anonymous message transmission. In *Proceedings of the 10th ACM Conference on Computer and Communications Security*, CCS '03, pages 122–130, New York, NY, USA, 2003. ACM.

[Wai89] M. Waidner. Unconditional sender and recipient untraceability in spite of active attacks. In J.-J. Quisquater and J. Vandewalle, editors, *EUROCRYPT*, volume 434 of *Lecture Notes in Computer Science*, pages 302–319. Springer, 1989.

[Zha11] B. Zhang. Generic constant-round oblivious sorting algorithm for mpc. In X. Boyen and X. Chen, editors, *ProvSec*, volume 6980 of *Lecture Notes in Computer Science*, pages 240–256. Springer, 2011.

Efficient Lock-free Binary Search Trees

Bapi Chatterjee, Nhan Nguyen and Philippas Tsigas
Chalmers University of Technology, Gothenburg, Sweden
{bapic, nhann, tsigas}@chalmers.se

ABSTRACT

In this paper we present a novel algorithm for concurrent lock-free internal binary search trees (BST) and implement a Set abstract data type (ADT) based on that. We show that in the presented lock-free BST algorithm the amortized step complexity of each set operation - ADD, REMOVE and CONTAINS - is $O(H(n)+c)$, where $H(n)$ is the height of the BST with n number of nodes and c is the contention during the execution. Our algorithm adapts to contention measures according to read-write load. If the situation is read-heavy, the operations avoid helping the concurrent REMOVE operations during traversal, and adapt to interval contention. However, for the write-heavy situations we let an operation help a concurrent REMOVE, even though it is not obstructed. In that case, an operation adapts to point contention. It uses single-word compare-and-swap (`CAS`) operations. We show that our algorithm has improved disjoint-access-parallelism compared to similar existing algorithms. We prove that the presented algorithm is linearizable. To the best of our knowledge, this is the first algorithm for any concurrent tree data-structure in which the modify operations are performed with an additive term of contention measure.

Categories and Subject Descriptors

E.1 [**data-structures**]: Distributed data-structures—*algorithm, complexity analysis*; D.1.3 [**Programming Techniques**]: Concurrent Programming - Parallel programming

Keywords

concurrent data-structures; binary search tree; amortized analysis; shared memory; lock-free; CAS

1. INTRODUCTION

With the wide and ever-growing availability of multi-core processors it is evermore compelling to design and develop more efficient concurrent data-structures. Being immune to deadlocks due to various fault-causing factors beyond the control of the data-structure designers, the non-blocking concurrent data-structures are more attractive than their blocking counterparts.

In literature, there are lock-free as well as wait-free singly linked-lists [11, 23], lock-free doubly linked-list [22], lock-free hash-tables [17] and lock-free skip-lists [11, 21]. However, not many performance-efficient non-blocking concurrent search trees are available. A multi-word compare-and-swap (`MCAS`) based lock-free BST implementation was presented by Fraser in [12]. However, `MCAS` is not a native atomic primitive provided by available multi-core chips and is very costly to be implemented using single-word `CAS`. Bronson et al. proposed an optimistic lock-based partially-external BST with relaxed balance [4]. Ellen et al. presented lock-free external binary search tree [10] based on co-operative helping technique presented by Barnes [3]. Though their work did not include an analysis of complexity or any empirical evaluation of the algorithm, the contention window of update operations in the data-structure is large. Also, because it is an external binary search tree, REMOVE is simpler at the cost of extra memory to maintain internal nodes without data. Howley et al. presented a lock-free internal BST [15] based on similar technique. A software transactional memory based approach was presented by Crain et al. [7] to design a concurrent red-black tree. While it seems to outperform some coarse-grained locking methods, it gets easily vanquished by a carefully tailored locking scheme as in [4]. Recently, two lock-free external BSTs [18, 5] and a lock-based internal BST [8] have been proposed. All of these works lack theoretical complexity analysis.

A common predicament for the existing lock-free BST algorithms is that if multiple modify operations contend at a leaf node, and, if a REMOVE operation among them succeeds then all other operations have to restart from the root. It results in the complexity of a modify operation to be $O(cH(n))$ where $H(n)$ is the height of the BST on n nodes and c is the measure of contention. It may grow dramatically with the growth in the size of the tree and the contention. In addition to that, CONTAINS operations have to be aware of an ongoing REMOVE of a node with two children, otherwise it may return an invalid result. Hence in the existing implementations of lock-free internal BST [15], a CONTAINS operation may have to restart from the root on realizing that the return may be invalid if more nodes are not scanned. The external or partially-external BSTs remain immune to this problem at the cost of extra memory for the routing internal nodes. Our algorithm solves both these problems elegantly. The CONTAINS operations in our BST enjoy oblivion of any

PODC'14, July 15–18, 2014, Paris, France.

ACM 978-1-4503-2944-6/14/07 ...$15.00.
http://dx.doi.org/10.1145/2611462.2611500 .

kind of modify operation as long as we do not make them help a concurrent REMOVE, which may be needed only in write-heavy situations. Also, the modify operations after helping a concurrent modify operation restart not from the root rather from a level in the vicinity of failure. It ensures that all the operations in our algorithm run in $O(H(n)+c)$[1]. This is our main contribution.

We always strive to exploit maximum possible disjoint-access-parallelism [16] in a concurrent data-structure. The lock-free methods for BST [10, 15], in order to use single-word `CAS` for atomically modifying the links outgoing from a node, and yet maintain correctness, store a flag as an operation field or some version indicator in the node itself, and hence a modify operation "holds" a node. This mechanism of holding a node, specifically for a REMOVE, can reduce the progress of two concurrent operations which may be otherwise non-conflicting. In [18], a flag is stored in a link instead of a node in an external BST. We found that even in an internal BST it is indeed possible that a REMOVE operation, instead of holding the node, just holds the links connected to and from a node in a predetermined order so that maximum possible progress of concurrent operations working at disjoint memory words corresponding to the links can be ensured. The design using "storing a flag" at a link instead of a node significantly improves the disjoint-access-parallelism. This is our next contribution.

Helping mechanism which ensures non-blocking progress may prove counterproductive to the performance if not used judiciously. However, in some situations the proportion of REMOVE operations may increase and they may need help to finish their pending steps. Then it is better to help them so that the traversal path does not contain large number of "under removal" nodes. Keeping that in view, we take helping to a level of adaptivity to the read-write load. In our algorithm, one may choose whether an operation helps a concurrent REMOVE operation during its traversal. We believe that this adaptive conservative helping in internal BSTs may be very useful in some situations. This is a useful contribution of this work.

Our algorithm requires only single-word atomic `CAS` primitives along with single-word atomic read and write which practically exist in all the widely available multi-core processors in the market. Based on our design, we implement a Set ADT. We prove that our algorithm is linearizable [14]. We also present complexity analysis of our implementation which is lacking in existing concurrent BST algorithms. This is another contribution in this paper.

The body of our paper will further consist of the following sections. In section 2, we present the basic tree terminologies. In section 3, the proposed algorithm is described. Section 4 presents a discussion on the correctness and the progress of our concurrent implementation along with an amortized analysis of its time complexity. The paper is concluded in section 5.

2. PRELIMINARIES

A *binary tree* is an ordered tree in which each *node* x has a *left-child* and a *right-child* denoted as $left(x)$ and $right(x)$ respectively, either or both of which may be *external*. When both the children are external the node is called a *leaf*, with one external child a *unary* node and with no external child a *binary* node, and all the non-external nodes are called *internal* nodes. We denote the parent of a node x by $p(x)$ and there is a unique node called *root* s.t. $p(root) = null$. Each parent is connected with its children via pointers as links (often we shall be using the terms pointer and link interchangeably when the context will be understood). We are primarily interested in implementing an ordered *Set* ADT - *binary search tree* using a binary tree in which each node is associated with a unique key k selected from a totally ordered universe. A node with a key k is denoted as $x(k)$ and x if the context is otherwise understood. Determined by the total order of the keys, each node x has a *predecessor* and a *successor*, denoted as $pre(x)$ and $suc(x)$, respectively. We denote height of x by $ht(x)$, which is defined as the distance of the deepest leaf in the *subtree* rooted at x from x. Height of a BST is $ht(root)$.

In an *internal BSTs*, all the internal nodes are *data-nodes* and the external nodes are usually denoted by `null`. There is a *symmetric order* of arranging the data - all the nodes in the *left subtree* of $x(k)$ have keys less than k and those in its *right subtree* have keys greater than k, and so no two nodes can have the same key. To query whether a BST CONTAINS a data with key k, at every *search-step* we utilize this order to look for the desired node either in the left or in the right subtree of the *current node* if the key not matched at it, unless we reach an external node. If the key matches at a node then we return `true` or address of the node if needed, otherwise `false`. To ADD data we query by its key k. If the query reaches an external node we replace this node with a new leaf node $x(k)$. To REMOVE a data-node corresponding to key k we check whether $x(k)$ is in the BST. If the BST does not contain $x(k)$, `false` is returned. On finding $x(k)$, we perform delete as following. If it is a leaf then we just replace it with an external node. In case of a unary node its only child is connected to its parent. For a binary node x, it is first replaced with $pre(x)$ or $suc(x)$ which may happen to be a leaf or a unary node, and then the replacer is removed.

In an alternate form - an *external BST*, all the internal nodes are *routing-nodes* and the external nodes are data-nodes. In this paper we focus on internal BSTs, and hence forward by a BST we shall mean an internal BST.

3. OUR ALGORITHM

3.1 The Efficient Lock-free BST Design

To implement a lock-free BST, we represent it in a threaded format [20]. In this format, if the left(right) child pointer at a node x is null and so corresponds to an external node, it is instead connected to $pre(x)(suc(x))$. An indicator is stored to indicate whether a child-link is used for such a connection. This is called *threading* of the child-links. In our design, we use the null child pointers at the leaf and unary nodes as following - right-child pointer, if null, is threaded and is used to point to the successor node, whereas a similar left-child pointer is threaded and pointed to the node itself, see Fig. 1(a). In this representation a binary tree can be viewed as an ordered list with exactly two outgoing and two incoming pointers per node, as shown in Fig. 1(b). Also among the two incoming pointers, exactly one is threaded and the other is not. In this representation, if $x(k_i)$ and $x(k_j)$ are

[1]A concurrent work by Ellen et al. [9] improving the external BST by Ellen et al. [10] achieves similar complexity as ours. This is to appear in the same proceedings and is independent from our work.

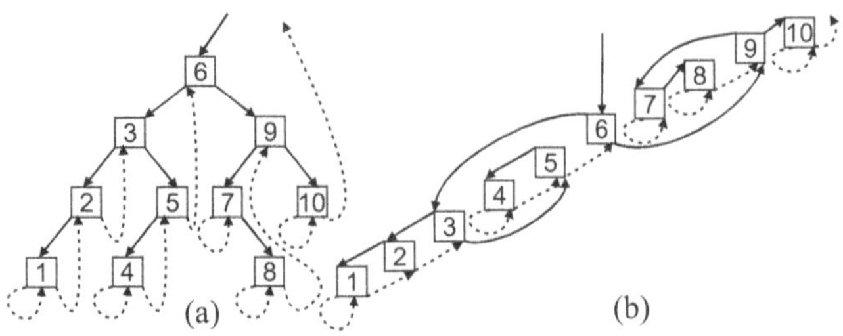

Figure 1: (a) Threaded BST (b) Equivalent ordered list.

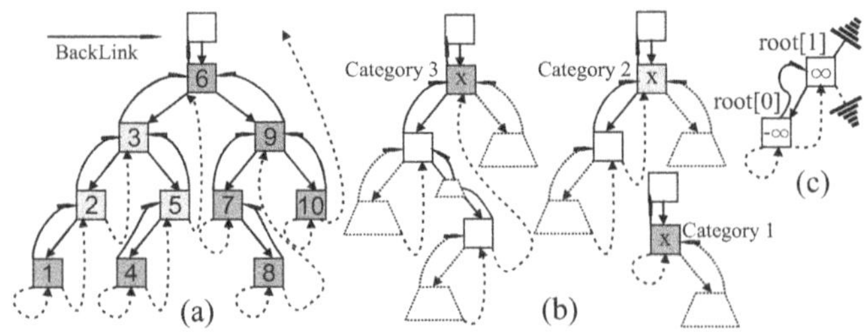

Figure 2: (a) Threaded BST with backlinks (b) Categorization of nodes for REMOVE (c) An empty tree.

two nodes in the BST and there is no node $x(k)$ such that $k_i \leq k \leq k_j$ then we call the interval $[k_i,\ k_j]$ *associated* with the threaded link incoming at k_j.

We exploit this symmetry of the equal number of incoming and outgoing pointers. A usual traversal in the BST following its symmetric order for a predecessor query, is equivalent to a traversal over a *subsequence* of the ordered-list produced by an in-order traversal of the BST, which is exactly the one shown in Fig. 1(b). This is made possible by the threaded right-links at leaf or unary nodes. Though in this representation, there are two pointers in both incoming and outgoing directions at each node, a single pointer needs to be modified to ADD a node in the list. To REMOVE a node we may have to modify up to four pointers. Therefore, ADD can be as simple as that in a lock-free single linked-list [11], and REMOVE is no more complex than that in a lock-free double linked-list [22]. A traversal in a lock-free linked-list may enjoy oblivion from a concurrent REMOVE of a node. In our design of internal BST also, a traversal can remain undeterred by any ongoing modification, unlike that in the existing lock-free implementations of internal BSTs [15, 12].

In all the existing designs of lock-free BSTs, when an operation fails at a link connected to an external node because of a concurrent modify operation, it retries from the scratch i.e. it restarts the operation from the root of the tree, after helping the obstructing concurrent operation. In our design an operation restarts from a node at the vicinity of the link where it fails, after the required helping. To achieve that, we need to get hold of the appropriate node(s) to restart at. For that, we use a *backlink* per node and ensure that it points to a node *present* in the tree from where the failure spot is a single link away. It should be noted that a backlink is not used for the tree traversal, see Fig. 2(a).

In designing an internal BST in a concurrent setup, the most difficult part is to perform an error-free REMOVE of a binary node. To remove a binary node we replace it with its predecessor, and hence, the incoming and outgoing links of the predecessor also need to be modified in addition to the incoming links of the node itself. According to the number of links needed to be modified in order to remove a node, unlike traditional categorization of nodes of a BST into leaf, unary and binary, we categorize them into three categories as shown in Fig. 2(b). The categorization characteristic is the origin of the threaded incoming link into the node. We call this link the *order-link*. Nodes belonging to category 1 are those whose order-link emanates from themselves; for a category 2 node, it emanates from its left-child; and for a category 3 node the incoming order-link emanates from the rightmost node in its left-subtree. We call the node where the order-link emanates from, the *order-node*. Note that, the order-node of a category 1 node is the node itself, whereas for category 2 and category 3 nodes it is its predecessor.

To remove a node of category 1, only the incoming parent-link needs to be modified to connect to the node pointed by the right-link. For a category 2 node, the parent-link is updated to connect to the node pointed by the left-link and the order-link is modified to point to the node which the right-link was pointing to. In order to remove a category 3 node, its predecessor replaces it and the incoming and outgoing links of the predecessor are updated to take the values of that of the removed node. Parent-link of the predecessor is connected to the node which its left-link was pointing to before it got shifted. Also, when a link is updated the thread indicator value of the link, which it updates to, is copied to it. Please note that in this categorization, a unary or a binary node whose left-child is left-unary (i.e. whose right-child is null) or a leaf, gets classified in to category 2. Category 1 includes conventional leaf and right-unary nodes (whose left-child is null).

Having categorized the nodes as above we describe the modifications of links associated with a node undergoing REMOVE. Storing an indicator bit in a pointer has been used in many previous papers [13, 11, 22, 18]. We use a similar technique as in [11]. Depending on the category, before swapping the pointers associated with a node we flag the incoming pointers to the node and its predecessor (for category 3 only) and mark the outgoing pointers from the same. Note that because a backlink is neither used for traversal nor for injecting a modify operation, we do not need to mark/flag it. Flagging ensures that an operation does not have to travel a long *chain* of backlinks for recovery from failure. Once a link is flagged or marked it can not be a *point of injection* of a *new* ADD or REMOVE. However, in the conflict between a REMOVE of a category 3 node, and therefore shifting its predecessor, and a concurrent REMOVE of the predecessor node itself, we give priority to the former. Also to guarantee a single pointer travelling for recovery from failure due to a concurrent modify operation, we use a *prelink* at each node. It connects a node to its order-node before any of the outgoing pointers are marked. The flagging and marking are performed in such a predetermined order so that a malformed structure of the BST is avoided and the required priorities between conflicting operations are ensured. The flag-mark order of links for a category 3 node is as following - (I) flag the incoming order-link, (II) set the prelink, (III) mark the outgoing right-link, (IV) flag the parent-link of the predecessor incoming to that, (V) flag the incoming parent-link, (VI) mark the outgoing left-link and finally (VII) mark the outgoing left-link of the predecessor. For a node belonging to category 1 or 2, because there is no node between its order-node and itself, steps (IV), (VI) and (VII) do not happen. Having performed the flagging and marking we update

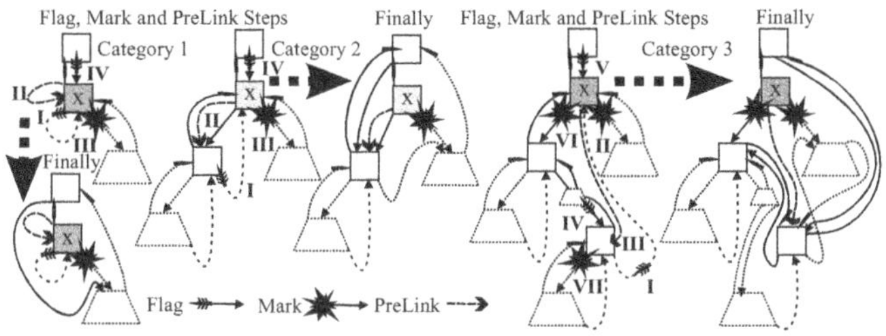

Figure 3: Remove steps of nodes

the flagged links according to the category of the node as described before. See Fig. 3.

Because we follow orderly modifications of the links, it never allows a node to be missed by a traversal in the BST unless both its incoming links are pointed away. However, because a node may shift "upward" to replace its successor, the interval associated with the order-link of its successor may shift "rightward" i.e. to the right subtree of the node after the successor is removed. Therefore, in order to terminate a traversal correctly, we use the stopping criterion given in Condition 1. It follows from the fact that the threaded left-link of a node is connected to the node itself and a traversal in the BST uses the order in the equivalent list.

CONDITION **1.** *Let k be the search key and k_{curr} be the key of the current node in the search path. If ($k = k_{curr}$) then stop. Else, if the next link is a threaded left-link then stop. Else, if the next link is a threaded right-link and the next node has key k_{next} then check if $k < k_{next}$. If true then stop, else continue.*

This stopping criterion not only solves the problem of synchronization between a concurrent REMOVE and a traversal for a predecessor query but also enables to achieve bound on the length of the traversal path. We shall explain that in section 4. A similar stopping criterion is used in [8] for conventional doubly-threaded BSTs.

We can observe that in our BST design, two modify operations that need to change two disjoint memory-words have significantly improved conditions for progress. For example, to REMOVE a category 2 node the left-link of its predecessor is never marked or flagged, therefore when such a node goes under REMOVE, a concurrent injection of ADD or REMOVE at the predecessor is possible. Also, because of the orderly flagging and marking of the links in more than one atomic steps, even after REMOVE of the node has commenced, a link at it that comes late in the order of flagging-marking can be modified for a concurrent ADD or REMOVE of another node. These progress conditions are not possible in the existing algorithms that use "node holding" [10, 15]. It shows that our algorithm has improved disjoint-access-parallelism.

3.2 The Implementation

We consider our concurrent setup as a shared memory machine in which processes are fully asynchronous and arbitrary failure halting is allowed. The read and write of a single memory-word is guaranteed to be atomic. The system provides atomic single-word `CAS` primitives. `CAS`(R, *old*, *new*) returns `true`, if (*old* $= R$), after updating R to *new*, else it returns `false` without any update. We steal three bits from a pointer, for (a) the thread indicator, (b) the mark-bit and (c) the flag-bit, see line 3. This is easily possible in high level languages such as C/C++. To prevent ABA problem in the implementation the standard technique of embedding a version tag using few bits in a pointer can be used. We also assume that the algorithm is implemented with a non-blocking safe memory reclamation scheme.

A typical node x in our BST implementation is represented by a structure consisting of five memory-words corresponding to - (a) a key k, (b) array $child[2]$ containing two child pointers : $child[0] := left(x)$ and $child[1] := right(x)$, (c) a $backLink$ and (d) a $preLink$. The bit sequence corresponding to boolean variables overlapping three stolen bits from a link is represented as (f, m, t). One or more bits together can be set or unset using a single atomic `CAS` operation over the pointer containing it. The node structure is shown in lines 1 to 6. We use two dummy nodes as global variables represented by a two member array of node-pointers called *root*. The keys $-\infty$ and ∞ are stored in the two members of *root* and they can never be deleted. Node $root[0]$ is left-child and predecessor of the node $root[1]$, see line 7 and figure 2 (c).

3.2.1 Locating a Node

The set operations - CONTAINS, ADD and REMOVE, need to perform a predecessor query using a given key k to locate an interval $[k_i,\ k_j]$, s.t. either $\{k_i \leq k < k_j\}$ or $\{k_i \geq k > k_j\}$, where $x(k_i)$ and $x(k_j)$ are two nodes in the BST. The function LOCATE is used for that, which starts from a specified set of two consecutive nodes {`prev`, `curr`} and follows the symmetric order of the internal BST to terminate at such a location $\{x(k_{prev}),\ x(k_{curr})\}$. The return value of LOCATE can be 0, 1 or 2 depending on whether the key k is less than, greater than or equal to the key k_{curr} at the termination point, line 10. If $k_{curr} \neq k$ then the desired interval is associated with the threaded outgoing link from $x(k_{curr})$ in the direction indicated by return value of LOCATE - 0 denotes left and 1 denotes right. The termination criterion for LOCATE implements Condition 1.

As we mentioned before, we can make a traversal eagerly help pending REMOVE operations, even though it is not obstructed by them, in the situations in which proportion of REMOVE increases. If that is done then a traversal cleans a node whose marked right-link it encounters during execution by calling the function CLEANMARK. This functionality can be enabled using a boolean variable as an input argument to every Set operation which is further passed to the LOCATE that it performs, see lines 14 to 20. To perform a CONTAINS operation for the key k, we start from the location $\{x(\infty),\ x(-\infty)\}$ represented by the global variables. Having performed LOCATE, the return value itself indicates whether the key k was present in the BST at the point of termination of LOCATE. If LOCATE returns 2 then CONTAINS returns `true` otherwise `false`, line 26 to 30.

3.2.2 Remove operation

To REMOVE a node $x(k)$, starting from $\{x(\infty),\ x(-\infty)\}$ we locate the link that the interval containing the key $(k-\epsilon)$ associates with, see line 33. If the LOCATE terminates at $\{x(k_{prev}),\ x(k_{curr})\}$ then $suc(x(k_{curr}))$ is the desired node to remove if k matches with its key. $suc(x(k_{curr}))$ is the node pointed by the threaded right-link of $x(k_{curr})$ and this link is indeed the order-link of $x(k)$. If $x(k)$ is located then we try to flag its order-link using TRYFLAG, line 37, in order to perform the step (I) of REMOVE.

```
1  struct Node {
2    KType k;
     // Three booleans overlap with three unused bits of the
     pointer ref.  left=child[0], right=child[1].
3    {NPtr ref, bool flag, bool mark, bool thread} child[2];
4    NPtr backLink;
5    NPtr preLink;
6  } *NPtr;
   // Global variable with the fixed value of members.
7  Node root[2] =
   {{-∞, {(&root[0], 0, 0, 1), (&root[1], 0, 0, 1)}, &root[1], null},
   {∞, {(&root[0], 0, 0, 0), (null, 0, 0, 1)}, null, null}};
```

```
   // LOCATE returns 2 if key is found otherwise 0 or 1 if the
   last visited link is left or right respectively.
8  int LOCATE(NPtr& prev, NPtr& curr, KType k)
9  while true do
     // Function cmp returns 2 := equal, 1 := greater than
     and 0 := less than
10   dir = cmp(k, curr→e);
11   if (dir = 2) then return dir;
12   else
13     (R, *, m, t) = curr→child[dir];
       /* If eager helping is required then help cleaning
       the current node if its right child pointer has been
       marked. */
14     if ((m = 1) and (dir = 1)) then
15       newPrev = prev→backLink;
16       CLEANMARKED(prev, curr, dir);
17       prev = newPrev;
18       pDir =cmp(k, prev→k);
19       curr = (prev→child[pDir])·ref;
20       continue;
21     if t then
         // Check the stopping criterion.
22       nextE = R→k;
23       if ((dir = 0) or (k < nextE)) then
24         return dir;
25       else prev = curr; curr = R;
```

```
26 bool CONTAINS(KType k)
   // Initialize the location variables with the global
   variables.
27 prev = &root[1]; curr = &root[0];
28 dir = LOCATE(prev, curr, k);
29 if (dir = 2) then return true;
30 else return false;
```

```
31 bool REMOVE(KType k)
   // Initialize the location variables as before.
32 prev = &root[1]; curr = &root[0];
33 dir = LOCATE(prev, curr, k- ϵ);                // locate order-link
34 (next, f, *, t) = curr→child[dir];
35 if (k ≠ next→k) then return false;
36 else
     // flag the order-link
37   result = TRYFLAG(curr, next, prev, true);
38   if (prev→child[dir].ref = curr) then
39     CLEANFLAG(curr, next, prev, true);
40 return result;
```

TRYFLAG, line 41 to 58, returns true only if the operation performing it could successfully flag the desired link at line 45. If the CAS step to atomically flag the link fails then it checks the reason of failure. If it fails because some other thread already had successfully flagged the link, false is returned, line 50. If it fails because the link was marked then it first helps the operation that marked the link, line 51. It could also fail to flag a threaded link because of an ADD of a new node. In both the latter cases it moves a step back and locates the node whose parent-link was desired to be flagged. The address for starting the recovery is saved in the variable back. If the node is not located then it implies that some other thread already removed the target node and so TRYFLAG just returns false, line 57.

```
41 bool TRYFLAG(NPtr& prev, NPtr& curr, NPtr& back, bool
   isThread)
42 while true do
43   pDir = cmp(curr→k, prev→k) & 1;  // If cmp returns 2 then
     curr is the left link of prev; so pDir is changed to 0.
44   t = isThread;
45   result = CAS(prev→child[pDir], (curr, 0, 0, t), (curr, 1, 0, t));
46   if result then return true;
47   else
       /* The CAS fails, check if the link has been marked,
       flagged or the curr node got deleted. If flagged,
       return false; if marked, first clean then proceed */
48     (newR, f, m, t) = prev→child[pDir];
49     if (newR = curr) then
50       if f then return false;
51       else if m then
52         CLEANMARKED(prev, pDir);
53       prev = back;
54       pDir =cmp(curr→k, prev→k);
55       newCurr = (prev→child[newPDir])·ref;
         LOCATE(prev, newCurr, curr→k);
56       if (newCurr ≠curr ) then
57         return false;
58       back = prev→backLink;
```

```
59 void TRYMARK(NPtr& curr, int dir)
60 while true do
61   back = curr→backLink;
62   (next, f, m, t) = curr→child[dir];
63   if (m == 1) then break;
64   else if (f == 1) then
65     if (t == 0) then
66       CLEANFLAG(curr, next, back, false); continue;
67     else if ((t == 1) and (dir == 1)) then
68       CLEANFLAG(curr, next, back, true); continue;
69   result = CAS(curr→child[dir], (next, 0, 0, t), (next,
     0, 1, t));          // Try atomically marking the child link.
70   if result then break;
```

Having performed the TRYFLAG, REMOVE checks whether the target node is still there, line 38. If the target node is found then REMOVE goes to clean the flag at the order-link of the target node, using the function CLEANFLAG, lines 71 to 117. The function CLEANFLAG is also used to clean the flag of the parent-link of a node, and therefore a boolean variable is passed to it to inform about the thread-bit of the flagged link. If the link is an order-link then for all categories of nodes, the next step is to set the prelink and then mark the right-link, see lines 72 to 87. If the CAS to mark the right-link fails because of its flagging, and if the right-link is threaded then it indicates that the node itself is being shifted to replace its successor by a concurrent REMOVE operation. We give priority to the shifting operation and therefore before proceeding it is helped. As before, we need to recover from failures and so the node back stores the address to restart the recovery from. Here one has to be careful that if back was pointed at the node under REMOVE then we need to change it before going to help, see lines 77 and 81. Having marked the right-link, REMOVE proceeds to take further steps in the function CLEANMARK. Also, before marking the right-link, the prelink gets pointed to the correct order-node, line 85.

If CLEANFLAG is performed on a link that is not threaded then the link must be the incoming parent-link of a node or of its predecessor. In that case it is determined whether the link is the parent-link of a node under REMOVE or that of its predecessor by checking the flag, mark and thread bits of the right-link. The right-link of a node being removed is marked, whereas that for the predecessor of the same is

```
71  void CleanFlag(NPtr& prev, NPtr& curr, NPtr& back, bool
    isThread)
72  if (isThread ) then
        // Cleaning a flagged order-link
73      while true do
            // To mark the right-child link
74          (next, f, m, t) = curr→child[1];
75          if (m) then break;
76          else if (f) then
                // Help cleaning if right-child is flagged
77              if (back = next) then
                    // If back is getting deleted then move back.
78                  back = back→backLink;
79              backNode = curr→backLink;
80              CleanFlag(curr, next, backNode, t);
81              if (back = next) then
82                  pDir =cmp(prev→k, backNode→k);
83                  prev = back→child[pDir];
84          else
85              if (curr→preLink ≠ prev) then curr→preLink =
                prev;
86              result = CAS(curr→child[1], (next, 0, 0, t),
                (next, 0, 1, t)) ;  // Try marking the right-link.
87              if result then break;
88      CleanMark(curr, 1);
89  else                              // Cleaning a flagged parent-link
90      (right, rF, rM, rT) = curr→child[1];
91      if (rM) then              // The node is to be deleted itself
92          (left, lF, lM, lT) = curr→child[0];
93          preNode = curr→preLink;
94          if (left ≠ preNode) then // A category 3 node
95              TryMark(curr, 0);
96              CleanMark(curr, 0);
97          else                      // This is a category 1 or 2 node
98              pDir =cmp(curr→k,prev→k);
99              if (left = curr) then            // A category 1 node
100                 CAS(prev→child[pDir], (curr
                    , f, 0, 0), (right, 0, 0, rT));
101                 if (!rT) then CAS(right→backLink, (curr
                    , 0, 0, 0), (prev, 0, 0, 0));
102             else                             // A category 2 node
103                 CAS(preNode→child[1], (curr
                    , 1, 0, 1), (right, 0, 0, rT));
104                 if (!rT) then CAS(right→backLink, (curr
                    , 0, 0, 0), (prev, 0, 0, 0));
105                 CAS(prev→child[pDir], (curr
                    , 1, 0, 0), (preNode, 0, 0, rT));
106                 CAS(preNode→backLink, (curr, 0, 0, 0), (prev
                    , 0, 0, 0));
107     else if (rt and rF) then
            // The node is moving to replace its successor
108         delNode = right;
109         while true do
110             parent = delNode→backLink;
111             pDir =cmp(curr→k, prev→k);
112             (*, pF, pM, pT) = parent→child[pDir];
113             if (pM) then CleanMark(parent, pDir);
114             else if (pF) then break;
115             else if (CAS(parent→child[pDir], (curr
                , 0, 0, 0), (curr, 1, 0, 0))) then
116                 break;
117         backNode = parent→backLink;
118         CleanFlag(parent, curr, backNode, true);
```

always flagged and threaded. Accordingly, either step (V) (lines 107 to 117) or step (VI) (lines 94) are performed. To perform the step (VI) the outgoing left-link of a category 3 node is marked, and for that the function TryMark is used. TryMark atomically sets the mark-bit at a link specified by its direction outgoing from a node, see lines 59 to 70. Note that, if the CAS to atomically mark a link fails due to a concurrent flagging of the link then TryMark helps the concurrent operation that flagged the link, except in the

```
119 void CleanMark(NPtr& curr, int markDir)
120 (left, lF, lM, lT) = curr→child[0];
121 (right, rF, rM, rT) = curr→child[1];
122 if (markDir   == 1) then
        /* The node is getting deleted itself.  if it is
        category 1 or 2 node, flag the incoming parent link; if
        it is a category 3 node, flag the incoming parent link
        of its predecessor.  */
123     while true do
124         preNode = delNode→preLink;
125         if (preNode == left) then // Category 1 or 2 node.
126             parent = delNode→backLink;
127             back = parent→backLink;
128             TryFlag(parent, curr, back, true);
129             if (parent→child[pDir].ref == curr) then
130                 CleanFlag(parent, curr, back, true);
131                 break;
132         else
                // Category 3 node.
133             preParent = preNode→backLink;
134             (*, pPF, pPM, pPT) = preParent→child[1];
135             backNode = preParent→backLink;
136             if (pM) then CleanMark(preParent, 1);
137             else if (pF) then
138                 CleanFlag(preParent, preNode, backNode, true
                    );break;
139             else if (CAS(parent→child[pDir], (curr
                , 0, 0, 0), (curr, 1, 0, 0))) then
140                 CleanFlag(preParent, preNode, backNode, true
                    );break;
141 else
        // The node is getting deleted (†) or moved to replace
        its successor (‡).
142     if (rM) then
            // (†) clean its left marked link.
143         preNode = curr→preLink;
144         TryMark(preNode, 0);
145         CleanMark(preNode, 0);
146     else if (rt and rF) then
            // (‡) change links accordingly
147         delNode = right;
148         delNodePa = delNode→backLink;
149         preParent = curr→backLink;
150         pDir =cmp(delNode→k, delNodePa→k);
151         (delNodeL, *, *, dlT) = delNode→child[0];
152         (delNodeR, *, *, drT) = delNode→child[1];
153         CAS(preParent→child[1], (curr
            , lF, 0, 0), (left, lF, 0, lT));
154         if (!lT) then CAS(left→backLink, (curr, 0, 0, 0),
            (preParent, 0, 0, 0));
155         CAS(curr→child[0], (left, 0, 1, lT), (delNodeL, 0, 0, 0));
156         CAS(delNodeL→backLink, (delNode, 0, 0, 0), (curr
            , 0, 0, 0));
157         CAS(curr→child[1], (right, 1, 0, 1), (delNodeR, 0, 0, drT));
158         if (!drT) then CAS(delNodeR→backLink,
            (delNode, 0, 0, 0), (curr, 0, 0, 0));
159         CAS(delNodePa→child[pDir], (delNode, 1, 0, 0), (curr
            , 0, 0, 0));
160         CAS(curr→backLink, (preParent, 0, 0, 0),
            (delNodePa, 0, 0, 0));
```

case when the link is a threaded left-link. This is because a flagged and threaded left-link of a node indicates that the node is a category 1 node under Remove and we give priority to the operation that must have already flagged its right link to shift it.

Because the last step for category 1 and category 2 nodes is flagging their parent-link before the pointers are appropriately swapped, CleanFlag also includes the final swapping of pointers for such nodes. Having determined that a node belongs to category 1 or 2 by checking the equality of left-node and order-node at line 97, it performs the pointer swapping for category 1 nodes in lines 100 and 101. Pointer swapping steps to clean a category 2 node is shown between lines 103 and 106.

The CLEANMARK function is used to help an operation that sets a mark-bit at a link. Depending on whether the link is a left- or a right-link, it takes different steps. If the link is a right-link, for category 1 and 2 nodes, the flagging of the parent-link is executed; otherwise for category 3 nodes the parent-link of its predecessor is flagged. On failing to flag the parent-link of predecessor of a category 3 node, because a concurrent operation already marked the link, it helps that operation. However, after helping it may be that the node under REMOVE changes from a category 3 to a category 2 node, so its status is checked again, see lines 123 to 139.

A set mark-bit at a left-link indicates that it is either coming out from a category 3 node under REMOVE or its predecessor. In the first case, the step (VII) to mark the left-link of the predecessor of the node is performed, line 142. In the second case the pointer swapping steps of the category 3 nodes are performed, see lines 147 to 160.

Return value of REMOVE is that of the absolutely first TRYFLAG that it performs if the node was located.

3.2.3 Add operation

To ADD a new data-node with key k in the BST, we LOCATE the target interval $[k_i,\ k_j]$ that k belongs to, associated with a threaded link. If LOCATE returns 2 then key is present in the BST and therefore ADD returns false. If it returns 0 or 1 then we create a new node containing the key k. Its left-link is threaded and connected to itself and right-link takes the value of the link to which it needs to be connected, line 171. Note that when a new node is added, both its children links are threaded. Also, its backlink is pointed to the node $x(k_i)$. The link which it needs to connect to is modified in one atomic step to point to the new node using a CAS. If the CAS succeeds then true is returned. On failure, it is checked whether the target link was flagged, marked or another ADD operation succeeded to insert a new node after we read the link. In case a new node is inserted, we start locating a new appropriate link starting with the location comprising nodes at the two ends of the changed link. On failure due to marking or flagging of the current link, the concurrent REMOVE operation is helped. Recovery from failure due to a flagging or marking by a concurrent REMOVE operation makes it to go one link back following the backlink of prev. After locating the new link, ADD is retried.

```
161 bool ADD(KType k)
162 prev = &root[1]; curr = &root[0];
    /* Initializing a new node with supplied key and left-link
    threaded and pointing to itself.  */
163 node = new Node(k);
164 node→child[0] = (node, 0, 0, 1);
165 while true do
166     dir = LOCATE(prev, curr, k);
167     if (dir = 2) then // key exists in the BST
168         return false;
169     else
170         (R, *, *, *) = curr→child[dir];
            /* The located link is threaded.  Set the right-link
            of the adding node to copy this value */
171         node→child[1] = (R, 0, 0, 1);
172         node→backLink = curr;
173         result = CAS(curr→child[dir], (R, 0, 0, 1),
            (node, 0, 0, 0));           // Try inserting the new node.
174         if result then return true;
175         else
                /* If the CAS fails, check if the link has been
                marked, flagged or a new node has been inserted.
                If marked or flagged, first help.  */
176             (newR, f, m, t) = curr→child[dir];
177             if (newR = R) then
178                 newCurr = prev;
179                 if m then CLEANMARKED(curr, dir);
180                 else if f then
181                     CLEANFLAGGED(curr, R, prev, true);
182                 curr = newCurr;
183                 prev = newCurr→backLink;
```

formed by our algorithm contains elements stored in regular nodes or logically removed nodes. Before we show that the return values of the set operations are consistent with this definition according to their linearizability, we have to show that the operations work as intended and the structure formed by the nodes operated with these operations maintains a valid BST. We present some invariants maintained by the operations and the nodes in lemmas 1 to 9.

4. CORRECTNESS AND COMPLEXITY

4.1 Correctness

Here we present a proof-sketch of correctness and defer a detailed proof to [6] due to space constraints. First, we give classification of nodes in a BST Υ implemented by our algorithm.

DEFINITION **1.** *A node $x\in\Upsilon$ is called logically removed if its right-link is marked and $\exists\ y\in\Upsilon$ s.t. either $left(y) = x$ or $right(y) = x$.*

DEFINITION **2.** *A node $x\in\Upsilon$ is called physically removed if $\nexists\ y\in\Upsilon$ s.t. either $left(y) = x$ or $right(y) = x$.*

DEFINITION **3.** *A node $x\in\Upsilon$ is called regular if it is neither logically removed nor physically removed.*

A node ever inserted in Υ has to fit in one of the above categories. At a point in the history of an execution, the BST

LEMMA **1.** *If a LOCATE(prev, curr, k) returns dir and terminates at $[x(k_{prev}),\ x(k_{curr})]$ then*

(a) If $k_{curr} \neq k$ then the link $x(k_{curr})\rightarrow child[dir]$ is threaded.

(b) $x(k_{prev})$ and $x(k_{curr})$ are not physically deleted.

LEMMA **2.** *A CONTAINS operation returns true if and only if the key is located at a non-physically removed node.*

LEMMA **3.** *An ADD always happens at an unmarked and unflagged threaded link.*

LEMMA **4.** *A REMOVE always starts by flagging the incoming order-link to a node.*

LEMMA **5.** *When a node is added, both its left- and right-links are threaded.*

LEMMA **6.** *Before a node is logically removed its incoming order-link is flagged and its prelink points to its correct order-node.*

LEMMA **7.** *Backlink of a node always points to a node which is a single link away.*

LEMMA **8.** *An unthreaded left-link and a right-link can not be both flagged and marked.*

LEMMA **9.** *If a node gets logically removed then eventually it will be physically removed.*

Lemma 1 follows from the lines 11 and 21. CONTAINS returns true only if LOCATE returns 2 and that happens only if curr is non-physically removed at line 10 during its execution, this proves lemma 2. In case the key of a node matches with the query key, ADD returns false, otherwise it tries adding the new node using an atomic CAS. If the CAS fails, it always uses LOCATE to find the desired link before retrying the CAS to add the new node. From this observation and using 1(a), lemma 3 follows. By lemma 1 if $x(k)$ is present in the tree then LOCATE(prev, curr, $(k - \epsilon)$) will always terminate at a location such that curr is order-node of $x(k)$ and that establishes lemma 4. Lemma 5 follows from lines 164 and 171. Line 153 ensures that even if the function CLEANFLAG helps a pending REMOVE, before it could successfully mark the right-link at line 86, the flag that was put on the order-link at line 45 is copied to the new order-link. Also, the line 85 inside the while loop ensures that prelink is always set to the order-node. That proves the correctness of lemma 6. When a node is added its backlink is pointed to curr at line 172. Before a REMOVE operation returns, the backlinks of the predecessor, left-child and right-child, if present for the node under REMOVE, are updated at lines 101, 104, 106, 154, 156, 158 and 160 only after the incoming parent-links of those nodes are updated. Hence, lemma 7 is proved. In our algorithm we always use an atomic CAS to set a flag or mark-bit in a pointer. Whenever a CAS fails we check the possible reason. The function TRYMARK on failing to mark a link because it is flagged, helps cleaning the flag in all cases except when the link has direction 0 and it is threaded, line 67. These observations prove lemma 8. Lemma 8 proves that once the right-link of a node is marked, it can not be flagged. By lemmas 3 and 4, a new ADD or REMOVE will be obstructed at this link. Therefore, if the thread invoking REMOVE to mark it becomes faulty then eventually another thread invoking a possible ADD or REMOVE, which gets obstructed, will help to complete the physical removal. That proves lemma 9. Having proved the lemmas listed above, it is trivial to observe that whenever a pointer is dereferenced it is not null. And, by the initialization of the global variable to ∞ and $-\infty$, at line 7, the two starting nodes are never deleted.

Hence, we state proposition 1 whose proof will follow by the above stated lemmas and the fact that a thread always takes a correct "turn" during traversal according to the symmetric order of the internal BST.

PROPOSITION **1.** *The union of the regular and logically removed nodes operated under the set operations in the algorithm Efficient Lock Free BST maintains a valid internal Binary Search Tree.*

An execution history in our implementation may consist of ADD, REMOVE and CONTAINS operations. We present the linearization point of the execution of these operations. Proving that a history consisting of concurrent executions of these operations is legal will be ordering these linearization points. The linearization points of the operations are as following:

ADD - For a successful ADD operation, execution of the CAS at line 173 will be the linearization point. For an unsuccessful one the linearization point will be at line 10 where a key in the tree is found matched.

REMOVE - For a successful REMOVE operation the linearization point will be the successful CAS that swaps the flagged parent link. For an unsuccessful one there may be two cases - (a) if the node is not located then it is treated as an unsuccessful CONTAINS and its linearization point will be accordingly (b) if the node is located but its order-link got flagged by another concurrent REMOVE then its linearization point is just after the linearization point of that REMOVE.

CONTAINS - Our algorithm varies according to the read-write load situation. In case we go for eager helping by a thread performing LOCATE, a successful CONTAINS shall always return a regular node. However, if we opt otherwise then a successful CONTAINS returns any non-physically removed node. In both situations a successful CONTAINS will be linearized at line 10. An unsuccessful one, if the node never existed in the BST, is linearized at the start point. And, if the node existed in the BST when the CONTAINS was invoked but got removed during its traversal by a concurrent REMOVE then the linearization point will be just after the linearization point of that REMOVE.

Following the linearization points as described above we have proposition 2:

PROPOSITION **2.** *The Set operations in the algorithm Efficient Lock Free BST are linearizable.*

4.2 Lock-Freedom

The lemmas 6, 8 and 9 imply the following lemma.

LEMMA **10.** *If* REMOVE(x) *and* REMOVE(y) *work concurrently on nodes x and y then without loss of generality*

(a) *If x is a child of y and the link $[y, x]$ is flagged then* REMOVE(x) *finishes before* REMOVE(y)*; otherwise if this link is marked,* REMOVE(y) *finishes before* REMOVE(x).
(b) *If x is the predecessor of y and the order-links of both x and y have been successfully flagged then* REMOVE(y) *finishes before* REMOVE(x)*; otherwise if x has been logically deleted then* REMOVE(x) *finishes before the order-link of y could be successfully flagged.*
(c) *If x is the left-child of the predecessor of y and the link $[pre(y), x]$ is flagged then* REMOVE(x) *finishes before* REMOVE(y)*; otherwise if this link is marked,* REMOVE(y) *finishes before* REMOVE(x).
(d) *In all other cases* REMOVE(x) *and* REMOVE(y) *do not obstruct each other.*

By the description of our algorithm, a non-faulty thread performing CONTAINS will always return unless its search path keeps on getting longer forever. If that happens, an infinite number of ADD operations would have successfully completed adding new nodes making the implementation lock-free. So, it will suffice to prove that the modify operations are lock-free. Suppose that a thread t performs an operation *op* on a BST Υ and takes infinite steps and no other modify operation completes after that. Now, if no modify operation completes then Υ remains unchanged forcing t to retract every time it wants to execute its own modification step on Υ. This is possible only if every time *op* finds its injection point flagged or marked. This implies that a REMOVE operation is pending. It is easy to observe in the function ADD that if it gets obstructed by a concurrent REMOVE then before retrying after recovery from failure it helps the pending REMOVE by executing all the remaining steps of that. Also from lemma 10, whenever two REMOVE operations obstruct each other, one finishes before the other. It implies that whenever two modify operations obstruct each other one finishes before the other and so Υ changes. It is contrary to our assumption. Hence, by contradiction we show that no non-faulty thread shall remain taking infinite steps if no other non-faulty thread is making progress. This proves the proposition 4.

PROPOSITION **3.** *Lock-freedom is guaranteed in the algorithm Efficient Lock Free BST.*

4.3 Complexity

Having proved that our algorithm guarantees lock-freedom, though we can not compute worst-case time complexity of an operation, we can definitely derive their amortized complexity. We derive the amortized step complexity of our implementation by the accounting method along the similar lines as in [11, 19].

In our algorithm, an ADD operation does not have to hold any pointer and so does not obstruct an operation for itself. We observe that after flagging the order-link of a node, a REMOVE operation op_r takes only a constant number of steps to flag, mark and swap pointers connected to the node and to its predecessor(if any) in addition to setting the prelink of the node under REMOVE. Also using lemma 7 and the fact that to access the predecessor of a node its prelink is used, recovery from failure due to a concurrent REMOVE operation needs only a constant number of links to traverse. Therefore, following lemma follows

LEMMA **11.** *An obstructing operation op makes an obstructed operation op′ take only a constant number of extra steps for recovery from failure in order to finish its execution.*

Now for an execution E, let $\mathcal{O}$ be the set of operations and let $\mathcal{S}$ be the set of steps taken by all $op{\in}\mathcal{O}$. Considering the *invocation point* $t_i(op)$ of op to be the time it reads the root, and *response point* $t_r(op)$ to be the time it reads or writes at the last link before it leaves the BST, its *interval contention* c_I is defined as the total number of operations whose execution overlaps the interval $[t_i(op),\ t_r(op)]$ [1]. We define a function $f : \mathcal{S} \mapsto \mathcal{O}$ such that if $f(s) = op$ then s is charged to the account of op and

(a) In case of no contention, all the essential steps s, representing read, write and CAS taken by an operation op is mapped to op by f.
(b) In case of contention, any failed CAS by an operation op is mapped by f to the operation op' whose successful CAS causes the failure.
(c) If an extra read is performed by a traversal due to an added node to the set of existing nodes by a concurrent ADD operation op then it is mapped by f to op.
(d) Any read, write or CAS step s taken by an operation op after the first failed CAS and before retrying at the same link i.e. during helping and recovery from failure is mapped by f to the operation op' that performed the successful CAS in order to make op help it, provided op' further does not help some op'' so that op helps op'' recursively. This includes resetting of prelink, if needed.
(e) In case of recursive helping, the extra steps by all the operations helping op is mapped by f to op.

Having identified the operations to map for a step, it is easy to observe that an operation op' to which a step s by an operation op is mapped, has its execution interval overlapping $[t_i(op),\ t_r(op)]$ and therefore op is counted in $c_I(op')$.

Next we bound the length of the traversal path for a predecessor query in our implementation. Note that, all the set operations have to perform a predecessor query by key k to LOCATE an interval $[k_i,\ k_j]$ associated with a link s.t. $x(k_i)$ and $x(k_j)$ are two nodes in the BST. Let us define the *access-node* of an interval as the node that the link which it associates with, emanates from. We define *distance* of an interval from an operation op as the number of links that op traverses from its current location (root $\forall\ t{\leq}t_i(op)$) to read the access-node of the interval. Suppose that at $t_i(op)$ there are n nodes in the BST Υ. Clearly, distance of any interval for op at $t_i(op)$ is $O(H(n))$. Now suppose that at $t_{ref}(op) \in [t_i(op),\ t_r(op)]$, $x(k_j)$ is a category 1 node and the distance of the interval $[k_i,\ k_j]$ associated with the order-link of $x(k_j)$ from op at $t_{ref}(op)$ is d. We can observe that if at $t \in [t_{ref}(op),\ t_r(op)]$, $x(k_j)$ is still a category 1 node and it is removed then the interval associated with its order-link gets subsumed by the interval associated with the order-link of the leftmost child in its right subtree or with the order-link emanating from its parent if the right subtree is null. In the former case the distance of $[k_i,\ k_j]$ from op becomes $d + ht(x(k_j))$ and in the latter it decreases by 1. Also if a node $x(k_l)$ is added by an operation op' then the extra distance except d traversed by op to access $[k_i,\ k_l]$ or $[k_l,\ k_j]$ is no more than c_I. Using the above observations, an inductive proof is derived to imply that op does not traverse more than $d + ht(x(k_j)) + c_I$ links to access a subinterval of $[k_i,\ k_j]$. Hence the lemma 12 follows whose detailed proof is deferred to [6].

LEMMA **12.** *If at $t_{ref}(op) \in [t_i(op),\ t_r(op)]$, $x(k_j)$ is a category 1 node and the distance of the interval $[k_i,\ k_j]$ associated with the order-link of $x(k_j)$ from op at $t_{ref}(op)$ is d then to access an interval $[k,\ k'] \subseteq [k_i,\ k_j]$ op traverses no more than $d + ht(x(k_j)) + c_I$ links.*

When op traverses in the left subtree of a category 3 node x and if x gets removed, the interval associated with its order-link gets subsumed by the interval associated with the order-link of the leftmost node in the right subtree of x which is a category 1 node. On removal of a category 2 node, the interval associated with its order-link is subsumed by the interval associated with the order-link of its parent which can be a category 2 or category 3 node. Because $(d + ht(x)) \leq 2H(n)\ \forall\ x{\in}\Upsilon$, lemma 12 along with these observations show that the path length of a traversal in our lock-free BST is bounded by $2H(n) + c_I$.

We have shown that (a) the traversal path is bounded by $O(H(n)+c_I)$, (b) a constant number of steps are needed for a modify operation after locating its target (node or link) and (c) to an operation op only a constant number of extra steps can be charged by any concurrent operation op' counted in c_I. Therefore, we can infer that the amortized step complexity for a set operation, which is the actual step complexity plus the number of steps charged by other operations minus the number of steps charged to other operations, in our lock-free BST algorithm is $O(H(n) + c_I)$. We also give choice of eager helping to operations according to the read-write load. Now if that happens, we do not need to count all the operations whose executions overlap the interval $[t_i(op),\ t_r(op)]$. We can then use a tighter notion of *point contention* c_P, which counts the maximum number of operations that execute concurrently at $t{\in}[t_i(op),\ t_r(op)]$ [2]. In that case, given the above discussion, along the similar lines as presented in [11], we can show that for any execution E, the average amortized step complexity of a set operation *op* in our algorithm will be

$$\hat{t}_{op \in E} \in O\left(\frac{\sum_{op \in E}(H(n(op)) + c_P(op))}{|\{op \in E\}|}\right)$$

where $n(op)$ is the number of nodes in the BST at the point of invocation of *op* and $c_P(op)$ is its point contention during E. That concludes the amortized analysis of our algorithm with the following proposition.

PROPOSITION **4.** *In a BST with n nodes at the start of an execution, the amortized step complexity of each operation in the algorithm Efficient Lock Free BST is* $O(H(n) + c)$, *where c is the measure of contention during the execution.*

It is straightforward to observe that the number of memory-words used by a BST with n nodes in our design is $5n$.

5. CONCLUSION AND FUTURE WORK

In this paper we proposed a novel algorithm for the implementation of a lock-free internal BST. Using amortized analysis we proved that all the operations in our implementation run in time $O(H(n) + c)$. We solved the existing problem of "retry from scratch" for modify operations after failure caused by a concurrent modify operation, which resulted into an amortized step complexity of $O(cH(n))$. This improvement takes care of an algorithmic design issue for which the time complexity of modify operations increases dramatically with the increase in the contention and the size of the data-structure. This is an important improvement over the existing algorithms. Our algorithm also comes with improved disjoint-access-parallelism compared to similar lock-free BST algorithms. We also proposed a conservative helping technique which adapts to read-write load on the implementation. We proved the correctness showing linearizability and lock-freedom of the proposed algorithm.

We plan to thoroughly evaluate our algorithm experimentally vis-a-vis existing concurrent set implementations.

Acknowledgments

This work is partially supported by the Swedish Research Council under grant number 37252706 as part of the project SCHEME (www.scheme-project.org).

6. REFERENCES

[1] Y. Afek, G. Stupp, and D. Touitou. Long lived adaptive splitter and applications. *Distributed Computing*, 15(2):67–86, 2002.

[2] H. Attiya and A. Fouren. Algorithms adapting to point contention. *Journal of the ACM*, 50(4):444–468, 2003.

[3] G. Barnes. A method for implementing lock-free shared-data structures. In *Proceedings of the 5th ACM SPAA*, pages 261–270, 1993.

[4] N. G. Bronson, J. Casper, H. Chafi, and K. Olukotun. A practical concurrent binary search tree. In *Proceedings of the 15th ACM PPoPP*, pages 257–268, 2010.

[5] T. Brown, F. Ellen, and E. Ruppert. A general technique for non-blocking trees. In *Proceedings of the 19th ACM PPoPP*, pages 329–342, 2014.

[6] B. Chatterjee, N. Nguyen, and P. Tsigas. Efficient lock-free binary search trees. Technical Report 2014:05, ISNN 1652-926X, Department of Computer Science and Engineering, Chalmers University of Technology, 2014.

[7] T. Crain, V. Gramoli, and M. Raynal. A speculation-friendly binary search tree. In *Proceedings of the 17th ACM PPoPP*, pages 161–170, 2012.

[8] D. Drachsler, M. Vechev, and E. Yahav. Practical concurrent binary search trees via logical ordering. In *Proceedings of the 19th ACM PPoPP*, pages 343–356, 2014.

[9] F. Ellen, P. Fatourou, J. Helga, and E. Rupert. The amortized complexity of non-blocking binary search trees. In *Proceedings of the 2013 ACM PODC*, 2014.

[10] F. Ellen, P. Fatourou, E. Ruppert, and F. van Breugel. Non-blocking binary search trees. In *Proceedings of the 29th ACM PODC*, pages 131–140, 2010.

[11] M. Fomitchev and E. Ruppert. Lock-free linked lists and skip lists. In *Proceedings of the 23rd ACM PODC*, pages 50–59, 2004.

[12] K. Fraser. *Practical lock-freedom*. PhD thesis, Cambridge University, Computer Laboratory, 2004.

[13] T. L. Harris. A pragmatic implementation of non-blocking linked-lists. In *Distributed Computing*, pages 300–314. Springer, 2001.

[14] M. P. Herlihy and J. M. Wing. Linearizability: A correctness condition for concurrent objects. *ACM Transactions on Programming Languages and Systems (TOPLAS)*, 12(3):463–492, 1990.

[15] S. V. Howley and J. Jones. A non-blocking internal binary search tree. In *Proceedinbgs of the 24th Annual ACM SPAA*, pages 161–171, 2012.

[16] A. Israeli and L. Rappoport. Disjoint-access-parallel implementations of strong shared memory primitives. In *Proceedings of the 13th ACM PODC*, pages 151–160, 1994.

[17] M. M. Michael. High performance dynamic lock-free hash tables and list-based sets. In *Proceedings of the 14th ACM SPAA*, pages 73–82, 2002.

[18] A. Natarajan and N. Mittal. Fast concurrent lock-free binary search trees. In *Proceedings of the 19th ACM PPoPP*, pages 317–328, 2014.

[19] R. Oshman and N. Shavit. The skiptrie: low-depth concurrent search without rebalancing. In *Proceedings of the 2013 ACM PODC*, pages 23–32, 2013.

[20] A. J. Perlis and C. Thornton. Symbol manipulation by threaded lists. *Communications of the ACM*, 3(4):195–204, 1960.

[21] H. Sundell and P. Tsigas. Fast and lock-free concurrent priority queues for multi-thread systems. *Journal of Parallel and Distributed Computing*, 65(5):609–627, 2005.

[22] H. Sundell and P. Tsigas. Lock-free and practical doubly linked list-based deques using single-word compare-and-swap. In *Principles of Distributed Systems*, pages 240–255. Springer, 2005.

[23] S. Timnat, A. Braginsky, A. Kogan, and E. Petrank. Wait-free linked-lists. In R. Baldoni, P. Flocchini, and R. Binoy, editors, *Principles of Distributed Systems*, volume 7702 of *LNCS*, pages 330–344. Springer Berlin Heidelberg, 2012.

The Amortized Complexity of Non-blocking Binary Search Trees

Faith Ellen
University of Toronto, Canada

Panagiota Fatourou
FORTH and University of Crete, Greece

Joanna Helga
Parahyangan Catholic University, Indonesia

Eric Ruppert
York University, Canada

ABSTRACT

We improve upon an existing non-blocking implementation of a binary search tree from single-word compare-and-swap instructions. We show that the worst-case amortized step complexity of performing a FIND, INSERT or DELETE operation op on the tree is $O(h(op) + \dot{c}(op))$ where $h(op)$ is the height of the tree at the beginning of op and $\dot{c}(op)$ is the maximum number of operations accessing the tree at any one time during op. This is the first bound on the complexity of a non-blocking implementation of a search tree.

Categories and Subject Descriptors

E.1 [**Data Structures**]: Trees; D.1.3 [**Programming Techniques**]: Concurrent Programming

Keywords

Binary search tree; amortized analysis; concurrent; asynchronous; non-blocking; lock-free; compare-and-swap

1. INTRODUCTION

Search trees are among the most fundamental data structures. Ellen et al. [7] described an implementation of a binary search tree (BST) from single-word compare-and-swap (CAS) instructions. They proved the implementation satisfies the non-blocking progress property, meaning that some operation is always guaranteed to complete if processes continue to take steps. However, they did not provide a bound on the complexity of their implementation. In the subsequent four years, there have been many novel non-blocking implementations of various types of search trees [3, 4, 5, 9, 11, 12, 14, 15]. Like [7], none have complexity analyses; instead, researchers have relied on experiments to evaluate and compare the performance of the search tree implementations. These experiments typically use microbenchmarks that measure the number of operations completed per second during runs where a collection of processes perform a sequence of FIND, INSERT and DELETE operations, in various ratios, using keys chosen randomly and uniformly. Although these experiments are valuable, they cannot provide information about the efficiency of the trees in applications where processes use the data structure intermittently (rather than continuously) or where the keys are not uniformly distributed.

We give the first analysis of the step complexity of a non-blocking implementation of a search tree. In a non-blocking implementation, an individual operation may run forever. Thus, we cannot bound the number of steps taken by an individual operation, but we can use an amortized analysis to establish an upper bound on the *average* number of steps taken per operation in an execution. We prove that the amortized complexity of performing a FIND, INSERT or DELETE operation op is $O(h(op) + \dot{c}(op))$ steps, where $h(op)$ is the height of the tree when op begins and $\dot{c}(op)$ is the *point contention* of op, i.e., the maximum number of operations accessing the tree at any one time during op. We prove the complexity bound for a modified version of the BST of Ellen et al. [7]. In Section 3, we show that the original implementation does not have the desired amortized complexity, so some small modifications were necessary. As in [7], we assume that a safe garbage collector (like the one provided by Java) is available to manage shared memory; our amortized analysis does not include the garbage collector's steps.

The amortized complexity bound is proved in two parts, one using the aggregate method and the other using the accounting method (or banker's view) [16]. The analysis is surprisingly intricate because, unlike previous applications of the accounting method in a sequential setting, we must cope with multiple concurrent operations. In particular, processes must help one another complete their operations in order to achieve the non-blocking progress property, and this complicates the amortized analysis. We believe that the techniques developed in our analysis could be useful for providing amortized analyses of many other non-blocking data structures.

2. RELATED WORK

In discussing related work, we focus on non-blocking data structures. (The non-blocking progress property is also sometimes called lock-freedom.) The non-blocking implementa-

PODC'14, July 15–18, 2014, Paris, France.

http://dx.doi.org/10.1145/2611462.2611486 .

tion of leaf-oriented BSTs by Ellen et al. [7] forms the basis of this work. It uses the cooperative technique that was originated by Turek, Shasha and Prakash [18] and Barnes [2]. Subsequently, this general approach was also used to implement k-ary search trees [5], node-oriented BSTs [9], and Patricia tries [14]. Recently, Brown, Ellen and Ruppert [4] generalized this approach by providing a template for implementing updates to any data structure based on a down-tree. They applied their template to obtain a non-blocking implementation of a chromatic tree, which is a version of a red-black tree with slightly weaker balance guarantees. Earlier, Tsay and Li [17] had given a template for wait-free implementations of down-trees, but it has very limited concurrency. A version of this technique was used to implement red-black trees [12]. Natarajan and Mittal [11] recently gave a different non-blocking implementation of leaf-oriented BSTs that is somewhat simpler than that of Ellen et al. Non-blocking implementations of a version of B-trees [15] and B+trees [3] have also appeared. None of these non-blocking search trees have been analyzed to provide bounds on their amortized step complexity.

Amortized analysis has been used to give upper bounds on the step complexity of a few other non-blocking data structures. Anderson and Woll gave an analysis of their union-find data structure [1]. Fomitchev and Ruppert [8] showed that their sorted singly-linked list, which supports insertions, deletions and searches, has amortized complexity of $O(n + \dot{c})$ steps per operation, where n is the length of the list. Their analysis has some similarities with the analysis presented here, but the more complex structure of BSTs involves some additional challenges. Moreover, their bound is proved using an ad hoc aggregate analysis, whereas here we use the accounting method. Oshman and Shavit [13] defined a data structure that combines a skiplist with a trie and uses randomization to implement an ordered subset of a finite universe U. It supports insertions, deletions, searches and predecessor queries. They gave a high-level outline of how to prove the expected amortized step complexity is $O(\log\log|U| + c_{OI})$ per operation, where the *overlapping interval contention* c_{OI} for an operation op is defined as the maximum number of operations overlapping any operation op' that itself overlaps with op. (Unlike point contention $\dot{c}$, the quantity c_{OI} can be arbitrarily large even when there is a fixed number of processes in the system.)

Valois's non-blocking singly-linked list [19] introduced the idea of storing a *backlink* pointer in a node before it is deleted. This allowed other concurrent operations with pointers to the deleted node to recover by tracing backlinks to return to a nearby undeleted node instead of having to return all the way to the beginning of the list. Fomitchev and Ruppert [8] refined this idea to produce a singly-linked list with good amortized complexity. In these proceedings, Chatterjee, Nguyen and Tsigas use a similar approach in their implementation of a threaded node-oriented BST [6], which they claim is linearizable and achieves the same complexity as our BST. In their implementation, each node stores additional pointers that can be followed to return to an active part of the tree from a deleted node. Maintaining consistency among the additional pointers is challenging. In this paper, we use a different, simpler approach of storing the search path locally so that an operation can easily backtrack to an undeleted node.

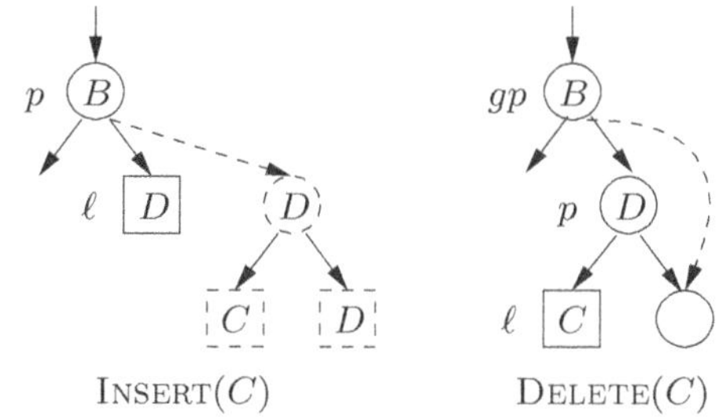

Figure 1: Updates to a leaf-oriented BST.

3. THE PREVIOUS IMPLEMENTATION

We first describe the non-blocking BST implementation of Ellen et al., and show it has poor amortized complexity.

In a leaf-oriented BST implementation, keys in the set being represented are stored in the leaves of the tree. Each internal node has exactly two children. The keys stored in internal nodes may or may not be in the set; they are simply used for directing searches to the appropriate leaf. The BST property requires that for each node x, keys in the subtree rooted at the left (right) child of x have keys that are strictly less than (greater than *or equal to*, respectively) x's key. Each operation with input key k begins by following the search path for the key k from the root until reaching a leaf ℓ. The modifications performed by update operations are illustrated in Figure 1. The new value of the child pointer is shown as a dashed arrow and newly created nodes are also dashed. Internal nodes are circles and leaves are squares. A key k can be inserted by changing a child pointer in ℓ's parent p from ℓ to a new internal node whose two children are a new copy of ℓ and a leaf containing the new key k. A leaf ℓ is deleted by changing a child pointer of the leaf's grandparent gp from ℓ's parent p to ℓ's sibling.

Even though each update operation can be achieved by changing a single child pointer, some coordination between operations is required to avoid problems that could arise, for example, if one operation changed the child pointer of a node while another concurrent deletion removed that node from the tree. To ensure that updates to the tree are performed atomically in the non-blocking implementation of Ellen et al., updates use CAS steps to temporarily *flag* nodes whose child pointers they want to change and to permanently *mark* internal nodes they want to remove from the tree. (A node cannot be simultaneously marked and flagged. A node that is neither marked nor flagged is said to be *clean*.) If an INSERT(k) finds the key k is already in leaf ℓ, it returns FALSE and terminates, since duplicate keys are not permitted. Otherwise, it attempts to temporarily flag the parent p of ℓ. If a DELETE(k) finds k in ℓ, it attempts to temporarily flag the grandparent gp and mark the parent p of ℓ. After these (*flag* and *mark*) CAS steps are successfully performed, the update operation applies the modification by performing a *child* CAS on a single child pointer of the node it flagged, and then removes that flag (by executing an *unflag* CAS) and terminates. If it fails to flag or mark a node (because some other operation has modified the node concurrently), the update restarts from scratch. (If a DELETE operation succeeds in flagging gp but then fails to mark p, it removes the flag from *gp* by executing a *back-off* CAS before restarting.)

When a node is successfully flagged, the flag is analogous to a lock: it guarantees that no other operation can modify the node or remove it from the tree until the flag is removed. Unlike locks, however, the flag belongs to an operation rather than a process. The implementation uses *helping* to ensure non-blocking progress. Two bits are used two indicate whether a node is clean, flagged, or marked. They are stored together with a pointer to an operation descriptor, which is a record that includes enough information so that a process that encounters the node when it is flagged or marked can attempt to complete the described operation. Once the operation is complete, the flag can be removed.

A detailed discussion of the implementation's correctness is given in [7]. Here, we highlight a few points that will be useful when we modify the algorithm. The algorithm is designed so that no CAS step ever stores a value in a location that has previously been there. This implies that a CAS step on a location succeeds only if no change has occurred since the old value was read there. This ensures that at most one of the processes helping an operation to complete can perform each of that operation's CAS steps successfully. It is also used in conjunction with the flagging scheme to show that updates take effect atomically, and that the data structure is therefore always a BST.

FIND is done just as in a sequential BST: it ignores concurrent updates. It may even pass through parts of the tree that have been deleted. A *configuration* is a snapshot of the system at some time during an execution; it consists of the values of all shared and local variables (including processes' programme counters). Let T_C be the tree defined by the child pointers in configuration C and let $height(T_C)$ denote its height. The *search path* for key k in configuration C is the sequence of nodes that would be visited by a BST search for k in T_C. The correctness of this search relies on the following key lemmas, which are proved in [7].

LEMMA 1. *If a node x is on the search path for key k in some configuration C and is still in the tree in some later configuration C', then x is still on the search path for k in C'.*

LEMMA 2. *If, during an execution, a search for key k visits node x, then there was a configuration C during the search when x was on the search path for k.*

Lemma 1 is used to prove Lemma 2. Lemma 2 establishes that FINDS can be linearized in a way that is consistent with linearizing updates at the time they modify the tree.

As remarked above, an update operation that finds a concurrent update operating on the same part of the tree helps that update and then restarts. This is wasteful, and leads to executions where the amortized cost per operation is $\Omega(h \cdot \dot{c})$. For example, let T be a tree of height h which has a key k stored in a leaf at depth h. Suppose m processes concurrently try to delete k. One process p succeeds, and the other $m-1$ processes fail in their attempt and restart. Then, before the other processes begin their next attempt, p quickly performs a complete reinsertion of the key k at its old location. This process can be repeated an arbitrary number of times. Every time two operations are completed, processes take a total of $\Theta(h \cdot m)$ steps and the point contention at all times is at most m, so the worst-case amortized complexity per operation of the implementation of Ellen et al. is $\Omega(h \cdot \dot{c})$.

4. THE MODIFIED IMPLEMENTATION

We modify the implementation of Ellen et al. in the following three ways to obtain one with better amortized complexity. Firstly, when an update operation fails because of a concurrent update, instead of restarting a search from the root (which is costly), the update recovers by backtracking up the tree until it reaches an unmarked node and then resumes the search from there. An operation stores the nodes it visits on a stack in its local memory, and backtracks by popping elements off of the stack. Secondly, while backtracking, a process helps complete any operations that have marked the nodes it encounters. This guarantees that the marked nodes will be removed from the tree before the search is resumed so that it will not be necessary for an operation to traverse nodes while searching for a key and then backtrack through them multiple times. Thirdly, the original algorithm included recursive helping, which turns out to be unnecessary, so it is omitted here.

The journal version of [7] will contain pseudocode for the modified version of the algorithm, along with a complete proof of its correctness as well as all of the details of the amortized analysis. A draft is available at `http://ics.forth.gr/~faturu/BSTproof.pdf`. The remainder of this section explains why the modifications we have made to the algorithm of [7] do not significantly change the proof of correctness in the original paper. Section 5 provides a sketch of the amortized analysis.

In the original implementation of [7], if an attempt to perform an update fails, the next attempt begins its search from the root of the tree. Lemma 1 and 2 imply that any undeleted node visited by the first attempt would also be visited by the second attempt. Since nodes are marked before being deleted, any node that is visited by the first attempt and remains unmarked will eventually be visited by the second attempt. So, instead of starting the second attempt's search from the root, it suffices to backtrack to the lowest unmarked node visited by the first attempt's search and continue the search from there, since the second attempt's search would pass through that node in this case.

Unfortunately, adding backtracking is not sufficient to achieve the required amortized complexity: there are still executions with amortized complexity $\Omega(h + \dot{c}^2)$ per operation. So, we make the two other modifications to the implementation, which simply change the criteria for deciding when to help other operations. This does not affect the proof of linearizability, since all of those arguments are made without knowing how many helpers an operation may have. It does however, have a significant impact on the proof of non-blocking progress. However, the new bound on the amortized complexity of operations that we provide in this paper directly implies that the implementation is non-blocking. (See Corollary 10.)

The modified algorithms for INSERT and DELETE are outlined in Figure 2. We refer to each box as an *action*. The dashed boxes show how to perform helping at a node: actions 4, 15, 17, 19 and 21, which each help a node, perform the actions inside one of those dashed boxes, depending on whether the node is flagged for an INSERT, flagged for a DELETE, or marked for a DELETE. To avoid recursive helping, action 21 is performed only by the process that initiated the deletion. (In other words, that action is skipped by any process that is helping another process's operation.) All of

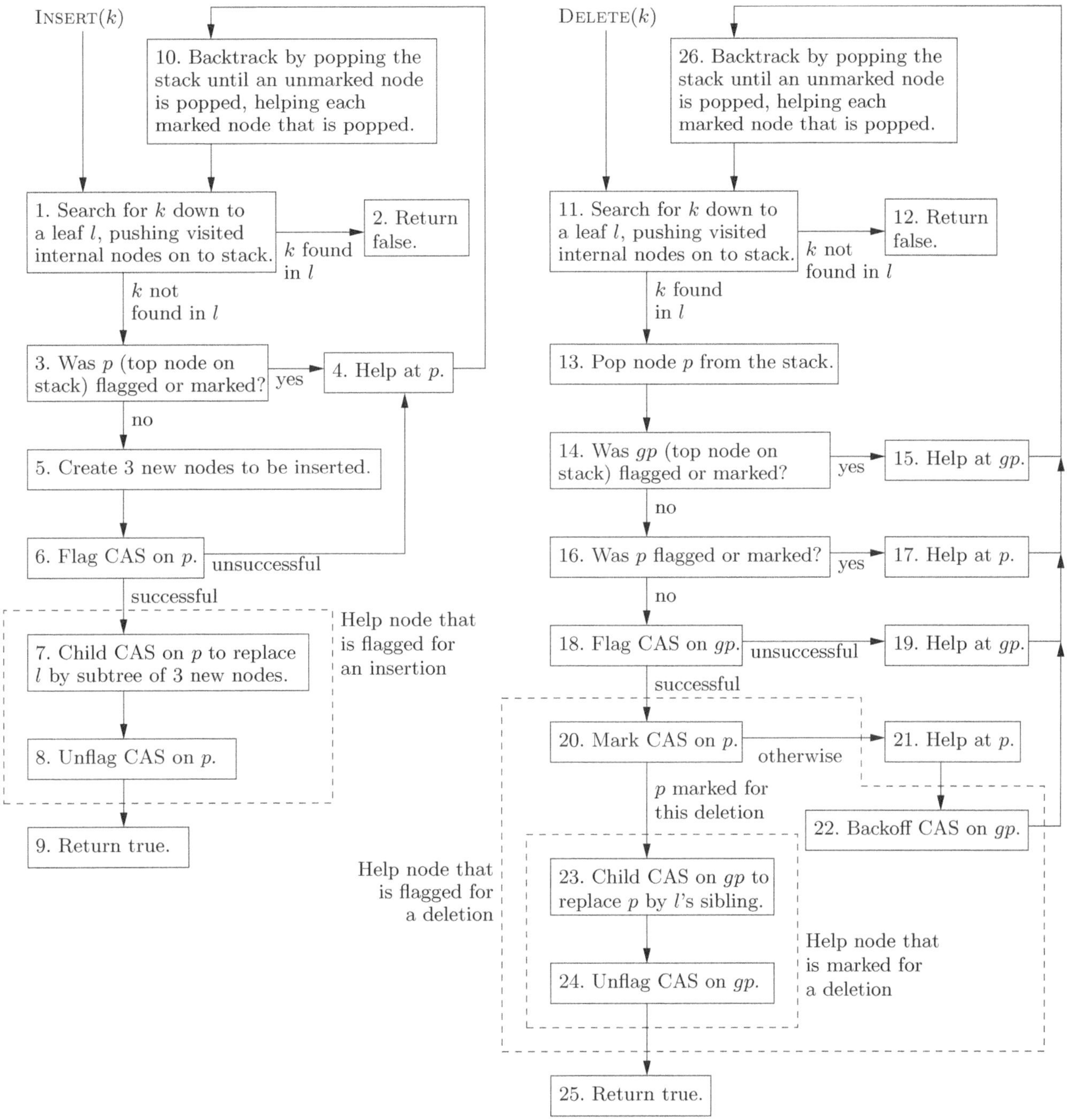

Figure 2: Flowcharts of INSERT and DELETE algorithms.

the information that is needed to carry out the actions inside one of these dashed boxes is stored inside the operation descriptor. A pointer to this descriptor is stored in a node when that node is flagged (action 6 or 18) or marked (action 20) so that helpers can access the information they require to help. When the node is unflagged (action 8 or 24) or when an attempt backs off (action 22) because it was unable to mark the node to be removed, the bits stored with the pointer to the operation are set to indicate that the node is clean and the pointer to the operation descriptor is inactive. A FIND still simply executes a BST search as it would in a sequential setting, ignoring all updates.

Among the information stored in the operation descriptors are the expected values to be used for all CAS steps performed by helpers. The expected values used for flag CAS and mark CAS steps are read from the nodes during the search actions (1 and 11) and stored along with the nodes on the stack. Moreover, these stored values are checked in actions 3, 14 and 16.

5. AMORTIZED ANALYSIS

Let α be any finite execution, starting from an initial configuration in which no operation is active and the BST is pre-loaded with an arbitrary set of keys. For each operation *op* that is performed during α, let $\dot{c}(op)$ be the maximum number of operations that are running at any one point in time during *op*'s execution interval and let $h(op)$ be the height of the BST when *op* is invoked. Our goal is to show that the amortized step complexity of *op* is $O(h(op)+\dot{c}(op))$, *i.e.*, that the total number of steps performed during α is $O(\sum_{op\in\alpha}(h(op)+\dot{c}(op)))$.

We divide each update operation into a sequence of *attempts*. A new attempt begins whenever the operation moves to action 10 or 26. The search actions (1 and 11) and the backtracking actions (10 and 26) each take time proportional to the number of nodes pushed onto the stack or popped from the stack, respectively. All other actions shown in Figure 2 can be performed in a constant number of steps. In particular, this depends on the fact that recursive helping is avoided by having helpers omit action 21. Moreover, each operation begins with an empty stack, and the number of pops from the stack (during action 10 or 26) is bounded by the number of nodes the operation has already pushed onto the stack. These observations imply the following lemma, which says we can bound the number of steps executed in α by counting the number of update attempts and the number of pushes onto stacks. For an update operation *op*, let $attempts(op)$ be the number of attempts *op* begins and let $pushes(op)$ be the number of nodes *op* pushes onto its stack. For a FIND operation *op*, we define $attempts(op)$ to be 1 and $pushes(op)$ to be the number of internal nodes it visits.

LEMMA 3. *The number of steps performed by an operation op is* $O(attempts(op) + pushes(op))$.

For the remainder of the analysis, we prove amortized bounds on $pushes(op)$ and $attempts(op)$.

5.1 Bounding the Number of Pushes

We use an aggregate analysis to obtain an amortized bound on $pushes(op)$.

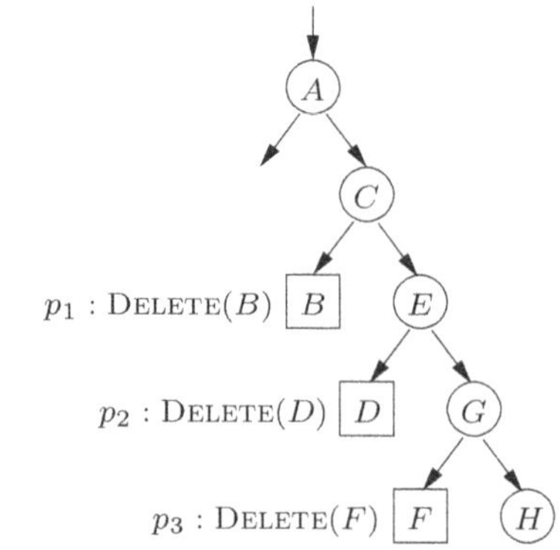

Figure 3: Example of a chain of deletion attempts.

LEMMA 4. *For any finite execution* α,

$$\sum_{op\in\alpha} pushes(op) \leq \sum_{op\in\alpha}(2\cdot attempts(op) + h(op) + \dot{c}(op)).$$

SKETCH OF PROOF. We divide the pushes into three categories, and prove a bound for each category.

Category 1: A push that is later popped by action 13 or the *last* pop inside action 10 or 26. By inspection of Figure 2, there are at most two such pops per attempt.

We prove each node is pushed onto the stack by an operation *op* at most once by a push that does not belong to Category 1. This argument uses the fact that *op* helps marked nodes as they are popped in action 10 or 26. This helping performs actions 23 and 24. Once *op* has performed action 23, the marked node is removed from the tree, ensuring that *op* will not push it back onto the stack by a later execution of action 1 or 11.

The pushes that do not belong to Category 1 are divided into the remaining two categories.

Category 2: A push by an operation *op* of a node that was reachable at all times during *op*. We prove that all of the nodes involved in these pushes were on a single path of the tree at the time *op* was invoked, so the number of such pushes is bounded by $h(op)$.

Category 3: A push by an operation *op* of a node x that was not reachable at some time during *op*. Then, the child CAS of the operation op' that inserted or deleted x must have occurred during *op*. Since the child CAS of op' inserts or deletes exactly one internal node x, and there is at most one category 3 push of x by each operation concurrent with the child CAS of op', it follows that there are at most $\dot{c}(op')$ pushes in Category 3 for each operation op'. □

5.2 Bounding the Number of Attempts: The Intuition

We use the accounting method to bound the amortized number of attempts per update operation. FINDS play no role in this analysis, since $attempts(op) = 1$ for each FIND operation *op* and FINDS cannot cause updates to perform any additional work. We first give some intuition for the analysis, before sketching the actual proof in Section 5.3.

Insertions only need to flag one node before performing their update. An attempt of an insertion succeeds if the CAS that flags that node succeeds and fails otherwise. In executions with no deletions, each failed attempt of an insertion can be charged to a concurrent successful insertion at the same location in the tree and it can be shown that each insertion causes $O(\dot{c})$ attempts of other insertions to fail, yielding the required bound.

When deletions are also considered, the situation becomes much more complex. This is because, unlike insertion attempts, a failed deletion attempt can be blocked by another deletion attempt that also fails. For example, consider the execution on the tree in Figure 3, where processes p_1, p_2 and p_3 attempt to delete keys B, D and F, respectively. Suppose p_1 and p_2 successfully flag the nodes A and C, respectively. Then, p_1's attempt fails because it cannot mark node C, which is already flagged by p_2. Next, p_3 successfully flags node E, causing p_2's attempt to fail. Finally, p_3's attempt succeeds. These chains of failed deletion attempts can be arbitrarily long, with only one attempt succeeding at the bottom of the chain. Note that this successful attempt might even start after all of the failed attempts have completed, except for the failed attempt immediately above it.

These chains make it difficult to charge for each failed attempt in such a way that each operation is only charged for $O(\dot{c})$ failed attempts. One approach is to charge only successful attempts for failed attempts, but with long chains of deletions, the successful attempt at the bottom of the chain that is ultimately responsible for all the failed attempts might not even be concurrent with some of the failed attempts. (This is because it was necessary to remove recursive helping from the implementation to achieve the desired amortized complexity.) The alternative approach of allowing some failed attempts to be charged is also problematic: a single operation can have arbitrarily many failed attempts. Thus, both approaches make it difficult to bound the amount charged to an operation by $\dot{c}$. The charging scheme is further complicated by the fact that the structure of the tree can change significantly between two attempts of the same operation. Consequently, the charging scheme that we had to devise to perform the amortized analysis is quite intricate.

Each operation *op* maintains three bank accounts which we call $D(op)$, $E_f(op)$ and $E_m(op)$. The amounts of money in these accounts in configuration C are denoted by $D(op, C)$, $E_f(op, C)$ and $E_m(op, C)$, respectively. Each operation adds money to its own bank accounts and the bank accounts of other operations when it makes some tangible progress. The amounts injected are chosen so that the total amount of money injected into the system by an operation *op* is $O(h(op) + \dot{c}(op))$. Each failed attempt performed by an operation will remove one dollar from one of its three bank accounts. We prove that bank account balances are always non-negative, so that the total number of failed attempts in the execution is bounded by the amount of money that has been injected, and it follows that the amortized number of attempts per operation is $O(h + \dot{c})$.

The idea behind the E_f and E_m accounts are fairly simple. Whenever an operation successfully performs a CAS on the child field of a node, it injects $O(1)$ dollars into each pending operation's E_f account and E_m account (a total contribution of $O(\dot{c})$ dollars). This means that we can use a dollar taken from these accounts to pay for any attempt that fails when the tree has changed "lately". This simplifies the analysis of the D accounts because we can assume that all the child pointers are static whenever we need to withdraw a dollar from a D account.

Consider any configuration C during the execution α. Define $target_f(op, C)$ to be the node that the operation *op* would try to flag if it were run by itself, starting from configuration C. (This is the last or second-last node on the search path for the key of *op*, depending on whether *op* is an INSERT or DELETE.) Similarly, if *op* is a DELETE, let $target_m(op, C)$ be the node that it would try to mark.

For any node x, let $depth(x)$ be the depth of node x, let $npa(x)$ be the set of all internal nodes in the tree that are not proper ancestors of x, and let $flag(x)$ be an indicator variable that is 1 if x is flagged and 0 otherwise. We also define an auxiliary variable for each node x called $pflag(x)$. It is initially 0, and is set to 1 if a successful flag CAS is performed on a child of x **and** x is the node that some operation would like to flag during its current attempt. This variable is reset to 0 when a successful backoff CAS is performed on x or when there is no longer any attempt that wishes to flag x. (The intuition is that $pflag(x)$ is 1 whenever a current attempt of a DELETE operation might have to perform a backoff CAS on x.) We denote the value of an auxiliary variable $v(x)$ for node x in configuration C by $v(x, C)$.

Let $\dot{c}(C)$ be the number of operations running in configuration C and let

$$\begin{aligned} F(x, C) &= \sum_{y \in npa(x,C)} [pflag(y, C) - flag(y, C)] \\ &\quad + \dot{c}(C) + height(T_C) - depth(x, C). \end{aligned}$$

The terms $\dot{c}(C)$ and $height(T_C)$ are included only to ensure that the value of F is positive.

We shall show that $F(target_f(op, C), C)$ is a lower bound on $D(op, C)$, when *op* is an INSERT and $F(target_f(op, C), C)+ F(target_m(op, C), C)$ is a lower bound when *op* is a DELETE. The main part of F is the sum, which does much of the work in accounting for failed deletion attempts. Consider such a failed attempt of a deletion *op* that manages to successfully flag a node *gp* (action 18), but then fails its mark CAS in action 20. (We may assume that the structure of the tree has not changed, since that situation is taken care of using a dollar from the E_f account.) The successful flag CAS increases $flag(gp)$ from 0 to 1 and therefore decreases the value of F at *gp* by 1. This decreases our lower bound on D for all operations that are targeting node *gp* for flagging or marking, including *op*. When the mark CAS of *op* on node p fails in action 20, it means that p has been flagged or marked by some other operation op' since *op* saw that p was clean at action 16. We prove that p could not have been marked by op', since this would require *gp* to have been flagged by op' and *gp* cannot be flagged by two different operations simultaneously. (This is one example of how we use the fact that the tree structure is static if we need to draw money from $D(op)$, rather than from $E_f(op)$ or $E_m(op)$.) Thus, the flag CAS by op' on p would have set $pflag(gp)$ to 1. Then, when *op*'s flag is later removed by a backoff CAS (action 22), both $pflag(gp)$ and $flag(gp)$ decrease from 1 to 0, so F's value at *gp* does not change. Hence, the net change to our lower bound on the account $D(op)$ during this attempt is a decrease of 1 caused by the successful flagging of *gp*. This allows us to remove one dollar from the account $D(op)$ to pay for this attempt without invalidating our lower bound.

So far, we have discussed attempts that successfully flag a node before aborting. Attempts that abort because a node is already flagged or marked when it is visited during the search (i.e., when the test in action 3, 14 or 16 is TRUE) or when the flag CAS in action 6 or 18 is unsuccessful are handled in a similar, but slightly different way. The main difference is that the CAS that wrote the value that blocks the attempt may have occurred before the attempt began. When that CAS occurs, we essentially set aside one dollar in the bank account of each concurrent operation to pay for an aborted attempt of that operation later.

To formalize this mechanism, we define one more auxiliary variable for each active update operation *op*. The boolean variable $lose_f(op)$ is 0 when *op* is invoked. It is set to 1 when there is a successful mark or flag CAS on *op*'s $target_f$ node that belongs to a different operation. It is set to 0 when *op* either reads (during action 1 or 11) a flagged or marked value in the node it must flag *or* performs an unsuccessful flag CAS(action 6 or 18). Similarly, we define an additional boolean auxiliary variable, $lose_m(op)$, for each active DELETE operation *op*. It is 0 when *op* is invoked and is set to 1 when there is a successful mark or flag CAS on *op*'s $target_m$ node that belongs to a different operation. It is set to 0 when *op* reads an unclean value in the last node visited during action 11 *after* reading a clean value in the second-last node visited. Intuitively, these are temporary holding locations for the dollar that has to be spent when an attempt loses because another operation flagged or marked a node it wants to flag or mark.

For each INSERT operation *op* that is active in configuration C, let

$$G(op, C) = F(target_f(op, C)) + lose_f(op, C)$$

and for each DELETE operation *op* that is active in configuration C, let

$$\begin{aligned} G(op, C) \quad &= \quad F(target_f(op, C)) + F(target_m(op, C)) \\ &\quad + lose_f(op, C) + lose_m(op, C). \end{aligned}$$

If *op* is inactive in C, we define $G(op, C) = 0$. We prove the credit invariant $D(op, C) \geq G(op, C)$.

5.3 Bounding the Number of Attempts: The Proof

Now we are ready to sketch the proof of the amortized complexity bound. The following two lemmas follow immediately from the definition of F and the fact that, in any configuration C, each update operation in progress has one node that it has flagged or wants to flag.

LEMMA 5. *For each configuration C and each node x, $0 \leq F(x, C) \leq 2\dot{c}(C) + height(T_C)$.*

LEMMA 6. *If y is a child of x in T_C, then $F(y, C) \leq F(x, C) \leq F(y, C) + 2$.*

Operations' bank accounts are initialized and modified according to the following 10 rules:

R1 **Initially**, all bank accounts are 0.

R2 The **invocation** of an update operation *op* at a configuration C adds $4\dot{c}(C) + 2 \cdot height(T_C)$ dollars to its own D account, 2 dollars to its own E_f account, 2 dollars to its own E_m account, and 2 dollars to the D account of each other active update operation.

R3 A **successful flag** CAS **by an** INSERT (action 6) adds 1 dollar to the D account of each active update operation.

R4 A **successful flag** CAS **by a** DELETE **that is not in its last attempt** (action 18) deducts 1 dollar from the operation's E_f account if the E_f account contains at least 2 dollars or there is a successful child CAS during the attempt; otherwise, it deducts 1 dollar from the operation's D account.

R5 A **successful flag** CAS **by a** DELETE **that is in its last attempt** (action 18) adds 1 dollar to the D account of each active update operation.

R6 A **successful mark** CAS (action 20) adds 1 dollar to the D account of each active update operation.

R7 A **successful child** CAS (action 7 or 23) adds 8 dollars to the D account of each active operation and 2 dollars to the E_f account and 2 dollars to the E_m account of each active update operation.

R8 A **successful unflag** CAS (action 8 or 24) adds 2 dollars to the D account of each active update operation.

R9 When an update operation either performs an **unsuccessful flag** CAS (action 6 or 18) or **reads an unclean value that will later cause action 3 or 14 to abort the attempt**, it deducts 1 dollar from its E_f account if the E_f account contains at least 2 dollars or there is a successful child CAS during the attempt; otherwise, it deducts 1 dollar from the operation's D account.

R10 When a DELETE operation **reads a flagged or marked value that will later cause action 16 to abort the attempt**, it deducts 1 dollar from the operation's E_m account if the E_m account contains at least 2 dollars or there is a successful child CAS during the attempt; otherwise, it deducts 1 dollar from the operation's D account.

The following lemma is the most difficult and important part of the analysis. Due to space restrictions, we can only give a very high-level proof sketch here.

INVARIANT 7. *For each configuration C, and each update operation op,*

1. *$E_f(op, C) \geq 0$ and $E_m(op, C) \geq 0$, and*
2. *$D(op, C) \geq G(op, C)$.*

SKETCH OF PROOF. The only rules that deduct money from E_f or E_m accounts are R4, R9 and R10 and at most one of these is applied in each attempt. To prove the first invariant, it is easy to see that these rules cannot drain money from the accounts faster than it is replenished by child CAS steps applying R7.

To prove the second invariant, consider the invocation of an update operation *op* or any step that is performed to help complete *op* (either by *op* itself or one of *op*'s helpers). We show that, for each active update operation op', the step results in a change, $\Delta G(op')$, in the G value for op' that is less than or equal to the change, $\Delta D(op')$, in $D(op')$. We consider each possible kind of step.

For the **invocation** of *op*, Rule R2 allocates enough money to initialize $D(op)$, by Lemma 5 and the fact that $lose_f(op) = lose_m(op) = 0$. For $op' \neq op$, $\Delta G(op') \leq 2$ and $\Delta D(op') = 2$ by Rule R2.

Next, we consider a **successful flag** CAS, **if** *op* **is an** INSERT, **or the last successful flag** CAS, **if** *op* **is a** DELETE, **or a successful mark** CAS (action 6, 18 or 20). We first argue that this step cannot increase the value of $F(x)$ for any node x. A mark CAS does not affect any of the terms used to define $F(x)$. A successful flag CAS on a node y may increase the value of $pflag(z)$ for y's parent z

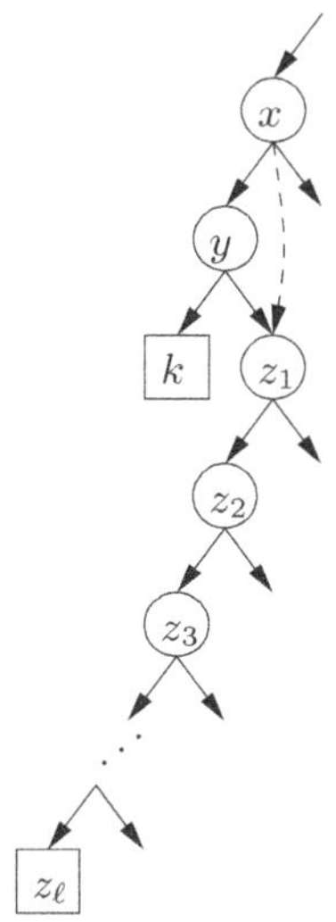

Figure 4: An example of a child CAS **that belongs to a** DELETE**.**

from 0 to 1, but if this term is included in the sum defining $F(x)$, then the sum also contains the term $-\mathit{flag}(y)$ which changes from 0 to -1, offsetting the change in $\mathit{pflag}(z)$. However, a successful flag or mark CAS step may increase one of $\mathit{lose}_f(op')$ or $\mathit{lose}_m(op')$ by 1. Thus, $\Delta G(op') \leq 1$ and $\Delta D(op') = 1$ by Rule R3, R5 or R6.

If *op* is an INSERT, a **successful child** CAS (action 7) can increase *height* by 1, and may add one term to the sum in the definition of F (for the newly inserted internal node). Thus, each node's F value can go up by at most 2. This step may also change each *target* of *op'* from one node to its child, but, by Lemma 6, this does not increase the contribution to $G(op')$. Thus $\Delta G(op') \leq 4$. $\Delta D(op') = 8$ by Rule R7.

If *op* is a DELETE, a **successful child** CAS (action 23) can change the *target* node of *op'* significantly. For example, if *op* deletes k in the tree shown in Figure 4, a *target* of *op'* can change from y to $z_{\ell-1}$ or from x to $z_{\ell-2}$. However, this change is offset in the computation of the F value for *target* by the increase in the depth of the target. (This is the reason the *depth* term is included in the definition of F.) It can be shown that the net change in the F value of each target is at most 4, so $\Delta G(op') \leq 8$. $\Delta D(op') = 8$ by Rule R7.

A **successful unflag** CAS (action 8 or 24) on node x decreases $\mathit{flag}(x)$ by 1, and this can increase each node's F value by 1. Hence, $\Delta G(op') \leq 2$ and $\Delta D(op') = 2$ by Rule R8.

A **successful flag** CAS on a node x (action 18) by a DELETE *op* that is **not in its last attempt** decreases the F value of x by 1 (since $\mathit{flag}(x)$ increases) and does not increase any other node's F value. If $op' \neq op$, one of $\mathit{lose}_f(op')$ or $\mathit{lose}_m(op')$ can increase from 0 to 1, but only if the corresponding *target* is x, so this increase is offset in the computation of $G(op')$ by the decrease in $F(x)$. Thus, $\Delta G(op') \leq 0$ and $\Delta D(op') = 0$ by Rule R4. It remains to show that $\Delta G(op) \leq \Delta D(op)$. If Rule R4 deducts one dollar from $E_f(op)$ then $\Delta D(op) = 0 \geq \Delta G(op)$. Otherwise, Rule R4 deducts one dollar from $\Delta D(op)$, because $E_f(op)$ was 0. In this case, there has been no successful child CAS during *op*'s current attempt, so $\mathit{target}_f(op)$ is still x. Therefore $\Delta G(op) = -1 = \Delta D(op)$.

A **successful backoff** CAS (action 22) on some node x decreases $\mathit{flag}(x)$ from 1 to 0. We prove, using a rather intricate argument that was sketched in Section 5.2, that $\mathit{pflag}(x)$ also decreases from 1 to 0. Hence, no F value is changed and $\Delta G(op') = 0 = \Delta D(op')$.

An **unsuccessful flag** CAS (action 6 or 18) by *op* or a **read** by *op* **of a flagged or marked value that later cause its current attempt to abort** does not increase any G value. Thus, for $op' \neq op$, $\Delta G(op') \leq 0 = \Delta D(op')$. It remains to prove $\Delta G(op) \leq \Delta D(op)$. If Rule R9 deducts a dollar from $E_f(op)$, or Rule R10 deducts a dollar from $E_m(op)$, then the invariant is satisfied. Otherwise, Rule R9 or Rule R10 deducts a dollar from $D(op)$. In this case, there has been no successful child CAS during *op*'s current and previous attempt, so $\mathit{target}_f(op)$ is still x. It follows that $\mathit{lose}_f(op)$ or $\mathit{lose}_m(op)$ decreases from 1 to 0, so $\Delta G(op) \leq -1 = \Delta D(op)$. □

LEMMA 8. *In any finite execution* α,
$\sum_{op\in\alpha} \mathit{attempts}(op) \leq \sum_{op\in\alpha} (22 \cdot \dot{c}(op) + 2 \cdot h(op) + 5)$.

SKETCH OF PROOF. Each operation has at most one successful attempt. Rules R4, R9 and R10 each deduct one dollar from the operation's bank accounts, and these cover all possible ways that an attempt can fail, so this ensures that all failed attempts are paid for from the operation's bank accounts. Invariant 7 ensures that all balances remain positive, so the number of failed attempts is bounded by the number of dollars injected into the system, since all account balances are initially 0.

The total number of dollars that can be injected into the system by an update operation *op* is $O(h(op) + \dot{c}(op))$: An INSERT (and its helpers) can apply each of Rules R2, R3, R7, R8 at most once for a total contribution of at most $21 \cdot \dot{c}(op) + 2 \cdot h(op) + 4$ dollars. A DELETE (and its helpers) can apply each of Rules R2, R5, R6, R7 and R8 once for a total contribution of at most $22 \cdot \dot{c}(op) + 2 \cdot h(op) + 4$ dollars. □

5.4 Summing Up

It follows immediately from Lemmas 3, 4 and 8 that the amortized step complexity of each operation *op* is $O(\dot{c}(op) + h(op))$.

THEOREM 9. *In any finite execution* α, *processes perform at most* $O(\sum_{op\in\alpha} (\dot{c}(op) + h(op)))$ *steps in total.*

COROLLARY 10. *The BST implementation is non-blocking.*

PROOF. To derive a contradiction, assume that there is some execution α where processes take infinitely many steps, but complete only finitely many operations. Then, since $\sum_{op\in\alpha} (\dot{c}(op) + h(op))$ is finite, Theorem 9 provides a finite upper bound B on the number of steps in any finite prefix of α. The prefix of α of length $B+1$ contradicts Theorem 9. □

6. DIRECTIONS FOR FUTURE WORK

This paper provides a good upper bound on the amortized complexity of non-blocking search trees. The bound is expressed in terms of h, the height of the tree, rather than n, the number of elements stored in it. For many applications, h will be small compared to n. Indeed, there are many results showing that the expected height of search trees built by sequential updates is $O(\log n)$ [10]. It is an interesting open question to extend these results to trees built by *concurrent* updates using random keys. Since the trees considered here are not necessarily balanced, h could be as large as $\Theta(n)$ in the worst case. Thus, the (extremely pessimistic) worst-case amortized bound on implementing the set abstract data type provided by this work is $O(n + \dot{c})$, which only matches the known bound for a sorted linked list implementation of a set [8]. Brown, Ellen and Ruppert [4] extended the approach of [7] to implement BSTs whose height is guaranteed to be $O(\log n + \dot{c})$. It would be interesting to see if the analysis here could likewise be extended to that more complex data structure to prove that the amortized complexity of a non-blocking set implementation is $O(\log n + \dot{c})$.

The recent alternative implementation of BSTs by Natarajan and Mittal [11] also provides an interesting opportunity for amortized analysis. However, unlike the approach used here, it is not clear whether their technique could be extended to balanced trees.

In this work, we have assumed an unlimited supply of memory. Can the amortized analysis be extended to include garbage collection?

Finally, lower bounds for non-blocking sets have not been studied. For example, is it possible to show that the $\dot{c}$ term in the amortized complexity is necessary for space-efficient representations of sets? (It is not necessary if the space can be proportional to the size of the universe from which keys are drawn. In this case, a simple bit vector allows each INSERT and DELETE to be performed by a single CAS step.)

Acknowledgements.

This research was supported by the Natural Sciences and Engineering Research Council of Canada, by the European Commission under the 7th Framework Program through the TransForm (FP7-MC-ITN-238639) project and by the ARISTEIA Action of the Operational Programme Education and Lifelong Learning which is co-funded by the European Social Fund (ESF) and National Resources through the GreenVM project. Part of this research was conducted while Eric Ruppert was working at FORTH ICS as a visiting scientist of TransForm.

7. REFERENCES

[1] Richard J. Anderson and Heather Woll. Wait-free parallel algorithms for the union-find problem. In *Proc. 23rd Annual ACM Symposium on Theory of Computing*, pages 370–380, 1991.

[2] Greg Barnes. A method for implementing lock-free data structures. In *Proc. 5th Annual ACM Symposium on Parallel Algorithms and Architectures*, pages 261–270, 1993.

[3] Anastasia Braginsky and Erez Petrank. A lock-free B+tree. In *Proc. 24th Annual ACM Symposium on Parallelism in Algorithms and Architectures*, pages 58–67, 2012.

[4] Trevor Brown, Faith Ellen, and Eric Ruppert. A general technique for non-blocking trees. In *Proc. 19th Annual ACM Symposium on Principles and Practice of Parallel Programming*, pages 329–342, 2014.

[5] Trevor Brown and Joanna Helga. Non-blocking k-ary search trees. In *Proc. 15th International Conference on Principles of Distributed Systems*, volume 7109 of *LNCS*, pages 207–221, 2011.

[6] Bapi Chatterjee, Nhan Nguyen, and Philippas Tsigas. Efficient lock-free binary search trees. In *Proc. 33rd Annual ACM Symposium on Principles of Distributed Computing*, 2014.

[7] Faith Ellen, Panagiota Fatourou, Eric Ruppert, and Franck van Breugel. Non-blocking binary search trees. In *Proc. 29th Annual ACM Symposium on Principles of Distributed Computing*, pages 131–140, 2010.

[8] Mikhail Fomitchev and Eric Ruppert. Lock-free linked lists and skip lists. In *Proc. 23rd Annual ACM Symposium on Principles of Distributed Computing*, pages 50–59, 2004.

[9] Shane V. Howley and Jeremy Jones. A non-blocking internal binary search tree. In *Proc. 24th Annual ACM Symposium on Parallelism in Algorithms and Architectures*, pages 161–171, 2012.

[10] Hosam H. Mahmoud. *Evolution of random search trees.* Wiley-Interscience, 1992.

[11] Aravind Natarajan and Neeraj Mittal. Fast concurrent lock-free binary search trees. In *Proc. 19th Annual ACM Symposium on Principles and Practice of Parallel Programming*, pages 317–328, 2014.

[12] Aravind Natarajan, Lee Savoie, and Neeraj Mittal. Concurrent wait-free red black trees. In *Proc. 15th International Symposium on Stabilization, Safety and Security of Distributed Systems*, volume 8255 of *LNCS*, pages 45–60, 2013.

[13] Rotem Oshman and Nir Shavit. The SkipTrie: Low-depth concurrent search without rebalancing. In *Proc. 32nd Annual ACM Symposium on Principles of Distributed Computing*, pages 23–32, 2013.

[14] Niloufar Shafiei. Non-blocking Patricia tries with replace operations. In *Proc. 33rd International Conference on Distributed Computing Systems*, pages 216–225, 2013.

[15] Michael Spiegel and Paul F. Reynolds, Jr. Lock-free multiway search trees. In *Proc. 39th International Conference on Parallel Processing*, pages 604–613, 2010.

[16] Robert Endre Tarjan. Amortized computational complexity. *SIAM Journal on Algebraic and Discrete Methods*, 6(2):306–318, April 1985.

[17] Jyh-Jong Tsay and H.-C. Li. Lock-free concurrent tree structures for multiprocessor systems. In *Proc. International Conference on Parallel and Distributed Systems*, pages 544–549, 1994.

[18] John Turek, Dennis Shasha, and Sundeep Prakash. Locking without blocking: Making lock based concurrent data structure algorithms nonblocking. In *Proc. 11th Annual ACM Symposium on Principles of Database Systems*, pages 212–222, 1992.

[19] John D. Valois. Lock-free linked lists using compare-and-swap. In *Proc. 14th ACM Symposium on Principles of Distributed Computing*, pages 214–222, 1995.

Brief Announcement: Gracefully Degrading Consensus and k-Set Agreement under Dynamic Link Failures

[Extended Abstract] *

Manfred Schwarz
ECS, TU Wien
Vienna, Austria
mschwarz@ecs.tuwien.ac.at

Kyrill Winkler
ECS, TU Wien
Vienna, Austria
kwinkler@ecs.tuwien.ac.at

Ulrich Schmid
ECS, TU Wien
Vienna, Austria
s@ecs.tuwien.ac.at

Martin Biely
EPFL
Lausanne, Switzerland
biely@ecs.tuwien.ac.at

Peter Robinson
National University of Singapore
robinson@comp.nus.edu.sg

ABSTRACT

We present a k-set agreement algorithm for synchronous dynamic distributed systems with unidirectional links controlled by an omniscient adversary. Our algorithm automatically adapts to the actual network properties: If the network is sufficiently well-connected, it solves consensus, while degrading gracefully to general k-set agreement in less well-behaved runs. The algorithm is oblivious to the maximum number of system-wide decision values k, which is bounded by the number of certain strongly connected components occurring in the dynamically changing network in a run. Related impossibility results reveal that this bound is close to the solvability border for k-set agreement. To the best of our knowledge, this is the first consensus algorithm that degrades in a graceful way in a dynamic network.

Categories and Subject Descriptors

C.2.1 [**Computer-Communication Networks**]: Network architecture and design—*network topology*;
F.2.m [**Analysis of Algorithms and Problem Complexity**]: Miscellanous

Keywords

Distributed algorithms; dynamic networks; k-set agreement; gracefully degrading consensus

*This work, a full version of which is available under [7], has been supported by the Austrian Science Fund (FWF) projects PSRTS (P20529) and RiSE (S11405), and the grant Fault-tolerant Communication Complexity in Wireless Networks from the Singapore MoE AcRF-2.

PODC'14, July 15–18, 2014, Paris, France.
ACM 978-1-4503-2944-6/14/07.
http://dx.doi.org/10.1145/2611462.2611506.

1. INTRODUCTION

In sharp contrast to conventional wireline networks, communication in *wireless dynamic networks* like sensor networks and mobile ad-hoc networks is adequately modeled only by time-varying directional links: Fading and interference phenomena such as capture effects and near-far problems are *local* effects, which affect the receiver but not the sender node of a particular message. Mobility and duty-cycling for energy saving purposes are additional causes for irregular communication patterns in dynamic networks. The simple synchronous system model of [2] also employed in this paper hence assumes *directed* communication graphs, where incoming and outgoing links of the processes can appear and disappear arbitrarily from round to round.

A natural approach to build robust services despite the dynamic nature of such systems is to use consensus to agree system-wide on (fundamental) parameters like schedules, frequencies, etc. Clearly, such solutions rest on the ability to (efficiently) reach consensus in dynamic systems. Unfortunately, solving consensus requires well-connected communication graphs: In [2], we provided a consensus algorithm that works under the assumption that, in every round, the communication graph is both (i) weakly connected and (ii) contains a single *root component*, i.e., a *strongly connected component* (SCC) without incoming links. The latter must eventually become *vertex stable*, in the sense that its processes remain the same (with possibly changing interconnection topology) for a certain number of rounds; such a SCC is called a *vertex-stable root component* (VSRC). Since these assumptions do not guarantee bidirectional reachability system-wide, the model in [2] falls between the weakest and second weakest class of models defined in [4]. Related impossibility results reveal that there is no hope for successfully weakening this model further.

However, in larger-scale dynamic networks, it is unrealistic to assume that the above properties can always be guaranteed. In this paper, we therefore provide a consensus algorithm that gracefully degrades to k-set agreement, for some k determined by the actual network properties, in case of less favorable conditions. Recall that, in the k-set agreement problem, processes may decide on one of at most k different values system-wide; 1-set agreement is equivalent to consensus. In sharp contrast to classic k-set agreement algorithms, our algorithm is k-*uniform*, i.e., the parameter k does not appear in its code. Rather, the number of system-wide decision values is bounded by the number k of (certain) vertex-stable root components occurring in the particular run. Thus, if the network partitions into k SCCs, for example, each partition would obtain its decision value (independently from other partitions). Whereas, if the network is particularly well-connected, the algorithm will guarantee a unique decision value.

Since our network properties have been defined so as to just circumvent certain impossibility results, they are reasonably close to the solvability border for k-set agreement. They can also be expected to have good coverage in real dynamic systems, even for small values of k, and make our algorithm indeed *gracefully* degrading, in the sense that it solves k-set agreement for some k reasonably close to the smallest value possible in a given network communication scenario.

2. MODEL

The *k-set agreement problem* [6] is defined as follows: Each process p_i starts with an initial value x_i taken from some set $\mathcal{V}$, where $|\mathcal{V}| > k$, and must irrevocably decide on some y_i, such that the following properties hold in all runs:

- At most k different decision values are obtained system-wide in any run.
- If $y_i = v$ then v is some p_j's initial value x_j.
- Eventually, every process p_i assigns a value to y_i.

Consensus is the special case of 1-set agreement. We call a k-set agreement algorithm k-*uniform*, if it does not require knowledge of k.

For our computing model, we use the same synchronous dynamic network model from [2, 3], which assumes a set $\Pi = \{p_1, \dots, p_n\}$ of processes that know their own id i but not necessarily n. Processes execute an infinite number of rounds $r = 1, 2, \dots$ (conceptually) in lock-step. In every round r, processes first broadcast a round r message of arbitrary content and then perform some deterministic local computation, based on the received round r messages and their current (local) state. The actual communication in the system is determined by the sequence of communication graphs $\mathcal{G}^r$, $r > 0$, fixed by the adversary. $\mathcal{G}^r$ contains a directed edge $(p \to q)$ from process p to q iff q receives p's round r broadcast in round r. Note that it also allows modeling of send and/or receive omission process failures (and thereby also crash failures) [5].

Since $\mathcal{G}^r$ can range arbitrarily from n isolated nodes to a fully connected graph, there is no hope to solve k-set agreement without restricting the adversary to some extent. We will provide two fairly weak conditions (Assumption 2 and Assumption 3), the conjunction of which is sufficient for this purpose. They rely on the pivotal concept of root components [2], which are SCCs in $\mathcal{G}^r$ without incoming edges from other components. By contracting the SCCs, it is easy to see that every weakly connected directed simple graph $\mathcal{G}$ has at least one root component. We require root components to be vertex-stable, i.e., their vertex sets must remain the same, albeit the edges between these vertices can change.

We say that a process p *causally influences* q *in round* r, denoted by $(p \overset{r}{\rightsquigarrow} q)$, iff either (i) q has an incoming edge $(p \to q)$ from p in $\mathcal{G}^r$, or (ii) if $q = p$. There exists a (causal) chain of length $k \geqslant 1$ starting from p in round r to q, denoted by $(p \overset{r[k]}{\rightsquigarrow} q)$, if there exists a sequence of not necessarily distinct processes $p = p_0, \dots, p_k = q$ such that $\forall 0 \leqslant i < k : p_i \overset{r+i}{\rightsquigarrow} p_{i+1}$. The *causal distance* $cd^r(p,q)$ at round r from process p to process q is the length of the shortest causal chain starting in p in round r and ending in q, formally, $cd^r(p,q) := min\{k|(p \overset{r[k]}{\rightsquigarrow} q)\}$.

Definition 1 (D-bounded I-vertex-stable root). *An I-vertex-stable root component R^I with $I = [r, s]$ is* D-bounded *if there exists some $D \leqslant s - r + 1$ such that for all but the last $D - 1$ rounds of I it is guaranteed that messages sent by any process in R reach all members of R within I, i.e., $\forall x \in [r, s - D + 1]$: $\max_{p,q \in R}\{cd^x(p,q)\} \leqslant D$.*

Note that we will sometimes write $|I|$-VSRC to denote an I-vertex-stable root component if only the length of I is important. In order to solve k-set agreement, we also need to guarantee information propagation from root components to the rest of the network. Since a process q outside any root component may be reachable from multiple root components, via different directed paths, our definitions will rely on a set S^I of $\ell \geqslant 1$ simultaneous I-vertex-stable root components $R_1^I, \dots, R_\ell^I$, all vertex-stable in the same interval $I = [r, s]$.

The round x *network causal height* h^x is the maximum, taken over all processes $q \in \Pi$, of the minimal causal distance $cd^x(p,q)$ from some process $p \in \bigcup_{i=1}^{\ell} R_i$ in round x. Formally, $h^x := \max_{q \in \Pi}\{\min_{p \in \bigcup_{i=1}^{\ell} R_i}\{cd^x(p,q)\}\}$.

Definition 2 (H-network-bounded roots). *A set S^I of $\ell \geqslant 1$ I-vertex-stable root components $R_1^I, \dots, R_\ell^I$ for some interval $I = [r, s]$ with $|I| \geqslant H$, where $H > 0$ is some integer, is H-network-bounded, if $\forall x \in [r, s - H + 1] : h^x \leqslant H$.*

Definition 2 will be used in the sequel to ensure that every process in the network receives a message from some member of at least one VSRC in $S^I = \{R_1^I, \dots, R_\ell^I\}$ within H rounds.

3. RESULTS

We now briefly summarize our main impossibility and possibility results from the full version of our paper [7]. A necessary assumption for the solvability of k-set agreement is Assumption 1.

Assumption 1. *$\forall r > 0$, $\mathcal{G}^r$ contains at most k root components.*

Yet, it turned out that under this assumption the generic impossibility theorem from [1] is applicable, resulting in the following impossibility Theorem 1.

Theorem 1. *There exists no algorithm that solves k-set agreement with $n > k + 1$ processes under Assumption 1, for any $1 \leqslant k < n$, even if there are $k - 1$ root components $R_1, \dots, R_{k-1}$ that are vertex-stable forever, and one root component R_k is vertex-stable for not more than $n-k-1$ rounds.*

Furthermore, and perhaps surprisingly, it turned out that k-set agreement remains impossible even under the assumption of eventually stable communication graphs, as revealed by Theorem 2.

THEOREM 2. *Suppose that in every run there is a stabilization round r_{GST} such that, for all $r \geqslant r_{\text{GST}}$, it holds that $\mathcal{G}^r = \mathcal{G}^{r+1}$ and there are no other restrictions on the communication graphs apart from Assumption 1. Then, there is no algorithm that solves k-set agreement for $1 < k < n$.*

We now provide two conditions, (Assumptions 2 and 3) the conjunction of which will be sufficient for k-set agreement. Note that choosing these constraints has been guided by just avoiding the impossibility results of Theorems 1 and 2.

To avoid non-terminating (i.e., forever undecided) executions as predicted by Theorem 1, we assume that the following *stable interval* constraint holds:

ASSUMPTION 2 (STABLE INTERVAL). *Let $H \geqslant D > 0$ be given. In every run, all vertex-stable root components R^I with $|I| \geqslant D+1$ are D-bounded. Moreover, there is some interval $I = [r_{GST}, r_{GST}+d]$ with $d \geqslant 3D+H$, where $\ell \leqslant k$ H-network-bounded vertex-stable root components $R_1^I, \ldots, R_\ell^I$ exist simultaneously.*

In order to also circumvent executions violating the k-agreement property, as established by Theorem 2, we introduce the *majority influence* constraint given in Assumption 3 below. Given some run ρ, we denote by $\mathbb{V}_d$ the set of all root components that are vertex-stable for at least d consecutive rounds in ρ. Let $R_{cur}^{I_{cur}} \in \mathbb{V}_1$ be vertex-stable in $I_{cur} = [r_{cur}, s_{cur}]$ and $R_{suc}^{I_{suc}} \in \mathbb{V}_1$ be vertex-stable in $I_{suc} = [r_{suc}, s_{suc}]$ with $r_{suc} > s_{cur}$; note that $\mathbb{V}_d \subseteq \mathbb{V}_1$ for every $d \geqslant 1$.

DEFINITION 3 ((WEAK) INFLUENCE). *Given $R_{cur}^{I_{cur}} \in \mathbb{V}_1$, $R_{suc}^{I_{suc}} \in \mathbb{V}_1$, we say that some process $p \in R_{cur}$* influences *some process $q \in R_{suc}$ and write $p \hookrightarrow q$ with $\hookrightarrow \subseteq \Pi^2$ iff there exists a causal chain from p to q that ends before $R_{suc}^{I_{suc}}$ begins, i.e., $cd^{s_{cur}+1}(p,q) \leqslant r_{suc} - s_{cur}$. In this case, we also say that $R_{cur}^{I_{cur}}$ (weakly) influences $R_{suc}^{I_{suc}}$ and write $R_{cur}^{I_{cur}} \hookrightarrow R_{suc}^{I_{suc}}$, using the relation $\hookrightarrow \subseteq \mathbb{V}_1^2$ here.*

DEFINITION 4 (INFLUENCE SETS). *Given $R_{cur}^{I_{cur}} \in \mathbb{V}_1$, $R_{suc}^{I_{suc}} \in \mathbb{V}_1$, their influence set is defined as $IS(R_{cur}, R_{suc}) := \{q \in R_{suc} \mid \exists p \in R_{cur} : p \hookrightarrow q\}$.*

DEFINITION 5 (MAJORITY INFLUENCE). *We say that $R_{cur}^{I_{cur}} \in \mathbb{V}_{2D+1}$ exercises* majority influence *on $R_{suc}^{I_{suc}} \in \mathbb{V}_{2D+1}$, denoted $R_{cur}^{I_{cur}} \hookrightarrow_{\mathtt{m}} R_{suc}^{I_{suc}}$ with $\hookrightarrow_{\mathtt{m}} \subseteq \mathbb{V}_{2D+1}^2$, iff $\forall R^I \in \mathbb{V}_{D+1}$ with $IS(R, R_{cur}) = \emptyset$ it holds that $|IS(R_{cur}, R_{suc})| > |IS(R, R_{suc})|$ and $\forall R^I \in \mathbb{V}_{D+1}$ with $IS(R, R_{cur}) \neq \emptyset$ it holds that $|IS(R_{cur}, R_{suc})| \geqslant |IS(R, R_{suc})|$.*

ASSUMPTION 3 (k-MAJORITY INFLUENCE). *$\exists K \subseteq \mathbb{V}_{2D+1}$ with $|K| \leqslant k$ s.t. $\forall \overline{R}^{\overline{I}} \in \mathbb{V}_{2D+1} \setminus K$ $\exists R^I \in \mathbb{V}_{2D+1}$ with $R^I \hookrightarrow_{\mathtt{m}} \overline{R}^{\overline{I}}$.*

We provided a an algorithm (see [7, Alg. 1] for the pseudocode), which allows to solve k-set agreement under Assumptions 2 and 3. It consists of two parts, a network approximation algorithm and the k-set agreement core algorithm.

Relying on the graph under-approximation provided by the network approximation algorithm, the core k-set agreement algorithm generates decisions only at members of $2D+1$-VSRCs, and disseminates those values throughout the remaining network. Note that the algorithm needs to know D, but not H (nor n). More specifically, the core algorithm causes process p_i to make a transition from the initially *undecided* state to a *locked* state when it detects some minimal "stability of its surroundings", namely, its membership in some $D+1$-VSRC D rounds in the past. If process p_i, while in the locked state, observes some period of stability that is sufficient for locally inferring a consistent view among *all* VSRC members (which occurs when the $D+1$-VSRC has actually extended to a $2D+1$-VSRC), p_i can safely make a transition to the *decided* state. An elaborate vector-clock-like mechanism is used for maintaining a lock history data structure for this purpose. Since locking is done optimistically, however, it may also happen that the $D+1$-VSRC does not extend to a $2D+1$-VSRC (or, even worse, is not recognized to have done so by some members) later on. In this case, p_i makes a transition from the locked state back to the undecided state.

Theorem 3 establishes that our algorithm indeed solves k-set agreement.

THEOREM 3. *There exists an algorithm that solves k-uniform k-set agreement in a dynamic network that adheres to the conjunction of Assumption 2 and Assumption 3.*

4. CONCLUSION

We introduced a consensus algorithm for synchronous dynamic networks with unidirectional communication links, which degrades gracefully to general k-set agreement in unfavorable runs. Related impossibility results show that the very weak model assumptions (eventual stability and majority influence of long-living vertex-stable root components) required by our algorithm are close to the solvability border of k-set agreement.

5. REFERENCES

[1] M. Biely, P. Robinson, and U. Schmid. Easy impossibility proofs for k-set agreement in message passing systems. In OPODIS'11, Springer LNCS 7109, pages 299–312, 2011.

[2] M. Biely, P. Robinson, and U. Schmid. Agreement in directed dynamic networks. In SIROCCO'12, LNCS 7355, pages 73–84. Springer-Verlag, 2012.

[3] M. Biely, P. Robinson, and U. Schmid. Agreement in directed dynamic networks. *arXiv:1204.0641*, Apr. 2012.

[4] A. Casteigts, P. Flocchini, W. Quattrociocchi, and N. Santoro. Time-varying graphs and dynamic networks. *IJPEDS*, 27(5):387–408, 2012.

[5] B. Charron-Bost and A. Schiper. The Heard-Of model: computing in distributed systems with benign faults. *Distributed Computing*, 22(1):49–71, Apr. 2009.

[6] S. Chaudhuri. More *choices* allow more *faults*: Set consensus problems in totally asynchronous systems. *Information and Control*, 105(1):132–158, July 1993.

[7] M. Schwarz, K. Winkler, U. Schmid, M. Biely, and P. Robinson. Gracefully degrading consensus and k-set agreement under dynamic link failures. Research Report TUW-220473, Technische Universität Wien, Institut für Technische Informatik, Treitlstr. 1-3/182-2, 1040 Vienna, Austria, 2013. http://publik.tuwien.ac.at/files/PubDat_220473.pdf.

Brief Announcement: Local Approximability of Minimum Dominating Set on Planar Graphs

Miikka Hilke
Helsinki Institute for Information Technology HIIT, Department of Computer Science, University of Helsinki, Finland
miikka.hilke@helsinki.fi

Christoph Lenzen
Computer Science and Artificial Intelligence Laboratory, MIT
clenzen@csail.mit.edu

Jukka Suomela
Helsinki Institute for Information Technology HIIT, Department of Information and Computer Science, Aalto University, Finland
jukka.suomela@aalto.fi

ABSTRACT

We show that there is no deterministic local algorithm (constant-time distributed graph algorithm) that finds a $(7-\epsilon)$-approximation of a minimum dominating set on planar graphs, for any positive constant ϵ. In prior work, the best lower bound on the approximation ratio has been $5-\epsilon$; there is also an upper bound of 52.

Categories and Subject Descriptors

C.2.4 [**Computer-Communication Networks**]: Distributed Systems; F.2.2 [**Analysis of Algorithms and Problem Complexity**]: Nonnumerical Algorithms and Problems

Keywords

Approximation algorithm; dominating set problem; local distributed algorithm; lower bound; planar graph

1. INTRODUCTION

This work studies one of the last uncharted corners in the area of deterministic local algorithms: planar graphs.

A *local algorithm* is a distributed graph algorithm that runs in $O(1)$ communication rounds, independently of the size of the network. While the theory of *randomised* local algorithms is still in its infancy, we have nowadays a good understanding of the capabilities of *deterministic* local algorithms.

For many classical graph problems, there are exactly matching upper and lower bounds on the best possible approximation ratio that can be achieved by a deterministic local algorithm [6]. In many cases, we can apply a straightforward two-step procedure to derive tight lower bounds:

1. Prove tight bounds for anonymous networks (without unique identifiers).
2. Apply a simulation argument [2] to show that unique identifiers do not help.

PODC'14, July 15–18, 2014, Paris, France.
ACM 978-1-4503-2944-6/14/07.
http://dx.doi.org/10.1145/2611462.2611504.

However, there are some isolated examples of natural questions in which the above two-step procedure fails badly. Perhaps the most intriguing example is *dominating sets on planar graphs*:

1. We do not have tight bounds for this problem in anonymous networks.
2. Planar graphs are not closed under lifts, and therefore the simulation argument [2] cannot be applied.

In this work we are interested in the smallest α such that there is a deterministic local algorithm that finds an α-approximation of a minimum dominating set in any planar graph. The current bounds are very far from being tight:

- $5-\epsilon < \alpha \leq 636$ for anonymous networks [1,7],
- $5-\epsilon < \alpha \leq 52$ in the LOCAL model [1,3,4,8].

In this work we give the first improvement on the lower bounds in six years: we prove a lower bound $\alpha > 7-\epsilon$ for both models, for any positive constant ϵ.

2. PROOF OVERVIEW

Let $\mathcal{A}$ be a deterministic distributed algorithm with running time $T = O(1)$ in the LOCAL model. Assume that $\mathcal{A}$ finds a dominating set $D = \mathcal{A}(G)$ in any planar graph G (that is, each node that is not in D is adjacent to at least one node of D).

Pick sufficiently large $m \gg T$ and r. Let $m' = m - 2T$. We will construct a planar graph G with $n = m^2 r$ nodes as shown in Figure 1a. There are r *blocks* with $m \times m$ nodes in each block. The nodes of each block are partitioned to *internal nodes* and *boundary nodes*: there are $m' \times m'$ internal nodes, and they are surrounded by boundary areas of width T. Let B_i be the set of nodes in block i, and let $I_i \subseteq B_i$ be the set of internal nodes in block B_i. We will prove the following lemma.

LEMMA 1. *For any m and any sufficiently large r, we can assign unique identifiers in G so that $I_i \subseteq \mathcal{A}(G)$ for all $1, 2, \dots, r-\ell$, for some $\ell = o(r)$.*

In other words, all internal nodes of blocks $1, 2, \dots, r-\ell$ are in the dominating set $D = \mathcal{A}(G)$ produced by algorithm $\mathcal{A}$. Now if we choose large enough m and r, we can make the contributions of the boundary nodes and the contributions of the remaining $o(r)$ blocks arbitrarily small. In particular, for any positive constant ϵ', we can pick m and r such that $|D| \geq (1-\epsilon')n$.

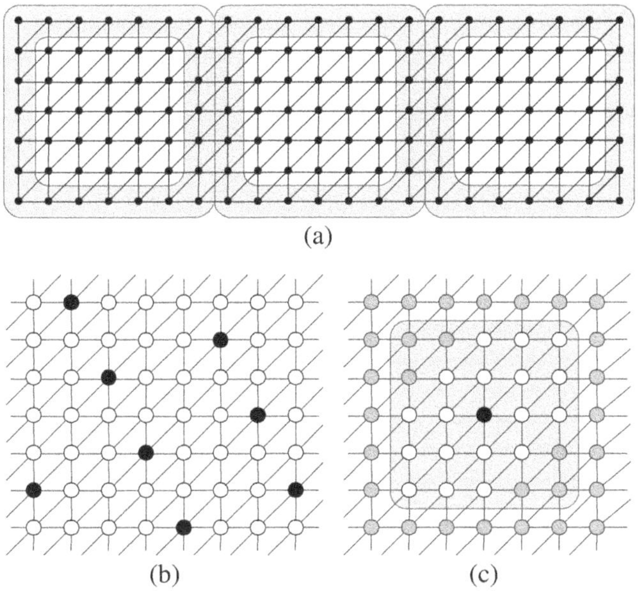

Figure 1: (a) Construction of graph G for $T = 1$, $m = 7$, and $r = 3$. There are 3 blocks. In each block there are 7×7 nodes: 5×5 internal nodes (white area), surrounded by a boundary area of width 1 (shaded). (b) A dominating set D^* of G that contains only a fraction $1/7$ of internal nodes—the figure shows only a part of a large triangular grid. (c) The local output of an internal node v (black node) only depends on its radius-T neighbourhood (white nodes, here $T = 2$). In particular, if we know the unique identifiers in the $k \times k$ region R_v around v (shaded area), we know the local output of node v.

On the other hand, there is a dominating set D^* which contains only a fraction $1/7$ of the internal nodes; see Figure 1b. Therefore $|D^*| \le (1/7 + \epsilon')n$, and the claim follows: for any positive constant ϵ we can show that algorithm $\mathcal{A}$ cannot find a factor $7 - \epsilon$ approximation of a minimum dominating set on planar graphs.

3. PROOF OF LEMMA 1

The proof uses the strategy of repeated applications of Ramsey's theorem; cf. Czygrinow et al. [1, Lemma 4]. We will use the notation $\mathcal{A}(G, v) \in \{0, 1\}$ to refer the *local output* of node v when we apply algorithm $\mathcal{A}$ to graph G; we have $\mathcal{A}(G, v) = 1$ if node v is in the dominating set computed by algorithm $\mathcal{A}$. By definition, $\mathcal{A}(G, v)$ only depends on the radius-T neighbourhood of v in G.

Let $k = 2T + 1$, $K = k^2$, and $M = m^2$. Consider any internal node $v \in I_i$ of any block B_i. The structure of graph G in the radius-T neighbourhood does not depend on the choice of v. The local output of node v only depends on the unique identifiers in the local neighbourhood. The local neighbourhood is contained within a rectangular $k \times k$ region $R_v \subseteq B_i$; see Figure 1c.

Let $V = \{1, 2, \ldots, n\}$ be the set of unique identifiers. Consider any K-subset of identifiers $X \subseteq V$, $|X| = K$. We will associate a *colour* $c(X) \in \{0, 1\}$ with each such set, as follows:

1. Pick an internal node v.
2. Assign the identifiers from X to region R_v in an increasing order by rows: the smallest k identifiers to the bottom row from left to right, etc. Assign the identifiers from $V \setminus X$ to the remaining nodes arbitrarily.
3. Apply algorithm $\mathcal{A}$, and set $c(X) = \mathcal{A}(G, v)$.

Now we have defined a colouring of all K-subsets of V; by restriction, we also have a colouring of all K-subsets of any $V' \subseteq V$. We say that $Y \subseteq V$ is *monochromatic* if $c(X_1) = c(X_2)$ for any K-subsets X_1 and X_2 of Y. By Ramsey's theorem [5] there exists an integer $N = N(K, M)$ such that the following holds: if V' is any N-subset of V, then there always exists a monochromatic subset $Y \subseteq V'$ of size M.

Now we will pick r and ℓ so that $\ell M > N$ and $\ell = o(r)$. Let $V_1 = V$. For each $i = 1, 2, \ldots, r - \ell$, we define the identifiers of block i as follows.

1. As $|V_i| \ge N$, we can find a monochromatic subset $Y_i \subseteq V_i$ of size M.
2. Assign the identifiers from Y_i to block B_i in an increasing order by rows: the smallest m identifiers to the bottom row from left to right, etc.
3. Set $V_{i+1} = V_i \setminus Y_i$.

Finally, assign the remaining ℓM identifiers from $V_{r-\ell+1}$ to blocks $r - \ell + 1, \ldots, r$ arbitrarily.

To complete the proof, consider a block i, where $1 \le i \le r - \ell$. Let $v \in I_i$ be an internal node of the block. Consider the $k \times k$ region R_v around v, and let X_v be the set of unique identifiers assigned to region R_v. Observe that the identifiers of X_v are assigned in an increasing order by rows. It follows that $\mathcal{A}(G, v) = c(X_v)$, i.e., the local output of the internal node v is simply the colour of subset X_v. Furthermore, $X_v \subseteq Y_i$ and Y_i was monochromatic. Hence all internal nodes of block i produce the same output. The common output cannot be 0; otherwise there would be nodes that are not dominated. Hence $I_i \subseteq \mathcal{A}(G)$.

4. ACKNOWLEDGEMENTS

Many thanks to Wojciech Wawrzyniak for discussions, and to anonymous reviewers for their helpful feedback. This work was supported in part by the Deutsche Forschungsgemeinschaft (DFG, reference number Le 3107/1-1), by the Academy of Finland, Grant 252018, and by the Research Funds of the University of Helsinki.

5. REFERENCES

[1] Andrzej Czygrinow, Michał Hańćkowiak, and Wojciech Wawrzyniak. Fast distributed approximations in planar graphs. In *Proc. 22nd International Symposium on Distributed Computing (DISC 2008)*, volume 5218 of *Lecture Notes in Computer Science*, pages 78–92. Springer, 2008. doi:10.1007/978-3-540-87779-0_6.

[2] Mika Göös, Juho Hirvonen, and Jukka Suomela. Lower bounds for local approximation. *Journal of the ACM*, 60(5):39:1–23, 2013. doi:10.1145/2528405. arXiv:1201.6675.

[3] Christoph Lenzen. *Synchronization and Symmetry Breaking in Distributed Systems*. PhD thesis, ETH Zurich, January 2011.

[4] Christoph Lenzen, Yvonne Anne Pignolet, and Roger Wattenhofer. Distributed minimum dominating set

approximations in restricted families of graphs. *Distributed Computing*, 26(2):119–137, 2013. doi:10.1007/s00446-013-0186-z.

[5] Frank P. Ramsey. On a problem of formal logic. *Proceedings of the London Mathematical Society*, 30:264–286, 1930. doi:10.1112/plms/s2-30.1.264.

[6] Jukka Suomela. Survey of local algorithms. *ACM Computing Surveys*, 45(2):24:1–40, 2013. doi:10.1145/2431211.2431223. http://www.cs.helsinki.fi/local-survey/.

[7] Wojciech Wawrzyniak. Brief announcement: a local approximation algorithm for MDS problem in anonymous planar networks. In *Proc. 32nd Annual ACM Symposium on Principles of Distributed Computing (PODC 2013)*, pages 406–408. ACM Press, 2013. doi:10.1145/2484239.2484281.

[8] Wojciech Wawrzyniak. A strengthened analysis of a local algorithm for the minimum dominating set problem in planar graphs. *Information Processing Letters*, 114(3):94–98, 2014. doi:10.1016/j.ipl.2013.11.008.

Beyond Geometry: Towards Fully Realistic Wireless Models*

Marijke H.L. Bodlaender
ICE-TCS, School of Computer Science
Reykjavik University, Iceland.
mbodlaender@gmail.com

Magnús M. Halldórsson
ICE-TCS, School of Computer Science
Reykjavik University, Iceland.
mmh@ru.is

ABSTRACT

Signal-strength models of wireless communications capture the gradual fading of signals and the additivity of interference. As such, they are closer to reality than other models. However, nearly all theoretic work in the SINR model depends on the assumption of smooth geometric decay, one that is true in free space but is far off in actual environments. The challenge is to model realistic environments, including walls, obstacles, reflections and anisotropic antennas, without making the models algorithmically impractical or analytically intractable.

We present a simple solution that allows the modeling of arbitrary static situations by moving from geometry to arbitrary *decay spaces*. The complexity of a setting is captured by a *metricity* parameter ζ that indicates how far the decay space is from satisfying the triangular inequality. All results that hold in the SINR model in general metrics carry over to decay spaces, with the resulting time complexity and approximation depending on ζ in the same way that the original results depends on the path loss term α. For distributed algorithms, that to date have appeared to necessarily depend on the planarity, we indicate how they can be adapted to arbitrary decay spaces at a cost in time complexity that depends on a *fading* parameter of the decay space. In particular, for decay spaces that are *doubling*, the parameter is constant-bounded.

Finally, we explore the dependence on ζ in the approximability of core problems. In particular, we observe that the capacity maximization problem has exponential upper and lower bounds in terms of ζ in general decay spaces. In Euclidean metrics and related growth-bounded decay spaces, the performance depends on the exact metricity definition, with a polynomial upper bound in terms of ζ, but an exponential lower bound in terms of a variant parameter ϕ. The upper bound result is the first approximation of a capacity-type SINR problem that is subexponential in α.

*Supported by Icelandic Research Fund grant-of-excellence no. 120032011.

PODC'14, July 15–18, 2014, Paris, France.

ACM 978-1-4503-2944-6/14/07 ...$15.00.
http://dx.doi.org/10.1145/2611462.2611476 .

Categories and Subject Descriptors

C.2.1 [**Computer-Communication Networks**]: Network Architecture and Design—*Wireless communication*; F.1.2 [**Computation by Abstract Devices**]: Modes of Computation—*Probabilistic computation*

General Terms

Algorithms, Design, Theory

Keywords

Wireless Networks, SINR, Capacity, Distributed Algorithms

1. INTRODUCTION

Signal-strength models of wireless communications capture the gradual fading of signals and the additivity of interference that are consistent with electro-magnetic theory. In spite of the apparent complexity of such models, various fundamental problems have been resolved analytically in recent years. These models also seem essential for studying certain properties of wireless networks, such as capacity [23], or connectivity and aggregation, which can be achieved in logarithmic rounds in worst case [48, 31].

Nearly all theoretic work in signal-strength models have been done in the GEO-SINR model that assumes that signals decay as a smooth polynomial function of distance. This assumption about decay (or *path-loss*) is true in free space, but turns out to be far off in actual environments, as shown by a long history of experimental studies (e.g., [45]). Quoting a recent meta-study, [3], "link quality is not correlated with distance." This questions the wisdom of studying "SINR models" analytically, given the added effort and complexity.

One hope might be that results in the "basic SINR model" could eventually carry some insights that would be of use in more detailed models that capture more of reality. However, real environments consist of assortments of walls, ceilings and obstacles, as well as complex interactions involving reflections, shadowing, multi-path signals, and anisotropic (or even directional) antennas. It might seem near impossible to capture all of that without making the resulting models hopelessly impractical for algorithm design and/or analytically intractable.

Various stochastic extensions of geometric path loss have been proposed to address the observed variability in signal propagation. The most common are *log-normal shadowing* and *Rayleigh fading* for addressing long- and short-distance variability, respectively. Both modify the signal strength multiplicatively by an exponentially distributed random variable. These models are highly useful both for generating instance (e.g., for simulations) and for average-case analysis. For handling actual instances, their utility necessarily depends on the suitability of the assumptions. The alternative view, with deep roots in computer science theory, is to allow for worst-case behavior and obtain guarantees that hold for *all* instances. The aim of this work is to make such "any-case" analysis feasible, while avoiding assumptions that may or may not be reflected in actual instances.

Our contributions. We present a simple solution that allows the modeling of arbitrary static situations by moving from geometry to arbitrary *decay spaces*. The decay between two ordered nodes is the relative reduction in the strength of a signal sent from the first node to the second. These decays can be obtained by signal-strength measurements – which almost any cheap widget can perform today – capturing the *truth on the ground*. The complexity of a setting is captured by a *metricity* parameter ζ that indicates how far the decay space is from satisfying the triangular inequality.

The simple metricity definition has wide-ranging implications: *All* results that hold in the SINR model in general metrics carry over to decay spaces; the resulting time complexity and approximation depending on ζ in the same way that the original results depends on the path-loss term α.

For distributed algorithms, that to date have appeared to necessarily depend on the planarity, we introduce a *fading* parameter of the decay space and indicate they can be adapted to arbitrary decay spaces at a cost in time complexity that depend on a *fading* parameter of the decay space. In particular, for decay spaces that are *doubling*, the parameter is constant-bounded.

Finally, we explore the dependence on ζ in the approximability of core problems. In particular, we observe that the CAPACITY problem has exponential upper and lower bounds in terms of ζ in general decay spaces. In Euclidean metrics and related growth-bounded decay spaces, the performance depends on the exact metricity definition, with a polynomial upper bound in terms of ζ, but an exponential lower bound in terms of a variant parameter ϕ.

One may ask if we are being led to yet another model that will later been shown unrealistic. Fortunately, numerous experimental studies have verified the remaining key assumptions in wide range of situations and technology [52, 47, 7, 51, 22]: additivity of interference, SINR capture effectiveness (the near-thresholding relationship between SINR level and packet reception rate), and invariability of wireless conditions in static environments. Thus, we may finally be reaching a wireless model that is a close approximation of the reality at the PHY/MAC layer, yet usable algorithmically and analytically. That said, one should not discount the value of abstractions or the potentially value of simple models. Also, modeling dynamic and mobile situations, which is outside the scope of our work, remains a highly important (and largely open) issue.

Related work. The "abstract SINR" model captures, like decay spaces, arbitrary pairwise path-loss. Some positive results hold in that model, e.g., distributed power assignment of feasible sets [46], reductions involving Rayleigh fading [8], and special cases of capacity maximization [26]. However, for most problems of interest, extremely strong inapproximability results hold [19, 44]. Thus, it is essential to use near-metric properties of the decay space.

The introduction of general metrics (apparently first in [15, 14]) was a significant step in extending SINR theory beyond geometric assumptions. Fading metrics [24] were identified to capture the main property required from the planar setting. The concept of *inductive independence* [43, 36] has heralded a more systematic approach to SINR analysis, and can by itself be seen as parameter of the decay space. Same holds for *C-independence* [1, 10] in the case of uniform power.

In a sibling paper [22], we introduced decay spaces and metricity with a focus on validation by measurements in two testbeds. We found that the metricity parameter did appear to reflect the "complexity" of the environment. We also examined the impact of the availability of multiple channels and found that this can significantly reduce the measured metricity. Additionally, we verified that the key properties of the SINR formula in decay spaces closely approximate reality, even in highly complex environments, in alignment with previous experimental results (e.g., [52, 47, 7, 51]).

Outline of the rest of the paper. In the next section, we introduce decay spaces (formal definitions and the metricity parameter), and indicate how previous results in metric spaces carry over. In Sec. 3, we address the core requirement of *fading* for distributed algorithms, introduce a parameter that extends their reach to arbitrary spaces, and prove constant upper bounds in spaces with bounded doubling dimension. The impact of metricity parameters on approximability is treated in Sec. 4, concluding with some observations and open issues in Sec. 5.

2. DECAY SPACES

2.1 Signal-strength models

The *abstract SINR* model has two key properties: **(i)** signal decays as it travels from a sender to a receiver, and **(ii)** interference – signals from other than the intended transmitter – accumulates. Transmission succeeds if and only if the interference is below a given threshold.

Formally, a *link* $l_v = (s_v, r_v)$ is given by a pair of nodes, sender s_v and a receiver r_v. The *channel gain* G_{uv} denotes the multiplicative decay in the signal of l_u as received at r_v. The *interference* I_{uv} of sender s_u (of link l_u) on the receiver r_v (of link l_v) is $P_u G_{uv}$, where P_v is the power used by s_v. When $u = v$, we refer to I_{vv} as the *signal strength* of link l_v. If a set S of links transmits simultaneously, then the *signal to noise and interference ratio* (SINR) at l_v is

$$\mathrm{SINR}_v := \frac{I_{vv}}{N + \sum_{u \in S} I_{uv}} = \frac{P_v G_{vv}}{N + \sum_{u \in S} P_v G_{uv}} , \quad (1)$$

where N is the ambient noise.

We refer to the standard signal-strength model as the GEO-SINR model, which adds to the SINR formula the assumption of *geometric path-loss*: that signal decays proportional to a fixed polynomial of the distance, *i.e.*, $G_{uv} = d(s_u, r_v)^{-\alpha}$, where the *path-loss term* α is assumed to be an arbitrary but fixed constant between 1 and 6. This assumption is valid with $\alpha = 2$ in in free space and perfect vacuum [18, Sec. 3.1].

The last assumption made in theoretical models is *thresholding*: the transmission of l_v is *successful* iff $\mathrm{SINR}_v \geq \beta$, where $\beta \geq 1$ is a hardware-dependent constant. We shall also make this assumption. It's been shown by Dams,

Kesselheim and Hoefer [8] that certain models that include a randomized filter in this decision can be efficiently simulated by thresholding algorithms.

2.2 Metrics and Decay Spaces

We seek to model arbitrary path-loss that is independent of distance. We capture this by a *decay* function f of pairs of points (or nodes) so that $G_{uv} = 1/f(s_u, r_v)$.

We shall formulate signal decay as *decay spaces.* Decays between distinct points are always positive. Exactly what happens at a given point (i.e., the value of $f(p,p)$) is immaterial to our consideration, since we may assume that all nodes are distinct.

Definition 1. A *decay space* is a pair $\mathcal{D} = (V, f)$, where V is a discrete set of nodes (or points) and f is a mapping (or matrix) $f : V \times V \to \mathbb{R}_{\geq 0}$ that associates values (*decays*) with ordered pairs of nodes. The decays satisfy: i) $f(p,q) \geq 0$ (non-negativity), and ii) $f(p,q) = 0$ if and only if $p = q$ (the identity of indiscernibles).

Decay spaces need not be symmetric ($f(p,q) = f(q,p)$) nor obey the triangular inequality ($f(p,q) \leq f(p,r)+f(r,q)$). Such spaces are known as *pre-metrics.* As shorthand, we write $f_{pq} = f(p,q)$.

Decay space can either represent the truth-on-the-ground, or its representation/approximation as data. Besides signal-strength measurements (typically available with precision of 1dB, or 26%), they can often be inferred by packet reception rates or predicted by heuristic or environmental models [18].

Metricity

We introduced in [22] a parameter that represents how close the decay matrix is to a distance metric.

Definition 2. The *metricity* $\zeta(\mathcal{D})$ of a decay space $\mathcal{D} = (V, f)$ is the smallest number such that, for every triplet $x, y, z \in V$,

$$f(x,y)^{1/\zeta} \leq f(x,z)^{1/\zeta} + f(z,y)^{1/\zeta} . \tag{2}$$

We note that ζ is well-defined. Namely, consider $\zeta = \zeta_0 := \log_2(f_{max}/f_{min})$, where $f_{max} = \max_{x,y} f(x,y)$ and $f_{min} = \min_{x \neq y} f(x,y)$. Then, we can see that the LHS of (2) is at most $f_{max}^{1/\zeta_0} = 2f_{min}^{1/\zeta_0}$, while the RHS is at least that value. In the case of geometric path-loss, $\zeta \leq \alpha$.

We define *quasi-distances* between nodes in a decay space by $d(p,q) = f_{pq}^{1/\zeta}$. Let $d_{pq} = d(p,q)$ for short. These quasi-distances induce a *quasi-metric* $\mathcal{D}' = (V, d)$, i.e., a metric except for the possible lack of symmetry. In the Euclidean setting, quasi-distances are simply the Euclidean distances.

2.3 Theory transfer

The lion share of the theoretic literature on signal-strength models can be converted to decay spaces with minimal effort. We aim here to clarify and substantiate that observation. Our objective is for the non-specialist to be able to determine with limited effort which results do hold in the decay model and which don't, and additionally, when the question arises, which properties of metric and/or decay spaces are necessary for correct functioning.

In this section, we focus on what is needed for results to hold in arbitrary decay spaces. In the following section, we deal with results that require special space properties, particularly in the context of distributed algorithms. By a *result*, we mean a combination of an algorithm or a protocol and its analysis.

The complexity of a result can be a function of the metric/space. Here, complexity refers to measures like time and message count, but also performance measures like approximability. In particular, these measures have nearly always been functions of the metric parameters, such as the path-loss term α, but this dependence is often hidden in big-oh notation.

We make the following sweeping observation:

PROPOSITION 2.1. *If a* GEO-SINR *result only requires metric properties (triangular inequality), then it holds equally well in arbitrary decay spaces. Symmetry is required of the decay space only if it was required in the original setting. The relevant complexity measure (time, approximation) grows with ζ in the same manner as for the original result in terms of α.*

PROOF. The quasi-distances d of a decay space $\mathcal{D} = (V, f)$ form a quasi-metric $\mathcal{D}' = (V, d)$, which becomes a metric iff $\mathcal{D}$ satisfies symmetry. Applying the original result to the metric $\mathcal{D}'$ with path loss constant $\zeta(\mathcal{D})$ gives an equivalent solution to the problem on the decay space $\mathcal{D}$. □

For example, the following results on the following problems carry over without change: capacity maximization [27, 41], scheduling [14, 15], weighted capacity [24, 30], spectrum auctions [36, 35], relationship between power control regimes [53, 25], dynamic packet scheduling [42, 25], distributed scheduling [43, 32], and distributed capacity maximization with regret-minimization [1] .

We remark that the resulting algorithms actually become *simpler* in decay spaces than in the standard setting. Namely, there is no longer any need to use or know the path-loss constant α. No known algorithms actually need ζ; it is used purely for analysis purposes.

We can also make an immediate observation regarding methods that hold for restricted metrics.

Observation 1. If a result holds in GEO-SINR for a given class $\mathcal{M}$ of (quasi-)metrics, then it holds equally in those decay spaces whose induced (quasi-)metric is contained in $\mathcal{M}$.

Results that do not carry over to decay spaces. There remains a significant body of work in GEO-SINR that depends on *positions* (or distributions thereof). Such results are necessarily tied to geometry, although with some work it may be possible to extend them to other decay spaces.

A common use of positional information is by partitioning the plane, so as to make simultaneous communication non-conflicting. This is particularly an issue for deterministic distributed algorithms. Examples of this include deterministic distributed broadcast [38, 39] and local broadcast [37, 16]. Also, some centralized approximation algorithms and heuristics for CAPACITY and SCHEDULING of [21, 58]. Occasionally, angles are used, e.g.[19], which does not carry over (but see Sec. 4.1).

There is also a large literature on average case analysis, typically assuming a uniform distribution of points in the plane, starting with an influential paper of Gupta and Kumar [23] that first introduced GEO-SINR.

Finally, SINR diagrams [2] (and follow-up work of subsets of the authors) use intrinsically topological properties of Euclidean metrics.

2.4 Additional definitions: Power, affectance, separability

We will work with a total order $\prec$ on the links, where $l_v \prec l_w$ implies that $f_{vv} \le f_{ww}$. A power assignment $\mathcal{P}$ is *monotone* if both $P_v \le P_w$ and $\frac{P_w}{f_{ww}} \le \frac{P_v}{f_{vv}}$ hold whenever $l_v \prec l_w$. [1] This captures the main power strategies, including uniform and linear power.

We modify the notion of *affectance* [19, 33, 43]: The affectance $a_w^{\mathcal{P}}(v)$ of link l_w on link l_v under power assignment $\mathcal{P}$ is the interference of l_w on l_v normalized to the signal strength (power received) of l_v, or

$$a_w(v) = \min\left(1, c_v \frac{P_w G_{wv}}{P_v G_{vv}}\right) = \min\left(1, c_v \frac{P_w}{P_v}\frac{f_{vv}}{f_{wv}}\right) ,$$

where $c_v = \frac{\beta}{1-\beta N/(P_v G_{vv})} > \beta$ is a factor depending only on universal constants and the signal strength G_{vv} of l_v, indicating the extent to which the ambient noise affects the transmission. We drop $\mathcal{P}$ when clear from context. Furthermore let $a_v(v) = 0$. For a set S of links and link l_v, let $a_v(S) = \sum_{l_w \in S} a_v(w)$ be the *out-affectance* of v on S and $a_S(v) = \sum_{l_w \in S} a_w(v)$ be the *in-affectance.* Assuming S contains at least two links we can rewrite Eqn. 1 as $a_S(v) \le 1$ and this is the form we will use. A set S of links is *feasible* if $a_S(v) \le 1$ and more generally *K-feasible* if $a_v(S) \le 1/K$.

Define $d_{vw} = \min(d(s_v, r_w), d(s_w, r_v), d(s_v, s_w), d(r_v, r_w)) = d(l_v, l_w)$ as the (quasi-)distance between two links l_v and l_w. Let $d_{vv} = d(s_v, r_v)$. A link l_v is said to be *η-separated* from a set L of links, for parameter η, if $d(l_v, l_w) \ge \eta d_{vv}$ for every $l_w \in L$. A set L is η-separated if each link in L is η-separated from the rest of the set.

Let e refer to the base of the natural logarithm and let lg denote the base-2 logarithm. Recall that $1+x \le e^x$, for any value x.

3. FADING PROPERTIES AND DISTRIBUTED ALGORITHMS

In the study of distributed algorithms in GEO-SINR in the plane, the standard assumption is that the path-loss constant α is strictly larger than 2. The reason is that this ensures that spatially well-separates nodes cannot affect each other too much, a property that does not hold when $\alpha \le 2$. This property is generalized to doubling metrics whose doubling dimension is strictly smaller than the path-loss constant α, dubbed *fading metrics* [24]. We call this property, that the sum of affectances from spatially separated transmitting nodes converges, the *fading* property. For the most common type of distributed algorithm to work, this has to be bounded.

We define a parameter γ that captures the fading effect. Let $\mathcal{X}(r)$ be the space of all r-separated subsets in V.

Definition 3. The *fading value* $\gamma_z(r)$ of a node z relative to a separation term r is

$$\gamma_z(r) = r \max_{X \in \mathcal{X}(r)} \sum_{x \in X} 1/f_{xz} .$$

[1]This corresponds to *length monotone* and *sub-linear* power assignments in GEO-SINR.

The *fading parameter* γ of a decay space is the maximum fading value of a node in the space, $\gamma = \gamma(r) = \max_{z \in V} \gamma_z(r)$, relative to a given separation term r.

That is, the total interference $I_S(z)$ experienced by a node z from an r-separated set S (of senders) using uniform power P is at most $\gamma(r) \cdot P/r$. Thus, if the intended signal has decay f_{zz} at most r, then the resulting affectance is bounded by $a_S(z) \le \frac{\gamma(r)P/r}{P/r} = \gamma(r)$.

Many distributed problems (e.g., broadcast, local broadcast) are primarily concerned with neighborhoods of particular size/radius; that radius then defines the separation term r and the fading value $\gamma(r)$ in consideration. Other problems (e.g., aggregation, capacity) are concerned with all possible distance (in a sense, "scale free"); in that case, we shall be interested in the fading term $\gamma = \max_r \gamma(r)$.

Until now, γ has been expected to be an absolute constant. However, we can now simply treat it as a parameter and thus handle arbitrary decay spaces by distributed algorithms, thus achieving significant increase in generality. The value of γ must naturally factor into the time complexity of the algorithms.

3.1 Fading spaces

We identify a large class of decay spaces for which the fading parameter is small. These are generalizations of fading metrics.

First, some additional notation. The *t-ball* $B(y,t) = \{x \in V | f(x,y) < t\}$ centered at y with radius t contains all points x for which decay to y is less than t. A set $Y \subseteq V$ is a *t-packing* if $f(x,y) > 2t$, for any $x, y \in V$. Thus, Y is a t-packing iff the set $\{B(y,t)\}_{y \in Y}$ of balls are disjoint. The *t-packing number* $\mathcal{P}(\mathcal{B}, t)$ is the size of the largest t-packing into the body $\mathcal{B}$.

Intuitively, a space is *doubling* if the number of mutually unit-separated points within a given distance from a center increases by at most a polynomial of the distance.

Definition 4. Let $\mathcal{D} = (V, f)$ be a decay space. Define $g_{\mathcal{D}}(q) = \max_{x \in V} \max_{r \in \mathbb{R}^+} \mathcal{P}(B(x,r), r/q)$, as the size of the densest q-packing in $\mathcal{D}$. The *Assouad (doubling) dimension A of $\mathcal{D}$ with parameter C* is given by

$$A(\mathcal{D}) = \max_q \log_q \left(\frac{g(q)}{C}\right) .$$

$A(\mathcal{D})$ is, in effect, the minimum k for which sizes of t-packings can be bounded by $O(t^k)$, for all t. Note that that $A(\mathbb{R}^k) = k$ [34].

Definition 5. A *fading space* is a decay space $\mathcal{D}$ with Assouad dimension strictly smaller than 1, $A(\mathcal{D}) < 1$, w.r.t. some absolute constant C.

Note that the (quasi-)distance metric of a decay space of doubling dimension A has doubling dimension $A \cdot \zeta$.

3.2 Annulus argument

Most randomized algorithms (e.g. in [4] and [62]) ensure that in any given neighborhood (defined as the set of nodes to which a given node can communicate directly), the expected number of transmissions in a slot is bounded above by a certain constant. This ensures that the total expected affectance from other nodes transmitting is also bounded by a (different) constant. By adjusting the constants appropriately, one can focus only on the local behavior. Some deterministic algorithms similarly ensure a spatial separation of sending (and thus possibly interfering) nodes and use this property to bound the total affectance from these nodes.

All proofs of the discussed sort use a common approach. They define some type of separation between interfering nodes which can be a (probabilistic) constant density, a hard minimum distance between nodes or links or similar. Then the interference at a node v is bounded, either directly or (if the node is the receiver of a predefined link) in terms of the (possibly probabilistic) affectance on the node. To do this we draw concentric circles around v, cutting the space around v up into annuli. Using the separation of the interferers, we argue that the number of interferers that can be packed in the annulus at distance i is bounded by a polynomial depending on i and the Assouad dimension of the space.

We argue that a general version of this 'annulus argument' still holds when directly used in fading decay spaces, after which we indicate how other different variations carry over.

Recall the Riemann $\hat{\zeta}$-function, $\hat{\zeta}(x) = \sum_{n\geq 1} n^{-x}$, which is known to converge for $x > 1$. We modify an earlier similar result for metric spaces [24].

THEOREM 3.1. *The fading parameter γ of a decay space $\mathcal{D} = (V, f)$ is bounded by $\gamma \leq C2^{A+1}(\hat{\zeta}(2-A) - 1)$, where $A < 1$ is the Assouad dimension and C is the related constant.*

PROOF. Let r be a value and $R = r/2$. Let S be an R-packing. Since $\mathcal{D}$ is doubling, there is a constant C such that for any $t > 0$, the maximal size of an R-packing in a ball of radius tR centered around a point x is,

$$\mathcal{P}(B(x, tR), R) \leq Ct^A \ . \tag{3}$$

We bound the received signal $I_S(x)$ at a listening node $x \in S$. Let g be a natural number. Let $S_g = \{y \in S_g : f(y,x) < gR\}$ and let $T_g = S_g \setminus S_{g-1}$. Then $S_2 = \emptyset$ since S is r-spaced.

We first note that since $S_{g-1} \subseteq S_g$ and $S_2 = \emptyset$,

$$\sum_{g\geq 3} \frac{|S_g \setminus S_{g-1}|}{g-1} = \sum_{g\geq 3} \frac{|S_g|}{g-1} - \sum_{g\geq 2} \frac{|S_g|}{g}$$
$$= \sum_{g\geq 3} |S_g| \left(\frac{1}{g-1} - \frac{1}{g}\right) = \sum_{g\geq 3} \frac{|S_g|}{g(g-1)} \ .$$

Since each sender $y \in T_g$ is of distance at least $(g-1)R$ from x the received signal from y on x is bounded by

$$I_y(x) = P/f(y,x) \leq \frac{P}{(g-1)R} \qquad \forall y \in T_g \ .$$

Then,

$$I_S(x) = \sum_{g\geq 3} I_{T_g}(x) \leq \sum_{g\geq 3} |S_g \setminus S_{g-1}| \frac{P}{(g-1)R}$$
$$\leq \frac{P}{R} \sum_{g\geq 3} |S_g| \frac{1}{(g-1)^2} \ .$$

By the doubling property of $\mathcal{D}$, the size of S_g is

$$|S_g| \leq \mathcal{P}(B(x, (g+1)R), R) \leq C(g+1)^A \ .$$

Thus, using that $g + 1 \leq 2(g-1)$, since $g \geq 3$,

$$\frac{|S_g|}{(g-1)^2} \leq \frac{C(g+1)^A}{(g-1)^2} = \frac{C2^A}{(g-1)^{2-A}} \ .$$

Continuing,

$$I_S(x) \leq \frac{P}{R} \sum_{g\geq 3} |S_g| \frac{1}{(g-1)^2} \leq \frac{2P}{r} \sum_{g\geq 3} \frac{C2^A}{(g-1)^{2-A}}$$
$$\leq \frac{2P}{r} C2^A \left(\hat{\zeta}(2-A) - 1\right) = \frac{\gamma(r) \cdot P}{r} \ ,$$

using the definitions of R and $\gamma(r)$. $\square$

3.3 Common usage of the annulus argument

We list some common types of lemmas in which the annulus argument is used and show how to use Theorem 3.1 in the proofs for these lemmas.

A common usage of the annulus argument is to prove the following: if L is a set of links, using a uniform power assignment P, with senders of a minimal mutual distance r and with the longest link of length at most a given constant times r, then L forms a q-feasible set. For sets as described in Theorem 3.1, where all *nodes* are r-separated and a maximum link decay f_{vv} at most constant r, the transition is straightforward. By the definition of affectance and Theorem 3.1, the affectance of L on link l_v with maximum decay f_{vv} is at most

$$a_L(v) \leq \frac{I_L(v)}{PG_{vv}} \leq \frac{f_{vv} \cdot \gamma(r)}{r} \ ,$$

where $I_L(v) = \sum_{l_w \in L} P/f_{wv}$. To obtain a q-feasible set, we simply set $r = f_{vv}\gamma(r)/q$.

However, if only a separation on senders is defined (e.g. [24]), we use the triangular inequality to bound the interference at r_v in terms of interference at s_v. Requiring $f_{vv} < R$, we obtain $I_L(r_v) \leq 2^\zeta I_L(s_v)$, since for any sender $s_x \in L$ by the triangle inequality

$$f(s_x, r_v)^{1/\zeta} \geq f(s_x, s_v)^{1/\zeta} - f(s_v, r_v)^{1/\zeta} \geq f(s_x, s_v)^{1/\zeta}/2 \ ,$$

using that $f_{vv} < R \leq f(s_x, s_v)^{1/\zeta}/2$. And thus $f_{xv} \geq f(s_x, s_v)/2^\zeta$, hence the argument holds as before by adjusting r with an extra 2^ζ factor. When $R \gg f_v$, the overhead factor is correspondingly smaller.

Examples of problems with centralized algorithms that use this form of annulus argument include: connectivity [48, 31], scheduling [5, 54], flow-based throughput [6], online capacity maximization [13], and bounds on the utility of conflict graphs [55].

For randomized algorithms, the annulus argument is used in a similar way to bound expected interference. The expected interference in a disk is bounded by arguments specific to the analyzed algorithm. These arguments may or may not translate to the decay space as discussed in Sec. 2.3. Instead of adjusting the separation term r, they typically adjust the transmission probabilities. Once the expected interference in a disk is bounded, however, the argumentation for bounding the total expected interference at a node x, $E(I_S(x))$, follows Theorem 3.1.

The probabilistic version of the annulus argument forms the core of the analysis for many randomized distributed algorithms which often carry over without any significant further adjustments. Example include (distributed) coloring

[61], local broadcast [20, 62, 29], broadcast [11] and multiple-message broadcast [59, 60], capacity [49], dominating set [50], and (multihop) connectivity [28, 4].

3.4 Beyond fading spaces

Fading spaces do not completely characterize spaces with a bounded fading parameter. One reason is that the definition of doubling metrics is scale-invariant in that the packing constraint holds for balls of any size, whereas we are often only interested in balls of a fixed size (or in a limited range of sizes).

Consider, for instance, the metric space formed by a star centered at node x_0 with k leaves $x_1, x_2, \ldots, x_k$ at distance k^2 and one leaf x_{-1} at distance r, where $r \ll k$. Suppose the decay f_{xy} equals the distance (so $\zeta = 1$). The doubling dimension of this space is k, so unbounded. Suppose also that we are interested how well we can transmit from x_0 to x_{-1} in the presence of transmissions from the other nodes; that is, what matters is fading w.r.t. separation term r. If $r = o(k)$, we find that the total interference at node x_{-1} is $\sum_{i=1}^{k} 1/k^2 = 1/k$, which is asymptotically smaller than the signal received from x_0. Thus, the fading property holds even if the metric is not doubling.

4. DEPENDENCE ON THE METRICITY IN APPROXIMATIONS

Having pinpointed the metricity parameter ζ as a key indicator of a decay space, the question arises how it affects the complexity of fundamental problems. This differs from GEO-SINR where the path-loss term α has traditionally been viewed as a constant.

We explore here the approximability of the CAPACITY problem as a function of innate properties of the decay space in question. Given a set L of links, the CAPACITY problem asks for maximum cardinality subset of L that is feasible. The CAPACITY problem is fundamental, not only because it addresses the basic question of how much wireless communication can coexist, but also because it has been the underlying core routine in other problems, including scheduling [19], throughput maximization (via flow) [56], spectrum auctions [36], spectrum sharing [30], and connectivity and aggregation [31, 28].

Our generic statement, Prop. 2.1, along with known approximation results [27, 41] in general metrics, implies that CAPACITY in decay spaces can be approximated within a function of ζ. Specifically, the approximation of [27] (for monotone power) is exponential in ζ, which was refined to 3^{ζ} in [22].

We can also observe that the known hardness construction for "abstract SINR" [19] (see also [27]) implies that $2^{\zeta(1-o(1))}$-approximation for CAPACITY is computationally hard.

THEOREM 4.1 ([19, 27]). CAPACITY *of equi-decay links is hard to approximate within* $2^{\zeta(1-o(1))}$ *factor. This holds even if the algorithm is allowed arbitrary power control against an adversary that uses uniform power.*

This leaves the question whether better results are possible in the Euclidean metric and comparable decay spaces. Surprisingly, the answer depends on the exact definition of the metricity parameter. Specifically, CAPACITY with uniform power is then approximable within a polynomial of ζ, while for a natural variant of the ζ-parameter, exponential dependence is still necessary.

4.1 Improved Approximations in Bounded Growth Decay Spaces

We show here that CAPACITY with uniform power can be approximated within polynomial factors of ζ in Euclidean metrics. More generally, this holds for decay spaces of bounded growth, as we shall define shortly. Interestingly, it does not rely on the fading behavior of the plane (i.e., that $\alpha > 2$). This appears to be the first instance in the signal-strength literature where better results are shown to be obtainable in the plane independent of α than for general metrics.

The intuitive reason why uniform power in the plane proves to be easier is two-fold. The main cause for exponential dependence on ζ comes from the use of the triangular inequality. If one can ensure that one angle is highly acute, the overhead of the inequality goes down accordingly. In particular, the overhead in switching the reference from a receiver to a sender of a link goes down if the length of the link relative to the other distances is small.

We shall allow any positive ζ (or α); for this purpose, we define $\underline{\zeta} = \max(1, \zeta)$ and $\underline{\alpha} = \max(1, \alpha)$.

Bounded Growth Decay Spaces. We shall consider decay spaces that have upper bounds on two measures that restrict growth: the doubling dimension (from Sec. 3), and the independence dimension, defined in [19] for metrics and adapted as follows to decay spaces.

Definition 6. ([19]) A set I of points in a decay space $\mathcal{D} = (V, f)$ is *independent* w.r.t. a point $x \in V$ if $B(z, f_{zx}) \cap I = \{x\}$ for each $z \in I$. The *independence dimension* of $\mathcal{D}$ is the size of the largest independent point set.

Spaces of bounded independence dimension D have the following useful property: for any point $x \in V$, there is a set $J_x \subset V$ of at most D points that *guard* x in the following sense: $\min_{y \in J_x} d(z, y) \leq d(z, x)$, for any point $z \in V \setminus \{x\}$. A node y *guards* node x *from* node z if $d(z, y) \leq d(z, y)$.

Welzl [57] has made a number of useful observations of metrics of bounded independence dimension. He showed that the number of guards needed in a metric is indeed exactly its independence dimension. In a Euclidean space $\mathbb{R}^n$, it equals the maximum number of unit vectors that form pairwise angles of more than 60°. Therefore, the independence is at most the so-called kissing number, the maximum number of disjoint open balls of radius 1 that can touch the unit ball. This number grows exponentially in the dimensions but its exact value is not known for most dimensions.

As a simple example, let us see how six guards suffice in the plane. Given a point x, divide the plane into six 60° sectors around x and partition V accordingly into sets $S_1, S_2, \ldots, S_6$. Let J_x consist of the nearest point to x in each of the six sectors. The guarding property follows from the fact that the angle $\angle g_i x y_i$ is at least 60°, for each point $y_i \in S_i$ and guard $g_i \in J_x$.

We define a decay space to be *bounded-growth* if it has bounded independence dimension and bounded doubling dimension.

The doubling and independence dimensions are actually incomparable. The uniform metric, with identical unit decays, is of independence dimension 1 but unbounded doubling dimension. The following curious construction of Welzl

[57] gives a metric of doubling dimension 1 whose independence dimension is unbounded: Let $V = \{v_{-1}, v_0, v_1, \ldots, v_n\}$ with $d(v_{-1}, v_i) = 2^i - \epsilon$, for $0 < \epsilon \leq 1/4$, and $d(v_j, v_i) = 2^i$, for $i, j \neq -1, j < i$. We leave it to the curious reader to verify that any ball (only those of radius 2^i or $2^i - \epsilon$ matter) can be covered with two balls of half the radius and that $V \setminus \{v_{-1}\}$ are independent with respect to v_{-1}.

Amicability. The following definition originates in [10] (with roots in [1]) as *C-independent conflict graphs.*

Definition 7. A set L of links is *h-amicable* if, for any feasible subset $S \subseteq L$, there is a subset $S' \subseteq S$ with $|S'| \geq 3|S|/4$ such that for any vertex $v \in S$, $a_v(S') \leq h$ (using uniform power).

It is known that instances of GEO-SINR in metric spaces are $2^{O(\alpha)}$-amicable [1]. Various decentralized capacity-type problems with uniform power have been treated with no-regret minimization techniques, relying only on the amicability property of the instances [12, 1, 9, 17, 10].

To bound amicability, we first show how to turn feasible sets in doubling spaces into well-separated sets at limited cost.

We shall make use of the following technique.

LEMMA 4.2 (SIGNAL-STRENGTHENING [33]). *There is a polynomial-time algorithm that, for any given p, q, partitions any p-feasible set into $\lceil 2q/p \rceil^2$ sets, all q-feasible.*

We first argue that feasible sets under uniform power must be at least $1/\zeta$-separated, independent of metric.

LEMMA 4.3. *Let S be an e^2/β-feasible set of links under uniform power. Then, S is $1/\zeta$-separated.*

PROOF. Suppose otherwise. Then, there are two links l_v, l_w in S that are not $1/\zeta$-separated. There are three cases, depending on which pairwise distance bound is violated.

Consider first the case when $d(s_v, r_w) < (1/\zeta) \max(d_{vv}, d_{ww})$. Since the two links co-exist in a $1/\beta$-feasible set, $a_v(w) = c_w f_{ww}/f_{vw} \leq \beta$, and since $c_w \geq \beta$, it follows that $P/f_{ww} \geq P/f_{vw}$, i.e., the signal received by r_w from s_w is at least as strong as that from the other sender s_v. So, $d_{ww} \leq d(s_v, r_w)$, implying that $d(s_v, r_w) < (1/\zeta) d_{vv}$. Then, by the triangular inequality and these bounds,

$$d(s_w, r_v) \leq d_{ww} + d(r_w, s_v) + d_{vv} \leq 2d(s_v, r_w) + d_{vv} < (1 + 2/\zeta) d_{vv} \; .$$

Thus, $f_{wv} < (1 + 2/\zeta)^\zeta f_{vv} \leq e^2 f_{vv}$. It follows that

$$a_w(v) = c_v \frac{f_{vv}}{f_{wv}} \geq \frac{c_v}{e^2} > \frac{\beta}{e^2} \; .$$

This contradicts the assumption that l_v and l_w coexist in the same e^2/β-feasible set.

Consider next the case when $d(r_v, r_w) < (1/\zeta) \max(d_{vv}, d_{ww})$. Without loss of generality, assume $d(r_v, r_w) < d_{vv}/\zeta$. By the triangular inequality, $d_{vw} \leq d_{vv} + d(r_v, r_w) < d_{vv}(1 + 1/\zeta)$, implying that $f_{vw} < (1 + 1/\zeta)^\zeta f_{vv} \leq e \cdot f_{vv}$, leading to a contradiction as before. Finally, the case when $d(s_v, s_w) < \max(d_{vv}, d_{ww})$ is symmetric to the previous one when swapping senders and receivers. Hence, the claim. □

We next show that in doubling metrics, the separation factor can be expanded at the cost of a polynomial factor.

LEMMA 4.4. *Let τ and η be positive parameters, $\tau < \eta$. Let S be a τ-separated set of links in a decay space whose quasi-distance metric has doubling dimension A'. Then, S can be partitioned into $O((\eta/\tau)^{A'})$ sets, each of which is η-separated.*

PROOF. Consider a link l_v in S. Let $R_v = \{r_u : \exists l_u = (s_u, r_u) \in S, d(l_u, l_v) \leq \eta d_{vv}, d_{uu} \geq d_{vv}\}$ be the set of links in S that are at least as long as l_v and whose receivers are within distance $\eta \cdot d_{vv}$ from r_v. We first bound the cardinality of R_v.

Draw a ball of radius $\tau d_{vv}/2$ around each receiver in R_v. Since S is τ-separated, and the links lengths are at least d_{vv}, the $|R_v|$ balls are disjoint; also, they are properly contained in a ball of radius of $(\eta + \tau/2) d_{vv}$ (around r_v). By the definition of the Assouad dimension,

$$|R_v| \leq C \left(\frac{\eta + \tau/2}{\tau/2} \right)^{A'} = C\left((2\eta + 1)/\tau\right)^{A'} \; . \quad (4)$$

We now form the graph $G_S = (V, E)$, where $V = S$ and $(l_v, l_w) \in E$ iff $l_v \in R_w$ or $l_w \in R_v$. Let $\rho = \max_{l_v \in S} |R_v| \leq C((2\eta + 1)/\tau)^{A'} = O((\eta/\tau)^{A'})$. Form a total order $\prec$ on the nodes by non-increasing link length. By (4), each node has at most ρ neighbors that follow it in the ordering (because if $d_{vv} < d_{ww}$ then $l_v \notin R_w$). That is, $\prec$ is a *ρ-inductive* (or, *ρ-degenerate*) ordering of G. Coloring the graph first-fit according to $\prec$ uses at most $\rho + 1$ colors. To complete the proof, we observe that a set of links is η-separated if and only if the corresponding set of vertices in the graph is independent (graph-theoretically). □

Put together, we obtain a sparsity-strengthening lemma in doubling spaces. Recall that $\underline{\zeta} = \max(1, \zeta)$.

LEMMA 4.5. *Let S be a feasible set of links in a decay space whose quasi-distance metric has doubling dimension A'. Then, S can be partitioned into $O(\underline{\zeta}^{2A'})$ sets, all of which are ζ-separated.*

PROOF. Recall that by the signal strengthening Lemma 4.2, S can be partitioned into at most $(2e^2/\beta + 1)^2$ sets each of which is e^2/β-feasible. Let S' be such a set. By Lemma 4.3, S' is $1/\zeta$-separated. If $\zeta \leq 1$, we are done. Otherwise, $\zeta = \underline{\zeta}$ and by Lemma 4.4, S' can be partitioned into $O(\underline{\zeta}^{2A'})$ sets, each of which is ζ-separated. □

We are now ready to prove the structural result of this section.

THEOREM 4.6. *Let L be a set of links in a decay space of independence dimension D and whose quasi-distance metric has doubling dimension A'. Then, L is $O(D\underline{\zeta}^{2A'})$-amicable.*

PROOF. Let $S \subseteq L$ be a feasible subset of L. By Lemma 4.5, there is a partition of S into ζ-separated sets $X_1, X_2, \ldots, X_s$, with $s = O(\underline{\zeta}^{2A'})$. Let i be an index, $1 \leq i \leq s$. Let $Y_i = \{l_v : a_v(X_i) \leq 4\}$ be the subset of links in X_i with low out-affectance. Note that $\sum_{l_v \in X_i} a_v(X_i) = \sum_{l_v \in X_i} a_{X_i}(v) \leq |X_i|$, by feasibility, so the average out-affectance of links in X_i is at most 1. By Markov's inequality, at least three fourths of the links in X_i will have out-affectance at most four times the average. Thus, $|Y_i| \geq 3|X_i|/4$.

Consider any link $l_v \in L$. Let $J_v = \{g_1, g_2, \ldots, g_t\}$ be the indices of senders in $|Y_i|$ that guard the sender s_v of l_v, where $t \le D$. Partition Y_i into sets $S_1, S_2, \ldots, S_t$, where s_{g_j} is contained in S_j and guards s_v from the senders of other links in S_j. Consider any set S_j and let l_x be a link in S_j. Since s_{g_j} guards s_v from s_x, $d(s_{g_j}, s_x) \le d(s_v, s_x)$. Then, additionally using the triangular inequality and that S_j is ζ-separated,

$$d(s_{g_j}, s_x) \le d(s_v, s_x) \le d_{vx} + d_{xx} \le (1 + 1/\zeta) d_{vx} .$$

So, $f(s_{g_j}, s_x) = d(s_{g_j}, s_x)^\zeta \le (1+1/\zeta)^\zeta f_{vx} \le e \cdot f_{vx}$. In a similar way, we obtain that $d_{g_j x} \le d(s_{g_j}, s_x) + d_{xx} \le (1 + 1/\zeta) d(s_{g_j}, s_x)$, so $f_{g_j x} \le e \cdot f(s_{g_j}, s_x)$. Combining, we get that $f_{g_j x} \le e \cdot f(s_{g_j}, s_x) \le e^2 f_{vx}$. We can then bound the out-affectance of l_v on S_j by

$$\begin{aligned} a_v(S_j) &= \sum_{l_x \in S_j} a_v(x) = \sum_{l_x \in S_j} c_x \cdot \frac{f_{xx}}{f_{vx}} \\ &\le a_v(g_j) + \sum_{l_x \in S_j \setminus \{l_{g_j}\}} c_x \cdot \frac{e^2 \cdot f_{xx}}{f_{g_j x}} \\ &\le 1 + e^2 \cdot a_{g_j}(S_j) \le 1 + 4e^2 , \end{aligned}$$

using the definition of Y_i in the last inequality. Then, $a_v(Y_i) = \sum_j a_v(S_j) \le (1+4e^2)D$. Let $S' = \cup_i Y_i$ and recall that $|S'| = \sum_i |Y_i| \ge \frac{3}{4} \sum_i |X_i| = \frac{3}{4}|S|$. Finally, $a_v(S') = \sum_i a_v(Y_i) \le (1+4e^2)D \cdot O(\underline{\zeta}^{2A'})$. Thus, L satisfies the definition of amicability with $h = O(D\underline{\zeta}^{2A'})$. □

This bound on amicability directly implies improved approximation for numerous distributed problems (from the previous, usually implicit, $\exp(O(\alpha))$ bounds). Note that for the plane $A' = 2$.

COROLLARY 4.7. *There is a distributed algorithm based on no-regret learning for* CAPACITY *with $O(\underline{\alpha}^4)$-approximation in the plane [12, 1]. This holds also in the presence of jamming [9], changing spectrum availability [10] and for online requests against stochastic adversaries [17].*

4.2 Inapproximability results for a variant of metricity

Metricity variant φ. Various alternative measures of the metric-like behavior of a space $\mathcal{D} = (V, f)$ can be concocted. A particularly natural one is the parameter φ that bounds the *multiplicative* factor within which f satisfies a relaxed triangular inequality:

$$\varphi = \max_{x,y,z \in V} \frac{f_{xy} + f_{yz}}{f_{xz}} .$$

So, φ is the smallest value such that $f_{xz} \le \varphi(f_{xy} + f_{yz})$, for every $x, y, z \in V$. For comparison with ζ, we define $\phi = \lg \varphi$.

Examining the proofs of the various results for CAPACITY and *inductive independence* [36], we find that the triangular inequality is applied to compare lengths that are within constant factor of each other, in which case the overhead is comparable to the case of ζ. Thus, the results hold also in terms of ϕ.

Observation 2. CAPACITY, both with monotone power [27, 22] and arbitrary power control [40], is approximable within $2^{O(\phi)}$. Other results with effective (exponential) approximations in terms of similar bounds hold for inductive independence [36, 25] and relationships between power control and monotone power [25].

Bounds on inductive independence also have numerous implications, including connectivity and aggregation [31, 28], spectrum auctions [36, 35], dynamic packet scheduling [42], and distributed scheduling [43, 32].

We can observe that $\zeta \le \phi$. Namely, for any nodes x, y, z, $f_{xz}^{1/\zeta} \le f_{xy}^{1/\zeta} + f_{yz}^{1/\zeta} \le 2\max(f_{xy}^{1/\zeta}, f_{yz}^{1/\zeta}) = 2(\max(f_{xy}, f_{yz}))^{1/\zeta} \le 2(f_{xy} + f_{yz})^{1/\zeta}$, using the definition of ζ. Thus, $f_{uv} \le 2^\zeta (f_{uw} + f_{wv})$. Hence, lower bounds in terms of ζ carry over to lower bounds in terms of $\phi = \log \varphi$, so exponential approximations in terms of ϕ are best possible in general metrics.

A converse relation between ζ and ϕ does not exist, however. Consider the instance on three points $V = \{a, b, c\}$ with $f_{ab} = 1$, $f_{bc} = q$ and $f_{ac} = 2q$, with $q \gg 1$. Then, one can verify that $\phi \le 2$, while $\zeta = \theta(\log q / \log\log q)$, which is unbounded.

Hardness in terms of φ. We find that CAPACITY in bounded-growth spaces is still exponentially hard in terms of ϕ. We give a construction that is embedded on a pair of lines, that holds for arbitrary values of a parameter α. For decays within the lines, it uses the usual distance function raised to power α, while between the lines, it uses two fixed decays: $n^{\alpha-1}$ and n^α. It then also shows that strong hardness holds even when none of the decay functions are particularly fast growing.

THEOREM 4.8 ([19]). CAPACITY *of equi-decay links in bounded-growth decay spaces is hard to approximate within $2^{\phi(1-o(1))}$-factor. This holds even if the algorithm is allowed arbitrary power control against an adversary that uses uniform power.*

PROOF. By reduction from the maximum independent set problem in graphs. Let α be arbitrary value satisfying $\alpha > 1$, denoting the maximum path-loss term and let $\alpha' = \alpha - 1$. Assume for simplicity that $N = 0$ and $\beta = 1$. Let $d_2(\cdot)$ refer to the standard Euclidean distance.

Given graph $G = (V, E)$, form a set L of links with link $l_i = (s_i, r_i)$ for each vertex $v_i \in V$ located in the plane. The senders are located on the vertical line segment $[(0,0),(0,n)]$ and the receivers on the segment $[(n,0),(n,n)]$: s_i at point $(0,i)$ and r_i at point (n,i).

Decays between points on the same line (both senders or both receivers) are set to their distance to the power of α'. For decays between points on different lines, we use two fixed decays: $n^{\alpha'}$ and $n^{\alpha'+1}$. Formally, for links l_i and l_j, let

$$f_{ij} = f(s_i, r_j) = \begin{cases} d_2(s_i, r_j)^{\alpha'} = n^{\alpha'} & \text{if } i = j \\ n^{\alpha'} - \delta & \text{if } v_i v_j \in E \\ n^{\alpha'+1} & \text{if } v_i v_j \notin E , \end{cases}$$

where $0 < \delta < 1/2$. Also, let $f(s_i, s_j) = f(r_i, r_j) = |i - j|^{\alpha'}$.

With uniform power P, we have that for each $i \ne j$,

$$a_i(j) = \frac{P/f_{ij}}{P/f_{jj}} = \frac{n^{\alpha'}}{f_{ij}} \begin{cases} > 1 & \text{if } v_i v_j \in E \\ \le 1/n & \text{if } v_i v_j \notin E. \end{cases}$$

Hence, a set $S \subset L$ of links is feasible iff $V_S = \{v_i \in V : l_i \in S\}$ is an independent set.

For the case of power control, consider a pair of links l_v, l_w and let $\mathcal{P}$ be any power assignment on the links. If $(v, w) \in E$, then $f_{vw} \cdot f_{wv} = (n^{\alpha'} - \delta)^2$, which implies that

$$a_v^{\mathcal{P}}(w) \cdot a_w^{\mathcal{P}}(v) \ge \beta^2 \frac{f_{vv} \cdot f_{ww}}{f_{vw} \cdot f_{wv}} = \beta^2 \frac{n^{2\alpha'}}{(n^{\alpha'} - \delta)^2} > \beta^2 = 1 .$$

So, at least one of $a_v^{\mathcal{P}}(w)$ and $a_w^{\mathcal{P}}(v)$ must be greater than one, implying that no power assignment allows l_v and l_w to be simultaneously feasible. Hence, any feasible set S must correspond to an independent set in G, and we know that any independent set in G can be made feasible in L using uniform power. Solutions to CAPACITY on L are therefore in one-one correspondence with solutions to MAX INDEPENDENT SET on G, preserving solution size.

Regarding φ, observe that $f(s_i, s_j) = f(r_i, r_j) \geq 1$. Then, we can verify that for any triplet x, y, z of points used in L,

$$f_{xz} \leq 2n \max(f_{xy}, f_{yz}) .$$

Thus, $\varphi = O(n)$. Hence, if CAPACITY is approximable within $f(\varphi)$ factor, then MAX INDEPENDENT SET is approximable within $O(f(n))$ factor. In particular, the $\Omega(n^{1-o(1)})$-computational hardness of MAX INDEPENDENT SET [44] implies equivalent $\Omega(\varphi^{1-o(1)})$-hardness for CAPACITY.

Finally, we examine the bounded-growth properties of the space. Any packing consists of packings in a smaller target ball in each of the two lines. A t-packing on the line within a target ball of size R has cardinality at most $(R/t)^{\alpha'}$. Thus, we find that the decay space is doubling with Assouad dimension $A = 1/\alpha' = 1/(\alpha - 1)$ and constant $C = 2$. As for independence, all nodes on a line are closer to each other than they are to any node on the other line. Thus, an independent set with respect to a point x contains at most two points from the same line as x and at most one point from the other line, for an independence dimension of 3. □

We note that the decays used in the construction were all in the range $d^{\alpha'}$ and $d^{\alpha'+1}$ between pairs of distance d. This result thus shows that huge decays (or, path-loss) are not needed *per se* to get large approximation hardness. Rather, it is the differences in decay among spatially related points that is the cause.

5. CONCLUSIONS

We have proposed studying wireless algorithms in abstract decay spaces to capture complex environments combined with parameters of closeness to a metric space. The wholesale theory transfer that follows appears to validate recent efforts to elucidate theoretical properties of the SINR model. The lesson for algorithm designers seems to be that GEO-SINR is fine but strictly Euclidean properties are to be avoided. Finally, our results may also indirectly strengthen the case for carrier sense or measurement mechanisms.

Several directions remain to be addressed. Different parameterizations, possibly tolerating local perturbations, is one. Capturing probabilistic behavior is another. Dynamic settings are extremely important yet lightly explored. Finally, recent advances at the physical layer (alignment, beamforming) open up completely new dimensions worth exploring analytically.

6. REFERENCES

[1] E. Ásgeirsson and P. Mitra. On a game theoretic approach to capacity maximization in wireless networks. In *INFOCOM*, 2011.

[2] C. Avin, Y. Emek, E. Kantor, Z. Lotker, D. Peleg, and L. Roditty. SINR diagrams: Convexity and its applications in wireless networks. *J. ACM*, 59(4), 2012.

[3] N. Baccour, A. Koubaa, L. Mottola, M. A. Zuniga, H. Youssef, C. A. Boano, and M. Alves. Radio link quality estimation in wireless sensor networks: a survey. *ACM Trans. Sensor Netw.*, 8(4):34, 2012.

[4] M. H. Bodlaender, M. M. Halldórsson, and P. Mitra. Connectivity and Aggregation in Multihop Wireless Networks. In *PODC*, 2013.

[5] D. Chafekar, V. Kumar, M. Marathe, S. Parthasarathy, and A. Srinivasan. Cross-layer latency minimization for wireless networks using SINR constraints. In *Mobihoc*, 2007.

[6] D. Chafekar, V. Kumar, M. Marathe, S. Parthasarathy, and A. Srinivasan. Approximation algorithms for computing capacity of wireless networks with SINR constraints. In *INFOCOM*, 2008.

[7] Y. Chen and A. Terzis. On the mechanisms and effects of calibrating RSSI measurements for 802.15.4 radios. In *EWSN*, pages 256–271, 2010.

[8] J. Dams, M. Hoefer, and T. Kesselheim. Scheduling in wireless networks with Rayleigh-fading interference. In *SPAA*, pages 327–335, 2012.

[9] J. Dams, M. Hoefer, and T. Kesselheim. Jamming-resistant learning in wireless networks. *arXiv:1307.5290*, 2013. To appear in *ICALP* 2014.

[10] J. Dams, M. Hoefer, and T. Kesselheim. Sleeping experts in wireless networks. In *DISC*, pages 344–357. Springer, 2013.

[11] S. Daum, S. Gilbert, F. Kuhn, and C. C. Newport. Broadcast in the ad hoc SINR model. In *DISC*, pages 358–372, 2013.

[12] M. Dinitz. Distributed algorithms for approximating wireless network capacity. In *INFOCOM*, 2010.

[13] A. Fanghänel, S. Geulen, M. Hoefer, and B. Vöcking. Online capacity maximization in wireless networks. *Journal of Scheduling*, 16(1):81–91, 2013.

[14] A. Fanghänel, T. Kesselheim, H. Räcke, and B. Vöcking. Oblivious interference scheduling. In *PODC*, pages 220–229, August 2009.

[15] A. Fanghänel, T. Kesselheim, and B. Vöcking. Improved algorithms for latency minimization in wireless networks. In *ICALP*, pages 447–458, 2009.

[16] F. Fuchs and D. Wagner. On local broadcasting schedules and CONGEST algorithms in the SINR model. In *ALGOSENSORS*, pages 170–184, 2013.

[17] O. Göbel, M. Hoefer, T. Kesselheim, T. Schleiden, and B. Vöcking. Online independent set beyond the worst-case: Secretaries, prophets, and periods. *CoRR*, abs/1307.3192, 2013. To appear in ICALP 2014.

[18] A. Goldsmith. *Wireless Communications*. Cambridge Univ. Press, 2005.

[19] O. Goussevskaia, M. M. Halldórsson, R. Wattenhofer, and E. Welzl. Capacity of Arbitrary Wireless Networks. In *INFOCOM*, pages 1872–1880, April 2009.

[20] O. Goussevskaia, T. Moscibroda, and R. Wattenhofer. Local Broadcasting in the Physical Interference Model. In *DialM-POMC*, August 2008.

[21] O. Goussevskaia, Y. A. Oswald, and R. Wattenhofer. Complexity in geometric SINR. In *Mobihoc*, 2007.

[22] H. Gudmundsdottir, E. I. Ásgeirsson, M. Bodlaender, J. T. Foley, M. M. Halldórsson, G. M. Jarvelä, H. Ulfarsson, and Y. Vigfusson. Measurement based

interference models for wireless scheduling algorithms. *arXiv:1401.1723*, 2014.
[23] P. Gupta and P. R. Kumar. The Capacity of Wireless Networks. *IEEE Trans. Information Theory*, 46(2):388–404, 2000.
[24] M. M. Halldórsson. Wireless scheduling with power control. *ACM Trans. Algorithms*, 9(1):7, 2012.
[25] M. M. Halldórsson, S. Holzer, P. Mitra, and R. Wattenhofer. The power of non-uniform wireless power. In *SODA*, 2013.
[26] M. M. Halldórsson and P. Mitra. Wireless capacity with arbitrary gain matrix. In *ALGOSENSORS*, pages 215–224, 2011.
[27] M. M. Halldórsson and P. Mitra. Wireless Capacity with Oblivious Power in General Metrics. In *SODA*, 2011.
[28] M. M. Halldórsson and P. Mitra. Distributed connectivity of wireless networks. In *PODC*, 2012.
[29] M. M. Halldórsson and P. Mitra. Towards tight bounds for local broadcasting. In *FOMC*, page 2, 2012.
[30] M. M. Halldórsson and P. Mitra. Wireless capacity and admission control in cognitive radio. In *INFOCOM*, pages 855–863, 2012.
[31] M. M. Halldórsson and P. Mitra. Wireless Connectivity and Capacity. In *SODA*, 2012.
[32] M. M. Halldórsson and P. Mitra. Nearly optimal bounds for distributed wireless scheduling in the SINR model. *Dist. Comput.*, 2014. To appear. CoRR abs/1107.4981. Earlier version in ICALP 2011.
[33] M. M. Halldórsson and R. Wattenhofer. Wireless Communication is in APX. In *ICALP*, 2009.
[34] J. Heinonen. *Lectures on Analysis in Metric Spaces*. Springer, 1999.
[35] M. Hoefer and T. Kesselheim. Secondary spectrum auctions for symmetric and submodular bidders. In *EC*, pages 657–671, 2012.
[36] M. Hoefer, T. Kesselheim, and B. Vöcking. Approximation algorithms for secondary spectrum auctions. In *SPAA*, 2011.
[37] T. Jurdzinski and D. R. Kowalski. Distributed backbone structure for algorithms in the SINR model of wireless networks. In *DISC*, pages 106–120, 2012.
[38] T. Jurdzinski, D. R. Kowalski, M. Rozanski, and G. Stachowiak. Distributed randomized broadcasting in wireless networks under the SINR model. In *DISC*, pages 373–387, 2013.
[39] T. Jurdzinski, D. R. Kowalski, and G. Stachowiak. Distributed deterministic broadcasting in uniform-power ad hoc wireless networks. In *FCT*, 2013.
[40] T. Kesselheim. A Constant-Factor Approximation for Wireless Capacity Maximization with Power Control in the SINR Model. In *SODA*, 2011.
[41] T. Kesselheim. Approximation algorithms for wireless link scheduling with flexible data rates. In *ESA*, 2012.
[42] T. Kesselheim. Dynamic packet scheduling in wireless networks. In *PODC*, pages 281–290, 2012.
[43] T. Kesselheim and B. Vöcking. Distributed contention resolution in wireless networks. In *DISC*, August 2010.
[44] S. Khot and A. K. Ponnuswami. Better inapproximability results for maxclique, chromatic number and min-3lin-deletion. In *ICALP*, 2006.
[45] D. Kotz, C. Newport, R. S. Gray, J. Liu, Y. Yuan, and C. Elliott. Experimental evaluation of wireless simulation assumptions. In *MSWiM*, 2004.
[46] Z. Lotker, M. Parter, D. Peleg, and Y. A. Pignolet. Distributed power control in the SINR model. In *INFOCOM*, pages 2525–2533, 2011.
[47] R. Maheshwari, S. Jain, and S. R. Das. A measurement study of interference modeling and scheduling in low-power wireless networks. In *SenSys*, pages 141–154, 2008.
[48] T. Moscibroda and R. Wattenhofer. The complexity of connectivity in wireless networks. In *INFOCOM*, 2006.
[49] G. Pei and A. K. S. Vullikanti. Distributed approximation algorithms for maximum link scheduling and local broadcasting in the physical interference model. In *INFOCOM*, 2013.
[50] C. Scheideler, A. W. Richa, and P. Santi. An $O(\log n)$ dominating set protocol for wireless ad-hoc networks under the physical interference model. In *MobiHoc*, pages 91–100, 2008.
[51] V. Sevani and B. Raman. SIR based interference modeling for wireless mesh networks: A detailed measurement study. In *COMSNETS*. IEEE, 2012.
[52] D. Son, B. Krishnamachari, and J. Heidemann. Experimental study of concurrent transmission in wireless sensor networks. In *SenSys*. ACM, 2006.
[53] T. Tonoyan. Algorithms for scheduling with power control in wireless networks. In *TAPAS*, 2011.
[54] T. Tonoyan. On some bounds on the optimum schedule length in the SINR model. In *ALGOSENSORS*, pages 120–131, 2012.
[55] T. Tonoyan. Comparing schedules in the SINR and conflict-graph models with different power schemes. In *ADHOC-NOW*, pages 317–328, 2013.
[56] P. Wan, O. Frieder, X. Jia, F. Yao, X. Xu, and S. Tang. Wireless link scheduling under physical interference model. In *INFOCOM*, 2011.
[57] E. Welzl. Blue-dominant centers. Unpublished memorandum, June 2008.
[58] X. Xu, J. Cao, and X.-Y. Li. MLLS: Minimum length link scheduling under physical interference model. *CoRR*, abs/1208.0627, 2012.
[59] D. Yu, Q.-S. Hua, Y. Wang, H. Tan, and F. C. M. Lau. Distributed multiple-message broadcast in wireless ad-hoc networks under the SINR model. In *SIROCCO*, pages 111–122, 2012.
[60] D. Yu, Q.-S. Hua, Y. Wang, J. Yu, and F. C. M. Lau. Efficient distributed multiple-message broadcasting in unstructured wireless networks. In *INFOCOM*, 2013.
[61] D. Yu, Y. Wang, Q.-S. Hua, and F. C. M. Lau. Distributed $(\Delta + 1)$-coloring in the physical model. In *ALGOSENSORS*, pages 145–160, 2011.
[62] D. Yu, Y. Wang, Q.-S. Hua, and F. C. M. Lau. An $O(\log n)$ distributed approximation algorithm for local broadcasting in unstructured wireless networks. In *DCOSS*, pages 132–139, 2012.

On the Impact of Geometry on Ad Hoc Communication in Wireless Networks*

Tomasz Jurdzinski
Institute of Computer Science
University of Wrocław, Poland

Dariusz R. Kowalski
Department of Computer Science
University of Liverpool, UK

Michal Rozanski
Institute of Computer Science
University of Wrocław, Poland

Grzegorz Stachowiak
Institute of Computer Science
University of Wrocław, Poland

ABSTRACT

In this work we address the question how important is the knowledge of geometric location and network density to the efficiency of (distributed) wireless communication in ad hoc networks. We study fundamental communication task of broadcast and develop well-scalable, randomized algorithms that do not rely on GPS information, and which efficiency formulas do not depend on how dense the geometric network is. We consider two settings: with and without spontaneous wake-up of nodes. In the former setting, in which all nodes start the protocol at the same time, our algorithm accomplishes broadcast in $O(D \log n + \log^2 n)$ rounds under the SINR model, with high probability (whp), where D is the diameter of the communication graph and n is the number of stations. In the latter setting, in which only the source node containing the original message is active in the beginning, we develop a slightly slower algorithm working in $O(D \log^2 n)$ rounds whp. Both algorithms are based on a novel distributed coloring method, which is of independent interest and potential applicability to other communication tasks under the SINR wireless model.

Categories and Subject Descriptors

C.2.1 [**Computer-Communication Networks**]: Network Architecture and Design; F.2.2 [**Analysis of Algorithms and Problem Complexity**]: Nonnumerical Algorithms and Problems

Keywords

Ad Hoc wireless networks; Signal-to-Interference-and-Noise-Ratio (SINR) model; Broadcast; Coloring; Distributed algorithms

1. INTRODUCTION

In this paper we study distributed communication problems in wireless networks, where interferences are resolved by the Signal-to-Interference-and-Noise Ratio (SINR) physical model. Specifically, but not exclusively, we concentrate on the broadcast problem, where a piece of information stored in a specified station/node (the source) is supposed to be delivered to all other stations in the network. The broadcast is a fundamental communication primitive, whose complexity is well understood in the previous models of wireless communication, such as radio networks. Closer to reality, models based on the SINR constraint attracted attention of algorithmic community much later than the radio network model. One of the key differences between models is that radio networks take into account only interference between stations in close neighborhood, while the SINR model relies on the physical assumptions that the strength of signals decrease gradually according to a continuous function and cumulate, which makes development of algorithms and their analysis much more complicated.

In this work we show that efficiency of wireless communication depends mainly on parameters of the communication graph, even for devices with limited knowledge and capabilities. In particular, we do not assume any carrier sensing capabilities, initial synchronization or any knowledge other than rough estimates of the number of nodes and physical SINR parameters. Despite of that, we develop almost optimal and well scalable solutions to the broadcast and wake-up problems. Moreover, as mentioned above, the worst-case performance of the considered communication tasks, and other problems building on them, depends only on the topology of the communication graph, also called a reachability graph, and not on specific location of nodes within reachability balls. One of the implications is that geometric properties of reachability regions studied in some previous works, c.f., [1], do not influence worst-case scenarios in ad hoc communication by more than $O(\log^2 n)$ factor - the factor by which our algorithms are far from lower bounds.

1.1 Model

We consider the model of a wireless network consisting of *stations*, also called *nodes*, deployed into a metric space with *bounded growth property* of degree γ.[1] All stations are identical, and therefore each of them has the same transmission power P (we call it a *uniform power model*).

There are three fixed model parameters: path loss $\alpha > \gamma$, threshold $\beta \geq 1$, ambient noise $\mathcal{N} > 0$. We also assume a connectivity graph parameter $\varepsilon \in (0, 1)$.

*This work was supported by the Polish National Science Centre grant DEC-2012/07/B/ST6/01534.

PODC'14, July 15–18, 2014, Paris, France.
Copyright 2014 ACM 978-1-4503-2944-6/14/07 ...$15.00.
http://dx.doi.org/10.1145/2611462.2611487.

[1]This notion generalizes the Euclidean R^γ space; its formal definition is provided later in this section.

The $SINR(v, u, \mathcal{T})$ ratio, for given stations u, v and a set of (transmitting) stations $\mathcal{T}$, is defined as follows:

$$SINR(v, u, \mathcal{T}) = \frac{P\text{dist}(v, u)^{-\alpha}}{\mathcal{N} + \sum_{w \in \mathcal{T} \setminus \{v\}} P_w \text{dist}(w, u)^{-\alpha}} \quad (1)$$

In the *Signal-to-Interference-and-Noise-Ratio (SINR) model* a station u successfully receives a message from a station v in a round if $v \in \mathcal{T}$, $u \notin \mathcal{T}$ and $SINR(v, u, \mathcal{T}) \geq \beta$, where $\mathcal{T}$ is the set of stations transmitting in that round.

Synchronization.

It is assumed that algorithms work synchronously in rounds. In general, we do not assume global clock ticking. Note, however, that some kind of global synchronization can be achieved by appending a counter to every message sent throughout broadcast algorithm; we use this property in algorithms developed in this work.

Carrier sensing.

We consider the model *without carrier sensing*, that is, a station u has no other feedback from the wireless channel than receiving or not receiving a message in a round t.

Knowledge of stations.

Each station knows the number of stations in the network, n. Our algorithms also work when stations share, instead of n, an estimate $\nu \geq n$ of this value which is $O(n^c)$ for a fixed constant c. We assume that nodes do not know the precise value of the SINR parameters α, β, and $\mathcal{N}$ but instead know only upper and lower bounds for the parameters (i.e., $\alpha_{\min}$ and $\alpha_{\max}$, $\beta_{\min}$ and $\beta_{\max}$, $\mathcal{N}_{\min}$ and $\mathcal{N}_{\max}$). For simplicity, in this version of the paper we perform calculations assuming that exact values of these parameters are known. In order to take into account uncertainty regarding those parameters, it is sufficient to choose their maximal/minimal values depending on the fact whether upper or lower estimates are provided.

Messages and initialization of stations.

We consider two variants of initialization of stations: without spontaneous wake-up and with spontaneous wake-up. In the former model each station (except some distinguished one(s)) sleeps till it obtains the message for the first time. In the latter variant, all nodes are woken up at the same time and start an execution of an algorithm simultaneously. (Observe that nodes can benefit from the spontaneous wake-up setting by performing a local preprocessing simultaneously for the whole network.)

Each station can either act as a sender or as a receiver during a round. A sender can transmit a broadcast message with attaching to it $O(\log n)$ additional bits. Our algorithms are described from a "global" perspective, i.e., we count rounds starting from the moment when the first message is sent. In order to synchronize stations in the model with non-spontaneous wake-up, we assume that each message contains the number of rounds elapsed from the beginning of the execution of the algorithm.

Ranges and uniformity.

The *communication range* r is the radius of the ball in which a message transmitted by a station is heard, provided no other station transmits at the same time. Note that $r = (P/(\mathcal{N}\beta))^{1/\alpha}$, where P is the transmission power of a station, c.f., Equation (1). Without loss of generality we assume that $r = 1$. (Note that this assumption implies the relationship $P = \mathcal{N}\beta$.)

Communication graph and graph notation.

The *communication graph* $G(V, E)$ of a given network consists of all network nodes and edges (v, u) such that $\text{dist}(v, u) \leq (1 - \varepsilon)r = 1 - \varepsilon$, where $0 < \varepsilon < 1$ is a fixed model parameter. The meaning of the communication graph is as follows: even though the idealistic communication range is r, it may be reached only in a very unrealistic case of single transmission in the whole network, c.f., [4]. In practice, however, many nodes located in different parts of the network often transmit simultaneously, and therefore it is reasonable to assume that we may only hope for a slightly smaller range to be achieved. The communication graph, through restricting connections to ranges at most $1 - \varepsilon$, envisions the network of such "reasonable reachability". It has become a classic tool in the analysis of ad hoc communication tasks under the SINR physical model c.f., [4, 13, 20].

Note that the communication graph is symmetric for uniform networks. By a *neighborhood* of a node u we mean the set of all neighbors of u in G, i.e., the set $\{w \mid (w, u) \in E(G)\}$. The *graph distance* from v to w is equal to the length of a shortest path from v to w in the communication graph, where the length of a path is equal to the number of its edges. The diameter D of a network is equal to the diameter of its communication graph (i.e., the largest graph distance between any pair of nodes), provided the graph is connected.

Metric space.

Given a metric space with a distance function dist, $B(v, r)$ for a point v from the space and $r > 0$ is equal to $\{w \mid \text{dist}(v, w) \leq r\}$ and is called a *ball* with radius r and center v. A *unit ball* is a ball with radius 1. Moreover, let $\chi(a, b)$ denote the number of balls with radius b sufficient to cover a ball with radius a. Nodes of a network are embedded (as points) in a general metric space with a distance function dist that satisfies the following *bounded growth property*: For every $d > 0$, $c \in \mathbb{N}$ and a point v in the metric space, the ball $B(v, c \cdot d)$ is included in a union of $O(c^\gamma)$ balls with radius d, where γ is a parameter called a *dimension* of the metric. (That is, $\chi(cd, d) = O(c^\gamma)$ for each $d > 0$ and $c \in \mathbb{N}$.) Note that this in particular implies that $B(v, (c+1) \cdot d) \setminus B(v, c \cdot d)$ can be covered by $O(c^{\gamma-1})$ balls with radius d; we will often rely on this property in our analysis when estimating the total strength of the interference received at a node.

Broadcast problem.

In the broadcast problem, there is one distinguished node, called the *source*, which initially holds a piece of information (also called a *source message* or a *broadcast message*). The goal is to disseminate this message to all other nodes in a network with connected communication graph. We are interested in minimizing the *time complexity* of this task being the minimum number of rounds after which, for all communication networks defined by some set of parameters, the broadcast occurs with high probability. This time is counted since the source is activated.

1.2 Previous and related work

The algorithmic research on communication in the SINR networks started around 10 years ago. Most papers concentrate on one-hop communication, which includes the local broadcast problem [8, 10, 21], link scheduling [17, 9], connectivity [2, 11] and others. Among them, the most related to this work are papers on local broadcast, in which each node has to transmit a message only to its neighbors in the corresponding communication graph. Using the local broadcast algorithm (e.g., from [10]) as a building block yields a solution for (global) broadcast that runs in

$O(D(\Delta+\log n)\log n)$ time, where Δ is the maximal degree of the communication graph. However, since there is only one message to be propagated in the global broadcast, we would like to avoid the dependence on potentially large parameter Δ (which could be necessary when all senders have different messages, but not in the case of a single source global broadcast).

In order to address obstacles for multi-hop communication, various authors take advantage of several features helping to design efficient algorithms. As for the broadcast problem in the SINR model, Scheideler at al. [19] solve the problem in $O(D+\log^2 n)$ rounds using a tunable collision detection and assuming that all stations start a protocol simultaneously, which allow them to build an overlay structure along which the message is then propagated. Yu et al. [20] solve the problem in $O(D+\log^2 n)$ rounds using power control, allowing stations to decide the strength of a transmitted signal in each step. Moreover, their results works merely for a restricted family of networks, excluding the most challenging scenarios. Specifically, their algorithm works under assumption that, for each node v, its closest neighbor is in distance at most $1/3$. Moreover, a possibility of filtering out messages received from large distances is necessary.

In [13] an $O(D\log n+\log^2 n)$ randomized algorithm and in [14] an $O(D\log^2 n)$ deterministic algorithm for networks deployed in the Euclidean space are presented, where stations know their own positions (e.g., thanks to GPS devices). Finally, Daum et al. [4] designed an algorithm working in $O((D\log n)\log^{\alpha+1} R_s)$ rounds, provided stations know only granularity R_s of the network (i.e., the maximum ratio between actual distances of stations connected by an edge in the communication graph) and do not use any other additional features.

If the model prevents successful direct transmissions between nodes which are not connected in the communication graph, so called *weak device model*, the lower bound $\Omega(D\Delta)$ holds even if stations know their positions on the plane [15], which separates that model from the one considered in this work. For other related problems in this more harsh model see e.g., [8, 12].

In a related radio network model, the complexity of broadcasting is much better understood. Its complexity in the model without collision detection is $\Theta((D+\log n)\log(n/D))$ [3, 18]. Interestingly, this lower bound was recently broken for the model with collision detection [7], in which a solution in $O(D+\text{polylog}(n))$ was designed. For the easier case where all nodes start during the same round, it is currently unknown whether or not formulas better than the ones in general graphs could be obtained, but in unit disk graphs a solution of the form $O(D+\log^2 n)$ is likely possible [4]. As shown e.g. in [6, 5], geometric graphs exhibit more efficient solutions than those possible in a general graph model of radio networks.

1.3 Our results

The results of this paper state that the broadcast problem can be accomplished in $O(D\log^2 n)$ rounds in the model without spontaneous wake-up and in $O(D\log n+\log^2 n)$ rounds in the model with spontaneous wake-up. Interestingly, this performance formulas does not depend on any geometric parameter related with specific locations of nodes, only on parameters of communication graph (expressing the relation whether nodes are within their transmission ranges or not). This improves the result of Daum et al. [4] for $R_s=\omega(2^{(\log n)^{1/(1+\alpha)}})$, where R_s is the maximum ratio between between actual distances in the metric space of stations which are connected by an edge in the communication graph. (Thus, in particular, for $R_s=\Omega(n^\delta)$, for any fixed $\delta>0$.) Moreover, our algorithm does not need information about parameter R_s. As R_s might be even exponential wrt to n,[2] this is the first solution with guaranteed $O(D\,\text{polylog}(n))$ complexity in the SINR networks without spontaneous wakeup, power assignment, carrier sensing (tuned collision detection), or any knowledge about location of nodes.

As the main tool, we design a specific coloring algorithm associating with each active station v the probability p_v which, when fixed, helps to solve other communication problems efficiently, including the consensus problem, the leader election and the alert protocol problem (due to limited space, these applications will be presented in the full version of the paper). This coloring plays a role similar to backbone structures in many other communication models (c.f., [12, 22]). In order to get rid of the dependence on the granularity parameter R_s, we use a different approach to [4]. They allow all stations to transmit with constant probability, which may generate a lot of noise but makes possible communication between stations within the smallest distance in the network. We, on the other hand, start from very low probabilities of the order $1/n$ and increase them gradually until stations can hear reasonable number of messages. Such a strategy reminds solutions to the local broadcast problem (e.g., in [10]); however, unlike in those solutions (which did not need it), the key and subtle issue in our approach is to somehow distinguish by a station v between the densities of the network in close neighborhood $B(v,\varepsilon/2)$ and in broader neighborhood $B(v,1)$. In order to tackle this issue without any geolocation information and other tools such as power control, we proceed by interleaving two kinds of phases serving different purposes: phases where stations transmit with some assigned probabilities (which intuitively grow up gradually) with phases where probabilities of transmissions are "scaled up" based on local statistics of successful transmissions with carefully probed transmission probabilities. This approach faces various technical obstacles, mainly due to the lack of geolocation information, which are addressed in the paper.

Organization of the paper.

Basic properties of simple transmission scenarios are given in Section 2. The main coloring tool, its details and construction can be found in Section 3. Its applications to broadcasting in non-spontaneous and spontaneous settings are presented in Section 4. Missing proofs can be found in the full version of the paper.

2. NOTATIONS AND TECHNICAL PRELIMINARIES

We say that an event happens in a network of n stations *with high probability (whp)* when the probability is at least $1-1/n^c$, for some constant $c>0$.[3] An event occurs with *negligible* probability if its negation occurs whp. In particular we prove in this paper that our algorithms succeed whp.

Given a metric space with the distance $\text{dist}(\cdot,\cdot)$, we use the notation $B(v,r)=\{v'\mid \text{dist}(v,v')\le r\}$. For a set of stations A, by $N(A)$ we denote the set of their neighbors in the communication graph, i.e., $N(A)=\{w\mid \text{dist}(v,w)\le 1-\varepsilon \text{ for some } v\in A\}$.

[2] Consider, for example, n stations $x_1,\ldots,x_n$ on a line such that $\text{dist}(x_i,x_{i+1})=1/2^i$.

[3] We often use union bounds to show that some undesirable events happen with small probability. Therefore, in order to carry on we usually require for some basic events occurring during the analysis to happen with probability at least $1-1/n^4$, when saying that they occur whp. This requirement will guarantee that after applying all union bound arguments within the analysis, the probability that our algorithms accomplish their tasks correctly within the given time bounds is at least $1-1/n$.

In order to simplify calculations, we assume that the constant hidden in the expressions $O(c^\gamma)$ determining the growth parameter of the metric space is equal to 1 (this does not change the asymptotic complexity of our algorithms).

Below, we formulate a basic property that a station transmitting successfully to a distance larger than $1-\varepsilon$ delivers its message to the neighbors of other stations in its close proximity.

FACT 1. *If a station v is transmitting in a round and its message can be successfully received at each point u such that $dist(u,v) \le 1-\varepsilon/2$, then the message is received by all neighbors of all nodes from $B(v,\varepsilon/2)$.*

Given a set of stations T transmitting in a round and a station u, the *interference* at u is equal to $I_u = \sum_{w\in T\setminus\{v\}} P/(\text{dist}(u,w))^\alpha$, where v is a station in the smallest distance from u among the elements of T.

FACT 2. *Let $x \le 1/2^{1/\alpha}$. If the interference at some receiver u is at most $\mathcal{N}/(2x^\alpha)$, then it can hear the transmitter v from the distance x.*

PROOF. Let us recall assumption that $P = \mathcal{N}\beta$. We have

$$SINR(v,u,T) \ge \frac{\beta\mathcal{N}}{x^\alpha}/(\mathcal{N} + \frac{\mathcal{N}}{2x^\alpha}) = \beta/(x^\alpha + 1/2) \ge \beta\,,$$

where the former inequality follows from the bound on the interference and the latter from the assumption $x \le 1/2^{1/\alpha}$. □

FACT 3. *If the interference at some receiver u is at most $\mathcal{N}\alpha x$, then it can hear the transmitter v from the distance $1-x$.*

PROOF. By the Bernoulli inequality we get $(1+x)^\alpha \ge 1+\alpha x$. Thus

$$SINR(v,u,T) \ge \frac{P/(1-x)^\alpha}{\mathcal{N}+\mathcal{N}\alpha x} \ge \frac{P}{\mathcal{N}(1+x)^\alpha(1-x)^\alpha}$$

$$= \frac{P}{\mathcal{N}(1-x^2)^\alpha} \ge \frac{P}{\mathcal{N}} = \beta\,.$$

□

Consider a scenario where every station v is assigned a variable p_v being its transmission probability.

FACT 4. *[16] Assume that $\sum_{v\in A} p_v = s \le 1/2$ for some set of stations A. Then the probability that exactly one element of A transmits is at least $s/2$ and at most s.*

FACT 5. *[16] Let $p_v \le 1/2$ for every station $v \in A$. Then the probability that no station from A transmits is at least $(1/4)^{\sum_{v\in A} p_v}$.*

3. NETWORK COLORING

The key ingredient of broadcasting algorithms presented in this paper is the procedure StabilizeProbability (Algorithm 1), which assigns probability ("color") p_v from the set

$$\{2^i p_{\text{start}} \mid i \in [0, \lceil\log(p_{\max}/p_{\text{start}})\rceil\}$$

to each station v participating in an execution, where $p_{\text{start}} = \Theta(1/n)$ and $p_{\max}$ is a constant which will be specified later. Thus, the number of colors is $O(\log n)$.

Before giving details of the procedure StabilizeProbability, we state the key properties that we want the procedure to satisfy. We express them as properties of the obtained coloring, described by the following lemmas. These lemmas are true for some constants C_1 and C_2 that depend on ε, γ, the parameters of the SINR model and constants chosen in the algorithm.

LEMMA 1. *After an execution of StabilizeProbability for a set of stations A, the inequality*

$$\sum_{\substack{w:p_w=p\\ w\in B}} p_w < C_1$$

holds for every color p and unit ball B whp.

LEMMA 2. *After an execution of StabilizeProbability on a set of stations A, for every $v \in A$ there exists a color p such that the following inequality holds whp:*

$$\sum_{\substack{w:p_w=p\\ w\in B(v,\varepsilon/2)}} p_w \ge C_2\,.$$

In this section we describe formally the algorithm StabilizeProbability and prove that it satisfies Lemma 1 and Lemma 2 for appropriate constants C_1 and C_2. Its pseudo-code is given as Algorithm 1. The pseudocode is missing information about the actual values of constants c_0, c_1, c_2, c_3, c', c_ε, C_2, and p_{start} used in the algorithm. We will choose the appropriate values for those constant in the analysis of the algorithm and its properties.

Algorithm StabilizeProbability performs two kinds of tests, defined by sub-routines DensityTest and Playoff, each of them taking $O(\log n)$ rounds. The while loop of StabilizeProbability is repeated $O(\log n)$ times, since each node v starts with $p_v = \Theta(1/n)$, increases p_v twice in each repetition of the loop and finishes either in line 6 or after achieving $p_v \ge p_{\max} = \Theta(1)$. Therefore, the following claim holds.

FACT 6. *Algorithm StabilizeProbability works in $O(\log^2 n)$ rounds whp.*

In Section 3.1, we give a general idea why StabilizeProbability satisfies Lemma 1 and Lemma 2.

In Section 3.2, the constants c_0, c_1 in the sub-routine DensityTest are set so that this procedure helps each station v to estimate whether density (i.e., the sum of probabilities assigned to stations) in $B(v,1)$ already achieved constant value. As a result, we also fix C_1 from Lemma 1.

Proofs of Lemma 1 and Lemma 2 are presented in separate sections. In Section 3.3, containing the proof of Lemma 1, the constants c_2, c_3 for sub-routine Playoff are chosen in order to guarantee that the regions (unit balls) with largest density will become sparser, i.e., some stations switch off (line 6 of Algorithm 1) in them in each execution of Playoff whp. Combined with the appropriate choice of the constant c' from Playoff, this will assure that Lemma 1 is satisfied.

In Section 3.4, dedicated to the proof of Lemma 2, the constant c_ε is chosen in order to make very unlikely the situations in which a station v switches off when the sum of probabilities of active stations in $B(v,\varepsilon/2)$ is very small. This property, combined with the fact that probabilities of "active" stations (i.e., stations which are not switched off in line 6 of Algorithm 1) grow up to the constant $p_{\max}$, will lead to the statement of Lemma 2.

3.1 Overview of the algorithm

The coloring algorithm assigns probability/color p_v to each active station $v \in A$ such that there are at most $\log n$ various colors and simultaneously the following two properties hold:

1. For each color, the sum of probabilities of stations in this color in each unit ball is at most C_1, for some constant C_1 (Lemma 1).

2. For each active station v, there exists a color such that the sum of probabilities of this color in the ball $B(v, \varepsilon/2)$ is at least C_2, for some constant C_2 (Lemma 2).

The former property assures that, when all stations transmit with assigned probabilities, the expected interference coming from the whole network is small at any station (this follows from the assumption that $\alpha > \gamma$, which implies $\sum_{i \in \mathbb{N}} i^{\gamma-1-\alpha} = O(1)$). Thanks to this property, if a station v is the only transmitter in $B(v, 2d)$ for a constant $d \leq 1 - \varepsilon$ then the message transmitted by v can be received in each point of $B(v, d)$ with constant probability. The latter property on the other hand guarantees that for each station v, the probability that a station from $B(v, \varepsilon/2)$ transmits is constant as well, for some color. Both properties combined imply that, each station from $N(A)$ receives a message with probability $\Omega(1/\log n)$ in a round if each station $v \in A$ transmits with probability $p_v/\log n$.

There is some intuition behind the coloring algorithm. The optimal probability for a station v to transmit is approximately $1/|\{w : \text{dist}(v, w) \leq \varepsilon/2\}|$. This would ensure that the sum $\sum_{B(v,\varepsilon/2)} p_v$ is limited from below by constant C_2 and C_1 is of the order of C_2/ε^γ. The algorithm starts from low probabilities (smaller than C_1/n), continuously increasing them. Once a station v starts receiving messages from others, it assumes that the sum of probabilities in $B(v, 1)$ is constant, which indicates that further increase of all probabilities in $B(v, 1)$ could break the property 1 (Lemma 1). When applied to the task of local broadcasting [10], this means that the "right" probability is reached (so, probabilities could be frozen). If stations are uniformly distributed, then this implies that the average sum of probabilities in balls of diameter ε is around C_1/ε^γ, which would also satisfy the property 2 (Lemma 2) for $C_2 \approx C_1/\varepsilon^\gamma$. In general, the constant sum of probabilities, around C_1, of stations in $B(v, 1)$ does not exclude that the sum of probabilities in $B(v, \varepsilon/2)$ is still very small.[4] Hence, our intuitive goal at this stage would be to distinguish those regions (balls of diameter ε) in which the sum of probabilities exceeds (say) half of the average from those where it is much smaller.

The main difficulty is to sense the actual sum of probabilities in $B(v, \varepsilon/2)$, without possibility of filtering out messages received from distance larger than $\varepsilon/2$ (as there is no geolocation). Imagine that stations in a network are uniformly distributed and the probabilities have reached such values that the sums in a unit ball are close to C_1. If one replaces p_v with $c_\varepsilon p_v$ for large enough c_ε (depending on the growth parameter of the metric, e.g., $c_\varepsilon \approx 1/\varepsilon^2$ in the Euclidean plane), then the average sum of probabilities in an ε-ball is around C_1. Hence, an "average" station still receives the number of messages similar to those received with the original probabilities p_v. If, however, the stations are not uniformly distributed, it is still the case that stations in the smallest ball with sum of probabilities at least C_1 could receive many message after probabilities p_v are scaled up to $c_\varepsilon p_v$. On the other hand, the situation in a (very) sparse ε-ball B is as follows (by "sparse ε-ball" we mean a ball with sum of probabilities much smaller than the average):

- The probability that $v \in B$ receives a message from other station from B is small (the sum is so small that usually no one is transmitting);
- The probability that $v \in B$ receives a message from $u \notin B$ is small as well (the sum in $B(v, 1)$ is as large after scaling up by constant c_ε that usually the interference prevents any successful transmission from distance larger than $\varepsilon/2$).

[4]Consider for example stations $v_1, \ldots, v_n$ on a line, where the distance between v_i and v_{i+1} is $1/2^i$, for $1 \leq i < n$.

Using this idea, our coloring algorithm works as follows. Procedure DensityTest verifies whether the sum of p_v's in a unit-disk around a station v is close to C_1 (i.e., whether v receives many messages when transmissions occur with probabilities p_v). If it is the case, procedure Playoff verifies if the density in close proximity of v is large (i.e., whether v still receives many messages when probabilities are scaled up). In the case of positive outcomes of both procedures, v is switched off, which decreases the sum of probabilities in the unit disk around v. If repeated sufficient number of times, Playoffs allow to preserve property 1 (Lemma 1), i.e., prevents the sums of probabilities in unit disks from going above C_1. On the other hand, as the positive result of Playoff cannot happen in (very) sparse areas while probabilities of stations (if not switched off) grow up to the constant $p_{\max}$, the property 2 (Lemma 2) is preserved at the end of an execution of StabilizeProbability.

```
procedure DENSITYTEST(v)
    for c0 log n rounds do transmit with prob. p_v
    if received at least c1 log n messages then return True
    else return False
```

```
procedure PLAYOFF(v)
    for c2 log n rounds do transmit with prob. p_v · c_ε
    if received at least c3 log n messages then return True
    else return False
```

Algorithm 1 StabilizeProbability(v)

```
p_v ← p_start                              ▷ p_start = C1/(2n)
p_max ← C2/c_ε
while p_v < p_max do
    for c' times do
        if DensityTest(v) and Playoff(v) then
            v quits with color p_v
    p_v ← 2p_v
v quits with color 2p_max
```

3.2 DensityTest

In this section we fix the constants C_1, c_0 and c_1 and state properties of DensityTest which are satisfied for this choice of constants.

We say that *bounded density property* is satisfied with the parameter $C > 0$ if $\sum_{w \in B} p_w \leq C$ for every unit ball B. The *effective communication property* is satisfied if the probability that a station v hears w when w is the only transmitting station in $B(v, 2/3)$ is at least $1/2$.

FACT 7. *For any network parameters $\alpha > \gamma$, $\beta \geq 1$, $\mathcal{N} > 0$ and $\varepsilon < 1$, there exists a constant $C > 0$ such that if the bounded density property is satisfied with any parameter $C_1 < C$, then the effective communication property is satisfied as well.*

PROOF. Assume that w is the only transmitter in $B(v, 2/3)$ and $\sum_{w \in B} p_w \leq C$ for every unit ball B and a constant C. Then, v receives the message from w by Fact 3, provided the interference from the remaining area is smaller than $\mathcal{N}\alpha \cdot \frac{1}{3}$. The expected value of this interference under the bounded density property with the parameter C is

$$
\begin{aligned}
E(I_v) &\leq C \sum_{i>0} \frac{P \cdot O(i^{\gamma-1})}{\mathcal{N} \cdot (\frac{2}{3} i)^\alpha} = \frac{CP(3/2)^\alpha}{\mathcal{N}} O(\textstyle\sum_{i>0} i^{\gamma-\alpha-1}) \\
&\leq C \cdot C'
\end{aligned}
$$

where C' is a constant depending on γ, α, β, $\mathcal{N}$. The first among the above inequalities follows from the bounded growth property and the last one from the assumption that $\gamma < \alpha$. Thus if $C < \frac{\frac{1}{6}\mathcal{N}\alpha}{C'}$ then $E(I_v) \leq C \cdot C' < \frac{1}{2} \cdot \frac{1}{3}\alpha$. Using Markov bound, we get $P(I_v > \mathcal{N}\alpha \cdot \frac{1}{3}) < 1/2$ and the probability that v receives a message from w is at least $1/2$ by Fact 3. □

From now on assume that C_1 is any value such that the bounded density property holds with such C_1 that the effective communication property is satisfied as well. The goal is to choose c_0 and c_1 such that the probability of receiving a successful transmission is around c_1/c_0 in a unit ball with the sum close to $C_1/2$ and it is much lower than c_1/c_0 if the sum is significantly smaller than $C_1/2$. As possibility of sensing stations in distance close to 1 heavily depends on network topology and because of some technical reasons, the actual properties (provably) guaranteed by our choice of c_0 and c_1 will be a bit different from this intuitive goal.

PROPOSITION 1. *Assume that bounded density property is satisfied with the parameter C_1 guarantying the effective communication property. Then, one can choose c_0, c_1 and c_d such that, for every node v, the following properties are satisfied:*

(1) *Let y be the number of balls of radius $1/6$ sufficient to cover a unit ball. If $1/2 \geq \sum_{w\in B(v,2/3)} p_w \geq C_1/(2y)$ then the routine DensityTest(v) returns True whp.*

(2) *There exists a constant c_d, such that if $\sum_{w\in B(v,1)} p_w < C_1 c_d$ then the routine DensityTest(v) returns False with high probability.*

The above proposition shows that DensityTest gives an opportunity to distinguish areas with large sums of probabilities from those with much smaller sums of probabilities. The proof can be found in full version of this paper.

3.3 Proof of Lemma 1

In this section we prove Lemma 1, assuming that C_1, c_0 and c_1 are the constants satisfying properties stated in Proposition 1. Moreover, we determine values of c_2 and c_3, which depend on c_ε (and c_ε can be arbitrary at this stage).

Recall that an execution of lines 4–7 of StabilizeProbability is called a *phase*. As the initial probabilities are set to p_{start}, we have $\sum_{w\in B(v,1)} p_w \leq C_1/2$ for each v at the beginning of the algorithm. Therefore, it suffices to show that $\sum_w p_w \leq C_1$ at the end of a phase, provided the same inequality is satisfied at the beginning of this phase, where the sum is taken over w that are active in a given round. As the probabilities of active stations are multiplied by 2 at the end of each phase, the above condition for correctness of Lemma 1 can be deduced from the following lemma.

LEMMA 3. *For every v, if before "For c' times" loop the following inequality holds*

$$\sum_{\substack{w \text{ is active} \\ w\in B(v,1)}} p_w < C_1$$

then after the loop

$$\sum_{\substack{w \text{ is active} \\ w\in B(v,1)}} p_w < \frac{C_1}{2}.$$

The remaining part of this section is devoted to the proof of Lemma 3, which in turn follows from the following property, provided c' is chosen large enough.

LEMMA 4. *There exists a constant q which satisfies the following statement. For every v if $\sum_{w\in B(v,1)} p_w \geq C_1/2$ then there is a set of stations $S \subseteq B(v,4/3)$ such that $\sum_{w\in S} p_w c_\varepsilon \geq q$ and every station from S is turned off in line 6 of the algorithm whp.*

Now, we prove Lemma 3 assuming correctness of Lemma 4 and then we give the proof of Lemma 4. By Lemma 4 the sum of probabilities in $B(v,4/3)$ will decrease by at least q/c_ε in every iteration of the "For c' times" loop. The maximal sum of probabilities in $B(v,4/3)$ is at most $\chi(1,\frac{4}{3})C_1$. Thus by performing $c' = \chi(1,\frac{4}{3})C_1 c_\varepsilon/q$ iterations we have the "opportunity" to reduce all the probabilities in $B(v,4/3)$, as long as $\sum_{w\in B(v,1)} p_w \geq C_1/2$. Thus after c' iterations of the loop we have $\sum_{w\in B(v,1)} p_w < C_1/2$.

It remains to prove Lemma 4; the proof is presented in the following part of this section. As we mainly analyze Playoff below, where stations transmit with probabilities scaled up by the factor c_ε, we use the notion of *mass of probability* of some set of stations A as $c_\varepsilon \sum_{w\in A} p_w$.

The proof of Lemma 4 requires to show that, close to each dense unit ball, a group of stations S with probability mass $\geq q$ exists, for which DensityTest and Playoff return true whp. The main effort in the proof is in ensuring that the elements of S can hear a message with constant probability p in each round of Playoff (i.e., when the probabilities are scaled up by c_ε) and with probability $\geq c_1/c_0$ in each round of DensityTest (i.e., with "standard" probabilities p_v's). (When this property is shown, one can adjust the value c_3/c_2 to p.) We show existence of such S by first proving that, in neighborhood of a dense unit ball, a ball with probability mass $\geq q$, center x and of radius r exists, which satisfies the following properties for some b (Lemma 5):

(a) the probability mass of each ball of radius r inside $B(x, br)$ is at most $z^\gamma q$;

(b) b is large enough to guarantee that the number of balls of radius r necessary to cover $B(x, br)$ is such that they can accumulate the whole probability mass C_1 of the unit ball, provided each of them has the (maximal) mass $z^\gamma q$, where $z > 2$ is some constant;

(c) $br \leq 1/6$;

(d) the sum of probabilities of stations in the ball of radius $2/3$ concentric with B is $\geq C_1/(2y)$, where $y = \chi(1/6, 1)$.

Using the above properties, the chances of receiving a message by a station during Playoff are estimated in Lemma 6. Then, c_2 and c_3 are chosen appropriately, to assure that Playoff returns true whp in S. On the other hand, (d) above guarantees that DensityTest returns true whp in S.

Before stating the following technical lemma sketched by (a)-(d) above, we estimate the value of b satisfying the condition (b). It is sufficient that $b^\gamma z^\gamma q \geq C_1 c_\varepsilon$ which means that $b \approx \frac{1}{z}(C_1 c_\varepsilon/q)^{1/\gamma}$ is suitable.

LEMMA 5. *For every v, whenever $\sum_{w\in B(v,1)} p_w \geq C_1/2$, there exists x such that $B(x,r) \subseteq B(v,4/3)$ and $r \leq (\frac{2q}{c_\varepsilon C_1})^{1/\gamma}$ such that if we denote*

$$D_0 = B(x,r)$$

$$D_1 = B(x,ar) \setminus D_0 \text{ for some } a \leq b$$

$$D_2 = B(x,br) \setminus (D_1 \cup D_0)$$

then

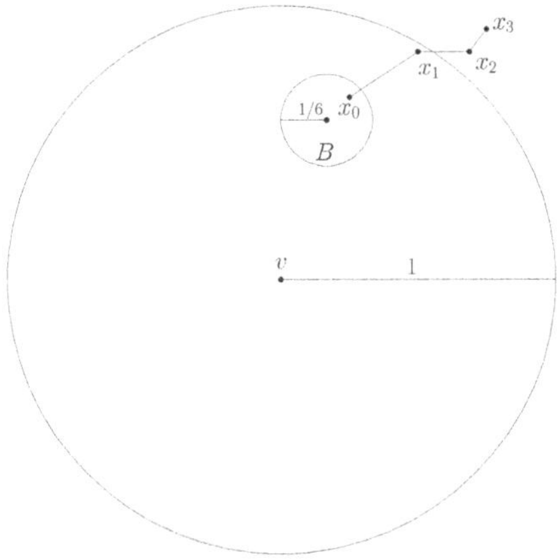

Figure 1: An illustration for the proof of Lemma 5. The distances $\mathrm{dist}(x_i, x_{i+1})$ form a geometric sequence $br, br/z, br/z^2, \ldots$ B is the ball with the largest probability mass among balls of radius $1/6$ included in $B(v, 1)$.

(1) The mass of probability in D_0 is at least q and at most $1/2$.

(2) For every $x' \in D_1 \cup D_2$ the mass of probability in $B(x', r)$ is bounded: $\sum_{w \in B(x',r)} p_w \leq z^\gamma q$.

(3) For all $w \in D_0$ we have $\sum_{u \in B(w, \frac{2}{3})} p_u \geq C_1/(2\chi(\frac{1}{6}, 1))$.

PROOF. (of Lemma 5) Let v be an arbitrary vertex such that $\sum_{w \in B(v,1)} p_w \geq C_1/2$. Let B be a ball with radius $1/6$ included in $B(v, 1)$ with the largest mass of probability. Thus, $\sum_{w \in B} p_w \geq C_1/(2y)$ (cf. Proposition 1), where $y = \chi(1/6, 1)$. Observe that, if x located in a ball of radius $2/3$ concentric with B satisfies (1) and (2), then (3) is satisfied for x as well. Therefore, the idea of our proof is to start looking for x satisfying (1)–(3) in B, as defined above (see Fig. 1).

Let r_0 be a number satisfying the relationship $C_1/2 = q/r_0^\gamma$. That is the average probability mass of a ball of radius r_0 in $B(v, 1)$ is at least q. As B is chosen to have the largest probability mass among balls of radius $1/6$ included in $B(v, 1)$, the average probability mass of a ball of radius r_0 in B is at least q as well. Then, B includes a ball $B_0 = B(x_0, r_0)$ with probability mass $\geq q$ such that $r_0 = (2q/(C_1 c_\varepsilon))^{1/\gamma}$. If (2) is satisfied for x_0, (3) holds as well by the choice of B. On the other hand, if (2) is not satisfied for x_0, there is a ball of radius r_0 and probability mass $\geq z^\gamma q$ in distance at most br_0 from x_0. Bounded growth property of the metric guarantees that this ball contains B_1 of radius $r_1 = r_0/z$ and probability mass $\geq q$.

One can build in such a way a sequence of balls $B_0, B_1, \ldots$ with probability mass larger than q, such that the radius of $B_i = B(x_i, r_i)$ is $r_i = r_{i-1}/z = r_0/z^i$ for $i > 0$, and the distance between (centers of) B_i and B_{i+1} is $\leq br_0(1 + 1/z + \cdots + 1/z^i)$, as long as (2) is not satisfied. If (2) is eventually satisfied for some x_i and $r_i = r_0/z^i$, we obtain a ball B_i of radius at most $r_0 = (2q/C_1)^{1/\gamma}$ with probability mass $\geq q$, whose center point is in distance at most $br_0 \sum_{i \geq 0} 1/z^i \leq 2br_0$ from x, provided $z > 2$. We call such an event *success*. Thus, the circle concentric with B_i of radius $2br_0 + 1/6$ contains the ball B with sum of probabilities $\geq C_1/(2\chi(\frac{1}{6}, 1))$, On the other hand,

$$br_0 \leq \frac{1}{z}(C_1 c_\varepsilon/q)^{1/\gamma} \cdot \left(\frac{2q}{c_\varepsilon C_1}\right)^{1/\gamma} \leq 1/z \leq 1/6$$

for $z \geq 6$. This implies that $2br_0 + 1/6 \leq 2/3$ and therefore (3) is satisfied as well for x_i and r_i.

It remains to show that *success* eventually appears in construction of the above sequence of balls. Note that if br_i is smaller than half of the smallest distance between stations, there is at most one station in a ball of radius br_i. This in turn implies that, if the probability mass of $B(x, r_i)$ is nonzero, then the probability mass of $B(x, br_i) \setminus B(x, r_i)$ is zero. Therefore (2) is satisfied for x and $r = r_i$. □

LEMMA 6. *Let D_0 be a ball satisfying assumptions of Lemma 5 and conditions (2) and (3) stated in this lemma. Then, for every $v \in D_0$ the probability of receiving a message $p(v)$ is at least $q/8 \cdot (1/4)^{a^\gamma z^\gamma q}$.*

PROOF. Now we analyze the probability that every station $v \in D_0$ receives a message. Let D denote the area around D_0, and $\mathcal{I}_0$ be the interference allowing for transmission on a distance $2r$, that is $D = D_0 \cup D_1 \cup D_2$ and by Fact 2 $\mathcal{I}_0 = \mathcal{N}/(2(2r)^\alpha)$. We also introduce four events that, when holds at the same time, allows for every station $v \in D_0$ to hear a message. Note that a station hears a message transmitted by itself.

(1) E_1 - exactly one station from D_0 transmits

(2) E_2 - no station from D_1 transmits

(3) E_3 - interference from D_2 is lower than $\mathcal{I}_0/2$

(4) E_4 - interference from stations outside D is at most $\mathcal{I}_0/2$

Observe that, since events are independent, we have Pr(every $v \in D_0$ hears something) $\geq Pr(E_1)Pr(E_2)Pr(E_3)Pr(E_4)$. Here we give only statement of claims that, when combined, give us the desired result. Details and proofs of this are given in the full version of the paper.

CLAIM 1. $Pr(E_1) \geq q/2$

CLAIM 2. $Pr(E_2) \geq (1/4)^{a^\gamma z^\gamma q}$

We choose such b that we can accommodate all the probability from an unit ball into D_2 without violating the condition (2) Lemma 5. This allows us for bounding interference in two stages. The first stage is bounding interference from close stations, and we do it more carefully as the close stations can introduce large noise. Then we bound the interference from far stations by using the fact that in every unit ball the mass of probability is at most C_1. By the properties of the metric $D_2 \cup D_1$ can be covered by b^γ balls of radius r, so we choose b as least integer that satisfy $b^\gamma z^\gamma q \geq C_1$. We also set $a = 2$ and $z = 6$ as a result of the previous observations.

CLAIM 3. $Pr(E_3) \geq 1/2$

CLAIM 4. $Pr(E_4) \geq 1/2$

Finally we set $q = 1/(z^\gamma 2^{\alpha+4} \beta \sum_{i \geq 1} i^{\gamma-\alpha-1})$ with respect to the bounds from previous two claims. By combining all the claims we get $p(v) \geq Pr$(every $w \in D_0$ hears a message) $\geq q/8 \cdot (1/4)^{a^\gamma z^\gamma q} = 2c_3/c_2$. □

Given the result of Lemma 5, we are ready to finish the proof of Lemma 4. Choose c_2 and c_3 such that $2c_3/c_2 = q/8 \cdot (1/4)^{a^\gamma z^\gamma q}$. Lemma 5 guarantees that there exists a ball D_0 satisfying conditions (1)–(3) from this lemma. Then, Lemma 6 guarantees that Playoff returns true whp, and (3) that DensityTest returns true whp for each active element of D_0. This concludes the proof of Lemma 4.

3.4 Proof of Lemma 2

Let $\varepsilon' = \varepsilon/2$. Here we prove Lemma 2 stating that for every station v the probability distributed among the stations from $B(v, \varepsilon')$ after execution of StabilizeProbability procedure is bounded from below by a constant. We show this for given C_1, c_2, c_3, we also fix the values of c_ε and C_2 to be respectively $c_\varepsilon \leftarrow 1/(\varepsilon^\alpha C_1 c_d) \cdot 8\ln(4c_2/c_3)$ and $C_2 \leftarrow \min(c_3/(8c_2), C_1c_d/(2c_d))/c_\varepsilon$, where c_d is the constant from Prop. 1.

Intuitively, c_ε is chosen large enough to make successful transmissions on distance larger than $\varepsilon/2$ very unlikely, provided the probability mass in a considered unit ball is large enough (close to C_1). Increased probabilities generate large noise preventing communication on distance larger than $\varepsilon/2$. Since the Playoff uses a constant probability scaled up by the factor of c_ε in the following proof we use the constant $C_2' = C_2 c_\varepsilon$ for the sake of clarity.

The main step in the proof is to show that, by our choice of C_2 and c_ε, a station whp does not quit if the mass of probability in its close proximity is small.

LEMMA 7. *For every node v if*

$$\sum_{\substack{w \text{ is active} \\ w\in B(v,\varepsilon')}} p_w c_\varepsilon < 2C_2'$$

then the probability that v turns off with color p_v is negligible.

First, we show that Lemma 2 follows from Lemma 7. Then, the proof of Lemma 7 will be provided. Let one execution of lines 4-7 in StabilizeProbability be a *phase* of the algorithm. Note that all stations switched off (by quitting in line 7) during a phase have the same color (probability). Consider any v participating in an execution of the protocol. If any $w \in B(v, \varepsilon')$ does not switch off until the end of the last phase then the final value of p_w is equal to $2p_{\max} = 2C_2'/c_\varepsilon$ and therefore $\sum_{\substack{w:p_w=2p_{\max} \\ w\in B(v,\varepsilon')}} p_w c_\varepsilon \geq C_2'/c_\varepsilon$ which in turn means that the statement of Lemma 2 is satisfied. Thus, consider the case that all elements of $B(v, \varepsilon')$ switch off before the last phase. Let j be the phase in which v quits and let B_i denote the set of stations from $B(v, \varepsilon')$ active after the ith phase. Then, by Lemma 7, $\sum_{w\in B_{j-1}} p_w c_\varepsilon \geq 2C_2'$ whp. Let k be the last phase such that $\sum_{w\in B_k} p_w c_\varepsilon \geq 2C_2'$. Such phase k exists because of our assumption that all stations eventually switch off. As the probabilities of active stations are multiplied by 2 after each phase, the condition $2\sum_{w\in B_{k+1}} p_w c_\varepsilon < 2C_2'$ due to the choice of k. Thus, the set $B_k \setminus B_{k+1}$ of stations quitting in the $(k+1)$st phase satisfies $\sum_{w\in B_k\setminus B_{k+1}} p_w' c_\varepsilon \geq C_2'$, where $p_w' = 2p_w$ is the probability assigned to w in phase $k+1$. This shows that the color assigned to stations in phase $k+1$ satisfies the inequality from Lemma 2.

Now, it remains to prove Lemma 7. Observe that v turns off only when it receives at least $c_3 \log n$ messages during the PlayOff and DensityTest(v) returns True. By Proposition 1 we only need to consider the case when

(a) $\sum_{w\in B(v,\varepsilon')} p_w c_\varepsilon < 2C_2'$ and

(b) $\sum_{w\in B(v,1)} p_w \geq C_1 c_d$.

In the remaining part of the proof we show that the probability of receiving $c_3 \log n$ messages during PlayOff is negligible for our choice of C_2' and c_ε, provided (a) and (b) hold.

Let $p(v)$ denote the probability that v receives a message if all active stations transmit with currently assigned probabilities. Below, we express a condition regarding $p(v)$ which is sufficient for correctness of Lemma 2.

FACT 8. *If $p(v) < c_3/(2c_2)$ then PlayOff(v) returns False with high probability.*

PROOF. The expected number of rounds in which v receives a message is $c_2 \log n \cdot p(v) \leq \frac{c_3 \log n}{2}$. Thus, by Chernoff Bound we can make the probability that PlayOff(v)=true (v receives at least $c_3 \log n$ messages) arbitrarily small by increasing c_2 and c_3 without changing the initial ratio c_3/c_2. □

In the following, let S_v be the sum of all signals received at node v, i.e.,

$$S_v = \sum_{w \text{ is transmitting}} \beta\mathcal{N}/(\text{dist}(v, w))^\alpha.$$

The next two facts show the way to bound the probability $p(v)$ of receiving a message by v in terms of the sum of probabilities in close neighborhood of v and of the interference from the whole network. These facts combined with Fact 8 give the property claimed in Lemma 2.

FACT 9. *If $S_v > \frac{2\beta\mathcal{N}}{\varepsilon'^\alpha}$ then v cannot receive a message from the outside of $B(v, \varepsilon')$.*

PROOF. The strength of signal from node in a distance at least ε' from v is at most $\beta\mathcal{N}/\varepsilon'^\alpha$ (since $P = \beta\mathcal{N}$), and the interference $\mathcal{I}$ is at least $S_v - \frac{\beta\mathcal{N}}{\varepsilon'^\alpha} > \frac{\beta\mathcal{N}}{\varepsilon'^\alpha}$. From these observations we have $SINR \leq \beta\mathcal{N}/(\varepsilon'^\alpha(\mathcal{N} + \mathcal{I})) < \beta/(\varepsilon'^\alpha + \beta) < \beta$, since $\beta \geq 1$. □

FACT 10. *The probability of receiving a message at v can be bounded as follows*

$$p(v) < Pr\left(S_v \leq \frac{2\mathcal{N}\beta}{\varepsilon^\alpha}\right) + \sum_{w\in B(v,\varepsilon')} p_w \cdot c_\varepsilon$$

PROOF. The former summand corresponds to the event of receiving a message from a station in a distance at least ε, thus by the Fact 9, the sum of signals at v should be at most $\frac{2\mathcal{N}\beta}{\varepsilon^\alpha}$. The latter is trivial upper bound on the probability of receiving a message from some station in $B(v, \varepsilon')$. □

Note that in the setting considered in the proof of Lemma 7 the quantity $\sum_{w\in B(v,\varepsilon')} p_w \cdot c_\varepsilon$ can be bounded by $2C_2'$. By our choice of $C_2' \leq c_3/(8c_2)$, in order to prove Lemma 7, it suffices to show that $Pr(S_v \leq \frac{2\mathcal{N}\beta}{\varepsilon^\alpha}) < c_3/(4c_2)$. Then, by Fact 10, if $\sum_{w\in B(v,\varepsilon')} p_w c_\varepsilon < 2C_2' = c_3/(4c_2)$ then $p(v) < c_3/(2c_2)$ which in turn gives the statement of Lemma 7 (by Fact 8).

From now on we focus on bounding the probability that interference at v allows for successful transmission on the distance ε or greater, i.e. that $S_v \leq \frac{2\mathcal{N}\beta}{\varepsilon^\alpha}$. As we already pointed out, it is sufficient to bound this probability from above by $c_3/(4c_2)$.

PROPOSITION 2. *Assuming that DensityTest(v) is satisfied the following inequality holds with high probability: $Pr(S_v \leq \frac{2\mathcal{N}\beta}{\varepsilon^\alpha}) < c_3/(4c_2)$.*

PROOF. In the proof, we take advantage of the fact that S_v is at least the sum of signals arriving from $B(v, 1) \setminus B(v, \varepsilon')$ and, according to (a), (b) and the fact that $C_2' \leq C_1 c_d/2$, the sum of probabilities in this area is at least $C_1 c_d/2$. As each transmitter in Playoff uses its probability scaled up by the factor c_ε,

$$\begin{aligned} E(S_v) &\geq c_\varepsilon \textstyle\sum_{w\in B(v,1)\setminus B(v,\varepsilon')} p_w \cdot \beta\mathcal{N}/(\text{dist}(w, v)^\alpha) \\ &\geq c_\varepsilon \textstyle\sum_{w\in B(v,1)\setminus B(v,\varepsilon')} p_w \cdot \beta\mathcal{N} \\ &\geq \beta\mathcal{N} c_\varepsilon C_1 c_d/2 \\ &= \frac{2\beta\mathcal{N}}{\varepsilon^\alpha} \cdot 4\ln(4c_2/c_3) \end{aligned}$$

where the second inequality follows from the fact that $\text{dist}(v, w) \leq 1$ for each $w \in B(v, 1)$, the third inequality from the fact that $\sum_{w \in B(v,1) \setminus B(v,\varepsilon')} p_w \geq C_1 c_d/2$.

On the other hand, the above estimation of S_v can be seen as the sum of independent random variables X_w equal either 0 or $\beta\mathcal{N}/\text{dist}(v, w)^\alpha$ over all $w \in B(v, 1) \setminus B(v, \varepsilon') = B$. Thus, each of these variables satisfies $X_w \leq \beta\mathcal{N}/\varepsilon^\alpha$ and $E(S_v) \geq E(\sum_{w \in B} X_w) \geq \frac{2\beta\mathcal{N}}{\varepsilon^\alpha} \cdot 4\ln(4c_2/c_3)$.

Now,we scale the variables X_w in order to apply the Chernoff bound. Let $Y_w = X_w/(\beta\mathcal{N}/\varepsilon^\alpha) \leq 1$, let $Y = \sum_{w \in B} Y_w$. Then,

$$E(Y) = E(\sum_{w \in B} X_w)/(\beta\mathcal{N}/\varepsilon^\alpha) \geq 2 \cdot 4\ln(4c_2/c_3).$$

Moreover,

$$\begin{aligned} Pr(S_v \leq \tfrac{2\mathcal{N}\beta}{\varepsilon^\alpha}) &< Pr(\textstyle\sum_{w \in B} X_w \leq \tfrac{2\mathcal{N}\beta}{\varepsilon^\alpha}) \\ &= Pr(Y \leq 2) \\ &\leq Pr(Y \leq \tfrac{1}{2}E(Y)) \\ &\leq \exp(-E(Y)/8) \leq c_3/(4c_2) \end{aligned}$$

where the third from last inequality follows from $4\ln(\frac{4c_2}{c_3}) \geq 2$, since $c_2 \geq c_3$. This finishes the proof of Proposition 2. □

4. BROADCAST

4.1 Broadcast with non-spontaneous wakeup

Algorithm NoSBroadcast.

For the model with non-spontaneous wake-up, we present the algorithm NoSBroadcast in which a message is disseminated over the network in time $O(D\log^2 n)$. The algorithm works in D phases. Each phase has $O(\log^2 n)$ rounds and consists of two parts. A node participates in the phase (is *active*) if it knows the source message at the beginning of the phase. The first part of a phase executes StabilizeProbability on the set of active stations. This execution takes $O(\log^2 n)$ rounds. As a result, it assigns a color p_v to each active node v. This coloring satisfies conditions from Lemma 1 and Lemma 2. In the second part, each active node transmits the message with probability $\frac{p_v}{c\varepsilon\log n}$, for some constant c, for $O(\log^2 n)$ rounds. Consider any shortest path $s = v_0, v_1, \ldots, v_k$ in the communication graph from the source s to a node v_k. Our construction guarantees that the i-th vertex v_i of the path knows the source message after the i-th phase of the algorithm whp.

THEOREM 1. *The NoSBroadcast algorithm solves the broadcast problem in the non-spontaneous wakeup model in $O(D\log^2 n)$ rounds whp.*

Theorem 1 follows directly from Fact 6 and the lemma below.

LEMMA 8. *There exists a constant c such that each neighbour in the communication graph of each active node v receives the source message whp in the second part of a phase.*

Let us recall that $\varepsilon' = \varepsilon/2$. In order to satisfy the claim of Lemma 8, it is sufficient that, for each active node v, an active station v' such that $\text{dist}(v, v') \leq \varepsilon'$ transmits and is heard in distance $1 - \varepsilon'$ during NoSBroadcast (see Fact 1). We show that this is actually the case in the following proposition, which concludes the proof of Lemma 8, and thus also Theorem 1.

PROPOSITION 3. *There exists a constant c such that for any node v active in a phase there exists a node $v' \in B(v, \varepsilon')$ which transmits in the second part of the phase and v' is heard anywhere in the distance $1 - \varepsilon'$ whp.*

PROOF. The sufficient condition for occurrence of the event from the proposition in a given round is that the following three assertions hold:

(1) exactly one station transmits in $B(v, \varepsilon')$,

(2) no other station in $B(v, 2)$ transmits,

(3) the interference from outside of $B(v, 2)$ in any point of $B(v, 1)$ is smaller, than $\mathcal{I} = \mathcal{N}\alpha\varepsilon'$ (which allows hearing transmissions from the distance $1 - \varepsilon'$).

Now, in a given round, we bound from below the probabilities of the events (1)–(3) by choosing sufficiently large c.

(1) The probability, that exactly one node in $B(v, \varepsilon')$ transmits is bigger than $\frac{C_2}{2c\varepsilon\log n}$ whp. This follows from Fact 4.

(2) The probability, that no one transmits in $B(v, 2) \setminus B(v, \varepsilon')$ is bigger than $3/4$ whp.

When restricting to stations w of the same color, the inequality $\sum_{w \in B} p_w \leq C_1$ holds for any unit ball B, by Lemma 1. Thus, using the bounded growth property, we know that for each color $\sum_{w \in B(v,2)} p_w = O(1)$. As there are at most $\log n$ colors, this sum over all colors fulfills

$$\sum_{w \in B(v,2)} \frac{p_w}{c\varepsilon\log n} = \log n \frac{O(1)}{c\varepsilon\log n} = O(1).$$

Thus, if c is sufficiently large, the average number of transmitters is smaller than $1/4$, and by Markov bound no one transmits with probability $3/4$. This holds whp.

(3) The probability, that in some point of $B(v, 1)$ the interference exceeds $\mathcal{I} = \mathcal{N}\alpha\varepsilon'$ is smaller than $1/4$ whp.

Once again, it is sufficient to choose c large enough so that the expected maximum of interference in $B(v, 1)$ from outside of $B(v, 2)$ is smaller than $\mathcal{I}/4 = \mathcal{N}\alpha\varepsilon'/4$. This follows from interference estimations similar as in Fact 7. Then this maximum interference is at most $\mathcal{I}$ with probability $3/4$ by the Markov bound.

As the events (1)–(3) are independent, the probability that exactly one node in $B(v, \varepsilon')$ transmits in a given round and it is heard in range $1 - \varepsilon'$ is bigger than

$$C_2/(2c\varepsilon\log n) \cdot \frac{3}{4} \cdot \left(1 - \frac{1}{4}\right) > C_2/(4c\varepsilon\log n) ;$$

For further references, we state it as a separate fact.

FACT 11. *There exists a constant c such that if each node v is transmitting with probability $\frac{p_v}{c\varepsilon\log n}$ in a round, the probability that exactly one node in $B(v, \varepsilon')$ transmits and it is heard in range $1 - \varepsilon'$ is at least $p = C_2/(4c\varepsilon\log n)$.*

Now, we take into account that the second part of a phase lasts for many subsequent rounds. Let the number of rounds be $T = (a\ln n)/p = O(\log^2 n)$, where a is an arbitrary constant. The probability that not all stations in range $1 - \varepsilon$ from a given active node v get the message during the second part is at most

$$(1-p)^{a\ln n/p} < e^{-a\ln n} = n^{-a} .$$

Hence, all neighbours of v in G get the source message whp during part two of the phase. □

4.2 Broadcast with spontaneous wakeup

Algorithm SBroadcast.

Now, we consider the model with spontaneous wake-up. We present an algorithm SBroadcast, which starts from a *single* execution of StabilizeProbability on all stations from the network for $\varepsilon'' = \varepsilon/3$. The color assignment made during StabilizeProbability might be viewed as a kind of a communication backbone.[5] When coloring is done, the source node transmits the message deterministically. Then, after receiving the source message, every node transmits it with probability $\frac{p_v}{c\varepsilon \log n}$ in each of next $O(\log^2 n)$ consecutive rounds. (The values of c and p are the same as in Fact 11.) This assures that in each round the broadcast message is propagated by one edge, say $\{v, u\}$, of the communication graph ie. $B(v, \varepsilon'')$ informs all nodes of $B(u, \varepsilon'')$ with probability p. Using standard concentration bounds for sums of independent random variables, one can assure that the source message is delivered to each station in the graph-distance at most D from the source in $O(D \log n + \log^2 n)$ rounds whp.

THEOREM 2. *The SBroadcast algorithm solves the broadcast problem in the spontaneous wake-up model in* $O(D \log n + \log^2 n)$ *rounds whp.*

PROOF. If $B(v, \varepsilon'')$ knowing the message informs any $B(u, \varepsilon'')$ for $\{v, u\} \in G$ whp which can be proved similarly to Proposition 3. Consider a shortest path from s to some node v. A sufficient condition for v to receive a message from s is D successful transmissions on this path. In each transmission a subsequent node v_i gets the message together with its neighbourhood $B(v_i, \varepsilon'')$. By Chernoff bound all these transmissions happen whp in time $t = (2D + C \log n)/p = O(D \log n + \log^2 n)$. □

[5] In Yu et al. [20] the backbone is obtained as a connected dominating set of the communication graph, by applying techniques from geometric radio networks. However, this result holds only for a restricted family of networks and the analysis requires that stations cannot receive signals from distance larger than $1 - \varepsilon$, i.e., their model assumes weak devices, and it is known that the power of that model is different than considered in our work (c.f., [15])

5. REFERENCES

[1] C. Avin, Y. Emek, E. Kantor, Z. Lotker, D. Peleg, and L. Roditty. SINR diagrams: Convexity and its applications in wireless networks. *J. ACM*, 59(4):18, 2012.

[2] C. Avin, Z. Lotker, F. Pasquale, and Y. A. Pignolet. A note on uniform power connectivity in the SINR model. In S. Dolev, editor, *ALGOSENSORS*, volume 5804 of *Lecture Notes in Computer Science*, pages 116–127. Springer, 2009.

[3] A. Czumaj and W. Rytter. Broadcasting algorithms in radio networks with unknown topology. In *FOCS*, pages 492–501. IEEE Computer Society, 2003.

[4] S. Daum, S. Gilbert, F. Kuhn, and C. C. Newport. Broadcast in the ad hoc SINR model. In *DISC*, pages 358–372, 2013.

[5] M. Farach-Colton, A. F. Anta, and M. A. Mosteiro. Optimal memory-aware sensor network gossiping (or how to break the broadcast lower bound). *Theor. Comput. Sci.*, 472:60–80, 2013.

[6] L. Gasieniec, D. R. Kowalski, A. Lingas, and M. Wahlen. Efficient broadcasting in known geometric radio networks with non-uniform ranges. In G. Taubenfeld, editor, *DISC*, volume 5218 of *Lecture Notes in Computer Science*, pages 274–288. Springer, 2008.

[7] M. Ghaffari, B. Haeupler, and M. Khabbazian. Randomized broadcast in radio networks with collision detection. In P. Fatourou and G. Taubenfeld, editors, *PODC*, pages 325–334. ACM, 2013.

[8] O. Goussevskaia, T. Moscibroda, and R. Wattenhofer. Local broadcasting in the physical interference model. In M. Segal and A. Kesselman, editors, *DIALM-POMC*, pages 35–44. ACM, 2008.

[9] M. M. Halldórsson and P. Mitra. Nearly optimal bounds for distributed wireless scheduling in the SINR model. In L. Aceto, M. Henzinger, and J. Sgall, editors, *ICALP (2)*, volume 6756 of *Lecture Notes in Computer Science*, pages 625–636. Springer, 2011.

[10] M. M. Halldórsson and P. Mitra. Towards tight bounds for local broadcasting. In F. Kuhn and C. C. Newport, editors, *FOMC*, page 2. ACM, 2012.

[11] M. M. Halldórsson and P. Mitra. Wireless connectivity and capacity. In Y. Rabani, editor, *SODA*, pages 516–526. SIAM, 2012.

[12] T. Jurdzinski and D. R. Kowalski. Distributed backbone structure for algorithms in the SINR model of wireless networks. In M. K. Aguilera, editor, *DISC*, volume 7611 of *Lecture Notes in Computer Science*, pages 106–120. Springer, 2012.

[13] T. Jurdzinski, D. R. Kowalski, M. Rozanski, and G. Stachowiak. Distributed randomized broadcasting in wireless networks under the SINR model. In *DISC*, pages 373–387, 2013.

[14] T. Jurdzinski, D. R. Kowalski, and G. Stachowiak. Distributed deterministic broadcasting in uniform-power ad hoc wireless networks. In L. Gasieniec and F. Wolter, editors, *FCT*, volume 8070 of *Lecture Notes in Computer Science*, pages 195–209. Springer, 2013.

[15] T. Jurdzinski, D. R. Kowalski, and G. Stachowiak. Distributed deterministic broadcasting in wireless networks of weak devices. In *ICALP (2)*, volume 7966 of *Lecture Notes in Computer Science*, pages 632–644. Springer, 2013.

[16] T. Jurdzinski and G. Stachowiak. Probabilistic algorithms for the wake-up problem in single-hop radio networks. *Theory Comput. Syst.*, 38(3):347–367, 2005.

[17] T. Kesselheim. Dynamic packet scheduling in wireless networks. In D. Kowalski and A. Panconesi, editors, *PODC*, pages 281–290. ACM, 2012.

[18] D. R. Kowalski and A. Pelc. Broadcasting in undirected ad hoc radio networks. *Distributed Computing*, 18(1):43–57, 2005.

[19] C. Scheideler, A. W. Richa, and P. Santi. An o(log n) dominating set protocol for wireless ad-hoc networks under the physical interference model, 2008.

[20] D. Yu, Q.-S. Hua, Y. Wang, H. Tan, and F. C. M. Lau. Distributed multiple-message broadcast in wireless ad-hoc networks under the SINR model. In G. Even and M. M. Halldórsson, editors, *SIROCCO*, volume 7355 of *Lecture Notes in Computer Science*, pages 111–122. Springer, 2012.

[21] D. Yu, Y. Wang, Q.-S. Hua, and F. C. M. Lau. Distributed local broadcasting algorithms in the physical interference model. In *DCOSS*, pages 1–8. IEEE, 2011.

[22] J. Yu, N. Wang, G. Wang, and D. Yu. Connected dominating sets in wireless ad hoc and sensor networks - a comprehensive survey. *Computer Communications*, 36(2):121–134, 2013.

On the Power of the Congested Clique Model

Andrew Drucker[*]
Institute for Advanced Study
Princeton, NJ, USA
andy.drucker@gmail.com

Fabian Kuhn[†]
University of Freiburg
Freiburg, Germany
kuhn@cs.uni-freiburg.de

Rotem Oshman[‡]
Princeton University
Princeton, NJ, USA
rotem.oshman@gmail.com

ABSTRACT

We study the computation power of the congested clique, a model of distributed computation where n players communicate with each other over a complete network in order to compute some function of their inputs. The number of bits that can be sent on any edge in a round is bounded by a parameter b. We consider two versions of the model: in the first, the players communicate by unicast, allowing them to send a different message on each of their links in one round; in the second, the players communicate by broadcast, sending one message to all their neighbors.

It is known that the unicast version of the model is quite powerful; to date, no lower bounds for this model are known. In this paper we provide a partial explanation by showing that the unicast congested clique can simulate powerful classes of bounded-depth circuits, implying that even slightly super-constant lower bounds for the congested clique would give new lower bounds in circuit complexity. Moreover, under a widely-believed conjecture on matrix multiplication, the triangle detection problem, studied in [8], can be solved in $O(n^{\epsilon})$ time for any $\epsilon > 0$.

The broadcast version of the congested clique is the well-known multi-party shared-blackboard model of communication complexity (with number-in-hand input). This version is more amenable to lower bounds, and in this paper we show that the subgraph detection problem studied in [8] requires polynomially many rounds for several classes of subgraphs. We also give upper bounds for the subgraph detection problem, and relate the hardness of triangle detection in the broadcast congested clique to the communication complexity of set disjointness in the 3-party number-on-forehead model.

[*]Supported by the NSF under agreements Princeton University Prime Award No. CCF-0832797 and Sub-contract No. 00001583.

[†]Supported by the ERC Grant No. 336495 (ACDC).

[‡]Supported by NSF Grants No. CCF-0832797 and CCF-1149888.

PODC'14, July 15–18, 2014, Paris, France.

http://dx.doi.org/10.1145/2611462.2611493 .

Categories and Subject Descriptors

F.1.1 [**Models of Computation**]: Relations between models; F.2.0 [**Analysis of Algorithms and Problem Complexity**]: General; G.2.2 [**Graph Theory**]: Graph algorithms

Keywords

Congested clique; lower bounds; subgraph detection

1. INTRODUCTION

The congested clique model, studied in [30, 32, 8, 28], features n players that communicate with each other in synchronous rounds over a complete network. In each round, each player can send b bits on each of its communication links, for a total of $\Theta(bn^2)$ bits sent per round. In the version of the model considered in [30, 32, 8, 28], players can send different messages on different links; we denote this version of the model by $\mathsf{CLIQUE\text{-}UCAST}_{n,b}$. In this paper we study the computation power of $\mathsf{CLIQUE\text{-}UCAST}_{n,b}$, and also of another variant, denoted $\mathsf{CLIQUE\text{-}BCAST}_{n,b}$, where in each round each player can only broadcast a single b-bit message over all its links. The $\mathsf{CLIQUE\text{-}BCAST}_{n,b}$ model is essentially the classical multi-party, number-in-hand model of communication complexity, with communication over a shared blackboard [27], since writing on the blackboard can be viewed as broadcasting a message to all players.

In both models we are interested in the round complexity of computing functions $f : \{0,1\}^{n^2} \to \{0,1\}$, where initially n^2 bits of input are equally partitioned between the players (with each player receiving n bits), and the goal is for some player to eventually output the value of f. We are especially interested in the *subgraph detection problem*, studied in [8]: here, the joint input to the players is interpreted as an undirected n-node graph G, with player i receiving the list of edges adjacent to the i-th node of G, and the goal is to determine whether G contains a particular subgraph H.

As noted in [28], part of what makes the $\mathsf{CLIQUE\text{-}UCAST}$ model interesting is that it does not have any "information bottlenecks", and it is therefore not amenable to the type of arguments typically used for restricted-bandwidth networks (e.g., [23, 39, 12, 26, 20]). For this reason, any lower bounds for $\mathsf{CLIQUE\text{-}UCAST}$ would have to rely on new, "bottleneck-free" lower bound techniques. To date, no such lower bounds have been proven, and in this paper we provide a partial explanation: we show that $\mathsf{CLIQUE\text{-}UCAST}$ is sufficiently strong to simulate some well-studied parallel circuit models, such as ACC and $\mathsf{TC0}$. Proving lower bounds for explicit functions in these models is a notoriously difficult and elusive goal in the theory of Boolean circuit complexity. Our results imply that even weak lower bounds for CLIQUE-UCAST would imply progress on these fundamental problems; specifically, even a slightly super-constant lower bound on the number of rounds required to compute some explicit function in $\mathsf{CLIQUE\text{-}UCAST}_{n,1}$ would imply a new lower bound on ACC, and an $\Omega(\log\log n)$ lower bound for $\mathsf{CLIQUE\text{-}UCAST}_{n,\log n}$ would imply new a lower bound for threshold circuits (the class TC). It seems, then, that "information bottlenecks" are essential to our ability to prove strong lower bounds, and without them we are subject to the same extremely difficult challenges facing the circuit complexity community.

We remark that, as with circuits, *non-explicit* lower bounds for the CLIQUE-UCAST model are not hard to show. In the full version we give a counting-based lower bound that shows that there exists a function that takes $(n-O(\log n))/b$ rounds to compute in $\mathsf{CLIQUE\text{-}UCAST}_{n,b}$. Since n/b rounds are sufficient for any node to learn the inputs of all other nodes (assuming n bits of input per node), this non-explicit lower bound is very close to optimal.

The other variant we consider, CLIQUE-BCAST, is used to study many areas in theoretical computer science, from streaming [1] to cryptology [14] and mechanism design [7]. Beyond being a fundamental model of communication complexity, it can also be viewed as a very abstract model of wireless communication over a single-hop network: although the theoretical distributed computing community typically assumes that in a wireless network only one node can successfully broadcast in each round, recent advances in coding (e.g., [15, 44] and others) can allow multiple packets to come through. Especially for the purpose of proving lower bounds, it seems reasonable to consider a model that allows *all* messages to be delivered.

From the perspective of lower bounds, a major difference between the $\mathsf{CLIQUE\text{-}UCAST}_{n,b}$ and $\mathsf{CLIQUE\text{-}BCAST}_{n,b}$ models is that in the broadcast model, only $\Theta(nb)$ "unique bits" (discounting duplicate messages) cross each balanced cut, compared to $\Theta(n^2b)$ in the unicast model. This difference restores our ability to apply bottleneck arguments, and we show that in CLIQUE-BCAST, the subgraph detection problem considered in [8] is polynomially hard for several classes of subgraphs. As is often the case when working with restricted-bandwidth models, our lower bounds are obtained by reduction from 2-party communication complexity. We also provide upper bounds showing that in some (though not all) cases our lower bounds are tight. Some of our upper and lower bounds also apply to general communication networks.

One major open problem left open by our work is the complexity of triangle detection, also studied in [8], where it is shown that the problem can be solved in time $\tilde{O}(n^{1/3}/T^{2/3})$ in $\mathsf{CLIQUE\text{-}UCAST}_{n,O(\log n)}$ when the input graph has at least T triangles. In Section 2.1 we show that if matrix multiplication can be solved by arithmetic circuits with size $O(n^{\delta})$, then we can solve triangle detection in $O(n^{\delta/n^2})$ rounds in $\mathsf{CLIQUE\text{-}UCAST}_{n,1}$. It is believed plausible that matrix multiplication can be solved in size $O(n^{2+\epsilon})$ for any $\epsilon > 0$, and this would imply an $O(n^{\epsilon})$-round triangle detection algorithm for $\mathsf{CLIQUE\text{-}UCAST}_{n,1}$.

In the CLIQUE-BCAST model, triangles are not amenable to our lower bound technique, because a triangle cannot be "partitioned" between two players — when the vertices are partitioned between the players, one of the two will always "see" all three edges of the triangle. Here we draw a connection to the 3-party number-on-forehead (NOF) model of communication complexity, in which each player can see the input of the other two players, but not its own input [27]. We show that a lower bound of $f(N)$ on the communication complexity of N-element set disjointness in the 3-party NOF model would imply a lower bound of $\Theta(f(n^2/e^{O(\sqrt{\log n})})/(nb))$ rounds for triangle detection in $\mathsf{CLIQUE\text{-}BCAST}_{n,b}$; currently the best unconditional lower bound on randomized 3-party NOF set disjointness with N elements is $\Omega(\sqrt{N})$ [41], which is not strong enough to yield a non-trivial bound on triangle detection. For deterministic algorithms, however, it has very recently been shown that $\Omega(N)$ bits are required for 3-party NOF set disjointness, yielding a lower bound of $\Omega(n/(e^{O(\sqrt{\log n})}b)$ for deterministic triangle detection. In addition, for the randomized case, we are able to obtain a conditional and restricted lower bound, through a connection made in [35] between 3-party NOF set disjointness and the computational hardness of SAT. Even a small polynomial improvement in the lower bound for randomized 3-party NOF set disjointness would yield an unconditional polynomial lower bound for randomized triangle detection.

Related work. The CONGEST model [33], introduced to study networks with restricted bandwidth, has received much attention recently [12, 13, 20, 23, 26, 39]. Most work on the model considers a setting where nodes communicate over some network graph G, and studies the complexity of detecting properties of G or computing various graph structures (e.g., minimum spanning trees [9, 34, 39]). Many of these results use reductions from two-player communication complexity, a technique we also use in Section 3.2.

Upper bounds for various problems in the congested clique are given in [30, 32, 8, 29, 28]. Of particular relevance to our work is [8], which gives an upper bound of $\tilde{O}(n^{(d-2)/d})$ on the round complexity of detecting a fixed d-vertex subgraph in $\mathsf{CLIQUE\text{-}UCAST}_{n,O(\log n)}$; we give upper and lower bounds on subgraph detection in the *broadcast* version of the congested clique in Section 3.

In [28] it is shown that any "balanced" routing demand, where the number of messages that must be routed between each pair of players does not exceed $O(n)$, can be scheduled deterministically in $O(1)$ rounds in $\mathsf{CLIQUE\text{-}UCAST}_{n,O(\log n)}$. We use the routing algorithm of [28] in our simulation of circuits in Section 2.

2. FROM CIRCUITS TO THE CONGESTED CLIQUE

In this section we show that the CLIQUE-UCAST model is powerful enough to simulate circuits with "simple" gates and a quasi-linear number of wires.

We model a circuit as a directed acyclic graph (DAG), where the nodes represent gates from some class $\mathcal{G}$ of Boolean functions. The complexity measures we are interested in are the *depth* of the circuit, which is the length of the longest path from any input (source node) to any output (sink node), and the *number of wires* (edges).

We now formalize what we mean by "simple gates". The following definition is a variant of *worst-partition communication complexity*, discussed in the textbook [27].

DEFINITION 1. *A function* $f : \{0,1\}^m \to \{0,1\}$ *is* b-*separable, for* $b \in [m]$, *if for any partition* $I = (I_1, \dots, I_k)$ *of* $[m]$ *there are functions* $\left\{g_j : \{0,1\}^{|I_j|} \to \{0,1\}^b\right\}_{j=1}^k$ *and* $h : \{0,1\}^{bk} \to \{0,1\}$ *s.t.* $f(x_1, \dots, x_m) = h(g_1(x_{I_1}), \dots, g_k(x_{I_k}))$.

We say that a gate G is *b-separable* if the function it computes is b-separable. We will analyze circuits whose gates are b-separable for small b; related restrictions on circuits have been studied previously in circuit complexity, e.g. in [24].

THEOREM 2. *Suppose that* $f : \{0,1\}^{n^2} \to \{0,1\}$ *is computed by a circuit* C *of depth* D, *comprising* b-*separable gates with unbounded fan-in and fan-out. Let* $N = n^2 \cdot s$ *be the number of wires in* C. *Then for any input partition which assigns to each player* p *no more than* $n(b+s)$ *input wires, there is an* $O(D)$-*round protocol* P *for the* CLIQUE-UCAST *model with* n *players and bandwidth* $O(b+s)$, *that computes* f *under the input partition.*

PROOF. For a gate $G \in C$, let $\mathsf{in}(G) \subseteq C$ and $\mathsf{out}(G) \subseteq C$ denote the set of inputs and outputs of G, respectively. We represent inputs to the circuit as gates that have no inputs ($\mathsf{in}(G) = \emptyset$) and outputs as gates that have no output ($\mathsf{out}(G) = \emptyset$).

We define the *weight* of G, denoted $w(G)$, to be the sum of its in-degree and its out-degree: $w(G) := |\mathsf{in}(G)| + |\mathsf{out}(G)|$. We say that G is *heavy* if $w(G) \geq n \cdot s$, otherwise we say that G is *light*. Let $C_H \subseteq C$ be the set of heavy gates in C, and let $C_L := C \setminus C_H$ be the light gates.

We construct an assignment $I : C \to [n]$ of gates (including inputs and outputs) to players, such that

(1) Each player p is assigned at most one heavy gate, that is, $|I^{-1}(p) \cap C_H| \leq 1$; and

(2) For each player p, the total weight of light gates assigned to p does not exceed $2n \cdot s$.

Here $I^{-1}(p) := \{G \in C \mid I(G) = p\}$. We say that player p *owns* a gate G or a wire incoming or outgoing from G if $I(G) = p$.

Construction of I. Since C has a total of $n^2 \cdot s$ wires, the number of heavy gates cannot exceed n, so we can assign each heavy gate to a unique player. As for the light gates, we go over them in arbitrary order, and assign each gate G to some player p that does not already own more than $2n \cdot s - w(G)$ wires. To see that there is always some such player, suppose for the sake of contradiction that we need to assign a light gate G, but each player already owns more than $2n \cdot s - w(G)$ wires. Since G is light we have $w(G) < n \cdot s$, so the total number of wires already assigned exceeds $n \cdot (2n \cdot s - w(G)) > n \cdot (2n \cdot s - n \cdot s) = n^2 \cdot s$, contradicting our assumption that C has a total of $n^2 \cdot s$ wires.

Evaluating the circuit. We partition the gates of C into layers $L_0, \dots, L_D$, where the first layer, defined by $L_0 := \{G \in C \mid \mathsf{in}(G) = \emptyset\}$, represents the inputs of C, and for each $r > 0$, $L_r := \left\{G \in C \mid \mathsf{in}(G) \subseteq \bigcup_{r'<r} L_{r'}\right\} \setminus \left(\bigcup_{r'<r} L_{r'}\right)$ are the gates whose inputs all belong to layers smaller than r, but which are not themselves in some smaller layer. Because the depth of the circuit is D, there are exactly D layers. We evaluate the circuit in D stages, each corresponding to one layer of the circuit and requiring $O(1)$ rounds.

The input layer, L_0, does not require any evaluation. Suppose that we have already evaluated the circuit up to layer L_{r-1}, and we now wish to evaluate L_r. For each $G \in L_r$ we proceed as follows:

(a) If G is heavy then we use the fact that G is b-separable. Let $p_1, \dots, p_k$ be the players that own inputs to G, and let $H = \{H_1, \dots, H_k\}$ be the partition of $\mathsf{in}(G)$ induced by I, where we have $H_i = \{G' \in \mathsf{in}(G) \mid I(G') = p_i\}$. Let $g_1, \dots, g_k$ and h be the functions from Definition 1 with respect to H. Each player p_i computes $g_i(H_i)$ and sends its b-bit value to player $I(G)$, who then applies h to obtain the value of G.

(b) If G is light and $G' \in \mathsf{in}(G)$ is heavy, then player $I(G')$ sends the value of G' to player $I(G)$, *unless it has already done so in the past.* (It is crucial to avoid duplication of heavy-gate outputs.)

(c) The remaining wires are both inputs and outputs of light gates. These wires induce a demand pattern, where each player $I(G)$ needs to learn all the values of "light inputs" $G' \in \mathsf{in}(G) \cap C_L$. Because each player is responsible for no more than $2n \cdot s$ incoming or outgoing wires for light gates, the demand pattern is balanced, with each player requiring no more than $2n \cdot s$ bits from any other player. We route all these wires in $O(1)$ rounds using Lenzen's algorithm [28].

It is not hard to see that since each player owns at most one heavy gate, the total number of bits sent from any player p to any other player q in stage r is $O(s+b)$.

Finally, to handle any input assignment which is roughly-balanced (each player receives at most $n(b+s)$ inputs), we can use Lenzen's algorithm to route the inputs from their originally-assigned players to the player assigned them under I, using no more than $O(b+s)$ bits per message and $O(1)$ rounds. □

REMARK 3. *Although the simulation is stated for functions, it is easy to see that it extends to* operators, *functions with multi-bit outputs. We partition the outputs between the players, such that no player is required to output more than* $O(b+s)$ *bits, and use Lenzen's algorithm to route the outputs to the correct players. This will be useful when we discuss matrix multiplication below.*

From the simulation above we conclude:

THEOREM 4. *For any* $s, b, R \geq 0$, *if* $f : \{0,1\}^{n^2} \to \{0,1\}$ *cannot be computed in* $\mathsf{CLIQUE\text{-}UCAST}_{n,O(b+s)}$ *in* R *rounds, then for some constant* $c > 1$, f *cannot be computed by circuits of depth* $c \cdot R$ *using* b-*separable gates and* $n^2 \cdot s$ *wires.*

This means that any attempt to prove lower bounds for this model runs up against the following open problems in bounded-depth circuit complexity:

Threshold circuits [31]. A threshold circuit is a circuit with unbounded fan-in, made up of gates that compute threshold functions — Boolean predicates of the form $a_1 x_1 + a_2 x_2 \dots + a_k x_k \geq b$, where $a_1, \dots, a_k, b \in \mathbf{Z}^+$ are called *weights*, and $x_1, \dots, x_k$ are the (Boolean) inputs to the gate. At present, the best lower bound known for bounded-depth threshold circuits that compute Boolean functions is from [21, 42], where it is shown that a threshold circuit of depth d that computes the parity of N-bit inputs requires $N^{1+cK^{-d}}$ wires, where $c > 0$ and $K \leq 3$ are explicit constants. This holds for circuits with arbitrary weights; however, despite extensive study, no better bounds are known for the unweighted case (where all weights are set to one) beyond depth 3 [16, 18, 37, 40].

The lower bound decays quickly with d, becoming trivial (linear) at $d = \Theta(\log\log n)$. Since unweighted threshold gates are $\Theta(\log n)$-separable, our simulation implies that for some fixed constants $\alpha, \beta > 0$, obtaining a lower bound of $\alpha \log\log n$ on the round complexity of some explicit function in $\mathsf{CLIQUE\text{-}UCAST}_{n,\beta\log n}$ would imply a better lower bound than that of [21, 42] for the number of wires in unweighted threshold circuits.

ACC *and* **CC** *[36].* Circuits in $\mathsf{ACC}[m]$ use unbounded fan-in AND, OR, NOT and MOD_m gates, where m is constant. MOD_m gates test whether or not $(x_1 + \ldots + \ldots x_k) \bmod m = 0$; for example, a MOD_2 gate computes the parity of its inputs. A $\mathsf{CC}[m]$ circuit is one comprising only unbounded fan-in MOD_m gates.

Although there are exponential lower bounds on the size of constant-depth $\mathsf{ACC}[m]$ circuits when m is prime or a prime power [43], the general case remains very challenging; even the possibility that all of NP has depth-3, poly-size circuits consisting only of MOD_6 gates, with a linear number of gates, has not been ruled out [17]. (In a recent breakthrough, Williams showed that the larger class NEXP does not have poly-size, constant-depth $\mathsf{ACC}[m]$ circuits for any m [46]; however only lower bounds for problems in NP are generally considered "explicit".)

Currently, the best explicit lower bound on the number of wires appears in [6], where it is shown that constant-depth $\mathsf{CC}[m]$ circuits (where m may be composite) require a superlinear number of wires to compute AND or MOD_q, where q is coprime to m. Specifically, the lower bound is the following: for depth 2, $\Omega(n \log n)$ wires are required; for depth 3, $\Omega(n \log^* n)$ wires; for depth 4, $\Omega(n \log^{**} n)$, and so on. In general, the bound for depth d is $\Omega(n \cdot \lambda_d(n))$, where $\lambda_1(n) = \lceil \log_2 n \rceil$ and $\lambda_{d+1}(n) = \min\left\{ i \in \mathbb{N} \mid \lambda_d^{(i)} \leq 1 \right\}$. Here $f^{(i)}$ denotes f iterated i times.

Let $\lambda^{-1}(n) := \min\{d \in \mathbb{N} \mid \lambda_d(n) \leq 1\}$. The lower bound of [6] becomes trivial at depth $\lambda^{-1}(n)$. Since MOD_6 gates are $O(1)$-separable, we get that for some constants $\alpha, \beta > 0$, a lower bound of $\alpha \cdot \lambda^{-1}(n)$ for $\mathsf{CLIQUE\text{-}UCAST}_{n,\beta}$ would imply a bound better than [6] on $\mathsf{ACC}[m]$ for composite m.

The circuit lower bounds referred to above are the best currently known in terms of asymptotic behavior as the depth increases. For fixed depths (typically 2 or 3), or for computing operators, some better bounds are known, but the asymptotic behavior remains the same (in the case of operators, up to a multiplicative constant in the depth).

2.1 Matrix Multiplication vs. Triangle Detection

The triangle detection problem received special attention in [8], which gives an elegant randomized algorithm that runs in time $\tilde{O}(n^{1/3}/T^{2/3})$ when the input graph has at least T triangles. In the full version we show that, under a certain widely-believed conjecture on the complexity of matrix multiplication, triangle detection can be solved in time $O(n^{\epsilon})$ for any $\epsilon > 0$ in $\mathsf{CLIQUE\text{-}UCAST}_{n,1}$.

We give an overview of the connection here. The connection between matrix multiplication and triangle detection is well-known [22, 45]: if one cubes the adjacency matrix of a graph over the Boolean semiring, triangles appear as non-zero entries on the diagonal. A simple randomized reduction due to Adi Shamir (described in [45, Thm. 4.1]) allows one to reduce this computation to a small number of matrix multiplications over the field $\mathbb{F}_2$. Now, it is widely conjectured (although there is no consensus) that for every $\epsilon > 0$, matrix multiplication over any field $\mathbb{F}$, and in particular over $\mathbb{F}_2$, can be computed (as a formal polynomial mapping) by arithmetic circuits of size $O(n^{2+\epsilon})$; and it is known [5] that such circuits also imply the existence of circuits for matrix multiplication with few wires *and* polylogarithmic depth. (This fact is shown by exploiting the block structure of matrix multiplication; see [5, Prop. 15.1] and the full version.)

By using the simulation from Theorem 2 (and Remark 3), we can translate small, shallow arithmetic circuits over $\mathbb{F}_2$ into a fast $\mathsf{CLIQUE\text{-}UCAST}_{n,1}$ protocol in which every entry of the output matrix is known to some player; each player can then announce whether or not it sees any non-zero diagonal entries, thereby solving triangle detection.

3. SUBGRAPH DETECTION IN THE CONGESTED CLIQUE WITH BROADCAST

We now turn our attention to the broadcast version of the congested clique, CLIQUE-BCAST, and study the problem of detecting whether a given fixed-size subgraph H is a subgraph of the input graph G. We assume that H is of fixed (constant) size, and we are interested in the complexity of the problem as the number of participants n grows. We start by describing a simple algorithm that solves the problem in the CLIQUE-BCAST model. We then describe lower bounds for subgraph detection in the CLIQUE-BCAST model; some of our lower bounds also hold for the CONGEST-UCAST model, where the communication topology is the same as the input graph G, rather than the clique.

Our bounds are based on Turán numbers for graphs, which are defined as follows.

Definition 5 (Turán Number). *For a graph H and an integer $n \geq 1$, the Turán number* $\mathrm{ex}(n, H)$ *for graph H is the maximal possible number of edges of an n-node graph G such that G does not contain a subgraph isomorphic to H.*

Of particular relevance to us in this section are the Turán numbers for any odd-length cycle (or in general for non-bipartite graphs), which is $\Theta(n^2)$, and for the 4-cycle C_4, which is $\Theta(n^{3/2})$.

3.1 Upper Bounds on Subgraph Detection

The *degeneracy* of a graph G is the smallest integer k such that every subgraph of G has a node of degree at most k. In [2], Becker et al. give a one-round algorithm for the CLIQUE-BCAST model that allows all players to learn the entire input graph, assuming it has known degeneracy of (at most) k. In the algorithm of [2], the players simultaneously each broadcast $O(k \log n)$ bits, and based on these messages they are able to completely reconstruct the input graph.

We can use the algorithm from [2] to solve subgraph detection in the $\mathsf{CLIQUE\text{-}BCAST}_{n,b}$ model. We first observe that the degeneracy of H-free graphs can be bounded from above in terms of the corresponding Turán number:

CLAIM 6. *Let H be a graph, and let G be an n-node H-free graph. Then the degeneracy of G is at most $4 \cdot \mathrm{ex}(n, H)/n$.*

PROOF. Consider an n'-node subgraph G' of G (for some $n' \leq n$). Since G' is also H-free, it has at most $\mathrm{ex}(n', H)$ edges, so one of the nodes of G' must have degree at most $2 \cdot \mathrm{ex}(n', H)/n'$. It therefore suffices to show that for all $n' \leq n$ we have $\mathrm{ex}(n', H)/n' \leq 2 \cdot \mathrm{ex}(n, H)/n$. This follows because $\mathrm{ex}(n, H)$ is non-decreasing in n, and because $\mathrm{ex}(2n, H) \geq 2 \cdot \mathrm{ex}(n, H)$, since we can take two disjoint copies of an extremal H-free n-node graph to obtain an H-free $2n$-node graph with $2 \cdot \mathrm{ex}(n, H)$ edges. □

Plugging this upper bound on the degeneracy into the algorithm of [2], we obtain the following upper bound for solving the H-subgraph problem in the CLIQUE-BCAST model.

THEOREM 7. *For any (fixed) graph H, the H-subgraph detection problem can be solved in the $\mathsf{CLIQUE\text{-}BCAST}_{n,b}$ model in $O(\frac{\mathrm{ex}(n,H)}{n} \cdot \frac{\log n}{b})$ rounds.*

The running time above is obtained by taking the single $O(\mathrm{ex}(n, H) \log(n)/n)$-bit message produced by each node in the algorithm of [2], dividing it into chunks of b bits each, and broadcasting the chunks over $O(\frac{\mathrm{ex}(n,H)}{n} \cdot \frac{\log n}{b})$ rounds.

If H has chromatic number $\chi(H) \geq 3$, the upper bound given by Theorem 7 is $O(n \log(n)/b)$; this is trivial to achieve by simply having each node broadcast its entire neighborhood. For bipartite graphs H, however, the theorem does give non-trivial upper bounds. For example, using known bounds on Turán numbers we get that the algorithm detects cycles of length 2ℓ for any $\ell \geq 2$ in time $O(n^{1/\ell} \log(n)/b)$ [4, 10], and for $2 \leq r \leq s$, $K_{r,s}$-subgraph detection can be solved in time $O(n^{2-1/r} \log(n)/b)$ [25]. If H is a tree or a forest of a fixed size, we have $\mathrm{ex}(n, H) = O(1)$, so Theorem 7 implies that the H-subgraph detection problem can be solved in time $O(\log(n)/b)$. In the full version we show that 4-cycle detection can also be solved in the same asymptotic time, $O(\sqrt{n} \log(n)/b)$, even when nodes can only communicate over the edges of the input graph G.

Detecting subgraphs of unknown Turán number. The simple algorithm above requires nodes to know $\mathrm{ex}(n, H)$. However, for most bipartite graphs H, even the asymptotic behavior of $\mathrm{ex}(n, H)$ is not known (although there are some upper and lower bounds). We now sketch how to adapt the algorithm such that even if $\mathrm{ex}(n, H)$ is not known to the nodes, the algorithm runs in time $\tilde{O}(\mathrm{ex}(n, H)/(nb))$, and with high probability it returns an H-subgraph of G if there is one. The modified algorithm is based on the observation that if G contains an H-subgraph, an appropriate random subgraph of G with $\Theta(\mathrm{ex}(n, H))$ edges still contains a copy of H, with high probability.

Let us recall the exact properties of the one-round algorithm $\mathcal{A}$ described in [2]. The algorithm is deterministic and has an integer parameter $k \geq 1$. When run on a graph G with parameter k, every node simultaneously writes an $O(k \log n)$-bit message on the blackboard. If the degeneracy of G is at most k, in the end, all nodes learn the complete topology of G. Otherwise, all nodes learn that the degeneracy of G is more than k. In the following, let $\mathcal{A}(G, k)$ denote algorithm $\mathcal{A}$ when applied to graph G and with parameter k.

Our algorithm will make exponentially-increasing guesses $k_i = 2^i$ for the degeneracy of G, where $i = 1, 2, \ldots, \lceil \log n \rceil$, and call $\mathcal{A}$ using the current guess. Let us first dispense with some easy cases. If G does *not* contain a copy of the subgraph H, then, as we saw in Claim 6, the degeneracy of G is at most $4\,\mathrm{ex}(n, H)/n$. Within at most $O(\log(\mathrm{ex}(n, H)/n)) = O(\log n)$ steps we will reach an appropriate guess for the degeneracy, and when we call $\mathcal{A}$ with this guess, all nodes will learn the entire topology of G, and detect that G is H-free. A similar case is when G does contain a copy of H, but its degeneracy is nevertheless bounded by $O(\mathrm{ex}(n, H)/n)$. In both cases the running time is bounded by $O(\mathrm{ex}(n, H) \log(n)/(nb))$, which we obtain by splitting the messages produced by $\mathcal{A}$ into chunks of b bits, such that each chunk can be broadcast in one round.

We therefore focus on the case where the degeneracy k of G satisfies $k \gg \mathrm{ex}(n, H)/n$. Our goal now is to reduce the degeneracy by sampling a subgraph of G, in such a way that the subgraph we sample will still contain a copy of H. By Claim 6, as long as we select a subgraph that is "not too sparse"— specifically, as long as our subgraph has degeneracy $4\,\mathrm{ex}(n, H)/n$ or greater—it will still contain a copy of H. However, we do want a subgraph with degeneracy at most $c \cdot \mathrm{ex}(n, H)/n$ for some constant $c > 4$, so that we can call $\mathcal{A}$ and obtain the desired running time.

It can be shown that if each edge of G is independently sampled with some probability $p \in [0, 1]$, then as long as $k \cdot p = \Omega(\log n)$, the random subgraph induced by all the sampled edges has degeneracy $\Theta(k \cdot p)$. Thus, a good strategy would be to sample each edge of G with probability $p = \Theta(\mathrm{ex}(n, H)/(kn))$, reducing the degeneracy to $\Theta(\mathrm{ex}(n, H)/n)$ but not less than $4\,\mathrm{ex}(n, H)/n$. Unfortunately, it is not clear how to quickly perform the sampling in a distributed way in the CLIQUE-BCAST model in such a way that each node will know which of its edges have been selected (which is necessary to run the algorithm from [2]). Indeed, when we sample each edge independently with probability $p < 1/2$, the entropy of the sample, viewed as a Boolean assignment to the edges of G, exceeds the expected number of edges in the sampled subgraph. Learning this information seems to require too much communication. We therefore use non-uniform sampling, and show that the degeneracy of the sampled subgraph still behaves as expected.

In addition to the above, we also do not know the "right" probability $p = \Theta(\mathrm{ex}(n, H)/(kn))$, because we know neither $\mathrm{ex}(n, H)$ nor the degeneracy k of G. As we said, we will be guessing the degeneracy, but in addition we will also make exponentially-decreasing guesses for p.

More specifically, the sampling is done as follows. Let n be the number of nodes of $G = (V, E)$. We define $\ell := \lfloor \log_2 n \rfloor$ and $N := 2^\ell$ to be the largest power of 2 not exceeding n. Each node $v \in V$ independently picks an integer X_v uniformly from $\{0, \ldots, N - 1\}$. For each integer $j \in \{0, \ldots, \ell\}$, we define a random subgraph $G_j = (V, E_j)$ of G, which roughly speaking corresponds to sampling each edge with probability $p = 2^{-j}$ (but the edges are not independent of each other). For each $j \in \{0, \ldots, \ell\}$, the edge set E_j is defined as follows:

$$E_j := \Big\{\{u,v\} \in E : X_u \equiv X_v \pmod{2^j}\Big\}.$$

The graphs $G_0, \ldots, G_\ell$ can be constructed simultaneously in $O(\log(n)/b)$ rounds: each node $v \in V$ broadcasts its random number X_v to all its neighbors, who can then determine which of their edges are in E_j for each $j \in \{0, \ldots, \ell\}$. Since $X_v \in [n]$, this requires $O(\log(n)/b)$ rounds.

For each edge $e \in E$, the probability that $e \in E_j$ is exactly 2^{-j}. In general, the edges are not independent, but for any specific node $v \in V$, the edges of node v *are* independent of each other; therefore, for any subset $S \subseteq V$, the number of nodes in S that are adjacent to v in E_j is binomially distributed with parameters $|S|$ and 2^{-j}.

We now show that the degeneracy of the sampled subgraphs behaves as expected: it is roughly $k \cdot p$, where $p = 2^{-j}$ is the sampling probability of an edge. In the following, for each $j \in \{0, \ldots, \ell\}$, let K_j be a random variable denoting the degeneracy of G_j.

LEMMA 8. *Let $c > 0$ be a sufficiently large constant. With high probability, for each $j \in \{0, \ldots, \ell\}$ such that $k \cdot 2^{-j} \geq c \log n$ we have $0.9k \cdot 2^{-j} \leq K_j \leq 1.1k \cdot 2^{-j}$.*

PROOF SKETCH. Fix $j \in \{0, \ldots, \ell\}$ such that $k \cdot 2^{-j} \geq c \log n$. First let us bound the degeneracy K_j of G_j from below, by exhibiting a subgraph of G_j that has minimal degree at least $0.9k \cdot 2^{-j}$ (w.h.p.). To this end, let $F = (V_F, E_F)$ be a subgraph of G that has some node $v \in V_F$ with degree k (we know that such a subgraph exists by definition of the degeneracy), and let $F_j := (V_F, E_F \cap E_j)$. As explained above, the distribution of the degree of v with respect to $E_F \cap E_j$ is binomial with expectation $2^{-j} \cdot k$, because each neighbor of v in F survives independently of the other neighbors with probability 2^{-j}. Since $k \cdot 2^{-j} \geq c \cdot \log n$, when we select c large enough a standard Chernoff bound implies that the degree of v in F_j is at least $0.9k \cdot 2^{-j}$ w.h.p., and therefore the degeneracy of G_j is also at least $0.9k \cdot 2^{-j}$.

Now let us show that w.h.p. the degeneracy K_j is also bounded from above by $1.1k \cdot 2^{-j}$. Because $G = (V, E)$ has degeneracy k, there is an ordering $v_1, \ldots, v_n$ of V such that for each $r \in [n]$, the degree of v_r in the subgraph $G[V_{\geq r}]$ induced by nodes $V_{\geq r} := \{v_r, \ldots, v_n\}$ is at most k. (To find such an ordering, start with a node that has degree at most k in all of G, then at each step consider the subgraph induced by the remaining nodes; since G has degeneracy k, some node has degree at most k in this subgraph, and we can select this node and continue.) By the same reasoning as above, for any $r \in [n]$, the expected degree of v_r in $G_j[V_{\geq r}]$ is at most $k \cdot 2^{-j}$. A standard Chernoff bound and a union bound over all $r \in [n]$ show that w.h.p. each node v_r has degree at most $1.1k \cdot 2^{-j}$ in $G_j[V_{\geq r}]$.

To show that G_j has degeneracy at most $1.1k \cdot 2^{-j}$, let $F = (V_F, E_F)$ be a subgraph of G_j; we must find some node with degree at most $1.1k \cdot 2^{-j}$ in F. Let r be the minimum index such that $v_r \in V_F$. Then F is a subgraph of $G_j[V_{\geq r}]$, and the degree of v_r in F is no greater than its degree in $G_j[V_{\geq r}]$, namely $1.1k \cdot 2^{-j}$. □

Combining all the ingredients above, we obtain the following algorithm for H-subgraph detection. We assume that calling $\mathcal{A}(G_j, k)$ sets a flag *success*, which indicates whether or not the parameter k was large enough for the nodes to learn the entire topology of G_j (i.e., at least as large as the true degeneracy G_j).

```
sample G_0, ..., G_ℓ;
for i = 1, 2, ..., ⌈log_2 n⌉ do
    k_i := 2^i;
    for j ∈ {0, ..., ℓ} do
        run algorithm A(G_j, k_i);
        if success and H-subgraph H' detected then
            return H'
        else if success then
            return "no H-subgraph"
```

THEOREM 9. *If G is H-free, the algorithm outputs "no H-subgraph" and terminates after $O(\operatorname{ex}(n, H) \log^2 n/(nb))$ rounds. If G contains a subgraph isomorphic to H, the algorithm finds such a subgraph with high probability after $O(\operatorname{ex}(n, H) \log^2 n/(nb) + \log^3 n/b)$ rounds.*

3.2 Lower Bounds

Our lower bounds on subgraph detection are obtained by reduction from the 2-party set disjointness problem. The reductions all use the same basic method: we split the nodes in $[n]$ into two sets A, B, "owned" by Alice and Bob respectively. We also fix an n-vertex "template graph" G' which contains many copies of H. The players then use their inputs X, Y to construct a subgraph G of G', with each player controlling the edges internal to the set of nodes it owns, in such a way that a copy of H appears in G iff X and Y are not disjoint.

The key technical challenge is designing G' in such a way that no copies of H appear inside the subgraphs G_A, G_B induced by A and B, so that the answer to the H-subgraph-detection problem always depends on both X and Y. We will now describe a family of graphs that achieve this requirement. In the following definition we introduce a second graph F, whose edges will serve as the elements of the set disjointness instance.

DEFINITION 10. *Let $H = (V_H, E_H)$ and $F = (V_F, E_H)$ be two graphs. We say that G' is a (H, F)-*lower bound graph *if G' satisfies the following properties:*

(1) G' contains two vertex-disjoint subgraphs $F_A = (V_A, E_A)$ and $F_B = (V_B, E_B)$ that are both isomorphic to F.

(2) There exist isomorphisms $\varphi_A : V_F \to V_A, \varphi_B : V_F \to V_B$ from F to F_A and F_B, respectively, such that

I. For every edge $\{u, v\} \in E_F$, G' contains a subgraph $H' = (V_{H'}, E_{H'})$, where

(a) H' is isomorphic to H,

(b) $\{\varphi_A(u), \varphi_A(v)\}$ and $\{\varphi_B(u), \varphi_B(v)\}$ are both edges of H',

(c) $V_{H'} \cap (V_A \cup V_B) = \{\varphi_A(u), \varphi_A(v), \varphi_B(u), \varphi_B(v)\}$.

II. The subgraphs described above are the only *subgraphs of G' isomorphic to H; that is, if H' is a subgraph of G' that is isomorphic to H, then there is an edge $\{u, v\} \in E_F$ such that (b) and (c) hold.*

We associate with each (H, F)-lower bound graph a fixed $F_A = (V_A, E_A), F_B = (V_B, E_B), \varphi_A$ and φ_B satisfying the requirements above (if there is more than one choice, we choose arbitrarily). For an edge $e = \{u, v\} \in E_F$ and a mapping φ, we let $\varphi(e) = \{\varphi(u), \varphi(v)\}$ denote the image of e under φ.

An essential property of Definition 10 is the following:

OBSERVATION 11. *Suppose that $G = (V, E)$ is a subgraph of an (H, F)-lower bound graph $G' = (V', E')$ such that $E' \setminus (E_A \cup E_B) \subseteq E$. Then G contains a copy of H iff for some edge $e \in E_F$ we have $\varphi_A(e), \varphi_B(e) \in E$.*

We will map this property into a set disjointness instance, with Alice controlling the edges of F_A and Bob controlling those of F_B. We will generally aim to have F be as dense as possible, to increase the size of the set disjointness instance.

In some cases we will be able to apply our reductions to show lower bounds for the more general CONGEST model, where the input graph G is also the communication network, and nodes communicate by unicast over the edges of G. We denote this model by CONGEST-UCAST. Here, the parameter determining the efficiency of the reduction will be the size of the cut between the nodes owned by each player.

DEFINITION 12. *We say that an (H, F)-lower bound graph $G' = (V', E')$ is δ-sparse, for $\delta > 0$, if there is a partition A, B of V' such that $V_A \subseteq A, V_B \subseteq B$ and the size of the cut (A, B) is at most $\delta \cdot |V'|$.*

Before describing how we can construct lower bound graphs for specific H and F, let us show how we can use these graphs to obtain a reduction from 2-party set disjointness to H-subgraph-detection.

LEMMA 13. *Suppose that for $H = (V_H, E_H)$ and $F = (V_F, H_F)$, there exists an n-node (H, F)-lower bound graph $G' = (V', E')$. Then the number of rounds required to solve H-subgraph-detection in CLIQUE-BCAST$_{n,b}$ with constant error probability is at least $\Omega(|E_F|/(nb))$.*

Further, if the (H, F)-lower bound graph G' is δ-sparse for some $\delta > 0$, the number of rounds required to solve H-subgraph-detection in CONGEST-UCAST$_{n,b}$ with constant error probability is at least $\Omega(|E_F|/(\delta nb))$.

PROOF SKETCH. The proof follows by reduction from 2-party set disjointness with $|E_F|$ elements, each representing an edge of F. We partition the nodes of G' between Alice and Bob, with each player simulating $\Theta(n)$ nodes, including all nodes of F_A (for Alice) or all nodes of F_B (for Bob). The players construct a subgraph of G', putting in edges of F_A or F_B only if the corresponding edge appears in their input, and then simulate the H-subgraph detection algorithm. By Observation 11, G' contains a copy of H iff the players' inputs are non-disjoint. □

We now show how to construct (H, F)-lower bound graphs for specific H and F. In the following, we derive lower bounds for the cases where H is a clique, a cycle, or a complete bipartite graph.

3.3 Detecting Cliques

Let $\ell \geq 4$ be an integer, and consider the problem of detecting whether a given network graph G contains K_ℓ, a clique of size ℓ.

LEMMA 14. *For any $\ell \geq 4, N \geq 4$, and $n \geq 1$ such that $4(N-1) + \ell \leq n$, there is a $(K_\ell, K_{N,N})$-lower bound graph $G' = (V', E')$ with n nodes. (Here $K_{N,N}$ is the complete bipartite graph on $2N$ nodes.)*

PROOF. First assume that $n = 4(N-1) + \ell$ nodes. Let $S_i := \{v_{i,1} \ldots, v_{i,N}\}$ for $i = 1, 2, 3, 4$, and let the vertices of G' be $V' := (\bigcup_{i=1}^{4} S_i) \cup \{u_1, \ldots, u_{\ell-4}\}$. The edges are defined as follows:

- For each $j \in [N]$, $\{v_{1,j}, v_{2,j}\} \in E'$ and $\{v_{3,j}, v_{4,j}\} \in E'$,
- For each $(i, i') \in \{1, 2\} \times \{3, 4\}$ and $j, j' \in [N]$, $\{v_{i,j}, v_{i',j'}\} \in E$, and finally,
- Each of the nodes $u_1, \ldots, u_{\ell-1}$ is connected to all other nodes of G'.

The proof that G' satisfies Definition 10 appears in the full version; intuitively, it is because any K_4-subgraph of G' must include exactly one node from each of the sets S_1, S_2, S_3, S_4 (these being independent sets of G'), and because S_1, $S2$ and S_3, S_4 are connected by perfect matchings, one must take four nodes of the form $v_{1,i}, v_{2,i}, v_{3,j}, v_{4,j}$, which requires the edge $\{i, j\}$ to exist in both players' inputs. □

THEOREM 15. *In the CLIQUE-BCAST$_{n,b}$ model, for every fixed $\ell \geq 4$, K_ℓ-subgraph detection requires at least $\Omega(n/b)$ rounds.*

PROOF. Fix n, and let $N = \lfloor (n-\ell)/4 \rfloor + 1 = \Theta(n)$. By Lemma 14, there is a $(K_\ell, K_{N,N})$-lower bound graph on n vertices. Because $K_{N,N}$ has $N^2 = \Theta(n^2)$ edges, Lemma 13 implies the theorem. □

REMARK 16. *Although we have assumed that the subgraph H we are trying to detect is of constant size, the proof above continues to work for cliques K_ℓ of size up to $(1-\epsilon)n$ for any constant $\epsilon \in (0, 1)$.*

3.4 Detecting Cycles

We now prove a lower bound on the H-subgraph-detection problem when H is a cycle C_ℓ of length $\ell \geq 4$. We will use the following definitions and notation from extremal graph theory:

DEFINITION 17. *For an integer $n > 0$ and a graph H, let $\text{ex}(n, H)$ denote the maximum number of edges of any graph on n vertices that does not contain H as a subgraph. We say that $G = (V, E)$ is an* extremal H-free graph *if $|E| = \text{ex}(|V|, H)$.*

LEMMA 18. *Fix $\ell \geq 4$, let N be an even integer, and let $n \geq \ell \cdot (N/2)$. Then for some extremal C_ℓ-free graph F on N vertices, there exists a (C_ℓ, F)-lower bound graph on n vertices.*

PROOF. Assume for simplicity that $n = \ell \cdot (N/2)$ (as in Lemma 14, it is straightforward to generalize to larger n by adding isolated nodes). If ℓ is odd, then $\text{ex}(N, \ell) = N^2/4$, and we let F be the complete bipartite graph $K_{N/2,N/2} = ([N], [N/2] \times ([N] \setminus [N/2]))$. If ℓ is even, then $\text{ex}(N, \ell) = \Omega(N^{3/2})$, and we let F be any extremal C_ℓ-free graph.

We construct $G' = (V', E')$ as follows. V' consists of two sets, $V_A = \{v_{A,1}, \ldots, v_{A,N}\}$ and $V_B = \{v_{B,1}, \ldots, v_{B,N}\}$, as well as $(\ell - 4)N/2$ additional nodes, which we denote by $u_{i,j}$ where either $i \in [N/2]$ and $0 \leq j \leq \lfloor \ell/2 \rfloor - 1$, or $i \in [N] \setminus [N/2]$ and $0 \leq j \leq \lceil \ell/2 \rceil - 1$. As for the edges, for any $i, j \in [N]$, $\{v_{A,i}, v_{A,j}\} \in E'$ iff $\{i, j\} \in E_F$, and similarly, $\{v_{B_i}, v_{B,j}\} \in E'$ iff $\{i, j\} \in E_F$. In addition, we connect each pair $v_{A,i}, v_{B,i}$ by a path P_i comprising all the nodes of the form $u_{i,j}$ for some j. The length of the path is $\lfloor \ell/2 \rfloor - 1$ if $i \leq N/2$, or $\lceil \ell/2 \rceil - 1$ if $i > N/2$. □

By Lemma 13, we obtain:

THEOREM 19. *For every fixed $\ell \geq 4$, C_ℓ-subgraph detection requires at least $\Omega(\text{ex}(n, C_\ell)/(nb))$ rounds, both in the CLIQUE-BCAST$_{n,b}$ and in the CONGEST-UCAST$_{n,b}$ models.*

A note on triangle detection. Theorems 15 and 19 both fail to address the complexity of detecting triangles; the technique we used cannot give any non-trivial lower bounds on C_3-subgraph detection. In our reductions, each node in the graph is simulated by at least one of the two players. (It is not hard to see that any *black-box reduction*, where we only access the distributed algorithm by executing it, must have this feature.) In order to simulate a node, the player must know the input edges adjacent to the node. In the case of triangles this means that for any three nodes a, b, c, some player simulates at least two of the nodes; even if this player does not simulate the third node, since each node "knows" the edges adjacent to it, the player can determine all by itself whether there is a triangle on a, b, c or not.

Since the problem is, informally, too much overlap between the players' inputs, it seems reasonable to turn to a model of communication complexity that features such overlaps; and this is exactly what we will do in Section 3.6.

3.5 Detecting Complete Bipartite Subgraphs

Finally, let us give a lower bound for detecting $K_{\ell,m}$, the complete bipartite subgraph with ℓ vertices on one side and m on the other. For this result we need the following fact from [11]:

OBSERVATION 20. **[11]** *If $\text{ex}(n, H) = k$ and H is bipartite, then there exists a* bipartite *H-free graph on n vertices with at least $k/2$ edges.*

Let F be a bipartite C_4-free graph on N vertices with at least $\text{ex}(N, C_4)/2$ edges.

LEMMA 21. *For every fixed $\ell, m \geq 2$, $N \geq 2$ and $n \geq 2N + \ell + m - 4$, there is a $(K_{\ell,m}, F)$-lower bound graph on n vertices.*

PROOF. As usual, assume for simplicity that $n = 4N + \ell + m - 4$, otherwise add isolated nodes to make up the difference. Let $F = (L \cup R, E_F)$, where $L, R \subseteq [N]$ are the vertices of F.

We construct $G' = (V', E')$ as follows. Define $V_A = \{u_1, \ldots, u_N\}$ and $V_B = \{v_1, \ldots, v_N\}$. We set $V' := V_A \cup V_B \cup W_L \cup W_R$, where $W_L := \{w_1^L, \ldots, w_{\ell-2}^L\}$ and $W_R := \{w_1^R, \ldots, w_{m-2}^R\}$, and in E' we include the following edges:

- For each $i, j \in [N]$, $\{u_i, u_j\} \in E'$ and $\{v_i, v_j\} \in E'$ iff $\{i, j\} \in F$. Let $\varphi_A(i) = u_i$ and $\varphi_B(i) = v_i$ be isomorphisms from F to F_A, F_B respectively.
- All nodes in W^L are connected to all nodes in $\varphi_A(R) \cup \varphi_B(L) \cup W^R$, and all nodes in W^R are connected to all nodes in $\varphi_A(L) \cup \varphi_B(R) \cup W^L$.
- We include all edges of the form $\{u_i, v_i\}$ for $i \in [N]$.

For each edge $\{i, j\} \in E_F$, the subgraph induced by the nodes $\{u_i, u_j, v_i, v_j\} \cup W$ is isomorphic to $K_{\ell,m}$: assume w.l.o.g. that $i \in L$ and $j \in R$. The sets $W^L \cup \{u_i, v_j\}$ and $W^R \cup \{u_j, v_i\}$ are of size ℓ and m respectively. The nodes in W^L are connected to all nodes in W^R as well as to $u_j \in \varphi_A(R), v_i \in \varphi_B(L)$, and similarly for the other side. Node u_i is connected to u_j (because of the isomorphism from F) and to v_i, and similarly v_j is connected to v_i and u_j, and there are no other edges in the induced subgraph. Therefore the induced subgraph is isomorphic to $K_{\ell,m}$.

Now suppose that H is a $K_{\ell,m}$-subgraph of G', and let L^H, R^H be the two sides of H. L^H and R^H must each include at least two nodes from $V_A \cup V_B$, as $|W^L| = \ell - 2$ and $|W^R| = m - 2$ (and no mixing between W^L, W^R is possible because $W^L \times W^R \in E'$). However, it cannot be that L^H and L^R both contain two nodes from the same set V_A or V_B, because F_A and F_B are both C_4-free. Therefore the following combinations are possible:

- L^H includes at least two distinct nodes $u_i, u_j \in V_A$, and L^R does not. Then L^R contains at least one node $v_k \in V_B$. But this is impossible, because each node in L^R must be connected to each node in L^H, but the only edges between V_A and V_B are of the form $\{u_s, v_s\}$ for some $s \in [N]$. We cannot have both $\{u_i, v_k\} \in E'$ and $\{u_j, v_k\} \in E'$.
- L^R includes at least two nodes from V_A, and L^H does not: similar. Also similar are the cases where either L^H or L^R include two nodes from V_B.
- L^H includes exactly one node $u_i \in V_A$ and one node $v_j \in V_B$, and L^R includes one node $u_p \in V_A$ and one node $v_q \in V_B$. Then either $W^L \subseteq L^H$ and $W^R \subseteq R^H$, or $W^R \subseteq L^H$ and $W^L \subseteq R^H$; assume that the first holds (otherwise rename L^H and L^R). This shows that condition (c) holds.

  In addition, since H is isomorphic to $K_{\ell,m}$, we must have $\{u_i, u_p\}, \{v_j, u_p\}, \{u_i, v_q\}, \{v_j, v_q\} \in E'$, which implies, by construction, that $\{i, p\} \in E_F, j = p, i = q$ and $\{j, q\} \in E_F$; in other words, we have one edge $\{i, j\} \in E_F$ such that $\varphi_A(\{i, j\})$ and $\varphi_B(\{i, j\})$ both appear in H, as required for (b).

□

Because $\text{ex}(N, C_4) = \Theta(N^{3/2})$, we obtain the following:

THEOREM 22. *For any $\ell, m \geq 1$, $K_{\ell,m}$-subgraph detection in CLIQUE-BCAST$_{n,b}$ requires $\Omega(\sqrt{n}/b)$ rounds.*

3.6 Lower Bounds on Triangle Detection

We will now show that the hardness of finding triangles in CLIQUE-BCAST is related to that of solving set disjointness in the 3-party number-on-forehead model and obtain a lower bound of $\Omega(n/(e^{O(\sqrt{n})}b))$ on deterministic triangle detection in CLIQUE-BCAST$_{n,b}$. For randomized algorithms, current lower bounds on 3-party NOF set disjointness are not strong enough to yield a non-trivial lower bound, but we can state a conditional and restricted lower bound assuming that SAT is computationally hard.

Our reduction from set disjointness uses a family of tripartite graphs with many edge-disjoint triangles. Such families can be easily obtained from dense graphs with many large disjoint induced matchings [38], which have been of interest to the theory community in various contexts including scheduling traffic in single-hop broadcast networks [3] and linearity testing [19]. The construction we will use is the following:

CLAIM 23 ([38]). *There is a family of graphs $\{G_n\}_{n>0}$ with the following properties:*

(1) G_n is a tripartite graph $G_n = (A \cup B \cup C, E)$, where $|A| = |B| = n$ and $|C| = n/3$,

(2) G_n contains $n^2/e^{O(\sqrt{\log n})}$ triangles, and each edge of G_n belongs to exactly one triangle.

Let $m(n)$ be the number of triangles in G_n (we have $m(n) \geq n^2/e^{O(\sqrt{\log n})}$), and let $R_\epsilon^{3\text{-NOF}}(\text{DISJ}_m)$ denote the randomized communication complexity of solving set disjointness with m elements and success probability $1-\epsilon$ in the 3-party NOF model.

THEOREM 24. *The number of rounds required to solve triangle detection in CLIQUE-BCAST$_{n,b}$ with error probability ϵ is at least $R_\epsilon^{3\text{-NOF}}(\text{DISJ}_m)/O(n \cdot b)$.*

PROOF. Fix n, and let $\mathcal{T} = \{t_1, \ldots, t_m\}$, where $m = m(n) = n^2/e^{O(\sqrt{\log n})}$, be the set of edge-disjoint triangles of G_n. Note that because G_n is tripartite, each triangle $t_i \in \mathcal{T}$ can be represented as $\{a_i, b_i, c_i\} \in A \times B \times C$. Moreover, since each edge of G_n belongs to exactly one triangle, for each edge e there is exactly one index $i(e) \in [m]$ such that e is part of the triangle $t_{i(e)}$.

Let $\mathcal{A}$ be a CLIQUE-BCAST$_{(7/3)n,b}$ algorithm for triangle-detection with a running time of R rounds. We use $\mathcal{A}$ to construct an 3-party number-on-forehead protocol P for DISJ_m as follows: given input $X_A, X_B, X_C \subseteq [m]$, the three parties construct a subgraph G_X of G_n, in which

- All nodes $A \cup B \cup C$ are present, with Alice simulating the nodes in A, Bob simulating the nodes in B, and Charlie simulating the nodes in C;
- An edge e of G_n is present in G_X iff $e \in A \times B$ and $i(e) \in X_C$, or $e \in B \times C$ and $i(e) \in X_A$, or $e \in C \times A$ and $i(e) \in X_B$.

Recall that since we are working with the number-on-forehead model, the set X_C is known to Alice and Bob, X_A is known to Bob and Charlie, and X_B is known to Alice and Charlie. Therefore each of the three players can tell whether an edge adjacent to any node it needs to simulate is present in G_X or not.

To simulate a run of $\mathcal{A}$ on input G_X, each player locally simulates the states of the nodes it "owns", and in each round it writes to the shared blackboard all the messages sent by these nodes. After reading the blackboard, each player feeds all messages to each of its nodes and computes their states for the next round.

The subgraph G_X contains a triangle iff there is some triangle $t_i \in \mathcal{T}$ whose edges all appear in G_X, and this occurs iff for some $i \in [m]$ we have $i \in X_A \cap X_B \cap X_C$. When $\mathcal{A}$ terminates, with probability at least $1-\epsilon$ there is at least one player that knows whether G_X contains a triangle, and hence also whether X_A, X_B and X_C are disjoint. This player then writes the answer on the blackboard.

The total cost of the simulation is $(7/3)n \cdot b \cdot R + 1$ bits, and since our protocol solves DISJ_m with error probability at most ϵ, we must have $R \geq R_\epsilon^{3\text{-NOF}}(\text{DISJ}_m)/O(n)$. □

At present, the best lower bounds on 3-NOF DISJ_N are the following: for randomized algorithms, the best bound is the $\Omega(\sqrt{N})$ bound due to Sherstov [41], and for deterministic algorithms, Rao and Yehudayoff have recently shown a lower bound of $\Omega(N)$. The deterministic lower bound gives us the following:

COROLLARY 25. *Deterministic triangle detection in the CLIQUE-BCAST$_{n,b}$ model requires $\Omega(n/(e^{O(\sqrt{\log n})}b))$ rounds.*

The randomized lower bound is just shy of yielding a non-trivial bound for randomized triangle detection. However, we do obtain a conditional lower bound: in [35], Pătraşcu and Williams discuss a strong form of the Exponential Time Hypothesis which asserts that there is no SAT algorithm with running time $O(2^{\delta n})$ for any $\delta < 1$. They show that under this assumption, there is no protocol for 3-NOF DISJ_n with communication complexity $o(n)$ in which the players' local computation is performed in time $2^{o(n)}$.

COROLLARY 26. *If for all $\delta < 1$ there is no SAT algorithm with running time $O(2^{\delta n})$, then there is no triangle detection algorithm for CLIQUE-BCAST$_{n,\text{polylog}(n)}$ with round complexity $O(n/e^{\sqrt{\log n}})$ in which the nodes' local computation is in time $2^{o(n)}$.*

4. ACKNOWLEDGMENTS

We would like to thank Mohsen Ghaffari for interesting discussions, particularly about the triangle detection lower bound, and for pointing out the reference [38] to us.

5. REFERENCES

[1] N. Alon, Y. Matias, and M. Szegedy. The space complexity of approximating the frequency moments. *J. Comput. and Syst. Sciences*, 58(1):137–147, 1999.

[2] F. Becker, M. Matamala, N. Nisse, I. Rapaport, K. Suchan, and I. Todinca. Adding a referee to an interconnection network: What can(not) be computed in one round. In *Proc. 25th Int. Symp. on Parallel and Dist. Processing (IPDPS)*, pages 508–514, 2011.

[3] Y. Birk, N. Linial, and R. Meshulam. On the uniform-traffic capacity of single-hop interconnections employing shared directional multichannels. *IEEE Trans. on Information Theory*, 39(1):186–191, 1993.

[4] J. A. Bondy and M. Simonovits. Cycles of even length in graphs. *J. Comb. Theory B*, 16:97–105, 1974.

[5] P. Bürgisser, M. Clausen, and M. A. Shokrollahi. *Algebraic complexity theory*, volume 315 of *Grundlehren der mathematischen Wissenschaften*. Springer, 1997.

[6] A. Chattopadhyay, N. Goyal, P. Pudlák, and D. Thérien. Lower bounds for circuits with MOD_m gates. In *Proc. 47th Symp. on Found. of Comp. Science (FOCS)*, pages 709–718, 2006.

[7] S. Dobzinski, N. Nisan, and S. Oren. Economic efficiency requires interaction. *CoRR*, abs/1311.4721, 2013.

[8] D. Dolev, C. Lenzen, and S. Peled. "Tri, tri agai": Finding triangles and small subgraphs in a distributed setting - (extended abstract). In *Proc. 25th Symp. on Distr. Comp. (DISC)*, pages 195–209, 2012.

[9] M. Elkin. Unconditional lower bounds on the time-approximation tradeoffs for the distributed minimum spanning tree problem. In *Proc. 36th Symp. on Theory of Comp. (STOC)*, pages 331–340, 2004.

[10] P. Erdős. Extremal problems in graph theory. *Theory of Graphs and its Applications*, pages 29–36, 1985.

[11] P. Erdős and M. Simonovits. Compactness results in extremal graph theory. *Combinatorica*, 2(3):275–288, 1982.

[12] S. Frischknecht, S. Holzer, and R. Wattenhofer. Networks cannot compute their diameter in sublinear time. In *Proc. 23rd Symp. on Discrete Alg. (SODA)*, pages 1150–1162, 2012.

[13] M. Ghaffari and F. Kuhn. Distributed minimum cut approximation. In *Proc. 26th Symp. on Distributed Comp. (DISC)*, pages 1–15, 2013.

[14] O. Goldreich and A. Warning. Secure multi-party computation. unpublished manuscript, 1998.

[15] S. Gollakota and D. Katabi. Zigzag decoding: combating hidden terminals in wireless networks. In *Proc. SIGCOMM*, pages 159–170, 2008.

[16] A. Hajnal, W. Maass, P. Pudlák, M. Szegedy, and G. Turán. Threshold circuits of bounded depth. *J. Comput. Syst. Sci.*, 46(2):129–154, 1993.

[17] K. A. Hansen and M. Koucký. A new characterization of ACC^0 and probabilistic CC^0. *Computational Complexity*, 19(2):211–234, 2010.

[18] J. Håstad and M. Goldmann. On the power of small-depth threshold circuits. *Computational Complexity*, 1:113–129, 1991.

[19] J. Håstad and A. Wigderson. Simple analysis of graph tests for linearity and PCP. *Random Struct. Algorithms*, 22(2):139–160, 2003.

[20] S. Holzer and R. Wattenhofer. Optimal distributed all pairs shortest paths and applications. In *Proc. 31st Symp. on Principles of Distr. Comp. (PODC)*, pages 355–364, 2012.

[21] R. Impagliazzo, R. Paturi, and M. E. Saks. Size-depth tradeoffs for threshold circuits. *SIAM J. Comput.*, 26(3):693–707, 1997.

[22] A. Itai and M. Rodeh. Finding a minimum circuit in a graph. *SIAM J. Comput.*, 7(4):413–423, 1978.

[23] A. Kipnis and B. Patt-Shamir. On the complexity of distributed stable matching with small messages. *Distributed Computing*, 23(3):151–161, 2010.

[24] M. Koucký, P. Pudlák, and D. Thérien. Bounded-depth circuits: separating wires from gates. In *Proc. 37th Symp. on Theory of Comp. (STOC)*, pages 257–265, 2005.

[25] T. Kövári, V. T. Sós, and P. Turán. On a problem of K. Zarankiewicz. *Colloq. Math.*, 3:50–57, 1954.

[26] F. Kuhn and R. Oshman. The complexity of data aggregation in directed networks. In *Proc. 25th Symp. on Distr. Comp. (DISC)*, pages 416–431, 2011.

[27] E. Kushilevitz and N. Nisan. *Communication complexity*. Cambridge University Press, 1997.

[28] C. Lenzen. Optimal deterministic routing and sorting on the congested clique. In *Proc. 32nd Symp. on Principles of Distr. Comp. (PODC)*, pages 42–50, 2013.

[29] C. Lenzen and R. Wattenhofer. Tight bounds for parallel randomized load balancing: extended abstract. In *Proc. 43rd Symp. on Theory of Comp. (STOC)*, pages 11–20, 2011.

[30] Z. Lotker, E. Pavlov, B. Patt-Shamir, and D. Peleg. MST construction in $O(\log \log n)$ communication rounds. In *Proc. 15th Symp. on Parallelism in Alg. and Architectures (SPAA)*, pages 94–100, 2003.

[31] I. Parberry and G. Schnitger. Parallel computation with threshold functions. *J. Comput. Syst. Sciences*, 36(3):278–302, 1988.

[32] B. Patt-Shamir and M. Teplitsky. The round complexity of distributed sorting: extended abstract. In *Proc. 30th Symp. on Principles of Distr. Comp. (PODC)*, pages 249–256, 2011.

[33] D. Peleg. *Distributed Computing: A Locality-sensitive Approach*. Society for Industrial and Applied Mathematics, 2000.

[34] D. Peleg and V. Rubinovich. A near-tight lower bound on the time complexity of distributed MST construction. *SIAM J. Comput.*, 30(5):1427–1442, 1999.

[35] M. Pătraşcu and R. Williams. On the possibility of faster SAT algorithms. In *Proc. 21st Symp. on Discrete Algorithms (SODA)*, pages 1065–1075, 2010.

[36] A. A. Razborov. Lower bounds for the size of circuits of bounded depth with basis $(\wedge,\oplus)$. *Mathematical Notes of the Academy of Science of the USSR*, 41(4):333–338, 1987.

[37] A. A. Razborov and A. Wigderson. $n^{\Omega(\log n)}$ lower bounds on the size of depth-3 threshold circuits with AND gates at the bottom. *Inf. Process. Lett.*, 45(6):303–307, 1993.

[38] I. Z. Ruzsa and E. Szemerédi. Triple systems with no six points carrying three triangles. *Combinatorica*, 1976.

[39] A. D. Sarma, S. Holzer, L. Kor, A. Korman, D. Nanongkai, G. Pandurangan, D. Peleg, and R. Wattenhofer. Distributed verification and hardness of distributed approximation. *SIAM J. Comput.*, 41(5):1235–1265, 2012.

[40] A. A. Sherstov. Separating AC^0 from depth-2 majority circuits. *SIAM J. Comput.*, 38(6):2113–2129, 2009.

[41] A. A. Sherstov. Communication lower bounds using directional derivatives. In *Proc. 45th Symp. on Theory of Comp. (STOC)*, pages 921–930, 2013.

[42] K.-Y. Siu, V. P. Roychowdhury, and T. Kailath. Computing with almost optimal size neural networks. In *Proc. Adv. in Neural Inf. Proc. Sys. (NIPS)*, pages 19–26, 1992.

[43] R. Smolensky. Algebraic methods in the theory of lower bounds for boolean circuit complexity. In *Proc. 19th Symp. on Theory of Comp. (STOC)*, pages 77–82, 1987.

[44] A. Tehrani, A. Dimakis, and M. Neely. Sigsag: Iterative detection through soft message-passing. *IEEE J. of Selected Topics in Signal Proc.*, 5(8):1512–1523, 2011.

[45] R. Williams. A new algorithm for optimal 2-constraint satisfaction and its implications. *Theor. Comput. Sci.*, 348(2-3):357–365, 2005.

[46] R. Williams. Nonuniform acc circuit lower bounds. *J. ACM*, 61(1):2, 2014.

Brief Announcement: Linial's Lower Bound Made Easy

Juhana Laurinharju
Helsinki Institute for Information Technology HIIT,
Department of Computer Science,
University of Helsinki, Finland
juhana.laurinharju@cs.helsinki.fi

Jukka Suomela
Helsinki Institute for Information Technology HIIT,
Department of Information and Computer Science,
Aalto University, Finland
jukka.suomela@aalto.fi

ABSTRACT

Linial's seminal result shows that any deterministic distributed algorithm that finds a 3-colouring of an n-cycle requires at least $\log^*(n)/2 - 1$ communication rounds. We give a new simpler proof of this theorem.

Categories and Subject Descriptors

C.2.4 [**Computer-Communication Networks**]: Distributed Systems; F.2.2 [**Analysis of Algorithms and Problem Complexity**]: Nonnumerical Algorithms and Problems

Keywords

Cycle; distributed algorithm; graph coloring; iterated logarithm; LOCAL model; lower bound

1. INTRODUCTION

Linial's lower bound for 3-colouring directed cycles [2] is one of the most celebrated results in the area of distributed graph algorithms. It is cited in hundreds of papers and the proof has been reproduced in textbooks and lecture notes [1, 3–5]. Yet it it seems that typical presentations of this result either follow the structure of Linial's original proof [1, 3, 5], or rely on some prior knowledge of Ramsey's theorem [4].

In this work we give a simpler, self-contained version of Linial's proof. This version of the proof is easy to explain to a student on a whiteboard in fifteen minutes. We do not need to refer to neighbourhood graphs, line graphs, and chromatic numbers.

2. PROBLEM FORMULATION

Fix a natural number n. We are interested in deterministic distributed algorithms that find a proper 3-colouring of any directed n-cycle. We use the LOCAL model [3]: in each round each node can send arbitrarily large messages to each of its neighbours. The nodes are labelled with unique identifiers from the set $\{1, 2, \ldots, n\}$. Each node must pick its own colour from the set $\{1, 2, 3\}$. The orientation of the edges is just auxiliary information that the algorithm can use; messages can be sent in both directions.

If we have a distributed algorithm with a running time of T communication rounds, then each node has to pick its own colour based on the information that is available within distance T from it; see Figure 1. Moreover, two nodes that are adjacent to each other must pick different colours. Hence the algorithm is a function A with $2T + 1$ arguments that satisfies

$$A(x_1, x_2, \ldots, x_{2T+1}) \in \{1, 2, 3\},$$
$$A(x_1, x_2, \ldots, x_{2T+1}) \neq A(x_2, x_3, \ldots, x_{2T+2})$$

whenever $x_1, x_2, \ldots, x_{2T+2}$ are distinct identifiers from the set $\{1, 2, \ldots, n\}$.

Function $\log^* x$ is the iterated logarithm of x, defined as follows: $\log^* x = 0$ if $x \leq 1$, and $\log^* x = 1 + \log^* \log_2 x$ otherwise. Linial's famous result shows that no matter which algorithm A we pick, we must have

$$T \geq \frac{1}{2} \log^*(n) - 1. \tag{1}$$

We will now give a simple proof of this theorem.

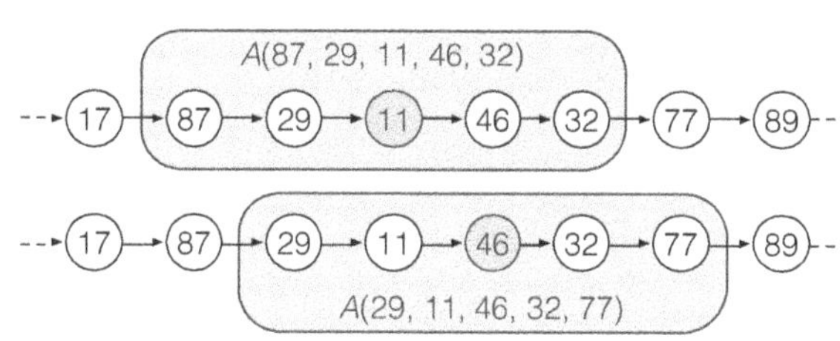

Figure 1: Colouring directed cycles in time $T = 2$. For example, the output of node 11 only depends on its radius-T neighbourhood, $(87, 29, 11, 46, 32)$. We can interpret algorithm A as a k-ary function, $k = 2T + 1 = 5$, that maps each local neighbourhood to a colour. As it is possible that adjacent nodes have neighbourhoods $(87, 29, 11, 46, 32)$ and $(29, 11, 46, 32, 77)$, function A must satisfy $A(87, 29, 11, 46, 32) \neq A(29, 11, 46, 32, 77)$.

PODC'14, July 15–18, 2014, Paris, France.
ACM 978-1-4503-2944-6/14/07.
http://dx.doi.org/10.1145/2611462.2611505.

3. COLOURING FUNCTIONS

The only concept that we need is a *colouring function*. We say that A is a k-ary c-colouring function if

$$\begin{aligned} &A(x_1, x_2, \ldots, x_k) \in \{1, 2, \ldots, c\} \\ &\text{for all } 1 \leq x_1 < x_2 < \ldots < x_k \leq n, \end{aligned} \tag{2}$$

$$\begin{aligned} &A(x_1, x_2, \ldots, x_k) \neq A(x_2, x_3, \ldots, x_{k+1}) \\ &\text{for all } 1 \leq x_1 < x_2 < \ldots < x_{k+1} \leq n. \end{aligned} \tag{3}$$

Any deterministic distributed algorithm A that finds a proper 3-colouring of an n-cycle defines a k-ary 3-colouring function for $k = 2T + 1$. (Note that the converse is not necessarily true. Colouring functions do not need to be valid algorithms. We do not care what happens if, e.g., $x_1 > x_2$.)

We will show that $k + 1 \geq \log^* n$ for any k-ary 3-colouring function. By plugging in $k = 2T + 1$, we obtain the main result (1).

4. PROOF

We begin with a trivial lemma: if a colouring function only sees 1 identifier, it cannot do much.

LEMMA 1. *If A is a 1-ary c-colouring function, we have $c \geq n$.*

PROOF. If $c < n$, by the pigeonhole principle there are some $x_1 < x_2$ with $A(x_1) = A(x_2)$, which contradicts (3). □

The key part of the proof is the following observation: given any colouring function A, we can always construct another colouring function B that is "faster" (smaller number of arguments) but "worse" (larger number of colours). Here it is crucial that colouring functions are well-defined for both odd and even values of k.

LEMMA 2. *If A is a k-ary c-colouring function, we can construct a $(k-1)$-ary 2^c-colouring function B.*

PROOF. We define B as follows:

$$\begin{aligned} &B(x_1, x_2, \ldots, x_{k-1}) \\ &\quad = \bigl\{A(x_1, x_2, \ldots, x_{k-1}, x_k) : x_k > x_{k-1}\bigr\}. \end{aligned}$$

There are only 2^c possible values of B: all possible subsets of $\{1, 2, \ldots, c\}$. These can be represented as integers $\{1, 2, \ldots, 2^c\}$, and hence (2) holds.

The interesting part is (3). Let $1 \leq x_1 < x_2 < \ldots < x_k \leq n$. By way of contradiction, suppose that

$$B(x_1, x_2, \ldots, x_{k-1}) = B(x_2, x_3, \ldots, x_k). \tag{4}$$

Let $\alpha = A(x_1, x_2, \ldots, x_k)$.

From the definition of B we have $\alpha \in B(x_1, x_2, \ldots, x_{k-1})$. By assumption (4), this implies $\alpha \in B(x_2, x_3, \ldots, x_k)$. But then we must have some $x_k < x_{k+1} \leq n$ such that

$$\alpha = A(x_2, x_3, \ldots, x_{k+1}).$$

That is, A cannot be a colouring function. □

To complete the proof, we will need power towers. Define

$$^{i}2 = 2^{2^{\cdot^{\cdot^{2}}}}$$

with i twos in the power tower. For example, $^{2}2 = 4$ and $^{3}2 = 16$. Now assume that A_1 is a k-ary 3-colouring function. Certainly it is also a k-ary $^{2}2$-colouring function. We can apply Lemma 2 iteratively to obtain

- a $(k-1)$-ary $^{3}2$-colouring function A_2,
- a $(k-2)$-ary $^{4}2$-colouring function A_3,

...

- a 1-ary $^{k+1}2$-colouring function A_k.

By Lemma 1, we must have $^{k+1}2 \geq n$, which implies $k + 1 \geq \log^* n$.

5. ACKNOWLEDGEMENTS

This work was supported in part by the Academy of Finland, Grant 252018, and by the Research Funds of the University of Helsinki. Many thanks to Barbara Keller, Stefan Schmid, Jara Uitto, and anonymous reviewers for comments and helpful feedback, and to all students and colleagues who have kindly served as guinea pigs.

6. REFERENCES

[1] Leonid Barenboim and Michael Elkin. *Distributed Graph Coloring: Fundamentals and Recent Developments.* Morgan & Claypool, 2013. doi:10.2200/S00520ED1V01Y201307DCT011.

[2] Nathan Linial. Locality in distributed graph algorithms. *SIAM Journal on Computing*, 21(1):193–201, 1992. doi:10.1137/0221015.

[3] David Peleg. *Distributed Computing: A Locality-Sensitive Approach.* SIAM Monographs on Discrete Mathematics and Applications. Society for Industrial and Applied Mathematics, Philadelphia, 2000.

[4] Jukka Suomela. *A Course on Deterministic Distributed Algorithms.* 2014. Online textbook. http://users.ics.aalto.fi/suomela/dda/.

[5] Roger Wattenhofer. Lecture notes on principles of distributed computing, 2013. http://dcg.ethz.ch/lectures/podc_allstars/.

Brief Announcement: Super-Fast t-Ruling Sets

Tushar Bisht Kishore Kothapalli
International Institute of Information Technology
Hyderabad, INDIA, 500032
tushar.bisht@research.iiit.ac.in,
kkishore@iiit.ac.in

Sriram V. Pemmaraju*
Department of Computer Science
The University of Iowa
Iowa City, IA 52242-1419
sriram-pemmaraju@uiowa.edu

ABSTRACT

A t-ruling set of a graph $G = (V, E)$ is a vertex-subset $S \subseteq V$ that is independent and satisfies the property that every vertex $v \in V$ is at a distance of at most t hops from some vertex in S. A *maximal independent set (MIS)* is a 1-ruling set. Extending results from Kothapalli et al. (FSTTCS 2012) this note presents a randomized algorithm for computing, with high probability, a t-ruling set in $O(t \cdot \log^{\frac{1}{t-1}} n)$ rounds for $2 \leq t \leq \sqrt{\log \log n}$ and in $\exp(O(\sqrt{\log \log n}))$ rounds for $t > \sqrt{\log \log n}$.

Categories and Subject Descriptors

F.2.2 [**Analysis of Algorithms and Problem Complexity**]: Nonnumerical Algorithms and Problems—*Computations on Discrete Structures*

Keywords

Distributed Algorithms; LOCAL Algorithms; Maximal Independent Sets; Ruling Sets; Symmetry Breaking

1. INTRODUCTION

Symmetry breaking is a fundamental theme in distributed computing and a classic example of symmetry breaking arises in the computation of a *maximal independent set* (MIS) of a given graph. There is a well known 25-year old randomized algorithm [6] that solves the MIS problem in $O(\log n)$ communication rounds. Since then, all attempts to devise an algorithm for MIS that runs in *sub-logarithmic* rounds (for general graphs) have failed. However, there has been some exciting recent progress on the problem. Barenboim et al. [1] present MIS algorithms that run in $O(\log \Delta \sqrt{\log n})$ rounds on arbitrary graphs (with n vertices and maximum degree Δ) and in $\exp(O(\sqrt{\log \log n}))$ rounds when $\Delta = \text{poly}(\log n)$.

A natural generalization of MIS is the problem of computing t-ruling sets. For $t \geq 1$, a *t-ruling set* of a graph $G = (V, E)$ is an independent subset S of vertices with the property that every vertex $v \in V$ is at a distance of at most t hops from some vertex in S. Thus an MIS is a 1-ruling set[1]. The main result of this paper is a t-ruling set algorithm that runs in $O(t \cdot \log^{\frac{1}{t-1}} n)$ rounds for $2 \leq t \leq \sqrt{\log \log n}$ and in $\exp(O(\sqrt{\log \log n}))$ rounds for $t > \sqrt{\log \log n}$. Our algorithms are designed to run in $\mathcal{LOCAL}$ model, which is a standard synchronous, message passing model of communication in which each node, in each round, can send a possibly distinct message of unbounded size along each incident edge. Our technique is randomized and involves an iterative, rapid sparsification of the graph while ensuring that nodes that are removed from further consideration are within one hop of some remaining node. When we complete all iterations of the algorithm, we can apply the MIS result due to Barenboim et al. [1], mentioned earlier, taking advantage of the low maximum degree of the graph that remains.

1.1 Related Work

In previous work [3], we showed how to compute a 2-ruling set in $O(\log^{3/4} n)$ rounds, with high probability. Our current work extends this result to $t \geq 3$.

Our results should also be viewed in the context of results by Gfeller and Vicari [2]. These authors showed how to compute, in $O(\log \log n)$ rounds, a vertex-subset T of a given n-vertex graph $G = (V, E)$ such that (i) every vertex is at most $O(\log \log n)$ hops from some vertex in T, and (ii) the subgraph induced by T has maximum degree $O(\log^5 n)$. One can use the MIS algorithm from Barenboim et al. [1] on $G[T]$ and sparsify T into an $O(\log \log n)$-ruling set in an additional $\exp(O(\sqrt{\log \log n}))$ rounds. Thus, by combining the Gfeller-Vicari algorithm with the Barenboim et al. algorithm one can compute an $O(\log \log n)$-ruling set in general graphs in $\exp(O(\sqrt{\log \log n}))$ rounds. Our current work improves on the Gfeller-Vicari result by allowing arbitrary t and also by being able to compute an $O(\sqrt{\log \log n})$-ruling set in $\exp(\sqrt{\log \log n})$ rounds.

Schneider et al. [7] consider the problem of computing an (α, β)-*ruling set*, which they define as a vertex-subset S of the input graph G such that (i) pairs of vertices in S are at distance at least α away from each other and (ii) every vertex in G is at distance at most β from some vertex in S. Thus a t-ruling set as per our definition is a $(2, t)$-ruling set as per their definition. These authors present an algorithm that can compute a $(2, t)$-ruling set in $t \cdot d^{1/t}$ rounds, given a

*The work of this author is supported in part by National Science Foundation grant CCF 1318166.

[1]In the definition of Gfeller and Vicari [2], a t-ruling set need not be independent, and what we call a t-ruling set, they call an *independent* t-ruling set.

PODC'14, July 15–18, 2014, Paris, France.
ACM 978-1-4503-2944-6/14/07.
http://dx.doi.org/10.1145/2611462.2611512.

d-coloring of the input graph. Preprocessing the input with a distributed graph coloring algorithm and then providing the colored graph as input to the above algorithm yields a $(2,t)$-ruling set algorithm. For example, using the classical distributed algorithm of Linial [5] that computes an $O(\Delta^2)$-coloring in $O(\log^* n)$ rounds, one can obtain a $(2,t)$-ruling set algorithm that runs in $O(t \cdot \Delta^{2/t} + \log^* n)$ rounds. For rather small Δ, i.e., $\Delta < \sqrt{\log n}$, this algorithm has smaller asymptotic running time relative to our algorithm, but not otherwise.

2. RAPID SPARSIFICATION

In this section we first describe Algorithm SPARSIFY-GG, that rapidly sparsifies a given graph. This algorithm was used in [3] as a step in computing a 2-ruling set and so the material in this section has largely appeared in [3]. Let f be some parameter that can be chosen later and i^* be the smallest positive integer such that $f^{i^*+1} \geq \Delta$. Thus $i^* = \lceil \log_f \Delta \rceil - 1$. The run-time of the algorithm depends on the parameter f. At the end of the algorithm, the following properties are satisfied: (i) all the vertices of the graph are labeled with one of {`inactive`, `active`} and every `inactive` node has an `active` neighbor, and (ii) the degree of the graph induced by the `active` vertices is bounded by $O(f \cdot \log n)$.

The algorithm proceeds in *stages* and there are i^* stages, indexed by $i = 1, 2, \ldots, i^*$. In Stage i every vertex independently joins a set M_i with probability $\frac{6 \log n \cdot f^i}{\Delta}$ and is marked `active` (Line 4). It is shown in [3] that any vertex that is in V at the start of Stage i has degree at most Δ/f^{i-1}, with high probability. Therefore, it is easy to see that any vertex in the graph induced by M_i has expected degree at most $O(f \cdot \log n)$. In fact, this is true with high probability and this fact can be shown by appealing to the fact that vertices join M_i independently and using Chernoff bounds. Following the identification of the set M_i, all neighbors of M_i that are outside M_i are placed in a set W_i and marked `inactive` (Line 7). Both sets M_i and W_i are then deleted from the vertex set V. The sets W_i play a critical role in our algorithm. Given the probability $\frac{6 \log n \cdot f^i}{\Delta}$ of joining M_i, we can show that with high probability every vertex with degree more than Δ/f^i ends up either in M_i or in W_i. This establishes the degree-bound needed for next iteration of the algorithm. Also, the sets W_i act as "buffers" between the M_i's ensuring that there are no edges between M_i and $M_{i'}$ for $i \neq i'$. As a result the graph induced by $\cup_i M_i$ has degree $O(f \cdot \log n)$.

Algorithm SPARSIFY-GG$(G = (V, E), f)$
1. **for** $i \leftarrow 1, 2, \ldots, i^*$ **do**
2. $\quad M_i \leftarrow \emptyset$; $W_i \leftarrow \emptyset$;
3. $\quad$ **for** each $v \in V$ *in parallel* **do**
4. $\qquad$ With probability $\frac{6 \log n \cdot f^i}{\Delta}$ add v to M_i and mark v as `active`
5. $\quad$ **for** each $v \in V$ *in parallel* **do**
6. $\qquad$ **if** $v \in$ Neighbors$(M_i) \setminus M_i$ **then**
7. $\qquad\quad$ Add v to W_i and mark v as `inactive`
8. $\quad V \leftarrow V \setminus (M_i \cup W_i)$
9. **end-for**(i)
10. Mark the vertices remaining in V as `active`
11. $S \leftarrow \{v \in V \mid v \text{ is } \texttt{active}\}$.
12. **return** S

The proof of the following theorem appears in [3].

THEOREM 1. *Let G be an arbitrary n-vertex graph with maximum degree Δ. With high probability, Algorithm Sparsify-GG with input G and f runs in $O(\log_f \Delta)$ rounds and produces a vertex-subset $S \subseteq V(G)$ such that $\Delta(G[S]) \in O(f \cdot \log n)$, and every vertex in V is either in S or has a neighbor in S.*

3. COMPUTING RULING SETS

The main idea behind out t-ruling set algorithm consists of iteratively sparsifying the given graph $t-1$ times using Algorithm SPARSIFY-GG and then computing an MIS. Let $G = (V, E)$ be the given graph and let $S_0 = V$. Let $f_0, f_1, \ldots$ be a sequence of parameters, whose values will be specified later. For $i = 1, 2, \ldots, t-1$, we execute SPARSIFY-GG$(G[S_{i-1}], f_{i-1})$ in order to compute S_i. Finally, we compute MIS on $G[S_{t-1}]$ and return this as the t-ruling set of G. It turns out that setting f_{i-1} to $2^{(\log n)^{(t-1-i)/(t-1)}}$ for $i = 1, 2, \ldots, t-2$ and then setting f_{t-2} to $\log n$ nicely balances the running time of all of the sparsification steps so that each call to SPARSIFY-GG takes $(\log n)^{1/(t-1)}$ rounds. Pseudocode of this algorithm appears below in Algorithm t-RULINGSET-GG. Correctness of the algorithm follows from the next lemma.

LEMMA 1. *For each i, $0 \leq i \leq t$, with high probability every vertex in V is at most i hops from some vertex in S_i. Thus, with high probability, S_t is a t-ruling set.*

PROOF. Every vertex in V is 0 hops away from some vertex in $S_0 = V$. Suppose that every vertex in V is i hops away from S_i, for some $0 \leq i < t$. From Theorem 1 we know that every vertex in S_i is at most one hop away from some vertex in S_{i+1}. The result follows by induction. □

Algorithm t-RULINGSET-GG$(G = (V, E))$ (for $t \geq 2$)

$S_0 \leftarrow V$
for $i \leftarrow 1$ **to** $t-2$ **do**
$\quad f_{i-1} \leftarrow 2^{(\log n)^{(t-1-i)/(t-1)}}$
$\quad S_i \leftarrow$ SPARSIFY-GG$(G[S_{i-1}], f_{i-1})$
$f_{t-2} \leftarrow \log n$
$S_{t-1} \leftarrow$ SPARSIFY-GG$(G[S_{t-2}], f_{t-2})$
$S_t \leftarrow \texttt{MIS}(G[S_{t-1}])$
return S_t

THEOREM 2. *With high probability, Algorithm t-RULINGSET-GG runs in time $O(t \cdot (\log n)^{1/(t-1)}) + \exp(O(\sqrt{\log \log n}))$.*

PROOF. For i, $0 \leq i \leq t$, let Δ_i be the maximum degree of a vertex in $G[S_i]$. Now consider i, $0 \leq i \leq t-2$. Since S_i is computed by calling SPARSIFY-GG$(G[S_{i-1}], f_{i-1})$ and the value of f_{i-1} is $2^{(\log n)^{(t-1-i)/(t-1)}}$, it follows from Theorem 1 that Δ_i is bounded above by

$$O\left(\log n \cdot 2^{(\log n)^{(t-1-i)/(t-1)}}\right).$$

Also from Theorem 1 it follows that the call to subroutine SPARSIFY-GG$(G[S_{i-1}], f_{i-1})$ takes $O(\log_{f_{i-1}} \Delta_{i-1})$ rounds. We obtain an upper bound on $\log_{f_{i-1}} \Delta_{i-1}$ as follows:

$$\begin{aligned} \log_{f_{i-1}} \Delta_{i-1} &\leq \frac{(\log n)^{(t-1-(i-1))/(t-1)} + \log \log n}{(\log n)^{(t-1-i)/(t-1)}} \\ &\leq (\log n)^{1/(t-1)} + \log \log n. \end{aligned}$$

Thus the call to SPARSIFY-GG$(G[S_{i-1}], f_{i-1})$ takes

$$O((\log n)^{1/(t-1)} + \log\log n)$$

rounds. Also note that $\Delta_{t-2} = O(\log n \cdot 2^{(\log n)^{1/(t-1)}})$ and thus the call (in Line 6) to SPARSIFY-GG$(G[S_{t-2}], f_{t-2})$ takes an additional

$$O(\log_{f_{t-2}} \Delta_{t-2}) = O((\log n)^{1/(t-1)} + \log\log n)$$

rounds. Thus all $t-1$ calls to the SPARSIFY-GG subroutine take a total of $O(t((\log n)^{1/(t-1)} + \log\log n))$ rounds. Now note that Δ_{t-1} is bounded by $O(f_{t-2} \cdot \log n) = O(\log^2 n)$ and therefore using the MIS algorithm (version 2) of Barenboim et al. (Theorem 4.3, [1]) we compute S_t in an additional $\exp(O(\sqrt{\log\log n}))$ rounds. The result follows. □

COROLLARY 1. *For $t \leq \sqrt{\log\log n}$, we can compute a t-ruling set in $O(t \cdot (\log n)^{1/(t-1)})$ rounds and if $t > \sqrt{\log\log n}$, we can compute a t-ruling set in $\exp(O(\sqrt{\log\log n}))$.*

4. CONCLUSIONS

Kuhn et al. [4] claim a $\Omega(\sqrt{\log n})$ lower bound on the computation of an MIS of an n-vertex input graph in the $\mathcal{LOCAL}$ model. Our results show that even for small constant t, one can compute a t-ruling set faster than it is possible to compute an MIS.

There are no known lower bounds for the t-ruling set problem in the $\mathcal{LOCAL}$ model and so it is possible that our results can be improved. In light of our results, it is interesting to explore whether the lower bound technique of Kuhn et al. [4] can be extended to derive a lower bound for t-rulings set

5. REFERENCES

[1] Leonid Barenboim, Michael Elkin, Seth Pettie, and Johannes Schneider. The locality of distributed symmetry breaking. In *Proc. of IEEE FOCS*, 2012.

[2] Beat Gfeller and Elias Vicari. A randomized distributed algorithm for the maximal independent set problem in growth-bounded graphs. In *Proc. ACM PODC*, pages 53–60, 2007.

[3] Kishore Kothapalli and Sriram V. Pemmaraju. Super-fast 3-ruling sets. In *In Proc. of Foundations of Software Technology and Theoretical Computer Science (FSTTCS)*, pages 136–147, 2012.

[4] Fabian Kuhn, Thomas Moscibroda, and Roger Wattenhofer. Local computation: Lower and upper bounds. *CoRR*, abs/1011.5470, 2010.

[5] N. Linial. Locality in distributed graph algorithms. *SIAM Journal of Computing*, 21:193–201, 1992.

[6] M. Luby. A simple parallel algorithm for the maximal independent set. *SIAM Journal on Computing*, 15:1036–1053, 1986.

[7] Johannes Schneider, Michael Elkin, and Roger Wattenhofer. Symmetry breaking depending on the chromatic number or the neighborhood growth. *Theor. Comput. Sci.*, 509:40–50, October 2013.

Brief Announcement: Almost-Tight Approximation Distributed Algorithm for Minimum Cut

Danupon Nanongkai*
Faculty of Computer Science
University of Vienna, Austria
danupon@gmail.com

ABSTRACT

In this short paper, we present an improved algorithm for approximating the minimum cut on distributed (CONGEST) networks. Let λ be the minimum cut. Our algorithm can compute λ exactly in $\tilde{O}((\sqrt{n} + D)\,\text{poly}(\lambda))$ time, where n is the number of nodes (processors) in the network, D is the network diameter, and $\tilde{O}$ hides poly $\log n$. By a standard reduction, we can convert this algorithm into a $(1+\epsilon)$-approximation $\tilde{O}((\sqrt{n} + D)/\,\text{poly}(\epsilon))$-time algorithm. The latter result improves over the previous $(2+\epsilon)$-approximation $\tilde{O}((\sqrt{n}+D)/\,\text{poly}(\epsilon))$-time algorithm of Ghaffari and Kuhn (DISC 2013). Due to the lower bound of $\tilde{\Omega}(\sqrt{n}+D)$ by Das Sarma et al. (SICOMP 2013), this running time is *tight* up to a poly $\log n$ factor. Our algorithm is an extremely simple combination of Thorup's tree packing theorem [Combinatorica 2007], Kutten and Peleg's tree partitioning algorithm [J. Algorithms 1998], and Karger's dynamic programming [JACM 2000].

Categories and Subject Descriptors

C.2.4 [**Computer Systems Organization**]: Computer Communication Networks — *Distributed Systems*; F.2.0 [**Analysis of Algorithms and Problem Complexity**]: General; G.2.2 [**Mathematics of Computing**]: Discrete Mathematics — *Graph Theory*

General Terms

Algorithms,Theory

Keywords

distributed computing; graph algorithms; minimum cut; time complexity; CONGEST model

*Work done while at Nanyang Technological University, Singapore, and Brown University, USA.

PODC'14, July 15–18, 2014, Paris, France.
ACM 978-1-4503-2944-6/14/07.
http://dx.doi.org/10.1145/2611462.2611511.

1. INTRODUCTION

Problem. In this paper, we study the time complexity of the fundamental problem of computing *minimum cut* on distributed network. Given a graph G, edge weight assignment w, and any set X of nodes in G, the cut $\mathscr{C}(X)$ is defined as

$$\mathscr{C}(X) = \sum_{(x,y)\in E(G), x\in X, y\notin X} w(x,y).$$

Our goal is to find $\lambda(G) = \min_{\emptyset\neq X\subsetneq V} \mathscr{C}(X)$.

Communication Model. We use a standard message passing network (the CONGEST model [7]). Throughout the paper, we let n be the number of nodes and D be the diameter of the network. Every node is assumed to have a unique ID, and initially knows the weights of edges incident to it. The execution in this network proceeds in synchronous rounds and in each round, each node can send a message of size $O(\log n)$ bits to each of its neighbors. The goal of the problem is find the minimum or approximately minimum cut X. (Every node outputs whether it is in X in the end of the process.) The time complexity is the number of rounds needed to compute this. (For more detail, see [3].)

Previous Work. The current best algorithm is by Ghaffari and Kuhn [3] which takes $\tilde{O}(\sqrt{n}+D)$ time with an approximation ratio of $(2+\epsilon)$. ($\tilde{O}(\cdot)$ hides the $O(\text{poly}\log n)$ factor.) The running time of this algorithm matches the lower bound of Das Sarma et al. [1] which showed that this problem cannot be computed faster than $\tilde{\Omega}(\sqrt{n} + D)$ even when we allow a large approximation ratio. (This lower bound was also shown to hold even when a quantum communication is allowed [2], and when a capacity of an edge is proportional to its weight [3].) For a more comprehensive literature review, see [3].

Our Results. Our main result is a distributed algorithm that can compute the minimum cut *exactly* in $\tilde{O}((\sqrt{n} + D)\,\text{poly}(\lambda))$ time. For the case where the minimum cut is small (i.e. $\tilde{O}(1)$), the running time of our algorithm matches the lower bound [1, 3]. When the minimum cut is large, Karger's edge sampling technique [4] can be used to reduce the minimum cut to $\tilde{O}(1)$ with the cost of $(1 + \epsilon)$ approximation factor (due to the space limit, we refer the readers to [9, Lemma 7] for the statement of Karger's sampling result). This makes our algorithm a $(1 + \epsilon)$-approximation $\tilde{O}(\sqrt{n} + D)$-time one, improving the previous algorithm of Ghaffari and Kuhn [3].

Techniques. Our algorithm is a simple combination of techniques from [9, 6, 5]. The starting point of our algorithm is Thorup's tree packing theorem, which shows that if we generate $\Theta(\lambda^7 \log^3 n)$ trees $T_1, T_2, \ldots$, where tree T_i is the minimum spanning tree with respect to the loads induced by $\{T_1, \ldots, T_{i-1}\}$, then one of these trees will contain exactly one edge in the minimum cut. (Due to the space limit, we refer the readers to [9, Theorem 9] for the full statement.) Since we can use the $\tilde{O}(\sqrt{n} + D)$-time algorithm of Kutten and Peleg [6] to compute the minimum spanning tree (MST), the problem of finding a minimum cut is reduced to finding the minimum cut that *1-respects a tree*; i.e., finding which edge in a given spanning tree defines a smallest cut (see the formal definition in Section 2). Solving this problem is our main result.

To solve this problem, we usea simple observation of Karger [5] which reduces the problem to computing the sum of degree and the number of edges contained in a subtree rooted at each node. We use this observation along with Kutten and Peleg's *tree partitioning* [6] to quickly compute these quantities. This requires several (elementary) steps, which we will discuss in more detail in Section 2.

Concurrent Result. Independent from our work, Su [8] also achieved a $(1 + \epsilon)$-approximation $\tilde{O}(\sqrt{n} + D)$-time algorithm for this problem. His starting point is, like ours, Thorup's theorem [9]. The way he finds the minimum cut that 1-respects a tree is, however, very different. In particular, he uses edge sampling to make the minimum cut of a certain graph be one and use Thurimella's algorithm [10] to find a bridge. (See Algorithm 2 in [8] for details.) This gives a nice and simple way to achieve essentially the same approximation result as ours, with a small drawback that minimum cut cannot be computed exactly, even when it is small.

2. DISTRIBUTED ALGORITHM FOR FINDING A CUT THAT 1-RESPECTS A TREE

In this section, we solve the following problem: Given a spanning tree T on a network G rooted at some node r, we want to find an edge in T such that when we cut it, the cut define by edges connecting the two connected component of T is smallest. To be precise, for any node v, define $v^{\downarrow}$ to be the set of nodes that are descendants of v in T, including v. The problem is then to compute $c^* = \min_{v \in V(G)} \mathscr{C}(v^{\downarrow})$.

THEOREM 2.1 (MAIN RESULT). *There is an $\tilde{O}(n^{1/2} + D)$-time distributed algorithm that can compute c^* as well as find a node v such that $c^* = \mathscr{C}(v^{\downarrow})$.*

In fact, at the end of our algorithm every node v knows $\mathscr{C}(v^{\downarrow})$. Our algorithm is inspired by the following observation used in Karger's dynamic programming [5]. For any node v, let $\delta(v)$ be the weighted degree of v, i.e. $\delta(v) = \sum_{u \in V(G)} w(u, v)$. Let $\rho(v)$ denote the total weight of edges whose endpoints' least common ancestor is v. Let $\delta^{\downarrow}(v) = \sum_{u \in v^{\downarrow}} \delta(u)$ and $\rho^{\downarrow}(v) = \sum_{u \in v^{\downarrow}} \rho(u)$.

LEMMA 2.2 ([5]). $\mathscr{C}(v^{\downarrow}) = \delta^{\downarrow}(v) - 2\rho^{\downarrow}(v)$.

Our algorithm will make sure that every node v knows $\delta^{\downarrow}(v)$ and $\rho^{\downarrow}(v)$. By Lemma 2.2, this will be sufficient for every node v to compute c^*. The algorithm is divided in several steps, as folows.

Step 1: Partition T into Fragments and Compute "Fragment Tree" T_F. We use the algorithm of Kutten and Peleg [6, Section 3.2] to partition nodes in tree T into $O(\sqrt{n})$ subtrees, where each subtree has $O(\sqrt{n})$ diameter[1] (every node knows which edges incident to it are in the subtree containing it). This algorithm takes $O(n^{1/2} \log^* n + D)$ time. We call these subtrees *fragments* and denote them by $F_1, \ldots, F_k$, where $k = O(\sqrt{n})$. For any i, let $\mathsf{id}(F_i) = \min_{u \in F_i} \mathsf{id}(u)$ be the *ID of F_i*. We can assume that every node in F_i knows $\mathsf{id}(F_i)$. This can be achieved in $O(\sqrt{n})$ time by a communication within each fragment.

Let T_F be a rooted tree obtained by contracting nodes in the same fragment into one node. This naturally defines the child-parent relationship between fragments (e.g. the fragments labeled (5), (6), and (7) in Figure 1b are children of the fragment labeled (0)). Let the *root* of any fragment F_i, denoted by r_i, be the node in F_i that is nearest to the root r in T. We now make every node know T_F: Every "inter-fragment" edge, i.e. every edge (u, v) such that u and v are in different fragments, either node u or v broadcasts this edge and the IDs of fragments containing u and v to the whole network. This step takes $O(\sqrt{n})$ time since there are $O(\sqrt{n})$ edges in T that link between different fragments. Note that this process also makes every node knows the roots of all fragments since, for every inter-fragment edge (u, v), every node knows the child-parent relationship between two fragments that contain u and v.

Step 2: Compute Fragments in Subtrees of Ancestors. For any node v let $F(v)$ be the set of fragments $F_i \subseteq v^{\downarrow}$. For any node v in any fragment F_i, let $A(v)$ be the set of ancestors of v in T that are in F_i or the parent fragment of F_i (also let $A(v)$ contain v). (For example, Figure 1c shows $A(15)$.) The goal of this step is to make every node v knows (i) $A(v)$ and (ii) $F(u)$ for all $u \in A(v)$.

First, we make every node v know $F(v)$: for every fragment F_i we aggregate from the leaves to the root of F_i (i.e. upcast) the list of child fragments of F_i. This takes $O(\sqrt{n})$ time since there are $O(\sqrt{n})$ fragments to aggregate. In this process every node v receives a list of child fragments of F_i that are contained in $v^{\downarrow}$. It can then use T_F to compute fragments that are descendants of these child fragments, and thus compute *all* fragments contained in $v^{\downarrow}$. Next, we make every node v in every fragment F_i know $A(v)$: every node u sends a message containing its ID down the tree T until this message reaches the leaves of the child fragments of F_i. Since each fragment has diameter $O(\sqrt{n})$, this process takes $O(\sqrt{n})$ time. With some minor modifications, we can also make every node v know $F(u)$ for all $u \in A(v)$: Initially every node u sends a message (u, F'), for every $F' \in F(u)$, to its children. Every node u that receives a message (u', F') from its parents sends this message further to its children *if* $F' \notin F(u)$. (A message (u', F') that a node u sends to its children should be interpreted as "u' is the lowest ancestor of u such that $F' \in F(u')$".)

Step 3: Compute $\delta^{\downarrow}(v)$. For every fragment F_i, we let $\delta(F_i) = \sum_{v \in F_i} \delta(v)$. For every node v in every fragment F_i, we will compute $\delta^{\downarrow}(v)$ by separately computing (i) $\sum_{u \in F_i \cap v^{\downarrow}} \delta(u)$

[1]To be precise, we compute a $(\sqrt{n} + 1, O(\sqrt{n}))$ *spanning forest.* Also note that we in fact do not need this algorithm since we obtain T by using Kutten and Peleg's MST algorithm, which already computes the $(\sqrt{n} + 1, O(\sqrt{n}))$ spanning forest as a subroutine. See [6] for details.

and (ii) $\sum_{F_j \in F(v)} \delta(F_j)$. The first quantity can be computed in $O(\sqrt{n})$ time by computing the sum within F_i (every node v sends the sum $\sum_{u \in F_i \cap v^\downarrow} \delta(u)$ to its parent). To compute the second quantity, it suffices to make every node know $\delta(F_i)$ for all i since every node v already knows $F(v)$. To do this, we make every root r_i know $\delta(F_i)$ in $O(\sqrt{n})$ time by computing the sum of degree of nodes within each F_i. Then, we can make every node know $\delta(F_i)$ for all i by letting r_i broadcast $\delta(F_i)$ to the whole network.

Step 4: Compute Merging Nodes and T'_F. We say that a node v is a *merging node* if there are two distinct children x and y of v such that both $x^\downarrow$ and $y^\downarrow$ contain some fragments (e.g. nodes 0 and 1 in Figure 1a). In other words, it is a point where two fragments "merge". Let T'_F be the following tree: Nodes in T'_F are both roots of fragments (r_i's) and merging nodes. The parent of each node v in T'_F is its lowest ancestor in T that appears in T'_F (see Figure 1d for an example). Note that every merging node has at least two children in T'_F. This shows that there are $O(\sqrt{n})$ merging nodes. The goal of this step is to let every node know T'_F.

First, note that every node v can easily know whether it is a merging node or not in one round by checking, for each child u, whether $u^\downarrow$ contains any fragment (i.e. whether $F(u) = \emptyset$). The merging nodes then broadcast their IDs to the whole network. (This takes $O(\sqrt{n})$ time since there are $O(\sqrt{n})$ merging nodes.) Note further that every node v in T'_F knows its parent in T'_F because its parent in T'_F is one of the ancestors in $A(v)$. So, we can make every node knows T'_F in $O(\sqrt{n})$ rounds by letting every node in T'_F broadcast the edge between itself and its parent in T'_F to the whole network.

Step 5: Compute $\rho^\downarrow(v)$. We now count, for every node v, the number of edges whose least common ancestor (LCA) of its end-nodes are v. For every edge (x, y) in G, we claim that x and y can compute the LCA of (x, y) by exchanging $O(\sqrt{n})$ messages through edge (x, y). Let z denote the LCA of (x, y). Consider three cases (see Figure 1e). *Case 1:* First, consider when x and y are in the same fragment, say F_i. In this case we know that z must be in F_i. Since x and y have the lists of their ancestors in F_i, they can find z by exchanging these lists. In the next two cases we assume that x and y are in different fragments, say F_i and F_j, respectively. *Case 2: z is not in F_i and F_j.* In this case, z is a merging node such that $z^\downarrow$ contains F_i and F_j. Since both x and y knows T'_F and their ancestors in T'_F, they can find z by exchanging the list of their ancestors in T'_F. *Case 3: z is in F_i* (the case where z is in F_j can be handled in a similar way). In this case $z^\downarrow$ contains F_j. Since x knows $F(x')$ for all its ancestors x' in F_i, it can compute its lowest ancestor x'' such that $F(x'')$ contains F_j. Such ancestor is the LCA of (x, y).

Now we compute $\rho^\downarrow(v)$ for every node v by splitting edges (x, y) whose LCA is v into two types (see Figure 1f): (i) those that x and y are in different fragments from v, and (ii) the rest. For (i), note that v must be a merging node. In this case one of x and y creates a message $\langle v \rangle$. We then count the number of messages of the form $\langle v \rangle$ for every merging node v by computing the sum along the breadth-first search tree of G. This takes $O(\sqrt{n} + D)$ time since there are $O(\sqrt{n})$ merging nodes. For (ii), the node among x and y that is in the same fragment as v creates and keeps a message $\langle v \rangle$. Now every node v in every fragment F_i counts the number

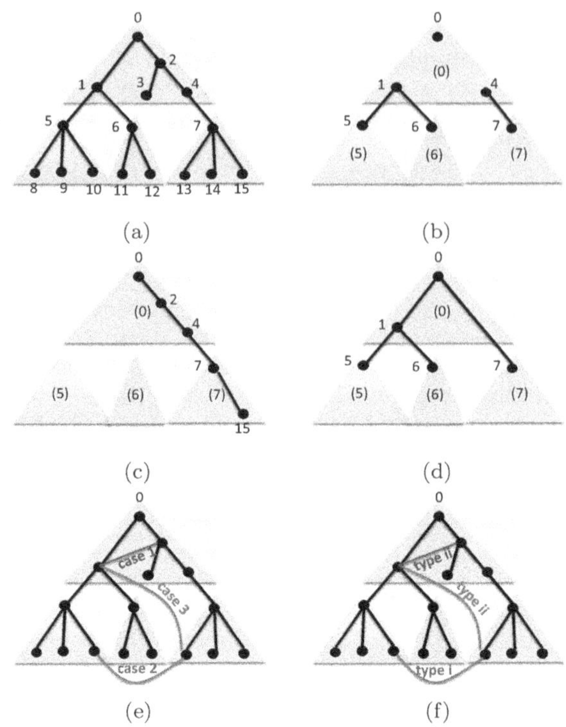

Figure 1

of messages of the form $\langle v \rangle$ in $v^\downarrow \cap F_i$ by computing the sum through the tree F_i. Note that, to do this, every node u has to send the number of messages of the form $\langle v \rangle$ to its parent, for all v that is an ancestor of u in the same fragment. There are $O(\sqrt{n})$ such ancestors, so we can compute the number of messages of the form $\langle v \rangle$ for every node v *concurrently* in $O(\sqrt{n})$ time (by pipelining).

Acknowledgment. I thank Thatchaphol Saranurak for bringing Thorup's tree packing theorem [9] to my attention.

References

[1] A. Das Sarma, S. Holzer, L. Kor, A. Korman, D. Nanongkai, G. Pandurangan, D. Peleg, and R. Wattenhofer. Distributed verification and hardness of distributed approximation. In *STOC*, pages 363–372, 2011.

[2] M. Elkin, H. Klauck, D. Nanongkai, and G. Pandurangan. Can quantum communication speed up distributed computation? In *PODC*, 2014.

[3] M. Ghaffari and F. Kuhn. Distributed minimum cut approximation. In *DISC*, pages 1–15, 2013.

[4] D. R. Karger. Random sampling in cut, flow, and network design problems. In *STOC*, pages 648–657, 1994.

[5] D. R. Karger. Minimum cuts in near-linear time. *J. ACM*, 47(1):46–76, 2000.

[6] S. Kutten and D. Peleg. Fast distributed construction of small k-dominating sets and applications. *J. Algorithms*, 28(1):40–66, 1998.

[7] D. Peleg. *Distributed Computing: A Locality-Sensitive Approach.* SIAM Society for Industrial and Applied Mathematics Monographs on Discrete Mathematics ans Applications, Philadelphia, 2000.

[8] H. Su. Brief announcement: A distributed minimum cut approximation scheme. In *SPAA*, 2014.

[9] M. Thorup. Fully-dynamic min-cut. *Combinatorica*, 27(1):91–127, 2007.

[10] R. Thurimella. Sub-linear distributed algorithms for sparse certificates and biconnected components. *J. Algorithms*, 23(1):160–179, 1997.

Making Objects Writable*

Zahra Aghazadeh
Dept. of Computer Science
University of Calgary
zaghazad@ucalgary.ca

Wojciech Golab
Dept. of Electrical and
Computer Engineering
University of Waterloo
wgolab@uwaterloo.ca

Philipp Woelfel
Dept. of Computer Science
University of Calgary
woelfel@ucalgary.ca

ABSTRACT

We devise a technique for augmenting shared objects in the standard n-process shared memory model with a linearizable `write()` operation, using bounded space and optimal worst-case step complexity. We provide a transformation of any shared object SW supporting only *sequential* `write()` operations into an object W that supports concurrent `write()` operations. This transformation requires $O(n^2)$ SW objects and $O(n^2)$ $O(\log n)$-bit registers, and each method (including `write()`) has, up to a constant additive term, the same time complexity as the corresponding method on object SW. Our implementation is deterministic, wait-free, and uses only shared registers (supporting atomic read and write operations). To the best of our knowledge, similarly efficient general constructions are not known even if stronger primitives such as CAS or LL/SC are available.

Applying our transformation, we obtain an implementation of a k-word register from $O(n^2 \cdot k)$ single-word registers. As another application we can transform one-time TAS objects (e.g., randomized wait-free implementations that use a bounded number of registers [8, 9]), into long-lived ones using also a bounded number of registers. The transformation preserves the time complexity of `TAS()` operations and allows resets in constant worst-case time.

Our transformation employs a novel memory reclamation technique, which can replace Hazard Pointers [20] and is more efficient.

Categories and Subject Descriptors

E.1 [**Data Structures**]: Distributed data structures; F.2.2 [**Analysis of Algorithms and Problem Complexity**]: Nonnumerical Algorithms and Problems; D.1.3 [**Programming Techniques**]: Concurrent Programming

*This research was undertaken, in part, thanks to funding from the Canada Research Chairs program and from the Discovery Grants program of the Natural Sciences and Engineering Research Council of Canada (NSERC).

PODC'14, July 15–18, 2014, Paris, France.

ACM 978-1-4503-2944-6/14/07 ...$15.00.
http://dx.doi.org/10.1145/2611462.2611483.

Keywords

Shared memory; writable objects; k-word registers; memory management; long-lived test-and-set

1. INTRODUCTION

For many years, it has been a focus of shared memory research to investigate what synchronization primitives can be implemented from other ones. This research is motivated by the fundamental desire to understand the relative power of shared memory model variants, and how the (non-)availability of certain primitives affects the limits of those models. The resulting algorithms and impossibility results have led to a rich theory and important insights that have shaped our understanding of concurrent computation.

The power of a shared memory model is determined by its ability to support solutions to synchronization problems, such as the problem of implementing concurrent data structures. Solving this problem on modern multi-core platforms remains an important task for theory and practice, as one size does not "fit all." Whereas wait-free implementations may be preferred in some application domains, such as real-time systems, lock-based solutions may offer better performance in other cases. As a result, a rich variety of concurrent data structures and algorithms have been presented in literature, representing a tremendous intellectual effort on the part of algorithm designers. Techniques that simplify the design and analysis of such implementations are attractive both in theory and in practice as they save time and reduce the amount of error-prone manual work associated with writing and verifying proofs of correctness. One such technique is augmenting a known implementation by adding support for additional operations while preserving existing correctness properties. For example, to support operations X, Y and Z, an algorithm designer might create a partial implementation that provides X and Y only, and then add Z in a manner that preserves the correctness of X and Y.

Designing general transformations that augment an implementation with new operations is as hard, or perhaps even harder than, designing such an implementation from first principles. However, once the transformation exists, ideally it can be applied easily in a variety of contexts provided that it works in a "black box" fashion—the transformation entails building a layer around the original input implementation rather than altering its delicate inner mechanisms. Ideally, such transformations add only wait-free code, as this guarantees that they can be universally applied to existing objects without weakening the objects' progress conditions. Of particular interest to us is the ability to make implementations *writable*. A reset operation is a special case of a write in that assigns an initial value to the implemented object. Supporting these operations efficiently is difficult in general as they need to overwrite a potentially large number of *base objects* internal to the implementation. A simple transformation that achieves this goal maintains an unbounded pool of objects of the input type, as well as a pointer that identifies among these a designated "current" object. Write and reset operations update (i.e., "swing") this pointer to a new object in the pool, and all other operations are applied on the designated object by first following the pointer. This transformation, while simple and wait-free, uses unbounded space and is neither practical nor interesting theoretically.

In this paper, we provide a transformation that makes any object writable provided that it is possible to write to the object non-concurrently, while preserving bounded space and wait-freedom. In fact, our transformation only increases the time complexity of operations on the original object by a constant additive term.

Our construction uses a method of bounding space complexity by recycling "spent" objects when they are no longer in use. Thus, we perform a form of memory management, which is a fundamental concern in its own right.

1.1 Results

We consider a shared memory system with n processes. We develop a general technique to augment linearizable objects with concurrent `write()` methods, provided that it is possible to write to the objects non-concurrently. A `write()` method is used to change the state of the object to any state, and can be used to simulate a `reset()`, which changes the state to an initial value. More concretely, our main contribution is the following: Suppose we are provided with an implementation SW of a type $\mathcal{T}$ that is linearizable only if no `write()` call overlaps any other method call. We show how to obtain a linearizable implementation W of type $\mathcal{T}$ using $O(n^2)$ SW objects, and $O(n^2)$ additional registers, such that the time complexity of all methods (including `write()`) changes only by a constant additive term.

Our only assumption on SW is linearizability in the special case when `write()` operations are executed in isolation. The original implementation can use any combination of primitives, including read-modify-write operations, while our transformation introduces only additional atomic registers. The transformation is also deterministic and wait-free, and therefore preserves worst-case time complexity. In particular, the `write()` operation in the transformed object, even when executed concurrently with another `write()` or with some other operation, takes the same number of steps (asymptotically) as a sequential `write()` operation on SW.

THEOREM 1. *Any wait-free sequentially writable object SW can be transformed into a wait-free writable object W that uses $O(n^2)$ instances of SW and $O(n^2)$ $(2\log n+O(1))$-bit registers, such that each method call on W has, up to a constant additive term, the same time complexity as the corresponding method call on SW.*

To obtain our transformation using a bounded pool of SW objects, we devise a novel memory management technique inspired by Michael's hazard pointers [20]. This technique can be applied in other domains, such as memory reclamation in concurrent dynamic data structures.

Our transformation has several interesting applications. For example, we can use it to obtain a linearizable k-word register from $O(k\cdot n^2)$ linearizable single-word registers, such that each k-word `read()` and `write()` operation runs in $O(k)$ steps (which is optimal).

COROLLARY 1. *There is a linearizable implementation of k-word registers from $O(n^2\cdot k)$ single word registers, such that each read and write operation of the k-word register takes $O(k)$ steps.*

The previously most time-efficient construction of k-word registers from single word registers has worst-case step and space complexity $\Theta(kn)$ [21]. Even if stronger primitives such Compare-And-Swap are available, it was previously not known how to obtain such a construction with optimal $O(k)$ worst-case step complexity.

Certain primitives such as atomic Compare-And-Swap (CAS) or Fetch-And-Add (FAA), trivially support sequential write operations. Thus, using our transformation we can implement writable CAS and writable FAA objects from $O(n^2)$ CAS respectively FAS objects and $O(n^2)$ registers, such that each `write()` or `CAS` respectively `FAA()` operation has constant step complexity. Moreover, whenever an object is implemented from registers, it trivially supports non-concurrent write operations, therefore such objects can be easily augmented with concurrent write operations.

As another application, we can transform randomized one-shot Test-And-Set (TAS) objects implemented from registers to resettable (long-lived) ones. The transformation preserves the time complexity of `TAS()` operations, allows resets in constant worst-case time, and increases the number of registers by a factor of $O(n^2)$. For example, in [8] a randomized one-shot TAS implementation from $O(\sqrt{n})$ registers is presented, which has $O(\log^* n)$ expected time complexity against an oblivious adversary. Using our transformation, we obtain a long-lived TAS object that can be reset in constant worst-case time, where `TAS()` operations have $O(\log^* n)$ expected time complexity against the oblivious adversary, and which uses $O(n^{5/2})$ registers.

1.2 Related Work

The problem of augmenting a type with a `reset()` or a `write()` operation, to the best of our knowledge, has not been studied in general, but only for some specific types. A long-lived implementation of a `TAS` object using registers was first discussed by Afek, Gafni, Tromp, and Vitányi [1]. Their construction uses unbounded registers, but they claim that they can make it bounded using a modified version of the Sequential Time Stamps System (STSS) by Israeli and Li [16]. Their long-lived implementation requires $\Theta(n)$ steps in the worst case. Alistarh and Aspnes [2] propose a simpler implementation of long-lived `TAS` by using an *infinite* array of one-shot `TAS` objects. Golab, Hadzilacos, Hendler, and Woelfel consider writable implementations of Compare-And-Swap (CAS) from atomic registers [12]. Their approach augments a non-writable CAS implementation with a `write()` operation using pointer swinging and dynamically allocated non-writable CAS base objects. The corresponding memory management technique, discussed in Golab's doctoral thesis [11], relies on a critical section and hence cannot be used in lock-free structures. Jayanti [17] shows how one can augment a non-writable CAS implementation with a wait-free `write()` operation.

Our results regarding multi-word atomic registers are related to wait-free register constructions. Peterson's construction of single-writer multi-reader (SWMR) k-word registers requires $\Theta(kn)$ SWMR single-word registers and provides $\Theta(kn)$ worst-case step complexity [21]. Using Fetch-And-Or and Swap in addition to single-word atomic registers, Larsson, Gidenstam, Ha, Papatriantafilou, and Tsigas propose a SWMR k-word atomic register implementation with $\Theta(kn)$ space complexity and $\Theta(k+n)$ worst-case step complexity [18]. In comparison, our construction (see Corollary 1) is multi-reader multi-writer (MRMW), requires $\Theta(kn^2)$ MRMW single-word atomic registers, and has $\Theta(k)$ worst-case step complexity (which is optimal).

The problem of memory management, which is of technical concern in our transformation, has been studied in the context of dynamic data structures, leading to a variety of solutions. In *reference counting*, the number of pointers or references held to a given object is recorded, and an object may be reclaimed when the reference count reaches zero. There have been many proposed techniques [23], [5], [6], [22], and [19], but they all use stronger primitives, such as CAS and FAA. Since reference counting in general deals poorly with cyclic references (i.e., when two or more objects refer to each other), several alternatives have been developed. Michael's *hazard pointer* technique is targeted at general lock-free algorithms, and does not require atomic read-modify-write primitives [20]. Object reclamation is wait-free and requires expected amortized $O(1)$ steps, but dereferencing a pointer safely is only lock-free. Hazard pointers impose a fixed bound on the number of shared objects a given process can reference. Herlihy, Luchangco, and Moir proposed a lock-free technique that overcomes this problem, but requires CAS [14]. Gidenstam, Papatriantafilou, Sundell, and Tsigas proposed a lock-free memory reclamation method that combines aspects of reference counting and hazard pointers, and requires both FAA and CAS [10].

2. PRELIMINARIES

2.1 Model and Definitions

We consider an asynchronous shared memory model with n processes with identifiers in $\{0, \ldots, n-1\}$. Processes communicate by executing operations on *shared objects*. A type specifies the behaviour of a shared object. A type $\mathcal{T}$ is a quintuple $(\mathcal{S}, s_0, \mathcal{O}, \mathcal{R}, \delta)$, where $\mathcal{S}$ is a set of *states*, $s_0 \in \mathcal{S}$ is the initial state, $\mathcal{O}$ is a set of operation types, and $\mathcal{R}$ is the set of responses. The set $\mathcal{R}$ contains the special value λ, which indicates that the operation does not return anything. The transition function $\delta : \mathcal{S} \times \mathcal{O} \to \mathcal{S} \times \mathcal{R}$ defines the behaviour of the object of type $\mathcal{T}$, when processes execute operations sequentially. If a process executes an operation $o \in \mathcal{O}$ on an object of type $\mathcal{T}$, when the object is in state $s \in \mathcal{S}$, then the operation returns the value $r \in \mathcal{R}$ and the state of the object changes to $s' \in \mathcal{S}$, if and only if $\delta(s, o) = (s', r)$.

We call a type *writable*, if there is a `write(s)` operation in $\mathcal{O}$ that changes the state of the object to state $s \in \mathcal{S}$, regardless of its current state. A `write()` operation returns nothing.

Processes execute shared memory operations on shared objects in the order determined by their program. A *step* is either an invocation or a response of an operation on a shared object. If an object is atomic, then invocation and

shared: `Array<`SW`>` $A[0 \ldots m-1]$, **int** $Ptr = \perp$

Method $\texttt{write}_p(v)$	**Method** $\texttt{exec}_q(op, arg)$
⋮	⋮
choose an appropriate write- index $f \in I_p$ that is not in use	determine an appropriate exec-index i
⋮	⋮
$A[f]$.`sWrite`(v)	$ret\_val := A[i].op(arg)$
⋮	⋮
$Ptr := (f, \ldots)$	**return** ret_val
⋮	

A and Ptr are only modified where indicated.

Figure 1: Writable object template

response occur at the same time, and therefore we usually identify the step with the operation on the object. The sequence of steps executed by all processes is called *history*.

An implemented object of some type is *linearizable*, if every history on that object is linearizable. (For the definition of linearizable histories see [15].) An implementation of a writable type is *sequentially writable*, if every history on that object in which no `write()` operation overlaps any other operation is linearizable.

Our aim is to augment objects with concurrent `write()` methods, provided that it is possible to write to the objects non-concurrently. More precisely, given a sequentially writable implementation SW of a writable type $\mathcal{T}$, we show how to implement a linearizable object W of type $\mathcal{T}$. For the sake of clarity, we provide two methods, `write()` and `exec()` that encapsulate the functionality of object W. Method `write`(v) changes the state of writable object W to state v, and method `exec`(op, arg) is used to execute any non-write operation `op`(arg) on object W.

We will denote `write()` methods on the sequentially writable object SW by `sWrite()`, to distinguish them from `write()` operations on W, and to emphasize that they are not allowed to overlap with any other method calls on SW.

2.2 The Standard Template

To motivate our wait-free bounded space implementation, we describe a simple lock-free construction based on standard techniques. All our implementations follow the same template depicted in Figure 1.

We use an array $A[0 \ldots m-1]$, $m \in \mathbb{N} \cup \{\infty\}$, of SW objects and a shared register *Ptr* that stores the index i of an array entry of A, and possibly some additional information. Each process p *owns* a distinct set $I_p \subseteq \{0, \ldots, m-1\}$ of array indices and the corresponding array entries $A[i]$, $i \in I_p$. Whenever an array index i is stored in *Ptr*, we say object $A[i]$ is *in use*. To execute a `write`(v) operation, the calling process p first chooses an appropriate *write-index* $f \in I_p$ that is not in use (what "appropriate" means, depends on the actual implementation), then it executes $A[f]$.`sWrite`(v), and later it *puts* $A[f]$ *into use* by writing f (and possibly some augmenting information) to *Ptr*. If $A[f']$ was in use immediately before $A[f]$ is put into use, then we say object $A[f']$ gets *retired* at that point. The writer, p, is not allowed to change array A or Ptr other than in the one `sWrite()` operation respectively when it puts $A[f]$ into use. In an `exec(`op, arg`)` operation e, the calling process q first determines an *exec-index* i such that object $A[i]$ is in use at some point during e, and then calls $A[i].op(arg)$, and returns the return value of that method call. Process q can only access A through this one operation, and it is not allowed to change Ptr. Implementations following this template differ only in how the write- and exec-indices are chosen.

A simple example is a straight-forward wait-free implementation that uses unbounded space: The array A and each set I_p are infinite, e.g., $I_p = \{i \geq 0 \mid i \bmod n = p\}$. In a `write()` operation, the calling process chooses a write-index that it owns and that it has never chosen before. In an `exec()` operation, the exec-index is obtained by reading Ptr. This way, each `sWrite()` operation on an object $A[j]$ is executed before j has ever been in use, and thus it does not overlap with any other operation on $A[j]$. Each `write()` operation with write-index i linearizes when the calling process puts object $A[i]$ into use, and each `exec()` operation with exec-index i can linearize at some point after the calling process read i from Ptr and before the `exec()` operation terminates and before any other object is put into use.

2.3 Lock-Free Implementation

Using standard memory reclamation techniques [14,20], it is easy to bound the space of an implementation of a writeable object by sacrificing wait-freedom. Here we sketch such a lock-free implementation. The aim is to demonstrate how this implementation fits our template, and it will motivate the wait-free construction presented in the next section.

To bound the size of array A, we need to reuse some of the previously used and then retired objects of A. The main challenge is to avoid inconsistent (unsafe) access to array entries that are used multiple times. This requires a memory management technique allowing each writer to identify a write-index f of an object $A[f]$ (which was possibly in use previously but is now retired), such that no process will access $A[f]$ before object $A[f]$ has been put back into use.

We use an array A of size $O(n^2)$, and the set of indices I_p of each process p is of size $O(n)$. Moreover, each process p keeps track of a local sequence number ctr_p that it increments modulo n at the end of every `write()` operation. Register Ptr now stores a pair (i, s), where i is an index of array A, and s is a sequence number that ensures that throughout any execution the same value (i, s) does not get written twice to Ptr.

In an `exec(`op, arg`)` operation, a process q first reads a pair (i, s) from Ptr. Then it *announces* index i by writing it to a single-writer multi-reader register $Ann[q]$ (similar to [13]). After that, q reads Ptr again. If Ptr has changed since q read it for the first time, q starts its `exec()` operation over. Otherwise, it uses i as its exec-index, i.e., it calls $A[i].op(arg)$ and returns the result.

To execute a `write(`v`)` operation, a process p first reads a pair (i, s) from Ptr. Then it reads an index from $Ann[ctr_p]$ (recall that ctr_p gets incremented modulo n with every `write()` operation). (Thus, p "lazily" scans the entire announce array during a sequence of n `write()` operations.) Next, p chooses a write-index $f \in I_p$, such that p did not read f from the announce array in the current and the preceding $n-1$ `write()` operations, and it also did not put f into use in any of the preceding $n-1$ `write()` operations. (Clearly, if $|I_p| = O(n)$ is large enough, such an index f must exist.) After that, p executes $A[f]$.`sWrite(`v`)`, and finally p writes the pair (f, ctr_p) to Ptr. The lazy scan of the announce array guarantees the following: If at some point t an index $i \in I_p$ is in use, and $Ann[q] = i$ throughout the interval $[t, t']$ for some $t' > t$, then throughout that interval $[t, t']$ process p will not choose i as a write-index, and in particular no $A[i]$.`sWrite()` operation will overlap with the interval $[t, t']$.

Now recall that in an `exec(`op, arg`)` operation e, a process q only executes $A[i].op(arg)$ if it read the same value (i, s) from Ptr twice, and announced index i in-between those two reads. This ensures that i is in use at the point t^* of the announcement. Hence, the owner, p of index i, will not choose i as a write-index again until q has announced a different index (overwritten $Ann[q]$ with a value different from i), and this does not happen during e. Thus, it follows that the interval starting with t^* and ending with the response of q's $A[i].op(arg)$ operation does not overlap with any `sWrite()` operation on $A[i]$. This property guarantees safe access and linearizability.

LEMMA 1. *An implementation of* `write()` *and* `exec()` *based on the template in Figure 1 is linearizable, if it guarantees the following: For each* `exec()` *method call e by process q that executes operation op on* $A[i]$*, there is a point* t^* *between the invocation of e and the invocation of op, such that*

(I) $A[i]$ *is in use at point* t^**, and*

(II) no `sWrite()` *operation on* $A[i]$ *overlaps with the interval starting at* t^* *and ending with the response of op.*

PROOF SKETCH. Consider a history H obtained by the implementation. Property (II) guarantees that each `sWrite()` operation on an object $A[j]$ does not overlap with any other operation on $A[j]$. Hence, the projection $H|A[j]$ of history H on any object $A[j]$ is linearizable. With each operation op on an object $A[j]$ we can associate a shared memory step $s_{lin}(op)$ on one of the base objects of $A[j]$ that is executed when op linearizes in $H|A[j]$.

To obtain a linearization of H, we let each `write()` operation that uses a write-index f linearize at the point when it puts object $A[f]$ into use (i.e., when it writes to Ptr). Now consider an `exec(`op, arg`)` operation e by process q, and let op, t^*, and i be as in the statement of the lemma. I.e., during e and after t^* process q executes $A[i].op(arg)$. By (I), $A[i]$ is in use at time t^*. If $A[i]$ gets retired after time t^*, let t' be the point when that happens, and otherwise let $t' = \infty$. Assume (w.l.o.g.) that op completes. If step $s_{lin}(op)$ (i.e., the step executed at the linearization point of op in the projected history $H|A[i]$) happens before t', we linearize op with this step, and otherwise we linearize op just before t'. By the assumptions of the lemma, $t' > t^*$ is after the invocation of e, so the linearization point chosen for e is also after the invocation of e, and by construction it is before the response of e.

Validity of the sequential history imposed by those linearization points follows from the two facts: First, all operations in H on an object $A[i]$ are linearized in the same order as in the linearization of $H|A[i]$ and while object $A[i]$

is in use. Second, at the point when $A[i]$ is put into use it is quiescent and is in some state v, and at that point a `write(v)` operation linearizes in $H|A[i]$ as well as in H. □

3. WAIT-FREE IMPLEMENTATION

It is challenging to bound space and sequence numbers, while maintaining wait-freedom, even if we are not concerned about the time complexity. We now propose an algorithm that uses registers of size $O(\log n)$ and is wait-free. Moreover, every operation has, up to a constant additive term, the same time complexity as the corresponding operation on *SW*. In the following we explain the high-level idea of the proposed implementation.

3.1 High Level Idea

This algorithm also follows the template in Figure 1. Recall that process p *owns* the indices in its set I_p, and the corresponding objects $A[i]$, $i \in I_p$. To execute `write(v)`, a process p needs to find a write-index $f \in I_p$ of an object $A[f]$ that is currently not in use, and that no process will access before p puts it into use. As in the lock-free algorithm discussed earlier, p lazily scans through the announce array by reading one array entry in each `write()` operation in a round-robin fashion, and it chooses a write-index $f \in I_p$ that it did not use or find in the announce array during the preceding $n-1$ `write()` operations.

In an `exec(op, arg)` operation, the calling process q needs to find an exec-index i and call $A[i]$.`op(arg)` such that properties (I) and (II) of Lemma 1 are satisfied for some point t^* that occurs after the invocation of the `exec()` operation and before the invocation of $A[i]$.`op(arg)`. Recall that in the lock-free `exec()` method explained above, a process q obtains a potential exec-index by reading a pair (i, s) from *Ptr*. Then it announces i by writing i to $Ann[q]$, to prevent the owner p of i from executing an `sWrite()` operation on $A[i]$ and from putting i into use again. In order to make sure that the announcement has been made "in time", process q has to check that *Ptr* has not changed. But if *Ptr* has changed, then q have to give up.

To achieve wait-freedom we will allow q to obtain an alternative exec-index in case the index it announces is not "safe" to use. This is based on two main ideas.

The first idea is that a process p does not use the same write-index $f \in I_p$ more than once during any $2n-1$ consecutive `write()` operations. We can easily achieve that by making array A large enough, so that each set I_p contains at least $2n$ elements. Hence, when p determines a write-index $f \in I_p$, during a `write()` operation, it chooses an index that it has not chosen during any of its preceding $2n-1$ `write()` operations. The reason for this is the following: Suppose a process q executes an `exec(op, arg)` method e during which it reads index i from *Ptr* at some point t, and at some point $t' > t$ it announces i as its exec-index. If $i \in I_p$, and p executes fewer than n `write()` method calls in the interval $[t, t']$, then it must execute at least n additional `write()` method calls before it can use write-index i again, and during at least one of them it will see q's announcement of index i. Hence, p will not use write-index i as long as q's `exec()` method e is pending. This ensures that assumptions (I) and (II) of Lemma 1 are satisfied.

The second idea deals with the case in which process p executes at least $2n$ `write()` method calls in this interval $[t, t']$. If p executes that many `write()` operations while q remains poised to announce index i, then p has enough time to provide an alternative exec-index to q. For that we utilize two *hint arrays* $H_p[0 \ldots n-1]$ and $H'_p[0 \ldots n-1]$ for every process p, as well as for each process q a single-writer multi-reader register S_q that stores a integer which q increments at the beginning of every `exec()` operation. For now, assume the counter S_q is unbounded; we will discuss later how we can bound it. Array entries $H_p[q]$ and $H'_p[q]$ are used to store a *hint* that process p can provide during a `write()` method to process q. Each time process p executes a `write()` operation with write-index f, it tries to provide a hint to process $q := ctr_p$ (recall that p increments ctr_p modulo n at the end of each `write()` operation). To do that, it first reads q's sequence number S_q into a local variable s, then it checks whether each of $H_p[q]$ and $H'_p[q]$ already contain a pair $(\cdot, s)$. If yes, then q does not provide a hint, i.e., it proceeds as before by simply putting object $A[f]$ into use. Otherwise, p provides hint f with sequence number S_q to process q by doing the following: It first writes the pair (f, s) to $H_p[q]$ then puts object $A[f]$ into use, and finally writes the pair (f, s) to $H'_p[q]$. It will be guaranteed that after that, p does not use write-index f again, as long as a pair $(f, \cdot)$ is stored in any of the hint arrays H_p and H'_p. (This is achieved by treating the hint arrays in a similar way as the announce array, i.e., process p scans them lazily in a round-robin fashion over n `write()` operations.)

Now consider again an `exec()` method e by process q. Recall that at the beginning of that method, q increments the value of its single-writer multi-reader register S_q. After that q reads an index i from *Ptr*, say at point t, and then it announces it at some point $t' > t$. Now q can determine the owner, p, of index i, i.e., p is such that $i \in I_p$. Then q reads the pairs stored in the hint array entries $H_p[q]$ and $H'_p[q]$, and compares them. If both entries store the same pair (j, s) and if $s = S_q$, then q uses hint j as its exec-index, and otherwise it uses index i.

The idea why this works is as follows: Suppose q finds the same pair (j, s), $s = S_q$, in both hint array entries. Since q incremented its sequence number at the beginning of its `exec()` method e, p must have written (j, s) to both hint array entries after q invoked e, and then p must have also put j into use at some point t^* after q invoked e and before it read $H'_p[q]$. Since the hint arrays also act as announce arrays, we can also be sure that process p does not use j again as a write-index in any subsequent `write()` operation, as long as the pair (j, s) remains in $H_p[q]$ or $H'_p[q]$. But recall that p does not provide a new hint to q until q has incremented its sequence number S_q. As a consequence, between t^* and the response of e, process p does not execute any `sWrite()` operation on $A[j]$. Therefore, properties (I) and (II) of Lemma 1 are satisfied.

Now suppose q reads pairs (j, s) and (j', s') from $H_p[q]$ respectively $H'_p[q]$, and either $(j, s) \neq (j', s')$ or $s \neq S_q$. Then during the interval $[t, t']$, where t is the point when q read index $i \in I_p$ from *Ptr*, and t' is the point when q announced that index, process p can have completed only fewer than n `write()` operations. (Otherwise, it would have provided a hint with sequence number S_q to q in the interval $[t, t']$). As discussed earlier, in this case it is safe for q to use exec-index i.

In order to bound the sequence number S_q, we increment S_q modulo $2n$. We deal with the ABA problem by ensuring that during any sequence of $2n$ `exec()` calls process q resets each hint array entry $H_r[q]$ and $H'_r[q]$, $r \in \{0,\ldots,n-1\}$, by writing $(\bot,\bot)$ to it, at least once.

However, this does not avoid the ABA problem completely. Suppose in some `write()` operation, $ctr_p = q$ and p reads the value s from S_q. Then, p falls asleep just before providing a hint f with sequence number s to q (i.e., before writing (f,s) to $H_p[q]$). In the meantime, q executes and finishes $2n-1$ `exec()` operations, thus resetting $H_p[q]$ and $H'_p[q]$, and incrementing S_q $2n-1$ times, so that $S_q = s-1$. Now p wakes up and provides the hint to q, i.e., it writes (f,s) to $H_p[q]$, f to Ptr, and then again (f,s) to $H'_p[q]$. Then it finishes its `write()` operation and starts another one in which it writes $f' \neq f$ to Ptr. Finally, q starts another `exec()` operation e in which it first increments S_q from $s-1$ to s, and later reads the pair (f,s) from both $H_p[q]$ and $H'_p[q]$. Therefore, q will use f as its exec-index of method e. But now it is possible that $A[f]$ is not in use at any point during e, and then clearly the assumptions of Lemma 1 are not satisfied. To avoid this case, the writer p has to read S_q twice, once before it writes to $H_p[q]$ and once before it writes to $H'_p[q]$. It then uses the latest sequence number it read from S_q in the corresponding write to the hint array. Our proofs show that this avoids any ABA problems.

Memory Management.

We equip our algorithm with a memory management technique that allows a process p in each `write()` operation to *recycle* an object, i.e., to identify a write-index $f \in I_p$ such that no other process is concurrently using f as an exec-index. Our technique is similar to that of Hazard Pointers [20], but more efficient: The deterministic version of the Hazard Pointers technique requires $O(\log n)$ amortized time per recycled object, and the randomized version expected $O(1)$ amortized time. Our technique allows us to recycle one object in constant worst-case time (not amortized). We believe that the technique is interesting by itself. It has already found other applications [3, 4, 7].

Recall that each time a process q wants to use an exec-index j in an `exec()` operation, it first announces that index by writing it to $Ann[q]$. Similarly, when a process p decides on a write-index f in a `write()` operation, it chooses one in I_p that is currently not announced and that it has not used as a write-index in any of its $n-1$ preceding `write()` operations. Similarly, that index f must not be stored in any of the hint arrays H_p or H'_p. To identify such an index, process p uses a method `recycle()` that takes one index as an argument. The `recycle()` method employs several queues, each of length $2n$. When p calls `recycle(`ℓ`)`, it adds ℓ to the end of a queue $retiredQ_p$, and then dequeues the front element from that queue. The idea is that by the time ℓ gets dequeued again, p has completed $2n$ `recycle()` and thus `write()` operations. During that time, p has already scanned the arrays Ann, H_p, and H'_p completely, and added the elements it found there to other queues. Using a simple data structure, p can then find out in constant time whether it can recycle ℓ or not. We describe the `recycle()` method in more detail in Section 3.2.

3.2 Detailed Description

We now describe our implementations of the `write()` and `exec()` methods in detail. Pseudocode is given in Figure 2.

To simplify the algorithm description and the proofs, we require that the first method call in any execution is a non-concurrent `write(`v_0`)` call, where v_0 is the initial state of the object. Clearly, one may easily obtain an implementation that does not require this assumption, by initializing all objects to the state they are in immediately after such an initial `write(`v_0`)` method.

We use an array A of $n(8n+1)$ instances of the sequentially writable object SW. Each process p owns a distinct set of indices $I_p \subseteq \{0,\ldots,n(8n+1)-1\}$, such that $|I_p| = 8n+1$ and $\bigcap_{p=0}^{n-1} I_p = \emptyset$.[1] E.g., $I_p = \{i \mid i \bmod n = p, 0 \leq i < n(8n+1)\}$. As discussed earlier, we use an announce array $Ann[0\ldots n-1]$, and for each process p two hint arrays $H_p[0\ldots n-1]$ and $H'_p[0\ldots n-1]$. Only process p writes register $Ann[p]$, and only processes p and q access $H_p[q]$ respectively $H'_p[q]$. Each element of H_p and H'_p is initialized to $(\bot,\bot)$, and each element of Ann to $\bot$. A shared register Ptr, which is initially $\bot$, stores the object in use. We also use a shared register S_p to store a sequence number for each process p. All registers need to store only $O(n^2)$ different values, and therefore $(2\log n + O(1))$-bit registers suffice.

Our implementation provides, in addition to the methods `write()` and `exec()`, a method `recycle()` that is used only internally and takes care of memory reclamation.

The Write() Method.

To execute `write(`v`)`, process p first needs to find a write-index f of a "free" SW object $A[i]$ to which it can first write using an `sWrite()` operation, and that it can then put into use. A local variable $lptr_p$ is used to keep track of the write-index that process p used in its preceding `write()` call (or $\bot$ if there was no such call). Process p first calls `recycle(`$lptr_p$`)` (line 14), which returns the index f that p will subsequently use as a write-index. The `recycle()` method also adds $lptr_p$ to a data structure that takes care of the memory reclamation. In lines 15-16 p writes the value v to $A[f]$, by executing `sWrite(`v`)`, and updates $lptr_p$ with the value f to indicate that f needs to be recycled in the subsequent `write()` operation. Then, in line 17 p reads the sequence number stored in S_{ctr_p} into a local variable s. (Recall that ctr_p is a local variable that gets incremented modulo n at the end of the `write()` operation.) In lines 18-19 p reads the second component of $H_p[ctr_p]$ and $H'_p[ctr_p]$ into $olds$, respectively $olds'$, to determine the sequence numbers associated with the hints currently stored in those registers. If $s = olds = olds'$, then the current hint is valid for process with identifier ctr_p, and p does not need to provide a new hint, and it can simply put $A[f]$ into use by writing f to Ptr (in line 26).

Otherwise, the current hint may not be valid, so in lines 21-24 process p provides a new hint to the process with identifier ctr_p. First, p writes the value (f,s) into $H_p[ctr_p]$. Then, p reads again the current sequence number of the process with identifier ctr_p into s', as the value might have changed since p has read it last. Next, p updates Ptr by writing value f into it, and finally, p writes (f,s') into $H'_p[ctr_p]$.

At the end of the `write()` method, in line 27, p increments the value of ctr_p (modulo n). This ensures that in n consecutive `write()` method calls, p attempts to provide at least one hint to each process.

[1] Applying some additional tricks, it may be possible to reduce the size of the sets I_p by a small constant factor. We did not attempt to do so, in order to not distract from the core ideas of this algorithm.

```
shared:
Array<SW> A[0...n(8n+1)-1]
Array<int> Ann[0...n-1] = (⊥,...,⊥)
int Ptr = ⊥
for i ∈ {0,...,n-1}:
  Array<int,int> H_i[0...n-1] = ((⊥,⊥),...,(⊥,⊥))
  Array<int,int> H'_i[0...n-1] = ((⊥,⊥),...,(⊥,⊥))
int S_0,...,S_{n-1} = -1

Method exec_q(op, arg)
1  x := (S_q + 1) mod 2n
2  S_q := x
3  i := Ptr
4  Ann[q] := i
5  p := owner(i)
6  (j, s) := H_p[q]
7  (j', s') := H'_p[q]
8  if s = s' = S_q ∧ j = j' then
9      i := j
10 ret_val := A[i].op(arg)
11 H_{S_q mod n}[q] := (⊥,⊥)
12 H'_{S_q mod n}[q] := (⊥,⊥)
13 return ret_val

Method write_p(v)
14 f = recycle_p(lptr_p)
15 A[f].sWrite(v)
16 lptr_p := f
17 s := S_{ctr_p}
18 (·, olds) := H_p[ctr_p]
19 (·, olds') := H'_p[ctr_p]
20 if s ≠ olds ∨ s ≠ olds' then
21     H_p[ctr_p] := (f, s)
22     s' := S_{ctr_p}
23     Ptr := f
24     H'_p[ctr_p] := (f, s')
25 else
26     Ptr := f
27 ctr_p := (ctr_p + 1) mod n

local:
Queue<int> retiredQ_p, announceQ_p, hintQ_p, hint'Q_p
/* 2n ⊥ values are initially enqueued to
each of the queues */
Set<int> free_p = I_p
Array<int> c_p[0...8n] = (0,...,0)
int lptr_p = ⊥
int ctr_p = 0

Method recycle_p(int ℓ)
28 if ℓ ≠ ⊥ then c_p[ℓ] := c_p[ℓ] + 1
29 retiredQ_p.enq(ℓ)
30 a := Ann[ctr_p]
31 if p = owner(a) then
32     c_p[a] := c_p[a] + 1
33     announceQ_p.enq(a)
34 else
35     announceQ_p.enq(⊥)
36 (h, .) := H_p[ctr_p]
37 if h ≠ ⊥ then c_p[h] := c_p[h] + 1
38 hintQ_p.enq(h)
39 (h', .) := H'_p[ctr_p]
40 if h' ≠ ⊥ then c_p[h'] := c_p[h'] + 1
41 hint'Q_p.enq(h')
42 r_0 := announceQ_p.deq()
43 r_1 := retiredQ_p.deq()
44 r_2 := hintQ_p.deq()
45 r_3 := hint'Q_p.deq()
46 for j = 0 to 3 do
47     if r_j ≠ ⊥ then
48         c_p[r_j] := c_p[r_j] - 1
49 for j = 0 to 3 do
50     if r_j ≠ ⊥ then
51         if c_p[r_j] = 0 then free_p.add(r_j)
52 f := free_p.remove()
53 return f
```

Figure 2: Implementation of the writable object

The Exec() Method.

Consider a call of `exec(op, arg)` by process q. In lines 1-2 q first increments (modulo $2n$) the value of its sequence number S_q. It then reads the index of the object that is in use from Ptr into a local variable i, announces i by writing it into $Ann[q]$, and determines the owner p of object $A[i]$ (lines 3-5). In lines 6-7 q reads the hint array entries $H_p[q]$ and $H'_p[q]$ into (j,s) respectively (j',s'). If it determines that the hint is valid, i.e., $(j,s) = (j,s')$ and s is stored in S_q, then q replaces index i with j (lines 8-9). Now, i is the exec-index that q will use, and so in line 10 q executes operation `op(arg)` on object $A[i]$. Finally, it writes $(\bot,\bot)$ to registers $H_{S_q \bmod n}[q]$ and $H'_{S_q \bmod n}[q]$, to prevent itself from using a very old hint in future `exec()` operations.

The Recycle() Method.

Operation `recycle()` takes as input an index i that p owns, and it returns an index of a free object that p owns. The `recycle()` method does not write to any shared objects. Most of the objects it uses are local to the calling process, p. In particular, it uses four local queues $retiredQ_p$, $announceQ_p$, $hintQ_p$, and $hint'Q_p$, and a local set data structure $free_p$. The set $free_p$ contains indices of p's free objects, i.e., those that p can use as write-indices. We assume that the data structure $free_p$ provides the operations `add()` and `remove()`, where $free_p$`.add(`i`)` adds value i to $free$ if it is not already in the set, and $free_p$`.remove()` removes one (arbitrary) element from $free_p$ and returns it. Since the domain of values stored in $free_p$ is I_p, which is of size $O(n)$, such a set data structure can be easily implemented from an array and a linked list in $O(n)$ space and with constant worst-case running time per per operation. The queues keep track of indices that p cannot use as write-indices. Initially, each queue contains $2n$ $\bot$ values, and $free_p$ contains all indices in I_p. Most of the time (except immediately before or after updating one of those data structures) each index $i \in I_p$ is either in one of p's queues or it is in $free_p$. A local counter array c_p keeps track for each index $i \in I_p$, of how many copies of i appear in p's queues.

To execute `recycle(ℓ)`, a process p first increments $c_p[\ell]$ and then adds ℓ to $retiredQ_p$ (lines 29). In lines 30-35 p reads a value a from $Ann[ctr_p]$, if p is the owner of index a, it increments $c_p[a]$ and enqueues a into $announceQ_p$, otherwise it enqueues $\bot$ to $announceQ$. In lines 36-41, p reads values h and h' from $H_p[ctr_p]$ and $H'_p[ctr_p]$, respectively. If h and h' are indices, p increments $c_p[h]$ and $c_p[h']$, and finally it enqueues the indices into $hintQ_p$ respectively $hint'Q_p$. (Every index h that p reads from H_p or H'_p is owned by p, so p does not have to test that before incrementing $c_p[h]$.)

In lines 42-51, p dequeues one value v from each of $retiredQ_p$, $announceQ_p$, $hintQ_p$, and $hint'Q_p$, and if that value is an index (i.e., it is not $\bot$), it decrements the counter $c_p[v]$. If the counter reaches 0, p adds value v to $free_p$. Finally, in line 52, p removes an (arbitrary) index f from $free_p$ and returns it. Note that in each `recycle()` operation one element is enqueued into and one element is dequeued from each queue, so as long as no `recycle()` by p is pending, the size of each queue is $2n$.

3.3 Analysis and Correctness

To prove correctness, we show that our algorithm satisfies the conditions of Lemma 1. We consider an arbitrary history H, generated by the implementation in Figure 2, that starts with a non-concurrent `write()` method call. Suppose process q executes $A[i^*]$.`op()` in line 10 during an `exec()` method call e, for some exec-index i^*. We say q obtains exec-index i^* *directly*, if q does not execute line 9 during e, and otherwise it obtains i^* *indirectly*.

Note that in all lines of the code, except for lines 10, 11, 12, 14, and 15, a process p executes at most one shared memory operation. Thus, we assume that each of those lines is executed instantaneously. For any method call m by process p and any line number $\ell \notin \{10, 11, 12, 14, 15\}$, we let $t^m_{p@\ell}$ denote the point in time when p executes line ℓ during method call m. Moreover, $t^m_{p@inv}$ denotes the point at which process p invokes method call m, and $t^m_{p@rsp}$ the point at which method call m by process p responds. Note that a method call uniquely identifies the process that executes that method call, so the symbol p in the notation $t^m_{p@\ell}$ is redundant, but we permit this redundancy in order to improve readability. We say a method call m by some process p *completes* in some interval $[t, t']$, if $[t^m_{p@inv}, t^m_{p@rsp}] \subseteq [t, t']$.

LEMMA 2. *For any process q and any index i^*, let t be the point when q invokes an* `exec()` *method call e, $t' > t$ be the point when q invokes an $A[i^*]$.*`op()` *operation during e, and $t'' > t'$ be the point when this operation responds during e. Then there exists a point $t^* \in [t, t']$, such that:*

(I) $Ptr = i^*$ at t^*, and

(II) no $A[i^*]$.`sWrite()` *overlaps with time interval $[t^*, t'']$.*

From this lemma and Lemma 1 it follows that our implementation is linearizable. In the following we partially prove Lemma 2. We have to rely on several claims that are stated in the appendix, but due to space constraints the proofs of some of those claims are omitted from this extended abstract.

PROOF OF LEMMA 2. Let p be the owner of index i^*, i.e. $i^* \in I_p$. We consider the following two cases:

Case 1. Process q obtains i^* directly. This implies that q must have read i^* from Ptr at $t^e_{q@3}$, and then it must have executed $Ann[q] := i^*$ at point $t^e_{q@4}$. Process q does not overwrite $Ann[q]$ before t'', thus,

$$Ann[q] = i^*, \text{ throughout } [t^e_{q@4}, t'']. \tag{1}$$

Let $t^* = t^e_{q@3}$, thus, $t^* \in [t, t']$. Then (I) is true, so it remains to show (II). Assume for the sake of contradiction, that there is an $A[i^*]$.`sWrite()` operation sw by p which overlaps with time interval $[t^*, t''] = [t^e_{q@3}, t'']$. It can be proved that no $A[i^*]$.`sWrite()` operation can be pending at $t^e_{q@3}$ (see Claim 6 in the appendix), thus, sw gets invoked at $t^{sw}_{p@inv} \in [t^e_{q@3}, t'']$.

Since $Ptr = i^*$ at $t^e_{q@3}$, it can be shown (see Claim 5 in the appendix) that process p must complete at least $2n$ `recycle()` calls $r_1, \ldots, r_{2n}$ (in this order) during $[t^e_{q@3}, t^{sw}_{p@inv})$, and it executes $free_p$.`add(`i^*`)` during r_{2n}. In the following, we first show that,

$$p \text{ can execute at most } n \texttt{ recycle()} \text{ calls during } [t^e_{q@3}, t^e_{q@6}] \subseteq [t^e_{q@3}, t^{sw}_{p@inv}). \tag{2}$$

This implies that p executes at least n `recycle()` calls during $(t^e_{q@6}, t^{sw}_{p@inv})$. Finally, we prove that this contradicts the assumption that p executes $free_p$.`add(`i^*`)` during r_{2n}.

Suppose (2) is not true, i.e. p completes more than n `recycle()` operations during $[t^e_{q@3}, t^e_{q@6}]$. This implies that p completes at least n `write()` operations during this time interval. In line 27 of each `write()` method call, p increments ctr_p modulo n. Hence, p completes at least one `write()` operation during $[t^e_{q@3}, t^e_{q@6}]$, such that $ctr_p = q$ at the invocation this `write()` operation. Let w' be the last such `write()` operation during $[t^e_{q@3}, t^e_{q@6}]$. As w' completes during this interval, $H_p[q] = H'_p[q] = (j, s^*)$ at the response of w', for some value j, where s^* is the value q writes to S_q at $t^e_{q@2}$. (This follows from Claim 4 in the appendix.) It can be shown that since $S_q = s^*$ at $t^{w'}_{p@rsp} \in [t^e_{q@3}, t^e_{q@6}]$, process p does not write to $H_p[q]$ and $H'_p[q]$ between $t^{w'}_{p@rsp}$ and the first point when the value stored in S_q has changed or q has written to $H_p[q]$ or $H'_p[q]$ (see Claim 2 in the appendix, using $t = t^{w'}_{p@rsp}$).

Process q does not write to any of $H_p[q]$ and $H'_p[q]$ during $[t^e_{q@3}, t^e_{q@7}]$ and the value stored in S_q does not change during the same interval. This means p does not write to $H_p[q]$ and $H'_p[q]$ during $[t^{w'}_{p@rsp}, t^e_{q@7}]$, hence $H_p[q] = H'_p[q] = (j, s^*)$ throughout this interval. Therefore, q reads the pair (j, s^*) from $H_p[q]$ and $H'_p[q]$ at $t^e_{q@6}$, respectively $t^e_{q@7}$. Thus, the if-condition in line 8 of e evaluates to true, and so q executes line 9. This is a contradiction, because we assumed q obtains i^* directly. This proves (2). Thus, there is an index $k \le n$, such that p executes operations $r_{k+1}, \ldots, r_{2n}$ during $(t^e_{q@6}, t^{sw}_{p@inv})$.

Consider these at least n `recycle()` method calls $r_{k+1}, \ldots, r_{2n}$, $1 \le k \le n$, executed by p during $(t^e_{q@6}, t^{sw}_{p@inv})$. In the following, we show that it is not possible that p executes $free_p$.`add(`i^*`)` during r_{2n}, which is a contradiction. Since during each `write()` call, and thus once per `recycle()` call, process p increments ctr_p modulo n,

$ctr_p = q$ at the invocation of at least one of the recycle() calls $r_{k+1}, \ldots, r_{2n}$. Let r_ℓ, $k+1 \le \ell \le 2n$, be the last recycle() call where $ctr_p = q$ at the invocation of r_ℓ. By (1) $Ann[q] = i^*$ throughout $(t^e_{q@6}, t^{sw}_{p@inv}) \subseteq [t^e_{q@4}, t'']$. Therefore, p reads i^* from $Ann[q]$ during r_ℓ. It is not hard to see that p does not add i^* to $free_p$ until some time after q writes a different value to $Ann[q]$ (see Claim 1 in the appendix), which by (1) can only happen after $t^{sw}_{p@inv} < t''$. Since p completes r_{2n} during $[t^e_{q@3}, t^{sw}_{p@inv})$, it cannot execute $free_p$.add(i^*) during r_{2n}—contradiction.

Case 2. Process q obtains i^* indirectly. Thus, it can be proved that there exists a write() operation w by process p during which p writes i^* into Ptr at point $t^w_{p@23}$ (see Claim 7 (a) in the appendix). We prove (I) and (II) for $t^* = t^w_{p@23}$. It follows from Claim 7 (b) in the appendix that $t^w_{p@23} \in [t^e_{q@2}, t^e_{q@7}] \subseteq [t, t']$, thus (I) is correct. To prove (II), we assume for the sake of contradiction that there is an $A[i^*]$.sWrite() operation sw by p which overlaps with time interval $[t^w_{p@23}, t'']$. Similar to the previous case, no $A[i^*]$.sWrite() operation can be pending at point $t^w_{p@23}$ (see Claim 6 in the appendix), thus, sw gets invoked at point $t^{sw}_{p@inv} \in [t^w_{p@23}, t'']$. Since $Ptr = i^*$ at $t^w_{p@23}$, it can be shown that process p must complete at least $2n$ recycle() calls $r_1, \ldots, r_{2n}$, all during $[t^w_{p@23}, t^{sw}_{p@inv})$, and it executes $free_p$.add(i^*) during r_{2n} (see Claim 5 in the appendix). Since p does not execute a recycle() call between lines 23 and 24 of w, all recycle() calls $r_1, \ldots, r_{2n}$ must complete during $[t^w_{p@24}, t^{sw}_{p@inv})$. In the following, we first show that,

$$H_p[q] = H'_p[q] = (i^*, s^*) \text{ throughout } [t^w_{p@24}, t^{sw}_{p@inv}], \quad (3)$$

where s^* is the value q writes to S_q at point $t^e_{q@2}$. Then we show that this contradicts the assumption that p executes $free_p$.add(i^*) during r_{2n}.

Here we show that (3) is true. We can show (see Claim 7 (c) in the appendix) that $H_p[q] = H'_p[q] = (i^*, s^*)$ at $t^w_{p@24}$. Moreover, $S_q = s^*$ at $t^w_{p@24}$, because it can be shown (see Claim 7 (b) in the appendix) that $t^w_{p@24} \in [t^e_{q@2}, t^e_{q@7}]$. Therefore, process p does not write to any of $H_p[q]$ and $H'_p[q]$ after point $t^w_{p@24}$ until either q has written to any of them or the value of S_q has changed (see Claim 2 in the appendix). Process q does not write to any of $H_p[q]$ and $H'_p[q]$ during $[t^e_{q@2}, t'']$, and $S_q = s^*$ during the same interval. Therefore, neither p nor q writes to any of $H_p[q]$ and $H'_p[q]$ during $(t^w_{p@24}, t'']$. By the assumption $t^{sw}_{p@inv} < t''$, thus (3) is true.

Now consider recycle() method calls $r_1, \ldots, r_{2n}$ executed by p during $[t^w_{p@23}, t^{sw}_{p@inv})$. Let r_ℓ be the last recycle() call among $r_1, \ldots, r_{2n}$, such that at its invocation $ctr_p = q$. In line 36 of r_ℓ, process p reads $H_p[q]$. By (3), process p reads i^* from the first component of $H_p[q]$ when it reads $H_p[q]$ during r_ℓ. Then, p does not add i^* to $free_p$ until some time after the value stored in $H_p[q]$ has changed (see Claim 1 in the appendix), which by (3) can only happen after $t^{sw}_{p@inv}$. Since p completes r_{2n} before $t^{sw}_{p@inv}$, it cannot execute $free_p$.add(i^*) during r_{2n}—contradiction. □

It is obvious from the implementation that write() and exec() operations are wait-free and need only constant time in addition to the time needed for one sWrite() respectively op() operation on an instance of a SW object. Moreover, it follows immediately from the data structures that $O(n^2)$ registers and $O(n^2)$ SW objects are used. Therefore, applying Lemma 1 and Lemma 2, yields our main result, Theorem 1.

4. LONG-LIVED TEST-AND-SET

Recently, randomized implementations of one-shot Test-And-Set (TAS) objects were provided [2, 8, 9] that are very efficient in the oblivious adversary model. For example, the implementation in [8] provides a one-shot TAS object from $k = O(\sqrt{n})$ registers, and TAS operations finish in $O(\log^* n)$ steps in expectation. Using our technique, we can implement a *resettable* TAS object from $O(n^{5/2})$ registers with the same (asymptotic) time complexity for TAS operations, and which can be reset in constant time.

This follows from a simple trick that allows us to *sequentially* reset any TAS object that is implemented from registers in constant time: We use a shared register *Ver*, to store a version number. To sequentially reset the entire TAS() object a process simply increments the version number stored in *Ver*. If some process wants to execute an implemented TAS() operation, it first reads the current version number from *Ver*. It then proceeds as in the original implementation, but whenever it writes some information to a register, it augments that information with the current version number. Whenever the process reads information together with an augmented version number from a register, it checks whether that version number matches the one stored in *Ver*. If yes, it can use the information stored in the register, otherwise it assumes the register is in an initial state. To bound register *Ver*, we can increment the version number modulo k, where k is the number of registers used in the TAS implementation. In order to avoid the ABA problem we "lazily" reset registers during a series of reset() operations (in each reset() we reset a constant number of registers), and thus ensure that during any sequence of k consecutive reset() executions, each register gets reset at least once.

Acknowledgments

The authors are grateful to Faith Ellen and Lisa Higham for insightful discussions and helpful comments on earlier drafts of the paper. The authors also thank the anonymous reviewers for their valuable comments.

5. REFERENCES

[1] Y. Afek, E. Gafni, J. Tromp, and P. Vitányi. Wait-free test-and-set (extended abstract). In *Proc. of 6th WDAG*, pages 85–94, 1992.

[2] D. Alistarh and J. Aspnes. Sub-logarithmic test-and-set against a weak adversary. In *Proc. of 25th DISC*, pages 97–109, 2011.

[3] T. Brown, F. Ellen, and E. Ruppert. Pragmatic primitives for non-blocking data structures. In *Proc. of 32th PODC*, pages 13–22, 2013.

[4] T. Brown, F. Ellen, and E. Ruppert. A general technique for non-blocking trees. In *Proc. of 19th PPoPP*, pages 329–342, 2014.

[5] D. Detlefs, P. Martin, M. Moir, and G. S. Jr. Lock-free reference counting. *Distr. Comp.*, 15(4):255–271, 2002.

[6] F. Ellen, Y. Lev, V. Luchangco, and M. Moir. Snzi: scalable nonzero indicators. In *Proc. of 26th PODC*, pages 13–22, 2007.

[7] F. Ellen and P. Woelfel. An optimal implementation of fetch-and-increment. In *Proc. of 27th DISC*, pages 284–298, 2013.

[8] G. Giakkoupis, M. Helmi, L. Higham, and P. Woelfel. An $O(\sqrt{n})$ space bound for obstruction-free leader election. In *Proc. of 27th DISC*, pages 46–60, 2013.

[9] G. Giakkoupis and P. Woelfel. On the time and space complexity of randomized test-and-set. In *Proc. of 31th PODC*, pages 19–28, 2012.

[10] A. Gidenstam, M. Papatriantafilou, H. Sundell, and P. Tsigas. Efficient and reliable lock-free memory reclamation based on reference counting. *IEEE Trans. Parallel Distrib. Syst.*, 20(8):1173–1187, 2009.

[11] W. Golab. *Constant-RMR Implementations of CAS and Other Synchronization Primitives Using Read and Write Operations.* PhD thesis, University of Toronto, 2010.

[12] W. Golab, V. Hadzilacos, D. Hendler, and P. Woelfel. RMR-efficient implementations of comparison primitives using read and write operations. *Distr. Comp.*, 25(2):109–162, 2012.

[13] M. Herlihy. Impossibility and universality results for wait-free synchronization. In *Proc. of 7th PODC*, pages 276–290, 1988.

[14] M. Herlihy, V. Luchangco, and M. Moir. The repeat offender problem: A mechanism for supporting dynamic-sized, lock-free data structures. In *Proc. of 16th DISC*, pages 339–353, 2002.

[15] M. Herlihy and J. Wing. Linearizability: A correctness condition for concurrent objects. *ACM Trans. Program. Lang. Syst.*, 12(3), 1990.

[16] A. Israeli and M. Li. Bounded time-stamps. In *Proc. of 28th FOCS*, pages 371–382, 1987.

[17] P. Jayanti. A complete and constant time wait-free implementation of CAS from LL/SC and vice versa. In *Proc. of 12th DISC*, pages 216–230, 1998.

[18] A. Larsson, A. Gidenstam, P. H. Ha, M. Papatriantafilou, and P. Tsigas. Multiword atomic read/write registers on multiprocessor systems. *ACM Journal of Experimental Algorithmics*, 13, 2008.

[19] H. Lee. Fast local-spin abortable mutual exclusion with bounded space. In *Proc. of 14th OPODIS*, pages 364–379, 2010.

[20] M. Michael. Hazard pointers: Safe memory reclamation for lock-free objects. *IEEE Trans. Parallel Distrib. Syst.*, 15(6):491–504, 2004.

[21] G. Peterson. Concurrent reading while writing. *ACM Trans. Program. Lang. Syst.*, 5(1):46–55, 1983.

[22] H. Sundell. Wait-free reference counting and memory management. In *Proc. of 19th IPDPS*, 2005.

[23] J. Valois. Lock-free linked lists using compare-and-swap. In *Proc. of 14th PODC*, pages 214–222, 1995.

APPENDIX

A. ADDITIONAL PROOFS

For any process p and q the following claims hold. Due to space constraints, some proofs are omitted.

CLAIM 1. *Consider some point t during some* `recycle()` *method call r by process p. If at point t, p reads some index $i^* \in I_p$ from $Ann[q]$, or from the first element of $H_p[q]$ (similarly $H'_p[q]$), then p does not add i^* to $free_p$ unless it has completed $2n-1$* `recycle()` *calls following r and the value stored in $Ann[q]$, respectively the first element of $H_p[q]$ (similarly $H'_p[q]$), has changed to some value different from i^*.*

(Proof omitted.)

CLAIM 2. *Let t be a point when p executes no* `write()` *call, or when p executes a* `write()` *method call w, but $t \notin [t^w_{p@17}, t^w_{p@24}]$. If $H_p[q] = (j_1, s^*)$, $H'_p[q] = (j_2, s^*)$, and $S_q = s^*$ at point t, for some values j_1, j_2, s^*, then process p does not write to any of $H_p[q]$ and $H'_p[q]$ during $[t, t')$, where $t' > t$ is the first point after t when q writes to at least one of these two registers or when S_q changes to $(s^*+1) \bmod 2n$.*

PROOF. Suppose for the sake of contradiction, that p writes to at least one of $H_p[q]$ and $H'_p[q]$ during $[t, t')$. We assume without loss of generality that p writes to $H_p[q]$ during this interval. Let $t^{w'}_{p@21}$ be the first point during $[t, t')$ at which p writes to $H_p[q]$ during a `write()` call w'. Since at point t, p's execution is not in lines 17-24, and since $t^{w'}_{p@21} \in [t, t')$, we have $[t^{w'}_{p@17}, t^{w'}_{p@21}] \subseteq [t, t')$.

At point t, we have $S_q = s^*$. Thus, if the value of S_q changes after t, it is because q writes $(s^*+1) \bmod 2n$ to it. Thus, $S_q = s^*$ throughout $[t, t')$. By the assumption, q does not write to any of $H_p[q]$ and $H'_p[q]$ during $[t, t')$, hence, $H_p[q] = (j_1, s^*)$, $H'_p[q] = (j_2, s^*)$ throughout $[t, t^{w'}_{p@21})$. Therefore, during method call w', $olds = s^*$, $olds' = s^*$, and $s = s^*$ at points $t^{w'}_{p@17}$, $t^{w'}_{p@18}$, and $t^{w'}_{p@19}$ respectively. Thus, the condition in line 8 evaluates to false, and p does not execute line 21 during w'—contradiction. □

CLAIM 3. *If process p's execution is not between lines 21-24 of a* `write()` *method, then either $H_p[q] = (\bot, \bot)$, or $H'_p[q] = (\bot, \bot)$, or the first components of $H_p[q]$ and $H'_p[q]$ are equal.*

PROOF. Recall that only processes p and q can write to $H_p[q]$ and $H'_p[q]$. Process p only writes to these two registers during its `write()` method call between lines 21-24 and by the implementation, if it writes some pair (j, s) to one of $H_p[q]$ and $H'_p[q]$, it writes pair (j, s') to the other one, for some value s'. Process q only writes $(\bot, \bot)$ to these two registers in lines 11 and 12 of its `exec()` method. Thus, if p's execution is not between lines 21-24, there are two possible cases: Either the last write operation to both $H_p[q]$ and $H'_p[q]$ was by process p, and thus the first components of $H_p[q]$ and $H'_p[q]$ are equal, or the last write to one of these two registers was by process q, and thus one of them stores value $(\bot, \bot)$. □

CLAIM 4. *For any two processes p and q, if p's* `write()` *method call w completes during $(t^e_{q@2}, t^e_{q@7}]$, where e is an* `exec()` *call by q, and $ctr_p = q$ at the invocation of w, then at the response of w, we have $H_p[q] = H'_q[q] = (j, s^*)$, for some j, where s^* is the value q writes to S_q at $t^e_{q@2}$.*

PROOF. Recall that only processes p and q can write to $H_p[q]$ and $H'_p[q]$. Process q does not write to any of these two registers during time interval $(t^e_{q@2}, t^e_{q@7}]$, and therefore during the execution of w. Now we consider the following two cases:

Case 1. At the invocation of w, $H_p[q] = (j_1, s^*)$ and $H'_p[q] = (j_2, s^*)$ for some values j_1 and j_2. By Claim 3, j_1 must be equal to j_2. Moreover, we know $S_q = s^*$ during time interval $(t^e_{q@2}, t^e_{q@7}]$, and therefore at the invocation of w. Hence, by Claim 2, p does not write to any of $H_p[q]$

and $H'_p[q]$ until some time after the value stored in S_q has changed to $(s^*+1) \bmod 2n$ or q writes to any of $H_p[q]$ and $H'_p[q]$. Note that only process q can change the value stored in S_q and it does so in line 2, and process q only writes to $H_p[q]$ and $H'_p[q]$ in lines 11 and 12, and none of them happens during $(t^e_{q@2}, t^e_{q@7}]$. Thus, p does not write to any of $H_p[q]$ and $H'_p[q]$ before $t^e_{q@7}$. Therefore, $H_p[q] = H'_q[q] = (j, s^*)$ at the response of w, where $j = j_1 = j_2$.

Case 2. At the invocation of w, either $H_p[q] = (j, s)$ or $H'_p[q] = (j, s)$, for some $s \neq s^*$ and some value j. Since process q does not write to any of $H_p[q]$ and $H'_p[q]$ during time interval $(t^e_{q@2}, t^e_{q@7}]$ and thus during w, and also p does not write to these two registers between the invocation and line 21 of w, then the second component stored in $H_p[q]$ or $H'_p[q]$ is $s \neq s^*$ when p reads them in lines 18 and 19. Therefore, the condition in line 20 is evaluated to true, and p writes to both $H_p[q]$ and $H'_p[q]$ in lines 21 respectively 24. However, as $S_q = s^*$ during time interval $[t^e_{q@3}, t^e_{q@7}]$, p reads s^* from S_q in lines 17 and 22 during w, thus it writes pair (j', s^*) to both $H_p[q]$ and $H'_p[q]$ in lines 21 respectively 24, for some value j'. As p does not write to any of these two registers any more during w, therefore, at the response of w, we have $H_p[q] = H'_q[q] = (j', s^*)$. □

CLAIM 5. *For any index $i^* \in I_p$, if $Ptr = i^*$ at some point t, and p invokes $A[i^*]$.sWrite(x) at point $t' > t$, then p completes at least $2n$ `recycle()` method calls $r_1, \ldots, r_{2n}$ (in this order) during time interval $[t, t')$, and p executes $free_p$.add(i^*) only during r_{2n}.*

(Proof omitted.)

CLAIM 6. *For any index i^*, if $Ptr = i^*$ at some point t, then no $A[i^*]$.sWrite() operation is pending at t.*

PROOF. For the sake of contradiction, suppose there is an $A[i^*]$.`sWrite()` operation sw by some process p, which is pending at t. Operation sw can only be executed in line 15 of a `write()` operation by p, during which the `recycle()` call in line 14 returned i^*. Since only the owner of object $A[i^*]$ can return index i^* from a `recycle()` call, p must be the owner of i^*. Hence, only p can have written i^* to Ptr. Let t' be the last time before t when p wrote i^* to Ptr. I.e. no process writes to Ptr during $(t', t]$. As sw gets invoked before t and is pending at t, and also p does not write to Ptr during the sw, point t' occurs before the invocation of sw.

By Claim 5, p must complete at least $2n$ `recycle()` operations after t' and before the invocation of sw. Hence, p completes at least $2n - 1$ `write()` operations between t' and the invocation of sw. As p writes at least once to Ptr during each `write()` call in line 23 or 26, p must write to Ptr at least once after t' and before the invocation of sw, thus before point t. This contradicts the assumption that this happens at t' for the last time before t. □

CLAIM 7. *For any index $i^* \in I_p$, the following holds. If q executes $A[i^*]$.op($args$) during its `exec()` method call e after it wrote s^* to S_q in line 2 and obtained i^* indirectly, then there exists a `write()` method call w executed by p, such that w has the following properties:*

(a) at $t^w_{p@23}$, process p writes i^* into Ptr,

(b) $t^w_{p@23}, t^w_{p@24} \in [t^e_{q@2}, t^e_{q@7}]$, and

(c) at $t^w_{p@24}$: $H_p[q] = H'_p[q] = (i^*, s^*)$.

PROOF. Process q obtains i^* indirectly, so the condition in line 8 of e evaluates to true. Hence, q reads (i^*, s^*) from both $H_p[q]$ and $H'_p[q]$ at $t^e_{q@6}$ respectively $t^e_{q@7}$. Therefore, process p must have previously written (i^*, s^*) to $H_p[q]$ and $H'_p[q]$ during some `write()` call(s) in lines 21 and 24 respectively. We define w and w' as follows:

$$w \text{ is the last } \texttt{write()} \text{ call by } p \text{, such that } t^w_{p@21} < t^e_{q@7}, \text{ and at } t^w_{p@21}, p \text{ writes } (i^*, s^*) \text{ to } H_p[q]. \quad (4)$$

$$w' \text{ is the last } \texttt{write()} \text{ call by } p \text{, such that } t^{w'}_{p@24} < t^e_{q@7}, \text{ and at } t^{w'}_{p@24}, p \text{ writes } (i^*, s^*) \text{ to } H'_p[q]. \quad (5)$$

Now we show that

$$\text{if } t^w_{p@21} < t^e_{q@6}, \text{ then } H_p[q] = (i^*, s^*) \text{ throughout } [t^w_{p@21}, t^e_{q@6}]. \quad (6)$$

For the sake of contradiction, suppose (6) is not true. This implies that some process writes some pair $(j, s) \neq (i^*, s^*)$ to $H_p[q]$ at some point t during $[t^w_{p@21}, t^e_{q@6}]$. As q reads $H_p[q] = (i^*, s^*)$ at $t^e_{q@6}$, p must write (i^*, s^*) to $H_p[q]$ during $(t, t^e_{q@6})$, and thus in $(t^w_{p@21}, t^e_{q@6})$. This contradicts (4).

We can prove that

$$w = w'. \quad (7)$$

(Due to lack of space, the proof is omitted.)

Proof of (a). By definition of method call w stated in (4), process p writes (i^*, s^*) to $H_p[q]$ in line 21 of w. Thus, in line 23 of w, process p writes i^* to Ptr at point $t^w_{p@23}$.

Proof of (b). By (5) and (7), we have $t^w_{p@23} < t^w_{p@24} < t^e_{q@7}$. Hence, it suffices to show that $t^w_{p@23} > t^e_{q@2}$. For the sake of contradiction, assume $t^w_{p@23} < t^e_{q@2}$. This implies that we also have $t^w_{p@23} < t^e_{q@6}$, so (6) holds. Moreover, the assumption implies that $t^w_{p@21} < t^w_{p@22} < t^e_{q@2}$. As process p writes the pair (i^*, s^*) to $H'_p[q]$ at $t^w_{p@24}$, it must have read value s^* from S_q at $t^w_{p@22}$. In line 1 of `exec()`, q increments modulo $2n$ the value stored in S_q, and in line 2, q writes the result to S_q, and S_q is not modified anywhere else. Thus just before $t^e_{q@2}$, $S_q \neq s^*$. As $S_q = s^*$ at $t^w_{p@22} < t^e_{q@2}$, therefore, lines 1 and 2 must be executed at least $2n$ times by q during time interval $[t^w_{p@22}, t^e_{q@2}]$. This implies that line 11 gets executed at least n times by q during $(t^w_{p@22}, t^e_{q@2})$. Thus, at least once when q executes line 11, $S_q \bmod n = p$, and so process q writes the pair $(\perp, \perp)$ into $H_p[q]$ at least once during $(t^w_{p@22}, t^e_{q@2})$, and therefore during $(t^w_{p@21}, t^e_{q@6})$. This contradicts (6).

Proof of (c). By (5) and (7), $H'_p[q] = (i^*, s^*)$ at point $t^w_{p@24}$. Now we show that $H_p[q] = (i^*, s^*)$ at the same point. Suppose for the purpose of contradiction, that $H_p[q] \neq (i^*, s^*)$ at point $t^w_{p@24}$. As by (4), $H_p[q] = (i^*, s^*)$ at point $t^w_{p@21}$, this implies that some process (p or q) writes to $H_p[q]$ during $(t^w_{p@21}, t^w_{p@24}]$. Process p does not write to $H_p[q]$ in lines 22-24. Therefore, process q writes $(\perp, \perp)$ to $H_p[q]$ in line 11 of an `exec()` call e', at some point $t \in (t^w_{p@21}, t^w_{p@24}]$. Both, e and e' are executed by q, and q executes line 11 of e' before $t^w_{p@24}$, and thus by (b) also before $t^e_{q@7}$. Hence, e' cannot be the same method call as e and it must be executed before e. Thus, we have $t^w_{p@21} < t < t^e_{q@inv} < t^e_{q@6}$. This contradicts (6) as q writes $(\perp, \perp)$ to $H_p[q]$ at $t \in (t^w_{p@21}, t^e_{q@6})$. □

Asynchronous Convex Hull Consensus in the Presence of Crash Faults*

Lewis Tseng
Department of Computer Science
Coordinated Science Laboratory
University of Illinois at Urbana-Champaign
ltseng3@illinois.edu

Nitin H. Vaidya
Department of Electrical and Computer Engineering
Coordinated Science Laboratory
University of Illinois at Urbana-Champaign
nhv@illinois.edu

ABSTRACT

This paper defines a new consensus problem, *convex hull consensus*. The input at each process is a d-dimensional vector of reals (or, equivalently, a point in the d-dimensional Euclidean space), and the output at each process is a *convex polytope* contained within the convex hull of the inputs at the fault-free processes. We explore the convex hull consensus problem under crash faults with *incorrect* inputs, and present an *asynchronous* approximate convex hull consensus algorithm with optimal fault tolerance that reaches consensus on an *optimal* output polytope.

Convex hull consensus can be used to solve other related problems. For instance, a solution for convex hull consensus trivially yields a solution for vector (multidimensional) consensus. More importantly, convex hull consensus can potentially be used to solve other more interesting problems, such as function optimization.

Categories and Subject Descriptors

C.2.4 [**Distributed Systems**]: [Distributed applications]

General Terms

Algorithm, Theory

Keywords

Convex hull consensus, vector inputs, asynchronous system, crash faults

1. INTRODUCTION

*This research is supported in part by National Science Foundation awards 1059540 and 1329681. Any opinions, findings, and conclusions or recommendations expressed here are those of the authors and do not necessarily reflect the views of the funding agencies or the U.S. government.

PODC'14, July 15–18, 2014, Paris, France.
Copyright 2014 ACM 978-1-4503-2944-6/14/07 ...$15.00.
http://dx.doi.org/10.1145/2611462.2611470.

The distributed *consensus* problem has received significant attention over the past three decades [3]. The traditional consensus problem formulation assumes that each process has a scalar input. As a generalization of this problem, recent work [13, 20, 19] has addressed *vector* consensus (also called multidimensional consensus) in the presence of Byzantine faults, wherein each process has a d-dimensional vector of reals as input, and the processes reach consensus on a d-dimensional vector within the convex hull of the inputs at fault-free processes ($d \geq 1$). In the discussion below, it will be more convenient to view a d-dimensional vector as a *point* in the d-dimensional Euclidean space.

This paper defines the problem of *convex hull consensus*. Similar to vector consensus, the input at each process is a point in the d-dimensional Euclidean space. However, for convex hull consensus, the output at each process is a *convex polytope* contained within the convex hull of the inputs at the fault-free processes. Intuitively, the goal is to reach consensus on the "largest possible" polytope within the convex hull of the inputs at fault-free processes, allowing the processes to estimate the domain of inputs at the fault-free processes. In some cases, the output convex polytope may consist of just a single point, but in general, it may contain an infinite number of points.

Convex hull consensus may be used to solve other related problems. For instance, a solution for convex hull consensus trivially yields a solution for vector consensus [13, 20]. More importantly, convex hull consensus can potentially be used to solve other more interesting problems, such as function optimization with the convex hull of the inputs at fault-free processes as the domain. We will discuss the application of convex hull consensus to function optimization in Section 7.

We first describe our fault and system models, and then formally define the convex hull consensus problem.

Fault model:

We assume the *crash faults with incorrect inputs* [6, 3] fault model. In this model, each faulty process have an *incorrect input*, and may crash. A faulty process performs the algorithm faithfully, using an incorrect input, until it (possibly) crashes. The implication of an incorrect input will be clearer when we formally define convex hull consensus below. We assume that at most f processes may be faulty. All fault-free processes have *correct inputs*. Since this model assumes incorrect inputs at faulty processes, the simulation techniques in [6, 3] can be used to transform an algorithm designed for this fault model to an algorithm for tolerating

Byzantine faults. For brevity, we do not discuss this transformation, which requires $n \geq 3f+1$. (A Byzantine convex hull consensus algorithm is also presented in our technical report [15].) Our results extend naturally to the more commonly used crash fault model wherein faulty processes also have correct inputs (we will refer to the latter model as crash faults with correct inputs). For brevity, the extension is presented in our technical report [16].

System model:
The system under consideration is *asynchronous*, and consists of n processes. Let the set of processes be denoted as $V = \{1, 2, \cdots, n\}$. All processes can communicate with each other. Thus, the underlying communication network is modeled as a complete graph. Similar to prior work (e.g., [7, 6, 20]), we assume that communication channels are reliable and FIFO (first-in first-out). Each message is delivered exactly once on each channel. The input at process i, denoted as x_i, is a point in the d-dimensional Euclidean space (equivalently, a d-dimensional vector of real numbers).

Convex hull consensus:
The FLP impossibility of reaching exact consensus in asynchronous systems with crash faults [9] extends to the problem of convex hull consensus as well. Therefore, we consider approximate convex hull consensus. An approximate convex hull consensus algorithm must satisfy the following properties:

- **Validity**: The *output* (or *decision*) at each fault-free process must be a convex polytope in the convex hull of correct inputs. Note that under the crash fault with incorrect inputs model, the input at any faulty process is incorrect.
- **ϵ-Agreement**: For a given constant $\epsilon > 0$, the Hausdorff distance (defined below) between the output polytopes at any two fault-free processes must be at most ϵ.
- **Termination:** Each fault-free process must terminate within a finite amount of time.

Moreover, the goal of the algorithm is to maximize the size of the output convex polytope at each fault-free process.

Distance metrics:

- $\mathbf{d}_E(p, q)$ denotes the Euclidean distance between points p and q. All points and polytopes in our discussion belong to a d-dimensional Euclidean space, for some $d \geq 1$, even if this is not always stated explicitly.
- For two convex polytopes h_1, h_2, the *Hausdorff distance* $\mathbf{d}_H(h_1, h_2)$ is defined as follows [11].

$$\mathbf{d}_H(h_1, h_2) = \max \{ \max_{p_1 \in h_1} \min_{p_2 \in h_2} \mathbf{d}_E(p_1, p_2), \max_{p_2 \in h_2} \min_{p_1 \in h_1} \mathbf{d}_E(p_1, p_2) \} \quad (1)$$

Optimality of approximate convex hull consensus:
The algorithm proposed in this paper is optimal in two ways. It requires an optimal number of processes to tolerate f faults, and it decides on a convex polytope that is optimal in a "worst-case sense", as elaborated below:

- Prior work on approximate vector consensus mentioned earlier [13, 20] showed that $n \geq (d+2)f+1$ is necessary to solve that problem in an asynchronous system consisting of n processes with at most f Byzantine faults. Although these prior papers dealt with Byzantine faults, it turns out that their proof of lower bound on n (i.e., lower bound of $(d+2)f+1$) is also directly applicable to approximate vector consensus under the crash fault with incorrect inputs model used in our present work. Thus, $n \geq (d+2)f+1$ is a necessary condition for vector consensus under this fault model. Secondly, it is easy to show that an algorithm for approximate convex hull consensus can be transformed into an algorithm for approximate vector consensus. Therefore, $n \geq (d+2)f+1$ is a necessary condition for approximate convex hull consensus as well. For brevity, we omit a formal proof of the lower bound, and our subsequent discussion under the crash faults with incorrect inputs model assumes that

$$n \geq (d+2)f+1 \quad (2)$$

Our algorithm is correct under this condition, and thus achieves optimal fault resilience. For crash faults with correct inputs, a smaller n suffices, as discussed in our technical report [16].

- In this paper, we only consider deterministic algorithms. A convex hull consensus algorithm A is said to be optimal if the following condition is true:

> Let F denote a set of up to f faulty processes. For a *given execution* of algorithm A with F being the set of faulty processes, let $y_i(A)$ denote the output polytope at process i at the end of the given execution. For any other convex hull consensus algorithm B, *there exists* an execution with F being the set of faulty processes, such that $y_i(B)$ is the output at fault-free process i, and $y_j(B) \subseteq y_j(A)$ for *each* fault-free process j.

The goal here is to decide on an output polytope that includes as much of the convex hull of *all* correct inputs as possible. However, since any process may be potentially faulty (with incorrect input), the output polytope can be smaller than the convex hull of all correct inputs. Intuitively speaking, the optimality condition says that an optimal algorithm should decide on a convex region that is *no smaller than that decided in a worst-case execution* of algorithm B. In Section 6, we will show that our proposed algorithm is optimal in the above sense.

Summary of main contributions of the paper:

- The paper introduces the problem of *convex hull consensus*. We believe that feasibility of convex hull consensus can be used to infer feasibility of other interesting problems as well, e.g., function optimization.
- We present an approximate convex hull consensus algorithm in asynchronous systems, and show that it achieves optimality in terms of its resilience, and also in terms of the convex polytope that it decides on.

- We apply convex hull consensus algorithm to solve the problem of optimizing a function over the convex hull of the inputs at fault-free processes. We also prove an impossibility result pertaining to function optimization with any arbitrary cost function under crash faults in asynchronous systems.

2. RELATED WORK

Many researchers in the decentralized control area, including Bertsekas and Tsitsiklis [4] and Jadbabaei, Lin and Morse [12], have explored approximate consensus in the absence of faults, using only near-neighbor communication in systems wherein the communication graph may be partially connected and time-varying. The structure of the proof of correctness of the algorithm presented in this paper, and our use of well-known matrix analysis results [21], is inspired by the above prior work. We have also used similar proof structures in our prior work on other (Byzantine) consensus algorithms [17, 19, 18]. With regards to the proof technique, this paper's contribution is to show how the above proof structure can be extended to the case when the process state consists of convex polytopes.

Dolev et al. addressed approximate Byzantine consensus in both synchronous and asynchronous systems [7] (with scalar input). Subsequently, Coan proposed a simulation technique to transform consensus algorithms that are resilient to crash faults into algorithms tolerating Byzantine faults [6, 3]. Abraham, Amit and Dolev proposed an algorithm for approximate Byzantine consensus [1]. The recent work of Mendes and Herlihy [13] and Vaidya and Garg [20] has addressed approximate vector consensus in the presence of Byzantine faults. This work has yielded lower bounds on the number of processes, and algorithms with optimal resilience for asynchronous [13, 20] as well as synchronous systems [20] modeled as complete graphs. Subsequent work [19] has explored the vector consensus problem in incomplete graphs.

Herlihy et al. [10] introduced the problem of Barycentric agreement. Barycentric agreement has some similarity to convex hull consensus, in that the output of Barycentric agreement is not limited to a single value (or a single point). However, the correctness conditions and assumptions on possible input values for Barycentric agreement are different from those of our convex hull consensus problem.

3. PRELIMINARIES

Some notations introduced in the paper are summarized in Appendix A. In this section, we introduce functions $\mathcal{H}$, $\mathbf{L}$, and a communication primitive used in our algorithm.

Definition 1. *For a multiset of points X, $\mathcal{H}(X)$ is the convex hull of the points in X.*

A multiset contain the same element more than once.

Definition 2. *Function $\mathbf{L}$: Suppose that ν non-empty convex polytopes $h_1, h_2, \cdots, h_\nu$, and ν weights $c_1, c_2, \cdots, c_\nu$ are given such that $0 \le c_i \le 1$ and $\sum_{i=1}^{\nu} c_i = 1$.* Linear combination *of these convex polytopes*

$$\mathbf{L}([h_1, h_2, \cdots, h_\nu] \ ; \ [c_1, c_2, \cdots, c_\nu])$$

is defined as follows:

$p \in \mathbf{L}([h_1, h_2, \cdots, h_\nu]; [c_1, c_2, \cdots, c_\nu])$ if and only if for $1 \le i \le \nu$, there exists

$$p_i \in h_i, \quad \textit{such that} \ \ p = \sum_{1 \le i \le \nu} c_i p_i \tag{3}$$

Because h_i's above are all convex and non-empty, $\mathbf{L}([h_1, h_2, \cdots, h_\nu] \ ; \ [c_1, c_2, \cdots, c_\nu])$ is also a convex non-empty polytope. (The proof is straightforward.) The parameters for $\mathbf{L}$ consist of two vectors, with the elements of the first vector being polytopes, and the elements of the second vector being the corresponding weights in the linear combination. With a slight abuse of notation, we will also specify the vector of polytopes as a multiset – in such cases, we will always assign an identical weight to all the polytopes in the multiset, and hence their ordering is not important.

Stable vector communication primitive:
As seen later, our algorithm proceeds in asynchronous rounds. In round 0 of the algorithm, the processes use a communication primitive called *stable vector* [2, 10], to try to learn each other's inputs. Stable vector was originally developed in the context of crash faults [2] and was later applied to solve Byzantine Barycentric agreement [10]. To achieve its desirable properties (listed below), stable vector requires at least $2f+1$ processes when each process either follows the algorithm faithfully or crashes. Since in our crash fault with incorrect inputs model, each process follows the algorithm unless it crashes, the properties of *stable vector* listed below will hold in our context, provided that $n \ge 2f+1$. As noted earlier in Section 1, $n \ge (d+2)f+1$ is a necessary condition for approximate convex hull consensus in the presence of crash faults with incorrect inputs. Then, with $d \ge 1$, we have $n \ge 3f+1$, and the properties of stable vector below will hold.

In round 0 of our algorithm, each process i first broadcasts a message consisting of the tuple $(x_i, i, 0)$, where x_i is process i's input. In this tuple, 0 indicates the (asynchronous) round index. Process i then waits for the stable vector primitive to return a set R_i containing round 0 messages. We will rely on the following properties of the stable vector primitive, which are implied by results proved in prior work [2, 10].

- **Liveness**: At each process i that does not crash before the end of round 0, stable vector returns a set R_i containing at least $n-f$ distinct tuples of the form $(x, k, 0)$.
- **Containment**: For processes i, j that do not crash before the end of round 0, let R_i, R_j be the set of messages returned to processes i, j by stable vector in round 0, respectively. Then, either $R_i \subseteq R_j$ or $R_j \subseteq R_i$. (Also, by the previous property, $|R_i| \ge n-f$ and $|R_j| \ge n-f$.)

Please refer to [2, 10] for the implementation of the *stable vector* primitive.

4. PROPOSED ALGORITHM

The proposed algorithm, named *Algorithm CC*, proceeds in asynchronous rounds. The input at each process i is named x_i. The initial round of the algorithm is called round 0. Subsequent rounds are named round 1, 2, 3, etc. In each round $t \ge 0$, each process i computes a state variable

h_i, which represents a convex polytope in the d-dimensional Euclidean space. We will refer to the value of h_i at the *end* of the t-th round performed by process i as $h_i[t]$, $t \geq 0$. Thus, for $t \geq 1$, $h_i[t-1]$ is the value of h_i at the *start* of the t-th round at process i. The algorithm terminates after t_{end} rounds, where t_{end} is a constant defined later in equation (19). The state $h_i[t_{end}]$ of each fault-free process i at the end of t_{end} rounds is its output (or decision) for the consensus algorithm.

X_i and $Y_i[t]$ defined on lines 4 and 13 of the algorithm below are both multisets. A given value may occur multiple times in a multiset. Also, the intersection in line 5 is over the convex hulls of the subsets of multiset X_i of size $|X_i| - f$ (note that each of these subsets is also a multiset). Elements of X_i are points in the d-dimensional Euclidean space, whereas elements of $Y_i[t]$ are convex polytopes. In line 14, $Y_i[t]$ specifies the multiset of polytopes whose linear combination is obtained using $\mathbf{L}$; all the weights specified as parameters to $\mathbf{L}$ here are equal to $1/|Y_i[t]|$

Algorithm CC: Steps performed at process i shown below.

Initialization: All sets used below are initialized to $\emptyset$.

Round 0 at process i:

- 1 On entering round 0:
  - 2 Send $(x_i, i, 0)$ to all the processes
- 3 When *stable vector* returns a set R_i:
  - 4 Multiset $X_i := \{\, x \mid (x, k, 0) \in R_i \}$
  - 5 $h_i[0] \;:=\; \cap_{C \subseteq X_i,\, |C| = |X_i| - f} \;\; \mathcal{H}(C)$
  - 6 Proceed to Round 1

Round $t \geq 1$ at process i:

- 7 On entering round $t \geq 1$:
  - 8 $\mathtt{MSG}_i[t] := \mathtt{MSG}_i[t] \cup (h_i[t-1], i, t)$
  - 9 Send $(h_i[t-1], i, t)$ to all other processes
- 10 When message (h, j, t) is received from $j \neq i$
  - 11 $\mathtt{MSG}_i[t] := \mathtt{MSG}_i[t] \cup \{(h, j, t)\}$
- 12 When $|\mathtt{MSG}_i[t]| \geq n - f$ for the first time:
  - 13 Multiset $Y_i[t] := \{h \mid (h, j, t) \in \mathtt{MSG}_i[t]\}$
  - 14 $h_i[t] \;:=\; \mathbf{L}(\; Y_i[t] \;;\; [\frac{1}{|Y_i[t]|}, \cdots, \frac{1}{|Y_i[t]|}])$
  - 15 If $t < t_{end}$, then proceed to Round $t+1$

Note that stable vector is only used in Round 0. As will be seen later in Section 6, to achieve optimality of the size of the output polytope, it is important for the intersection of multiset X_i (at line 4) at each fault-free process i to be as large as possible. This property is ensured by receiving messages using stable vector. In later rounds, the goal is to achieve convergence, and in this case, exchanging messages over the reliable channels is enough.

5. CORRECTNESS OF *ALGORITHM CC*

In this section, we prove that *Algorithm CC* satisfies Validity, ϵ-Agreement, and Termination properties. The use of matrix representation in our correctness proof below is inspired by the prior work on non-fault-tolerant consensus (e.g., [12, 4]). We have also used such a proof structure in our work on Byzantine consensus [17, 19, 18]. The main differences in this proof are: (i) the state at each process is now a convex polytope (instead of a point), and (ii) the multiplication operation on a vector of convex polytopes and a vector of scalar is now defined using function $\mathbf{L}$ (introduced in Section 3).

We now introduce more notations (some of the notations are summarized in Appendix A) and two lemmas:

- For a *given* execution of the proposed algorithm, let F denote the *actual* set of faulty processes in that execution. Processes in F have incorrect inputs, and they may potentially crash.
- For round $r \geq 0$, let $\mathcal{F}[r]$ denote the set of faulty processes that have crashed before sending any round r messages. Since the algorithm terminates after round t_{end}, we define for $t > t_{end}$, $\mathcal{F}[t] = \mathcal{F}[t_{end}]$. Note that $\mathcal{F}[r] \subseteq \mathcal{F}[r+1] \subseteq F$.

LEMMA 1. *Algorithm CC ensures* progress*: (i) all the fault-free processes will eventually progress to round 1; and, (ii) if all the fault-free processes progress to the start of round t ($t_{end} \geq t \geq 1$), then all the fault-free processes will eventually progress to the start of round $t+1$.*

Proof of Lemma 1 is trivial and is presented in [16].

LEMMA 2. *For each process $i \in V - \mathcal{F}[1]$, the polytope $h_i[0]$ is non-empty and convex.*

Proof of Lemma 2 is presented in Appendix B.

5.1 Matrix Preliminaries

We now introduce some matrix notation and terminology to be used in our proof. Boldface upper case letters are used below to denote matrices, rows of matrices, and their elements. For instance, $\mathbf{A}$ denotes a matrix, $\mathbf{A}_i$ denotes the i-th row of matrix $\mathbf{A}$, and $\mathbf{A}_{ij}$ denotes the element at the intersection of the i-th row and the j-th column of matrix $\mathbf{A}$. A vector is said to be *stochastic* if all its elements are non-negative, and the elements add up to 1. A matrix is said to be row stochastic if each row of the matrix is a stochastic vector [12]. For matrix products, we adopt the "backward" product convention below, where $a \leq b$,

$$\Pi_{\tau=a}^{b} \mathbf{A}[\tau] = \mathbf{A}[b]\mathbf{A}[b-1] \cdots \mathbf{A}[a] \tag{4}$$

Let $\mathbf{v}$ be a column vector of size n whose elements are convex polytopes. The i-th element of $\mathbf{v}$ is $\mathbf{v}_i$. Let $\mathbf{A}$ be a $n \times n$ row stochastic square matrix. We define the product of $\mathbf{A}_i$ (the i-th row of $\mathbf{A}$) and $\mathbf{v}$ as follows using function $\mathbf{L}$ defined in Section 3.

$$\mathbf{A}_i \mathbf{v} \;=\; \mathbf{L}(\mathbf{v}^T \;;\; \mathbf{A}_i) \tag{5}$$

where ^{T} denotes the transpose operation. The above product is a polytope in the d-dimensional Euclidean space. Product of matrix $\mathbf{A}$ and $\mathbf{v}$ is then defined as follows:

$$\mathbf{A}\mathbf{v} = [\; \mathbf{A}_1\mathbf{v} \quad \mathbf{A}_2\mathbf{v} \quad \cdots \quad \mathbf{A}_n\mathbf{v} \;]^T \tag{6}$$

Due to the transpose operation above, the product $\mathbf{Av}$ is a column vector consisting of n polytopes.

We describe how to represent Algorithm CC using a matrix form. Let $\mathbf{v}[t]$ ($t_{end} \geq t \geq 0$), denote a column vector of length n. In the remaining discussion, we will refer to $\mathbf{v}[t]$ as the state of the system at the end of round t. In particular, $\mathbf{v}_i[t]$ for $i \in V$ is viewed as the state of process i at the end of round t. We define $\mathbf{v}[0]$ as follows as *initialization* of the state vector:

(I1) For each process $i \in V - \mathcal{F}[1]$, $\mathbf{v}_i[0] := h_i[0]$. Recall that $h_i[0]$ is the convex hull computed at process i at line 5 in *Algorithm CC*.

(I2) For each process $k \in \mathcal{F}[1]$, first pick any one fault-free process $m \in V - F \subseteq V - \mathcal{F}[1]$, and then $\mathbf{v}_k[0]$ is *arbitrarily* defined to be equal to $h_m[0]$. Such an arbitrary choice suffices because the state $\mathbf{v}_k[0]$ for $k \in \mathcal{F}[1]$ does not impact future state of any other process (by definition, processes in $\mathcal{F}[1]$ do not send any messages in round 1 and beyond).

We will show that the state evolution of *Algorithm CC* can be expressed using matrix form as in (7) below, where $\mathbf{M}[t]$ is an $n \times n$ matrix with certain desirable properties. The state $\mathbf{v}_k[t]$ of process $k \in \mathcal{F}[t]$ is not meaningful, since process k has crashed before sending any round t messages. However, (7) assigns it a value for convenience of analysis. $\mathbf{M}[t]$ is said to be the *transition matrix* for round t.

$$\mathbf{v}[t] = \mathbf{M}[t]\ \mathbf{v}[t-1], \qquad t_{end} \geq t \geq 1 \tag{7}$$

In particular, given an execution of the algorithm, we construct the transition matrix $\mathbf{M}[t]$ for round $t \geq 1$ of that execution using the two rules below (*Rule 1* and *Rule 2*). Elements of row $\mathbf{M}_i[t]$ will determine the state $\mathbf{v}_i[t]$ of process i (specifically, $\mathbf{v}_i[t] = \mathbf{M}_i[t]\mathbf{v}[t-1]$). Note that *Rule 1* applies to processes in $V - \mathcal{F}[t+1]$. Each process $i \in V - \mathcal{F}[t+1]$ survives at least until the start of round $t+1$, and sends at least one message in round $t+1$. Therefore, its state $\mathbf{v}_i[t]$ at the end of round t is of consequence. On the other hand, processes in $\mathcal{F}[t+1]$ crash sometime before sending any messages in round $t+1$ (possibly crashing in previous rounds). Thus, their states at the end of round t are not relevant to the fault-free processes anymore, and hence *Rule 2* defines the entries of the corresponding rows of $\mathbf{M}[t]$ somewhat arbitrarily.

Construction of Transition Matrix $\mathbf{M}[t]$ for $t_{end} \geq t \geq 1$:

In the matrix specification below, $\texttt{MSG}_i[t]$ is the message set at the point where $Y_i[t]$ is defined on line 13 of the algorithm. Thus, $Y_i[t] := \{h \mid (h, j, t) \in \texttt{MSG}_i[t]\}$, and $|\texttt{MSG}_i[t]| = |Y_i[t]|$.

- *Rule 1*: For each process $i \in V - \mathcal{F}[t+1]$, and each $k \in V$:

  If a round t message from process k (of the form $(*, k, t)$) is in $\texttt{MSG}_i[t]$, then

  $$\mathbf{M}_{ik}[t] := \frac{1}{|\texttt{MSG}_i[t]|} \tag{8}$$

  Otherwise,

  $$\mathbf{M}_{ik}[t] := 0 \tag{9}$$

- *Rule 2*: For each process $j \in \mathcal{F}[t+1]$, and each $k \in V$,

  $$\mathbf{M}_{jk}[t] \quad := \quad \frac{1}{n} \tag{10}$$

Observe that by design, $\mathbf{M}[t]$ is a row stochastic matrix.

THEOREM 1. *For $t \geq 1$, define $\mathbf{v}[t] = \mathbf{M}[t]\mathbf{v}[t-1]$, with $\mathbf{M}[t]$ as specified above. Then, for $\tau \geq 0$, and for all $i \in V - \mathcal{F}[\tau+1]$, $\mathbf{v}_i[\tau]$ equals $h_i[\tau]$.*

The proof is presented in Appendix C. The above theorem states that, for $t_{end} \geq t \geq 1$, equation (7), that is, $\mathbf{v}[t] = \mathbf{M}[t]\mathbf{v}[t-1]$, correctly characterizes the state of the processes that have not crashed before the end of round t. For processes that have crashed, their states are not relevant, and could be assigned any arbitrary value for analytical purposes (this is what *Rule 2* above effectively does). Given the matrix product definition in (6), and by repeated application of the state evolution equation (7), we obtain

$$\mathbf{v}[t] \quad = \quad \left(\Pi_{\tau=1}^{t}\mathbf{M}[\tau]\right)\mathbf{v}[0], \qquad t \geq 1 \tag{11}$$

Recall that we adopt the "backward" matrix product convention presented in (4). Then, (11) follows from the observation that $\mathbf{M}[\tau](\mathbf{M}[\tau-1]\mathbf{v}[\tau-2]) = (\mathbf{M}[\tau]\mathbf{M}[\tau-1])\mathbf{v}[\tau-2]$.

5.2 Correctness Proof

DEFINITION 3. *A polytope is* valid *if it is contained in the convex hull of the inputs of fault-free processes.*

Now, we present three lemmas that are used in the correctness proof below. The following lemma specifies the properties of the multiplication of a series of transition matrices $\mathbf{M}[\tau]$ constructed using the procedure above.

LEMMA 3. *For $t \geq 1$, let $\mathbf{P}[t] = \Pi_{\tau=1}^{t}\mathbf{M}[\tau]$. Then,*

- *$\mathbf{P}[t]$ is a row stochastic matrix.*
- *For $i, j \in V - F$, and $k \in V$,*

$$\|\,\mathbf{P}_{ik}[t] - \mathbf{P}_{jk}[t]\,\| \leq \left(1 - \frac{1}{n}\right)^t \tag{12}$$

where $\|a\|$ denotes absolute value of real number a.

Proof Sketch: First observe that (i) $\mathbf{M}[\tau]$ is a row stochastic matrix by construction, and (ii) due to the assumption that $n \geq 3f+1$, for $i, j \in V - \mathcal{F}[t+1]$, there exists a fault-free process $g(i,j)$ such that $\mathbf{M}_{ig(i,j)}[t] \geq 1/n$ and $\mathbf{M}_{jg(i,j)}[t] \geq 1/n$. Then, from these two observations, Lemma 3 can be proved using the convergence analysis of multiplication of row stochastic matrices based on the coefficients of ergodicity [12, 21]. The proof is omitted due to lack of space, and is presented in [16]. □

LEMMA 4. *$h_i[0]$ for each process $i \in V - \mathcal{F}[1]$ is valid.*

LEMMA 5. *Suppose non-empty convex polytopes $h_1, \cdots, h_\nu$ are all valid. Consider ν constants $c_1, c_2, \cdots, c_\nu$ such that $0 \leq c_i \leq 1$ and $\sum_{i=1}^{\nu} c_i = 1$. Then the linear combination of these convex polytopes, $\boldsymbol{L}([h_1, h_2, \cdots, h_\nu]\,;\,[c_1, c_2, \cdots, c_\nu])$, is convex, non-empty, and valid.*

The proofs of Lemmas 4 and 5 are trivial, and are presented in [16].

THEOREM 2. *Algorithm CC satisfies the* validity, ϵ-agreement *and* termination *properties.*

PROOF. We prove that Algorithm CC satisfies the *validity*, *ϵ-agreement* and *termination* properties after a large enough number of asynchronous rounds.

Repeated applications of Lemma 1 ensures that the fault-free processes will progress from round 0 through round r, for any $r \geq 0$, allowing us to use (11). Consider round $t \geq 1$. Let

$$\mathbf{P}[t] \quad = \quad \Pi_{\tau=1}^{t}\mathbf{M}[\tau] \tag{13}$$

Validity:

We prove validity using the series of observations below:

- *Observation 1*: By Lemma 2 and Lemma 4, $h_i[0]$ for each $i \in V - \mathcal{F}[1]$ is non-empty and valid. Also, each such $h_i[0]$ is convex by construction (line 5 of Algorithm CC).
- *Observation 2*: As per the initialization step (I1) in Section 5, for each $i \in V - \mathcal{F}[1]$, $\mathbf{v}_i[0] := h_i[0]$; thus, by Observation 1 above, for each such process i, $\mathbf{v}_i[0]$ is convex, valid and non-empty. Also, in initialization step (I2), for each process $k \in \mathcal{F}[1]$, we set $\mathbf{v}_k[0] := h_m[0]$, where m is a fault-free process; thus, by Observation 1, for each such process k, $\mathbf{v}_k[0]$ is convex, valid and non-empty. Therefore, each element of $\mathbf{v}[0]$ is a non-empty, convex and valid polytope.
- *Observation 3*: By Lemma 3, $\mathbf{P}[t]$ is a *row stochastic* matrix. Thus, elements of each row of $\mathbf{P}[t]$ are non-negative and add up to 1. Therefore, by Observation 2 above, and Lemma 5, $\mathbf{P}_i[t]\mathbf{v}[0]$ for each $i \in V - F$ is valid, convex and non-empty. Also, by Theorem 1, and equation (11), $h_i[t] = \mathbf{P}[t]\mathbf{v}[0]$ for $i \in V - F$. Thus, $h_i[t]$ is valid, convex and non-empty for $t \geq 1$.

Therefore, *Algorithm CC* satisfies the validity property.

ϵ-Agreement and Termination:

Processes in $\mathcal{F}[1]$ do not send any messages to any other process in round 1 and beyond. Thus, by the construction of $\mathbf{M}[t]$, for each $a \in V - \mathcal{F}[1]$ and $b \in \mathcal{F}[1]$, $\mathbf{M}_{ab}[t] = 0$ for all $t \geq 1$; it then follows that $\mathbf{P}_{ab}[t] = 0$ as well.[1]

Consider fault-free processes $i, j \in V - F$. The previous paragraph implies that, for any point q_i in $h_i[t] = \mathbf{v}_i[t] = \mathbf{P}_i[t]\mathbf{v}[0]$, there must exist, for all $k \in V - \mathcal{F}[1]$, $p_k \in h_k[0]$, such that

$$q_i = \sum_{k \in V - \mathcal{F}[1]} \mathbf{P}_{ik}[t] p_k \tag{14}$$

Using points p_k in the above equation, now choose point q_j in $h_j[t]$ defined as follows.

$$q_j = \sum_{k \in V - \mathcal{F}[1]} \mathbf{P}_{jk}[t] p_k \tag{15}$$

For points p_k, denote by $p_k(l)$ the value of p_k's l-th coordinate. Then, (14) and (15) imply the following equalities for $d \geq l \geq 1$, respectively:

$$q_i(l) = \sum_{k \in V - \mathcal{F}[1]} \mathbf{P}_{ik}[t] p_k(l) \tag{16}$$

and

$$q_j(l) = \sum_{k \in V - \mathcal{F}[1]} \mathbf{P}_{jk}[t] p_k(l) \tag{17}$$

Recall that the Euclidean distance between q_i and q_j is $\mathbf{d}_E(q_i, q_j)$. From Lemma 3, (16) and (17), we have the following:

$$\begin{aligned}
\mathbf{d}_E(q_i, q_j) &= \sqrt{\sum_{l=1}^{d} (q_i(l) - q_j(l))^2} \\
&= \sqrt{\sum_{l=1}^{d} \left(\sum_{k \in V - \mathcal{F}[1]} \mathbf{P}_{ik}[t] p_k(l) - \sum_{k \in V - \mathcal{F}[1]} \mathbf{P}_{jk} p_k(l) \right)^2} \\
&= \sqrt{\sum_{l=1}^{d} \left(\sum_{k \in V - \mathcal{F}[1]} (\mathbf{P}_{ik}[t] - \mathbf{P}_{jk}[t]) p_k(l) \right)^2} \\
&\leq \sqrt{\sum_{l=1}^{d} \left[\left(1 - \frac{1}{n}\right)^{2t} \left(\sum_{k \in V - \mathcal{F}[1]} \|p_k(l)\| \right)^2 \right]} \\
&= \left(1 - \frac{1}{n}\right)^{t} \sqrt{\sum_{l=1}^{d} \left(\sum_{k \in V - \mathcal{F}[1]} \|p_k(l)\| \right)^2}
\end{aligned}$$

The second equality above is due to (16) and (17), and the fourth inequality is due to Lemma 3.

Define

$$\Omega = \max_{p_k \in h_k[0], k \in V - \mathcal{F}[1]} \sqrt{\sum_{l=1}^{d} \Big(\sum_{k \in V - \mathcal{F}[1]} \|p_k(l)\|\Big)^2}$$

Therefore, $\mathbf{d}_E(q_i, q_j)$ is upper bounded by

$$\left(1 - \frac{1}{n}\right)^{t} \sqrt{\sum_{l=1}^{d} \left(\sum_{k \in V - \mathcal{F}[1]} \|p_k(l)\| \right)^2} \leq \left(1 - \frac{1}{n}\right)^{t} \Omega \tag{18}$$

Because the $h_k[0]$'s in the definition of Ω are all valid (by Lemma 4), Ω can itself be upper bounded by a function of the input vectors at the fault-free processes. In particular, under the assumption that each element of fault-free processes' input vectors is upper bounded by U and lower bounded by μ, Ω is upper bounded by $\sqrt{dn^2 \max(U^2, \mu^2)}$. Observe that the upper bound on the right-hand-side of (18) monotonically decreases with t, because $1 - \frac{1}{n} < 1$. Define t_{end} as the smallest positive integer t for which

$$\left(1 - \frac{1}{n}\right)^{t} \sqrt{dn^2 \max(U^2, \mu^2)} < \epsilon \tag{19}$$

Recall that the algorithm terminates after t_{end} rounds. Since t_{end} is finite, the algorithms satisfies the *termination* condition.

[1]Claim 1 in Appendix D relates to this observation.

(18) and (19) together imply that, for fault-free processes i, j and for each point $q_i \in h_i[t_{end}]$, there exists a point $q_j[t] \in h_j[t_{end}]$, such that $\mathbf{d}_E(q_i, q_j) < \epsilon$ (and, similarly, vice-versa). Thus, by Definition of Hausdorff distance, $\mathbf{d}_H(h_i[t_{end}], h_j[t_{end}]) < \epsilon$. Since this holds true for any pair of fault-free processes i, j, the ϵ-agreement property is satisfied at termination. □

Even though we only show that validity and ϵ-agreement properties hold for fault-free processes, these two properties hold for all processes that do not crash before completing the algorithm.

6. OPTIMALITY OF ALGORITHM CC

Due to the *Containment* property of stable vector mentioned in Section 3, the set Z defined below contains at least $n - f$ messages. Recall that set R_i is defined on line 3 of Algorithm CC.

$$Z \quad := \quad \cap_{i \in V-F} R_i \qquad (20)$$

Define multiset $X_Z := \{x \mid (x, k, 0) \in Z\}$. Then, define a convex polytope I_Z as follows.

$$I_Z \quad := \quad \cap_{D \subset X_Z, |D| = |X_Z| - f} \mathcal{H}(D) \qquad (21)$$

Now we establish a "lower bound" on output at the fault-free processes.

LEMMA 6. *For all $i \in V - \mathcal{F}[t+1]$ and $t \geq 0$, $I_Z \subseteq h_i[t]$.*

Lemma 6 is proved in Appendix D. The following theorem is proved in Appendix E using Lemma 6.

THEOREM 3. Algorithm CC *is optimal under the notion of optimality in Section 1.*

Degenerate cases:

In some cases, the output polytope at fault-free processes may be a single point, making the output equivalent to that obtained from vector consensus [13, 20]. As a trivial example, this occurs when all the fault-free processes have identical input. It is possible to identify scenarios when the number of processes is exactly equal to the lower bound, i.e., $n = (d+2)f+1$ processes, when the output polytope consists of just a single point. However, in general, particularly when n is larger than the lower bound, the output polytopes will contain infinite number of points. In any event, as shown in Theorem 3, our algorithm achieves optimality in all cases. Thus, any other algorithm can also produce such degenerate outputs for the same inputs.

7. CONVEX HULL FUNCTION OPTIMIZATION

The goal of *convex hull function optimization* is to minimize a cost function, say function c, over a domain consisting of the convex hull of the correct inputs. Formally, the following four properties must be satisfied by the function optimization algorithm:

- **Validity**: output y_i at fault-free process i is a point in the convex hull of the correct inputs.
- **ϵ-Agreement**: for any constant $\epsilon > 0$, for any fault-free processes i, j, $\mathbf{d}_E(y_i, y_j) < \epsilon$.
- **Weak β-Optimality**: (i) for any constant $\beta > 0$, for any fault-free processes i, j, $\|c(y_i) - c(y_j)\| < \beta$, and (ii) if at least $2f + 1$ processes (faulty or fault-free) have an identical input, say x, then for any fault-free process i, $c(y_i) \leq c(x)$.
- **Termination:** each fault-free process must terminate within a finite amount of time.

The intuition behind part (ii) of the weak optimality condition above is as follows. When $2f + 1$ processes have an identical input, say x^*, even if f of them are slow (or crash), each fault-free process must be able to learn that $f + 1$ processes have input x^*, and at least one of these $f+1$ processes must be fault-free. Therefore, each fault-free process would know that the minimum value of the cost function over the convex hull of the correct inputs is at most $c(x^*)$.

It turns out that it is not feasible to simultaneously reach (approximate) consensus on a point, and to ensure that the cost function at that point is "small enough" for any arbitrary cost function.[2] The theorem below states this observation more formally.

THEOREM 4. *The four properties of convex hull function optimization cannot be satisfied simultaneously in an asynchronous system in the presence of crash faults with incorrect inputs for $n \geq 4f + 1$ and $d \geq 1$.*

The proof of Theorem 4 is presented in Appendix F. We know that even without the weak β-optimality, we need $n \geq (d + 2)f + 1$. Thus, the impossibility result is complete for $d \geq 2$. Whether the impossibility extends to $3f+1 \leq n \leq 4f$ and $d = 1$ is presently unknown.

The natural question then is "What function optimization problem can we solve?" Suppose that the cost function satisfies b-Lipschitz continuity. That is, for any points x, y, $\|c(x) - c(y)\| \leq b\,\mathbf{d}_E(x, y)$. Below, we present an algorithm that achieves validity, weak β-optimality and termination, but not ϵ-agreement. The proposed algorithm has two simple steps:

- Step 1: First solve convex hull consensus with parameter ϵ. Let h_i be the output polytope of convex hull consensus at process i.
- Step 2: The output of function optimization is the tuple $(y_i, c(y_i))$, where $y_i = \arg\min_{x \in h_i} c(x)$. When there are multiple points in h_i minimizing $c(x)$, break tie arbitrarily.

The ϵ-agreement property of the convex hull consensus together with the assumption of b-Lipschitz continuity imply that for fault-free processes i, j, $\|c(y_i) - c(y_j)\| < \epsilon b$. Thus, the fault-free processes find approximately equal minimum value for the function. Therefore, for any $\beta > 0$, we can achieve $\|c(y_i) - c(y_j)\| < \beta$ by choosing $\epsilon = \beta/b$ for convex hull consensus in Step 1. Validity and termination follow directly form the properties of the convex hull consensus algorithm. Note that since in step 2, processes break tie arbitrarily, we are not able to guarantee that $\mathbf{d}_E(y_i, y_j)$ is

[2]Impossibility result can be easily extended to the case when condition (ii) is relaxed as follows: $c(y_i) \leq c(x) + \beta'$ for some $\beta' > 0$. For brevity, we consider only the case when $c(y_i) \leq c(x)$ in this work.

small. That is, ϵ-agreement may not hold. However, we believe that when the cost function is D-strongly convex [5] and differentiable, it can be shown that the 2-step algorithm above not only achieves validity, weak β-optimality and termination, but also ensures that $\mathbf{d}_E(y_i, y_j)$ is bounded by a function of ϵ, b and D. We have some preliminary analysis, but a formal proof has not been developed.

Notion of Optimality:

Observe that in the 2-step algorithm above, $c(y_i)$ at process i may not be minimum over the *entire* convex hull of the inputs of fault-free processes. For instance, even when all the processes are fault-free, each subset of f processes is viewed as *possibly* faulty with incorrect inputs. We can extend the notion of optimality from Section 1 to function optimization as follows. An algorithm A for function optimization is said to be optimal if the following condition is true.

> Let F denote a set of up to f faulty processes. For a *given execution* of algorithm A with F being the set of faulty processes, let $y_i(A)$ denote the output at process i at the end of the given execution. For any other algorithm B, *there exists* an execution with F being the set of faulty processes, such that $y_i(B)$ is the output at fault-free process i, and $c(y_j(A)) \leq c(y_j(B))$ for *each* fault-free process j.

The intuition behind the above formulation is as follows. A goal of function optimization here is to allow the processes to "learn" the smallest value of the cost function over the convex hull of the inputs at the fault-free processes. The above condition implies that an optimal algorithm will learn a function value that is no larger than that learned in a worst-case execution of any other algorithm.

The 2-step function optimization algorithm above is optimal in the above sense. This is a direct consequence of Theorem 3.

8. SUMMARY

We introduce the *convex hull consensus* problem under crash faults with incorrect inputs model, and present an asynchronous approximate convex hull consensus algorithm with optimal fault tolerance that reaches consensus on an optimal output polytope. We also consider the use of convex hull consensus algorithm to solve the problem of optimizing a function over the convex hull of the inputs at fault-free processes. An impossibility result for asynchronous function optimization for arbitrary cost functions is also presented.

9. ACKNOWLEDGMENTS

We acknowledge Eli Gafni for his comments on our previous work [20] that inspired us to reduce the convex hull consensus algorithm from Byzantine [15] to crash faults. We also thank anonymous reviewers for their insightful comments.

10. REFERENCES

[1] I. Abraham, Y. Amit, and D. Dolev. Optimal resilience asynchronous approximate agreement. In *OPODIS*, pages 229–239, 2004.

[2] H. Attiya, A. Bar-Noy, D. Dolev, D. Peleg, and R. Reischuk. Renaming in an asynchronous environment. *Journal of the ACM*, July 1990.

[3] H. Attiya and J. Welch. *Distributed Computing: Fundamentals, Simulations, and Advanced Topics.* Wiley Series on Parallel and Distributed Computing, 2004.

[4] D. P. Bertsekas and J. N. Tsitsiklis. *Parallel and Distributed Computation: Numerical Methods.* Optimization and Neural Computation Series. Athena Scientific, 1997.

[5] S. Boyd and L. Vandenberghe. Convex Optimization. *Cambridge University Press*, New York, NY, USA, 2011.

[6] B. A. Coan. A compiler that increases the fault tolerance of asynchronous protocols. *IEEE Trans. Comput.*, 37(12):1541–1553, Dec. 1988.

[7] D. Dolev, N. A. Lynch, S. S. Pinter, E. W. Stark, and W. E. Weihl. Reaching approximate agreement in the presence of faults. *J. ACM*, 33:499–516, May 1986.

[8] M. J. Fischer, N. A. Lynch, and M. Merritt. Easy impossibility proofs for distributed consensus problems. In *Proceedings of the fourth annual ACM symposium on Principles of distributed computing*, PODC '85, pages 59–70, New York, NY, USA, 1985. ACM.

[9] M. J. Fischer, N. A. Lynch, and M. S. Paterson. Impossibility of distributed consensus with one faulty process. *J. ACM*, 32:374–382, April 1985.

[10] M. Herlihy, D. Kozlov, and S. Rajsbaum. *Distributed Computing Through Combinatorial Topology.* Elsevier Science, 2013.

[11] D. Huttenlocher, G. Klanderman, and W. Rucklidge. Comparing images using the Hausdorff distance. *Pattern Analysis and Machine Intelligence, IEEE Transactions on*, 15(9):850–863, 1993.

[12] A. Jadbabaie, J. Lin, and A. Morse. Coordination of groups of mobile autonomous agents using nearest neighbor rules. *Automatic Control, IEEE Transactions on*, 48(6):988 – 1001, june 2003.

[13] H. Mendes and M. Herlihy. Multidimensional approximate agreement in Byzantine asynchronous systems. In *STOC '13*, 2013.

[14] M. A. Perles and M. Sigorn. A generalization of Tverberg's theorem. *CoRR*, abs/0710.4668, 2007.

[15] L. Tseng and N. H. Vaidya. Byzantine convex consensus: An optimal algorithm. *CoRR*, abs/1307.1332, 2013.

[16] L. Tseng and N. H. Vaidya. Asynchronous convex consensus in the presence of crash faults. *CoRR*, abs/1403.3455, 2014.

[17] L. Tseng and N. H. Vaidya. Iterative approximate Byzantine consensus under a generalized fault model. In *In International Conference on Distributed Computing and Networking (ICDCN)*, January 2013.

[18] N. H. Vaidya. Matrix representation of iterative approximate Byzantine consensus in directed graphs. *CoRR*, Mar. 2012.

[19] N. H. Vaidya. Iterative Byzantine vector consensus in incomplete graphs. In *In International Conference on*

Distributed Computing and Networking (ICDCN), January 2014.

[20] N. H. Vaidya and V. K. Garg. Byzantine vector consensus in complete graphs. In *Proceedings of the 2013 ACM Symposium on Principles of Distributed Computing*, PODC '13, pages 65–73, New York, NY, USA, 2013. ACM.

[21] J. Wolfowitz. Products of indecomposable, aperiodic, stochastic matrices. In *Proceedings of the American Mathematical Society*, volume 14, pages 733–737, 1963.

APPENDIX

A. NOTATIONS

This appendix summarizes some of the notations and terminology introduced throughout the paper.

- d = dimension of the input vector at each process.
- n = number of processes. We assume that $n \geq (d+2)f+1$.
- f = maximum number of faulty processes.
- $V = \{1, 2, \cdots, n\}$ is the set of all processes.
- $\mathbf{d}_E(p, q)$ = Euclidean distance between points p and q.
- $\mathbf{d}_H(h_1, h_2)$ = the Hausdorff distance between convex polytopes h_1, h_2.
- $\mathcal{H}(C)$ = the convex hull of a multiset C.
- $\mathbf{L}([h_1, h_2, \cdots, h_k]; [c_1, c_2, \cdots, c_k])$, defined in Section 3, is a linear combination of convex polytopes $h_1, h_2, ..., h_k$ with weights $c_1, c_2, \cdots, c_k$, respectively.
- $|X|$ = the size of a *multiset* or *set* X.
- $\|a\|$ = the absolute value of a real number a.
- F denotes the *actual* set of faulty processes in an execution of the algorithm.
- $\mathcal{F}[t]$ $(t \geq 0)$, defined in Section 4, denotes the set of (faulty) processes that do not send any messages in round t. Thus, each process in $\mathcal{F}[t]$ must have crashed before sending any message in round t (it may have possibly crashed in an earlier round). Note that $\mathcal{F}[r] \subseteq \mathcal{F}[r+1] \subseteq F$ for $r \geq 1$.
- We use boldface upper case letters to denote matrices, rows of matrices, and their elements. For instance, $\mathbf{A}$ denotes a matrix, $\mathbf{A}_i$ denotes the i-th row of matrix $\mathbf{A}$, and $\mathbf{A}_{ij}$ denotes the element at the intersection of the i-th row and the j-th column of matrix $\mathbf{A}$.

B. PROOF OF LEMMA 2

The proof of Lemma 2 uses the following theorem by Tverberg [14]:

THEOREM 5. *(Tverberg's Theorem [14]) For any integer $f \geq 0$, for every multiset T containing at least $(d+1)f+1$ points in a d-dimensional space, there exists a partition $T_1, .., T_{f+1}$ of T into $f+1$ non-empty multisets such that $\cap_{l=1}^{f+1} \mathcal{H}(T_l) \neq \emptyset$.*

Now, we prove Lemma 2.

PROOF. Consider any $i \in V - \mathcal{F}[1]$. Consider the computation of polytope $h_i[0]$ on line 5 of the algorithm as

$$h_i[0] \;:=\; \cap_{C \subseteq X_i,\, |C|=|X_i|-f} \;\; \mathcal{H}(C), \tag{22}$$

where $X_i := \{x \mid (x, k, 0) \in R_i\}$ (lines 4-5). Convexity of $h_i[0]$ follows directly from (22), because $h_i[0]$ is an intersection of convex hulls.

Recall that, due to the lower bound on n discussed in Section 1, we assume that $n \geq (d+2)f+1$. Thus, $|X_i| \geq n - f \geq (d+1)f+1$. By Theorem 5 above, there exists a partition $T_1, T_2, \cdots, T_{f+1}$ of X_i into multisets (T_j's) such that $\cap_{j=1}^{f+1} \mathcal{H}(T_j) \neq \emptyset$. Let us define

$$J = \cap_{j=1}^{f+1} \mathcal{H}(T_j) \tag{23}$$

Thus, by Tverberg's theorem above, J is non-empty. Now, each multiset C used in (22) to compute $h_i[0]$ excludes only f elements of X_i, whereas there are $f+1$ multisets in the partition $T_1, T_2, \cdots, T_{f+1}$ of multiset X_i. Therefore, each multiset C will fully contain at least one multiset from the partition. It follows that $\mathcal{H}(C)$ will contain J defined above. Since this property holds true for each multiset C used to compute $h_i[0]$, J is contained in the convex polytope $h_i[0]$ computed as per (22). Since J is non-empty, $h_i[0]$ is non-empty. □

C. PROOF OF THEOREM 1

PROOF. The proof of the above theorem is by induction on τ. Recall that we defined $\mathbf{v}_i[0]$ to be equal to $h_i[0]$ for all $i \in V - \mathcal{F}[1]$ in the initialization step (I1) in Section 5. Thus, the theorem trivially holds for $\tau = 0$.

Now, for some $\tau \geq 0$, and for all $i \in V - \mathcal{F}[\tau+1]$, suppose that $\mathbf{v}_i[\tau] = h_i[\tau]$. Recall that processes in $V - \mathcal{F}[\tau+2]$ surely survive at least till the end of round $\tau+1$ (by definition of $\mathcal{F}[\tau+2]$). Therefore, in round $\tau+1 \geq 1$, each process in $i \in V - \mathcal{F}[\tau+2]$ computes its new state $h_i[\tau+1]$ at line 14 of Algorithm CC, using function $\mathbf{L}(\, Y_i[\tau+1] \,;\, [\frac{1}{|Y_i[\tau+1]|}, \cdots, \frac{1}{|Y_i[\tau+1]|}])$, where $Y_i[\tau+1] := \{h \mid (h, j, \tau+1) \in \texttt{MSG}_i[\tau+1]\}$. Also, if $(h, j, \tau+1) \in \texttt{MSG}_i[\tau+1]$, then process j must have sent round $\tau+1$ message $(h_j[\tau], j, \tau+1)$ to process i – in other words, h above (in $(h, j, \tau+1) \in \texttt{MSG}_i[\tau+1]$) must be equal to $h_j[\tau]$. Also, since j did send a round $\tau+1$ message, $j \in V - \mathcal{F}[\tau+1]$. Thus, by induction hypothesis, $\mathbf{v}_j[\tau] = h_j[\tau]$.

Now observe that, by definition of $Y_i[\tau+1]$ at line 13 of the algorithm, $|Y_i[\tau+1]| = |\texttt{MSG}_i[\tau+1]|$. Thus, the definition of the matrix elements in (8) and (9) ensures that $\mathbf{M}_i[\tau+1]\mathbf{v}[\tau]$ equals $\mathbf{L}(\, Y_i[\tau+1] \,;\, [\frac{1}{|Y_i[\tau+1]|}, \cdots, \frac{1}{|Y_i[\tau+1]|}])$, i.e., $h_i[\tau+1]$. Thus, $\mathbf{v}_i[\tau+1]$ defined as $\mathbf{M}_i[\tau+1]\mathbf{v}[\tau]$ also equals $h_i[\tau+1]$. This holds for all $i \in V - \mathcal{F}[\tau+2]$, completing the induction. □

D. PROOF OF LEMMA 6

We first present a claim that will be used in the proof of Lemma 6.

CLAIM 1. *For $t \geq 1$, let $\mathbf{P}[t] = \Pi_{\tau=1}^{t} \mathbf{M}[\tau]$. Then, for all processes $j \in V - \mathcal{F}[t+1]$, and $k \in \mathcal{F}[1]$, $\mathbf{P}_{jk}[t] = 0$.*

PROOF. The claim is intuitively straightforward. For completeness, we present a formal proof here. The proof is by induction on t.

Induction Basis: Consider the case when $t = 1$, $j \in V - \mathcal{F}[2]$, and $k \in \mathcal{F}[1]$. Then by definition of $\mathcal{F}[1]$, $(*, k, 0) \notin \texttt{MSG}_j[1]$. Then, due to (9), $\mathbf{M}_{jk}[1] = 0$, and hence $\mathbf{P}_{jk}[1] = \mathbf{M}_{jk}[1] = 0$.

Induction: Consider $t \geq 2$. Assume that the claim holds true through round $t-1$. Then, $\mathbf{P}_{jk}[t-1] = 0$ for all $j \in V - \mathcal{F}[t]$ and $k \in \mathcal{F}[1]$. Recall that $\mathbf{P}[t-1] = \Pi_{\tau=1}^{t-1}\mathbf{M}[\tau]$.

Now, we will prove that the claim holds true for round t. Consider $j \in V - \mathcal{F}[t+1]$ and $k \in \mathcal{F}[1]$. Note that $\mathbf{P}[t] = \Pi_{\tau=1}^{t}\mathbf{M}[\tau] = \mathbf{M}[t]\Pi_{\tau=1}^{t-1}\mathbf{M}[\tau] = \mathbf{M}[t]\mathbf{P}[t-1]$. Thus, $\mathbf{P}_{jk}[t]$ can be non-zero only if there exists a $q \in V$ such that $\mathbf{M}_{jq}[t]$ and $\mathbf{P}_{qk}[t-1]$ are both non-zero.

For any $q \in \mathcal{F}[t-1]$, $(*, q, t-1) \notin \texttt{MSG}_j[t]$. Then, due to (9), $\mathbf{M}_{jq}[t] = 0$ for all $q \in \mathcal{F}[t-1]$, and hence all $q \in \mathcal{F}[1]$ (note that $\mathcal{F}[r-1] \subseteq \mathcal{F}[r]$ for $r \geq 2$). Additionally, by the induction hypothesis, for all $q \in V - \mathcal{F}[t]$ and $k \in \mathcal{F}[1]$, $\mathbf{P}_{qk}[t-1] = 0$. Thus, these two observations together imply that there does not exist any $q \in V$ such that $\mathbf{M}_{jq}[t]$ and $\mathbf{P}_{qk}[t-1]$ are both non-zero. Hence, $\mathbf{P}_{jk}[t] = 0$. □

Now, we are ready to prove Lemma 6 in Section 6.

PROOF. Recall that Z and I_Z are defined in (20) and (21), respectively. We first prove that for all $j \in V - \mathcal{F}[1]$, $I_Z \subseteq h_j[0]$. We make the following observations for each process $i \in V - \mathcal{F}[1]$:

- *Observation 1*: By the definition of multiset X_i at line 4 of round 0 at process i, and the definition of X_Z in Section 6, we have $X_Z \subseteq X_i$.
- *Observation 2*: Let A and B be sets of points in the d-dimensional space, where $|A| \geq n-f$, $|B| \geq n-f$ and $A \subseteq B$. Define $h_A := \cap_{C_A \subseteq A, |C_A| = |A|-f}\ \mathcal{H}(C_A)$ and $h_B := \cap_{C_B \subseteq B, |C_B| = |B|-f}\ \mathcal{H}(C_B)$. Then $h_A \subseteq h_B$. This observation follows directly from the fact that every multiset C_A in the computation of h_A is contained in some multiset C_B used in the computation of h_B, and the property of function $\mathcal{H}$.

Now, consider the computation of $h_i[0]$ at line 5. By Observations 1 and 2, and the definitions of $h_i[0]$ and I_Z, we have that $I_Z \subseteq h_i[0] = \mathbf{v}_i[0]$, where $i \in V - \mathcal{F}[1]$. Also, by initialization step (I2) (in Section 5), for $k \in \mathcal{F}[1]$, $\mathbf{v}_k[0] = h_m[0]$, for some fault-free process m. Thus, all the elements of $\mathbf{v}[0]$ contain I_Z. Then, due to row stochasticity of $\Pi_{\tau=1}^{t}\mathbf{M}[\tau]$, it follows that each element of $\mathbf{v}[t] = \left(\Pi_{\tau=1}^{t}\mathbf{M}[\tau]\right)\mathbf{v}[0]$ also contain I_Z. Recalling that $h_i[t] = \mathbf{v}_i[t]$ for each fault-free process, proves the lemma. □

E. PROOF OF THEOREM 3

PROOF. Consider multiset X_Z defined in Section 6. Recall that $|X_Z| = |Z|$, and that Z contains at least $n-f$ tuples. Thus, X_Z contains at least $n-f$ points, and of these, at least $n-2f$ points must be the inputs at fault-free processes. Let V_Z denote the set of fault-free processes whose inputs appear in X_Z.

Now consider the following execution of any algorithm ALGO that correctly solves approximate convex hull consensus. Suppose that the faulty processes in F do not crash, and have incorrect inputs. Consider the case when processes in $V - X_Z$ are so slow that the other fault-free processes must terminate before receiving any messages from the processes in $V - X_Z$. This is possible, since we assume that faulty processes do not crash, and $|V - X_Z| \leq f$ (due to $|X_Z| \geq n-f$). The fault-free processes in V_Z cannot determine whether the processes in $V - X_Z$ are just slow, or they have crashed.

Processes in V_Z must be able to terminate without receiving any messages from the processes in $V - X_Z$. Thus, their output must be in the convex hull of inputs at the fault-free processes whose inputs are included in X_Z. However, any f of the processes whose inputs are in X_Z may potentially be faulty and have incorrect inputs. Therefore, the output obtained by ALGO must be contained in I_Z as defined in Section 6. On the other hand, by Lemma 6, the output obtained using Algorithm CC contains I_Z. This proves the theorem. □

F. PROOF OF THEOREM 4

PROOF. We will prove the result for $d = 1$. It should be obvious that impossibility with $d = 1$ implies impossibility for larger d (since we can always choose inputs that have 0 coordinates in all dimensions except one).

The proof is by contradiction. Suppose that there exists an algorithm, say Algorithm $\mathcal{A}$, that achieves the above four properties for $n \geq 4f+1$ and $d = 1$.

Let the cost function be given by $c(x) = 4 - (2x-1)^2$ for $x \in [0,1]$ and $c(x) = 3$ for $x \notin [0,1]$. For future reference, note that within the interval $[0,1]$, function $c(x)$ has the smallest value at $x = 0, 1$ both.

Now, suppose that all the inputs (correct and incorrect) are restricted to be binary, and must be 0 or 1. We will prove impossibility under this restriction on the inputs at faulty and fault-free processes both, which suffices to prove that the four properties cannot *always* be satisfied. Suppose that the output of Algorithm $\mathcal{A}$ at fault-free process i is y_i. Due to the validity property, and because the inputs are restricted to be 0 or 1, we know that $y_i \in [0,1]$.

Since $\lceil \frac{n}{2} \rceil \geq \lceil \frac{4f+1}{2} \rceil = 2f+1$, at least $2f+1$ processes will have either input 0, or input 1. Without loss of generality, suppose that at least $2f+1$ processes have input 0.

Consider a fault-free process i. By weak β-Optimality, $c(y_i) \leq c(0)$, that is, $c(y_i) \leq 3$. However, the minimum value of the cost function is 3 over all possible inputs. Thus, $c(y_i) = 3$. Similarly, for any other fault-free process j as well, $c(y_j)$ must equal 3. Now, due to validity, $y_j \in [0,1]$, and the cost function is 3 in interval $[0,1]$ only at $x = 0, 1$. Therefore, we must have y_i equal to 0 or 1, and y_j also equal to 0 or 1. However, because algorithm $\mathcal{A}$ satisfies the ϵ-agreement condition, $\mathbf{d}_E(y_i, y_j) = \|y_i - y_j\| < \epsilon$ (recall that dimension $d = 1$). If $\epsilon < 1$, then y_i and y_j must be identical (because we already know that they are either 0 or 1). Since this condition holds for any pair of fault-free processes, it implies *exact* consensus. Also, y_i and y_j will be equal to the input at a fault-free process due to the validity property above, and because the inputs are restricted to be 0 or 1. In other words, Algorithm $\mathcal{A}$ can be used to solve exact consensus in the presence of crash faults with incorrect inputs when $n \geq 4f+1$ in an asynchronous system. This contradicts the well-known impossibility result by Fischer, Lynch, and Paterson [8]. □

Distributed Computing Building Blocks for Rational Agents

Yehuda Afek, Yehonatan Ginzberg, Shir Landau Feibish, and Moshe Sulamy
Blavatnik School of Computer Science, Tel-Aviv University, Israel
afek@cs.tau.ac.il, jhonathe@mail.tau.ac.il, shirl11@post.tau.ac.il,
moshesulamy@mail.tau.ac.il

ABSTRACT

Following [4] we extend and generalize the game-theoretic model of distributed computing, identifying different utility functions that encompass different potential preferences of players in a distributed system. A good distributed algorithm in the game-theoretic context is one that prohibits the agents (processors with interests) from deviating from the protocol; any deviation would result in the agent losing, i.e., reducing its utility at the end of the algorithm. We distinguish between different utility functions in the context of distributed algorithms, e.g., utilities based on communication preference, solution preference, and output preference. Given these preferences we construct two basic building blocks for game theoretic distributed algorithms, a wake-up building block resilient to any preference and in particular to the communication preference (to which previous wake-up solutions were not resilient), and a knowledge sharing building block that is resilient to any and in particular to solution and output preferences. Using the building blocks we present several new algorithms for consensus, and renaming as well as a modular presentation of the leader election algorithm of [4].

Categories and Subject Descriptors

C.4 [**Computer Systems Organization**]: Performance Of Systems—*Fault-Tolerance*; F.2.2 [**Analysis of Algorithms and Problem Complexity**]: Nonnumerical Algorithms and Problems

General Terms

Algorithms, Reliability, Theory

Keywords

distributed computing; game theory; message passing; consensus; renaming; leader election; knowledge sharing; rational agents

This research was supported by the Ministry of Science and Technology, Israel, and by the Israel Science Foundation (grants 6693/11 and 1386/11)

PODC'14, July 15–18, 2014, Paris, France.
Copyright 2014 ACM 978-1-4503-2944-6/14/07 ...$15.00.
http://dx.doi.org/10.1145/2611462.2611481 .

1. INTRODUCTION

A central issue in distributed computing, if not the main point, is multi-processor computing in the face of faulty processors. Many different faults are considered, from fail-stop to Byzantine faults. Recently, a new model, that of distributed game theory has emerged, in which processors, now called rational agents, are not faulty but may cheat in order to increase their profit according to some utility function [4, 1, 18, 2, 5].

For example, if an agent can cheat and cause an election algorithm to elect itself as a leader the agent profits one dollar, or if it can cheat causing a consensus algorithm to agree on 1 although its input was 0, then its profit is again some positive value. A basic property of the utility function considered in all cases, which is called *solution preference*, captures the notion that agents cannot gain if the algorithm fails (a zero profit is assigned to all the agents if the algorithm fails). As a result, though agents have preferences, they have no incentive to fail the algorithm.

The challenge for distributed algorithms in the context of game theory is to design algorithms that reach equilibrium, i.e., such algorithms in which the players, agents, have no incentive to cheat. That is, for any utility function materializing any combination of preferences, the algorithm should ensure that in any run the agents lose, or gain absolutely nothing, by deviating from the algorithm (trying to cheat). The algorithm, therefore, needs to govern the behavior of the rational agents and to punish agents (reducing their profit) for any deviation from it.

We present a comprehensive examination of the preferences and utilities of rational agents in a distributed network setting, building on the results presented in [4]. We take a closer look at factors that might affect the utilities of such agents in a distributed setting, and the actions that they may take as a result of these factors. Based on this examination, we provide a refined game-theoretic model which encompasses these preferences and gives insight to natural utilities that rational agents in a distributed setting may have. Specifically, we examine factors such as an agent's possible preference for a certain output or an agent's desire to send fewer messages.

Having identified the major factors which could influence the agents' utilities and modeled them, we go on to present building blocks for solving common problems in distributed computing which are resilient to this rational behavior. Such operations include performing wake-up and knowledge sharing in a variety of network topologies. In a network with n agents, our protocols achieve $(n-1)$-*strong equilibrium* for synchronous networks and $\frac{n}{2}$-*strong equilibrium* for asynchronous networks. Informally, a protocol which achieves k-*strong equilibrium* is a protocol in which no coalition of size at most k can improve its utility by deviating from the protocol. These protocols are in fact building blocks which can be used to construct many other distributed algorithms for rational agents.

Finally, we demonstrate the usefulness of the two building blocks in the construction of new algorithms that achieve strong equilibrium for consensus, renaming, and reconstructing the leader election algorithms of [4].

1.1 Related Work

The work of Abraham, Dolev and Halpern [4] goes back and questions the fundamental problems in distributed computing, under the assumption that processors may behave as rational agents. In their work they have examined, among other things, protocols for various settings of the leader-election problem that not only deal with acquiescent or Byzantine processors but also with the *rational* processors.

It seems that the connection between distributed computing and algorithmic game-theory stemmed from the problem of secret sharing. One such example, where k-out-of-n secret sharing [28] comes in handy, is when participants do not fully trust each other with a secret, yet they would like to reconstruct it using their private parts of the secret, when there is an acceptance of more than k participants. It seems that known solution to the secret sharing problem do not handle the reconstruction phase, that can be modeled as a synchronous network of n processors, where each of them wants to learn the secret and also prefers that as few other processors as possible will learn the secret. This raises an interesting question: is there a protocol with a fixed running time that solves the problem? Halpern and Teague showed [18], among other things, that the problem cannot be solved with a bounded distributed protocol for the solution concept of iterated admissibility (i.e., iterated deletion of weakly dominated strategies). Further works continued the research on secret sharing and multiparty computation when both Byzantine and rational agents are present [2, 8, 13, 16, 23, 17]. At the same time, another line of research has shown applicative and theoretical results for cooperative services for what is known as the BAR model (Byzantine, acquiescent [33] and rational) [5, 26, 33] . Another related line of research asks whether a problem that can be solved with a mediator can be converted to a cheap talk based solution [2, 3, 6, 7, 9, 11, 21, 22, 24, 29, 30, 31]. This approach is very strong because there are many results that are based on a mediator, which other players cannot trust under the rationality assumption, if we can convert mediator based protocols to be based on cheap talk, many of the previous works that do not assume rationality may become relevant under this assumption.

2. MODEL

Our model consists of n processors in a distributed network. Each processor is a rational agent, and thus has *preferences* over the outcome of the protocol. Whenever a processor can increase its *expected utility*, it will deviate from any given protocol, in order to benefit itself. For protocols to be resilient to rational agents, we require them to reach *equilibrium*, such that agents have no incentive to deviate from the protocol. To reach this, we require agents to have a utility function satisfying the *solution preference*, such that agents do not prefer an outcome of the protocol where there is no solution to the problem, over an outcome in which there is a solution.

Following [4] we use the standard message-passing model, where all the processors are *rational agents*. The network is a simple, strongly-connected, finite graph. Each node represents an agent (i.e., a processor), and the edges represent communication links through which pairs of agents exchange messages. Agents may send messages through their outgoing links, and can identify the link an incoming message is received over. Denote n the total number of agents in the network. Each agent is assigned a unique *id* taken from a common name space, assumed to be the set of natural numbers. We assume that the topology of the network and n are common information, thus they are a-priori known to all. Each agent additionally knows its *id* and input, if it received any input as part of the protocol, but not the *id* or input of any other agent.

In this paper, both the synchronous and asynchronous network models are considered. In a synchronous network, agents execute the protocol in rounds. Each round r consists of agents receiving all messages sent on their incoming links in round $r-1$ (if $r>0$), performing any computations and updating internal variables, and sending messages on their outgoing links. In the asynchronous network we assume the standard asynchronous event driven communication model - in which message transmission delay is unbounded but finite [15].

Three fundamental distributed computing problems are considered here; *renaming*, *consensus* and *leader election*.

The *consensus* problem: each agent p start with an input i_p, and its output o_p is initialized to $\perp$. The processors must then agree on the output. That is, the processors communicate, and at the end of the protocol run (after all processors stop, assuming no processor fails) $\forall i \in \{1,..,n\}, o_i \neq \perp$ and: *(1)* **Agreement**: for each processor p, $o_p = v$ for some value v; *(2)* **Validity**: if $\exists j$ s.t. $o_j = v$, then there is some processor k for which $i_k = v$.

The *leader election* problem is the same as the consensus problem where the input of each agent is its *id*.

The *tight renaming* problem: each agent has a unique *id* and needs to choose a unique name from the tight range $1 \ldots n$. Denote o_p to be the agent's output. Each agent p writes its new name in o_p, satisfying the following requirements: *(1)* **Agreement**: No two processors obtain the same new name. $\forall_{x,y}\, o_x \neq o_y$; *(2)* **Validity**: Each new name is an integer in the set $[1 \ldots n]$.

2.1 Game Theoretic Model

Unlike processors in the standard fail-stop or Byzantine models, rational agents are not faulty. Instead, agents have preferences over the outcome of the protocol. If an agent can improve upon its preferences, it will deviate from the protocol (i.e., cheat).

For example, a rational agent p might prefer to send fewer messages in the protocol. In such a case, it might be lazy and not fully participate in the protocol, or otherwise deviate from it in any way in which its expected number of messages sent is as few as possible, so long as it does not cause the protocol to fail.

Formally, each agent p has a utility function u_p on the final states of the protocol. The final state of the protocol encompasses the execution leading to the state as visible by p and the output of the protocol in this final state. The utility function represents how good or profitable the result is, from p's point of view. The higher the utility, the better. An agent can have *any* utility function representing any preference; it can have a preference over the output of the algorithm, the number of messages it has sent, the amount of computation it does, or any other preference or combination of preferences, so long as the algorithm terminates in a legal global state, satisfying the solution preference (definition 2.1, below).

Let c be the state of p in the protocol execution, and let S_p be the set of all possible final states that may be reachable and are consistent with the current state of p, assuming all agents other than p follow the given protocol and the next step of p is op, which may be deviating from the protocol (i.e., cheating). For each final state $s \in S_p$, let x_s be the probability, estimated by p, that s is reached by taking the step op. The *expected* utility of p after taking step op in state c is then:

$$\mathbb{E}_{c,op}[u_p] = \sum_{\forall s \in S_p} x_s \cdot u_p(s)$$

If by deviating from the protocol by taking a step op, p can increase its expected utility, we then say that agent p has an *incentive* to deviate from the protocol (i.e., cheat).

For example, in the consensus problem, an agent p might have a preference over the agreement value, such that it prefers an agreement on 1 over an agreement on 0. Its utility function u_p might look as follows:

$$u_p = \begin{cases} 1 & \text{1 is decided} \\ 0 & \text{0 is decided or no agreement is reached} \end{cases}$$

At every point during the protocol execution, p estimates the probability for each possible outcome of the protocol, according to its knowledge while assuming all other agents follow the given protocol. Let x be the probability, estimated by p, that the protocol outcome results in an agreement on 1, then the expected utility of p is the following:

$$\mathbb{E}[u_p] = x * u_p(1) + (1-x) * u_p(0)$$

Since p is a rational agent, it will deviate from the protocol whenever it can increase its expected utility by any positive value.

To prevent rational agents from deliberately failing the algorithm (i.e., becoming *Byzantine* rational agents), we assume agents have utility functions that penalize the agents if the protocol errs. The *solution preference* guarantees that an agent never has an incentive for the protocol to fail.

DEFINITION 2.1 (SOLUTION PREFERENCE). *Let O be the set of all possible executions of the protocol. Let $o_L \in O$ be a legal execution of the protocol (e.g., producing a legal output), and let $o_E \in O$ be an erroneous execution of the protocol (e.g., producing an illegal output). To satisfy the solution preference, the utility function u_p of an agent p must satisfy the following:*

$$\forall o_L, o_E : u_p(o_L) \geq u_p(o_E)$$

Meaning, the utility function u_p of an agent p never assigns a higher utility to an outcome of the protocol in which there is either no solution or an erroneous solution than to an outcome in which there is a legal global solution.

We say that a protocol is resilient to rational behavior if it reaches *Nash equilibrium*. A protocol that reaches Nash equilibrium is guaranteed to execute correctly in the face of rational agents, with no agent being able to improve its utility by deviating from the protocol.

DEFINITION 2.2 (NASH EQUILIBRIUM PROTOCOL). *A protocol is said to reach Nash equilibrium if no agent can unilaterally increase its expected utility by deviating from it while assuming that all other agents follow the given protocol.*

While Nash equilibrium deals with a single agent deviating from the protocol, sometimes agents are in coalitions, working together to improve their utilities. We define a coalition of size t as a set of t rational agents.

We say that a protocol is resilient in the face of coalitions if it reaches *strong equilibrium*. A protocol that reaches t-strong equilibrium is guaranteed to execute correctly, with no coalition of k agents, where $k \leq t$, being able to improve its utility by deviating from the protocol, even in a coordinated way.

DEFINITION 2.3 (t-STRONG EQUILIBRIUM PROTOCOL). *A protocol reaches t-strong equilibrium if no coalition of size $k \leq t$ can increase the expected utility of one or more agents in the coalition by deviating from the protocol, assuming all agents not in the coalition follow the given protocol.*

In game theory, a game requires three things: players, the players' utilities, and the strategies available for each player. The distributed model with rational agents that we discuss in this paper, fulfills this paradigm in the following manner: 1) The set of players P is the set of all agents (i.e., processors) in the network. 2) Each player $p \in P$ has a utility function u_p, which can be any function that satisfies the solution preference (definition 2.1). 3) The strategy of each player p determines the messages that p sends. Player p can choose to send none, one, or several messages at any point in the protocol, and by that it executes its selected strategy.

2.2 Truthfulness

Consider a consensus protocol which reaches agreement by deciding on the maximum value of all agents. Consider an agent p with the utility function u_p from the consensus example in the previous subsection. Agent p has an incentive to lie about its input: provided it received an input of 0, it benefits by claiming an input of 1, since it raises the probability of 1 to be decided, thus raising its expected utility. In an execution where all agents start with an input of 0, agreement of 1 is reached, and thus the consensus fails since the validity requirement is violated. This shows that, even though each agent satisfies the solution preference, it is not enough in order to solve protocols in the game-theoretic model.

To overcome this, in game theory we design mechanisms that are *truthful*, such that agents do not have an incentive to lie about their input, regardless of any a-priori knowledge they may have of the input or strategies of other players.

However, in distributed protocols, though we assume no a-priori knowledge exists, such a requirement is not enough. Distributed protocols allow agents to deviate by lying about the values of other agents. Thus, even though we might design a truthful mechanism in which an agent does not have an incentive to lie about its input, in a distributed environment it might still have an incentive to lie about the values of other agents.

For example, a well-known mechanism in game theory is second price auction [32]. In it, the players are bidders submitting bids for an item. Each player has a private value v_i which is its value for the item, and submits a bid b_i to the auctioneer. The winner of the item is the player who sent the highest bid, and he pays a value equal to the second-highest bid. Let b_j be the second-highest bid, then the utility of the winner i is defined as $v_i - b_j$. The utility of all other players is 0.

This mechanism is known to be truthful, such that players have no incentive to bid any value other than $b_i = v_i$, even if they know the values and submitted bids of all other players.

However, in a distributed network, not all agents are necessarily directly linked to the auctioneer in the network. Thus, they may need to communicate through other agents in the network. These agents may lie regarding their input. An agent p, separating some bidders from the auctioneer, has a clear incentive to send $b_i = 0$ for each agent i sending its bid in the network through p, thus increasing p's chances of winning the item, and possibly also decreasing the amount paid for it. This is true even if p is truthful with regard to its own input, having no incentive to send a bid other than its true value for the item, i.e., $b_p = v_p$.

Following this example, we can clearly see that the existing definition of a truthful mechanism is not enough. For distributed protocol to be truthful, we require agents to have no incentive to lie regarding not only their input, but also the input of other agents.

DEFINITION 2.4 (TRUTHFUL PROTOCOL). *A protocol is said to be* truthful *if no agent participating in the protocol has incentive to lie about its input, or any other data it shares as part of the protocol. Meaning, an agent's utility for an outcome achieved by lying is no greater than its utility achieved by telling the truth.*

3. AGENTS WAKE-UP

In many distributed computing protocols, we assume that all agents start the protocol at the same time. However, this is usually not the case. Usually, processors are either woken up spontaneously at arbitrary points of time by the scheduler, or when receiving the first message over one of their input links.

The *agents wake-up* building block deals with waking up all agents. The building block can be executed as the first phase of any protocol, thus ensuring all agents are awake and start together.

A protocol for the building block starts by having agents wake-up at arbitrary points of time by the scheduler. The agents need to communicate so that, at the end of the protocol, all agents are awake. The protocol makes sure that, upon termination, agents also know the *id*s of all other agents. In addition, the protocol needs to succeed in the face of rational agents—the building block reaches t-strong equilibrium for $t < n$.

A wake-up procedure was included within each of the leader election protocols presented in [4]. However, it does not reach Nash equilibrium. The protocol fails in the presence of lazy rational agents, that prefer sending fewer messages, in the following way:

Consider a wake-up procedure that requires agents to send and forward messages around the ring, where only messages of the agent with the highest *id* are forwarded. Consider an agent p with a preference for sending fewer messages having, for example, the following utility function, where m_p denotes the number of messages p sends:

$$u_p = \begin{cases} 1 - \frac{m_p}{n} & \text{wake-up is successful} \\ 0 & \text{wake-up is unsuccessful} \end{cases}$$

In the procedure, each agent sends no more than n messages, thus u_p satisfies the solution preference (definition 2.1).

When p wakes up, it prefers not to send any wake-up message. It relies on another agent to wake up the others, doing the work for it—thus raising p's expected utility. In addition, if p is the only agent to wake-up spontaneously, no solution will be reached and the protocol will fail.

Even though it is possible that no solution will be reached, the utility u_p satisfies the solution preference (definition 2.1). This is because only the *expected* utility of p is raised, so p will "take the chance" of failing the protocol, given the positive probability that it will not fail and p will benefit.

The wake-up protocol must be resilient to the utility function discussed in the above example, and to any other utility function satisfying the solution preference (definition 2.1).

Another possible preference an agent might have is a preference over properties of its *id*. While the building block itself is oblivious to the agents' *id*s, it might be used by a protocol that is not.

For example, consider a leader election protocol that is run over the wake-up building block, where the agent with the highest *id* is elected leader. If we execute the protocol, an agent might have an incentive to lie about its *id*. Consider an agent p with the following utility function:

$$u_p = \begin{cases} 1 & p \text{ is elected leader} \\ 0 & p \text{ is } \textbf{not} \text{ elected leader, or no leader is elected} \end{cases}$$

Agent p will deviate from the building block by lying about its *id*. It prefers to send messages and pretend to have the highest *id*. While it is possible that another agent will have the same *id* that p lied about, according to u_p it still raises its expected utility by raising its chances to be elected leader.

Following this example, for the building block we assume that the protocols built on top of the wake-up building block are oblivious to the agents' *id*s. Indeed, in [4], a leader election protocol is suggested which elects the leader by choosing a random *id*. This ensures that an agent's specific *id* has no affect on the outcome of the protocol (the elected leader), and thus it can be preceded by the wake-up building block proposed here.

With these possible utilities in mind, we present protocols for the wake-up building block. In a synchronous network, all agents complete the protocol in the same round. The protocols reach t-strong equilibrium for $t < n$, for n rational agents with any utility function that satisfies the solution preference (definition 2.1).

The idea behind our procedure in order to achieve these properties, and prevent an agent from not sending wake-up messages when it should, is to require *all* agents to send wake-up messages. An agent does not finish the protocol before receiving wake-up messages from all other agents. Thus, an agent that does not send a wake-up message causes the protocol to fail, in contradiction to the solution preference (definition 2.1). A detailed description of the protocols and full proofs are provided in the full paper.

3.1 Ring Wake-Up Protocol

The protocol for wake-up in a ring is as follows: upon waking up, each agent sends a wake-up message that goes around the ring. An agents finishes the protocol when it has received a wake-up message from all other agents.

The wake-up message contains both the *id* of the originator of the message, and a hop counter k—initialized to $n-1$ by the originator, and decremented by each successor. This counter k represents the distance from the current recipient to the originator, in the direction of the message.

For a bidirectional un-oriented ring, each agent arbitrarily decides on a direction for its wake-up message. When agents receive messages on one link, they forward it on the other link. When finished, the ring orientation can be decided according to the direction chosen by the highest *id*. Thus, for a bidirectional ring, we further assume that the direction of the messages is irrelevant, and no agent has a preference on the direction (i.e., clockwise or counterclockwise).

3.2 Complete Network Wake-Up Protocol

The protocol in a complete network is as follows: upon waking up, each agent sends a wake-up message containing its *id* to all agents. An agent finishes the protocol when it has received a wake-up message from all other agents, and has sent wake-up messages to all other agents.

3.3 General Network Wake-Up Protocol

The protocol for a general network is as follows: upon waking up, each agent broadcasts a message containing its *id* through the network. An agent finishes the protocol when it has received a wake-up message from all other agents, i.e., n wake-up messages, as n is known a-priori.

In a synchronous network, this protocol is not enough. Since this is usually a preliminary building block, we require agents to finish the protocol in the same round, i.e., start together the next step of the protocol using this building block. To this end, a hop counter k is attached to each broadcast message, initialized to 0 and incremented in each hop. When a wake-up message is received by an agent, it can determine from the hop counter the round in which the originator of the wake-up started broadcasting. Once an agent receives all n wake-up messages, it can tell the earliest round at which an agent woke up. To end in the same round, an agent terminates $2n$ rounds after that first round.

Unlike the previous wake-up protocols, the protocol for a general network has an additional requirement.

CLAIM 1. *To reach t-strong equilibrium for $t < n$, the underlying topology must be at least $(t+1)$-connected.*

Sketch of proof: Assume by contradiction that the network is not $(t+1)$-connected, then a coalition of t agents might separate two parts of the network. Such a coalition can be lazy and decide not to wake up one of the separated parts, instead making up *ids* for that part and sending it to the rest of the network, essentially faking the participation of agents in that part of the network, thus saving itself from sending some messages. The protocol thus does not reach equilibrium. That is a contradiction, thus the network must be at least $(t+1)$-connected.

4. KNOWLEDGE SHARING

In many distributed algorithms, each process needs to know the private values of all other processes in order to perform the desired computation. The *knowledge sharing* building block deals with sharing the private values among all agents.

Facing rational agents poses a problem that an agent, once it knows all other values, might lie about its own value to increase its utility. Thus, the presented protocols for the building block make sure that each agent commits to its own value before learning the values of all other agents.

Each agent p starts with a value v_p, and needs to learn the values of all other agents $V = \{v_1, \dots, v_n\}$. For this building block, we assume agents know the *id*s of all other agents. If not, we can simply precede it with the agents wake-up building block.

A solution for knowledge sharing seems trivial: each agent broadcasts its value to all other agents. Once an agent receives the values V of all other agents, it terminates. However, this solution does not reach equilibrium. An agent can easily cheat regarding its value in order to increase its utility.

For example, consider a leader election protocol executed using this building block, where the leader is elected in the following way: Each agent's value is a random number, and the sum of all numbers *mod n* is the rank of the *id* elected leader. If we execute the protocol in the game-theoretic model, an agent might have an incentive to lie about its value.

Consider an agent p with the following utility function:

$$u_p = \begin{cases} 1 & p \text{ is elected leader} \\ 0 & p \text{ is \textbf{not} elected leader, or no leader is elected} \end{cases}$$

Agent p might prefer to delay its participation in the protocol, so that it knows the values of all other agents. Once p knows all values V, it can then lie about its own value v_p—ensuring that it is elected as a leader.

Adapting the same techniques used in [4] to overcome this issue, we ensure that no agent learns the values of other agents before sending its own value. In addition, when facing coalitions, the protocols make sure that agents outside the coalition learn the values of all agents in the coalition before agents in the coalition learn the values of all other agents.

No matter how protocols for the building block are built, if it is used by a protocol that is not truthful (definition 2.4), an agent can have an incentive to lie about its value, regardless of the knowledge sharing protocol.

For example, consider a consensus protocol built on top of this building block, that decides on the maximum value of all agents. If we execute the protocol in the game-theoretic model, an agent might have an incentive to lie about its value. Consider an agent p with value $v_p \in \{0,1\}$, with the following utility:

$$u_p = \begin{cases} 1-d & \text{the consensus decision is } d \\ 0 & \text{no consensus is reached} \end{cases}$$

In an execution where $v_p = 1$, agent p prefers broadcasting $v_p = 0$. In case p is the only agent with an input of 1, the protocol decides 0 instead of 1 and p benefits. Otherwise, the decision remains the same and p does not benefit, but does not lose, either. Therefore, p raises its expected utility by deviating from the protocol, and thus it does not reach equilibrium.

In addition, consider an execution where all agents have the utility u_p, but all received 1 as input—the agents all broadcast the value 0, which is decided. It was not the input of any agent, and thus the validity requirement is violated.

This shows that, while the knowledge sharing building block does not violate truthfulness, it is dependent upon the *full knowledge property* of the protocols that use it. Therefore, according to 4.1, any protocol that uses the knowledge sharing building block must make sure that it satisfies the full knowledge property for the entire algorithm to be truthful.

DEFINITION 4.1 (FULL KNOWLEDGE PROPERTY). *For each agent that does not know the values of all other agents $V = \{v_1, \dots, v_n\}$, any output of the protocol is still equally possible.*

For example, even though the previous example shows that the consensus protocol fails with this building block, it is possible to achieve agreement with this building block. The consensus protocol shown in that example does not satisfy 4.1, since an agent can lie about its value in order to affect the outcome of the protocol, without knowing the values of other agents, thus raising its expected utility. In 5.3, however, we show a protocol that reaches agreement while satisfying 4.1, thus using the knowledge sharing building block properly.

With these utilities in mind, we present protocols for the knowledge sharing building block. The building block assumes the following: each agent p starts with a value v_p, agents know the *ids* of all other agents, and, in synchronous networks, all agents start the protocol together.

The protocols reach t-strong equilibrium, where $t < n$ for synchronous networks and $t < \frac{n}{2}$ for asynchronous networks, for n rational agents with any preference that satisfies the solution preference (definition 2.1), and any value that satisfies the full knowledge property (definition 4.1). In a synchronous network, all agents complete the protocol in the same round. A detailed description of the protocols and full proofs are provided in the full paper.

4.1 Knowledge Sharing in a Synchronous Ring Network

In round 1, each agent p sends a message with its value v_p. These messages are passed around the ring by all the agents, until each message returns to its originator. At this point, all the agents have received all of the data. If an agent p does not receive a single message from its predecessor each round, or receives a duplicate message it received before, it sets $o_p = \bot$, thus ensuring the correct participation of all due to the solution preference (definition 2.1). The message complexity of the protocol is n^2, and the time complexity is n rounds.

4.2 Knowledge Sharing in a Synchronous Complete Network

The protocol consists of a single round, in which each agent sends its value to all other agents, and receives the values of all other agents. If an agent p does not receive messages from all agents, it sets $o_p = \bot$, thus ensuring the correct participation of all due to the solution preference (definition 2.1). The message complexity of the protocol is n^2, and the time complexity is 1 round.

4.3 Knowledge Sharing in an Asynchronous Ring Network

The synchronous ring solution does not work in an asynchronous ring. Agents can not determine when to send and forward messages, and we can reach a state in which an agent might learn the values of all other agents before sending its own value to its successor. The agent might then have an incentive to lie about its value, as described in the leader election example, above.

To solve this issue, we propose a protocol similar to the one suggested in [4] for leader election in an asynchronous ring. We have the agent p with the lowest *id* be the *originator*, which starts the protocol by sending its value to its successor. Its successor then sends a message with its own value to its own successor, and so forth.

Messages are passed around the entire ring in the same manner. When the originator receives a message from its predecessor, this is an indication that the first cycle, in which each agent learned the value of its predecessor, has completed and the initiator begins the second round of messages by sending the value of its predecessor to its successor. Messages are passed around the entire ring again, in the same manner, where each agent sends the data of its predecessor. From cycles 2 to $n-1$, each agent sends the value it has received in the previous cycle, s.t., in round v agent u sends the input value of agent $u-v+1 \mod n$. It is easy to see that the message and time complexity of the protocol is $n(n-1)$.

4.4 Knowledge Sharing in an Asynchronous Complete Network

For an asynchronous complete network, we can use the protocol presented in 4.3 for knowledge sharing in an asynchronous ring by embedding a unidirectional ring in the network. We embed the ring by sorting the *id*s of all agents from lowest to highest. Each agent's successor is the agent with the *id* following its own on the list. The successor of the agent with the highest *id* is the agent with the lowest *id*, thus forming a ring.

However, the added connectivity of a complete network hurts the coalition resiliency of the protocol in 4.3. While a coalition of size $t < \frac{n}{2}$ still must commit to its data before learning the data of all other agents, it can still break the protocol in 4.3.

Since the network is completely connected, any two agents in the network can communicate directly with each other, even if they are not neighbors in the embedded ring. Splitting the ring into two (or more) parts, agents in a coalition can share information and thus lie to the split parts of the ring regarding the input of the other part. This way, the coalition can make sure that the protocol succeeds (all agents have a valid output); however, the coalition has control over the outputs and can therefore alter the input messages sent in order to reach an output they prefer.

To prevent this, we use the added connectivity to our benefit. Upon finishing the protocol in 4.3, each agent sends its value to all other agents. This prevents agents from being able to lie regarding the values of other agents, thus making agents are truthful regarding the values that they send.

4.5 Knowledge Sharing in a Synchronous General Network

For a synchronous general network, we use a similar protocol to 3.3 for wake-up in a general network. Each agent p broadcasts its value v_p through the network. Once p receives the values of all other agents, it terminates.

If an agent p receives contradicting messages, or does not receive all values after n rounds, it sets $o_p = \bot$ and terminates, thus ensuring the correct participation of all due to the solution preference (definition 2.1).

As in the wake-up protocol in 3.3, the knowledge sharing protocol for a synchronous general network has an additional requirement:

CLAIM 2. *To reach t-strong equilibrium for $t < n$, the underlying topology must be at least $(t+1)$-connected.*

Sketch of proof: Assume by contradiction that the network is not $(t+1)$-connected, then there is a group of no more than t agents that split the graph. Assume that these agents form a coalition. Then, for any knowledge sharing protocol, the agents can cheat by lying on the input values of agents connected in the network only through the coalition.

The message complexity of the protocol is n^2, and the time complexity is n rounds.

5. USING THE BUILDING BLOCKS

Here we demonstrate the building blocks approach [14] by presenting Leader election, Renaming and Consensus algorithms that are truthful and reach Nash equilibrium building on the agents wake-up and knowledge sharing building blocks.

The protocol for leader election mostly borrows the ideas presented in [4]. However, it demonstrates how to adjust a problem to meet the requirements of the building blocks. In the protocols for renaming and consensus, we demonstrate how to use the building blocks further, for more complicated problems with less trivial solutions.

5.1 Leader Election

Here is a building blocks construction of the leader election algorithm of [4]:

PROTOCOL 5.1 (GAME-THEORETIC LEADER ELECTION). *For each agent p:*

(1) Initiate the wake-up building block.

(2) Let $v_p = random(1, \ldots, n)$.

(3) Knowledge sharing to learn $V = \{v_1, \dots, v_n\}$.

(4) For any k, if $(v_k < 1)$ or $(v_k > n)$, set $o_p = \perp$ and terminate.

(5) Calculate $(N = \sum_{k=1}^{n} v_k \mod n)$, and output: $o_p \leftarrow$ (the N-th rank id).

It is easy to see that protocol 5.1 follows the requirements of our building blocks, and correctly elects a leader while reaching equilibrium.

5.2 Renaming

Having a solution to the leader election problem that reaches equilibrium under the game-theoretic model, there seems to be a naive renaming protocol: execute leader election, then the leader randomizes the new names and sends them to all agents. However, this naive protocol does not reach equilibrium; the leader might have a preference for a certain assignment of names, and can assign them as it sees fit.

With that in mind, another possible protocol is to execute the leader election protocol n times. Each execution, the leader is given a name from $[1 \dots n]$, in order, and removed from the list of possible leaders for the next execution. While this protocol solves the problem, it has a very high message and time complexities. In addition, perhaps requirement 2.1 is too strong? We can think of a case where an agent cares only about certain names (or a single name), and not the entire solution.

For example, consider an agent p with the following utility:

$$u_p = \begin{cases} 1 - \frac{m_p}{n^2} & p \text{ knows its new name and sent } m_p \text{ messages} \\ 0 & p \text{ does not know its new name} \end{cases}$$

While u_p does not satisfy the solution preference (definition 2.1), it is still a reasonable utility to consider. Thus, once the agents have chosen a new name for p, it will stop sending messages and no longer participate in the protocol, thus raising its utility. Thus, the protocol does not reach equilibrium. In addition, the protocol fails and chooses no new names after the new name of p.

To solve this issue, we propose a protocol for one-shot renaming—where either all new names are chosen, or none is. With one-shot renaming, an agent can learn its new name only if all new names are assigned to all agents. Thus, the protocol reaches equilibrium, even when facing an agent with the preference presented in the above example.

The protocol is similar to the protocol presented in 5.1. However, instead of randomizing a single number, each agent randomizes n numbers, essentially running n leader elections simultaneously. The agents then share all n^2 numbers, and assign new names accordingly. The protocol works as follows:

PROTOCOL 5.2 (GAME-THEORETIC RENAMING). *For each agent p:*

(1) Initiate the wake-up building block.

(2) Choose a set of n random numbers as value:
$\forall k \in \{1, \dots, n\} : v_p[k] \leftarrow random(1, \dots, k)$.

(3) Knowledge sharing to learn $V = \{v_1, \dots, v_n\}$.

(4) For any k, j, if $(v_k[j] < 1)$ or $(v_k[j] > j)$, set $o_p = \perp$ and terminate.

(5) Calculate the set of sums:
$\forall j \in \{1, \dots, n\} : N_j = \sum_{k=1}^{n} v_k[j] \pmod j$.
The agent with the N_n^{th} highest id is assigned the new name n, and then removed from the list of ids, thus it is ignored in the following iterations. The agent with the N_{n-1}^{th} highest id is then assigned the new name $(n-1)$ and removed from the list of ids, and so on.

(6) Set o_p to p's new name as calculated in the previous step.

This randomization makes sure that each name chosen is random, thus satisfying the full knowledge property (definition 4.1). Again, it is easy to see that it satisfies all of the requirements for the building blocks, and assigns new names while reaching equilibrium.

5.3 Consensus

In [4], it is implied that the consensus problem can be solved in the presence of rational agents by electing a leader, and having the leader choose the consensus value as its input. However, this algorithm does not reach equilibrium, and may not uphold the validity requirement even if only one rational agent is present. The elected leader may have a preference over the agreement value, and thus has an incentive to lie about its input. It takes the chance of reaching no agreement, but its expected utility is raised overall, thus it benefits.

We can execute the building blocks, where the value for knowledge sharing is each agent's input to the consensus problem. However, how we calculate the decided value after the knowledge sharing is critical.

For example, agreeing on the maximum value of all agents does not work in the presence of ration agents, and does not reach equilibrium. An agent p with a preference for agreement on 1 has a clear incentive to share a value $v_p = 1$, even if its input to consensus was 0. Thus, we propose the following protocol for truthful consensus:

PROTOCOL 5.3 (GAME-THEORETIC CONSENSUS). *For each agent p:*

(1) Initiate the wake-up building block.

(2) Knowledge sharing to learn $V = \{v_1, \dots, v_n\}$.

(3) For any k, if $v_k \notin \{0, 1\}$, set $o_p = \perp$ and terminate.

(4) If the total number of 1's is odd or equals n, set $o_p = 1$, else set $o_p = 0$.

First, it is clear that without rational agents, the protocol solves consensus. In addition, since deciding according to the parity of all of the values, agents can not affect the outcome. An agent might learn the values of all agents but 1, and still has no incentive to lie about its value, as it can not determine what influence it will have on the decision, thus it satisfies the full knowledge property (definition 4.1).

When the number of agents n is odd, the protocol is truthful (definition 2.4), since no agent can benefit by lying about its input. However, when n is even, it is not satisfied. If, for example, a coalition of $(n-1)$ agents have a preference to agree on 1, each agent p in the coalition can lie such that $v_p = 1$. In such a case, the agreement will be 1, regardless of the remaining agent's input, and thus we do not reach equilibrium, and do not satisfy the validity requirement in the case that the input of all agents is 0. To handle it, for networks where n is even, each agent's input for the knowledge sharing also includes a random number, as in the leader election protocol 5.1, thereby electing a leader at the same time. The input of the leader is then considered *twice* in the computation, thus making the protocol truthful for even size networks as well.

The protocol satisfies all of the requirements for the building blocks, and reaches agreement while reaching equilibrium.

6. EXTENSIONS AND TRADEOFFS

6.1 Improving the Message Complexity of Knowledge Sharing

In most of the protocols presented in this work, our main aim was to obtain algorithms which would be most resilient to coalitions, even at the cost of increased message or time complexity. To illustrate the tradeoff between the two approaches, we present an alternative knowledge sharing protocol for a synchronous bi-directional ring network. The protocol significantly improves the message complexity, at the cost of reduced coalition resiliency.

The protocol *KSP* works as follows: We have the agent p with the lowest *id* (after the wake-up) be the *originator*, which starts the protocol by sending a message containing its value $\langle v_p \rangle$ both to its right and to its left neighbors, i.e., both clockwise and counter-clockwise accordingly. Each agent q that receives a message concatenates its own value to the message such that the message is now $\langle v_p; v_q \rangle$ and sends it to its neighbor in the direction in which the message was travelling, i.e., clockwise or counter-clockwise. Each message is sent one time completely around the ring until it gets back to the initiator. This ensures that all agents receive all data. However, messages are sent on both sides of the ring, thus agents send their value before receiving the values of all other agents and, due to the full knowledge property (definition 4.1), are guaranteed to be truthful.

If the number n of agents in the network is odd, the protocol works as-is. If n is even, the initiator sends the message to the right in round 1, and to the left in round 2. This is needed to prevent the possibility of some agent receiving both messages at the same round which could allow that agent to modify the values in the message in order to increase its utility.

The message complexity of the algorithm is $O(n)$ rather than $O(n^2)$ of the protocol presented in 4.1. The protocol is, however, a lot less resilient to coalitions, as it can not withstand even a coalition of 2 agents.

Furthermore, in some cases the bit-complexity of the above algorithm can be further reduced. One such example is a protocol for solving binary consensus. Our binary consensus protocol is based on parity and can therefore be computed in an *on-the-fly* manner using the following protocol: Two messages are initiated by the agent with the lowest *id*, as described in the *KSP* protocol, but now the messages contain 2 bits b_1 and b_2. Bit b_1 is used to indicate whether all inputs so far have only been 1 and is initialized to 1. Bit b_2 is initialized according to the value v_p of the initiator, meaning, if $v_p = 0$, b_2 is initialized to 0 otherwise b_2 is initialized to 1. Each agent q that receives a message does the following: if v_q equals 0, set $b_1 = 0$, otherwise, switch the value of b_2, that is, set $b_2 = !b_2$. Continue to send the message as described above. Once each agent has received both a message from the left and a message from the right, it can compute the output of the consensus based on those 2 messages alone.

6.2 Fail-Stop Model

We extend our model to a *fail-stop* model with rational agents, where an agent can fail by stopping (i.e., crashing) at any point in the protocol. From that point on it does not participate in the protocol—the agent can not send messages or perform computations, and any messages sent to it are discarded. A protocol is said to be *k-fault-tolerant* if it can withstand up to k faulty agents, and still produce a correct output for each of the non-faulty agents.

This model poses new challenges for solving problems in our game theoretic model. In previous protocols, when an agent does not participate, we "punish" it by failing the algorithm. Thus, we ensure its correct participation, due to the solution preference (definition 2.1). However, in the presence of faulty agents, such a solution will not work. An agent can fail-stop, stopping its participation and preventing the protocol from reaching a solution to the problem. Thus, our previous protocols are not even 1-fault-tolerant.

A possible solution might be to proceed with the protocol, regardless of which agents participate. However, this solution is clearly not in equilibrium. For example, an agent preferring to send fewer messages benefits by not participating. Thus, the agent pretends to fail-stop and we do not (and can not) "punish" it. The protocol thus does not reach equilibrium and, if all agents have that utility, none participate and no solution is reached.

For this reason, in the fail-stop model we require agents to have a *knowledge preference*. The knowledge preference makes sure that agents not only prefer the protocol not to fail, but additionally prefer to know at least part of the protocol's output.

DEFINITION 6.1 (KNOWLEDGE PREFERENCE). *Each agent p prefers knowing some output of the problem (o_q for some agent q) to not knowing any of the output, in the weak sense that it never assigns a higher utility to an outcome where it does not know o_q (for all q) to one in which it knows o_q (for some q).*

However, we are now faced with another problem. An agent can "bail-out" of the knowledge sharing building block. According to the protocol presented in 4.2, it will receive all data in the first round, and thus know the output while saving itself the messages it sends to other agents, thus raising its expected utility. Thus, we also require the input i_p of an agent p in the knowledge sharing building block to be determined randomly, such that we can choose to restart the protocol, and the input will be different. What this means is, we can only execute our protocol for the fail-stop model to solve problems in which the input for the knowledge sharing building block is random. This means that consensus, for example, can not be solved by this protocol, but leader election and renaming can.

The protocols for the agents wake-up and knowledge sharing building blocks are similar to those presented in 3.2 and 4.2, for a synchronous complete network. However, whenever an agent p stops sending messages when it is expected to, we "restart" the protocol without it—executing the agents wake-up or knowledge sharing building block again from the beginning, as if p is not part of the network. Whenever we restart the protocol, all inputs are randomized, as described above. Thus, an agent p not participating in the protocol does not know any output of the protocol, thus ensuring its correct participation due to the knowledge preference (definition 6.1). After at most k restarts, we are guaranteed to have an execution where no processor fail-stopped, and thus the protocol is k-fault-resilient for $k < n$.

While the fail-stop protocol reaches Nash equilibrium, it does not reach even 2-strong equilibrium. Any coalition can benefit by having some of its agents stop sending messages, while others continue to participate in the protocol. When the protocol is finished, the participating agents can send the results to the non-participating agents, thus satisfying the knowledge preference. Thus, it is not possible to reach k-strong equilibrium for $k \geq 2$.

It is worth noting that, while the protocol does not reach k-strong equilibrium for $k \geq 2$, coalitions will not harm the result of the protocol. Even when facing coalitions, the protocol still outputs a legal result.

6.3 Anonymous Networks

Sometimes, distributed computing problems need to be solved in anonymous networks—where agents have no *id*s.

While our protocols use the *id*s of the agents in the wake-up and output computation protocols, this is actually not always necessary. In synchronous networks, for problems which don't require *id*s or distinction among agents (such as the *consensus* problem), we can use the paradigm in an anonymous network.

The protocols are mostly the same for both ring and complete network. The only difference is that any messages with *id*s are sent without *id*s, and the *id* part of the message is ignored.

This allows both the wake-up and the knowledge sharing protocols to execute in much the same way, and then the output computation protocol is executed on the data of the agents $(d_1, \ldots, d_n)$ alone, without the *id*s.

7. CONCLUSIONS AND FUTURE WORK

In this paper, we presented building blocks that are useful for many common distributed problems. Additionally, we presented a refined game-theoretic model for a distributed network. Our building blocks are built with this model in mind, such that the protocols for these building blocks are all resilient in the face of rational agents, and coalitions of rational agents to some extent.

One natural question that arises is how this model can be applied to dealing with general graphs in an asynchronous network. General graphs pose some interesting challenges in the presence of rational agents, especially if some agent or group of agents can disconnect parts of the network. In 3.3 we proposed a protocol for solving *wake-up* in general graphs, and in 4.5 we proposed a protocol for solving *knowledge sharing* in general graphs in synchronous networks. We leave open the question of how the other building blocks and algorithms presented in this paper can be adapted to work in an asynchronous general graph network.

An additional network model which would be of interest is anonymous networks. In 6.3 we give some initial thoughts on solving the *wake-up* and *consensus* problems in these types of networks and it would be interesting to see how these can be improved.

We are currently exploring the problem of finding a *minimum spanning tree* in networks with rational agents, and what might be the natural preferences of rational agents in this problem setting. Other fundamental problems of distributed computing might be of interest, finding the natural preferences for each problem and developing new protocols, which are resilient to rational agents, for these known problems.

Additionally, we are looking into devising algorithms for the *fail-stop* model (left as an open question in [4]) which are resilient to both the presence of rational agents and faulty agents which can fail by stopping. An initial analysis of this model can be found in 6.2. Another model of interest is that of *Byzantine* rational agents (also left as an open question in [4]) in which an agent has a preference on the outcome, but does not satisfy the solution preference and prefers to fail the protocol if it does not benefit otherwise.

Acknowledgments

We are grateful to Michal Feldman for helpful discussions and for her enlightening course on Algorithmic Game Theory which has inspired this research, and to Eyal Itkin and the PODC reviewers of this paper for their helpful comments.

8. REFERENCES

[1] I. Abraham, L. Alvisi, and J. Y. Halpern. Distributed computing meets game theory: combining insights from two fields. *SIGACT News*, 42(2):69–76, 2011.

[2] I. Abraham, D. Dolev, R. Gonen, and J. Y. Halpern. Distributed computing meets game theory: robust mechanisms for rational secret sharing and multiparty computation. In *PODC*, pages 53–62, 2006.

[3] I. Abraham, D. Dolev, and J. Y. Halpern. Lower bounds on implementing robust and resilient mediators. In *TCC*, pages 302–319, 2008.

[4] I. Abraham, D. Dolev, and J. Y. Halpern. Distributed protocols for leader election: A game-theoretic perspective. In *DISC*, pages 61–75, 2013.

[5] A. S. Aiyer, L. Alvisi, A. Clement, M. Dahlin, J.-P. Martin, and C. Porth. Bar fault tolerance for cooperative services. In *SOSP*, pages 45–58, 2005.

[6] I. Bárány. Fair distribution protocols or how the players replace fortune. *Math. Oper. Res.*, 17(2):327–340, May 1992.

[7] E. Ben-Porath. Cheap talk in games with incomplete information. *J. Economic Theory*, 108(1):45–71, 2003.

[8] V. Dani, M. Movahedi, Y. Rodriguez, and J. Saia. Scalable rational secret sharing. In *PODC*, pages 187–196, 2011.

[9] Y. Dodis, S. Halevi, and T. Rabin. A cryptographic solution to a game theoretic problem. In *CRYPTO*, pages 112–130, 2000.

[10] M. J. Fischer, N. A. Lynch, and M. Paterson. Impossibility of distributed consensus with one faulty process. *J. ACM*, 32(2):374–382, 1985.

[11] F. Forges. Universal mechanisms. *Econometrica*, 58(6):1341–64, November 1990.

[12] G. N. Frederickson and N. A. Lynch. Electing a leader in a synchronous ring. *J. ACM*, 34(1):98–115, 1987.

[13] G. Fuchsbauer, J. Katz, and D. Naccache. Efficient rational secret sharing in standard communication networks. In *TCC*, pages 419–436, 2010.

[14] E. Gafni. Perspectives on distributed network protocols: A case for building blocks. 1:1.1.1–1.1.5, Oct 1986.

[15] R. G. Gallager, P. A. Humblet, and P. M. Spira. A distributed algorithm for minimum-weight spanning trees. *ACM Trans. Program. Lang. Syst.*, 5(1):66–77, 1983.

[16] S. D. Gordon and J. Katz. Rational secret sharing, revisited. In *SCN*, pages 229–241, 2006.

[17] A. Groce, J. Katz, A. Thiruvengadam, and V. Zikas. Byzantine agreement with a rational adversary. In *ICALP (2)*, pages 561–572, 2012.

[18] J. Y. Halpern and V. Teague. Rational secret sharing and multiparty computation: extended abstract. In *STOC*, pages 623–632, 2004.

[19] Y. Heller. Minority-proof cheap-talk protocol. *Games and Economic Behavior*, 69(2):394–400, 2010.

[20] J. Hendler and D. Subramanian, editors. *Proceedings of the Sixteenth National Conference on Artificial Intelligence and Eleventh Conference on Innovative Applications of Artificial Intelligence, July 18-22, 1999, Orlando, Florida, USA.* AAAI Press / The MIT Press, 1999.

[21] S. Izmalkov, M. Lepinski, and S. Micali. Perfect implementation. *Games and Economic Behavior*, 71(1):121–140, 2011.

[22] M. Lepinski, S. Micali, C. Peikert, and A. Shelat. Completely fair sfe and coalition-safe cheap talk. In *PODC*, pages 1–10, 2004.

[23] A. Lysyanskaya and N. Triandopoulos. Rationality and adversarial behavior in multi-party computation. In *CRYPTO*, pages 180–197, 2006.

[24] R. McGrew, R. Porter, and Y. Shoham. Towards a general theory of non-cooperative computation. In *TARK*, pages 59–71, 2003.

[25] D. Monderer and M. Tennenholtz. Distributed games: From mechanisms to protocols. In *AAAI/IAAI*, pages 32–37, 1999.

[26] T. Moscibroda, S. Schmid, and R. Wattenhofer. When selfish meets evil: byzantine players in a virus inoculation game. In *PODC*, pages 35–44, 2006.

[27] S. A. Plotkin. Sticky bits and universality of consensus. In P. Rudnicki, editor, *PODC*, pages 159–175. ACM, 1989.

[28] A. Shamir. How to share a secret. *Commun. ACM*, 22(11):612–613, 1979.

[29] Y. Shoham and M. Tennenholtz. Non-cooperative computation: Boolean functions with correctness and exclusivity. *Theoretical Computer Science*, 343(1âĂŞ2):97 – 113, 2005.

[30] A. Urbano and J. E. Vila. Computational complexity and communication: Coordination in two-player games. *Econometrica*, 70(5):1893–1927, September 2002.

[31] A. Urbano and J. E. Vila. Computationally restricted unmediated talk under incomplete information. *Economic theory*, 2004.

[32] W. Vickrey. Counterspeculation, auctions and competitve sealed tenders. pages 8–37, 1961.

[33] E. L. Wong, I. Levy, L. Alvisi, A. Clement, and M. Dahlin. Regret freedom isn't free. In *OPODIS*, pages 80–95, 2011.

Near-Optimal Communication-Time Tradeoff in Fault-Tolerant Computation of Aggregate Functions

Yuda Zhao
National University of Singapore
Republic of Singapore
yuda@comp.nus.edu.sg

Haifeng Yu
National University of Singapore
Republic of Singapore
haifeng@comp.nus.edu.sg

Binbin Chen
Advanced Digital Sciences Center
Republic of Singapore
binbin.chen@adsc.com.sg

ABSTRACT

This paper considers the problem of computing general *commutative and associative aggregate functions* (such as SUM) over distributed inputs held by nodes in a distributed system, while tolerating failures. Specifically, there are N nodes in the system, and the topology among them is modeled as a general undirected graph. Whenever a node sends a message, the message is received by all of its neighbors in the graph. Each node has an input, and the goal is for a special *root* node (e.g., the base station in wireless sensor networks or the gateway node in wireless ad hoc networks) to learn a certain commutative and associate aggregate of all these inputs. All nodes in the system except the root node may experience crash failures, with the total number of edges incidental to failed nodes being upper bounded by f. The timing model is synchronous where protocols proceed in rounds. Within such a context, we focus on the following question:

Under any given constraint on time complexity, what is the lowest communication complexity, in terms of the number of bits sent (i.e., locally broadcast) by each node, needed for computing general commutative and associate aggregate functions?

This work, for the first time, reduces the gap between the upper bound and the lower bound for the above question from *polynomial* to *polylog*. To achieve this reduction, we present significant improvements over both the existing upper bounds and the existing lower bounds on the problem.

Categories and Subject Descriptors

F.1.3 [**Computation by Abstract Devices**]: Complexity Measures and Classes; F.2.2 [**Analysis of Algorithms and Problem Complexity**]: Nonnumerical Algorithms and Problems

Keywords

Communication complexity, time complexity, communication-time tradeoff, fault tolerance, aggregate functions

PODC'14, July 15–18, 2014, Paris, France.

ACM 978-1-4503-2944-6/14/07 ...$15.00.
http://dx.doi.org/10.1145/2611462.2611475.

1. INTRODUCTION

The problem of fault-tolerant aggregation. In recent years, there has been a line of research (e.g., [1, 4–6, 8, 9, 13, 14, 16, 17]) on computing aggregates over distributed inputs held by nodes in a distributed system. This paper focuses on the following specific fault-tolerant version of the problem (formally defined in Section 2): There are N nodes in the system, and the topology among them is modeled as a general undirected graph. Whenever a node sends a message, the message is received by all of its neighbors in the graph. (In other words, each "send" is a local broadcast.) Each node has a non-negative integer input that is no larger than some polynomial of N. The goal is for a special *root* node to compute a certain aggregate function over all these inputs. For example, the root can be the base station in wireless sensor networks or the gateway node in wireless ad hoc networks. We will focus on the SUM function first, and then trivially generalize to arbitrary *commutative and associative aggregate functions* (or CAAFs in short — see definition in Section 2). All nodes in the system except the root may experience crash failures. For convenience, we say that an edge *fails*, iff at least one of its end points experiences a crash failure. We use f to denote an upper bound on the total number of edge failures. We consider a synchronous timing model where protocols proceed in *rounds*.

We consider randomized protocols for computing SUM (or general CAAFs) that always generate a *correct* result. A sum result is *correct* [1] iff it falls between the sum of the inputs of all nodes and the sum of the inputs of all nodes that are still alive and are not partitioned from the root at the end of the protocol's execution.[1] We similarly define result *correctness* for general CAAFs. The *time complexity* (TC) of a protocol is defined to be the number (denoted as b) of *flooding rounds* needed for the protocol to terminate. Here each flooding round consists of d rounds where d is the diameter of the network. The *communication complexity* (CC) of a protocol is the maximum number of bits that a node needs to send (i.e., locally broadcast) in the entire execution of the protocol. Here the maximum is taken across all nodes in the system. Given such a context, this paper focuses on the following question:

Under any given constraint on TC, what is the lowest CC needed for computing SUM *(or general CAAFs)?*

Existing lower/upper bounds. The only known non-trivial lower bound so far on the CC of SUM protocols, in the fault-tolerant setting, was from our own previous work [4]. Specifically, there we

[1]For example, if a node fails or gets partitioned from the root (due to the failure of other nodes) right before the SUM protocol starts, incorporating the node's input into the final sum would not be possible.

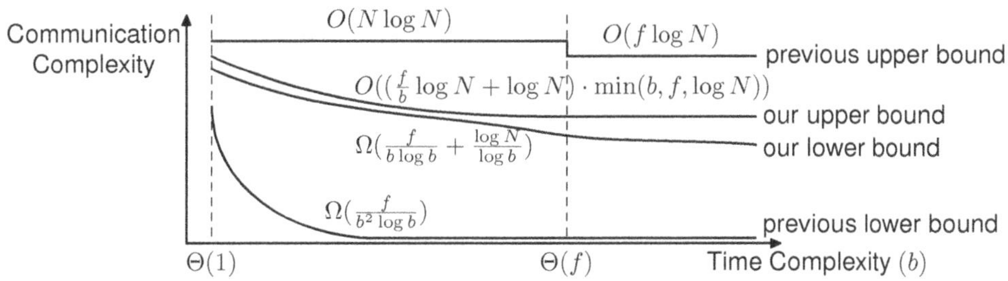

Figure 1: Summary of results on the SUM problem. Here b is the time complexity, and f is an upper bound on the total number of edges incident to failed nodes. Since the communication complexity depends on three parameters b, f, and N, the two-dimensional curves here are for illustration purposes only. Note that $O((\frac{f}{b} \log N + \log N) \cdot \min(b, f, \log N)) = O(\frac{f}{b} \log^2 N + \log^2 N)$.

proved that the CC is lower bounded by $\Omega(\frac{f}{b^2 \log b})$.[2] This lower bound indicates that the CC might be able to decrease polynomially with the TC (i.e., with b). There have been only a few upper bounds on the problem. Well-known tree-aggregation protocols [12] for computing SUM cannot tolerate failures. A brute-force SUM protocol, which has every node flood its id together with its value to the whole network, can tolerate arbitrary number of failures, while incurring $O(1)$ TC and $O(N \log N)$ CC. In comparison, under such TC, the current lower bound of $\Omega(\frac{f}{b^2 \log b})$ on CC is only $\Omega(f)$. There is also a folklore SUM protocol that tolerates failures by repeatedly invoking the naive tree-aggregation protocol until it experiences a failure-free run. This incurs $O(f)$ TC and $O(f \log N)$ CC. Under such TC, the current lower bound of $\Omega(\frac{f}{b^2 \log b})$ on CC is $\Omega(\frac{1}{f \log f})$. To summarize, the two fault-tolerant SUM protocols here both have fixed TC, and preclude the possibility of trading off TC with CC. Furthermore, even under that fixed TC, their CC is still a *polynomial* factor away from the lower bound (Figure 1).

Researchers have also studied the SUM problem when bounded errors are allowed in the final answer (e.g., [1, 4, 5, 8, 13, 14]), in either fault-tolerant or failure-free setting. Those results and their approaches are less related to this work. Nevertheless even there, in the fault-tolerant setting, a *polynomial* gap exists between the upper bound and lower bound as long as $b \geq 2$ [4].

For protocols that can compute general CAAFs, obviously existing lower bounds on SUM protocols directly carry over, since those protocols need to at least be able to compute SUM. It happens that the two existing (zero-error) SUM upper bound protocols work, without modification, for general CAAFs as well. We are not aware of any better lower/upper bounds on zero-error protocols for general CAAFs.

There have also been research efforts (e.g., [6,9,16,17]) on computing aggregate functions (such as SELECTION) that are not CAAFs. But none of these efforts consider failures. Finally, some researchers (e.g., [10]) have studied the token dissemination problem in *dynamic networks*. In comparison, this paper considers i) the aggregation problem where the "tokens" can be aggregated, and ii) node failures in static networks. With these differences, their techniques/results have limited relevance to our setting.

Our results. This work reduces the gap between the upper and lower bound for the above SUM problem from *polynomial* to *polylog*, over the entire time complexity spectrum. Improvements over both the existing upper bound and lower bound turn out to be necessary to achieve this significant reduction. Specifically, we present a novel upper bound of $O(\frac{f}{b} \log^2 N + \log^2 N)$ as well as a novel lower bound of $\Omega(\frac{f}{b \log b} + \frac{\log N}{\log b})$, for the CC of SUM protocols whose TC is within b flooding rounds (Figure 1)[3]. Note that our upper bound is at most $\log^2 N \log b$ factor away from our improved lower bound.

Our upper bound protocol also, for the first time, allows a tunable tradeoff between CC and TC where the CC can decrease polynomially with the TC. Using the standard doubling trick, the full version of this paper [18] further shows that the protocol can be easily extended to settings with unknown f, while only increasing the CC by a $\log N$ factor. Doing so will achieve a property similar to *early termination* — namely, the overhead of the protocol will automatically vary depending on the actual number of failures occurred during its execution.

Finally, same as some existing SUM protocols, our SUM protocol and its guarantees trivially generalizes to arbitrary CAAFs as well. This gives an $O(\frac{f}{b} \log^2 N + \log^2 N)$ upper bound on general CAAFs. By our lower bound, within polylog factors, this upper bound is the best that one can hope for.

Our main techniques. Our upper bound is non-trivial and involves the synthesis of two novel building blocks:

- We first propose a novel deterministic aggregation protocol AGG, parameterized by $t \geq 0$, with TC of $O(1)$ flooding rounds and CC of $O((t + 1) \log N)$ bits. If the actual number of edge failures is no more than t, AGG always generates a correct result. Note that setting $t = f$ directly gives us $O(1)$ TC and $O(f \log N)$ CC, which is already much better than the two existing SUM protocols mentioned earlier. The key technique in AGG is to take *speculative* actions to save time, instead of waiting for failures to be detected and then falling back to a second plan. We further carefully design a distributed mechanism to determine which speculative actions' effects should be retained or discarded, while using only local information.

- If the number of edge failures exceeds t, AGG may *unknowingly* generates a wrong result. We hence design a novel deterministic distributed verification protocol VERI, which aims to tell whether AGG's result is correct. VERI is also parameterized by t and incurs $O(1)$ TC and $O((t + 1) \log N)$ CC. The key technique in VERI is that we allow it to have one-sided error. Specifically, we allow VERI to sometimes

[2] The model in [4] slightly differs from the model in this paper. But the results there can still be trivially adapted to this paper. Such trivial adaptation will be rigorously described in the full version of this paper [18].

[3] We have actually proved an upper bound of $O((\frac{f}{b} \log N + \log N) \cdot \min(b, f, \log N))$. But for clarity, this paper uses the simpler form of $O(\frac{f}{b} \log^2 N + \log^2 N)$ in most places. The main novelty in our lower bound is the $\frac{f}{b \log b}$ term. The $\frac{\log N}{\log b}$ term comes, in a relatively straightforward way, from applying the results in [7] to the output domain size of $\Omega(N)$.

N	number of nodes in the system	b	SUM protocol's TC, in terms of flooding rounds
n	size of two-party problems	d	diameter of the topology $\mathcal{G}$
f	upper bound on the number of edge failures	c	diameter of the topology never exceeds cd due to failures
t	parameter in AGG and VERI	l	a node's level in the aggregation tree

Table 1: Key notations.

err when AGG does not err. VERI also employs a similar distributed mechanism to the one in AGG to avoid the need for global information in its execution.

Our upper bound protocol is eventually obtained by executing multiple pairs of AGG and VERI in a proper way.

Our new lower bound builds upon our previous lower bound [4], which was obtained via information cost arguments. To obtain this new result, we first introduce a new two-party problem EQUALITYCP, and then leverage a strong result on the Sperner capacity of general directed graphs [3] (instead of relying on information cost arguments). The possibility of leveraging the Sperner capacity of the cyclic q-gon [2] was hinted in a single footnote, but without any further details or any final result, in our previous paper [4]. This paper not only presents the specific lower bound obtained via that approach, but also slightly strengthens that approach — The approach in this paper yields a slightly better constant (specifically in Lemma 11) than the originally hinted approach.

2. MODEL AND DEFINITIONS

Commutative and associative aggregate functions. A binary operator $\diamond$ is *commutative and associative* if for all operands o_1, o_2, and o_3, we have $o_1 \diamond o_2 = o_2 \diamond o_1$ and $(o_1 \diamond o_2) \diamond o_3 = o_1 \diamond (o_2 \diamond o_3)$. A function $\mathcal{F}$ is called a *commutative and associative aggregate function*, or *CAAF* in short, if i) there exists a commutative and associative binary operator $\diamond$ such that $\mathcal{F}(o_1, o_2, ..., o_N) = o_1 \diamond o_2 \diamond ... \diamond o_N$, and ii) the domain size of $o_{i_1} \diamond o_{i_2} \diamond ... \diamond o_{i_k}$ is at most polynomial with respect to N, for all $1 \leq k \leq N$ where i_1 through i_k are arbitrary distinct indices. The second requirement stems from the "aggregate" nature of the function — "aggregating" o_{i_1} through o_{i_k} should generate a concise output. CAAF covers a wide range of common aggregate functions such as SUM and COUNT. Many other aggregate functions such as AVERAGE, MEDIAN, and SELECTION are related to CAAFs. For example, it is known [16] that MEDIAN and SELECTION can be solved using COUNT by doing a binary search over the output domain.

Our novel upper bound applies to all CAAFs. But for the sake of clarity, the rest of the paper will prove the upper bound only for SUM. This allows us to conveniently use natural phrases such as "the sum of these 4 inputs". None of our arguments there rely on the specifics of the addition operator. Hence generalizing to other CAAFs is entirely trivial – one only needs to replace the addition operator with $\diamond$.

Network model. There are N nodes in the system, where N is known by the protocol. (See Table 1 for notation summary.) Each node has a unique id of $\log N$ bits (log in this paper is always base 2). Node i has an integer *input* o_i, whose domain size is polynomial of N. The goal is for a special *root* node, whose id is known by all nodes, to learn the sum of all these inputs. The topology among the N nodes is modeled as an undirected graph $\mathcal{G}$. A node knows neither $\mathcal{G}$ nor its neighbors in $\mathcal{G}$. We impose no restriction on $\mathcal{G}$ except that it needs to be connected. We consider a synchronous timing model where protocols proceed in *rounds*. In each round, each node first receives all the messages sent by its neighbors in $\mathcal{G}$ in the previous round. Next it does some local computation and then may choose to send (i.e., locally broadcast) a single message, which will be received by all its neighbors in $\mathcal{G}$ in the next round. To make our results as strong as possible, we assume that all nodes start execution at round 1 for our lower bound. For our upper bound, we assume that the root initiates the protocol at round 1. Upon receiving the first message, a non-root node gets "activated" and joins the execution.

Failure model. All nodes in the system, except the root, may experience crash failures. A node that is disconnected from the root (i.e., has no path to the root) due to the failures of other nodes is also considered as failed. We consider only oblivious failure adversaries that adversarially decide beforehand (i.e., before the protocol flips any coins) which nodes fail at what time. For convenience, we say that an edge *fails*, iff at least one of its end points experiences a crash failure. We use f to denote an upper bound on the total number of edge failures, ranging from 1 to $\Theta(N)$.[4] We assume that f is known to the protocol.[5]

Let s_2 be the set of the inputs of all nodes, and s_1 be the set of the inputs of all nodes that have not failed by the end of the protocol's execution. Following [1, 4], we say that a sum result is *correct* if it is in the interval of $[\sum_{o \in s_1} o, \sum_{o \in s_2} o]$. We naturally generalize such result *correctness* definition to any CAAF: Here the result is *correct* if it is between $\min_{s_1 \subseteq s \subseteq s_2}(\diamond_{o \in s} o)$ and $\max_{s_1 \subseteq s \subseteq s_2}(\diamond_{o \in s} o)$.[6] We only consider randomized protocols for computing SUM (or general CAAFs) that always generate a correct result.

Time complexity and communication complexity. Most of the definitions here directly follow from [4]. To make our results as strong as possible, our upper bound only uses private coins, while our lower bound allows public coins.

With respect to a topology $\mathcal{G}$, the *time complexity* (TC) of a SUM protocol describes the number of rounds needed for it to terminate, under the worst-case inputs of nodes in $\mathcal{G}$, the worst-case failure adversary (parameterized by f), and the worst-case coin flips. The shape of $\mathcal{G}$ has a large impact on TC. Hence similar to [4], we will always describe TC in terms of *flooding rounds*. Here each flooding round consists of d rounds, where d is $\mathcal{G}$'s diameter and is assumed to be known to the protocol. We use b to denote the TC in terms of flooding rounds (i.e., the total number of rounds would be bd).

At any given point of time between round 1 and round bd, let $\mathcal{H}$ be the same as $\mathcal{G}$ except that all the failed nodes and their incidental edges have been deleted. $\mathcal{H}$'s diameter may be larger or smaller than $\mathcal{G}$. For a flooding round to remain meaningful in such a context, we assume that the failures do not substantially increase the network's diameter. Specifically, we assume that the diameter of $\mathcal{H}$ is no larger than $c \cdot d$, where c is some constant known to the protocol. As part of our future work, we are currently working on

[4]Certain graphs may have more than $\Theta(N)$ edges. But we focus on f between 1 and $\Theta(N)$ which applies to all graphs.

[5]The full version of this paper [18] explains how to remove this assumption using a simple doubling trick.

[6]Alternatively, one could define a result to be *correct* iff the result equals $\diamond_{o \in s} o$ for some s where $s_1 \subseteq s \subseteq s_2$. All our theorems and proofs hold, without any modification, under such an alternative definition.

Algorithm 1 Our upper bound protocol. Here b, c, and f are input parameters with $b \geq 21c$.

1: $x = \lfloor \frac{b-2c}{19c} \rfloor$; the root uses private coins to select $\log N$ integers, with replacement, from the range of $[1, x]$;
   let the selected integers be $y_1, y_2, ..., y_{\log N}$, in non-decreasing order;
2: **for all** integer $i \in [1, \log N]$ **where** ($i = 1$ **or** $y_i \neq y_{i-1}$) **do**
3:     at the beginning of flooding round $((y_i - 1) \times 19c + 1)$, root initiates a pair of AGG and VERI executions, both with $t = \lfloor \frac{2f}{x} \rfloor$;
       // this pair of executions will end by flooding round $(y_i \times 19c)$;
4:     **if** (AGG does not abort **and** VERI outputs `true`) **then** output AGG's result and terminate;
5: **end for**
6: at the beginning of the last $2c$ flooding rounds, root initiates the brute-force SUM protocol, outputs its result, and terminates;

a new lower bound proof that aims to show the necessity of this requirement, which is however beyond the scope of this paper.

With respect to $\mathcal{G}$, we define a node i's *communication complexity* (denoted as a_i) when running a SUM protocol to be the total number of bits it sends (i.e., locally broadcasts) when running the protocol, under the worst-case inputs of nodes in $\mathcal{G}$, the worst-case failure adversary (parameterized by f), and the average-case coin flips. A SUM protocol's *communication complexity* (CC) is the maximum a_i across all i's. Note that here we define CC over the bottleneck node instead of over the average node, which is appropriate in our distributed setting with a general topology and consistent with prior work [16].

Let $a_{\mathcal{G}}$ be the smallest CC under the topology $\mathcal{G}$ with at most f edge failures, across all SUM protocols whose TC is at most b flooding rounds. We define $\text{FT}_0(\text{SUM}_N, f, b)$ to be the maximum $a_{\mathcal{G}}$ across all $\mathcal{G}$ where $\mathcal{G}$ is connected and has exactly N nodes. Here "FT" stands for "fault-tolerant" and the subscript "0" stands for "zero-error".

Communication complexity of two-party problems. In Section 7, we will need to reason about the communication complexity of certain two-party problems. In those problems, Alice and Bob have inputs X and Y respectively, and they aim to compute a certain function $\Pi(X, Y)$. We only require Alice to learn the final result. We use n to denote the size of these two-party problems (with N being reserved to denote the number of nodes in $\mathcal{G}$). Unless otherwise noted, by a protocol for solving Π, we mean a public coin Las Vegas protocol. We define the *communication complexity* (CC) of Π (denoted as $\mathcal{R}_0(\Pi)$) to be smallest expected (with expectation taken over the coin flips) number of bits sent by Alice and Bob combined, across all protocols for solving Π.

3. SUMMARY OF RESULTS

The following two theorems summarize our main results:

THEOREM 1. *For any $b \geq 21c$ and $1 \leq f \leq N$, we have:*

$$\begin{aligned} \text{FT}_0(\text{SUM}_N, f, b) &= O((\frac{f}{b}\log N + \log N) \cdot \min(b, f, \log N)) \\ &= O(\frac{f}{b}\log^2 N + \log^2 N). \end{aligned}$$

THEOREM 2. *For any $b \geq 1$ and $1 \leq f \leq N$, we have:*

$$\text{FT}_0(\text{SUM}_N, f, b) = \Omega(\frac{f}{b \log b} + \frac{\log N}{\log b}).$$

The rest of the paper proves the two theorems above. Here we give an overview of the structure of our upper bound protocol (Algorithm 1) that is used to prove Theorem 1. Given total b flooding rounds as a constraint on TC, we divide the first $b - 2c$ flooding rounds into $x = \Theta(b)$ *intervals*, with each interval having $19c = \Theta(1)$ flooding rounds. Thanks to the small TC of AGG and VERI, running AGG followed by VERI will take at most one interval. If the edge failures were evenly distributed across all the intervals, then each interval would have at most $\frac{f}{x}$ edge failures. In such a case, running AGG parameterized with $t = \frac{f}{x}$ in any single interval would already produce a correct result, while incurring a desirable CC of $O((\frac{f}{b} + 1)\log N)$. Here recall that t is the number of edge failures that AGG intends to tolerate, and the CC of AGG is $O((t + 1)\log N)$.

Since the edge failures are not always evenly distributed, we need a more complex design. Specifically, the root uses private coins to select $\log N$ intervals uniformly randomly. In each selected interval, the root initiates a pair of AGG and VERI executions, both with $t = \lfloor \frac{2f}{x} \rfloor$. One can easily see that with probability at least $\frac{1}{2}$, a random interval has no more than t edge failures. Hence with probability at least $1 - \frac{1}{N}$, the number of edge failures in *some* selected interval is small enough for AGG to tolerate. But if there have been more than t edge failures in an interval, then AGG may *unknowingly* produce a wrong result. A difficulty here is that we cannot easily determine the number of edge failures that have occurred in a given interval, since it involves counting while tolerating potential additional failures during counting. Hence instead of checking the number of edge failures in a given interval, our protocol invokes VERI after AGG, and then checks the condition at Line 4 of Algorithm 1. If the condition is met, the protocol outputs AGG's result and terminates. By Theorem 5 and 7 later, such a result must be correct. Furthermore by Theorem 4 and 7 later, if the number of edge failures in an interval is no more than t, then the condition at Line 4 is guaranteed to be met.

Having given an intuitive overview on the protocol's correctness, we move on to look at its CC. Since there can be at most x intervals in total and f intervals with failures, AGG and VERI will be executed at most $\min(x, f + 1, \log N)$ times. The CC incurred by each AGG and VERI invocation is $O((t + 1)\log N)$ bits, resulting in total $O((\frac{f}{b}\log N + \log N) \cdot \min(b, f, \log N))$ bits in all the intervals. Next, the probability of reaching Line 6 is at most $\frac{1}{N}$. As explained in Section 1, the CC of the brute-force SUM protocol is $O(N \log N)$. Hence the CC incurred at Line 6, over average coin-flips, is $O(\log N)$.

Next in Section 4 and 5, we focus on AGG and VERI, and prove their properties. Section 6 then provides the full proof for Theorem 1. Theorem 2 will be discussed in Section 7.

4. THE AGG PROTOCOL

Overview. Algorithm 2 at the end of this paper provides the pseudocode for AGG. AGG has an input parameter t ($t \geq 0$), which is the number of edge failures that it intends to tolerate. When running AGG, a node will flood[7] a special symbol to abort AGG once it has sent $(11t + 14)(\log N + 5)$ bits. Such a mechanism will never be

[7]Throughout this paper, a node *floods* a certain message by first sending the message to its neighbors, and then the other nodes simply forward that message upon first receiving it.

triggered (as we prove later) if the actual number of edge failures is no larger than t. If the actual number of edge failures exceeds t, aborting before the CC gets too large enables AGG to properly bound its CC.

AGG first constructs a spanning tree and does a standard tree-based aggregation, where each non-root node sends its *partial sum* upstream (i.e., towards the root) along the tree. The *partial sum* of a node (either non-root or root) is the sum of the node's own input and all the partial sums received from its children. A key impact of failures is that they may block and prevent certain partial sums from propagating upstream. If a partial sum from a node B is blocked, a natural solution is to have B flood its partial sum, since flooding has the maximum resilience against failures. If the flooding does reach the root, the root can then incorporate B's partial sum to the final result. A second thought, however, shows that even with flooding, B's partial sum may still fail to reach the root if B's entire neighborhood fails immediately after B initiates the flooding. When this happens, the system needs to fall back and flood the partial sums of B's children, or B's descendants if B's children have also failed.

The key challenge here is that we need to do this within $O(1)$ flooding rounds. We cannot afford to wait to see whether B's partial sums get successfully flooded, and then fall back to flooding some other partial sums if things did not go well. To save time, we will have to do floodings *speculatively*, before knowing which floodings will be needed. This in turn leads to a second challenge: There will be overlap (or duplicates) in the partial sums received by the root (e.g., partial sums from both B and some of B's descendants). We need a careful mechanism to avoid double counting, which is non-trivial, especially without global knowledge about the tree topology.

The following sections present the details of AGG. At a high-level, AGG has 3 sequential phases: i) spanning tree construction and tree-aggregation (Section 4.1), ii) identifying potentially blocked partial sums and (speculatively) flooding them (Section 4.2), and iii) using a distributed mechanism based on *witnesses* to avoid double counting (Section 4.3). To facilitate understanding, the discussion here will be intuitive — we leave the formal proofs to the full version of this paper [18].

4.1 Tree Construction/Aggregation and Some Key Concepts

This section first describes the tree construction/aggregation phase in AGG, which is largely standard. Next we formalize a number of new concepts that are key for our later design.

Tree construction and aggregation. To construct the tree, the root first sends a tree_construct message, together with a hop count. A node B waits for the first tree_construct message it receives. Note that this message easily enables B to figure out the current round, and synchronize its round counter with the root. Let A denote the sender of that message. B sends an ack message indicating to A that B is A's child, and then sends a tree_construct message itself to continue constructing the tree. B's failing before sending ack will be equivalent to B not being present in the network. The failure of B after sending ack will be dealt with later in AGG. From now on in this paper, the notions of "parent", "child", "ancestor", and "descendant" will always be with respect to this tree.

Next AGG does standard tree-aggregation. Consider a given node B, and let l be its *level* (i.e., its distance from the root). Node B acts in the $(cd-l+1)$th round during tree-aggregation, by summing up its own input with all the partial sums received from its children so far, and then sending the new partial sum to B's parent. Note that B does not necessarily wait for a message from each of its children, since some may have failed. Each partial sum thus is the sum of inputs from a subset of the nodes, and we also say that the partial sum *includes* those inputs.

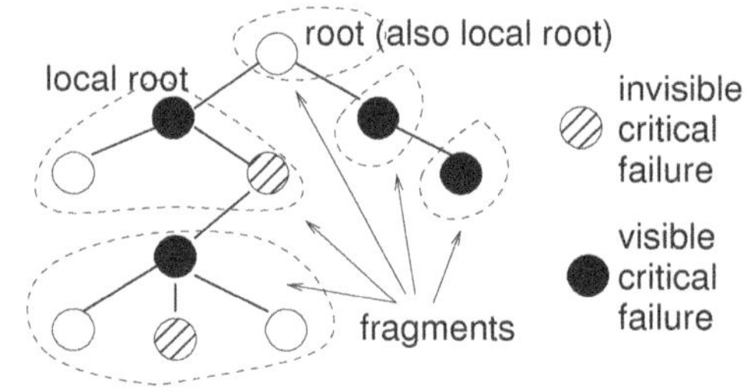

Figure 2: Example aggregation tree and fragments.

Some key concepts. We say that a node B at level l experiences a *critical failure* if it fails after sending ack during tree construction and before taking its action in the $(cd - l + 1)$th round during tree-aggregation. Such a critical failure can be easily detected by B's parent A (if A is alive) during that round, when A does not receive the scheduled message from B. We want critical failure to become global knowledge when possible. To do so, A will flood a message claiming that B experiences a critical failure. We say that a flooding is *successful* if the flooded message eventually reaches the root. One can easily see that a successful flooding must reach all live nodes within cd rounds. We say that a critical failure is *visible* if it is eventually seen by the root. Otherwise it is *invisible*. To help understanding, the next will first assume that all critical failures are visible, and then remove that assumption in Section 4.4.

Imagine that we remove all those edges connecting visible critical failures with their corresponding parents. Doing so partitions the aggregation tree into many smaller trees which we call *fragments* (Figure 2). A node's *local ancestors (descendants)* are all its ancestors (descendants) within the node's fragment. Each fragment also has its own *local root*. A fragment has a clean property: The partial sum of a node never includes inputs from nodes outside of its fragment, since those inputs have been blocked by the visible critical failures. Hence we can restrict most of our discussions to within a fragment.

A node A's partial sum is a *representative* of a node B iff i) A is either B itself or A is B's local ancestor, and ii) the tree path from A to B (excluding A and B) contains no invisible critical failures. Intuitively, B's representative must include B's input. A *representative set* is a set of partial sums with the following property: For any node B, if B is alive at (has failed by) the end of the VERI execution that immediately follows AGG, then a representative set contains exactly one (at most one) representative of B. Intuitively, if we obtain a representative set and sum up all the partial sums there, we get a correct sum result.

4.2 Identify and Flood Potentially Blocked Partial Sums

With the above notion of representative set, our goal in the remainder of AGG is for the root to obtain a representative set. If there were no critical failures at all, then the root's partial sum by itself is already a representative set. With critical failures, a representative set will contain not only the root's partial sum but also those blocked partial sums. Consider the example in Figure 3. Here, the root's partial sum, A's partial sum, and F's partial sum form a representative set. Imagine that we have A and F flood their partial sums, so that the root can get those and add those to the final result. However, A, B, and C all fail right before A intends to flood. Hence A's partial sum is lost and we now need D and E to flood their partial sums, which will form a second representative

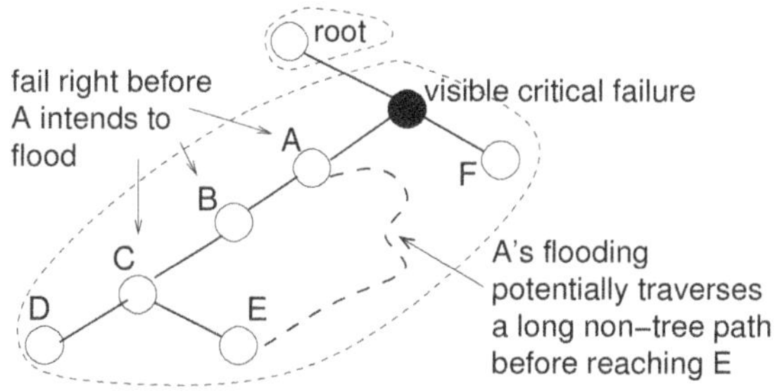

Figure 3: Why speculative flooding is needed.

set together with the root's and F's partial sum. Ideally, D and E should do so after they know that A's flooding has failed. Unfortunately, it can take one flooding round before such determination can be made, since A's flooding could traverse a long non-tree path before reaching E (Figure 3). Similarly, if E's flooding also fails, then E's local descendants (if any) may need to wait one more flooding round before taking action.

This example shows that to have small TC, nodes need to flood speculatively, before knowing that the flooding is needed. AGG uses the following elegant design to decide which node initiates flooding at what time: The root always floods its partial sum in the first round of the partial sum flooding phase. A non-root node B at level l floods its partial sum in the $(l+1)$th round of the phase, iff in that round it does not receive any flooding message (containing any partial sums) from its parent A. Here A may or may not be the *initiator* of the corresponding flooding. This design has two important features. First, the design never does excessive floodings: If A has not failed by the $(l+1)$th round, B must receive some message from A and will not initiate its own flooding. This implies that the total number of floodings is linear with the number of edge failures. Second, the full version of this paper [18] proves that the design always floods a superset of those partial sums that need to be flooded. Namely, if B did not flood its own partial sum, then B must have forwarded a "better" partial sum that includes all those inputs included by B's partial sum.

4.3 Avoid Double Counting While Using Only Limited Information

The root potentially receives many flooded partial sums, and it needs to pick a representative set to avoid double counting. The partial sums seen by the root can be classified into three mutually-exclusive categories: The partial sum of a node B is *dominated* if the root also sees A's partial sum where A is B's local ancestor. A non-dominated partial sum of a node B is *compulsory* if either B or at least one of B's local descendants is still alive at the end of the VERI execution that immediately follows AGG, otherwise the non-dominated partial sum is called *optional*. The full version of this paper [18] proves that the union of all compulsory partial sums and any subset of optional partial sums forms a representative set.

Without knowledge of the global tree topology for labeling each partial sum, AGG maintains distributed topology information to do so. Specifically, when initially constructing the tree, AGG lets each node learn the ids of its nearest $2t$ ancestors. Interestingly, such limited information is already sufficient for AGG to select a representative set, in the following way via *witnesses*.

Having witnesses label partial sums. A node B's *witness* is either B itself or some local descendant of B whose distance to B is at most t. Let the local root of B's fragment be X and consider B's witness C. First, if C sees X among its $2t$ ancestors, then its $2t$ ancestors must contain all of B's local ancestors. Note that partial sums seen by the root must be seen by all live nodes as well. Hence if C sees a partial sum from some local ancestor of B's, C knows that B's partial sum is dominated and will thus flood its determination $\langle$dominated, $B\rangle$ to inform the root. Otherwise C floods its determination $\langle$compulsory$\|$optional, $B\rangle$. When B has multiple witnesses, such determination may be flooded multiple times. This does not increase CC since all the determinations are identical, and a node only needs to participate in one such flooding.

Second, if C does not see X among its $2t$ ancestors, then there must be at least $2t - t = t$ nodes on the tree path from B to X (excluding B and X). If the number of edge failures is no more than t, then there must be at least one live node on that tree path between B and X. That live node must have successfully flooded a partial sum of either itself or one of its local ancestors. This implies that B's partial sum must be dominated. C will thus flood the determination $\langle$dominated, $B\rangle$. If the number of edge failures exceeds t, such determination might be wrong, which will be dealt with later by VERI.

Finally, it is possible for all of B's witnesses to fail (or for their floodings to fail to reach the root). In such a case, B's farthest local descendant must be no more than t hops away from B, since otherwise the number of edge failures will be more than t. (Again, the case where the number of edge failures exceeds t will be dealt with by VERI.) This implies that B and its local descendants must have all failed, since they are all B's witnesses. Hence if the root does not receive any determination on B's partial sum, the root knows that the partial sum cannot be compulsory, and must be either dominated or optional.

Take all three cases into account, to form a representative set, the root simply includes in the set a partial sum from a node B iff $\langle$compulsory$\|$optional, $B\rangle$ has been received.

4.4 Complexity and Correctness of AGG

We have been assuming no invisible critical failures. The full version of this paper [18] proves that all the local ancestors of an invisible critical failure must have failed by the end of the tree-aggregation phase. Leveraging such observation, there we show that invisible critical failures does not affect any of our arguments earlier.

The following two theorems prove the complexity and correctness guarantees of AGG:

THEOREM 3. *The time complexity and communication complexity of* AGG *are no more than* $11c$ *flooding rounds and* $O((t+1)\log N)$ *bits, respectively.*

Proof: The pseudo-code in Algorithm 2 obviously shows that AGG terminates within $7cd + 4$ rounds, which are at most $11c$ flooding rounds. For communication complexity, recall that in AGG, a node will flood a special symbol to abort AGG once it has sent $(11t + 14)(\log N + 5)$ bits. □

THEOREM 4. *If there are at most t edge failures during the execution of* AGG*, then* AGG *never aborts and always outputs a correct result.*

Proof: See the full version of this paper [18]. □

5. THE VERI PROTOCOL

We again focus on intuitions here, and leave the formal proofs to the full version of this paper [18].

Overview. Algorithm 3 at the end of this paper provides the pseudo-code for VERI. VERI aims to determine whether AGG's output is correct. The natural approach is for VERI to determine whether

scenario	AGG	VERI
1. no more than t edge failures (implying no LFC)	output correct result	output `true`
2. more than t edge failures and no LFC	output correct result or abort	no guarantee
3. more than t edge failures and exists LFC	no guarantee	output `false`

Table 2: Guarantees of AGG and VERI under different scenarios.

there have been more than t edge failures. This turns out to be difficult since it involves counting while tolerating potential additional failures during counting. Instead, our approach is to i) identify a weaker requirement that is nevertheless sufficient for AGG not to err, and ii) allow VERI to sometimes err when AGG does not err. Such a weaker requirement on VERI eventually makes an efficient design possible.

Specifically, with respect to a pair of AGG and VERI execution (both with parameter t), a *long failure chain* (LFC) is a chain of t nodes $A_1, A_2, ..., A_t$ within the same fragment such that i) A_i is the parent of A_{i+1} ($1 \leq i \leq t-1$), ii) all of them have failed by the end of the AGG execution, and iii) A_t has at least one local descendant that is alive at the end of the VERI execution. Here the notions of fragment, parent, and etc are all defined based on the AGG execution. A_1 and A_t are called the *head* and *tail* of the LFC, respectively. Note that having no more than t edge failures implies no LFC, while the reverse is not true. The following theorem claims that regardless of the number of edge failures, AGG will not err as long as there is no LFC.

THEOREM 5. *If there is no LFC, then* AGG *either outputs a correct result or aborts.*

Proof: See the full version of this paper [18]. □

The theorem implies that VERI may safely err in the 2nd scenario in Table 2, where there are more than t edge failures but no LFC. Table 2 also summarizes the guarantees of AGG and VERI in all other possible scenarios.

5.1 Design of The VERI Protocol

By the above discussion, we design VERI by focusing on detecting LFCs. Similar to AGG, in VERI once a node has sent $(5t+7)(3\log N+10)$ bits, it will flood a special symbol to cause VERI to output `false`.

Strawman design assuming no additional failures. To help understanding, we first describe a strawman design while assuming that there are no additional failures occurring during VERI's execution. A simple way to detect LFCs is for each node to ping its parent and children on the (aggregation) tree, and to flood the information about detected failures to all other nodes. Those *failed parents* and *failed children* are potentially tails and heads of LFCs. Without knowing the global tree topology, we will leverage the same witnesses as in Section 4.3 to determine whether they are indeed tails and heads of LFCs. Consider a failed parent B and a witness C of B's. Recall that B's witness is either B itself or some local descendant of B whose distance to B is at most t. C finds, among its $2t$ ancestors, B's nearest ancestor A such that A is either a failed child or a fragment boundary. One can easily see that B is the tail of an LFC iff A is at least $t-1$ hops away from B. Thus C can precisely determine whether B is the tail of an LFC, and can flood such determination to inform the root.

Failures of the witnesses. We now move on to the actual VERI design, by explaining how different kinds of failures during VERI's execution are addressed. We first consider the failures of the witnesses: In the earlier example, it is possible for all of B's witnesses to fail, so that no node can make a proper determination. We overcome this key challenge precisely by allowing VERI to err, as explained below.

First, we need AGG to maintain some additional information: During AGG's aggregation phase, we have each node learn the maximum level among its local descendants. This can be easily done by having nodes propagate upstream, along with the partial sum, the maximum level it has seen among its local descendants. Now in VERI, imagine that we can infer the distance x from B to B's farthest local descendants.[8] If the root does not receive any determination on whether B is the tail of some LFC (implying that all of B's witnesses have failed), the root applies the following rule: If $x \leq t$, it claims that B is not the tail of an LFC. Otherwise it claims that B is the tail of an LFC, and outputs `false`.

To see when the above rule gives a correct/wrong determination, we separately consider two cases. First, $x \leq t$ implies that all of B's local descendants are B's witnesses. They must have all failed since all witnesses have failed. In turn, by definition B must not be the tail of an LFC. Second, $x > t$ implies that B has at least t witnesses and all of them have failed. We still cannot determine whether there exists an LFC. But since VERI is allowed to make one-sided error when there are more than t edge failures (i.e., the 2nd and 3rd scenario in Table 2), VERI can simply output `false` in such a case.

When to detect failures. We move on to consider additional failures during the detection of failed parents/children. Those failures may prevent the floodings of information about failed parents/children from reaching the root. This is similar to flooded partial sums getting lost in Section 4.2 and Figure 3. To deal with this, VERI uses the following design similar to the one in AGG: The root floods a single bit. If a node at level l does not receive this bit or any message (claiming the detection of failed parents) from its own parent within $l+1$ rounds, it floods a message claiming that its own parent is a failed parent. If B is the tail of an LFC, such design guarantees (see the full version of this paper [18] for a proof) to inform the root that either B or some of B's local descendant is a failed parent.

Detection of failed children is similarly done by propagating a single bit upstream along all the tree edges. Finally, VERI always detects failed parents first and then detects failed children. This is necessary for correctness, if additional failures may occur during VERI. We leave the details on how this ordering is leveraged in our proofs to the full version of this paper [18].

5.2 Complexity and Correctness of VERI

THEOREM 6. *The time complexity and communication complexity of* VERI *are no more than* $8c$ *flooding rounds and* $O((t+1)\log N)$ *bits, respectively.*

Proof: The pseudo-code in Algorithm 3 clearly shows that VERI always terminates within $5cd+3$ rounds, which are at most $8c$

[8] Since B may have failed early on, we may not be able to actually get x. Nevertheless, one can achieve a similar functionality by using the maximum level information from B's descendants. See the full version of this paper [18] for details.

flooding rounds. For communication complexity, recall that in VERI, a node will flood a special symbol to terminate VERI once it has sent over $(5t+7)(10+3\log N)$ bits. □

THEOREM 7. *Consider a pair of* AGG *and* VERI *execution, both parameterized by t. If there exists an LFC, then* VERI *must output* `false`. *If there are at most t edge failures, then* VERI *must output* `true`.

Proof: See the full version of this paper [18].□

6. PROOF FOR THEOREM 1

THEOREM 1 (RESTATED). *For any $b \geq 21c$ and $1 \leq f \leq N$, we have:*

$$\begin{aligned} \mathrm{FT}_0(\mathrm{SUM}_N, f, b) &= O((\frac{f}{b}\log N + \log N)\cdot \min(b, f, \log N)) \\ &= O(\frac{f}{b}\log^2 N + \log^2 N). \end{aligned}$$

Proof: We prove the theorem by constructing an upper bound protocol as in Algorithm 1. The following proves the time complexity, communication complexity, and correctness of Algorithm 1.

For TC, Theorem 3 and 6 tell us that a pair of AGG and VERI executions take no more than $19c$ flooding rounds, and hence Line 3 of Algorithm 1 can complete in time. At Line 6, the root will flood a single bit to all nodes to initiate a brute-force protocol, taking c flooding rounds. Upon receiving this bit, a node floods its id and its input to all other nodes. Within c flooding rounds, the root is guaranteed to receive all flooded messages initiated by nodes that are still alive at the end of the protocol. The root then adds up the input for each id, and outputs the sum. Hence Line 6 takes at most $2c$ flooding rounds. Putting it all together, the time complexity of Algorithm 1 is no more than b flooding rounds.

For CC, by Theorem 4 and 7, if there are no more than $t = \lfloor \frac{2f}{x} \rfloor$ edge failures within an interval, then AGG will not abort and VERI will output `true`. This will then allow Algorithm 1 to terminate immediately after that interval at Line 4. Thus AGG and VERI will be executed at most $\min(x, f+1, \log N)$ times at Line 3 of Algorithm 1, since there are (i) total at most x intervals, (ii) at most f edge failures and hence at most $f+1$ intervals with failures, and (iii) at most $\log N$ intervals selected. By Theorem 3 and 6, the CC of AGG and VERI are both $O((t+1)\log N)$. Hence the total CC incurred at Line 3 is $O((t+1)\cdot \min(b, f, \log N)\cdot \log N)$.

Next consider the CC incurred at Line 6. Since there are at most f edge failures in all the x intervals, with probability at least $\frac{1}{2}$, a uniformly random interval contains no more than $\lfloor \frac{2f}{x} \rfloor$ edge failures. Hence with probability at least $\frac{1}{2}$, by Theorem 4 and 7, AGG will not abort and VERI will output `true`, causing Algorithm 1 to terminate in that interval. The probability of reaching Line 6 is thus at most $1/2^{\log N} = 1/N$. The brute-force protocol at Line 6 itself has a CC of $O(N \log N)$, implying that the CC (over average-case coin flips) incurred at Line 6 is at most $O(\frac{1}{N}\cdot N\log N) = O(\log N)$.

Putting everything together, the CC of Algorithm 1 is:

$$\begin{aligned} & O((t+1)\cdot \min(b, f, \log N)\cdot \log N) + O(\log N) \\ =\ & O((\frac{f}{b}\log N + \log N)\cdot \min(b, f, \log N)) \\ =\ & O(\frac{f}{b}\log^2 N + \log^2 N). \end{aligned}$$

Finally, we prove that Algorithm 1 always produces a correct sum result. If it outputs a sum at Line 6 from the brute-force protocol, the result is trivially correct. If it outputs the result generated by AGG, then we know that AGG did not abort and VERI outputted `true`. By Theorem 7, we know that there must have been no LFC. In turn by Theorem 5, we know that the result generated by AGG (if it did not abort) must be correct. □

7. A NEW $\Omega(\frac{f}{b\log b} + \frac{\log N}{\log b})$ LOWER BOUND ON THE CC OF SUM(THEOREM 2)

Review of previous lower bound. Our previous work [4] obtained a lower bound on SUM's CC by reducing a two-party communication complexity problem UNIONSIZECP to SUM. In UNIONSIZECP$_{n,q}$, Alice has a string X of length n as her input. Each character in the string is an integer in $[0, q-1]$ where $q \geq 2$. Bob similarly has a string Y as his input. X and Y satisfy the *cycle promise*,[9] in the sense that for all $1 \leq i \leq n$, either $Y_i = X_i$ or $Y_i = (X_i + 1) \bmod q$. Here X_i and Y_i are the ith character of X and Y respectively. Alice and Bob aim to determine the quantity $|\{i | X_i \neq 0 \text{ or } Y_i \neq 0\}|$. Our previous work [4] proved a lower bound of $\Omega(\frac{n}{q^2}) - O(\log n)$ on the CC of UNIONSIZECP$_{n,q}$, and then obtained a lower bound on SUM via a reduction from UNIONSIZECP. Trivially adapting that lower bound to the model in this paper gives us a lower bound of $\Omega(\frac{f}{b^2\log b})$ in this paper's setting.

Our new lower bound. This section presents a new lower bound of $\Omega(\frac{f}{b\log b} + \frac{\log N}{\log b})$ for SUM, and this factor-b improvement is necessary to bring down the gap between the upper and lower bound to polylog. The key to achieving this improvement is a stronger lower bound of $\Omega(\frac{n}{q}) - O(\log n)$ on UNIONSIZECP. This lower bound on UNIONSIZECP is almost tight, given the existing $O(\frac{n}{q}\log n + \log q)$ upper bound [4].

To obtain this lower bound on UNIONSIZECP, we introduce a new two-party problem called EQUALITYCP$_{n,q}$, which is the same as UNIONSIZECP$_{n,q}$ except that in EQUALITYCP$_{n,q}$, Alice and Bob aim to determine whether X equals Y. We are interested in EQUALITYCP$_{n,q}$ because its rectangular properties are easier to study. The following theorem establishes a reduction from EQUALITYCP to UNIONSIZECP, based on the following observation: Knowing the result of UNIONSIZECP, Alice and Bob can infer whether there exists j such that $X_j = q-1$ and $Y_j = 0$. If there exists such j, then $X \neq Y$ and we are done. Otherwise for $1 \leq i \leq n$, we must have $Y_i = X_i$ or $Y_i = X_i + 1$ (note that there is no longer "mod q"). This implies that $X = Y$ iff $\sum_{i=1}^n X_i = \sum_{i=1}^n Y_i$.

THEOREM 8. $\mathcal{R}_0(\text{EQUALITYCP}_{n,q}) \leq \mathcal{R}_0(\text{UNIONSIZECP}_{n,q}) + O(\log q) + O(\log n)$.

Proof: To solve EQUALITYCP, Alice and Bob first invoke the oracle UNIONSIZECP protocol on their inputs X and Y. Bob next sends Alice $\sum_{i=1}^n Y_i$, using $\log n + \log q$ bits, and the occurrence count (denoted as z) of the character 0 in Y, using $\log n$ bits. Alice finally outputs that X equals Y iff $\sum_{i=1}^n X_i = \sum_{i=1}^n Y_i$ and UNIONSIZECP(X, Y) equals $n - z$.

To show the correctness of the above protocol, note that if $X = Y$, then the two conditions trivially hold. We next prove the reverse direction. Since UNIONSIZECP$(X, Y) = n - z$, for all i where $Y_i = 0$, we have $X_i = 0$. In turn, there does not exist i such that $X_i = q-1$ and $Y_i = 0$. With this additional property, together with the cycle promise, we know that for $1 \leq i \leq n$, either $Y_i = X_i$ or $Y_i = X_i + 1$ (note that there is no longer "mod q"). Hence X must equal to Y since otherwise $\sum_{i=1}^n Y_i$ would be larger than $\sum_{i=1}^n X_i$. □

[9]The cycle promise described here is called the "alternative form" of the cycle promise in [4].

Next we apply an existing strong result on the Sperner capacity of directed graphs [3] to obtain a lower bound on the CC of EQUALITYCP. That result was originally stated in the context of a directed coding graph, and the following instantiates it in our specific context:

THEOREM 9. (Adapted from Theorem 3.2 in [3].) *Let S be a subset of $\{0, 1, 2, ..., q-1\}^n$ with the following property: For all $V, W \in S$ where $V \neq W$, there i) exists i such that $V_i \neq W_i$ and $V_i \neq (W_i + 1)$ mod q, and ii) exists j such that $W_j \neq V_j$ and $W_j \neq (V_j + 1)$ mod q. Then $|S| \leq (rank(\mathbb{M}))^n$ for any $q \times q$ matrix $\mathbb{M}$, where $\mathbb{M}_{i,i} = 1$ for all i, $\mathbb{M}_{i,j} = 0$ for all $(j - i)$ mod $q \in \{2, 3, ..., q-1\}$, and all other entries in $\mathbb{M}$ (i.e., $\mathbb{M}_{1,2}$, $\mathbb{M}_{2,3}$, ..., $\mathbb{M}_{q-1,q}$, and $\mathbb{M}_{q,1}$) can be arbitrary real numbers.*

THEOREM 10.

$$\mathcal{R}_0(\text{EQUALITYCP}_{n,q}) = \Omega(\frac{n}{q} - \log n - \log\log q).$$

Proof: Our definition of $\mathcal{R}_0$ allows public coins and only requires Alice to know the result. We define $\mathcal{R}_0^{\text{pri}}$ to be the same as $\mathcal{R}_0$ except that only private coins are allowed and both Alice and Bob are required to know the result. Using arguments based on rectangles [11], Lemma 11 next proves that $\mathcal{R}_0^{\text{pri}}(\text{EQUALITYCP}_{n,q}) \geq \frac{n}{q-1}$. The theorem follows since i) only one bit is needed for Alice to inform Bob the result, and ii) a public coin protocol using k bits here can always be simulated via private coins while using $O(k + \log\log(q^n \cdot q^n)) = O(k + \log n + \log\log q)$ bits [15]. □

LEMMA 11. $\mathcal{R}_0^{\text{pri}}(\text{EQUALITYCP}_{n,q}) \geq \frac{n}{q-1}$.

Proof sketch: It is well known [11][10] that for any (partial) function $h : X \times Y \rightarrow \{0, 1\}$, $\mathcal{R}_0^{\text{pri}}(h) \geq N(h) \geq \log C^1(h)$. Here $N(h)$ is the non-deterministic communication complexity, and $C^1(h)$ is the smallest number of monochromatic rectangles needed to cover (possibly with intersections) all the 1-entries in the matrix corresponding to h. The matrix $\mathbb{Z}$ corresponding to $\text{EQUALITYCP}_{n,q}$ is a $q^n \times q^n$ matrix. All 1-entries in $\mathbb{Z}$ are on the main diagonal. The remainder of $\mathbb{Z}$ consists of 0-entries and undefined entries that correspond to input pairs not satisfying the cycle promise. In any given covering of all the 1-entries using monochromatic rectangles, consider any two 1-entries $\mathbb{Z}_{V,V}$ (i.e., the entry for $X = V$ and $Y = V$) and $\mathbb{Z}_{W,W}$ in any rectangle used in the covering. For the rectangle to be monochromatic, $\mathbb{Z}_{W,V}$ and $\mathbb{Z}_{V,W}$ must not be 0-entries and hence must be undefined entries. This means that there i) exists i such that $V_i \neq W_i$ and $V_i \neq (W_i + 1)$ mod q, and ii) exists j such that $W_j \neq V_j$ and $W_j \neq (V_j + 1)$ mod q.

Applying Theorem 9 tells us that the number of 1-entries in such a monochromatic rectangle is upper bounded by $(rank(\mathbb{M}))^n$ for any $q \times q$ matrix $\mathbb{M}$ satisfying the properties specified in Theorem 9. We want to find such an $\mathbb{M}$ with a small rank, by properly choosing the values of $\mathbb{M}_{1,2}, \mathbb{M}_{2,3}, ..., \mathbb{M}_{q-1,q}$, and $\mathbb{M}_{q,1}$. We set all of them to be -1. We claim that the rank of such an $\mathbb{M}$ is exactly $q - 1$. To see why, note that adding up all the q rows gives us an all-zero row, and hence $rank(\mathbb{M}) \leq q - 1$. It is also easy to verify that the first $q - 1$ rows are linearly independent. Hence $rank(\mathbb{M}) = q - 1$, implying that the number of 1-entries in a monochromatic rectangle of $\mathbb{Z}$ is upper bounded by $(q-1)^n$. Finally, because the total number of 1-entries in $\mathbb{Z}$ is q^n, we have $\mathcal{R}_0^{\text{pri}}(\text{EQUALITYCP}_{n,q}) \geq \log(q^n/(q-1)^n) = n\log(1 + \frac{1}{q-1}) \geq \frac{n}{q-1}$. □

[10]The result was originally stated for functions, though it trivially applies to partial functions as well.

THEOREM 12. $\mathcal{R}_0(\text{UNIONSIZECP}_{n,q}) = \Omega(\frac{n}{q}) - O(\log n)$.

Proof: The equation trivially holds for $n \leq q$. For $n > q$, combining Theorem 8 and 10 directly yields the result. □

The $\Omega(\frac{f}{b\log b})$ term in Theorem 2 then follows naturally from Theorem 12 and the known reduction [4] from UNIONSIZECP to SUM. The extra $\Omega(\frac{\log N}{\log b})$ term in Theorem 2 comes from the $\Omega(N)$ domain size of the sum result. By results in [7], sending $\Omega(\log N)$ bits of information to the root within b flooding rounds (and hence within b rounds under the worst-case topology) requires sending $\Omega(\frac{\log N}{\log b})$ actual bits. We defer the full proof of Theorem 2 to the full version of this paper [18].

8. ACKNOWLEDGMENTS

We thank Faith Ellen and the PODC anonymous reviewers for many helpful comments on this paper. This work is partly supported by Singapore Ministry of Education Academic Research Fund Tier 2 grant MOE2011-T2-2-042, and partly supported by the research grant for the Human Sixth Sense Programme at the Advanced Digital Sciences Center from Singapore's Agency for Science, Technology and Research (A*STAR).

9. REFERENCES

[1] M. Bawa, A. Gionis, H. Garcia-Molina, and R. Motwani. The price of validity in dynamic networks. *Journal of Computer and System Sciences*, 73(3):245–264, May 2007.

[2] A. Blokhuis. On the sperner capacity of the cyclic triangle. *Journal of Algebraic Combinatorics*, 2(2):123–124, June 1993.

[3] A. R. Calderbank, P. Frankl, R. L. Graham, W.-C. W. Li, and L. A. Shepp. The sperner capacity of linear and nonlinear codes for the cyclic triangle. *Journal of Algebraic Combinatorics*, 2(1):31–48, March 1993.

[4] B. Chen, H. Yu, Y. Zhao, and P. B. Gibbons. The Cost of Fault Tolerance in Multi-Party Communication Complexity. *Journal of the ACM*, 2014.

[5] J. Considine, F. Li, G. Kollios, and J. Byers. Approximate aggregation techniques for sensor databases. In *ICDE*, March 2004.

[6] G. Frederickson. Tradeoffs for selection in distributed networks. In *PODC*, 1983.

[7] R. Impagliazzo and R. Williams. Communication complexity with synchronized clocks. In *CCC*, June 2010.

[8] D. Kempe, A. Dobra, and J. Gehrke. Gossip-based computation of aggregate information. In *FOCS*, October 2003.

[9] F. Kuhn, T. Locher, and R. Wattenhofer. Tight bounds for distributed selection. In *SPAA*, 2007.

[10] F. Kuhn, N. Lynch, and R. Oshman. Distributed computation in dynamic graphs. In *STOC*, 2010.

[11] E. Kushilevitz and N. Nisan. *Communication Complexity*. Cambridge University Press, 1996.

[12] S. Madden, M. Franklin, J. Hellerstein, and W. Hong. Tag: a tiny aggregation service for ad-hoc sensor networks. In *OSDI*, December 2002.

[13] D. Mosk-Aoyama and D. Shah. Computing separable functions via gossip. In *PODC*, July 2006.

[14] S. Nath, P. B. Gibbons, S. Seshany, and Z. Anderson. Synopsis diffusion for robust aggregation in sensor networks. *ACM Transactions on Sensor Networks*, 4(2), March 2008.

[15] I. Newman. Private vs. common random bits in communication complexity. *Information Processing Letters*, 39(2):67–71, July 1991.

[16] B. Patt-Shamir. A note on efficient aggregate queries in sensor networks. In *PODC*, 2004.

[17] L. Shrira, N. Francez, and M. Rodeh. Distributed k-selection: From a sequential to a distributed algorithm. In *PODC*, 1983.

[18] Y. Zhao, H. Yu, and B. Chen. Near-optimal communication-time tradeoff in fault-tolerant computation of aggregate functions. Technical report, School of Computing, National University of Singapore, 2014. Also available at `http://www.comp.nus.edu.sg/~yuhf/optimalagg-nustr.pdf`.

Algorithm 2 The AGG Protocol. Following are some additional comments on the pseudo-code. By default, the sender of a message always attaches its id on the message (not shown in the pseudo-code), allowing the receiver to infer the sender. A "__" field in a received message means that we do not care about the value of that field. The pseudo-code allows a node to send multiple messages in a single round. In actual implementation, all these messages should be combined into one, and can thus be sent in one round. The pseudo-code invokes the **flood** primitive in several places, whose (trivial) implementation is not included in the pseudo-code. For a node to flood a message, the node sends the message to its neighbors. Any node receiving a flooded message simply forwards that message upon first receiving that message. The initiating node is called the *source* of the flooding. Note that if a node receives a second flooded message (potentially initiated by a different source) with the same content, the node will *not* forward it again. Finally, each node in AGG keeps track of the total number of bits it has sent. Once the number reaches $(11t + 14)(\log N + 5)$, a node will flood a special symbol to cause all nodes to abort AGG. This mechanism is not shown in the pseudo-code, for clarity.

/* **Tree Construction Phase (total** $2cd + 1$ **rounds)** */
if (I am the root) **then**
    $level = 0$; $parent = \texttt{null}$; $children = \emptyset$; $ancestor[i] = \texttt{null}$ for all $i \in [1, 2t]$;
    send $\langle$tree_construct, $level, ancestor\rangle$ in round 1 of this phase;
else
    wait to receive the first message (with arbitrary tie breaking if multiple messages received in the same round) in the form of $\langle$tree_construct, $sender\_level$, $sender\_ancestor\rangle$ from any node u;
    // the node is now activated, and knows that the current round is round $sender\_level + 2$ of this phase;
    // the node can then determine the starting round of all the remaining phases in AGG and VERI;
    let $r = sender\_level + 2$ be the current round of this phase;
    $level = sender\_level + 1$; $parent = u$; $children = \emptyset$;
    $ancestor[1] = parent$; $ancestor[i] = sender\_ancestor[i-1]$ for all $i \in [2, 2t]$;
    send $\langle$ack, $parent\rangle$ in round r of this phase;
    send $\langle$tree_construct, $level, ancestor\rangle$ in round $r + 1$ of this phase;
end if
upon receiving message in the form of $\langle$ack, $my\_id\rangle$ from any node v: $children = children \bigcup \{v\}$;

/* **Aggregation Phase (total** $2cd + 1$ **rounds)** */
$psum = my\_input$; $max\_level = level$; // $psum$ is for "partial sum"
for all $v \in children$ **do**
    if (in round $cd - level + 1$ of this phase, receive message $\langle$aggregation, $sender\_psum$, $sender\_max\_level\rangle$ from node v) **then**
        $psum = psum + sender\_psum$; $max\_level = \max(max\_level, sender\_max\_level)$;
    else
        flood $\langle$critical_failure, $v\rangle$ in round $cd - level + 1$ of this phase;
    end if
end for
send $\langle$aggregation, $psum$, $max\_level\rangle$ in round $cd - level + 1$ of this phase;

/* **Speculative Flooding Phase (total** $2cd + 1$ **rounds)** */
if (I am the root) **then flood** $\langle$flooded_psum, my_id, $psum\rangle$ in round 1 of this phase;
if (I am not the root **and** no message from $parent$ is received in round $level + 1$ of this phase) **then**
    flood $\langle$flooded_psum, my_id, $psum\rangle$ in round $level + 1$ of this phase;
end if

/* **Partial Sum Selection Phase (total** $cd + 1$ **rounds)** */
$ancestor[0] = my\_id$;
for all message received in the form of $\langle$flooded_psum, $source\_id$, __$\rangle$ **do**
    let $i \in [0, 2t]$ be the smallest i such that $ancestor[i] = source\_id$; let $i = \infty$ if such i does not exist;
    let $j \in [0, 2t]$ be the smallest j such that $ancestor[j]$ is the root or $\langle$critical_failure, $ancestor[j]\rangle$ has been received; let $j = \infty$ if such j does not exist;
    dom = I have received a message $\langle$flooded_psum, $ancestor[k]$, __$\rangle$ with $k \in [i+1, j]$; // dom is for "dominated"
    if $(i \le t)$ **and** $(i \le j)$ **then** // I am a witness
        if $(j = \infty)$ **then flood** $\langle$dominated, $source\_id\rangle$ in round 1 of this phase;
        if $(j \ne \infty$ **and** $dom)$ **then flood** $\langle$dominated, $source\_id\rangle$ in round 1 of this phase;
        if $(j \ne \infty$ **and** $(!dom))$ **then flood** $\langle$compulsory||optional, $source\_id\rangle$ in round 1 of this phase;
    end if
end for

/* **Output Phase (only executed by the root)** */
$sum = 0$;
for all received message in the form of $\langle$flooded_psum, $source\_id$, $source\_psum\rangle$ **do**
    if ($\langle$compulsory||optional, $source\_id\rangle$ has been received) **then** $sum = sum + source\_psum$;
    // messages $\langle$dominated, $source\_id\rangle$ are not actually needed, and we sent those only for clarity
end for
output sum;

Algorithm 3 The VERI Protocol. The initial values of the variables $parent$, $children$, $ancestor$, $level$, and max_level are all from the previous AGG execution. All the comments in the caption of Algorithm 2 apply to Algorithm 3 as well, except the following: In VERI, once a node has sent $(5t + 7)(10 + 3 \log N)$ bits, it will flood a special symbol to terminate VERI and cause the root to output `false`.

```
/* Failed Parent Detection Phase (total 2cd + 1 rounds) */
if (I am the root) then
    flood ⟨detect_failed_parent⟩ in round 1 of this phase;
else
    if (no message from parent is received in round level + 1 of this phase) then
        flood ⟨failed_parent, parent, max_level − level + 1⟩ in round level + 1 of this phase;
    end if
end if

/* Failed Child Detection Phase (total 2cd + 1 rounds) */
if (children = ∅) then // I am a leaf
    flood ⟨detect_failed_child⟩ in round cd − level + 1 of this phase;
else
    for all node v ∈ children do
        if (no message from node v is received in round cd − level + 1 of this phase) then
            flood ⟨failed_child, v⟩ in round cd − level + 1 of this phase;
        end if
    end for
end if

/* LFC Detection Phase (total cd + 1 rounds) */
for all received messages in the form of ⟨failed_parent, v, __⟩ do
    let i ∈ [0, 2t] be the smallest i such that ancestor[i] = v; let i = ∞ if such i does not exist;
    let j ∈ [0, 2t] be the smallest j such that ancestor[j] is either the root or ⟨critical_failure, ancestor[j]⟩ was previously received in
    AGG; let j = ∞ if such j does not exist;
    if (i ≤ t and i ≤ j) then // I am a witness
        let k ∈ [i, 2t] be the smallest k such that i) ⟨failed_child, ancestor[k]⟩ has been received, or ii) ancestor[k] is the root, or
        iii) ⟨critical_failure, ancestor[k]⟩ was previously received in AGG; let k = ∞ if such k does not exist;
        if (k − i + 1 ≥ t) then
            flood ⟨LFC_tail, v⟩ in round 1 of this phase;
        else
            flood ⟨not_LFC_tail, v⟩ in round 1 of this phase;
        end if
    end if
end for

/* Output Phase (only executed by the root) */
if (I have received message ⟨LFC_tail, v⟩ for any node v) then output false; // LFC exists
for all received message in the form of ⟨failed_parent, v, x⟩ where x ≥ t do
    if (⟨not_LFC_tail, v⟩ has not been received) then output false; // LFC may exist — VERI may have one-sided error here
end for
output true; // no LFC
```

Author Index

www.ingramcontent.com/pod-product-compliance
Ingram Content Group UK Ltd.
Pitfield, Milton Keynes, MK11 3LW, UK
UKHW051412290926
15471UKWH00009B/1562

9 781450 329446